with MyAccounting

- **Hallmark Features**—Personalized Learning Aids, like Help Me Solve This, Demo Docs, and instant feedback are available for further practice and mastery when students need the help most!

- **Learning Catalytics**—Generates classroom discussion, guides lecture, and promotes peer-to-peer learning with real-time analytics. Now, students can use any device to interact in the classroom.

- **Adaptive Study Plan**—Assists students in monitoring their own progress by offering them a customized study plan powered by Knewton, based on Homework, Quiz, and Test results. Includes regenerated exercises with unlimited practice and the opportunity to prove mastery through quizzes on recommended learning objectives.

- **Worked Solutions**—Provide step-by-step explanations on how to solve select problems using the exact numbers and data that were presented in the problem. Instructors will have access to the Worked Out Solutions in preview and review mode.

PEARSON

Prepare, Apply, and Confirm with MyAccountingLab®

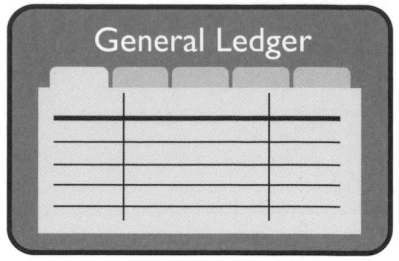

- **General Ledger**—Students can launch General Ledger software in MyAccountingLab, where they will be able to record transactions and adjusting entries, post to the ledger, close periods, and see the effects in the ledger accounts. Their work will be auto-graded, and grades will then automatically flow to the MyAccountingLab Gradebook.

- **Algorithmic Test Bank**—Instructors have the ability to create multiple versions of a test or extra practice for students.

- **Reporting Dashboard**—View, analyze, and report learning outcomes clearly and easily. Available via the Gradebook and fully mobile-ready, the Reporting Dashboard presents student performance data at the class, section, and program levels in an accessible, visual manner.

- **LMS Integration**—Link from any LMS platform to access assignments, rosters, and resources, and synchronize MyLab grades with your LMS gradebook. For students, new direct, single sign-on provides access to all the personalized learning MyLab resources that make studying more efficient and effective.

- **Mobile Ready**—Students and instructors can access multimedia resources and complete assessments right at their fingertips, on any mobile device.

Accounting in the Headlines.

One of the biggest challenges for accounting instructors is that students often feel disengaged from the course material, which can seem abstract and unrelated to their personal experiences. But by incorporating real-life examples, instructors can spark student interest and engagement, especially when teaching accounting at the introductory level.

Accounting in the Headlines, an award-winning blog by renowned author Wendy Tietz, does just that with stories about real companies and events that can be used in the accounting classroom to illustrate introductory financial and managerial accounting concepts.

Concise, tailorable, and updated on a weekly basis, these articles easily fit into the typical introductory accounting curriculum, whether the course is delivered in-person or online. **Accounting in the Headlines articles, along with multiple-choice and polling questions, can be assigned through** MyAccountingLab **and Learning Catalytics™. Instructors are also provided with discussion questions, PowerPoint slides, and handout files, to support learning initiatives.**

http://accountingintheheadlines.com

Dear Valued Colleagues,

Welcome to the Eleventh Edition of *Financial Accounting*. We are grateful for your support as an adopter of our text as we celebrate over 30 years of success in the market. The Eleventh Edition of *Financial Accounting* has been improved in many respects, as explained below.

Several editions ago, we shifted the focus of *Financial Accounting* more toward meeting the needs of users of accounting information for a more balanced presentation. Despite this shift, we still cover the "basic nuts-and-bolts of financial accounting"—the accounting cycle and financial statement preparation. In this edition, we added more discussion of key financial ratios, detailing what those ratios measure and how they are used.

Try It in Excel®. As educators, we often have conversations with those who recruit our students. Based on these conversations, we found that students often complete their study of financial accounting without sufficient knowledge of how to use Excel to perform accounting tasks. To respond to this concern, we have adapted most of the illustrations of key accounting tasks in the book to Excel format and have added new sections in key chapters entitled "Try It in Excel," which describe line-by-line how to retrieve and prepare accounting information (such as adjusted trial balance worksheets, ratio computations, depreciation schedules, bond discount and premium amortization schedules, and financial statement analysis) in Excel format.

Student success. We feel we have the most advanced student learning materials in the market with MyAccountingLab. These include automatically graded homework, DemoDocs, and learning aid videos. We believe that the use of MyAccountingLab homework will greatly enhance student understanding of accounting with its instantaneous feedback. MyAccountingLab makes the study of financial accounting a more interactive and fun experience for students. In addition, we have adopted a scaffolding approach in the book and its resources. Chapter content and the end-of-chapter material builds from the basic short exercise featuring one basic single concept to more advanced problems featuring multiple learning objectives. The student can practice at the basic level and then build upon that success to advance on to more challenging problems.

Professor expectations. As professors, we know that you want a book that contains the most relevant and technically correct content available. We also know that you want excellent end-of-chapter material that is as up-to-date and error-free as possible. We reviewed and created the end-of-chapter questions, exercises, problems, and cases taking into account the types of assignments we ourselves use in class and assign as homework. Based on comments from adopters, we have thoroughly reviewed every end-of-chapter exercise and problem, with the goal of eliminating redundancy and adding relevance. The textbook and solutions manual have been put through a rigorous accuracy check to ensure that they are as complete and error-free as possible.

We welcome your comments and suggestions. Please don't hesitate to send feedback about this book to HorngrensAccounting@pearson.com

Bill Thomas
Wendy Tietz

Financial
Accounting

ELEVENTH EDITION

Walter T. Harrison Jr.
Baylor University

Charles T. Horngren
Stanford University

C. William (Bill) Thomas
Baylor University

Wendy M. Tietz
Kent State University

PEARSON

Boston   Columbus   Indianapolis   New York   San Francisco
Amsterdam   Cape Town   Dubai   London   Madrid   Milan   Munich   Paris   Montréal   Toronto
Delhi   Mexico City   São Paulo   Sydney   Hong Kong   Seoul   Singapore   Taipei   Tokyo

Vice President, Business Publishing: Donna Battista
Editor-in-Chief: Adrienne D'Ambrosio
Senior Acquisitions Editor: Lacey Vitetta
Editorial Assistant: Christine Donovan
Vice President, Product Marketing: Maggie Moylan
Director of Marketing, Digital Services and Products: Jeanette Koskinas
Field Marketing Manager: Natalie Wagner
Product Marketing Assistant: Jessica Quazza
Team Lead, Program Management: Ashley Santora
Program Manager: Mary Kate Murray
Team Lead, Project Management: Jeff Holcomb

Project Manager: Heather Pagano
Operations Specialist: Carol Melville
Creative Director: Blair Brown
Art Director: Jonathan Boylan
Vice President, Director of Digital Strategy and Assessment: Paul Gentile
Manager of Learning Applications: Paul DeLuca
Digital Editor: Sarah Peterson
Director, Digital Studio: Sacha Laustsen
Digital Studio Manager: Diane Lombardo
Digital Studio Project Manager: Andra Skaalrud
Digital Studio Project Manager: Robin Lazrus

Digital Content Team Lead: Noel Lotz
Digital Content Project Lead: Martha LaChance
Full-Service Project Management and Composition: Cenveo® Publishing Services
Interior Designer: Cenveo® Publishing Services
Cover Designer: Cenveo® Publishing Services
Cover Art: somchaiP/Shutterstock
Printer/Binder: RR Donnelley/Kendallville
Cover Printer: Phoenix Color/Hagerstown

Library of Congress Cataloging-in-Publication Data
Names: Harrison, Walter T., author. | Horngren, Charles T., author. | Thomas, C. William, author.
Title: Financial accounting / Walter T. Harrison Jr., Baylor University, Charles T. Horngren, Stanford University, C. William (Bill) Thomas, Baylor University, Wendy M. Tietz, Kent State University.
Description: Eleventh Edition. | Boston : Pearson, 2016. | Revised edition of Financial accounting, 2015. | Includes index.
Identifiers: LCCN 2015043663 | ISBN 9780134127620
Subjects: LCSH: Accounting.
Classification: LCC HF5636 .H37 2016 | DDC 657—dc23
LC record available at http://lccn.loc.gov/2015043663

10 9 8 7 6 5 4 3 2 1

PEARSON

ISBN 10: 0-13-412762-5
ISBN 13: 978-0-13-412762-0

ABOUT THE AUTHORS

Walter T. Harrison Jr. is professor emeritus of accounting at the Hankamer School of Business, Baylor University. He received his BBA from Baylor University, his MS from Oklahoma State University, and his PhD from Michigan State University.

Professor Harrison, recipient of numerous teaching awards from student groups as well as from university administrators, has also taught at Cleveland State Community College, Michigan State University, the University of Texas, and Stanford University.

A member of the American Accounting Association and the American Institute of Certified Public Accountants, Professor Harrison has served as chairman of the Financial Accounting Standards Committee of the American Accounting Association, on the Teaching/Curriculum Development Award Committee, on the Program Advisory Committee for Accounting Education and Teaching, and on the Notable Contributions to Accounting Literature Committee.

Professor Harrison has lectured in several foreign countries and published articles in numerous journals, including *Journal of Accounting Research*, *Journal of Accountancy*, *Journal of Accounting and Public Policy*, *Economic Consequences of Financial Accounting Standards*, *Accounting Horizons*, *Issues in Accounting Education*, and *Journal of Law and Commerce*.

Professor Harrison has received scholarships, fellowships, and research grants or awards from PricewaterhouseCoopers, Deloitte & Touche, the Ernst & Young Foundation, and the KPMG Foundation.

Charles T. Horngren (1926–2011) was the Edmund W. Littlefield Professor of Accounting, emeritus, at Stanford University. A graduate of Marquette University, he received his MBA from Harvard University and his PhD from the University of Chicago. He was also the recipient of honorary doctorates from Marquette University and DePaul University.

A certified public accountant, Horngren served on the Accounting Principles Board for six years, the Financial Accounting Standards Board Advisory Council for five years, and the Council of the American Institute of Certified Public Accountants for three years. For six years he served as a trustee of the Financial Accounting Foundation, which oversees the Financial Accounting Standards Board and the Government Accounting Standards Board.

Horngren is a member of the Accounting Hall of Fame. As a member of the American Accounting Association, Horngren was its president and its director of research. He received its first annual Outstanding Accounting Educator Award. The California Certified Public Accountants Foundation gave Horngren its Faculty Excellence Award and its Distinguished Professor Award. He was the first person to have received both awards. The American Institute of Certified Public Accountants presented its first Outstanding Educator Award to Horngren. Horngren was named Accountant of the Year, in Education, by the national professional accounting fraternity, Beta Alpha Psi. Professor Horngren was also a member of the Institute of Management Accountants, from whom he received its Distinguished Service Award. He was a member of the institute's Board of Regents, which administers the certified management accountant examinations.

Horngren is an author of these other accounting books published by Pearson: *Cost Accounting: A Managerial Emphasis*, Fifteenth Edition, 2015 (with Srikant M. Datar and Madhav V. Rajan); *Introduction to Financial Accounting*, Eleventh Edition, 2014 (with Gary L. Sundem, John A. Elliott, and Donna Philbrick); *Introduction to*

Management Accounting, Sixteenth Edition, 2014 (with Gary L. Sundem, Jeff Schatzberg, and Dave Burgstahler); *Horngren's Financial & Managerial Accounting*, Fifth Edition, 2016 (with Tracie L. Miller-Nobles, Brenda L. Mattison, and Ella Mae Matsumura); and *Horngren's Accounting*, Eleventh Edition, 2016 (with Tracie L. Miller-Nobles, Brenda L. Mattison, and Ella Mae Matsumura). Horngren was the consulting editor for Pearson's Charles T. Horngren Series in Accounting.

C. William (Bill) Thomas is the J.E. Bush Professor of Accounting and a Master Teacher at Baylor University. A Baylor University alumnus, he received both his BBA and MBA there and went on to earn his PhD from The University of Texas at Austin.

With primary interests in the areas of financial accounting and auditing, Bill Thomas has served as the J.E. Bush Professor of Accounting since 1995. He has been a member of the faculty of the Accounting and Business Law Department of the Hankamer School of Business since 1971 and served as chair of the department for 12 years. He has been recognized as an Outstanding Faculty Member of Baylor University as well as a Distinguished Professor for the Hankamer School of Business. Dr. Thomas has received many awards for outstanding teaching, including the Outstanding Professor in the Executive MBA Programs as well as the designation of Master Teacher.

Thomas is the author of textbooks in auditing and financial accounting, as well as many articles in auditing, financial accounting and reporting, taxation, ethics, and accounting education. His scholarly work focuses on the subject of fraud prevention and detection, as well as ethical issues among accountants in public practice. He presently serves as the accounting and auditing editor of *Today's CPA*, the journal of the Texas Society of Certified Public Accountants, with a circulation of approximately 28,000.

Thomas is a certified public accountant in Texas. Prior to becoming a professor, Thomas was a practicing accountant with the firms of KPMG, LLP, and BDO Seidman, LLP. He is a member of the American Accounting Association, the American Institute of Certified Public Accountants, and the Texas Society of Certified Public Accountants.

For my wife, Mary Ann.
C. William (Bill) Thomas

Wendy M. Tietz is a professor in the Department of Accounting in the College of Business Administration at Kent State University, where she has taught since 2000. She teaches introductory financial and managerial accounting in a variety of formats, including large sections, small sections, and web-based sections. She has received numerous college and university teaching awards while at Kent State University. Most recently she was named the Beta Gamma Sigma Professor of the Year for the College of Business Administration.

Dr. Tietz is a certified public accountant, a certified management accountant, and a chartered global management accountant. She is a member of the American Accounting Association (AAA), the Institute of Management Accountants (IMA), and the American Institute of Certified Public Accountants (AICPA). She has published articles in such journals as *Issues in Accounting Education, Accounting Education: An International Journal*, and *Journal of Accounting & Public Policy*. She received the 2014 Bea Sanders/AICPA Innovation in Teaching Award for her accounting educator blog entitled "Accounting in the Headlines." She regularly presents at AAA regional and national meetings. Dr. Tietz is also the coauthor of a managerial accounting textbook, *Managerial Accounting*, with Dr. Karen Braun.

Dr. Tietz received her PhD from Kent State University. She received both her MBA and BSA from the University of Akron. She worked in industry for several years, both as a controller for a financial institution and as the operations manager and controller for a recycled plastics manufacturer.

To my husband, Russ, who steadfastly supports me in every endeavor.
Wendy M. Tietz

BRIEF CONTENTS

CONTENTS

Chapter 3
Accrual Accounting & Income   121

Chapter 4
Internal Control & Cash   199

Chapter 9

Liabilities   492

SPOTLIGHT | Southwest Airlines: Flying High!   492

Chapter 10

Stockholders' Equity   564

SPOTLIGHT | The Home Depot: Building Toward Success   564

Chapter 11

Evaluating Performance: Earnings Quality, the Income Statement, & the Statement of Comprehensive Income 631

Chapter 12

The Statement of Cash Flows 678

Chapter 13

Financial Statement Analysis   750

SPOTLIGHT | Under Armour, Inc., Is a
"Red-Hot" Competitor!   750

PREFACE

Financial Accounting gives readers a solid foundation in the fundamentals of accounting and the basics of financial statements, and then builds upon that foundation to offer more advanced and challenging concepts and problems. This scaffolded approach helps students to better understand the meaning and relevance of financial information, see its significance within a real-world context, as well as develop the skills needed to analyze financial information in both their courses and career.

Financial Accounting has a long-standing reputation in the marketplace for being readable and easy to understand. It drives home fundamental concepts using relevant examples from real-world companies in a reader-friendly way without adding unnecessary complexity. While maintaining hallmark features of accuracy, readability, and ease of understanding, the Eleventh Edition includes updated explanations, coverage, and ratio analysis with decision-making guidelines. These time-tested methodologies with the latest technology ensures that students learn basic concepts in accounting in a way that is relevant, stimulating, and fun, while exercises and examples from real-world companies help students gain a better grasp of the course material.

CHANGES FOR THE ELEVENTH EDITION

1. The first three chapters of the book cover the accounting cycle and how financial statements are constructed. In previous editions of the book, we used separate companies in each of Chapters 1, 2, and 3 to illustrate various phases of the accounting cycle. In the Eleventh Edition, we switched to using *a single, very familiar* company (The Walt Disney Company) to illustrate all phases of the accounting cycle. In Chapter 1, we give an overview of the company's financial statements and explain what each contains. In Chapter 2, we cover transactions—how they impact the accounting equation and how they are journalized, posted, and summarized. In Chapter 3, we discuss the latter stages of the accounting cycle for the same company and what goes on at the end of the cycle to convert the books into financial statements—adjusting entries, closing entries, and financial statement preparation. Thus, the Eleventh Edition should have more continuity in the early chapters; tell a more integrated, unified story; and cover the accounting cycle in a chronological sequence. The hypothetical company (Alladin Travel, Inc.) that we have created in Chapter 1 and carried through Chapter 3 is a company that conceivably fits into Disney's business model.

2. A scaffolding approach has been implemented in the book and its resources. Chapter content and the end-of-chapter material builds from the basic short exercise featuring one basic concept to more advanced problems featuring multiple learning objectives. This allows the student to practice at the basic level and then build upon that success to advance to more challenging problems.

3. The ethical component of accounting has been enhanced in the Eleventh Edition by adding a section on the AICPA's Code of Professional Conduct, located at the end of Chapter 1. The principles section of the code is included, explaining CPAs' responsibilities to act in the public interest, to have integrity and objectivity, and to exercise due professional care. In each chapter, there are short exercises that demonstrate the application of these principles.

4. Short exercises, exercises, and problems are more clearly labeled by learning objective (LO). Short exercises have been shortened and simplified in this edition to cover only one LO each. They can be used better to briefly cover single concepts as illustrations or class exercises. Exercises might cover two or three LOs, and problems cover multiple LOs.

5. In Chapters 3, 5, and 11, we have updated and provided complete coverage of the revised FASB accounting standard on revenue recognition, impacting the accounting for sales returns and sales discounts. We provide the most accurate up-to-the-minute information available for this critical area. End-of-chapter short exercises, exercises, and problems have also been revised to reflect application of the new revenue recognition standard at an appropriate and understandable level for beginning students in accounting.

6. Chapter 4 contains a new hypothetical case study to introduce the concepts of fraud and how it can be prevented by internal control. This fictionalized case study is based on an actual company in Texas whose highly trusted and loyal controller and his wife systematically stole $16 million over the space of 10 years by issuing company checks to pay off their personal credit card bills. The scheme was enabled by weak internal controls. Executives of the company allowed the controller to have access to the check-signing

machine and electronic signature of the company president. Chapter 4 also contains updated illustrations of electronic bank statements.

7. In Chapter 5, using Apple Inc. as the book's Appendix A focus company, we emphasize proper revenue recognition, accounting for accounts and notes receivable, and measuring and evaluating collectability through the allowance for doubtful accounts. The coverage of the days' sales outstanding (DSO) ratio has been updated, improved, and made more consistent with the coverage of days' inventory outstanding (DIO) in Chapter 6 and days' payable outstanding (DPO) in Chapter 9. We first introduce the computation of accounts receivable turnover (net sales/average accounts receivable) and explain its meaning. We then convert the turnover to DSO by dividing the turnover by 365. In previous editions, the primary computation was average daily sales (net sales/365), followed by division of average AR by average daily sales.

8. In Chapter 6, the coverage of inventory and cost of goods sold has been updated, using Under Armour, Inc., the textbook's Appendix B focus company. The products sold by Under Armour should be highly familiar to college students, and the study of inventory is made more interesting by applying it to this fascinating and fast-growing company.

9. In Chapter 9, based on feedback we received from adopters who only have time to cover straight-line amortization for bond premium or discount, we added a new self-contained section at the beginning of the coverage for bonds payable: Accounting for Bonds Payable Using Straight-Line Amortization. We moved the coverage of amortization by the effective-interest method back one section. Thus, users who only want to cover issuance of bonds and recognition of interest expense based on straight-line amortization of bond premium or discount may use only that section. Separate problems using the straight-line method or amortization at the end of the chapter allow these users to easily skip the more complex effective-interest method altogether.

10. In every chapter, after relevant concepts are covered, a text box labeled "Try it" is introduced. This employs the following learning philosophy: 1. read it; 2. try it; 3. practice it.

11. In many cases, we add "Try It in Excel" to illustrate use of Excel and a business problem-solving tool. We feel that students should be exposed early and frequently in their business education to Excel applications. At the beginning of every chapter, we give students instructions as to how to access the most current financial statements of the chapter's focus company in Excel format from the Securities and Exchange Commission (SEC) website (**http://www.sec.gov**). Throughout the book, most exhibits and journal entries are formatted as Excel worksheets. In addition, at certain points throughout the text, we include examples that show students step-by-step how to build Excel templates to facilitate the solutions of specific accounting problems. The following provides examples of these applications by chapter:

Chapter 1: Preparing basic financial statements (income statement, retained earnings statement, balance sheet)

Chapter 2: Processing business transactions, preparation of trial balance

Chapter 3: Adjusting journal entries, preparation of adjusted trial balance, final financial statements

Chapter 4: Preparation of bank reconciliation, cash budget

Chapter 5: Accounts receivable aging analysis

Chapter 6: Computation of cost of goods sold and gross profit

Chapter 7: Calculation of depreciation expense and accumulated depreciation by three methods: straight-line, units-of-production, and double-declining balance

Chapter 8: Calculation of present value

Chapter 9: Calculation of bond discount and premium amortization tables using effective-interest method

Chapter 13: Horizontal and vertical analysis of financial statements

12. Ethics is a vital part of accounting. Several sections of the text are dedicated to discussing potential ethical problems that can arise in dealing with that particular subject matter and how they should be properly handled.

13. In all chapters, we emphasize how accounting information covered in that chapter is analyzed and used to help managers make various kinds of business decisions. User-relevant information and key ratios that are covered in various chapters include the following:

> Chapter 3: Debt-paying ability: net working capital, current ratio, debt ratio
>
> Chapter 4: Internal control: importance of internal control to preserve the integrity of financial information; the significance of cash and cash flow
>
> Chapter 5: Liquidity: quick (acid-test) ratio, accounts receivable turnover, days' sales in receivables
>
> Chapter 6: Profitability: gross profit percentage, inventory turnover, days' inventory outstanding
>
> Chapter 7: Profitability: introduction rate of return on total assets (ROA) using Du Pont Analysis (profit margin $\times$ asset turnover)
>
> Chapter 8: Time value: time value of money and how it impacts investing and lending decisions
>
> Chapter 9: Liquidity: accounts payable turnover, days' payable outstanding, cash collection cycle (days' sales in receivables $+$ days inventory outstanding $-$ days' payable outstanding). Leverage: continuation of Du Pont Analysis by introducing leverage ratio (average total assets/average stockholders' equity)
>
> Chapter 10: Profitability: rate of return on common stockholders' equity using expanded Du Pont Analysis Model (ROA [introduced in Chapter 7] $\times$ leverage ratio [introduced in Chapter 9])
>
> Chapter 11: Evaluating performance: earnings quality, earnings per share, book value per share, dividend yield, capitalization of earnings from operations to estimate future profitability and stock price
>
> Chapter 12: Cash flow: use of cash flow information by creditors and investors; free cash flow
>
> Chapter 13: Statement analysis: comprehensive financial statement analysis, incorporating all of the ratios covered in the previous chapters, applying them to the book's two appendix focus companies, Under Armour, Inc. and Apple Inc.

VISUAL WALK-THROUGH

Try It in Excel

Describes line-by-line how to retrieve and prepare accounting information (such as adjusted trial balance worksheets, ratio computations, depreciation schedules, bond discount and premium amortization schedules, and financial statement analysis) in Excel.

 Formatting comparative financial statements for horizontal analysis when the financial statements are in Excel format is quite easy. Try reconstructing Exhibit 13-2 in Excel.

1. Start with the Consolidated Statements of Operations in the opening figure of the chapter.
2. Change the labels to correspond with Exhibit 13-2. Your spreadsheet might be slightly different from Exhibit 13-2, so the cells in which you start to enter formulas might have to be modified accordingly.
3. Insert one column between the 2014 and 2013 columns and another column between the 2013 and 2012 columns. Label these "% change."
4. Compute the percentage change as follows. We start in cell C4 (blank). Change the format of the data in the cell to % by clicking on the % box in the number field in the top toolbar. In cell C4, type the following: =(B4–D4)/D4. The result of 32.3% should appear in the cell. Copy this cell formula through line 13 of the sheet to perform this computation for all other income and expenses.
5. Repeat the process in (4) using blank cell E4 and using the formula: =(D4–F4)/F4. Copy this formula through line 13.
6. Pat yourself on the back. You've just performed horizontal analysis using Excel!

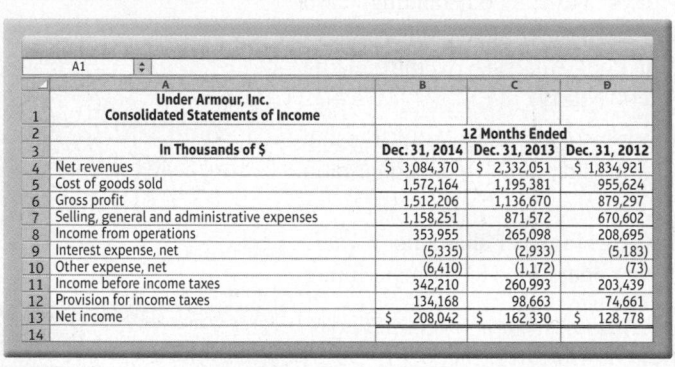

Excel Integrated Throughout Text!

Excel-based financial statements are used so that students will familiarize themselves with the accounting information format actually used in the business world.

Try It

Found at various points in a chapter, this tool includes a question-and-answer snapshot asking students to apply what they just learned.

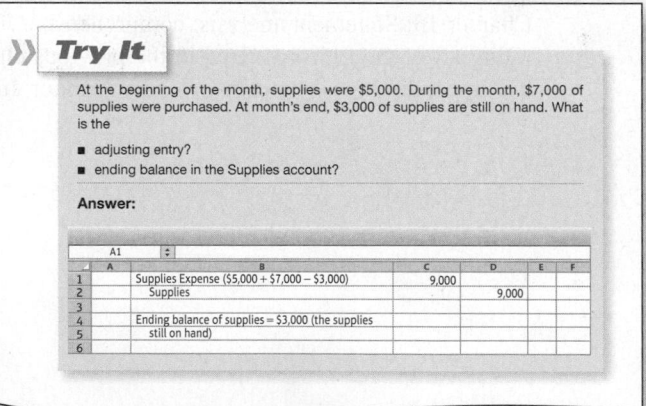

Try It

At the beginning of the month, supplies were $5,000. During the month, $7,000 of supplies were purchased. At month's end, $3,000 of supplies are still on hand. What is the

- adjusting entry?
- ending balance in the Supplies account?

Answer:

 In contrast to U.S. GAAP, with its mechanical, or "bright line," tests for capitalization of leases, IFRS adopts a much broader approach. Rather than rules, IFRS employs "guidance" that focuses on the overall substance of the transaction, rather than on the mechanical form, and that leaves more to the judgment of the preparer of the financial statement. If, in the judgment of the company's accountants, the lease transfers "substantially all of the risks and rewards of ownership to the lessee," IFRS says the lease should be capitalized. Otherwise, the lease should be expensed as an operating lease.

As of the date of this text, the FASB and IASB have issued a final exposure draft for a new standard on long-term leases that will, for the great majority of such agreements, require capital lease treatment. This will essentially end the practice of operating leases and off-balance-sheet financing for leased property. The new standard is expected to take effect sometime after 2016. When that happens, Southwest Airlines and many other companies with long-term operating leases for fixed assets could be forced to add billions of dollars to their long-term assets, as well as their long-term liabilities, with results as we just showed on their debt and other ratios.

Global View

Offers students an international perspective on accounting issues and integrates the International Financial Reporting Standards (IFRS) with corresponding concepts throughout the text.

Decision Guidelines

Illustrates how financial statements are used and how accounting information aids companies in decision making.

 DECISION GUIDELINES

USING THE INCOME STATEMENT AND RELATED NOTES IN INVESTMENT ANALYSIS

Suppose you've completed your studies, taken a job, and have been fortunate to save $10,000. Now you are ready to start investing. These guidelines provide a framework for using accounting information for investment analysis.

Decision	Factors to Consider		Decision Variable or Model
Which measure of profitability should be used for investment analysis?	Are you interested in accounting income? →	Income, including all revenues, expenses, gains, and losses?	Net income (bottom line)
		Income that can be expected to repeat from year to year?	Income from continuing operations
	Are you interested in cash flows?		Net cash flow from operating activities (Chapter 12)

Note: A conservative strategy may use both income and cash flows and compare the two sets of results.

Ethics Check

EC10-1. Identify ethical principle violated
For each of the situations listed, identify which of three principles (integrity, objectivity and independence, or due care) from the AICPA Code of Professional Conduct that is violated. Assume all persons listed in the situations are members of the AICPA. (Note: Refer to the AICPA Code of Professional Conduct contained on pages 29–30, Chapter 1 for descriptions of the principles.)
   a. Henry is the CFO for Front Street Coffee Corporation and is going to take the company public within the next six months. In an effort to make the stock look more appealing and therefore sell at a higher price, Henry overrides the system controls and records fictitious sales entries.
   b. Heather is a senior auditor for Lenardi & Calwell and has worked on its client, New Iron, Inc., for the past few years. A few months ago, New Iron, Inc., offered Heather a position in its internal audit department. Heather accepted the position and works very closely with the external auditors. In fact, she often prepares the work papers for the external auditor since she knows the systems better than the new auditors.

Ethics Check **NEW!**

This new end-of-chapter feature presents students with several ethical business situations and asks them to identify which of the principles from the AICPA Code of Professional Conduct is violated.

Ethical Issue

This end-of-chapter feature presents students with ethical situations and has them work through the decision framework for making ethical judgments. Finally, they are asked to come to a decision and support it.

 Ethical Issue

Media One owns 18% of the voting stock of Web Talk, Inc. The remainder of the Web Talk stock is held by numerous investors with small holdings. Austin Cohen, president of Media One and a member of Web Talk's board of directors, heavily influences Web Talk's policies.

Under the fair value method of accounting for investments, Media One's net income increases as it receives dividend revenue from Web Talk. Media One pays President Cohen a bonus computed as a percentage of Media One's net income. Therefore, Cohen can control his personal bonus to a certain extent by influencing Web Talk's dividends.

A recession occurs in 2016, and Media One's income is low. Cohen uses his power to have Web Talk pay a large cash dividend. The action requires Web Talk to borrow in order to pay the dividend.

Requirements
1. What are the ethical issues in the Media One case?
2. Who are the stakeholders? What are the possible consequences to each?
3. What are the alternatives for Austin Cohen to consider? Analyze each alternative from the following standpoints: (a) economic, (b) legal, (c) ethical.
4. If you were Cohen, what would you do?
5. Discuss how using the equity method of accounting for the investment would decrease Cohen's potential for manipulating his bonus.

Challenge Exercises and Problem

E5-67. *(Learning Objective 6: Show how to speed up cash from receivables)* Ripley Shirt Company sells on credit and manages its own receivables. Average experience for the past three years has been the following: **LO 6**

	Cash	Credit	Total
Sales	$350,000	$350,000	$700,000
Cost of goods sold	175,000	175,000	350,000
Uncollectible-account expense	—	20,000	20,000
Other expenses	89,000	89,000	178,000

Jack Rivers, the owner, is considering whether to accept bankcards (VISA, MasterCard). Rivers expects total sales to increase by 12% but cash sales to remain unchanged. If Rivers switches to bankcards, the business can save $10,000 on other expenses, but VISA and MasterCard charge

Critical Thinking Challenge Problems Increased!

Additional problems have been developed to provide students with the opportunity for applied critical thinking.

DIGITAL WALK-THROUGH

 **Pearson eText**

The Pearson eText, available through MyAccountingLab, gives students access to their textbook anytime, anywhere. In addition to note taking, highlighting, and bookmarking, the Pearson eText offers interactive and sharing features. Rich media options let students watch lecture and example videos as they read or do their homework. Instructors can share their comments or highlights, and students can add their own, creating a tight community of learners in your class.

The Pearson eText companion app (**http://www.pearsonhighered.com/etextmobile/**) allows existing subscribers to access their titles on an iPad or Android tablet for either online or offline viewing.

- Now available on smartphones and tablets
- Seamlessly integrated videos and other rich media
- Accessible (screen-reader ready)
- Configurable reading settings, including resizable type and night-reading mode
- Instructor and student note taking, highlighting, bookmarking, and search

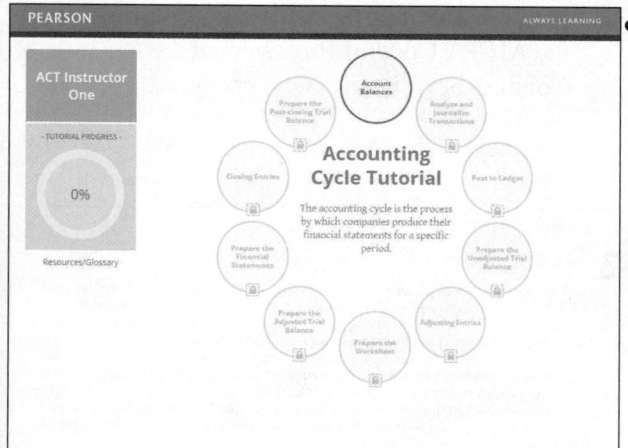

Accounting Cycle Tutorial (ACT) *NEW!*

MyAccountingLab's new interactive tutorial helps students master the accounting cycle for early and continued success in the Introduction to Accounting course. The tutorial, accessed by computer, Smartphone, or tablet, provides students with brief explanations of each concept of the accounting cycle through engaging videos and animations. Students are immediately assessed on their understanding, and their performance is recorded in the MyAccountingLab grade book. Whether the Accounting Cycle Tutorial is used as a remediation self-study tool or course assignment, students have yet another resource within MyAccountingLab to help them be successful with the accounting cycle.

Learning Catalytics *NEW!*

Learning Catalytics, available through MyAccountingLab, is a "bring your own device" assessment and classroom activity system that expands the possibilities for student engagement. Using Learning Catalytics, you can deliver a wide range of automatically graded or open-ended questions that test content knowledge and build critical thinking skills. Eighteen different answer types provide great flexibility, including graphical, numerical, textual input, and more.

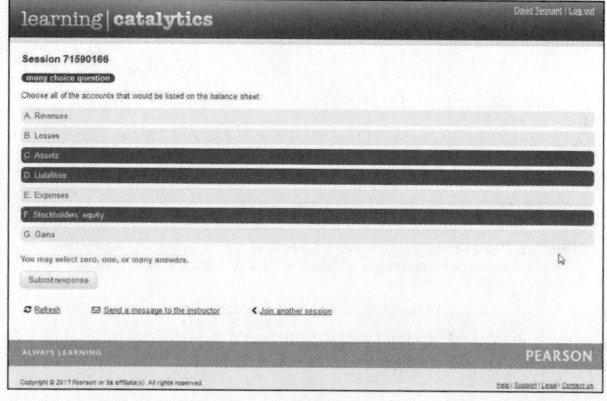

Try It Videos

These videos, offered only in MyAccountingLab, guide students step-by-step through key exhibits in the text.

STUDENT AND INSTRUCTOR RESOURCES

For Students

MyAccountingLab online Homework and Assessment Manager includes:

- Pearson eText
- Student PowerPoint® Presentations
- Accounting Cycle Tutorial
- Videos
- Demo Docs
- Flash Cards
- Dynamic Study Modules
- QuickBooks Data Files
- Excel in Practice Data Files
- Working Papers
- Directed Reading
- Questions You Should be Able to Answer

Student resource website: http://www.pearsonhighered.com/harrison
This website contains the following:

- The QuickBooks Data Files and the Excel in Practice Data Files, related to select end-of-chapter problems

- Working Papers, for completing end-of-chapter questions in preformatted templates

- Directed Reading, help direct students to what is content in the chapter is important.

- Student PowerPoint® Presentations

For Instructors

Instructor Resource Center: http://www.pearsonhighered.com/harrison
For the instructor's convenience, the instructor resources can be downloaded from the textbook's catalog page and MyAccountingLab. Available resources include the following:

- **NEW!** *Discussion Board Prompts*: Get the most out of online and in class discussions and promote interaction and engagement with your financial accounting students. This supplement will aid instructors in facing the challenges of utilizing discussion prompts effectively in the accounting classroom.

  Discussion Prompts for each chapter includes: sample discussion prompts for introductory financial accounting, engaging discussion prompts to promote critical thinking, effective facilitation strategies, possible sources of potential online discussion sources, and examples of grading rubrics for online discussions.

- **NEW!** *Directed Reading*: Encourage students to actively read the textbook BEFORE coming to class and help direct them to what is important. Students should hand in these directed reading worksheets at the beginning of class before starting the corresponding chapter.

- *Instructor's Resource Manual*: Includes chapter outlines, suggested in-class activities, topics with which students struggle, as well as the following:

  - The *Questions You Should Be Able To Answer* feature presented in a table format. This is an interactive feature students can find in the MyAccountingLab eText.

  - Assignment grid that outlines all end-of-chapter exercises, problems, and cases; the topic being covered in that particular exercise, problem, or cases; estimated completion time; level of difficulty; and availability in General Ledger, QuickBooks, or Excel templates.

– Ten-minute quizzes that quickly assess students' understanding of the chapter material.

– **NEW!** Flipping Your Classroom Guide: Tips for each chapter on how to take your course from a traditional/in-class course to a hybrid, blended, or fully online format. Includes links to the discussion board prompts.

■ *Instructor's Solutions Manual*: Contains solutions to all end-of-chapter questions, including short exercises, exercises, problems and cases.

■ *Test Bank*: Includes more than 2,000 questions. Both objective-based questions and computational problems are available. Algorithmic test bank is available in MyAccountingLab.

■ *PowerPoint Presentations*: These presentations help facilitate classroom discussion.

– Instructor PowerPoint Presentations with lecture notes

– Student PowerPoint Presentations

■ *Working Paper Templates and Solutions* in Excel and PDF Format

■ *Image Library*

■ *Data and Solution Files*: The QuickBooks Data Files and the Excel in Practice Data Files, related to select end-of-chapter problems. Corresponding solution files are also provided.

ACKNOWLEDGMENTS

We sincerely thank the many friends and colleagues who have helped in the process of writing and revising this book. Betsy Willis deserves special mention for her dedication, feedback, and hard work throughout this project. We thank Carolyn Streuly for her amazing accuracy checking. We are also deeply grateful to Lacey Vitetta and Heather Pagano for their endless patience and support. Thank you to Donna Battista, Natalie Wagner, Mary Kate Murray, Sarah Peterson, Kathy Smith, and Martha LaChance for their continued help and support. Thanks also to Sheila Ammons for preparing the Test Bank, to Betsy Willis for preparing the *Instructor's Resource Manual*, and to Michelle Franz for preparing the PowerPoint presentation. Thank you also to the many professors and students who have used the book and provided feedback for improving it.

We would like to thank the following reviewers for the Eleventh Edition for their valuable input: Patricia Derrick, Drexel University; Shuai Ma, American University; Susan Machuga, University of Hartford; Dorothy Thompson, Ave Maria University; Gary Olsen, Carroll University; Reed Easton, Seton Hall University; Randall Serrett, University of Houston–Downtown; Ada Duffey, University of Wisconsin-Waukesha; Alesha Graves, Mount St. Joseph University; Brian Routh, University of Southern Indiana; Regan Garey, Lock Haven University; Michelle Watts, Boise State University; David Parker, Saint Xavier University; Brian Porter, Hope College; Rosemary Nurre, College of San Mateo.

In revising previous editions of *Financial Accounting*, we had the help of instructors from across the country who have participated in online surveys, chapter reviews, and focus groups. Their comments and suggestions for both the text and the supplements have been a great help in planning and carrying out revisions, and we thank them for their contributions.

Past Reviewer Participants

Shawn Abbott, College of the Siskiyous
Linda Abernathy, Kirkwood Community College
Sol Ahiarah, SUNY College at Buffalo (Buffalo State)
M. J. Albin, University of Southern Mississippi
Gary Ames, Brigham Young University, Idaho
Elizabeth Ammann, Lindenwood University
Brenda Anderson, Brandeis University
Kim Anderson, Indiana University of Pennsylvania
Florence Atiase, University of Texas at Austin
Walter Austin, Mercer University, Macon
Brad Badertscher, University of Iowa
Sandra Bailey, Oregon Institute of Technology
Patrick Bauer, DeVry University, Kansas City
Barbara A. Beltrand, Metropolitan State University
Jerry Bennett, University of South Carolina–Spartanburg
Peg Beresewski, Robert Morris College
Lucille Berry, Webster University
John Bildersee, New York University, Stern School
Brenda Bindschatel, Green River Community College
Candace Blankenship, Belmont University
Charlie Bokemeier, Michigan State University
Patrick Bouker, North Seattle Community College
Amy Bourne, Oregon State University
Scott Boylan, Washington and Lee University
Robert Braun, Southeastern Louisiana University
Linda Bressler, University of Houston–Downtown
Michael Broihahn, Barry University
Rada Brooks, University of California, Berkeley
Carol Brown, Oregon State University
Elizabeth Brown, Keene State College
Helen Brubeck, San Jose State University
Scott Bryant, Baylor University
Marcus Butler, University of Rochester
Marci Butterfield, University of Utah
Mark Camma, Atlantic Cape Community College
Kay Carnes, Gonzaga University
Brian Carpenter, University of Scranton
Sandra Cereola, James Madison University
Kam Chan, Pace University
Hong Chen, Northeastern Illinois University
C. Catherine Chiang, Elon University
Freddy Choo, San Francisco State University
Charles Christy, Delaware Tech and Community College, Stanton Campus
Lawrence Chui, Opus College of Business, University of St. Thomas
Shifei Chung, Rowan University
Bryan Church, Georgia Tech at Atlanta
Carolyn Clark, Saint Joseph's University
Dr. Paul Clikeman, University of Richmond
Charles Coate, St. Bonaventure University
Dianne Conry, University of California State College Extension–Cupertino
Ellen D. Cook, University of Louisiana at Lafayette

John Coulter, Western New England College
Sue Counte, Saint Louis Community College–Meramec
Julia Creighton, American University
Sue Cullers, Buena Vista University
Donald Curfman, McHenry County College
Alan Czyzewski, Indiana State University
Laurie Dahlin, Worcester State College
Bonita Daly, University of Southern Maine
Kreag Danvers, Clarion University
Betty David, Francis Marion University
Patricia Derrick, George Washington University
Peter DiCarlo, Boston College
Charles Dick, Miami University
Barbara Doughty, New Hampshire Community Technical College
Allan Drebin, Northwestern University
Carolyn Dreher, Southern Methodist University
Emily Drogt, Grand Valley State University
Carol Dutton, South Florida Community College
James Emig, Villanova University
Ellen Engel, University of Chicago
Mary Ewanechko, Monroe Community College
Alan Falcon, Loyola Marymount University
Janet Farler, Pima Community College
Dr. Andrew Felo, Penn State Great Valley
Ken Ferris, Thunderbird College
Dr. Mary Fischer, The University of Texas at Tyler
Dr. Caroline Ford, Baylor University
Clayton Forester, University of Minnesota
Lou Fowler, Missouri Western State College
Timothy Gagnon, Northeastern University
Terrie Gehman, Elizabethtown College
Lucille Genduso, Nova Southeastern University
Frank Gersich, Monmouth College
Bradley Gillespie, Saddleback College
Lisa Gillespie, Loyola University, Chicago
Marvin Gordon, University of Illinois at Chicago
Brian Green, University of Michigan at Dearborn
Anthony Greig, Purdue University
Ronald Guidry, University of Louisiana at Monroe
Konrad Gunderson, Missouri Western State College
Dr. Geoffrey J. Gurka, Colorado Mesa University
William Hahn, Southeastern College
Jack Hall, Western Kentucky University
Gloria Halpern, Montgomery College
Penny Hanes, Mercyhurst College
Dr. Heidi Hansel, Kirkwood Community College
Kenneth Hart, Brigham Young University, Idaho
Al Hartgraves, Emory University
Michael Haselkorn, Bentley University
Thomas Hayes, University of North Texas
Larry Hegstad, Pacific Lutheran University
Candy Heino, Anoka-Ramsey Community College
Mary Hollars, Vincennes University

Anit Hope, Tarrant County College
Thomas Huse, Boston College
Fred R. Jex, Macomb Community College
Grace Johnson, Marietta College
Celina Jozsi, University of South Florida
John Karayan, Woodbury University
Beth Kern, Indiana University, South Bend
Irene Kim, The George Washington University
Hans E. Klein, Babson College
Robert Kollar, Duquesne University
Willem Koole, North Carolina State University
Emil Koren, Hillsborough Community College
Dennis Kovach, Community College of Allegheny County–
   North Campus
Maria U. Ku, Ohlone College & Diablo Valley College
Ellen Landgraf, Loyola University Chicago
Howard Lawrence, Christian Brothers University
Barry Leffkov, Regis College
Elliott Levy, Bentley University
Chao-Shin Liu, Notre Dame
Barbara Lougee, University of California, Irvine
Heidemarie Lundblad, California State University,
   Northridge
Joseph Lupino, Saint Mary's College of California
Anna Lusher, West Liberty State College
Harriet Maccracken, Arizona State University
Constance Malone Hylton, George Mason University
Carol Mannino, Milwaukee School of Engineering
Herb Martin, Hope College
Aziz Martinez, Harvard University, Harvard Business
   School
Anthony Masino, Queens University/NC Central
Lizbeth Matz, University of Pittsburgh, Bradford
Bruce Maule, College of San Mateo
Michelle McEacharn, University of Louisiana
   at Monroe
Molly McFadden-May, Tulsa Community College
Nick McGaughey, San Jose State University
Allison McLeod, University of North Texas
Cathleen Miller, University of Michigan–Flint
Cynthia J. Miller, Gatton College of Business & Economics,
   University of Kentucky
Mark Miller, University of San Francisco
Mary Miller, University of New Haven
Scott Miller, Gannon University
Frank Mioni, Madonna University
Dr. Birendra (Barry) K. Mishra, University of California,
   Riverside
Theodore D. Morrison III, Wingate University
Lisa Nash, Vincennes University
Rosemary Nurre, College of San Mateo
Bruce L. Oliver, Rochester Institute of Technology
Stephen Owen, Hamilton College
Charles Pedersen, Quinsigamond Community College

Richard J. Pettit, Mountain View College
George Plesko, Massachusetts Institute of Technology
David Plumlee, University of Utah
Gregory Prescott, University of South Alabama
Rama Ramamurthy, College of William and Mary
Craig Reeder, Florida A&M University
Barb Reeves, Cleary University
Bettye Rogers-Desselle, Prairie View A&M University
Darren Roulstone, University of Chicago
Norlin Rueschhoff, Notre Dame
Anwar Salimi, California State Polytechnic University,
   Pomona
Philippe Sammour, Eastern Michigan University
Angela Sandberg, Jacksonville State University
George Sanders, Western Washington University
Betty Saunders, University of North Florida
Albert A Schepanski, University of Iowa
William Schmul, Notre Dame
Arnie Schnieder, Georgia Tech at Atlanta
Gim Seow, University of Connecticut
Itzhak Sharav, CUNY–Lehman Graduate School of
   Business
Allan Sheets, International Business College
Lily Sieux, California State University, East Bay
Alvin Gerald Smith, University of Northern Iowa
James Smith, Community College of Philadelphia
Virginia Smith, Saint Mary's College of California
Beverly Soriano, Framingham State College
Vic Stanton, Stanford University
Carolyn R. Stokes, Frances Marion University
J. B. Stroud, Nicholls State University
Gloria J. Stuart, Georgia Southern University
Al Taccone, Cuyamaca College
Diane Tanner, University of North Florida
Martin Taylor, University of Texas at Arlington
Howard Toole, San Diego State University
Vincent Turner, California State Polytechnic University,
   Pomona
Sue Van Boven, Paradise Valley Community College
Marcia Veit, University of Central Florida
Bruce Wampler, Louisiana State University, Shreveport
Suzanne Ward, University of Louisiana at Lafayette
Craig Weaver, University of California, Riverside
Frederick Weis, Claremont McKenna College
Frederick Weiss, Virginia Wesleyan College
Betsy Willis, Baylor University
Ronald Woan, Indiana University of Pennsylvania
Allen Wright, Hillsborough Community College
Dr. Jia Wu, University of Massachusetts, Dartmouth
Yanfeng Xue, George Washington University
Barbara Yahvah, University of Montana–Helena
Myung Yoon, Northeastern Illinois University
Lin Zeng, Northeastern Illinois University
Tony Zordan, University of St. Francis

⦿ SPOTLIGHT | The Walt Disney Company

Where is the happiest place on earth? Walt Disney World or Disneyland, of course! The Disney theme parks in Orlando, Florida, and Anaheim, California, are famous for providing the ultimate family entertainment experience. However, these two theme parks are actually only a small part of the worldwide entertainment empire that is The Walt Disney Company.

From rather humble beginnings in the American Midwest, Walt Disney first began to display his extraordinary talents as an animation artist in the 1920s. Walt and his brother Roy pooled their resources and set up a cartoon studio in Hollywood, California, in 1923. Their early work focused on animated short cartoon films featuring animal characters. The best known of these is Mickey Mouse, invented in the early 1930s. Mickey became an instant success in the first cartoon "short" with sound called *Steamboat Willie*, earning Disney his first Academy Award in 1932. The studio soon launched spin-offs for supporting characters: Mickey's friends Donald Duck and Goofy, and Mickey's beloved hound Pluto.

Thankfully, Walt Disney's dreams didn't end with the short animated cartoon. In 1937, the studio released its first-ever full-length feature animated film, *Snow White and the Seven Dwarfs*. Considered quite a risky venture at the time, the film became the most successful motion picture of 1938, earning over $8 million on its initial release, the equivalent of over $134 million today. This led to numerous other animated features such as *Pinocchio, Fantasia, Bambi, Cinderella, Peter Pan,* and *Dumbo*.

Fueled by imagination, the empire continued to grow. The opening of Disneyland in 1955 signaled a new era in development for the Disney name, which has become synonymous with family entertainment worldwide. Sixty years later, among The Walt Disney Company's assets are sole ownership or interests in 5 vacation resorts, 11 theme parks, 2 water parks, 39 hotels, 8 motion picture studios, 6 record labels, and 11 cable television networks (including ESPN and ABC). The company also sells billions of dollars of branded merchandise through its retail, online, and wholesale distribution channels (Disney Stores and DisneyStore.com). As shown in The

Martin Beddall/Alamy

	A	B	C	D	E
1	**The Walt Disney Company** **Consolidated Statements of Income**	**12 Months Ended**			
2	**Adapted, in millions of $**	**Sep. 27, 2014**	**Sep. 28, 2013**		
3	Services revenue	$ 40,246	$ 37,280		
4	Products revenue	8,567	7,761		
5	Total revenues	48,813	45,041		
6	Cost of services (exclusive of depreciation and amortization)	(21,356)	(20,090)		
7	Cost of products (exclusive of depreciation and amortization)	(5,064)	(4,944)		
8	Selling, general, administrative, and other	(8,565)	(8,365)		
9	Depreciation and amortization	(2,288)	(2,192)		
10	Total costs and expenses	(37,273)	(35,591)		
11	Income from operations	11,540	9,450		
12	Other income (expense), net	706	170		
13	Income before income taxes	12,246	9,620		
14	Income taxes	(4,242)	(2,984)		
15	Net income	8,004	6,636		
16	Less: Net income attributable to noncontrolling interests	(503)	(500)		
17	Net income attributable to The Walt Disney Company (Disney)	$ 7,501	$ 6,136		
18					

Walt Disney Company Consolidated Statement of Income for the year ended September 27, 2014, the company had annual revenues of $48.8 billion (line 5) and net income attributable to The Walt Disney Company of $7.5 billion (line 17). The Walt Disney Company today stands as an example of just how far a dream and a little imagination can take you!

The terms *revenue* and *net income* may be unfamiliar to you now, but after you read this chapter, you'll be able to use these and other business terms. Welcome to the world of accounting! ●

Most chapters of this book begin with an actual financial statement. In Chapters 1–3, our reference is the Consolidated Financial Statements of The Walt Disney Company, for the two years ended September 27, 2014, and September 28, 2013. The core of financial accounting revolves around these basic financial statements:

- Income statement (sometimes known as the statement of operations)
- Statement of retained earnings (usually included in the statement of stockholders' equity)
- Balance sheet (sometimes known as the statement of financial position)
- Statement of cash flows

Financial statements are the business documents that companies use to report the results of their activities to various user groups, which can include managers, investors, creditors, and regulatory agencies. In turn, these parties use the reported information to make a variety of decisions, such as whether to invest in or loan money to the company. To learn accounting, you must learn to focus on decisions.

In this chapter, we explain generally accepted accounting principles, their underlying assumptions and concepts, and the bodies responsible for issuing accounting standards. We discuss the judgment process that is necessary for making good accounting decisions. We also discuss the contents of the four basic financial statements that report the results of those decisions. In later chapters, we will explain in more detail how to construct the financial statements, as well as how user groups typically use the information contained in them to make business decisions.

LEARNING | OBJECTIVES

① **Explain** why accounting is the language of business

② **Explain and apply** underlying accounting concepts, assumptions, and principles

③ **Apply** the accounting equation to business organizations

④ **Evaluate** business operations through the financial statements

⑤ **Construct** financial statements and **analyze** the relationships among them

⑥ **Evaluate** business decisions ethically

» Try It in Excel®

You can access the most current annual report of The Walt Disney Company in Excel® format at **http://www.sec.gov**. Using the "FILINGS" link on the toolbar at the top of the home page, select "Company Filings Search." This will take you to the "EDGAR Company Filings" page. Type "Walt Disney" in the company name box, and select "Search." This will produce the "EDGAR Search Results" page showing the company name. Click on the "CIK" link beside the company name. This will pull up a list of the reports the company has filed with the Securities and Exchange Commission (SEC). Under the "Filing Type" box, type "10-K," and click the "Search" box. Form 10-K is the SEC form for the company's annual report. Find the year that you wish to view. Click on the "Interactive Data" box, which takes you to the "View Filing Data" page. Find and click on the "View Excel Document" link at the top of this page, and download the Excel file containing the selected 10-K report. Alternatively, you can click the listed section of the 10-K you would like to open.

The Walt Disney Company's managers make lots of decisions. What new ideas will bring about a new feature film? How can those ideas be incorporated into new features in the company's theme parks? Should the company acquire another television network or sell a radio network? Which character dolls are the hottest sellers—Mickey, Pluto, Donald, or Elsa from *Frozen*? Which theme parks are most and least profitable? Accounting information helps companies make these decisions.

Take a look at The Walt Disney Company's Consolidated Statements of Income on page 2. Focus on Net income attributable to The Walt Disney Company (line 17). Net income (profit) is the excess of revenues (net sales) over expenses. You can see that The Walt Disney Company earned $7,501 million of net income in the year ended September 27, 2014. That's good news because it means that The Walt Disney Company had $7.5 billion more revenues than expenses for the year.

The Walt Disney Company's Consolidated Statements of Income present more interesting news. Total revenue (line 5) increased by about 8.4% during the period compared with the previous year (from $45,041 million to $48,813 million). Furthermore, net income attributable to The Walt Disney Company increased by 22.2% (from $6,136 million to $7,501 million).

Suppose you have $10,000 to invest. What information would you need before deciding to invest that money in stock of The Walt Disney Company? Let's see how accounting works.

EXPLAIN WHY ACCOUNTING IS THE LANGUAGE OF BUSINESS

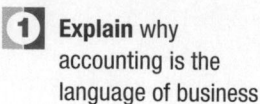

1 **Explain** why accounting is the language of business

Accounting is an information system. It measures business activities, processes data into reports, and communicates results to decision makers. Accounting is "the language of business." The better you understand the language, the better you can manage your finances, as well as those of your business.

Accounting produces financial statements, which report information about a business. The financial statements measure performance and communicate where a business stands in financial terms. In this chapter, as well as Chapters 2 and 3, we focus on The Walt Disney Company. After completing this chapter, you'll begin to understand the nature of financial statements and the relationships between them. By the end of Chapter 3, you'll understand the process by which a company's financial statements are prepared, called the **accounting cycle**.

Don't confuse bookkeeping and accounting. Bookkeeping is a mechanical part of accounting, just as arithmetic is a part of mathematics. Exhibit 1-1 below illustrates the flow of accounting information and helps illustrate accounting's role in business. The accounting process begins and ends with people making decisions.

Who Uses Accounting Information?

Decision makers use many types of information; a banker needs information to decide who gets a loan or The Walt Disney Company uses accounting information, along with designs and plans from its "imagineers" (designers and engineers) to decide the size and location of a new theme park attraction. Let's see how decision makers use accounting information.

- *Individuals.* People like you manage their personal bank accounts, decide whether to rent an apartment or buy a house, and budget the monthly income and expenditures of their businesses. Accounting provides the necessary information to allow individuals to make these decisions.

- *Investors and creditors.* Investors and creditors provide the money to finance The Walt Disney Company. Investors want to know how much income they can expect to earn on an investment. Creditors want to know when and how The Walt Disney Company is going to pay them back. These decisions also require accounting information.

- *Regulatory bodies.* All kinds of regulatory bodies use accounting information. For example, the Internal Revenue Service (IRS) and various state and local governments require businesses, individuals, and other types of organizations to pay income, property, excise,

Exhibit 1-1 | The Flow of Accounting Information

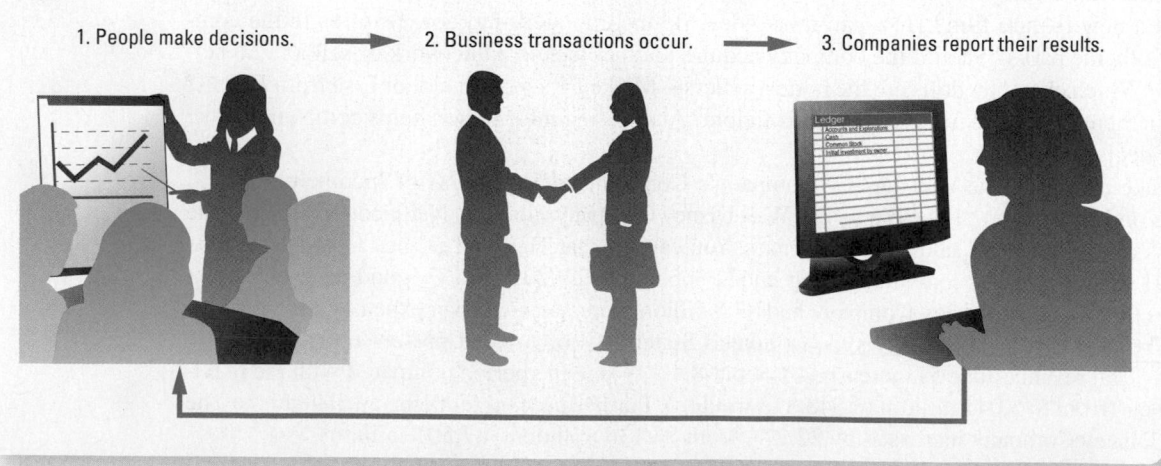

1. People make decisions. → 2. Business transactions occur. → 3. Companies report their results.

and other taxes. The SEC requires companies with publicly-traded stock to provide it with many kinds of periodic financial reports. All of these reports contain accounting information.

■ *Nonprofit organizations.* Nonprofit organizations—churches, hospitals, and charities such as Habitat for Humanity and the Red Cross—base many of their operating decisions on accounting data. In addition, these organizations have to file periodic reports of their activities with the IRS and state governments, even though they may owe no taxes.

Two Kinds of Accounting: Financial Accounting and Management Accounting

Both *external* and *internal users* of accounting information exist. We can therefore classify accounting into two branches.

Financial accounting provides information for decision makers outside the entity, such as investors, creditors, government agencies, and the public. This information must be relevant for the needs of decision makers and must faithfully give an accurate picture of the entity's economic activities. This textbook focuses on financial accounting.

Management accounting provides information for managers of The Walt Disney Company. Examples of management accounting information include budgets, forecasts, and projections that are used in making the strategic decisions of the entity. Internal information must still be accurate and relevant for the decision needs of managers. Management accounting is covered in a separate course that usually follows this one.

Organizing a Business

Accounting is used in every type of business. A business generally takes one of the following forms:

■ Proprietorship

■ Partnership

■ Limited-liability company (LLC)

■ Corporation

Exhibit 1-2 compares different ways to organize a business.

Exhibit 1-2 | The Various Forms of Business Organization

	Proprietorship	Partnership	LLC	Corporation
1. *Owner(s)*	Proprietor—one owner	Partners—two or more owners	Members	Stockholders—generally many owners
2. *Personal liability of owner(s) for business's debts*	Proprietor is personally liable	General partners are personally liable; limited partners are not	Members are *not* personally liable	Stockholders are *not* personally liable

Proprietorship. A **proprietorship** has a single owner, called the proprietor. Walt Disney started his work as a sole-proprietor animator working out of his home. Proprietorships tend to be small retail stores or solo providers of professional services—physicians, attorneys, artists, or accountants. Legally, the business *is* the proprietor, and the proprietor is personally liable for all the business's debts. But for accounting purposes, a proprietorship is a distinct entity, separate from its proprietor. Thus, the business records should not include the proprietor's personal finances.

Partnership. A **partnership** has two or more parties as co-owners, and each owner is a partner. Individuals, corporations, partnerships, or other types of entities can be partners. Income and losses of the partnership "flow through" to the partners, and they recognize them based on their agreed-upon percentage interest in the business. The partnership is not a tax-paying entity. Instead, each partner takes a proportionate share of the entity's taxable income and pays tax according to that partner's individual or corporate rate. Many retail establishments, professional service firms (law, accounting, etc.), real estate, and oil and gas exploration companies operate as partnerships. Many partnerships are small or medium-sized, but some are gigantic, with thousands of partners. Partnerships are governed by agreement, usually spelled out in writing in the form of a contract between the partners. General partnerships have mutual agency and unlimited liability, meaning that each partner may conduct business in the name of the entity and can make agreements that legally bind all partners without limit for the partnership's debts. Partnerships are therefore quite risky because an irresponsible partner can create large debts for the other general partners without their knowledge or permission. This feature of general partnerships has spawned the creation of limited-liability partnerships (LLPs).

A *limited-liability partnership* is one in which a wayward partner cannot create a large liability for the other partners. In LLPs, each partner is liable for partnership debts only up to the extent of his or her investment in the partnership. Each LLP, however, must have one general partner with unlimited liability for all partnership debts.

Limited-Liability Company. A **limited-liability company (LLC)** is one in which the business (and not the owner) is liable for the company's debts. An LLC may have one owner or many owners, called *members*. Unlike a proprietorship or a general partnership, the members of an LLC do *not* have unlimited liability for the LLC's debts. An LLC pays no business income tax. Instead, the LLC's income "flows through" to the members, and they pay income tax at their own tax rates, just as they would if they were partners. Today, many multiple-owner businesses are organized as LLCs, because members of an LLC effectively enjoy limited liability while still being taxed like members of a partnership.

Corporation. A **corporation** is a business owned by the **stockholders**, or **shareholders**, who own **stock** representing shares of ownership in the corporation. One of the major advantages of doing business in the corporate form is the ability to raise large sums of capital from the issuance of stock to the public. All types of entities (individuals, partnerships, corporations, or other types) may be shareholders in a corporation. Even though proprietorships and partnerships are more numerous, corporations transact much more business and are larger in terms of assets, income, and number of employees. Most well-known companies, such as The Walt Disney Company, Amazon.com, Inc., Google, Inc., General Motors Company, Toyota Motor Corporation, and Apple Inc., are corporations. Their full names include *Corporation* or *Incorporated* (abbreviated as *Corp.* and *Inc.*) to indicate that they are corporations—for example, Starbucks Corporation. A few bear the name *Company*, such as Ford Motor Company or The Walt Disney Company.

A corporation is formed under state law. Unlike proprietorships and partnerships, a corporation is legally distinct from its owners. The corporation is like an artificial person and possesses many of the same rights that a person has. The stockholders have no personal obligation for the corporation's debts. So, stockholders of a corporation have limited liability, as do limited partners and members of an LLC. However, unlike partnerships or LLCs, a corporation pays a business income tax as well as many other types of taxes. Furthermore, the shareholders of a corporation are effectively taxed twice on distributions received from the corporation (called dividends). Thus, one of the major disadvantages of the corporate form of business is *double taxation of distributed profits.*

Ultimate control of a corporation rests with the stockholders, who generally get one vote for each share of stock they own. Stockholders elect the **board of directors**, which sets policy and appoints officers. The board elects a chairperson, who holds the most power in the corporation and often carries the title chief executive officer (CEO); it also appoints the president as chief operating officer (COO). Corporations have vice presidents in charge of sales, accounting, finance (the chief financial officer or CFO), and other key areas.

EXPLAIN AND APPLY UNDERLYING ACCOUNTING CONCEPTS, ASSUMPTIONS, AND PRINCIPLES

Accountants follow professional frameworks for measurement and disclosure of financial information. The most common of these frameworks is called **generally accepted accounting principles (GAAP)**. In the United States, the **Financial Accounting Standards Board (FASB)** formulates GAAP. The **International Accounting Standards Board (IASB)** sets global—or international—financial reporting standards (IFRS), as discussed later in this section.

Exhibit 1-3 gives an overview of the joint conceptual framework of accounting developed by the FASB and the IASB. Financial reporting standards (whether U.S. or international), at the bottom, follow this conceptual framework. The overall *objective* of accounting is to provide financial information about the reporting entity that is useful to existing and potential investors, lenders, and other creditors in making decisions about providing resources to the entity.

To be useful, information must have the fundamental qualitative characteristics, which include

- relevance, and
- faithful representation.

To be relevant, information must be capable of making a difference to the decision maker, in helping them to predict or confirm value. In addition, the information must be *material*, which means it must be important enough to the informed user so that, if it were omitted or incorrect, it would make a difference in the user's decision. Only information that is material needs to be separately *disclosed* (listed or discussed) in the financial statements. If not material, it does not need separate disclosure but may be combined with other information. To make a faithful representation, the information must be complete, neutral (free from bias), and free from error (accurate). Accounting information must focus on the *economic substance* of a transaction, event, or circumstance, which may or may not always be the same as its legal form. Faithful representation makes the information *reliable* to users.

2 **Explain and apply** underlying accounting concepts, assumptions, and principles

Exhibit 1-3 | Conceptual Foundation of Accounting

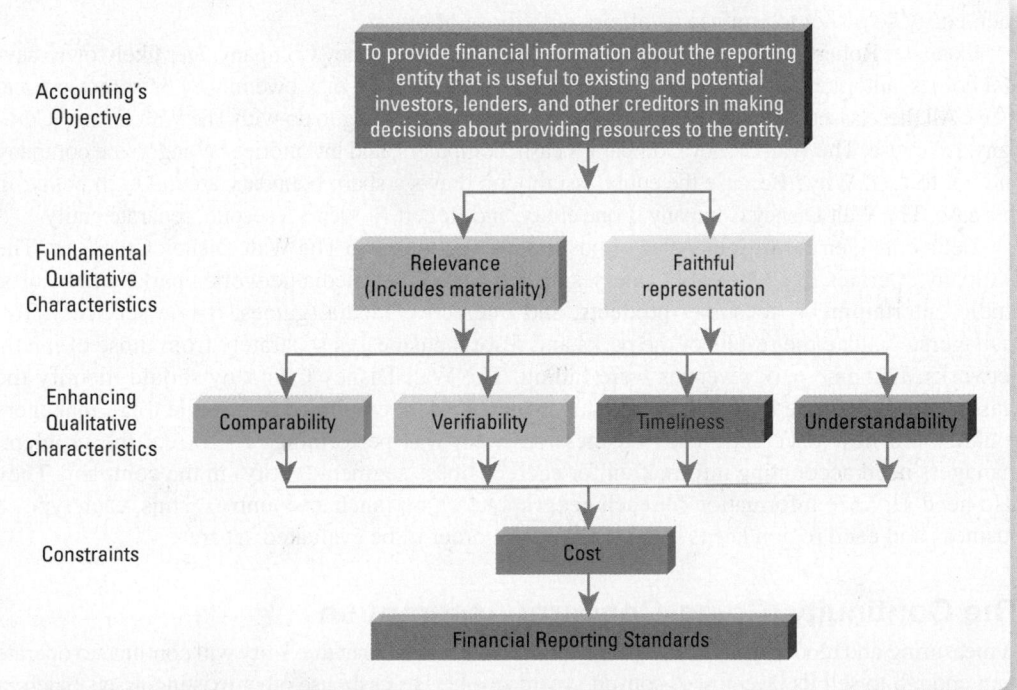

Based on Financial Accounting Standards Board (FASB) and International Accounting Standards Board (IASB), *Joint Conceptual Framework for Reporting* (2010).

Accounting information must also have a number of *enhancing or supplementary qualitative characteristics*. These include

- comparability,
- verifiability,
- timeliness, and
- understandability.

Comparability means that the accounting information for a company must be prepared in such a way as to be capable of being compared with information from other companies in the same period; it should also be *consistent* with similar information for that company in previous periods. *Verifiability* means that the information must be capable of being checked for accuracy, completeness, and reliability. The process of verifying information is often done by *internal* as well as *external auditors*. Verifiability enhances the reliability of information and thus makes the information more representative of economic reality. *Timeliness* means that the information must be made available to users early enough to help them make decisions, thus making the information more relevant to their needs. *Understandability* means the information must be sufficiently transparent so that it makes sense to reasonably informed users of the information (investors, creditors, regulatory agencies, and managers).

Accounting information is costly to produce. A primary constraint in the decision to disclose accounting information is that the *cost of disclosure should not exceed the expected benefits* to users. The management of an entity is primarily responsible for preparing accounting information. Managers must exercise judgment in determining whether the information is necessary for a complete understanding of economic facts and is not excessively costly to provide.

This course will expose you to GAAP as well as to relevant IFRS. We summarize GAAP in Appendix D and IFRS in Appendix E. In the following section, we briefly summarize some of the basic assumptions and principles that underlie the application of these standards.

The Entity Assumption

The most basic accounting assumption (underlying idea) is the **entity**, which is any organization (or person) that stands apart as a separate economic unit. Sharp boundaries are drawn around each entity so as not to confuse its affairs with those of others.

Consider Robert A. Iger, chairman and CEO of The Walt Disney Company. Iger likely owns several homes, automobiles, and other personal assets. In addition, he may owe money on some personal loans. All these assets and liabilities belong to Iger and have nothing to do with The Walt Disney Company. Likewise, The Walt Disney Company's cash, computers, and inventories belong to the company and not to Iger. Why? Because the entity assumption draws a sharp boundary around each entity; in this case, The Walt Disney Company is one entity, and Robert A. Iger is a second, separate entity.

Let's consider the various types of businesses that make up The Walt Disney Company. The company operates five types of businesses, called **segments**: media networks, parks and resorts, studio entertainment, consumer products, and interactive media (games, online services). Top managers evaluate the results of the parks and resorts businesses separately from those of media networks. If theme park revenues were falling, The Walt Disney Company should identify the reason. But if revenue figures from all the businesses were combined in a single total, managers couldn't tell how differently each business segment was performing. To correct the problem, managers need accounting information for each business segment (entity) in the company. They also need separate information for each geographic region (such as country). Thus, each type of business and each region keeps its own records in order to be evaluated separately.

The Continuity (Going-Concern) Assumption

In measuring and reporting accounting information, we assume that the entity will continue to operate long enough to sell its inventories, convert any receivables to cash, use other existing assets (such as land, buildings, equipment, and supplies) for their intended purposes, and settle its obligations in the normal course of business. This is called the **continuity (or going-concern) assumption**.

Consider the alternative to the **going-concern assumption**: the quitting concern, or going out of business assumption. An entity that is not continuing would have to sell all of its assets in the process. In that case, the most *relevant* measure of the value of the assets would be their liquidating values (or the amount the company can receive for the assets when sold in order to go out of business). But going out of business is the exception rather than the rule. Therefore, the continuity assumption says that a business should stay in business long enough to convert its inventories and receivables to cash and pay off its obligations in the ordinary course of business, and to continue this process of operating into the future.

The Historical Cost Principle

The **historical cost principle** states that assets should be recorded at their *actual cost*, measured on the date of purchase as the amount of cash paid plus the fair market value of all noncash considerations (other assets, privileges, or rights) also given in exchange. For example, suppose The Walt Disney Company purchases a building for a new Disney Store. The building's current owner is asking $6,000,000 for the building. The management of The Walt Disney Company believes the building is worth $5,850,000 and offers the present owner that amount. Two real estate professionals appraise the building at $6,100,000. The buyer and seller compromise and agree on a price of $5,900,000 for the building. The historical cost principle requires The Walt Disney Company to initially record the building at its actual cost of $5,900,000—not at $5,850,000, $6,000,000, or $6,100,000, even though those amounts were what some people believed the building was worth. At the point of purchase, $5,900,000 is both the *relevant* amount for the building's worth and the amount that *faithfully represents* a reliable figure for the price the company paid for it.

The *historical cost principle* and the *continuity assumption* (discussed previously) also maintain that The Walt Disney Company's accounting records should continue to use historical cost to value the asset for as long as the business holds it. Why? Because cost is a *verifiable* measure that is relatively *free from bias*. Suppose that The Walt Disney Company owns the building for six years. Real estate prices increase during this period. As a result, at the end of the period, the building can be sold for $6,500,000. Should The Walt Disney Company increase the carrying value of the building on the company's books to $6,500,000? No. According to the historical cost principle, the building remains on The Walt Disney Company's books at its historical cost of $5,900,000, less accumulated depreciation. According to the continuity assumption, The Walt Disney Company intends to stay in business and use the building, not to sell it, so its historical cost is the most relevant and the most faithful representation of its carrying value. It is also the most easily verifiable (auditable) amount. Should the company decide to sell the building later at a price above or below its carrying value, it will record the cash received, remove the carrying value of the building from the books, and record a gain or a loss for the difference at that time.

Although the historical cost principle is used widely in the United States to value certain assets, accounting is moving in the direction of reporting more assets and liabilities at their fair values. **Fair value** is the amount that the business could sell the asset for, or the amount that the business could pay to settle the liability. The FASB has issued guidance for companies to report many assets and liabilities at fair values.[1] Moreover, in recent years, the FASB has agreed to "harmonize" GAAP with IFRS. IFRS generally allow for broader measurement of different types of assets with fair values than GAAP, which may cause more assets to be revalued periodically to fair market values. We will discuss the trend toward globalization of accounting standards on the next page, and we will illustrate it in later chapters throughout the book.

The Stable-Monetary-Unit Assumption

In the United States, we record transactions in dollars because that is our medium of exchange. British accountants record transactions in pounds sterling, Japanese in yen, and some continental Europeans in euros.

---

[1] In 2013, the American Institute of Certified Public Accountants (AICPA) adopted a separate "financial reporting framework for small and medium-sized entities" (FRF-SME) that avoids some of the complexities of full-blown GAAP. Many SMEs are owner managed and prepare financial statements mostly for the use of their bankers, who do not require all of the complex disclosures of GAAP. FRF-SME is less complicated than GAAP, and, while it requires accrual accounting, it emphasizes use of historical cost more than fair values for assets. Most of the principles we employ in this text are applicable to both FRF-SMEs and GAAP. Accrual accounting is discussed in Chapter 3.

Unlike a liter or a mile, the value of a dollar changes over time. A rise in the general price level is called *inflation*. During inflation, a dollar will purchase less food, less toothpaste, and less of other goods and services. When prices are stable—there is little inflation—a dollar's purchasing power is also stable.

Under the **stable-monetary-unit assumption**, accountants assume that the dollar's purchasing power is stable over time. We ignore inflation, and this allows us to add and subtract dollar amounts as though the dollar over successive years has a consistent amount of purchasing power. This is important because businesses that report their financial information publicly usually report comparative financial information (that is, the current year along with one or more prior years). If we could not assume a stable monetary unit, assets and liabilities denominated in prior years' dollars would have to be adjusted to current year price levels. Inflation has been at very low levels in developed countries for several decades and is expected to remain so for the foreseeable future. Thus, inflation adjustments to accounting information to make it comparable over time are not considered necessary.

GLOBAL VIEW

International Financial Reporting Standards We live in a global economy! Investors in the United States can easily trade stocks on the Hong Kong, London, and Brussels stock exchanges over the Internet. Each year, American companies such as Starbucks Corporation, The Gap, Inc., McDonalds Corp., Microsoft Corp., and The Walt Disney Company conduct billions of dollars of business around the globe. Conversely, foreign companies such as Nokia, Samsung, Toyota, and Nestlé conduct billions of dollars of business in the United States. American companies have merged with foreign companies to create international conglomerates such as Pearson (the publisher of this textbook) and Anheuser-Busch InBev (producers of alcoholic beverages). No matter where your career starts, it is very likely that it will eventually take you into global markets.

Until recently, one of the major challenges of conducting global business has been the fact that different countries have adopted different accounting standards for business transactions. Historically, the major developed countries in the world (United States, United Kingdom, Japan, Germany, etc.) have all had their own versions of GAAP. As investors seek to compare financial results across entities from different countries, they have had to restate and convert accounting data from one country to the next in order to make them comparable. This takes time and can be expensive.

The solution to this problem lies with the IASB, which has developed the International Financial Reporting Standards (IFRS). These standards are now being used by most countries around the world. For years, accountants in the United States did not pay much attention to IFRS because our GAAP was considered to be the strongest single set of accounting standards in the world. In addition, the application of GAAP for public companies in the United States is overseen carefully by the SEC, a body that at present has no global counterpart.

Nevertheless, in order to promote consistency in global financial reporting, the SEC is studying whether and how to require all U.S. public companies to adopt some version of IFRS within the next decade. The advantage to adopting a uniform set of high-quality global accounting standards is that financial statements from a U.S. company (say, Hershey Corporation in Pennsylvania) will be comparable to those of a foreign company (say, Nestlé in Switzerland). Using these standards, it will be easier for investors and businesspeople to evaluate information of various companies in the same industries from across the globe, and companies will have to prepare only one set of financial statements instead of multiple versions. Thus, in the long run, a uniform set of high-quality global accounting standards should significantly reduce costs of doing business globally.

Does this mean that the accounting information you are studying in this textbook will eventually become outdated? Fortunately, no. For one thing, the vast majority of the introductory material you learn from this textbook, including the underlying conceptual framework outlined in this section, is *already* part of IFRS as well. The most commonly used accounting practices are essentially the same under both U.S. GAAP and IFRS. Additionally, the FASB is working hand-in-hand with the IASB toward the *convergence* of standards, that is, gradually adjusting both sets of standards to more closely align them over time so that, if transition to IFRS in the United States ever occurs, it will occur smoothly. At the time of the publication of this text, there are still some areas of disagreement between U.S. GAAP and IFRS. For example, certain widely accepted U.S. practices, such as the use of the last-in, first-out (LIFO) inventory costing method (discussed in Chapter 6), are disallowed under IFRS. Other differences exist as well, which must be resolved before IFRS can be fully adopted in the United States.

In general, the main difference between U.S. GAAP and IFRS is that U.S. GAAP has become rather "rules based" over its long history, while IFRS (not in existence as long) allows more professional judgment on the part of companies. One other major difference between IFRS and U.S. GAAP lies in the valuation of long-term assets (plant assets and intangibles) and liabilities. In U.S. GAAP, the historical cost principle tells us to value assets at historical cost. In contrast, IFRS prefers a more fair-value approach, which reports assets and liabilities on the balance sheet at their up-to-date values rather than at historical cost. This may seem like a big difference, but U.S. GAAP already allows for a partial fair-value approach with rules such as lower-of-cost-or-market, accounting for the impairment of long-term assets, and adjusting certain investments to fair values. We cover these concepts in more depth in later chapters.

Throughout the remainder of this textbook, in chapters that cover concepts where major differences between U.S. GAAP and IFRS exist, we will discuss those differences. Because this is an introductory textbook in financial accounting, our discussion will be brief in order to focus on the differences that are relevant for this course. Appendix E includes a table, cross-referenced by chapter, that summarizes all of these differences, as well as their impacts on financial statements once IFRS is fully adopted.

You can expect to hear more about the global harmonization of accounting standards in the future. When you do, the most important things to remember will be that these changes will be beneficial for financial statement users in the long run and that most of what you learned in this accounting course will still apply. Remember that there are far more areas of common ground than of disagreement. Whatever may come, your knowledge of international accounting principles will benefit you in the future. The globalization of the world economy provides a wonderful opportunity for you to succeed in the business world.

APPLY THE ACCOUNTING EQUATION TO BUSINESS ORGANIZATIONS

The Walt Disney Company's financial statements tell us how the business is performing and where it stands. But how do we arrive at the financial statements? Let's examine the *elements of financial statements*, which are the building blocks from which statements are made.

 Apply the accounting equation to business organizations

Assets and Liabilities

The financial statements are based on the **accounting equation**. This equation presents the resources of a company and the claims to those resources.

■ **Assets** are economic resources that are expected to produce a benefit in the future. The Walt Disney Company's cash, receivables, inventory, attractions, buildings, and equipment are examples of assets.

Claims on assets come from two sources:

■ **Liabilities** are "outsider claims." They are debts that are payable to outsiders, called *creditors*. For example, a creditor who has loaned money to The Walt Disney Company has a claim—a legal right—to a part of The Walt Disney Company's assets until the company repays the debt.

■ **Owners' equity** (also called **capital**, **equity**, or **stockholders' equity** for a corporation) represents the "insider claims" of a business. Equity means ownership, so The Walt Disney Company's equity is the stockholders' interest in the assets of the corporation.

The accounting equation shows the relationship among assets, liabilities, and owners' equity. Assets appear on the left side and liabilities and owners' equity on the right. As Exhibit 1-4 shows, the two sides must be equal:

Exhibit 1-4 | The Accounting Equation

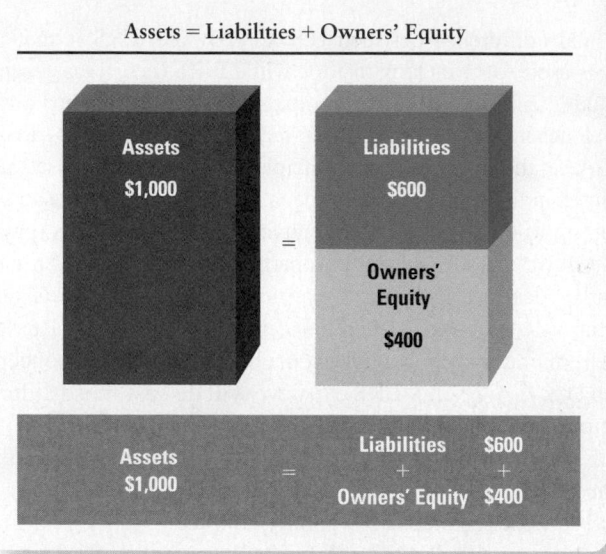

What are some of The Walt Disney Company's assets? The first asset is *cash and cash equivalents*, the liquid assets that are the medium of exchange. Another important asset is merchandise inventory (often called inventories)—the consumer products—that The Walt Disney Company's stores sell. The Walt Disney Company also has assets in the form of *parks*, *resorts*, and *equipment*, or *fixed assets*. These are the long-lived assets the company uses to do business—theme park attractions (rides), buildings, computers, and other equipment.

The Walt Disney Company's liabilities include a number of payables, such as accounts payable and accrued liabilities. The word *payable* always signifies a liability. An account payable is a liability for goods or services purchased on credit and supported by the credit standing of the purchaser. Accounts payable typically have to be paid within 30 to 60 days. **Long-term debt** (borrowings) is a liability that's payable beyond one year from the date of the financial statements. The *current portion of long-term debt (borrowings)* is the amount due within the next year, and it has to be disclosed separately in current liabilities.

Owners' Equity

The owners' equity of any business is its assets minus its liabilities. We can write the accounting equation to show that owners' equity is what's left over when we subtract liabilities from assets.

$$\text{Assets} - \text{Liabilities} = \text{Owners' Equity}$$

A corporation's equity—called stockholders' equity—has two main subparts:

- Paid-in capital
- Retained earnings

The accounting equation can be written as

$$\text{Assets} = \text{Liabilities} + \text{Stockholders' Equity}$$
$$\text{Assets} = \text{Liabilities} + \text{Paid-in Capital} + \text{Retained Earnings}$$

- **Paid-in capital** is the amount the stockholders have invested in the corporation. The basic component of paid-in capital is **common stock**, which the corporation issues to the stockholders as evidence of their ownership. All corporations have common stock.

- **Retained earnings** is the amount earned by income-producing activities and kept for use in the business. Three major types of transactions affect retained earnings: revenues, expenses, and dividends.

- **Revenues** are inflows of resources that increase retained earnings by delivering goods or services to customers. For example, sales of admissions to theme parks brings in revenue and increases The Walt Disney Company's retained earnings.

- **Expenses** are resource outflows that decrease retained earnings due to operations. For example, the wages that The Walt Disney Company pays employees are an expense and decrease retained earnings. Expenses represent the costs of doing business; they are the opposite of revenues. Expenses include cost of services or products sold, building rent, salaries, and utility payments. Expenses also include the depreciation of attractions and buildings held as fixed assets, and other equipment.

- **Dividends** decrease retained earnings, because they are distributions to stockholders of assets (usually cash) generated by operating activities. A successful business may pay dividends to shareholders as a return on their investments. Remember: **dividends are not expenses. Dividends never affect net income. Instead of being subtracted from revenues to compute net income, dividends are recorded as direct reductions of retained earnings.**

Businesses strive for *profits,* the excess of revenues over expenses.

- When total revenues exceed total expenses, the result is called **net income**, **net earnings**, or **net profit**.

- When total expenses exceed total revenues, the result is a **net loss**.

- Net income or net loss is the "bottom line" on an income statement. The Walt Disney Company's bottom line reports net income attributable to The Walt Disney Company for the year ended September 27, 2014, of $7,501 million (line 17 on the Consolidated Statements of Income on page 15).

Exhibit 1-5 shows the relationships among the following:

- Retained earnings
- Revenues − Expenses = Net income (or net loss)
- Dividends

Exhibit 1-5 | The Components of Retained Earnings

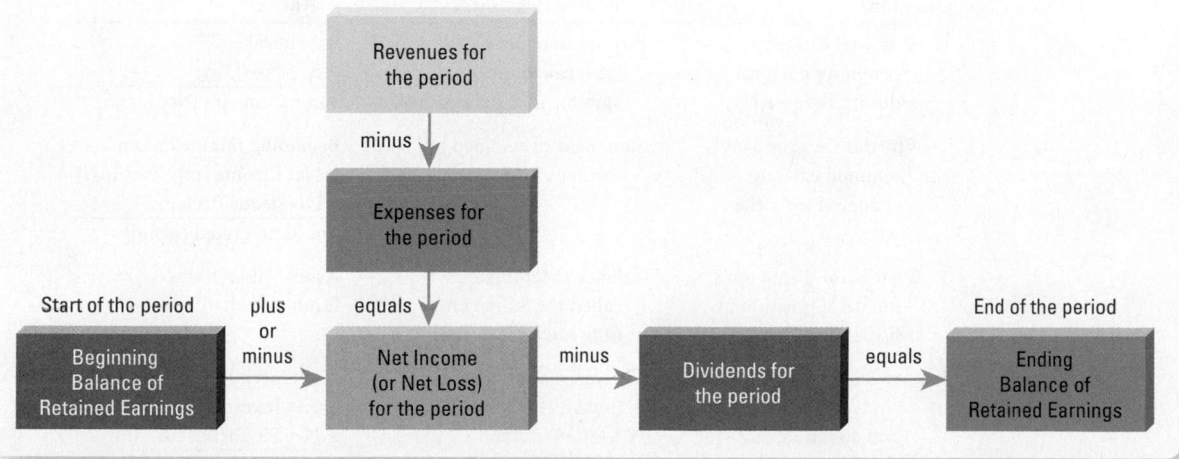

The owners' equity of proprietorships and partnerships is different from that of corporations. Proprietorships and partnerships don't identify paid-in capital and retained earnings separately. Instead, they use a single heading: Capital. Examples include "Randall Waller, Capital" (for a proprietorship) and "Powers, Capital" and "Salazar, Capital" (for a partnership).

(1) If the assets of a business are $480,000 and the liabilities are $160,000, how much is the owners' equity?

(2) If the owners' equity in a business is $160,000 and the liabilities are $100,000, how much are the assets?

(3) A company reported monthly revenues of $365,000 and monthly expenses of $225,000. What is the result of operations for the month?

(4) If the beginning balance of retained earnings is $180,000, revenue is $85,000, expenses total $35,000, and the company declares and pays a $20,000 dividend, what is the ending balance of retained earnings?

Answers:

(1) $320,000 ($480,000 − $160,000)

(2) $260,000 ($160,000 + $100,000)

(3) Net income of $140,000 ($365,000 − $225,000); revenues minus expenses

(4) $210,000 [$180,000 beginning balance + net income $50,000 ($85,000 − $35,000) − dividends $20,000]

EVALUATE BUSINESS OPERATIONS THROUGH THE FINANCIAL STATEMENTS

4 Evaluate business operations through the financial statements

The financial statements present a company to the public in financial terms. Each financial statement relates to a specific date or time period. What would investors want to know about The Walt Disney Company at the end of its fiscal year? Exhibit 1-6 lists four questions that decision makers may ask. Each answer comes from one of the financial statements.

Exhibit 1-6 | Information Reported in the Financial Statements

Question	Financial Statement	Answer
1. How well did the company perform during the year?	Income statement (also called the Statement of operations)	Revenues − Expenses Net income (or Net loss)
2. Why did the company's retained earnings change during the year?	Statement of retained earnings	Beginning retained earnings + Net income (or − Net loss) − Dividends declared Ending retained earnings
3. What is the company's financial position at fiscal year end?	Balance sheet (also called the Statement of financial position)	Assets = Liabilities + Owners' Equity
4. How much cash did the company generate and spend during the year?	Statement of cash flows	Net Operating cash flows ± Net Investing cash flows ± Net Financing cash flows Increase (decrease) in cash

To learn how to use financial statements, let's work through The Walt Disney Company's financial statements for the year ended September 27, 2014. The following diagram shows how the data flow from one financial statement to the next. The order is important.

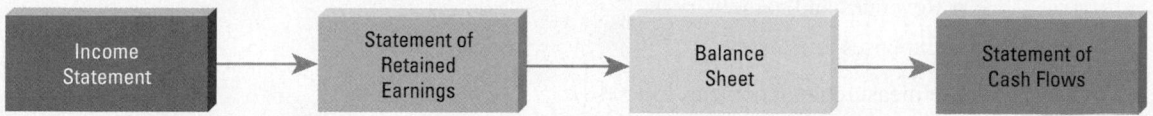

We begin with the income statement in Exhibit 1-7.

The Income Statement Measures Operating Performance

The **income statement**, or **statement of operations**, reports revenues and expenses for the period. The bottom line is net income or net loss *for the period*. At the top of Exhibit 1-7 is the company's name: The Walt Disney Company. On the second line is the term "Consolidated Statements of Income."

The Walt Disney Company is actually made up of several corporations that are owned by a common group of shareholders. Commonly controlled corporations like this are required to combine, or consolidate, all of their revenues, expenses, assets, liabilities, and stockholders' equity and to report them all as one.

The dates of The Walt Disney Company's Consolidated Statements of Income are 12 months ended September 27, 2014, and 12 months ended September 28, 2013. The Walt Disney Company, like many retailers, uses a *fiscal year* consisting of the 52 weeks ending closest to September 30 as the accounting year. This is because the summer vacation season is the busiest time of the year for the company, while September is typically a slower month, allowing the company time to get its books in order. Companies often adopt a fiscal year that ends at the low point of their operations. Whole Foods Market, Inc., uses a fiscal year consisting of the 52 weeks ending closest to September 30. FedEx Corp.'s fiscal year-end falls on May 31. Alternatively, about 60% of the largest companies, such as Amazon.com, Inc., use a fiscal year corresponding to the calendar year.

The Walt Disney Company's Consolidated Statements of Income in Exhibit 1-7 report the results of its operations for two fiscal years in order to show trends for revenues, expenses, and

Exhibit 1-7 | The Walt Disney Company, Consolidated Statements of Income

	A	B	C	D	E
	The Walt Disney Company	Fiscal 2014	Fiscal 2013		
1	Consolidated Statements of Income	12 Months Ended			
2	Adapted, in millions of $	Sep. 27, 2014	Sep. 28, 2013		
3	Services revenue	$ 40,246	$ 37,280		
4	Products revenue	8,567	7,761		
5	Total revenues	48,813	45,041		
6	Cost of services (exclusive of depreciation and amortization)	(21,356)	(20,090)		
7	Cost of products (exclusive of depreciation and amortization)	(5,064)	(4,944)		
8	Selling, general, administrative, and other	(8,565)	(8,365)		
9	Depreciation and amortization	(2,288)	(2,192)		
10	Total costs and expenses	(37,273)	(35,591)		
11	Income from operations	11,540	9,450		
12	Other income (expense), net	706	170		
13	Income before income taxes	12,246	9,620		
14	Income taxes	(4,242)	(2,984)		
15	Net income	8,004	6,636		
16	Less: Net income attributable to noncontrolling interests	(503)	(500)		
17	Net income attributable to The Walt Disney Company (Disney)	$ 7,501	$ 6,136		
18					

net income. To avoid clutter, The Walt Disney Company reports its results in millions of dollars. Some relatively simple analysis of the company's consolidated statements of income will help us evaluate how well the company performed in fiscal 2014 in comparison with fiscal 2013.

An income statement reports two main categories:

- Revenues and gains
- Expenses and losses

We measure net income as follows:

$$\text{Net Income} = \text{Total Revenues and Gains} - \text{Total Expenses and Losses}$$

In accounting, the word *net* refers to an amount after a subtraction. *Net* income is the profit left over after subtracting expenses and losses from revenues and gains. **Net income is the single most important item in the financial statements.**

Overall, during the fiscal year ended September 27, 2014, The Walt Disney Company earned total revenues of $48,813 million (line 5). The company earned net income attributable to The Walt Disney Company (line 17) of $7,501 million.

Revenues. The Walt Disney Company earns significant revenues from performing services as well as selling products. Services revenue is generated in its media networks, parks and resorts, studio entertainment, and interactive divisions. Product sales revenue is generated in its consumer products division. In order to present a clearer picture of its results of operations, the company reports each of these revenue streams separately. For the fiscal year ended September 27, 2014, services revenue (line 3) accounts for 82.4% of the company's total revenue ($40,246 million ÷ $48,813 million, on line 5). Products revenue (line 4) comprises 17.6% of total revenue for the year ($8,567 million ÷ $48,813 million). During the fiscal year ended September 27, 2014, services revenue increased about 8% over fiscal 2013, from $37,280 million to $40,246 million. Products revenue increased about 10.4% over fiscal 2013, from $7,761 million to $8,567 million. From these computations you can tell that services revenue dominates the total revenue stream of the company, but products revenue has grown faster over the last year than services revenue.

Expenses. Not all expenses have the word *expense* in their titles. For example, The Walt Disney Company's largest expenses are for cost of services and cost of products (lines 6 and 7, respectively). In line 6, The Walt Disney Company includes the direct cost of providing services (exclusive of depreciation and amortization) through its media networks, parks and resorts, studio entertainment, and interactive business segments. Examples of cost of services include labor and materials directly related to each service segment's revenue. Line 6 reports that cost of services in fiscal 2014 was $21,356 million (up 6.3% from the 2013 cost of services of $20,090 million). Comparing the year-to-year increase in services revenue discussed in the preceding paragraph, we see that service revenue in fiscal 2014 increased at a faster pace (about 8%) than the cost of those services (about 6.3%). This means that the services business segments of The Walt Disney Company were more profitable in 2014 than they were in 2013. Although not shown separately in Exhibit 1-7, you can measure the **gross profit** from services by subtracting cost of services from services revenue. In fiscal 2014, the gross profit from services was $18,890 million ($40,246 million − $21,356 million). In fiscal 2013, the gross profit from services was $17,190 million ($37,280 million − $20,090 million). Thus, gross profit of the services segment rose by $1,700 million or 9.9%.

Line 7 reports that the cost of products in fiscal 2014 was $5,064 million (up $120 million, or 2.4%) from $4,944 million in fiscal 2013. Comparing this small increase of 2.4% in costs with the 10.4% increase in product revenue, we can see why the company's profits from the sale of products increased more dramatically than those from services during the year. Gross profit from sale of products (products revenue minus related cost of products) increased from $2,817 million ($7,761 million − $4,944 million) in fiscal 2013 to $3,503 million ($8,567 million − $5,064 million) in fiscal 2014, an increase of $686 million, or 24.4%. From this analysis, we can conclude that, although the services segments of the business dominated in terms of the company's total revenue (82.4% vs. 17.6%), gross profits from the products segments grew at a much faster pace during 2014 than those from the services segment (24.4% vs. 9.9%).

Pat yourself on the back! You're beginning to understand financial statement analysis! The Walt Disney Company has some other categories of expenses.

- **Selling, general, administrative and other expenses** (line 8) are the costs of everyday operations that are not directly related to performing services or selling products. Many expenses may be included in this category, including salaries paid to administrative employees, information technology, warehousing expenses, executive salaries, and other general operating expenses. These expenses amounted to $8,565 million during fiscal 2014, up about 2.4% from fiscal 2013 ($8,365 million).

- **Depreciation and amortization** (line 9). The Walt Disney Company has invested billions of dollars in fixed assets (which the company calls attractions, buildings, and equipment). Examples are all of the buildings and attractions (rides) at Disney's 11 theme parks, as well as the 39 hotels that it owns. These assets are reported at historical cost on the company's balance sheet (see Exhibit 1-9, line 11). **Depreciation** is a process that allocates a portion of the cost of these assets over their estimated useful lives against the revenues the assets help to generate. Depreciation is discussed in greater depth in Chapters 3 and 7. **Amortization** is a process similar to depreciation, except that it applies to certain other long-term tangible and intangible assets, as well as certain liabilities. These amounts are initially recorded as assets and liabilities on the balance sheet, and are allocated as amortization expense to the time periods affected by them. Amortization is discussed in greater depth in Chapters 7 and 9. Depreciation and amortization was $2,288 million in fiscal 2014 and $2,192 million in fiscal 2013.

- **Income from Operations** (line 11). The difference between all operating revenues and all operating expenses is called income from operations. This is a very important number on the income statement because it communicates whether the company's core business operations were profitable or not. Income from operations is the best predictor of future profitability of the company. If income from operations is trending on a steady path upward, it is a sign that the company's earnings are of high quality. We will study this concept further in Chapter 11.

- **Other income (expense), net** (line 12) was $706 million for fiscal 2014 and $170 million for fiscal 2013. This line includes some items that are too small for the company to report separately. According to the financial statement footnotes, these include gains and losses from transactions in foreign currencies, as well as gains and losses from dispositions of fixed assets.

- **Income taxes** (Exhibit 1-7, line 14) are expenses levied on The Walt Disney Company's taxable income by the federal government. This is often one of a corporation's largest expenses. The Walt Disney Company's income tax expense for the 12 months ended September 27, 2014, was a whopping $4,242 million (34.6% of its net income before taxes)!

- **Less: Net Income Attributable to Noncontrolling Interests** (Exhibit 1-7, line 16). As discussed in the opening section of this chapter, The Walt Disney Company owns various percentage interests of other corporations around the world. Whenever the percentage interest owned in another company is 20% to 50%, GAAP require use of the **equity method** of accounting, under which the investor company increases its investment and income by its proportionate share of ownership in the investee company, and reduces its investment by the dividends it receives. In contrast, whenever the percentage interest owned in the investee exceeds 50%, the investor or parent company is said to own a controlling interest in the investee. The proper accounting for controlling interests is **consolidation** of the financial statements of all entities (parent and subsidiaries) under common control. The consolidation method of accounting requires that the parent company report the entire amount of income of all entities in which it owns an interest. That amount is $8,004 million in fiscal 2014 and $6,636 million in fiscal 2013 (line 15). Next, the parent company is required to subtract the portion of net income of all consolidated subsidiaries that is *not* owned. This is called **net income attributable to noncontrolling interests**. The amount of net income of those subsidiaries was $503 million in fiscal 2014 and $500 million in fiscal 2013 (line 16). The equity method of accounting for investments and issues related to consolidated financial statements are discussed briefly in Chapter 8, although most of these issues are beyond the scope of this text.

■ **Net income attributable to The Walt Disney Company** (line 17). The "bottom line" of the Consolidated Statements of Income (all revenues less all expenses) is net income attributable to The Walt Disney Company. Those amounts are $7,501 million in fiscal 2014 and $6,136 million in fiscal 2013.

Now let's examine the Statement of Retained Earnings in Exhibit 1-8.

The Statement of Retained Earnings Shows
What a Company Did with Its Net Income

Retained earnings means exactly what the term implies, which is that portion of net income the company has kept over a period of years. If, historically, revenues exceed expenses, the result will be a positive balance in retained earnings. On the other hand, if, historically, expenses have exceeded sales revenues, the accumulation of these losses will result in an accumulated **deficit** in retained earnings (usually shown in parentheses). Net income attributable to The Walt Disney Company (lines 4 and 8 in Exhibit 1-8) flows from the income statement (line 17 of Exhibit 1-7) to the **statement of retained earnings**.

Exhibit 1-8 | The Walt Disney Company, Consolidated Statements of Retained Earnings

	A	B
	A1	
1	**The Walt Disney Company Consolidated Statements of Retained Earnings For the Two Years Ending September 27, 2014**	
2	Adapted, in millions of $	
3	Retained earnings, Sep. 29, 2012	$ 42,965
4	Net income attributable to The Walt Disney Company, year ended Sep. 28, 2013	6,136
5	Dividends declared, year ended Sep. 28, 2013	(1,342)
6	Other reductions, year ended Sep. 28, 2013	(1)
7	Retained earnings, Sep. 28, 2013	47,758
8	Net income attributable to The Walt Disney Company, year ended Sep. 27, 2014	7,501
9	Dividends declared, year ended Sep. 27, 2014	(1,525)
10	Retained earnings, Sep. 27, 2014	$ 53,734
11		

Net income increases retained earnings, and net losses and dividends decrease retained earnings. A positive balance in retained earnings indicates that a corporation has been able to accumulate earnings over its lifetime in order to expand, as well as to return a portion of its assets in the form of dividends to shareholders, if the corporation distributes dividends.

Let's review The Walt Disney Company's Consolidated Statements of Retained Earnings for the two-year period ending September 27, 2014. This statement was excerpted from the company's Consolidated Statements of Stockholders' Equity, which analyze all of the increases and decreases in every account in the stockholders' equity section of the balance sheet. At the beginning of fiscal 2013 (September 29, 2012), The Walt Disney Company had $42,965 million in retained earnings (line 3). During fiscal 2013, the company earned net income attributable to The Walt Disney Company of $6,136 million (line 4) and declared dividends of $1,342 million ($1,324 million in cash and $18 million in stock) to shareholders (line 5). It made another small negative adjustment to retained earnings of $1 million (line 6). It ended the 2013 fiscal year with a retained earnings balance of $47,758 million, which carried over and became the beginning balance of retained earnings in fiscal 2014 (line 7).

During fiscal 2014, the company earned net income attributable to The Walt Disney Company of $7,501 million (line 8). As shown on line 9, it then declared dividends to shareholders in the amount of $1,525 million. Of this amount, $1,508 million was distributed in cash, and another $17 million was distributed in the form of the company's common stock. We will discuss cash and stock dividends in greater depth in Chapter 10. The company ended the 2014 fiscal year with a retained earnings balance of $53,734 million (line 10).

Which item on the statement of retained earnings comes directly from the income statement? It is net income attributable to The Walt Disney Company. Lines 4 and 8 of the retained earnings statement come directly from line 17 of the income statement (see Exhibit 1-7) for fiscal 2013 and 2014, respectively. Take a moment to trace this amount from one statement to the other. Then give yourself another pat on the back—You've learned more about how to analyze financial statements!

After a company earns net income, the board of directors decides whether to pay a dividend to the stockholders. Corporations are not obligated to pay dividends unless their boards decide to pay (i.e., declare) them. Usually, companies that are in a development stage or growth mode elect not to pay dividends, opting instead to plow resources back into the company to expand operations or purchase property, plant, and equipment. However, established companies like The Walt Disney Company, usually have enough accumulated retained earnings (and cash) to pay dividends. Dividends decrease retained earnings because they represent a distribution of a company's assets (usually cash) to its stockholders.

The Balance Sheet Measures Financial Position

A company's **balance sheet**, also called the **statement of financial position**, reports three items: assets (line 14), liabilities (line 23), and equity (line 30). The Walt Disney Company's Consolidated Balance Sheets, shown in Exhibit 1-9, are dated at the *moment in time* when the accounting periods end (September 27, 2014, and September 28, 2013).

Assets. There are two main categories of assets: current and long-term. **Current assets** are assets that are expected to be converted to cash, sold, or consumed during the next 12 months or within the business's operating cycle if longer than a year. Current assets typically include cash

Exhibit 1-9 | The Walt Disney Company, Consolidated Balance Sheets

	A	B	C	D
	A1			
1	The Walt Disney Company Consolidated Balance Sheets	**Fiscal 2014**	**Fiscal 2013**	
2	**Adapted, in millions of $**	**Sep. 27, 2014**	**Sep. 28, 2013**	
3	**Current assets:**			
4	Cash and cash equivalents	$ 3,421	$ 3,931	
5	Receivables	7,822	6,967	
6	Inventories	1,574	1,487	
7	Other current assets	2,359	1,724	
8	**Total current assets**	15,176	14,109	
9	Film and television costs	5,325	4,783	
10	Investments	2,696	2,849	
11	Parks, resorts, and other property, net	23,332	22,380	
12	Intangible assets	35,315	34,694	
13	Other long-term assets	2,342	2,426	
14	**Total assets**	$ 84,186	$ 81,241	
15	**Current liabilities:**			
16	Accounts payable and accrued liabilities	$ 7,595	$ 6,803	
17	Current portion of long-term borrowings	2,164	1,512	
18	Unearned royalties and other advances	3,533	3,389	
19	**Total current liabilities**	13,292	11,704	
20	Long-term borrowings	12,676	12,776	
21	Other long-term liabilities	10,040	8,611	
22	Commitments and contingencies (note 14)			
23	**Total liabilities**	36,008	33,091	
24	**Equity:**			
25	Common stock and additional paid-in capital	34,301	33,440	
26	Retained earnings	53,734	47,758	
27	Accumulated other comprehensive loss	(1,968)	(1,187)	
28	Treasury stock at cost	(41,109)	(34,582)	
29	Noncontrolling interests	3,220	2,721	
30	**Total equity**	48,178	48,150	
31	**Total liabilities and equity**	$ 84,186	$ 81,241	
32				

and cash equivalents, short-term investments, accounts and notes receivable, merchandise inventory, and other current assets like prepaid expenses. The Walt Disney Company's current assets at September 27, 2014, total $15,176 million (line 8). Let's examine each current asset that The Walt Disney Company holds.

- *Cash and cash equivalents* (line 4). All companies have cash. Cash is the liquid asset that's the medium of exchange, and *cash equivalents* include U.S. Treasury securities or other financial instruments that are easily convertible to cash. The Walt Disney Company owns $3,421 million in cash and cash equivalents at September 27, 2014. This is down from $3,931 million at September 28, 2013. We will explain this further when we discuss the statement of cash flows later.

- *Receivables* (line 5) are monetary claims that a company has against outsiders (customers), acquired mainly by performing services for them, selling goods to them, or loaning money to them. In the case of The Walt Disney Company, these claims include amounts receivable from advertisers on Disney-owned television networks, travel agencies that book vacations at Disney-owned resorts, and retailers who sell Disney trademark merchandise, among many other things. Receivables account for the largest single current asset of The Walt Disney Company as of September 27, 2014 ($7,822 million), up from $6,967 million the year before. The company expects to convert these receivables to cash within the next fiscal year.

- *Inventories* (line 6) are a merchandising company's most important, and often its largest, current asset. As we emphasized earlier, The Walt Disney Company's revenue comes mostly from services rather than sales of merchandise, so inventories are not the company's largest current asset. However, inventories are still significant, totaling $1,574 million at September 27, 2014, up from $1,487 million at September 28, 2013. The company expects to sell these inventories and convert them to cash within the next fiscal year.

- *Other current assets* (line 7) may include *prepaid expenses*, which represent amounts paid in advance for advertising, rent, insurance, taxes, and supplies. These are current assets because the company will benefit from these expenditures within the next year. The Walt Disney Company owns $2,359 million in other current assets as of September 27, 2014, up from $1,724 million the previous year.

- An asset always represents a future benefit.

Long-term (non-current) assets are expected to benefit the company for long periods of time, beyond just the next fiscal year. Let's look at The Walt Disney Company's long-term assets.

- *Film and television costs* (line 9) include production costs such as labor, materials, and overhead for Disney's movies, television, and stage programs. As an example, consider the costs that the company incurred to produce the feature film *Frozen*. Many of these costs are initially recorded ("capitalized") as assets of the company and are transferred over time to expenses through the process of amortization, to be matched against the revenue recognized from the film in the same periods those revenues are earned. The amount of these unamortized costs was $5,325 million as of September 27, 2014, and $4,783 million as of September 28, 2013.

- *Investments* (line 10) represent mostly the amounts that The Walt Disney Company has invested in *equity method investments* of other media companies. These include A&E Television Networks, LLC; Seven TV, CTV Specialty Television; Hulu, LLC; and Fusion. As mentioned previously in the discussion of the income statement, these investments comprise 20% to 50% of the voting stock of other companies. The equity method requires the investor company to record the initial investment at cost and, in subsequent periods, increase (or decrease) its investment by its proportionate share of the investee company's earnings (losses), and also to decrease the investment by its proportionate share of the investees' dividends. The amount of The Walt Disney Company's equity investment in these companies was $2,696 million as of September 27, 2014, and $2,849 million as of September 28, 2013. These types of investments are discussed in greater depth in Chapter 8.

- *Parks, resorts, and other property, net* (line 11) includes The Walt Disney Company's land, buildings, furniture, and equipment (*fixed assets*) that make up its theme parks, resorts, hotels, and studios. The Walt Disney Company reports these assets on one line, *net*, meaning that the historical acquisition cost of the assets has been reduced by *accumulated depreciation*. Accumulated depreciation represents the amount of the historical cost of fixed assets that has been allocated to expense in the income statement over time as the assets have been used in producing revenue. Thus, accumulated depreciation represents the used-up portion of the fixed asset. We subtract accumulated depreciation from the cost of parks, resorts, and other property to determine their net book values ($23,332 million at the end of fiscal 2014 and $22,380 million at the end of fiscal 2013 on line 11). We will discuss the concept of depreciation further in Chapters 3 and 7.

- *Intangible assets* (line 12) are assets that have no physical substance. That is, you can neither see them nor touch them, but nevertheless they represent resources that have a future benefit to the company. Examples are copyrights, trademarks, patents, franchises, and licenses. The vast majority of this largest category of assets for The Walt Disney Company is comprised of **goodwill**, which is the excess of the cost of an acquired company over the sum of the market values of its net assets (assets minus liabilities). Intangible assets were $35,315 million as of September 27, 2014, and $34,694 million as of September 28, 2013. Intangible assets are discussed in greater depth in Chapter 7.

- *Other long-term assets* (line 13) is a catchall category for assets that are difficult to classify. The Walt Disney Company owned about $2,342 million of these assets as of September 27, 2014, compared with $2,426 million at September 28, 2013. These primarily represent long-term receivables, and long-term prepaid expenses.

- Overall, The Walt Disney Company reported total assets (line 14) of $84,186 million at September 27, 2014, compared with $81,241 million at September 28, 2013.

Liabilities. Liabilities are also divided into current and long-term categories. **Current liabilities** (lines 16–18) are debts generally payable within one year of the balance sheet date. Chief among the current liabilities are accounts payable and accrued liabilities, current portion of long-term borrowings, and unearned royalties and other advances. *Long-term liabilities* are payable after one year.

- *Accounts payable and accrued liabilities* (line 16) of $7,595 million at the end of fiscal 2014 and $6,803 million at the end of 2013 represent amounts owed to The Walt Disney Company's vendors and suppliers for purchases of inventory, as well as for accrued liabilities such as salaries and taxes as of those respective year-ends.

- *Current portion of long-term borrowings* (line 17) represents the portion of long-term borrowings (usually notes payable) that the company will have to pay off within the next year. Notice on line 20 that, at September 27, 2014, the company had about $12,676 million in long-term borrowings, which was virtually unchanged from the prior year. In addition to that, another $2,164 million was due and payable within 12 months (line 17), making a total of $14,840 million in long-term borrowings. GAAP requires companies to segregate and report the portion of long-term debt due and payable within 12 months of the balance sheet date as a current liability, rather than long-term. We'll discuss this in more depth in Chapter 9.

- *Unearned royalties and other advances* (line 18). The Walt Disney Company collects royalties in advance for use of its corporate name, as well as for movie and television rights. Whenever cash is received in advance, in periods before services are rendered or goods are shipped, the amount received is required to be added to a liability account. In other words, the company is obligated to its customers to perform those services or ship those products in future periods. As of September 27, 2014, customers had paid The Walt Disney Company $3,533 million in advance for future services and shipment of goods. During fiscal 2015, the company will make adjusting entries to its books to transfer amounts from the unearned account to services revenue or products revenue as those services are performed or goods are shipped, which is the point at which revenues may be recognized as earned. We will discuss this topic in more depth in Chapters 3 and 9.

- At September 27, 2014, The Walt Disney Company's current liabilities total $13,292 million, up from $11,704 million as of September 28, 2013 (line 19). The company also owes

$12,676 million in long-term borrowings (line 20) and $10,040 million in other long-term liabilities. These liabilities are due one year or more after the balance sheet date.

- At September 27, 2014, total liabilities are $36,008 million (line 23). This represents about 42.8% of total assets and indicates a very strong financial position from a debt standpoint. The previous year's debt ratio (total liabilities/total assets) of 40.7% was slightly stronger.

Equity (Stockholders' Equity). The accounting equation states that

$$\text{Assets} - \text{Liabilities} = \text{Owners' Equity}$$

The assets (resources) and the liabilities (debts) of The Walt Disney Company are fairly easy to understand. Owners' equity is harder to pin down. Owners' (stockholders') equity is simple to calculate, but what does it *mean*?

The Walt Disney Company, calls its owners' equity merely *Equity* (line 24) and this title is appropriately descriptive. Remember that a corporation's owners' equity represents the stockholders' ownership of the business's assets. The Walt Disney Company's equity consists of the following:

- *Common stock and additional paid-in capital* (line 25), represented by shares issued to stockholders for about $34,301 million at September 27, 2014, and $33,440 million at September 28, 2013. This account represents the face amount (par value) of the stock issued to shareholders, plus additional amounts paid in excess of the stock's par value. We discuss this topic in greater depth in Chapter 10.

- *Retained earnings* (line 26) are $53,734 million and $47,758 million at September 27, 2014, and September 28, 2013, respectively. We saw these figures on the statement of retained earnings in Exhibit 1-8 (lines 7 and 10). Retained earnings' final resting place is the stockholders' equity section of the balance sheet.

- The Walt Disney Company's equity holds three other items. *Treasury stock* at cost (line 28) represents amounts paid by the company to repurchase its own stock. *Accumulated other comprehensive income (loss)* (line 27) represents items of gain or loss that are allowed by the FASB to bypass the income statement and be recorded directly into stockholders' equity. We will discuss the reasons for this in Chapters 8 and 11. **Noncontrolling interests** (line 29) represent the amount of consolidated earnings attributable to noncontrolling interests (see line 16 of Exhibit 1-7) that have accumulated over time. The amounts of $3,220 million as of September 27, 2014, and $2,721 million as of September 28, 2013, represent the portion of The Walt Disney Company's consolidated net assets that are not owned by The Walt Disney Company. This topic is also discussed in Chapter 8.

- At September 27, 2014, The Walt Disney Company has total equity of $48,178 million (line 30). We can now prove that The Walt Disney Company's total assets equal total liabilities and equity at September 27, 2014 (amounts in millions):

Total assets (line 14)	$84,186
Total liabilities (line 23)	$36,008
+ Total equity (line 30)	$48,178
Total liabilities and equity (line 31)	$84,186

Must equal

The statement of cash flows is the fourth required financial statement.

The Statement of Cash Flows Measures
Cash Receipts and Payments

Companies engage in three basic types of activities:

- **Operating activities**
- **Investing activities**
- **Financing activities**

The **statement of cash flows** reports cash receipts and cash payments in each of these categories.

- *Companies operate by selling goods and services to customers.* **Operating activities** result in net income or net loss, and they either increase or decrease cash. The income statement of The Walt Disney Company reveals whether the company is profitable. The statement of cash flows reports whether operations increased the company's cash balance. Operating activities are most important, and they should be the company's main source of cash. Continuing negative net cash flow from operations can lead to bankruptcy.

- *Companies invest in long-term assets.* The Walt Disney Company buys property for amusement parks and resorts, as well as other long-term assets for which it must spend cash. When these assets wear out, the company might sell them, which often increases cash. Both purchases and sales of long-term assets are investing cash flows. Investing cash flows are the next most important after operations.

- *Companies need money for financing.* Financing activities include issuing stock, paying dividends, borrowing, and repayments of borrowed funds. The Walt Disney Company issues stock to its shareholders and borrows from banks, which are cash inflows from financing activities. The company may also pay loans, pay dividends, and repurchase its own stock, which are cash outflows from financing activities.

Overview. Each category of cash flows—operating, investing, and financing—either increases or decreases cash. On a statement of cash flows, cash receipts appear as positive amounts. Cash payments are negative amounts and are enclosed by parentheses.

In Exhibit 1-10, which shows The Walt Disney Company's Consolidated Statements of Cash Flows, operating activities provided net cash of $9,780 million in the 12 months ended September 27, 2014 (line 7). Notice that this is $1,776 million more than net income ($8,004 million in line 5), caused primarily by depreciation and amortization expenses, which were deducted from total revenues in order to compute net income, but which did not use cash. Investing activities for the fiscal year (mostly purchase of parks, resorts, and other property) used cash of about $3,345 million (line 12). That signals expansion.

Exhibit 1-10 | The Walt Disney Company, Consolidated Statements of Cash Flows

	A	B	C	D	E
	A1				
1	The Walt Disney Company Consolidated Statements of Cash Flows	Fiscal 2014	Fiscal 2013		
2	Adapted, in Millions of $	12 Months Ended			
3		Sep. 27, 2014	Sep. 28, 2013		
4	**OPERATING ACTIVITIES**				
5	Net income	$ 8,004	$ 6,636		
6	Adjustments to reconcile net income to net cash provided by operating activities	1,776	2,816		
7	Net cash provided by operating activities	9,780	9,452		
8	**INVESTING ACTIVITIES**				
9	Investments in parks, resorts, and other property	(3,311)	(2,796)		
10	Sales of investments/proceeds from dispositions	395	479		
11	Acquisitions and other investing activities	(429)	(2,359)		
12	Net cash used in investing activities	(3,345)	(4,676)		
13	**FINANCING ACTIVITIES**				
14	Net proceeds from borrowing	2,281	1,881		
15	Reductions of borrowings	(1,648)	(1,502)		
16	Repurchases of common stock	(6,527)	(4,087)		
17	Dividends	(1,508)	(1,324)		
18	Proceeds from exercise of stock options and other	692	818		
19	Net cash used in financing activities	(6,710)	(4,214)		
20	Effect of foreign exchange rate fluctuations on cash	(235)	(18)		
21	Net increase (decrease) in cash and cash equivalents	(510)	544		
22	Cash and cash equivalents at beginning of period	3,931	3,387		
23	Cash and cash equivalents at end of period	$ 3,421	$ 3,931		
26					

Financing activities used another $6,710 million (line 19). Examining the details, we find that The Walt Disney Company used a whopping $6,527 million in cash to repurchase its common stock from existing shareholders during the year (line 16). This represents the largest single transaction reflected on the cash flow statement, besides net income. In addition, the company paid another $1,508 million in cash dividends to shareholders (line 17). We will discuss the reasons why companies repurchase stock from their shareholders and pay dividends in Chapter 10.

Overall, The Walt Disney Company's cash and cash equivalents decreased by $510 million during the 12 months ended September 27, 2014 (line 21) and ended the year at $3,421 million (line 23). Trace ending cash and cash equivalents back to the balance sheet in Exhibit 1-9 (line 4). Cash and cash equivalents links the statement of cash flows to the balance sheet. You've just performed more financial statement analysis!

CONSTRUCT FINANCIAL STATEMENTS AND ANALYZE THE RELATIONSHIPS AMONG THEM

5 **Construct** financial statements and **analyze** the relationships among them

Exhibit 1-11 summarizes the relationships among the financial statements of The Walt Disney Company for the fiscal year ending September 27, 2014. These statements are condensed, so the details of Exhibits 1-7 through 1-10 are omitted. Study the exhibit carefully because these relationships apply to all organizations. Specifically, note the following:

1. The income statement for the 12 months ended September 27, 2014

    a. Reports total revenues and expenses of the year. Revenues and expenses are reported *only* on the income statement.

    b. Reports net income if total revenues exceed total expenses. If total expenses exceed total revenues, there is a net loss.

2. The statement of retained earnings for the 12 months ended September 27, 2014

    a. Opens with the beginning retained earnings balance.

    b. Adds net income (or subtracts net loss). Net income comes directly from the income statement (arrow 1 in Exhibit 1-11).

    c. Subtracts dividends declared.

    d. Reports the retained earnings balance at the end of the year.

3. The balance sheet at September 27, 2014, end of the accounting year

    a. Reports assets, liabilities, and stockholders' equity at the end of the year. Only the balance sheet reports assets and liabilities.

    b. Reports that assets equal the sum of liabilities plus stockholders' equity. This balancing feature follows the accounting equation and gives the balance sheet its name.

    c. Reports retained earnings, which comes from the statement of retained earnings (arrow 2 in Exhibit 1-11).

4. The statement of cash flows for the 12 months ended September 27, 2014

    a. Reports cash flows from operating, investing, and financing activities. Each category results in net cash provided (an increase) or used (a decrease).

    b. Reports whether cash and cash equivalents increased (or decreased) during the year. The statement shows the ending cash and cash equivalents balance, as reported on the balance sheet (arrow 3 in Exhibit 1-11).

Exhibit 1-11 | Relationships among the Financial Statements (in millions of $)

	A	B	C	D	E
1	**The Walt Disney Company** **Consolidated Statement of Income (Adapted)** **12 Months Ended September 27, 2014**				
2	Total revenues	$ 48,813			
3	Total expenses	40,809			
4	Net income	8,004			
5	Less: Net income attributable to noncontrolling interests	(503)			
6	Net income attributable to The Walt Disney Company	$ 7,501			
7					

	A	B	C	D	E
1	**Consolidated Statement of Retained Earnings (Adapted)**				
2	Beginning retained earnings	$ 47,758			
3	Net income attributable to The Walt Disney Company	7,501			
4	Dividends declared*	(1,525)			
5	Ending retained earnings	$ 53,734			
6					

* Cash dividends $1,508; stock dividends $17

	A	B	C	D	E
1	**Consolidated Balance Sheet (Adapted)**				
2	Assets				
3	Cash and cash equivalents	$ 3,421			
4	All other assets	80,765			
5	Total assets	$ 84,186			
6	Liabilities				
7	Total liabilities	$ 36,008			
8	Equity				
9	Common stock and additional paid-in capital	34,301			
10	Retained earnings	53,734			
11	Other equity	(39,857)			
12	Total equity	48,178			
13	Total liabilities and equity	$ 84,186			
14					

	A	B	C	D	E
1	**Consolidated Statement of Cash Flows (Adapted)**				
2	Net cash provided by operating activities	$ 9,780			
3	Net cash used in investing activities	(3,345)			
4	Net cash used in financing activities	(6,710)			
5	Effect of foreign exchange rate fluctuations on cash	(235)			
6	Net increase (decrease) in cash and cash equivalents	(510)			
7	Cash and cash equivalents, beginning of year	3,931			
8	Cash and cash equivalents, end of year	$ 3,421			
9					

DECISION GUIDELINES

IN EVALUATING A COMPANY, WHAT DO DECISION MAKERS LOOK FOR?

These Decision Guidelines illustrate how people use financial statements. Decision Guidelines appear throughout the book to show how accounting information aids decision making.

Suppose you are considering an investment in The Walt Disney Company stock. How do you proceed? Where do you get the information you need? What do you look for?

Decision	Guidelines
1. Can the company sell its services or products?	1. Net revenue on the income statement. Are revenues growing or falling?
2. What are the main income measures to watch for trends?	2. a. Gross profit (sales – cost of goods sold) b. Operating income (gross profit – operating expenses) c. Net income (bottom line of the income statement) All three income measures should be increasing over time.
3. What percentage of revenue ends up as profit?	3. Divide net income by sales revenue. Examine the trend of the net income percentage from year to year.
4. Can the company collect its receivables?	4. From the balance sheet, compare the percentage increase in accounts receivable to the percentage increase in sales. If receivables are growing much faster than sales, collections may be too slow, and a cash shortage may result.
5. Can the company pay its a. current liabilities? b. current and long-term liabilities?	5. From the balance sheet, compare a. current assets to current liabilities. Current assets should be somewhat greater than current liabilities. b. total assets to total liabilities. Total assets must be somewhat greater than total liabilities.
6. Where is the company's cash coming from? How is cash being used?	6. On the cash flows statement, operating activities should provide the bulk of the company's cash during most years. Otherwise, the business will fail. Examine investing cash flows to see if the company is purchasing long-term assets—property, plant, and equipment and intangibles (this signals growth).

EVALUATE BUSINESS DECISIONS ETHICALLY

6 **Evaluate** business decisions ethically

Good business requires decision making, which in turn requires the exercise of good judgment, both at the individual and corporate levels. For example, you may work for or eventually run a company like Starbucks Corp. that has decided to plow back a portion of its profits to support social development projects in the communities that produce its coffee, tea, and cocoa. Can that be profitable in the long run?

Perhaps as an accountant, you may have to decide whether to report a $50,000 expenditure for a piece of equipment as an asset on the balance sheet or an expense on the income statement. Alternatively, as a sales manager for a company like IBM, you may have to decide whether $25 million of goods and services shipped to customers in 2016 would be more appropriately recorded as revenue in 2016 or 2017. Depending on the type of business, the facts and circumstances surrounding accounting decisions may not always make them clear-cut, and yet the decision may determine whether the company shows a profit or a loss in a particular period! What are the factors that influence business and accounting decisions, and how should these factors be weighed? Generally, three types of factors influence business and accounting decisions: *economic, legal,* and *ethical.*

The *economic* factor states that the decision being made should *maximize the economic benefits* to the decision maker. Based on economic theory, every rational person faced with a decision will choose the course of action that maximizes his or her own welfare, without regard to how that decision impacts others. In summary, the combined outcome of each person acting in his or her own self-interest will maximize the benefits to society as a whole.

The *legal* factor is based on the proposition that free societies are governed by laws. Laws are written to provide clarity and to prevent abuse of the rights of individuals or society. Democratically enacted laws both contain and express society's moral standards. Legal analysis involves applying the relevant laws to each decision and then choosing the action that complies with those laws. A complicating factor for a global business may be that what is legal in one country might not be legal in another. In that case, it is usually best to abide by the laws of the most restrictive country.

The *ethical* factor recognizes that while certain actions might be both economically profitable and legal, they may still not be right. Therefore, most companies, and many individuals, have established standards for themselves to enforce a higher level of conduct than that imposed by law. These standards govern how we treat others and the way we restrain our selfish desires. This behavior and its underlying beliefs are the essence of ethics. **Ethics** are shaped by our cultural, socioeconomic, and religious backgrounds. An *ethical analysis* is needed to guide judgments when making decisions.

The decision rule in an ethical analysis is to choose the action that fulfills ethical duties—responsibilities of the members of society to each other. The challenge in an ethical analysis is to identify specific ethical duties and stakeholders to whom you owe these duties. As with legal issues, a complicating factor in making global ethical decisions may be that what is considered ethical in one country is not considered ethical in another.

Among the questions you may ask in making an ethical analysis are the following:

- *Which options are most honest, open, and truthful?*
- *Which options are most kind and compassionate and will build a sense of community?*
- *Which options create the greatest good for the greatest number of stakeholders?*
- *Which options result in treating others as I would want to be treated?*

Ethical training starts at home and continues throughout our lives. It is reinforced by the teaching that we receive in our church, synagogue, or mosque; the schools we attend; and by the persons and companies we associate with.

A thorough understanding of ethics requires more study than we can accomplish in this book. However, remember that when you are making accounting decisions, you should not check your ethics at the door!

In the business setting, ethics work best when modeled "from the top." Ethisphere Institute (**http://www.ethisphere.com**) has recently established the Business Ethics Leadership Alliance (BELA), aimed at "reestablishing ethics as the foundation of everyday business practices." BELA members agree to embrace and uphold four core values that incorporate ethics and integrity into all their practices: (1) legal compliance, (2) transparency, (3) conflict identification, and (4) accountability.

Each year, Ethisphere Institute publishes a list of the World's Most Ethical Companies. The 2014 list includes corporations like United Parcel Service, Inc., Starbucks Corp., Pepsico, Inc., and The Gap, Inc. Excerpts from some of these companies' financial statements will be featured in later chapters of this text. As you begin to make your decisions about future employers, put these companies on your list! It's easier to act ethically when you work for companies that recognize the importance of ethics in business practices. These companies have learned from experience that, in the long run, ethical conduct pays big rewards—not only socially, morally, and spiritually, but economically as well!

DECISION GUIDELINES

DECISION FRAMEWORK FOR MAKING ETHICAL JUDGMENTS

Weighing tough ethical judgments in business and accounting requires a decision framework. Answering the following four questions will guide you through tough decisions:

Decision	Guidelines
1. What is the issue?	1. The issue will usually deal with making a judgment about an accounting measurement or disclosure that results in economic consequences, often to numerous parties.
2. Who are the stakeholders, and what are the consequences of the decision to each?	2. Stakeholders are anyone who might be impacted by the decision—you, your company, and potential users of the information (investors, creditors, and regulatory agencies). Consequences can be economic, legal, or ethical in nature.
3. Weigh the alternatives.	3. Analyze the impact of the decision on all stakeholders, using economic, legal, and ethical criteria. Ask "Who will be helped or hurt, whose rights will be exercised or denied, and in what way?"
4. Make the decision and be prepared to deal with the consequences.	4. Exercise the courage to either defend the decision or to change it, depending on its positive or negative impact. How does your decision make you feel afterward?

To simplify, we might ask three questions:

1. Is the action legal? If not, steer clear, unless you want to go to jail or pay monetary damages to injured parties. If the action is legal, go on to questions 2 and 3.

2. Who will be affected by the decision and how? Be as thorough about this analysis as possible, and analyze it from all three standpoints (economic, legal, and ethical).

3. How will this decision make me feel afterward? How would it make me feel if my family reads about it in the newspaper?

In later chapters throughout the book, we will apply this model to different accounting decisions.

American Institute of Certified Public Accountants
Code of Professional Conduct

The decision framework for making ethical judgments provides general guidance for everyone, regardless of profession or industry. Many professional organizations, businesses, and other entities adopt their own ethical guidelines or codes of conduct so that their members have more specific guidance.

The American Institute of Certified Public Accountants (AICPA) is one such organization. The AICPA has a code of professional conduct that applies to all of its members. This code provides guidance to all members in the performance of their professional duties and is composed of several principles that form the basic building blocks of ethical and professional conduct. The code also contains extensive interpretations and other guidance; the actual code is almost 200 pages in length.

Even though you may not be an accounting major and may never be a member of the AICPA and covered by the AICPA Code of Professional Conduct, the basic principles contained in its code can be applied to a wide range of professions and organizations. In addition, you may in your future career have interactions with CPAs, and it is helpful to understand the code of conduct to which CPAs adhere if they are members of the AICPA.

Excerpts from the description of the basic principles of the AICPA Code of Professional Conduct[2] are as follows:

- **Responsibilities principle.** In carrying out their responsibilities as professionals, members should exercise sensitive professional and moral judgments in all their activities.

  As professionals, members perform an essential role in society. Consistent with that role, members of the American Institute of Certified Public Accountants have responsibilities to all those who use their professional services. Members also have a continuing responsibility to cooperate with each other to improve the art of accounting, maintain the public's confidence, and carry out the profession's special responsibilities for self-governance. The collective efforts of all members are required to maintain and enhance the traditions of the profession.

- **The public interest principle.** Members should accept the obligation to act in a way that will serve the public interest, honor the public trust, and demonstrate a commitment to professionalism.

  A distinguishing mark of a profession is acceptance of its responsibility to the public. The accounting profession's public consists of clients, credit grantors, governments, employers, investors, the business and financial community, and others who rely on the objectivity and integrity of members to maintain the orderly functioning of commerce. This reliance imposes a public interest responsibility on members. The public interest is defined as the collective well-being of the community of people and institutions that the profession serves.

  In discharging their professional responsibilities, members may encounter conflicting pressures from each of those groups. In resolving those conflicts, members should act with integrity, guided by the precept that when members fulfill their responsibility to the public, clients' and employers' interests are best served.

- **Integrity principle.** To maintain and broaden public confidence, members should perform all professional responsibilities with the highest sense of integrity.

  Integrity is an element of character fundamental to professional recognition. It is the quality from which the public trust derives and the benchmark against which a member must ultimately test all decisions. Integrity requires a member to be, among other things, honest and candid within the constraints of client confidentiality. Service and the public trust should not be subordinated to personal gain and advantage. Integrity can accommodate the inadvertent error and honest difference of opinion; it cannot accommodate deceit or subordination of principle.

  Integrity is measured in terms of what is right and just. In the absence of specific rules, standards, or guidance or in the face of conflicting opinions, a member should test decisions and deeds by asking: "Am I doing what a person of integrity would do? Have I retained my integrity?"

  Integrity requires a member to observe both the form and the spirit of technical and ethical standards; circumvention of those standards constitutes subordination of judgment.

- **Objectivity and independence principle.** A member should maintain objectivity and be free of conflicts of interest in discharging professional responsibilities. A member in public practice should be independent in fact and appearance when providing auditing and other attestation services.

  Objectivity is a state of mind, a quality that lends value to a member's services. It is a distinguishing feature of the profession. The principle of objectivity imposes the obligation to be impartial, intellectually honest, and free of conflicts of interest. Independence precludes relationships that may appear to impair a member's objectivity in rendering attestation services.

- **Due care principle.** A member should observe the profession's technical and ethical standards, strive continually to improve competence and the quality of services, and discharge professional responsibility to the best of the member's ability.

  The quest for excellence is the essence of due care. Due care requires a member to discharge professional responsibilities with competence and diligence. It imposes the obligation to perform professional services to the best of a member's ability, with concern for the

---

[2] © 2015, AICPA. All rights reserved. Used by permission.

best interest of those for whom the services are performed, and consistent with the profession's responsibility to the public.

Competence is derived from a synthesis of education and experience. It begins with a mastery of the common body of knowledge required for designation as a certified public accountant. The maintenance of competence requires a commitment to learning and professional improvement that must continue throughout a member's professional life. It is a member's individual responsibility. In all engagements and in all responsibilities, each member should undertake to achieve a level of competence that will assure that the quality of the member's services meets the high level of professionalism required by these Principles.

Competence represents the attainment and maintenance of a level of understanding and knowledge that enables a member to render services with facility and acumen. It also establishes the limitations of a member's capabilities by dictating that consultation or referral may be required when a professional engagement exceeds the personal competence of a member or a member's firm. Each member is responsible for assessing his or her own competence of evaluating whether education, experience, and judgment are adequate for the responsibility to be assumed.

- **Scope and nature of services.** A member in public practice should observe the Principles of the Code of Professional Conduct in determining the scope and nature of services to be provided.

End-of-Chapter Summary Problem

Alladin Travel, Inc., began operations on April 1, 2016. During April, the business provided services for customers. It is now April 30 and Starr Williams, majority shareholder and manager, is trying to determine how well Alladin Travel, Inc., performed during its first month. Ms. Williams also wants to know the company's financial position at the end of April and its cash flows during the month.

The following data are listed in alphabetical order.

Accounts payable	$ 1,800	Land	$18,000
Accounts receivable	2,000	Payments of cash:	
Adjustments to reconcile net income to net cash provided by operating activities	(3,900)	Acquisition of land	40,000
		Dividends	2,100
		Rent expense	1,100
Cash balance at beginning of April	0	Retained earnings at beginning of April	0
Cash balance at end of April	?	Retained earnings at end of April	?
Cash receipts:			
Issuance (sale) of stock to owners	50,000	Salary expense	1,200
Sale of land	22,000	Service revenue	10,000
Common stock	50,000	Supplies	3,700
		Utilities expense	400

Requirements

1. Prepare the income statement, the statement of retained earnings, and the statement of cash flows for the month ended April 30, 2016, and the balance sheet at April 30, 2016. Draw arrows linking the statements.
2. Answer the following questions:
   a. How well did Alladin Travel, Inc., perform during its first month of operations?
   b. Where does Alladin Travel, Inc., stand financially at the end of April?

Answers

Requirement 1

Financial Statements of Alladin Travel, Inc.

A1

	A	B	C	D
1	**Alladin Travel, Inc.** **Income Statement** **Month Ended April 30, 2016**			
2	**Revenue:**			
3	Service revenue		$ 10,000	
4	**Expenses:**			
5	Salary expense	$ 1,200		
6	Rent expense	1,100		
7	Utilities expense	400		
8	Total expenses		2,700	
9	Net Income		$ 7,300	
10				

①

A1

	A	B	C	D
1	**Alladin Travel, Inc.** **Statement of Retained Earnings** **Month Ended April 30, 2016**			
2	Retained earnings, April 1, 2016		$ 0	
3	Net income for period		7,300	
4			$ 7,300	
5	Less dividends declared		(2,100)	
6	Retained earnings, April 30, 2016		$ 5,200	
7				

②

A1

	A	B	C	D
1	**Alladin Travel, Inc.** **Balance Sheet** **April 30, 2016**			
2	**Assets**		**Liabilities**	
3	Cash	$ 33,300	Accounts payable	$ 1,800
4	Accounts receivable	2,000	**Stockholders' equity**	
5	Supplies	3,700	Common Stock	50,000
6	Land	18,000	Retained earnings	5,200
7			Total stockholders' equity	55,200
8			Total liabilities and	
9	Total assets	$ 57,000	stockholders' equity	$ 57,000
10				

③

A1

	A	B	C
1	**Alladin Travel, Inc.** **Statement of Cash Flows** **Month Ended April 30, 2016**		
2	**Cash flows from operating activities:**		
3	Net income		$ 7,300
4	Adjustments to reconcile net income to net cash provided by operating activities		(3,900)
5	Net cash provided by operating activities		3,400
6	**Cash flows from investing activities:**		
7	Acquisition of land	$ (40,000)	
8	Sale of land	22,000	
9	Net cash used for investing activities		(18,000)
10	**Cash flows from financing activities:**		
11	Issuance (sale) of stock	$ 50,000	
12	Payment of dividends	(2,100)	
13	Net cash provided by financing activities		47,900
14	Net increase in cash		$ 33,300
15	Cash balance, April 1, 2016		0
16	Cash balance, April 30, 2016		$ 33,300
17			

Requirement 2

a. Alladin Travel, Inc., performed rather well in April. Net income was $7,300—very good in relation to service revenue of $10,000. The company was able to pay cash dividends of $2,100.

b. Alladin Travel, Inc., ended April with cash of $33,300. Total assets of $57,000 far exceed total liabilities of $1,800. Stockholders' equity of $55,200 provides a good cushion for borrowing. The business's financial position at April 30, 2016, is strong.

≫ Try It in Excel®

If you've had a basic course in Excel, you can prepare financial statements easily using an Excel spreadsheet! In this chapter, you learned the accounting equation (see Exhibit 1-4 on page 12). In Exhibit 1-5 you learned the formulas for net income as well as how to compute the ending balance of retained earnings. Using the balance sheet for Alladin Travel, Inc., in the End-of-Chapter Summary Problem, it is easy to prepare an Excel template for a balance sheet by programming cells for total assets (cell B9) and total liabilities and stockholders' equity (cell D9). Then, as long as you know what accounts belong in each category, you can use the insert function to insert individual assets, liabilities, and stockholders' equity accounts from a list into various cells of the spreadsheet (don't forget to include both description and amounts). You can insert subtotals for current assets, non-current assets, current liabilities, non-current liabilities, and stockholders' equity. You can also build a basic Excel template for the income statement for Alladin Travel, Inc., by listing and totaling revenues and listing and totaling expenses, then subtracting total expenses from total revenues to compute net income (cell C9). You can build an Excel template for the statement of retained earnings by programming a cell for the ending balance of retained earnings (beginning balance + net income (loss) − dividends) (cell C6). Then merely insert the individual amounts, and bingo, your spreadsheet does all the math for you.

Don't forget the proper order of financial statement preparation: (1) income statement, (2) statement of retained earnings, (3) balance sheet, and (4) statement of cash flows. If you have to prepare all four statements, it's best to follow that order so that you can link the income statement cell containing net income to the corresponding cell in the statement of retained earnings; link the value of the ending balance of retained earnings to the cell containing the retained earnings amount in the balance sheet; and link the ending balance of cash on the statement of cash flows to the balance of cash on the balance sheet as of the year-end. These links correspond to the amounts connected by arrows (1, 2, and 3) on page 31.

The beauty of this approach is that once you build a set of basic templates, you can save and use them over and over again as you progress through the course.

REVIEW | The Financial Statements

Quick Check (Answers are given on page 59.)

1. Suppose you are starting a medical data analytics firm. Which form of business will limit your liability for the business to the amount you have invested?
   a. Proprietorship
   b. Partnership
   c. Corporation
   d. None of the above.

2. Rosenbaum Enterprises buys a warehouse for $500,000 to use for its East Coast distribution operations. On the date of the purchase, a professional appraisal shows a value of $550,000 for the warehouse. The seller had originally purchased the building for $475,000. Rosenbaum has a similar warehouse on the West Coast that has a book value of $510,000. Under the historical cost principle, Rosenbaum should record the building for
   a. $475,000.
   b. $500,000.
   c. $510,000.
   d. $550,000.

3. The accounting equation can be expressed as
   a. Assets − Liabilities = Owners' equity.
   b. Owners' equity − Assets = Liabilities.
   c. Assets − Liabilities − Owners' equity.
   d. Assets + Liabilities = Owners' equity.

4. The nature of an asset is best described as
   a. something with physical form that's valued at cost in the accounting records.
   b. an economic resource that's expected to benefit future operations.
   c. an economic resource representing cash or the right to receive cash in the future.
   d. something owned by a business that has a ready market value.

5. Sarah Zocki is interviewing next week for a job at Rainbow Inks Corporation. Which financial statement should she examine to evaluate how well Rainbow Inks Corporation performed last year?
   a. Balance sheet
   b. Income statement
   c. Statement of cash flows
   d. Statement of retained earnings

6. How would net income be most likely to affect the accounting equation?
   a. Increase assets and increase liabilities
   b. Decrease assets and decrease liabilities
   c. Increase assets and increase stockholders' equity
   d. Increase liabilities and decrease stockholders' equity

7. During the year, Snowtown Corporation has $320,000 in revenues, $115,000 in expenses, and $8,000 in dividend declarations and payments. Stockholders' equity changed by
   a. +$205,000.
   b. −$197,000.
   c. +$213,000.
   d. +$197,000.

8. Snowtown Corporation in question 7 had
   a. net income of $123,000.
   b. net income of $205,000.
   c. net income of $435,000.
   d. net loss of $135,000.

9. Jammer Corporation holds cash of $8,000 and owes $21,000 on accounts payable. Jammer has accounts receivable of $33,000, inventory of $28,000, and land that cost $42,000. How much are Jammer's total assets and liabilities?

	Total Assets	Liabilities
a.	$83,000	$49,000
b.	$69,000	$63,000
c.	$111,000	$49,000
d.	$111,000	$21,000

10. Which item(s) is(are) reported on the balance sheet?
    a. Inventory
    b. Accounts payable
    c. Retained earnings
    d. All of the listed choices.

11. During the year, McKenna Company's stockholders' equity increased from $99,000 to $115,000. McKenna earned net income of $25,000. Assume no changes in the capital stock accounts. How much in dividends did McKenna declare during the year?
    a. $25,000
    b. $0
    c. $9,000
    d. $16,000

12. Noonan Company had total assets of $145,000 and total stockholders' equity of $75,000 at the beginning of the year. During the year, assets increased by $47,000 and liabilities increased by $14,000. Stockholders' equity at the end of the year is
    a. $136,000.
    b. $122,000.
    c. $108,000.
    d. $142,000.

13. Which of the following is a true statement about International Financial Reporting Standards?
    a. They are not needed for U.S. businesses since the United States already has the strongest accounting standards in the world.
    b. They are more exact (contain more rules) than U.S. generally accepted accounting principles.
    c. They are converging gradually with U.S. standards.
    d. They are not being applied anywhere in the world yet, but soon they will be.

14. Which of the following is the most accurate statement regarding ethics as applied to decision making in accounting?
    a. Ethics has no place in accounting, since accounting deals purely with numbers.
    b. It is impossible to learn ethical decision making, since it is just something you decide to do or not to do.
    c. Ethics is becoming less and less important as a field of study in business.
    d. Ethics involves making difficult choices under pressure and should be kept in mind in making every decision, including those involving accounting.

Accounting Vocabulary

accounting (p. 4) The information system that measures business activities, processes that information into reports and financial statements, and communicates the results to decision makers.

accounting cycle (p. 4) The process by which financial statements are prepared.

accounting equation (p. 11) The most basic tool of accounting: Assets = Liabilities + Owners' equity.

amortization (p. 17) Allocation of the cost of an intangible asset to expense over its useful life.

asset (p. 11) An economic resource that is expected to be of benefit in the future.

balance sheet (p. 19) List of an entity's assets, liabilities, and owners' equity as of a specific date. Also called the *statement of financial position*.

board of directors (p. 6) Group elected by the stockholders to set policy for a corporation and to appoint its officers.

capital (p. 11) Another name for the *owners' equity* of a business.

common stock (p. 13) The most basic form of capital stock.

consolidation (p. 17) The method of accounting used for multiple entities that are under common ownership (more than 50% of the voting interests are owned by the same parties).

continuity assumption (p. 8) See going-concern assumption.

corporation (p. 6) A business owned by stockholders. A corporation is a legal entity, an "artificial person" in the eyes of the law.

current asset (p. 19) An asset that is expected to be converted to cash, sold, or consumed during the next 12 months, or within the business's normal operating cycle if longer than a year.

current liability (p. 21) A debt due to be paid within one year or within the entity's operating cycle if the cycle is longer than a year.

deficit (p. 18) Negative balance in retained earnings caused by net losses over a period of years.

depreciation (p. 17) Allocation of the cost of a plant asset to expense over its useful life.

dividends (p. 13) Distributions (usually cash) by a corporation to its stockholders.

entity (p. 8) An organization or a section of an organization that, for accounting purposes, stands apart from other organizations and individuals as a separate economic unit.

equity (p. 11) See owners' equity and stockholders' equity.

equity method (p. 17) Method of accounting required for investments where 20% to 50% of voting interest is owned.

ethics (p. 27) Standards of right and wrong that transcend economic and legal boundaries. Ethical standards deal with the way we treat others and restrain our own actions because of the desires, expectations, or rights of others, or because of our obligations to them.

expenses (p. 13) Decrease in retained earnings that results from operations; the cost of doing business; opposite of revenues.

fair value (p. 9) The amount that a business could sell an asset for, or the amount that a business could pay to settle a liability.

financial accounting (p. 5) The branch of accounting that provides information to people outside the firm.

Financial Accounting Standards Board (FASB) (p. 7) The regulatory body in the United States that formulates generally accepted accounting principles (GAAP).

financial statements (p. 2) Business documents that report financial information about a business entity to decision makers.

financing activities (p. 22) Activities that obtain from investors and creditors the cash needed to launch and sustain the business; a section of the statement of cash flows.

generally accepted accounting principles (GAAP) (p. 7) Accounting guidelines, formulated by the Financial Accounting Standards Board, that govern how accounting is practiced.

going-concern assumption (p. 8) Holds that the entity will remain in operation for the foreseeable future.

goodwill (p. 21) The excess of cost of an acquired company over the sum of the market values of its net assets (assets minus liabilities).

gross profit (p. 16) Revenue from a particular activity minus the direct costs associated with earning that revenue.

historical cost principle (p. 9) Principle that states that assets should be recorded at their actual cost.

income statement (p. 15) A financial statement listing an entity's revenues, expenses, and net income or net loss for a specific period. Also called the *statement of operations*.

intangible assets (p. 21) Assets with no tangible form that represent resources that have a value and future benefit.

International Financial Reporting Standards (IFRS) (p. 7) Accounting guidelines, formulated by the International Accounting Standards Board (IASB).

investing activities (p. 22) Activities that increase or decrease the long-term assets available to the business; a section of the statement of cash flows.

liability (p. 11) An economic obligation (a debt) payable to an individual or an organization outside the business.

limited-liability company (p. 6) A business organization in which the business (not the owner) is liable for the company's debts.

long-term assets (p. 20) Assets that are expected to benefit the entity for long periods of time, beyond the end of the next fiscal year. These usually include investments, property and equipment (plant assets), and intangible assets.

long-term debt (p. 12) A liability that falls due beyond one year from the date of the financial statements.

management accounting (p. 5) The branch of accounting that generates information for the internal decision makers of a business, such as top executives.

net earnings (p. 13) Another name for *net income*.

net income (p. 13) Excess of total revenues over total expenses. Also called *net earnings* or *net profit*.

net loss (p. 13) Excess of total expenses over total revenues.

net profit (p. 13) Another name for *net income*.

noncontrolling interests (p. 22) Interests in consolidated entities that are more than 50% but less than 100% owned.

operating activities (p. 22) Activities that create revenue or expense in the statement of cash flows. Operating activities affect the income statement.

owners' equity (p. 11) The claim of the owners of a business to the assets of the business. Also called *capital, stockholders' equity,* or *net assets.*

paid-in capital (p. 13) The amount of stockholders' equity that stockholders have contributed to the corporation. Also called *contributed capital.*

partnership (p. 6) An association of two or more persons who co-own a business for profit.

proprietorship (p. 5) A business with a single owner.

retained earnings (p. 13) The amount of stockholders' equity that the corporation has earned through profitable operations and has not given back to stockholders.

revenues (p. 13) Increase in retained earnings from delivering goods or services to customers or clients.

segment (p. 8) A division or subset of a business's operations.

shareholder (p. 6) Another name for *stockholder.*

stable-monetary-unit assumption (p. 10) The reason for ignoring the effect of inflation in the accounting records,

based on the assumption that the dollar's purchasing power is relatively stable.

statement of cash flows (p. 23) Reports cash receipts and cash payments classified according to the entity's major activities: operating, investing, and financing.

statement of financial position (p. 19) Another name for the *balance sheet.*

statement of operations (p. 15) Another name for the *income statement.*

statement of retained earnings (p. 18) Summary of the changes in the retained earnings of a corporation during a specific period.

stock (p. 6) Shares into which the owners' equity of a corporation is divided.

stockholder (p. 6) A person who owns stock in a corporation. Also called a *shareholder.*

stockholders' equity (p. 11) The stockholders' ownership interest in the assets of a corporation.

ASSESS YOUR PROGRESS

Some of the following exercises and problems are available as Excel questions in MyAccountingLab®.

Ethics Check

EC1-1. *(Learning Objective 6: Identify ethical principle violated)*

For each of the situations listed, identify which of three principles (integrity, objectivity and independence, or due care) from the AICPA Code of Professional Conduct is violated. Assume all persons listed in the situations are members of the AICPA. (Note: Refer to the AICPA Code of Professional Conduct contained on pages 29–30 in Chapter 1 for descriptions of the principles.)

    a. This year Marcus's company incurred higher cost of goods sold than expected, which resulted in an overall net loss for the company. Marcus does not want the company to lose investors due to the net loss so he adjusts cost of goods sold so that the company has a positive net income.

    b. Bethany is eager to please her supervisor and wants to earn a promotion. When Bethany puts together the financial statements and related information for the past year, she buries unfavorable results deep in the report and presents the good news prominently. She figures that by making the company look good, it will make her case for promotion stronger.

    c. Jennelle receives a large year-end bonus if her company's sales grow by 8% this year. Sales only grew by 7.5% so Jennelle created false sales documentation to make it appear that the sales growth goal was met.

    d. Andrew is in charge of putting together his company's financial statements, but does not understand the newest financial reporting standard that went into effect last year. He decides to do the best he can with interpreting and applying the new standard, since he does not have time right now to learn about the new standard in depth.

Short Exercises

S1-1. (*Learning Objective 1: Explain accounting language*) Accounting definitions are precise, and you must understand the vocabulary to properly use accounting. Sharpen your understanding of key terms by answering the following questions:

LO **1**

1. How do the assets and owners' equity of Nike, Inc., differ from each other? Which one (assets or owners' equity) must be at least as large as the other? Which one can be smaller than the other?
2. How are Nike, Inc.'s, liabilities and owners' equity similar? Different?

S1-2. (*Learning Objective 4: Evaluate business activity*) Consider Walmart, a large retailer. Classify the following items as an asset (A), a liability (L), or stockholders' equity (S) for Walmart:

LO **4**

a. _____ Accounts receivable	**g.** _____ Notes payable
b. _____ Long-term debt	**h.** _____ Retained earnings
c. _____ Merchandise inventory	**i.** _____ Land
d. _____ Prepaid expenses	**j.** _____ Accounts payable
e. _____ Accrued expenses payable	**k.** _____ Common stock
f. _____ Equipment	**l.** _____ Supplies

S1-3. (*Learning Objective 5: Construct an income statement*)

LO **5**

1. Identify the two basic categories of items on an income statement.
2. What do we call the bottom line of the income statement?

S1-4. (*Learning Objective 1: Explain and differentiate between business organizations*) Regal Signs, Inc., needs funds, and Megan Regal, the president, has asked you to consider investing in the business. Answer the following questions about the different ways that Regal might organize the business. Explain each answer.

LO **1**

    a. What forms of organization will enable the owners of Regal Signs, Inc., to limit their risk of loss to the amounts they have invested in the business?

    b. What form of business organization will give Megan Regal the most freedom to manage the business as she wishes?

    c. What form of organization will give creditors the maximum protection in the event that Regal Signs, Inc., fails and cannot pay its debts?

S1-5. (*Learning Objective 2: Explain underlying accounting concepts, assumptions, and principles of accounting*) Mason Olson is chairman of the board of Healthy Fast Foods, Inc. Suppose Olson has just founded Healthy Fast Foods, and assume that he treats his home and other personal assets as part of Healthy Fast Foods. Answer these questions about the evaluation of Healthy Fast Foods, Inc.

LO **2**

1. Which accounting assumption governs this situation?
2. How can the proper application of this accounting assumption give Olson and others a realistic view of Healthy Fast Foods, Inc.? Explain in detail.

S1-6. (*Learning Objective 2: Apply underlying accounting concepts, assumptions, and principles*) Identify the accounting concept, assumption, or principle that best applies to each of the following situations:

LO **2**

    a. Burger King, the restaurant chain, sold a store location to McDonald's. How can Burger King determine the sale price of the store—by a professional appraisal, Burger King's original cost, or the amount actually received from the sale?

    b. General Motors wants to determine which division of the company—Chevrolet or GMC—is more profitable.

    c. Inflation has been around 5.5% for some time. Woodlake Realtors is considering measuring its land values in inflation-adjusted amounts.

    d. You get an especially good buy on a laptop, paying only $300 when it normally costs $800. What is your accounting value for this laptop?

LO 3   **S1-7.** *(Learning Objective 3: Apply the accounting equation)* Suppose you manage a Thai restaurant. Identify the missing amount for each situation:

	Total Assets	=	Total Liabilities	+	Stockholders' Equity
a.	$?		$270,000		$340,000
b.	95,000		70,000		?
c.	420,000		?		350,000

LO 3   **S1-8.** *(Learning Objective 3: Apply the accounting equation)*
1. If you know the assets and the owners' equity of a business, how can you measure its liabilities? Give the equation.
2. Use the accounting equation to show how to determine the amount of a company's owners' equity. How would your answer change if you were analyzing your own household or a single IHOP restaurant?

LO 4   **S1-9.** *(Learning Objective 4: Evaluate business activity)* Suppose you are analyzing the financial statements of Bartelle, Inc. Identify each item with its appropriate financial statement, using the following abbreviations: Income statement (I), Statement of retained earnings (R), Balance sheet (B), and Statement of cash flows (C). Three items appear on two financial statements, and one item shows up on three statements.

a. _____ Accounts payable

b. _____ Inventory

c. _____ Interest revenue

d. _____ Long-term debt

e. _____ Net cash used for financing activities

f. _____ Salary expense

g. _____ Cash

h. _____ Dividends

i. _____ Increase or decrease in cash

j. _____ Net income

k. _____ Net cash provided by operating activities

l. _____ Retained earnings

m. _____ Sales revenue

n. _____ Common stock

LO 2 4   **S1-10.** *(Learning Objectives 2, 4: Apply accounting concepts; evaluate business activity)* Apply your understanding of the relationships among the financial statements to answer these questions.
a. How can a business earn large profits but have a small balance of retained earnings?
b. Give two reasons why a business can have a steady stream of net income over a five-year period and still experience a cash shortage.
c. If you could pick a single source of cash for your business, what would it be? Why?
d. How can a business be unprofitable several years in a row and still have plenty of cash?

LO 4   **S1-11.** *(Learning Objective 4: Evaluate business activity)* For each of the following questions, indicate which financial statement would most likely be used to provide the information. Use the following abbreviations: Income statement (I), Statement of retained earnings (R), Balance sheet (B), and Statement of cash flows (C).
a. How well did the company perform during the year?
b. Why did the company's retained earnings change during the year?
c. Did the company declare a dividend during the year?
d. How much in total debt does the company have?
e. How much cash did the company generate and spend during the year?
f. What assets does the company have?
g. How much cash was generated by operating activities?
h. What were the company's net sales for the year?
i. What is the company's financial position at the end of the year?

LO 5   **S1-12.** *(Learning Objective 5: Construct an income statement)* O'Conner Services, Inc., began 2016 with total assets of $235 million and ended 2016 with assets of $355 million. During 2016, O'Conner Services earned revenues of $397 million and had expenses of $164 million. O'Conner Services paid dividends of $29 million in 2016. Prepare the company's income statement for the year ended December 31, 2016, complete with an appropriate heading.

S1-13. *(Learning Objective 5: Construct a statement of retained earnings)* Roam Corporation began 2016 with retained earnings of $230 million. Revenues during the year were $490 million, and expenses totaled $340 million. Roam declared dividends of $54 million. What was the company's ending balance of retained earnings? To answer this question, prepare Roam's statement of retained earnings for the year ended December 31, 2016, complete with its proper heading.

LO 5

S1-14. *(Learning Objective 5: Construct a balance sheet)* At December 31, 2016, Aloha Enterprises has cash of $50 million, accounts receivable of $19 million, and long-term assets of $39 million. The company owes accounts payable of $13 million and has a long-term note payable of $25 million. Aloha Enterprises has common stock of $20 million and retained earnings of $50 million. Prepare Aloha Enterprises's balance sheet at December 31, 2016, complete with its proper heading.

LO 5

S1-15. *(Learning Objective 5: Solve for retained earnings and construct a balance sheet)* Harmon Corporation ended its fiscal year on September 30, 2016, with cash of $75 million, accounts receivable of $22 million, property and equipment of $28 million, and other long-term assets of $17 million. The company's liabilities consist of accounts payable of $33 million and long-term notes payable of $15 million. Harmon Corporation has total stockholders' equity of $94 million; of this total, common stock is $30 million. Solve for the company's ending retained earnings and then prepare Harmon Corporation's balance sheet at September 30, 2016. Use a proper heading on the balance sheet.

LO 5

S1-16. *(Learning Objective 5: Construct a statement of cash flows)* Avalon Legal Services, Inc., ended 2015 with cash of $18,000. During 2016, Avalon earned net income of $105,000 and had adjustments to reconcile net income to net cash provided by operations totaling $10,000 (this is a negative amount). Avalon paid $32,000 to purchase equipment during 2016. During 2016, the company paid dividends of $80,000. Prepare Avalon's statement of cash flows for the year ended December 31, 2016, complete with its proper heading.

LO 5

S1-17. *(Learning Objective 5: Construct an income statement, statement of retained earnings, and balance sheet)* Following are partially completed financial statements (income statement, statement of retained earnings, and balance sheet) for Masterton Corporation. Complete the financial statements. All amounts are in millions.

LO 5

A1				B	C	D	E
	Masterton Corporation						
	Income Statement						
1	**for Year Ended December 31, 2016**						
2	Net sales		$	184			
3	Expenses			103			
4	Net income		$	a			
5							

A1				B	C	D	E
	Masterton Corporation						
	Statement of Retained Earnings						
1	**for Year Ended December 31, 2016**						
2	Beginning retained earnings		$	67			
3	Net income			b			
4	Cash dividends declared			(5)			
5	Ending retained earnings		$	c			
6							

S1-17 (continued)

	A	B	C	D	E
1	**Masterton Corporation** **Balance Sheet** **December 31, 2016**				
2	Assets				
3	Cash	$ 112			
4	All other assets	d			
5	Total assets	$ e			
6	Liabilities				
7	Total liabilities	$ 40			
8	Stockholders' equity				
9	Common stock	25			
10	Retained earnings	f			
11	Total stockholders' equity	g			
12	Total liabilities and stockholders' equity	$ h			
13					

LO 6

S1-18. (*Learning Objective 6: Evaluate business decisions ethically*) Good business and accounting practices require the exercise of good judgment. How should ethics be incorporated into making accounting judgments? Why is ethics important?

Exercises MyAccountingLab

Group A

LO 3 4

E1-19A. (*Learning Objectives 3, 4: Apply the accounting equation; evaluate business operations*) Compute the missing amount in the accounting equation for each company (amounts in billions):

	Assets	Liabilities	Stockholders' Equity
Presto Drycleaners	$?	$52	$37
First Street Bank	26	?	17
Pam's Florals	36	10	?

Which company appears to have the strongest financial position? Explain your reasoning.

LO 3 4

E1-20A. (*Learning Objectives 3, 4: Apply the accounting equation; evaluate business operations*) Hooper, Inc., has current assets of $200 million; property, plant, and equipment of $350 million; and other assets totaling $160 million. Current liabilities are $170 million and long-term liabilities total $320 million.

Requirements

1. Use these data to write Hooper's accounting equation.
2. How much in resources does Hooper have to work with?
3. How much does Hooper owe creditors?
4. How much of the company's assets do the Hooper stockholders actually own?

E1-21A. *(Learning Objectives 3, 4: Apply the accounting equation; evaluate business operations)* Franklin Company's comparative balance sheet at January 31, 2017, and 2016, reports the following (in millions):

LO 3 4

	2017	2016
Total assets	$75	$53
Total liabilities	23	15

Requirements

Three situations about Franklin Company's issuance of stock and declaration and payment of dividends during the year ended January 31, 2017, follow. For each situation, use the accounting equation and the statement of retained earnings to compute the amount of Franklin's net income or net loss during the year ended January 31, 2017.

1. Franklin issued $12 million of stock and declared no dividends.
2. Franklin issued no stock but declared dividends of $12 million.
3. Franklin issued $88 million of stock and declared dividends of $30 million.

E1-22A. *(Learning Objective 4: Identify financial statement by type of information)* Assume Malcolm Tech, Inc., is expanding into China. The company must decide where to locate and how to finance the expansion. Identify the financial statement where these decision makers can find the following information about Malcolm Tech, Inc. In some cases, more than one statement will report the needed data.

LO 4

a. Revenue
b. Dividends
c. Ending cash balance
d. Total assets
e. Selling, general, and administrative expense
f. Adjustments to reconcile net income to net cash provided by operations

g. Cash spent to acquire the building
h. Current liabilities
i. Income tax expense
j. Net income
k. Common stock
l. Ending balance of retained earnings
m. Income tax payable
n. Long-term debt

E1-23A. *(Learning Objective 5: Construct a balance sheet)* At December 31, 2016, Womack Products has cash of $23,000, receivables of $15,000, and inventory of $77,000. The company's equipment totals $184,000. Womack owes accounts payable of $24,000 and long-term notes payable of $165,000. Common stock is $32,500. Prepare Womack's balance sheet at December 31, 2016, complete with its proper heading. Use the accounting equation to compute retained earnings.

LO 5

E1-24A. *(Learning Objectives 3, 5: Apply the accounting equation; construct a balance sheet)* Amounts of the assets and liabilities of Ellen Samuel Realty Company, as of May 31, 2016, are given as follows. Also included are revenue, expense, and selected stockholders' equity figures for the year ended on that date (amounts in millions):

LO 3 5

Total revenue	$ 37.9	Investment assets (long-term)	$135.7
Receivables	0.5	Property and equipment, net	1.7
Current liabilities	2.6	Other expenses	5.4
Common stock	27.7	Retained earnings, beginning	16.8
Interest expense	0.4	Retained earnings, ending	?
Salary and other employee expenses	13.6	Cash	1.6
Long-term liabilities	102.8	Other assets (long-term)	10.5

Requirement

1. Construct the balance sheet of Ellen Samuel Realty Company at May 31, 2016. Use the accounting equation to compute ending retained earnings.

LO 4   **E1-25A.** *(Learning Objective 4: Construct an income statement and a statement of retained earnings)* This exercise should be used with Exercise 1-24A. Refer to the data of Ellen Samuel Realty Company in Exercise 1-24A.

Requirements

1. Prepare the income statement of Ellen Samuel Realty Company for the year ended May 31, 2016.
2. What amount of dividends did Ellen Samuel declare during the year ended May 31, 2016? (*Hint*: Prepare a statement of retained earnings.)

LO 5   **E1-26A.** *(Learning Objective 5: Construct an income statement and a statement of retained earnings)* Assume the Carson Coffee Roasters Corp. ended the month of August 2017 with these data:

Payments of cash:				
Acquisition of equipment	$200,400		Cash balance, August 1, 2017	$ 0
Dividends	2,300		Cash balance, August 31, 2017	5,900
Retained earnings			Cash receipts:	
August 1, 2017	0		Issuance (sale) of stock	
Retained earnings			to owners	13,200
August 31, 2017	?		Rent expense	1,900
Utilities expense	5,400		Common stock	13,200
Adjustments to reconcile			Equipment	200,400
net income to net cash			Office supplies	7,500
provided by operations	1,500		Accounts payable	9,000
Salary expense	78,400		Service revenue	279,600

Requirement

1. Prepare the income statement and the statement of retained earnings of Carson Coffee Roasters Corp., for the month ended August 31, 2017.

LO 5   **E1-27A.** *(Learning Objective 5: Construct a balance sheet)* Refer to the data in Exercise 1-26A.

Requirement

1. Prepare the balance sheet of Carson Coffee Roasters Corp., for August 31, 2017.

LO 5   **E1-28A.** *(Learning Objective 5: Construct a statement of cash flows)* Refer to the data in Exercises 1-26A and 1-27A.

Requirement

1. Prepare the statement of cash flows of Carson Coffee Roasters Corp., for the month ended August 31, 2017. Using Exhibit 1-11 as a model, show with arrows the relationships among the income statement, statement of retained earnings, balance sheet, and statement of cash flows.

LO 4   **E1-29A.** *(Learning Objective 4: Evaluate business operations through the financial statements)* This exercise should be used in conjunction with Exercises 1-26A through 1-28A.

The owner of Carson Coffee Roasters Corp. seeks your advice as to whether he should cease operations or continue the business. Complete the report, giving him your opinion of net income, dividends, financial position, and cash flows during his first month of operations. Cite specifics from the financial statements to support your opinion. Conclude your memo with advice on whether to stay in business or cease operations.

LO 5   **E1-30A.** *(Learning Objective 5: Construct an income statement, statement of retained earnings, and balance sheet)* During 2016, McFall Company earned revenues of $140 million. McFall incurred, during that same year, salary expense of $31 million, rent expense of $16 million, and utilities expense of $22 million. McFall declared and paid dividends of $12 million during the year. At December 31, 2016, McFall has cash of $150 million, accounts receivable of $55 million, property and equipment of $32 million, and other long-term assets of $17 million. At December 31, 2016, the company owes accounts payable of $60 million and has a long-term note payable of $27 million. McFall began 2016 with a balance in retained earnings of $68 million. At December 31, 2016, McFall has total stockholders' equity of $167 million, which consists of common stock and retained earnings. McFall has a year-end of December 31. Prepare the following financial statements (with proper headings) for 2016:

1. Income statement,
2. Statement of retained earnings,
3. Balance sheet.

Group B

E1-31B. *(Learning Objectives 3, 4: Apply the accounting equation; evaluate business operations)* Compute the missing amount in the accounting equation for each company (amounts in billions):

	Assets	Liabilities	Stockholders' Equity
Corner Grocery	$?	$51	$37
Sixth Street Bank	21	?	20
Valerie's Gifts	29	13	?

Which company appears to have the strongest financial position? Explain your reasoning.

E1-32B. *(Learning Objectives 3, 4: Apply the accounting equation; evaluate business operations)* Blackwell Services, Inc., has current assets of $240 million; property, plant, and equipment of $350 million; and other assets totaling $170 million. Current liabilities are $150 million, and long-term liabilities total $360 million.

Requirements

1. Use these data to write Blackwell Services, Inc.'s, accounting equation.
2. How much in resources does Blackwell Services have to work with?
3. How much does Blackwell Services owe creditors?
4. How much of the company's assets do the Blackwell Services stockholders actually own?

E1-33B. *(Learning Objectives 3, 4: Apply the accounting equation; evaluate business operations)* Cranberry, Inc.'s, comparative balance sheet at January 31, 2017, and 2016, reports the following (in millions):

	2017	2016
Total assets	$77	$51
Total liabilities	19	12

Requirements

Three situations about Cranberry's issuance of stock and declaration and payment of dividends during the year ended January 31, 2017, follow. For each situation, use the accounting equation and the statement of retained earnings to compute the amount of Cranberry's net income or net loss during the year ended January 31, 2017.

1. Cranberry issued $13 million of stock and declared no dividends.
2. Cranberry issued no stock but declared dividends of $20 million.
3. Cranberry issued $66 million of stock and declared dividends of $20 million.

LO 4

E1-34B. *(Learning Objective 4: Identify financial statement by type of information)* Assume Flurrish, Inc., is expanding into India. The company must decide where to locate and how to finance the expansion. Identify the financial statement where these decision makers can find the following information about Flurrish, Inc. In some cases, more than one statement will report the needed data.

a. Net income
b. Current liabilities
c. Cash spent to acquire the building
d. Adjustments to reconcile net income to net cash provided by operations
e. Selling, general, and administrative expenses
f. Ending cash balance
g. Ending balance of retained earnings
h. Income tax expense
i. Long-term debt
j. Revenue
k. Total assets
l. Dividends
m. Income tax payable
n. Common stock

LO 5

E1-35B. *(Learning Objective 5: Construct a balance sheet)* At December 31, 2016, Robinson Products has cash of $18,000, receivables of $20,000, and inventory of $82,000. The company's equipment totals $183,000. Robinson owes accounts payable of $29,000 and long-term notes payable of $171,000. Common stock is $29,500. Prepare Robinson's balance sheet at December 31, 2016, complete with its proper heading. Use the accounting equation to compute retained earnings.

LO 3 5

E1-36B. *(Learning Objectives 3, 5: Apply the accounting equation; construct a balance sheet)* Amounts of the assets and liabilities of David Austin Realty Company, as of January 31, 2016, are as follows. Also included are revenue, expense, and selected stockholders' equity figures for the year ended on that date (amounts in millions):

Total revenue	$ 37.2	Investment assets (long-term)	$135.6
Receivables	0.7	Property and equipment, net	1.8
Current liabilities	2.1	Other expenses	5.6
Common stock	25.1	Retained earnings, beginning	16.9
Interest expense	0.5	Retained earnings, ending	?
Salary and other employee expenses	13.5	Cash	1.3
Long-term liabilities	102.1	Other assets (long-term)	9.9

Requirement

1. Construct the balance sheet of David Austin Realty Company at January 31, 2016. Use the accounting equation to compute ending retained earnings.

LO 5

E1-37B. *(Learning Objective 5: Construct an income statement and a statement of retained earnings)* This exercise should be used with Exercise 1-36B.

Requirements

1. Prepare the income statement of David Austin Realty Company for the year ended January 31, 2016.
2. What amount of dividends did David Austin Realty Company declare during the year ended January 31, 2016? (*Hint*: Prepare a statement of retained earnings.)

E1-38B. *(Learning Objective 5: Construct an income statement and a statement of retained earnings)* Assume Earl Coffee Roasters Corporation ended the month of August 2016 with these data:

Payments of cash:			
Acquisition of equipment	$202,100	Cash balance, August 1, 2016....	$ 0
Dividends.............................	3,000	Cash balance, August 31, 2016..	5,300
Retained earnings		Cash receipts:	
August 1, 2016......................	0	Issuance (sale) of stock	
Retained earnings		to owners	24,600
August 31, 2016....................	?	Rent expense...........................	1,900
Utilities expense	5,900	Common stock.........................	24,600
Adjustments to reconcile		Equipment................................	202,100
net income to net cash		Office supplies.........................	7,300
provided by operations...........	1,500	Accounts payable	8,800
Salary expense..........................	78,700	Service revenue........................	270,800

Requirement

1. Prepare the income statement and the statement of retained earnings of Earl Coffee Roasters Corporation for the month ended August 31, 2016.

E1-39B. *(Learning Objective 5: Construct a balance sheet)* Refer to the data in Exercise 1-38B.

Requirement

1. Prepare the balance sheet of Earl Coffee Roasters Corporation at August 31, 2016.

E1-40B. *(Learning Objective 5: Construct a statement of cash flows)* Refer to the data in Exercises 1-38B and 1-39B.

Requirement

1. Prepare the statement of cash flows of Earl Coffee Roasters Corporation for the month ended August 31, 2016. Using Exhibit 1-11 as a model, show with arrows the relationships among the income statement, statement of retained earnings, balance sheet, and statement of cash flows.

E1-41B. *(Learning Objective 4: Evaluate business operations through the financial statements)* This exercise should be used in conjunction with Exercises 1-38B through 1-40B.

The owner of Earl Coffee Roasters Corporation now seeks your advice as to whether she should cease operations or continue the business. Complete the report giving her your opinion of net income, dividends, financial position, and cash flows during her first month of operations. Cite specifics from the financial statements to support your opinion. Conclude your memo with advice on whether to stay in business or cease operations.

E1-42B. *(Learning Objective 5: Construct an income statement, statement of retained earnings, and balance sheet)* During 2016, Young Company earned revenues of $150 million. Young incurred, during that same year, salary expense of $30 million, rent expense of $14 million, and utilities expense of $29 million. Young declared and paid dividends of $10 million during the year. At December 31, 2016, Young has cash of $160 million, accounts receivable of $62 million, property and equipment of $34 million, and other long-term assets of $19 million. At December 31, 2016, the company owes accounts payable of $63 million and has a long-term note payable of $25 million. Young began 2016 with a balance in retained earnings of $75 million. At December 31, 2016, Young has total stockholders' equity of $187 million, which consists of common stock and retained earnings. Young has a year-end of December 31. Prepare the following financial statements (with proper headings) for 2016:

1. Income statement,
2. Statement of retained earnings, and
3. Balance sheet.

Quiz

Test your understanding of the financial statements by answering the following questions. Select the best choice from among the possible answers given.

Q1-43. The *primary* objective of financial reporting is to provide information
   a. on the cash flows of the company.
   b. to the federal government.
   c. useful for making investment and credit decisions.
   d. about the profitability of the enterprise.

Q1-44. Which type of business organization provides the least amount of protection for bankers and other creditors of the company?
   a. Proprietorship
   b. Corporation
   c. Partnership
   d. Both a and c

Q1-45. Assets are usually reported at their
   a. current market value.
   b. historical cost.
   c. appraised value.
   d. none of the above (fill in the blank) _____.

Q1-46. During February, assets increased by $87,000 and liabilities increased by $31,000. Stockholders' equity must have
   a. increased by $56,000.
   b. decreased by $56,000.
   c. increased by $118,000.
   d. decreased by $118,000.

Q1-47. The amount a company expects to collect from customers appears on the
   a. balance sheet in the stockholders' equity section.
   b. income statement in the expenses section.
   c. balance sheet in the current assets section.
   d. statement of cash flows.

Q1-48. All of the following are current assets except
   a. accounts payable.
   b. inventory.
   c. accounts receivable.
   d. prepaid expenses.

Q1-49. Revenues are
   a. increases in paid-in capital resulting from the owners investing in the business.
   b. increases in retained earnings resulting from selling products or performing services.
   c. decreases in liabilities resulting from paying off loans.
   d. all of the above.

Q1-50. The financial statement that reports revenues and expenses is called the
   a. income statement.
   b. balance sheet.
   c. statement of retained earnings.
   d. statement of cash flows.

Q1-51. Another name for the balance sheet is the
   a. statement of financial position.
   b. statement of earnings.
   c. statement of operations.
   d. statement of profit and loss.

Q1-52. Dobson Corporation began the year with cash of $143,000 and land that cost $41,000. During the year, Dobson earned service revenue of $230,000 and had the following expenses: salaries, $185,000; rent, $83,000; and utilities, $26,000. At year-end, Dobson's cash balance was down to $56,000. How much net income (or net loss) did Dobson experience for the year?
   a. $45,000
   b. ($38,000)
   c. ($151,000)
   d. ($64,000)

Q1-53. Thompson Instruments had retained earnings of $340,000 at December 31, 2015. Net income for 2016 totaled $185,000, and dividends declared for 2016 were $85,000. How much retained earnings should Thompson report at December 31, 2016?
   a. $425,000
   b. $340,000
   c. $525,000
   d. $440,000

Q1-54. Net income appears on which financial statement(s)?

a. Balance sheet

b. Statement of retained earnings

c. Income statement

d. Both b and c

Q1-55. Cash paid to purchase a building appears on the statement of cash flows among the

a. stockholders' equity.

b. operating activities.

c. financing activities.

d. investing activities.

Q1-56. The stockholders' equity of Voronsky Company at the beginning and end of 2016 totaled $119,000 and $138,000, respectively. Assets at the beginning of 2016 were $144,000. If the liabilities of Voronsky Company increased by $74,000 in 2016, how much were total assets at the end of 2016? Use the accounting equation.

a. $218,000

b. $51,000

c. $237,000

d. $208,000

Q1-57. Smith Company had the following on the dates indicated:

	12/31/16	12/31/15
Total assets	$ 560,000	$ 330,000
Total liabilities	35,000	25,000

Smith had no stock transactions in 2016; thus, the change in stockholders' equity for 2016 was due to net income and dividends. If dividends were $70,000, how much was Smith's net income for 2016? Use the accounting equation and the statement of retained earnings.

a. $220,000

b. $150,000

c. $290,000

d. $360,000

Problems MyAccountingLab

Group A

P1-58A. *(Learning Objectives 3, 4: Apply the accounting equation; evaluate business operations)* Compute the missing amount (?) for each company—amounts in millions.

LO 3 4

	Crystal Co.	Lowell, Inc.	Broom Corp.
Beginning			
Assets..................................	$83	$ 43	$?
Liabilities	43	14	7
Common stock...................	6	3	7
Retained earnings..............	?	26	1
Ending			
Assets..................................	$?	$ 61	$18
Liabilities	45	26	?
Common stock...................	6	?	9
Retained earnings..............	38	?	?
Income statement			
Revenues............................	$228	?	$22
Expenses	222	156	?
Net income........................	?	?	?
Statement of retained earnings			
Beginning RE	$ 34	$ 26	$ 1
+ Net income.......................	?	10	2
− Dividends declared.............	(2)	(13)	(0)
= Ending RE.........................	$ 38	$ 23	$ 3

At the end of the year, which company has the

■ highest net income?

■ highest percent of net income to revenues?

P1-59A. *(Learning Objectives 1, 3, 4, 5: Explain accounting language; apply the accounting equation; evaluate business operations; construct a balance sheet)* The manager of Salem News, Inc., prepared the company's balance sheet as of October 31, 2016, while the accountant was ill. The balance sheet contains numerous errors. In particular, the manager knew that the balance sheet should balance, so she plugged in the stockholders' equity amount needed to achieve this balance. The stockholders' equity amount is *not* correct. All other amounts are accurate.

A1			
A	**B**	**C**	**D**
Salem News, Inc. **Balance Sheet** **October 31, 2016**			
Assets		**Liabilities**	
Cash	$ 10,500	Notes receivable	$ 15,500
Equipment	35,000	Interest expense	2,000
Accounts payable	5,000	Office supplies	1,300
Utilities expense	1,100	Accounts receivable	2,800
Advertising expense	900	Note payable	55,000
Land	84,000	Total	76,600
Salary expense	2,500	**Stockholders' Equity**	
		Stockholders' equity	62,400
Total assets	$ 139,000	Total liabilities	$ 139,000

Requirements

1. Prepare the correct balance sheet and date it properly. Compute total assets, total liabilities, and stockholders' equity.
2. Is Salem News actually in better (or worse) financial position than the erroneous balance sheet reports? Give the reason for your answer.
3. Identify the accounts listed on the incorrect balance sheet that should not be reported on the balance sheet. State why you excluded them from the correct balance sheet you prepared for Requirement 1. On which financial statement should these accounts appear?

P1-60A. *(Learning Objectives 2, 4, 5: Apply underlying accounting concepts; evaluate business operations; construct a balance sheet)* Caden Healey is a realtor. He organized the business as a corporation on December 16, 2017. The business received $60,000 cash from Healey and issued common stock. Consider the following facts as of December 31, 2017:

a. Healey has $12,000 in his personal bank account and $48,000 in the business bank account.
b. Healey owes $6,800 on a personal charge account at a local department store.
c. Healey acquired business furniture for $23,400 on December 24. Of this amount, the business owes $2,000 on accounts payable at December 31.
d. Office supplies on hand at the real estate office total $2,000.
e. Healey's business owes $132,000 on a note payable for some land acquired for a total price of $168,000.
f. Healey's business spent $15,000 for a Realty First franchise, which entitles him to represent himself as an agent. Realty First is a national affiliation of independent real estate agents. This franchise is a business asset.
g. Healey owes $190,000 on a personal mortgage on his personal residence, which he acquired in 2012 for a total price of $405,000.

Requirements

1. Prepare the balance sheet of the real estate business of Caden Healey Realtor, Inc., at December 31, 2017.
2. Does it appear that the realty business can pay its debts? How can you tell?
3. Identify the personal items given in the preceding facts that should not be reported on the balance sheet of the business.

P1-61A. (*Learning Objectives 4, 5: Evaluate business operations; construct and analyze an income statement, a statement of retained earnings, and a balance sheet*) The assets and liabilities of Beckwith Garden Supply, Inc., as of December 31, 2016, and revenues and expenses for the year ended on that date follow:

Equipment............................	$119,000	Land.....................................	$ 27,000
Interest expense....................	10,200	Note payable.......................	99,500
Interest payable....................	2,500	Property tax expense..........	7,300
Accounts payable................	24,000	Rent expense.......................	40,600
Salary expense......................	108,500	Accounts receivable............	84,600
Building...............................	401,000	Service revenue...................	457,600
Cash....................................	41,000	Supplies...............................	6,800
Common stock....................	12,700	Utilities expense	8,500

Beginning retained earnings was $364,200, and dividends declared totaled $106,000 for the year.

Requirements

1. Prepare the income statement of Beckwith Garden Supply, Inc., for the year ended December 31, 2016.
2. Prepare the company's statement of retained earnings for the year.
3. Prepare the company's balance sheet at December 31, 2016.
4. Analyze Beckwith Garden Supply, Inc., by answering these questions:
   a. Was Beckwith Garden Supply profitable during 2016? By how much?
   b. Did retained earnings increase or decrease? By how much?
   c. Which is greater, total liabilities or total stockholders' equity? Who has a greater claim to Beckwith Garden Supply's assets, creditors of the company or the Beckwith Garden Supply stockholders?

P1-62A. (*Learning Objectives 4, 5: Evaluate business operations; construct a statement of cash flows*) The following data come from the financial statements of Riley Company for the year ended March 31, 2017 (in millions):

Purchases of property,		Other investing cash	
plant, and equipment for cash....	$ 3,505	payments..	$ 170
Net income......................................	3,040	Accounts receivable..........................	800
Adjustments to reconcile net		Payment of dividends	270
income to net cash provided		Common stock..................................	4,880
by operating activities	2,410	Issuance of common stock................	165
Revenues...	60,000	Cash proceeds on sale of	
Cash, beginning of year..................	210	property, plant, and equipment.....	45
end of year	1,925	Retained earnings.............................	12,930
Cost of goods sold..........................	37,400		

Requirements

1. Prepare a cash flow statement for the year ended March 31, 2017. Not all items given appear on the cash flow statement.
2. What activities provided the largest source of cash? Is this a sign of financial strength or weakness?

LO 5   **P1-63A.** *(Learning Objective 5: Construct financial statements)* Summarized versions of Santos Corporation's financial statements are given for two recent years.

	A	B	C	D
		A1		
1				
2		2017	2016	
3	**Income Statement**	**(in Thousands)**		
4	Revenues	$ k	$ 15,000	
5	Cost of goods sold	11,000	a	
6	Other expenses	1,210	1,180	
7	Income before income taxes	1,500	2,000	
8	Income taxes (35%)	l	700	
9	Net income	$ m	$ b	
10	**Statement of Retained Earnings**			
11	Beginning balance	$ n	$ 2,650	
12	Net income	o	c	
13	Dividends declared	(90)	(110)	
14	Ending balance	$ p	$ d	
15	**Balance Sheet**			
16	**Assets**			
17	Cash	$ q	$ e	
18	Property, plant, and equipment	1,507	1,346	
19	Other assets	r	11,799	
20	Total assets	$ s	$ 14,465	
21	**Liabilities**			
22	Current liabilities	$ t	$ 5,650	
23	Long-term debt	4,450	3,380	
24	Other liabilities	975	1,120	
25	Total liabilities	$ 9,050	$ f	
26	**Stockholders' equity:**			
27	Common stock	$ 275	$ 275	
28	Retained earnings	u	g	
29	Other stockholders' equity	150	200	
30	Total stockholders' equity	v	4,315	
31	Total liabilities and stockholders' equity	$ w	$ h	
32	**Cash Flow Statement**			
33	Net cash provided by operating activities	$ x	$ 975	
34	Net cash used in investing activities	(260)	(375)	
35	Net cash used in financing activities	(570)	(540)	
36	Increase (decrease) in cash	(180)	i	
37	Cash at beginning of year	y	1,260	
38	Cash at end of year	$ z	$ j	
39				

Requirement

1. Complete Santos Corporation's financial statements by determining the missing amounts denoted by the letters.

Group B

P1-64B. *(Learning Objectives 3, 4: Apply the accounting equation; evaluate business operations)* Compute the missing amount (?) for each company—amounts in millions.

	Pearl Co.	Loomis Co.	Bryant Corp.
Beginning			
Assets	$ 82	$42	$?
Liabilities	44	20	10
Common stock	3	2	3
Retained earnings	?	20	4
Ending			
Assets	$?	$62	$ 19
Liabilities	46	33	?
Common stock	3	?	7
Retained earnings	37	?	?
Income statement			
Revenues	$223	$?	$ 26
Expenses	216	160	?
Net income	?	?	?
Statement of retained earnings			
Beginning RE	$ 35	$20	$ 4
+ Net income	?	10	1
− Dividends declared	(5)	(16)	(2)
= Ending RE	$ 37	$14	$ 3

Which company has the
- highest net income?
- highest percent of net income to revenues?

P1-65B. *(Learning Objectives 1, 3, 4, 5: Explain accounting language; apply the accounting equation; evaluate business operations; construct a balance sheet)* The manager of Candace Design, Inc., prepared the company's balance sheet as of June 30, 2016, while the accountant was ill. The balance sheet contains numerous errors. In particular, the manager knew that the balance sheet should balance, so she plugged in the stockholders' equity amount needed to achieve this balance. The stockholders' equity amount is *not* correct. All other amounts are accurate.

	A1			
	A	B	C	D
1	**Candace Design, Inc.** **Balance Sheet** **June 30, 2016**			
2	**Assets**		**Liabilities**	
3	Cash	$ 8,500	Notes receivable	$ 13,000
4	Equipment	35,600	Interest expense	2,200
5	Accounts payable	2,500	Office supplies	1,000
6	Utilities expense	1,800	Accounts receivable	3,800
7	Advertising expense	300	Note payable	54,500
8	Land	76,000	Total	74,500
9	Salary expense	2,500	**Stockholders' Equity**	
10			Stockholders' equity	52,700
11	Total assets	$ 127,200	Total liabilities	$ 127,200
12				

Requirements

1. Prepare the correct balance sheet and date it properly. Compute total assets, total liabilities, and stockholders' equity.
2. Is Candace Design, Inc., in better (or worse) financial position than the erroneous balance sheet reports? Give the reason for your answer.
3. Identify the accounts listed on the incorrect balance sheet that should *not* be reported on the balance sheet. State why you excluded them from the correct balance sheet you prepared for Requirement 1. On which financial statement should these accounts appear?

 **P1-66B.** *(Learning Objectives 2, 4, 5: Apply underlying accounting concepts; evaluate business operations; construct a balance sheet)* Billy Higgins is a realtor. He organized his business as a corporation on June 16, 2017. The business received $65,000 from Higgins and issued common stock. Consider these facts as of June 30, 2017.

   a. Higgins has $14,000 in his personal bank account and $58,000 in the business bank account.
   b. Higgins owes $5,200 on a personal charge account with a local department store.
   c. Higgins acquired business furniture for $19,600 on June 24. Of this amount, the business owes $4,000 on accounts payable at June 30.
   d. Office supplies on hand at the real estate office total $4,000.
   e. Higgins' business owes $136,000 on a note payable for some land acquired for a total price of $157,000.
   f. Higgins' business spent $15,000 for an American Realty franchise, which entitles him to represent himself as an agent. American Realty is a national affiliation of independent real estate agents. This franchise is a business asset.
   g. Higgins owes $151,000 on a personal mortgage on his personal residence, which he acquired in 2012 for a total price of $423,000.

Requirements

1. Prepare the balance sheet of the real estate business of Billy Higgins Realtor, Inc., at June 30, 2017.
2. Does it appear that the realty business can pay its debts? How can you tell?
3. Identify the personal items given in the preceding facts that should not be reported on the balance sheet of the business.

 **P1-67B.** *(Learning Objectives 4, 5: Evaluate business operations; construct and analyze an income statement, a statement of retained earnings, and a balance sheet)* The assets and liabilities of Blue Moon Products, Inc., as of December 31, 2016, and revenues and expenses for the year ended on that date follow:

Equipment..........................	$ 111,000	Land..................................	$ 28,000
Interest expense..................	10,800	Note payable.....................	99,700
Interest payable..................	2,300	Property tax expense..........	7,900
Accounts payable	27,000	Rent expense.....................	40,200
Salary expense....................	108,300	Accounts receivable............	84,500
Building.............................	402,000	Service revenue..................	458,600
Cash...................................	41,000	Supplies.............................	6,100
Common stock...................	3,800	Utilities expense	8,100

Beginning retained earnings was $364,500, and dividends declared totaled $108,000 for the year.

Requirements

1. Prepare the income statement of Blue Moon Products, Inc., for the year ended December 31, 2016.
2. Prepare the company's statement of retained earnings for the year.
3. Prepare the company's balance sheet at December 31, 2016.
4. Analyze Blue Moon Products, Inc., by answering these questions:
   a. Was Blue Moon Products profitable during 2016? By how much?
   b. Did retained earnings increase or decrease? By how much?
   c. Which is greater, total liabilities or total stockholders' equity? Who has a greater claim to Blue Moon Products' assets, creditors of the company or Blue Moon Products' stockholders?

P1-68B. *(Learning Objectives 4, 5: Evaluate business operations; construct a statement of cash flows)* The following data come from the financial statements of Salem Water Company for the year ended March 31, 2017 (in millions):

Purchases of property, plant, and equipment for cash....	$ 3,515	Other investing cash payments............................	$ 190
Net income...........................	3,060	Accounts receivable...............	550
Adjustments to reconcile net income to net cash provided by operating activities	2,350	Payment of dividends	285
		Common stock.......................	4,810
		Issuance of common stock......	205
Revenues..............................	59,000	Cash proceeds on sale of property, plant, and equipment	
Cash, beginning of year........	230		
end of year	1,910		55
Cost of goods sold...............	37,410	Retained earnings..................	13,000

Requirements

1. Prepare a cash flow statement for the year ended March 31, 2017. Not all the items given appear on the cash flow statement.
2. Which activities provided the largest source of cash? Is this a sign of financial strength or weakness?

LO 5 **P1-69B.** *(Learning Objective 5: Construct financial statements)* Summarized versions of Nettleton Corporation's financial statements are given for two recent years:

	A	B	C	D
1				
2		2017	2016	
3	**Income Statement**	**(in Thousands)**		
4	Revenues	$ k	$ 16,175	
5	Cost of goods sold	11,020	a	
6	Other expenses	1,200	1,210	
7	Income before income taxes	1,510	1,820	
8	Income taxes (35%)	l	637	
9	Net income	$ m	$ b	
10	**Statement of Retained Earnings**			
11	Beginning balance	$ n	$ 2,740	
12	Net income	o	c	
13	Dividends declared	(82)	(140)	
14	Ending balance	$ p	$ d	
15	**Balance Sheet**			
16	**Assets**			
17	Cash	$ q	$ e	
18	Property, plant, and equipment	1,567	1,306	
19	Other assets	r	10,872	
20	Total assets	$ s	$ 13,398	
21	**Liabilities**			
22	Current liabilities	$ t	$ 5,660	
23	Long-term debt	4,300	3,370	
24	Other liabilities	35	180	
25	Total liabilities	$ 9,200	$ f	
26	**Stockholders' equity:**			
27	Common stock	$ 225	$ 225	
28	Retained earnings	u	g	
29	Other stockholders' equity	120	180	
30	Total stockholders' equity	v	4,188	
31	Total liabilities and stockholders' equity	$ w	$ h	
32	**Cash Flow Statement**			
33	Net cash provided by operating activities	$ x	$ 900	
34	Net cash used in investing activities	(210)	(350)	
35	Net cash used in financing activities	(590)	(550)	
36	Increase (decrease) in cash	(80)	i	
37	Cash at beginning of year	y	1,220	
38	Cash at end of year	$ z	$ j	
39				

Requirement

1. Complete Nettleton Corporation's financial statements by determining the missing amounts denoted by the letters.

APPLY YOUR KNOWLEDGE

Decision Cases

Case 1. *(Learning Objectives 1, 4: Explain accounting language; evaluate business operations through financial statements)* Two businesses, Queens Service Corp. and Insley Sales Co., have sought business loans from you. To decide whether to make the loans, you have requested their balance sheets.

 LO 1 4

	A	B	C	D
1	**Queens Service Corp.** **Balance Sheet** **August 31, 2017**			
2	**Assets**		**Liabilities**	
3	Cash	$ 5,000	Accounts payable	$ 50,000
4	Accounts receivable	10,000	Note payable	80,000
5	Land	75,000	Total liabilities	130,000
6	Furniture	15,000	**Stockholders' Equity**	
7	Equipment	45,000	Stockholders' equity	20,000
8			Total liabilities and	
9	Total assets	$ 150,000	stockholders' equity	$ 150,000
10				

	A	B	C	D
1	**Insley Sales Co.** **Balance Sheet** **August 31, 2017**			
2	**Assets**		**Liabilities**	
3	Cash	$ 5,000	Accounts payable	$ 6,000
4	Accounts receivable	10,000	Note payable	9,000
5	Merchandise inventory	15,000	Total liabilities	15,000
6	Building	35,000	**Stockholders' Equity**	
7			Stockholders' equity	50,000
8			Total liabilities and	
9	Total assets	$ 65,000	stockholders' equity	$ 65,000
10				

Requirement

1. Using only these balance sheets, to which entity would you be more comfortable lending money? Explain fully, citing specific items and amounts from the respective balance sheets. (Challenge)

Case 2. (*Learning Objectives 4, 5: Evaluate business operations through financial statements; correct errors; construct financial statements*) A year out of college, you have $10,000 to invest. A friend has started Flowers Unlimited, Inc., and he asks you to invest in his company. You obtain the company's financial statements, which are summarized at the end of the first year as follows:

	A1			B	C
	A			**B**	**C**
1	**Flowers Unlimited, Inc.** **Income Statement** **Year Ended December 31, 2016**				
2	Revenues				$ 100,000
3	Expenses				80,000
4	Net income				$ 20,000
5					

	A1			
	A	**B**	**C**	**D**
1	**Flowers Unlimited, Inc.** **Balance Sheet** **December 31, 2016**			
2	Cash	$ 6,000	Liabilities	$ 60,000
3	Other assets	100,000	Stockholders' equity	46,000
4	Total assets	$ 106,000	Total liabilities and stockholders' equity	$ 106,000
5				

Visits with your friend turn up the following facts:

a. Flowers Unlimited delivered $140,000 of services to customers during 2016 and collected $100,000 from customers for those services.

b. Flowers Unlimited recorded a $50,000 cash payment for software as an asset. This cost should have been an expense.

c. To get the business started, your friend borrowed $10,000 from his parents at the end of 2015. The proceeds of the loan were used to pay salaries for the first month of 2016. Since the loan was from his parents, your friend did not reflect the loan or the salaries in the accounting records.

Requirements

1. Prepare corrected financial statements.
2. Use your corrected statements to evaluate Flowers Unlimited's results of operations and financial position. (Challenge)
3. Will you invest in Flowers Unlimited? Give your reason. (Challenge)

Ethical Issue

(*Learning Objective 6: Evaluate ethical decisions*) You are studying frantically for an accounting exam tomorrow. You are having difficulty in this course, and the grade you make on this exam can make the difference between receiving a final grade of B or C. If you receive a C, it will lower your grade point average to the point that you could lose your academic scholarship. An hour ago, a friend, also enrolled in the course but in a different section under the same professor, called you with some unexpected news. In her sorority test files, she has just found a copy of an old exam from the previous year. In looking at the exam, it appears to contain questions that come right from the class notes you have taken, even the very same numbers. She offers to make a copy for you and bring it over.

You glance at your course syllabus and find the following: "You are expected to do your own work in this class. Although you may study with others, giving, receiving, or obtaining information pertaining to an examination is considered an act of academic dishonesty, unless such action is authorized by the instructor giving the examination. Also, divulging the contents of an essay or objective examination designated by the instructor as an examination is considered an act of academic dishonesty. Academic dishonesty is considered a violation of the student honor code and will subject the student to disciplinary procedures, which can include suspension from the university." Although you have heard a rumor that fraternities and sororities have cleared their exam files with professors, you are not sure.

Requirements

1. What is the ethical issue in this situation?
2. Who are the stakeholders? What are the possible consequences to each?
3. Analyze the alternatives from the following standpoints: (a) economic, (b) legal, and (c) ethical.
4. What would you do? How would you justify your decision? How would your decision make you feel afterward?
5. How is this similar to a business situation?

Focus on Financials | Apple Inc.

(Learning Objectives 3, 4: Apply the accounting equation; evaluate business operations)
This and similar cases in succeeding chapters are based on the consolidated financial statements of **Apple Inc.**, given in Appendix A and online in the filings section of **http://www.sec.gov**. As you work with Apple Inc. throughout this course, you will develop the ability to use the financial statements of actual companies.

LO 3 4

Requirements

1. Go on the Internet and do some research on Apple Inc. and its industry. Use one or more popular websites such as Yahoo! Finance or Google Finance. Write a paragraph (about 100 words) that describes the industry, some current developments, and a projection for future growth.
2. Read Part I, Item 1 (Business) of Apple Inc.'s annual report. What do you learn here and why is it important?
3. Name at least one of Apple Inc.'s competitors. Why is this information important in evaluating Apple Inc.'s financial performance?
4. Suppose you own stock in Apple Inc. If you could pick one item on the company's Consolidated Statements of Operations to increase year after year, what would it be? Why is this item so important? Did this item increase or decrease during fiscal 2014? Is this good news or bad news for the company?
5. What was Apple Inc.'s largest expense in 2012–2014? In your own words, explain the meaning of this item. Give specific examples of items that make up this expense. The chapter gives another title for this expense. What is it?
6. Use the Consolidated Balance Sheets of Apple Inc., in Appendix A to answer these questions: At the end of fiscal 2014, how much in total resources did Apple Inc., have to work with? How much did the company owe? How much of its assets did the company's stockholders actually own? Use these amounts to write Apple Inc.'s accounting equation at September 27, 2014.
7. How much cash and cash equivalents did Apple Inc., have at September 28, 2013? How much cash and cash equivalents did Apple Inc., have at September 27, 2014?

Focus on Analysis | Under Armour, Inc.

(Learning Objectives 3, 4: Apply the accounting equation; evaluate business operations)
This and similar cases in each chapter are based on the consolidated financial statements of
Under Armour, Inc., given in Appendix B and online in the filings section of **http://www.sec
.gov**. As you work with Under Armour, Inc., you will develop the ability to analyze the financial
statements of actual companies.

Requirements

1. Go on the Internet and do some research on Under Armour, Inc., and its industry. Use one
   or more popular websites such as Yahoo! Finance or Google Finance. Write a paragraph
   (about 100 words) that describes the industry, some current developments, and a projection
   for where the industry is headed.
2. Read Note 1—(Description of Business) of Under Armour, Inc.'s, annual report. What do
   you learn here and why is it important?
3. Name two of Under Armour, Inc.'s, competitors. Why is this information important in evaluating Under Armour, Inc.'s, financial performance?
4. Write Under Armour, Inc.'s, accounting equation at December 31, 2014 (express all items
   in millions and round to the nearest $1 million). Does Under Armour, Inc.'s, financial con-
   dition look strong or weak? How can you tell?
5. What was the result of Under Armour, Inc.'s, operations during 2014? Identify both the
   name and the dollar amount of the result of operations for 2014. Does an increase (or
   decrease) signal good news or bad news for the company and its stockholders?
6. Examine retained earnings in the Consolidated Statements of Stockholders' Equity. What
   caused retained earnings to increase during 2014? (*Note*: Comprehensive income is based
   on net income and will be covered in Chapter 11.)
7. Which statement reports cash and cash equivalents as part of Under Armour, Inc.'s, financial position? Which statement tells *why* cash and cash equivalents increased (or decreased)
   during the year? Which activities caused Under Armour, Inc.'s, cash and cash equivalents
   to change during 2014, and how much did each activity provide or use?

Group Projects

*Project 1. As instructed by your professor, obtain the annual report of a well-known
company.*

Requirements

1. Take the role of a loan committee of Bank of America Corporation, a large banking company headquartered in Charlotte, North Carolina. Assume a company has requested a loan
   from Bank of America. Analyze the company's financial statements and any other information you need to reach a decision regarding the largest amount of money you would be
   willing to lend. Go as deeply into the analysis and the related decision as you can. Specify
   the following:
   a. The length of the loan period—that is, over what period will you allow the company to
      pay you back?
   b. The interest rate you will charge on the loan. Will you charge the prevailing interest rate,
      a lower rate, or a higher rate? Why?
   c. Any restrictions you will impose on the borrower as a condition for making the loan.

Note: The long-term debt note to the financial statements gives details of the company's existing liabilities.

2. Write your group decision in a report addressed to the bank's board of directors. Limit your
   report to two double-spaced typed pages (400 to 600 words).
3. If your professor directs, present your decision and your analysis to the class. Limit your
   presentation to 10 to 15 minutes.

Project 2. You are the owner of a company that is about to "go public," that is, issue its stock to outside investors. You wish to make your company look as attractive as possible to raise $1 million of cash to expand the business. At the same time, you want to give potential investors a realistic picture of your company.

Requirements

1. Design a booklet to portray your company in a way that will enable outsiders to reach an informed decision as to whether to buy some of your stock. The booklet should include the following:
   a. Name and location of your company.
   b. Nature of the company's business (be as detailed as possible).
   c. How you plan to spend the money you raise.
   d. The company's comparative income statement, statement of retained earnings, balance sheet, and statement of cash flows for two years: the current year and the preceding year. Make the data as realistic as possible with the intent of receiving $1 million.
2. Create your booklet using Word, Pages, or other similar tool. Do not exceed five pages.
3. If directed by your professor, make a copy for each member of your class. Distribute copies to the class and present your case with the intent of interesting your classmates in investing in the company. Limit your presentation to 10 to 15 minutes.

Quick Check Answers

1. *c*

2. *b*

3. *a* [This is not the typical way the accounting equation is expressed (Assets − Liabilities = Owners' equity), but it may be rearranged this way.]

4. *b*

5. *b*

6. *c*

7. *d* ($320,000 − $115,000 − $8,000 = $197,000)

8. *b* ($320,000 − $115,000 = $205,000)

9. *d* [Total assets = $111,000 ($8,000 + $33,000 + $28,000 + $42,000). Liabilities = $21,000]

10. *d*

11. *c* ($99,000 + Net income $25,000 − Dividends $9,000 = $115,000)

12. *c*

	Assets	=	Liabilities	+	Equity
Beginning	$145,000	=	$70,000*	+	$75,000
Increase	$47,000	=	$14,000	+	$33,000*
Ending	$192,000*	=	$84,000*	+	$108,000*

Must solve for these amounts.

13. *c*

14. *d*

Transaction Analysis

⬙ SPOTLIGHT | The Walt Disney Company Records Millions of Transactions a Year!

In 2013, an estimated 132.6 million people purchased either single-day or multiday tickets to 1 of 11 Disney theme parks. The Disney live-action feature motion picture *Cinderella* opened in about 4,000 theaters worldwide in March 2015, with gross revenues of $159 million in its first week. At an average price of $8 per ticket, that amounts to about 19.9 million tickets sold in just one week. Each park admission and each movie ticket sold involves a business transaction. And that's just the tip of the iceberg. If you log on to the Disney website (**http://www.disney .com**), as millions of people do every day, you can go almost anywhere within the bounds of your imagination. Besides the purchase of tickets to a Disney theme park, you can book a reservation at a Disney Resort, reserve a table for an elegant dinner at a Disney hotel, buy merchandise at the online Disney Store, play Disney video games, view Disney movies that have been released and review planned future releases, or even book a cruise to the Caribbean, Mediterranean, or Alaska on the Disney Cruise Line—all for a price. You may use the Disney Movies Anywhere app on your smart phone to purchase or rent the Disney movie of your choice. Beyond these, log on to the ESPN website (**http://espn.go.com**) and you will see logos of various other companies such as The Walt Disney Company that purchase space to advertise their products or services on the website. If you subscribe to a cable television service or DIRECTV, ESPN, The

Andrew Holbrooke/Corbis

Disney Channel, or ABC Family Network, all of these cable television networks are accessed by subscription. As we showed in Chapter 1, in total, The Walt Disney Company made $48.8 billion in revenues and incurred $41.3 billion in expenses of various types, to earn net income attributable to The Walt Disney Company of $7.5 billion in 2014. Where did those figures come from? Millions and millions of transactions! ●

Chapter 1 introduced the financial statements. In Chapters 2 and 3, we introduce you to the accounting cycle that is the process by which financial statements are prepared.

The first four steps in the accounting cycle are recognizing transactions, analyzing their impact on the accounting equation, entering those transactions in the "books," and posting them to the accounts.

LEARNING	OBJECTIVES

① **Explain** what a transaction is

② **Define** "account," and **list** and **differentiate** between different types of accounts

③ **Show** the impact of business transactions on the accounting equation

④ **Analyze** the impact of business transactions on accounts

⑤ **Record** (journalize and post) transactions in the books

⑥ **Construct and use** a trial balance

Try It

Read more about the businesses of The Walt Disney Company by accessing "Description of the Business and Segment Information" in the footnotes to its annual report. You can access the most current annual report of The Walt Disney Company at **http://www.sec.gov**. Using the "FILINGS" link on the toolbar at the top of the home page, select "Company Filings Search." This will take you to the "EDGAR Company Filings" page. Type "Walt Disney" in the company name box, and select "Search." This will produce the "EDGAR Search Results" page showing the company name. Click on the "CIK" link beside the company name. This will pull up a list of the reports the company has filed with the Securities and Exchange Commission (SEC). Under the "Filing Type" box, type "10-K," and click the "Search" box. Form 10-K is the SEC form for the company's annual report. Find the year that you wish to view. Click on the "Interactive Data" box, which takes you to the "View Filing Data" page. In the yellow left-hand toolbar of the page, click on "Notes to Financial Statements." A gray toolbar will appear listing the various footnotes. Click on "Description of the Business and Segment Information."

EXPLAIN WHAT A TRANSACTION IS

A **transaction** is any event that has a financial impact on the business and can be measured reliably. For example, The Walt Disney Company purchases fresh produce and meat for its restaurants, and supplies for its hotels and resorts. The Walt Disney Company provides entertainment services through its television networks, sells Disney merchandise, borrows money, and repays the loan—all separate transactions.

But not all events qualify as transactions. The Disney Cruise Line may be featured in a travel brochure, or a person planning a vacation may see a Disney theme park advertisement on television. These events may create awareness and, ultimately, new business for The Walt Disney Company. However, no transaction occurs until someone actually buys tickets to the theme park, stays as a guest at a Disney resort, purchases Disney products, or otherwise engages in an

① **Explain** what a transaction is

exchange with The Walt Disney Company. Transactions provide objective information about the financial impact of an exchange on an entity:

- It gives something.
- It receives something in return.

In accounting, we always record both sides of a transaction. We must be able to measure the financial impact of the event on the business before recording it as a transaction.

DEFINE "ACCOUNT," AND LIST AND DIFFERENTIATE BETWEEN DIFFERENT TYPES OF ACCOUNTS

② Define "account," and list and **differentiate** between different types of accounts

As we saw in Chapter 1, the accounting equation expresses the basic relationship of accounting:

$$\text{Assets} = \text{Liabilities} + \text{Stockholders' (Owners') Equity}$$

For each asset, each liability, and each element of stockholders' equity, we use a record called the account. An **account** is the record of all the changes in a particular asset, liability, or stockholders' equity during a period. The account is the basic summary device of accounting. Before launching into transaction analysis, let's review some of the accounts used by a company such as The Walt Disney Company.

Assets

Assets are economic resources that provide a future benefit for a business. Most firms use the following asset accounts:

Cash. Cash is money and any medium of exchange including bank account balances, paper currency, coins, certificates of deposit, and checks.

Accounts Receivable. The Walt Disney Company, like most other companies, sells its goods and services and receives a promise for future collection of cash. The accounts receivable account holds these amounts.

Inventory. An important current asset of The Walt Disney Company is its inventory—the branded merchandise that The Walt Disney Company sells to customers. It also includes assets like vacation time-share units that the company sells on a daily, weekly, or monthly basis to vacationers. Other titles for this account include *Merchandise* and *Merchandise Inventory*.

Prepaid Expenses. The Walt Disney Company pays certain expenses in advance, such as insurance and rent. A prepaid expense is an asset because the payment provides a *future* benefit for the business. Prepaid Rent, Prepaid Insurance, and Supplies are prepaid expenses.

Film and Television Costs. These costs include production costs, production overhead, interest, and development costs for Disney films and television programs. These are accumulated in an asset account and are eventually amortized as expenses as the films and television programs are shown. These costs are unique to media companies like The Walt Disney Company.

Investments. As explained in Chapter 1, The Walt Disney Company has purchased interests in other companies that operate all over the world. Because these investments have a long-term future use to the company, they are listed among the company's long-term assets.

Parks, Resorts, and Other Property. This account shows the cost of the land, buildings, and equipment used by The Walt Disney Company in its operations to earn revenue. Within this category, the company segregates each asset by type and eventually allocates much of the cost associated with each asset through depreciation to the periods of time that the asset helps earn revenue. Most other companies call this account Property, Plant, and Equipment.

Liabilities

Recall that a *liability* is a debt. A payable is always a liability. The most common types of liabilities include the following:

Accounts Payable. The accounts payable account is the direct opposite of accounts receivable. The Walt Disney Company's promise to pay a debt (perhaps arising from a credit purchase of inventory or from a utility bill) appears in the accounts payable account.

Notes Payable (borrowings). The notes payable account includes the amounts The Walt Disney Company must *pay* because it signed notes promising to pay a future amount. Notes payable, like notes receivable in the assets section of the balance sheet, also bear interest.

Accrued Liabilities. An **accrued liability** is a liability for an expense you have not yet paid. Interest payable and salary payable are accrued liability accounts for most companies. Income tax payable is another accrued liability.

Stockholders' (Owners') Equity

The owners' claims to the assets of a corporation are called *stockholders' equity*, *shareholders' equity*, or simply *owners' equity*. A corporation such as The Walt Disney Company uses common stock, retained earnings, and dividend accounts to record the company's stockholders' equity. In a proprietorship, there is a single capital account. For a partnership, each partner has a separate owner's equity account.

Common Stock. The common stock account shows the owners' investment in the corporation. The Walt Disney Company receives cash and issues common stock to its stockholders. A company's common stock is its most basic element of equity. All corporations have common stock.

Retained Earnings. The retained earnings account shows the cumulative net income earned by The Walt Disney Company over the company's lifetime, minus its cumulative net losses and dividends.

Dividends. Dividends are optional; they are decided (declared) by the board of directors. After profitable operations, the board of directors of The Walt Disney Company may declare and pay a cash dividend. The corporation may keep a separate account titled *dividends*, which indicates a decrease in retained earnings.

Revenues. The increase in stockholders' equity from delivering goods or services to customers is called *revenue*. The company uses as many revenue accounts as needed. The Walt Disney Company uses a products revenue account for revenue earned by selling its products and a services revenue account for the revenue it earns by providing services to customers. A lawyer provides legal services for clients and also uses a service revenue account. A business that loans money to an outsider needs an interest revenue account. If the business rents a building to a tenant, the business needs a rent revenue account.

Name two things that

(1) increase The Walt Disney Company's stockholders' equity, and

(2) decrease The Walt Disney Company's stockholders' equity.

Answers:

(1) Increases in stockholders' equity: Sale of stock and net income (revenues greater than expenses).

(2) Decreases in stockholders' equity: Dividends and net loss (expenses greater than revenues).

Expenses. The cost of operating a business is called an *expense*. Expenses *decrease* stockholders' equity, the opposite effect of revenues. A business needs a separate account for each type of expense, such as cost of goods or services sold, salary expense, rent expense, advertising expense, insurance expense, utilities expense, and income tax expense. Businesses strive to minimize expenses and thereby maximize net income.

SHOW THE IMPACT OF BUSINESS TRANSACTIONS ON THE ACCOUNTING EQUATION

Example: Alladin Travel, Inc.

③ Show the impact of business transactions on the accounting equation

To illustrate the accounting for transactions, let's return to Alladin Travel, Inc. In Chapter 1's End-of-Chapter Problem, primary shareholder and manager Starr Williams opened Alladin Travel, Inc., in April 2016.

We will consider 11 transactions and analyze each in terms of its effect on Alladin Travel. We will begin by using the accounting equation to build the financial statements in spreadsheet format. In the second half of the chapter, we will record transactions using the journal and ledger of the business.

》 *Try It in* **Excel®**

As you review the 11 transactions, build an Excel template. Use the accounting equation on page 62 as a model. Remember that each transaction has either an equal effect on both the left- and right-hand sides of the accounting equation, or an offsetting effect (both positive and negative) on the same side of the equation. Recreate the spreadsheet in Exhibit 2-1, Panel B (page 70), step by step, as you go along. In Excel, open a new blank spreadsheet.

Step 1 Format the worksheet. Label cell A2 "Trans." You will put transaction numbers corresponding to the transactions below in the cells in column A. Row 1 will contain the elements of the accounting equation. Enter "Assets" in cell D1. Enter an "=" sign in cell F1. Enter "Liabilities + Stockholders' Equity" in cell G1. Enter "Type of SE (abbreviation for stockholders' equity) Transaction" in cell J1. Highlight cells B1 through E1 and click "merge and center" on the top toolbar. Highlight cells G1 through I1 and click "merge and center." Now you will have a spreadsheet organized around the elements of the accounting equation: "Assets = Liabilities + Stockholders' Equity" and, for all transactions impacting stockholders' equity, you will be able to enter the type (capital stock, revenue, expense, or dividends). This will be important later when you construct the financial statements (Exhibit 2-2, page 72).

Step 2 Continue formatting. In cells B2 through E2, enter the asset account titles that transactions 1–11 deal with. B2: Cash; C2: AR (an abbreviation for accounts receivable); D2: Supplies; E2: Land. In cells G2 through I2, enter the liability and stockholders' equity account titles that Alladin Travel, Inc.'s, transactions deal with: G2: AP (an abbreviation for accounts payable); H2: C Stock (an abbreviation for common stock); and I2: RE (abbreviation for retained earnings; this is where all transactions impacting revenue, expenses, and dividends will go for now).

Step 3 In row 15, enter the formula to sum each column from B through E and G through I. For example, the formula in cell B15 should be "=sum(B3:B14)." In cell A15, enter "Bal." This will allow you to keep a running sum of the accounts in the balance sheet as you enter each transaction.

Step 4 In cell A16, enter "Totals." In cell C16, enter "=sum(B15:E15)." In cell H16, enter "=sum(G15:I15)." You can use the short cut symbol "Σ" followed by highlighting

> the respective cells. Excel allows you to keep a running sum of the column totals on each side of the equation. You should find that the running sum of the column totals on the left-hand side of the equation always equals the running sum of the column totals on the right-hand side, so the accounting equation always stays in balance. As a final formatting step, highlight cells B3 through I16. Using the "number" tab on the toolbar at the top of the spreadsheet, select "Accounting" for format with no $ sign, and select "decrease decimal" to zero places. Now you're ready to process the transactions.

Transaction 1. On April 1, Starr Williams and a few friends invest $50,000 to open Alladin Travel, Inc., and the business issues common stock to the stockholders. The effect of this transaction on the accounting equation of Alladin Travel, Inc., is a receipt of cash and issuance of common stock:

Assets		Liabilities	+	Stockholders' Equity	Type of Stockholders' Equity Transaction
Cash	=			Common Stock	
(1) + 50,000				+ 50,000	Issued common stock

Every transaction's net amount on the left side of the accounting equation must equal the net amount on the right side. The first transaction increases both the cash and the common stock of the business. If you're following along in Excel, enter 1 in cell A3 of the spreadsheet you are creating. Enter 50000 in cell B3 (under Cash) and 50000 in cell H3 (under C Stock). To the right of the transaction in cell J3 write "Issued common stock" to show the reason for the increase in stockholders' equity. You don't have to enter commas; Excel will do that for you. Notice that the sum of Cash (cell B15) is now 50,000 and the sum of Common Stock (cell H15) is also 50,000. The total of accounts on the left side of the accounting equation is 50,000 (cell C16) and it equals the total of accounts on the right side of the accounting equation (cell H16).

Every transaction affects the financial statements of the business, and we can prepare financial statements after one, two, or any number of transactions. For example, Alladin Travel, Inc., could create the company's balance sheet from our spreadsheet after its first transaction, shown here.

	A	B	C	D	E	F
		A1				
1	Alladin Travel, Inc. Balance Sheet April 1, 2016					
2	**Assets**			**Liabilities**		
3	Cash		$ 50,000	None		
4				**Stockholders' Equity**		
5				Common stock	$ 50,000	
6				Total stockholders' equity	50,000	
7				Total liabilities and		
8	Total assets		$ 50,000	stockholders' equity	$ 50,000	
9						

This balance sheet shows that the business holds cash of $50,000 and owes no liabilities. The company's equity (ownership) is denoted as *Common stock* on the balance sheet. A bank would look favorably on this balance sheet because the business has $50,000 cash and no debt—a strong financial position.

As a practical matter, most entities report their financial statements at the end of the accounting period, and not after each transaction. But an accounting system based on a structure similar to our Excel spreadsheet can produce statements whenever managers need to know where the business stands.

Transaction 2. Alladin purchases land for a new location and pays cash of $40,000. The effect of this transaction on the accounting equation is as follows:

	Assets				Liabilities	+	Stockholders' Equity	Type of Stockholders' Equity Transaction
	Cash	+	Land				Common Stock	
(1)	50,000						50,000	Issued common stock
(2)	− 40,000		+ 40,000					
Bal	10,000		40,000	=			50,000	
		50,000					50,000	

The purchase increases one asset (Land) and decreases another asset (Cash) by the same amount. If you're following along in Excel, enter a 2 in cell A4. Enter –40000 in cell B4 and 40000 in cell E4. The spreadsheet automatically updates, showing that after the transaction is completed, Alladin has cash of $10,000, land of $40,000, total assets of $50,000, and no liabilities. Stockholders' equity is unchanged at $50,000. Note that, as shown in cells C16 and H16, total assets must always equal total liabilities plus stockholders' equity.

Transaction 3. The business buys supplies on account, agreeing to pay $3,700 within 30 days. This transaction increases both the assets and the liabilities of the business. Its effect on the accounting equation follows:

	Assets						Liabilities	+	Stockholders' Equity
	Cash	+	Supplies	+	Land		Accounts Payable	+	Common Stock
Bal	10,000				40,000				50,000
(3)			+ 3,700			=	+ 3,700		
Bal	10,000		3,700		40,000		3,700		50,000
			53,700					53,700	

The new asset is Supplies, and the liability is an Account Payable. Alladin signs no formal promissory note, so the liability is an account payable, not a note payable. If you're following along in Excel, enter 3 in cell A5, 3700 in cell D5 under the account "Supplies," and 3700 in cell G5 under "AP" (accounts payable). Notice that the spreadsheet now reflects three assets in row 15: cash with a balance of $10,000 (cell B15), supplies with a balance of $3,700 (cell D15), and land with a balance of $40,000 (cell E15), for total assets of $53,700 (cell C16). On the right-hand side of the accounting equation, Alladin now has accounts payable (a liability) of $3,700 (cell G15) and common stock (cell H15) of $50,000, for a total of $53,700 (cell H16).

Transaction 4. Alladin earns $7,000 of service revenue by providing services for customers. The business collects the cash. The effect on the accounting equation is an increase in the asset Cash and an increase in Retained Earnings, as follows:

	Assets				Liabilities	+	Stockholders' Equity			Type of Stockholders' Equity Transaction
	Cash	+	Supplies	+	Land		Accounts Payable	+	Common Stock	+	Retained Earnings	
Bal	10,000		3,700		40,000	=	3,700		50,000			
(4)	+ 7,000										+ 7,000	Service revenue
Bal	17,000		3,700		40,000		3,700		50,000		7,000	
			60,700						60,700			

In the Excel spreadsheet on line 6, we enter 7000 under Cash (cell B6) and 7000 under Retained Earnings (cell I6). In cell J6, we enter "Service revenue" to show where the $7,000 of increase in retained earnings came from. Our grand totals on the bottom of the spreadsheet now show $60,700 for total assets as well as $60,700 for total liabilities and stockholders' equity.

Transaction 5. Alladin performs services on account, which means that Alladin lets some customers pay later. Alladin earns revenue but doesn't receive the cash immediately. In transaction 5, Alladin arranges travel for several large corporate customers, and they agree to pay Alladin $3,000 within one month. This promise is an account receivable—an asset—of Alladin Travel. The transaction record is:

	Assets								Liabilities	+	Stockholders' Equity			Type of Stockholders' Equity Transaction
	Cash	+	Accounts Receivable	+	Supplies	+	Land		Accounts Payable	+	Common Stock	+	Retained Earnings	
Bal	17,000				3,700		40,000	=	3,700		50,000		7,000	
(5)			+ 3,000										+ 3,000	Service revenue
Bal	17,000		3,000		3,700		40,000		3,700		50,000		10,000	
				63,700							63,700			

It's performing the service that earns the revenue—not collecting the cash. Therefore, Alladin records revenue when it performs the service—regardless of whether Alladin receives cash now or later. In your Excel spreadsheet, enter 3000 under Accounts Receivable on the left-hand side (cell C7) and 3000 under Retained Earnings on the right-hand side (cell I7). Also enter "Service revenue" in cell J7 to keep a record of the type of transaction (revenue) that affects stockholders' equity (SE).

Transaction 6. During the month, Alladin Travel, Inc., pays $2,700 for the following expenses: rent, $1,100; employee salaries, $1,200; and utilities, $400. The effect on the accounting equation is:

	Assets								Liabilities	+	Stockholders' Equity			Type of Stockholders' Equity Transaction
	Cash	+	Accounts Receivable	+	Supplies	+	Land		Accounts Payable	+	Common Stock	+	Retained Earnings	
Bal	17,000		3,000		3,700		40,000	=	3,700		50,000		10,000	
(6)	− 2,700												− 1,100	Rent expense
													− 1,200	Salary expense
													− 400	Utilities expense
Bal	14,300		3,000		3,700		40,000		3,700		50,000		7,300	
				61,000							61,000			

This transaction will take up lines 8, 9, and 10 of the Excel spreadsheet. Enter −2700 under Cash (cell B8); −1100 under Retained Earnings (cell I8); −1200 under Retained Earnings (cell I9); and −400 under Retained Earnings (cell I10). Enter the type of transaction (rent expense, salary expense, utilities expense) to account for the type of transaction impacting stockholders' equity (SE). These expenses decrease Alladin Travel, Inc.'s, Cash and Retained Earnings. List each expense separately to keep track of its amount and to facilitate the preparation of the income statement later.

Transaction 7. Alladin pays $1,900 on account, which means to make a payment toward an account payable. In this transaction Alladin pays the store from which it purchased supplies in transaction 3. The transaction decreases Cash (cell B11 on the Excel spreadsheet) and also decreases Accounts Payable (cell G11):

	Assets									Liabilities	+	Stockholders' Equity		
	Cash	+	Accounts Receivable	+	Supplies	+	Land		=	Accounts Payable	+	Common Stock	+	Retained Earnings
Bal	14,300		3,000		3,700		40,000			3,700		50,000		7,300
(7)	− 1,900									− 1,900				
Bal	12,400		3,000		3,700		40,000			1,800		50,000		7,300
				59,100								59,100		

Transaction 8. Starr Williams, the major stockholder of Alladin Travel, paid $30,000 out of her personal (not business) bank account to remodel her home. This event is a personal transaction of the Williams family. It is not recorded by Alladin Travel, Inc. We focus solely on the business entity, not on its owners. This transaction illustrates the entity assumption from Chapter 1.

Transaction 9. In transaction 5, Alladin performed travel services for customers on account. The business now collects $1,000 from a customer. We say that Alladin *collects the cash on account*, which means that Alladin will record an increase in Cash and a decrease in Accounts Receivable. This is not service revenue because Alladin already recorded the revenue in transaction 5. The effect of collecting cash on account is:

	Assets									Liabilities	+	Stockholders' Equity		
	Cash	+	Accounts Receivable	+	Supplies	+	Land		=	Accounts Payable	+	Common Stock	+	Retained Earnings
Bal	12,400		3,000		3,700		40,000			1,800		50,000		7,300
(9)	+ 1,000		− 1,000											
Bal	13,400		2,000		3,700		40,000			1,800		50,000		7,300
				59,100								59,100		

This transaction is entered on line 12 of the Excel spreadsheet as an increase in Cash (cell B12) and a decrease in AR (cell C12).

Transaction 10. Alladin sells some land for $22,000, which is the same amount that Alladin paid for the land. Alladin receives $22,000 cash, and the effect on the accounting equation is:

	Cash	+	Accounts Receivable	+	Supplies	+	Land			Accounts Payable	+	Common Stock	+	Retained Earnings
					Assets				=	**Liabilities**	+	**Stockholders' Equity**		
Bal	13,400		2,000		3,700		40,000			1,800		50,000		7,300
(10)	+22,000						−22,000							
Bal	35,400		2,000		3,700		18,000			1,800		50,000		7,300
				59,100								59,100		

Note that the company did not sell all its land; Alladin still owns $18,000 worth of land. This transaction is entered in the Excel spreadsheet as an increase in Cash (cell B13) and a decrease in Land (cell E13).

Transaction 11. Alladin Travel, Inc., declares a dividend and pays the stockholders $2,100 cash. The effect on the accounting equation is:

	Cash	+	Accounts Receivable	+	Supplies	+	Land			Accounts Payable	+	Common Stock	+	Retained Earnings	Type of Stockholders' Equity Transaction
				Assets				=		**Liabilities**	+	**Stockholders' Equity**		
Bal	35,400		2,000		3,700		18,000			1,800		50,000		7,300	
(11)	−2,100													−2,100	Dividend
Bal	33,300		2,000		3,700		18,000			1,800		50,000		5,200	
				57,000								57,000			

The dividend decreases both Cash (cell B14) and the Retained Earnings (cell I14) of the business. *However, dividends are not an expense.* They are a separate type of reduction of stockholders' equity. Therefore, enter "Dividend" in cell J14. We should now have all of the transactions impacting stockholders' equity labeled properly, which will facilitate the preparation of the financial statements later.

Transactions and Financial Statements

Exhibit 2-1 summarizes the 11 preceding transactions. Panel A gives the details of the transactions, and Panel B shows the transaction analysis. If you prepared an Excel spreadsheet as you followed the discussion of the 11 transactions, it should look very similar to Panel B. As you study the exhibit, note that every transaction maintains the equality:

$$\text{Assets} = \text{Liabilities} + \text{Stockholders' Equity}$$

Exhibit 2-1 | Transaction Analysis: Alladin Travel, Inc.

PANEL A—Transaction Details

(1) Received $50,000 cash and issued stock to the owners

(2) Paid $40,000 cash for land

(3) Bought $3,700 of supplies on account

(4) Received $7,000 cash from customers for service revenue earned

(5) Performed services for customers on account, $3,000

(6) Paid cash expenses: rent, $1,100; employee salary, $1,200; utilities, $400

(7) Paid $1,900 on the account payable created in transaction 3

(8) Major stockholder paid personal funds to remodel home, *not* a transaction of the business

(9) Received $1,000 on account

(10) Sold land for cash at the land's cost of $22,000

(11) Declared and paid a dividend of $2,100 to the stockholders

---

PANEL B—Transaction Analysis

	A	B	C	D	E	F	G	H	I	J
					A1 ⬍					
1			**Assets**			**=**	**Liabilities**	**+Stockholders' Equity**		**Type of SE Transaction**
2	**Trans**	**Cash**	**AR**	**Supplies**	**Land**		**AP**	**C Stock**	**RE**	
3	1	50,000						50,000		Issued common stock
4	2	(40,000)			40,000					
5	3			3,700			3,700			
6	4	7,000							7,000	Service revenue
7	5		3,000						3,000	Service revenue
8	6	(2,700)							(1,100)	Rent expense
9									(1,200)	Salary expense
10									(400)	Utilities expense
11	7	(1,900)					(1,900)			
12	9	1,000	(1,000)							
13	10	22,000			(22,000)					
14	11	(2,100)							(2,100)	Dividend
15	Bal	33,300	2,000	3,700	18,000		1,800	50,000	5,200	
16	Totals		57,000					57,000		
17										

Statement of Cash Flows Data

Income Statement Data

Statement of Retained Earnings Data

Balance Sheet Data

Panel B of Exhibit 2-1 provides the data for Alladin Travel, Inc.'s, financial statements:

- *Income statement* data appear as revenues and expenses under Retained Earnings. The revenues increase retained earnings; the expenses decrease retained earnings.

- The *balance sheet* data are composed of the ending balances of the assets, liabilities, and stockholders' equities shown at the bottom of the exhibit. The accounting equation shows that total assets ($57,000) equal total liabilities plus stockholders' equity ($57,000).

- The *statement of retained earnings* repeats net income (or net loss) from the income statement. Dividends are subtracted. Ending retained earnings is the final result.

- Data for the *statement of cash flows* are aligned under the Cash account. Cash receipts increase cash, and cash payments decrease cash. *Note: We did not reproduce the statement of cash flows in Exhibit 2-2.*

Exhibit 2-2 shows the Alladin Travel, Inc.'s, income statement, statement of retained earnings, and balance sheet at the end of April, the company's first month of operations. Follow the flow of data to observe the following:

1. The income statement reports revenues, expenses, and either a net income or a net loss for the period. During April, Alladin Travel, Inc., earned net income of $7,300. From the transaction analysis spreadsheet in Exhibit 2-1, Panel B, service revenue consists of the sum of cells I6 and I7 ($7,000 for cash and $3,000 on account). Expenses (salary $1,200 from cell I9, rent $1,100 from cell I8, and utilities $400 from cell I10) are listed separately in the income statement. The sum of these expenses is $2,700. Net income consists of the difference between service revenue and total expenses ($10,000 − $2,700 = $7,300). This is known as a "single-step" income statement. Compare Alladin Travel's income statement with that of The Walt Disney Company, at the beginning of Chapter 1. Alladin's income statement includes only two types of accounts: revenues and expenses. In contrast, The Walt Disney Company's consolidated statement of income illustrated in the chapter opening includes multiple types of revenue (services, products, other income) and several types of expenses (cost of services, cost of products, selling, general and administrative expenses, depreciation and amortization, etc.), segregated by type. It has important subheadings that segregate different types of income (operating income, income before income taxes, net income). This is known as a "multistep" income statement. You will learn more about it in Chapters 3 and 11.

2. The statement of retained earnings starts with the beginning balance of retained earnings (zero for a new business). Add net income for the period from the income statement (arrow ①), subtract dividends ($2,100 from cell I14 of the transaction analysis spreadsheet in Exhibit 2-1, Panel B), and compute the ending balance of retained earnings ($5,200).

3. The balance sheet lists the assets, liabilities, and stockholders' equity of the business at the end of the period. The assets consist of the totals of cash, accounts receivable, supplies, and land (see cells B15 through E15 in Exhibit 2-1, Panel B). Liabilities consist of only accounts payable (cell G15). Common stock carries over from cell H15. Also included in stockholders' equity is retained earnings, which comes from the statement of retained earnings (arrow ②). It has also been accumulated in cell I15 of Exhibit 2-1, Panel B.

Exhibit 2-2 | Financial Statements of Alladin Travel, Inc.

	A	B	C	D
1	**Alladin Travel, Inc.** **Income Statement** **Month Ended April 30, 2016**			
2	**Revenues**			
3	Service revenue ($7,000 + $3,000)		$ 10,000	
4	**Expenses**			
5	Salary expense	$ 1,200		
6	Rent expense	1,100		
7	Utilities expense	400		
8	Total expenses		2,700	
9	Net income		$ 7,300	
10				

①

	A	B	C	D
1	**Alladin Travel, Inc.** **Statement of Retained Earnings** **Month Ended April 30, 2016**			
2	Retained earnings, April 1, 2016		$ 0	
3	Add: Net income for the month		7,300	
4	Subtotal		7,300	
5	Less: Dividends declared		(2,100)	
6	Retained earnings, April 30, 2016		$ 5,200	
7				

②

	A	B	C	D	E	F
1	**Alladin Travel, Inc.** **Balance Sheet** **April 30, 2016**					
2	**Assets**			**Liabilities**		
3	Cash		$ 33,300	Accounts payable	$ 1,800	
4	Accounts receivable		2,000	**Stockholders' Equity**		
5	Supplies		3,700	Common stock	50,000	
6	Land		18,000	Retained earnings	5,200	
7				Total stockholders' equity	55,200	
8				Total liabilities and		
9	Total assets		$ 57,000	stockholders' equity	$ 57,000	
10						

≫ Try It in Excel®

If you are familiar with Excel, a quick look at Exhibit 2-2 should convince you of how easy it is to prepare the income statement, statement of retained earnings, and balance sheet in Excel. If you have not already prepared them in Chapter 1 (see page 32), prepare three simple templates for each of these financial statements for Alladin Travel, Inc. You may use these templates again, and add to them, in Chapter 3 as you learn the adjusting entry process. Selected problems in MyAccountingLab have already prepared these templates for you. The mid-chapter summary problem will illustrate with another small company.

Let's put into practice what you have learned so far.

Shelly Richmond opens a research service near a college campus. She names the corporation Richmond Researchers, Inc. During the first month of operations, July 2016, the business engages in these transactions:

a. Richmond Researchers, Inc., issues its common stock to Shelly Richmond, who invests $25,000 to open the business.

b. The company purchases on account office supplies costing $350.

c. Richmond Researchers pays cash of $20,000 to acquire a lot next to the campus. The company intends to use the land as a building site for a business office.

d. Richmond Researchers performs research for clients and receives cash of $1,900.

e. Richmond Researchers pays $100 on the account payable that it created in transaction b.

f. Richmond pays $2,000 of personal funds for a vacation.

g. Richmond Researchers pays cash expenses for office rent ($400) and utilities ($100).

h. The business sells a small parcel of the land for its cost of $5,000.

i. The business declares and pays a cash dividend of $1,200.

Requirements

1. Using Excel, build a spreadsheet to analyze the preceding transactions in terms of their effects on the accounting equation of Richmond Researchers, Inc. Use Exhibit 2-1, Panel B, as a guide.

2. Using Excel, prepare the income statement, statement of retained earnings, and balance sheet of Richmond Researchers, Inc., after recording the transactions. Draw arrows linking the statements. Use Exhibit 2-2 as a guide.

Answers

Requirement 1
PANEL B—Transaction Analysis: Richmond Researchers, Inc.

	A	B	C	D	E	F	G	H	I
1			**Assets**		=	**Liabilities**	**+Stockholders' Equity**		**Type of SE transaction**
2	**Trans**	**Cash**	**Office Supplies**	**Land**		**AP**	**C Stock**	**RE**	
3	a	25,000					25,000		Issued common stock
4	b		350			350			
5	c	(20,000)		20,000					
6	d	1,900						1,900	Service revenue
7	e	(100)				(100)			
8	f (n/a)								
9	g	(400)						(400)	Rent expense
10		(100)						(100)	Utilities expense
11	h	5,000		(5,000)					
12	i	(1,200)						(1,200)	Dividend
13	Bal	10,100	350	15,000		250	25,000	200	
14	Totals		25,450				25,450		
15									

Requirement 2

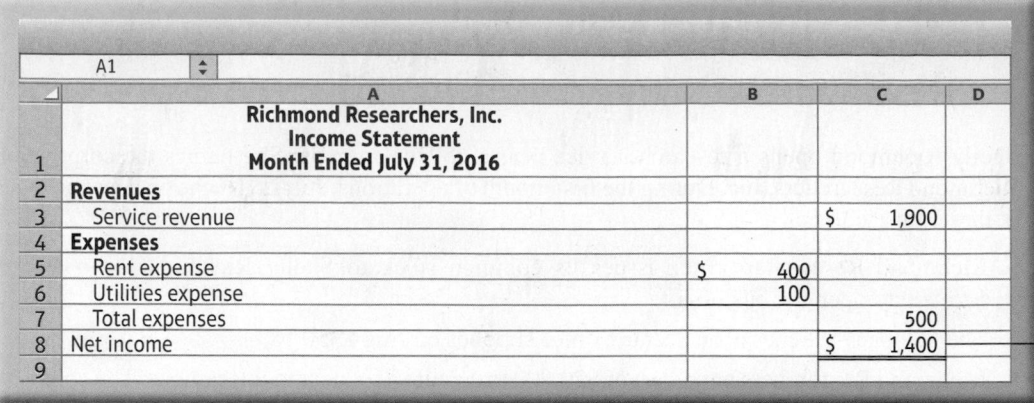

Richmond Researchers, Inc.
Income Statement
Month Ended July 31, 2016

	A	B	C	D
2	**Revenues**			
3	Service revenue		$ 1,900	
4	**Expenses**			
5	Rent expense	$ 400		
6	Utilities expense	100		
7	Total expenses		500	
8	Net income		$ 1,400	
9				

Richmond Researchers, Inc.
Statement of Retained Earnings
Month Ended July 31, 2016

	A	B	C	D
2	Retained earnings, July 1, 2016		$ 0	
3	Add: Net income for the month		1,400	
4	Subtotal		1,400	
5	Less: Dividends declared		(1,200)	
6	Retained earnings, July 31, 2016		$ 200	
7				

Richmond Researchers, Inc.
Balance Sheet
July 31, 2016

	A	B	C	D	E	F
2	**Assets**			**Liabilities**		
3	Cash		$ 10,100	Accounts payable	$ 250	
4	Office supplies		350	**Stockholders' Equity**		
5	Land		15,000	Common stock	25,000	
6				Retained earnings	200	
7				Total stockholders' equity	25,200	
8				Total liabilities and		
9	Total assets		$ 25,450	stockholders' equity	$ 25,450	
10						

The analysis in the first half of this chapter can be used, but even in Excel, it can be cumbersome. The Walt Disney Company has hundreds of accounts and millions of transactions. The spreadsheet to account for The Walt Disney Company's transactions would be huge! In the second half of this chapter we discuss double-entry accounting as it is actually used in business.

ANALYZE THE IMPACT OF BUSINESS TRANSACTIONS ON ACCOUNTS

Every business transaction involves an exchange of at least two things:

- You give something.
- You receive something in return.

Accounting is, therefore, based on a double-entry system, which records the *dual effects* on the entity. *Each transaction affects at least two accounts*. For example, Alladin Travel, Inc., received $50,000 cash in exchange for the issuance of stock. This transaction increased both Cash and Common Stock by $50,000. It would be incomplete to record only the increase in Cash or only the increase in Common Stock.

4 **Analyze** the impact of business transactions on accounts

The T-Account

An account can be represented by the letter T. We call this a *T-account*. The vertical line in the letter T represents the division of the account into its two sides: left and right. The account title appears at the top of the T. For example, the Cash account can appear as follows:

Cash	
(Left side)	(Right side)
Debit	*Credit*

The left side of each account is called the **debit** side, and the right side is called the **credit** side. Often, students are confused by the words *debit* and *credit*. To become comfortable using these terms, remember that *every business transaction involves both a debit and a credit*. You should remember that *debit* means "left-hand side" and *credit* means "right-hand side."

Debit – Left side	Credit = Right side

Increases and Decreases in the Accounts:
The Rules of Debit and Credit

The type of account determines how we record increases and decreases. *The rules of debit and credit* are illustrated in Exhibit 2-3.

- Increases in *assets* are recorded on the left (debit) side of the account. Decreases in *assets* are recorded on the right (credit) side. You receive cash and debit the Cash account. You pay cash and credit the Cash account.
- Conversely, increases in *liabilities* and *stockholders' equity* are recorded by credits. Decreases in *liabilities* and *stockholders' equity* are recorded by debits.

Exhibit 2-3 | Accounting Equation and the Rules of Debit and Credit

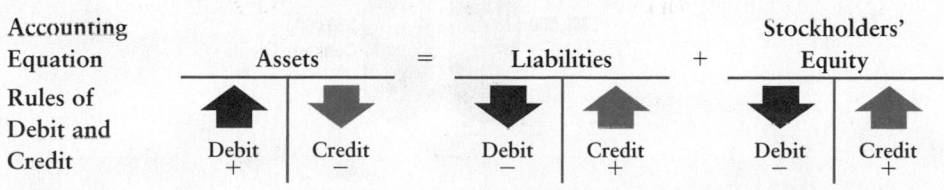

To illustrate the ideas diagrammed in Exhibit 2-3, let's review the first transaction. Alladin Travel, Inc., received $50,000 and issued (gave) stock. Which accounts are affected? The Cash account and the Common Stock account will hold these amounts:

Exhibit 2-4 | The Accounting Equation after Alladin Travel, Inc.'s, First Transaction

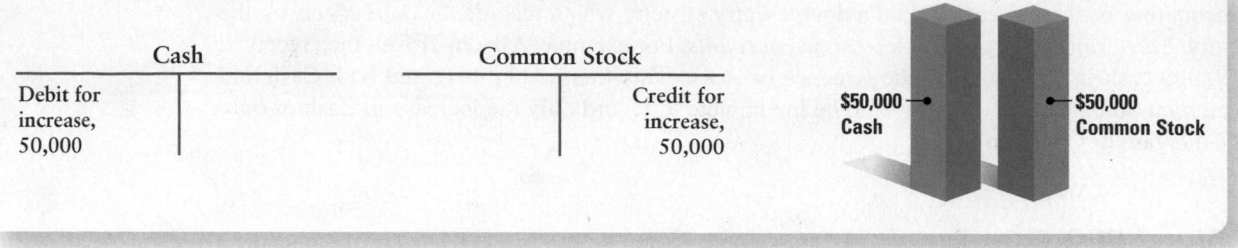

The amount remaining in an account is called its *balance*. This first transaction gives Cash a $50,000 debit balance and Common Stock a $50,000 credit balance. Exhibit 2-4 shows this relationship.

Alladin's second transaction is a $40,000 cash purchase of land. This transaction decreases Cash with a credit and increases Land with a debit, as shown in the following T-accounts (focus on Cash and Land):

	Cash				Common Stock	
Bal	50,000	Credit for decrease, 40,000			Bal	50,000
Bal	10,000					

Land	
Debit for increase, 40,000	
Bal 40,000	

After this transaction, Cash has a $10,000 debit balance, Land has a debit balance of $40,000, and Common Stock has a $50,000 credit balance, as shown in Exhibit 2-5.

Exhibit 2-5 | The Accounting Equation after Alladin Travel, Inc.'s, First Two Transactions

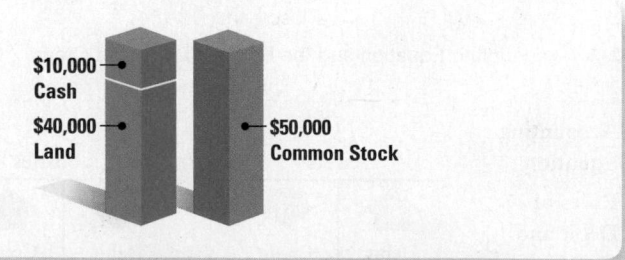

Additional Stockholders' Equity Accounts:
Revenues and Expenses

Stockholders' equity also includes the two categories of income statement accounts, Revenues and Expenses:

- *Revenues* are increases in stockholders' equity that result from delivering goods or services to customers.
- *Expenses* are decreases in stockholders' equity due to the cost of operating the business.

Therefore, the accounting equation may be expanded as shown in Exhibit 2-6. Revenues and expenses appear in parentheses because their net effect—revenues minus expenses—equals net income, which increases stockholders' equity. If expenses exceed revenues, there is a net loss, which decreases stockholders' equity.

Exhibit 2-6 | Expansion of the Accounting Equation

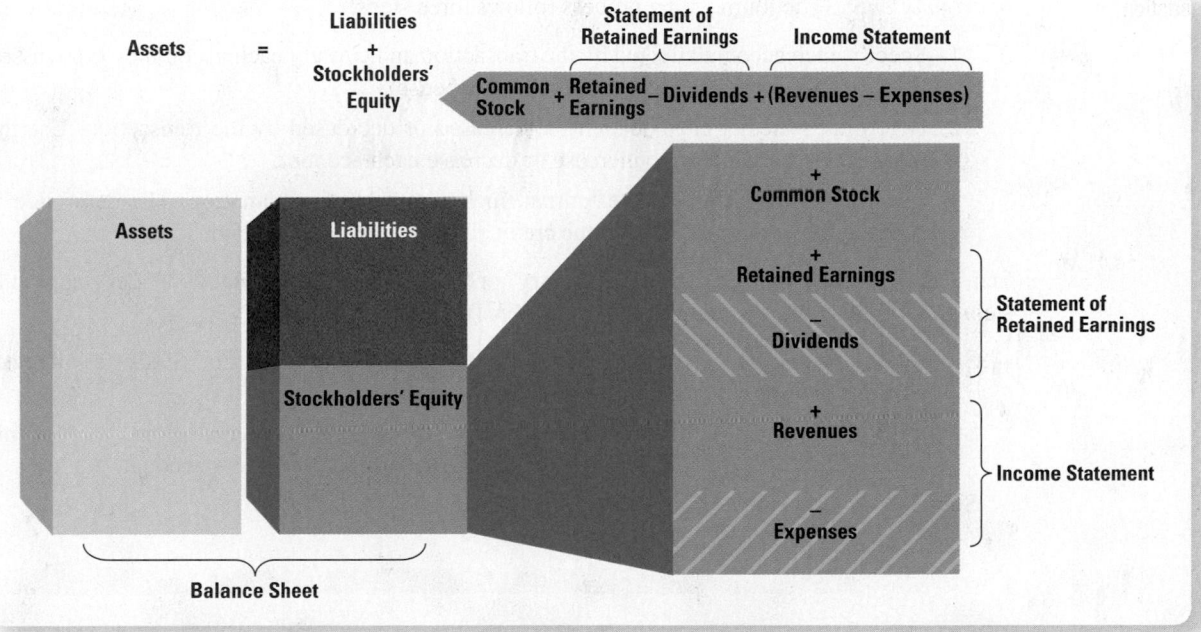

We can now express the final form of the rules of debit and credit, as shown in Exhibit 2-7. *You should not proceed until you have learned these rules.* For example, you must remember that

- a debit increases an asset account;
- a credit decreases an asset account.

Exhibit 2-7 | Final Form of the Rules of Debit and Credit

| ASSETS | = | LIABILITIES | + | STOCKHOLDERS' EQUITY | | | | | |

Assets		Liabilities		Common Stock		Retained Earnings		Dividends	
Debit	Credit	Debit	Credit	Debit	Credit	Debit	Credit	Debit	Credit
+	−	−	+	−	+	−	+	+	−

						Revenues		Expenses	
						Debit	Credit	Debit	Credit
						−	+	+	−

Liabilities and stockholders' equity are the opposite.

- A credit increases a liability or stockholders' equity account.
- A debit decreases a liability or stockholders' equity account.

Dividends and Expense accounts are exceptions to the rule. Dividends and Expenses are equity accounts that are increased by a debit. Dividends and Expense accounts are negative (or *contra*) equity accounts.

Revenues and expenses are treated as separate account categories because users of financial statements need to keep track of each separately. Exhibit 2-7 shows revenues and expenses below the other equity accounts.

RECORD (JOURNALIZE AND POST) TRANSACTIONS IN THE BOOKS

5 Record (journalize and post) transactions in the books

Accountants use a chronological record of transactions called a **journal**, also known as the *book of original entry*. The journalizing process follows three steps:

1. Specify each account affected by the transaction and classify each account by type (asset, liability, stockholders' equity, revenue, or expense).

2. Determine whether each account is increased or decreased by the transaction. Use the rules of debit and credit to increase or decrease each account.

3. Record the transaction in the journal, including a brief explanation. The debit side is entered on the left margin, and the credit side is indented to the right.

Step 3 is also called "booking the journal entry" or "journalizing the transaction." Let's apply the steps to journalize the first transaction of Alladin Travel, Inc.

Step 1 The business receives cash and issues stock. Cash and Common Stock are affected. Cash is an asset, and Common Stock is stockholders' equity.

Step 2 Both Cash and Common Stock increase. Debit Cash to record an increase in this asset. Credit Common Stock to record an increase in this equity account.

Step 3 Journalize the transaction:

	A1	⬍				
	A	B	C	D	E	F
		JOURNAL				
1	**Date**	**Accounts and Explanation**	**Debit**	**Credit**		
2	Apr 1	Cash	50,000			
3		Common Stock		50,000		
4		*Issued common stock.*				
5						

When analyzing a transaction, first pinpoint the effects (if any) on Cash. Did Cash increase or decrease? Typically, it is easiest to identify Cash effects. Then identify the effects on the other accounts.

Exhibit 2-8 | The Ledger (Asset, Liability, and Stockholders' Equity Accounts)

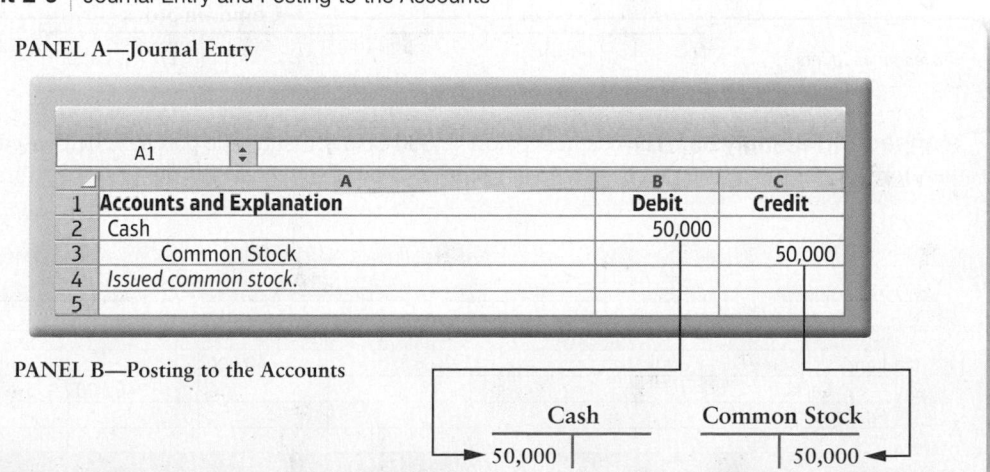

Copying Information (Posting) from the Journal to the Ledger

The journal is a chronological record of all company transactions listed by date. But the journal does not indicate how much cash or accounts receivable the business has.

The **ledger** is a grouping of all the T-accounts, with their balances. For example, the balance of the Cash T-account shows how much cash the business has. The balance of Accounts Receivable shows the amount due from customers. Accounts Payable shows how much the business owes suppliers on open account, and so on.

In the phrase "keeping the books," *books* refers to the journals as well as the accounts in the ledger. In most accounting systems, the ledger is computerized. Exhibit 2-8 shows how asset, liability, and stockholders' equity accounts are grouped in the ledger. Revenue and expense accounts also appear in the general ledger, which may contain hundreds or even thousands of accounts.

Entering a transaction in the journal does not get the data into the ledger. Data must be copied to the ledger—a process called **posting**. Debits in the journal are always posted as debits in the accounts, and likewise for credits. Exhibit 2-9 shows how Alladin Travel, Inc.'s, stock issuance transaction is posted to the accounts.

Exhibit 2-9 | Journal Entry and Posting to the Accounts

PANEL A—Journal Entry

	A	B	C
	A1		
	A	**B**	**C**
1	**Accounts and Explanation**	**Debit**	**Credit**
2	Cash	50,000	
3	Common Stock		50,000
4	*Issued common stock.*		
5			

PANEL B—Posting to the Accounts

Cash		Common Stock	
50,000			50,000

Exhibit 2-10 | Flow of Accounting Data

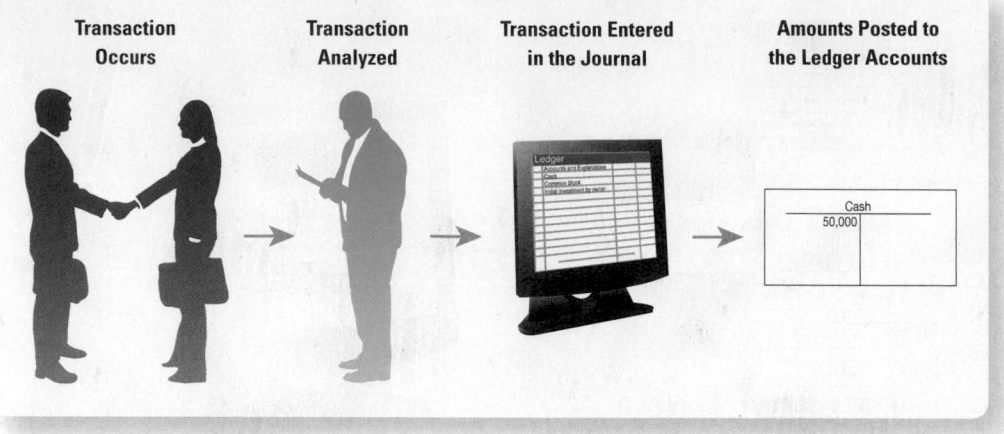

The Flow of Accounting Data

Exhibit 2-10 summarizes the flow of accounting data from the business transaction to the ledger. Let's continue the example of Alladin Travel, Inc., and account for the same 11 transactions we illustrated earlier. Here we use the journal and the accounts. Each journal entry posted to the accounts is keyed by date or by transaction number. This linking allows you to locate any information you may need.

Transaction 1 Analysis. Alladin Travel, Inc., received $50,000 cash from the stockholders and in turn issued common stock to them. The journal entry, accounting equation, and ledger accounts follow:

	A	B	C	D	E
	A1				
1	Cash	50,000			
2	Common Stock		50,000		
3	Issued common stock.				
4					

	Assets	=	Liabilities	+	Stockholders' Equity
Accounting equation	+50,000	=	0	+	50,000

	Cash		Common Stock
The ledger accounts	(1) 50,000		(1) 50,000

Transaction 2 Analysis. The business paid $40,000 cash for land. The purchase decreased cash; therefore, credit Cash. The purchase increased the asset land; to record this increase, debit Land.

	A	B	C	D	E
	A1				
1	Land	40,000			
2	Cash		40,000		
3	Paid cash for land.				
4					

	Assets	=	Liabilities	+	Stockholders' Equity
Accounting equation	+ 40,000	=	0	+	0
	− 40,000				

	Cash			Land	
The ledger accounts	(1) 50,000	(2) 40,000	(2) 40,000		

Transaction 3 Analysis. The business purchased supplies for $3,700 on accounts payable. The purchase increased Supplies, an asset, and Accounts Payable, a liability.

	A1					
		A	B	C	D	E
1	Supplies		3,700			
2	Accounts Payable			3,700		
3	Purchased office supplies on account.					
4						

	Assets	=	Liabilities	+	Stockholders' Equity
Accounting equation	+ 3,700	=	+ 3,700	+	0

	Supplies			Accounts Payable	
The ledger accounts	(3) 3,700			(3) 3,700	

Transaction 4 Analysis. The business performed services for clients and received cash of $7,000. The transaction increased cash and service revenue. To record the revenue, credit Service Revenue.

	A1					
		A	B	C	D	E
1	Cash		7,000			
2	Service Revenue			7,000		
3	Performed services for cash.					
4						

	Assets	=	Liabilities	+	Stockholders' Equity	+	Revenues
Accounting equation	+ 7,000	=	0			+	7,000

	Cash			Service Revenue	
The ledger accounts	(1) 50,000	(2) 40,000		(4) 7,000	
	(4) 7,000				

Transaction 5 Analysis. Alladin performed services for other customers on account. These customers did not pay immediately, so Alladin billed them for $3,000. The transaction increased accounts receivable; therefore, debit Accounts Receivable. Service revenue also increased, so credit the Service Revenue account.

	A	B	C	D	E
	A1 ⬍				
1	Accounts Receivable	3,000			
2	Service Revenue		3,000		
3	*Performed services on account.*				
4					

	Assets	=	Liabilities	+	Stockholders' Equity	+	Revenues
Accounting equation	+ 3,000	=	0			+	3,000

	Accounts Receivable		Service Revenue
The ledger accounts	(5) 3,000		(4) 7,000
			(5) 3,000

Transaction 6 Analysis. The business paid $2,700 for the following expenses: rent, $1,100; employee salary, $1,200; and utilities, $400. Credit Cash for the sum of the expense amounts. The expenses increased, so debit each expense account separately.

	A	B	C	D	E
	A1 ⬍				
1	Rent Expense	1,100			
2	Salary Expense	1,200			
3	Utilities Expense	400			
4	Cash		2,700		
5	*Paid expenses.*				
6					

	Assets	=	Liabilities	+	Stockholders' Equity	−	Expenses
Accounting equation	− 2,700	=	0			−	2,700

	Cash			Rent Expense
The ledger accounts	(1) 50,000	(2) 40,000	(6) 1,100	
	(4) 7,000	(6) 2,700		

	Salary Expense		Utilities Expense
	(6) 1,200	(6) 400	

Transaction 7 Analysis. The business paid $1,900 on the account payable created in transaction 3. Credit Cash for the payment. The payment decreased a liability, so debit Accounts Payable.

	A	B	C	D	E
	A1 ⬍				
1	Accounts Payable	1,900			
2	Cash		1,900		
3	Paid cash on account.				
4					

	Assets	=	Liabilities	+	Stockholders' Equity
Accounting equation	− 1,900	=	− 1,900	+	0

	Cash				Accounts Payable		
The ledger accounts	(1)	50,000	(2)	40,000	(7) 1,900	(3)	3,700
	(4)	7,000	(6)	2,700			
			(7)	1,900			

Transaction 8 Analysis. Starr Williams, the major stockholder of Alladin Travel, Inc., remodeled her personal residence. This is not a transaction of the business, so the business does not record the transaction.

Transaction 9 Analysis. The business collected $1,000 cash on account from the client in transaction 5. Cash increased, so debit Cash. The asset accounts receivable decreased; therefore, credit Accounts Receivable.

	A	B	C	D	E
	A1 ⬍				
1	Cash	1,000			
2	Accounts Receivable		1,000		
3	Collected cash on account.				
4					

	Assets	=	Liabilities	+	Stockholders' Equity
Accounting equation	+ 1,000	=	0	+	0
	− 1,000				

	Cash				Accounts Receivable		
The ledger accounts	(1)	50,000	(2)	40,000	(5) 3,000	(9)	1,000
	(4)	7,000	(6)	2,700			
	(9)	1,000	(7)	1,900			

Transaction 10 Analysis. The business sold land for its cost of $22,000, receiving cash. The asset cash increased; debit Cash. The asset land decreased; credit Land.

	A	B	C	D	E
1	Cash	22,000			
2	Land		22,000		
3	*Sold land.*				
4					

	Assets	=	Liabilities	+	Stockholders' Equity
Accounting equation	+ 22,000	=	0	+	0
	− 22,000				

	Cash				Land		
The ledger accounts	(1)	50,000	(2)	40,000	(2)	40,000 (10)	22,000
	(4)	7,000	(6)	2,700			
	(9)	1,000	(7)	1,900			
	(10)	22,000					

Transaction 11 Analysis. Alladin Travel, Inc., declared and paid its stockholders cash dividends of $2,100. Credit Cash for the payment. The transaction also decreased stockholders' equity and requires a debit to an equity account. Therefore, debit Dividends.

	A	B	C	D	E
1	Dividends	2,100			
2	Cash		2,100		
3	*Declared and paid dividends.*				
4					

	Assets	=	Liabilities	+	Stockholders' Equity	−	Dividends
Accounting equation	− 2,100	=	0			−	2,100

	Cash				Dividends	
The ledger accounts	(1)	50,000	(2)	40,000	(11)	2,100
	(4)	7,000	(6)	2,700		
	(9)	1,000	(7)	1,900		
	(10)	22,000	(11)	2,100		

Accounts After Posting to the Ledger

Exhibit 2-11 shows the accounts after all transactions have been posted to the ledger. Group the accounts under assets, liabilities, and stockholders' equity.

Each account has a balance, denoted as Bal, which is the difference between the account's total debits and its total credits. For example, the Accounts Payable balance of $1,800 is the difference between the credit ($3,700) and the debit ($1,900). Cash has a debit balance of $33,300.

Exhibit 2-11 | Alladin Travel, Inc.'s, Ledger Accounts after Posting

Assets	=	Liabilities	+	Stockholders' Equity

Cash

(1)	50,000	(2)	40,000
(4)	7,000	(6)	2,700
(9)	1,000	(7)	1,900
(10)	22,000	(11)	2,100
Bal	33,300		

Accounts Receivable

(5)	3,000	(9)	1,000
Bal	2,000		

Supplies

(3)	3,700	
Bal	3,700	

Land

(2)	40,000	(10)	22,000
Bal	18,000		

Accounts Payable

(7)	1,900	(3)	3,700
		Bal	1,800

Common Stock

		(1)	50,000
		Bal	50,000

Revenue

Service Revenue

		(4)	7,000
		(5)	3,000
		Bal	10,000

Dividends

(11)	2,100	
Bal	2,100	

Expenses

Rent Expense

(6)	1,100	
Bal	1,100	

Salary Expense

(6)	1,200	
Bal	1,200	

Utilities Expense

(6)	400	
Bal	400	

A horizontal line separates the transaction amounts from the account balance. If an account's debits exceed its total credits, that account has a debit balance, as for Cash. If the sum of the credits is greater than the debits, the account has a credit balance, as for Accounts Payable.

CONSTRUCT AND USE A TRIAL BALANCE

A **trial balance** lists all accounts with their balances—assets first, then liabilities and stockholders' equity (including revenue and expense accounts). The trial balance summarizes all the account balances for the financial statements and *shows whether total debits equal total credits*. A trial balance may be taken at any time, but the most common time is at the end of the period. Exhibit 2-12 is the trial balance of Alladin Travel, Inc., after all transactions have been journalized and posted at the end of April.

6 Construct and use a trial balance

Exhibit 2-12 | Trial Balance

Alladin Travel, Inc. Trial Balance April 30, 2016	Balance	
Account Title	Debit	Credit
Cash	$33,300	
Accounts receivable	2,000	
Supplies	3,700	
Land	18,000	
Accounts payable		$ 1,800
Common stock		50,000
Dividends	2,100	
Service revenue		10,000
Rent expense	1,100	
Salary expense	1,200	
Utilities expense	400	
Total	$61,800	$61,800

The trial balance *facilitates the preparation of the financial statements*. It is possible to prepare an income statement, statement of retained earnings, and balance sheet from the data shown in a trial balance such as the one in Exhibit 2-12. For Alladin Travel, Inc., the financial statements would appear exactly as shown in Exhibit 2-2 on page 72. However, the financial statements are normally not constructed at this point, because they do not yet contain end-of-period adjustments, which are covered in Chapter 3.

>> **Try It in Excel®**

A trial balance can be one of the most simple and useful applications of Excel. Try building Exhibit 2-12 in Excel. Open a new blank worksheet. Format the title (company name, trial balance, and date), and provide column headings (account title, balance, debit, and credit) exactly as shown in Exhibit 2-12. Then on successive lines enter account titles and amounts from the general ledger accounts, being careful to enter amounts in the proper debit or credit columns. Finally, sum both debit and credit columns. The total amounts of debits and credits should agree.

Analyzing Accounts

You can often tell what a company did by analyzing its accounts. This is a powerful tool for a manager who knows accounting. For example, if you know the beginning and ending balances of Cash, and if you know total cash receipts, you can compute your total cash payments during the period.

In our chapter example, suppose Alladin Travel began May with cash of $1,000. During May, Alladin received cash of $8,000 and ended the month with a cash balance of $3,000. You can compute total cash payments by analyzing Alladin's Cash account:

Cash			
			$x = $ beginning balance + cash receipts − ending balance
			$= 1{,}000 + 8{,}000 - 3{,}000$
Beginning balance	1,000		
Cash receipts	8,000	Cash payments	$x = 6{,}000$
Ending balance	3,000		

Or, if you know Cash's beginning and ending balances and total payments, you can compute cash receipts during the period—for any company!

You can compute either sales on account or cash collections on account by analyzing the Accounts Receivable account (using assumed amounts):

Accounts Receivable			
			$x = $ beginning balance + sales on account − ending balance
			$= 6{,}000 + 10{,}000 - 5{,}000$
Beginning balance	6,000		
Sales on account	10,000	Collections on account	$x = 11{,}000$
Ending balance	5,000		

Also, you can determine how much you paid on account by analyzing Accounts Payable (using assumed amounts):

Accounts Payable

x = beginning balance + purchases on account − ending balance = 9,000 + 6,000 − 11,000	
	Beginning balance 9,000
Payments on account x = 4,000	Purchases on account 6,000
	Ending balance 11,000

Please master this powerful technique. It works for any company and for your personal finances! You will find this tool very helpful when you become a manager.

Correcting Accounting Errors

Accounting errors can occur even in computerized systems. Input data may be wrong, or they may be entered twice or not at all. A debit may be entered as a credit and vice versa. You can detect the reason or reasons behind many out-of-balance conditions by computing the difference between total debits and total credits in the trial balance. Then perform one or more of the following actions:

1. Search the records for a missing account. Trace each account back and forth from the journal to the ledger. A $200 transaction may have been recorded incorrectly in the journal or posted incorrectly to the ledger. Search the journal for a $200 transaction.

2. Divide the out-of-balance amount by 2. A debit treated as a credit, or vice versa, doubles the amount of error. Suppose Alladin Travel, Inc., added $300 to Cash instead of subtracting $300. The out-of-balance amount is $600, and dividing by 2 identifies $300 as the amount of the transaction. Search the journal for the $300 transaction and trace to the account affected.

3. Divide the out-of-balance amount by 9. If the result is an integer (no decimals), the error may be one of the following:

   - a *slide* (e.g., writing $400 as $40). The accounts would be out of balance by $360 ($400 − $40 = $360). Dividing $360 by 9 yields $40. Scan the trial balance in Exhibit 2-12 for an amount similar to $40. Utilities Expense (balance of $400) is the misstated account.

   - a *transposition* (e.g., writing $2,100 as $1,200). The accounts would be out of balance by $900 ($2,100 − $1,200 = $900). Dividing $900 by 9 yields $100. Trace all amounts on the trial balance back to the T-accounts. Dividends (balance of $2,100) is the misstated account.

Chart of Accounts

As you know, the ledger contains the accounts grouped under these headings:

1. **Balance sheet accounts: Assets, Liabilities, and Stockholders' Equity**

2. **Income statement accounts: Revenues and Expenses**

Organizations use a **chart of accounts** to list all their accounts and account numbers. Account numbers usually have two or more digits. Asset account numbers may begin with 1, liabilities with 2, stockholders' equity with 3, revenues with 4, and expenses with 5. The second, third, and higher digits in an account number indicate the position of the individual account within the category. For example, Cash may be account number 101, which is the first asset account. Accounts Payable may be number 201, the first liability. All accounts are numbered by using this system.

Organizations with many accounts use lengthy account numbers. For example, the chart of accounts of The Walt Disney Company, may use 10-digit account numbers. The chart of accounts for Alladin Travel, Inc., appears in Exhibit 2-13. The gap between account numbers 111 and 141

Exhibit 2-13 | Chart of Accounts—Alladin Travel, Inc.

Balance Sheet Accounts		
Assets	**Liabilities**	**Stockholders' Equity**
101 Cash	201 Accounts Payable	301 Common Stock
111 Accounts Receivable	231 Notes Payable	311 Retained Earnings
141 Supplies		312 Dividends
151 Land		
191 Office Furniture		

Income Statement Accounts (Part of Stockholders' Equity)	
Revenues	**Expenses**
401 Service Revenue	501 Rent Expense
	502 Salary Expense
	503 Utilities Expense

leaves room to add another category of receivables, for example, Notes Receivable, which may be numbered 121.

Appendix C to this book gives two expanded charts of accounts that you will find helpful as you work through this course. The first chart lists the typical accounts that a service corporation, such as Alladin Travel, Inc., would have after a period of growth. The second chart is for a *merchandising* corporation, one that sells a product instead of a service.

The Normal Balance of an Account

An account's *normal balance* falls on the side of the account—debit or credit—where increases are recorded. The normal balance of assets is on the debit side, so assets are *debit-balance accounts*. Conversely, liabilities and stockholders' equity usually have a credit balance, so these are *credit-balance accounts*. Exhibit 2-14 illustrates the normal balances of all the assets, liabilities, and stockholders' equities, including revenues and expenses.

As explained earlier, stockholders' equity usually contains several accounts. Dividends and expenses carry debit balances because they represent decreases in stockholders' equity. In total, the equity accounts show a normal credit balance.

Exhibit 2-14 | Normal Balances of the Accounts

Assets...	Debit	
Liabilities		Credit
Stockholders' Equity—overall		Credit
Common stock..................................		Credit
Retained earnings............................		Credit
Dividends...	Debit	
Revenues..		Credit
Expenses	Debit	

Account Formats

So far we have illustrated accounts in a two-column T-account format, with the debit column on the left and the credit column on the right. Another format has four *amount* columns, as illustrated for the Cash account in Exhibit 2-15. The first pair of amount columns on the left are for the debit and credit amounts of individual transactions. The last two columns are for the account

Exhibit 2-15 | Account in Four-Column Format

Account: Cash					Account No. 101

				Balance	
Date	Item	Debit	Credit	Debit	Credit
2016					
Apr 2		50,000		50,000	
3			40,000	10,000	

balance. This four-column format keeps a running balance in the two right columns. The format of the accounts is determined by the type of computer software that the company uses.

Analyzing Transactions Using Only T-Accounts

Businesspeople must often make decisions without the benefit of a complete accounting system. For example, the managers of Alladin Travel, Inc., may consider borrowing $100,000 to buy equipment. To see how the two transactions [(a) borrowing cash and (b) buying equipment] affect Alladin Travel, Inc., the manager can go directly to T-accounts (for these purposes, assume these transactions occur on September 30, 2016, and that no other transactions occur):

T-accounts:

Cash		Note Payable	
(a) 100,000			(a) 100,000

T-accounts:

Cash		Equipment		Note Payable	
(a) 100,000	(b) 100,000	(b) 100,000			(a) 100,000

This informal analysis shows immediately that Alladin Travel, Inc., will add $100,000 of equipment and a $100,000 note payable. Assuming that Alladin Travel, Inc., began with zero balances, the equipment and note payable transactions would result in the following balance sheet (date assumed for illustration only):

	A	B	C	D
A1				
1	Alladin Travel, Inc. Balance Sheet September 30, 2016			
2	Assets		Liabilities	
3	Cash	$ 0	Note payable	$100,000
4	Equipment	100,000		
5			Stockholders' Equity	0
6			Total liabilities and	
7	Total assets	$100,000	stockholders' equity	$100,000
8				

Companies don't actually keep records in this shortcut fashion. But a decision maker who needs information quickly may not have time to journalize, post to the accounts, take a trial balance, and prepare the financial statements. A manager who knows accounting can analyze the transaction and make the decision quickly.

Now apply what you've learned. Study the Decision Guidelines, which summarize the chapter.

 # DECISION GUIDELINES

HOW TO MEASURE RESULTS OF OPERATIONS AND FINANCIAL POSITION

Any entrepreneur must determine whether the venture is profitable. To do this, he or she needs to know its results of operations and financial position. If a shareholder of The Walt Disney Company wants to know whether the business is making money, the guidelines that follow will help:

Decision	Guidelines
Has a transaction occurred?	If the event affects the entity's financial position and can be reliably recorded—Yes If either condition is absent—No
Where to record the transaction?	In the *journal*, the chronological record of transactions
How to record an increase or decrease in the following accounts?	Rules of *debit* and *credit*:

	Increase	Decrease
Assets	Debit	Credit
Liabilities	Credit	Debit
Stockholders' equity	Credit	Debit
Revenues	Credit	Debit
Expenses	Debit	Credit

Decision	Guidelines
Where to store all the information for each account?	In the *ledger*, the book of accounts
Where to list all the accounts and their balances?	In the *trial* balance
Where to report the following:	
Results of operations?	In the income statement (Revenues − Expenses = Net income or net loss)
Financial position?	In the balance sheet (Assets = Liabilities + Stockholders' equity)

The trial balance of Dunn Service Center, Inc., on March 1, 2016, lists the entity's assets, liabilities, and stockholders' equity on that date.

Account Title	Balance Debit	Balance Credit
Cash...	$26,000	
Accounts receivable...............	4,500	
Accounts payable		$ 2,000
Common stock.......................		10,000
Retained earnings...................		18,500
Total	$30,500	$30,500

During March, the business completed the following transactions:

a. Borrowed $45,000 from the bank, with Dunn signing a note payable in the name of the business.

b. Paid cash of $40,000 to a real estate company to acquire land.

c. Performed service for a customer and received cash of $5,000.

d. Purchased supplies on credit, $300.

e. Performed customer service and earned revenue on account, $2,600.

f. Paid $1,200 on account.

g. Paid the following cash expenses: salaries, $3,000; rent, $1,500; and interest, $400.

h. Received $3,100 on account.

i. Received a $200 utility bill that will be paid next week.

j. Declared and paid a dividend of $1,800.

Requirements

1. Make the following accounts, with the balances indicated, in the ledger of Dunn Service Center, Inc. Use the T-account format.

   ■ Assets—Cash, $26,000; Accounts Receivable, $4,500; Supplies, no balance; Land, no balance

   ■ Liabilities—Accounts Payable, $2,000; Note Payable, no balance

   ■ Stockholders' Equity—Common Stock, $10,000; Retained Earnings, $18,500; Dividends, no balance

   ■ Revenues—Service Revenue, no balance

   ■ Expenses—(none have balances) Salary Expense, Rent Expense, Interest Expense, Utilities Expense

2. Journalize the preceding transactions. Key journal entries by transaction letter.
3. Post the transactions from the journal to the ledger and compute the balance in each account after all the transactions have been posted.
4. Prepare the trial balance of Dunn Service Center, Inc., at March 31, 2016.
5. To determine the net income or net loss of the entity during the month of March, prepare the single-step income statement for the month ended March 31, 2016. List expenses in order from the largest to the smallest.

Answers

Requirement 1

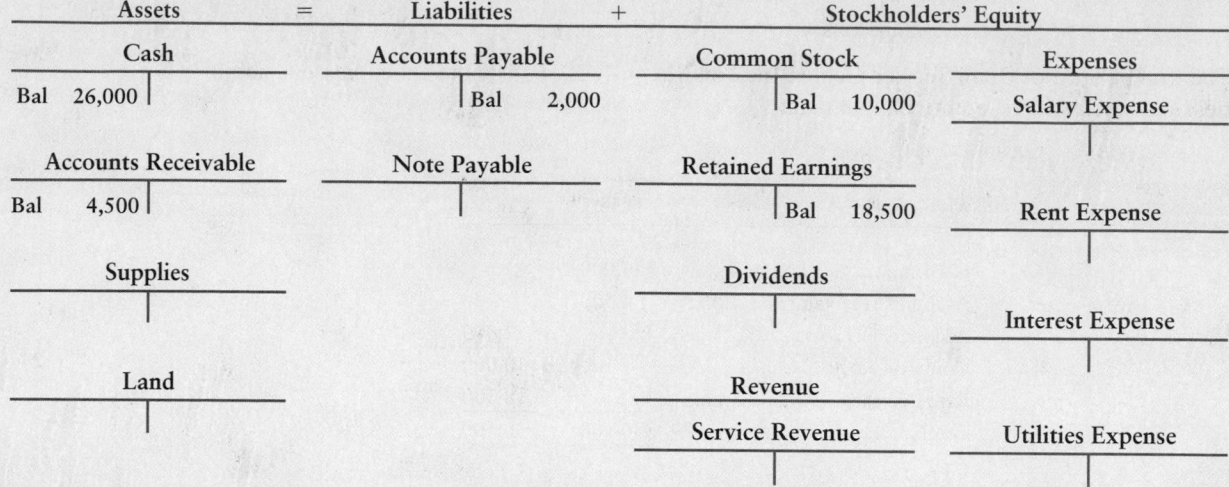

	Assets	=	Liabilities	+	Stockholders' Equity

Cash
Bal   26,000

Accounts Payable
Bal   2,000

Common Stock
Bal   10,000

Expenses

Salary Expense

Accounts Receivable
Bal   4,500

Note Payable

Retained Earnings
Bal   18,500

Rent Expense

Supplies

Dividends

Interest Expense

Land

Revenue

Service Revenue

Utilities Expense

Requirement 2

Accounts and Explanation	Debit	Credit		Accounts and Explanation	Debit	Credit
a. Cash...........................	45,000		g.	Salary Expense.............................	3,000	
Note Payable		45,000		Rent Expense	1,500	
Borrowed cash on note payable.				Interest Expense	400	
b. Land..	40,000			Cash		4,900
Cash		40,000		Paid cash expenses.		
Purchased land for cash.			h.	Cash...	3,100	
c. Cash..	5,000			Accounts Receivable		3,100
Service Revenue		5,000		Received cash on account.		
Performed service and received cash.			i.	Utilities Expense...........................	200	
d. Supplies....................................	300			Accounts Payable...................		200
Accounts Payable................		300		Received utility bill to be paid later.		
Purchased supplies on account.			j.	Dividends.....................................	1,800	
e. Accounts Receivable.................	2,600			Cash		1,800
Service Revenue		2,600		Declared and paid dividends.		
Performed service on account.						
f. Accounts Payable	1,200					
Cash		1,200				
Paid on account.						

Requirement 3

| Assets | = | Liabilities | + | Stockholders' Equity |

Cash

Bal	26,000	(b)	40,000
(a)	45,000	(f)	1,200
(c)	5,000	(g)	4,900
(h)	3,100	(j)	1,800
Bal	31,200		

Accounts Receivable

Bal	4,500	(h)	3,100
(e)	2,600		
Bal	4,000		

Supplies

| (d) | 300 | |
| Bal | 300 | |

Land

| (b) | 40,000 | |
| Bal | 40,000 | |

Accounts Payable

(f)	1,200	Bal	2,000
		(d)	300
		(i)	200
		Bal	1,300

Note Payable

| | | (a) | 45,000 |
| | | Bal | 45,000 |

Common Stock

| | Bal | 10,000 |

Retained Earnings

| | Bal | 18,500 |

Dividends

| (j) | 1,800 | |
| Bal | 1,800 | |

Revenue

Service Revenue

		(c)	5,000
		(e)	2,600
		Bal	7,600

Expenses

Salary Expense

| (g) | 3,000 | |
| Bal | 3,000 | |

Rent Expense

| (g) | 1,500 | |
| Bal | 1,500 | |

Interest Expense

| (g) | 400 | |
| Bal | 400 | |

Utilities Expense

| (i) | 200 | |
| Bal | 200 | |

Requirement 4

A1					
	A	**B**	**C**	**D**	**E**
1	**Dunn Service Center, Inc.** **Trial Balance** **March 31, 2016**				
2		**Balance**			
3	**Account Title**	**Debit**	**Credit**		
4	Cash	$ 31,200			
5	Accounts receivable	4,000			
6	Supplies	300			
7	Land	40,000			
8	Accounts payable		$ 1,300		
9	Notes payable		45,000		
10	Common stock		10,000		
11	Retained earnings		18,500		
12	Dividends	1,800			
13	Service revenue		7,600		
14	Salary expense	3,000			
15	Rent expense	1,500			
16	Interest expense	400			
17	Utilities expense	200			
18	Total	$ 82,400	$ 82,400		
19					

Requirement 5

	A	B	C	D	E
1	**Dunn Service Center, Inc.** **Income Statement** **Month Ended March 31, 2016**				
2	**Revenues**				
3	Service revenue		$ 7,600		
4					
5	**Expenses**				
6	Salary expense	$ 3,000			
7	Rent expense	1,500			
8	Interest expense	400			
9	Utilities expense	200			
10	Total expenses		5,100		
11	Net income		$ 2,500		
12					

REVIEW | Transaction Analysis

Quick Check (Answers are given on page 120.)

1. A debit entry to an account
   - **a.** increases assets.
   - **b.** increases liabilities.
   - **c.** increases stockholders' equity.
   - **d.** both b and c.

2. Which account types normally have a debit balance?
   - **a.** Expenses
   - **b.** Revenues
   - **c.** Liabilities
   - **d.** Both b and c

3. An attorney performs services of $1,100 for a client and receives $400 cash, with the remainder on account. The journal entry for this transaction would
   - **a.** debit Cash, debit Service Revenue, credit Accounts Receivable.
   - **b.** debit Cash, debit Accounts Receivable, credit Service Revenue.
   - **c.** debit Cash, credit Service Revenue.
   - **d.** debit Cash, credit Accounts Receivable, credit Service Revenue.

4. Accounts Payable had a normal beginning balance of $1,300. During the period, there were debit postings of $700 and credit postings of $900. What was the ending balance?
   - **a.** $1,100 debit
   - **b.** $1,500 credit
   - **c.** $1,100 credit
   - **d.** $1,500 debit

5. The list of all accounts with their balances is the
   - **a.** chart of accounts.
   - **b.** balance sheet.
   - **c.** journal.
   - **d.** trial balance.

6. The basic summary device of accounting is the
   - **a.** account.
   - **b.** trial balance.
   - **c.** journal.
   - **d.** ledger.

7. The beginning Cash balance was $6,000. At the end of the period, the balance was $7,000. If total cash paid out during the period was $20,000, the amount of cash receipts was
   a. $26,000.
   c. $19,000.
   b. $21,000.
   d. $27,000.

8. In a double-entry accounting system,
   a. half of all the accounts have a normal credit balance.
   b. liabilities, owners' equity, and revenue accounts all have normal debit balances.
   c. a debit entry is recorded on the left side of a T-account.
   d. both a and b are correct.

9. Which accounts appear on which financial statement?

Balance sheet	Income statement
a. Cash, revenues, land	Expenses, payables
b. Cash, receivables, payables	Revenues, expenses
c. Expenses, payables, cash	Revenues, receivables, land
d. Receivables, land, payables	Revenues, supplies

10. A doctor purchases medical supplies of $640 and pays $290 cash with the remainder on account. The journal entry for this transaction would be which of the following?
   a. Supplies
          Accounts Payable
              Cash
   b. Supplies
          Accounts Receivable
              Cash
   c. Supplies
          Accounts Receivable
              Cash
   d. Supplies
          Accounts Payable
              Cash

11. Which is the correct sequence for recording transactions and preparing financial statements?
   a. Ledger, trial balance, journal, financial statements
   b. Financial statements, trial balance, ledger, journal
   c. Journal, ledger, trial balance, financial statements
   d. Ledger, journal, trial balance, financial statements

12. The error of posting $50 as $500 can be detected by
   a. totaling each account's balance in the ledger.
   b. dividing the out-of-balance amount by 2.
   c. dividing the out-of-balance amount by 9.
   d. examining the chart of accounts.

Accounting Vocabulary

account (p. 62) The record of the changes that have occurred in a particular asset, liability, or stockholders' equity during a period. The basic summary device of accounting.

accrued liability (p. 63) A liability for an expense that has not yet been paid by the company.

cash (p. 62) Money and any medium of exchange that a bank accepts at face value.

chart of accounts (p. 87) List of a company's accounts and their account numbers.

credit (p. 75) The right side of an account.

debit (p. 75) The left side of an account.

journal (p. 78) The chronological accounting record of an entity's transactions.

ledger (p. 79) The book of accounts and their balances.

posting (p. 79) Copying amounts from the journal to the ledger.

transaction (p. 61) Any event that has a financial impact on the business and can be measured reliably.

trial balance (p. 85) A list of all the ledger accounts with their balances.

ASSESS YOUR PROGRESS

Some of the following exercises and problems are available as Excel questions in MyAccountingLab.

Ethics Check

EC2-1. Identify ethical principle violated

For each of the situations listed, identify which of three principles (integrity, objectivity and independence, or due care) from the AICPA Code of Professional Conduct that is violated. Assume all persons listed in the situations are members of the AICPA. (Note: Refer to the AICPA Code of Professional Conduct contained on pages 29–30 in Chapter 1 for descriptions of the principles.)

 a. Michael is in charge of entering accounts receivable journal entries. Michael is notorious for transposing the numbers in his journal entries so his supervisor requires him to review his work at the end of each day. Michael is annoyed by this policy and leaves work without reviewing his journal entries.

 b. Sara sets up a fake supplier account and then creates false invoices and bills her company for work done by this fictitious supplier. Once the check is cut for the fake supplier, Sara deposits it in her own bank account.

 c. Shawna recently received a promotion and is required to do more complex journal entries than in her previous position. Since Shawna is embarrassed that she does not know how to do the journal entries, she does not attend a training session at her company. She figures that she can figure it out on her own; after all, the company promoted her.

 d. Corbin, the managing partner of a CPA firm, received two tickets to the upcoming Alabama versus LSU football game from an accounting software vendor. The CPA firm is currently conducting an audit of that accounting software vendor. These football tickets sell for over $500 each.

Short Exercises

LO 1

S2-1. (*Learning Objective 1: Explain what a transaction is*) For each of the following items, indicate whether or not that item would be considered to be a transaction at Highpoint Lawn Maintenance.

 a. Highpoint Lawn Maintenance files its articles of incorporation with the state.

 b. Highpoint Lawn Maintenance acquires a new lawn tractor by signing a note payable with the lawn equipment company.

 c. Molly Anderson, a customer, signs a contract for next season's lawn service with Highpoint Lawn Maintenance.

 d. Highpoint Lawn Maintenance pays its employees an annual bonus on December 31.

 e. A customer, Billy Harrison, gives Highpoint Lawn Maintenance a check for $540 to prepay for his lawn maintenance contract for the upcoming season.

 f. Highpoint Lawn Maintenance pays $250 for last month's electric bill.

 g. Highpoint Lawn Maintenance selects a new supplier for its lawn chemicals.

 h. The controller for Highpoint Lawn Maintenance pays the bill for a catered lunch at its annual training event for employees.

LO 2

S2-2. (*Learning Objective 2: Differentiate between different types of accounts*) For each of the following accounts, identify whether that item is an asset, liability, or equity account.

 a. Accounts payable
 b. Sales revenue
 c. Cash
 d. Bonds payable
 e. Common stock
 f. Accounts receivable
 g. Equipment
 h. Salaries payable
 i. Inventory
 j. Retained earnings

S2-3. (*Learning Objective 2: Define accounting terms*) Accounting has its own vocabulary and basic relationships. Match the accounting terms at the left with the corresponding definition or meaning at the right.

LO 2

_____ 1. Debit	A. The cost of operating a business; a decrease in
_____ 2. Expense	stockholders' equity
_____ 3. Net income	B. Assets − Liabilities
_____ 4. Ledger	C. Grouping of accounts
_____ 5. Posting	D. Copying data from the journal to the ledger
_____ 6. Normal balance	E. Record of transactions
_____ 7. Payable	F. Revenues − Expenses
_____ 8. Journal	G. Left side of an account
_____ 9. Receivable	H. Always an asset
_____10. Owners' equity	I. Side of an account where increases are recorded
	J. Always a liability

S2-4. (*Learning Objective 2: Differentiate between different types of accounts*) Carcy Anderson opened a software consulting firm that immediately paid $21,000 for a computer system. Was Anderson's computer system an expense of the business? If not, explain.

LO 2

S2-5. (*Learning Objective 3: Show the impact of transactions on the accounting equation*) LeVon Fashions specializes in imported clothing. During March, LeVon completed a series of transactions. For each of the following items, give an example of a transaction that has the described effect on the accounting equation of LeVon Fashions.

LO 3

a. Increase an asset and increase a liability.

b. Decrease an asset and decrease owners' equity.

c. Decrease an asset and decrease a liability.

d. Increase an asset and increase owners' equity.

e. Increase one asset and decrease another asset.

S2-6. (*Learning Objective 3: Show the impact of transactions on the accounting equation*) Fill out the following chart to show the impact on the accounting equation from each transaction.

LO 3

Date	Description	Assets		Liabilities		Stockholders' equity	
		Increase	Decrease	Increase	Decrease	Increase	Decrease
Jan 2	Purchased office supplies on account for $500						
Jan 4	Issued common stock for cash for $5,000						
Jan 10	Sold services on account for $2,000						
Jan 15	Paid amount owed to vendor for the office supplies purchased on account on January 2						
Jan 18	Sold services for cash $200						
Jan 21	Received cash for payment on account from sale on January 10						
Jan 31	Paid employees for monthly payroll $1,500						

S2-7. (*Learning Objective 4: Analyze the impact of business transactions on accounts*) Greene's Catering began with cash of $17,000. Greene then bought supplies for $2,200 on account. Separately, Greene paid $4,600 for equipment. Answer these questions.

LO 4

a. How much in total assets does Greene have?

b. How much in liabilities does Greene owe?

S2-8. (*Learning Objective 4: Analyze the impact of business transactions on accounts*) Seventh Investments, Inc., began by issuing common stock for cash of $250,000. The company immediately purchased computer equipment on account for $106,000.

LO 4

1. Set up the following T-accounts of Seventh Investments, Inc.: Cash, Computer Equipment, Accounts Payable, and Common Stock.

2. Record the first two transactions of the business directly in the T-accounts without using a journal.
3. Show that total debits equal total credits.

LO 4 **S2-9.** (*Learning Objective 4: Analyze the impact of business transactions on accounts*)
Gloria Varay, MD, opened a medical practice. The business completed the following transactions:

July 1	Varay invested $29,000 cash to start her medical practice. The business issued common stock to Varay.
2	Purchased medical supplies on account totaling $9,200.
3	Paid monthly office rent of $4,000.
6	Recorded $7,100 revenue (in cash) for service rendered to patients.

After these transactions, how much cash does the business have to work with? Use a T-account to show your answer.

LO 5 **S2-10.** (*Learning Objective 5: Record [journalize] transactions*) After operating for several months, architect Mark Meecham completed the following transactions during the latter part of January:

Jan 15	Borrowed $31,000 from the bank, signing a note payable.
22	Performed service for clients on account totaling $16,800.
28	Received $12,000 cash on account from clients.
29	Received and paid a utility bill of $1,400.
31	Paid monthly salaries of $9,000 to employees.

Journalize the transactions of Mark Meecham, Architect. Include an explanation with each journal entry.

LO 5 **S2-11.** (*Learning Objective 5: Record [journalize and post] transactions in the books*)
Consultant Dina Delorme purchased supplies on account for $5,200. Later Delorme paid $1,750 on account.
1. Journalize the two transactions on the books of Dina Delorme, Consultant. Include an explanation for each transaction.
2. Open a T-account for Accounts Payable and post to Accounts Payable. Compute the balance and denote it as Bal.
3. How much does the business owe after both transactions? In which account does this amount appear?

LO 5 **S2-12.** (*Learning Objective 5: Record [journalize and post] transactions in the books*)
Borland Consulting performed service for a client who could not pay immediately. Borland expected to collect the $4,900 the following month. A month later, Borland received $2,300 cash from the client.
1. Record the two transactions on the books of Borland Consulting. Include an explanation for each transaction.
2. Post to these T-accounts: Cash, Accounts Receivable, and Service Revenue. Compute each account balance and denote it as Bal.

LO 5 **S2-13.** (*Learning Objective 5: Record [journalize] transactions*) Journalize the following transactions. Include dates and a brief explanation for each journal entry.
July 1: Issued common stock for $10,000
July 5: Sold services on account for $5,000
July 9: Purchased office supplies on account for $500
July 10: Sold services for cash of $2,100
July 12: Received payment in full for services sold on account from July 5
July 24: Paid in full for office supplies purchased on July 9

July 25: Received and paid monthly electric bill of $200

July 30: Signed a note payable to purchase office furniture for $3,500

July 31: Paid monthly payroll of $3,000

S2-14. *(Learning Objective 6: Construct and use a trial balance)* Assume that Navy Port Company reported the following summarized data at December 31, 2016. Accounts appear in no particular order; dollar amounts are in millions.

LO 6

Other liabilities	$ 1	Revenues	$39
Other assets	23	Cash	4
Expenses	24	Accounts payable	5
Stockholders' equity	6		

Prepare the trial balance of Navy Port Company at December 31, 2016. List the accounts in their proper order. How much was Navy Port Company's net income or net loss?

S2-15. *(Learning Objective 6: Use a trial balance)* Yellowberry, Inc.'s, trial balance follows:

LO 6

	A	B	C	D	E
	Yellowberry, Inc.				
	Trial Balance				
1	**December 31, 2016**				
2		**Balance**			
3	**Account Title**	**Debit**	**Credit**		
4	Cash	$ 4,000			
5	Accounts receivable	14,000			
6	Supplies	1,000			
7	Land	48,000			
8	Equipment	27,000			
9	Accounts payable		$ 54,000		
10	Note payable		26,000		
11	Common stock		13,000		
12	Retained earnings		9,000		
13	Service revenue		31,600		
14	Salary expense	29,000			
15	Rent expense	9,000			
16	Utilities expense	1,600			
17	Total	$ 133,600	$ 133,600		
18					

Compute these amounts for the business:

1. Total assets
2. Total liabilities
3. Net income or net loss during December

S2-16. *(Learning Objective 6: Use a trial balance)* Refer to Yellowberry, Inc.'s, trial balance in Short Exercise 2-15. The purpose of this exercise is to help you learn how to correct three common accounting errors.

LO 6

> *Error 1.* Slide. Suppose the trial balance lists Land as $4,800 instead of $48,000. Recompute column totals, take the difference, and divide by 9. The result is an integer (no decimals), which suggests that the error is either a transposition or a slide.
>
> *Error 2.* Transposition. Assume the trial balance lists Accounts Receivable as $41,000 instead of $14,000. Recompute column totals, take the difference, and divide by 9. The result is an integer (no decimals), which suggests that the error is either a transposition or a slide.
>
> *Error 3.* Mislabeling an item. Assume that Yellowberry, Inc., accidentally listed Accounts Receivable as a credit balance instead of a debit. Recompute the trial balance totals for debits and credits. Then take the difference between total debits and total credits and divide the difference by 2. You get back to the original amount of Accounts Receivable.

Exercises MyAccountingLab

Group A

LO 1 4

E2-17A. *(Learning Objectives 1, 4: Explain what a transaction is; analyze the impact of transactions on accounts)* Assume Designs Unlimited opened a store in Columbus, Ohio, starting with cash and common stock of $98,000. Laura Sprague, the store manager, then signed a note payable to purchase land for $76,000 and a building for $199,000. Sprague also paid $36,000 for equipment and $6,600 for supplies to use in the business.

Suppose the home office of Designs Unlimited requires a weekly report from store managers. Write Sprague's memo to the home office to report on her purchases. Include the store's balance sheet as the final part of your memo. Prepare a T-account to compute the balance for Cash.

LO 4

E2-18A. *(Learning Objective 4: Analyze the impact of business transactions on accounts)* The following selected events were experienced by either Knox Eldercare Services, Inc., a corporation, or Steve Knox, the major stockholder. State whether each event (1) increased, (2) decreased, or (3) had no effect on the total assets of the business. Identify any specific asset affected.

    a. Sold land and received cash of $69,000 (the land was carried on the company's books at $69,000).
    b. Received $15,400 cash from customers on account.
    c. Made cash purchase of land for a building site for the business, $89,000.
    d. Borrowed $62,000 from the bank for use in the business.
    e. Knox used personal funds to purchase a flat-screen TV for his home.
    f. Purchased medical equipment and signed a $90,000 promissory note in payment.
    g. Purchased office supplies on account for $1,200.
    h. Received $12,000 cash and issued stock to a stockholder.
    i. Paid $400 cash on accounts payable.
    j. The business paid Knox a cash dividend of $4,000.

LO 3

E2-19A. *(Learning Objective 3: Show the impact of business transactions on the accounting equation)* Dr. Kristine Cohen opened a medical practice specializing in physical therapy. During the first month of operation (July), the business, titled Dr. Kristine Cohen, Professional Corporation (P.C.), experienced the following events:

Jul	6	Cohen invested $148,000 in the business, which in turn issued its common stock to her.
	9	The business paid cash for land costing $66,000. Cohen plans to build an office building on the land.
	12	The business purchased medical supplies for $2,000 on account.
	15	Dr. Kristine Cohen, P.C., officially opened for business.
	15–31	During the rest of the month, Cohen treated patients and earned service revenue of $9,200, receiving cash for half the revenue earned.
	15–31	The business paid cash expenses: employee salaries, $2,900; office rent, $1,500; utilities, $700.
	31	The business sold supplies to another physician for cost of $600 and received cash.
	31	The business borrowed $36,000, signing a note payable to the bank.
	31	The business paid $1,500 on account.

Requirements

1. Analyze the effects of these events on the accounting equation of the medical practice of Dr. Kristine Cohen, P.C.
2. After completing the analysis, answer these questions about the business.
    a. How much are total assets?
    b. How much does the business expect to collect from patients?

c. How much does the business owe in total?

d. How much of the business's assets does Cohen really own?

e. How much net income or net loss did the business experience during its first month of operations?

E2-20A. *(Learning Objective 5: Record [journalize] transactions in the books)* Refer to Exercise 2-19A.

Requirement

1. Record the transactions in the journal of Dr. Kristine Cohen, P.C. List the transactions by date and give an explanation for each transaction.

E2-21A. *(Learning Objectives 4, 5, 6: Analyze the impact of business transactions on accounts; record [post] transactions in the books; construct and use a trial balance)* Refer to Exercises 2-19A and 2-20A.

Requirements

1. After journalizing the transactions of Exercise 2-19A, post the entries to the ledger, using T-accounts. Key transactions by date.
2. Prepare the trial balance of Dr. Kristine Cohen, P.C., at July 31, 2016.
3. From the trial balance, determine total assets, total liabilities, and total stockholders' equity on July 31.

E2-22A. *(Learning Objectives 1, 4, 5: Explain what a transaction is; analyze the impact of business transactions on the accounts; record [journalize] transactions)* The first seven transactions of Fournier Advertising, Inc., have been posted to the company's accounts:

LO **1 4 5**

	Cash				Supplies			Land			Equipment	
(1)	8,900	(4)	12,000	(3)	1,000	(5)	75	(4)	36,000	(7)	3,700	
(2)	10,000	(6)	300									
(5)	75	(7)	3,700									

	Accounts Payable				Note Payable			Common Stock	
(6)	300	(3)	1,000		(2)	10,000		(1)	8,900
					(4)	24,000			

Requirement

1. Prepare the journal entries that served as the sources for the seven transactions. Include an explanation for each entry. As Fournier moves into the next period, how much cash does the business have? How much does Fournier owe in total liabilities?

E2-23A. *(Learning Objective 6: Construct and use a trial balance)* The accounts of Custom Patio Service, Inc., follow with their normal balances at April 30, 2016. The accounts are listed in no particular order.

LO **6**

Account	Balance	Account	Balance
Dividends............................	$ 3,400	Common stock..................	$ 16,800
Utilities expense	2,200	Accounts payable	4,900
Accounts receivable...........	5,100	Service revenue..................	21,100
Delivery expense	600	Equipment.........................	30,400
Retained earnings..............	2,400	Note payable.....................	24,000
Salary expense...................	8,800	Cash..................................	18,700

Requirements

1. Prepare the company's trial balance at April 30, 2016, listing accounts in proper sequence, as illustrated in the chapter. For example, Accounts Receivable comes before Equipment. List the expense with the largest balance first, the expense with the next largest balance second, and so on.
2. Prepare the financial statement for the month ended April 30, 2016, which will tell the company the results of operations for the month.

LO 6   **E2-24A.** *(Learning Objective 6: Construct and use a trial balance)* The trial balance of Harper, Inc., at September 30, 2016, does not balance:

Cash...	$ 14,500	
Accounts receivable...............	12,600	
Inventory...............................	16,800	
Supplies.................................	200	
Land..	50,000	
Accounts payable		$12,000
Common stock........................		47,100
Sales revenue		40,000
Salary expense........................	2,400	
Rent expense	900	
Utilities expense	800	
Total	$98,200	$99,100

The accounting records hold the following errors:
   a. Recorded a $500 cash revenue transaction by debiting Accounts Receivable. The credit entry was correct.
   b. Posted a $3,000 credit to Accounts Payable as $300.
   c. Did not record utilities expense or the related account payable in the amount of $240.
   d. Understated Common Stock by $100.
   e. Omitted Insurance Expense of $3,700 from the trial balance.

Requirement

1. Prepare the correct trial balance at September 30, 2016, complete with a heading. Journal entries are not required.

LO 4   **E2-25A.** *(Learning Objective 4: Analyze the impact of business transactions on accounts)* Set up the following T-accounts: Cash, Accounts Receivable, Office Supplies, Office Furniture, Accounts Payable, Common Stock, Dividends, Service Revenue, Salary Expense, and Rent Expense. Record the following transactions directly in the T-accounts without using a journal. Use the letters to identify the transactions.
   a. Leigh Hampton opened a law firm by investing $22,500 cash and office furniture with a fair value of $9,000. Organized as a professional corporation, the business issued common stock to Hampton.
   b. Paid monthly rent of $1,600.
   c. Purchased office supplies on account, $1,400.
   d. Paid employees' salaries of $3,300.
   e. Paid $850 of the account payable created in transaction c.
   f. Performed legal service on account, $10,100.
   g. Declared and paid dividends of $2,300.

LO 6   **E2-26A.** *(Learning Objective 6: Construct and use a trial balance)* Refer to Exercise 2-25A.
   1. After recording the transactions in Exercise 2-25A, and assuming they all occurred in the month of January 2016, prepare the trial balance of Leigh Hampton, Attorney, at January 31, 2016. Use the T-accounts that have been prepared for the business.

2. How well did the business perform during its first month? Compute net income (or net loss) for the month.

E2-27A. *(Learning Objective 6: Construct and use a trial balance)* Assume that New Towne Company reported the following summarized data at September 30, 2016. Accounts appear in no particular order; dollar amounts are in millions.

Stockholders' equity, September 1, 2016*..	$ 5	Revenues............................	$ 37
Accounts payable	7	Expenses	30
Other assets..	21	Cash.................................	?
Other liabilities	6		

*Stockholders' equity does not include the current period net income.

Requirements

1. Solve for Cash.
2. Prepare the trial balance of New Towne at September 30, 2016. List the accounts in their proper order. How much was New Towne Company's net income or net loss?

Group B

E2-28B. *(Learning Objectives 1, 4: Explain what a transaction is; analyze the impact of transactions on accounts)* Assume Summertime Fashions opened a store in Orlando, starting with cash and common stock of $108,000. Gary Breen, the store manager, then signed a note payable to purchase land for $79,000 and a building for $200,000. Breen also paid $42,000 for equipment and $5,700 for supplies to use in the business.

Suppose the home office of Summertime Fashions requires a weekly report from store managers. Write Breen's memo to the head office to report on his purchases. Include the store's balance sheet as the final part of your memo. Prepare a T-account to compute the balance for Cash.

E2-29B. *(Learning Objective 4: Analyze the impact of business transactions on accounts)* The following selected events were experienced by either Bishop Industries, Inc., a corporation, or Kate Bishop, the major stockholder. State whether each event (1) increased, (2) decreased, or (3) had no effect on the total assets of the business. Identify any specific asset affected.

a. Sold land and received a note receivable of $43,000 (the land was carried on the company's books at $43,000).
b. Received $140,000 cash and issued stock to a stockholder.
c. Purchased equipment for the business for $81,000 cash.
d. Received $37,000 cash from customers for services performed.
e. Purchased land for a building site for the business and signed a $98,000 promissory note to the bank.
f. Earned $15,000 in revenue for services performed. The customer promises to pay Bishop Industries in one month.
g. Paid $12,000 cash on accounts payable.
h. Purchased supplies on account for $4,000.
i. Bishop used personal funds to purchase a pool table for her home.
j. The business paid Bishop a cash dividend of $4,500.

E2-30B. *(Learning Objective 3: Show the impact of business transactions on the accounting equation)* Sue Smith opened a medical practice specializing in surgery. During the first month of operation (May), the business, titled Dr. Sue Smith, Professional Corporation (P.C.), experienced the following events:

May	6	Smith invested $148,000 in the business, which in turn issued its common stock to her.
	9	The business paid cash for land costing $59,000. Smith plans to build an office building on the land.
	12	The business purchased medical supplies for $1,700 on account.
	15	Sue Smith, P.C., officially opened for business.
	15–31	During the rest of the month, Smith treated patients and earned service revenue of $9,000, receiving cash for half the revenue earned.
	15–31	The business paid cash expenses: employee salaries, $3,200; office rent, $1,100; utilities, $1,200.
	31	The business sold supplies to another physician for cost of $300 and received cash.
	31	The business borrowed $32,000, signing a note payable to the bank.
	31	The business paid $1,300 on account.

Requirements

1. Analyze the effects of these events on the accounting equation of the medical practice of Dr. Sue Smith, P.C.
2. After completing the analysis, answer these questions about the business.
   a. How much are total assets?
   b. How much does the business expect to collect from patients?
   c. How much does the business owe in total?
   d. How much of the business's assets does Smith really own?
   e. How much net income or net loss did the business experience during its first month of operations?

LO 5

E2-31B. *(Learning Objective 5: Record [journalize] transactions in the books)* Refer to Exercise 2-30B.

Requirement

1. Record the transactions in the journal of Dr. Sue Smith, P.C. List the transactions by date and give an explanation for each transaction.

LO 4 5 6

E2-32B. *(Learning Objectives 4, 5, 6: Analyze the impact of business transactions on accounts; record [post] transactions in the books; construct and use a trial balance)* Refer to Exercises 2-30B and 2-31B.

Requirements

1. Post the entries to the ledger, using T-accounts. Key transactions by date.
2. Prepare the trial balance of Dr. Sue Smith, P.C., at May 31, 2016.
3. From the trial balance, determine total assets, total liabilities, and total stockholders' equity on May 31.

LO 1 4 5

E2-33B. *(Learning Objectives 1, 4, 5: Explain what a transaction is; analyze the impact of business transactions on accounts; record [journalize] transactions in the books)* The first seven transactions of Big Horn Advertising, Inc., have been posted to the company's accounts:

Cash				Supplies				Land			Equipment	
(1)	8,600	(4)	7,000	(3)	800	(5)	70	(4)	36,000		(7)	3,500
(2)	7,500	(6)	230									
(5)	70	(7)	3,500									

Accounts Payable				Note Payable			Common Stock	
(6)	230	(3)	800		(2)	7,500		(1)	8,600
					(4)	29,000			

Requirement

1. Prepare the journal entries that served as the sources for the seven transactions. Include an explanation for each entry. As Big Horn moves into the next period, how much cash does the business have? How much does Big Horn owe in total liabilities?

E2-34B. *(Learning Objective 6: Construct and use a trial balance)* The accounts of Deluxe Deck Service, Inc., follow with their normal balances at April 30, 2016. The accounts are listed in no particular order.

 LO 6

Account	Balance	Account	Balance
Dividends...........................	$ 3,900	Common stock..................	$ 16,800
Utilities expense	1,400	Accounts payable	4,900
Accounts receivable...........	5,800	Service revenue.................	21,200
Delivery expense	750	Equipment........................	30,000
Retained earnings..............	3,450	Note payable....................	22,500
Salary expense...................	8,500	Cash.................................	18,500

Requirements

1. Prepare the company's trial balance at April 30, 2016, listing accounts in proper sequence, as illustrated in the chapter. For example, Accounts Receivable comes before Land. List the expense with the largest balance first, the expense with the next largest balance second, and so on.
2. Prepare the financial statement for the month ended April 30, 2016, which will tell the company the results of operations for the month.

E2-35B. *(Learning Objective 6: Construct and use a trial balance)* The trial balance of Carver, Inc., at September 30, 2016, does not balance.

 LO 6

Cash..	$ 14,100	
Accounts receivable...............	12,600	
Inventory...............................	17,200	
Supplies..................................	800	
Land.......................................	52,000	
Accounts payable		$12,100
Common stock.......................		47,600
Service revenue......................		41,000
Salary expense........................	2,100	
Rent expense..........................	500	
Utilities expense	200	
Total......................................	$99,500	$100,700

The accounting records hold the following errors:

    a. Recorded a $200 cash revenue transaction by debiting Accounts Receivable. The credit entry was correct.

    b. Posted a $2,000 credit to Accounts Payable as $200.

    c. Did not record utilities expense or the related account payable in the amount of $650.

    d. Understated Common Stock by $300.

    e. Omitted Insurance Expense of $3,300 from the trial balance.

Requirement

1. Prepare the correct trial balance at September 30, 2016, complete with a heading. Journal entries are not required.

LO 4

E2-36B. *(Learning Objective 4: Analyze the impact of business transactions on accounts)*
Set up the following T-accounts: Cash, Accounts Receivable, Office Supplies, Office Furniture, Accounts Payable, Common Stock, Dividends, Service Revenue, Salary Expense, and Rent Expense. Record the following transactions directly in the T-accounts without using a journal. Use the letters to identify the transactions.

    a. Eric Newton opened a law firm by investing $23,000 cash and office furniture with a fair value of $9,400. Organized as a professional corporation, the business issued common stock to Newton.

    b. Paid monthly rent of $1,000.

    c. Purchased office supplies on account, $700.

    d. Paid employee salaries of $2,500.

    e. Paid $150 of the accounts payable created in transaction c.

    f. Performed legal service on account, $10,900.

    g. Declared and paid dividends of $2,000.

LO 6

E2-37B. *(Learning Objective 6: Construct and use a trial balance)* Refer to Exercise 2-36B.

Requirements

    1. After recording the transactions in Exercise E2-36B, and assuming they all occurred in the month of December 2016, prepare the trial balance of Eric Newton, Attorney, at December 31, 2016. Use the T-accounts that have been prepared for the business.

    2. How well did the business perform during its first month? Compute net income (or net loss) for the month.

LO 6

E2-38B. *(Learning Objective 6: Construct and use a trial balance)* Assume that Wolf Products Company reported the following summarized data at May 31, 2016. Accounts appear in no particular order; dollar amounts are in millions.

Stockholders' equity, May 1, 2016*......	$ 6	Revenues............................	$ 38
Accounts payable	7	Expenses	25
Other assets...	20	Cash....................................	?
Other liabilities	3		

*Stockholders' equity does not include the current period net income.

Requirements

    1. Solve for Cash.

    2. Prepare the trial balance of Wolf Products at May 31, 2016. List the accounts in their proper order. How much was Wolf Products Company's net income or net loss?

Serial Exercise

Exercise 2-39 begins an accounting cycle that will be completed in Chapter 3.

LO 1 4 5 6

E2-39. *(Learning Objectives 1, 4, 5, 6: Explain what a transaction is; analyze the impact of business transactions on accounts; record [journalize and post] transactions in the books; construct and use a trial balance)* Barbara Miracle, Certified Public Accountant, operates as a professional corporation (P.C.). The business completed these transactions during the first part of August 2016:

Aug 2	Received $10,000 cash from Miracle, and issued common stock to her.	
2	Paid monthly office rent, $600.	
3	Paid cash for a Dell computer, $2,700, with the computer expected to remain in service for five years.	
4	Purchased office furniture on account, $4,500, with the furniture projected to last for five years.	
5	Purchased supplies on account, $800.	
9	Performed tax services for a client and received cash for the full amount of $1,400.	
12	Received and paid utility expenses, $300.	
18	Performed consulting services for a client on account, $1,900.	

Requirements

1. Journalize the transactions for Barbara Miracle, Certified Public Accountant. Explanations are not required.
2. Post to the T-accounts. Key all items by date and determine the ending balance in each account. Denote an account balance on August 18, 2016, as Bal.
3. Using Excel, prepare a trial balance at August 18, 2016. In the Serial Exercise of Chapter 3, we add transactions for the remainder of August and will require a trial balance at August 31.

Quiz

Test your understanding of transaction analysis by answering the following questions. Select the best choice from among the possible answers.

Q2-40. An investment of cash by stockholders into the business will
   a. increase stockholders' equity.
   b. decrease total liabilities.
   c. have no effect on total assets.
   d. decrease total assets.

Q2-41. Purchasing a laptop computer on account will
   a. increase total assets.
   b. have no effect on stockholders' equity.
   c. increase total liabilities.
   d. All of the listed choices are correct.

Q2-42. Performing a service on account will
   a. increase total assets.
   b. increase stockholders' equity.
   c. increase total liabilities.
   d. accomplish both a and b.

Q2-43. Receiving cash from a customer on account will
   a. decrease liabilities.
   b. have no effect on total assets.
   c. increase stockholders' equity.
   d. increase total assets.

Q2-44. Purchasing computer equipment for cash will
   a. decrease both total liabilities and stockholders' equity.
   b. increase both total assets and total liabilities.
   c. have no effect on total assets, total liabilities, or stockholders' equity.
   d. decrease both total assets and stockholders' equity.

Q2-45. Purchasing a building for $80,000 by paying cash of $25,000 and signing a note payable for $55,000 will
   a. decrease total assets and increase total liabilities by $25,000.
   b. increase both total assets and total liabilities by $55,000.
   c. increase both total assets and total liabilities by $80,000.
   d. decrease both total assets and total liabilities by $25,000.

Q2-46. What is the effect on total assets and stockholders' equity of paying the telephone bill as soon as it is received each month?

	Total assets	**Stockholders' equity**
a.	Decrease	Decrease
b.	No effect	Decrease
c.	Decrease	No effect
d.	No effect	No effect

Q2-47. Which of the following transactions will increase an asset and increase a liability?
    a. Payment of an account payable   **c.** Issuing stock
    b. Purchasing office equipment for cash   **d.** Buying equipment on account

Q2-48. Which of the following transactions will increase an asset and increase stockholders' equity?
    a. Performing a service on account for a customer
    b. Borrowing money from a bank
    c. Collecting cash from a customer on an account receivable
    d. Purchasing supplies on account

Q2-49. Where do we first record a transaction?
    a. Ledger   **c.** Journal
    b. Account   **d.** Trial balance

Q2-50. Which of the following is not an asset account?
    a. Salary Expense   **c.** Service Revenue
    b. Common Stock   **d.** None of the listed accounts is an asset.

Q2-51. Which statement is false?
    a. Dividends are increased by credits.   **c.** Assets are increased by debits.
    b. Liabilities are decreased by debits.   **d.** Revenues are increased by credits.

Q2-52. The journal entry to record the receipt of land and a building and issuance of common stock
    a. debits Land and Building and credits Common Stock.
    b. debits Land, Building, and Common Stock.
    c. debits Common Stock and credits Land and Building.
    d. debits Land and credits Common Stock.

Q2-53. The journal entry to record the purchase of supplies on account
    a. debits Supplies Expense and credits Supplies.
    b. credits Supplies and debits Cash.
    c. credits Supplies and debits Accounts Payable.
    d. debits Supplies and credits Accounts Payable.

Q2-54. If the credit to record the purchase of supplies on account is not posted,
    a. liabilities will be understated.   **c.** stockholders' equity will be understated.
    b. assets will be understated.   **d.** expenses will be overstated.

Q2-55. The journal entry to record a payment on account will
    a. debit Accounts Payable and credit Retained Earnings.
    b. debit Cash and credit Expenses.
    c. debit Expenses and credit Cash.
    d. debit Accounts Payable and credit Cash.

Q2-56. If the credit to record the payment of an account payable is not posted,
    a. expenses will be understated.
    b. cash will be understated.
    c. liabilities will be understated.
    d. cash will be overstated.

Q2-57. Which statement is false?
   a. A trial balance can verify the equality of debits and credits.
   b. A trial balance lists all the accounts with their current balances.
   c. A trial balance can be taken at any time.
   d. A trial balance is the same as a balance sheet.

Q2-58. A business's receipt of a $115,000 building, with a $75,000 mortgage payable, and issuance of $40,000 of common stock will
   a. increase assets by $40,000.
   b. increase stockholders' equity by $115,000.
   c. increase stockholders' equity by $40,000.
   d. decrease assets by $75,000.

Q2-59. NextTalk, a new company, completed these transactions.
   1. Stockholders invested $51,000 cash and inventory with a fair value of $30,000.
   2. Sales on account, $22,000.
   What will NextTalk's total assets equal?
   a. $51,000   c. $81,000
   b. $103,000   d. $73,000

Problems MyAccountingLab

Group A

P2-60A. *(Learning Objective 6: Construct and use a trial balance)* The trial balance of Amusement Specialties, Inc., follows:

LO 6

	A	B	C	D	E
A1					
1	**Amusement Specialties, Inc.** **Trial Balance** **December 31, 2016**				
2	Cash	$ 14,000			
3	Accounts receivable	40,000			
4	Prepaid expenses	4,500			
5	Building	96,000			
6	Equipment	239,000			
7	Accounts payable		$ 51,300		
8	Note payable		96,000		
9	Common stock		35,000		
10	Retained earnings		91,200		
11	Dividends	19,000			
12	Service revenue		270,000		
13	Rent expense	47,000			
14	Advertising expense	2,000			
15	Wage expense	79,000			
16	Supplies expense	3,000			
17	Total	$ 543,500	$ 543,500		
18					

Vicki Gutierrez, your best friend, is considering investing in Amusement Specialties, Inc. Vicki seeks your advice in interpreting the company's information. Specifically, she asks how to use this trial balance to compute the company's total assets, total liabilities, and net income or net loss for the year.

Requirement

1. Write a short note to answer Vicki's questions. In your note, state the amounts of Amusement Specialties' total assets, total liabilities, and net income or net loss for the year. Also show how you computed each amount.

LO 3 4

P2-61A. *(Learning Objectives 3, 4: Show the impact of business transactions on the accounting equation; analyze the impact of business transactions on accounts)* The following amounts summarize the financial position of Rodriguez Computing, Inc., on September 30, 2016:

	Cash	+	Accounts Receivable	+	Supplies	+ Equipment	=	Accounts Payable	+	Common Stock	+	Retained Earnings
			Assets				**=**	**Liabilities**	**+**	**Stockholders' Equity**		
Bal	2,200		3,600			12,000		7,700		6,200		3,900

During October 2016, Rodriguez Computing completed these transactions:
  a. The business received cash of $3,800 and issued common stock.
  b. Performed services for a customer and received cash of $6,000.
  c. Paid $4,300 on accounts payable.
  d. Purchased supplies on account, $500.
  e. Collected cash from a customer on account, $2,000.
  f. Consulted on the design of a computer system and billed the customer for services rendered, $4,000.
  g. Recorded the following business expenses for the month: (1) paid office rent—$1,300; (2) paid advertising—$700.
  h. Declared and paid a cash dividend of $2,800.

Requirements

  1. Analyze the effects of the preceding transactions on the accounting equation of Rodriguez Computing, Inc.
  2. Prepare the income statement of Rodriguez Computing, Inc., for the month ended October 31, 2016. List expenses in decreasing order by amount.
  3. Prepare the entity's statement of retained earnings for the month ended October 31, 2016.
  4. Prepare the balance sheet of Rodriguez Computing, Inc., at October 31, 2016.

LO 4 5

P2-62A. *(Learning Objectives 4, 5: Analyze the impact of business transactions on accounts; record [journalize and post] transactions in the books)* This problem can be used in conjunction with Problem 2-61A. Refer to Problem 2-61A.

Requirements

  1. Journalize the October transactions of Rodriguez Computing, Inc. Explanations are not required.
  2. Prepare T-Accounts for each account. Insert in each T-account its September 30 balance as given (example: Cash $2,200). Then, post the October transactions to the T-accounts.
  3. Compute the balance in each account.

LO 4 5 6

P2-63A. *(Learning Objectives 4, 5, 6: Analyze the impact of business transactions on accounts; record [journalize and post] transactions in the books; construct and use a trial balance)* During the first month of operations, Martinson Services, Inc., completed the following transactions:

May	2	Martinson Services received $65,000 cash and issued common stock to the stockholders.
	3	Purchased supplies, $600, and equipment, $11,700, on account.
	4	Performed services for a customer and received cash, $5,600.
	7	Paid cash to acquire land, $37,000.
	11	Performed services for a customer and billed the customer, $2,900. Martinson expects to collect within one month.
	16	Paid for the equipment purchased May 3 on account.
	17	Paid for newspaper advertising, $610.
	18	Received partial payment from customer on account, $800.
	22	Received and paid the water and electricity bills, $440.
	29	Received $2,500 cash for servicing the heating unit of a customer.
	31	Paid employee salaries, $2,400.
	31	Declared and paid dividends of $2,000.

Requirements

1. Record each transaction in the journal. Be sure to record the date in each entry. Explanations are not required.
2. Post the transactions to the T-accounts, using transaction dates as posting references. Label the ending balance of each account Bal, as shown in the chapter.
3. Prepare the trial balance of Martinson Services, Inc., at May 31 of the current year.
4. Adam Martinson, the manager, asks you how much in total resources the business has to work with, how much it owes, and whether May was profitable (and by how much).

P2-64A. *(Learning Objectives 4, 6: Analyze the impact of business transactions on accounts; construct and use a trial balance)* During the first month of operations (April 2016), Stein Music Services Corporation completed the following selected transactions:

  a. The business received cash of $44,000 and a building with a fair value of $106,000. The corporation issued common stock to the stockholders.
  b. Borrowed $63,000 from the bank; signed a note payable.
  c. Paid $49,000 for music equipment.
  d. Purchased supplies on account, $230.
  e. Paid employees' salaries, $6,000.
  f. Received $3,710 for music services performed for customers.
  g. Performed services for customers on account, $13,300.
  h. Paid $100 of the account payable created in transaction d.
  i. Received an $800 bill for utility expense that will be paid in the near future.
  j. Received cash on account, $1,200.
  k. Paid the following cash expenses: (1) rent, $1,100; (2) advertising, $700.

Requirements

1. Record each transaction directly in the T-accounts without using a journal. Use the letters to identify the transactions.
2. Prepare the trial balance of Stein Music Services Corporation at April 30, 2016.

Group B

P2-65B. *(Learning Objective 6: Construct and use a trial balance)* The trial balance of Larrabee Design, Inc., follows:

	A1					
	A	B	C	D	E	
1	**Larrabee Design, Inc.** **Trial Balance** **December 31, 2016**					
2	Cash	$ 13,000				
3	Accounts receivable	47,000				
4	Prepaid expenses	5,500				
5	Building	103,000				
6	Equipment	224,000				
7	Accounts payable		$ 50,400			
8	Note payable		98,000			
9	Common stock		80,000			
10	Retained earnings		96,100			
11	Dividends	23,000				
12	Service revenue		220,000			
13	Rent expense	33,000				
14	Advertising expense	15,000				
15	Wage expense	79,000				
16	Supplies expense	2,000				
17	Total	$ 544,500	$ 544,500			
18						

Amy Swoboda, your best friend, is considering making an investment in Larrabee Design, Inc. Amy seeks your advice in interpreting the company's information. Specifically, she asks how to use this trial balance to compute the company's total assets, total liabilities, and net income or net loss for the year.

Requirement

1. Write a short note to answer Amy's questions. In your note, state the amounts of Larrabee Design's total assets, total liabilities, and net income or net loss for the year. Also show how you computed each amount.

LO 3 4

P2-66B. *(Learning Objectives 3, 4: Show the impact of business transactions on the accounting equation; analyze the impact of business transactions on accounts)* The following amounts summarize the financial position of Willis Computing, Inc., on October 31, 2016:

			Assets				=	Liabilities	+	Stockholders' Equity		
	Cash	+	Accounts Receivable	+	Supplies	+ Equipment =		Accounts Payable	+	Common Stock	+	Retained Earnings
Bal	2,100		3,400			12,400		7,500		5,600		4,800

During November 2016, the business completed these transactions:
   a. The business received cash of $3,900 and issued common stock.
   b. Performed services for a customer and received cash of $6,000.
   c. Paid $4,800 on accounts payable.
   d. Purchased supplies on account, $900.
   e. Collected cash from a customer on account, $1,100.
   f. Consulted on the design of a computer system and billed the customer for services rendered, $4,500.
   g. Recorded the following expenses for the month: (1) paid office rent, $1,700; (2) paid advertising, $1,300.
   h. Declared and paid a cash dividend of $2,300.

Requirements

1. Analyze the effects of the preceding transactions on the accounting equation of Willis Computing, Inc.
2. Prepare the income statement of Willis Computing, Inc., for the month ended November 30, 2016. List expenses in decreasing order by amount.
3. Prepare the statement of retained earnings of Willis Computing, Inc., for the month ended November 30, 2016.
4. Prepare the balance sheet of Willis Computing, Inc., at November 30, 2016.

LO 4 5

P2-67B. *(Learning Objectives 4, 5: Analyze the impact of business transactions on accounts; record [journalize and post] transactions in the books)* This problem can be used in conjunction with Problem 2-66B. Refer to Problem 2-66B.

Requirements

1. Journalize the transactions of Willis Computing, Inc. Explanations are not required.
2. Prepare T-accounts for each account. Insert in each T-account its October 31 balance as given (example: Cash $2,100). Then, post the November transactions to the T-accounts.
3. Compute the balance in each account.

LO 4 5 6

P2-68B. *(Learning Objectives 4, 5, 6: Analyze the impact of business transactions on accounts; record [journalize and post] transactions in the books; construct and use a trial balance)* During the first month of operations, Gagne Services, Inc., completed the following transactions:

Jul	2	Gagne received $62,000 cash and issued common stock to the stockholders.
	3	Purchased supplies, $800, and equipment, $12,100, on account.
	4	Performed services for a customer and received cash, $5,600.
	7	Paid cash to acquire land, $39,000.
	11	Performed services for a customer and billed the customer, $2,900. Gagne expects to collect within one month.
	16	Paid for the equipment purchased July 3 on account.
	17	Received and paid the telephone bill, $590.
	18	Received partial payment from customer on account, $800.
	22	Received and paid the water and electricity bills, $420.
	29	Received $2,300 cash for servicing the heating unit of a customer.
	30	Paid employee salaries, $2,500.
	30	Declared and paid dividends of $2,000.

Requirements

1. Record each transaction in the journal. Be sure to record the date in each entry. Explanations are not required.
2. Post the transactions to the T-accounts, using transaction dates as posting references.
3. Prepare the trial balance of Gagne Services, Inc., at July 31 of the current year.
4. John Gagne, the manager, asks you how much in total resources the business has to work with, how much it owes, and whether July was profitable (and by how much).

P2-69B. *(Learning Objectives 4, 6: Analyze the impact of business transactions on accounts; construct and use a trial balance)* During the first month of operations (May 2016), Spahr Music Corporation completed the following selected transactions:

    a. The business received cash of $50,000 and a building with a fair value of $106,000. The corporation issued common stock to the stockholders.
    b. Borrowed $63,000 from the bank; signed a note payable.
    c. Paid $44,000 for music equipment.
    d. Purchased supplies on account, $210.
    e. Paid employees' salaries, $5,900.
    f. Received $3,700 for music service performed for customers.
    g. Performed service for customers on account, $13,100.
    h. Paid $200 of the account payable created in transaction d.
    i. Received a $600 bill for utilities expense that will be paid in the near future.
    j. Received cash on account, $1,700.
    k. Paid the following cash expenses: (1) rent, $1,200; (2) advertising, $300.

Requirements

1. Record each transaction directly in the T-accounts without using a journal. Use the letters to identify the transactions.
2. Prepare the trial balance of Spahr Music Corporation at May 31, 2016.

Challenge Exercises and Problem

E2-70. *(Learning Objective 4: Analyze the impact of business transactions on accounts)*
The manager of Sadie Industries Furniture needs to compute the following amounts:
    a. Total cash paid during December.
    b. Cash collections from credit customers during December. Analyze Accounts Receivable.
    c. Cash paid on a note payable during December. Analyze Notes Payable.

Here's the additional data you need to analyze the accounts:

	Balance		
Account	Nov 30	Dec 31	Additional Information for the Month of December
1. Cash..............................	$16,500	$ 8,250	Cash receipts, $91,000
2. Accounts Receivable.......	23,000	21,000	Sales on account, $42,000
3. Notes Payable	11,500	19,500	New borrowing, $31,000

Requirement

1. Prepare a T-account to compute each amount, *a* through *c*.

LO 4 6

E2-71. *(Learning Objectives 4, 6: Analyze the impact of business transactions on accounts; construct and use a trial balance)* The trial balance of 4AC, Inc., at October 31, 2016, does not balance.

Cash....................................	$ 3,900	Common stock.....................	$24,100
Accounts receivable.............	7,100	Retained earnings...............	1,700
Land..................................	30,100	Service revenue....................	9,400
Accounts payable	6,200	Salary expense.....................	2,900
Note payable......................	5,900	Advertising expense.............	1,400

Requirements

1. Prepare a trial balance for the ledger accounts of 4AC, Inc., as of October 31, 2016.
2. Determine the out-of-balance amount. The error lies in the Accounts Receivable account. Add the out-of-balance amount to, or subtract it from, Accounts Receivable to determine the correct balance of Accounts Receivable. After correcting Accounts Receivable, advise the top management of 4AC, Inc., on the company's
   a. total assets.
   b. total liabilities.
   c. net income or net loss for October.

LO 4

E2-72. *(Learning Objective 4: Analyze the impact of business transactions on accounts)* This question concerns the items and the amounts that two entities, Henderson Co. and Goodland Hospital, should report in their financial statements.

During November, Goodland provided Henderson with medical exams for Henderson employees and sent a bill for $38,000. On December 7, Henderson sent a check to Goodland for $27,000. Henderson began November with a cash balance of $57,000; Goodland began with cash of $0.

Requirements

1. For this situation, show everything that both Henderson and Goodland will report on their November and December income statements and on their balance sheets at November 30 and December 31.
2. After showing what each company should report, briefly explain how the Henderson and Goodland data relate to each other.

LO 3 4 5

E2-73. *(Learning Objectives 3, 4, 5: Show the impact of business transactions; Analyze the impact of errors and compute correct amounts; Record [journalize and post] transactions in the books)* Frontland Advertising creates, plans, and handles advertising campaigns in a three-state area. Recently, Frontland had to replace an inexperienced office worker in charge of bookkeeping because of some serious mistakes that had been uncovered in the accounting records. You have been hired to review these transactions to determine any corrections that might be necessary. In all cases, the bookkeeper made an accurate description of the transaction.

	A		B	C	D
	A		**B**	**C**	**D**
1	May	1	Accounts receivable	100	
2			Service revenue		100
3			*Collected an account receivable.*		
4					
5		2	Rent expense	20,000	
6			Cash		20,000
7			*Paid monthly rent, $2,000.*		
8					
9		5	Cash	2,800	
10			Accounts receivable		2,800
11			*Collected cash for services provided.*		
12					
13		10	Supplies	3,100	
14			Accounts payable		3,100
15			*Purchased office equipment on account.*		
16					
17		16	Dividends	5,600	
18			Cash		5,600
19			*Paid salaries.*		
20					
21		25	Accounts receivable	5,400	
22			Cash		5,400
23			*Paid for supplies purchased earlier on account.*		
24					

Requirements

1. For each of the preceding entries, indicate the effect of the error on cash, total assets, and net income. The answer for the first transaction has been provided as an example.

Date	Effect on Cash	Effect on Total Assets	Effect on Net Income
May 1	Understated $100	Overstated $100	Overstated $100

2. What is the correct balance of cash if the balance of cash on the books before correcting the preceding transactions was $6,400?
3. What is the correct amount of total assets if the total assets on the books before correcting the preceding transactions was $28,000?
4. What is the correct net income for May if the reported income before correcting the preceding transactions was $8,000?

APPLY YOUR KNOWLEDGE

Decision Cases

Case 1. (*Learning Objectives 4, 6: Analyze the impact of transactions on business accounts; construct and use a trial balance*) A friend named Jay Barlow has asked what effect certain transactions will have on his company. Time is short, so you cannot apply the detailed procedures of journalizing and posting. Instead, you must analyze the transactions without the use of a journal. Barlow will continue the business only if he can expect to earn monthly net income of at least $5,000. The following transactions occurred this month:

LO 4 6

    a. Barlow deposited $7,000 cash in a business bank account, and the corporation issued common stock to him.
    b. Borrowed $6,000 cash from the bank and signed a note payable due within 1 year.
    c. Paid $1,300 cash for supplies.
    d. Purchased advertising in the local newspaper for cash, $1,800.

e. Purchased office furniture on account, $5,400.

f. Paid the following cash expenses for one month: employee salary—$2,000; office rent— $1,200.

g. Earned revenue on account, $8,000.

h. Earned revenue and received $2,500 cash.

i. Collected cash from customers on account, $1,200.

j. Paid on account, $1,000.

Requirements

1. Set up the following T-accounts: Cash, Accounts Receivable, Supplies, Furniture, Accounts Payable, Notes Payable, Common Stock, Service Revenue, Salary Expense, Advertising Expense, and Rent Expense.

2. Record the transactions directly in the accounts without using a journal. Key each transaction by letter.

3. Construct a trial balance for Barlow Networks, Inc., at the current date. List expenses with the largest amount first, the next largest amount second, and so on.

4. Compute the amount of net income or net loss for this first month of operations. Why or why not would you recommend that Barlow continue in business?

LO 4

Case 2. (*Learning Objective 4: Analyze the impact of transactions on business accounts; correct erroneous financial statements; decide whether to expand a business*) Will Gardner opened an Italian restaurant. Business has been good, and Gardner is considering expanding the restaurant. Gardner, who knows little accounting, produced the following financial statements for Little Italy, Inc., at December 31, 2016, the end of the first month of operations:

	A	B	C
	A1		
1	**Little Italy, Inc.** **Income Statement** **Month Ended December 31, 2016**		
2	Sales revenue		$ 42,000
3	Common stock		10,000
4	Total revenue		52,000
5			
6	Accounts payable		8,000
7	Advertising expense		5,000
8	Rent expense		6,000
9	Total expenses		19,000
10	Net income		$ 33,000
11			

	A	B	C
	A1		
1	**Little Italy, Inc.** **Balance Sheet** **December 31, 2016**		
2	Assets		
3	Cash		$ 12,000
4	Cost of sales (expense)		22,000
5	Food inventory		5,000
6	Furniture		10,000
7	Total Assets		$ 49,000
8	Liabilities		
9	None		
10	Owners' Equity		$ 49,000
11			

In these financial statements all *amounts* are correct, except for Owners' Equity. Gardner heard that total assets should equal total liabilities plus owners' equity, so he plugged in the amount of owners' equity at $49,000 to make the balance sheet come out even.

Requirement

1. Will Gardner has asked whether he should expand the restaurant. His banker says Gardner may be wise to expand if (a) net income for the first month reached $10,000 and (b) total assets are at least $35,000. It appears that the business has reached these milestones, but Gardner doubts whether the financial statements tell the true story. He needs your help in making this decision. Prepare a corrected income statement and balance sheet. (Remember that Retained Earnings, which was omitted from the balance sheet, should equal net income for the first month; there were no dividends.) After preparing the statements, give Will Gardner your recommendation as to whether he should expand the restaurant.

Ethical Issues

Issue 1. Scruffy Murphy is the president and principal stockholder of Scruffy's Bar & Grill, Inc. To expand, the business is applying for a $350,000 bank loan. To get the loan, Murphy is considering two options for beefing up the owners' equity of the business:

> *Option 1.* Issue $200,000 of common stock for cash. A friend has wanted to invest in the company. This may be the right time to extend the offer.
> *Option 2.* Transfer $200,000 of Murphy's personal land to the business, and issue common stock to Murphy. Then, after obtaining the loan, Murphy can transfer the land back to himself and zero out the common stock.

Requirements

Use the ethical decision model in Chapter 1 to answer the following questions:
1. What is the ethical issue?
2. Who are the stakeholders? What are the possible consequences to each?
3. Analyze the alternatives from the following standpoints: (a) economic, (b) legal, and (c) ethical.
4. What would you do? How would you justify your decision? How would your decision make you feel afterward?

Issue 2. Part a. You have received your grade in your first accounting course, and to your amazement, it is an A. You feel the instructor must have made a big mistake. Your grade was a B going into the final, but you are sure that you really "bombed" the exam, which is worth 30% of the final grade. In fact, you walked out after finishing only 50% of the exam, and the grade report says you made 99% on the exam!

Requirements

1. What is the ethical issue?
2. Who are the stakeholders? What are the possible consequences to each?
3. Analyze the alternatives from the following standpoints: (a) economic, (b) legal, and (c) ethical.
4. What would you do? How would you justify your decision? How would it make you feel afterward?

Part b. Now assume the same facts that were just provided, except that you have received your final grade for the course and the grade is a B. You are confident that you "aced" the final. In fact, you stayed to the very end of the period and checked every figure twice! You are confident that the instructor must have made a mistake grading the final.

Requirements

1. What is the ethical issue?
2. Who are the stakeholders and what are the consequences to each?
3. Analyze the alternatives from the following standpoints: (a) economic, (b) legal, and (c) ethical.
4. What would you do? How would you justify your decision? How would it make you feel?

Part c. How is this situation like a financial accounting misstatement? How is it different?

Focus on Financials | Apple Inc.

 *(Learning Objectives 3, 4: Record transactions; compute net income)* Refer to **Apple Inc.'**s financial statements in Appendix A and online in the filings section of **http://www.sec.gov**. Assume that Apple completed the following selected transactions during 2014:

    a. Made company sales (revenue) of $182,795 million, all on account (debit Accounts Receivable, net; credit Net Sales).

    b. Collected cash on accounts receivable, $178,437 million.

    c. Purchased inventories on account, $112,605 million (credit Accounts Payable).

    d. Incurred cost of sales in the amount of $112,258 million. Debit the Cost of Sales (expense) account. Credit the Inventories account.

    e. Paid accounts payable in cash, $104,776 million.

    f. Paid operating expenses in cash, $18,034 million.

    g. Received cash from Other Income/(Expense), net, $980 million.

    h. Paid income taxes, $13,973 million in cash (debit Provision for Income Taxes).

    i. Received cash from sale of other assets, $1,382 million.

    j. Paid cash of $4,027 million for purchase of Property, Plant, and Equipment, net.

Requirements

1. Set up T-accounts for beginning balances of Cash ($0* balance); Accounts Receivable, net (debit balance of $13,102 million); Inventories (debit balance of $1,764 million); Property, Plant, and Equipment, net (debit balance of $16,597 million); Other Assets (debit balance of $ 5,146 million); Accounts Payable (credit balance of $22,367 million); Net Sales ($0 balance); Cost of Sales ($0 balance); Operating Expenses ($0 balance); Other Income/(Expense), net ($0 balance); Provision for Income Taxes ($0 balance).
2. Journalize Apple's transactions a–j. Explanations are not required.
3. Post to the T-accounts, and compute the balance for each account. Key postings by transaction letters a–j.
4. For each of the following accounts, compare your computed balance to Apple Inc.'s, actual balance as shown on its 2014 Consolidated Statement of Operations or Consolidated Balance Sheet in Appendix A at the end of the book. Your amounts should agree with the actual figures.

    a. Accounts Receivable, net

    b. Inventories

    c. Property, Plant, and Equipment, net (assume no other activity in these assets than given in the problem)

    d. Other Assets

    e. Accounts Payable

    f. Net Sales

    g. Cost of Sales

    h. Operating Expenses

    i. Other Income/(Expense), net

    j. Provision for Income Taxes

---

*To keep this exercise at an appropriate level of difficulty, we are using a hypothetical beginning balance of zero for Cash.

5. Use the relevant accounts from requirement 4 to prepare a summary, single-step income statement for Apple Inc., for 2014. Compare the net income (loss) you computed to Apple Inc.'s actual net income (loss). The two amounts should be equal.

Focus on Analysis | Under Armour, Inc.

(Learning Objective 4: Analyze financial statements) Refer to **Under Armour, Inc.'s,** financial statements in Appendix B and online in the filings section of **http://www.sec.gov.** Suppose you are an investor considering buying Under Armour, Inc.'s, common stock. The following questions are important. Show amounts in millions.

LO 4

Requirements

1. Which was larger for Under Armour, Inc., during 2014: (1) net revenues or (2) cash collected from customers? Why? Show computation. (Challenge)
2. Investors are vitally interested in a company's sales and profits and its trends of sales (net revenues) and profits over time. Consider Under Armour, Inc.'s, net revenues and net income (net loss) during the period from 2012 through 2014. Compute the percentage increase or decrease in net revenues and also in net income (net loss) from 2012 to 2014. Which item grew faster during this two-year period—net revenues or net income (net loss)? Can you offer a possible explanation for these changes? (Challenge)

Group Projects

Project 1. You are promoting a rock concert in your area. Your purpose is to earn a profit, so you need to establish the formal structure of a business entity. Assume you organize as a corporation.

Requirements

1. Make a detailed list of 10 factors you must consider as you establish the business.
2. Describe 10 of the items your business must arrange to promote and stage the rock concert.
3. Identify the transactions that your business can undertake to organize, promote, and stage the concert. Journalize the transactions, and post to the relevant T-accounts. Set up the accounts you need for your business ledger. Refer to the chart of accounts in Appendix C at the end of the book if needed.
4. Prepare the income statement, statement of retained earnings, and balance sheet immediately after the rock concert—that is, before you have had time to pay all the business bills and to collect all receivables.
5. Assume that you will continue to promote rock concerts if the venture is successful. If it is unsuccessful, you will terminate the business within three months after the concert. Discuss how to evaluate the success of your venture and how to decide whether to continue in business.

Project 2. Contact a local business and arrange with the owner to learn what accounts the business uses.

Requirements

1. Obtain a copy of the business's chart of accounts.
2. Prepare the company's financial statements for the most recent month, quarter, or year. You may use either made-up account balances or balances supplied by the owner.

If the business has a large number of accounts within a category, combine related accounts and report a single amount on the financial statements. For example, the company may have several cash accounts. Combine all cash amounts and report a single Cash amount on the balance sheet.

You will probably encounter numerous accounts that you have not yet learned. Deal with these as best you can. The charts of accounts given in Appendix C at the end of the book could be helpful.

Quick Check Answers

1. *a*	6. *a*	10. *d*
2. *a*	7. *b* ($6,000 + x − $20,000	11. *c*
3. *b*	= $7,000; *x* = $21,000)	12. *c*
4. *b* ($1,300 + $900 − $700)	8. *c*	
5. *d*	9. *b*	

3 Accrual Accounting & Income

After Labor Day weekend in September of each year, the weather gets a little cooler, the kids are back in school, and things start to slow down a bit at the Disney theme parks. However, The Walt Disney Company has chosen September as the last month in its fiscal year, so when September rolls around, things start to heat up at the company's world headquarters in Burbank, California. There's lots of work to be done. The millions of transactions reflecting the huge company's worldwide operations over the course of a year will be compiled over the next 50 to 60 days and processed into the company's financial statements, which are included in the company's annual report (form 10-K) submitted to the Securities and Exchange Commission (SEC), during the last two weeks of November. This involves adjusting certain accounts in the financial statements to bring them up-to-date as of the last day of the last full week in September in order to clearly and transparently reflect the company's financial position and results of operations in accordance with generally accepted accounting principles (GAAP). It also involves closing the books: zeroing out the balances in the temporary accounts, and transferring the amounts in those accounts to the retained earnings account, which is where the permenant earnings record of the company is stored. ●

Heeb Christian/Prisma Bildagentur AG/Alamy

121

This chapter completes our coverage of the accounting cycle, covering adjusting entries, construction of the financial statements, and closing the books. It also covers the first three items in a long list of key relationships that are essential to your understanding of the information in financial statements: net working capital, the current ratio, and the debt ratio.

LEARNING OBJECTIVES

1 **Explain** how accrual accounting differs from cash-basis accounting

2 **Apply** the revenue and expense recognition principles

3 **Adjust** the accounts

4 **Construct** the financial statements

5 **Close** the books

6 **Analyze** and evaluate a company's debt-paying ability

 **Try It**

For deeper understanding, you may access the most current annual report of The Walt Disney Company at **http://www.sec.gov**. Using the "FILINGS" link on the toolbar at the top of the home page, select "Company Filings Search." This will take you to the "Edgar Company Filings" page. Type "Walt Disney" in the company name box, and select "Search." This will produce the "EDGAR Search Results" page showing the company name. Click on the "CIK" link beside the company name. This will pull up all of the reports the company has filed with the SEC. In the "Filing Type" box, type "10-K" and click the search box. Form 10-K is the SEC form for the company's annual report. You will find the most recent 19 years of annual reports listed. The most recent 6 years have interactive data, meaning that they may be accessed with EXCEL. Examine the "Filing Date" column for those years. Notice that the dates of filing for the 10-K are usually in the last two weeks of November each year. This chapter describes what happens between the last day of the last full week in September and the date the annual reports are filed with the SEC.

EXPLAIN HOW ACCRUAL ACCOUNTING DIFFERS FROM CASH-BASIS ACCOUNTING

1 **Explain** how accrual accounting differs from cash-basis accounting

Managers want to earn a profit. Investors search for companies with stock prices that will increase. Banks seek borrowers who will pay their debts. Accounting provides the information these people use for decision making. Accounting can be based on either the

- accrual basis, or the
- cash basis.

Accrual accounting records the impact of a business transaction as it occurs. When the business performs a service, makes a sale, or incurs an expense, the accountant records the transaction, even if the business receives or pays no cash.

Cash-basis accounting records only cash transactions—cash receipts and cash payments. Cash receipts are treated as revenues, and cash payments are handled as expenses.

Generally Accepted Accounting Principles (GAAP) Require Accrual Accounting. Under accrual accounting, a business records revenues as the revenues are earned and expenses as the expenses are incurred—not necessarily when cash changes hands. Suppose you sell inventory that cost you $500, for $800 on account, and that you collect the $800 from the customer 30 days later. The sale and the subsequent cash collection are actually two separate transactions. Which transaction increases your wealth—making an $800 sale on account, or collecting the $800 cash 30 days later? Making the sale increases your wealth by $300 because you gave up inventory that cost you $500 and you got a receivable worth $800. Collecting cash later merely swaps your $800 receivable for $800 cash—no wealth is created by this transaction. Making the sale—not collecting the cash—increases your wealth.

The basic defect of cash-basis accounting is that the cash basis ignores important information. That makes the financial statements incomplete. The result? People using the statements make decisions based on incomplete information, which can lead to mistakes.

Suppose your business makes a sale on account. The cash basis does not record the sale because you received no cash. You may be thinking, "Let's wait until we collect cash and then record the sale. After all, we pay the bills with cash, so let's ignore transactions that don't affect cash."

What's wrong with this argument? There are two defects—one on the balance sheet and the other on the income statement.

Balance-Sheet Defect. If we fail to record a sale on account, the balance sheet reports no account receivable. Why is this so bad? The receivable represents a claim to receive cash in the future, which is a real asset, and it should appear on the balance sheet. Without this information, assets are understated on the balance sheet.

Income Statement Defect. A sale on account provides revenue that increases the company's wealth. Ignoring the sale understates revenue and net income on the income statement.

The take-away lessons from this discussion are as follows:

■ Companies that use the cash basis of accounting do not follow GAAP. Their financial statements omit important information.

■ All but the smallest businesses use the accrual basis of accounting.

Accrual Accounting and Cash Flows

Accrual accounting is more complex—and, in terms of the Conceptual Foundations of Accounting (see Exhibit 1-3), is a more faithful representation of economic reality—than cash-basis accounting. To be sure, accrual accounting records cash transactions, such as the following:

■ Collecting cash from customers

■ Receiving cash from interest earned

■ Paying salaries, rent, and other expenses

■ Borrowing money

■ Paying off loans

■ Issuing stock

But accrual accounting also records *noncash* transactions, such as the following:

■ Sales on account

■ Purchases of inventory on account

■ Accrual of expenses incurred but not yet paid

■ Depreciation expense

■ Usage of prepaid rent, insurance, and supplies

■ Earning of revenue when cash was collected in advance

Accrual accounting is based on a framework of concepts and principles additional to those we discussed in Chapter 1. We turn now to the time-period concept, the revenue principle, and the expense recognition principle.

The Time-Period Concept

The only way for a business to know for certain how well it performed is to shut down, sell the assets, pay the liabilities, and return any leftover cash to the owners. This process, called liquidation, means going out of business. Ongoing companies can't wait until they go out of business to measure income! Instead, they need regular progress reports. Accountants, therefore, prepare financial statements for specific periods. The **time-period concept** ensures that accounting information is reported at regular intervals.

The basic accounting period is one year, and virtually all businesses prepare annual financial statements. Around 60% of large companies—including Amazon.com, eBay, and Under Armour, Inc.—use the calendar year from January 1 through December 31.

A *fiscal* year may end on a date other than December 31. Most retailers, including Walmart, The Gap Inc., and J.C. Penney, use a fiscal year that ends on or near January 31 because the low point in their business activity falls in January, after Christmas. The Walt Disney Company uses a 52-week fiscal year that ends on the last day of the last full week in September.

Companies also prepare financial statements for interim periods of less than a year, such as a month, a quarter (three months), or a semiannual period (six months). Most of the discussions in this text are based on an annual accounting period.

APPLY THE REVENUE AND EXPENSE RECOGNITION PRINCIPLES

2 Apply the revenue and expense recognition principles

The Revenue Principle

The **revenue principle** deals with two issues:

1. When to record (recognize) revenue
2. What amount of revenue to record

When should you record (recognize) revenue? After it has been earned—and not before. In most cases, revenue is earned when the business has delivered a good to, or has performed a service for, a customer. Revenue is recognized when the business transfers promised goods or services to a customer in an amount that reflects the cash (or fair market value of other consideration) that the entity expects to receive in exchange for those goods or services.

GLOBAL VIEW

The FASB and IASB have recently issued a joint new standard that provides a globally consistent, converged, and simplified way to recognize revenue. The standard is based on the idea that all business transactions involve contracts that exchange goods or services for cash or claims to receive cash. The selling entity must do the following: (1) identify the contract with the customer, (2) identify the separate performance obligations in the contract, (3) determine the transaction price, (4) allocate the transaction price to the separate performance obligations in the contract, and (5) recognize revenue when (or as) the entity satisfies the performance obligation. This text deals mostly with the retail industry, where businesses enter into relatively simple and straightforward contracts to purchase and sell largely finished goods and render services. In other industries, such as computer software, long-term construction, motion pictures, natural resources, or real estate, contracts can be more complex, making the issue of how and when to recognize revenue more complicated. Fortunately, in the retail industry, U.S. GAAP and international financial reporting standards (IFRS) have historically been consistent with respect to general principles of revenue recognition, so the issuance of the new standard has not substantially changed the rules by which revenue is recognized in the retail industry.

Exhibit 3-1 provides guidance on when to record revenue for The Walt Disney Company. In the picture you see people enjoying a stroll through Downtown Disney. There is no admission charge to Downtown Disney, and window shopping is free. No transactions have occurred, so no contract exists, and The Walt Disney Company records nothing. Now suppose a person in the crowd walks into a Disney Store, selects a Disney character doll from a display, and purchases it at the counter. Now a transaction has occurred, producing a contract that both parties are obligated to fulfill. Disney recognizes revenue when the store delivers the product, satisfying its contractual obligation and entitling it to collect cash. The customer receives the product and pays, satisfying the customer's contractual obligation.

By contrast, suppose that a plumbing company (a service-type business) signs a contract to perform plumbing services for a customer who is remodeling a home. The value of the services is $50,000. In signing the contract, the plumbing company becomes obligated to complete the plumbing services by a certain date. Revenue may not be recognized until the plumbing company has substantially completed its obligation and has finished performing the services for the customer.

The *amount* of revenue to record is the amount of cash or its equivalent that is transferred from the customer to the seller. For example, suppose that in order to promote business, The Disney Store runs a promotion and sells character dolls that regularly sell for $20 for the discount price of $15. How much revenue should The Disney Store record? The answer is $15—the current fair (cash) value of the transaction. The amount of the sale, $15, is the amount of revenue earned—not the regular price of $20.

Exhibit 3-1 | When to Record Revenue

Eric James/Alamy

The Expense Recognition Principle

The **expense recognition principle** is the basis for recording expenses. Expenses are the costs of assets used up and of liabilities created in earning revenue. Expenses have no future benefit to the company. The expense recognition principle includes two steps:

1. Identify all the expenses incurred during the accounting period.
2. Measure the expenses and recognize them in the same period in which any related revenues are earned.

To *recognize* expenses along with related revenues means to subtract expenses from related revenues to compute net income or net loss. Exhibit 3-2 illustrates the expense recognition (sometimes referred to as matching) principle.

Exhibit 3-2 │ The Expense Recognition Principle

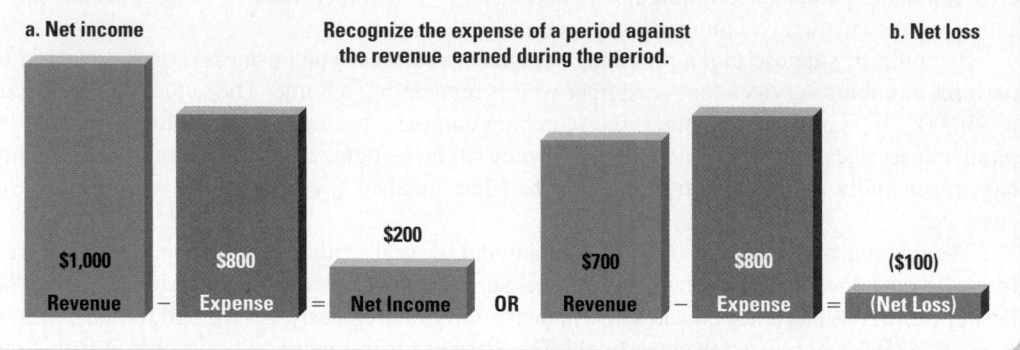

Some expenses are paid in cash. Other expenses arise from using up an asset such as supplies. Still other expenses occur when a company creates a liability. For example, The Walt Disney Company's salary expense occurs when employees work for the company. The company may pay the salary expense immediately, or it may record a liability for the salary to be paid later. In either case, the company has salary expense. The critical event for recording an expense is the employees' working for the company, not the payment of cash.

≫ *Try It*

(1) A customer pays $3,133 on March 15 via the Disney World website for ten 4-day passes to Disney World for a vacation on the days of June 1–4. Has The Walt Disney Company earned revenue on March 15? When will the company earn the revenue?

(2) The Walt Disney Company pays $60,000 on July 1 for advance rental on a Disney Store building for the next six months. Has The Walt Disney Company incurred an expense on July 1? When will the company recognize rent expense?

Answers:

(1) No. The Walt Disney Company has received the cash in March but will not perform the services until June. The company will earn the revenue when the customers go through the gates and a park employee scans the barcode on the tickets on June 1, 2, 3, and 4. Until this happens, The Walt Disney Company must recognize a liability to the customer for 4 days of admission to Disneyworld (unearned revenue).

(2) No. The Walt Disney Company has paid cash for rent in advance. No expense has yet been incurred because the company has not yet occupied the space. This prepaid rent is an asset because The Walt Disney Company has acquired the use of a store location in the future. Rent expense in the amount of $10,000 will be recognized during each of the next six months as the store is occupied.

Ethical Issues in Accrual Accounting

Accrual accounting provides some ethical challenges that cash accounting avoids. For example, suppose that in 2016 The Walt Disney Company prepays a $4.5 million advertising campaign to be conducted by a large advertising agency. The advertisements are scheduled to run during September, October, and November. In this case, Disney is buying an asset, a prepaid expense.

Suppose The Walt Disney Company pays for the advertisements on September 1 and the ads start running immediately. Under accrual accounting, the company should record one-third of the expense ($1.5 million) during the year ended September 24, 2016, and two-thirds ($3 million) during October and November, which are part of fiscal 2017.

Suppose fiscal 2016 is a great year for the company—net income is better than expected. However, top managers believe that fiscal 2017 will not be as profitable as 2016. In this case, the company has a strong incentive to expense the full $4.5 million during fiscal 2016 in order to report all the advertising expense in the fiscal 2016 income statement. This unethical action would keep $3 million of advertising expense off the fiscal 2017 income statement and make 2017's net income look $3 million better than it actually is.

ADJUST THE ACCOUNTS

At the end of the period, the business reports its financial statements. This process begins with the trial balance introduced in Chapter 2. We refer to this trial balance as unadjusted because the accounts are not yet ready for the financial statements. In most cases, the simple label "Trial Balance" means "unadjusted."

3 **Adjust** the accounts

Which Accounts Need to Be Updated (Adjusted)?

The stockholders and management need to know how well Alladin Travel, Inc., is performing. The financial statements report this information, and all accounts must be up-to-date. That means some accounts must be adjusted. Exhibit 3-3 gives the unadjusted trial balance of Alladin Travel, Inc., at June 30, 2016.

This trial balance reflects the same accounts as those in Chapter 2 (see Exhibit 2-12), except for two additional months of transaction activity—May and June 2016. Still, the trial balance is unadjusted. That means it's not completely up-to-date. It's not quite ready for preparing the financial statements for presentation to the public.

Exhibit 3-3 | Unadjusted Trial Balance

Alladin Travel, Inc. Unadjusted Trial Balance June 30, 2016	Debit	Credit
Cash	$36,800	
Accounts receivable	2,200	
Supplies	700	
Prepaid rent	3,000	
Land	18,000	
Equipment	24,000	
Accounts payable		$13,100
Unearned service revenue		400
Common stock		50,000
Retained earnings		18,800
Dividends	3,200	
Service revenue		7,000
Salary expense	900	
Utilities expense	500	
Total	$89,300	$89,300

Cash, Land, Equipment, Accounts Payable, Common Stock, and Dividends are up-to-date and need no adjustment at the end of the period. Why? Because the day-to-day transactions provide all the data for these accounts.

Accounts Receivable, Supplies, Prepaid Rent, and the other accounts are another story. These accounts are not yet up-to-date on June 30. Why? Because certain transactions have not yet been recorded. Consider Supplies. During June, Alladin Travel, Inc., used cleaning supplies to clean their office building. But Alladin didn't make a journal entry for supplies used every time it used them. That would waste time and money. Instead, Alladin waits until the end of the period and then records the supplies used up during the entire month.

The cost of supplies used up is an expense. An adjusting entry at the end of June updates both Supplies (an asset) and Supplies Expense. We must adjust all accounts whose balances are not yet up-to-date.

Categories of Adjusting Entries

Accounting adjustments fall into three basic categories: deferrals, depreciation, and accruals.

Deferrals. A **deferral** is an adjustment for payment of an item or receipt of cash in advance. The Walt Disney Company purchases supplies for use in its operations. During the period, some supplies (assets) are used up and become expenses. At the end of the period, an adjustment is needed to decrease the Supplies account for the supplies used up. This is Supplies Expense. Prepaid Rent, Prepaid Insurance, and all other prepaid expenses require deferral adjustments.

There are also deferral adjustments for liabilities. The Walt Disney Company collects cash for park admission several months in advance of earning the revenue. When the company receives cash up front, it has a liability to provide future park admission to the customer. This liability is called Unearned (or deferred) Services Revenue. Then, each time the customers with paid admission tickets actually visit the park, the company earns Service Revenue as those tickets are scanned at the park entrance. This earning process requires an adjustment at the end of the period. The adjustment decreases the liability and increases the revenue for the revenue earned. The Walt Disney Company also collects royalties in advance for use of its film and media products that it earns later as those products are used. The company must make adjusting entries as these revenues are earned later.

Depreciation. **Depreciation** allocates the cost of a plant asset to expense over the asset's useful life. Depreciation is the most common long-term deferral. The Walt Disney Company buys buildings and equipment. As the company uses the assets, it records depreciation for wear-and-tear and obsolescence. The accounting adjustment records Depreciation Expense and decreases the asset's book value over its life. The process is identical to a deferral-type adjustment; the only difference is the type of asset involved.

Accruals. An **accrual** is the opposite of a deferral. For an accrued *expense*, The Walt Disney Company records the expense before paying cash. For an accrued *revenue*, Disney records the revenue before collecting cash.

Salary Expense can create an accrual adjustment. As employees work for The Walt Disney Company, the company's salary expense accrues with the passage of time. At September 27, 2014, The Walt Disney Company owed employees some salaries to be paid after year-end. At September 27, The Walt Disney Company recorded Salary Expense and Salary Payable for the amount owed. Other examples of expense accruals include interest expense and income tax expense.

An accrued revenue is a revenue that the business has earned and will collect next year. At year-end, The Walt Disney Company must accrue the revenue. The adjustment debits a receivable and credits a revenue. For example, accrual of interest revenue debits Interest Receivable and credits Interest Revenue.

Let's see how the adjusting process actually works for Alladin Travel, Inc., at June 30. We start with prepaid expenses.

Prepaid Expenses

A **prepaid expense** is an expense paid in advance. Therefore, prepaid expenses are assets because they provide a future benefit for the owner. Let's make the adjustments for prepaid rent and supplies.

Prepaid Rent. Companies pay rent in advance. This prepayment creates an asset for the renter, who can then use the rented item in the future. Suppose Alladin Travel, Inc., prepays three months' store rent ($3,000) on June 1. The entry for the prepayment of three months' rent debits Prepaid Rent as follows:

	A	B	C	D	E	F
1	Jun 1	Prepaid Rent ($1,000 × 3)	3,000			
2		Cash		3,000		
3		*Paid three months' rent in advance.*				
4						

The accounting equation shows that one asset increases and another decreases. Total assets are unchanged.

Assets	=	Liabilities	+	Stockholders' Equity
3,000	=	0	+	0
− 3,000				

After posting, the Prepaid Rent account appears as follows:

Prepaid Rent

Jun 1	3,000

Throughout June, the Prepaid Rent account carries this beginning balance, as shown in Exhibit 3-3. The adjustment transfers $1,000 from Prepaid Rent to Rent Expense as follows:*

Adjusting entry a

	A	B	C	D	E	F
1	Jun 30	Rent Expense ($3,000 × 1/3)	1,000			
2		Prepaid Rent		1,000		
3		*To record rent expense.*				
4						

Both assets and stockholders' equity decrease.

Assets	=	Liabilities	+	Stockholders' Equity	−	Expenses
− 1,000	=	0				− 1,000

After posting, Prepaid Rent and Rent Expense appear as follows (with the adjustment highlighted):

Prepaid Rent			**Rent Expense**	
Jun 1 3,000	Jun 30 1,000 →		Jun 30 1,000	
Bal 2,000			Bal 1,000	

This adjusting entry illustrates application of the expense recognition principle. We record an expense when incurred in order to measure net income.

---

*See Exhibit 3-8 (p. 138) for a summary of adjustments a–g.

Supplies. Supplies are another type of prepaid expense. On June 2, Alladin Travel paid cash of $700 for cleaning supplies:

	A	B	C	D	E	F
1	Jun 2	Supplies	700			
2		Cash		700		
3		*Paid cash for supplies.*				
4						

	Assets	=	Liabilities	+	Stockholders' Equity
	700	=	0	+	0
	− 700				

The cost of the supplies Alladin Travel used is Supplies Expense. To measure June's supplies expense, the business counts the supplies on hand at the end of the month. The count shows that $400 of supplies remain. Subtracting the $400 of supplies on hand from the supplies available ($700) measures supplies expense for the month ($300):

Asset Available During the Period	−	Asset on Hand at the End of the Period	=	Asset Used (Expense) During the Period
$700	−	$400	=	$300

The June 30 adjusting entry debits the expense and credits the asset:

Adjusting entry b

	A	B	C	D	E	F
1	Jun 30	Supplies Expense ($700 − $400)	300			
2		Supplies		300		
3		*To record supplies expense.*				
4						

	Assets	=	Liabilities	+	Stockholders' Equity	−	Expenses
	− 300	=	0				− 300

After posting, the Supplies and Supplies Expense accounts appear as follows. The adjustment is highlighted for emphasis.

	Supplies					Supplies Expense		
Jun 2	700	Jun 30	300	→	Jun 30	300	
Bal	400				Bal	300	

At the start of July, Supplies has a $400 balance, and the adjustment process is repeated each month.

At the beginning of the month, supplies were $5,000. During the month, $7,000 of supplies were purchased. At month's end, $3,000 of supplies are still on hand. What is the

- adjusting entry?
- ending balance in the Supplies account?

Answer:

	A	B	C	D	E	F
1		Supplies Expense ($5,000 + $7,000 − $3,000)	9,000			
2		Supplies		9,000		
3						
4		Ending balance of supplies = $3,000 (the supplies				
5		still on hand)				
6						

Depreciation of Plant Assets

Plant assets are long-lived tangible assets, such as land, buildings, furniture, and equipment. All plant assets except land decline in usefulness, and this decline is an expense. Accountants spread the cost of each plant asset, except land, over its useful life. **Depreciation** is the process of allocating cost to expense for a long-term plant asset.

To illustrate depreciation, consider Alladin Travel. Suppose that on June 3 Alladin Travel purchased equipment on account for $24,000:

	A	B	C	D	E	F
1	Jun 3	Equipment	24,000			
2		Accounts Payable		24,000		
3		Purchased equipment on account.				
4						

Assets	=	Liabilities	+	Stockholders' Equity
24,000	=	24,000	+	0

After posting, the Equipment account appears as follows:

Equipment	
Jun 3 24,000	

Alladin Travel records an asset when it purchases machinery and equipment. Then, as the asset is used, a portion of the asset's cost is transferred to Depreciation Expense. The machinery and equipment are being used to produce revenue. The cost of the machinery and equipment should be allocated (matched) against that revenue. This is another illustration of the expense recognition principle. Computerized systems program the depreciation for automatic entry each period.

Alladin Travel's equipment will remain useful for five years and then be worthless. One way to compute the amount of depreciation for each year is to divide the cost of the asset ($24,000 in our example) by its expected useful life (five years). This procedure—called the straight-line depreciation method—gives annual depreciation of $4,800. The depreciation amount is an estimate. (Chapter 7 covers plant assets and depreciation in more detail.)

$$\text{Annual depreciation} = \$24,000/5 \text{ years} = \$4,800 \text{ per year}$$

Depreciation for June is $400.

$$\text{Monthly depreciation} = \$4,800/12 \text{ months} = \$400 \text{ per month}$$

The Accumulated Depreciation Account. Depreciation expense for June is recorded as follows:

	Adjusting entry c					
	A1					
	A	B	C	D	E	F
1	Jun 30	Depreciation Expense—Equipment	400			
2		Accumulated Depreciation—Equipment		400		
3		*To record depreciation.*				
4						

Total assets decrease by the amount of the expense:

Assets	=	Liabilities	+	Stockholders' Equity	−	Expenses
− 400	=	0				− 400

The Accumulated Depreciation—Equipment account (not Equipment) is credited to preserve the original cost of the asset in the Equipment account. Managers can then refer to the Equipment account if they ever need to know how much the asset cost.

The **Accumulated Depreciation** account shows the sum of all depreciation expense from using the asset. Therefore, the balance in the Accumulated Depreciation account increases over the asset's life.

Accumulated Depreciation is a contra asset account—an asset account with a normal credit balance. A **contra account** has two distinguishing characteristics:

1. It always has a companion account.
2. Its normal balance is opposite that of the companion account.

In this case, Accumulated Depreciation—Equipment is the contra account to Equipment, so it appears directly after Equipment on the balance sheet. A business carries an accumulated depreciation account for each depreciable asset, for example, Accumulated Depreciation—Building and Accumulated Depreciation—Equipment.

After posting, the plant asset accounts of Alladin Travel, Inc., are as follows—with the adjustment highlighted:

Equipment		Accumulated Depreciation—Equipment		Depreciation Expense—Equipment	
Jun 3 24,000			Jun 30 400	Jun 30 400	
Bal 24,000			Bal 400	Bal 400	

Book Value. The net amount of a plant asset (cost minus accumulated depreciation) is called that asset's **book value (of a plant asset)**, or carrying amount. Exhibit 3-4 shows how Alladin Travel would report the book value of its land and equipment at June 30.

Exhibit 3-4 | Plant Assets on the Balance Sheet of Alladin Travel

	A1					
	A	B	C	D	E	
1	**Alladin Travel, Inc.** **Plant Assets at June 30**					
2	Land		$18,000			
3	Equipment	$24,000				
4	Less: Accumulated Depreciation	(400)	23,600			
5						
6	Book value of plant assets		$41,600			
7						

At June 30, the book value of equipment is $23,600.

Try It

What will be the book value of Alladin's equipment at the end of July?

Answer:

$24,000 − $400 − $400 = $23,200.

Exhibit 3-5 shows how The Walt Disney Company reports its parks, resorts, and other property, net, in its September 27, 2014, annual report. Line 8 gives the amount of accumulated depreciation, and line 11 shows the assets' book value ($23,332 million and $22,380 million at the end of the current and prior periods, respectively).

Exhibit 3-5 | The Walt Disney Corporation's Reporting of Parks, Resorts, and Other Property, Net (Adapted, in millions)

	A1					
	A	B	C	D	E	
1	**The Walt Disney Company's reporting of parks,** **resorts and other property, net**					
2	Adapted in millions of $	September 27, 2014	September 28, 2013			
3	Attractions, buildings, and improvements	$ 21,539	$ 21,195			
4	Leasehold improvements	757	697			
5	Furniture, fixtures and equipment	15,701	15,135			
6	Land improvements	4,266	4,165			
7		42,263	41,192			
8	Accumulated depreciation	(23,722)	(22,459)			
9	Projects in progress	3,553	2,476			
10	Land	1,238	1,171			
11	Parks, resorts and other property, net	$ 23,332	$ 22,380			
12						

Accrued Expenses

Businesses may incur expenses before they pay cash. Consider an employee's salary. Alladin's expense and payable grow as the employee works, so the liability is said to accrue. Another example is interest expense on a note payable. Interest accrues as the clock ticks. The term **accrued expense** refers to a liability that arises from an expense that has not yet been paid.

Companies don't record accrued expenses daily or weekly. Instead, they wait until the end of the period and use an adjusting entry to update each expense (and related liability) for the financial statements. Let's look at salary expense.

Most companies pay their employees at set times. Suppose Alladin Travel, Inc., pays its employee a monthly salary of $1,800, half on the 15th and half on the last day of the month. The following calendar for June has the paydays circled:

June						
Sun.	Mon.	Tue.	Wed.	Thur.	Fri.	Sat.
						1
2	3	4	5	6	7	8
9	10	11	12	13	14	⑮
16	17	18	19	20	21	22
23	24	25	26	27	28	29
㉚						

Assume that if a payday falls on a Sunday, Alladin Travel pays the employee on the following Monday. During June, Alladin Travel paid its employee the first half-month salary of $900 and made the following entry:

	A	B	C	D	E	F
1	Jun 15	Salary Expense	900			
2		Cash		900		
3		To pay salary.				
4						

Assets	=	Liabilities	+	Stockholders' Equity	−	Expenses
− 900	=	0				− 900

After posting, the Salary Expense account appears as follows:

Salary Expense	
Jun 15 900	

The trial balance at June 30 (Exhibit 3-3, p. 127) includes Salary Expense with its debit balance of $900. Because June 30, the second payday of the month, falls on a Sunday, the second half-month amount of $900 will be paid on Monday, July 1. At June 30, therefore, Alladin Travel adjusts for additional salary expense and salary payable of $900:

Adjusting entry d

	A	B	C	D	E	F
1	Jun 30	Salary Expense	900			
2		Salary Payable		900		
3		To accrue salary expense.				
4						

An accrued expense increases liabilities and decreases stockholders' equity:

Assets	=	Liabilities	+	Stockholders' Equity	−	Expenses
0	=	900				− 900

After posting, the Salary Payable and Salary Expense accounts appear as follows (adjustment highlighted):

Salary Payable		
	Jun 30	900
	Bal	900

Salary Expense		
Jun 15	900	
Jun 30	900	
Bal	1,800	

The accounts now hold all of June's salary information. Salary Expense has a full month's salary, and Salary Payable shows the amount owed at June 30. All accrued expenses are recorded this way—debit the expense and credit the liability.

Computerized systems contain a payroll module. Accrued salaries can be automatically journalized and posted at the end of each period.

Accrued Revenues

Businesses often earn revenue before they receive the cash. A revenue that has been earned but not yet collected is called an **accrued revenue**.

Assume that on June 15 a luxury resort hotel agrees to pay Alladin Travel a commission of $600 for booking 100 clients into its hotel over the next 30 days. Alladin books 50 clients into the resort in June and 50 customers in July. During June, Alladin Travel will earn half a month's fee, $300, for work done June 15 through June 30. On June 30, Alladin makes the following adjusting entry:

Adjusting entry e

	A	B	C	D	E	F
1	Jun 30	Accounts Receivable ($600 × 1/2)	300			
2		Service Revenue		300		
3		*To accrue service revenue.*				
4						

Revenue increases both total assets and stockholders' equity:

Assets	=	Liabilities	+	Stockholders' Equity	+	Revenues
300	=	0				+ 300

Recall that Accounts Receivable has an unadjusted balance of $2,200, and Service Revenue's unadjusted balance is $7,000 (Exhibit 3-3, p. 127). This June 30 adjusting entry has the following effects (adjustment highlighted):

Accounts Receivable		
	2,200	
Jun 30	300	
Bal	2,500	

Service Revenue		
		7,000
	Jun 30	300
	Bal	7,300

All accrued revenues are accounted for similarly—debit a receivable and credit a revenue.

Suppose Alladin Travel, Inc., holds a note receivable as an investment. At the end of June, $100 of interest revenue has been earned. Journalize the accrued revenue adjustment at June 30.

Answer:

	A1					
	A	B	C	D	E	F
1	Jun 30	Interest Receivable	100			
2		Interest Revenue		100		
3		*To accrue interest revenue.*				
4						

Unearned Revenues

Some businesses collect cash from customers before earning the revenue. This creates a liability called **unearned revenue**. Only when the job is completed does the business earn the revenue. Suppose the **Disneyworld Resort** in Orlando, Florida, engages a large group of travel agencies, including Alladin Travel, Inc., paying them commissions in advance to book clients in Disney resort hotels. Assume Disneyworld Resort pays Alladin Travel, Inc., $400 monthly, beginning immediately, if it books up to eight clients into the resort within a 30-day period. If Alladin Travel collects the first amount on June 15, then Alladin Travel records this transaction as follows:

	A1					
	A	B	C	D	E	F
1	Jun 15	Cash	400			
2		Unearned Service Revenue		400		
3		*Received cash for revenue in advance.*				
4						

Assets	=	Liabilities	+	Stockholders' Equity
400	=	400	+	0

After posting, the liability account appears as follows:

Unearned Service Revenue	
	Jun 15 400

Unearned Service Revenue is a liability because Alladin Travel is obligated to perform services (i.e., book clients) for Disneyworld Resort. The June 30 unadjusted trial balance (Exhibit 3-3, p. 127) lists Unearned Service Revenue with a $400 credit balance. During the last 15 days of the month, Alladin Travel books four clients into Disneyworld Resort to earn one-half of the $400, or $200. On June 30, Alladin Travel, Inc., makes the following adjustment:

	Adjusting entry f					

	A1	⬍				

◢	A	B	C	D	E	F
1	Jun 30	Unearned Service Revenue ($400 × 1/2)	200			
2		Service Revenue		200		
3		*To record unearned service revenue that has been earned.*				
4						
5						

Assets	=	Liabilities	+	Stockholders' Equity	+	Revenues
0	=	− 200				+ 200

This adjusting entry shifts $200 of the total amount received ($400) from liability to revenue. After posting, Unearned Service Revenue is reduced to $200, and Service Revenue is increased by $200, as follows (adjustment highlighted):

Unearned Service Revenue			
Jun 30	200	Jun 15	400
		Bal	200

Service Revenue		
		7,000
	Jun 30	300
	Jun 30	200
	Bal	7,500

All revenues collected in advance are accounted for this way. An unearned revenue is a liability, not a revenue.

One company's prepaid expense is the other company's unearned revenue. For example, Disneyworld Resort's prepaid expense is Alladin Travel, Inc.'s, liability for unearned revenue.

Exhibit 3-6 diagrams the distinctive timing of prepaids and accruals. Study prepaid expenses all the way across. Then study unearned revenues across, and so on.

Exhibit 3-6 | Prepaid and Accrual Adjustments

PREPAIDS—Cash First

	First		Later	

Prepaid expenses	*Pay cash and record an asset:*
	Prepaid Expense...... XXX
	    Cash.............. XXX
			Record an expense and decrease the asset:
			Expense............................. XXX
			    Prepaid Expense......... XXX	

Unearned revenues	*Receive cash and record*
	unearned revenue:
	Cash........................ XXX
	    Unearned Revenue XXX
			Record revenue and decrease
			unearned revenue:
			Unearned Revenue XXX
			    Revenue XXX	

ACCRUALS—Cash Later

	First		Later	

Accrued expenses	*Accrue expense and a payable:*
	Expense.................. XXX
	    Payable........... XXX
			Pay cash and decrease the payable:
			Payable.............................. XXX
			    Cash........................... XXX	

Accrued revenues	*Accrue revenue and a receivable:*
	Receivable............... XXX
	    Revenue XXX
			Receive cash and decrease the receivable:
			Cash................................... XXX
			    Receivable.................. XXX	

Summary of the Adjusting Process

Two purposes of the adjusting process are to

- measure income, and
- update the balance sheet.

Therefore, every adjusting entry affects both of the following:

- Revenue or expense—to measure income
- Asset or liability—to update the balance sheet

Exhibit 3-7 summarizes the standard adjustments.

Exhibit 3-7 | Summary of Adjusting Entries

	Type of Account	
Category of Adjusting Entry	**Debit**	**Credit**
Prepaid expense...................	Expense	Asset
Depreciation.......................	Expense	Contra asset
Accrued expense.................	Expense	Liability
Accrued revenue.................	Asset	Revenue
Unearned revenue...............	Liability	Revenue

Exhibit 3-8 summarizes the adjustments of Alladin Travel, Inc., at June 30—the adjusting entries we've examined over the past few pages.

- Panel A repeats the data for each adjustment.
- Panel B gives the adjusting entries.
- Panel C, on the following page, shows the accounts after posting the adjusting entries. The adjustments are keyed by letter.

Exhibit 3-8 | The Adjusting Process of Alladin Travel, Inc.

PANEL A—Information for Adjustments at June 30, 2016	PANEL B—Adjusting Entries		
(a) Prepaid rent expired, $1,000.	(a) Rent Expense	1,000	
	Prepaid Rent		1,000
	To record rent expense.		
(b) Supplies used, $300.	(b) Supplies Expense......................................	300	
	Supplies...		300
	To record supplies used.		
(c) Depreciation on equipment, $400.	(c) Depreciation Expense—Equipment	400	
	Accumulated Depreciation—Equipment		400
	To record depreciation.		
(d) Accrued salary expense, $900.	(d) Salary Expense	900	
	Salary Payable		900
	To accrue salary expense.		
(e) Accrued service revenue, $300.	(e) Accounts Receivable.................................	300	
	Service Revenue.....................................		300
	To accrue service revenue.		
(f) Amount of unearned service revenue that has been earned, $200.	(f) Unearned Service Revenue.........................	200	
	Service Revenue.....................................		200
	To record unearned revenue that has been earned.		
(g) Accrued income tax expense, $600.	(g) Income Tax Expense	600	
	Income Tax Payable..............................		600
	To accrue income tax expense.		

PANEL C—Ledger Accounts

Assets	Liabilities	Stockholders' Equity

Cash

Bal 36,800	

Accounts Payable

	Bal 13,100

Common Stock

	Bal 50,000

Expenses

Rent Expense

(a) 1,000	
Bal 1,000	

Accounts Receivable

2,200	
(e) 300	
Bal 2,500	

Salary Payable

	(d) 900
	Bal 900

Retained Earnings

	Bal 18,800

Salary Expense

900	
(d) 900	
Bal 1,800	

Supplies

700	(b) 300
Bal 400	

Unearned Service Revenue

(f) 200	400
	Bal 200

Dividends

Bal 3,200	

Supplies Expense

(b) 300	
Bal 300	

Prepaid Rent

3,000	(a) 1,000
Bal 2,000	

Income Tax Payable

	(g) 600
	Bal 600

Depreciation Expense—Equipment

(c) 400	
Bal 400	

Land

Bal 18,000	

Utilities Expense

Bal 500	

Equipment

Bal 24,000	

Revenue

Service Revenue

	7,000
	(e) 300
	(f) 200
	Bal 7,500

Income Tax Expense

(g) 600	
Bal 600	

Accumulated Depreciation— Equipment

	(c) 400
	Bal 400

Exhibit 3-8 includes an additional adjusting entry that we have not yet discussed—the accrual of income tax expense. Like individual taxpayers, corporations are subject to income tax. They typically accrue income tax expense and the related income tax payable as the final adjusting entry of the period. Alladin Travel, Inc., accrues income tax expense with adjusting entry g:

Adjusting entry g

A1					
	A	B	C	D	E	F
1	Jun 30	Income Tax Expense	600			
2		Income Tax Payable		600		
3		To accrue income tax expense.				
4						

The income tax accrual follows the pattern for accrued expenses.

The Adjusted Trial Balance

This chapter began with the unadjusted trial balance (see Exhibit 3-3, p. 127). After the adjustments are journalized and posted, the accounts appear as shown in Exhibit 3-8, Panel C. A useful step in preparing the financial statements is to list the accounts, along with their adjusted balances, on an **adjusted trial balance**. This document lists all the accounts and their final balances in a single place. Exhibit 3-9 shows the worksheet for preparing the adjusted trial balance of Alladin Travel, Inc.

Exhibit 3-9 | Trial Balance Worksheet

A1

	A	B	C	D	E	F	G	H
1	Alladin Travel, Inc. Trial Balance Worksheet June 30, 2016							
2		Trial Balance		Adjustments		Adjusted Trial Balance		
3	Account Title	Debit	Credit	Debit	Credit	Debit	Credit	
4	Cash	36,800				36,800		←
5	Accounts receivable	2,200		(e) 300		2,500		
6	Supplies	700			(b) 300	400		
7	Prepaid rent	3,000			(a) 1,000	2,000		
8	Land	18,000				18,000		
9	Equipment	24,000				24,000		
10	Accumulated depreciation–equipment				(c) 400		400	Balance sheet
11	Accounts payable		13,100				13,100	(Exhibit 3-12)
12	Salary payable				(d) 900		900	
13	Unearned service revenue		400	(f) 200			200	
14	Income tax payable				(g) 600		600	
15	Common stock		50,000				50,000	←
16	Retained earnings		18,800				18,800	← Statement of retained
17	Dividends	3,200				3,200		← earnings (Exhibit 3-11)
18	Service revenue		7,000		(e) 300		7,500	←
19					(f) 200			
20	Rent expense			(a) 1,000		1,000		Income statement
21	Salary expense	900		(d) 900		1,800		(Exhibit 3-10)
22	Supplies expense			(b) 300		300		
23	Depreciation expense–equipment			(c) 400		400		
24	Utilities expense	500				500		
25	Income tax expense			(g) 600		600		←
26	Totals	89,300	89,300	3,700	3,700	91,500	91,500	
27								

Note how clearly this worksheet presents the data. The Account Title and the Trial Balance data come from the unadjusted trial balance. The two Adjustments columns summarize the adjusting entries. The Adjusted Trial Balance columns then give the final account balances. Each adjusted amount in Exhibit 3-9 is the unadjusted balance plus or minus the adjustments. For example, Accounts Receivable starts with a balance of $2,200. Add the $300 debit adjustment to get Accounts Receivable's ending balance of $2,500. Spreadsheets are designed for this type of analysis.

Envision Exhibit 3-9 as an Excel spreadsheet. By preparing one, you can use it as a template to solve future problems just by changing the initial trial balance data. To prepare the template, follow these steps:

1. Open a blank Excel spreadsheet. Format the spreadsheet header and column headings exactly as you see in Exhibit 3-9.
2. Enter the account titles and account balances from the unadjusted trial balance (Exhibit 3-3).
3. Calculate a sum for both the debit and credit columns labeled "Trial Balance."

4. Enter adjusting journal entries (a) through (g) one at a time in the "adjustments" columns. For example, for adjusting journal entry (a) enter 1,000 in the debit column on the "Rent expense" line, and 1,000 in the credit column of the "Prepaid rent" line. Do not enter the letters (a) through (g); use only the amounts.
5. In the adjusted trial balance debit and credit columns, enter formulas as follows:
   - For asset, dividend, and expense accounts: = + (debit amounts from "Trial Balance" and "Adjustments" columns) − (credit amounts from "Adjustments" columns).
   - For contra asset, liability, common stock, retained earnings, and service revenue accounts: = + (credit amounts from "Trial Balance" and "Adjustments" columns) − (debit amounts from "Adjustments" columns)
6. Sum the Adjustments debit and credit columns.
7. Sum the Adjusted Trial Balance debit and credit columns.

Formatted spreadsheets for adjusting journal entries are provided for you in selected problems in MyAccountingLab.

CONSTRUCT THE FINANCIAL STATEMENTS

The June financial statements of Alladin Travel, Inc., can be prepared from the adjusted trial balance. At the far right, Exhibit 3-9 shows how the accounts are distributed to the financial statements.

4 Construct the financial statements

- The income statement (Exhibit 3-10) lists the revenue and expense accounts.
- The statement of retained earnings (Exhibit 3-11) shows the changes in retained earnings.
- The balance sheet (Exhibit 3-12) reports assets, liabilities, and stockholders' equity.

The arrows in Exhibits 3-10, 3-11, and 3-12 (all on the following page) show the flow of data from one statement to the next.

>> **Try It** in **Excel®**

If you have already prepared Excel templates for the income statement, statement of retained earnings, and balance sheet for Alladin Travel, Inc., in Chapter 2 (see Exhibit 2-2), or Chapter 1 (see page 32), you may update these, inserting additional amounts, and copying and pasting values from cells in the worksheet in Exhibit 3-9 to the appropriate cells in the financial statements. The value of Excel is that once you have prepared the templates for the worksheet and financial statements, you can reuse them multiple times for different sets of facts.

Why is the income statement prepared first and the balance sheet last?

1. The income statement reports net income or net loss, the result of revenues minus expenses. Revenues and expenses affect stockholders' equity, so net income is then transferred to retained earnings. The first arrow (1) tracks net income.
2. Retained Earnings is the final balancing element of the balance sheet. To solidify your understanding, trace the $18,500 retained earnings figure from Exhibit 3-11 to Exhibit 3-12. Arrow 2 tracks retained earnings.

Exhibit 3-10 | Income Statement

	A	B	C	D	E
1	**Alladin Travel, Inc.** **Income Statement** **Month ended June 30, 2016**				
2	Revenue:				
3	Service revenue		$7,500		
4	Expenses:				
5	Salary expense	$1,800			
6	Rent expense	1,000			
7	Utilities expense	500			
8	Depreciation expense—equipment	400			
9	Supplies expenses	300	4,000		
10	Income before tax		3,500		
11	Income tax expense		600		
12	Net income		$2,900		
13					

①

Exhibit 3-11 | Statement of Retained Earnings

	A	B	C	D	E
1	**Alladin Travel, Inc.** **Statement of Retained Earnings** **Month ended June 30, 2016**				
2	Retained earnings, May 31, 2016	$18,800			
3	Add: Net income	2,900			
4	Subtotal	21,700			
5	Less: Dividends declared	(3,200)			
6	Retained earnings, June 30, 2016	$18,500			
7					

②

Exhibit 3-12 | Balance Sheet

	A	B	C	D	E	F
1	**Alladin Travel, Inc.** **Balance Sheet** **June 30, 2016**					
2	**Assets**			**Liabilities**		
3	Cash		$36,800	Accounts payable	$13,100	
4	Accounts receivable		2,500	Salary payable	900	
5	Supplies		400	Unearned service revenue	200	
6	Prepaid rent		2,000	Income tax payable	600	
7	Land	$18,000		Total liabilities	14,800	
8	Equipment	24,000				
9	Less: Accumulated			**Stockholders' Equity**		
10	depreciation	(400)	41,600	Common stock	50,000	
11				Retained earnings	18,500	
12				Total stockholders' equity	68,500	
13				Total liabilities and		
14	Total assets		$83,300	stockholders' equity	$83,300	
15						

Mid-Chapter | Summary Problem

The given trial balance of Badger Ranch Company pertains to December 31, 2016, which is the end of its year-long accounting period. Data needed for the adjusting entries include:

a. Supplies on hand at year-end, $2,000.

b. Depreciation on furniture and fixtures, $20,000.

c. Depreciation on building, $10,000.

d. Salaries owed but not yet paid, $5,000.

e. Accrued service revenue, $12,000.

f. Of the $45,000 balance of unearned service revenue, $32,000 was earned during the year.

g. Accrued income tax expense, $35,000.

A1	◆				
	A	B	C	D	E
1	**Badger Ranch Company** **Trial Balance** **December 31, 2016**				
2	Cash	$ 198,000			
3	Accounts receivable	370,000			
4	Supplies	6,000			
5	Building	250,000			
6	Accumulated depreciation—building		$ 130,000		
7	Furniture and fixtures	100,000			
8	Accumulated depreciation—furniture and fixtures		40,000		
9	Accounts payable		380,000		
10	Salary payable				
11	Unearned service revenue		45,000		
12	Income tax payable				
13	Common stock		100,000		
14	Retained earnings		193,000		
15	Dividends	65,000			
16	Service revenue		286,000		
17	Salary expense	172,000			
18	Supplies expense				
19	Depreciation expense—building				
20	Depreciation expense—furniture and fixtures				
21	Income tax expense				
22	Miscellaneous expense	13,000			
23	Total	$1,174,000	$1,174,000		
24					

Requirements

1. Open the ledger accounts with their unadjusted balances. We show the accounts receivable account as an example:

Accounts Receivable
370,000

2. Journalize the Badger Ranch Company adjusting entries at December 31, 2016. Key entries by letter, as in Exhibit 3-8 (p. 139).

3. Post the adjusting entries to the accounts.

4. Using an Excel spreadsheet, prepare a worksheet for the adjusted trial balance, as shown in Exhibit 3-9 (p. 140).

5. Prepare the income statement, the statement of retained earnings, and the balance sheet. (At this stage, it is not necessary to classify assets or liabilities as current or long term.) Draw arrows linking these three financial statements.

Answers

Requirements 1 and 3

Assets

Cash

| Bal | 198,000 | |

Accounts Receivable

	370,000	
(e)	12,000	
Bal	382,000	

Supplies

| | 6,000 | (a) | 4,000 |
| Bal | 2,000 | | |

Building

| Bal | 250,000 | |

Accumulated Depreciation—Building

			130,000
		(c)	10,000
		Bal	140,000

Furniture and Fixtures

| Bal | 100,000 | |

Accumulated Depreciation— Furniture and Fixtures

			40,000
		(b)	20,000
		Bal	60,000

Liabilities

Accounts Payable

| | | Bal | 380,000 |

Salary Payable

| | | (d) | 5,000 |
| | | Bal | 5,000 |

Unearned Service Revenue

| (f) | 32,000 | | 45,000 |
| | | Bal | 13,000 |

Income Tax Payable

| | | (g) | 35,000 |
| | | Bal | 35,000 |

Stockholders' Equity

Common Stock

| | | Bal | 100,000 |

Retained Earnings

| | | Bal | 193,000 |

Dividends

| Bal | 65,000 | |

Revenues

Service Revenue

			286,000
		(e)	12,000
		(f)	32,000
		Bal	330,000

Expenses

Salary Expense

	172,000	
(d)	5,000	
Bal	177,000	

Supplies Expense

| (a) | 4,000 | |
| Bal | 4,000 | |

Depreciation Expense— Building

| (c) | 10,000 | |
| Bal | 10,000 | |

Depreciation Expense— Furniture and Fixtures

| (b) | 20,000 | |
| Bal | 20,000 | |

Income Tax Expense

| (g) | 35,000 | |
| Bal | 35,000 | |

Miscellaneous Expense

| Bal | 13,000 | |

Requirement 2

	A	B	C	D	E	F	G
1	(a)	Dec 31	Supplies Expense ($6,000 − $2,000)	4,000			
2			Supplies		4,000		
3			*To record supplies used.*				
4							
5	(b)	31	Depreciation Expense—Furniture and Fixtures	20,000			
6			Accumulated Depreciation—Furniture and Fixtures		20,000		
7			*To record depreciation expense on furniture and fixtures.*				
8							
9	(c)	31	Depreciation Expense—Building	10,000			
10			Accumulated Depreciation—Building		10,000		
11			*To record depreciation expense on building.*				
12							
13	(d)	31	Salary Expense	5,000			
14			Salary Payable		5,000		
15			*To accrue salary expense.*				
16							
17	(e)	31	Accounts Receivable	12,000			
18			Service Revenue		12,000		
19			*To accrue service revenue.*				
20							
21	(f)	31	Unearned Service Revenue	32,000			
22			Service Revenue		32,000		
23			*To record unearned service revenue that has been earned.*				
24							
25	(g)	31	Income Tax Expense	35,000			
26			Income Tax Payable		35,000		
27			*To accrue income tax expense.*				
28							

Requirement 4

	A1						
	A	**B**	**C**	**D**	**E**	**F**	**G**
1	**Badger Ranch Company** **Trial Balance Worksheet** **December 31, 2016**						
2		**Trial Balance**		**Adjustments**		**Adjusted Trial Balance**	
3	**Account title**	**Debit**	**Credit**	**Debit**	**Credit**	**Debit**	**Credit**
4	Cash	198,000				198,000	
5	Accounts receivable	370,000		(e) 12,000		382,000	
6	Supplies	6,000			(a) 4,000	2,000	
7	Building	250,000				250,000	
8	Accumulated depreciation—building		130,000		(c) 10,000		140,000
9	Furniture and fixtures	100,000				100,000	
10	Accumulated depreciation—furniture and fixtures		40,000		(b) 20,000		60,000
11	Accounts payable		380,000				380,000
12	Salary payable				(d) 5,000		5,000
13	Unearned service revenue		45,000	(f) 32,000			13,000
14	Income tax payable				(g) 35,000		35,000
15	Common stock		100,000				100,000
16	Retained earnings		193,000				193,000
17	Dividends	65,000				65,000	
18	Service revenue		286,000		(e) 12,000		330,000
19					(f) 32,000		
20	Salary expense	172,000		(d) 5,000		177,000	
21	Supplies expense			(a) 4,000		4,000	
22	Depreciation expense—building			(c) 10,000		10,000	
23	Depreciation expense—furniture and fixtures			(b) 20,000		20,000	
24	Income tax expense			(g) 35,000		35,000	
25	Miscellaneous expense	13,000				13,000	
26		1,174,000	1,174,000	118,000	118,000	1,256,000	1,256,000
27							

Requirement 5

	A	B	C	D	E
1	**Badger Ranch Company** **Income Statement** **Year ended December 31, 2016**				
2	Revenue:				
3	Service revenue		$330,000		
4	Expenses:				
5	Salary expense	$177,000			
6	Depreciation expense—furniture and fixtures	20,000			
7	Depreciation expense—building	10,000			
8	Supplies expense	4,000			
9	Miscellaneous expenses	13,000	224,000		
10	Income before tax		106,000		
11	Income tax expense		35,000		
12	Net income		$ 71,000		
13					

①

	A	B	C	D	E
1	**Badger Ranch Company** **Statement of Retained Earnings** **Year ended December 31, 2016**				
2	Retained earnings, December 31, 2015	$193,000			
3	Add: Net income	71,000			
4	Subtotal	264,000			
5	Less: Dividends declared	(65,000)			
6	Retained earnings, December 31, 2016	$199,000			
7					

②

	A	B	C	D	E	F
1	**Badger Ranch Company** **Balance Sheet** **December 31, 2016**					
2	**Assets**			**Liabilities**		
3	Cash		$198,000	Accounts payable	$380,000	
4	Accounts receivable		382,000	Salary payable	5,000	
5	Supplies		2,000	Unearned service revenue	13,000	
6	Building	$250,000		Income tax payable	35,000	
7	Less: Accumulated			Total liabilities	433,000	
8	depreciation	(140,000)	110,000			
9				**Stockholders' Equity**		
10	Furniture and fixtures	$100,000		Common stock	100,000	
11	Less: Accumulated			Retained earnings	199,000	
12	depreciation	(60,000)	40,000	Total stockholders' equity	299,000	
13				Total liabilities and		
14	Total assets		$732,000	stockholders' equity	$732,000	
15						

5 Close the books

CLOSE THE BOOKS

It is now June 30, the end of the month. Starr Williams, the manager, will continue to run Alladin Travel, Inc., into July, August, and beyond. But wait—the revenue and the expense accounts still hold amounts for June. At the end of each accounting period, it is necessary to close the books in order to make an accurate measurement of revenue, expenses, and dividends for that period before proceeding to the next.

Closing the books means to prepare the accounts for the next period's transactions. The **closing entries** set the revenue, expense, and dividends balances back to zero at the end of the period. The idea is the same as setting the scoreboard back to zero after a game.

The closing process is obviously handled by computers, but it must be carefully overseen by managers in the accounting department. Recall that the income statement for a particular year reports only one year's income. For example, net income for The Walt Disney Company in fiscal 2014 relates exclusively to the year ended September 27, 2014. All of the accounts that relate to net income, as well as other accounts such as dividends, only relate to one period.

Temporary Accounts. Because revenues and expenses relate to a limited period, they are called **temporary accounts**. The Dividends account is also temporary. The closing process applies only to temporary accounts (revenues, expenses, and dividends).

Permanent Accounts. Let's contrast the temporary accounts with the **permanent accounts**: assets, liabilities, and stockholders' equity. The permanent accounts are not closed at the end of the period because they carry over to the next period. Consider Cash, Receivables, Equipment, Accounts Payable, Common Stock, and Retained Earnings. Their ending balances at the end of one period become the beginning balances of the next period.

Closing entries transfer revenue, expense, and dividends balances to Retained Earnings, where they will reside on a permanent basis. Here are the steps to close the books of a company such as The Walt Disney Company or Alladin Travel, Inc.:

1. Debit each revenue account for the amount of its credit balance. Credit Retained Earnings for the sum of the revenues. This process transfers the sum of all revenues into Retained Earnings, thereby increasing Retained Earnings.

2. Credit each expense account for the amount of its debit balance. Debit Retained Earnings for the sum of the expenses. This process transfers the sum of the expenses into Retained Earnings, thereby decreasing Retained Earnings.

3. Credit the Dividends account for the amount of its debit balance. Debit Retained Earnings. This entry places the dividends amount in the debit side of Retained Earnings. Remember that dividends are not expenses, but represent a permanent reduction of retained earnings.

Assume that Alladin Travel, Inc., closes the books at the end of June. Exhibit 3-13 presents the complete closing process for the business. Panel A gives the closing journal entries, and Panel B shows the accounts after closing.

After closing the books, the Retained Earnings account of Alladin Travel, Inc., appears as follows (data from Exhibit 3-13 on p. 149):

		Retained Earnings	
		Beginning balance	18,800
Expenses	4,600	Revenues	7,500
Dividends	3,200		
		Ending balance	18,500

Exhibit 3-13 | Journalizing and Posting the Closing Entries

PANEL A—Journalizing the Closing Entries   Page 5

		Closing Entries		
①	Jun 30	Service Revenue..	7,500	
		Retained Earnings		7,500
②	30	Retained Earnings	4,600	
		Rent Expense		1,000
		Salary Expense		1,800
		Supplies Expense.................................		300
		Depreciation Expense–Equipment.......		400
		Utilities Expense..................................		500
		Income Tax Expense		600
③	30	Retained Earnings	3,200	
		Dividends...		3,200

PANEL B—Posting to the Accounts

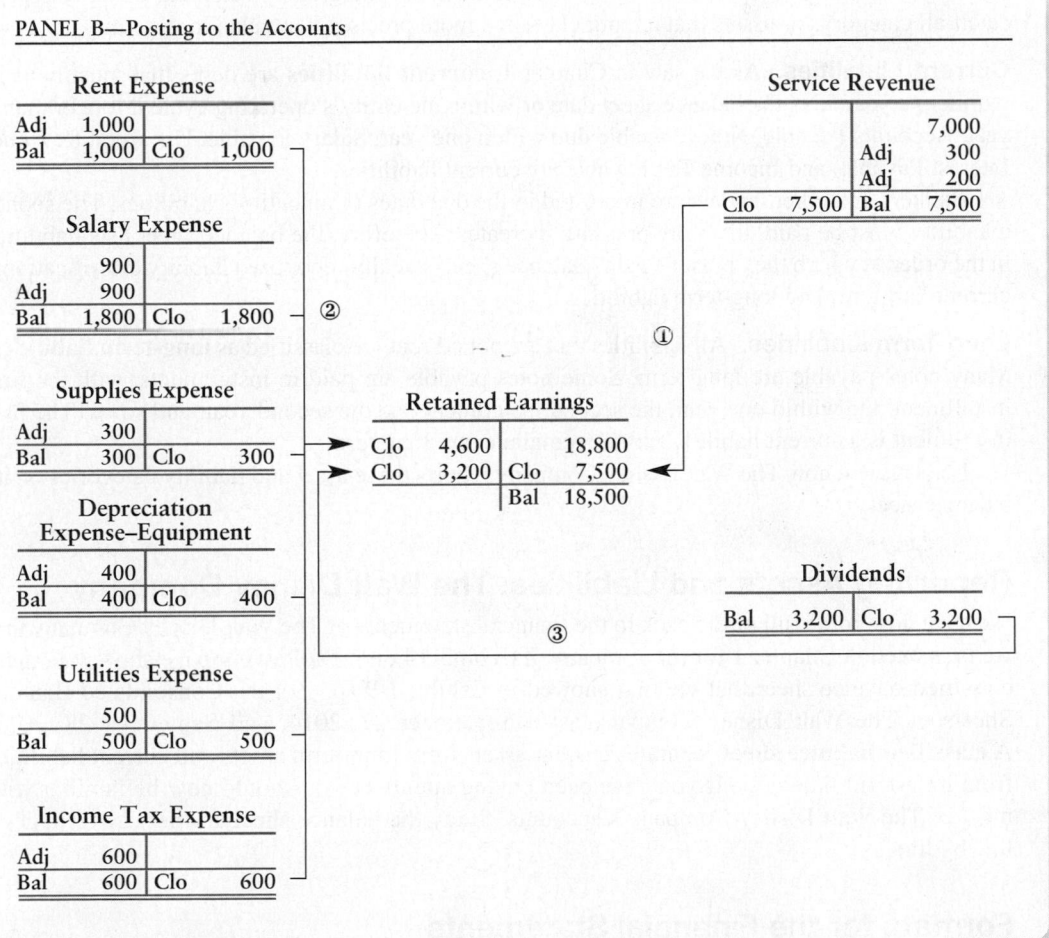

Adj = Amount posted from an adjusting entry
Clo = Amount posted from a closing entry
Bal = Balance
As arrow ② in Panel B shows, we can make a compound closing entry for all the expenses.

Classifying Assets and Liabilities Based on Their Liquidity

On the balance sheet, assets and liabilities are classified as current or long term to indicate their relative liquidity. **Liquidity** measures how quickly an item can be converted to cash. Cash is the most liquid asset. Accounts receivable are relatively liquid because cash collections usually follow quickly. Inventory is less liquid than accounts receivable because the company must first sell the goods. Equipment and buildings are even less liquid because these assets are held for use and not for sale. A balance sheet lists assets and liabilities in the order of relative liquidity.

Current Assets. As we saw in Chapter 1, **current assets** are the most liquid assets. They will be converted to cash, sold, or consumed during the next 12 months after the balance sheet date or within the business's normal operating cycle if longer than a year. The **operating cycle** is the time span during which cash is paid for goods and services, and these goods and services are sold to bring in cash.

For most businesses, the operating cycle is a few months. Cash, Short-Term Investments, Accounts Receivable, Merchandise Inventory, and Prepaid Expenses are the typical current assets.

Long-Term Assets. **Long-term assets** are all assets not classified as current assets. One category of long-term assets is plant assets, often labeled Property, Plant, and Equipment. Land, Buildings, Furniture and Fixtures, and Equipment are plant assets. Of these, Alladin Travel, Inc., has only Land and Equipment. Long-Term Investments, Intangible Assets, and Other Assets (a catch-all category for assets that are not classified more precisely) are also long-term.

Current Liabilities. As we saw in Chapter 1, **current liabilities** are debts that must be paid within one year after the balance sheet date or within the entity's operating cycle if longer than a year. Accounts Payable, Notes Payable due within one year, Salary Payable, Unearned Revenue, Interest Payable, and Income Tax Payable are current liabilities.

Bankers and other lenders are interested in the due dates of an entity's liabilities. The sooner a liability must be paid, the more pressure it creates. Therefore, the balance sheet lists liabilities in the order in which they must be paid. Balance sheets usually report two liability classifications: current liabilities and long-term liabilities.

Long-Term Liabilities. All liabilities that are not current are classified as **long-term liabilities**. Many notes payable are long term. Some notes payable are paid in installments, with the first installment due within one year, the second installment due the second year, and so on. The first installment is a current liability, and the remainder are long term.

Let's review how The Walt Disney Company reports these asset and liability categories on its balance sheet.

Reporting Assets and Liabilities: The Walt Disney Company

We have now come full circle back to the financial statements of The Walt Disney Company that we presented in Chapter 1 for the company. Exhibit 3-14 on the following page shows the same classified balance sheet that we first showed in Exhibit 1-9 (p. 19): the Consolidated Balance Sheets of The Walt Disney Company as of September 27, 2014, and September 28, 2013. A **classified balance sheet** separates current assets from long-term assets and current liabilities from long-term liabilities. If you have been paying attention, you should now be familiar with most of The Walt Disney Company's accounts. Study the balance sheet all the way through—line by line.

Formats for the Financial Statements

Companies can format their financial statements in different ways. Both the balance sheet and the income statement can be formatted in two basic ways.

Balance-Sheet Formats. The **report format** lists the assets at the top, followed by the liabilities and stockholders' equity below. The comparative Consolidated Balance Sheets of The Walt Disney Company in Exhibit 3-14 illustrate the report format. The report format is more popular, with approximately 60% of large companies using it.

Exhibit 3-14 | Classified Balance Sheet of The Walt Disney Company

	A	B	C	D	E
1	**The Walt Disney Company** **Consolidated Balance Sheets**				
2	**Adapted, In millions of $**	**Sep. 27, 2014**	**Sep. 28, 2013**		
3	**Current assets:**				
4	Cash and cash equivalents	$ 3,421	$ 3,931		
5	Receivables	7,822	6,967		
6	Inventories	1,574	1,487		
7	Other current assets	2,359	1,724		
8	**Total current assets**	15,176	14,109		
9	Film and television costs	5,325	4,783		
10	Investments	2,696	2,849		
11	Parks, resorts and other property, net	23,332	22,380		
12	Intangible assets	35,315	34,694		
13	Other long-term assets	2,342	2,426		
14	**Total assets**	$ 84,186	$ 81,241		
15	**Current liabilities:**				
16	Accounts payable and accrued liabilities	$ 7,595	$ 6,803		
17	Current portion of long-term borrowings	2,164	1,512		
18	Unearned royalties and other advances	3,533	3,389		
19	**Total current liabilities**	13,292	11,704		
20	Long term borrowings	12,676	12,776		
21	Other long-term liabilities	10,040	8,611		
22	Commitments and contingencies (Note 14)				
23	**Total liabilities**	36,008	33,091		
24	**Equity:**				
25	Common stock and additional paid-in capital	34,301	33,440		
26	Retained earnings	53,734	47,758		
27	Accumulated other comprehensive loss	(1,968)	(1,187)		
28	Treasury stock at cost	(41,109)	(34,582)		
29	Noncontrolling interests	3,220	2,721		
30	**Total equity**	48,178	48,150		
31	**Total liabilities and equity**	$ 84,186	$ 81,241		
32					

The **account format** lists the assets on the left and the liabilities and stockholders' equity on the right in the same way that a T-account does, with assets (debits) on the left and liabilities and equity (credits) on the right. Exhibit 3-12 (p. 142) shows an account format balance sheet for Alladin Travel, Inc. Either format is acceptable.

Income Statement Formats. A **single-step income statement** (statement of earnings) lists all the revenues together under a heading such as Revenues, or Revenues and Gains. The expenses are listed together in a single category titled Expenses, or Expenses and Losses. There is only one step, the subtraction of the sum of Expenses and Losses from the sum of Revenues and Gains, in arriving at income before income tax expense. Alladin Travel, Inc.'s single-step statement of earnings in Exhibit 3-10 appears in single-step format.

A **multistep income statement** reports a number of subtotals to highlight important relationships between revenues and expenses. Exhibit 3-15 restates Exhibit 1-7 and shows The Walt Disney Company's comparative Consolidated Statements of Income in multistep format. We have modified Exhibit 3-15 slightly from Exhibit 1-7 to subtotal the cost of services and products and to show the company's total gross profit ($22,393 million for fiscal 2014, up from $20,007 million for fiscal 2013). Gross profit is an important piece of information for a company like The Walt Disney Company, because it shows the amount of "pure profit" that results from subtracting the cost of services and products directly from the revenue generated by those services and products, respectively. A few extra quick computations can reveal some other valuable information. Total gross profit for fiscal 2014 ($22,393 million) can be further divided between gross profit from services of $18,890 million ($40,246 million − $21,356 million) and gross profit from products of $3,503 million ($8,567 million − $5,064 million). We can then compute the gross profit percentage from both services and products (gross profit ÷ revenue) to reveal the percentage of each type of revenue dollar that represents profits. For services, the gross profit percentage is 46.9% ($18,890 million ÷ $40,246 million). For products, the gross profit percentage is 40.9% ($3,503 million ÷ $8,567 million). These ratios can be compared with those of the prior period as well as competitors to evaluate how well The Walt Disney Company is performing. We will cover the gross profit percentage in more detail in Chapter 6. Exhibit 3-15 also shows various levels of income, such as operating income, other income, income before taxes, and net income.

Exhibit 3-15 | The Walt Disney Company Income Statement in Multistep Format

	A	B	C	D	E
	A1				
1	**The Walt Disney Company** **Consolidated Multistep Statements of Income**				
2		**12 months ended**			
3	**Adapted, in millions of $**	**Sep. 27, 2014**	**Sep. 28, 2013**		
4	Services revenue	$ 40,246	$ 37,280		
5	Products revenue	8,567	7,761		
6	**Total revenues**	48,813	45,041		
7	Cost of services (exclusive of depreciation and amortization)	(21,356)	(20,090)		
8	Cost of products (exclusive of depreciation and amortization)	(5,064)	(4,944)		
9	**Total cost of services and products**	(26,420)	(25,034)		
10	**Gross profit on services and products**	22,393	20,007		
11	Selling, general, administrative and other	(8,565)	(8,365)		
12	Depreciation and amortization	(2,288)	(2,192)		
13	**Income from operations**	11,540	9,450		
14	Equity in the income of investees	854	688		
15	Other income (expense), net	(148)	(518)		
16	**Income before income taxes**	12,246	9,620		
17	Income taxes	(4,242)	(2,984)		
18	**Net income**	8,004	6,636		
19	Less: Net income attributable to noncontrolling interests	(503)	(500)		
20	Net income attributable to The Walt Disney Company (Disney)	$ 7,501	$ 6,136		
21					

In particular, operating income ($11,540 million) is separated from other types of income (i.e., Equity in the income of investees, Other income (expense), net) that The Walt Disney Company did not earn by performing entertainment services or selling products. Operating income reflects the earnings from the company's core business activities. The other income consists mainly of interest income and other investment income. Most investors consider it important for the companies they own to report operating income separately from nonoperating income such as interest and dividends so that they can evaluate the profitability of the company's core business activities.

Most companies' income statements do not conform to either a pure single-step format or a pure multistep format. Business operations are too complex for all companies to conform to rigid reporting formats. We will discuss the components of the income statement in more detail in Chapter 11.

ANALYZE AND EVALUATE A COMPANY'S DEBT-PAYING ABILITY

6 **Analyze** and evaluate a company's debt-paying ability

As we've seen, accounting provides information for decision making. A bank considering lending money must predict whether the borrower can repay the loan. If the borrower already has a lot of debt, the probability of repayment may be low. If the borrower owes little, the loan may go through. To analyze a company's financial position, decision makers use data and ratios computed from various items in the financial statements. Let's see how this process works.

Net Working Capital

Net working capital is computational data that represents operating liquidity. Its computation is simple:

$$\text{Net working capital} = \text{Total current assets} - \text{Total current liabilities}$$

For The Walt Disney Company, at September 27, 2014 (amounts in millions in Exhibit 3-14),

$$\text{Net working capital} = \$15,176 - \$13,292 = \$1,884$$

Generally, to be considered sufficiently liquid, entities should have a sufficient excess of current assets over current liabilities. The amount of that excess is usually expressed in terms of the current ratio discussed below, and the amount considered "sufficient" varies with the industry. The Walt Disney Company's current assets exceed its current liabilities by $1,884 million, meaning that after the company pays all of its current liabilities, it will still have about $1.9 billion in cash and other assets that can be converted into cash. Thus, The Walt Disney Company is considered highly "liquid."

Current Ratio

Another means of expressing operating liquidity through the relationship between current assets and current liabilities is the **current ratio**, which divides total current assets by total current liabilities.

$$\text{Current ratio} = \frac{\text{Total current assets}}{\text{Total current liabilities}}$$

For The Walt Disney Company, at September 27, 2014 (amounts in millions from Exhibit 3-14),

$$\text{Current ratio} = \frac{\text{Total current assets}}{\text{Total current liabilities}} = \frac{\$15,176}{\$13,292} = 1.14$$

Like net working capital, the current ratio measures the company's ability to pay current liabilities with current assets. A company prefers a high current ratio, which means that the business has plenty of current assets to pay current liabilities. An increasing current ratio from period to period indicates improvement in liquidity.

As a rule of thumb, a strong current ratio is 1.50, which indicates that the company has $1.50 in current assets for every $1.00 in current liabilities. A company with a current ratio of 1.50 would probably have little trouble paying its current liabilities. Many successful businesses operate with current ratios between 1.20 and 1.50. A current ratio of less than 1.00 is considered low. That would mean that current liabilities exceed current assets.

The Walt Disney Company's current ratio of 1.14, although it is below the "benchmarks" mentioned in the previous paragraph, does not indicate a weak current position for several reasons. First, the computation of the current ratio assumes the worst-case scenario, that the company will have to liquidate all of its current assets (turn them into cash), pay off all its current liabilities at once, and go out of business. That is far from a realistic assumption for a company like The Walt Disney Company. Second, The Walt Disney Company generated a huge amount of cash through its operating activities (over $9.8 billion in fiscal 2014, according to its Consolidated Statements of Cash Flows in Exhibit 1-10 on page 23), certainly enough to pay off accounts payable and accrued liabilities ($7.6 billion) and the current portion of long-term borrowings ($2.2 billion) as they become due. The remainder of current liabilities consists of unearned income, which has been collected in advance. In summary, it is necessary to evaluate each company on its own merits based on an understanding of its entire financial picture and a thorough knowledge of its business model, rather than attempt to adopt a "one size fits all" benchmark or to limit the evaluation merely to one ratio.

Debt Ratio

Still another measure of debt-paying ability is the **debt ratio**, which is the ratio of total liabilities to total assets.

$$\text{Debt ratio} = \frac{\text{Total liabilities}}{\text{Total assets}}$$

For The Walt Disney Company, at September 27, 2014 (amounts in millions from Exhibit 3-14),

$$\text{Debt ratio} = \frac{\text{Total liabilities}}{\text{Total assets}} = \frac{\$36,008}{\$84,186} = 0.43$$

The debt ratio indicates the proportion of a company's assets that is financed with debt. This ratio measures a business's ability to pay both current and long-term debts (total liabilities).

A low debt ratio is safer than a high debt ratio. Why? Because a company with few liabilities has low required debt payments. This company is unlikely to get into financial difficulty. By contrast, a business with a high debt ratio may have trouble paying its liabilities, especially when sales are low and cash is scarce.

The Walt Disney Company's debt ratio of 43% (0.43) is low compared to most companies in the United States. The norm for the debt ratio ranges from 60% to 70%. This indicates to creditors that the company is a low credit risk, meaning that there is a high probability that borrowed money will be paid back on time, along with interest.

When a company fails to pay its debts, some of its creditors might be in a position to take the company away from its owners. Most bankruptcies result from high debt ratios. Companies that continue in this pattern are often forced out of business.

How Do Transactions Affect the Ratios?

Companies such as The Walt Disney Company are aware of how transactions affect their ratios. Lending agreements often require that a company's current ratio not fall below a certain level. Another loan requirement is that the company's debt ratio may not rise above a threshold, such as 0.70. When a company fails to meet one of these conditions, it is said to default on its lending agreements. The penalty can be severe: The lender can require immediate payment of the loan. The Walt Disney Company has a sufficiently small amount of debt that the company is not in danger of default. But many companies are. To help keep debt ratios within normal limits, companies might adopt one or more of the following strategies:

- Increase revenue and decrease costs, thus increasing current assets, net income, and retained earnings without increasing liabilities
- Sell stock, thus increasing cash and stockholders' equity
- Choose to borrow less money

Let's use The Walt Disney Company to examine the effects of some transactions on the company's current ratio and debt ratio. As shown in the preceding section, The Walt Disney Company's ratios are as follows (dollar amounts in millions):[1]

$$\text{Current ratio} = \frac{\$15,176}{\$13,292} = 1.142$$

$$\text{Debt ratio} = \frac{\$36,008}{\$84,186} = 0.428$$

---

[1]Because of the relatively small amounts of these particular illustrative transactions compared to the original components, we have chosen to carry current ratio and debt ratio computations to three or four decimal places in order to illustrate the impact of individual transactions on the current ratio and debt ratio. The larger the individual transaction in comparison with the original components (for example, see the End-of-Chapter Summary Problem), the less necessary this will be.

The managers of any company would be concerned about how inventory purchases, payments on account, expense accruals, and depreciation would affect its ratios. Let's see how The Walt Disney Company would be affected by some typical transactions. For each transaction, the journal entry helps identify the effects on the company.

   a. Issued stock and received cash of $50 million.

	A	B	C	D	E	F
		A1				
1	Journal entry:	Cash	50			
2		Common Stock		50		
3						

Cash, a current asset, affects both the current ratio and the debt ratio as follows:

$$\text{Current ratio} = \frac{\$15,176 + \$50}{\$13,292} = 1.146 \qquad \text{Debt ratio} = \frac{\$36,008}{\$84,186 + \$50} = 0.427$$

The issuance of stock improves both ratios slightly.

   b. Paid cash to purchase buildings for $20 million.

	A	B	C	D	E	F
		A1				
1	Journal entry:	Buildings	20			
2		Cash		20		
3						

Cash, a current asset, decreases, but total assets stay the same. Liabilities are unchanged.

$$\text{Current ratio} = \frac{\$15,176 - \$20}{\$13,292} = 1.140 \qquad \text{Debt ratio} = \frac{\$36,008}{\$84,186 + \$20 - \$20} = 0.428; \text{ no change}$$

A cash purchase of a building hurts the current ratio but doesn't affect the debt ratio.

   c. Made a $30 million sale on account.

	A	B	C	D	E	F
		A1				
1	Journal entry:	Accounts Receivable	30			
2		Sales Revenue		30		
3						

The increase in Accounts Receivable increases current assets and total assets, as follows:

$$\text{Current ratio} = \frac{\$15,176 + \$30}{\$13,292} = 1.144 \qquad \text{Debt ratio} = \frac{\$36,008}{\$84,186 + \$30} = 0.4276$$

A sale on account improves both ratios slightly.

d. Collected the account receivable, $30 million.

	A	B	C	D	E	F
1	*Journal entry:*	Cash	30			
2		Accounts Receivable		30		
3						

This transaction has no effect on total current assets, total assets, or total liabilities. Both ratios are unaffected.

e. Accrued expenses at year-end, $40 million.

	A	B	C	D	E	F
1	*Journal entry:*	Expenses	40			
2		Expenses Payable		40		
3						

$$\text{Current ratio} = \frac{\$15,176}{\$13,292 + \$40} = 1.138 \qquad \text{Debt ratio} = \frac{\$36,008 + \$40}{\$84,186} = 0.4282$$

Most expenses hurt both ratios.

f. Recorded depreciation, $80 million.

	A	B	C	D	E	F
1	*Journal entry:*	Depreciation Expense	80			
2		Accumulated Depreciation		80		
3						

No current accounts are affected, so only the debt ratio is affected.

$$\text{Current ratio} = \frac{\$15,176}{\$13,292} = 1.142 \qquad \text{Debt ratio} = \frac{\$36,008}{\$84,186 - \$80} = 0.4281$$

Depreciation decreases total assets and therefore hurts the debt ratio.

g. Earned interest revenue and collected cash, $40 million.

	A	B	C	D	E	F
1	*Journal entry:*	Cash	40			
2		Interest Revenue		40		
3						

Cash, a current asset, affects both the current ratio and the debt ratio as follows:

$$\text{Current ratio} = \frac{\$15,176 + \$40}{\$13,292} = 1.145 \qquad \text{Debt ratio} = \frac{\$36,008}{\$84,186 + \$40} = 0.4275$$

A revenue improves both ratios.

Now, let's wrap up the chapter by seeing how to use net working capital, the current ratio, and the debt ratio for decision making. The Decision Guidelines feature offers some clues.

DECISION GUIDELINES

EVALUATE DEBT-PAYING ABILITY USING NET WORKING CAPITAL, THE CURRENT RATIO, AND THE DEBT RATIO

In general, a larger amount of net working capital is preferable to a smaller amount. Similarly, a *high* current ratio is preferable to a low current ratio. *Increases* in net working capital and increases in the current ratio improve financial position. By contrast, a *low* debt ratio is preferable to a high debt ratio. Improvement is indicated by a *decrease* in the debt ratio.

No single ratio gives the whole picture about a company. Therefore, lenders and investors use many ratios to evaluate a company. Let's apply what we have learned. Suppose you are a loan officer at Bank of America and The Walt Disney Company has asked you for a $20 million loan to launch a new theme park ride. How will you make this loan decision? The Decision Guidelines show how bankers and investors use two key ratios.

▶ USING NET WORKING CAPITAL AND THE CURRENT RATIO

Decision	Guidelines
How can you measure a company's ability to pay current liabilities with current assets?	Net working capital = Total current assets − Total current liabilities $$\text{Current ratio} = \frac{\text{Total current assets}}{\text{Total current liabilities}}$$
Who uses net working capital and the current ratio for decision making?	*Lenders and other creditors*, who must predict whether a borrower can pay its current liabilities. *Stockholders*, who know that a company that cannot pay its debts is not a good investment because it may go bankrupt. *Managers*, who must have enough cash to pay the company's current liabilities.
What is a good value of net working capital and the current ratio?	There is no correct answer for this. It depends on the industry as well as the individual entity's ability to generate cash quickly and primarily from operations. An entity with strong operating cash flow can operate successfully with a low amount of net working capital as long as cash comes in through operations at least as fast as accounts payable become due. A current ratio of, say, 1.10–1.20 is sometimes sufficient. An entity with relatively slow cash flow from operations needs a higher current ratio of, say, 1.30–1.50. Traditionally, a current ratio of 2.00 was considered ideal. Recently, acceptable values have decreased as companies have been able to operate more efficiently; today, a current ratio of 1.50 is considered strong. Although not ideal, cash-rich companies like The Walt Disney Company can operate with a current ratio at or near 1.0.

> **USING THE DEBT RATIO**

Decision	Guidelines
How can you measure a company's ability to pay total liabilities?	$$\text{Debt ratio} = \frac{\text{Total liabilities}}{\text{Total assets}}$$
Who uses the debt ratio for decision making?	*Lenders and other creditors*, who must predict whether a borrower can pay its debts.
	Stockholders, who know that a company that cannot pay its debts is not a good investment because it may go bankrupt.
	Managers, who must have enough assets to pay the company's debts.
What is a good value of the debt ratio?	It depends on the industry:
	A company with strong cash flow can operate successfully with a high debt ratio of, say, 0.70–0.80.
	A company with weak cash flow needs a lower debt ratio of, say, 0.50–0.60.
	Traditionally, a debt ratio of 0.50 was considered ideal. Recently, values have increased as companies have been able to operate more efficiently; today, a normal value of the debt ratio is around 0.60–0.70.

End-of-Chapter | Summary Problem

Refer to the Mid-Chapter Summary Problem that begins on page 143. The adjusted trial balance appears on page 146.

Requirements

1. Make Badger Ranch Company's closing entries at December 31, 2016. Explain what they accomplish and why they are necessary.

2. Post the closing entries to Retained Earnings and compare Retained Earnings' ending balance with the amount reported on the balance sheet on page 147. The two amounts should be the same.

3. Prepare Badger Ranch Company's classified balance sheet to identify the company's current assets and current liabilities. (Badger Ranch Company has no long-term liabilities.) Use the account format. Then compute the company's net working capital, current ratio, and debt ratio at December 31, 2016.

4. The top management of Badger Ranch Company has asked you for a $500,000 loan to expand the business. Badger Ranch proposes to pay off the loan over a 10-year period. Recompute Badger Ranch Company's debt ratio assuming you make the loan. Use the company financial statements plus the ratio values to decide whether to grant the loan at an interest rate of 8%, 10%, or 12%. Badger Ranch Company's cash flow is strong. Give the reasoning underlying your decision.

Answers

Requirement 1

2016			
Dec 31	Service Revenue..	330,000	
	Retained Earnings		330,000
31	Retained Earnings	259,000	
	Salary Expense		177,000
	Depreciation Expense—		
	Furniture and Fixtures............................		20,000
	Depreciation Expense—Building		10,000
	Supplies Expense		4,000
	Income Tax Expense		35,000
	Miscellaneous Expense...............................		13,000
31	Retained Earnings	65,000	
	Dividends..		65,000

Explanation of Closing Entries

The closing entries set the balance of each revenue, expense, and dividend account back to zero for the start of the next accounting period. We must close these accounts because their balances relate only to one accounting period.

Requirement 2

Retained Earnings

				193,000
Clo	259,000	Clo	330,000
Clo	65,000		
		Bal	199,000

The balance in the Retained Earnings account agrees with the amount reported on the balance sheet, as it should.

Requirement 3

	A	B	C	D	E
1	**Badger Ranch Company** **Balance Sheet** **December 31, 2016**				
2	**Assets**			**Liabilities**	
3	Current assets:			Current liabilities:	
4	Cash		$198,000	Accounts payable	$380,000
5	Accounts receivable		382,000	Salary payable	5,000
6	Supplies		2,000	Unearned service revenue	13,000
7	Total current assets		582,000	Income tax payable	35,000
8	Building	$250,000		Total current liabilities	433,000
9	Less: Accumulated			**Stockholders' Equity**	
10	depreciation	(140,000)	110,000	Common stock	100,000
11	Furniture and fixtures	$100,000		Retained earnings	199,000
12	Less: Accumulated			Total stockholders' equity	299,000
13	depreciation	(60,000)	40,000	Total liabilities and	
14	Total assets		$732,000	stockholders' equity	$732,000
15					

$$\text{Net working capital} = \$582,000 - \$433,000 = \$149,000$$

$$\text{Current ratio} = \frac{\$582,000}{\$433,000} = 1.34$$

$$\text{Debt ratio} = \frac{\$433,000}{\$732,000} = 0.59$$

Requirement 4

$$\text{Debt ratio assuming the loan is made} = \frac{\$433,000 + \$500,000}{\$732,000 + \$500,000} = \frac{\$933,000}{\$1,232,000} = .76$$

Decision: Make the loan at 10%.

Reasoning: Prior to the loan, the company's financial position and cash flow are strong. The current ratio is in a middle range, and the debt ratio is not too high. Net income (from the income statement) is high in relation to total revenue. Therefore, the company should be able to repay the loan.

The loan will increase the company's debt ratio from 59% to 76%, which is more risky than the company's financial position at present. On this basis, a midrange interest rate appears reasonable—at least as the starting point for the negotiation between Badger Ranch Company and the bank.

REVIEW | Accrual Accounting & Income

Quick Check (Answers are given on p. 198.)

1. On September 1, Seaside Apartments received $2,800 from a tenant for four months' rent. The receipt was credited to Unearned Rent Revenue. Seaside's year-end is December 31, which is when it makes its adjusting entries for the year. What adjusting entry needs to be made by Seaside on December 31?

a. Cash   700
    Rent Revenue   700
b. Unearned Rent Revenue   2,800
    Rent Revenue   2,800
c. Unearned Rent Revenue   700
    Rent Revenue   700
d. Rent Revenue   700
    Unearned Rent Revenue   700

2. The following normal balances appear on the *adjusted* trial balance of Portland Company:

Equipment..	$70,000
Accumulated depreciation, equipment...............	18,000
Depreciation expense, equipment......................	6,000

The book value of the equipment is

a. $64,000.   **c.** $52,000.
b. $46,000.   **d.** $34,000.

3. Barlow, Inc., purchased supplies for $1,100 during 2016. At year-end, Barlow had $500 of supplies left. The adjusting entry should

a. debit Supplies $500.   **c.** debit Supplies Expense $600.
b. credit Supplies $500.   **d.** debit Supplies $600.

4. The accountant for Trumbull Corp. failed to make the adjusting entry to record depreciation for the current year. The effect of this error is which of the following?

a. Assets are overstated; stockholders' equity and net income are understated.
b. Net income is overstated and liabilities are understated.
c. Assets and expenses are understated; net income is understated.
d. Assets, net income, and stockholders' equity are all overstated.

5. Interest earned on a note receivable at December 31 equals $375. What adjusting entry is required to accrue this interest?

a. Interest Receivable   375
    Interest Revenue   375
b. Interest Expense   375
    Cash   375
c. Interest Expense   375
    Interest Payable   375
d. Interest Payable   375
    Interest Expense   375

6. If a real estate company fails to accrue commission revenue,

a. revenues are understated, and net income is overstated.
b. liabilities are overstated, and owners' equity is understated.
c. assets are understated, and net income is understated.
d. net income is understated, and stockholders' equity is overstated.

7. All of the following statements are true except one. Which statement is false?

   a. Adjusting entries are required for a business that uses the cash basis.

   b. Accrual accounting produces better information than cash-basis accounting.

   c. A fiscal year may end on some date other than December 31.

   d. The expense recognition principle directs accountants to identify and measure all expenses incurred and deduct them from revenues earned during the same period.

8. The account Unearned Revenue is a(n)

   a. asset.   **c.** expense.

   b. revenue.   **d.** liability.

9. Adjusting entries

   a. update the accounts.

   b. do not debit or credit Cash.

   c. are needed to measure the period's net income or net loss.

   d. all of the above.

10. An adjusting entry that debits an expense and credits a liability is which type?

    a. Prepaid expense   **c.** Depreciation expense

    b. Accrued expense   **d.** Cash expense

    Use the following data for questions 11 and 12.

    Here are key figures from the balance sheet of Atwood, Inc., at the end of 2016 (amounts in thousands):

	December 31, 2016
Total assets (of which 30% are current)	$4,000
Current liabilities	600
Bonds payable (long-term)	800
Common stock	500
Retained earnings	2,100
Total liabilities and stockholders' equity	4,000

11. Atwood's current ratio at the end of 2016 is

    a. 6.67.   **c.** 0.86.

    b. 2.00.   **d.** 0.57.

12. Atwood's debt ratio at the end of 2016 is (all amounts are rounded)

    a. 15%.   **c.** 20%.

    b. 29%.   **d.** 35%.

13. On a trial balance, which of the following would indicate that an error has been made?

    a. Unearned Revenue has a credit balance.

    b. Salary Expense has a debit balance.

    c. Service Revenue has a debit balance.

    d. All of the above indicate errors.

14. The entry to close Management Fee Revenue would be which of the following?

    a. Retained Earnings
           Management Fee Revenue

    b. Management Fee Revenue
           Retained Earnings

    c. Management Fee Revenue
           Service Revenue

    d. Management Fee Revenue does not need to be closed.

15. Which of the following accounts is not closed?
    a. Accumulated Depreciation   **c.** Depreciation Expense
    b. Interest Revenue   **d.** Dividends

16. United Parcel Service earns service revenue of $650,000. How does this transaction affect UPS's current and debt ratios?
    a. Improves both ratios
    b. Hurts the current ratio and improves the debt ratio
    c. Improves the current ratio and doesn't affect the debt ratio
    d. Hurts both ratios

17. Suppose Frederick Corporation borrows $20 million on a 10-year note payable. How does this transaction affect Frederick's current ratio and debt ratio?
    a. Improves the current ratio and hurts the debt ratio
    b. Hurts both ratios
    c. Improves both ratios
    d. Hurts the current ratio and improves the debt ratio

Accounting Vocabulary

account format (p. 151) A balance-sheet format that lists assets on the left and liabilities and stockholders' equity on the right.

accrual (p. 128) An expense or a revenue that occurs before the business pays or receives cash. An accrual is the opposite of a deferral.

accrual accounting (p. 122) Accounting that records the impact of a business event as it occurs, regardless of whether the transaction affected cash.

accrued expense (p. 134) An expense incurred but not yet paid in cash.

accrued revenue (p. 135) A revenue that has been earned but not yet received in cash.

accumulated depreciation (p. 132) The cumulative sum of all depreciation expense from the date of acquiring a plant asset.

adjusted trial balance (p. 140) A list of all the ledger accounts with their adjusted balances.

book value (of a plant asset) (p. 133) The asset's cost minus accumulated depreciation.

cash-basis accounting (p. 122) Accounting that records only transactions in which cash is received or paid.

classified balance sheet (p. 150) A balance sheet that shows current assets separate from long-term assets and current liabilities separate from long-term liabilities.

closing the books (p. 148) The process of preparing the accounts to begin recording the next period's transactions. Closing the accounts consists of journalizing and posting the closing entries to set the balances of the revenue, expense, and dividends accounts to zero. Also called closing the accounts.

closing entries (p. 148) Entries that transfer the revenue, expense, and dividends balances from these respective accounts to the Retained Earnings account.

contra account (p. 132) An account that always has a companion account and whose normal balance is opposite that of the companion account.

current asset (p. 150) An asset that is expected to be converted to cash, sold, or consumed during the next 12 months or within the business's normal operating cycle if longer than a year.

current liability (p. 150) A debt due to be paid within one year or within the entity's operating cycle if the cycle is longer than a year.

current ratio (p. 153) Current assets divided by current liabilities. Measures a company's ability to pay current liabilities with current assets.

debt ratio (p. 154) Ratio of total liabilities to total assets. States the proportion of a company's assets that is financed with debt.

deferral (p. 128) An adjustment for which the business paid or received cash in advance. Examples include prepaid rent, prepaid insurance, and supplies.

depreciation (p. 131) Allocation of the cost of a plant asset to expense over its useful life.

expense recognition principle (p. 125) The basis for recording expenses. Directs accountants to identify all expenses incurred during the period, to measure the expenses, and to match them against the revenues earned during that same period.

liquidity (p. 150) Measure of how quickly an item can be converted to cash.

long-term asset (p. 150) An asset that is not a current asset.

long-term liability (p. 150) A liability that is not a current liability.

multistep income statement (p. 151) An income statement that contains subtotals to highlight important relationships between revenues and expenses.

net working capital (p. 153) A measure of liquidity; current assets – current liabilities.

operating cycle (p. 150) Time span during which cash is paid for goods and services that are sold to customers who pay the business in cash.

permanent accounts (p. 148) Asset, liability, and stockholders' equity accounts that are not closed at the end of the period.

plant assets (p. 131) Long-lived assets, such as land, buildings, and equipment, used in the operation of the business. Also called fixed assets.

prepaid expense (p. 128) A category of miscellaneous assets that typically expire or get used up in the near future. Examples include prepaid rent, prepaid insurance, and supplies.

report format (p. 150) A balance-sheet format that lists assets at the top, followed by liabilities and stockholders' equity below.

revenue principle (p. 124) The basis for recording revenues; tells accountants when to record revenue and the amount of revenue to record.

single-step income statement (p. 151) An income statement that lists all the revenues together under a heading such as Revenues or Revenues and Gains. Expenses appear in a separate category called Expenses or perhaps Expenses and Losses.

temporary accounts (p. 148) The revenue and expense accounts that relate to a limited period and are closed at the end of the period are temporary accounts. For a corporation, the Dividends account is also temporary.

time-period concept (p. 124) Ensures that accounting information is reported at regular intervals.

unearned revenue (p. 136) A liability created when a business collects cash from customers in advance of earning the revenue. The obligation is to provide a product or a service in the future.

ASSESS YOUR PROGRESS

Some of the following exercises and problems are available as Excel questions in MyAccountingLab.

Ethics Check

EC3-1. Identify ethical principle violated

For each of the situations listed, identify which of three principles (integrity, objectivity and independence, or due care) from the AICPA Code of Professional Conduct is violated. Assume all persons listed in the situations are members of the AICPA. (Note: Refer to the AICPA Code of Professional Conduct contained on pages 29–30 in Chapter 1 for descriptions of the principles.)

    a. Maggie's company determines year-end bonuses based on company revenue growth. Maggie records the sales of gift cards during this month as revenue rather than as unearned revenue. None of these gift cards have been used by customers as of the end of the current month. By recording the gift card sales as revenue in the current period, revenue will be higher and Maggie's bonus will, as a result, be higher as well.

    b. A new revenue recognition standard has been issued by the Financial Accounting Standards Board (FASB) and the International Accounting Standards Board (IASB). Tony does not attend training on the new revenue recognition standard because he is busy dealing with the accounting impact of a merger.

    c. Patrick purposely excludes a large amount of accrued salaries payable from this year's financial statements so his company's debt-to-equity ratio appears lower to investors.

    d. Kyle, a CPA, is an associate at a regional public accounting firm. Kyle's firm is auditing a local payroll company. Kyle does not disclose that his wife is a manager at the payroll company.

Short Exercises

S3-1. *(Learning Objective 1: Explain how accrual accounting differs from cash-basis accounting)* Carter Corporation made sales of $900 million during 2016. Of this amount, Carter collected cash for $871 million. The company's cost of goods sold was $280 million, and all other expenses for the year totaled $325 million. Also during 2016, Carter paid $375 million for its inventory and $285 million for everything else. Beginning cash was $115 million. Carter's top management is interviewing you for a job and they ask two questions:

LO **1**

 a. How much was Carter's net income for 2016?

 b. How much was Carter's cash balance at the end of 2016?

You will get the job only if you answer both questions correctly.

S3-2. *(Learning Objective 1: Explain how accrual accounting differs from cash-basis accounting)* Riverside Corporation began 2016 owing notes payable of $3.5 million. During 2016, Riverside borrowed $1.7 million on notes payable and paid off $1.6 million of notes payable from prior years. Interest expense for the year was $0.4 million, including $0.2 million of interest payable accrued at December 31, 2016.

LO **1**

Show what Riverside should report for these facts on the following financial statements:
1. Income statement for 2016
 a. Interest expense
2. Balance sheet as of December 31, 2016
 a. Notes payable
 b. Interest payable

S3-3. *(Learning Objective 2: Apply the revenue and expense recognition principles)* As the controller of Newton Consulting, you have hired a new employee, whom you must train. She objects to making an adjusting entry for accrued salaries at the end of the period. She reasons, "We will pay the salaries soon. Why not wait until payment to record the expense? In the end, the result will be the same." Write a reply to explain to the employee why the adjusting entry is needed for accrued salary expense.

LO **2**

S3-4. *(Learning Objective 2: Apply the revenue and expense recognition principles)* A large auto manufacturer sells large fleets of vehicles to auto rental companies, such as Budget and Hertz. Suppose Budget is negotiating with the auto manufacturer to purchase 827 vehicles. Write a short paragraph to explain to the auto manufacturer when the company should, and should not, record this sales revenue and the related expense for cost of goods sold. Mention the accounting principles that provide the basis for your explanation.

LO **2**

S3-5. *(Learning Objective 2: Apply the expense recognition principle)* Write a short paragraph in your own words to explain the concept of depreciation as used in accounting.

LO **2**

S3-6. *(Learning Objective 2: Apply the revenue and expense recognition principles)* Identify the accounting concept or principle that gives the most direction on how to account for each of the following situations:

LO **2**

 a. Salary expense of $48,000 is accrued at the end of the period to measure income properly.

 b. March has been a particularly slow month, and the business will have a net loss for the second quarter of the year. Management is considering not following its customary practice of reporting quarterly earnings to the public.

 c. A physician performs a surgical operation and bills the patient's insurance company. It may take three months to collect from the insurance company. Should the physician record revenue now or wait until cash is collected?

 d. A construction company is building a highway system, and construction will take four years. When should the company record the revenue it earns?

 e. A utility bill is received on December 27 and will be paid next year. When should the company record utility expense?

LO 3 **S3-7.** *(Learning Objective 3: Adjust the accounts)* Answer the following questions about prepaid expenses:

    a. On July 1, Davis Tree Service prepaid $12,000 for six months' rent. Give the adjusting entry to record rent expense at July 31. Include the date of the entry and an explanation. Then post all amounts to the two accounts involved, and show their balances at July 31. Davis adjusts the accounts only at July 31, the end of its fiscal year.

    b. On July 1, Davis Tree Service paid $850 for supplies. At July 31, Davis has $400 of supplies on hand. Make the required journal entry at July 31. Then post all amounts to the accounts and show their balances at July 31.

LO 3 **S3-8.** *(Learning Objective 3: Adjust the accounts for depreciation)* Suppose that on January 1 Coddington Travel Company paid cash of $30,000 for equipment that is expected to remain useful for five years. At the end of five years, the equipment's value is expected to be zero.

    1. Make journal entries to record (a) purchase of the equipment on January 1 and (b) annual depreciation on December 31. Include dates and explanations, and use the following accounts: Equipment, Accumulated Depreciation—Equipment, and Depreciation Expense—Equipment.

    2. Post to the accounts and show their balances at December 31.

    3. What is the equipment's book value at December 31?

LO 2 **S3-9.** *(Learning Objective 2: Apply the revenue and expense recognition principles)* During 2016, Quanta Airlines paid salary expense of $41.2 million. At December 31, 2016, Quanta accrued salary expense of $2.4 million. Quanta then paid $2.6 million to its employees on January 3, 2017, the company's next payday after the end of the 2016 year. For this sequence of transactions, show what Quanta would report on its 2016 income statement and on its balance sheet at the end of 2016.

LO 3 **S3-10.** *(Learning Objective 3: Adjust the accounts for interest expense)* Laziza Restaurant borrowed $80,000 on October 1 by signing a note payable to First State Bank. The interest expense for each month is $433. The loan agreement requires Laziza to pay interest on January 2 for October, November, and December.

    1. Make Laziza's adjusting entry to accrue monthly interest expense at October 31, at November 30, and at December 31. Date each entry and include its explanation.

    2. Post all three entries to the Interest Payable account. You do not need to calculate the balance of the account at the end of each month.

    3. Record the payment of three months' interest at on January 2.

LO 3 **S3-11.** *(Learning Objective 3: Adjust the accounts for interest revenue)* Return to the situation in Short Exercise 3-10. Here you are accounting for the same transactions on the books of First State Bank, which lent the money to Laziza Restaurant.

    1. Make First State Bank's adjusting entry to accrue monthly interest revenue at October 31, at November 30, and at December 31. Date each entry and include its explanation.

    2. Post all three entries to the Interest Receivable account. You do not need to calculate the balance of the account at the end of each month.

    3. Record the receipt of three months' interest at on January 2.

LO 3 **S3-12.** *(Learning Objective 3: Adjust the accounts for unearned revenue)* Write a paragraph to explain why unearned revenues are liabilities instead of revenues. In your explanation, use the following actual example: *The New York Times*, a national newspaper, collects cash from subscribers in advance and later provides news content via print newspapers and online access to subscribers over a one-year period. Explain what happens to the unearned revenue over the course of a year as *The New York Times* delivers papers and online content to subscribers. Into what account does the earned subscription revenue go as *The New York Times* delivers papers and online content? Give the journal entries that *The New York Times* would make to (a) collect $65,000 of subscription revenue in advance and (b) record earning $55,000 of subscription revenue. Include an explanation for each entry, as illustrated in the chapter.

S3-13. *(Learning Objective 3: Adjust the accounts for prepaid rent)* Due to the terms of its lease, Peachtree Services, Inc., pays the rent for its new office space in one annual payment of $24,000 on August 1, 2016. The lease covers the period of August 1, 2016, through July 31, 2017. Peachtree Services has a year-end of December 31. Assume that Peachtree Services had no other prepaid rent transactions, nor did it have a Prepaid Rent beginning balance in 2016. Give the journal entries that Peachtree Services would make for (a) the annual rent payment of $24,000 on August 1 and (b) the adjusting entry for rent expense on December 31, 2016. What is the balance of Prepaid Rent at December 31, 2016?

LO 3

S3-14. *(Learning Objective 3: Adjust the accounts for accrued and unearned revenue)* Gerbig, Inc., collects cash from customers in advance and from other customers after the sale. Journalize the following transactions for Gerbig:

LO 3

    a. Accrued revenue. Some customers pay Gerbig after Gerbig has performed service for the customer. During 2016, Gerbig performed services for $22,000 on account and later received cash of $7,000 on account from these customers.

    b. Unearned revenue. A few customers pay Gerbig in advance, and Gerbig later performs the service for the customer. During 2016, Gerbig collected $5,500 cash in advance and later earned $4,000 of this amount.

S3-15. *(Learning Objective 4: Construct the financial statements)* Suppose Tree City Sporting Goods Company reported the following data at July 31, 2016, with amounts in thousands:

LO 4

Retained earnings, July 31, 2015	$ 36,900	Cost of goods sold	$136,200
Accounts receivable	28,500	Cash	43,100
Net revenues	184,500	Property and equipment, net	17,400
Total current liabilities	60,000	Common stock	30,800
All other expenses	28,000	Inventories	37,000
Other current assets	5,400	Long-term liabilities	12,000
Other assets	28,600	Dividends	0

Use these data to prepare Tree City Sporting Goods Company's single-step income statement for the year ended July 31, 2016; statement of retained earnings for the year ended July 31, 2016; and classified balance sheet at July 31, 2016. Use the report format for the balance sheet. Draw arrows linking the three statements.

S3-16. *(Learning Objective 5: Close the books)* Use the Tree City Sporting Goods Company data in Short Exercise 3-15 to make the company's closing entries at July 31, 2016. Then set up a T-account for Retained Earnings and post to that account. Compare Retained Earnings' ending balance to the amount reported on Tree City's statement of retained earnings and balance sheet. What do you find?

LO 5

S3-17. *(Learning Objective 6: Analyze and evaluate liquidity and debt-paying ability)* Tree City Sporting Goods reported the following data at July 31, 2016, with amounts adapted in thousands:

LO 6

	A	B	C	D	E
1	**Tree City Sporting Goods Company** **Income Statement** **Year ended July 31, 2016**				
2	*(Amounts in thousands)*				
3	Net revenues	$184,500			
4	Cost of goods sold	136,200			
5	All other expenses	28,000			
6	Net income	$ 20,300			
7					

	A	B	C	D	E
	A1 ⬥				
1	**Tree City Sporting Goods Company** **Statement of Retained Earnings** **Year ended July 31, 2016**				
2	*(Amounts in thousands)*				
3	Retained earnings, July 31, 2015		$36,900		
4	Add: Net income		20,300		
5	Retained earnings, July 31, 2016		$57,200		
6					

	A	B	C	D	E
	A1 ⬥				
1	**Tree City Sporting Goods Company** **Balance Sheet** **July 31, 2016**				
2	*(Amounts in thousands)*				
3	**Assets**				
4	Current:				
5	Cash	$ 43,100			
6	Accounts receivable	28,500			
7	Inventories	37,000			
8	Other current assets	5,400			
9	Total current assets	114,000			
10	Property and equipment, net	17,400			
11	Other assets	28,600			
12	Total assets	$160,000			
13	**Liabilities**				
14	Total current liabilities	$ 60,000			
15	Long-term liabilities	12,000			
16	Total liabilities	72,000			
17	**Stockholders' Equity**				
18	Common stock	30,800			
19	Retained earnings	57,200			
20	Total stockholders' equity	88,000			
21	Total liabilities and stockholders' equity	$160,000			
22					

1. Compute Tree City's net working capital.
2. Compute Tree City's current ratio. Round to two decimal places.
3. Compute Tree City's debt ratio. Round to two decimal places.

Do these values and ratios look strong, weak, or middle-of-the-road?

LO 6   **S3-18.** (*Learning Objective 6: Analyze and evaluate liquidity and debt-paying ability*) Refer to the Tree City Sporting Goods Company data in Short Exercise 3-17.

At July 31, 2016, Tree City Sporting Goods Company's current ratio was 1.90 (rounded) and its debt ratio was 0.45 (rounded). Compute Tree City's (a) net working capital, (b) current ratio, and (c) debt ratio after each of the following transactions (all amounts in thousands, as in the Tree City financial statements):

1. Tree City earned revenue of $12,000 on account.
2. Tree City paid off accounts payable of $12,000.

When calculating the revised ratios, treat each of the above scenarios independently. Round ratios to two decimal places.

Exercises MyAccountingLab

Group A

E3-19A. *(Learning Objectives 1, 2: Explain how accrual accounting differs from cash-basis accounting; apply the revenue and expense recognition principles)* During 2016, Nicholson Network, Inc., which designs network servers, earned revenues of $800 million. Expenses totaled $570 million. Nicholson collected all but $21 million of the revenues and paid $600 million on its expenses. Nicholson's top managers are evaluating 2016, and they ask you the following questions:

    a. Under accrual accounting, what amount of revenue should Nicholson Network report for 2016? How does the revenue principle help to answer these questions?

    b. Under accrual accounting, what amount of total expense should Nicholson Network report for 2016? Which accounting principle helps to answer this question?

    c. Redo parts a and b using the cash basis. Explain how the accrual basis differs from the cash basis.

    d. Which financial statement reports revenues and expenses? Which statement reports cash receipts and cash payments?

E3-20A. *(Learning Objectives 1, 3: Explain how accrual accounting differs from cash-basis accounting; adjust the accounts)* An accountant made the following adjustments at December 31, the end of the accounting period:

    a. Prepaid insurance, beginning, $300. Payments for insurance during the period, $2,900. Prepaid insurance, ending, $600.

    b. Interest revenue accrued, $2,400.

    c. Unearned service revenue, beginning, $1,600. Unearned service revenue, ending, $300.

    d. Depreciation, $5,500.

    e. Employees' salaries owed for two days of a five-day work week; weekly payroll, $13,000.

    f. Income before income tax, $20,000. Income tax rate is 35%.

Requirements

1. Journalize the adjusting entries.

2. Suppose the adjustments were not made. Compute the overall overstatement or understatement of net income as a result of the omission of these adjustments.

E3-21A. *(Learning Objectives 2, 3: Apply the revenue and expense recognition principles; adjust the accounts)* Rankle Corporation experienced four situations for its supplies. Compute the amounts that have been left blank for each situation. For situations 1 and 2, journalize the needed transaction. Consider each situation separately.

	Situation			
	1	2	3	4
Beginning supplies.....................................	$2,500	$ 600	$ 700	$ 700
Purchases of supplies during the year........	?	500	?	900
Total amount to account for	3,500	?	?	1,600
Ending supplies	(1,030)	(300)	(400)	?
Supplies Expense.......................................	$2,470	$?	$2,200	$1,000

E3-22A. *(Learning Objective 3: Adjust the accounts)* Dellroy Rentals Company faced the following situations. Journalize the adjusting entry needed at December 31, 2016, for each situation. Consider each fact separately.

    a. The business has interest expense of $3,200 that it must pay early in January 2017.

    b. Interest revenue of $4,100 has been earned but not yet received.

    c. On July 1, 2016, when the business collected $12,000 rent in advance, it debited Cash and credited Unearned Rent Revenue. The tenant was paying for two years' rent.

d. Salary expense is $6,100 per day—Monday through Friday—and the business pays employees each Friday. This year, December 31 falls on a Thursday.

e. The unadjusted balance of the Supplies account is $3,200. The total cost of supplies on hand is $1,300.

f. Equipment was purchased on January 1 of this year at a cost of $180,000. The equipment's useful life is five years. There is no residual value. Record depreciation for this year and then determine the equipment's book value.

LO 3 4   **E3-23A.** *(Learning Objectives 3, 4: Adjust the accounts for prepaid expenses; construct the financial statements)* Childtime Toys prepaid three years' rent ($54,000) on January 1, 2016. At December 31, 2016, Childtime prepared a trial balance and then made the necessary adjusting entry at the end of the year. Childtime adjusts its accounts once each year—on December 31.

What amount appears for Prepaid Rent on
a. Childtime's *unadjusted* trial balance at December 31, 2016?
b. Childtime's *adjusted* trial balance at December 31, 2016?
What amount appears for Rent Expense on
c. Childtime's *unadjusted* trial balance at December 31, 2016?
d. Childtime's *adjusted* trial balance at December 31, 2016?

LO 4   **E3-24A.** *(Learning Objective 4: Construct the financial statements)* The adjusted trial balance of Honeybell, Inc., follows.

A1		

	A	B	C	D	E
1	**Honeybell, Inc.** **Adjusted Trial Balance** **December 31, 2016**				
2	*(Amounts in thousands)*				
3	**Account**	**Debit**	**Credit**		
4	Cash	$ 3,900			
5	Accounts receivable	1,400			
6	Inventories	2,200			
7	Prepaid expenses	1,800			
8	Property, plant, and equipment	16,700			
9	Accumulated depreciation—property, plant, and equipment		$ 2,800		
10	Other assets	9,500			
11	Accounts payable		7,400		
12	Income tax payable		400		
13	Other liabilities		2,500		
14	Common stock		14,600		
15	Retained earnings (beginning, December 31, 2015)		5,900		
16	Dividends	1,300			
17	Sales revenue		41,200		
18	Cost of goods sold	25,500			
19	Selling, administrative, and general expenses	10,500			
20	Income tax expense	2,000			
21					
22	Total	$74,800	$74,800		
23					

Requirement

1. Prepare Honeybell, Inc.'s single-step income statement and statement of retained earnings for the year ended December 31, 2016, and its balance sheet on that date.

LO 3 4   **E3-25A.** *(Learning Objectives 3, 4: Adjust the accounts; construct the financial statements)* The adjusted trial balances of Victory Corporation at August 31, 2016, and August 31, 2015, include these amounts (in millions):

	2016	2015
Receivables..	$470	$290
Prepaid insurance	380	460
Accrued liabilities payable (for other operating expenses)	760	650

Victory Corporation completed these transactions (in millions) during the year ended August 31, 2016.

Collections from customers...	$20,800
Payment of prepaid insurance	460
Cash payments for other operating expenses...............	4,600

Compute the amount of sales revenue, insurance expense, and other operating expenses to report on the income statement for the year ended August 31, 2016.

E3-26A. *(Learning Objective 5: Close the books)* Prepare the closing entries from the following selected accounts from the records of Wolf Enterprises at December 31, 2016:

LO 5

Cost of services sold............	$14,300	Service revenue........................	$32,100
Accumulated depreciation...	40,800	Depreciation expense	4,600
Selling, general, and		Other revenue	200
administrative expenses....	6,300	Dividends declared.................	300
Retained earnings,		Income tax expense	300
December 31, 2015	2,400	Income tax payable	700

How much net income did Wolf Enterprises earn during 2016? Prepare a T-account for Retained Earnings to show the December 31, 2016, balance of Retained Earnings.

E3-27A. *(Learning Objectives 3, 5: Adjust the accounts; close the books)* The unadjusted trial balance and income statement amounts from the December 31 adjusted trial balance of Winwood Production Company follow.

LO 3 5

	A	B	C	D	E	F
	A1					
1	**Winwood Production Company**					
2	**Account**	**Unadjusted Trial Balance**		**From the Adjusted Trial Balance**		
3	Cash	13,300				
4	Prepaid rent	1,600				
5	Equipment	45,000				
6	Accumulated depreciation—equipment		3,300			
7	Accounts payable		4,900			
8	Salary payable					
9	Unearned service revenue		9,200			
10	Income tax payable					
11	Notes payable, long-term		16,000			
12	Common stock		8,400			
13	Retained earnings		11,400			
14	Dividends	1,300				
15	Service revenue		13,600		19,900	
16	Salary expense	4,500		5,200		
17	Rent expense	1,100		1,900		
18	Depreciation expense—equipment			400		
19	Income tax expense			1,200		
20	Total	66,800	66,800	8,700	19,900	
21						

Requirement

1. Journalize the adjusting and closing entries of Winwood Production Company at December 31. There was only one adjustment to Service Revenue.

LO 4 6   **E3-28A.** *(Learning Objectives 4, 6: Construct the financial statements; analyze and evaluate liquidity and debt-paying ability)* Refer to Exercise 3-27A.

Requirements

1. Use the data in the partial worksheet to prepare Winwood Production Company's classified balance sheet at December 31 of the current year. Use the report format. First you must compute the adjusted balance for several of the balance-sheet accounts.
2. Compute Winwood Production Company's net working capital, current ratio, and debt ratio at December 31. A year ago, net working capital was $3,900, the current ratio was 1.40, and the debt ratio was 0.64. Indicate whether the company's ability to pay its debts—both current and total—improved or deteriorated during the current year.

LO 6   **E3-29A.** *(Learning Objective 6: Analyze and evaluate liquidity and debt-paying ability)*
Landry Company reported these ratios at December 31, 2016 (dollar amounts in millions):

$$\text{Current ratio} = \frac{\$20}{\$10} = 2.00$$

$$\text{Debt ratio} = \frac{\$20}{\$50} = 0.40$$

Landry Company completed these transactions during 2017:
  a. Purchased equipment on account, $7
  b. Paid long-term debt, $10
  c. Collected cash from customers in advance, $5
  d. Accrued interest expense, $6
  e. Made cash sales, $8

Determine whether each transaction improved or hurt Landry's current ratio and debt ratio.

Group B

LO 1 2   **E3-30B.** *(Learning Objectives 1, 2: Explain how accrual accounting differs from cash-basis accounting; apply the revenue and expense recognition principles)* During 2016, Gibson Network, Inc., which designs network servers, earned revenues of $720 million. Expenses totaled $520 million. Gibson collected all but $20 million of the revenues and paid $570 million on its expenses. Gibson's top managers are evaluating 2016, and they ask you the following questions:
  a. Under accrual accounting, what amount of revenue should Gibson Network report for 2016? How does the revenue principle help to answer these questions?
  b. Under accrual accounting, what amount of total expense should Gibson report for 2016? Which accounting principle helps to answer this question?
  c. Redo parts a and b using the cash basis. Explain how the accrual basis differs from the cash basis.
  d. Which financial statement reports revenues and expenses? Which statement reports cash receipts and cash payments?

LO 1 3   **E3-31B.** *(Learning Objectives 1, 3: Explain how accrual accounting differs from cash-basis accounting; adjust the accounts)* An accountant made the following adjustments at December 31, the end of the accounting period:
  a. Prepaid insurance, beginning, $600. Payments for insurance during the period, $2,000. Prepaid insurance, ending, $1,200.
  b. Interest revenue accrued, $2,100.

  c. Unearned service revenue, beginning, $1,800. Unearned service revenue, ending, $400.

  d. Depreciation, $5,200.

  e. Employees' salaries owed for two days of a five-day work week; weekly payroll, $18,000.

  f. Income before income tax, $25,000. Income tax rate is 35%.

Requirements

1. Journalize the adjusting entries.
2. Suppose the adjustments were not made. Compute the overall overstatement or understatement of net income as a result of the omission of these adjustments.

E3-32B. *(Learning Objectives 2, 3: Apply the revenue and expense recognition principles; adjust the accounts)* Henry Corporation experienced four situations for its supplies. Compute the amounts that have been left blank for each situation. For situations 1 and 2, journalize the needed transaction. Consider each situation separately.

	Situation			
	1	2	3	4
Beginning supplies.....................................	$2,400	$ 700	$ 600	$ 600
Purchases of supplies during the year........	?	400	?	900
Total amount to account for	3,400	?	?	1,500
Ending supplies	(1,020)	(800)	(300)	?
Supplies Expense......................................	$2,380	$?	$ 1,700	$ 900

E3-33B. *(Learning Objective 3: Adjust the accounts)* Rockwell Company faced the following situations. Journalize the adjusting entry needed at December 31, 2016, for each situation. Consider each fact separately.

  a. The business has interest expense of $3,300 that it must pay early in January 2017.

  b. Interest revenue of $4,500 has been earned but not yet received.

  c. On July 1, 2016, when the business collected $13,900 rent in advance, it debited Cash and credited Unearned Rent Revenue. The tenant was paying for two years' rent.

  d. Salary expense is $5,500 per day—Monday through Friday—and the business pays employees each Friday. This year, December 31 falls on a Thursday.

  e. The unadjusted balance of the Supplies account is $2,800. The total cost of supplies on hand is $1,600.

  f. Equipment was purchased on January 1 of this year at a cost of $60,000. The equipment's useful life is five years. There is no residual value. Record depreciation for this year and then determine the equipment's book value.

E3-34B. *(Learning Objectives 3, 4: Adjust the accounts for prepaid expenses; construct the financial statements)* McCool Floral Co. prepaid three years' rent ($36,000) on January 1, 2016. At December 31, 2016, McCool prepared a trial balance and then made the necessary adjusting entry at the end of the year. McCool adjusts its accounts once each year—on December 31.

What amount appears for Prepaid Rent on

  a. McCool's *unadjusted* trial balance at December 31, 2016?

  b. McCool's *adjusted* trial balance at December 31, 2016?

What amount appears for Rent Expense on

  c. McCool's *unadjusted* trial balance at December 31, 2016?

  d. McCool's *adjusted* trial balance at December 31, 2016?

LO **4**   **E3-35B.** *(Learning Objective 4: Construct the financial statements)* The adjusted trial balance of Marshall, Inc., follows:

	A	B	C
	A1		
1	Marshall, Inc. Adjusted Trial Balance December 31, 2016		
2	(Amounts in thousands)		
3	**Account**	**Debit**	**Credit**
4	Cash	$ 4,300	
5	Accounts receivable	1,400	
6	Inventories	2,400	
7	Prepaid expenses	1,600	
8	Property, plant, and equipment	16,700	
9	Accumulated depreciation—property, plant, and equipment		$ 2,400
10	Other assets	9,300	
11	Accounts payable		7,500
12	Income tax payable		800
13	Other liabilities		2,700
14	Common stock		14,500
15	Retained earnings (beginning, December 31, 2015)		5,100
16	Dividend	1,500	
17	Sales revenue		42,400
18	Cost of goods sold	25,500	
19	Selling, administrative, and general expenses	10,500	
20	Income tax expense	2,200	
21			
22	Total	$ 75,400	$ 75,400
23			

Requirement

1. Prepare Marshall, Inc.'s, single-step income statement and statement of retained earnings for the year ended December 31, 2016, and its balance sheet on that date. Draw the arrows linking the three statements.

LO **3** **4**   **E3-36B.** *(Learning Objectives 3, 4: Adjust the accounts; construct the financial statements)* The adjusted trial balances of Bova Corporation at August 31, 2016, and August 31, 2015, include these amounts (in millions):

	2016	2015
Receivables..	$460	$290
Prepaid insurance...	320	450
Accrued liabilities payable (for other operating expenses)	730	610

Bova completed these transactions (in millions) during the year ended August 31, 2016.

Collections from customers..	$20,600
Payment of prepaid insurance	480
Cash payments for other operating expenses...............	4,500

Compute the amount of sales revenue, insurance expense, and other operating expenses to report on the income statement for the year ended August 31, 2016.

E3-37B. *(Learning Objective 5: Close the books)* Prepare the closing entries from the following selected accounts from the records of Hector, Inc., at December 31, 2016:

Cost of services sold............	$14,600	Service revenue........................	$32,300
Accumulated depreciation...	41,400	Depreciation expense	4,100
Selling, general, and		Other revenue	1,000
administrative expenses....	6,500	Dividends declared................	700
Retained earnings,		Income tax expense................	600
December 31, 2015.........	2,100	Income tax payable	700

How much net income did Hector earn during 2016? Prepare a T-account for Retained Earnings to show the December 31, 2016, balance of Retained Earnings.

E3-38B. *(Learning Objectives 3, 5: Adjust the accounts; close the books)* The unadjusted trial balance and income statement amounts from the December 31 adjusted trial balance of Emerson Production Company follow:

	A	B	C	D	E
		A1			
1	**Emerson Production Company**				
2	**Account**	**Unadjusted** **Trial Balance**		**From the Adjusted** **Trial Balance**	
3	Cash	13,690			
4	Prepaid rent	1,500			
5	Equipment	42,000			
6	Accumulated depreciation—equipment		3,200		
7	Accounts payable		4,300		
8	Salary payable				
9	Unearned service revenue		9,100		
10	Income tax payable				
11	Notes payable, long-term		11,000		
12	Common stock		8,300		
13	Retained earnings		15,090		
14	Dividends	1,400			
15	Service revenue		13,400		19,700
16	Salary expense	4,500		5,300	
17	Rent expense	1,300		1,800	
18	Depreciation expense—equipment			800	
19	Income tax expense			1,400	
20	Total	64,390	64,390	9,300	19,700
21					

Requirement

1. Journalize the adjusting and closing entries of Emerson Production Company at December 31. There was only one adjustment to Service Revenue.

E3-39B. *(Learning Objectives 4, 6: Construct the financial statements; analyze and evaluate liquidity and debt-paying ability)* Refer to Exercise 3-38B.

Requirements

1. Use the data in the partial worksheet to prepare Emerson Production Company's classified balance sheet at December 31 of the current year. Use the report format. First you must compute the adjusted balance for several of the balance-sheet accounts.
2. Compute Emerson Production Company's net working capital, current ratio, and debt ratio at December 31. A year ago, the net working capital was $5,790, the current ratio was 1.61, and the debt ratio was 0.23. Indicate whether the company's ability to pay its debts—both current and total—improved or deteriorated during the current year.

LO 6

E3-40B. *(Learning Objective 6: Analyze and evaluate liquidity and debt-paying ability)*
Halston Consulting Company reported these ratios at December 31, 2016 (dollar amounts in millions):

$$\text{Current ratio} = \frac{\$40}{\$30} = 1.33$$

$$\text{Debt ratio} = \frac{\$40}{\$70} = 0.57$$

Halston Consulting completed these transactions during 2017:
   a. Purchased equipment on account, $8
   b. Paid long-term debt, $10
   c. Collected cash from customers in advance, $5
   d. Accrued interest expense, $2
   e. Made cash sales, $12

Determine whether each transaction improved or hurt the business's current ratio and debt ratio.

Serial Exercise

Exercise 3-41 continues the Barbara Miracle, Certified Public Accountant, P.C., situation begun in Exercise 2-39 of Chapter 2.

LO 3 4 5 6

E3-41. *(Learning Objectives 3, 4, 5, 6: Adjust the accounts; construct the financial statements; close the books; analyze and evaluate liquidity and debt-paying ability)* Refer to Exercise 2-39 of Chapter 2. Start from the trial balance and the posted T-accounts that Barbara Miracle, Certified Public Accountant, Professional Corporation (P.C.), prepared for her accounting practice at August 18. A professional corporation is not subject to income tax. Later in August, the business completed these transactions:

Aug 21	Received $2,700 in advance for tax work to be performed over the next 30 days.
22	Hired a secretary to be paid on the 15th day of each month.
26	Paid $800 for the supplies purchased on August 5.
28	Collected $1,900 from the client on August 18.
31	Declared and paid dividends of $1,400.

Requirements

1. Journalize the transactions of August 21 through 31.
2. Post the August 21 to 31 transactions to the T-accounts, keying all items by date.
3. Prepare an Excel spreadsheet showing the unadjusted trial balance at August 31.
4. At August 31, Miracle gathers the following information for the adjusting entries:
   a. Accrued service revenue, $1,800.
   b. Earned $900 of the service revenue collected in advance on August 21.
   c. Supplies on hand, $400.
   d. Depreciation expense equipment, $45; furniture, $75.
   e. Accrued expense for secretary's salary, $600.

Refer to the Excel spreadsheet you prepared in Requirement 3. Make these adjustments in the adjustments columns and complete the adjusted trial balance at August 31.
5. Journalize and post the adjusting entries. Denote each adjusting amount as Adj and an account balance as Bal.
6. Prepare the single-step income statement and statement of retained earnings of Barbara Miracle, Certified Public Accountant, P.C., for the month ended August 31 and the classified balance sheet at that date.

7. Journalize and post the closing entries at August 31. Denote each closing amount as Clo and an account balance as Bal.

8. Compute the net working capital, current ratio, and the debt ratio of Barbara Miracle, Certified Public Accountant, P.C., and evaluate these values as indicative of a strong or weak financial position.

Quiz

Test your understanding of accrual accounting by answering the following questions. Select the best choice from among the possible answers given.

Questions 42–44 are based on the following facts: Kelsey Allerton began a music business in July 2016. Allerton prepares monthly financial statements and uses the accrual basis of accounting. The following transactions are Allerton Company's only activities during July through October:

Jul 14	Bought music on account for $25, with payment to the supplier due in 90 days.
Aug 3	Performed a job on account for Jimmy Jones for $40, collectible from Jones in 30 days. Used up all the music purchased on July 14.
Sep 16	Collected the $40 receivable from Jones.
Oct 22	Paid the $25 owed to the supplier from the July 14 transaction.

Q3-42. In which month should Allerton record the cost of the music as an expense?
- **a.** August
- **b.** July
- **c.** September
- **d.** October

Q3-43. In which month should Allerton report the $40 revenue on its income statement?
- **a.** July
- **b.** September
- **c.** October
- **d.** August

Q3-44. If Allerton Company uses the *cash* basis of accounting instead of the accrual basis, in what month will Allerton report revenue and in what month will it report expense?

	Revenue	Expense
a.	August	August
b.	September	October
c.	September	July
d.	August	October

Q3-45. Using the accrual basis, in which month should revenue be recorded?
- **a.** In the month that goods are shipped to the customer
- **b.** In the month that the invoice is mailed to the customer
- **c.** In the month that goods are ordered by the customer
- **d.** In the month that cash is collected from the customer

Q3-46. On January 1 of the current year, Bamber Company paid $1,500 rent to cover six months (January–June). Bamber recorded this transaction as follows:

	A	B	C	D	E	F
	A1					
1		Journal Entry				
2	Date	Accounts	Debit	Credit		
3	Jan 1	Prepaid Rent	1,500			
4		Cash		1,500		
5						

Bamber adjusts the accounts at the end of each month. Based on these facts, the adjusting entry at the end of January should include
   a. a debit to Prepaid Rent for $250.
   b. a credit to Prepaid Rent for $1,250.
   c. a debit to Prepaid Rent for $1,250.
   d. a credit to Prepaid Rent for $250.

Q3-47. Assume the same facts as in question 3-46. Bamber's adjusting entry at the end of February should include a debit to Rent Expense in the amount of
   a. $0.   c. $500.
   b. $1,500.   d. $250.

Q3-48. What effect does the adjusting entry in question 3-47 have on Bamber's net income for February?
   a. Decrease by $500   c. Decrease by $250
   b. Increase by $500   d. Increase by $250

Q3-49. An adjusting entry recorded June salary expense that will be paid in July. Which statement best describes the effect of this adjusting entry on the company's accounting equation?
   a. Assets are not affected, liabilities are increased, and stockholders' equity is increased.
   b. Assets are decreased, liabilities are not affected, and stockholders' equity is decreased.
   c. Assets are decreased, liabilities are increased, and stockholders' equity is decreased.
   d. Assets are not affected, liabilities are increased, and stockholders' equity is decreased.

Q3-50. On April 1, 2016, Jiminee Insurance Company sold a one-year insurance policy covering the year ended March 31, 2017. Jiminee collected the full $1,800 on April 1, 2016. Jiminee made the following journal entry to record the receipt of cash in advance:

	A	B	C	D	E	F
1		Journal Entry				
2	Date	Accounts	Debit	Credit		
3	Apr 1	Cash	1,800			
4		Unearned Revenue		1,800		
5						

Nine months have passed, and Jiminee has made no adjusting entries. Based on these facts, the adjusting entry needed by Jiminee at December 31, 2016, is

	A	B	C	D	E	F
1	a.	Insurance Revenue	450			
2		Unearned Revenue		450		
3	b.	Unearned Revenue	1,350			
4		Insurance Revenue		1,350		
5	c.	Insurance Revenue	1,350			
6		Unearned Revenue		1,350		
7	d.	Unearned Revenue	450			
8		Insurance Revenue		450		
9						

Q3-51. The Unearned Revenue account of Berry Incorporated began 2016 with a normal balance of $3,000 and ended 2016 with a normal balance of $19,000. During 2016, the Unearned Revenue account was credited for $22,000 that Berry will earn later. Based on these facts, how much revenue did Berry earn in 2016?
   a. $38,000   c. $6,000
   b. $22,000   d. $0

Q3-52. What is the effect on the financial statements of recording depreciation on equipment?
  a. Net income is not affected, but assets and stockholders' equity are decreased.
  b. Net income, assets, and stockholders' equity are all decreased.
  c. Net income and assets are decreased, but stockholders' equity is not affected.
  d. Assets are decreased, but net income and stockholders' equity are not affected.

Q3-53. For 2016, Nestor Company had revenues in excess of expenses. Which statement describes Nestor's closing entries at the end of 2016 (assume there is only one closing entry for both revenue and expenses)?
  a. Revenues will be debited, expenses will be credited, and retained earnings will be debited.
  b. Revenues will be debited, expenses will be credited, and retained earnings will be credited.
  c. Revenues will be credited, expenses will be debited, and retained earnings will be credited.
  d. Revenues will be credited, expenses will be debited, and retained earnings will be debited.

Q3-54. Which of the following accounts would *not* be included in the closing entries?
  a. Retained Earnings   **c.** Service Revenue
  b. Depreciation Expense   **d.** Accumulated Depreciation

Q3-55. A major purpose of preparing closing entries is to
  a. zero out the liability accounts.
  b. adjust the asset accounts to their correct current balances.
  c. close out the Supplies account.
  d. update the Retained Earnings account.

Q3-56. Selected data for the Dublin Company follow:

Current assets..............	$ 25,200	Current liabilities	$ 21,000
Long-term assets	175,000	Long-term liabilities	102,000
Total revenues.............	194,000	Total expenses.................	160,000

Based on these facts, what are Dublin's current ratio and debt ratio?

Current ratio	Debt ratio
a. 1.213	0.206
b. 1.200	0.614
c. 1.628	0.614
d. 9.533	0.833

Q3-57. Unadjusted net income equals $5,000. Calculate what net income will be after the following adjustments:
  1. Salaries payable to employees, $700
  2. Interest due on note payable at the bank, $130
  3. Unearned revenue that has been earned, $750
  4. Supplies used, $175

Q3-58. Salary Payable at the beginning of the month totals $28,000. During the month, salaries of $126,000 were accrued as expense. If ending Salary Payable is $12,000, what amount of cash did the company pay for salaries during the month?
  a. $166,000   **c.** $86,000
  b. $139,000   **d.** $142,000

Problems MyAccountingLab

Group A

LO **1**

P3-59A. *(Learning Objective 1: Explain how accrual accounting differs from cash-basis accounting)* Masters Consulting had the following selected transactions in October:

October	1	Prepaid insurance for October through December, $3,900.
	4	Purchased office furniture for cash, $4,500.
	5	Performed services and received cash, $1,000.
	8	Paid advertising expense, $500.
	11	Performed service on account, $3,200.
	19	Purchased computer on account, $1,900.
	24	Collected for October 11 service.
	26	Paid account payable from October 19.
	29	Paid salary expense, $800.
	31	Adjusted for October insurance expense (see October 1).
	31	Earned revenue of $800 that was collected in advance back in September.
	31	Recorded October depreciation expense on all fixed assets, $460.

Requirements

1. Show how each transaction would be handled (in terms of recognizing revenues and expenses) using the cash basis and the accrual basis.
2. Compute October income (loss) before tax under each accounting method.
3. Indicate which measure of net income or net loss is preferable. Use the transactions on October 11 and October 24 to explain.

LO **3**

P3-60A. *(Learning Objective 3: Adjust the accounts)* Journalize the adjusting entry needed on December 31, the end of the current accounting period, for each of the following independent cases affecting Woolton Corporation. Include an explanation for each entry.

a. Details of Prepaid Insurance are shown in the account:

Prepaid Insurance	
Jan 1 Bal 2,300	
Mar 31 3,200	

Woolton prepays insurance on March 31 each year. At December 31, $800 is still prepaid.

b. Woolton pays employees each Friday. The amount of the weekly payroll is $5,900 for a five-day work week. The current accounting period ends on a Tuesday.
c. Woolton has a note receivable. During the current year, Woolton has earned accrued interest revenue of $500 that it will collect next year.
d. The beginning balance of supplies was $3,100. During the year, Woolton purchased supplies costing $6,200, and at December 31 supplies on hand total $2,300.
e. Woolton is providing services for Orca Investments, and the owner of Orca paid Woolton $11,400 as the annual service fee. Woolton recorded this amount as Unearned Service Revenue. Woolton estimates that it has earned 60% of the total fee during the current year.
f. Depreciation for the current year includes Office Furniture, $3,200, and Equipment, $5,800. Make a compound entry.

P3-61A. *(Learning Objectives 3, 4: Adjust the accounts; construct the financial statements)*  LO **3 4**
Consider the unadjusted trial balance of Spateness, Inc., at December 31, 2016, and the related
month-end adjustment data.

	A1						
	A	**B**	**C**	**D**	**E**	**F**	**G**
1	**Spateness, Inc.** **Trial Balance Worksheet** **December 31, 2016**						
2		**Trial Balance**		**Adjustments**		**Adjusted Trial Balance**	
3	**Account**	**Debit**	**Credit**	**Debit**	**Credit**	**Debit**	**Credit**
4	Cash	8,300					
5	Accounts receivable	1,400					
6	Prepaid rent	3,000					
7	Supplies	2,200					
8	Furniture	54,000					
9	Accumulated depreciation—furniture		3,200				
10	Accounts payable		3,600				
11	Salary payable						
12	Common stock		13,000				
13	Retained earnings		29,070				
14	Dividends	3,900					
15	Service revenue		27,400				
16	Salary expense	3,000					
17	Rent expense						
18	Utilities expense	470					
19	Depreciation expense—furniture						
20	Supplies expense						
21	Total	76,270	76,270				
22							

Adjustment data at December 31, 2016:
   a. Accrued service revenue at December 31, $3,960.
   b. Prepaid rent expired during the month. The unadjusted prepaid balance of $3,000 relates
   to the period December 1, 2016, through February 28, 2017.
   c. Supplies used during December, $1,880.
   d. Depreciation on furniture for the month. The estimated useful life of the furniture is five
   years.
   e. Accrued salary expense at December 31 for Monday, Tuesday, and Wednesday. The
   five-day weekly payroll of $20,000 will be paid on Friday.

Requirements

1. Using Exhibit 3-9 as an example, prepare the adjusted trial balance of Spateness, Inc., at
   December 31, 2016. Key each adjusting entry by letter.
2. Prepare the single-step monthly income statement, the statement of retained earnings, and
   the classified balance sheet. Draw arrows linking the three statements.

LO 3 **P3-62A.** *(Learning Objective 3: Adjust the accounts)* Lemontree Rentals, Inc.'s, unadjusted and adjusted trial balances at June 30, 2016, follow.

A1				

	A	B	C	D	E
1	**Lemontree Rentals, Inc.** **Trial Balance Worksheet** **June 30, 2016**				
2		**Trial Balance**		**Adjusted Trial Balance**	
3	**Account**	**Debit**	**Credit**	**Debit**	**Credit**
4	Cash	$ 8,000		$ 8,000	
5	Accounts receivable	6,000		6,810	
6	Interest receivable			300	
7	Note receivable	4,500		4,500	
8	Supplies	1,400		700	
9	Prepaid insurance	2,600		900	
10	Building	63,000		63,000	
11	Accumulated depreciation—building		$ 7,900		$ 9,500
12	Accounts payable		6,500		6,500
13	Wages payable				840
14	Unearned rental revenue		1,800		1,380
15	Common stock		23,000		23,000
16	Retained earnings		41,400		41,400
17	Dividends	3,600		3,600	
18	Rental revenue		10,300		11,530
19	Interest revenue		700		1,000
20	Depreciation expense—building			1,600	
21	Supplies expense			700	
22	Utilities expense	400		400	
23	Wage expense	1,400		2,240	
24	Property tax expense	700		700	
25	Insurance expense			1,700	
26	Total	$91,600	$91,600	$95,150	$95,150
27					

Requirements

1. Make the adjusting entries that account for the differences between the two trial balances.
2. Compute Lemontree Rentals' total assets, total liabilities, net income, and total equity.

P3-63A. *(Learning Objectives 4, 6: Construct the financial statements; analyze and evalu-ate debt-paying ability)* The adjusted trial balance for the year of Nicholl Corporation at October 31, 2016, follows.

	A	B	C
	A1 ⬍		
	A	B	C
1	**Nicholl Corporation** **Adjusted Trial Balance** **October 31, 2016**		
2	**Account**	**Debit**	**Credit**
3	Cash	$ 15,000	
4	Accounts receivable	18,600	
5	Supplies	2,500	
6	Prepaid rent	1,800	
7	Equipment	36,000	
8	Accumulated depreciation—equipment		$ 4,700
9	Accounts payable		8,800
10	Interest payable		600
11	Unearned service revenue		200
12	Income tax payable		2,500
13	Note payable		18,000
14	Common stock		16,000
15	Retained earnings		2,900
16	Dividends	4,000	
17	Service revenue		93,200
18	Depreciation expense—equipment	1,700	
19	Salary expense	40,500	
20	Rent expense	10,400	
21	Interest expense	2,600	
22	Insurance expense	3,800	
23	Supplies expense	2,500	
24	Income tax expense	7,500	
25	Total	$ 146,900	$ 146,900
26			

Requirements

1. Prepare Nicholl Corporation's 2016 single-step income statement, statement of retained earnings, and balance sheet. List expenses (except for income tax) in decreasing order on the income statement, and show total liabilities on the balance sheet. Draw arrows linking the three financial statements.
2. Nicholl's lenders require that the company maintain a debt ratio no higher than 0.50. Compute Nicholl's debt ratio at October 31, 2016, to determine whether the company is in compliance with this debt restriction. If not, suggest a way that Nicholl could have avoided this difficult situation.

LO 5   **P3-64A.** *(Learning Objective 5: Close the books, and evaluate retained earnings)* The accounts of Granger Services, Inc., at January 31, 2016, are listed in alphabetical order.

Accounts payable	$12,200	Interest expense...............	$ 500
Accounts receivable...............	17,000	Note payable, long term...	16,000
Accumulated depreciation,		Other assets, long-term	13,700
equipment	6,500	Prepaid expenses	5,900
Advertising expense...............	11,300	Retained earnings,	
Cash..	17,400	January 31, 2015	13,300
Common stock.......................	5,300	Salary expense..................	26,100
Current portion of long-term		Salary payable..................	3,400
note payable......................	1,900	Service revenue.................	95,000
Depreciation expense—equipment	1,900	Supplies............................	3,500
Dividends declared.................	12,500	Supplies expense..............	4,600
Equipment.............................	42,000	Unearned service revenue ...	2,800

Requirements

1. All adjustments have been journalized and posted, but the closing entries have not yet been made. Journalize Granger's closing entries at January 31, 2016.
2. Set up a T-account for Retained Earnings and post to that account. Then compute Granger's net income for the year ended January 31, 2016. What is the ending balance of Retained Earnings?
3. Did Retained Earnings increase or decrease during the year? What caused the increase or the decrease?

LO 4 6   **P3-65A.** *(Learning Objectives 4, 6: Construct the financial statements; analyze and evaluate liquidity and debt-paying ability)* Refer back to Problem 3-64A.

Requirements

1. Use the Granger Services data in Problem 3-64A to prepare the company's classified balance sheet at January 31, 2016. Show captions for total assets, total liabilities, and total liabilities and stockholders' equity.
2. Compute Granger's net working capital, current ratio, and debt ratio at January 31, 2016, rounding to two decimal places. At January 31, 2015, net working capital was $22,600, the current ratio was 1.90, and the debt ratio was 0.15. Did Granger's ability to pay both current and total debts improve or deteriorate during fiscal 2016? Evaluate Granger's debt position as strong or weak and give your reason.

LO 6   **P3-66A.** *(Learning Objective 6: Analyze and evaluate liquidity and debt-paying ability)* This problem demonstrates the effects of transactions on the current ratio and the debt ratio of Hartford Company. Hartford's condensed and adapted balance sheet at December 31, 2016, follows:

	(In millions)
Total current assets	$15.4
Properties, plant, equipment, and other assets...............	16.0
	$31.4
Total current liabilities...	$ 8.6
Total long-term liabilities...	5.8
Total stockholders' equity...	17.0
	$31.4

Assume that during the first quarter of the following year, 2017, Hartford completed the following transactions:

    a. Earned revenue, $2.5 million, on account.
    b. Borrowed $3.0 million on long-term debt.
    c. Paid half the current liabilities.
    d. Paid selling expense of $3.0 million.
    e. Accrued general expense of $0.9 million. Credit General Expense Payable, a current liability.
    f. Purchased equipment for $4.6 million, paying cash of $1.8 million, and signing a long-term note payable for $2.8 million.
    g. Recorded depreciation expense of $0.9 million.

Requirements

1. Compute Hartford's current ratio and debt ratio at December 31, 2016. Round to two decimal places.
2. Consider each transaction separately. Compute Hartford's current ratio and debt ratio after each transaction during 2017—that is, seven times. Round ratios to two decimal places.
3. Based on your analysis, you should be able to readily identify the effects of certain transactions on the current ratio and the debt ratio. Test your understanding by completing these statements with either "increase" or "decrease":
    a. Revenues usually _____ the current ratio.
    b. Revenues usually _____ the debt ratio.
    c. Expenses usually _____ the current ratio. (*Note:* Depreciation is an exception to this rule.)
    d. Expenses usually _____ the debt ratio.
    e. If a company's current ratio is greater than 1.0, as it is for Hartford, paying off a current liability will always _____ the current ratio.
    f. Borrowing money on long-term debt will always _____ the current ratio and the debt ratio.

Group B

P3-67B. (*Learning Objective 1: Explain how accrual accounting differs from cash-basis accounting*) Whittaker Consulting had the following selected transactions in July:

LO **1**

July	1	Prepaid insurance for July through September, $750.
	4	Purchased office furniture for cash, $3,500.
	5	Performed services and received cash, $1,200.
	8	Paid advertising expense, $200.
	11	Performed service on account, $3,300.
	19	Purchased computer on account, $2,500.
	24	Collected for July 11 service.
	26	Paid account payable from July 19.
	29	Paid salary expense, $1,500.
	31	Adjusted for July insurance expense (see July 1).
	31	Earned revenue of $400 that was collected in advance back in June.
	31	Recorded July depreciation expense on all fixed assets, $260.

Requirements

1. Show how each transaction would be handled (in terms of recognizing revenues and expenses) using the cash basis and the accrual basis.
2. Compute July income (loss) before tax under each accounting method.
3. Indicate which measure of net income or net loss is preferable. Use the transactions on July 11 and July 24 to explain.

LO 3 **P3-68B.** *(Learning Objective 3: Adjust the accounts)* Journalize the adjusting entry needed on December 31, the end of the current accounting period, for each of the following independent cases affecting Tiger Corp. Include an explanation for each entry.

a. Details of Prepaid Insurance are shown in the account:

Prepaid Insurance			
Jan 1	Bal	2,900	
Mar 31		4,000	

Tiger prepays insurance on March 31 each year. At December 31, $1,800 is still prepaid.

b. Tiger pays employees each Friday. The amount of the weekly payroll is $5,900 for a five-day work week. The current accounting period ends on Thursday.

c. Tiger has a note receivable. During the current year, Tiger has earned accrued interest revenue of $500 that it will collect next year.

d. The beginning balance of supplies was $3,100. During the year, Tiger purchased supplies costing $6,100, and at December 31 supplies on hand total $2,300.

e. Tiger is providing services for Dolphin Investments, and the owner of Dolphin paid Tiger $11,500 as the annual service fee. Tiger recorded this amount as Unearned Service Revenue. Tiger estimates that it has earned 70% of the total fee during the current year.

f. Depreciation for the current year includes Office Furniture, $3,800, and Equipment, $6,100. Make a compound entry.

LO 3 4 **P3-69B.** *(Learning Objectives 3, 4: Adjust the accounts; construct the financial statements)* Consider the unadjusted trial balance of Edison, Inc., at December 31, 2016, and the related month-end adjustment data.

A1							
	A	**B**	**C**	**D**	**E**	**F**	**G**
1	Edison, Inc. Trial Balance Worksheet December 31, 2016						
2		**Trial Balance**		**Adjustments**		**Adjusted Trial Balance**	
3	**Account**	**Debit**	**Credit**	**Debit**	**Credit**	**Debit**	**Credit**
4	Cash	8,600					
5	Accounts receivable	1,300					
6	Prepaid rent	3,000					
7	Supplies	1,800					
8	Furniture	81,000					
9	Accumulated depreciation—furniture		3,900				
10	Accounts payable		3,500				
11	Salary payable						
12	Common stock		10,000				
13	Retained earnings		65,390				
14	Dividends	4,500					
15	Service revenue		21,400				
16	Salary expense	3,500					
17	Rent expense						
18	Utilities expense	490					
19	Depreciation expense—furniture						
20	Supplies expense						
21	Total	104,190	104,190				
22							

Adjustment data at December 31, 2016, include the following:

a. Accrued service revenue at December 31, $2,780.

b. Prepaid rent expired during the month. The unadjusted prepaid balance of $3,000 relates to the period December 1, 2016, through February 28, 2017.

    c. Supplies used during December, $1,330.

    d. Depreciation on furniture for the month. The furniture's expected useful life is five years.

    e. Accrued salary expense at December 31 for Monday, Tuesday, and Wednesday. The five-day weekly payroll is $14,000 and will be paid on Friday.

Requirements

  1. Using Exhibit 3-9 as an example, prepare the adjusted trial balance of Edison, Inc., at December 31, 2016. Key each adjusting entry by letter.

  2. Prepare the single-step income statement, the statement of retained earnings, and the classified balance sheet. Draw arrows linking the three statements.

P3-70B. *(Learning Objective 3: Adjust the accounts)* Peppertree Rentals, Inc.'s, unadjusted and adjusted trial balances at June 30, 2016, follow:

LO 3

A1 ⬍				
A	**B**	**C**	**D**	**E**
Peppertree Rentals, Inc. **Trial Balance Worksheet** **June 30, 2016**				
	Trial Balance		**Adjusted Trial Balance**	
Account	**Debit**	**Credit**	**Debit**	**Credit**
Cash	$ 8,300		$ 8,300	
Accounts receivable	6,300		6,880	
Interest receivable			200	
Note receivable	4,100		4,100	
Supplies	1,500		900	
Prepaid insurance	2,800		1,400	
Building	68,000		68,000	
Accumulated depreciation—building		$ 8,500		$10,000
Accounts payable		7,200		7,200
Wages payable				1,190
Unearned rental revenue		2,200		1,900
Common stock		21,000		21,000
Retained earnings		44,500		44,500
Dividends	3,300		3,300	
Rental revenue		12,500		13,380
Interest revenue		900		1,100
Depreciation expense—building			1,500	
Supplies expense			600	
Utilities expense	400		400	
Wage expense	1,500		2,690	
Property tax expense	600		600	
Insurance expense			1,400	
Total	$ 96,800	$96,800	$100,270	$100,270

Requirements

  1. Make the adjusting entries that account for the differences between the two trial balances.

  2. Compute Peppertree Rentals's total assets, total liabilities, net income, and total equity.

LO 4 6

P3-71B. *(Learning Objectives 4, 6: Construct the financial statements; analyze and evaluate debt-paying ability)* The adjusted trial balance for the year of Schneider Corporation at December 31, 2016, follows:

	A	B	C
	A1		
1	**Schneider Corporation** **Adjusted Trial Balance** **December 31, 2016**		
2	**Account**	**Debit**	**Credit**
3	Cash	$ 12,400	
4	Accounts receivable	19,500	
5	Supplies	2,300	
6	Prepaid rent	1,200	
7	Equipment	36,000	
8	Accumulated depreciation—equipment		$ 4,100
9	Accounts payable		8,700
10	Interest payable		800
11	Unearned service revenue		800
12	Income tax payable		2,200
13	Note payable		18,500
14	Common stock		16,000
15	Retained earnings		3,000
16	Dividends	5,000	
17	Service revenue		91,500
18	Depreciation expense—equipment	1,700	
19	Salary expense	39,800	
20	Rent expense	10,400	
21	Interest expense	3,500	
22	Insurance expense	3,800	
23	Supplies expense	2,700	
24	Income tax expense	7,300	
25	Total	$ 145,600	$ 145,600
26			

Requirements

1. Prepare Schneider Corporation's 2016 single-step income statement, statement of retained earnings, and balance sheet. List expenses (except for income tax) in decreasing order on the income statement, and show total liabilities on the balance sheet.
2. Schneider's lenders require that the company maintain a debt ratio no higher than 0.50. Compute Schneider's debt ratio at December 31, 2016, to determine whether the company is in compliance with this debt restriction. If not, suggest a way Schneider Corporation could have avoided this difficult situation.

LO 5

P3-72B. *(Learning Objective 5: Close the books, evaluate retained earnings)* The accounts of Spa View Service, Inc., at January 31, 2016, are listed in alphabetical order.

Accounts payable	$ 12,700	Interest expense	$ 800
Accounts receivable	16,600	Note payable, long-term...	15,900
Accumulated depreciation,		Other assets, long-term	13,500
equipment	6,500	Prepaid expenses	5,800
Advertising expense	10,800	Retained earnings,	
Cash	17,500	January 31, 2015	13,700
Common stock	8,900	Salary expense	27,700
Current portion of long term		Salary payable	3,400
note payable	1,000	Service revenue	94,100
Depreciation expense—equipment	1,700	Supplies	3,300
Dividends declared	15,000	Supplies expense	4,200
Equipment	43,000	Unearned service revenue ...	3,700

Requirements

1. All adjustments have been journalized and posted, but the closing entries have not yet been made. Journalize Spa View's closing entries at January 31, 2016.
2. Set up a T-account for Retained Earnings and post to that account. Then compute Spa View's net income for the year ended January 31, 2016. What is the ending balance of Retained Earnings?
3. Did Retained Earnings increase or decrease during the 2016 fiscal year? What caused the increase or decrease?

P3-73B. *(Learning Objectives 4, 6: Construct the financial statements; analyze and evaluate liquidity and debt-paying ability)* Refer back to Problem 3-72B.

Requirements

1. Use the Spa View Services data in Problem 3-72B to prepare the company's classified balance sheet at January 31, 2016. Show captions for total assets, total liabilities, and stockholders' equity.
2. Compute Spa View's net working capital, current ratio, and debt ratio at January 31, 2016, rounding to two decimal places. At January 31, 2015, the net working capital was $21,600, the current ratio was 1.70, and the debt ratio was 0.15. Did Spa View's ability to pay both current and total liabilities improve or deteriorate during fiscal 2016? Evaluate Spa View's debt position as strong or weak and give your reason.

P3-74B. *(Learning Objective 6: Analyze and evaluate liquidity and debt-paying ability)* This problem demonstrates the effects of transactions on the current ratio and the debt ratio of Digger Company. Digger's condensed and adapted balance sheet at December 31, 2015, follows:

LO 6

	(In millions)
Total current assets	$15.2
Properties, plant, equipment, and other assets	15.8
	$31.0
Total current liabilities	$ 8.6
Total long-term liabilities	5.8
Total shareholders' equity	16.6
	$31.0

Assume that during the first quarter of the following year, 2016, Digger completed the following transactions:

a. Earned revenue of $2.7 million, on account.
b. Borrowed $7.0 million on long-term debt.
c. Paid half of the current liabilities.
d. Paid selling expense of $0.6 million.
e. Accrued general expense of $0.7 million. Credit General Expense Payable, a current liability.
f. Purchased equipment for $4.2 million, paying cash of $1.7 million and signing a long-term note payable for $2.5 million.
g. Recorded depreciation expense of $0.3 million.

Requirements

1. Compute Digger's current ratio and debt ratio at December 31, 2015. Round to two decimal places.
2. Consider each transaction separately. Compute Digger's current ratio and debt ratio after each transaction during 2016—that is, seven times. Round ratios to two decimal places.

3. Based on your analysis, you should be able to readily identify the effects of certain transactions on the current ratio and the debt ratio. Test your understanding by completing these statements with either "increase" or "decrease."
   a. Revenues usually _____ the current ratio.
   b. Revenues usually _____ the debt ratio.
   c. Expenses usually _____ the current ratio. (*Note:* Depreciation is an exception to this rule.)
   d. Expenses usually _____ the debt ratio.
   e. If a company's current ratio is greater than 1.0, as for Digger, paying off a current liability will always _____ the current ratio.
   f. Borrowing money on long-term debt will always _____ the current ratio and _____ the debt ratio.

Challenge Exercises and Problems

LO 6

E3-75. (*Learning Objective 6: Analyze and evaluate liquidity and debt-paying ability*)
Satterfield Corporation reported the following current accounts at December 31, 2016 (amounts in thousands):

Cash..	$1,500
Receivables.......................................	5,900
Inventory...	2,700
Prepaid expenses	1,000
Accounts payable	2,600
Unearned revenue.............................	1,600
Accrued expenses payable	1,900

During January 2017, Satterfield completed these selected transactions:
- Sold services on account, $9,000
- Depreciation expense, $400
- Paid for expenses, $7,300
- Collected from customers on account, $8,100
- Accrued expenses, $500
- Paid on account, $1,400
- Used up prepaid expenses, $700

Compute Satterfield's net working capital and current ratio at December 31, 2016, and again at January 31, 2017. Did the net working capital and current ratio improve or deteriorate during January 2017? Comment on the level of the company's net working capital and current ratio.

E3-76. *(Learning Objectives 3, 4: Adjust the accounts; compute financial statement amounts)* LO 3 4
The accounts of United Digital Services Company prior to the year-end adjustments follow:

Cash	$ 7,300	Common stock	$ 14,000
Accounts receivable	7,500	Retained earnings	46,000
Supplies	4,600	Dividends declared	16,000
Prepaid insurance	3,500	Service revenue	161,000
Building	110,000	Salary expense	37,000
Accumulated depreciation—		Depreciation expense—	
building	15,600	building	
Land	53,000	Supplies expense	
Accounts payable	6,100	Insurance expense	
Salary payable		Advertising expense	7,300
Unearned service revenue	5,500	Utilities expense	2,000

Adjusting data at the end of the year include the following:
a. Unearned service revenue that has been earned, $1,650
b. Accrued service revenue, $32,200
c. Supplies used in operations, $3,100
d. Accrued salary expense, $3,500
e. Prepaid insurance expired, $1,500
f. Depreciation expense—building, $2,600

Megan Hodge, the principal stockholder, has received an offer to sell United Digital Services Company. She needs to know the following information within one hour:
a. Net income for the year covered by these data
b. Total assets
c. Total liabilities
d. Total stockholders' equity
e. Proof that Total assets = Total liabilities + Total stockholders' equity after all items are updated

Requirement

Without opening any accounts, making any journal entries, or using a work sheet, provide Ms. Hodge with the requested information. The business is not subject to income tax.

LO 4   **P3-77.** *(Learning Objective 4: Construct a balance sheet from given financial data)* Tidy Car, Inc., provides mobile detailing to its customers. The Income Statement for the month ended January 31, 2016, the Balance Sheet for December 31, 2015, and details of postings to the Cash account in the general ledger for the month of January 2016 follow:

A1						
	A			**B**	**C**	**D** **E**
1	Tidy Car, Inc. Income Statement Month ended January 31, 2016					
2	Revenue:					
3	Detailing revenue			$36,500		
4	Gift certificates redeemed			700	$37,200	
5	Expenses:					
6	Salary expense			$10,000		
7	Depreciation expense—equipment			6,800		
8	Supplies expense			3,100		
9	Advertising expense			3,000	22,900	
10	Net income				$ 14,300	
11						

A1						
	A	**B**	**C**	**D**	**E**	**F**
1	Tidy Car, Inc. Balance Sheet December 31, 2015					
2	**Assets**			**Liabilities**		
3	Cash		$ 1,900	Accounts payable	$ 3,500	
4	Accounts receivable		2,600	Salary payable	1,700	
5	Supplies		1,800	Unearned service revenue	1,200	
6	Equipment	$34,000		Total liabilities	6,400	
7	Less: Accumulated			**Stockholders' Equity**		
8	depreciation	(6,800)	27,200	Common stock	10,000	
9				Retained earnings	17,100	
10				Total stockholders' equity	27,100	
11				Total liabilities and		
12	Total assets		$33,500	stockholders' equity	$33,500	
13						

Cash

Bal 12/31/2015	1,900			
Cash collections from customers	38,700	Salaries paid	11,400	
Issuance of common stock	12,000	Dividends paid	1,300	
		Purchase of equipment	6,000	
		Payments of accounts payable	1,800	
		Advertising paid	2,800	
Bal 1/31/2016	?			

The following additional information is also available:

1. $1,100 of the cash collected from customers in January 2016 was for gift certificates for detailing services to be performed in the future. As of January 31, 2016, $1,600 of gift certificates were still outstanding.
2. $3,300 of supplies were purchased on account.
3. Employees are paid monthly during the first week after the end of the pay period.

Requirement

Based on these statements, prepare the Balance Sheet for January 31, 2016.

APPLY YOUR KNOWLEDGE

Decision Cases

Case 1. *(Learning Objectives 3, 6: Adjust the accounts; analyze and evaluate liquidity)*
The unadjusted trial balance of Rock City Services, Inc., at January 31, 2017, does not balance.
The list of accounts and their balances is given below. The trial balance needs to be prepared
and adjusted before the financial statements at January 31, 2017, can be prepared. The manager
of Rock City Services also needs to know the business's current ratio.

Cash	$ 8,000
Accounts receivable	4,200
Supplies	800
Prepaid rent	1,200
Land	43,000
Accounts payable	12,000
Salary payable	0
Unearned service revenue	700
Note payable, due in three years	23,400
Common stock	5,000
Retained earnings	9,300
Service revenue	9,100
Salary expense	3,400
Rent expense	0
Advertising expense	900
Supplies expense	0

Requirements

1. How much *out of balance* is the trial balance? Notes Payable (the only error) is
   understated.
2. Rock City Services needs to make the following adjustments at January 31:
   a. Supplies of $400 were used during January.
   b. The balance of prepaid rent was paid on January 1 and covers the entire calendar year of
      2017. No adjustment was made on January 31.
   c. At January 31, Rock City Services owed employees $1,000.
   d. Unearned service revenue of $500 was earned during January.

   Prepare a corrected, adjusted trial balance. Give Notes Payable its correct balance.

3. After the error is corrected and after these adjustments are made, compute the current
   ratio of Rock City Services, Inc. If your business had this current ratio, could you sleep at
   night?

LO 4 6

Case 2. *(Learning Objectives 4, 6: Construct the financial statements; analyze and evaluate liquidity and debt-paying ability)* On October 1, 2016, Hilda Petrochuck opened Hilda's Coffee Shop, Inc. Petrochuck is now at a crossroads. The October financial statements paint a glowing picture of the business, and Petrochuck has asked you whether she should expand the business. To expand the business, Petrochuck wants to be earning net income of $10,000 per month and have total assets of $50,000. Petrochuck believes she is meeting both goals.

To start the business, Petrochuck invested $25,000, not the $15,000 amount reported as "Common stock" on the balance sheet. The business issued $25,000 of common stock to Petrochuck. The bookkeeper "plugged" the $15,000 "Common stock" amount into the balance sheet (entered the amount necessary without any support) to make it balance. The bookkeeper made some other errors, too. Petrochuck shows you the following financial statements that the bookkeeper prepared:

A1						
	A		**B**	**C**	**D**	**E**
1	**Hilda's Coffee Shop** **Income Statement** **Month ended October 31, 2016**					
2	**Revenue:**					
3	Investments by owner		$25,000			
4	Unearned banquet sales revenue		3,000			
5				$28,000		
6	**Expenses:**					
7	Wages expense		$ 5,000			
8	Rent expense		4,000			
9	Dividends		3,000			
10	Depreciation expense—fixtures		1,000			
11				13,000		
12	**Net income**			$ 15,000		
13						

A1					
	A	**B**	**C**	**D**	**E**
1	**Hilda's Coffee Shop** **Balance Sheet** **October 31, 2016**				
2	**Assets**		**Liabilities**		
3	Cash	$ 8,000	Accounts payable	$ 7,000	
4	Prepaid insurance	1,000	Sales revenue	32,000	
5	Insurance expense	1,000	Accumulated depreciation—		
6	Food inventory	5,000	fixtures	1,000	
7	Cost of goods sold (expense)	12,000		40,000	
8	Fixtures (tables, chairs, etc.)	24,000	**Stockholders' Equity**		
9	Dishes and silverware	4,000	Common stock	15,000	
10		$55,000		$55,000	
11					

Requirement

1. Prepare corrected financial statements for Hilda's Coffee Shop, Inc.: single-step Income Statement, Statement of Retained Earnings, and Balance Sheet. Then, based on Petrochuck's goals and your corrected statements, recommend to Petrochuck whether she should expand the restaurant.

Case 3. *(Learning Objectives 3, 4: Adjust the accounts; construct the financial statements; evaluate a business based on financial statements)* Rachel Gambol has owned and operated Gambol Advertising, Inc., since it began 10 years ago. Recently, Gambol mentioned that she would consider selling the company for the right price.

LO **3** **4**

Assume that you are interested in buying this business. You obtain its most recent monthly trial balance, which follows. Revenues and expenses vary little from month to month, and June is a typical month. Your investigation reveals that the trial balance does not include the effects of monthly revenues of $4,000 and expenses totaling $1,100. If you were to buy Gambol Advertising, you would hire a manager so you could devote your time to other duties. Assume that your manager would require a monthly salary of $5,000.

	A1	B	C
	Gambol Advertising, Inc.		
	Trial Balance		
1	**June 30, 2016**		
2	Cash	$ 12,000	
3	Accounts receivable	6,900	
4	Prepaid expenses	3,200	
5	Land	158,000	
6	Plant assets	125,000	
7	Accumulated depreciation—plant assets		$ 81,500
8	Accounts payable		13,800
9	Salary payable		
10	Unearned advertising revenue		58,700
11	Common stock		50,000
12	Retained earnings		93,000
13	Dividends	9,000	
14	Advertising revenue		22,000
15	Rent expense		
16	Salary expense	4,000	
17	Utilities expense	900	
18	Depreciation expense—plant assets		
19	Supplies expense		
20	Total	$319,000	$319,000
21			

Requirements

1. Assume that the most you would pay for the business is 16 times the amount of monthly net income *you could expect to earn* from it. Compute this possible price.
2. Gambol states that the least she will take for the business is two times its stockholders' equity on June 30. Compute this amount.
3. Under these conditions, how much should you offer Gambol? Give your reason. (Challenge)

Ethical Issues

Issue 1. Green Horizons Energy Co. is in its third year of operations, and the company has grown. To expand the business, Green Horizons borrowed $15 million from Bank of Ravenna. As a condition for making this loan, the bank required that Green Horizons maintain a current ratio of at least 1.50 and a debt ratio of no more than 0.50.

Business recently has been worse than expected. Expenses have brought the current ratio down to 1.47 and the debt ratio up to 0.51 at December 15. Dana McCoy, the general manager, is considering the result of reporting this current ratio to the bank. McCoy is considering recording this year some revenue on account that Green Horizons will earn next year. The contract for this job has been signed, and Green Horizons will deliver the natural gas during January of next year.

Requirements

1. Journalize the revenue transaction (without dollar amounts), and indicate how recording this revenue in December would affect the current ratio and the debt ratio.
2. Analyze this transaction according to the Decision Framework for Making Ethical Judgments in Chapter 1:
   a. What is the issue?
   b. Who are the stakeholders, and what are the alternatives? Weigh them from the standpoint of economic, legal, and ethical implications.
   c. What decision would you make?
3. Propose an ethical course of action for Green Horizons.

Issue 2. The net income of Dusek Photography Company decreased sharply during 2016. Patty Dusek, owner of the company, anticipates the need for a bank loan in 2017. Late in 2016, Dusek instructed Tim Loftus, the accountant and a personal friend of yours, to record a $15,000 sale of portraits to the Dusek family, even though the photos will not be shot until January 2017. Dusek also told Loftus *not* to make the following December 31, 2016, adjusting entries:

Salaries owed to employees	$14,000
Prepaid insurance that has expired	$2,000

Requirements

1. Compute the overall effect of these transactions on the company's reported income for 2016. Is reported net income overstated or understated?
2. Why did Dusek take these actions? Are they ethical? Give your reason, identifying the parties helped and the parties harmed by Dusek's action. Consult the Decision Framework for Making Ethical Judgments in Chapter 1. Which factor (economic, legal, or ethical) seems to be taking precedence? Identify the stakeholders and the potential consequences to each.
3. As a personal friend of Tim's, what advice would you give him?

Focus on Financials | Apple Inc.

(Learning Objectives 3, 4, 6: Adjust the accounts; construct financial statements; evaluate debt-paying ability) **Apple Inc.**—like all other businesses—adjusts accounts prior to year-end to get correct amounts for the financial statements. Examine Apple Inc.'s Consolidated Balance Sheets in Appendix A and online in the filings section of **http://www.sec.gov.**, and pay particular attention to "Accrued expenses."

Requirements

1. Why does a company have accrued expenses payable at year-end?
2. See Apple Inc.'s Consolidated Balance Sheets for 2013 and 2014. What was the balance of Accrued expenses at the end of each of those balance sheet years? What type of account is "Accrued expenses"?
3. See Note 3—Consolidated Financial Statement Details. Go to the section of that note for Accrued expenses. What expenses does Apple Inc. accrue according to this note? Verify that the total of the accrued expenses for each year is the same as the balance of Accrued expenses on the balance sheet for each of the two balance sheet years.
4. Compute net working capital, the current ratio, and the debt ratio for Apple Inc., at September 28, 2013, and September 27, 2014. Did the amount of net working capital and ratio values improve, deteriorate, or hold steady during fiscal 2014? Do Apple Inc.'s ratio values indicate relative financial strength or weakness?

Focus on Analysis | Under Armour, Inc.

(Learning Objective 1: Explain accruals and deferrals) Refer to the consolidated financial statements of **Under Armour, Inc.**, in Appendix B and online in the filings section of **http://www.sec.gov**. During 2014, the company reported net revenues of $3,084 million in its consolidated statement of income. In addition, the company had numerous accruals and deferrals. As a new member of Under Armour, Inc.'s, accounting staff, it is your job to explain the company's revenue recognition policy, as well as the effects of accruals and deferrals on net income for 2014. *(Note that all amounts in this activity are rounded to the nearest million.)*

LO 1

Requirements

1. Examine Note 2, Summary of Significant Accounting Policies. Explain the company's policy for recognizing each type of revenue that is included in the Consolidated Statements of Income.
2. Examine Under Armour, Inc.'s, consolidated balance sheets at December 31, 2014, and December 31, 2013, as well as Note 2, Summary of Significant Accounting Policies. Ending net accounts receivable for 2013 (beginning balance for 2014) were $210 million. Ending net receivables for 2014 were $280 million (all amounts are rounded to the nearest million). Explain the source of these receivables. Were all of these amounts considered collectible (see Allowance for Doubtful Accounts under Note 2)? Why or why not?
3. Refer to Under Armour, Inc.'s, comsolidated balance sheets at December 31, 2014, and December 31, 2013, and examine the balances of the account entitled "Prepaid expenses and other current assets." What specific accounts might be included in this balance sheet line item? The beginning balance is $64 million, and the ending balance is $87 million. Construct a journal entry or entries that might account for the change.
4. View Note 4, Property and Equipment, Net. Notice that accumulated depreciation and amortization stood at $172 million at the end of 2013 and at $217 million at year-end 2014. Assume that depreciation and amortization expense for 2014 was $72 million. Explain what must have happened to account for the remainder of the change in the accumulated depreciation account during 2014. (Challenge)
5. In Note 2 Summary of Significant Accounting Policies, locate the paragraph entitled "Accrued Expenses." What are the primary categories of items in Accrued Expenses? What type of account is Accrued Expenses? Did the company's Accrued Expenses increase, decrease, or stay the same from 2013 to 2014? How would this change have impacted the company's overall net income in 2014?

Group Projects

Upon graduation from Texas State Technical College in Waco, Texas, your neighbor John Abel immediately accepted a position as an electrician's assistant for a large electrical repair company in Austin, Texas. After three years of hard work, John received a master electrician's license and decided to open his own business. John had saved $10,000, which he invested in the business, transferring the money from his personal savings account. His attorney advised him to set up the business as a corporation. He received 10,000 shares of capital stock in exchange for this transfer.

On October 1, 2016, John purchased a used panel truck for $6,000 cash and some used tools for $1,200 cash. That same day, he signed a lease on a small shop building at 4240 East Oltorf in Austin and paid $3,000 in advance for the first six months' rent. Also on October 1, 2016, he obtained an iPhone on a two-year contract, paying a $100 deposit, which he will get back at the end of the contract term. He also placed a small advertisement on Craigslist that day. Finally, John opened the doors of Abel Electronics, Inc., on October 1, 2016.

John's telephone immediately began ringing, with potential customers requesting small repairs and construction projects. After the first month, John was so busy that he had to employ an assistant.

Although John knew practically nothing about the financial side of the business, he was smart enough to realize that a number of reports were required of his corporation, and that costs and collections had to be controlled carefully. At the end of the year, prompted in part by concern about his income tax situation (corporations have to pay taxes as well as their employees) and partly by a $15,000 loan application at South Congress Bank for some new tools and shop expansion, John realizes that he needs to prepare financial statements. Knowing that you, his neighbor, are attending the University of Texas at Austin's business program, he comes to you for some help. After all, anyone trained in business should be able to prepare a set of financial statements to help a buddy out, right? He has brought all of his records (kept in a shoe box) to you, from which you gather the following information for the three months ended December 31, 2016:

- Bank account deposits for collections from customers for services totaled $33,000.
- Services billed to customers but not yet collected totaled $3,000.
- Checks written included: John's salary $5,000; his assistant's salary $3,500 (he still owes the assistant $500); payroll taxes $575; supplies purchased $9,500 (count of supplies still on hand on December 31 is $1,000); fuel and maintenance on truck $1,200; insurance $700; utilities including telephone $825; advertising $600 (he still owes $100).
- According to the Internal Revenue Service, the estimated life of the truck is five years and the estimated life of the tools is three years. These assets have no estimated salvage value and you recommend that John use the straight-line method of depreciation.
- You plug Abel Electronics, Inc.'s, revenue and expenses for the quarter into Excel and it computes an estimated quarterly income tax payable of $1,680.

Requirements

1. Analyze the paragraphs above for evidence of business transactions. As you do so, prepare an Excel spreadsheet that includes every financial statement account involved (e.g., cash, accounts receivable, supplies, property & equipment, etc.). Use the spreadsheet format from Exhibit 2-1 as a model. (*Hint:* To make sure you enter the transactions correctly and completely, number the transactions consecutively as you recognize them.)
2. From the spreadsheet you created in Requirement 1, prepare the single-step income statement of Abel Electronics, Inc., using generally accepted accounting principles, for the three months ended December 31, 2016.
3. From the spreadsheet you created in Requirement 1, prepare the statement of retained earnings of Abel Electronics, Inc., for the three months ended December 31, 2016.
4. From the spreadsheet you created in Requirement 1, prepare the balance sheet for Abel Electronics, Inc., as of December 31, 2016.
5. Analyze the account "cash" that you created in Requirement 1, and prepare a statement of cash flows for Abel Electronics, Inc., for the three months ended December 31, 2016. Divide the various increases and decreases to the account into three categories: operating, investing, and financing. Discuss among your team members what these categories mean. (Challenge)
6. Thoroughly analyze Abel Electronics, Inc.'s, creditworthiness for the loan at South Congress Bank. For this purpose, assume that the term of the loan is 5 years and that the principal balance is not due and payable until the end of the term of the loan. Only interest is payable yearly. Use all of the ratios you have learned so far. Consider not only Abel's present position but also its position should the loan be granted. If you were a loan officer for the bank, would you approve Abel's request for the loan? Why or why not?

Quick Check Answers

1. *b*	7. *a*	13. *c*
2. *c*	8. *d*	14. *b*
3. *c*	9. *d*	15. *a*
4. *d*	10. *b*	16. *a*
5. *a*	11. *b*	17. *a*
6. *c*	12. *d*	

4 Internal Control & Cash

 SPOTLIGHT | Cooking the Books at Green Valley Coffee Company: $10 million Is a Lot of Beans!

This account is modeled on a true story:

"I've never been so shocked in my life!" exclaimed Frank Roberts, CEO of the **Green Valley Coffee Company** in Littleton, Colorado. "I never thought this could happen to us. We are such a close-knit organization where everyone trusts everyone else. Why, people at Green Valley feel like family! I feel betrayed, violated."

Roberts had just returned from the trial of Joe Johnson, who had been convicted of embezzling over $10,000,000 from Green Valley Coffee Company over a nine-year period. The company, though located in a Denver suburb, had achieved a worldwide reputation over its 30-year history for its delicious, premium roasted and uniquely flavored coffees as well as syrups, candies, and confections. They had started with just one small store in Littleton, but had achieved meteoric sales growth since the advent of the Internet in the 1990s. They now operated 100 stores in upscale shopping areas across the Midwest. During the past year, the company had opened ten new locations from Colorado to Missouri, along busy interstate highways. The company's regular customer base had become fiercely loyal. Store sales had more than doubled over the last year from $2,000,000 to over $5,000,000. Internet sales had opened up a new world, adding an additional $5,000,000 in sales of all types of coffees, which the company was beginning to ship to customers all over the world.

Johnson had been one of Green Valley Coffee Company's most trusted employees for 12 years. He had been a graduate of a small religiously-affiliated university in Oklahoma and had worked for a large corporation before moving to Littleton to become controller of the company. Pillars of the community, Johnson and his wife were well-known figures around town, members of a posh country club, which, according to its website, strives to attract members of the "highest caliber." Johnson had a reputation of public acts of generosity, including large donations to school

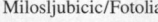
Milosljubicic/Fotolia

and arts programs and large donations to his church. He often demonstrated generosity by hosting lavish parties at his estate-sized home with its own wine cellar. Although Johnson earned a salary of only $100,000 per year, he quietly and strategically spread the good news that he and his wife had inherited a great deal of money in oil and mining interests from deceased wealthy family. No one questioned it.

As controller, Johnson was given the job of writing checks to company vendors (suppliers). He also had access to the supply of unused company checks, the electronic signature of Roberts, CEO, and the accounting records. Johnson soon discovered that this combination of incompatible duties gave him access to a virtually unlimited treasure chest full of cash, which he used as an opportunity to embezzle money from the company. Johnson and his wife would run up vast amounts of charges (often exceeding $20,000 per month) on their personal credit cards. The credit cards allowed the Johnsons to maintain a lavish lifestyle, which included financing and maintenance of a vacation home in Santa Fe, New Mexico, their palatial home in Littleton, a multimillion dollar watch and jewelry collection, numerous luxury automobiles, a 600-bottle wine collection, a Steinway grand piano, and multiple trips aboard a chartered private jet out of a small airport on the southern edge of Denver. When the credit card bills came to his house, Johnson would process company checks made out to the banks. To hide the fact that these checks were to his personal creditors and not to approved vendors (suppliers) of Green Valley Coffee Company, he recorded the checks as "voided" (canceled) in the company's cash disbursements (payments) journal. He then issued duplicate checks for the same amounts written to the company's legitimate creditors. Almost 900 such checks were written. Thus, for nine years, the company's cash payments processed by its banks were overstated by the amount of Johnson's personal bills. Roberts, whose signature was on the checks, never bothered to review the checks that had gone out under his electronic signature. Johnson also had the responsibility of reconciling the company's bank statement, giving him a convenient way to make sure month-end bank statements always agreed with the books, even if Johnson had to manipulate the outstanding checks list to make it balance.

The company's top management had begun to suspect that something was amiss. They had noticed that, over the past five years, in spite of the company's expansion plans that produced huge increases in sales, the company's cash balances and profits were declining. However, the company's sales growth had been so explosive and had generated so much cash that these declines were considered relatively minor. The company had not been audited by an independent auditor in the entire 12-year period Johnson was controller. Top management had, however, initiated an internal review, looking for inventory theft, increased labor costs, mismanagement, and inefficiency. As they would later discover, they were overlooking the "elephant in the room." The shortages could only be traced to one "trusted employee"—good old loyal Joe. One June day, an accounting clerk named Elizabeth Warner, a conscientious former bank teller who had been with the company for less than a year, brought some questionable entries to Joe's (her boss's) attention. She happened to find a $20,000 check that had been issued for only a $10,000 postage bill. The amount on the check was double the amount of the bill! Joe initially lied and called the discrepancy a computer error. This led Elizabeth to review 8 months of accounts payable records to other vendors (suppliers). She found the same discrepancies in many of them. She brought this to the attention of Roberts and other executives, who called the police and the FBI, bringing Joe's embezzlement scheme to an abrupt end. ●

The excerpt from the Green Valley Coffee Company balance sheet below reports the company's assets. Focus on the top line, Cash and cash equivalents. At December 31, 2016, Green Valley reported cash and cash equivalents of $6,000,000. Due to Johnson's scheme, the company had been cheated of $10 million over several years that it could have used to buy new equipment, expand operations, or pay off debts.

Green Valley Coffee Company has now reformed its internal controls. The company has hired a separate person, with no access to cash, to keep vendor accounts payable records in the controller's department. Only approved vendors may be paid by company check. The controller's department no longer has access to the supply of unused checks or to the CEO's electronic signature. Once checks are prepared to approved vendors in the accounts payable department, they are sent to the treasurer's department for final review, along with supporting documentation, which must include a purchase order, receiving report, and approved vendor invoice. Persons processing the checks with Roberts's electronic signature review the supporting documents to determine that all documents are in order before affixing the signature. Checks exceeding $10,000 in amount require dual signatures of Roberts and another company executive. Once a check is signed, the supporting documents are marked "paid" to prevent them being reused as support for another check. Signed checks are mailed out directly from the treasurer's department to vendors, rather than being returned to the controller's office. Another employee, who has neither cash handling nor customer bookkeeping responsibilities, reconciles Green Valley Coffee Company's monthly bank statement and reconciles the total checks written with the total amount of approved vendor invoices processed.

	A	B	C
	Green Valley Coffee Company		
	Balance Sheet (Partial, Adapted)		
1	**December 31, 2016**		
2	**Assets**		
3	Cash and cash equivalents		$ 6,000,000
4	Marketable securities		2,000,000
5	Accounts receivable		8,000,000
6	Inventories		36,200,000
7	Prepaid expenses		1,400,000
8	Investments (long-term)		10,000,000
9	Equipment and facilities (net of accumulated depreciation of $2,400)		13,170,000
10	Other assets		3,930,000
11	Total assets		$80,700,000
12			

Creating false vendors is a type of fraud known as "misappropriation of assets." Although it doesn't take a genius to accomplish, it requires some *motivation* and is usually *rationalized* by distorted and unethical thinking. The *opportunity* to commit this type and other types of fraud arises through a weak internal control system. In this case, Johnson's access to Roberts's electronic signature as well as access to the accounting records such as accounts payable, along with Roberts's failure to monitor Johnson's activities, proved to be the deadly combination that provided the opportunity for fraud.

This chapter begins with a discussion of fraud, its types, and common characteristics. We then discuss internal controls, which are the primary means by which fraud, as well as unintentional financial statement errors, are prevented. We also discuss how to account for cash. These three topics—fraud, internal control, and cash—go together. Internal controls help prevent fraud. Cash is the asset that is most often misappropriated through fraud.

LEARNING OBJECTIVES

1 **Describe** fraud and its impact

2 **Explain** the objectives and components of internal control

3 **Design** and **use** a bank reconciliation

4 **Evaluate** internal controls over cash receipts and cash payments

5 **Construct** and **use** a cash budget

6 **Report** cash on the balance sheet

DESCRIBE FRAUD AND ITS IMPACT

1 **Describe** fraud and its impact

Fraud is an intentional misrepresentation of facts, made for the purpose of persuading another party to act in a way that causes injury or damage to that party. Fraud is a huge problem and is getting bigger, not only in the United States but across the globe. In its 2014 survey titled *Report to the Nations on Occupational Fraud and Abuse*,[1] the Association for Certified Fraud Examiners (ACFE) revealed:

- A typical organization loses 5% of its revenue each year to fraud. Applied to the 2011 gross world product, this translates to a projected annual fraud loss of over $3.7 trillion. In the United States alone, this amounts to about $4,500 per employee.
- The median loss in occupational fraud cases is $145,000; these tended to be cases involving employee theft.
- Of reported fraud cases, 22% percent caused losses of at least $1 million; these larger cases tended to involve misleading financial statements.
- Occupational fraud is a significant risk for small business.
- Industries most commonly victimized by fraudsters include banking and financial services, government and public administration, and manufacturing.
- The longer a perpetrator has worked for an organization, the higher the fraud losses tend to be.
- The majority (77%) of reported frauds are perpetrated by employees in one of six departments: accounting, operations, sales, executive/upper management, customer service, and purchasing.
- Most occupational fraudsters are one-time offenders with clean employment histories.
- In most reported cases, fraudsters exhibit one or more behavioral red flags, including (a) living beyond one's means; (b) financial difficulties; and (c) unusually close associations with vendors or customers.

Fraud has exploded with the expansion of e-commerce via the Internet. In addition, studies have shown that the percentage of losses related to fraud from transactions originating in "third-world" or developing countries via the Internet is even higher than in economically-developed countries.

What are the most common types of fraud? What causes fraud? What can be done to prevent it?

---

[1]Association for Certified Fraud Examiners. *Report to the Nations on Occupational Fraud and Abuse.* Austin, TX: ACFE, 2014. http://www.acfe.com/rttn/docs/2014-report-to-nations.pdf.

There are many types of fraud. Some of the most common types are insurance fraud, check forgery, Medicare fraud, credit card fraud, and identity theft. The two most common types of fraud that impact financial statements are the following:

- **Misappropriation of assets** *This type of fraud is committed by employees of an entity who steal money from the company and cover it up* through erroneous entries in the books. The Green Valley Coffee Company case is an example. Other examples of asset misappropriation include employee theft of inventory, bribery or kickback schemes in the purchasing function, or employee overstatement of expense reimbursement requests.

- **Fraudulent financial reporting** *This type of fraud is committed by company managers who make false and misleading entries in the books*, making financial results of the company appear to be better than they actually are. The purpose of this type of fraud is to deceive investors and creditors into investing or loaning money to the company that they might not otherwise have invested or loaned.

Both of these types of fraud involve making false or misleading entries in the books of the company. We call this *cooking the books*. Of these two types, asset misappropriation is the most common, but fraudulent financial reporting is by far the most expensive. Perhaps the two most notorious cases in recent history involving fraudulent financial reporting in the United States involved **Enron Corporation** in 2001 and **WorldCom Inc.** in 2002. These two scandals alone rocked the U.S. economy and impacted financial markets across the world. Enron (discussed in Chapter 8) committed fraudulent financial reporting by overstating profits through bogus sales of nonexistent assets with inflated values. When Enron's banks found out, they stopped loaning the company money to operate, causing it to go out of business almost overnight. WorldCom (discussed in Chapter 7) reported expenses as plant assets and overstated both profits and assets. The company's internal auditor blew the whistle on WorldCom, resulting in the company's eventual collapse. Sadly, the same international accounting firm, Arthur Andersen, LLP, had audited both companies' financial statements. Because of these and other failed audits, the once mighty firm of Arthur Andersen was forced to close its doors in 2002.

Each of these frauds, and many others revealed about the same time, involved losses in billions of dollars and thousands of jobs when the companies went out of business. Widespread media coverage sparked adverse market reaction, loss of confidence in the financial reporting system, and losses through declines in stock values that ran in the trillions of dollars! We will discuss some of these cases throughout the remaining chapters of the text as examples of how accounting principles were deliberately misapplied through cooking the books in environments characterized by *weak internal controls*.

Exhibit 4-1 explains in graphic form the elements that make up virtually every fraud. We call it the **fraud triangle**.

Exhibit 4-1 | The Fraud Triangle

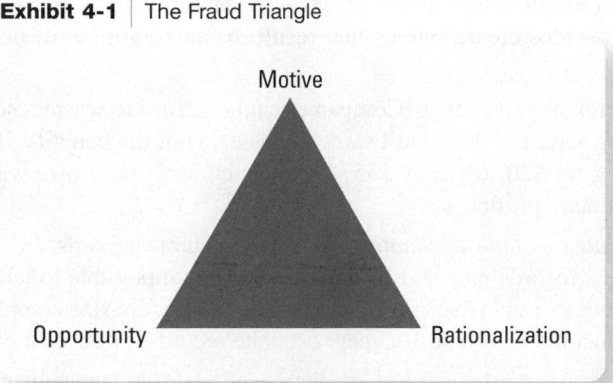

The first element in the fraud triangle is *motive*. This usually results from either critical need or greed on the part of the person who commits the fraud (the perpetrator). Sometimes it is a matter of just never having enough (because some persons who commit fraud are already rich by most people's standards). Other times the perpetrator of the fraud might have a legitimate financial need, such as a medical emergency, but he or she uses illegitimate means to meet that need. In any case, the prevailing attitude on the part of the perpetrator is, "I want it, and someone else has it, so I'm going to do whatever I have to do to get it."

The second element in the fraud triangle is *opportunity*. As in the case of Green Valley Coffee Company, the opportunity to commit fraud usually arises through weak internal controls. It might be a breakdown in a key element of controls, such as improper *segregation of duties* and/or *improper access to assets*. Or it might result from a weak *control environment*, such as a domineering CEO, a weak or conflicted board of directors, or lax ethical practices, allowing top management to override whatever controls the company has placed in operation for other transactions.

The third element in the triangle is *rationalization*. The perpetrator engages in distorted thinking, such as "I deserve this"; "Nobody treats me fairly"; "No one will ever know"; "Just this once, I won't let it happen again"; or "Everyone else is doing it."

Fraud and Ethics

As we pointed out in our decision model for making ethical accounting and business judgments introduced in Chapter 1, the decision to engage in fraud is an act with economic, legal, and ethical implications. The perpetrators of fraud usually do so for their own short-term *economic gain*, while others incur *economic losses* that may far outstrip the gains of the fraudsters. Moreover, fraud is defined by state, federal, and international law as *illegal*. Those who are caught and found guilty of fraud ultimately face penalties that include imprisonment, fines, and monetary damages. Finally, from an *ethical* standpoint, fraud violates the rights of many for the temporary betterment of a few and for the ultimate betterment of no one. At the end of the day, everyone loses! **Fraud is the ultimate unethical act in business!**

EXPLAIN THE OBJECTIVES AND COMPONENTS OF INTERNAL CONTROL

2 **Explain** the objectives and components of internal control

The primary way that fraud, as well as unintentional error, is prevented, detected, or corrected in an organization is through a proper system of internal control. **Internal control** is a plan of organization and a system of procedures implemented by company management and the board of directors designed to accomplish the following five objectives:

1. *Safeguard assets.* A company must safeguard its assets against waste, inefficiency, and fraud. As in the case of Green Valley Coffee Company, if management fails to safeguard assets such as cash or inventory, those assets will slip away.

2. *Encourage employees to follow company policies.* Everyone in an organization—managers and employees—needs to work toward the same goals. A proper system of controls provides clear policies that result in fair treatment of both customers and employees.

3. *Promote operational efficiency.* Companies cannot afford to waste resources. They work hard to make a sale, and they don't want to waste any of the benefits. If the company can buy something for $30, why pay $35? Effective controls minimize waste, which lowers costs and increases profits.

4. *Ensure accurate, reliable accounting records.* Accurate records are essential. Without proper controls, records may be unreliable, making it impossible to tell which part of the business is profitable and which part needs improvement. A business could be losing money on every product it sells—unless it keeps accurate records for the cost of its products.

5. *Comply with legal requirements.* Companies, like people, are subject to laws, such as those of regulatory agencies like the Securities and Exchange Commission (SEC); the IRS; and state, local, and international governing bodies. When companies disobey the law, they are subject to fines, or in extreme cases, their top executives may even go to prison. Effective internal controls help ensure compliance with the law and avoidance of legal difficulties.

How critical are internal controls? They're so important that the U.S. Congress has passed a law to require public companies—those that sell their stock to the public—to maintain a system of internal controls and to require that their auditors examine those controls and issue audit reports as to their reliability. Exhibit 4-2 is an excerpt from a typical public company's annual report expressing management's responsibility for its internal controls.

Exhibit 4-2 | Excerpt from Public Company Management Report on Internal Controls

> Management is responsible for establishing and maintaining adequate internal control over financial reporting. . . . The Company's internal control over financial reporting includes the maintenance of records that . . . accurately and fairly reflect the transactions and . . . assets of the Company . . . provide reasonable assurance that transactions are recorded as necessary to permit preparation of financial statements in accordance with generally accepted accounting principles, and that receipts and expenditures of the Company are being made only in accordance with authorizations of management and directors of the Company. . . .
>
> Under the supervision and with the participation of management, including our principal executive officer and principal financial officer, we conducted an evaluation of the effectiveness of our internal control over financial reporting. . . . Based on our evaluation . . . management concluded that our internal control over financial reporting was effective as of December 31, 2016.

The Sarbanes-Oxley Act (SOX)

To address public concerns about the quality of financial reporting and corporate governance over public companies, the United States Congress passed the Sarbanes-Oxley Act of 2002 (SOX). SOX revamped corporate governance in the United States and profoundly affected the way that accounting and auditing is done in public companies. Here are some of the SOX provisions:

1. Public companies must issue an internal control report, and the outside auditor must evaluate and report on the soundness of the company's internal controls.

2. A special body, the Public Company Accounting Oversight Board, has been created to oversee the audits of public companies.

3. An accounting firm may not both audit a public client and also provide certain consulting services for the same client.

4. Stiff penalties await violators—25 years in prison for securities fraud, 20 years for an executive making false sworn statements.

The former CEO of WorldCom was convicted of securities fraud and sentenced to 25 years in prison. The top executives of Enron were also sent to prison. You can see that a lack of internal controls and related matters can have serious consequences.

Exhibit 4-3 diagrams the shield that internal controls provide for an organization. Protected by this shield, which provides protection from fraud, waste, and inefficiency, companies can do business in a trustworthy manner that ensures public confidence—an extremely important element in maintaining the stability of financial markets around the world.

How does a business achieve good internal controls? The next section identifies the components of internal control.

Exhibit 4-3 | The Shield of Internal Controls

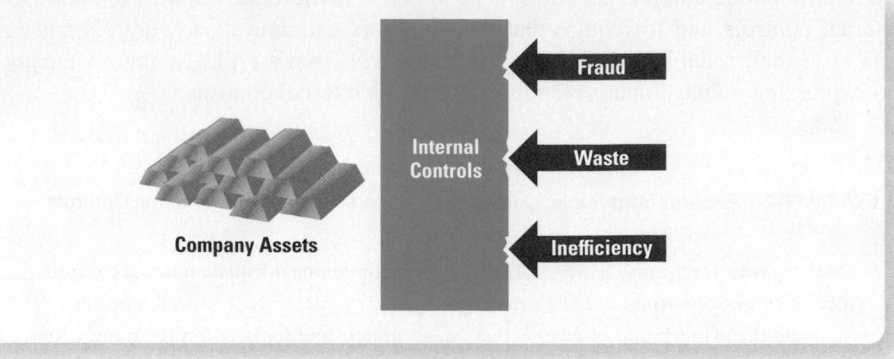

The Components of Internal Control

Internal control can be broken down into five components:

- Control environment
- Risk assessment
- Information system
- Control procedures
- Monitoring of controls

Exhibit 4-4 diagrams the components of internal control.

Exhibit 4-4 | The Components of Internal Control

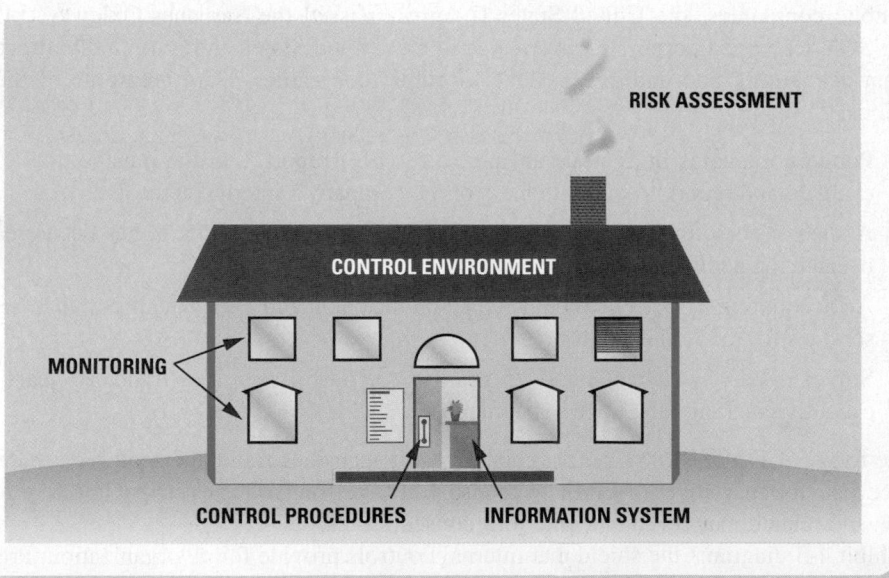

Control Environment. The control environment, symbolized by the roof over the building in Exhibit 4-4, is the "tone at the top" of the business. It starts with the owner and the top managers. They must behave honorably to set a good example for company employees. The owner must demonstrate the importance of internal controls if he or she expects employees to take the controls seriously. A key ingredient in the control environment of many companies is a corporate code of ethics, modeled by top management, which includes such provisions as prohibition against giving or taking bribes or kickbacks from customers or suppliers, prohibition of transactions that involve conflicts of interest, and provisions that encourage good citizenship and corporate social responsibility.

Risk Assessment. Symbolized by the smoke rising from the chimney, assessment of risks that a company faces offers hints of where mistakes or fraud might arise. A company must be able to identify its business risks, as well as to establish procedures for dealing with those risks to minimize their impacts on the company. For example, Kraft Foods faces the risk that its food products may harm people. Southwest Airlines' planes may crash. And all companies face the risk of bankruptcy. The managements of companies, supported by their boards, have to identify these risks and do what they can to prevent those risks from causing financial or other harm to the company, its employees, its owners, and its creditors.

Information System. Symbolized by the door of the building, the information system is the means by which accounting information enters and exits. The owner of a business needs accurate information to keep track of assets and measure profits and losses. Every system within the business that processes accounting data should have the ability to capture transactions as they occur, record (journalize) those transactions in an accurate and timely manner, summarize (post) those transactions in the books (ledgers), and report those transactions in the form of account balances or footnotes in the financial statements.

Control Procedures. Also symbolized by the door, control procedures built into the control environment and information system are the means by which companies gain access to the five objectives of internal controls discussed previously. Examples include proper separation of duties, comparison and other checks, adequate records, proper approvals, and physical safeguards to protect assets from theft. The next section discusses internal control procedures.

Monitoring of Controls. Symbolized by the windows of the building, monitoring provides "eyes and ears" so that no one person or group of persons can process a transaction completely without being seen and checked by another person or group. With modern computerized systems, much of the monitoring of day-to-day activity is done through controls programmed into a company's information technology. Computer programs dealing with such systems as cash receipts and cash disbursements can be automatically programmed to generate *exception reports* for transactions that exceed certain predefined guidelines (such as disbursements in excess of $15,000 in a payroll) for special management scrutiny. In addition, companies hire auditors to monitor their controls. Internal auditors monitor company controls from the inside to safeguard the company's assets, and external auditors test the controls from the outside to ensure that the accounting records are accurate and reliable. Audits are discussed more fully in the next section.

Internal Control Procedures

Whether the business is Green Valley Coffee Company, Microsoft, or a Disney Store, every major class of transactions needs to have the following *internal control procedures*.

Smart Hiring Practices and Separation of Duties. In a business with good internal controls, no important duty is overlooked. Each person in the information chain is important. The chain should start with hiring. Background checks should be conducted on job applicants. Proper training and supervision, as well as paying competitive salaries, helps ensure that all employees are sufficiently competent for their jobs. Employee responsibilities should be laid out clearly in position descriptions. For example, the **treasurer**'s department should be in charge of cash handling, as well as signing and approving checks. Warehouse personnel should be in charge of storing and keeping track of inventory. With clearly assigned responsibilities, all important jobs get done.

In processing transactions, smart management *separates three key duties: asset handling, record keeping, and transaction approval.* For example, in the case of Green Valley Coffee Company, separation of the duties of cash handling from record keeping for vendor accounts payable would have removed Joe Johnson's incentive to engage in fraud. It would have made it impossible for Joe to use company checks to pay his own bills if he had been denied access to signed company checks.

The accounting department should be completely separate from the operating departments, such as production and sales. What would happen if sales personnel who are compensated based on a percentage of the amount of sales they make approved the company's sales transactions to customers? Sales figures could be inflated and might not reflect the eventual amount collected from customers.

At all costs, accountants must not handle cash, and cash handlers must not have access to the accounting records. If one employee has both cash-handling and accounting duties, that person can steal cash and conceal the theft. This is what happened at Green Valley Coffee Company.

For companies that are *too small* to hire separate persons to do all of these functions, the key to good internal control is *getting the owner involved*, usually by approving all large transactions, making bank deposits, or reconciling the monthly bank account.

Comparisons and Compliance Monitoring. No person or department should be able to completely process a transaction from beginning to end without being cross-checked by another person or department. For example, one division of the treasurer's department should be responsible for signing checks. The **controller**'s department should be responsible for recording company purchases and payments to suppliers. A third and separate employee who reconciles the bank statement should compare canceled (paid) checks with supporting invoices and with payments recorded in the journal and payments posted to individual vendor accounts payable by the controller's department.

One of the most effective tools for monitoring compliance with management's policies is the use of **operating budgets** and **cash budgets**. A **budget** is a quantitative financial plan that helps control day-to-day management activities. Management may prepare these budgets on a yearly, quarterly, monthly, or more frequent basis. Operating budgets are budgets of future periods' net income. They are prepared by line item of the income statement. Cash budgets, discussed in depth later in this chapter, are budgets of future periods' cash receipts and cash disbursements. Often, these budgets are "rolling," being constantly updated by adding a time period a year away while dropping the time period that has just passed. Computer systems are programmed to prepare exception reports for data that are out of line with expectations. This data can include variances for each account from budgeted amounts. Department managers are required to explain the variances and to take corrective actions in their operating plans to keep the budgets in line with expectations. This is an example of the use of **exception reporting**.

To validate the accounting records and monitor compliance with company policies, most companies have an audit. An **audit** is an examination of the company's financial statements and its accounting system, including its controls.

Audits can be internal or external. *Internal auditors* are employees of the business. They ensure that employees are following company policies and that operations are running efficiently. Internal auditors also determine whether the company is following legal requirements.

External auditors are completely independent of the business. They are hired to determine whether or not the company's financial statements are in compliance with generally accepted accounting principles. Auditors examine the client's financial statements and the underlying transactions in order to form a professional opinion on the accuracy and reliability of the company's financial statements.

Adequate Records. *Accounting records* provide the details of business transactions. The general rule is that all major groups of transactions should be supported by either hard copy documents or electronic records. Examples of documents include sales invoices, shipping records, customer remittance advices, purchase orders, vendor invoices, receiving reports, and canceled (paid) checks. Documents should be prenumbered to ensure completeness of processing and proper transaction cutoff and to prevent theft and inefficiency. A gap in the numbered document sequence draws attention to the possibility that transactions might have been omitted from processing.

Limited Access. To complement segregation of duties, company policy should limit access to assets only to those persons or departments that have custodial responsibilities. For example, access to cash should be limited to persons in the treasurer's department. The supply of unused checks should be kept under lock and key. Cash receipts might be processed through a lock-box system. Access to inventory should be limited to persons in the company warehouse where inventories are stored or to persons in the shipping and receiving functions. Likewise, the company should limit access to records to those persons who have record-keeping responsibilities. All manual records of the business should be protected by lock and key, and electronic records including the electronic signature of the check signer should be limited only to authorized persons and should be protected by passwords. Individual computers in the business should be protected by user identification and password. Electronic data files should be encrypted (processed through a special code) to prevent their recognition if accessed by a "hacker" or other unauthorized person.

Proper Approvals. No transaction should be processed without management's general or specific approval. The bigger the transaction, the more specific approval it should have. For individual small transactions, management might delegate approval to a specific department, such as in the following examples:

- Sales to customers on account should all be approved by a separate *credit department* that reviews all customers for creditworthiness before goods are shipped to customers on credit. This helps ensure that the company doesn't make sales to customers who cannot afford to pay their bills.
- Purchases of all items on credit should be approved by a separate *purchasing department* that specializes in that function. Among other things, a purchasing department should only buy from approved vendors, on the basis of competitive bids, to ensure that the company gets the highest quality products for the most competitive prices.
- All personnel decisions, including hiring, firing, and pay adjustments, should be handled by a separate *human resources (HR) department* that specializes in personnel-related matters.

Very large (material) transactions should generally be approved by top management and may even go to the board of directors.

What's an easy way to remember the basic control procedures for any class of transactions? Look at the first letters of each of the headings in this section:

Smart hiring practices and **S**eparation of duties

Comparisons and compliance monitoring

Adequate records

Limited access to both assets and records

Proper approvals (either general or specific) for each class of transaction

So, if you can remember SCALP and how to apply each of these attributes, you can have great controls in your business!

Information Technology

Accounting systems are relying less on manual procedures and more on information technology (IT) than ever before for record keeping, asset handling, approval, and monitoring, as well as for physically safeguarding the assets. For example, retailers such as Target Stores and Macy's control inventory by attaching an *electronic sensor* to merchandise. The cashier must remove the sensor before the customer can walk out of the store. If a customer tries to leave the store with the sensor attached, an alarm sounds. According to Checkpoint Systems, these devices reduce theft by as much as 50%. *Bar codes* speed checkout at retail stores, performing multiple operations in a single step. When the sales associate scans the merchandise at the register, the computer records the sale, removes the item from inventory, and computes the amount of cash to be tendered.

When a company employs sophisticated IT, the basic attributes of internal control (SCALP) do not change, but the procedures by which these attributes are implemented change substantially. For example, segregation of duties is often accomplished by separating mainframe computer departments from other user departments (i.e., controller, sales, purchasing, receiving, credit, HR, and treasurer) and restricting access to the IT department to only authorized personnel. Within the computer department, programmers should be

David R. Frazier Photolibrary, Inc/Science Source

separated from computer operators and data librarians. Access to sensitive data files is protected by **password** and data encryption. Electronic records must be saved routinely, or they might be written over or erased. Comparisons of data (such as cash receipts with total credits to customer accounts) that might otherwise be done by hand are performed by the computer. Computers can monitor inventory levels by item, generating a purchase order for inventory when it reaches a certain level.

The use of computers has the advantage of speed and accuracy (when programmed correctly). However, a computer that is *not* programmed correctly can corrupt *all* the data, making it unusable. It is therefore important to hire experienced and competent people to run the IT department, to restrict access to sensitive data (and the IT department) to only authorized personnel, to check data entered into and retrieved from the computer for accuracy and completeness, and to test and retest programs on a regular basis to ensure data integrity and accuracy.

Safeguard Controls

Businesses keep important documents in *fireproof vaults*. *Burglar alarms* safeguard buildings, and *security cameras* safeguard other property. *Loss-prevention specialists* train employees to spot suspicious activity.

Employees who handle cash are in a tempting position. Many businesses purchase **fidelity bonds** on cashiers. The bond is an insurance policy that reimburses the company for any losses due to employee theft. Before issuing a fidelity bond, the insurance company investigates the employee's background.

Mandatory vacations and *job rotation* improve internal control. Companies move employees from job to job. This improves morale by giving employees a broad view of the business. Also, knowing someone else will do your job next month keeps you honest.

Internal Controls for E-Commerce

E-commerce creates its own risks. Hackers may gain access to confidential information such as account numbers and passwords. E-commerce pitfalls include

- stolen credit card numbers,
- computer viruses and Trojan Horses, and
- phishing expeditions.

Stolen Credit Card Numbers. Suppose you buy CDs from emusic.com. To make the purchase, your credit card number must travel through cyberspace. Wireless networks (Wi-Fi) are creating new security hazards.

Amateur hacker Carlos Salgado, Jr., used his home computer to steal 100,000 credit card numbers with a combined limit exceeding $1 billion. Salgado was caught when he tried to sell the numbers to an undercover FBI agent.

Computer Viruses and Trojan Horses. A **computer virus** is a malicious program that enters program code without consent and performs destructive actions in the victim's computer files or programs. A **Trojan horse** is a malicious computer program that hides inside a legitimate program and works like a virus. Viruses can destroy or alter data, make bogus calculations, and infect files. Most firms have found a virus in their system at some point.

Suppose the U.S. Department of Defense takes bids for a missile system. Raytheon and Lockheed-Martin are competing for the contract. A hacker infects Raytheon's system and alters Raytheon's design. The government would label the Raytheon design as flawed and award the contract to Lockheed. The success of a business can be seriously affected by technological fraud.

Phishing Expeditions. Thieves **phish** by creating bogus websites, such as AOL4Free.com and AmericaBank.com. The almost-authentic-sounding website attracts lots of visitors, and the thieves obtain account numbers and passwords from unsuspecting people. The thieves then use the data for illicit purposes.

Security Measures

To address the risks posed by e-commerce, companies have devised a number of security measures, including

- encryption and
- firewalls.

Encryption. The server holding confidential information may not be secure. One technique for protecting customer data is encryption. **Encryption** rearranges messages by a mathematical process. The encrypted message can't be read by those who don't know the code. An accounting example uses check-sum digits for account numbers. Each account number has its last digit equal to the sum of the previous digits. For example, consider Customer Number 2237, where $2 + 2 + 3 = 7$. Any account number that fails this test triggers an error message.

Firewalls. **Firewalls** limit access into a local network. Members can access the network but nonmembers can't. Usually, several firewalls are built into the system. Think of a fortress with multiple walls protecting the company's computerized records in the center. At the point of entry, passwords, personal identification numbers (PINs), and signatures are used. More sophisticated firewalls are placed deeper in the network. Start with Firewall 1 and work toward the center.

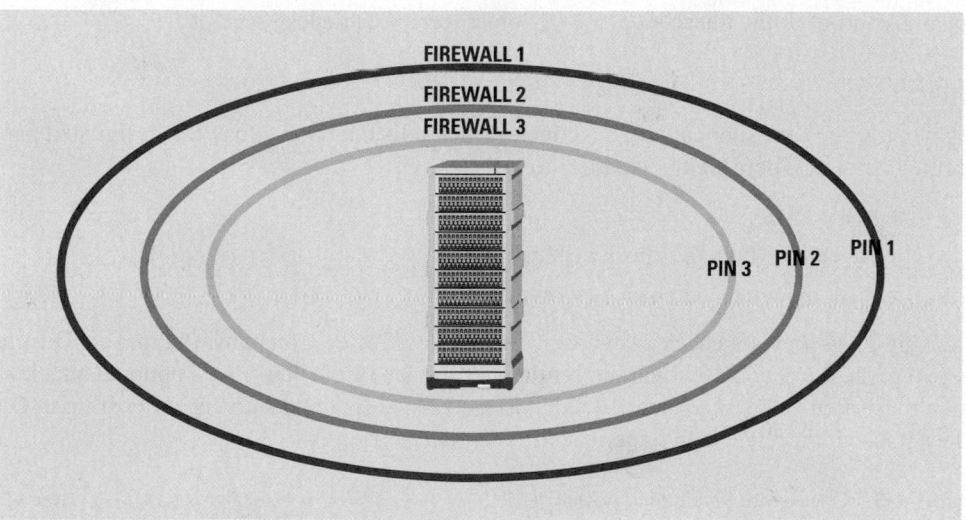

The Limitations of Internal Control—Costs and Benefits

Unfortunately, most internal controls can be circumvented. Collusion—two or more people working together—can beat internal controls. Consider Green Valley Coffee Company's situation. Even if Roberts were to hire a new person to approve cash payments, if that person had a relationship with Johnson and they conspired with each other, they could design a scheme identical to the one Johnson designed, and split the takings. Other ways to circumvent a good system of internal controls include management override, human limitations such as fatigue and negligence, and gradual deterioration over time due to neglect. Because of the cost/benefit principle, discussed in the next paragraph, internal controls are not generally designed to detect these types of breakdowns. The best a company can do in this regard is to exercise care in hiring honest people who have no conflicts of interest with existing employees and to exercise constant diligence in monitoring the system to ensure it continues to work properly.

The stricter the internal control system, the more it costs. An overly complex system of internal control can strangle the business with red tape. How tight should the controls be? Internal controls must be judged in light of their costs and benefits. Here is an example of a good cost/benefit relationship: A part-time security guard at a **Walmart** store costs about $28,000 a year. On average, each part-time guard prevents about $50,000 of theft. The net savings to Walmart is $22,000. Most people would say the extra guard is well worth the cost!

3 **Design** and **use** a bank reconciliation

DESIGN AND USE A BANK RECONCILIATION

Cash is the most liquid asset because it's the medium of exchange. Cash is easy to conceal and relatively easy to steal. As a result, most businesses create specific controls for cash.

Keeping cash in a bank account helps control cash because banks have established practices for safeguarding customers' money. The documents used to control a bank account include

- a signature card,
- a deposit ticket,
- a check,
- a bank statement, and
- a bank reconciliation.

Signature Card

Banks require each person authorized to sign on an account to provide a *signature card*. This protects against forgery.

Deposit Ticket

Banks supply standard forms such as *deposit tickets*. The customer fills in the amount of each deposit. As proof of the transaction, the customer receives a deposit receipt.

Check

To pay cash, the depositor can write a **check**, which tells the bank to pay the designated party a specified amount. There are three parties to a check:

- The maker, who signs the check
- The payee, to whom the check is paid
- The bank on which the check is drawn

Exhibit 4-5 shows a check drawn by Green Valley Coffee Company, the maker. The check has two parts, the check itself and the **remittance advice** (see below). This optional attachment, which may often be scanned electronically, is used as the source document for posting to Green Valley's account receivable in Superior Office Products' records.

Exhibit 4-5 | Check with Remittance Advice

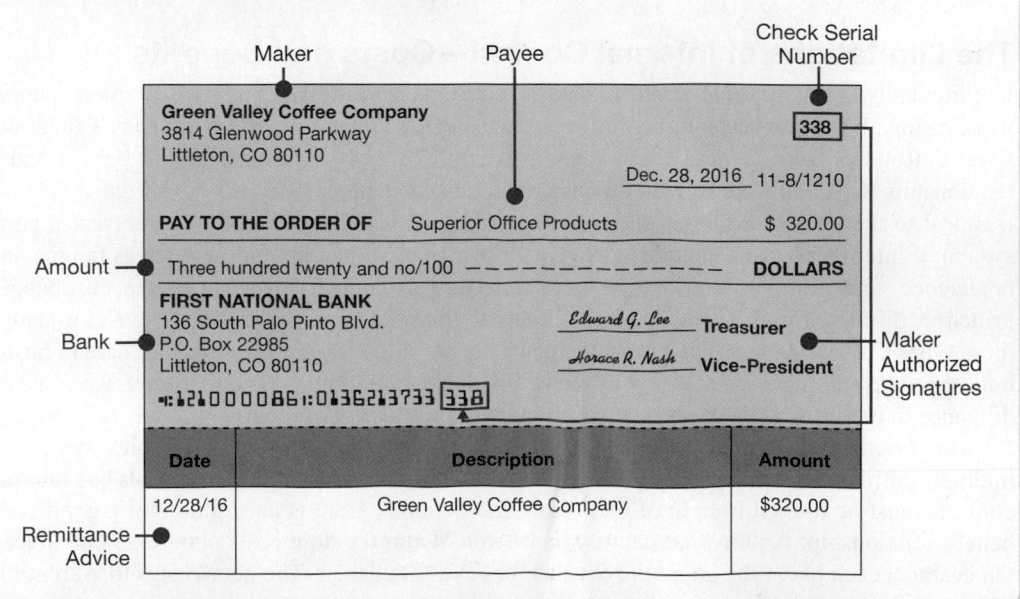

Bank Statement

Banks send monthly statements to customers. A **bank statement** reports what the bank did with the customer's cash. The statement shows the account's beginning and ending balances, cash receipts, and payments. Included with the statement is a list, and often visual images, of the maker's *canceled checks* (or the actual paid checks). Most companies have multiple bank accounts in different banks. Exhibit 4-6 is the December bank statement for one of the smaller bank accounts of the Green Valley Coffee Company at the First National Bank.

Electronic funds transfer (EFT) moves cash by electronic communication. It is cheaper to pay without having to mail a check, so many businesses and individuals pay their mortgages, rent, utilities, and insurance by EFT.

Exhibit 4-6 | Bank Statement

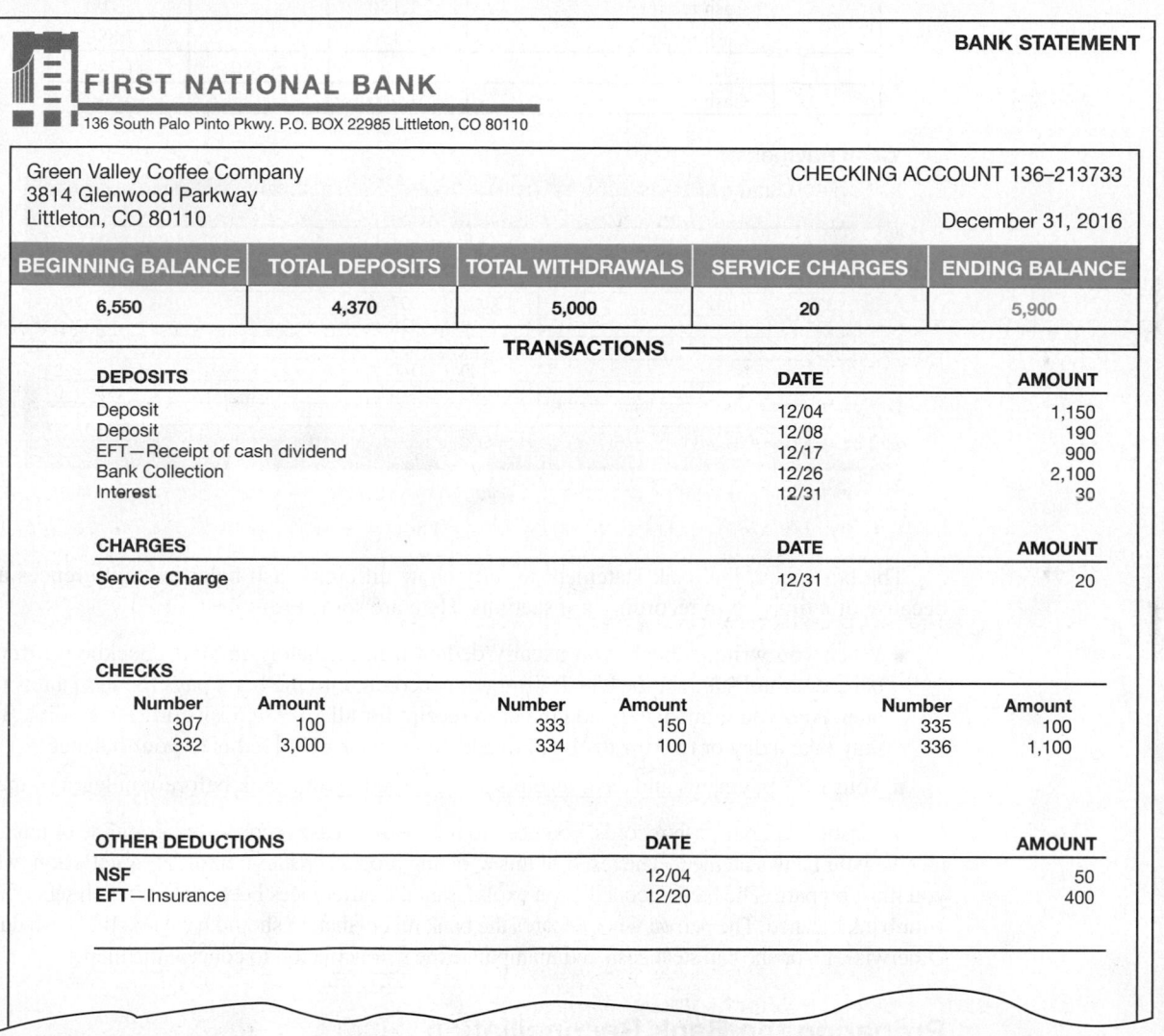

BANK STATEMENT

FIRST NATIONAL BANK
136 South Palo Pinto Pkwy. P.O. BOX 22985 Littleton, CO 80110

Green Valley Coffee Company
3814 Glenwood Parkway
Littleton, CO 80110

CHECKING ACCOUNT 136–213733

December 31, 2016

BEGINNING BALANCE	TOTAL DEPOSITS	TOTAL WITHDRAWALS	SERVICE CHARGES	ENDING BALANCE
6,550	4,370	5,000	20	5,900

TRANSACTIONS

DEPOSITS	DATE	AMOUNT
Deposit	12/04	1,150
Deposit	12/08	190
EFT—Receipt of cash dividend	12/17	900
Bank Collection	12/26	2,100
Interest	12/31	30

CHARGES	DATE	AMOUNT
Service Charge	12/31	20

CHECKS

Number	Amount	Number	Amount	Number	Amount
307	100	333	150	335	100
332	3,000	334	100	336	1,100

OTHER DEDUCTIONS	DATE	AMOUNT
NSF	12/04	50
EFT—Insurance	12/20	400

Bank Reconciliation

There are two records of a business's cash:

1. The Cash account in the company's general ledger. Exhibit 4-7 shows that Green Valley Coffee Company's ending cash balance in the checking account at First National Bank is $3,340.

2. The bank statement for the same checking account, which shows the cash receipts and payments transacted through this account at the bank. In Exhibit 4-6, the bank shows an ending balance of $5,900 for this account of Green Valley Coffee Company.

Exhibit 4-7 | Cash Records of Green Valley Coffee Company

General Ledger:

ACCOUNT Cash: Checking Account First National Bank				
Date	Item	Debit	Credit	Balance
2016				
Dec 1	Balance			6,550
2	Cash receipt	1,150		7,700
7	Cash receipt	190		7,890
31	Cash payments		6,150	1,740
31	Cash receipt	1,600		3,340

Cash Payments:

	A1				
	A	**B**	**C**		**D**
1	Check No.	Amount	Check No.		Amount
2	332	$3,000	337		$ 280
3	333	510*	338		320
4	334	100	339		250
5	335	100	340		490
6	336	1,100	Total		$6,150
7					

*Correct amount of check #333 is $150. See bank reconciliation in Exhibit 4-8 for correction.

The books and the bank statement usually show different cash balances. Differences arise because of a time lag in recording transactions. Here are some examples:

- When you write a check, you usually deduct it immediately in your checkbook. But the bank does not subtract the check from your account until the bank pays the item a few days later. And you immediately add the cash receipt for all your deposits or EFT credits. But it may take a day or two for the bank to add deposits or EFT credits to your balance.

- Your EFT payments and cash receipts are recorded by the bank before you learn of them.

To ensure accurate cash records, you need to update your cash record—either online or after you receive your bank statement. The result of this updating process creates a **bank reconciliation**, which you must prepare. The bank reconciliation explains all the differences between your cash records and your bank balance. The person who prepares the bank reconciliation should have no other cash duties. Otherwise, he or she can steal cash and manipulate the reconciliation to conceal the theft.

Preparing the Bank Reconciliation

Panel B of Exhibit 4-8 illustrates a typical bank reconciliation. It lists items that account for differences between the bank balance and the book balance. We call the cash record (also known as a "checkbook") the "Books."

Bank Side of the Reconciliation

1. Items to show on the Bank side of the bank reconciliation include the following:

    a. **Deposits in transit** (outstanding deposits). You have recorded these deposits, but the bank has not. Add deposits in transit on the bank reconciliation.

b. **Outstanding checks**. You have recorded these checks, but the bank has not yet paid them. Subtract outstanding checks.

c. **Bank errors**. Correct all bank errors on the Bank side of the reconciliation. For example, the bank may erroneously subtract from your account a check written by someone else.

Book Side of the Reconciliation

1. Items to show on the Book side of the bank reconciliation include the following:

    a. **Bank collections**. Bank collections are cash receipts that the bank has recorded for your account, but you haven't recorded the cash receipt yet. Many businesses have their customers send payments to a post office box belonging to their bank. This is called a **lock-box system** and it reduces theft. An example is a bank collecting an account receivable for you. Add bank collections on the bank reconciliation.

    b. **Electronic funds transfers**. The bank may receive or pay cash on your behalf. An EFT may be a cash receipt or a cash payment. Add EFT receipts and subtract EFT payments.

    c. **Service charge**. This cash payment is the bank's fee for processing your transactions. Subtract service charges.

    d. **Interest revenue on your checking account**. On certain types of bank accounts, you earn interest if you keep enough cash in your account. The bank statement tells you of this cash receipt. Add interest revenue.

    e. **Nonsufficient funds (NSF) checks**. These are cash receipts from customers for which there are not sufficient funds in the bank to cover the amount. NSF checks (sometimes called hot checks) are treated as cash payments on your bank reconciliation. Subtract NSF checks.

    f. **The cost of printed checks**. This cash payment is handled like a service charge. Subtract this cost.

    g. **Book errors**. Correct all book errors on the Book side of the reconciliation. For example, you may have recorded a $150 check that you wrote as $510.

Bank Reconciliation Illustrated. The bank statement in Exhibit 4-6 shows that the December 31 bank balance of Green Valley Coffee Company's checking account at First National Bank is $5,900 (upper right corner). However, the company's record of this account shows a balance of $3,340, as shown in Exhibit 4-7. This situation calls for a bank reconciliation. Exhibit 4-8, Panel A, lists the reconciling items for easy reference, and Panel B shows the completed reconciliation.

Exhibit 4-8 | Bank Reconciliation

PANEL A—Reconciling Items

Bank side:

1. Deposit in transit, $1,600.
2. Bank error: The bank deducted $100 for a check written by another company. Add $100 to the bank balance.
3. Outstanding checks—total of $1,340.

Book side:

4. EFT receipt of your dividend revenue earned on an investment, $900.
5. Bank collection of your account receivable, $2,100.
6. Interest revenue earned on your bank balance, $30.
7. Book error: You recorded check no. 333 for $510. The amount you actually paid on account was $150. Add $360 to your book balance.
8. Bank service charge, $20.
9. NSF check from a customer, $50. Subtract $50 from your book balance.
10. EFT payment of insurance expense, $400.

	A	⬍		
	A		**B**	
1	**Check No.**		**Amount**	
2	337		$280	
3	338		320	
4	339		250	
5	340		490	
6				

PANEL B—Bank Reconciliation

	A	B	C	D	E	F
1	**Green Valley Coffee Company Bank Reconciliation: First National Bank Checking Account December 31, 2016**					
2	**Bank**			**Books**		
3	**Balance, December 31**		$ 5,900	**Balance, December 31**		$ 3,340
4	Add:			Add:		
5	1. Deposit in transit		1,600	4. EFT receipt of dividend revenue		900
6	2. Correction of bank error		100	5. Bank collection of account		
7			7,600	receivable		2,100
8				6. Interest revenue earned on		
9				bank balance		30
10				7. Correction of book error—		
11				overstated our check no. 333		360
12	Less:					6,730
13	3. Outstanding checks					
14	No. 337	$280		Less:		
15	No. 338	320		8. Service charge	$ 20	
16	No. 339	250		9. NSF check	50	
17	No. 340	490	(1,340)	10. EFT payment of insurance expense	400	(470)
18	**Adjusted bank balance**		$ 6,260	**Adjusted book balance**		$ 6,260
19						

These amounts should agree.

SUMMARY OF THE VARIOUS RECONCILING ITEMS:

BANK BALANCE—ALWAYS

- *Add* deposits in transit.
- *Subtract* outstanding checks.
- *Add* or *subtract* corrections of bank errors.

BOOK BALANCE—ALWAYS

- *Add* bank collections, interest revenue, and EFT receipts.
- *Subtract* service charges, NSF checks, and EFT payments.
- *Add* or *subtract* corrections of book errors.

Journalizing Transactions from the Bank Reconciliation. The bank reconciliation is an accountant's tool separate from the journals and ledgers. It does *not* account for transactions in the journal. To get the transactions into the accounts, we must make journal entries and post to the ledger. All items on the Book side of the bank reconciliation require journal entries.

The bank reconciliation in Exhibit 4-8 requires Green Valley Coffee Company to make journal entries to bring the Cash account up-to-date. The numbers in red correspond to the reconciling items listed in Exhibit 4-8, Panel A.

	A1	⬦			
	A	**B**	**C**	**D**	**E**
1	4.	Dec 31	Cash	900	
2			Dividend Revenue		900
3			*Receipt of dividend revenue earned on investment.*		
4					
5	5.	31	Cash	2,100	
6			Accounts Receivable		2,100
7			*Account receivable collected by bank.*		
8					
9	6.	31	Cash	30	
10			Interest Revenue		30
11			*Interest earned on bank balance.*		
12					
13	7.	31	Cash	360	
14			Accounts Payable		360
15			*Correction of check no. 333.*		
16					
17	8.	31	Miscellaneous Expense[1]	20	
18			Cash		20
19			*Bank service charge.*		
20					
21	9.	31	Accounts Receivable	50	
22			Cash		50
23			*NSF check returned by bank.*		
24					
25	10.	31	Insurance Expense	400	
26			Cash		400
27			*Payment of monthly insurance.*		
28					

[1]Miscellaneous Expense is debited for the bank service charge because the service charge pertains to no particular expense category.

The entry for the NSF check (entry 9) requires explanation. Upon learning that a customer's $50 check was not good, Cash must be credited to update the Cash account. Unfortunately, there is still a receivable from the customer, so Accounts Receivable must be debited to reinstate the receivable.

Online Banking

Online banking allows you to pay bills and view your account electronically. You don't have to wait until the end of the month to get a bank statement. With online banking, you can reconcile transactions at any time and keep your account current whenever you wish. Exhibit 4-9 shows a page from the account history of Toni Anderson's bank account.

The account history—like a bank statement—lists deposits, checks, EFT payments, ATM withdrawals, and interest earned on your bank balance. It also often lists the running balance in the account (the updated balance after each addition and subtraction).

Exhibit 4-9 | Online Banking—Account History

Account History for Toni Anderson Checking # 5401-632-9
as of Close of Business 07/27/2016

Account Details

Current Balance $4,136.08

Date ↓	Description	Withdrawals	Deposits	Balance
	Current Balance			$4,136.08
07/27/16	DEPOSIT		1,170.35	
07/26/16	28 DAYS INTEREST		2.26	
07/25/16	Check #6131 View Image	443.83		
07/24/16	Check #6130 View Image	401.52		
07/23/16	EFT PYMT CINGULAR	61.15		
07/22/16	EFT PYMT CITICARD PAYMENT	3,172.85		
07/20/16	Debit card payment, Anthropologie Stores	550.00		
07/19/16	Debit card payment, CEPCO Convenience Stores	50.00		
07/16/16	Debit card payment, Haverty's Furniture Stores	2,056.75		
07/15/16	Debit card payment, Dillard's Department Stores	830.00		
07/13/16	Debit card payment, HEB Stores	150.00		
07/11/16	ATM 4900 SANGER AVE	200.00		
07/09/16	Debit card payment, CEPCO Convenience Stores	30.00		
07/05/16	Debit card payment, Warren University	2,500.00		
07/04/16	ATM 4900 SANGER AVE	100.00		
07/01/16	DEPOSIT		9,026.37	
07/01/16	Beginning Balance			$4,483.20

FDIC
FEDERAL DEPOSIT INSURANCE CORPORATION
EQUAL HOUSING LENDER

▢ E-Mail

Try It

The bank statement balance is $4,500 and shows a service charge of $15, interest earned of $5, and an NSF check for $300. Deposits in transit total $1,200; outstanding checks are $575. The bookkeeper recorded as $152 a check of $125 in payment of an account payable. This created a book error of $27 (positive amount to correct the error).

(1) What is the adjusted bank balance?

(2) What was the book balance of cash before the reconciliation?

Answers:

(1) $5,125 ($4,500 + $1,200 − $575).

(2) $5,408 ($5,125 + $15 − $5 + $300 − $27). The adjusted book and bank balances are the same. The answer can be determined by working backward from the adjusted balance.

Using the Bank Reconciliation to Control Cash. The bank reconciliation can be a powerful control device. Tim Bosworth is a certified public accountant (CPA) in New Orleans, Louisiana. He owns several apartment complexes that are managed by his aunt. His aunt signs up tenants, collects the monthly rents, arranges maintenance work, hires and fires employees, writes the checks, and performs the bank reconciliation. In short, she does it all. This concentration of duties in one person is evidence of weak internal control. Bosworth's aunt could be stealing from him and, as a CPA, he is aware of this possibility.

Bosworth trusts his aunt because she is a member of the family. Nevertheless, Bosworth exercises some controls over his aunt's management of his apartments. Bosworth periodically drops by the apartments to see whether the maintenance staff is keeping the property in good condition. To control cash, Bosworth occasionally examines the bank reconciliation that his aunt has performed. Bosworth would know immediately if his aunt were writing checks to herself. By examining the copy of each check, Bosworth establishes control over cash payments.

Bosworth has a simple method for controlling cash receipts. He knows the occupancy level of his apartments. He also knows the monthly rent he charges. Bosworth multiplies the number of apartments—say 20—by the monthly rent (which averages $500 per unit) to arrive at expected monthly rent revenue of $10,000. By tracing the $10,000 revenue to the bank statement, Bosworth can tell if all his rent money went into his bank account. To keep his aunt on her toes, Bosworth lets her know that he periodically audits her work.

Control activities such as these are critical. If there are only a few employees, separation of duties may not be feasible. The manager must control operations, or the assets will slip away.

Mid-Chapter | Summary Problem

The cash account of Ayers Associates at February 28, 2016, follows:

Cash

Feb 1	Bal 3,995	Feb 3		400
6	800	12		3,100
15	1,800	19		1,100
23	1,100	25		500
28	2,400	27		900
Feb 28	Bal 4,095			

Ayers Associates received the bank statement on February 28, 2016 (negative amounts are in parentheses):

	A1	A	B	C
1		**Bank Statement for February 2016**		
2		Beginning balance		$ 3,995
3		Deposits:		
4		Feb 7	$ 800	
5		15	1,800	
6		24	1,100	3,700
7		Checks (total per day):		
8		Feb 8	$ 400	
9		16	3,100	
10		23	1,100	(4,600)
11		Other items:		
12		Service charge		(10)
13		NSF check from M. E. Crown		(700)
14		Bank collection of note receivable for the company		1,000
15		EFT—monthly rent expense		(330)
16		Interest revenue earned on account balance		15
17		Ending balance		$ 3,070
18				

Additional data: Ayers deposits all cash receipts in the bank and makes all payments by check.

Requirements

1. Prepare the bank reconciliation of Ayers Associates at February 28, 2016.
2. Journalize the entries based on the bank reconciliation.

Answers
Requirement 1

	A	B	C
	Ayers Associates		
	Bank Reconciliation		
1	**February 28, 2016**		
2	**Bank:**		
3	Balance, February 28, 2016		$ 3,070
4	Add: Deposit of February 28 in transit		2,400
5			5,470
6			
7	Less: Outstanding checks issued on Feb 25 ($500)		
8	and Feb 27 ($900)		(1,400)
9	Adjusted bank balance, February 28, 2016		$ 4,070
10			
11	**Books:**		
12	Balance, February 28, 2016		$ 4,095
13	Add: Bank collection of note receivable		1,000
14	Interest revenue earned on bank balance		15
15			5,110
16	Less: Service charge	$ 10	
17	NSF check	700	
18	EFT—Rent expense	330	(1,040)
19	Adjusted book balance, February 28, 2016		$ 4,070
20			

equal

Requirement 2

	A	C	D	G
1	Feb 28	Cash	1,000	
2		Note Receivable		1,000
3		*Note receivable collected by bank.*		
4				
5	28	Cash	15	
6		Interest Revenue		15
7		*Interest earned on bank balance.*		
8				
9	28	Miscellaneous Expense	10	
10		Cash		10
11		*Bank service charge.*		
12				
13	28	Accounts Receivable–M.E. Crown	700	
14		Cash		700
15		*NSF check returned by bank.*		
16				
17	28	Rent Expense	330	
18		Cash		330
19		*Monthly rent expense.*		
20				

EVALUATE INTERNAL CONTROLS OVER CASH RECEIPTS AND CASH PAYMENTS

Cash requires some specific internal controls because it is relatively easy to steal and it is easy to convert to other forms of wealth. Moreover, all transactions ultimately affect cash. That's why cash is called the "eye of the needle." Let's see how to control cash receipts.

All cash receipts should be deposited for safekeeping in the bank—quickly. Companies receive cash over the counter and through the mail. Each source of cash has its own security measures.

4 Evaluate internal controls over cash receipts and cash payments

Cash Receipts over the Counter

Exhibit 4-10 illustrates the purchase of products in a grocery store. The point-of-sale terminal provides control over the cash receipts, while also recording the sale and reducing inventory for the appropriate cost of the goods sold. Consider a **Whole Foods Market** store. For each transaction, the Whole Foods sales associate issues a receipt to the customer as proof of purchase. The cash drawer opens when the sales associate enters a transaction, and the machine electronically transmits a record of the sale to the store's main computer. At the end of each shift, the sales associate delivers the cash drawer to the office, where it is combined with cash from all other terminals and delivered by armored car to the bank for deposit. Later, a separate employee in the accounting department reconciles the electronic record of the sales per terminal to the record of the cash turned in. These measures, coupled with oversight by a manager, discourage theft.

Exhibit 4-10 | Cash Receipts over the Counter

Photos.com/Getty Images

Point-of-sale terminals also provide effective control over inventory. For example, in a restaurant, these devices track sales by menu item and total sales by cash, type of credit card, gift card redeemed, etc. They create the daily sales journal for that store, which, in turn, interfaces with the general ledger. Managers can use records produced by point-of-sale terminals to check inventory levels and compare them against sales records for accuracy. For example, in a restaurant, an effective way to monitor sales of expensive wine is for a manager to perform a quick count of the bottles on hand at the end of the day and compare it with the count at the end of the previous day, plus the record of any purchased. The count at the end of the previous day, plus the record of bottles purchased, minus the count at the end of the current day should equal the amount sold as recorded by the point-of-sale terminals in the restaurant.

An effective control for many chain retail businesses, such as restaurants, grocery stores, or clothing stores, to prevent unauthorized access to cash as well as to allow for more efficient management of cash, is the use of "depository bank accounts." Cash receipts for an individual store are deposited into a local bank account (preferably delivered by armored car for security reasons) on a daily basis. The corporate headquarters arranges for its centralized bank to draft the local depository accounts on a frequent (perhaps daily) basis to get the money concentrated into the company's centralized account, where it can be used to pay the corporation's bills. Depository accounts are "one-way" accounts where the local management may only make deposits; local management has no authority to write checks on the account or take money out of the store's account.

Cash Receipts by Mail

Many companies receive cash by mail. Exhibit 4-11 shows how companies control cash received by mail. All incoming mail is opened by a mailroom employee. The mailroom then sends all customer checks to the treasurer, who has the cashier deposit the checks in the bank. The remittance advices go to the accounting department for journal entries to Cash and customer Accounts Receivable. As a final step, the controller compares the records for the day:

- Bank deposit amount from the treasurer
- Debit to Cash from the accounting department

The debit to Cash should equal the amount deposited in the bank. All cash receipts are safe in the bank, and the company books are up-to-date.

Exhibit 4-11 | Cash Receipts by Mail

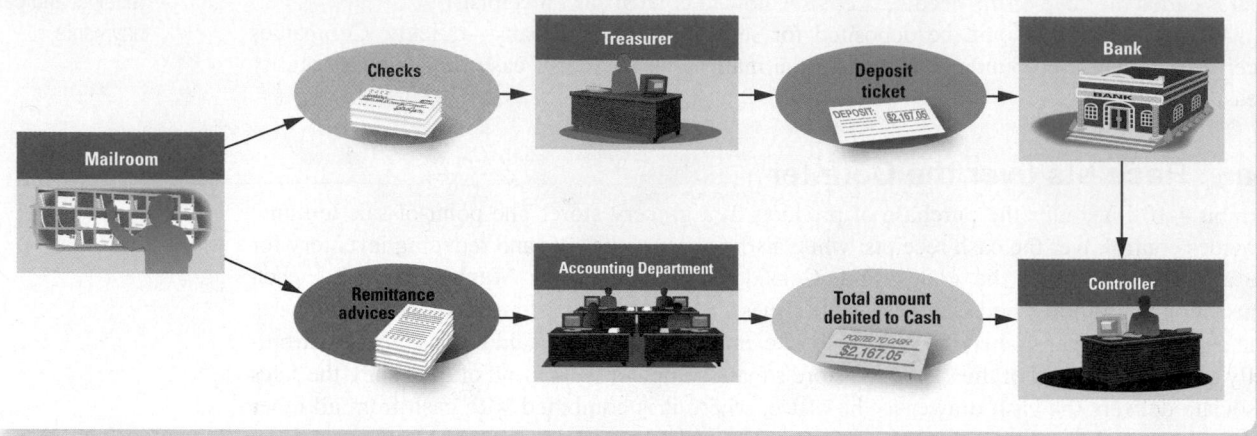

To prevent unauthorized access to cash, many companies use a bank lock-box system rather than risk processing checks through the mailroom. Customers send their checks by return mail directly to a post office box controlled by the company's bank. The bank sends a detailed record of cash received, by customer, to the company for use in posting collections to Accounts Receivable. Internal control is tight because company personnel never touch incoming cash. The lock-box system also gets the cash to the bank in a more timely manner, allowing the company to put the cash to work faster than would be possible if it were processed by the company's mailroom.

Controls over Payment by Check

Companies make most payments by check or EFT. As we have seen, a company needs good separation of duties between (a) operations and (b) writing checks or authorizing EFTs for cash payments. Payment by check or EFT is an important internal control, as follows:

- The check or EFT provides a record of the payment.
- The check must be signed by an authorized official. The EFT must be approved by an authorized official.
- Before signing the check or authorizing the EFT, the official should study the evidence supporting the payment.

Controls over Purchase and Payment.   To illustrate the internal control over cash payments by check, suppose Green Valley Coffee Company buys some of its flavoring syrup from Sysco Foods. The purchasing and payment process follows these steps, as shown in Exhibit 4-12. Start with the box for Green Valley Coffee Company on the left side.

1. Green Valley Coffee Company faxes or e-mails an electronic *purchase order* to Sysco Foods. Green Valley Coffee Company says, "Please send us 2,000 16-ounce bottles of syrup."

2. Sysco ships 2,000 bottles of syrup and sends an electronic or paper *invoice* back to Green Valley Coffee Company. Sysco sent the inventory.

3. Green Valley Coffee Company receives 2,000 16-ounce bottles of syrup (*inventory*) and prepares a *receiving report* to list the inventory received.

4. After making sure all documents agree and approving payment, Green Valley sends a *check* to Sysco or authorizes an EFT directly from its bank to Sysco's bank. By this action, Green Valley Coffee Company says, "Okay, we'll pay you."

Exhibit 4-12 | Cash Payments by Check or EFT

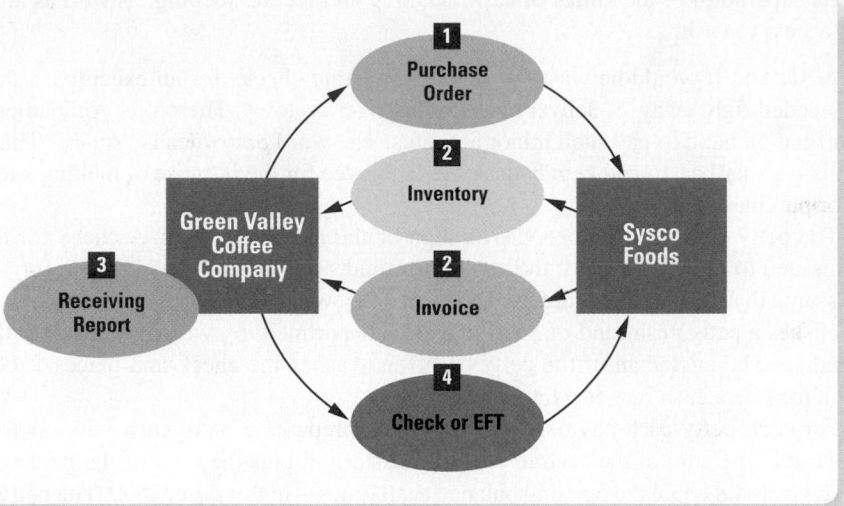

For good internal control, the purchasing agent should neither receive the goods nor approve the payment. If these duties aren't separated, a purchasing agent can buy goods and have them shipped to his or her home. Or a purchasing agent can spend too much on purchases, approve the payment, and split the excess with the supplier. To avoid these problems, companies split the following duties among different employees:

- Purchasing goods
- Receiving goods
- Preparing check or EFT for payment
- Approval of payment

Exhibit 4-13 shows Green Valley Coffee Company's payment packet of documents. Before signing the check or approving the EFT, the treasurer's department should examine the packet to prove that all the documents agree. Only then does the company know that

1. it received the goods ordered, and
2. it is paying only for the goods received.

Exhibit 4-13 | Payment Packet

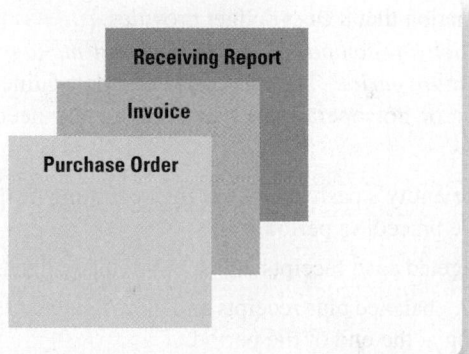

After payment, the person in the treasurer's department who has authorized the payment stamps the payment packet "paid" or punches a hole through it to prevent it from being submitted a second time. Dishonest people have tried to run a bill through twice for payment. The stamp or hole shows that the bill has been paid. If checks are used, they should then be mailed directly to the payee without being allowed to return to the department that prepared them. To do so would violate separation of the duties of cash handling and record keeping, as well as allow unauthorized access to cash.

Petty Cash. It would be wasteful to write separate checks for an executive's taxi fare, name tags needed right away, or delivery of a package across town. Therefore, companies keep a **petty cash** fund on hand to pay such minor amounts. The word *petty* means "small." That's what petty cash is—a small cash fund kept by a single employee for the purpose of making such on-the-spot minor purchases.

The petty cash fund is opened with a particular amount of cash. A check for that amount is then issued to the custodian of the petty cash fund, who is solely responsible for accounting for it. Assume that on February 28, **Cisco Systems**, the worldwide leader in networks for the Internet, establishes a petty cash fund of $500 in a sales department by writing a check to the designated custodian. The custodian of the petty cash fund cashes the check and places $500 in the fund, which may be a cash box or other device.

For each petty cash payment, the custodian prepares a petty cash voucher to list the item purchased. The sum of the cash in the petty cash fund plus the total of the paid vouchers in the cash box should equal the opening balance at all times—in this case, $500. The petty cash account keeps its $500 balance at all times. Maintaining the petty cash account at this balance, supported by the fund (cash plus vouchers), is how an **imprest system** works. The control feature is that it clearly identifies the amount for which the custodian is responsible.

In recent years, banks have instituted the practice of *debit cards*, which are used to make cash purchases of relatively small amounts. A company employee who needs to make a small purchase may obtain permission from a supervisor to use a company debit card. Supervisors require receipts for all such purchases and compare them with EFT amounts on the bank statement. Debit cards are taking the place of petty cash systems in many companies.

CONSTRUCT AND USE A CASH BUDGET

5 **Construct** and **use** a cash budget

As mentioned earlier in the chapter, a budget is a financial plan that helps coordinate business activities. Managers control operations with an operating budget. They also control cash receipts and cash payments, as well as ending cash balances, through use of a cash budget.

How, for example, does Green Valley Coffee Company decide when to invest in new inventory-tracking technology? How will Green Valley Coffee Company decide how much to spend? Will borrowing be needed, or can the company finance the purchase with internally generated cash? What do ending cash balances need to be in order to provide a "safety margin" so the company won't unexpectedly run out of cash? A cash budget for a business works on roughly the same concept as a personal budget. By what process do you decide how much to spend on your education? On an automobile? On a house? All these decisions depend to some degree on the information that a cash budget provides.

A *cash budget helps a company or an individual manage cash by planning receipts and payments during a future period*. The company must determine how much cash it will need and then decide whether or not operations will bring in the needed cash. Managers proceed as follows:

1. Start with the entity's cash balance at the beginning of the period. This is the amount left over from the preceding period.

2. Add the budgeted cash receipts and subtract the budgeted cash payments.

3. The beginning balance plus receipts and minus payments equals the cash available before new financing at the end of the period.

4. Compare the cash available before new financing to the budgeted cash balance at the end of the period. Managers know the minimum amount of cash they need (the budgeted balance). If the budget shows excess cash, managers can invest the excess. But if the cash available falls below the budgeted balance, the company will need additional financing. The company may need to borrow the shortfall amount. The budget is a valuable tool for helping the company plan for the future.

Exhibit 4-14 | Cash Budget

	A	B	C
1	**Green Valley Coffee Company** **Cash Budget** **For the Year Ended December 31, 2017**		
2	Cash balance, December 31, 2016		$ 6,000,000
3	Budgeted cash receipts:		
4	Collections from customers		55,990,000
5	Dividends on investments		1,200,000
6	Sale of equipment		5,700,000
7			68,890,000
8	Budgeted cash payments:		
9	Purchases of inventory	$ 33,720,000	
10	Operating expenses	11,530,000	
11	Construction of new stores	12,000,000	
12	Payment of long-term debt	5,000,000	
13	Payment of dividends	3,000,000	65,250,000
14	Cash available (needed) before new financing		$ 3,640,000
15	Budgeted cash balance, December 31, 2017		(5,000,000)
16	Cash available for additional investments, or		
17	(New financing needed)		$ (1,360,000)
18			

The budget period can span any length of time—a day, a week, a month, or a year. Exhibit 4-14 shows a cash budget for Green Valley Coffee Company, Inc., for the year ended December 31, 2017. Study it carefully because, at some point, you will use a cash budget.

Green Valley Coffee Company's cash budget in Exhibit 4-14 begins with $6,000,000 of cash at the end of 2016 (line 2). Then add budgeted cash receipts and subtract budgeted payments for the next year. In this case, Green Valley Coffee Company expects to have $3,640,000 of cash available at next year-end (line 14). Green Valley Coffee Company's managers need to maintain a cash balance of at least $5,000,000 (line 15). Line 17 shows that Green Valley Coffee Company must arrange $1,360,000 of financing in order to achieve its goals for 2017.

Try It in Excel®

The cash budget represents a perfect opportunity to use your Excel skills. Usually, budgeted cash receipts and budgeted cash payments (step 2 in the list on page 224) are derived by starting with cash receipts and cash payments of the current period and multiplying them by estimated percentage changes for next period. For example, assume that the current year's actual collections from customers are $1,000,000 and that, because of improved policies, management estimates a 10% increase in collections next year. Budgeted collections for next year will be $1,100,000 ($1,000,000 × 1.10). Similarly, assume that current-year expenditures for employee salaries are $500,000 and that the company grants all employees a 2% cost-of-living raise. Assuming no change in personnel next year, budgeted cash payments for employee salaries will be $510,000 ($500,000 × 1.02). Following the format of Exhibit 4-14, prepare an Excel spreadsheet using formulas based on accurate estimates for next year. This can make preparation of the cash budget a breeze for next year as well as every year thereafter!

REPORT CASH ON THE BALANCE SHEET

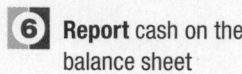

6 Report cash on the balance sheet

Most companies have numerous bank accounts, but they usually combine all cash amounts into a single total called "Cash and Cash Equivalents." **Cash equivalents** include liquid assets such as time deposits, certificates of deposit, and high-grade U.S. or foreign government securities that are very close to maturity (three months or less at the time of purchase). Time deposits are interest-bearing accounts that can be withdrawn for immediate use. Slightly less liquid than cash, cash equivalents are sufficiently similar to be reported along with cash. The balance sheet of Green Valley Coffee Company reported the following:

	A	B	C
1	**Green Valley Coffee Company** **Balance Sheet (Excerpts, adapted)** **December 31, 2016**		
2	**Assets**		
3	Cash and cash equivalents		$ 6,000,000
4			

Most public companies include additional information about cash and cash equivalents in the footnotes to their financial statements. For example, Note 1 (Summary of Significant Accounting Policies) of Apple Inc.'s 2014 financial statements contains the following brief comment about cash equivalents:

> ### Cash equivalents . . .
>
> All highly liquid investments with maturities of three months or less at the date of purchase are classified as cash equivalents.

Compensating Balance Agreements

The Cash account on the balance sheet reports the liquid assets available for day-to-day use. None of the Cash balance is restricted in any way. Any restricted amount of cash should be separately disclosed as such on the balance sheet. Banks often lend money under a compensating balance agreement. The borrower agrees to maintain a minimum balance in a checking account at all times. This minimum balance becomes a long-term asset and is therefore not cash in the normal sense. For example, suppose Green Valley Coffee Company borrowed $10,000 at 8% from First National Bank but agreed to keep 20% ($2,000) on deposit at all times. The net result of the compensating balance agreement is that Green Valley Coffee Company actually is permitted to use only $8,000 of the $10,000 borrowed. By paying 8% interest on the full $10,000, Green Valley Coffee Company's actual (effective) interest rate on the available balance ($8,000) is really 10%, as shown here:

$$\$10,000 \times .08 = \$800 \text{ interest}$$
$$\$800/\$8,000 = .10 \text{ interest rate}$$

End-of-Chapter | Summary Problem

Assume the following financial data for Petco, Inc.:

Petco ended 2016 with cash of $200 million. At December 31, 2016, Bob Detmer, the CFO of Petco, is preparing the cash budget for 2017.

During 2017, Detmer expects Petco to collect $26,400 million from customers and $80 million from interest earned on investments. Petco expects to pay $12,500 million for its inventories and $5,400 million for operating expenses. To remain competitive, Petco plans to spend $2,200 million to upgrade production facilities and an additional $350 million to acquire other companies. Petco also plans to sell older assets for approximately $300 million and to collect $220 million of this amount in cash. Petco is budgeting dividend payments of $550 million during the year. Finally, the company is scheduled to pay off $1,200 million of long-term debt plus the $6,600 million of current liabilities left over from 2016.

Because of the growth planned for 2017, Detmer budgets the need for a minimum cash balance of $300 million.

Requirement

1. How much must Petco borrow during 2017 to keep its cash balance from falling below $300 million? Prepare the 2017 cash budget to answer this important question. You may want to use Excel to streamline this task.

Answer

	A	B	C
	A1		
1	**Petco, Inc.** **Cash Budget** **For the Year Ended December 31, 2017**		
2	(In millions)		
3	Cash balance, December 31, 2016		$ 200
4	Estimated cash receipts:		
5	Collections from customers		26,400
6	Receipt of interest		80
7	Sales of assets		220
8			26,900
9	Estimated cash payments:		
10	Purchases of inventory	$ 12,500	
11	Payment of operating expenses	5,400	
12	Upgrading of production facilities	2,200	
13	Acquisition of other companies	350	
14	Payment of dividends	550	
15	Payment of long-term debt and other liabilities ($1,200 + $6,600)	7,800	(28,800)
16	Cash available (needed) before new financing		$ (1,900)
17	Budgeted cash balance, December 31, 2017		(300)
18	Cash available for additional investments, or		
19	(New financing needed)		$ (2,200)
20			

Petco must borrow $2.2 billion.

REVIEW | Internal Control & Cash

Quick Check (Answers are given on page 248.)

1. Internal control has its own terminology. On the left are some key internal control concepts. On the right are some key terms. Match each internal control concept with its term by writing the appropriate letter in the space provided. Not all letters are used.

_____ Internal control cannot always safeguard against this problem.	**a.** Fidelity bond
_____ This is often mentioned as the cornerstone of a good system of internal control.	**b.** Supervision
_____ Pay employees enough to require them to do a good job.	**c.** Separation of duties
	d. Encryption
_____ This procedure limits access to sensitive data.	**e.** Competent personnel
_____ This type of insurance policy covers losses due to employee theft.	**f.** Articles of incorporation
	g. Collusion
_____ Trusting your employees can lead you to overlook this procedure.	**h.** Safeguarding assets
_____ This is the most basic purpose of internal control.	**i.** External audits

2. Each of the following is an example of a control procedure, *except*
   a. sound personnel procedures.
   b. a sound marketing plan.
   c. limited access to assets.
   d. separation of duties.

3. Which of the following is an example of poor internal control?
   a. Rotate employees through various jobs.
   b. The accounting department compares goods received with the related purchase order.
   c. The mailroom clerk records daily cash receipts in the journal.
   d. Employees must take vacations.

Trisha Corporation has asked you to prepare its bank reconciliation at the end of the current month. Answer questions 4–8 using the following code letters to indicate how the item described would be reported on the bank reconciliation.

   a. Deduct from the bank balance
   b. Add to the book balance
   c. Does not belong on the bank reconciliation
   d. Deduct from the book balance
   e. Add to the bank balance

4. The bank statement showed interest earned of $50.

5. The bank statement showed that the bank had credited Trisha's account for a $500 deposit made by Tryon Company.

6. A check for $753 written by Trisha during the current month was erroneously recorded as a $375 payment.

7. The bank statement included a check from a customer that was marked NSF.

8. A $600 deposit made on the last day of the current month did not appear on this month's bank statement.

9. Which of the following reconciling items does not require a journal entry?
   a. NSF check
   b. Bank collection of note receivable
   c. Bank service charge
   d. Deposit in transit

10. A check was written for $295 to purchase supplies. The check was recorded in the journal as $259. The entry to correct this error would
    a. increase Supplies, $36.
    b. decrease Cash, $36.
    c. decrease Supplies, $36.
    d. both a and b.

11. A cash budget helps control cash by
    a. ensuring accurate cash records.
    b. helping to determine whether additional cash is available for investments or new financing is needed.
    c. developing a plan for increasing sales.
    d. all of the above.

Accounting Vocabulary

audit (p. 208) A periodic examination of a company's financial statements and the accounting systems, controls, and records that produce them. Audits may be either external or internal. External audits are usually performed by certified public accountants (CPAs).

bank collections (p. 215) Collection of money by the bank on behalf of a depositor.

bank reconciliation (p. 214) A document explaining the reasons for the difference between a depositor's records and the bank's records about the depositor's cash.

bank statement (p. 213) Document showing the beginning and ending balances of a particular bank account listing the month's transactions that affected the account.

budget (p. 208) A quantitative expression of a plan that helps managers coordinate the entity's activities.

cash budget (p. 208) A budget that projects the entity's future cash receipts and cash disbursements.

cash equivalent (p. 226) Investments such as time deposits, certificates of deposit, or high-grade government securities that are considered so similar to cash that they are combined with cash for financial disclosure purposes on the balance sheet.

check (p. 212) Document instructing a bank to pay the designated person or business the specified amount of money.

computer virus (p. 210) A malicious program that enters a company's computer system by e-mail or other means and destroys program and data files.

controller (p. 208) The chief accounting officer of a business.

deposits in transit (p. 214) A deposit recorded by the company but not yet by its bank.

electronic funds transfer (EFT) (p. 213) System that transfers cash by electronic communication rather than by paper documents.

encryption (p. 211) Mathematical rearranging of data within an electronic file to prevent unauthorized access to information.

exception reporting (p. 208) Identifying data that is not within "normal limits" so that managers can follow up and take corrective action. Exception reporting is used in operating and cash budgets to keep company profits and cash flow in line with management's plans.

fidelity bond (p. 210) An insurance policy taken out on employees who handle cash.

firewall (p. 211) An electronic barrier, usually provided by passwords, around computerized data files to protect local area networks of computers from unauthorized access.

fraud (p. 202) An intentional misrepresentation of facts, made for the purpose of persuading another party to act in a way that causes injury or damage to that party.

fraud triangle (p. 203) The three elements that are present in almost all cases of fraud. These elements are motive, opportunity, and rationalization on the part of the perpetrator.

fraudulent financial reporting (p. 203) Fraud perpetrated by management by preparing misleading financial statements.

imprest system (p. 224) A way to account for petty cash by maintaining a constant balance in the petty cash account, supported by the fund (cash plus payment tickets) totaling the same amount.

internal control (p. 204) Organizational plan and related measures adopted by an entity to safeguard assets, encourage adherence to company policies, promote operational efficiency, ensure accurate and reliable accounting records, and ensure compliance with legal requirements.

lock-box system (p. 215) A system of handling cash receipts by mail whereby customers remit payment directly to the bank's post office box, rather than through the entity's mail system.

misappropriation of assets (p. 203) Fraud committed by employees by stealing assets from the company.

nonsufficient funds (NSF) check (p. 215) A "hot" check, one for which the payer's bank account has insufficient money to pay the check. NSF checks are cash receipts that turn out to be worthless.

operating budget (p. 208) A budget of future net income. The operating budget projects a company's future revenue and expenses. It is usually prepared by line item of the company's income statement.

outstanding check (p. 215) A check issued by the company and recorded on its books but not yet paid by its bank.

password (p. 210) A special set of characters that must be provided by the user of a computerized program or data files to prevent unauthorized access to those files.

petty cash (p. 224) Fund containing a small amount of cash that is used to pay minor amounts.

phish (p. 210) Creating bogus websites for the purpose of stealing unauthorized data, such as names, addresses, Social Security numbers, and bank account and credit card numbers.

remittance advice (p. 212) An optional attachment to a check (sometimes a perforated tear-off document and sometimes capable of being electronically scanned) that indicates the payer, date, and purpose of the cash payment. The remittance advice is often used as the source documents for posting cash receipts or payments.

treasurer (p. 207) In a large company, the individual in charge of the department that has final responsibility for cash handling and cash management. Duties of the treasurer's department include cash budgeting, cash collections, writing checks, investing excess funds, and making proposals for raising additional cash when needed.

Trojan horse (p. 210) A malicious program that hides within legitimate programs and acts like a computer virus.

ASSESS YOUR PROGRESS

Some of the following exercises and problems are available as Excel questions in MyAccountingLab.

Ethics Check

EC4-1. Identify ethical principle violated

For each of the situations listed, identify which of three principles (integrity, objectivity and independence, or due care) from the AICPA Code of Professional Conduct is violated. Assume all persons listed in the situations are members of the AICPA. (Note: Refer to the AICPA Code of Professional Conduct contained on pages 29–30 in Chapter 1 for descriptions of the principles.)

   a. Sally, an accounts payable clerk, must have her manager sign off on all checks over $10,000. Her manager is out of the office this week so Sally forges her signature to make sure the check is sent out on time.

   b. Angelica is a first-year auditor for a large public accounting firm. She is assigned to audit Bike Tyme, a regional travel agency specializing in bike tours. Angelica does not disclose to her firm that her mom is a co-owner of Bike Tyme, since Angelica knows that she will not allow herself to be influenced by her mom.

   c. Mark, the CEO of his company, has the authority to approve all transactions. As a result, he uses company funds to purchase a new couch for his home.

   d. Joe has been working for his company for ten years and is required to attend internal control training annually. Joe does not attend the training this year because he feels he already understands the policies. Significant policy updates have occurred during the past year.

Short Exercises

LO 1 **S4-1.** (*Learning Objective 1: Define fraud and its impact*) Define "fraud." List and briefly discuss the three major components of the fraud triangle.

LO 1 **S4-2.** (*Learning Objective 1: Describe fraud and its impact*) Dorthea Alston, an accountant for Fun Tymes Limited, discovers that her supervisor, Eli Golden, made several errors last year.

Overall, the errors overstated the company's net income by 20%. It is not clear whether the errors were deliberate or accidental. What should Alston do?

S4-3. *(Learning Objective 2: Describe objectives and components of internal control)* How do computer viruses, Trojan horses, and phishing expeditions work? How can these e-commerce pitfalls hurt you? Be specific.

S4-4. *(Learning Objective 2: Describe objectives and components of internal control)* List the components of internal control. Briefly describe each component.

S4-5. *(Learning Objective 2: Explain the objectives and components of internal control)* Explain why separation of duties is often described as the cornerstone of internal control for safeguarding assets. Describe what can happen if the same person has custody of an asset and also accounts for the asset.

S4-6. *(Learning Objective 2: Explain the objectives and components of internal control)* Identify the other control procedures usually found in a company's system of internal control besides separation of duties, and tell why each is important.

S4-7. *(Learning Objective 2: Explain the objectives and components of internal control)* Cash may be a small item on the financial statements. Nevertheless, internal control over cash is very important. Why is this true?

S4-8. *(Learning Objective 2: Explain the objectives and components of internal control)* Cardinal Company requires that all documents supporting a check be canceled by punching a hole through the packet. Why is this practice required? What might happen if it were not?

S4-9. *(Learning Objective 3: Design and use a bank reconciliation)* The Cash account of Rampart Corp. reported a balance of $3,530 at August 31, 2016. Included were outstanding checks totaling $1,700 and an August 31 deposit of $400 that did not appear on the bank statement. The bank statement, which came from Park State Bank, listed an August 31 balance of $5,483. Included in the bank balance was an August 30 collection of $691 on account from a customer who pays the bank directly. The bank statement also shows a $13 service charge, $20 of interest revenue that Rampart earned on its bank balance, and an NSF check for $45.

Prepare a bank reconciliation to determine how much cash Rampart actually has at August 31.

S4-10. *(Learning Objective 3: Design and use a bank reconciliation)* After preparing Rampart Corp.'s bank reconciliation in Short Exercise 4-9, make the company's journal entries for transactions that arise from the bank reconciliation. Date each transaction August 31, 2016, and include an explanation with each entry.

S4-11. *(Learning Objective 3: Design and use a bank reconciliation)* Claire Hunter manages Sunshine Manufacturing. Hunter fears that a trusted employee has been stealing from the company. This employee receives cash from clients and also prepares the monthly bank reconciliation. To check up on the employee, Hunter prepares her own bank reconciliation, as follows:

	A	B	C	D	E
	A1				
1	**Sunshine Manufacturing Bank Reconciliation May 31, 2016**				
2	**Bank**		**Books**		
3	Balance, May 31	$ 4,400	Balance, May 31		$ 3,780
4	Add:		Add:		
5	Deposits in transit	350	Bank collections		950
6			Interest revenue		50
7	Less:		Less:		
8	Outstanding checks	(760)	Service charge		(25)
9	Adjusted bank balance	$ 3,990	Adjusted book balance		$ 4,755
10					

Does it appear that the employee has stolen from the company? If so, how much? Explain your answer. Which side of the bank reconciliation shows the company's true cash balance?

LO 4

S4-12. *(Learning Objective 4: Evaluate internal control over cash receipts and cash payments)* Victor Albert sells memberships to the Orlando Symphony Association in Orlando. The symphony's procedure requires Albert to write a patron receipt for all memberships sold. The receipt forms are pre-numbered. Albert is having personal financial problems, and he stole $600 received from a customer. To hide his theft, Albert destroyed the company copy of the receipt that he gave the patron. What will alert manager Jennifer Schwab that something is wrong?

LO 4

S4-13. *(Learning Objective 4: Evaluate internal control over cash receipts and cash payments)* Answer the following questions about internal control over cash payments:
1. Payment by check carries three controls over cash. What are they?
2. Suppose a purchasing agent receives the goods that he purchases and also approves payment for the goods. How could a dishonest purchasing agent cheat the company? How do companies avoid this internal control weakness?

LO 5

S4-14. *(Learning Objective 5: Construct and use a cash budget)* Kent Market (KM) is a major food cooperative. Suppose KM begins 2017 with cash of $5 million. KM estimates cash receipts during 2017 will total $103 million. Planned payments will total $93 million. To meet daily cash needs next year, KM must maintain a cash balance of at least $11 million. Prepare the organization's cash budget for 2017.

LO 6

S4-15. *(Learning Objective 6: Report cash on the balance sheet)* Describe the types of assets that are typically included under the heading "cash and cash equivalents" on the balance sheet. What is a "cash equivalent"?

Exercises MyAccountingLab

Group A

LO 1 2

E4-16A. *(Learning Objectives 1, 2: Describe fraud and its impact; Explain the objectives and components of internal control)* Identify the internal control weakness in the following situations. State how the person can hurt the company.
   a. Julie Sweitzer works as a security guard at SPEEDY parking in Denver. Sweitzer has a master key to the cash box where customers pay for parking. Each night Sweitzer prepares the cash report that shows (a) the number of cars that parked on the lot and (b) the day's cash receipts. Hallie Donovan, the SPEEDY treasurer, checks Sweitzer's figures by multiplying the number of cars by the parking fee per car. Donovan then deposits the cash in the bank.
   b. Wei Li is the purchasing agent for Targhee Sports Equipment. Li prepares purchase orders based on requests from division managers of the company. Li faxes the purchase order to suppliers, who then ship the goods to Targhee. Li receives each incoming shipment and checks it for agreement with the purchase order and the related invoice. She then routes the goods to the respective division managers and sends the receiving report and the invoice to the accounting department for payment.

LO 4

E4-17A. *(Learning Objective 4: Evaluate internal controls over cash receipts and cash payments)* The following situations describe two cash payment situations and two cash receipt situations. In each pair, one set of internal controls is better than the other. Evaluate the internal controls in each situation as strong or weak, and give the reason for your answer.

Cash payments:
   a. Garrett Colton Construction policy calls for construction supervisors to request the equipment needed for their jobs. The home office then purchases the equipment and has it shipped to the construction site.
   b. Sellers, Inc., policy calls for project supervisors to purchase the equipment needed for jobs. The supervisors then submit the paid receipts to the home office for

reimbursement. This policy enables supervisors to get the equipment quickly and keep construction jobs moving.

Cash receipts:

a. At Gopherton Auto Parts, cash received by mail goes straight to the accountant, who debits Cash and credits Accounts Receivable to record the collections from customers. The Gopherton accountant then deposits the cash in the bank.

b. Cash received by mail at Markley Dermatology Clinic goes to the mailroom, where a mail clerk opens envelopes and totals the cash receipts for the day. The mail clerk forwards customer checks to the cashier for deposit in the bank and forwards the remittance advices to the accounting department for posting credits to customer accounts.

E4-18A. *(Learning Objectives 1, 2, 4: Describe fraud and its impact; explain the objectives and components of internal control; evaluate internal controls over cash receipts and cash payments)* Rhonda Dunbar served as executive director of Downtown Forest Lake, an organization created to revitalize Forest Lake, Minnesota. Over the course of 11 years, Dunbar embezzled $444,000. How did Dunbar do it? By depositing subscriber cash receipts in her own bank account, writing Downtown Forest Lake checks to herself, and creating phony entities to which Downtown Forest Lake wrote checks.

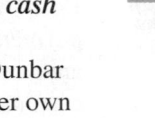

Downtown Forest Lake was led by a board of directors comprised of civic leaders. Dunbar's embezzlement went undetected until Downtown Forest Lake couldn't pay its bills.

Give four ways Dunbar's embezzlement could have been prevented.

E4-19A. *(Learning Objective 3: Design and use a bank reconciliation)* F. L. Hardy's checkbook lists the following:

Date	Check No.	Item	Check	Deposit	Balance
10/1					$ 515
4	622	Landry's Cafe	$ 25		490
9		Dividends received		$ 125	615
13	623	City Tire Co.	160		455
14	624	Jiffy Lube	68		387
18	625	Cash	65		322
26	626	Shalom Baptist Church	75		247
28	627	Greenside Apartments	175		72
31		Paycheck		1,225	1,297

The October bank statement shows:

Balance			$515
Add: Deposits			125
Debit checks:	No.	Amount	
	622	$25	
	623	160	
	624	86*	
	625	65	(336)
Other charges:			
NSF check		$20	
Service charge		5	(25)
Balance			$279

*This is the correct amount for check number 624.

Requirement

1. Prepare Hardy's bank reconciliation at October 31, 2017.

LO 3

E4-20A. *(Learning Objective 3: Use a bank reconciliation)* Dean White operates a roller skating center, Rinkland USA. He has just received the monthly bank statement at March 31 from Peoples National Bank, and the statement shows an ending balance of $740. Listed on the statement are an EFT rent collection of $320, a service charge of $8, two NSF checks totaling $110, and a $10 charge for printed checks. In reviewing his cash records, White identifies outstanding checks totaling $610 and a March 31 deposit in transit of $1,790. During March, he recorded a $280 check for the salary of a part-time employee as $28. White's Cash account shows a March 31 cash balance of $1,980. How much cash does White actually have at March 31, 2016?

LO 3

E4-21A. *(Learning Objective 3: Use a bank reconciliation)* Use the data from Exercise 4-20A to make the journal entries that White should record on March 31 to update his Cash account. Include an explanation for each entry.

LO 4

E4-22A. *(Learning Objective 4: Evaluate internal control over cash receipts and cash payments)* Orchard Stores use point-of-sale terminals as cash registers. The register shows the amount of each sale, the cash received from the customer, and any change returned to the customer. The machine also produces a customer receipt but keeps no record of transactions. At the end of the day, the clerk counts the cash in the register and gives it to the cashier for deposit in the company bank account.

Write a memo to convince the store manager that there is an internal control weakness over cash receipts. Identify the weakness that gives an employee the best opportunity to steal cash, and state how to prevent such a theft.

LO 4

E4-23A. *(Learning Objective 4: Evaluate internal control over cash payments)* Linus Manufacturing Company manufactures a popular line of work clothes. Linus Manufacturing employs 125 workers and keeps their employment records on time sheets that show how many hours the employee works each week. On Friday the shop foreman collects the time sheets, checks them for accuracy, and delivers them to the payroll department for preparation of paychecks. The treasurer signs the paychecks and returns the checks to the payroll department for distribution to the employees.

Identify the main internal control weakness in this situation, state how the weakness can hurt Linus Manufacturing, and propose a way to correct the weakness.

LO 5

E4-24A. *(Learning Objective 5: Construct and use a cash budget)* Byer Communications, Inc., is preparing its cash budget for the year ending December 31, 2017. Byer ended 2016 with cash of $65 million and managers need to keep a cash balance of at least $68 million for operations.

Collections from customers are expected to total $11,283 million during 2017, and payments for the cost of services and products should reach $6,194 million. Operating expense payments are budgeted at $2,556 million.

During 2017, Byer expects to invest $1,823 million in new equipment and sell older assets for $137 million. Debt payments scheduled for 2017 will total $564 million. The company forecasts net income of $887 million for 2017 and plans to pay dividends of $325 million.

Prepare Byer Communications' cash budget for 2017. Will the budgeted level of cash receipts leave Byer with the desired ending cash balance of $68 million, or will the company need additional financing? If so, how much?

Group B

LO 1 2

E4-25B. *(Learning Objectives 1, 2: Describe fraud and its impact; Explain the objectives and components of internal control)* Identify the internal control weakness in the following situations. State how the person can hurt the company.

    a. Mandy Morrison works as a security guard at POST parking in Oklahoma City. Morrison has a master key to the cash box where customers pay for parking. Each night Morrison prepares the cash report that shows (a) the number of cars that parked on the lot and (b) the day's cash receipts. Judy Gibson, the POST treasurer, checks Morrison's figures by multiplying the number of cars by the parking fee per car. Gibson then deposits the cash in the bank.

b. Sophie Peterson is the purchasing agent for Pinkerton Sports Equipment. Peterson prepares purchase orders based on requests from division managers of the company. Peterson faxes the purchase order to suppliers, who then ship the goods to Pinkerton. Peterson receives each incoming shipment and checks it for agreement with the purchase order and the related invoice. She then routes the goods to the respective division managers and sends the receiving report and the invoice to the accounting department for payment.

E4-26B. *(Learning Objective 4: Evaluate internal controls over cash receipts and cash payments)* The following situations describe two cash payment situations and two cash receipt situations. In each pair, one set of internal controls is better than the other. Evaluate the internal controls in each situation as strong or weak, and give the reason for your answer.

`LO 4`

Cash payments:

a. Thomas Giles Construction policy calls for construction supervisors to request the equipment needed for their jobs. The home office then purchases the equipment and has it shipped to the construction site.

b. Chumton Buildings, Inc., policy calls for project supervisors to purchase the equipment needed for jobs. The supervisors then submit the paid receipts to the home office for reimbursement. This policy enables supervisors to get the equipment quickly and keep construction jobs moving.

Cash receipts:

a. At Tallmadge Auto Parts, cash received by mail goes straight to the accountant, who debits Cash and credits Accounts Receivable to record the collections from customers. The Tallmadge accountant then deposits the cash in the bank.

b. Cash received by mail at Nelson Heart Clinic goes to the mailroom, where a mail clerk opens envelopes and totals the cash receipts for the day. The mail clerk forwards customer checks to the cashier for deposit in the bank and forwards the remittance slips to the accounting department for posting credits to customer accounts.

E4-27B. *(Learning Objectives 1, 2, 4: Describe fraud and its impact; explain the objectives and components of internal control; evaluate internal controls over cash receipts and cash payments)* Sue Valentine served as executive director of Downtown Wooster, an organization created to revitalize Wooster, Ohio. Over the course of 14 years, Valentine embezzled $236,000. How did Valentine do it? She did it by depositing subscriber cash receipts in her own bank account, writing Downtown Wooster checks to herself, and creating phony entities to which Downtown Wooster wrote checks.

`LO 1 2 4`

Downtown Wooster was led by a board of directors comprised of civic leaders. Valentine's embezzlement went undetected until Downtown Wooster couldn't pay its bills.

Give four ways Valentine's embezzlement could have been prevented.

E4-28B. *(Learning Objective 3: Design and use a bank reconciliation)* F.L. Hill's checkbook lists the following:

`LO 3`

Date	Check No.	Item	Check	Deposit	Balance
7/1					$ 525
4	622	Sun Cafe	$ 20		505
9		Dividends received		$ 125	630
13	623	Hartford Co.	160		470
14	624	FastMobil	18		452
18	625	Cash	60		392
26	626	First Baptist Church	80		312
28	627	Willow Tree Apartments	280		32
31		Paycheck		1,220	1,252

The October bank statement shows:

Balance				$525
Add: Deposits				125
Debit checks:	No.	Amount		
	622	$20		
	623	160		
	624	81*		
	625	60		(321)
Other charges:				
NSF check			$25	
Service charge			10	(35)
Balance				$294

*This is the correct amount for check number 624.

Requirement

1. Prepare Hill's bank reconciliation at July 31, 2016.

LO 3

E4-29B. *(Learning Objective 3: Use a bank reconciliation)* Rick Neal operates a roller skating center, Neal's Rinks. He has just received the monthly bank statement at October 31 from Sandstone National Bank, and the statement shows an ending balance of $750. Listed on the statement are an EFT rent collection of $330, a service charge of $10, two NSF checks totaling $110, and an $11 charge for printed checks. In reviewing his cash records, Neal identifies outstanding checks totaling $603 and an October 31 deposit in transit of $1,770. During October, he recorded a $310 check for the salary of a part-time employee as $31. Neal's Cash account shows an October 31 cash balance of $1,997. How much cash does Neal actually have at October 31, 2016?

LO 3

E4-30B. *(Learning Objective 3: Use a bank reconciliation)* Use the data from Exercise 4-29B to make the journal entries that Neal should record on October 31 to update his Cash account. Include an explanation for each entry.

LO 4

E4-31B. *(Learning Objective 4: Evaluate internal controls over cash receipts and cash payments)* Rally Stores use point-of-sale terminals as cash registers. The register shows the amount of each sale, the cash received from the customer, and any change returned to the customer. The machine also produces a customer receipt but keeps no record of transactions. At the end of the day, the clerk counts the cash in the register and gives it to the cashier for deposit in the company bank account.

Write a memo to convince the store manager that there is an internal control weakness over cash receipts. Identify the weakness that gives an employee the best opportunity to steal cash, and state how to prevent such a theft.

LO 4

E4-32B. *(Learning Objective 4: Evaluate internal control over cash payments)* Greentown Company manufactures a popular brand of footballs. Greentown employs 142 workers and keeps its employment records on time sheets that show how many hours the employee works each week. On Friday the shop foreman collects the time sheets, checks them for accuracy, and delivers them to the payroll department for preparation of paychecks. The treasurer signs the paychecks and returns the checks to the payroll department for distribution to the employees.

Identify the main internal control weakness in this situation, state how the weakness can hurt Greentown, and propose a way to correct the weakness.

LO 5

E4-33B. *(Learning Objective 5: Construct and use a cash budget)* Ayers Communications, Inc., is preparing its cash budget for the year ending December 31, 2017. Ayers ended 2016 with cash of $62 million and managers need to keep a cash balance of at least $71 million for operations.

Collections from customers are expected to total $11,339 million during 2017, and payments for the cost of services and products should reach $6,193 million. Operating expense payments are budgeted at $2,544 million.

During 2017, Ayers expects to invest $1,823 million in new equipment and sell older assets for $132 million. Debt payments scheduled for 2017 will total $552 million. The company forecasts net income of $893 million for 2017 and plans to pay dividends of $355 million.

Prepare Ayers Communications' cash budget for 2017. Will the budgeted level of cash receipts leave Ayers with the desired ending cash balance of $71 million, or will the company need additional financing? If so, how much?

Quiz

Test your understanding of internal control and cash by answering the following questions. Answer each question by selecting the best choice from among the options given.

Q4-34. All of the following are objectives of internal control *except*
    a. to comply with legal requirements.
    b. to ensure accurate and reliable accounting records.
    c. to maximize net income.
    d. to safeguard assets.

Q4-35. All of the following are internal control procedures *except*
    a. Sarbanes-Oxley reforms.   **c.** assignment of responsibilities.
    b. adequate records.   **d.** internal and external audits.

Q4-36. Requiring that an employee with no access to cash do the accounting is an example of which characteristic of internal control?
    a. Competent and reliable personnel   **c.** Assignment of responsibility
    b. Monitoring of controls   **d.** Separation of duties

Q4-37. All of the following are controls for cash received over the counter *except*
    a. a printed receipt must be given to the customer.
    b. the customer should be able to see the amounts entered into the cash register.
    c. the sales clerk must have access to the cash register tape.
    d. the cash drawer should open only when the sales clerk enters an amount on the keys.

Q4-38. In a bank reconciliation, an outstanding check is
    a. added to the bank balance.   **c.** deducted from the bank balance.
    b. deducted from the book balance.   **d.** added to the book balance.

Q4-39. In a bank reconciliation, an EFT cash payment is
    a. deducted from the bank balance.   **c.** added to the book balance.
    b. deducted from the book balance.   **d.** added to the bank balance.

Q4-40. If a bookkeeper mistakenly recorded a $34 deposit as $43, the error would be shown on the bank reconciliation as a
    a. $9 addition to the book balance.   **c.** $43 addition to the book balance.
    b. $43 deduction from the book balance.   **d.** $9 deduction from the book balance.

Q4-41. If a bank reconciliation included a deposit in transit of $790, the entry to record this reconciling item would include
    a. a credit to Prepaid insurance for $790.   **c.** a credit to Cash for $790.
    b. a debit to Cash for $790.   **d.** No entry is required.

Q4-42. In a bank reconciliation, interest revenue earned on your bank balance is
    a. deducted from the book balance.   **c.** added to the book balance.
    b. added to the bank balance.   **d.** deducted from the bank balance.

Q4-43. Before paying an invoice for goods received on account, the controller or treasurer should ensure that
    a. the company is paying for the goods it actually received.
    b. the company has not already paid this invoice.
    c. the company is paying for the goods it ordered.
    d. all of the above.

Q4-44. Jubilee's Bakery is budgeting cash for 2017. The cash balance at December 31, 2016, was $6,000. Jubilee's Bakery budgets 2017 cash receipts at $81,000. Estimated cash payments include $44,000 for inventory, $34,000 for operating expenses, and $15,000 to expand the store. Jubilee's Bakery needs a minimum cash balance of $13,000 at all times. Jubilee's Bakery expects to earn net income of $76,000 during 2017. What is the final result of the company's cash budget for 2017?

    a. Must arrange new financing for $19,000.

    b. Pay off $38,000 of debt.

    c. There is $38,000 available for additional investments.

    d. There is $19,000 available for additional investments.

Q4-45. Which of the following assets are *not* included in "cash equivalents" in a typical balance sheet?

    a. U.S. government securities

    b. Foreign government securities

    c. Time deposits

    d. Certain very low-risk equity securities

    e. All of the above might be included in "cash equivalents."

Problems MyAccountingLab

Group A

LO 1 4

P4-46A. *(Learning Objectives 1, 4: Describe fraud and its impact; evaluate internal controls over cash receipts and cash payments)* Irish Imports is an importer of silver, brass, and furniture items from Ireland. Patricia O'Malley is the general manager of Irish Imports. O'Malley employs two other people in the business. Maureen Kennedy serves as the buyer for Irish Imports. In her work, Kennedy travels throughout Ireland to find interesting new products. When Kennedy finds a new product, she arranges for Irish Imports to purchase and pay for the item. She helps the artisans prepare their invoices and then faxes the invoices to O'Malley in the company office.

O'Malley operates out of an office in Boston, Massachusetts. The office is managed by Lesley Luck, who handles the mail, keeps the accounting records, makes bank deposits, and prepares the monthly bank reconciliation. Virtually all of Irish Imports' cash receipts arrive by mail—from sales made to Target, Pier 1 Imports, and specialty shops.

Luck also prepares checks for payment based on invoices that come in from the suppliers who have been contacted by Kennedy. To maintain control over cash payments, O'Malley examines the paperwork and signs all checks.

Requirement

    1. Identify all the major internal control weaknesses in Irish Imports' system and how the resulting action could hurt Irish Imports. Also state how to correct each weakness.

LO 2 4

P4-47A. *(Learning Objectives 2, 4: Explain the objectives and components of internal control; evaluate internal controls)* Each of the following situations reveals an internal control weakness:

    a. In evaluating the internal control over cash payments of Judd Manufacturing, an auditor learns that the purchasing agent is responsible for purchasing diamonds for use in the company's manufacturing process, approving the invoices for payment, and signing the checks. No supervisor reviews the purchasing agent's work.

    b. Krysta Pesarchick owns an architectural firm. Pesarchick's staff consists of 16 professional architects, and Pesarchick manages the office. Often, Pesarchick's work requires her to travel to meet with clients. During the past six months, Pesarchick has observed that when she returns from a business trip, the architecture jobs in the office have not progressed satisfactorily. Pesarchick learns that when she is away, two of her senior architects take over office management and neglect their normal duties. One employee could manage the office.

    c. Ian Holt has been an employee of the city of Streetsboro for many years. Because the city is small, Holt performs all accounting duties, in addition to opening the mail, preparing the bank deposit, and preparing the bank reconciliation.

Requirements

1. Identify the missing internal control characteristic in each situation.
2. Identify each firm's possible problem.
3. Propose a solution to the problem.

P4-48A. *(Learning Objective 3: Design and use a bank reconciliation)* The cash data of Dunlap Automotive for June 2016 follow:

LO 3

Cash					Account No. 101
Date	Item	Jrnl. Ref.	Debit	Credit	Balance
June 1	Balance				7,450
30		CR6	9,478		16,928
30		CP11		10,397	6,531

Cash Receipts (CR)		Cash Payments (CP)	
Date	Cash Debit	Check No.	Cash Credit
June 2	$ 2,930	3113	$ 1,509
8	532	3114	1,869
10	1,696	3115	1,830
16	837	3116	87
22	355	3117	871
29	885	3118	149
30	2,243	3119	453
Total	$9,478	3120	1,013
		3121	208
		3122	2,408
		Total	$10,397

Dunlap Automotive received the following bank statement on June 30, 2016:

	A	B	C
	A1 ⬍		
	A	B	C
1	**Bank Statement for June 2016**		
2	Beginning balance		$ 7,450
3	Deposits and other additions:		
4	June 1	$ 625 EFT	
5	4	2,930	
6	9	532	
7	12	1,696	
8	17	837	
9	22	355	
10	23	1,275 BC	8,250
11	Checks and other deductions:		
12	June 7	$ 1,509	
13	13	1,380	
14	14	489 US	
15	15	1,869	
16	18	87	
17	21	382 EFT	
18	26	871	
19	30	149	
20	30	30 SC	(6,766)
21	Ending balance		$ 8,934
22			

Explanation: BC—bank collection of note receivable from customer, EFT—electronic funds transfer, US—unauthorized signature, SC—service charge

Additional data for the bank reconciliation include the following:

a. The EFT deposit was a receipt of monthly rent. The EFT debit was a monthly insurance payment.

b. The unauthorized signature check was received from a customer and returned by the bank unpaid.

c. The correct amount of check number 3115, a payment on account, is $1,380. (Dunlap Automotive's accountant mistakenly recorded the check as $1,830.)

Requirements

1. Prepare the Dunlap Automotive bank reconciliation at June 30, 2016.
2. Prepare the journal entries required at June 30, 2016.
3. Describe how a bank account and the bank reconciliation help the general manager control Dunlap Automotive's cash.

LO 5

P4-49A. *(Learning Objective 5: Construct and use a cash budget)* Julia Beecher, chief financial officer of Keller Wireless, is responsible for the company's budgeting process. Beecher's staff is preparing the Keller Wireless cash budget for 2017. A key input to the budgeting process is last year's statement of cash flows, which follows (amounts in thousands):

	A	B	C
	A1		
1	**Keller Wireless** **Statement of Cash Flows** **For the Year Ended December 31, 2016**		
2			(In thousands)
3	**Cash Flows from Operating Activities**		
4	Collections from customers		$ 66,000
5	Interest received		600
6	Cash payments for inventory		(45,000)
7	Cash payments for operating expenses		(13,600)
8	Net cash provided by operating activities		8,000
9	**Cash Flows from Investing Activities**		
10	Purchases of equipment		(4,600)
11	Purchases of investments		(200)
12	Sales of investments		900
13	Net cash used for investing activities		(3,900)
14	**Cash Flows from Financing Activities**		
15	Payment of long-term debt		(400)
16	Issuance of stock		1,400
17	Payment of cash dividends		(300)
18	Net cash provided by financing activities		700
19	**Cash**		
20	Increase (decrease) in Cash		4,800
21	Cash, beginning of year		3,300
22	Cash, end of year		$ 8,100
23			

Requirements

1. Prepare the Keller Wireless cash budget for 2017. Date the budget simply "2017," and denote the beginning and ending cash balances as "beginning" and "ending." Assume the company expects 2017 to be the same as 2016, but with the following changes:

a. In 2017, the company expects a 14% increase in collections from customers and a 20% increase in cash payments for inventory.

b. There will be no sales of investments in 2017.

c. Keller Wireless plans to issue no stock in 2017.

d. Keller Wireless plans to end the year with a cash balance of $3,500 (thousand).

Group B

P4-50B. *(Learning Objectives 1, 4: Describe fraud and its impact; evaluate internal controls over cash receipts and cash payments)* Swedish Imports is an importer of silver, brass, and furniture items from Sweden. Sandra Gustafson is the general manager of Swedish Imports. Gustafson employs two other people in the business. Mandy Martin serves as the buyer for Swedish Imports. In her work, Martin travels throughout Sweden to find interesting new products. When Martin finds a new product, she arranges for Swedish Imports to purchase and pay for the item. She helps the artisans prepare their invoices and then faxes the invoices to Gustafson in the company office.

LO **1** **4**

Gustafson operates out of an office in Brooklyn, New York. The office is managed by Sandra Moore, who handles the mail, keeps the accounting records, makes bank deposits, and prepares the monthly bank reconciliation. Virtually all of Swedish Imports' cash receipts arrive by mail—from sales made to Target, Crate and Barrel, and Williams-Sonoma.

Moore also prepares checks for payment based on invoices that come in from the suppliers who have been contacted by Martin. To maintain control over cash payments, Gustafson examines the paperwork and signs all checks.

Requirement

1. Identify all the major internal control weaknesses in Swedish Imports' system and how the resulting action could hurt Swedish Imports. Also state how to correct each weakness.

P4-51B. *(Learning Objectives 2, 4: Explain the objectives and components of internal control; evaluate internal controls)* Each of the following situations reveals an internal control weakness:

LO **2** **4**

Situation a.   In evaluating the internal control over cash payments of Arlington Manufacturing, an auditor learns that the purchasing agent is responsible for purchasing diamonds for use in the company's manufacturing process, approving the invoices for payment, and signing the checks. No supervisor reviews the purchasing agent's work.

Situation b.   Kelly Hixson owns an architectural firm. Hixson's staff consists of 19 professional architects, and Hixson manages the office. Often, Hixson's work requires her to travel to meet with clients. During the past six months, Hixson has observed that when she returns from a business trip, the architecture jobs in the office have not progressed satisfactorily. Hixson learns that when she is away, two of her senior architects take over office management and neglect their normal duties. One employee could manage the office.

Situation c.   Ron Lucas has been an employee of the city of Scandia for many years. Because the city is small, Lucas performs all accounting duties, in addition to opening the mail, preparing the bank deposit, and preparing the bank reconciliation.

Requirements

1. Identify the missing internal control characteristic in each situation.
2. Identify each firm's possible problem.
3. Propose a solution to the problem.

LO 3

P4-52B. *(Learning Objective 3: Design and use a bank reconciliation)* The cash data of Duffy Automotive for July 2016 follow:

Cash					Account No. 101
Date	Item	Jrnl. Ref.	Debit	Credit	Balance
July 1	Balance				7,450
31		CR 6	9,693		17,143
31		CP 11		9,885	7,258

Cash Receipts (CR)			Cash Payments (CP)	
Date	Cash Debit		Check No.	Cash Credit
July 2	$ 2,850		3113	$ 1,532
8	560		3114	1,615
10	1,693		3115	1,830
16	890		3116	70
22	409		3117	790
29	915		3118	97
30	2,376		3119	477
Total	$9,693		3120	990
			3121	183
			3122	2,301
			Total	$9,885

Duffy Automotive received the following bank statement on July 31, 2016:

	A	B	C
	A1		
1	**Bank Statement for July 2016**		
2	Beginning balance		$ 7,450
3	Deposits and other additions:		
4	July 1	$ 800 EFT	
5	4	2,850	
6	9	560	
7	12	1,693	
8	17	890	
9	22	409	
10	23	1,275 BC	8,477
11	Checks and other deductions:		
12	July 7	$1,532	
13	13	1,380	
14	14	430 US	
15	15	1,615	
16	18	70	
17	21	351 EFT	
18	26	790	
19	30	97	
20	30	10 SC	(6,275)
21	Ending balance		$ 9,652
22			

Explanation: BC—bank collection of note receivable from customer, EFT—electronic funds transfer, US—unauthorized signature, SC—service charge

Additional data for the bank reconciliation include the following:
a. The EFT deposit was a receipt of monthly rent. The EFT debit was a monthly insurance payment.
b. The unauthorized signature check was received from a customer and returned by the bank unpaid.

c. The correct amount of check number 3115, a payment on account, is $1,380. (Duffy Automotive's accountant mistakenly recorded the check as $1,830.)

d. The bank collected a note receivable for Duffy Automotive.

Requirements

1. Prepare the Duffy Automotive bank reconciliation at July 31, 2016.
2. Prepare the journal entries required at July 31, 2016.
3. Describe how a bank account and the bank reconciliation help the general manager control Duffy Automotive's cash.

P4-53B. *(Learning Objective 5: Construct and use a cash budget)* Mark Farmer, chief financial officer of Carvel Wireless, is responsible for the company's budgeting process. Farmer's staff is preparing the Carvel cash budget for 2017. A key input to the budgeting process is last year's statement of cash flows, which follows (amount in thousands):

	A	B	C
A1			
1	**Carvel Wireless** **Statement of Cash Flows** **For the Year Ended December 31, 2016**		
2			(In thousands)
3	**Cash Flows from Operating Activities**		
4	Collections from customers		$ 65,000
5	Interest received		300
6	Cash payments for inventory		(44,000)
7	Cash payments for operating expenses		(13,900)
8	Net cash provided by operating activities		7,400
9	**Cash Flows from Investing Activities**		
10	Purchases of equipment		(4,400)
11	Purchases of investments		(400)
12	Sales of investments		900
13	Net cash used for investing activities		(3,900)
14	**Cash Flows from Financing Activities**		
15	Payment of long-term debt		(500)
16	Issuance of stock		1,800
17	Payment of cash dividends		(200)
18	Net cash provided by financing activities		1,100
19	**Cash**		
20	Increase (decrease) in Cash		4,600
21	Cash, beginning of year		3,300
22	Cash, end of year		$ 7,900
23			

Requirements

1. Prepare the Carvel Wireless cash budget for 2017. Date the budget simply "2017," and denote the beginning and ending cash balances as "beginning" and "ending." Assume the company expects 2017 to be the same as 2016, but with the following changes:

   a. In 2017, the company expects a 12% increase in collections from customers and a 20% increase in cash payments for inventory.

   b. There will be no sales of investments in 2017.

   c. Carvel Wireless plans to issue no stock in 2017.

   d. Carvel Wireless plans to end the year with a cash balance of $3,500 (thousand).

Challenge Exercises and Problem

LO 1 4

E4-54 (*Learning Objectives 1, 4: Describe fraud and its impact; evaluate internal controls over cash receipts and cash payments*) Julie Brown, the owner of Julie's Party Sandwiches, has delegated management of the business to Stacie Wood, a friend. Brown drops by to meet customers and check up on cash receipts, but Wood buys the merchandise and handles cash payments. Business has been very good lately, and cash receipts have kept pace with the apparent level of sales. However, for a year or so, the amount of cash on hand has been too low. When asked about this, Wood explains that suppliers are charging more for goods than in the past. During the past year, Wood has taken two expensive vacations, and Brown wonders how Wood can afford these trips on her $52,000 annual salary and commissions.

List at least three ways Wood could be defrauding Brown of cash. In each instance, also identify how Brown can determine whether Wood's actions are ethical. Limit your answers to the store's cash payments. The business pays all suppliers by check (no EFTs).

LO 5

E4-55 (*Learning Objective 5: Construct and use a cash budget*) Megan Williams, the chief financial officer, is responsible for Dollar Depot's cash budget for 2017. The budget will help Williams determine if long-term borrowing is needed to end the year with a cash balance of $175,000 or if the company will have excess cash to end the year. Williams' assistants have assembled budget data for 2017, which the computer printed in alphabetical order. Not all the data items reproduced below are used in preparing the cash budget.

(Assumed Data)	(In thousands)
Actual cash balance, December 31, 2016	$ 100
Budgeted total assets, December 31, 2017	22,177
Budgeted total current assets, December 31, 2017	7,476
Budgeted total current liabilities, December 31, 2017	4,760
Budgeted total liabilities, December 31, 2017	11,588
Budgeted total stockholders' equity, December 31, 2017	7,197
Collections from customers	20,400
Dividend payments	257
Issuance of stock	647
Net income	1,163
Payment of long-term and short-term debt	950
Payment of operating expenses	2,349
Payments for inventory items	14,445
Purchase of property and equipment with cash	1,548

Requirements

1. Construct the cash budget of Dollar Depot, Inc.
2. Compute Dollar Depot's budgeted current ratio and debt ratio at December 31, 2017.
3. Williams plans to end the year with a cash balance of $175,000. Determine whether she will need to arrange additional financing or will have excess cash to invest.

LO 3

P4-56. (*Learning Objective 3: Design and use a bank reconciliation*) The president of The Parkview Company has recently become concerned that the bookkeeper has embezzled cash from the company. She asks you, confidentially, to look over the bank reconciliation that the bookkeeper has prepared to see if you discover any discrepancies between the books and the bank statement. She provides you with the Cash account from the general ledger, the bank statement, and the bank reconciliation as of December 31. You learn from the November bank reconciliation that the following checks were outstanding on November 30: No. 1560 for $184, No. 1880 for $549, No. 1882 for $122, and No. 1883 for $467. There was one deposit in transit on November 30 for $1,275. An examination of the actual deposit slips revealed no bank errors. Assume the cash deposit of $2,375 on December 24 is the correct amount. The January bank statement showed that a $670 deposit cleared the bank on January 2.

	A	B	C	D	E	F
1	**Parkview Company Bank Reconciliation December 31**					
2	**Bank**			**Books**		
3	Balance, 12/31		$ 3,936	Balance, 12/31		$ 10,747
4	Add:			Add:		
5	Deposits in transit		3,170	EFT receipt from customer		55
6	Subtotal		7,106	Interest revenue		13
7	Less:			Subtotal		10,815
8	Outstanding checks			Less:		
9	No. 1560	$ 184		Book error	$ 4,000	
10	No. 1901	849		NSF check	155	
11	No. 1902	168	(1,201)	EFT payment of utilities	755	(4,910)
12	Adjusted bank balance		$ 5,905	Adjusted book balance		$ 5,905
13						

General Ledger
Cash

Bal 12/1	7,291			
Cash receipt 12/7	1,600	No. 1880		549
Cash receipt 12/15	4,165	No. 1882		122
Cash receipt 12/23	6,375	No. 1883		467
Cash receipt 12/30	670	No. 1884		1,285
		No. 1885		1,332
		No. 1886		720
		No. 1887		2,430
		No. 1888		1,012
		No. 1889		420
		No. 1901		849
		No. 1902		168
Bal 12/31	10,747			

	A	B	C
1	**Bank Statement for December 31**		
2	Bal 12/1		$ 3,700
3	Deposits		
4	Dec 1	$ 1,275	
5	8	1,600	
6	16	4,165	
7	24	2,375	
8	31	13	
9	31	55	
10	Total deposits		9,483
11	Checks and other debits:		
12	No. 1880	549	
13	No. 1882	122	
14	No. 1883	467	
15	No. 1884	1,285	
16	No. 1885	1,332	
17	No. 1886	720	
18	No. 1887	2,430	
19	No. 1888	1,012	
20	No. 1889	420	
21	NSF	155	
22	EFT	755	
23	Total checks and other debits		(9,247)
24	Bal 12/31		$ 3,936
25			

Explanation: BC—bank collection, EFT—electronic funds transfer, US—unauthorized signature, SC—service charge

Requirement

1. Prepare a corrected bank reconciliation. Show the unexplained difference as an adjustment to the book balance. Include in your analysis the amount of the theft and how the bookkeeper attempted to conceal the theft.

APPLY YOUR KNOWLEDGE
Decision Cases

Case 1. *(Learning Objectives 1, 3, 4: Describe fraud and its impact; design and use a bank reconciliation; evaluate internal controls over cash receipts and cash payments)* Environmental Concerns, Inc., has poor internal control. Recently, Oscar Benz, the manager, has suspected the bookkeeper of stealing. Details of the business's cash position at September 30 follow.

a. The Cash account shows a balance of $10,402. This amount includes a September 30 deposit of $3,794 that does not appear on the September 30 bank statement.

b. The September 30 bank statement shows a balance of $8,224. The bank statement lists a $200 bank collection, an $8 service charge, and a $36 NSF check. The bookkeeper has not recorded any of these items.

c. At September 30, the following checks are outstanding:

Check No.	Amount
154	$116
256	150
278	853
291	990
292	206
293	145

d. The bookkeeper receives all incoming cash and makes the bank deposits. He also reconciles the monthly bank statement. Here is his September 30 reconciliation:

Balance per books, September 30...............		$10,402
Add: Outstanding checks		1,460
Bank collection....................................		200
Subtotal..		12,062
Less: Deposits in transit............................	$3,794	
Service charge	8	
NSF check..	36	(3,838)
Balance per bank, September 30................		$ 8,224

Requirement

1. Benz has requested that you determine whether the bookkeeper has stolen cash from the business and, if so, how much. He also asks you to explain how the bookkeeper attempted to conceal the theft. To make this determination, you perform a proper bank reconciliation. There are no bank or book errors. Benz also asks you to evaluate the internal controls and to recommend any changes needed to improve them.

Case 2. *(Learning Objectives 1, 4: Describe fraud and its impact; evaluate internal controls over cash receipts and cash payments)* This case is based on an actual situation experienced by one of the authors. Gilead Construction, headquartered in Topeka, Kansas, built a motel in Kansas City. The construction foreman, Slim Pickins, hired the workers for the project. Pickins had his workers fill out the necessary tax forms and sent the employment documents to the home office.

 LO 1 4

Work on the motel began on May 1 and ended in December. Each Thursday evening, Pickins filled out a time card that listed the hours worked by each employee during the five-day work week ended at 5 p.m. on Thursday. Pickins faxed the time sheets to the home office, which prepared the payroll checks on Friday morning. Pickins drove to the home office after lunch on Friday, picked up the payroll checks, and returned to the construction site. At 5 p.m. on Friday, Pickins distributed the paychecks to the workers.

    a. Describe in detail the internal control weakness in this situation. Specify what negative result could occur because of the internal control weakness.

    b. Describe what you would do to correct the internal control weakness.

Ethical Issues

Requirements

For each of the following situations, answer the following questions:

1. What is the ethical issue in this situation?
2. What are the alternatives?
3. Who are the stakeholders? What are the possible consequences to each? Analyze from the following standpoints: (a) economic, (b) legal, and (c) ethical.
4. Place yourself in the role of the decision maker. What would you do? How would you justify your decision?

Issue 1. Sunrise Bank recently appointed the accounting firm of Smith, Godfroy, and Hannaford as the bank's auditor. Sunrise quickly became one of Smith, Godfroy, and Hannaford's largest clients. Subject to banking regulations, Sunrise must provide for any expected losses on notes receivable that Sunrise may not collect in full.

During the course of the audit, Smith, Godfroy, and Hannaford determined that three large notes receivable of Sunrise seem questionable. The auditors discussed these loans with Susan Carter, controller of Sunrise. Carter assured the auditors that these notes were good and that the makers of the notes will be able to pay their notes after the economy improves.

Smith, Godfroy, and Hannaford stated that Sunrise must record a loss for a portion of these notes receivable to account for the likelihood that Sunrise may never collect their full amount. Carter objected and threatened to dismiss the auditors if they demanded that the bank record the loss. Smith, Godfroy, and Hannaford wants to keep Sunrise as a client. In fact, the firm was counting on the revenue from the Sunrise audit to finance an expansion.

Issue 2. Barry Galvin is executive vice president of Community Bank. Active in community affairs, Galvin serves on the board of directors of The Salvation Army. The Salvation Army is expanding rapidly and is considering relocating. At a recent meeting, The Salvation Army decided to buy 250 acres of land on the edge of town. The owner of the property is Olga Nadar, a major depositor in Community Bank. Nadar is completing a bitter divorce, and Galvin knows that Nadar is eager to sell her property. In view of Nadar's difficult situation, Galvin believes Nadar would accept a low offer for the land. Realtors have appraised the property at $3.6 million.

Issue 3. Community Bank has a loan receivable from IMS Chocolates. IMS is six months late in making payments to the bank, and Jan French, a Community Bank vice president, is assisting IMS to restructure its debt.

French learns that IMS is depending on landing a contract with Snicker Foods, another Community Bank client. French also serves as Snicker Foods' loan officer at the bank. In this capacity, French is aware that Snicker is considering bankruptcy. No one else outside Snicker Foods knows this. French has been a great help to IMS and IMS's owner is counting on French's expertise in loan workouts to advise the company through this difficult process. To help the bank collect on this large loan, French has a strong motivation to alert IMS of Snicker's financial difficulties.

Focus on Financials | Apple Inc.

LO 6

(Learning Objective 6: Report cash on the balance sheet) Refer to the **Apple Inc.** consolidated financial statements in Appendix A and online in the filings section of **http://www.sec.gov**. The cash and cash equivalents section of the Consolidated Balance Sheet shows a balance of $13,844 million as of September 27, 2014.

Requirements

1. What are the general criteria for an asset to be classified as a "cash equivalent"?
2. Refer to the Financial Instruments section of Note 1—Summary of Significant Accounting Policies. What types of assets does the company generally include in the category of "cash equivalents"?
3. Does the company include any more detailed description of "cash equivalents"? Where? Describe the categories.

Focus on Analysis | Under Armour, Inc.

LO 2 5

(Learning Objectives 2, 5: Analyze internal controls and cash flows) Refer to the **Under Armour, Inc.**, Financial Statements in Appendix B and online in the filings section of **http://www.sec.gov**.

Requirements

1. Focus on cash and cash equivalents. Why did cash and cash equivalents change during 2014? The statement of cash flows holds the answer to this question. Analyze the seven largest *individual* items on the statement of cash flows (not the summary subtotals such as "net cash provided by operating activities"). For each of the seven individual items, state how Under Armour's actions affected cash. Show amounts in millions and round to the nearest $1 million. (Challenge)
2. Refer to Exhibit 4-2 on page 205 that contains the Report of Management on Internal Control over Financial Reporting. Under Armour, Inc. has a similar report included in its annual report. Show how this report corresponds to the objectives of internal control included in this chapter. (Challenge)

Group Project

You are promoting a rock concert in your area. Assume you organize as a partnership, with each member of your group contributing $5,000 in exchange for an ownership interest and a share in the profits. Therefore, each of you is risking some hard-earned money on this venture. Assume it is April 1 and that the concert will be performed on June 30. Your promotional activities begin immediately, and ticket sales start on May 1. You expect to sell all of the firm's assets, pay all the liabilities, and distribute all remaining cash to the group members by July 31.

Requirements

Write an internal control manual that will help to safeguard the assets of the business. The manual should address the following aspects of internal control:

1. Assign responsibilities among the group members.
2. Authorize individuals, including group members and any outsiders that you need to hire to perform specific jobs.
3. Separate duties among the group and any employees.
4. Describe all documents needed to account for and safeguard the business's assets.

Quick Check Answers

1. *g, c, e, d, a, b, h;* *Unused: f and i*	5. *a*	9. *d*
2. *b*	6. *d*	10. *d*
3. *c*	7. *d*	11. *b*
4. *b*	8. *e*	

5 Short-Term Investments & Receivables

 SPOTLIGHT | Amazing Apple! Short-Term Investments and Accounts Receivable Are 14 Times as Large as Inventories!

How do you manage your busy life? You may use any of thousands of applications ("Apps") on a device made by Apple Inc. Apple is a U.S.-based multinational corporation that designs, manufactures, and markets highly innovative and reliable consumer electronics and related peripheral equipment and software. The company sells its products worldwide through its retail stores, online stores, and direct sales force, as well as through third-party cellular network carriers, wholesalers, retailers, and value-added resellers. Sales of iPad, iPhone, iPod, Apple Watches, and AppleTV products, along with the company's popular Macbook Pro and iMac notebook computers, have generated hundreds of billions of dollars in profits for the company over the past decade, much of it in cold hard cash! You may be surprised to find that Apple Inc., has not spent a great deal of this cash. In fact, according to the company's balance sheet at September 27, 2014 (see excerpt on the next page), much of that cash ($11.2 billion) went no further than the next category down the balance sheet—short-term investments in marketable securities. In addition, company sales have also generated almost $17.5 billion in net accounts receivable. The company holds another $13.8 billion in cash and cash equivalents (another kind of very short-term investment discussed in Chapter 4).

As Apple is a manufacturer, you might expect that inventories would compose the largest single current asset account on its balance sheet, as is the case for many manufacturing companies. However, a closer look at the balance sheet shows that cash and cash equivalents, short-term marketable securities, and accounts receivable account for over $42 billion of its $68.5 billion in current assets. That's about 61%. These liquid assets literally dwarf inventories. Short-term marketable securities and net accounts receivable ($28.7 billion) together are about 14 times as large as inventories ($2.1 billion)! ●

LEARNING OBJECTIVES

① **Account for** short-term investments

② **Apply** GAAP for proper revenue recognition

③ **Account for and control** accounts receivable

④ **Evaluate** collectibility using the allowance for uncollectible accounts

⑤ **Account for** notes receivable

⑥ **Show** how to speed up cash flow from receivables

⑦ **Evaluate** liquidity using three new ratios

	A	B	C	D
1	**Apple, Inc.** **Balance Sheet (Excerpt, Adapted)**			
2	(In Millions of $)	Sep. 27, 2014	Sep. 28, 2013	
3	Current assets:			
4	Cash and cash equivalents	$ 13,844	$ 14,259	
5	Short-term marketable securities	11,233	26,287	
6	Accounts receivable, less allowances of $86 and $99,			
7	respectively	17,460	13,102	
8	Inventories	2,111	1,764	
9	Deferred tax assets	4,318	3,453	
10	Vendor non-trade receivables	9,759	7,539	
11	Other current assets	9,806	6,882	
12	Total current assets	68,531	73,286	
13	Long-term marketable securities	130,162	106,215	
14	Property, plant, and equipment, net	20,624	16,597	
15	Goodwill	4,616	1,577	
16	Acquired intangible assets, net	4,142	4,179	
17	Other assets	3,764	5,146	
18	Total assets	$ 231,839	$ 207,000	
19				

》》 Try It in Excel®

You can access the most current annual report of Apple Inc., in Excel format at **http://www.sec.gov**. Using the "FILINGS" link on the toolbar at the top of the home page, select "Company Filings Search." This will take you to the "EDGAR Company Filings" page. Type "Apple" in the company name box, and select "Search." This will produce the "EDGAR Search Results" page showing the company name. Click on the "CIK" link beside the company name. This will pull up a list of the reports the company has filed with the SEC. Under the "Filing Type" box, type "10-K," and click on the search box. Form 10-K is the SEC form for the company's annual report. Find the year that you wish to view. Click on the "Interactive Data" box, which takes you to the "View Filing Data" page. Find and click on the "View Excel Document" link at the top of this page. You may choose to either open or download the Excel files containing the company's most recent financial statements.

This chapter shows how to account for short-term investments and receivables. We cover short-term investments along with receivables to emphasize their relative liquidity. Short-term investments are the next-most-liquid current assets after cash and cash equivalents. (Recall that *liquid* means "close to cash.")

ACCOUNT FOR SHORT-TERM INVESTMENTS

Reasons to Invest in Other Companies

Companies invest in debt or equity securities of other companies for at least two reasons:

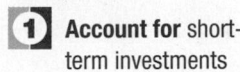

1 **Account for** short-term investments

1. They may have excess cash that they do not need immediately and so they invest on a short-term basis in equity or debt securities in other companies, hoping to earn additional income to eventually use in operations.

2. They may have long-term strategic reasons for investing, such as obtaining the ability to influence another company. For example, a company might acquire an investment in a supplier in order to obtain a steady stream of good-quality, reasonably priced raw material to use in production.

Investments in debt or equity securities may be classified as either short-term or long-term. Short-term investments are reported as current assets on a company's balance sheet, and long-term investments are classified as long-term assets. To be classified as a current asset, an investment must meet *both* of the following criteria:

- investment must be *liquid* (easily convertible to cash); and
- investor must *intend* to either convert the investment to cash within one year or current operating cycle, whichever is longer, or use it to pay a current liability.

Otherwise, the investment is classified as a long-term asset.

Investments in securities are classified into three categories, as shown in Exhibit 5-1. These categories are (1) **trading securities**, (2) **held-to-maturity securities**, and (3) **available-for-sale securities**.

- *Trading securities* are debt (bonds, notes, etc.) or equity (stock) investments purchased and expected to be sold within the near term through active trading. These securities generate gains or losses on a day-to-day basis through changes in their prices.
- *Available-for-sale securities* are debt or equity securities that are not classified as either trading or held-to-maturity. They are held with the intent of selling them some time in the future.

Exhibit 5-1 | Categories of Investments in Securities

Type of security	Trading (1)	Available-for-Sale (2)	(3)	Held-to-Maturity (4)	(5)
Asset classification	Current	Current	Long-term	Current	Long-term
Initial measurement	Cost	Cost	Cost	Cost	Cost
Subsequent measurement	Fair value	Fair value	Fair value	Amortized cost	Amortized cost
Unrealized gains/losses	Income statement (other income, gains and losses)	Other comprehensive income (OCI)	Other comprehensive income (OCI)	N/A	N/A
Chapter	5	5	8	8	8

■ *Held-to-maturity securities* are debt securities (bonds, notes, or other instruments with established maturity dates) that the investor has the intent and ability to hold until they mature.

Any of these categories of investments may be classified as a current asset, as long as it meets both of the stated criteria on page 251. However, of the three categories, only trading securities are always classified as current assets.

Let's examine how Apple Inc., describes its investments (from Note 1, *Summary of Significant Accounting Policies*):

Cash Equivalents and Marketable Securities

All highly liquid investments with maturities of three months or less at the date of purchase are classified as cash equivalents. The Company's marketable debt and equity securities have been classified and accounted for as available-for-sale. Management determines the appropriate classification of its investments at the time of purchase and reevaluates the designations at each balance sheet date. The Company classifies its marketable debt securities as either short-term or long-term based on each instrument's underlying contractual maturity date. Marketable debt securities with maturities of 12 months or less are classified as short-term and marketable debt securities with maturities greater than 12 months are classified as long-term. The Company classifies its marketable equity securities, including mutual funds, as either short-term or long-term based on the nature of each security and its availability for use in current operations. The Company's marketable debt and equity securities are carried at fair value, with the unrealized gains and losses, net of taxes, reported as a component of shareholders' equity. The cost of securities sold is based upon the specific identification method.

Source: From Apple Inc., Annual Report 2014, http://www.sec.gov/Archives/edgar/data/320193/000119312514383437/d783162d10k.htm.

Applying this explanation to the line items in the balance sheet, notice that it encompasses securities in three of the line items:

■ Line 4, "cash and cash equivalents," $13,844 million, includes a portfolio of debt securities with maturities of three months or less. These were discussed in Chapter 4.

■ Line 5, "short-term marketable securities," $11,233 million, includes a portfolio of both debt and equity securities that are classified as available-for-sale, as described in Note 1 above. These are current assets because they meet the criteria of being both highly liquid and the company intends to convert them to cash within the next fiscal year. However, the company has chosen not to treat them as trading securities because they do not trade them on a daily basis.

■ Line 13, "long-term marketable securities," $130,162 million, includes a portfolio of investment assets that does not meet at least one of the criteria for being classified as current. The company has made these investments for long-term strategic purposes. It does not plan to sell these investments within the next fiscal year and/or the investments are not liquid.

Notice that cash and investment assets on these three line items together total $155.2 billion, or 67% of Apple Inc.'s total assets as of September 27, 2014.

In this chapter, we discuss how companies measure and report investments in trading securities and available-for-sale securities that meet the criteria for inclusion in current assets. These are listed in columns (1) and (2) of Exhibit 5-1. We reserve the discussion of long-term available-for-sale securities, as well as long-term held-to-maturity securities, until Chapter 8.

Trading Securities

Suppose that, on June 18, 2016, Apple Inc., purchases 5,000 shares of **Intel** stock as a trading security, intending to trade (sell) the stock on the active market within a few months. If the fair value of the Intel stock increases, Apple Inc., will have a gain; if Intel's stock price drops, Apple Inc., will have a loss. Along the way, Apple Inc., will receive dividend revenue from Intel.

For simplicity, suppose first that the Intel stock is Apple Inc.'s only short-term investment. Apple Inc., buys the Intel stock for $20 per share, paying $100,000 cash. Apple Inc., records the purchase of the investment at cost:

	A1	◆			
	A	**B**		**C**	**D**
1	2016				
2	June 18	Investment in Trading Securities		100,000	
3		Cash			100,000
4		*Purchased investment.*			
5					

Investment in Trading Securities

100,000 |

Assume that, on June 30, Apple Inc., receives a cash dividend of $4,000 from Intel. Apple Inc., records the dividend revenue as:

	A1	◆			
	A	**B**		**C**	**D**
1	June 30	Cash		4,000	
2		Dividend Revenue			4,000
3		*Received cash dividend.*			
4					

Assets	=	Liabilities	+	Stockholders' Equity	+	Revenues
+4,000	=				+	4,000

Unrealized Gains and Losses. Apple Inc.'s 2016 fiscal year ends on September 24, and Apple Inc., prepares financial statements. On this date, the fair market value of Intel's stock is $22. The Intel stock has risen in value, and on September 24, Apple Inc.'s investment has a current fair value of $110,000. Fair (market) value is the amount for which the owner can sell the securities. Apple Inc., has an **unrealized gain** on the investment:

- *Gain* because the fair value ($110,000) of the portfolio of securities is greater than Apple Inc.'s cost of the securities ($100,000). A gain has the same effect as a revenue.

- *Unrealized gain* because Apple Inc., has not yet sold the securities.

Trading securities are reported on the balance sheet at current fair value, because fair (market) value is the amount the investor can receive by selling the securities. Prior to preparing financial statements on September 24, 2016, Apple Inc., adjusts the investment in Intel securities to its current fair value with this year-end journal entry:

	A1	◆			
	A	**B**		**C**	**D**
1	Sept 24	Investment in Trading Securities		10,000	
2		Unrealized Gain on Trading Securities			10,000
3		*Adjusted investment to fair value.*			
4					

Investment in Trading Securities

100,000	
10,000	
110,000	

Unrealized Gain on Trading Securities (other income)

	10,000

After the adjustment, Apple Inc.'s Investment in Trading Securities account, reflecting its investment in Intel stock, is ready to be reported on the balance sheet at the current fair value of $110,000.

Suppose that Apple Inc., decides to keep the Intel stock for another year, even though the company still regards the stock as a trading security. During 2017, the Intel stock declines in value. On September 30, 2017, the end of Apple Inc.'s fiscal year, the fair value of Intel stock is $21 per share. In preparation for its 2017 balance sheet, Apple Inc., makes the following adjusting entry:

	A	B	C	D
	A1			
1	2017			
2	Sept 30	Unrealized Loss on Trading Securities	5,000	
3		Investment in Trading Securities		5,000
4		Adjusted investment to fair value.		
5				

Investment in Trading Securities

100,000	5,000
10,000	
105,000	

Unrealized Loss on Trading Securities

5,000	

Unrealized gains and losses on trading securities are reported as elements of "other income or losses" in the income statement, as shown in Exhibit 5-1.

At the end of each period, because they are reported on the income statement, unrealized gains and losses on trading securities are closed along with other revenue and expense accounts and eventually become a part of retained earnings on the balance sheet. In our case, an unrealized gain of $10,000 is reported on 2016's income statement and is closed to retained earnings at the end of that year. In 2017, an unrealized loss is reported on 2017's income statement and is closed to retained earnings at the end of that year. Thus, the company's retained earnings balance at the end of 2017 includes a net $5,000 unrealized gain from the Intel stock ($10,000 unrealized gain in 2016 − $5,000 unrealized loss in 2017).

Realized Gains and Losses. A *realized* gain or loss occurs only when the investor sells an investment. This gain or loss is different from the unrealized gain that we just reported for Apple Inc. The result may be:

- Realized gain = Sale price is *greater than* the investment carrying amount.
- Realized loss = Sale price is *less than* the investment carrying amount.

Suppose Apple Inc., sells its Intel stock on June 19, 2018. The sale price is $107,000, and Apple Inc., makes this journal entry:

	A	B	C	D
	A1			
1	2018			
2	June 19	Cash	107,000	
3		Investment in Trading Securities		105,000
4		Gain on Sale of Trading Securities (other income)		2,000
5		Sold investments at a gain.		
6				

Accountants rarely use the word *realized* in the account title. A gain (or a loss) is understood to be a realized gain (or loss) arising from a sale transaction. Unrealized gains and losses are clearly labeled as *unrealized*.

Available-for-Sale Securities. Exhibit 5-2, Part A, contrasts the journal entries for Apple Inc.'s hypothetical investment in Intel stock under two alternative sets of assumptions: (1) the securities are treated as trading securities; and (2) the securities are treated as available-for-sale securities.

We have already illustrated the journal entries under the assumption of the Intel stock being treated as a trading security. Now focus on the right-hand side of Exhibit 5-2. Entry 1 in 2016 for the initial purchase of available-for-sale securities is the same as it is for trading securities, except for the investment account title. In addition, accounting for periodic dividend revenue (entry 2) in 2016 for available-for-sale securities is identical to the entry for trading securities. However, the year-end adjustment in 2016 and 2017 to fair value (entries 3 and 4) for available-for-sale securities is different than it is for trading securities. Although the investment adjustment (a debit

Exhibit 5-2 | Accounting and Reporting for Short-Term Investments and Related Revenues, Gains, and Losses

Entry	Trading Securities (TS)			Available-for-Sale Securities (AFSS)		
	Part A. Journal Entries					
1	Purchase in 2016	Investment in TS..........................	100,000	Investment in AFSS..........................	100,000	
	($100,000 cash)	Cash.....................................		100,000	Cash.....................................		100,000
2	Receipt of dividends	Cash.....................................	4,000	Cash.....................................	4,000	
	$ 4,000	Dividend Revenue.................		4,000	Dividend Revenue....................		4,000
3	Year-end adjustment 2016 (unrealized gain $10,000)					
		Investment in TS*.......................	10,000	Investment in AFSS*......................	10,000	
		Unrealized Gain on TS (other income)......................		10,000	Unrealized Gain on Investment in AFSS (OCI).........		10,000
4	Year-end adjustment 2017 (unrealized loss $5,000)					
		Unrealized Loss on TS (other loss)................................	5,000	Unrealized Gain on Investment in AFSS (OCI)................	5,000	
		Investment in TS.................		5,000	Investment in AFSS..................		5,000
5	Sale in 2018	Cash...	107,000	Cash...	107,000	
	($107,000 cash)	Investment in TS.................		105,000	Unrealized Gain on Investment in AFSS (OCI)................	5,000	
		Gain on Sale of TS (other income)......................		2,000	Investment in AFSS..................		105,000
					Gain on Sale of Investment in AFSS................................		7,000

	Part B. Financial Reporting						
	Trading Securities (TS)				Available-for-Sale Securities (AFSS)		
Balance sheet	2016	2017	2018		2016	2017	2018
Assets				Assets			
Investment in TS......................................	110,000	105,000	0	Investment in AFSS......................	110,000	105,000	0
				Stockholders' equity			
				Accumulated OCI (other comprehensive income)......	10,000	5,000	0
Income statement	2016	2017	2018		2016	2017	2018
Dividend revenue.......................	4,000	0	0		4,000	0	0
Unrealized gain (loss)................	10,000	(5,000)	0		0	0	0
Realized gain on sale................	0	0	2,000		0	0	7,000

*Many companies use an allowance account to record upward and downward movements in fair value of the investment, enabling them to maintain the original cost information for the security. The allowance account is added to (subtracted from) cost to reflect fair value on the balance sheet.

of $10,000 in 2016 and a credit of $5,000 in 2017) is the same, the offsetting unrealized gains and losses on available-for-sale securities are not reported as other income or other loss in the income statement for those years. Instead, they are reported as **other comprehensive income (loss)** for each period and are accumulated separately over time as **accumulated other comprehensive income (loss)**, which is a separate component of stockholders' equity. This is because an available-for-sale security, even if it is classified as short-term, is typically not sold as quickly or frequently as a trading security. So, prior to the actual sale, it is more likely that previously recorded unrealized gains and losses may be reversed for available-for-sale securities. These unrealized gains and losses are kept separate and are not reflected as part of net income of any period, as long as the securities remain unsold.

When the securities are sold in 2018 (entry 5), the unrealized gain or loss account remaining for the available-for-sale securities is eliminated from both the investment account and accumulated other comprehensive income. This entry returns the investment back to its original cost, which is then matched against the sales proceeds to calculate the realized gain or loss on the sale (in this case, a $7,000 gain). The terms "other comprehensive income" and "accumulated other comprehensive income" are discussed more thoroughly in Chapters 8, 10, and 11.

Reporting on the Balance Sheet and the Income Statement

Exhibit 5-2, Part B, illustrates the proper way to report investments in both trading and available-for-sale securities on the balance sheet and income statement.

The Balance Sheet.   Short-term investments are current assets. They appear on the balance sheet immediately after cash because short-term investments are almost as liquid as cash. Report both short-term trading investments and short-term available-for-sale investments at their *current fair (market) values*.

For available-for-sale investments, report unrealized gains and losses as an element of other comprehensive income, which, over time, is accumulated in a separate section of stockholders' equity. In our simple case with only one stock, the balance in accumulated other comprehensive income at the end of 2017 is $5,000 and is the result of a $10,000 increase in 2016 offset by a $5,000 decrease in 2017. This balance is zeroed out when the securities are sold in 2018. The investment account ($105,000) is restored to original cost ($100,000) at this point so that it may be matched against the proceeds of the sale to reflect the realized gain ($7,000).

Income Statement.   Investments in debt and equity securities earn interest revenue and dividend revenue. Investments also create both unrealized and realized gains and losses. For trading investments, these items are reported on the income statement as other revenue, gains, and losses, reported in the periods in which they occur. For available-for-sale investments, dividends are reported in the same way as for trading securities, and realized gains and losses are recognized in other revenue, gains, and losses as the securities are sold. Notice that, regardless of whether the securities are treated as trading or available-for-sale, the impact on reported earnings over the three-year period is the same (+14,000, − $5,000, and + $2,000 in 2016, 2017, and 2018, respectively, for trading versus +$4,000 in 2016 and +$7,000 in 2018 for available-for-sale). The only difference between the two classification methods is in the timing (the period in which the net gains or losses are recognized on the income statement).

Ethics and the Current Ratio

Recall that the current ratio is computed as follows:

$$\text{Current ratio} = \frac{\text{Total current assets}}{\text{Total current liabilities}}$$

Lending agreements often require the borrower to maintain a current ratio at some specified level, say 1.50 or greater. What happens when the borrower's current ratio falls below 1.50? The consequences can be severe:

- The lender can call the loan for immediate payment.
- If the borrower cannot pay, then the lender may take over the company.

Suppose it's December 10 and it looks like Health Corporation of America's (HCA's) current ratio will end the year at a value of 1.48. That would put HCA in default on the lending agreement and create a bad situation. With three weeks remaining in the year, how can HCA improve its current ratio?

There are several strategies for increasing the current ratio, such as the following:

1. Launch a major sales effort. The increase in cash and receivables will more than offset the decrease in inventory, total current assets will increase, and the current ratio will improve.

2. Pay off some current liabilities before year-end. Both current assets in the numerator and current liabilities in the denominator will decrease by the same amount. The proportionate impact on current liabilities in the denominator will be greater than the impact on current assets in the numerator, and the current ratio will increase. This strategy increases the current ratio when the current ratio is already above 1.0, as it is for HCA.

3. A third strategy reveals one of the accounting games that companies with questionable ethics sometimes play. Suppose HCA owns some investments that it clearly plans to hold for strategic reasons for longer than a year. Suppose the company chooses to reclassify a sufficient amount of these as current assets for the sole purpose of increasing the current ratio to an acceptable level. This strategy would be acceptable if HCA does in fact plan to sell the investments within the next year. However, such a strategy would be unethical if HCA does it solely for the purpose of beefing up its current ratio.

From this example you can see that accounting is not all black and white. It takes good judgment—which includes a strong sense of ethics—to become a successful accountant.

Mid-Chapter | Summary Problem

The largest current asset on Waverly Corporation's balance sheet at December 31, 2016, is Investment in Trading Securities. The investments consist of stock in other corporations and cost Waverly $8,660 (amounts in millions). At the balance sheet date, the fair value of these securities is $9,000.

Suppose Waverly holds the stock investments in the hope of trading them actively for a profit and converting them to cash within four to six months. How will Waverly classify the investments? What will Waverly report on the balance sheet at December 31, 2016? What will Waverly report on its 2016 income statement? Show a T-account for Investment in Trading Securities.

Answer

Investment in Trading Securities

	8,660	
	340	
Balance	9,000	

These investments in trading securities are *current assets* as reported on the 2016 balance sheet, and Waverly's 2016 income statement will report as follows (amounts in millions):

Balance sheet		Income statement	
Current assets:		Other revenue and expense:	
Cash.....................................	$ XX	Unrealized Gain on Trading Securities	
Investment in		($9,000 − $8,660)......................	$ 340
Trading Securities...........	9,000		

Suppose Waverly sells the investment in securities for $8,700 in 2017. Journalize the sale and then show the Investment in Trading Securities T-account as it appears after the sale.

Answer

	(In millions)
Cash	8,700
Loss on Sale of Trading Securities..	300
Investment in Trading Securities	9,000
Sold investments at a loss.	

Investment in Trading Securities

	8,660		
	340	9,000	
Balance	-0-		

APPLY GENERALLY ACCEPTED ACCOUNTING PRINCIPLES (GAAP) FOR PROPER REVENUE RECOGNITION

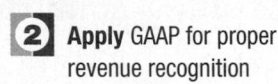

Apply GAAP for proper revenue recognition

A study of accounts and notes receivable would not be complete without a brief review of the revenue recognition principle that is the basis for measurement and reporting in this critical area. Recall from Chapters 1 and 3 that **revenue** is the inflow of resources (or reduction of liabilities) resulting from delivering goods to or rendering services for customers. Revenue should be recognized when it is earned, and not before.

The core principle for **revenue recognition** is that revenue should be recognized when an entity transfers goods or services to customers in an amount that reflects the cash or fair market value of other assets that the entity expects to receive in exchange for those goods or services. The process of revenue recognition is based on contracts that the entity has with outsiders. A **contract** is an agreement (either written or oral) between two parties that creates enforceable rights or performance obligations. The following five-step model applies in sequential order (that is, you cannot proceed to step 2 unless step 1 is satisfied; you cannot proceed to step 3 unless steps 1 and 2 are satisfied, etc.).

1. Identify the contract(s) with the customer.
2. Identify the performance obligations in the contract.
3. Determine the transaction price.
4. Allocate the transaction price to the performance obligation(s) in the contract.
5. Recognize revenue when (or as) the entity satisfies the performance obligations.

To satisfy a performance obligation means that the selling entity has done everything required to earn the revenue. If the sale of products is involved, the performance obligation is generally satisfied when the goods have been transferred to the customer and when the customer has assumed ownership and control over goods. When services are involved, the performance obligation is generally satisfied when the provider has substantially completed the service for the customer. In addition, the price of the goods or services must be fixed or determinable, and collection must be reasonably assured. The amount of the revenue to be recognized by the seller is the amount of cash or fair market value of other assets received from the buyer to satisfy the buyer's obligation to purchase the goods or services.

Sometimes revenue recognition occurs as the result of a simple contract that may not even be written. For example, a retailer may sell groceries over the counter to customers who pay cash to purchase them. The contract is implied, based on the customer taking delivery of the products and transferring cash to the retailer. The entity has a single performance obligation: to transfer goods in exchange for cash received. Revenue is recognized when that event takes place. However, business transactions are often not that simple. Large businesses often engage in complex, multifaceted contracts, some of which have multiple performance obligations to deliver multiple products and/or services for prices that may be variable or contingent on future events. In these cases, application of the revenue recognition model can become quite complex and might require the exercise of a great deal of judgment on the part of management. This text deals only with simple and straightforward contracts with single performance obligations. The more complex applications of the revenue recognition model are reserved for more advanced courses in accounting.

Exhibit 5-3 shows an excerpt from footnote 1 of Apple Inc.'s financial statements containing Apple Inc.'s revenue recognition policy. The first two paragraphs state the company's relatively simple policy for recognizing revenue related to the sale of products alone. Revenue for these sales is generally recorded at the point the products are shipped to the customer. The last paragraph describes how the company records revenue from contracts with multiple deliverables, including hardware, software, and service and support contracts. These types of revenues are more complex in nature, requiring more computations and the exercise of more judgment on the part of management. We do not discuss these types of revenues in this text.

Exhibit 5-3 | Excerpt of Footnote from Apple, Inc.'s Financial Statements Describing Its Revenue Recognition Policy

Net sales consist primarily of revenue from the sale of hardware, software, digital content and applications, accessories and service and support contracts. The Company recognizes revenue when persuasive evidence of an arrangement exists, delivery has occurred, the sales price is fixed or determinable and collection is probable. Product is considered delivered to the customer once it has been shipped and title, risk of loss and rewards of ownership have been transferred. For most of the Company's product sales, these criteria are met at the time the product is shipped. For online sales to individuals, for some sales to education customers in the U.S., and for certain other sales, the Company defers revenue until the customer receives the product because the Company retains a portion of the risk of loss on these sales during transit.

...

The Company records reductions to revenue for estimated commitments related to price protection and other customer incentive programs. For transactions involving price protection, the Company recognizes revenue net of the estimated amount to be refunded... The Company also records reductions to revenue for expected future product returns based on the Company's historical experience...

Revenue Recognition for Arrangements with Multiple Deliverables

For multi-element arrangements that include hardware products containing software essential to the hardware product's functionality, undelivered software elements that relate to the hardware product's essential software, and undelivered non-software services, the Company allocates revenue to all deliverables based on their relative selling prices...

Source: From Apple Inc, Financial Statement, Revenue Recognition Policy, http://www.sec.gov/Archives/edgar/data/320193/000119312514383437/d783162d10k.htm.

Let's look at a simple example. Suppose Apple Inc., enters into a contract to deliver a truckload of iPhones to an AT&T Wireless warehouse in Florida. On the truck are 30,000 iPhones, each of which Apple Inc., sells to AT&T Wireless for $100 on account. Each phone costs Apple Inc., $60. The terms of the contract provide that if AT&T Wireless pays for the product within 30 days, Apple Inc., will allow them a 2% discount off the purchase price. Let's apply the five-step revenue recognition model to this set of facts.

1. Identify the contract. Apple agrees to ship 30,000 iPhones to AT&T, its customer, in exchange for a promise from AT&T to pay for the phones in cash within 30 days.

2. Identify the performance obligations. Apple Inc.'s only obligation in this contract is to ship the products to AT&T, who, on receipt, will then package them with various service contracts and sell them to its customers.

3. Determine the transaction price. Apple agrees to invoice AT&T for at the agreed-upon price of the phones, to be paid to Apple Inc., within 30 days. AT&T's obligation is to pay for the phones within an agreed time period. The gross agreed-upon price is $100 per unit for the 30,000 units. The gross amount of the sale is therefore $3,000,000. However, Apple Inc., like most other large businesses, offers customers an incentive of a **sales discount** for early payment in order to speed up cash flow. A typical sales discount incentive might be stated as **2/10, n/30**. This expression means that the seller is willing to discount the order by 2% if the buyer pays the invoice within 10 days of the invoice date. After that time, the seller withdraws the discount offer. Regardless, the buyer *must* pay within 30 days. In the case of Apple Inc.'s sale to AT&T Wireless, if AT&T Wireless pays the invoice within 10 days, it is entitled to a $2 per unit discount ($100 selling price less 2% discount), for a total $60,000 discount on the order, making the full amount due to settle Apple Inc.'s invoice, and the full amount it expects to collect, $2,940,000 rather than $3,000,000.

4. Allocate the transaction price to the performance obligation(s) in the contract. According to Apple Inc.'s revenue recognition policy as stated in Exhibit 5-3, at the point when Apple, Inc., ships the phones to AT&T, it performs its obligation to supply the products, and simultaneously, AT&T Wireless assumes ownership and acquires the obligation to pay for the iPhones.

5. Recognize revenue as the performance obligation is fulfilled. Apple Inc., records the sales transaction to AT&T Wireless with two entries[1]:

	A	B	C	D
1		Accounts Receivable	2,940,000	
2		Sales Revenue		2,940,000
3		To record sale of 30,000 iPhones for $98 each		
4		($100 - 2% discount)		
5				

	A	B	C	D
1		Cost of Goods Sold	1,800,000	
2		Inventory		1,800,000
3		To record cost of products sold ($60 × 30,000)		
4				

[1]We assume that Apple Inc., uses a perpetual inventory system, which requires continual accounting for all inventories purchased and sold as those transactions take place. Thus, every sales transaction requires two entries: (1) to record the receivable and sale at the net amount the company expects to collect and (2) to record cost of goods sold (an expense) and to reduce (credit) inventory for the cost of the products. Inventory and cost of goods sold are the subjects of Chapter 6.

Shipping Terms

The proper time to recognize sales revenue is when ownership of goods changes hands between the seller and the buyer. This point is determined by the **shipping terms** in the sales contract. When goods are shipped **FOB (free on board)** *shipping point*, ownership changes hands and revenue is recognized at the point when the goods leave the seller's shipping dock. When goods are shipped FOB *destination*, ownership changes hands and revenue is recognized at the point of delivery to the customer. As specified in its revenue recognition policy (Exhibit 5-3), Apple Inc., records most product sales as FOB shipping point, which means that the company recognizes revenue and cost of goods sold at the point the goods leave its shipping dock. Goods in transit are regarded as the property of the purchaser (in the case of our example, AT&T Wireless). However, for online sales and sales to education customers in the U.S., Apple Inc., recognizes revenue as FOB destination, because the company retains a portion of the risk of loss on these sales during transit.

Collection Within (vs. Outside) the Discount Period

Assuming AT&T fulfills its obligation to pay the discounted price within the 10-day discount period, the transaction to record the collection of this receivable would be as follows:

	A	B	C	D
1		Cash	2,940,000	
2		Accounts Receivable		2,940,000
3		*To record collection of credit sale less 2% discount.*		
4				
5				

If for some reason, AT&T does not pay its discounted invoice within the prescribed time period of 10 days, it forfeits its contractual right to the sales discount and would be obligated to pay Apple Inc., the full amount. In that event, collection of the account receivable would be recorded as follows:

	A	B	C	D
1		Cash	3,000,000	
2		Accounts Receivable		2,940,000
3		Sales Discounts Forfeited (other revenue)		60,000
4		*To record collection of credit sale including forfeiture*		
5		*of 2% discount.*		
6				

Sales Refunds, Returns, and Allowances

Customers usually have a right to return unsatisfactory or damaged merchandise to sellers for refund, credit, or exchange. This is called a **sales return** or **allowance**. In these cases, the seller is obligated to accept the returned product if the customer chooses to return it. In the case of cash sales, customers are entitled to a cash refund for returned merchandise. Companies that sell on credit generate accounts receivable from customers, so when a customer returns a product, the seller will issue a **credit memo**, which is a document authorizing a credit to the customer's account receivable on the seller's books. Returned merchandise means lost profits. For companies like Apple Inc., that have extensive business experience, events like product returns tend to follow rather predictable patterns over time. Thus, the company can make reasonably accurate estimates of the amount of sales returns from customers based on historical experience and, following the expense recognition principle (discussed in Chapter 3), make end-of-period adjustments to sales, receivables, and inventories for returns and refunds. Refer to Apple Inc.'s revenue recognition policy in Exhibit 5-3, second paragraph, last sentence for an explanation of its treatment of product returns.

Remember that the revenue recognition principle requires that revenue be recorded only for the net amount that the company expects to eventually realize. Therefore, sales revenue recognized in a particular period must be reduced (debited) by an amount for estimated sales returns. For goods sold for cash, a refund liability account should be credited for the amount of the estimated returns. For goods sold on account, an allowance for sales returns (contra asset) account should be credited for the amount of the estimated returns. Cost of goods sold must also be reduced by the estimated cost of goods returned, and an offsetting account called estimated returns inventory debited for the same amount. Later, when the returns actually take place, if the inventory is saleable, the actual cost of goods returned is debited to the inventory account, and the estimated returns inventory is reduced for the same amount. For goods originally sold for cash, the refund liability account should be debited to offset the credit to cash for the refund. For goods originally sold on credit, the allowance for sales returns should be debited, offset with a credit to accounts receivable.

For example, suppose that Cox's Department Store has a policy that allows customers to return merchandise for up to 60 days for a full refund. In June, the store's total sales are $2,000,000, all for cash. The cost of the merchandise sold is $1,200,000. The company makes the following entries:

	A1				
	A	**B**		**C**	**D**
1	June 30	Cash		2,000,000	
2		Sales Revenue			2,000,000
3		*To record monthly sales for June*			
4		Cost of Goods Sold		1,200,000	
5		Inventory			1,200,000
6		*To record cost of merchandise sold for June*			
7					

Based on the store's past experience, approximately 5% of merchandise sold will be returned. At the end of June, the company must record the following adjusting entries:

	A1				
	A	**B**		**C**	**D**
1	June 30	Sales Revenue		100,000	
2		Refund Liability			100,000
3		*To record estimated refunds for June sales*			
4		Estimated Returns Inventory		60,000	
5		Cost of Goods Sold			60,000
6		*To record cost of estimated returns for June sales*			
7					

In July, within the allowable return period, customers return merchandise that retailed for $90,000 and that cost $54,000 for refund. The company makes the following entries:

	A1				
	A	**B**		**C**	**D**
1	July	Refund Liability		90,000	
2		Cash			90,000
3		*To record merchandise returned in July*			
4		Inventory		54,000	
5		Estimated Returns Inventory			54,000
6		*To record cost of merchandise returned in July*			
7					

Retailers, wholesalers, and manufacturers typically disclose sales revenue at the *net* amount, which means after sales discounts and sales returns and allowances have been subtracted. Apple Inc.'s net sales revenue for 2014, compared with the last two years, is:

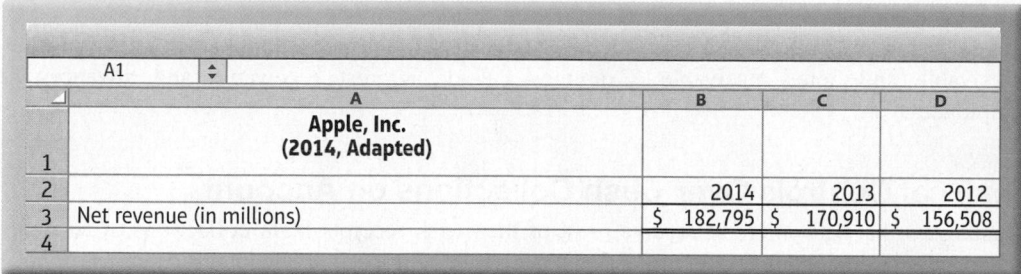

A1					
	A		**B**	**C**	**D**
1	**Apple, Inc.** **(2014, Adapted)**				
2			2014	2013	2012
3	Net revenue (in millions)		$ 182,795	$ 170,910	$ 156,508
4					

ACCOUNT FOR AND CONTROL ACCOUNTS RECEIVABLE

Receivables are the third most-liquid asset—after cash and short-term investments. Most of the remainder of this chapter shows how to account for receivables.

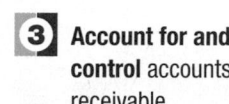

3 Account for and control accounts receivable

Types of Receivables

Receivables are monetary claims against others. Receivables are acquired mainly by selling goods and services (accounts receivable) and by lending money (notes receivable). The journal entries to record the receivables are

Performing a Service on Account		Lending Money on a Note Receivable	
Accounts Receivable.................. XXX		Notes Receivable........................ XXX	
Service Revenue.......................	XXX	Cash..	XXX
Performed a service on account.		*Loaned money to another company.*	

The two major types of receivables are accounts receivable and notes receivable. A business's *accounts receivable* are the amounts collectible from customers from the sale of goods and services. Accounts receivable, which are *current assets*, are sometimes called *trade receivables* or merely *receivables*.

The Accounts Receivable account in the general ledger serves as a *control account* that summarizes the total amount receivable from all customers. Companies also keep a *subsidiary ledger* of accounts receivable with a separate account for each customer:

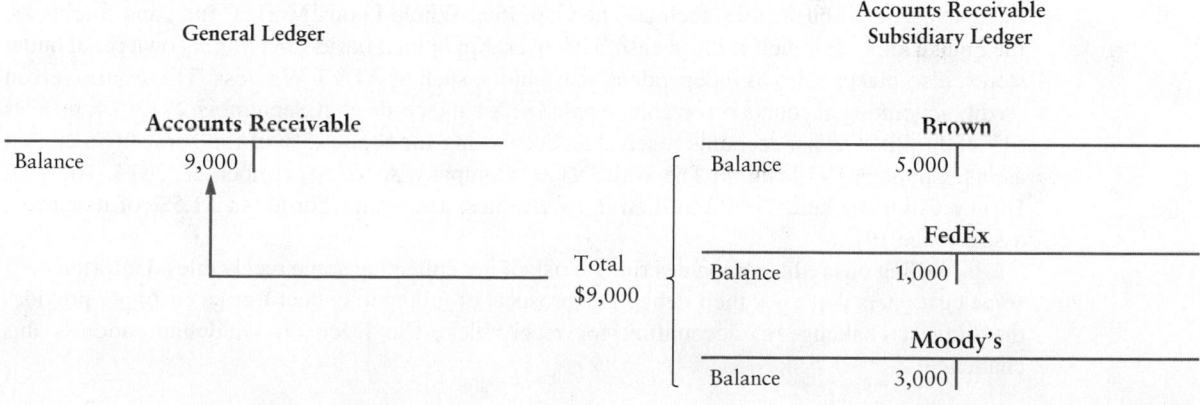

Notes receivable are more formal contracts than accounts receivable. For a note, the borrower signs a written promise to pay the lender a definite sum at the maturity date, plus interest. This is why notes are also called promissory notes. The note may require the borrower to pledge *security* for the loan. This means that the borrower gives the lender permission to claim certain assets, called *collateral*, if the borrower fails to pay the amount due. We cover the details of notes receivable later in this chapter.

Other receivables is a miscellaneous category for all receivables other than accounts receivable and notes receivable. Examples include interest receivable and advances to employees.

Internal Controls Over Cash Collections on Account

Businesses that sell on credit receive most of their cash receipts from collections of accounts receivable. Internal control over collections on account is important. Chapter 4 discusses control procedures for cash receipts, but another element of internal control deserves emphasis here—the separation of cash-handling and cash-accounting duties. Consider the following case:

> Central Paint Company is a small, family-owned business that takes pride in the loyalty of its workers. Most employees have been with Central for 10 or more years. The company makes 90% of its sales on account and receives most of its cash by mail.
>
> The office staff consists of a bookkeeper and an office supervisor. The bookkeeper maintains the general ledger and a subsidiary record of individual customer accounts receivable. The bookkeeper also makes the daily bank deposit.
>
> The supervisor prepares monthly financial statements and any special reports the company needs. The supervisor also takes sales orders from customers and serves as office manager.

Can you identify the internal control weakness here? The problem is that the bookkeeper makes the bank deposit. With this cash-handling duty, the bookkeeper could steal an incoming customer check and write off the customer's account as uncollectible. The customer doesn't complain because the bookkeeper wrote off the customer's account, and Central therefore stops pursuing collection.

How can this weakness be corrected? The supervisor—not the bookkeeper—could open incoming mail and make the daily bank deposit. The bookkeeper should *not* be allowed to handle cash. Only the remittance advices should be forwarded to the bookkeeper to credit customer accounts receivable. Removing cash handling from the bookkeeper and keeping the accounts away from the supervisor separates duties and strengthens internal control.

Using a bank lockbox achieves the same separation of duties. Customers send their payments directly to a post office box owned by Central Paint Company's bank, which records cash as the cash goes into Central's bank account. The bank then forwards the remittance advice to Central's bookkeeper, who credits the customer account. No Central Paint employee even touches incoming cash.

How Do We Manage the Risk of Not Collecting?

Exclusively retail businesses such as The Gap, Inc., Whole Foods Market, Inc., and Starbucks, Inc., make almost all their sales in cash. However, Apple Inc., besides having its own retail outlet stores, also makes sales to independent distributors, such as AT&T Wireless. These sales are on credit, generating accounts receivable. Apple Inc.'s balance sheet at September 27, 2014, reflects $17,460 million in net accounts receivable, accounting for about 25% of the company's current assets. Chapters 1–3 featured The Walt Disney Company. As of September 27, 2014, The Walt Disney Company held $7,822 million in receivables, accounting for about 51.5% of its current assets (page 19).

By selling on credit, companies run the risk of not collecting some receivables. Unfortunately, some customers don't pay their debts. The prospect of failing to collect from a customer provides the biggest challenge in accounting for receivables. The Decision Guidelines address this challenge.

 **DECISION GUIDELINES**

MANAGING AND ACCOUNTING FOR RECEIVABLES

Here are the management and accounting issues a business faces when the company extends credit to customers. For each issue, the Decision Guidelines propose a plan of action. Let's look at a business situation: Suppose you open a health club near your college. Assume you will let customers use the club and bill them for their monthly dues. What challenges will you encounter by extending credit to customers?

The main issues in *managing* receivables, along with plans of action, are the following:

Issues	Plan of Action
1. What are the benefits and the costs of extending credit to customers?	1. Benefit—Increase in sales. Cost—Risk of not collecting.
2. Run a credit check on prospective customers.	2. Extend credit only to creditworthy customers.
3. Design the internal control system to separate duties.	3. Separate cash-handling and accounting duties to keep employees from stealing the cash collected from customers.
4. Keep a close eye on customer payment habits. Send second and third statements to slow-paying customers, if necessary.	4. Pursue collection from customers to maximize cash flow.

The main issues in accounting for receivables (amounts are assumed), and the related plans of action, are the following:

Issues

1. Measure and report receivables on the balance sheet at net realizable value, the amount you expect to collect. This is the appropriate amount to report for receivables.

2. Measure and report the expense associated with failure to collect receivables. This expense is called *uncollectible-account expense* and is reported on the income statement.

Plan of Action

Report receivables at net realizable value:

Balance sheet

Receivables...	$1,000
Less: Allowance for uncollectible accounts...	(80)
Receivables, net...	$ 920

Measure the expense of not collecting from customers:

Income statement

Sales (or service) revenue..............................	$8,000
Expenses:	
Uncollectible-account expense..................	190

These guidelines lead to our next topic, accounting for uncollectible receivables.

EVALUATE COLLECTIBILITY USING THE ALLOWANCE FOR UNCOLLECTIBLE ACCOUNTS

4 Evaluate collectibility using the allowance for uncollectible accounts

A company acquires an account receivable only when it sells its product or service on credit (on account). You'll recall that the entry to record the earning of revenue on account is (amount assumed):

	A	B	C	D
1		Accounts Receivable	1,000	
2		Sales Revenue (or Service Revenue)		1,000
3		*Earned revenue on account.*		
4				

Ideally, the company would collect cash for all of its receivables. But unfortunately the entry to record cash collections on account is for only $950.

	A	B	C	D
1		Cash	950	
2		Accounts Receivable		950
3		*Collections on account.*		
4				

You can see that companies rarely collect all of their accounts receivable. So companies must account for their uncollectible accounts—$50 in this example. Selling on credit creates both a benefit and a cost:

- *Benefit:* Customers who cannot pay cash immediately can buy on credit, so sales and profits increase.
- *Cost:* The company cannot collect from some customers. Accountants label this cost **uncollectible-account expense**, **doubtful-account expense**, or **bad-debt expense**.

Apple Inc., reports accounts receivable as follows on its 2014 balance sheet (in millions):

	Sep. 27, 2014	Sep. 28, 2013
Accounts receivable, less allowances of $86 and $99, respectively	$17,460	$13,102

The phrase "less allowances" means that a relatively small amount ($86 million, or less than 1/2% of the total) has been subtracted from total accounts receivable, representing the amount that Apple Inc., does *not* expect to collect.[2] Sometimes the amount of the allowance is not considered sufficiently material to separately disclose in the line item, so it is disclosed in an explanatory financial statement footnote and the line item in the balance sheet simply says "accounts receivable, net." Apple Inc.'s net amount of the receivables ($17,460 million) is the amount that Apple Inc., *does* expect to collect in cash receipts. Notice that the net amount of receivables increased by about 33% during the current year (from $13,102 million to $17,460 million) while the allowance actually went down (from $99 million to $86 million).

---

[2]Apple Inc., like many other large manufacturing and marketing companies, makes allowances for sales returns (see discussion on pages 261 through 263) as well as uncollectible accounts. To illustrate accounting for both of these types of allowances simultaneously adds a level of complexity that we consider beyond the scope of this text, and appropriate only for more advanced courses. Therefore, in the discussion of the computation of the allowance for uncollectible accounts in the pages that follow, as well as related exercise and problem material, we assume that the figures used for both accounts receivable and sales have already been reduced by allowances for sales returns.

Uncollectible-account expense is an operating expense in the selling, general, and administrative category along with salaries, rent, and utilities. To measure uncollectible-account expense, companies that follow GAAP use the allowance method.

Allowance Method

The best way to measure uncollectible accounts expense (bad debts) is by the **allowance method**. This method records losses from failure to collect receivables based on estimates developed from the company's collection experience. Apple Inc., doesn't wait to see which customers will not pay. Instead, it records the estimated amount as Uncollectible-Account Expense and also sets up a contra-account to accounts receivable called **Allowance for Uncollectible Accounts**. In doing so, Apple follows the expense recognition principle discussed in Chapter 3 by matching the expense related to noncollection in the same period that the related sales revenue is recognized. On the balance sheet, the Allowance for Uncollectible Accounts reduces gross receivables to their net realizable value. Other titles for this account are **Allowance for Doubtful Accounts** and *Allowance for Bad Debts*. The allowance shows the amount of the receivables the business expects *not* to collect.

In Chapter 3 we used the Accumulated Depreciation account to show the amount of a plant asset's cost that has been expensed—the portion of the asset that's no longer a benefit to the company. Allowance for Uncollectible Accounts serves a similar purpose for Accounts Receivable. The allowance shows how much of the receivable has been expensed. You'll find this diagram helpful (amounts are assumed):

Equipment............................	$100,000	Accounts receivable....................	$10,000
Less: Accumulated		Less: Allowance for	
depreciation	(40,000)	uncollectible accounts	(900)
Equipment, net....................	60,000	Accounts receivable, net.............	9,100

Focus on Accounts Receivable. Customers owe this company $10,000, but it expects to collect only $9,100. The *net realizable value* of the receivables is therefore $9,100. Another way to report these receivables is as follows:

| Accounts receivable, less allowance of $900................. | $9,100 |

You can work backward to determine the full amount of the receivables, $10,000 (net realizable value of $9,100 plus the allowance of $900).

The income statement reports Uncollectible-Account Expense among the operating expenses, using assumed figures, as:

Income statement (partial):

Expenses:

Uncollectible-account expense:................ $2,000

» Try It

Refer to the Apple Inc., balance sheet at the beginning of the chapter. At September 27, 2014, how much in total did customers owe Apple Inc.? How much did Apple Inc., expect *not* to collect? How much did Apple Inc., expect to collect? What was the net realizable value of Apple Inc.'s receivables?

Answer:

	Millions
Customers owed Apple, Inc.	$17,546 ($17,460 + $86)
Apple, Inc. expected not to collect the allowance of....	(86)
Apple, Inc. expected to collect—net realizable value ...	$17,460

Notice that to determine the *total* (*gross*) amount customers owed, you have to add the amount of the allowance back to the "net realizable value" ($17,460 million + $86 million = $17,546 million). Of this amount, $86 million was expected not to be collected, leaving $17,460 million that the company expected to collect (i.e., its net realizable value). Although the gross amount is not shown in the financial statements, it is useful for analysis purposes, as shown on pages 272–273.

The best way to estimate uncollectibles uses the company's history of collections from customers. There are two basic ways to estimate uncollectibles:

- Percent-of-sales method
- Aging-of-receivables method

Percent-of-Sales. The **percent-of-sales method** computes uncollectible-account expense as a percent of revenue.[3] This method takes an *income-statement approach* because it focuses on the amount of expense to be reported on the income statement. Assume it is September 27, 2014, and Apple, Inc.,'s accounts have these balances *before the year-end adjustments* (amounts in millions):

Accounts Receivable		Allowance for Uncollectible Accounts	
$17,546			$10

Customers owe Apple Inc. $17,546 million, and the Allowance amount on the books is $10 million. But Apple Inc.'s top managers know that the company will fail to collect more than $10 million. Suppose Apple Inc.'s credit department estimates that uncollectible-account expense is 0.0004 (1/25 of 1%) of total revenues, which are $182,795 million. The entry that records uncollectible-account expense for the year also updates the allowance as follows (using Apple Inc., figures):

	A	B	C	D
1	Sep. 27	Uncollectible-Account Expense ($182,795 × .0004)	73	
2		Allowance for Uncollectible Accounts		73
3		*Recorded uncollectible account expense for the year.*		
4		*Calculations rounded to nearest million.*		
5				

The expense decreases Apple Inc.'s assets, as shown by the accounting equation.

Assets	=	Liabilities	+	Stockholders' Equity	−	Expenses
− 73	=	0			−	73

The percent-of-sales method employs the expense recognition (matching) concept to estimate, probably on a monthly or quarterly basis, the cost that has been incurred in order to earn a certain amount of revenue and to recognize both in the same time period.

---

[3]In this text, we assume that all sales are on account, unless it is specifically stated that they are in cash.

Accounts Receivable		Allowance for Uncollectible Accounts		Uncollectible-Account Expense	
17,546			10	73	
		Adj	73		
		End Bal	83		

Net accounts receivable, $17,463

Using the percent-of-sales method, the net realizable value of accounts receivable, or the amount ultimately expected to be collected from customers, would be $17,463 ($17,546 − $83). This method will usually result in a different amount of estimated uncollectible-accounts expense and net realizable value of accounts receivable than would be produced by the aging method, discussed next.

Aging-of-Receivables. The other popular method for estimating uncollectibles is called **aging-of-receivables**. The aging method is a *balance-sheet approach* because it focuses on what should be the most relevant and faithful representation of accounts receivable as of the balance-sheet date. In the aging method, individual receivables from specific customers are analyzed based on how long they have been outstanding.

Suppose it is September 27, 2014, and Apple Inc.'s receivables accounts show the following before the year-end adjustment (amounts in millions):

Accounts Receivable		Allowance for Uncollectible Accounts	
17,546			10

These accounts are not yet ready for the financial statements because the allowance balance is not realistic.

Apple Inc.'s computerized accounting package ages the company's accounts receivable. Exhibit 5-4 shows a representative aging schedule at September 27, 2014. Apple Inc.'s gross receivables total $17,546. Of this amount, the aging schedule shows that the company will *not* collect $86 (lower right corner).

Exhibit 5-4 | Aging Accounts Receivable of Apple Inc.

Customer	Age of Account (Dollar amounts rounded to the nearest million)				
	1–30 Days	31–60 Days	61–90 Days	Over 90 Days	Total Balance
Best Buy					
Walmart					
Totals...	$16,682	$ 600	$ 200	$ 64	$17,546
Estimated percent uncollectible...............................	× 0.383%	× 1%	× 5%	× 10%	
Allowance for Uncollectible Accounts balance should be	$ 64* +	$ 6 +	$ 10 +	$ 6* =	$ 86

*Computations are rounded

The aging method will bring the balance of the allowance account ($10) to the needed amount as determined by the aging schedule ($86). The lower right corner of the aging schedule gives the needed balance in the allowance account. To update the allowance, Apple Inc., would make this adjusting entry at year-end:

	A	B	C	D
	A1			
1	2014			
2	Sep. 27	Uncollectible-Account Expense	76	
3		Allowance for Uncollectible Accounts ($86 – $10)		76
4		*Recorded uncollectible accounts expense for the year.*		
5				

The expense decreases Apple, Inc.'s assets and net income, as shown by the accounting equation.

$$\text{Assets} \quad = \quad \text{Liabilities} \quad + \quad \overset{\text{Stockholders'}}{\text{Equity}} \quad - \quad \text{Expenses}$$

$$-76 \quad = \quad 0 \qquad\qquad - \qquad 76$$

Now the balance sheet can report the amount that Apple Inc., actually expects to collect from customers: $17,460 ($17,546 − $86). This is the net realizable value of Apple Inc.'s accounts receivable.

Accounts Receivable		Allowance for Uncollectible Accounts		Uncollectible-Account Expense
17,546				76
		Beg. bal. 10		
		Adj. 76		
		End Bal 86		

Net accounts receivable, $17,460

Writing Off Uncollectible Accounts. Assume that at the beginning of fiscal 2015, Apple Inc., had these accounts receivable (amounts in millions):

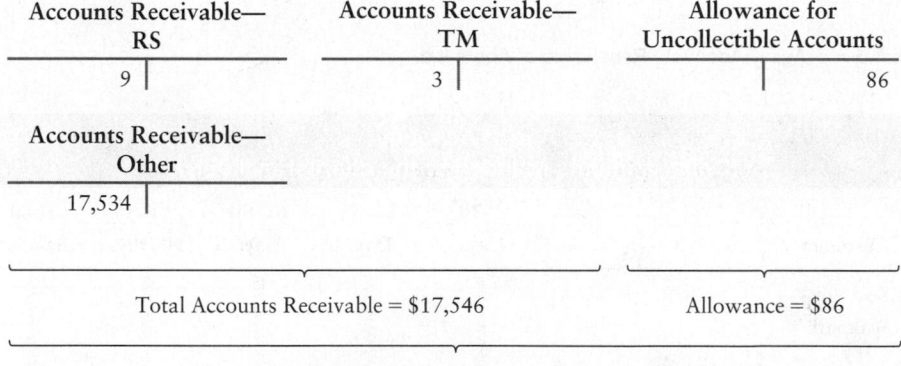

Accounts Receivable—RS	Accounts Receivable—TM	Allowance for Uncollectible Accounts
9	3	86

Accounts Receivable—Other
17,534

Total Accounts Receivable = $17,546   Allowance = $86

Accounts Receivable, Net = $17,460

Suppose that, early in fiscal 2015, Apple Inc.'s credit department determines that Apple Inc., cannot collect from customers RS and TM. Apple Inc., then writes off the receivables from these customers with the following entry:

	A	B	C	D
	A1			
1	2015			
2	Jan 31	Allowance for Uncollectible Accounts	12	
3		Accounts Receivable—RS		9
4		Accounts Receivable—TM		3
5		*Wrote off uncollectible receivables.*		
6				

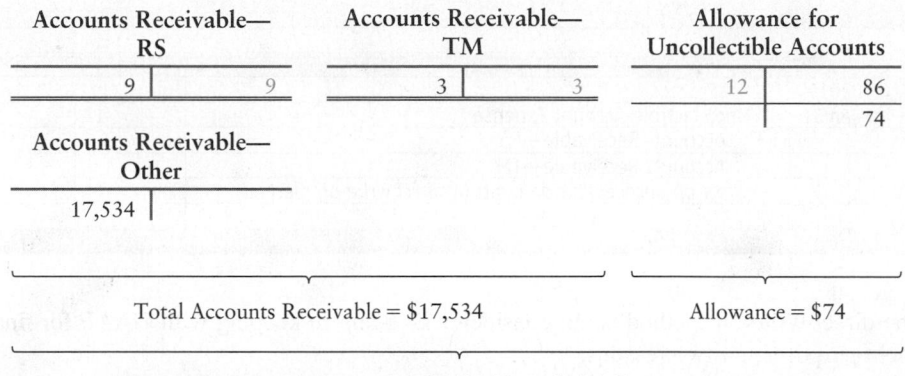

Assets	=	Liabilities	+	Stockholders' Equity
+ 12 − 12	=	0	+	0

After the write-off, Apple Inc.'s accounts show these amounts:

Accounts Receivable— RS		Accounts Receivable— TM		Allowance for Uncollectible Accounts	
9	9	3	3	12	86
					74

Accounts Receivable— Other
17,534

Total Accounts Receivable = $17,534   Allowance = $74

Accounts Receivable, Net = $17,460

The accounting equation shows that the write-off of uncollectibles has no effect on Apple Inc.'s total assets, no effect on current assets, and no effect on net accounts receivable. Notice that Accounts Receivable, Net is still $17,460. There is no effect on net income either. Why is there no effect on net income? Net income is unaffected because the write-off of uncollectibles affects no expense account. If the company uses the allowance method, as discussed in the previous section, expenses would have been properly recognized in the period they were incurred, which is the same period in which the related sales took place.

Combining the Percent-of-Sales and the Aging Methods. Most companies use the percent-of-sales and aging-of-accounts methods together:

- For *interim statements* (monthly or quarterly), companies often use the percent-of-sales method because it is easier and quicker to apply. The percent-of-sales method focuses on the uncollectible-account *expense*, but that is not enough.

- At the end of the year, companies use the aging method to ensure that Accounts Receivable is reported at *net realizable value* on the balance sheet. The aging method focuses on the amount of the receivables that is uncollectible.

- Using the two methods together provides good measures of both the *expense* and the *asset*. Exhibit 5-5 compares the two methods.

Exhibit 5-5 | Comparing the Percent-of-Sales and Aging Methods for Estimating Uncollectible Accounts

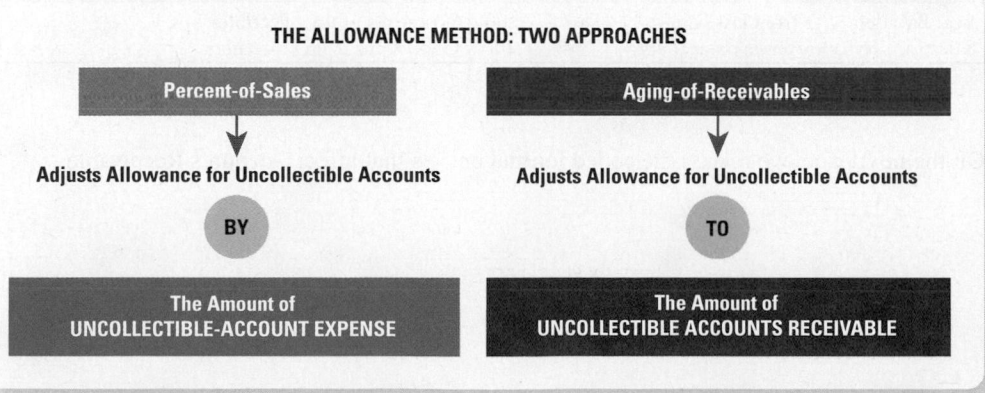

Direct Write-Off Method

There is another, less preferable way to account for uncollectible receivables. Under the **direct write-off method**, the company waits until a specific customer's receivable proves uncollectible. Then, the accountant writes off the customer's account and records Uncollectible-Account Expense (using assumed data):

	A	B	C	D
1	2015			
2	Jan 31	Uncollectible-Account Expense	12	
3		Accounts Receivable—RS		9
4		Accounts Receivable—TM		3
5		*Wrote off uncollectible accounts by direct write-off method.*		
6				

The direct write-off method is not considered as being in keeping with GAAP for financial statement purposes, for two reasons:

1. It uses no allowance for uncollectibles. As a result, receivables are always reported at their full amount, which is more than the business expects to collect. *Assets on the balance sheet may be overstated.*

2. It fails to recognize the expense of uncollectible accounts in the same period in which the related sales revenue is earned. In this example, Apple Inc., made the sales to RS and TM in 2014 and should have recorded the uncollectible-account expense during 2014, not in 2015 when it wrote off the accounts.

Because of these deficiencies, Apple Inc., and virtually all other large companies use the allowance method for preparing their financial statements.

The direct write-off method is the *required* method of accounting for uncollectible accounts for federal income tax purposes. It is one of several sources of timing differences that may arise between net income for financial reporting purposes and net income for federal income tax purposes. We will discuss other differences between book and taxable income in later chapters.

Computing Cash Collections From Customers

A company earns revenue and then collects the cash from customers. For Apple Inc., and most other companies, there is usually a time lag between earning the revenue and collecting the cash. Collections from customers are the single most important source of cash for any business. You can compute a company's collections from customers by analyzing its Accounts Receivable account. Receivables typically hold only five items, as reflected in the five elements of the following Accounts Receivable account balance (amounts assumed):

Accounts Receivable

Beg. Bal. (left over from last period)	200	Write-offs of uncollectibles	100**
Sales (or service) revenue on account	1,800*	Collections from customers	$X = 1,500$†
End. Bal. (carries over to next period)	400		

On the next page, we review the coded journal entries that affect Accounts Receivable.

*The journal entry that places revenue into the accounts receivable account is:

	A	B	C
1	Accounts Receivable	1,800	
2	Sales (or Service) Revenue		1,800
3			

**The journal entry for write-offs of uncollectible accounts is:

	A	B	C
1	Allowance for Uncollectible Accounts	100	
2	Accounts Receivable		100
3			

†The journal entry that records cash collections of accounts receivable is:

	A	B	C
1	Cash	1,500	
2	Accounts Receivable		1,500
3			

Suppose you know all these amounts *except* collections from customers. You can compute collections by solving for X in the T-account.[4] Often, write-offs are unknown and must be omitted. Then the computation of collections becomes an approximation.

ACCOUNT FOR NOTES RECEIVABLE

As stated earlier, notes receivable are more formal than accounts receivable. Notes receivable due within one year or less are current assets. Notes due beyond one year are *long-term receivables* and are reported as long-term assets. Some notes receivable are collected in installments. The portion due within one year is a current asset and the remainder is long-term. A company may hold a $20,000 note receivable from a customer, but only the $6,000 that the customer must pay within one year is a current asset.

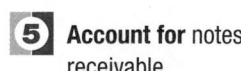 **Account for** notes receivable

Before exploring accounting for notes receivable, let's define some key terms:

Creditor. The party to whom money is owed. The creditor is also called the *lender*.

Debtor. The party that borrowed and owes money on the note. The debtor is also called the *maker* of the note or the *borrower*.

Interest. Interest is the cost of borrowing money. The interest is stated in an annual percentage rate.

Maturity date. The date on which the debtor must pay the note.

Maturity value. The sum of principal and interest on the note.

Principal. The amount of money borrowed by the debtor and lent by the creditor.

Term. The length of time from when the note was signed by the debtor to when the debtor must pay the note.

---

[4]An equation may help you solve for X. The equation is $\$200 + \$1,800 - X - \$100 = \$400$. $X = \$1,500$.

There are two parties to a note:

- The *creditor* has a note receivable.
- The *debtor* has a note payable.

Exhibit 5-6 is a typical promissory note.

Exhibit 5-6 | Promissory Note

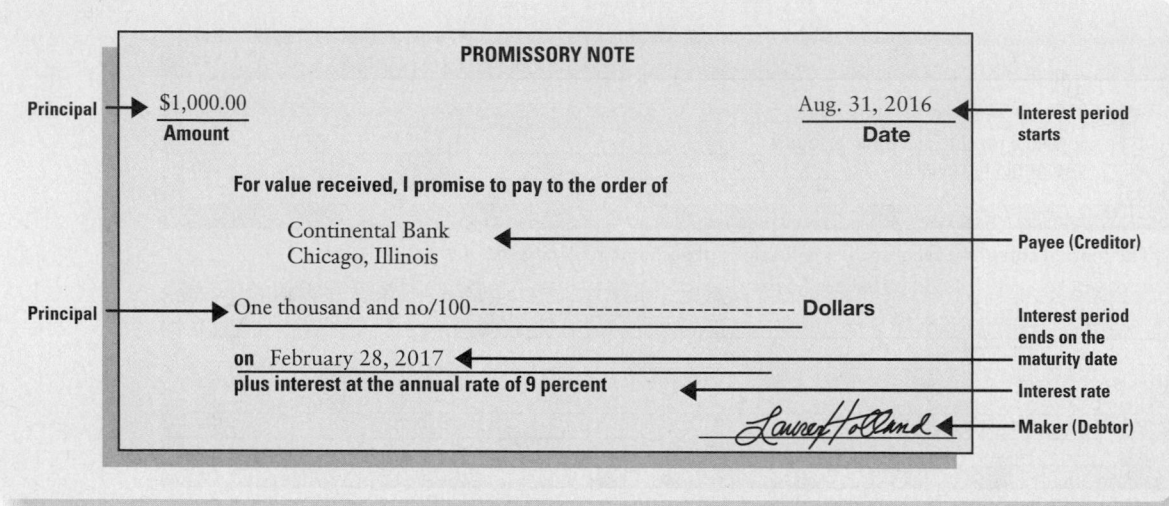

The **principal** amount of the note ($1,000) is the amount borrowed by the debtor and lent by the creditor. This six-month note receivable runs from August 31, 2016, to February 28, 2017, when Lauren Holland (the maker) promises to pay Continental Bank (the creditor) the principal of $1,000 plus 9% interest. Interest is revenue to the creditor (Continental Bank, in this case).

Accounting for Notes Receivable

Consider the promissory note in Exhibit 5-6. After Lauren Holland signs the note, Continental Bank gives her $1,000 cash. The bank's entries follow, assuming a December 31 year-end for Continental Bank:

	A	B	C	D
1	2016			
2	Aug 31	Note Receivable—L. Holland	1,000	
3		Cash		1,000
4		*Made a loan.*		
5				

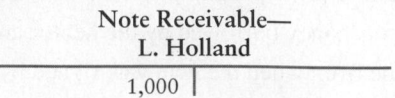

Note Receivable—
L. Holland

The bank gives one asset, cash, in exchange for another asset, a note receivable; so total assets do not change.

Continental Bank earns interest revenue during September, October, November, and December. At December 31, 2016, the bank accrues 9% interest revenue for four months:

	A		B	C	D
	A1	▲			
	A		**B**	**C**	**D**
1	Dec 31		Interest Receivable ($1,000 × .09 × 4/12)	30	
2			Interest Revenue		30
3			*Accrued interest revenue.*		
4					

The bank's assets and revenues increase.

Continental Bank reports these amounts in its financial statements at December 31, 2016:

Balance sheet

Current assets:

Note receivable $1,000

Interest receivable................ 30

Income statement

Interest revenue.................. $ 30

The bank collects the note on February 28, 2017, and records the following:

	A		B	C	D
	A1	▲			
	A		**B**	**C**	**D**
1	2017				
2	Feb 28		Cash	1,045	
3			Note Receivable—L. Holland		1,000
4			Interest Receivable		30
5			Interest Revenue ($1,000 × .09 × 2/12)		15
6			*Collected note at maturity.*		
7					

This entry zeroes out Note Receivable and Interest Receivable and also records the interest revenue earned in 2017.

Note Receivable—
L. Holland

1,000	1,000

In its financial statements for the year ended December 31, 2017, the only item that Continental Bank will report is the interest revenue of $15 that was earned in 2017. There's no note receivable or interest receivable on the balance sheet because those items were zeroed out when the bank collected the note at maturity.

Three aspects of the interest computation deserve mention:

1. Interest rates are always for an annual period, unless stated otherwise. In this example, the annual interest rate is 9%. At December 31, 2016, Continental Bank accrues interest revenue for four months. The interest computation is:

Principal	×	Interest Rate	×	Time	=	Amount of Interest
$1,000	×	.09	×	4/12	=	$30

2. The time element (4/12) is the fraction of the year that the note has been in force during 2016.

3. Interest is often computed for a number of days. For example, suppose you loaned out $10,000 on April 10. The note receivable runs for 90 days and specifies interest at 8%.

   a. Interest starts accruing on April 11 and runs for 90 days, ending on the due date, July 9:

Month	Number of Days That Interest Accrues
April	20
May	31
June	30
July	9
Total	90

   b. The interest computation is
   $$\$10,000 \times 0.08 \times 90/365 = \$197$$

Some companies sell goods and services on notes receivable (versus selling on accounts receivable). This often occurs when the payment term extends beyond the customary accounts receivable period of 30 to 60 days.

Suppose that on March 20, 2017, Apple Inc., sells a large number of iPads to Walmart. Apple Inc., gets Walmart's three-month promissory note plus 10% annual interest. At the outset, Apple Inc., would debit Notes Receivable and credit Sales Revenue.

A company may also accept a note receivable from a trade customer whose account receivable is past due. The company then debits Notes Receivable and credits Accounts Receivable. We would say the company "received a note receivable on account." Now let's examine some strategies to speed up the cash flow from receivables.

SHOW HOW TO SPEED UP CASH FLOW FROM RECEIVABLES

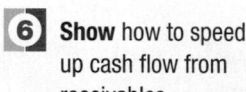

6 **Show** how to speed up cash flow from receivables

CASH FLOW

All companies want speedy cash receipts. Rapid cash flow means companies have the ability to pay off current liabilities faster, as well as to finance new products, research, and development. Thus, companies such as Apple Inc., develop strategies to shorten the credit cycle and collect cash more quickly. For example, they might offer sales discounts for early payment, as discussed earlier. They might also charge interest on customer accounts that exceed a certain age. They adopt more effective credit and collection procedures. In recent years, as electronic banking has become more popular, a common strategy has been to emphasize credit card or bankcard sales.

Credit Card or Bankcard Sales

The merchant sells merchandise and lets the customer pay with a credit card, such as Discover or American Express, or with a bankcard, such as VISA or MasterCard. This strategy may increase sales dramatically, but the added revenue comes at a cost, which is typically about 2% to 3% of the total amount of the sale. Let's see how credit cards and bankcards work from the seller's perspective.

Suppose Apple Inc., sells a computer and peripheral devices for $5,000 at one of its stores, and the customer pays with a VISA card. VISA's fee is 2%. Apple Inc., records the sale, ignoring cost of goods sold:

A1				
	A		**B**	**C**
1	Cash		4,900	
2	Credit Card Discount Expense		100	
3	Sales Revenue			5,000
4	*Recorded bankcard sales.*			
5				

Assets	=	Liabilities	+	Stockholders' Equity	+	Revenues	−	Expenses
+ 4,900	=	0	+			+ 5,000		− 100

Apple enters the transaction in its accounting system via a point-of-sale terminal. The terminal, linked to a VISA server, automatically credits Apple Inc.'s bank account for a discounted portion, say $4,900, of the $5,000 sale amount. Two percent ($100) goes to VISA. To Apple Inc., the credit card discount is similar to interest expense and is therefore recorded on the income statement separately from operating income as other income (expense).

Selling (Factoring) Receivables

Apple Inc., makes some large sales to big-box electronics stores on account, debiting Accounts Receivable and crediting Sales Revenue. Apple Inc., might then sell these accounts receivable to another business, called a *factor*. The factor earns revenue by paying a discounted price for the receivable and then, it is hoped, collecting the full amount from the customer. The benefit to Apple Inc., is the immediate receipt of cash. The biggest disadvantage of factoring is that it is often quite expensive when compared to the costs of retaining the receivable on the books and ultimately collecting the full amount. In addition, the company that factors its receivables loses control over the collection process. For these reasons, factoring is not often used by companies who have other, less costly means to raise cash, such as short-term borrowing from banks. Factoring may be used by start-up companies with insufficient credit history to obtain loans at a reasonable cost, by companies with weak credit history, or by companies that are already saddled with a significant amount of debt.

To illustrate selling, or *factoring*, accounts receivable, suppose a company wishes to speed up cash flow and therefore sells $100,000 of accounts receivable, receiving cash of $95,000. The company would record the sale of the receivables:

	A	B	C
	A1		
1	Cash	95,000	
2	Financing Expense	5,000	
3	Accounts Receivable		100,000
4	*Sold accounts receivable.*		
5			

Again, Financing Expense is reported on the income statement as other expense (separate from operating expense). Some companies may debit a Loss account. Discounting a note receivable is similar to selling an account receivable. However, the credit is to Notes Receivable (instead of Accounts Receivable).

Notice the high price (5% of the face amount, or $5,000) the company has had to pay in order to collect the cash immediately, as opposed to waiting 30–60 days to collect the full amount. Therefore, if the company can afford to wait, it will probably not engage in factoring to collect the full amount of the receivables.

Reporting on the Statement of Cash Flows

Receivables and short-term investments appear on the balance sheet as current assets. We saw these in Apple Inc.'s balance sheet at the beginning of the chapter. We've also seen how to report the related revenues, expenses, gains, and losses on the income statement. Because receivable and investment transactions affect cash, their effects must also be reported on the statement of cash flows.

Receivables bring in cash when the business collects from customers. These transactions are reported as *operating activities* on the statement of cash flows because they result from sales. Investment transactions show up as *investing activities* on the statement of cash flows. Chapter 12 shows how companies report their cash flows on the statement of cash flows. In that chapter, we will see exactly how to report cash flows related to receivables and investment transactions.

EVALUATE LIQUIDITY USING THREE NEW RATIOS

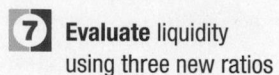

Investors and creditors use ratios to evaluate the financial health of a company. We introduced the current ratio in Chapter 3. Other ratios, including the **quick ratio** (or **acid-test ratio**), **accounts receivable turnover** and the number of **days' sales outstanding (DSO)**, help investors measure liquidity.

Quick (Acid-Test) Ratio

The balance sheet lists assets in the order of relative liquidity:

1. Cash and cash equivalents
2. Short-term investments
3. Accounts (or notes) receivable

Apple Inc.'s balance sheet in the chapter-opening story lists these accounts in order.

Managers, stockholders, and creditors care about the liquidity of a company's assets. The current ratio measures ability to pay current liabilities with current assets. A more stringent measure of the ability to pay current liabilities is the quick (or *acid-test*) ratio:

Apple, Inc. 2014

(Dollars in millions, taken from Apple, Inc. balance sheet)

$$\text{Quick (acid-test) ratio} = \frac{\overset{\text{Cash and cash}}{\text{equivalents}} + \overset{\text{Short-term}}{\text{investments}} + \overset{\text{Net current}}{\text{receivables}}}{\text{Total current liabilities}} = \frac{\$13,844 + \$11,233 + \$17,460}{\$63,448} = 0.67$$

The higher the quick ratio, the easier it is to pay current liabilities. Apple Inc.'s quick ratio of 0.67 means that it has only $0.67 of quick assets to pay each $1 of current liabilities. In many cases, this ratio value would be considered sub-par. But remember our observation about the current ratio in Chapter 3. The computation of both the current and quick ratios assume the worst case scenario: that the company might be forced to go out of business, liquidate, and pay off all of its current liabilities immediately. That assumption is obviously not applicable to a company like Apple, which generates a ton of cash from its operations. That helps alleviate our concerns about what otherwise would be a low value for the quick ratio. What is considered an acceptably high quick ratio? The answer depends on the industry. Auto dealers can operate smoothly with a quick ratio of 0.20, less than one-third of Apple Inc.'s quick ratio value. How can auto dealers survive with so low a quick ratio? The auto manufacturers help finance their dealers' inventory. Most dealers, therefore, have a financial safety net provided through the manufacturers. Retail stores and high-volume integrated design, manufacturing, and marketing companies like Apple Inc., often have relatively low quick ratios as well, but compensate for it with high inventory turnover and virtually 100% cash sales, which keeps the cash flowing in fast enough to pay creditors.

Accounts Receivable Turnover and Days' Sales Outstanding

After a business makes a credit sale, the *next* step is collecting the receivable. Two important ratios, **accounts receivable turnover** and **days' sales outstanding (DSO)** (also called *days' sales in receivables* or the *collection period*) tell a company how long it takes to collect its average level of receivables. The accounts receivable turnover ratio measures the ratio of net credit sales to average net accounts receivable. The result, expressed as a decimal fraction, shows the number of times per year the company completely collects its average accounts receivable. A larger number is better than a smaller number for this ratio. Once the turnover ratio is computed, it is converted to DSO by dividing it into 365 (days per year). For DSO, shorter is better because it shows that cash is coming in quickly. Notice that high turnover translates to a smaller number for DSO, and low turnover translates to a larger number for DSO.

Apple Inc.'s accounts receivable turnover for fiscal 2014 is computed as follows:

(Dollars in millions, taken from Apple, Inc.'s financial statements)

$$\text{Accounts receivable turnover} = \frac{\text{Net credit sales}}{\text{Average net accounts receivable}}$$

$$= \frac{\$182,795}{(\$17,460 + \$13,102)/2}$$

$$= 11.96 \text{ times}$$

$$\text{Days' sales outstanding (DSO)} = \frac{365}{11.96} = 30.5 \text{ days}$$

Accounts receivable turnover was 11.96 times per year. This means that the company converted its average accounts receivable to cash 11.96 times during fiscal 2014. Converted to days, it took Apple Inc., an average of 30.5 days (365 ÷ 11.96) to collect the average customer account.

To evaluate Apple Inc.'s collection period, we need to compare 30.5 days to the credit terms that Apple Inc., offers customers when the company makes a sale, as well as the number of days on average that creditors typically allow Apple Inc., to pay them without penalty. Suppose Apple Inc., makes sales on "net 30" terms, which means that customers should pay Apple Inc., within 30 days of the sale. That makes Apple Inc.'s DSO acceptable in comparison to its credit terms. With regard to its credit terms for payables, if Apple, Inc.'s short-term creditors expect payment of their accounts payable within 30 days, Apple Inc.'s DSO is also acceptable.

Companies watch their collection periods closely. Whenever collections slow down, the business must find other sources of financing, such as borrowing or selling receivables. During recessions, customers pay more slowly and a longer collection period may be unavoidable.[5]

---

[5]Another way to compute DSO is to follow two logical steps. First, compute average daily sales (or average revenue for one day). Then divide average daily sales into average net receivables for the period. Following this method, we can calculate days' sales in receivables for Apple Inc., as follows:

(Dollars in millions, taken from Apple, Inc.'s financial statements)

Days' Sales in Receivables	(In millions)
1. $\dfrac{\text{Average daily sales}}{} = \dfrac{\text{Net sales}}{365 \text{ days}}$	$\dfrac{\$182,795}{365 \text{ days}} = \$500.80 \text{ per day}$
2. $\dfrac{\text{Days' sales in receivables}}{} = \dfrac{\text{Average net receivables*}}{\text{Average daily sales}}$	$\dfrac{\$15,281^*}{\$500.80 \text{ per day}} = 30.5 \text{ days}$
*$\dfrac{\text{Average net receivables}}{} = \dfrac{\text{Beginning net receivables} + \text{Ending net receivables}}{2}$	$= \dfrac{\$17,460 + \$13,102}{2} = \$15,281$

You can see that this method merely rearranges the equations in the body of the text, "going through the back door" to achieve the same result.

End-of-Chapter | Summary Problem

Excelsior Technical Resources' (ETR's) balance sheet at December 31, 2016, reported the following:

	(In millions)
Accounts receivable.....................................	$382
Allowance for doubtful accounts................	(52)

ETR uses both the percent-of-sales and the aging approaches to account for uncollectible receivables.

Requirements

1. How much of the December 31, 2016, balance of accounts receivable did ETR expect to collect? Stated differently, what was the net realizable value of ETR's receivables?

2. Journalize, without explanations, 2017 entries for ETR:

   a. Estimated doubtful-account expense of $40 million, based on the percent-of-sales method, all during the year.

   b. Write-offs of uncollectible accounts receivable totaling $58 million. Prepare a T-account for Allowance for Doubtful Accounts and post to this account. Show its unadjusted balance at December 31, 2017.

   c. December 31, 2017, aging-of-receivables, which indicates that $47 million of the total receivables of $409 million is uncollectible at year-end. Post to Allowance for Doubtful Accounts, and show its adjusted balance at December 31, 2017.

3. Show how ETR's receivables and the related allowance will appear on the December 31, 2017, balance sheet.

4. Show what ETR's income statement for the year ending December 31, 2017, will report for the transactions detailed.

Answers

Requirement 1

	(In millions)
Net realizable value of receivables ($382 − $52)	$330

Requirement 2

	A	B	C	D
1			(In millions)	
2	a.	Doubtful-Account Expense	40	
3		Allowance for Doubtful Accounts		40
4				
5	b.	Allowance for Doubtful Accounts	58	
6		Accounts Receivable		58
7				

Allowance for Doubtful Accounts

	Dec 31, 2016	52
2017 Write-offs 58	2017 Expense	40
	Unadjusted balance at Dec 31, 2017	34

	A1	⬍				
◢	A	B			C	D
1					(In millions)	
2	c.	Doubtful-Account Expense ($47 – $34)			13	
3		Allowance for Doubtful Accounts				13
4						

Allowance for Doubtful Accounts

Dec 31, 2017 Unadj bal	34
2017 Expense	13
Dec 31, 2017 Adj bal	47

Requirement 3

	(In millions)
Accounts receivable.....................................	$409
Allowance for doubtful accounts...............	(47)
Accounts receivable, net............................	$362

Requirement 4

	(In millions)
Expenses: Doubtful-account expense for 2017 ($40 + $13)	$53

REVIEW │ Short-Term Investments and Receivables

Quick Check (Answers are given on page 307.)

1. Dazzle Productions held investments in trading securities with a fair value of $35,000 at December 31, 2016. These investments cost Dazzle Productions $25,000 on January 1, 2016. What is the appropriate amount for Dazzle Productions to report for these investments on the December 31, 2016, balance sheet?

   a. $10,000 gain
   b. $35,000
   c. $25,000
   d. Cannot be determined from the data given

2. Return to Dazzle Productions in question 1. What should appear on the Dazzle Production's income statement for the year ended December 31, 2016, for the trading securities?

   a. $25,000

   b. $35,000

   c. $10,000 unrealized gain

   d. Cannot be determined from the data given

Use the following information to answer questions 3–7.

Marshall Company had the following information in 2016:

Accounts receivable 12/31/16	$ 14,000
Allowance for uncollectible accounts 12/31/16 (before adjustment)	800
Credit service revenue during 2016	35,000
Cash service revenue during 2016	16,000
Collections from customers on account during 2016	47,000

3. Uncollectible accounts are determined by the percent-of-sales method to be 2% of credit sales. How much is uncollectible-account expense for 2016?

   a. $320   c. $700

   b. $1,010   d. $800

4. Uncollectible account expense for 2016 is $1,450. What is the adjusted balance in the Allowance account at year-end for 2016?

   a. $800   c. $2,250

   b. $650   d. $1,450

5. If uncollectible accounts are determined by the aging-of-receivables method to be $1,200, the uncollectible-account expense for 2016 would be

   a. $1,200.   c. $700.

   b. $2,000.   d. $400.

6. Refer to Question 5. Using the aging-of-receivables method, the balance of the Allowance account after the adjusting entry at year-end 2016 would be

   a. $1,200.   c. $400.

   b. $700.   d. $2,000.

7. Refer to Question 5. Using the aging-of-receivables method, the net realizable value of accounts receivable on the December 31, 2016, balance sheet would be

   a. $12,800.   c. $14,000.

   b. $14,800.   d. $15,200.

8. Accounts Receivable has a debit balance of $2,400, and the Allowance for Uncollectible Accounts has a credit balance of $300. A $40 account receivable is written off. What is the amount of net receivables (net realizable value) after the write-off?

   a. $2,100   c. $2,140

   b. $2,360   d. $2,060

9. Birchwood Corporation began 2016 with Accounts Receivable of $600,000. Service revenue, all on account, for the year totaled $1,600,000. Birchwood ended the year with accounts receivable of $800,000. Birchwood's bad-debt losses are nonexistent. How much cash did Birchwood collect from customers in 2016?

   a. $1,800,000   c. $1,600,000

   b. $2,400,000   d. $1,400,000

10. Carey Ltd. received a four-month, 6%, $2,400 note receivable on March 1. The adjusting entry on March 31 will include

a. a debit to Cash for $144.

c. a debit to Interest Receivable for $144.

b. a credit to Interest Revenue for $12.00.

d. a debit to Interest Receivable for $48.

11. What is the maturity value of a $80,000, 14%, six-month note?

a. $85,600

c. $80,000

b. $91,200

d. $74,400

12. If the adjusting entry to accrue interest on a note receivable is omitted, then

a. assets, net income, and stockholders' equity are overstated.

b. assets are overstated, net income is understated, and stockholders' equity is understated.

c. liabilities are understated, net income is overstated, and stockholders' equity is overstated.

d. assets, net income, and stockholders' equity are understated.

13. Net credit sales total $584,000. Beginning and ending accounts receivable are $46,000 and $50,000, respectively. Calculate days' sales outstanding.

a. 27 days

c. 36 days

b. 31 days

d. 30 days

14. From the following list of accounts, calculate the quick ratio.

Cash	$ 7,000	Accounts payable	$ 9,000
Accounts receivable	13,600	Salary payable	3,000
Inventory	10,000	Notes payable (due in two years)	9,000
Prepaid insurance	2,000	Short-term investments	1,000

a. 1.6

c. 2.7

b. 2.4

d. 1.8

Accounting Vocabulary

acid-test ratio (p. 278) Ratio of the sum of cash plus short-term investments plus net current receivables to total current liabilities. Tells whether the entity can pay all its current liabilities if they come due immediately. Also called the *quick ratio*.

accounts receivable turnover (p. 278) Net sales divided by average net accounts receivable.

accumulated other comprehensive income (p. 256) The cumulative amount of items reported as other comprehensive income; a separate category in the stockholders' equity section of the balance sheet.

aging-of-receivables (p. 269) A way to estimate bad debts by analyzing individual accounts receivable according to the length of time they have been receivable from the customer.

Allowance for Doubtful Accounts (p. 267) Another name for *Allowance for Uncollectible Accounts*.

Allowance for Uncollectible Accounts (p. 267) The estimated amount of collection losses on accounts receivable. Another name for *Allowance for Doubtful Accounts*.

allowance method (p. 267) A method of recording collection losses based on estimates of how much money the business will not collect from its credit customers.

available-for-sale securities (p. 251) Securities that are not classified as held-to-maturity or trading securities.

bad-debt expense (p. 266) Another name for *uncollectible-account expense*.

contract (p. 258) An agreement between two parties that creates enforceable rights or obligations.

credit memo (p. 261) A document issued to a credit customer for merchandise returned, authorizing a credit to the customer's account receivable for the amount of the sale.

creditor (p. 273) The party to whom money is owed.

days' sales outstanding (DSO) (p. 278) 365 ÷ accounts receivable turnover. Indicates how many days' sales remain in Accounts Receivable awaiting collection. Also called *days' sales in receivables* or the *collection period*.

debtor (p. 273) The party who owes money.

direct write-off method (p. 272) A method of accounting for bad debts in which the company waits until a customer's account receivable proves uncollectible and then debits Uncollectible-Account Expense and credits the customer's Account Receivable.

doubtful-account expense (p. 266) Another name for *uncollectible-account expense*.

FOB (p. 261) Acronym for "free on board"; used in quoting shipping terms. See also *shipping terms*.

held-to-maturity securities (p. 251) Securities in which the investor has the intent and ability to hold until a maturity date stated on the face of the security.

interest (p. 273) The borrower's cost of renting money from a lender. Interest is revenue for the lender and expense for the borrower.

maturity date (p. 273) The date on which the debtor must pay the note.

maturity value (p. 273) The sum of principal and interest on the note.

other comprehensive income (p. 256) Certain types of revenue, expenses, gains, and losses that are allowed to bypass the income statement. These items are reported either in a separate statement or in a combined statement of net income and comprehensive income. At the end of a period, items of comprehensive income for that period are reported as accumulated other comprehensive income, a separate category of stockholders' equity.

percent-of-sales method (p. 268) Computes uncollectible-account expense as a percentage of net credit sales. Also called the *income-statement approach* because it focuses on the amount of expense to be reported on the income statement.

principal (p. 273) The amount borrowed by a debtor and lent by a creditor.

quick ratio (p. 278) Another name for *acid-test ratio*.

receivables (p. 263) Monetary claims against a business or an individual, acquired mainly by selling goods or services and by lending money.

revenue (p. 258) Inflows of resources to an entity that result from delivering goods or rendering services to customers.

revenue recognition (p. 258) The process of recording revenue to depict the transfer of promised goods or services to customers in an amount that reflects the consideration to which the entity expects to be entitled to receive in exchange for those goods or services.

sales discount (p. 260) Percentage reduction of sales price by the seller as an incentive for early payment before the due date. A typical way to express sales discount is "2/10, n/30." This means the seller will grant a 2% discount if the invoice is paid within 10 days, and the entire amount is due within 30 days.

shipping terms (p. 261) Terms provided by the seller of merchandise that dictate the date on which title transfers to the buyer. A typical way to express shipping terms is through FOB terms. For example, "FOB destination" means title to the goods passes to the buyer when the goods are delivered and the buyer assumes control over them. "FOB shipping point" means title passes on the date the goods are shipped from the seller's warehouse.

term (p. 273) The length of time from inception to maturity for a note.

trading securities (p. 251) Debt or equity investments that are to be sold in the near future with the intent of generating profits on the sale.

uncollectible-account expense (p. 266) Cost to the seller of extending credit. Arises from the failure to collect from credit customers. Also called *doubtful-account expense* or *bad-debt expense*.

unrealized gain/loss (p. 253) Gains and losses that occur on investments through fluctuations in market values, rather than through sales.

ASSESS YOUR PROGRESS

Some of the following exercises and problems are available as Excel questions in MyAccountingLab.

Ethics Check

EC5-1. Identify ethical principle violated

For each of the situations listed, identify which of three principles (integrity, objectivity and independence, or due care) from the AICPA Code of Professional Conduct that is violated. Assume all persons listed in the situations are members of the AICPA. (Note: Refer to the AICPA Code of Professional Conduct contained on pages 29–30 in Chapter 1 for descriptions of the principles.)

a. Bryan is on the audit staff of Crawley & Co, CPAs. He is assigned to the audit of Farley Holdings, a fast-growing technology firm that is run by his stepmother. He is excited to be assigned to this exciting audit because he feels it will help to advance his career. He does not disclose the relationship to anyone, nor does his stepmother.

b. Smythe Corporation has a large unrealized gain on the trading securities it holds. Norbert, the controller for Smythe, records the gain as a realized gain. This action by Norbert causes the net income of Smythe to be significantly higher than it would have otherwise been.

c. Sheila is the treasurer of Morrison Company. She knows that her company plans to keep its investment in Apple stock for several years (it has actually been pledged as collateral for a loan that Morrison has at a local bank.) However, she decides to classify the Apple stock as a trading security. The classification of the stock as a trading security makes it a current asset and increases Morrison's current ratio, making the company look more favorable to investors.

d. Marguerite, a staff accountant for Brown & Co., is confused by the rules for short-term investments; she struggled with this topic when she was in her accounting program in college. When she is given the responsibility for reviewing the entries related to her company's short-term investments, she compares this period to the prior period and does not do any further review or analysis as is needed.

Short Exercises

S5-1. *(Learning Objective 1: Report trading investments)* Answer these questions about investments.

LO 1

1. What is the amount to report on the balance sheet for a trading security?
2. Why is a trading security always a current asset? Explain.

S5-2. *(Learning Objective 1: Account for short-term investments)* Slocomb Corp. holds a portfolio of trading securities. Suppose that on January 15, Slocomb paid $80,000 for an investment in Turok Co. shares to add to its portfolio. At October 31, the market value of Turok Co. shares is $97,000. For this situation, show everything that Slocomb would report on its October 31 balance sheet and on its income statement for the year ended October 31.

LO 1

S5-3. *(Learning Objective 1: Account for short-term investments)* Barfield Investments purchased Melnick Corp. shares as a trading security on December 16 for $109,000.

LO 1

1. Suppose the Melnick Corp. shares decreased in value to $92,000 at December 31. Make the Barfield journal entry to adjust the Investment in Trading Securities account to market value.
2. Show how Barfield would report the Investment in Trading Securities on its balance sheet and the unrealized gain or loss on its income statement.

S5-4. *(Learning Objective 2: Apply GAAP for proper revenue recognition)* On December 23, 2016, Robertson Sports Manufacturing sells a truckload of sporting goods to the Sports R Us store in Columbus, Ohio. The terms of the sale are FOB destination. The truck runs into bad weather on the way to Columbus and doesn't arrive until January 2, 2017. Robertson Sports Manufacturing's invoice totals $150,000 including sales tax. The company's year-end is December 31. What should Robertson Sports Manufacturing reflect in its 2016 income statement for this sale?

LO 2

S5-5. *(Learning Objective 2: Apply GAAP for proper revenue recognition)* Costello Company purchases inventory from Terry Pool Supplies on June 1. The sales terms on the invoice from Terry Pool Supplies are 4/20, net 30. What does this mean? What is Costello's potential savings, if any? How much time does the company have to take advantage of these savings?

LO 2

S5-6. *(Learning Objective 2: Apply GAAP for proper revenue recognition)* In August, Landeau Designs sold $500,000 of merchandise; all sales were in cash. The cost of sales for August was $320,000. Based on past experience, Landeau uses an estimated refund rate of 4% of sales. Record the journal entries for the monthly sales, cost of sales, estimated refunds, and cost of estimated returns for August.

LO 2

LO 3   **S5-7.** *(Learning Objective 3: Account for accounts receivable)* On April 3, Parker Company sold $5,000 of merchandise to Wheeler Corporation, terms 2/10, n/30, FOB shipping point. Parker Company's cost of sales for this merchandise was $4,000. The merchandise left Parker Company's facility on April 4 and arrived at Wheeler Corporation on April 10. Wheeler Corporation paid the invoice for the merchandise on April 11.

Requirements

1. Prepare the journal entries for Parker Company for the sale of the merchandise, the cost of the sale, and the related receipt of payment from Wheeler Corporation. Assume that Wheeler Corporation takes the discount if payment is within the discount period. (You do not need to record any estimated returns/refunds for this exercise.)
2. Indicate which company (Parker Company or Wheeler Corporation) owns the merchandise at the end of each of the following dates:
   a. April 3
   b. April 4
   c. April 10

LO 3   **S5-8.** *(Learning Objective 3: Account for accounts receivable)* Perform the following accounting for the receivables of Bronson and Moore, a law firm, at December 31, 2016.

Requirements

1. Set up T-accounts for Cash, Accounts Receivable, and Service Revenue. Start with the beginning balances as follows: Cash $27,000; Accounts Receivable $98,000; and Service Revenue $0. Post the following 2016 transactions to the T-accounts:
   a. Service revenue of $703,000, all on account
   b. Collections on account, $720,000
2. What are the ending balances of Cash, Accounts Receivable, and Service Revenue?

LO 3   **S5-9.** *(Learning Objective 3: Apply internal controls to accounts receivable)* As a recent college graduate, you land your first job in the customer collections department of Silktown Publishing. Alicia Donovan, the manager, asked you to propose a system to ensure that cash received from customers by mail is handled properly. Draft a short memorandum to explain the essential element in your proposed plan; explain why this element is important.

LO 4   **S5-10.** *(Learning Objective 4: Evaluate collectibility using the allowance for uncollectible accounts)* During its first year of operations, Old Tyme Furniture Restoration, Inc., had sales of $461,000, all on account. Industry experience suggests that Old Tyme's uncollectibles will amount to 4% of credit sales. At December 31, 2016, accounts receivable total $56,000. The company uses the allowance method to account for uncollectibles. (Assume that there are no expected sales refunds or sales returns for this exercise.)

1. Make Old Tyme's journal entry for uncollectible-account expense using the percent-of-sales method.
2. Show how Old Tyme should report accounts receivable on its balance sheet at December 31, 2016.

LO 4   **S5-11.** *(Learning Objective 4: Evaluate collectibility using the allowance for uncollectible accounts)* At the end of the current year (before adjusting entries), Holliday Corporation had a balance of $75,000 in Accounts Receivable and a credit balance of $4,000 in Allowance for Uncollectible Accounts. Service revenue (all on credit) for the year totaled $450,000.

Requirements

Consider each of the following two independent situations.

1. Using the percent-of-sales method, calculate the amount of Uncollectible-Account Expense if Holliday Corporation estimates its uncollectible-account expense using a rate of 2% of credit sales. What is the ending balance of the Allowance for Uncollectible-Accounts under this scenario?
2. Now assume that Holliday Corporation uses the aging-of-receivables method. Holliday Corporation estimates that its Allowance for Uncollectible Accounts should have a credit

balance of $14,000. Calculate the amount of its Uncollectible-Account Expense. What is the ending balance of the Allowance for Uncollectible Accounts under this scenario?

S5-12. *(Learning Objective 5: Account for notes receivable)*   LO **5**
1. Compute the amount of interest during 2016, 2017, and 2018 for the following note receivable: On May 31, 2016, Charter Bank lent $220,000 to Laurie Walker on a two-year, 10% note.
2. Which party has a (an)
   a. note receivable?
   b. note payable?
   c. interest revenue?
   d. interest expense?
3. How much in total would Charter Bank collect if Laurie Walker paid off the note early—say, on November 30, 2016?

S5-13. *(Learning Objective 5: Account for notes receivable)* On August 31, 2016, Diane   LO **5**
Fields borrowed $4,000 from Ferris State Bank. Fields signed a note payable, promising to pay the bank principal plus interest on August 31, 2017. The interest rate on the note is 9%. The accounting year of Ferris State Bank ends on June 30, 2017. Journalize Ferris State Bank's (a) lending money on the note receivable at August 31, 2016, (b) accrual of interest at June 30, 2017, and (c) collection of principal and interest at August 31, 2017, the maturity date of the note.

S5-14. *(Learning Objective 6: Record a credit card sale)* Collins Woodworking accepts   LO **6**
credit cards at its store. Collins' credit card processor charges a fee of 3% of the total amount of any credit sale. Assume that Russell Knight purchases $8,000 of custom furniture and pays with a VISA card. Make the entry that Collins would make to record the sale to Knight. (You do not need to make the cost of goods sold entry in this exercise. Also assume that since this is a custom order, no refunds or returns are allowed.)

S5-15. *(Learning Objective 7: Evaluate liquidity using the quick [acid-test] ratio and days'*   LO **7**
sales in receivables) Highland Products reported the following amounts in its 2017 financial statements. The 2016 amounts are given for comparison.

		2017		2016
Current assets:				
Cash..		$ 9,700		$ 9,700
Short-term investments................		15,000		11,500
Accounts receivable.....................	$87,500		$77,000	
Less: Allowance for				
uncollectibles........................	(8,200)	79,300	(6,200)	70,800
Inventory......................................		193,000		195,000
Prepaid insurance........................		2,400		2,400
Total current assets		299,400		289,400
Total current liabilities.................		100,000		109,000
Net sales (all on account)		777,450		733,000

Requirements

1. Compute Highland's quick (acid-test) ratio at the end of 2017. Round to two decimal places. How does the quick ratio compare with the industry average of 0.92?
2. Compare days' sales outstanding for 2017 with the company's credit terms of net 30 days.

S5-16. *(Learning Objectives 2, 3, 4, 5, 6: Apply GAAP for revenue recognition; account for*   LO **2 3 4 5 6**
accounts receivable, uncollectible accounts, and notes receivable; show how to speed up cash flow from receivables) Answer these questions about receivables and uncollectibles. For the true-false questions, explain any answers that turn out to be false.
1. True or false? Credit sales increase receivables. Collections and write-offs decrease receivables.
2. True or false? A proper way to express credit terms is "FOB shipping point."
3. Which receivables figure—the *total* amount that customers *owe* the company, or the *net* amount the company expects to collect—is more interesting to investors as they consider buying the company's stock? Give your reason.
4. Show how to calculate the amount of sales revenue when a sales discount is offered to speed up payment.

5. Show how to determine net accounts receivable.
6. True or false? The direct write-off method of accounting for uncollectibles understates assets.
7. Iowa State Bank lent $150,000 to Mason Company on a six-month, 6% note. Which party has interest receivable? Which party has interest payable? Interest expense? Interest revenue? How much interest will these organizations record one month after Mason Company signs the note?
8. When Iowa State Bank accrues interest on the Mason Company note, show the directional effects on the bank's assets, liabilities, and equity (increase, decrease, or no effect).
9. True or false? Credit card sales increase accounts receivable.
10. True or false? Companies with strong liquidity usually factor receivables.

Exercises MyAccountingLab

Group A

LO 1

E5-17A. *(Learning Objective 1: Apply GAAP for short-term investments)* Riverton Corporation, the investment banking company, often has extra cash to invest. Suppose Riverton buys 1,000 shares of Switzer, Inc., stock at $48 per share. Assume Riverton expects to hold the Switzer stock for one month and then sell it. The purchase occurs on December 15, 2016. At December 31, the market price of a share of Switzer stock is $58 per share.

Requirements

1. What type of investment is this to Riverton? Give the reason for your answer.
2. Record Riverton's purchase of the Switzer stock on December 15 and the adjustment to market value on December 31.
3. Show how Riverton would report this investment on its balance sheet at December 31 and any gain or loss on its income statement for the year ended December 31, 2016.
4. Suppose Riverton did *not* intend to treat the Switzer stock as a trading security, but still intended to treat it as a short-term investment. How do your answers for parts 1–3 change? Follow Exhibit 5-2.

LO 2 3

E5-18A. *(Learning Objectives 2, 3: Apply GAAP for sales, sales discount, and sales returns; account for accounts receivable)* Chic Interiors reported the following transactions in November:

Nov 2	Sold merchandise on account to Ella Barron, $1,300, terms 1/10, n/30.
10	Sold merchandise on account to Amanda O'Connor, $2,500, terms 2/10, n/30.
11	Collected payment from Ella Barron for the November 2 sale.
15	O'Connor returned $1,700 of the merchandise purchased on November 10.
19	Collected payment from Amanda O'Connor for the balance of the November 10 sale.

Requirements

1. Record the foregoing transactions in the journal of Chic Interiors. (You do not need to make the cost of sales, estimated refunds, or cost of estimated returns journal entries; assume that these entries will be made by the company when it makes its other adjusting entries at period end.)
2. Prepare a computation of net sales for the month of November.

LO 3 4

E5-19A. *(Learning Objectives 3, 4: Account for accounts receivable and uncollectible accounts)* Perform the following accounting for the receivables of Bronson and Moore, a law firm, at December 31, 2016.

Requirements

1. Set up T-accounts and start with the beginning balances for these T-accounts:
   - Accounts Receivable, $97,000
   - Allowance for Uncollectible Accounts, $13,000

Post the following 2016 transactions to the T-accounts:
a. Service revenue of $702,000, all on account
b. Collections on account, $716,000
c. Write-offs of uncollectible accounts, $9,000
d. Uncollectible-account expense (allowance method), $7,000

2. What are the ending balances of Accounts Receivable and Allowance for Uncollectible Accounts?
3. Show how Bronson and Moore will report accounts receivable on its balance sheet at December 31, 2016.

E5-20A. *(Learning Objective 4: Apply GAAP for uncollectible receivables)* At December 31, 2016, Fako Travel Agency has an Accounts Receivable balance of $96,000. Allowance for Doubtful Accounts has a credit balance of $830 before the year-end adjustment. Service revenue (all on account) for 2016 was $550,000. Fako estimates that doubtful-account expense for the year is 2% of service revenue. Make the year-end entry to record doubtful-account expense. Show how Accounts Receivable and Allowance for Doubtful Accounts are reported on the balance sheet at December 31, 2016.

LO **4**

E5-21A. *(Learning Objectives 2, 3, 4: Apply GAAP for revenue recognition, accounts receivable, and uncollectible receivables)* On June 30, Paisley Party Planners had a $35,000 balance in Accounts Receivable and a $3,252 credit balance in Allowance for Uncollectible Accounts. During July, Paisley made credit sales of $198,000. July collections on account were $169,000, and write-offs of uncollectible receivables totaled $2,890. Uncollectible-accounts expense is estimated as 4% of credit sales. No sales returns are expected.

LO **2 3 4**

Requirements

1. Journalize sales, collections, write-offs of uncollectibles, and uncollectible-account expense by the allowance method during July. Explanations are not required.
2. Show the ending balances in Accounts Receivable, Allowance for Uncollectible Accounts, and *Net* Accounts Receivable at July 31. How much does Paisley expect to collect?
3. Show how Paisley Party Planners will report accounts receivable and net sales on its July 31 balance sheet and income statement for the month ended July 31.

E5-22A. *(Learning Objective 4: Apply GAAP to uncollectible receivables)* At December 31, 2016, before any year-end adjustments, the Accounts Receivable balance of Turf Trimmers, Inc., is $350,000. The Allowance for Doubtful Accounts has an $18,700 credit balance. Turf Trimmers prepares the following aging schedule for Accounts Receivable:

LO **4**

| | Age of Accounts | | | |
Total Balance	1–30 Days	31–60 Days	61–90 Days	Over 90 Days
$350,000	$140,000	$110,000	$70,000	$30,000
Estimated uncollectible	0.5%	4.0%	9.0%	40.0%

Requirements

1. Based on the aging of Accounts Receivable, is the unadjusted balance of the allowance account adequate? Too high? Too low?
2. Make the entry required by the aging schedule. Prepare a T-account for the allowance.
3. Show how Turf Trimmers will report Accounts Receivable on its December 31 balance sheet.

LO 4 **E5-23A.** *(Learning Objective 4: Apply GAAP for uncollectible accounts)* Assume Birch Foods, Inc., experienced the following revenue and accounts receivable write-offs:

Month	Service Revenue	January	February	March	Totals
		Accounts Receivable Write-Offs in Month			
January	$ 4,400	$54	$ 89		$143
February	3,900		103	$31	134
March	4,100			112	112
	$12,400	$54	$192	$143	$389

Suppose Birch estimates that 4% of (gross) revenues will become uncollectible. Assume all revenues are on credit.

Requirement

1. Journalize service revenue (all on account), bad-debt expense, and write-offs during March. Include explanations.

LO 5 **E5-24A.** *(Learning Objective 5: Apply GAAP for notes receivable)* Record the following note receivable transactions in the journal of Celtic Services. How much interest revenue did Celtic earn this year? *Use a 365-day year* for interest computations, and round interest amounts to the nearest dollar. Celtic Services has a December 31 fiscal year-end.

Oct 1	Loaned $11,000 cash to Carroll Fadal on a one-year, 6% note.
Dec 6	Performed service for Fairway Masters, receiving a 90-day, 8% note for $9,000.
16	Received a $4,000, six-month, 12% note on account from Warren, Inc.
31	Accrued interest revenue for the year.

LO 6 7 **E5-25A.** *(Learning Objectives 6, 7: Show how to speed up cash flow from receivables; evaluate liquidity through ratios)* Marshall, Inc., reported the following items at December 31, 2016, and 2015:

	A	B	C	D	E	F
				A1		
1	**Balance Sheets (Summarized)**					
2						
3		Year-end			Year-end	
4		**2016**	**2015**		**2016**	**2015**
5	**Current assets:**			**Current liabilities:**		
6	Cash	$ 15,000	$ 11,000	Accounts payable	$ 16,000	$ 17,500
7	Marketable securities	22,000	11,000	Other current liabilities	107,000	109,000
8	Accounts receivable, net	54,000	68,000	Long-term liabilities	20,000	21,000
9	Inventory	194,000	190,000			
10	Other current assets	6,000	6,000	Stockholders' equity	148,000	148,500
11	Long-term assets		10,000			
12	Total assets	$ 291,000	$ 296,000	Total liabilities and equity	$ 291,000	$ 296,000
13						
14	**Income statement (partial):**	**2016**				
15	Sales Revenue	$ 727,000				
17						

Requirements

1. Compute Marshall's (a) quick (acid-test) ratio and (b) days' sales outstanding for 2016. Evaluate each ratio value as strong or weak. All sales are on account with terms of net 30 days.
2. Recommend two ways for Marshall to speed up its cash flow from receivables.

E5-26A. *(Learning Objectives 6, 7: Show how to speed up cash flow from receivables; evaluate liquidity through ratios)* Stark Co., Inc., an electronics and appliance chain, reported these figures in millions of dollars:

	2017	2016
Net sales*..	$565,750	$607,725
Receivables at end of year..............	3,820	4,710

*All sales are on account.

Requirements

1. Compute Stark's days' sales in receivables or days' sales outstanding (DSO) during 2017.
2. Is Stark's DSO long or short? Viflex Networks takes 39 days to collect its average level of receivables. Donahue Freight, the overnight shipper, takes 33 days. What causes Stark's collection period to be so different?

Group B

E5-27B. *(Learning Objective 1: Apply GAAP for short-term investments)* Northern Corporation, the investment banking company, often has extra cash to invest. Suppose Northern buys 1,000 shares of Twister, Inc., stock at $46 per share. Assume Northern expects to hold the Twister stock for one month and then sell it. The purchase occurs on December 15, 2016. At December 31, the market price of a share of Twister stock is $69 per share.

Requirements

1. What type of investment is this to Northern? Give the reason for your answer.
2. Record Northern's purchase of the Twister stock on December 15 and the adjustment to market value on December 31.
3. Show how Northern would report this investment on its balance sheet at December 31 and any gain or loss on its income statement for the year ended December 31, 2016.
4. Suppose Northern did *not* intend to treat the Twister stock as a trading security, but still intended to treat it as a short-term investment. How do your answers for parts 1–3 change? Follow Exhibit 5-2.

E5-28B. *(Learning Objectives 2, 3: Apply GAAP for sales, sales discount, and sales returns; account for accounts receivable)* Wolford Interiors reported the following transactions in November:

Nov 2	Sold merchandise on account to Maxine Holder, $1,000, terms 2/10, n/30.
10	Sold merchandise on account to Alexis Pinney, $2,600, terms 3/10, n/30.
11	Collected payment from Maxine Holder for November 2 sale.
15	Pinney returned $1,500 of the merchandise purchased on November 10.
19	Collected payment from Alexis Pinney for the balance of the November 10 sale.

Requirements

1. Record the foregoing transactions in the journal of Wolford Interiors. (You do not need to make the cost of sales, estimated refunds, or cost of estimated returns journal entries; assume that these entries will be made by the company when it makes its other adjusting entries at period end.)
2. Prepare a computation of net sales for the month of November.

LO **3** **4** **E5-29B.** *(Learning Objectives 3, 4: Account for accounts receivable and uncollectible accounts)* Perform the following accounting for the receivables of Laksmana and Li, a CPA firm, at December 31, 2016.

Requirements

1. Set up T-accounts and start with the beginning balances for these T-accounts:
   - Accounts Receivable, $303,000
   - Allowance for Uncollectible Accounts, $26,000

   Post the following 2016 transactions to the T-accounts:
   a. Service revenue of $1,978,000, all on account
   b. Collections on account, $2,010,000
   c. Write-offs of uncollectible accounts, $29,000
   d. Uncollectible-account expense (allowance method), $35,000
2. What are the ending balances of Accounts Receivable and Allowance for Uncollectible Accounts?
3. Show how Laksmana and Li will report accounts receivable on its balance sheet at December 31, 2016.

LO **4** **E5-30B.** *(Learning Objective 4: Apply GAAP for uncollectible receivables)* At December 31, 2016, Canning Travel Agency has an Accounts Receivable balance of $89,000. Allowance for Doubtful Accounts has a credit balance of $840 before the year-end adjustment. Service revenue (all on account) for 2016 was $600,000. Canning estimates that doubtful-account expense for the year is 2% of service revenue. Make the year-end entry to record doubtful-account expense. Show how Accounts Receivable and Allowance for Doubtful Accounts are reported on the balance sheet at December 31, 2016.

LO **2** **3** **4** **E5-31B.** *(Learning Objectives 2, 3, 4: Apply GAAP for revenue recognition, accounts receivable, and uncollectible receivables)* On June 30, Maloney Party Planners had a $43,000 balance in Accounts Receivable and a $2,493 credit balance in Allowance for Uncollectible Accounts. During July, Maloney made credit sales of $200,000. July collections on account were $169,000, and write-offs of uncollectible receivables totaled $2,910. Uncollectible-account expense is estimated as 1% of credit sales. No sales returns are expected.

Requirements

1. Journalize sales, collections, write-offs of uncollectibles, and uncollectible-account expense by the allowance method during July. Explanations are not required.
2. Show the ending balances in Accounts Receivable, Allowance for Uncollectible Accounts, and *Net* Accounts Receivable at July 31. How much does Maloney expect to collect?
3. Show how Maloney Party Planners will report Accounts Receivable and net sales on its July 31 balance sheet and income statement for the month ended July 31.

LO **4** **E5-32B.** *(Learning Objective 4: Apply GAAP for uncollectible receivables)* At December 31, 2016, before any year-end adjustments, the Accounts Receivable balance of Foley Distribution Service is $320,000. The Allowance for Doubtful Accounts has a $22,200 credit balance. Foley Distribution Service prepares the following aging schedule for Accounts Receivable:

	Age of Accounts			
Total Balance	1–30 Days	31–60 Days	61–90 Days	Over 90 Days
$320,000	$130,000	$100,000	$60,000	$30,000
Estimated uncollectible	0.4%	5.0%	7.0%	60.0%

Requirements

1. Based on the aging of Accounts Receivable, is the unadjusted balance of the allowance account adequate? Too high? Too low?
2. Make the entry required by the aging schedule. Prepare a T-account for the allowance.
3. Show how Foley Distribution Service will report Accounts Receivable on its December 31 balance sheet.

E5-33B. *(Learning Objective 4: Apply GAAP for uncollectible receivables)* Assume Olson Foods, Inc., experienced the following revenue and accounts receivable write-offs:

LO 4

	Service	Accounts Receivable Write-Offs in Month			
Month	Revenue	March	April	May	Totals
March	$ 3,300	$53	$ 87		$140
April	4,400		100	$ 26	126
May	4,100			100	100
	$11,800	$53	$187	$126	$366

Suppose Olson estimates that 4% of (gross) revenues will become uncollectible. Assume all revenues are on credit.

Requirement

1. Journalize service revenue (all on account), bad-debt expense, and write-offs during May. Include explanations.

E5-34B. *(Learning Objective 5: Applying GAAP for notes receivable)* Record the following note receivable transactions in the journal of Caribou Golf. How much interest revenue did Caribou earn this year? *Use a 365-day year* for interest computations, and round interest amounts to the nearest dollar. Caribou Golf has an October 31 fiscal year-end.

LO 5

Aug 1	Loaned $19,000 cash to Carl Fajar on a one-year, 7% note.
Oct 6	Performed service for Green Pro, receiving a 90-day, 6% note for $6,000.
16	Received a $5,000, six-month, 11% note on account from Voeron, Inc.
31	Accrued interest revenue for the year.

E5-35B. *(Learning Objectives 6, 7: Show how to speed up cash flow from receivables; evaluate liquidity through ratios)* Saybrooke, Inc., reported the following items at December 31, 2016, and 2015:

LO 6 7

	A	B	C	D	E	F
	A1					
	Balance Sheets (Summarized)					
1						
2						
3		Year-end			Year-end	
4		**2016**	**2015**		**2016**	**2015**
5	**Current assets:**			**Current liabilities:**		
6	Cash	$ 16,000	$ 12,000	Accounts payable	$ 19,000	$ 20,500
7	Marketable securities	23,000	12,000	Other current liabilities	107,000	109,000
8	Accounts receivable, net	58,000	72,000	Long-term liabilities	20,000	21,000
9	Inventory	195,000	191,000			
10	Other current assets	2,000	2,000	Stockholders' equity	148,000	148,500
11	Long-term assets		10,000			
12	Total assets	$ 294,000	$ 299,000	Total liabilities and equity	$ 294,000	$ 299,000
13						
14	**Income statement (partial):**	**2016**				
15	Sales Revenue	$ 732,000				
16						

Requirements

1. Compute Saybrooke's (a) quick (acid-test) ratio and (b) days' sales outstanding for 2016. Evaluate each ratio value as strong or weak. All sales are on account with terms of net 30 days.
2. Recommend two ways for Saybrooke to speed up its cash flow from receivables.

LO 6 7 **E5-36B.** *(Learning Objectives 6, 7: Show how to speed up cash flow from receivables; evaluate liquidity through ratios)* Iverson Co., Inc., an electronics and appliance chain, reported these figures in millions of dollars:

	2017	2016
Net sales*...	$578,525	$613,200
Receivables at end of year	3,880	4,610

*All sales are on account.

Requirements

1. Compute Iverson's days' sales in receivables or days' sales outstanding (DSO) during 2017.
2. Is Iverson's DSO long or short? Dartex Networks takes 39 days to collect its average level of receivables. Defranco, the overnight shipper, takes 33 days. What causes Iverson's collection period to be so different?

Quiz

Test your understanding of receivables by answering the following questions. Select the best choice from among the possible answers given.

Q5-37. USA National Bank, the nationwide banking company, owns many types of investments. Assume that USA National Bank paid $650,000 for trading securities on December 5. Two weeks later, USA National Bank received a $40,000 cash dividend. At December 31, these trading securities were quoted at a market price of $657,000. USA National Bank's December income statement would include an

    a. unrealized loss of $7,000.   **c.** unrealized gain of $7,000.
    b. unrealized loss of $2,000.   **d.** unrealized gain of $47,000.

Q5-38. Refer to the USA National Bank data in Q5-37. At December 31, USA National Bank's balance sheet should report

    a. investment in trading securities of $650,000.
    b. unrealized gain of $7,000.
    c. investment in trading securities of $657,000.
    d. dividend revenue of $40,000.

Q5-39. Under the allowance method for uncollectible receivables, the entry to record uncollectible-account expense has what effect on the financial statements?

    a. Decreases net income and decreases assets
    b. Increases expenses and increases owners' equity
    c. Decreases assets and has no effect on net income
    d. Decreases owners' equity and increases liabilities

Q5-40. Snead Company uses the aging method to adjust the allowance for uncollectible accounts at the end of the period. At December 31, 2016, the balance of accounts receivable is $210,000 and the allowance for uncollectible accounts has a credit balance of $3,000 (before adjustment). An analysis of accounts receivable produced the following age groups:

Current	$160,000
60 days past due........................	43,000
Over 60 days past due...............	7,000
	$210,000

Based on past experience, Snead estimates that the percentage of accounts that will prove to be uncollectible within the three age groups is 4%, 10%, and 18%, respectively. Based on these facts, the adjusting entry for uncollectible accounts should be made in the amount of

    a. $14,960.   **c.** $8,960.
    b. $11,960.   **d.** $15,960.

Q5-41. Refer to **Q5-40**. The net receivables on the balance sheet as of December 31, 2016, are _____.

Q5-42. Milo Company uses the percent-of-sales method to estimate uncollectibles. Net credit sales for the current year amount to $100,000, and management estimates 4% will be uncollectible. Allowance for Doubtful Accounts prior to adjustment has a credit balance of $3,000. The amount of expense to report on the income statement will be

    a. $7,000.   **c.** $6,000.
    b. $4,000.   **d.** $1,500.

Q5-43. Refer to Q5-42. The balance of Allowance for Doubtful Accounts, after adjustment, will be

    a. $1,000.   **c.** $3,000.
    b. $4,000.   **d.** $7,000.

Q5-44. Refer to questions 5-42 and 5-43. The following year, Milo Company wrote off $2,000 of old receivables as uncollectible. What is the balance in the Allowance account now?

Questions 5-45 through 5-49 use the following data:

On August 1, 2016, Azore, Inc., sold equipment and accepted a six-month, 8%, $30,000 note receivable. Azore's year-end is December 31.

Q5-45. How much interest revenue should Azore accrue on December 31, 2016?

    a. $1,550   **c.** $1,200
    b. $2,400   **d.** $1,000

Q5-46. If Azore, Inc., fails to make an adjusting entry for the accrued interest on December 31, 2016,

    a. net income will be overstated and assets will be overstated.
    b. net income will be understated and assets will be understated.
    c. net income will be understated and liabilities will be overstated.
    d. net income will be overstated and liabilities will be understated.

Q5-47. How much interest does Azore, Inc., expect to collect on the maturity date (February 1, 2017)?

    a. $1,200   **c.** $200
    b. $2,400   **d.** $2,000

Q5-48. Which of the following accounts will Azore, Inc., credit in the journal entry at maturity on February 1, 2017, assuming collection in full?

    a. Cash   **c.** Interest Payable
    b. Note Payable   **d.** Interest Receivable

Q5-49. Write the journal entry on the maturity date (February 1, 2017).

Q5-50. Which of the following is included in the calculation of the quick (acid-test) ratio?

    a. Inventory and prepaid expenses
    b. Prepaid expenses and cash
    c. Inventory and short-term investments
    d. Cash and accounts receivable

Q5-51. A company with net credit sales of $1,017,000, beginning net receivables of $90,000, and ending net receivables of $120,000 has days' sales outstanding of

    a. 48 days.   **c.** 41 days.
    b. 44 days.   **d.** 38 days.

Q5-52. A company sells on credit terms of 2/10, n/30 and has days' sales in accounts receivable of 31 days. Its days' sales outstanding is

    a. about right.

    b. too high.

    c. too low.

    d. not able to be evaluated from the data given.

Problems MyAccountingLab

Group A

 P5-53A. (*Learning Objective 1: Apply GAAP to short-term investments*) During the fourth quarter of 2016, Abbott, Inc., generated excess cash, which the company invested in trading securities as follows:

2016	
Nov 16	Purchased 900 common shares as an investment in trading securities, paying $9 per share.
Dec 16	Received cash dividend of $0.35 per share on the trading securities.
Dec 31	Adjusted the trading securities to fair value of $5 per share.

Requirements

1. Open T-accounts for Cash (including its beginning balance of $19,000), Investment in Trading Securities, Dividend Revenue, and Unrealized Gain (Loss) on Trading Securities.
2. Journalize the foregoing transactions and post to the T-accounts.
3. Show how to report the short-term investment on Abbott's balance sheet at December 31, 2016.
4. Show how to report whatever should appear on Abbott's income statement for the year ended December 31, 2016.
5. Abbott sold the trading securities for $6,300 on January 14, 2017. Journalize the sale.
6. Assume that the securities were classified as available-for-sale. Further, assume that the fair value was $10 per share on December 31, 2017, and $10.50 per share on January 1, 2018, when they were sold. Repeat steps 3–4 for 2016 and 2017, and journalize the sale of the securities on January 1, 2018. Follow the example in Exhibit 5-2.

P5-54A. (*Learning Objective 3: Apply controls to cash receipts from customers*) Bogoda Industries makes all sales on account. Ian Holt, accountant for the company, receives and opens incoming mail. Company procedure requires Holt to separate customer checks from the remittance slips, which list the amounts that Holt posts as credits to customer accounts receivable. Holt deposits the checks in the bank. At the end of each day, he computes the day's total amount posted to customer accounts and matches this total to the bank deposit slip. This procedure ensures that all receipts are deposited in the bank.

Requirement

1. As a consultant hired by Bogoda Industries, write a memo to management evaluating the company's internal controls over cash receipts from customers. If the system is effective, identify its strong features. If the system has flaws, propose a way to strengthen the controls.

P5-55A. (*Learning Objectives 2, 3, 4, 5: Apply GAAP for revenue, receivables, collections, and uncollectibles using the percent-of-sales method; account for notes receivable*) This problem takes you through the accounting for sales, receivables, uncollectibles, and notes receivable for Bates Delivery Corp., the overnight shipper. By selling on credit, the company cannot expect to collect 100% of its accounts receivable. At October 31, 2016, and 2017, respectively, Bates Delivery Corp. reported the following on its balance sheet (in millions of dollars):

	October 31,	
	2017	2016
Accounts receivable...	$3,900	$3,600
Less: Allowance for uncollectible accounts...............	(160)	(230)
Accounts receivable, net..	$3,740	$3,370

During the year ended October 31, 2017, Bates Delivery Corp. earned service revenue and collected cash from customers. Assume uncollectible-account expense for the year was 4% of service revenue on account and that Bates Delivery wrote off uncollectible receivables and made other adjustments as necessary (see below). At year-end, Bates Delivery ended with the foregoing October 31, 2017, balances.

Requirements

1. Prepare T-accounts for Accounts Receivable and Allowance for Uncollectible Accounts, and insert the October 31, 2016, balances as given.
2. Journalize the following transactions of Bates Delivery Corp. for the year ended October 31, 2017 (explanations are not required):
   a. Service revenue was $32,900 million, of which 7% is cash and the remainder is on account.
   b. Collections from customers on account were $28,860 million.
   c. Uncollectible-account expense was 4% of service revenue on account.
   d. Write-offs of uncollectible accounts receivable were $1,294 million.
   e. On October 1, Bates Delivery received a 2-month, 7%, $185 million note receivable from a large corporate customer in exchange for the customer's past due account; Bates Delivery made the proper year-end adjusting entry for the interest on this note.
   f. Bates Delivery's October 31, 2017, year-end bank statement reported $42 million of NSF checks from customers.
3. Post your entries to the Accounts Receivable and the Allowance for Uncollectible Accounts T-accounts.
4. Compute the ending balances for Accounts Receivable and the Allowance for Uncollectible Accounts and compare your balances to the actual October 31, 2017, amounts. They should be the same. How much does Bates Delivery expect to collect from its customers after October 31, 2017?
5. Show the net effect of these transactions on Bates Delivery's net income for the year ended October 31, 2017.

P5-56A. *(Learning Objective 4: Apply GAAP for uncollectible receivables)* The September 30, 2017, records of First Data Communications include these accounts:

LO 4

Accounts Receivable....................................	$243,000
Allowance for Doubtful Accounts...............	(8,200)

During the year, First Data Communications estimates doubtful-account expense at 1% of credit sales. At year-end (December 31), the company ages its receivables and adjusts the balance in Allowance for Doubtful Accounts to correspond to the following aging schedule.

Accounts Receivable	Age of Accounts			
	1–30 Days	31–60 Days	61–90 Days	Over 90 Days
$231,000	$134,000	$45,000	$16,000	$36,000
Estimated percent uncollectible	0.2%	2%	15%	35%

During the last quarter of 2017, the company completed the following selected transactions:

Nov 30	Wrote off as uncollectible the $1,600 account receivable from Black Carpets and the $600 account receivable from Rare Antiques.
Dec 31	Adjusted the Allowance for Doubtful Accounts and recorded doubtful-account expense at year-end, based on the aging of receivables.

Requirements

1. Record the transactions for the last quarter of 2017 in the journal. Explanations are not required.
2. Prepare a T-account for Allowance for Doubtful Accounts with the appropriate beginning balance. Post the entries from requirement 1 to that account.
3. Show how First Data Communications will report its accounts receivable in a comparative balance sheet for 2016 and 2017. Use the three-line reporting format. At December 31, 2016, the company's Accounts Receivable balance was $215,000, and the Allowance for Doubtful Accounts stood at $4,500.

P5-57A. *(Learning Objectives 1, 4, 7: Apply GAAP for short-term investments and uncollectible receivables; evaluate liquidity through ratios)* Assume Williams & Sellers, the accounting firm, advises Ocean Mist Seafood that its financial statements must be changed to conform to GAAP. At December 31, 2016, Ocean Mist's accounts include the following:

Cash	$50,000
Investment in trading securities, at cost	26,000
Accounts receivable	42,000
Inventory	62,000
Prepaid expenses	11,000
Total current assets	$191,000
Accounts payable	$66,000
Other current liabilities	40,000
Total current liabilities	$106,000

The accounting firm advised Ocean Mist of the following:
- Cash includes $18,000 that is deposited in a compensating balance account that is tied up until 2018.
- The market value of the trading securities is $17,000. Ocean Mist purchased the investments a couple of weeks ago.
- Ocean Mist has been using the direct write-off method to account for uncollectible receivables. During 2016, Ocean Mist wrote off bad receivables of $4,000. The aging of Ocean Mist's receivables at year-end indicated uncollectibles of $26,500.
- Ocean Mist reported net income of $94,000 in 2016.

Requirements

1. Restate Ocean Mist's current accounts to conform to GAAP. (Challenge)
2. Compute Ocean Mist's current ratio and quick (acid-test) ratio both before and after your corrections.
3. Determine Ocean Mist's correct net income for 2016. (Challenge)

P5-58A. *(Learning Objective 5: Apply GAAP for notes receivable)* Hughes Foods completed the following selected transactions.    LO 5

2016	
Oct 31	Sold goods to BiLo's Foods, receiving a $36,000, three-month, 4.5% note. (You do not need to make the cost of goods sold journal entry for this transaction.)
Dec 31	Made an adjusting entry to accrue interest on the BiLo's Foods note.
2017	
Jan 31	Collected the BiLo's Foods note.
Feb 18	Received a 90-day, 7.00%, $7,000 note from Dutton Market on account.
19	Sold the Dutton Market note to Seabrook Bank, receiving cash of $6,800. (Debit the difference to financing expense.)
Nov 11	Loaned $15,600 cash to Sauble Co., receiving a 90-day, 9.50% note.
Dec 31	Accrued the interest on the Sauble Co. note.

Requirements

1. Record the transactions in Hughes Foods' journal. Assume that no sales returns are expected. Round all amounts to the nearest dollar. Explanations are not required.
2. Show what Hughes Foods will report on its comparative classified balance sheet at December 31, 2017, and December 31, 2016.

P5-59A. *(Learning Objectives 6, 7: Show how to speed up cash flow from receivables; evaluate liquidity using ratios)* The comparative financial statements of Kenmore Pools, Inc., for 2017, 2016, and 2015 included the following select data: LO 6 7

	(In millions)		
	2017	2016	2015
Balance sheet			
Current assets:			
Cash..	$ 70	$ 80	$ 40
Investment in trading securities......	130	165	125
Receivables, net of allowance for doubtful accounts of $7, $6, and $4, respectively	270	260	230
Inventories	350	325	300
Prepaid expenses............................	65	30	50
Total current assets	$ 885	$ 860	$ 745
Total current liabilities......................	$ 560	$ 620	$ 660
Income statement			
Net sales (all on account)	$7,665	$5,110	$4,015

Requirements

1. Compute these ratios for 2017 and 2016:
   a. Current ratio
   b. Quick (acid-test) ratio
   c. Days' sales outstanding
2. Which ratios improved from 2016 to 2017 and which ratios deteriorated? Is this trend favorable or unfavorable?
3. Recommend two ways for Kenmore Pools to improve cash flows from receivables.

Group B

P5-60B. *(Learning Objective 1: Apply GAAP to short-term investments)* During the fourth quarter of 2016, Zinner, Inc., generated excess cash, which the company invested in trading securities as follows:

2016	
Nov 17	Purchased 1,300 common shares as an investment in trading securities, paying $9 per share.
Dec 19	Received cash dividend of $0.48 per share on the trading securities.
Dec 31	Adjusted the trading securities to fair value of $6 per share.

Requirements

1. Open T-accounts for Cash (including its beginning balance of $15,000), Investment in Trading Securities, Dividend Revenue, and Unrealized Gain (Loss) on Trading Securities.
2. Journalize the foregoing transactions and post to the T-accounts.
3. Show how to report the short-term investment on Zinner's balance sheet at December 31, 2016.
4. Show how to report whatever should appear on Zinner's income statement for the year ended December 31, 2016.
5. Zinner sold the trading securities for $10,400 on January 11, 2017. Journalize the sale.
6. Assume that the securities were classified as available-for-sale. Further, assume that the fair value was $10 per share on December 31, 2017, and $10.50 per share on January 1, 2018, when they were sold. Repeat steps 3–4 for 2016 and 2017, and journalize the sale of the securities on January 1, 2018. Follow the example in Exhibit 5-2.

P5-61B. *(Learning Objective 3: Apply controls to cash receipts from customers)* Carson Computer Solutions makes all sales on account, so virtually all cash receipts arrive in the mail. Jeannette Carson, the company president, has just returned from a trade association meeting with new ideas for the business. Among other things, Carson plans to institute stronger internal controls over cash receipts from customers.

Requirement

1. Take the role of Jeannette Carson, the company president. Write a memo to employees outlining procedures to ensure that all cash receipts are deposited in the bank and that the total amounts of each day's cash receipts are posted to customer accounts receivable.

P5-62B. *(Learning Objectives 2, 3, 4, 5: Apply GAAP for revenue, receivables, collections, and uncollectibles using the percent-of-sales method; account for notes receivable)* This problem takes you through the accounting for sales, receivables, uncollectibles, and notes receivable for Henderson Shipping Corp., the overnight shipper. By selling on credit, the company cannot expect to collect 100% of its accounts receivable. At August 31, 2016, and 2017, respectively, Henderson Shipping Corp. reported the following on its balance sheet (in millions of dollars):

	August 31,	
	2017	**2016**
Accounts receivable	$4,300	$3,500
Less: Allowance for uncollectible accounts	(180)	(240)
Accounts receivable, net	$4,120	$3,260

During the year ended August 31, 2017, Henderson Shipping Corp. earned service revenue and collected cash from customers. Assume uncollectible-account expense for the year was 4% of service revenue on account and Henderson Shipping wrote off uncollectible receivables and made other adjustments as necessary (see below). At year-end, Henderson Shipping ended with the foregoing August 31, 2017, balances.

Requirements

1. Prepare T-accounts for Accounts Receivable and Allowance for Uncollectible Accounts, and insert the August 31, 2016, balances as given.
2. Journalize the following transactions of Henderson Shipping for the year ended August 31, 2017 (explanations are not required):
   a. Service revenue was $32,600 million, of which 6% is cash and the remainder is on account.
   b. Collections from customers on account were $28,395 million.
   c. Uncollectible-account expense was 4% of service revenue on account.
   d. Write-offs of uncollectible accounts receivable were $1,286 million.
   e. On August 1, Henderson Shipping received a 2-month, 8%, $210 million note receivable from a large corporate customer in exchange for the customer's past due account; Henderson Shipping made the proper year-end adjusting entry for the interest on this note.
   f. Henderson Shipping's August 31, 2017, year-end bank statement reported $47 million of NSF checks from customers.
3. Post your entries to the Accounts Receivable and Allowance for Uncollectible Accounts T-accounts.
4. Compute the ending balances for Accounts Receivable and Allowance for Uncollectible Accounts and compare your balances to the actual August 31, 2017, amounts. They should be the same. How much does Henderson Shipping expect to collect from its customers after August 31, 2017?
5. Show the net effect of these transactions on Henderson Shipping's net income for the year ended August 31, 2017.

P5-63B. *(Learning Objective 4: Apply GAAP for uncollectible receivables)* The September 30, 2017, records of Media Communications include these accounts:

LO 4

Accounts Receivable......................................	$242,000
Allowance for Doubtful Accounts..............	(8,400)

During the year, Media Communications estimates doubtful-account expense at 1% of credit sales. At year-end (December 31), the company ages its receivables and adjusts the balance in Allowance for Doubtful Accounts to correspond to the following aging schedule:

Accounts Receivable	Age of Accounts			
	1–30 Days	31–60 Days	61–90 Days	Over 90 Days
$230,000	$132,000	$54,000	$17,000	$27,000
Estimated percent uncollectible	0.2%	2%	15%	35%

During the last quarter of 2017, the company completed the following selected transactions:

Nov 30	Wrote off as uncollectible the $1,300 account receivable from Blue Carpets and the $400 account receivable from Rare Antiques.
Dec 31	Adjusted the Allowance for Doubtful Accounts and recorded doubtful-account expense at year-end, based on the aging of receivables.

Requirements

1. Record the transactions for the last quarter of 2017 in the journal. Explanations are not required.
2. Prepare a T-account for Allowance for Doubtful Accounts with the appropriate beginning balance. Post the entries from requirement 1 to that account.
3. Show how Media Communications will report its accounts receivable in a comparative balance sheet for 2016 and 2017. Use the three-line reporting format. At December 31, 2016, the company's Accounts Receivable balance was $215,000 and the Allowance for Doubtful Accounts stood at $4,200.

 **P5-64B.** *(Learning Objectives 1, 4, 7: Apply GAAP for short-term investments and uncollectible receivables; evaluate liquidity through ratios)* Assume Spahr and Kennedy, the accounting firm, advises Arctic Seafood that its financial statement must be changed to conform to GAAP. At December 31, 2016, Arctic's accounts include the following:

Cash...	$55,000
Investment in trading securities, at cost...........	22,000
Accounts receivable..	36,000
Inventory..	63,000
Prepaid expenses	18,000
Total current assets	$194,000
Accounts payable	$62,000
Other current liabilities	37,000
Total current liabilities...............................	$99,000

The accounting firm advised Arctic of the following:
- Cash includes $22,000 that is deposited in a compensating balance account that is tied up until 2018.
- The market value of the trading securities is $16,000. Arctic purchased the investments a couple of weeks ago.
- Arctic has been using the direct write-off method to account for uncollectible receivables. During 2016, Arctic wrote off bad receivables of $8,500. The aging of Arctic's receivables at year-end indicated uncollectibles of $22,000.
- Arctic reported net income of $95,000 for 2016.

Requirements

1. Restate Arctic's current accounts to conform to GAAP. (Challenge)
2. Compute Arctic's current ratio and quick (acid-test) ratio both before and after your corrections.
3. Determine Arctic's correct net income for 2016. (Challenge)

 P5-65B. *(Learning Objective 5: Apply GAAP for notes receivable)* Quick Meals completed the following selected transactions:

2016		
Oct 31	Sold goods to Dorsey Foods, receiving a $38,000, three-month 5.75% note. (You do not need to make the cost of goods sold journal entry for this transaction.)
Dec 31	Made an adjusting entry to accrue interest on the Dorsey Foods note.
2017		
Jan 31	Collected the Dorsey Foods note.
Feb 18	Received a 90-day, 7.00%, $7,600 note from Barb's Market on account.
19	Sold the Barb's Market note to Glen Cove Bank, receiving cash of $7,400. (Debit the difference to financing expense.)
Nov 11	Loaned $15,600 to Master Foods, receiving a 90-day, 9.00% note.
Dec 31	Accrued the interest on the Master Foods note.

Requirements

1. Record the transactions in Quick Meals' journal. Assume that no sales returns are expected. Round all amounts to the nearest dollar. Explanations are not required.
2. Show what Quick Meals will report on its comparative classified balance sheet at December 31, 2017, and December 31, 2016.

P5-66B. *(Learning Objectives 6, 7: Show how to speed up cash flow from receivables; evaluate liquidity using ratios)* The comparative financial statements of Gold Pools, Inc., for 2017, 2016, and 2015 included the following select data:

	(In millions)		
	2017	2016	2015
Balance sheet			
Current assets:			
Cash..	$ 70	$ 60	$ 50
Investment in trading securities......	150	175	110
Receivables, net of allowance			
for doubtful accounts of $7, $6,			
and $4, respectively	270	260	240
Inventories	350	345	300
Prepaid expenses............................	70	20	45
Total current assets........................	$ 910	$ 860	$ 745
Total current liabilities......................	$ 560	$ 620	$ 650
Income statement			
Net sales (all on account)	$6,570	$5,110	$5,110

Requirements

1. Compute these ratios for 2017 and 2016:
   a. Current ratio
   b. Quick (acid-test) ratio
   c. Days' sales outstanding
2. Which ratios improved from 2016 to 2017 and which ratios deteriorated? Is this trend favorable or unfavorable?
3. Recommend two ways for Gold Pools to improve cash flow from receivables.

Challenge Exercises and Problem

E5-67. *(Learning Objective 6: Show how to speed up cash from receivables)* Ripley Shirt Company sells on credit and manages its own receivables. Average experience for the past three years has been the following:

	Cash	Credit	Total
Sales...	$350,000	$350,000	$700,000
Cost of goods sold............................	175,000	175,000	350,000
Uncollectible-account expense...........	—	20,000	20,000
Other expenses...................................	89,000	89,000	178,000

Jack Rivers, the owner, is considering whether to accept bankcards (VISA, MasterCard). Rivers expects total sales to increase by 12% but cash sales to remain unchanged. If Rivers switches to bankcards, the business can save $10,000 on other expenses, but VISA and MasterCard charge

2% on bankcard sales. Rivers figures that the increase in sales will be due to the increased volume of bankcard sales.

Requirement

1. Should Ripley Shirt Company start selling on bankcards? Show the computations of net income under the present plan and under the bankcard plan. (Ignore estimated sales returns and refunds for this exercise.)

LO 3 4 **E5-68.** *(Learning Objectives 3, 4: Apply GAAP for receivables and uncollectible receivables)* Suppose Carat, Inc., reported net receivables of $2,584 million and $2,265 million at January 31, 2017, and 2016, respectively, after subtracting allowances of $68 million and $65 million at these respective dates. Carat earned total revenue of $46,667 million (all on account) and recorded doubtful-account expense of $14 million for the year ended January 31, 2017.

Requirement

1. Use this information to measure the following amounts for the year ended January 31, 2017:
   a. Write-offs of uncollectible receivables
   b. Collections from customers

LO 2 3 4 **P5-69.** *(Learning Objectives 2, 3, 4: Analyze accounts receivable)* The balance sheet of Libra, Inc., a world leader in the design and sale of telescopic equipment, reported the following information on its balance sheets for 2016 and 2015 (figures are in thousands):

(In thousands)	December 31, 2016	December 31, 2015
Accounts receivable (net of allowance of $1,050 and $990, respectively)	$8,650	$8,910

In 2016, Libra recorded $13,200 (gross) in sales (all on account), of which $1,200 (gross) was returned for credit. The cost of sales was $7,260; the cost of the merchandise returned was $660. Libra offers its customers credit terms of 2/10, n/30. Sixty percent of collections on accounts receivable were made within the discount period. Libra wrote off uncollectible accounts receivable in the amount of $200 (net) during 2016. Sales returns are estimated to be 5% of sales.

Requirements

1. Compute the amount of uncollectible accounts expense recorded by Libra in 2016.
2. Compute Libra's cash collections from customers in 2016.
3. Open T-accounts for Accounts Receivable and Allowance for Uncollectible Accounts. Enter the beginning balances into each of these accounts. Prepare summary journal entries in the T-accounts to record the following for 2016:
   a. Sales revenue
   b. Cost of goods sold
   c. Estimated refunds
   d. Cost of estimated returns
   e. Merchandise returned
   f. Cost of merchandise returned
   g. Collections including sales discounts forfeited
   h. Write-offs of uncollectible accounts
   i. Uncollectible-Accounts Expense

APPLY YOUR KNOWLEDGE

Decision Cases

Case 1. *(Learning Objectives 2, 3, 4: Apply GAAP for revenue, accounts receivable, and uncollectible receivables)* A fire during 2016 destroyed most of the accounting records of Sinclair Entertainment, Inc. The only accounting data for 2016 that Sinclair can come up with are the following balances at December 31, 2016. The general manager also knows that bad-debt expense should be 5% of service revenue on credit.

 LO **2** **3** **4**

Accounts receivable, December 31, 2016	$180,000
Less: Allowance for bad debts	(22,000)
Total expenses, excluding bad-debt expense............	670,000
Collections from customers	840,000
Write-offs of bad receivables	30,000
Accounts receivable, December 31, 2015	110,000

Prepare a summary income statement for Sinclair Entertainment, Inc., for the year ended December 31, 2016. The stockholders want to know whether the company was profitable in 2016. Use a T-account for Accounts Receivable to compute service revenue. Assume that all revenues are on credit.

Case 2. *(Learning Objectives 4, 7: Apply GAAP for uncollectible receivables; evaluate liquidity through ratios)* Suppose you work in the loan department of Second National Bank. Brian Evert, owner of Evert Beauty Solutions, has come to you seeking a loan for $500,000 to expand operations. Evert proposes to use accounts receivable as collateral for the loan and has provided you with the following information from the company's most recent financial statements:

LO **4** **7**

	2017	2016	2015
	(In thousands)		
Sales (all on account).........................	$1,475	$1,001	$902
Cost of goods sold.............................	876	647	605
Gross profit.......................................	599	354	297
Other expenses..................................	518	287	253
Net profit or (loss) before taxes.........	$ 81	$ 67	$ 44
Accounts receivable...........................	$ 128	$ 107	$ 94
Allowance for doubtful accounts........	13	11	9

Requirement

1. Analyze the trends of sales, days' sales outstanding, and cash collections from customers for 2017 and 2016. Would you make the loan to Evert? Support your decision with facts and figures.

Ethical Issue

Rockville Loan Company is in the consumer loan business. Rockville borrows from banks and loans out the money at higher interest rates. Rockville's bank requires Rockville to submit quarterly financial statements to keep its line of credit. Rockville's main asset is Notes Receivable. Therefore, Uncollectible-Account Expense and Allowance for Uncollectible Accounts are important accounts for the company.

Rachel Laber, the company's owner, prefers that net income reflect a steady increase in a smooth pattern, rather than an increase in some periods and a decrease in other periods. To report smoothly increasing net income, Laber underestimates Uncollectible-Account Expense in some periods. In other periods, Laber overestimates the expense. She reasons that the income over-statements roughly offset the income understatements over time.

Requirements

1. What is the ethical issue in this situation?
2. Who are the stakeholders? What are the possible consequences to each?
3. Analyze the alternatives from the following standpoints: (a) economic, (b) legal, (c) ethical.
4. What would you do? How would you justify your decision?

Focus on Financials | Apple Inc.

LO 1 2

(Learning Objectives 1, 2: Account for short-term investments; apply GAAP for proper revenue recognition) Refer to **Apple Inc.'s** consolidated financial statements in Appendix A and online in the filings section of **http://www.sec.gov**.

Requirements

1. Examine the account "Short-term marketable securities" in the consolidated balance sheets, as well as related information in Note 2 to the Consolidated Financial Statements for Apple Inc. (See the section for "Cash, Cash Equivalents and Marketable Securities.")
   a. What does this account consist of?
   b. Why do you think the company has made these investments?
   c. What percentage change has occurred in Short-term marketable securities from September 28, 2013, to September 27, 2014? What management business strategy might this reveal?
   d. Using the financial statement Note 1 for reference, explain how Apple Inc., accounts for marketable securities.
   e. Has the company profited from holding its portfolio of marketable securities during the year ended September 27, 2014? How do you know?
2. Using the Revenue Recognition section of Note 1 as a reference, describe how Apple Inc., recognizes revenue. From what types of activities does Apple earn its revenue?
3. The third account listed on Apple's Consolidated Balance Sheet is called "Accounts receivable, less allowances." To what does the "allowances" refer?
4. Refer to the Accounts Receivable section of Note 2. What kinds of accounts receivable are included in Apple Inc.'s receivables?
5. How much is the allowance for doubtful accounts in 2014 and 2013?
6. Calculate the current ratio, quick (acid-test) ratio, and net working capital for Apple Inc., for 2014 and 2013. Evaluate Apple Inc.'s liquidity trend over the two years. What other information might be helpful in evaluating these statistics?

Focus on Analysis | Under Armour, Inc.

LO 2 3

(Learning Objectives 2, 3: Apply GAAP for revenue recognition; account for and control accounts receivable) This case is based on **Under Armour, Inc.'s**, consolidated balance sheets, consolidated statements of income, and Note 2 of its financial statements (Significant Accounting Policies) in Appendix B and online in the filings section of **http://www.sec.gov**.

Requirements

1. Describe Under Armour, Inc.'s, revenue recognition policy. According to the Concentration of Credit Risk section of Note 2, from what sources does it earn most of its revenue?
2. Since Under Armour, Inc., is a consumer retail business, most of its retail sales are cash sales. However, accounts receivable still comprise about 18% ($280/$1,549) of its current assets. What type of customers do business with Under Armour, Inc., on account? Why is this necessary? Use Note 2, Concentration of Credit Risk section.

3. Compute the following for 2014:
   a. Average daily sales, using total revenues.
   b. Days' sales outstanding. Assume all sales are on account.
4. Calculate the current ratio, quick (acid-test) ratio, and net working capital for Under Armour, Inc., for 2014 and 2013. Evaluate the two-year trend in Under Armour, Inc.'s, liquidity. What other information might be helpful in evaluating these statistics?

Group Project

Jillian Michaels and Dee Childress worked for several years as sales representatives for Xerox Corporation. During this time, they became close friends as they acquired expertise with the company's full range of copier equipment. Now they see an opportunity to put their expertise to work and fulfill lifelong desires to establish their own business. Navarro Community College, located in their city, is expanding, and there is no copy center within five miles of the campus. Business in the area is booming, office buildings and apartments are springing up, and the population of the Navarro section of the city is growing.

Michaels and Childress want to open a copy center, similar to FedEx Kinko's, near the Navarro campus. A small shopping center across the street from the college has a vacancy that would fit their needs. Michaels and Childress each have $35,000 to invest in the business, but they forecast the need for $200,000 to renovate the store and purchase some equipment. Xerox Corporation will lease two large copiers to them at a total monthly rental of $6,000. With enough cash to see them through the first six months of operation, they are confident they can make the business succeed. The two women work very well together, and both have excellent credit ratings. Michaels and Childress must borrow $130,000 to start the business, advertise its opening, and keep it running for its first six months.

Requirements

Assume two roles: (1) Michaels and Childress, the partners who will own Navarro Copy Center; and (2) loan officers at Synergy Bank.
1. As a group, visit a copy center to familiarize yourselves with its operations. If possible, interview the manager or another employee. Then write a loan request that Michaels and Childress will submit to Synergy Bank with the intent of borrowing $130,000 to be paid back over three years. The loan will be a personal loan to the partnership of Michaels and Childress, not to Navarro Copy Center. The request should specify all the details of the plan that will motivate the bank to grant the loan. Include a budget for each of the first six months of operation of the proposed copy center.
2. As a group, interview a loan officer in a bank. Write Synergy Bank's reply to the loan request. Specify all the details that the bank should require as conditions for making the loan.
3. If necessary, modify the loan request or the bank's reply in order to reach agreement between the two parties.

Quick Check Answers

1. *b*
2. *c*
3. *c* ($35,000 × 0.02)
4. *c* ($1,450 + $800)
5. *d* ($1,200 − $800)
6. *a*
7. *a* ($14,000 − $1,200)
8. *a* ($2,400 − $40) − ($300 − $40)
9. *d* ($600,000 + $1,600,000 − $800,000)
10. *b* ($2,400 × 0.06 × 4/12 × 1/4)
11. *a* [$80,000 + ($80,000 × 0.14 × 6/12)]
12. *d*
13. *d* [($46,000 + $50,000)/2] ÷ ($584,000/365)
14. *d* ($7,000 + $13,600 + $1,000) ÷ ($9,000 + $3,000)

6

Inventory & Cost of Goods Sold

Are you into fitness? If so, chances are that you may have recently purchased some Under Armour products. Based in Baltimore, Maryland, Under Armour, Inc.'s, principal business activities are the development, marketing, and distribution of branded performance apparel, footwear, and accessories for men, women, and youth. The brand's moisture-wicking fabrications are engineered in many designs and styles for wear in nearly every climate to provide a performance alternative to traditional products. Under Armour, Inc.'s, products are sold worldwide and are worn by athletes at all levels, from youth to professional, on playing fields around the globe, as well as by consumers with active lifestyles. Not surprisingly, on its 2014 Consolidated Balance Sheets (page 309), inventories composed about 35% of its current assets ($536.7 million ÷ $1.55 billion). Inventory balances as of December 31, 2014, were 114.4% of their 2013 levels ($536.7 million ÷ $469 million). This signals that the company is gearing up for growth in sales for their product lines in 2015. Under Armour, Inc.'s, goal is to be more to the aspiring athlete than merely clothing. The company has recently made big investments in other companies that develop "apps" to monitor personal fitness, not only to wear as separate items, but also as "futuristic" gear actually built into clothing to monitor pulse

Don Feria/Getty Images

and blood pressure and to count calories, steps, and miles, hoping to convert the current obsessions of "fitness fanatics" into future sales revenue.

Speaking of sales revenue, Under Armour, Inc.'s, Consolidated Statements of Income for the year ended December 31, 2014 (page 310), show net revenues of slightly over $3 billion, an increase of about 32.3% over the previous year ($2.3 billion). Revenues are generated primarily from the wholesale of products to national, regional, independent, and specialty retailers. The company also generates revenue from the sale of products through its direct to consumer sales channel, which includes its brand and factory house stores and websites, and from product licensing. Although the majority of Under

Armour, Inc.'s, products are sold in North America, the company is aiming to expand its product lines to appeal to athletes and consumers with active lifestyles around the globe. Virtually all of Under Armour, Inc.'s, products are purchased from unaffiliated manufacturing companies operating in 13 countries outside of the United States.

Cost of Goods Sold, the largest expense on the Consolidated Statements of Income, was $1.57 billion for 2014, an increase of about 31.5% over 2013 ($1.195 billion). Consequently, gross profit (Net revenues − Cost of goods sold) of $1.512 billion was up by about 33% over 2013 ($1.137 billion). Gross profit percentage (Gross profit ÷ net sales) increased from 48.7% in fiscal 2013 to slightly more than 49% in fiscal 2014. That means the company was more profitable on sales of its products in 2014 than it was in 2013 by 0.3%. Although 0.3% doesn't look like much, when multiplied by $3 billion in revenue, it amounts to approximately a $9 million increase in gross profit in fiscal 2014.

We feature Under Armour, Inc., as one of this textbook's focus companies in Appendix B. Check them out, if you haven't already done so. Next time you visit your favorite sporting goods store, you'll understand more about this exciting company than just what you see on the shelves.

	A1			
	A	**B**	**C**	**D**
1	**Under Armour, Inc.** **Consolidated Balance Sheets**			
2	**In Thousands, unless otherwise specified**			
3	**Assets**	**Dec. 31, 2014**	**Dec. 31, 2013**	
4	**Current Assets:**			
5	Cash and cash equivalents	$ 593,175	$ 347,489	
6	Accounts receivable, net	279,835	209,952	
7	Inventories	536,714	469,006	
8	Prepaid expenses and other current assets	87,177	63,987	
9	Deferred income taxes	52,498	38,377	
10	Total current assets	1,549,399	1,128,811	
11	Property and equipment, net	305,564	223,952	
12	Goodwill	123,256	122,244	
13	Intangible assets, net	26,230	24,097	
14	Deferred income taxes	33,570	31,094	
15	Other long-term assets	57,064	47,543	
16	**Total assets**	$ 2,095,083	$ 1,577,741	
17	**Liabilities and Stockholders' Equity**			
18	**Current Liabilities:**			
19	Revolving credit facility	$ -	$ 100,000	
20	Accounts payable	210,432	165,456	
21	Accrued expenses	147,681	133,729	
22	Current maturities of long-term debt	28,951	4,972	
23	Other current liabilities	34,563	22,473	
24	Total current liabilities	421,627	426,630	
25	Long-term debt, net of current maturities	255,250	47,951	
26	Other long-term liabilities	67,906	49,806	
27	**Total liabilities**	744,783	524,387	
28	Commitments and contingencies (see Note 7)			
29	**Stockholders' equity**			
30	Common stock	59	57	
31	Convertible common stock	12	13	
32	Additional paid-in capital	508,350	397,248	
33	Retained earnings	856,687	653,842	
34	Accumulated other comprehensive income (loss)	(14,808)	2,194	
35	**Total stockholders' equity**	1,350,300	1,053,354	
36	**Total liabilities and stockholders' equity**	$ 2,095,083	$ 1,577,741	
37				

	A	B	C	Đ
1	**Under Armour, Inc.** **Consolidated Statements of Income**			
2			**12 Months Ended**	
3	**In Thousands of $**	**Dec. 31, 2014**	**Dec. 31, 2013**	**Dec. 31, 2012**
4	Net revenues	$ 3,084,370	$ 2,332,051	$ 1,834,921
5	Cost of goods sold	1,572,164	1,195,381	955,624
6	Gross profit	1,512,206	1,136,670	879,297
7	Selling, general and administrative expenses	1,158,251	871,572	670,602
8	Income from operations	353,955	265,098	208,695
9	Interest expense, net	(5,335)	(2,933)	(5,183)
10	Other expense, net	(6,410)	(1,172)	(73)
11	Income before income taxes	342,210	260,993	203,439
12	Provision for income taxes	134,168	98,663	74,661
13	Net income	$ 208,042	$ 162,330	$ 128,778
14				

Merchandise *inventory* is the heart of a merchandising business, and *cost of goods sold* is the most important expense for a company that sells goods rather than services. *Gross profit* (or gross margin) is the difference between net sales and cost of goods sold. *Gross profit percentage* is gross profit expressed as a percentage of net sales. It shows how profitable a company's products are when they are sold. *Inventory turnover* and *days' inventory outstanding* show how fast products are sold. All of these are important measures of success for a merchandising company.

This chapter covers the accounting for inventory and cost of goods sold. It also shows you how to analyze the impact of changes in this asset and expense on the financial statements.

LEARNING OBJECTIVES

1 **Show** how to account for inventory

2 **Apply and compare** various inventory cost methods

3 **Explain and apply** underlying GAAP for inventory

4 **Compute and evaluate** gross profit (margin) percentage, inventory turnover, and days' inventory outstanding (DIO)

5 **Use** the cost-of-goods-sold (COGS) model to make management decisions

6 **Analyze** effects of inventory errors

>> Try It in Excel®

You can access the most current annual report of Under Armour, Inc., in Excel format at **http://www.sec.gov**. Using the "FILINGS" link on the toolbar at the top of the page, select "Company Filings Search." This will take you to the "EDGAR Company Filings" page. Type "Under Armour" in the company name box, and select "Search." This will produce the "EDGAR Search Results" page showing the company name. Click on the "CIK" link beside the company name. This will pull up a list of the reports that the company has filed with the SEC. Under the "Filing Type" box, type "10-K." Form

≽ 10-K is the SEC form for the company's annual report. Find the year that you wish to view. Click on the "Interactive Data" box, which takes you to the "View Filing Data" page. You may choose to either open or download the Excel files containing the company's selected financial statements.

SHOW HOW TO ACCOUNT FOR INVENTORY

We begin by showing how the financial statements of a merchandiser such as Under Armour, Inc., differs from those of service entities such as Century 21 Real Estate. The financial statements in Exhibit 6-1 highlight how service entities differ from merchandisers.

1 **Show** how to account for inventory

Exhibit 6-1 | Contrasting a Service Company with a Merchandising Company

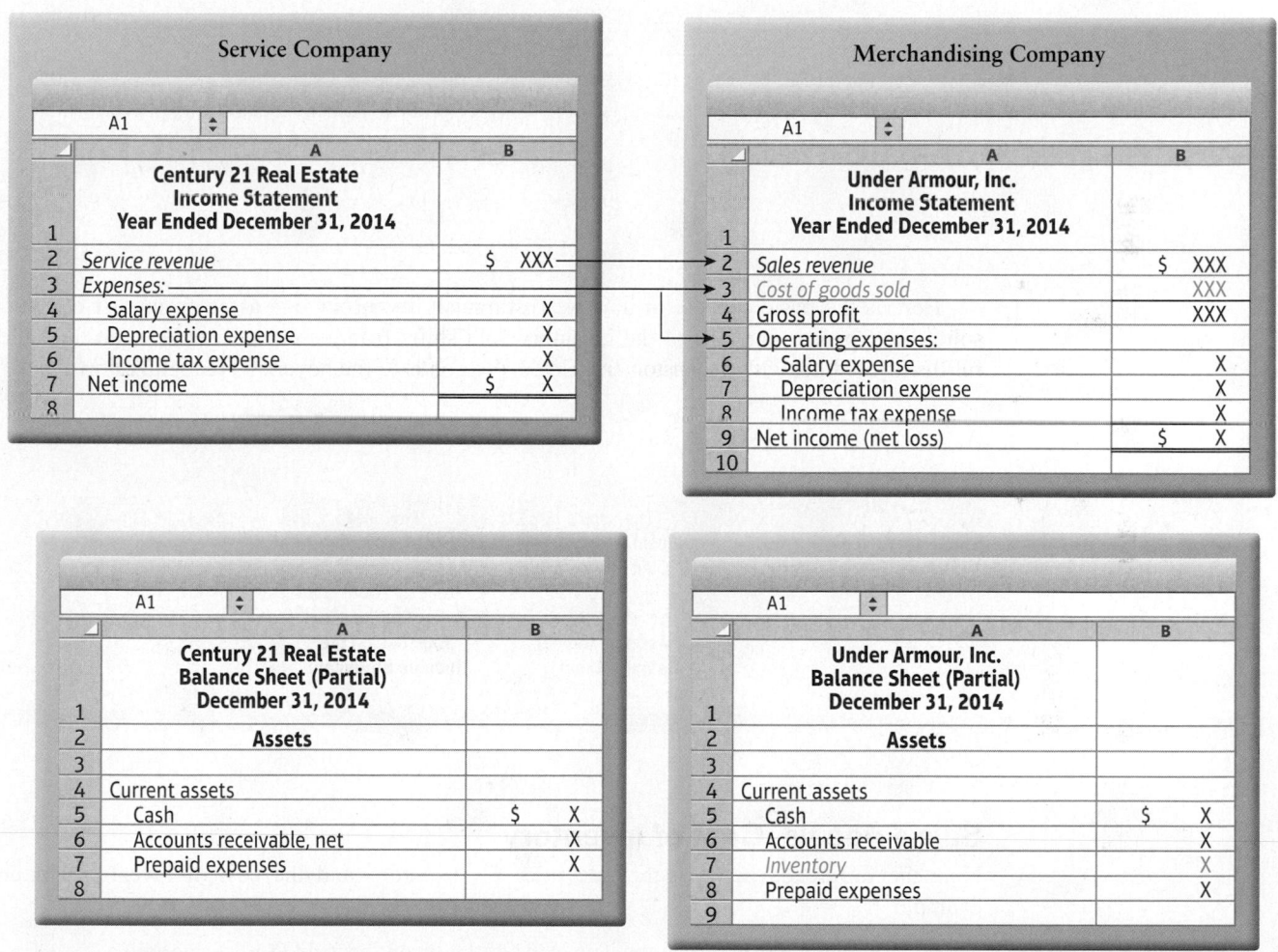

Merchandisers have two accounts that service entities don't need:
- Cost of goods sold on the income statement
- Inventory on the balance sheet

The basic concept of accounting for merchandise inventory can be illustrated with an example. Suppose that an Under Armour Outlet store has in stock 300 men's Under Armour fleece hoodies that cost $30 each. The store marks each hoodie up by $20 and sells 200 of the hoodies for $50 each. After the sale of 200 hoodies:

- The store's balance sheet reports the 100 hoodies that the company still holds in inventory.
- The income statement reports both the revenue from and the cost of the 200 hoodies sold, as shown in Exhibit 6-2.

Exhibit 6-2 | Inventory and Cost of Goods Sold When Inventory Cost Is Constant

Balance Sheet (partial)		Income Statement (partial)	
Current assets		Sales revenue	
Cash..	$XXX	(200 hoodies @ $50 each)......................	$10,000
Accounts receivable...............................	XXX	Cost of goods sold	
Inventory (100 hoodies @ $30 each).....	3,000	(200 hoodies @ $30 each)......................	6,000
Prepaid expenses....................................	XXX	Gross profit...	$ 4,000

Here is the basic concept of how we distinguish **inventory**, the asset, from **cost of goods sold**, the expense. The cost of the inventory sold shifts from asset to expense when the seller fulfills its contract with the customer, delivers the goods to the buyer and recognizes revenue.

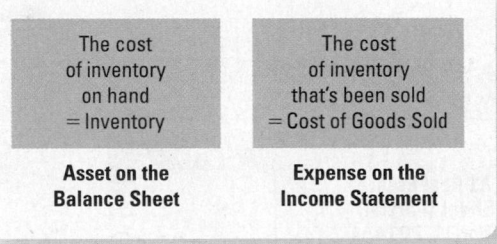

Sale Price vs. Cost of Inventory

Note the difference between the sale price of inventory and the cost of inventory. In our example,

- sales revenue is based on the *sale price* of the inventory sold ($50 per hoodie);
- cost of goods sold is based on the *cost* of the inventory sold ($30 per hoodie);
- inventory on the balance sheet is based on the *cost* of the inventory still on hand ($30 per hoodie).

Exhibit 6-2 shows these items.

Gross profit, also called **gross margin**, is the excess of sales revenue over cost of goods sold. It is called *gross* profit (margin) because operating expenses have not yet been subtracted. Exhibit 6-3 shows actual inventory and cost-of-goods-sold data adapted from the financial statements of Under Armour, Inc.

Exhibit 6-3 | Under Armour, Inc., Inventory and Cost of Sales

	A	B	C
	A1 ◆		
1	**Under Armour, Inc.** **Consolidated Balance Sheet (Partial, Adapted)** **December 31, 2014**		
2	**Assets**		
3	**(in millions)**		
4	Current assets		
5	Cash and cash equivalents		$ 593.2
6	Accounts receivable, net		279.8
7	Inventories		536.7
8			

	A	B	C
	A1 ◆		
1	**Under Armour, Inc.** **Consolidated Statement of Income (Partial, Adapted)** **Year Ended December 31, 2014**		
2	**(In millions)**		
3	Net (sales) revenues		$ 3,084.4
4	Cost of goods sold		1,572.2
5	Gross profit (margin)		$ 1,512.2
6			

Under Armour, Inc.'s, inventory of $536.7 million represents

$$\frac{\text{Inventory}}{\text{(balance sheet)}} = \frac{\text{Number of units of}}{\text{inventory } on \ hand} \times \frac{\text{Cost per unit}}{\text{of inventory}}$$

Under Armour, Inc.'s, cost of goods sold ($1,572.2 million) represents

$$\frac{\text{Cost of goods sold}}{\text{(income statement)}} = \frac{\text{Number of units of}}{\text{inventory } sold} \times \frac{\text{Cost per unit}}{\text{of inventory}}$$

Let's see what "units of inventory" and "cost per unit" mean.

Number of Units of Inventory. The number of inventory units on hand is determined from the accounting records, backed up by a physical count of the goods at year-end. Companies do not include in inventory any goods they hold on **consignment** because those goods belong to another company. But they do include their own inventory that is out on consignment and held for sale by another company. As discussed in Chapter 5, companies include inventory in transit from suppliers or in transit to customers that, according to shipping terms, legally belong to them as of the year-end. Shipping terms, otherwise known as *FOB (free on board) terms*, indicate who owns the goods at a particular time and, therefore, who must pay for the shipping costs. When the vendor invoice specifies *FOB shipping point* (the most common business practice), legal title to the goods passes from the seller to the purchaser when the inventory leaves the seller's place of business. The purchaser therefore owns the goods while they are in transit and must pay the transportation costs. In the case of goods purchased FOB shipping point, the company purchasing the goods must include goods in transit from suppliers as units in inventory as of the year-end. In the case of goods purchased *FOB destination*, title to the goods does not pass from the seller to the purchaser until the goods arrive at the purchaser's receiving dock. Therefore, these goods while in transit are not counted in year-end inventory of the purchasing company. Rather, the cost of these goods is included in inventory of the seller until the goods reach their destination.

Cost per Unit of Inventory. The cost per unit of inventory poses a challenge because companies purchase goods at different prices throughout the year. Which unit costs go into ending inventory? Which unit costs go to cost of goods sold?

Starting on page 317, we discuss how the selection between different accounting methods determines reported amounts on the balance sheet and the income statement. First, however, let's take a step back and cover how inventory accounting systems work.

Accounting for Inventory in the Perpetual System

There are two main types of inventory accounting systems: the periodic system and the perpetual system. The **periodic inventory system**, discussed in more detail in Appendix 6A, is used for inexpensive goods. A fabric store or a hardware store won't keep a running record of every bolt of fabric or every ten-penny nail. Instead, these stores count their inventory periodically—at least once a year—to determine the quantities on hand. Businesses such as restaurants and hometown nurseries also use the periodic system because the accounting cost of a periodic system is low.

A **perpetual inventory system** uses computer software to keep a running record of inventory on hand. This system achieves control over goods such as furniture, automobiles, jewelry, apparel, and most other types of inventory. Most businesses use the perpetual inventory system.

Even with a perpetual system, the business still counts the inventory on hand annually. The physical count establishes the correct amount of ending inventory for the financial statements and also serves as a check on the perpetual records. Here is a quick summary of the two main inventory accounting systems.

Perpetual Inventory System	Periodic Inventory System
• Used for all types of goods	• Used for inexpensive goods
• Keeps a running record of all goods bought, sold, and on hand	• Does *not* keep a running record of all goods bought, sold, and on hand
• Inventory counted at least once a year	• Inventory counted at least once a year

How the Perpetual System Works. Let's use an everyday situation to show how a perpetual inventory system works. When you check out at an Under Armour Outlet store, Walmart, or Whole Foods Market store, the clerk scans the bar codes on the labels of the items you buy. Exhibit 6-4 illustrates a typical bar code. Suppose you are buying a hoodie from an Under Armour Outlet store. The bar code on the product label holds lots of information. The optical scanner reads the bar code, and the computer records the sale and updates the inventory records.

Exhibit 6-4 | Bar Code for Electronic Scanner

0 72512 06581 5

Recording Transactions in the Perpetual System. All accounting systems record each purchase of inventory. When an Under Armour Outlet store makes a sale, two entries are needed in the perpetual system:

- The company records the sale—debits Cash or Accounts Receivable and credits Sales Revenue for the sale price of the goods.

- The Under Armour Outlet store also debits Cost of Goods Sold and credits Inventory for the cost of the inventory sold.

Exhibit 6-5 shows the accounting for inventory in a perpetual system. Panel A gives the journal entries and the T-accounts, and Panel B shows the income statement and the balance sheet. All amounts are assumed. (Appendix 6A illustrates the accounting for these same transactions for a periodic inventory system.)

Exhibit 6-5 | Recording and Reporting Inventory—Perpetual System

PANEL A—Recording Transactions and the T-accounts (All amounts are assumed)

Journal Entry

	A	C	D	G
1	1. Inventory		560,000	
2	Accounts Payable			560,000
3	Purchased inventory on account.			
4				
5	2. Accounts Receivable		900,000	
6	Sales Revenue			900,000
7	Sold inventory on account.			
8	Cost of Goods Sold		540,000	
9	Inventory			540,000
10	Recorded cost of goods sold.			
11				

Inventory

Beginning balance	100,000*		
Purchases	560,000	Cost of goods sold	540,000
Ending balance	120,000		

*Beginning inventory was $100,000

Cost of Goods Sold

Cost of goods sold	540,000

PANEL B—Reporting in the Financial Statements

Income Statement (partial)

Sales revenue	$900,000
Cost of goods sold	540,000
Gross profit	$360,000

Ending Balance Sheet (partial)

Current assets:	
Cash	$ XXX
Short-term investments	XXX
Accounts receivable	XXX
Inventory	120,000
Prepaid expenses	XXX

In Exhibit 6-5 (panel A), the first entry to Inventory summarizes in one entry what, in practice, may actually be several entries. The cost of the inventory, $560,000, is the *net* amount of the purchases, determined as follows (using assumed amounts):

Purchase price of the inventory	$600,000
+ **Freight in** (the cost to transport the goods from the seller to the buyer)	4,000
− **Purchase returns** for unsuitable goods returned to the seller	(25,000)
− **Purchase allowances** granted by the seller	(5,000)
− **Purchase discounts** for early payment by the buyer	(14,000)
= Net purchases of inventory—Cost to the buyer	$560,000

Freight in is the transportation cost, paid by the buyer under terms FOB shipping point, to move goods from the seller to the buyer. Freight in is accounted for as part of the cost of inventory. Freight out is paid by the *seller*, under shipping terms FOB destination, and is not part of the cost of inventory. Instead, freight out is considered a delivery expense. It's the seller's expense of delivering merchandise to customers.

A **purchase return** represents a decrease in inventory and a corresponding decrease in accounts payable because the buyer returned the goods to the seller (vendor). With a **purchase allowance**, the buyer keeps the inventory but decreases its cost of inventory held because the buyer is granted an allowance (a deduction) from the amount owed. These terms are similar to the concept of the seller's *sales return* and *sales allowance* discussed in Chapter 5, but are accounted for differently. To document approval of purchase returns, management issues a **debit memorandum**, meaning that accounts payable are reduced (debited) for the amount of the return. The offsetting credit is to inventory as the goods are shipped back to the seller (vendor). Purchase returns and allowances are usually documented on the final invoice received from the vendor. Throughout this book, we often refer to net purchases simply as *Purchases*.

A **purchase discount** (similar to the concept of a sales discount discussed in Chapter 5) is a decrease in the buyer's cost of inventory earned by paying quickly. Many companies offer payment terms of "2/10 n/30." This means the buyer can take, and the seller grants, a 2% discount for payment within 10 days, with the final amount due within 30 days. Another common credit term is "net 30," which tells the customer to pay the full amount within 30 days. In summary,

$$\text{Net purchases} = \text{Purchases}$$
$$- \text{Purchase returns and allowances}$$
$$- \text{Purchase discounts}$$
$$+ \text{Freight in}$$

The journal entries for purchase returns and purchase discounts are as follows (assuming a purchase return of $500 in merchandise and a purchase of $1,000 in merchandise with terms of 2/10, n/30):

	A	B	C	D
			Debit	**Credit**
1		Purchase returns:		
2		Accounts payable	500	
3		Inventory		500
4		*To record purchase return of merchandise that cost $500.*		
5				
6		Purchase discounts:		
7		Original purchase:		
8		Inventory (1,000 × 1)	1,000	
9		Accounts payable (1,000 × 1)		1,000
10		*To record a gross purchase of $1,000 in merchandise.*		
11				
12		Payment 10 days later (within discount period):		
13		Accounts payable	1,000	
14		Inventory		20
15		Cash		980
16		*To record payment for merchandise within 10 days at 2% discount.*		
17				

APPLY AND COMPARE VARIOUS INVENTORY COST METHODS

2 Apply and compare various inventory cost methods

Inventory is the first asset for which a manager can decide which accounting method to use. The accounting method selected affects the profits to be reported, the amount of income tax to be paid, and the values of the inventory turnover and gross margin percentage ratios derived from the financial statements.

What Goes into Inventory Cost?

The cost of inventory on Under Armour, Inc.'s, balance sheet represents all the costs that the company incurred to bring its inventory to the point of sale. The following cost principle applies to all assets:

The cost of any asset, such as inventory, is the sum of all the costs incurred to bring the asset to its intended use, less any discounts.

The cost of inventory includes its basic purchase price, plus freight in, insurance while in transit, and any fees or taxes paid to get the inventory ready to sell, less returns, allowances, and discounts.

After an Under Armour t-shirt is sitting on the shelf in the store, other costs, such as advertising and sales commissions, are *not* included as the cost of inventory. Advertising, sales commissions, and delivery costs are selling expenses that go in the income statement rather than in the balance sheet.

Apply the Various Inventory Costing Methods

Determining the cost of inventory is easy when the unit cost remains constant, as in Exhibit 6-2. But the unit cost of merchandise usually fluctuates. For example, prices of products sometimes rise along with fuel prices that increase transportation costs of merchandise to retail stores. The t-shirt that cost Under Armour, Inc., $10 in January may cost $14 in June and $18 in October. Suppose an Under Armour Outlet store sells 1,000 t-shirts in November. How many of those t-shirts cost $10, how many cost $14, and how many cost $18?

To compute cost of goods sold and the cost of ending inventory still on hand, we must assign a unit cost to the items. Accounting uses four generally accepted inventory methods:

1. **Specific unit cost**
2. **Average cost**
3. **First-in, first-out (FIFO) cost**
4. **Last-in, first-out (LIFO) cost**

A company can use any of these methods. The methods can have very different effects on reported profits, income taxes, and cash flow. Therefore, companies select their inventory method with great care.

Specific Unit Cost. Some businesses deal in unique inventory items, such as automobiles, antique furniture, jewels, and real estate. These businesses cost their inventories at the specific cost of the particular unit. For instance, a Toyota dealer may have two vehicles in the showroom—a "stripped-down" model that cost the dealer $19,000 and a "loaded" model that cost the dealer $30,000. If the dealer sells the loaded model, the cost of goods sold is $30,000. The stripped-down auto will be the only unit left in inventory, and so ending inventory is $19,000.

The **specific-unit-cost method** is also called the *specific identification method*. This method is too expensive to use for inventory items that have common characteristics, such as bushels of wheat, gallons of paint, or auto tires.

The other inventory accounting methods—average, FIFO, and LIFO—are fundamentally different. These other methods do not use the specific cost of a particular unit. Instead, they assume different flows of inventory costs. To illustrate average, FIFO, and LIFO costing, we use a common set of data given in Exhibit 6-6.

Exhibit 6-6 | Inventory Data Used to Illustrate the Various Inventory Costing Methods

		Inventory		
Beg bal	(10 units @ $10)	100		
Purchases:			Cost of goods sold	
No. 1	(25 units @ $14)	350	(40 units @ ?)	?
No. 2	(25 units @ $18)	450		
End bal	(20 units @ ?)	?		

In Exhibit 6-6, an Under Armour Outlet store began the period with 10 t-shirts that cost $10 each; the beginning inventory was therefore $100. During the period, Under Armour bought 50 more t-shirts, sold 40 t-shirts, and ended the period with 20 t-shirts.

Goods Available		Number of Units	Total Cost
Goods available	=	10 + 25 + 25 = 60 units	$100 + $350 + $450 = $900
Cost of goods sold	=	40 units	?
Ending inventory	=	20 units	?

The big accounting questions are as follows:

1. What is the cost of goods sold for the income statement?
2. What is the cost of the ending inventory for the balance sheet?

The answers to these questions depend on which inventory method Under Armour uses. Let's look at average costing first.

Average Cost. The **average-cost method**, sometimes called the **weighted-average method**, is based on the average cost of inventory during the period. Using data from Exhibit 6-6, the average cost per unit is determined as

$$\text{Average cost per unit} = \frac{\text{Cost of goods available}^1}{\text{Number of units available}} = \frac{\$900}{60} = \$15$$

$$
\begin{aligned}
\text{Cost of goods sold} &= \text{Number of units sold} \times \text{Average cost per unit} \\
&= \quad 40 \text{ units} \quad \times \quad \$15 \quad = \$600
\end{aligned}
$$

$$
\begin{aligned}
\text{Ending inventory} &= \text{Number of units on hand} \times \text{Average cost per unit} \\
&= \quad 20 \text{ units} \quad \times \quad \$15 \quad = \$300
\end{aligned}
$$

The following T-account shows the effects of average costing:

Inventory (at Average Cost)

Beg bal	(10 units @ $10)	100		
Purchases:				
No. 1	(25 units @ $14)	350		
No. 2	(25 units @ $18)	450	Cost of goods sold (40 units	
			@ average cost of $15 per unit)	600
End bal	(20 units @ average cost of $15 per unit)	300		

Average costing

Purchases

Cost of goods sold

FIFO Cost. Under the FIFO method, the first costs into inventory are the first costs assigned to cost of goods sold—hence the name *first-in, first-out*. The diagram on the next page shows the

---

[1]Cost of Goods Available (used synonymously with Cost of Goods Available for Sale throughout the chapter) = Beginning inventory + Purchases.

effect of FIFO costing. The following T-account shows how to compute FIFO cost of goods sold and ending inventory for the Under Armour t-shirts (data from Exhibit 6-6):

Inventory (at FIFO cost)

Beg bal	(10 units @ $10)	100				
Purchases:			Cost of goods sold (40 units):			
No. 1	(25 units @ $14)	350	(10 units @ $10)	100		
No. 2	(25 units @ $18)	450	(25 units @ $14)	350	}	540
			(5 units @ $18)	90		
End bal	(20 units @ $18)	360				

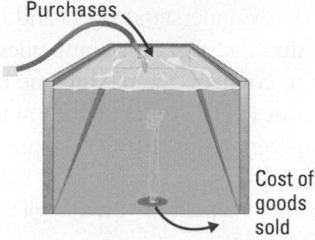

First-in, first-out (FIFO) costing

Under FIFO, the cost of ending inventory is always based on the latest costs incurred—in this case, $18 per unit.

LIFO Cost. LIFO (*last-in, first-out*) costing is the opposite of FIFO. Under LIFO, the last costs into inventory go immediately to cost of goods sold, as shown in the diagram below. Compare LIFO and FIFO, and you will see a vast difference.

The following T-account shows how to compute the LIFO inventory amounts for the Under Armour t-shirts (data from Exhibit 6-6):

Inventory (at LIFO cost)

Beg bal	(10 units @ $10)	100				
Purchases:			Cost of goods sold (40 units):			
No. 1	(25 units @ $14)	350	(25 units @ $18)	450	}	660
No. 2	(25 units @ $18)	450	(15 units @ $14)	210		
End bal	(10 units @ $10) (10 units @ $14)	} 240				

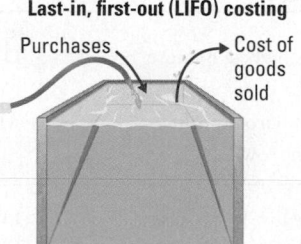

Last-in, first-out (LIFO) costing

Under LIFO, the cost of ending inventory is always based on the oldest costs—from beginning inventory plus the earliest purchases of the period $10 and $14 per unit.

Compare the Effects of FIFO, LIFO, and Average Cost on Cost of Goods Sold, Gross Profit, and Ending Inventory

When inventory unit costs change, the various inventory methods produce different cost-of-goods-sold figures. Exhibit 6-7 summarizes the income effects (Sales − Cost of goods sold = Gross profit) of the three inventory methods (remember that prices are rising). Study Exhibit 6-7 carefully, focusing on cost of goods sold and gross profit.

Exhibit 6-7 | Income Effects of the FIFO, LIFO, and Average Inventory Methods; Increasing Costs

	FIFO	LIFO	Average
Sales revenue (assumed)	$1,000	$1,000	$1,000
Cost of goods sold.........................	540 (lowest)	660 (highest)	600
Gross profit.................................	$ 460 (highest)	$ 340 (lowest)	$ 400

Exhibit 6-8 shows the impact of both FIFO and LIFO costing methods on cost of goods sold and inventories during both increasing costs (Panel A) and decreasing costs (Panel B). Study this exhibit carefully; it will help you *really* understand FIFO and LIFO.

Financial analysts search the stock markets for companies with good prospects for income growth. Analysts sometimes need to compare the net income of a company that uses LIFO with the net income of a company that uses FIFO. Appendix 6B, at the end of this chapter, shows how to convert a LIFO company's net income to the FIFO basis in order to compare the companies.

Exhibit 6-8 | Cost of Goods Sold and Ending Inventory—FIFO and LIFO; Increasing Costs and Decreasing Costs

PANEL A—When Inventory Costs Are Increasing

	Cost of Goods Sold (COGS)	Ending Inventory (EI)
FIFO	FIFO COGS is lowest because it's based on the oldest costs, which are low. Gross profit is, therefore, the highest.	FIFO EI is highest because it's based on the most recent costs, which are high.
LIFO	LIFO COGS is highest because it's based on the most recent costs, which are high. Gross profit is, therefore, the lowest.	LIFO EI is lowest because it's based on the oldest costs, which are low.

PANEL B—When Inventory Costs Are Decreasing

	Cost of Goods Sold (COGS)	Ending Inventory (EI)
FIFO	FIFO COGS is highest because it's based on the oldest costs, which are high. Gross profit is, therefore, the lowest.	FIFO EI is lowest because it's based on the most recent costs, which are low.
LIFO	LIFO COGS is lowest because it's based on the most recent costs, which are low. Gross profit is, therefore, the highest.	LIFO EI is highest because it's based on the oldest costs, which are high.

Keeping Track of Perpetual Inventories under LIFO and Weighted-Average-Cost Methods

The LIFO cost-flow assumption does not follow the logical flow of goods. Therefore, when costs are changing, it is physically impossible to apply LIFO unit costs to units purchased and sold as the transactions are happening using a perpetual inventory accounting system. Similarly, for large companies with millions of purchases and sales transactions, although it might be physically possible to do so, keeping track of perpetual inventories using weighted-average cost can be quite challenging, requiring sophisticated computer software to make constant updates to both changing quantities and changing unit prices on a daily basis. Therefore, many companies that use these methods keep track of perpetual inventories in quantities only during the period, making adjusting journal entries at the end of the period to apply either LIFO or weighted-average cost to both ending inventory and cost of goods sold. The details of this topic are reserved for more advanced accounting courses.

The Tax Advantage of LIFO

The Internal Revenue Service requires all U.S. companies to use the same method of costing inventories for tax purposes that they use for financial reporting purposes. Thus, the choice of inventory methods directly affects income taxes, which must be paid in cash. When costs are rising, LIFO results in the *lowest taxable income* and thus the *lowest income taxes*. Let's use the gross profit data of Exhibit 6-7 to illustrate.

	FIFO	LIFO
Gross profit (from Exhibit 6-7)	$460	$340
Operating expenses (assumed)................	260	260
Income before income tax	$200	$ 80
Income tax expense (40%).....................	$ 80	$ 32

Income tax expense is lowest under LIFO by $48 ($80 − $32). **This is the most attractive feature of LIFO—low income tax payments**—which is why about one-third of all U.S. companies use LIFO. During periods of inflation, companies that can justify it may switch to LIFO for its tax and cash-flow advantages.

Let's compare the FIFO and LIFO inventory methods from a couple of different standpoints.

1. *Measuring cost of goods sold.* How well does each method match inventory expense—cost of goods sold—against revenue? LIFO results in the most realistic net income figure because LIFO assigns the most recent inventory costs to expense. In contrast, FIFO matches old inventory costs against revenue—a poor measure of expense. FIFO income is therefore less realistic than LIFO income.

2. *Measuring ending inventory.* Which method reports the most up-to-date inventory cost on the balance sheet? FIFO. LIFO can value inventory at very old costs because LIFO leaves the oldest costs in ending inventory.

LIFO and Managing Reported Income. LIFO allows managers to manipulate net income by timing their purchases of inventory. When inventory costs are rising rapidly and a company wants to show less income (in order to pay less taxes), managers can buy a large amount of inventory near the end of the year. Under LIFO, these high inventory costs go straight to cost of goods sold. As a result, net income is decreased.

If the business is having a bad year, management may wish to report higher income. The company can delay the purchase of high-cost inventory until next year. This avoids decreasing current year income. In the process, the company draws down inventory quantities, a practice known as *LIFO inventory liquidation*.

LIFO Liquidation. When LIFO is used and ending inventory quantities fall below the level of the previous period, the situation is called a *LIFO liquidation*. To compute cost of goods sold, the company must dip into older layers of inventory cost. Under LIFO, and when prices are rising, that action shifts older, lower costs into cost of goods sold. The result is higher net income. Managers try to avoid a LIFO liquidation because it increases reported income as well as income taxes.

International Perspective Many U.S. companies that currently use LIFO for their U.S. operations must use another method if they have operations in foreign countries. Why? International Financial Reporting Standards (IFRS) do not permit the use of LIFO, although they do permit FIFO and other methods.

These differences can create comparability problems for financial analysts when comparing a U.S. company against a foreign competitor. As discussed earlier, Appendix 6B illustrates how analysts convert reported income to income under FIFO for a company that uses LIFO.

If U.S. generally accepted accounting principles (GAAP) and IFRS become fully integrated in the future, U.S. companies that use LIFO might be forced to convert their inventory pricing to another method. As we discussed earlier in the chapter, in periods of rising prices, the use of LIFO inventories results in the lowest amount of reported income and, thus, the lowest amount of income taxes. If, as stated previously, about a third of U.S. companies continue to use LIFO through the next few years, conversion of inventories to methods other than LIFO may substantially increase income for them. This change has potentially far-reaching implications. For example, if the Internal Revenue Service were to continue to require companies to use the same inventory pricing methods for income tax purposes and financial statement purposes, conversion of LIFO inventories to another method would greatly increase the tax burden on many U.S. companies, including some small- and medium-sized businesses that can least afford it.

The disallowance of LIFO inventories under IFRS is only one of several rather thorny issues that must be resolved before the United States can adopt IFRS. Resolution of these differences will likely have political as well as financial implications. We will cover other key differences between U.S. GAAP and IFRS in later chapters. Appendix E summarizes all of these differences.

Mid-Chapter | Summary Problem

Suppose a division of **Texas Instruments Incorporated** that sells computer microchips has these inventory records for January 2016:

Date		Item	Quantity	Unit Cost	Total Cost
Jan	1	Beginning inventory	100 units	$ 8	$ 800
	6	Purchase	60 units	9	540
	21	Purchase	150 units	9	1,350
	27	Purchase	90 units	10	900

Company accounting records show sales of 310 units for revenue of $6,770. Operating expense for January was $1,900.

Requirements

1. Prepare the January, multistep income statement, showing amounts for LIFO, average, and FIFO cost. Label the bottom line "Operating income." Round average cost per unit to three decimal places and all other figures to whole-dollar amounts. Show your computations.

2. Suppose you are the financial vice president of Texas Instruments. Which inventory method will you use if your motive is to

   a. minimize income taxes?

   b. report the highest operating income?

   c. report operating income between the extremes of FIFO and LIFO?

   d. report inventory on the balance sheet at the most current cost?

   e. attain the best measure of net income for the income statement?

State the reason for each of your answers.

Answers

Requirement 1

A1	◆				
	A		**B**	**C**	**D**
1	**Texas Instruments Incorporated** **Income Statement for Microchip** **Month Ended January 31, 2016**				
2			LIFO	Average	FIFO
3	Sales revenue		$ 6,770	$ 6,770	$ 6,770
4	Cost of goods sold		2,870	2,782	2,690
5	Gross profit		3,900	3,988	4,080
6	Operating expenses		1,900	1,900	1,900
7	Operating income		$ 2,000	$ 2,088	$ 2,180
8					

Cost of goods sold computations:

LIFO: $(90 @ \$10) + (150 @ \$9) + (60 @ \$9) + (10 @ \$8) = \$2,870$

Average: $310 \times \$8.975* = \$2,782$

FIFO: $(100 @ \$8) + (60 @ \$9) + (150 @ \$9) = \$2,690$

$$* \ \frac{(\$800 + \$540 + \$1,350 + \$900)}{(100 + 60 + 150 + 90)} = \$8.975$$

Requirement 2

a. Use LIFO to minimize income taxes. Operating income under LIFO is lowest when inventory unit costs are increasing, as they are in this case (from $8 to $10). (If inventory costs were decreasing, income under FIFO would be lowest.)

b. Use FIFO to report the highest operating income. Income under FIFO is highest when inventory unit costs are increasing, as in this situation.

c. Use the average-cost method to report an operating income amount between the FIFO and LIFO extremes. This is true in this situation and in others when inventory unit costs are increasing or decreasing.

d. Use FIFO to report inventory on the balance sheet at the most current cost. The oldest inventory costs are expensed as cost of goods sold, leaving in ending inventory the most recent (most current) costs of the period.

e. Use LIFO to attain the best measure of net income. LIFO produces the best current expense recognition by matching the most current expense with current revenue. The most recent (most current) inventory costs are expensed as cost of goods sold.

EXPLAIN AND APPLY UNDERLYING GAAP FOR INVENTORY

3 Explain and apply underlying GAAP for inventory

Several accounting principles have special relevance to inventories:

- Consistency
- Disclosure
- Representational faithfulness

Disclosure Principle

The **disclosure principle** holds that a company's financial statements should report enough information for outsiders to make informed decisions about the company. The company should report *relevant* and *representationally faithful* information about itself. That means properly disclosing inventory accounting methods, as well as the substance of all material transactions impacting the existence and proper valuation of inventory. It also requires the use of *comparable* methods for *consistency* of presentation from period to period. The financial statements typically contain a footnote describing the inventory pricing method used, as well as the fact that inventory was valued at the lower of that method or market. The lower-of-cost-or-market rule is described next. Without knowledge of the accounting method and without clear, complete disclosures in the financial statements, a banker could make an unwise lending decision. Suppose the banker is comparing two companies—one using LIFO and the other, FIFO. The FIFO company reports higher net income but only because it uses FIFO. Without knowing this, the banker could loan money to the wrong business.

Lower-of-Cost-or-Market Rule

The **lower-of-cost-or-market rule** (abbreviated as **LCM**) is based on the principles of relevance and representational faithfulness. LCM requires that inventory be reported in the financial statements at whichever is lower—the inventory's historical cost or its market value. Applied to inventories, *market value* generally means *current replacement cost* (that is, how much the business would have to pay now to replace its inventory). If the replacement cost of inventory falls below its historical cost, the business must write down the value of its goods to market value, which is the most relevant and representationally faithful measure of its true worth to the business. **The business reports ending inventory at its LCM value on the balance sheet.** All this can be done automatically by a computerized accounting system. How is the write-down accomplished?

Suppose Under Armour, Inc., paid $3,000,000 for inventory on November 1. By December 31, its fiscal year-end, the inventory can be replaced for $2,000,000. Under Armour's year-end balance sheet must report this inventory at the LCM value of $2,000,000. Exhibit 6-9 presents the effects of LCM on the balance sheet and the income statement. Before any LCM effect, cost of goods sold is $9,000,000. An LCM write-down decreases Inventory and increases Cost of Goods Sold:

	A	B	C	D
1	Dec. 31	Cost of Goods Sold	1,000,000	
2		Inventory		1,000,000
3		*Wrote inventory down to market value.*		
4				

Exhibit 6-9 | Lower-of-Cost-or-Market (LCM) Effects on Inventory and Cost of Goods Sold

Balance Sheet

Current assets:

Cash	$ XXX,XXX
Short-term investments	XXX,XXX
Accounts receivable	XXX,XXX
Inventories, at market (which is lower than $3,000,000 cost)	2,000,000
Prepaid expenses	XXX,XXX
Total current assets	$X,XXX,XXX

Income Statement

Sales revenue	$21,000,000
Cost of goods sold ($9,000,000 + $1,000,000)	10,000,000
Gross profit	$11,000,000

If the market value of Under Armour, Inc.'s inventory had been above cost, it would have made no adjustment for LCM. In that case, simply report the inventory at cost, which is the lower of cost or market.

Companies disclose the method(s) they use to value inventory, as well as the fact that they use LCM, in notes to their financial statements. LCM is not optional. It is required by GAAP.

To illustrate how companies follow the disclosure principle for inventories, here is an excerpt from Note 2 of the financial statements of Under Armour, Inc. regarding inventories:

Summary of Significant Accounting Policies

Inventories. The Company values its inventory at standard cost which approximates landed cost, using the first-in, first-out method of cost determination. Market value is estimated based upon assumptions made about future demand and retail market conditions. If the Company determines that the estimated market value of its inventory is less than the carrying value of such inventory, it records a charge to cost of goods sold to reflect the lower of cost or market.

Another IFRS Difference IFRS defines "market" differently from U.S. GAAP. Under IFRS, "market" is always defined as "net realizable value," which, for inventories, is selling price minus disposal costs. If IFRS is adopted in the United States, inventory write-downs may become less common than they are now, due to the fact that selling prices are usually greater than replacement cost.

Under U.S. GAAP, once the LCM rule is applied to write inventories down to current replacement cost, the write-downs may never be reversed. In contrast, under IFRS, some LCM write-downs may be reversed, and inventory may be subsequently written up again, not to exceed original cost. This may cause more fluctuations in the reported incomes of companies that sell inventories than we currently see.

GLOBAL VIEW

COMPUTE AND EVALUATE GROSS PROFIT (MARGIN) PERCENTAGE, INVENTORY TURNOVER, AND DAYS' INVENTORY OUTSTANDING (DIO)

4 **Compute and evaluate** gross profit (margin) percentage, inventory turnover, and days' inventory outstanding

Owners, managers, and investors use ratios to evaluate a business. Two ratios relate directly to inventory: gross profit percentage and the rate of inventory turnover.

Gross Profit Percentage

Gross profit—sales minus cost of goods sold—is a key indicator of a company's ability to sell inventory at a profit. Merchandisers strive to increase **gross profit percentage**, also called the **gross margin percentage**. Gross profit percentage is gross profit stated as a percentage of sales. Gross profit percentage is computed as follows for Under Armour, Inc. for the year ended December 31, 2014. Figures (in thousands) are taken from the company's Consolidated Statements of Income on page 310.

$$\text{Gross profit percentage} = \frac{\text{Gross profit}}{\text{Net sales revenue}} = \frac{\$1,512,206}{\$3,084,370} = 0.490 = 49.0\%$$

The gross profit percentage is watched carefully by managers and investors. A 49.0% gross margin percentage means that each dollar of sales generates about $0.49 of gross profit. On average, cost of goods sold consumes $0.51 of each sales dollar for Under Armour, Inc. For most firms, the gross profit percentage changes little from year to year, so a small downturn may signal trouble, and an upturn by a small percentage can mean millions of dollars in additional profits. Under Armour, Inc.'s, gross profit percentage for fiscal years 2012, 2013, and 2014 was 47.9%, 48.7%, and 49.0%, respectively. These figures reflect steady increases in gross profit percentage over the three-year period. A 1.1% increase in gross profit from 2012 through 2014, when multiplied by 2014 sales of $3.1 billion, computes to an increase in gross profits of about $34 million over three years. Is Under Armour, Inc.'s, gross profit percentage strong, weak, or neither compared to a competitor? The other two big players in the athletic wear space are Nike and Adidas AG, each of which has tremendous leverage and buying power. All three companies are competing on a global scale for the business of the sports enthusiast. Based on gross profit percentage and inventory turnover ratios, Under Armour, Inc., competes favorably with both of these larger competitors.

Exhibit 6-10 graphs the 2014 gross profit percentage of Under Armour, Inc., against its chief competitor, Nike, Inc. Under Armour, Inc.'s, gross profit percentage of 49.0% is greater than that of Nike, Inc. (44.8%). Knowing a few more facts can help you figure out why. Under Armour, Inc., has only been a public company since 2005. Eighty percent of its customer base is made up of 20,000 retail stores like Dick's Sporting Goods, Foot Locker, and Modell's. These chains are characterized by relatively small stores that sell specialized (and higher priced) athletic wear. Under Armour, Inc.'s, franchise products are athletic wear made of a synthetic fabric that wicks

Exhibit 6-10 | Gross Profit Percentages of Two Competing Athletic Apparel Companies in 2014

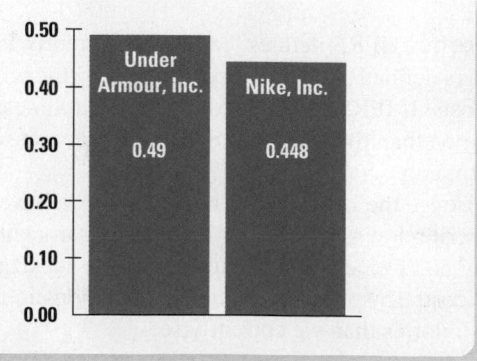

away perspiration, rather than plain cotton that absorbs it. The company has only recently entered the athletic shoe market that has been dominated by Nike, Inc., for years. In contrast, Nike, Inc., is a much more mature company in terms of years in business, as well as much more diverse in terms of product offerings and price ranges than Under Armour, Inc. Although Nike sells competing products to specialty stores, it has a much larger customer base than Under Armour, Inc., also selling some lower-end branded products to budget retailers like Walmart, Target, and Dollar General Stores. These stores are capable of leveraging their buying power with Nike, thus purchasing its products at lower prices in order to pass the savings on to their customers. Thus, Nike would be expected to have a lower gross profit percentage than Under Armour, Inc. However, because of its volume of sales ($27.8 billion in fiscal 2014) and greater diversity of customers (discount chains as well as specialty athletic wear retailers), Nike generates a larger amount of gross profit in terms of absolute dollars (about $12.4 billion) than Under Armour, Inc.

Inventory Turnover

Under Armour, Inc., strives to sell its inventory as quickly as possible because the goods generate no profit until they're sold. The faster the sales, the higher the income, and the reverse is true for slow-moving goods. Ideally, a business could operate with zero inventory, but most businesses, especially retailers, must keep some goods on hand. **Inventory turnover**, the ratio of cost of goods sold to average inventory, indicates how rapidly inventory is sold. The comparative inventory turnover statistics for 2014 and 2013 for Under Armour, Inc., follow (data in thousands from the Consolidated Balance Sheets and Statements of Income) on pages 309 and 310:

$$\text{Inventory turnover} = \frac{\text{Cost of goods sold}}{\text{Average inventory}} = \frac{\text{Cost of goods sold}}{\left(\dfrac{\text{Beginning}}{\text{inventory}} + \dfrac{\text{Ending}}{\text{inventory}}\right) \div 2}$$

for year ended December 31, 2014:

$$= \frac{\$1,572,164}{(\$536,714 + \$469,006)/2} = \begin{array}{l}\text{3.13 times per year}\\ \text{(every 117 days)}\end{array}$$

for year ended December 31, 2013:

$$= \frac{\$1,195,381}{(\$469,006 + \$319,286^*)/2} = \begin{array}{l}\text{3.03 times per year}\\ \text{(every 120 days)}\end{array}$$

*Beginning inventory for 2013 from 2013 annual report (not shown)

The inventory turnover statistic shows how many times the company sold (or turned over) its average level of inventory during the year. Inventory turnover varies from industry to industry. During the year ended December 31, 2014, Under Armour, Inc.'s, inventory turned over 3.13 times. As with all turnover ratios, inventory turnover can be converted to **days' inventory outstanding (DIO)** by dividing it into 365. Therefore, DIO during 2014 was 117 days. This means that, on average, items of inventory sat on the shelves for 117 days before being sold. How can we evaluate these results as strong or weak? By comparing with the results of the preceding year as well as those of a major competitor. The calculations above also show Under Armour's inventory turnover for the year ended December 31, 2013. It was 3.03 times, or every 120 days. Therefore, although 2014's turnover of 3.13 (117 days) seems slow, it is faster when compared with 2013's ratio of 3.03 (120 days). Therefore, 2014's results were better. On average, it took three fewer days to sell an item of inventory in 2014 than it did in 2013.

Another way to evaluate Under Armour's inventory turnover is to compare it with a competitor. Exhibit 6-11 graphs the rate of inventory turnover for Under Armour, Inc., against that of its major competitor, Nike, Inc. in 2014. You can see that Nike, Inc., turns inventory over 4.13 times a year (every 88 days) compared with Under Armour, Inc.'s, turnover of 3.13 times a year (every 117 days). The reason for this is the same as we discussed above for the two companies' comparative gross profit figures. Nike, Inc., is a much larger company, selling a much wider variety and volume of products to a much wider array of customers, including discount stores. Thus, they carry some less expensive lines that sell for cheaper prices. Naturally, these items will sell faster. Thus, on average, a Nike product moves off the shelves almost a full month (29 days) before the more expensive Under Armour product.

Exhibit 6-11 | Inventory Turnover Rates of Under Armour, Inc. and Nike, Inc. in 2014

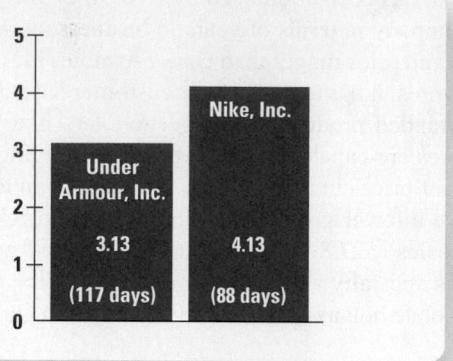

Examine Exhibits 6-10 and 6-11. What do those ratio values say about the merchandising (pricing) strategies of Under Armour, Inc., vs. Nike, Inc.?

Answer:

It's obvious that Under Armour, Inc. sells high-end merchandise. Under Armour, Inc.'s gross profit percentage is higher than Nike, Inc.'s. However, Nike has a much faster rate of inventory turnover. The lower the price, the faster the turnover, and vice versa.

USE THE COGS MODEL TO MAKE MANAGEMENT DECISIONS

5 **Use** the cost-of-goods-sold (COGS) model to make management decisions

Exhibit 6-12 presents the **cost-of-goods-sold (COGS) model**. Some may view this model as related to the periodic inventory system. But the COGS model is used by all companies, regardless of their accounting systems. The model is extremely powerful because it captures all the inventory information for an entire accounting period. Study this model carefully (all amounts are assumed).

Exhibit 6-12 | The Cost-of-Goods-Sold Model

	A	B
1	**Cost of goods sold (in thousands):**	
2	Beginning inventory	$1,200
3	+ Purchases	6,300
4	= Cost of goods available	7,500
5	− Ending inventory	(1,500)
6	= Cost of goods sold	$6,000
7		

Assume that Exhibit 6-12 represents the cost of goods sold for an Under Armour, Inc. outlet store. Because outlet store sales prices are discounted, the gross profit percentage is 35% rather than 49% as reflected in the company's overall consolidated statement of income, illustrated earlier. Let's see how the store manager can use the COGS model to manage the business effectively.

Computing Budgeted Purchases

1. What's the single most important question for Under Armour, Inc., to address?

   - What merchandise should Under Armour, Inc., offer to its customers? This is a *marketing* question that requires market research. If Under Armour continually stocks up on the wrong merchandise, sales will suffer and profits will drop.

2. What's the second most important question for Under Armour, Inc.?

   - How much inventory should Under Armour, Inc., buy? This is an accounting question faced by all merchandisers. If Under Armour, Inc., buys too much merchandise, it will have to lower prices, the gross profit percentage will suffer, and the company may lose money. Buying the right quantity of inventory is critical for success. This question can be answered with the COGS model. Let's see how it works.

We must rearrange the COGS model on the prior page. Then we can help an Under Armour, Inc., outlet store manager know how much inventory to buy, as follows (using amounts from Exhibit 6-12):

1	Cost of goods sold (based on the plan for the next period).....................	$6,000
2 +	Ending inventory (based on the plan for the next period).....................	1,500
3 =	Cost of goods available as planned...	7,500
4 −	Beginning inventory (actual amount left over from the prior period)......	(1,200)
5 =	Purchases (how much inventory the manager needs to buy)..................	$6,300

In this case, the manager should buy $6,300 of merchandise to work his plan for the upcoming period.

Estimating Inventory by the Gross Profit Method

Often a business must *estimate* the value of its goods. For example, suppose a fire destroys the warehouse, all inventory, and all records. The insurance company requires an estimate of the loss. In this case, the business must estimate the cost of ending inventory because the records have been destroyed.

The **gross profit method**, also known as the **gross margin method**, is widely used to estimate ending inventory. This method uses the familiar COGS model (amounts are assumed).

Beginning inventory	$ 4,000
+ Purchases	16,000
= Cost of goods available	20,000
− Ending inventory...................................	(5,000)
= Cost of goods sold.................................	$15,000

For the gross profit method, we rearrange *ending inventory* and *cost of goods sold* as follows:

Beginning inventory	$ 4,000
+ Purchases	16,000
= Cost of goods available	20,000
− Cost of goods sold.................................	(15,000)
= Ending inventory...................................	$ 5,000

Suppose a fire destroys some of the Under Armour, Inc. outlet store's inventory as well as the computer system on which the records are kept, which prevents the manager from physically reconstructing the records of the inventory lost. To collect insurance, the company must estimate the cost of the ending inventory lost. Using its *gross profit percentage* of 35%, you can estimate the store's cost of goods sold. Then subtract cost of goods sold from cost of goods available to estimate the amount of ending inventory. Exhibit 6-13 shows the calculations for the gross profit method, with new amounts assumed for the illustration.

You can also use the gross profit method to test the overall reasonableness of an ending inventory amount. This method also helps to detect large errors.

Exhibit 6-13 | Gross Profit Method of Estimating Inventory

	A	B	C
	A1		
1	Beginning inventory		$ 38,000
2	Purchases		72,000
3	Cost of goods available		110,000
4	Estimated cost of goods sold:		
5	Net sales revenue	$ 100,000	
6	Less estimated gross profit of 35%	35,000	
7	Estimated cost of goods sold		65,000
8	Estimated cost of ending inventory lost		$ 45,000
9			

Try It

Beginning inventory is $70,000, net purchases total $365,000, and net sales are $500,000. With a normal gross profit rate of 40% of sales (cost of goods sold = 60%), how much is ending inventory?

Answer:

$$\$135{,}000 = [\$70{,}000 + \$365{,}000 - (0.60 \times \$500{,}000)]$$

ANALYZE EFFECTS OF INVENTORY ERRORS

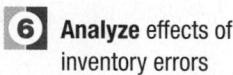

6 **Analyze** effects of inventory errors

Inventory errors sometimes occur. An error in ending inventory creates errors for two accounting periods. In Exhibit 6-14, start with period 1 in which ending inventory is *overstated* by $10,000 and cost of goods sold is therefore *understated* by $10,000. Then compare period 1 with period 3, which is correct. *Period 1 should look exactly like period 3*.

Inventory errors counterbalance in two consecutive periods. Why? Recall that period 1's ending inventory becomes period 2's beginning amount. Thus, the period 1 error carries over into period 2. Trace the ending inventory of $20,000 from period 1 to period 2. Then compare periods 2 and 3. *All three periods should look exactly like period 3*. The Exhibit 6-14 amounts in color are incorrect.

Exhibit 6-14 | Inventory Errors: An Example

	A	B	C	D	E	F	G
	A1						
1		**Period 1** **Ending Inventory** **Overstated by $10,000**		**Period 2** **Beginning Inventory** **Overstated by $10,000**		**Period 3** **Correct**	
2	Sales revenue		$ 100,000		$100,000		$ 100,000
3	Cost of goods sold:						
4	Beginning inventory	$ 10,000		$ 20,000		$ 10,000	
5	Purchases	50,000		50,000		50,000	
6	Cost of goods available	60,000		70,000		60,000	
7	Ending inventory	(20,000)		(10,000)		(10,000)	
8	Cost of goods sold		40,000		60,000		50,000
9	Gross profit		$ 60,000		$ 40,000		$ 50,000
10							
11				$ 100,000			
12							

Beginning inventory and ending inventory have opposite effects on cost of goods sold (beginning inventory is added; ending inventory is subtracted). Therefore, after two periods, an inventory error washes out (counterbalances). Notice that total gross profit is correct for periods 1 and 2 combined ($100,000) even though each year's gross profit is off by $10,000. The correct gross profit is $50,000 for each period, as shown in period 3.

We must have accurate information for all periods. Exhibit 6-15 summarizes the effects of inventory accounting errors.

Exhibit 6-15 | Effects of Inventory Errors

A1				
A	B	C	D	E
	Period 1		**Period 2**	
1	Cost of Goods Sold	Gross Profit and Net Income	Cost of Goods Sold	Gross Profit and Net Income
2 Period 1				
3 Ending inventory overstated	Understated	Overstated	Overstated	Understated
4 Period 1				
5 Ending inventory understated	Overstated	Understated	Understated	Overstated
6				

COOKING THE BOOKS
With Inventory

Crazy Eddie

It is one thing to make honest mistakes in accounting for inventory, but quite another to use inventory to commit fraud. The two most common ways to "cook the books" with inventory are

1. inserting fictitious inventory, thus overstating quantities, and

2. deliberately overstating unit prices used in the computation of ending inventory amounts.

Either one of these tricks has exactly the same effect on income as inventory errors, discussed in the previous section. The difference is that honest inventory errors are often corrected as soon as they are detected, thus minimizing their impact on income. In contrast, deliberate overstatement of inventories tends to be repeated over and over again throughout the course of months, or even years, thus causing the misstatement to grow ever higher until it is discovered. By that time, it can be too late for the company.

Crazy Eddie, Inc.,[3] was a retail consumer electronics store in 1987, operating 43 retail outlets in the New York City area, with $350 million in reported sales and reported profits of $10.5 million. Its stock was a Wall Street "darling," with a collective market value of $600 million. The only problem was that the company's reported profits had been grossly overstated since 1984, the year that the company went public.

Eddie Antar, the company's founder and major stockholder, became preoccupied with the price of his company's stock in 1984. Antar realized that the company, in an extremely competitive retail market in the largest city in the United States, had to keep posting impressive operating profits in order to maintain the upward trend in the company's stock price.

Within the first six months, Antar ordered a subordinate to double-count about $2 million of inventory in the company's stores and warehouses. Using Exhibits 6-14 and 6-15, you can see that the impact of this inventory overstatement went straight to the "bottom line," overstating profits by the same amount, ignoring income tax effects. Unfortunately, the company's auditors failed to detect the inventory overstatement. The following year, emboldened by the audit error, Antar ordered subordinates (now accomplices) to bump the overstatement to $9 million. In addition, he ordered employees to destroy incriminating documents to conceal the inventory

[3]Michael C. Knapp, *Contemporary Auditing: Real Issues and Cases*, 6th edition, Mason, Ohio: Thomson Southwestern, 2009.

shortage. When auditors asked for these documents, employees told them they had been lost. Antar also ordered that the company scrap its sophisticated computerized perpetual inventory system and return to an outdated manual system that was easier to manipulate. The auditors made the mistake of telling Antar which company stores and warehouses they were going to visit in order to observe the year-end physical count of inventory. Antar shifted sufficient inventory to those locations just before the counts to conceal the shortages. By 1988, when the fraud was discovered, the inventory shortage (overstatement) was larger than the total profits the company had reported since it went public in 1984.

In June 1989, Crazy Eddie, Inc., filed for Chapter 11 bankruptcy protection. Later that year, the company closed its stores and sold off its assets. Eddie Antar became a fugitive from justice, moved to Israel, and took an assumed name. He was arrested in 1992, extradited to the United States, and convicted on 17 counts of fraudulent financial reporting in 1993. He was ordered to pay $121 million in restitution to former stockholders and creditors.

A series of missteps by the courts led to a plea bargain agreement in 1996, a condition of which was Antar's admission, for the first time, that he had defrauded investors by manipulating the company's accounting records. One of the prosecuting attorneys was quoted as saying, "Crazy Eddie wasn't crazy, just crooked."

The following Decision Guidelines summarize the situations that call for (a) a particular inventory system and (b) the motivation for using each costing method.

 # DECISION GUIDELINES

ACCOUNTING FOR INVENTORY

Suppose a Williams-Sonoma store stocks two basic categories of merchandise:

- High-end cookware, small electric appliances, cutlery, and kitchen furnishings
- Small items of low value, near the checkout stations, such as cupholders and bottle openers

Jacob Stiles, the store manager, is considering how accounting will affect the business. Let's examine several decisions Stiles must make to properly account for the store's inventory.

Decision	Guidelines	System or Method
Which inventory system to use?	• Expensive merchandise • Cannot control inventory by visual inspection	Perpetual system for high-unit-cost items
	• Can control inventory by visual inspection	Periodic system for the small, low-value items
	• Unique inventory items	Specific unit cost for one-of-a-kind objects because they are unique
Which costing method to use?	• Most current cost of ending inventory • Maximizes reported income when costs are rising	FIFO
	• Most current measure of cost of goods sold and net income • Minimizes income tax when costs are rising	LIFO
	• Middle-of-the-road approach for income tax and reported income	Average

The Gift Horse began in 2016 with 60,000 units of inventory that cost $36,000. During 2016, The Gift Horse purchased merchandise on account for $352,500:

Purchase 1	100,000 units costing	$ 65,000
Purchase 2	270,000 units costing	175,500
Purchase 3	160,000 units costing	112,000

Cash payments on account totaled $326,000 during the year (ignore purchase discounts).

The Gift Horse's sales during 2016 consisted of 520,000 units of inventory for $660,000, all on account. The company uses the FIFO inventory method.

Cash collections from customers were $630,000. Operating expenses totaled $240,500, of which The Gift Horse paid $211,000 in cash. The Gift Horse credited Accrued Liabilities for the remainder. At December 31, The Gift Horse accrued income tax expense at the rate of 35% of income before tax.

Requirements

1. Make summary journal entries to record The Gift Horse's transactions for the year, assuming the company uses a perpetual inventory system. Explanations are not required.
2. Determine the FIFO cost of The Gift Horse's ending inventory at December 31, 2016, two ways:
   a. Use a T-account.
   b. Multiply the number of units on hand by the unit cost.
3. Show how The Gift Horse would compute cost of goods sold for 2016. Follow the FIFO example on pages 318–319.
4. Prepare The Gift Horse's income statement for 2016. Show subtotals for the gross profit and income before tax.
5. Determine The Gift Horse's gross profit percentage, rate of inventory turnover, and net income as a percentage of sales for the year. In The Gift Horse's industry, a gross profit percentage of 40%, an inventory turnover of six times per year, and a net income percentage of 7% are considered excellent. How well does The Gift Horse compare to these industry averages?

Answers

Requirement 1

	A	B	C	D
1		Inventory ($65,000 + $175,500 + $112,000)	352,500	
2		Accounts Payable		352,500
3				
4		Accounts Payable	326,000	
5		Cash		326,000
6				
7		Accounts Receivable	660,000	
8		Sales Revenue		660,000
9				
10		Cost of Goods Sold (see Requirement 3)	339,500	
11		Inventory		339,500
12				
13		Cash	630,000	
14		Accounts Receivable		630,000
15				
16		Operating Expenses	240,500	
17		Cash		211,000
18		Accrued Liabilities		29,500
19				
20		Income Tax Expense (see Requirement 4)	28,000	
21		Income Tax Payable		28,000
22				

Requirement 2

Inventory

Beg bal	36,000		
Purchases	352,500	Cost of goods sold	339,500
End bal	49,000		

Number of units in ending inventory (60,000 + 100,000 + 270,000 + 160,000 − 520,000).............	70,000
Unit cost of ending inventory at FIFO ($112,000 ÷ 160,000 from Purchase 3).....	× $ 0.70
FIFO cost of ending inventory......................	$49,000

Requirement 3

Cost of goods sold (520,000 units):	
60,000 units costing...	$ 36,000
100,000 units costing..	65,000
270,000 units costing..	175,500
90,000 units costing $0.70 each*	63,000
Cost of goods sold..	$339,500

*From Purchase 3: $112,000/160,000 units = $0.70 per unit.

Requirement 4

A1		

	A	B	C
1	**The Gift Horse** **Income Statement** **Year Ended December 31, 2016**		
2	Sales revenue	$ 660,000	
3	Cost of goods sold	339,500	
4	Gross profit	320,500	
5	Operating expenses	240,500	
6	Income before tax	80,000	
7	Income tax expense (35%)	28,000	
8	Net income	$ 52,000	
9			

Requirement 5

		Industry Average
Gross profit percentage:	$320,500 ÷ $660,000 = 48.6%	40%
Inventory turnover:	$\dfrac{\$339,500}{(\$36,000 + \$49,000)/2} = 8$ times	6 times
Net income as a percent of sales:	$52,000 ÷ $660,000 = 7.9%	7%

The Gift Horse's statistics are better than the industry averages.

REVIEW | Inventory & Cost of Goods Sold

Quick Check (Answers are given on page 366.)

1. Which statement is true?
   a. Gross profit is the excess of sales revenue over cost of goods sold.
   b. Purchase returns and allowances increase the net amount of purchases.
   c. The Sales account is used to record only sales on account.
   d. A service company purchases products from suppliers and then sells them.

2. Cost of goods sold will appear on which financial statement?
   a. statement of retained earnings
   b. balance sheet
   c. statement of cash flows
   d. income statement

3. How is inventory classified in the financial statements?
   a. As an expense
   b. As a contra account to Cost of Goods Sold
   c. As a revenue
   d. As a liability
   e. As an asset

Questions 4–6 use the following data of Tortoise Sales, Inc.:

	Units	Unit Cost	Total Cost	Units Sold
Beginning inventory	25	$6	$150	
Purchase on Apr 25	39	8	312	
Purchase on Nov 16	12	9	108	
Sales	60	?	?	

4. Tortoise Sales uses a FIFO inventory system. Cost of goods sold for the period is
   a. $450.   c. $420.
   b. $430.   d. $540.

5. Tortoise Sales' LIFO cost of ending inventory would be
   a. $120.   c. $96.
   b. $360.   d. $430.

6. Tortoise Sales' cost of ending inventory using the average cost method is
   a. $540.   c. $120.
   b. $140.   d. $150.

7. When applying the lower-of-cost-or-market rule to inventory, "market" generally means
   a. resale value.   c. current replacement cost.
   b. original cost, less physical deterioration.   d. original cost.

8. During a period of rising prices, the inventory method that will yield the highest net income and asset value is
   a. LIFO.   c. specific identification.
   b. average cost.   d. FIFO.

9. Which statement is true?
   a. Application of the lower-of-cost-or-market rule often results in a lower inventory value.
   b. An error overstating ending inventory in 2016 will understate 2016 net income.
   c. When prices are rising, the inventory method that results in the lowest ending inventory value is FIFO.
   d. The inventory method that best matches current expense with current revenue is FIFO.

10. The ending inventory of Cape Harbor Co. is $46,000. If beginning inventory was $64,000 and goods available (cost of goods available for sale) totaled $117,000, the cost of goods sold is
    a. $135,000.   c. $71,000.
    b. $64,000.   d. $53,000.

11. Chime Company had cost of goods sold of $150,000. The beginning and ending inventories were $13,000 and $28,000, respectively. Purchases for the period must have been

a. $178,000.

b. $165,000.

c. $163,000.

d. $135,000.

Use the following information for questions 12–14.

Wedge Company had a $26,000 beginning inventory and a $29,000 ending inventory. Net sales were $160,000; purchases, $80,000; purchase returns and allowances, $8,000; and freight in, $3,000.

12. Cost of goods sold for the period is

a. $78,000.

b. $88,000.

c. $72,000.

d. $69,000.

13. What is Wedge's gross profit percentage (rounded to the nearest percentage)?

a. 55%

b. 18%

c. 45%

d. 16%

14. What is Wedge's rate of inventory turnover?

a. 2.9 times

b. 5.5 times

c. 2.6 times

d. 2.5 times

15. Beginning inventory is $110,000, purchases are $220,000, and sales total $500,000. The normal gross profit percentage is 35%. Using the gross profit method, how much is ending inventory?

a. $175,000

b. $215,000

c. $5,000

d. $280,000

16. An overstatement of ending inventory in one period results in

a. an understatement of the beginning inventory of the next period.

b. no effect on net income of the next period.

c. an overstatement of net income of the next period.

d. an understatement of net income of the next period.

Accounting Vocabulary

average-cost method (p. 318) Inventory costing method based on the average cost of inventory during the period. Average cost is determined by dividing the cost of goods available by the number of units available. Also called the *weighted-average method*.

consignment (p. 313) An inventory arrangement where the seller sells inventory that belongs to another party. The seller does not include consigned merchandise on hand in its balance sheet, because the seller does not own this inventory.

cost of goods sold (p. 312) Cost of the inventory the business has sold to customers.

cost-of-goods-sold (COGS) model (p. 328) Formula that brings together all the inventory data for the entire accounting period: Beginning inventory + Purchases = Cost of goods available (i.e., cost of goods available for sale). Then, Cost of goods available − Ending inventory = Cost of goods sold.

days' inventory outstanding (DIO) (p. 327) The DIO is calculated as 365 ÷ inventory turnover (defined on the next page).

Converts inventory turnover to days to show how many days an average item of inventory remains on the shelves before being sold.

debit memorandum (p. 316) A document issued to the seller (vendor) when an item of inventory that is unwanted or damaged is returned. This document authorizes a reduction (debit) to accounts payable for the amount of the goods returned.

disclosure principle (p. 324) A business's financial statements must report enough information for outsiders to make knowledgeable decisions about the business. The company should report relevant and representationally faithful information about its economic affairs.

first-in, first-out (FIFO) (p. 318) Inventory costing method by which the first costs into inventory are the first costs out to cost of goods sold. Ending inventory is based on the costs of the most recent purchases.

gross margin (p. 312) Another name for *gross profit*.

gross margin method (p. 329) Another name for the *gross profit method*.

gross margin percentage (p. 326) Another name for the *gross profit percentage*.

gross profit (p. 312) Sales revenue minus cost of goods sold. Also called *gross margin*.

gross profit method (p. 329) A way to estimate ending inventory based on a rearrangement of the cost-of-goods-sold model: Beginning inventory + Net purchases = Cost of goods available − Cost of goods sold = Ending inventory. Also called the *gross margin method*.

gross profit percentage (p. 326) Gross profit divided by net sales revenue. Also called the *gross margin percentage*.

inventory (p. 312) The merchandise that a company sells to customers.

inventory turnover (p. 327) Ratio of cost of goods sold to average inventory. Indicates how rapidly (in terms of times per year) inventory is sold out.

last-in, first-out (LIFO) cost (p. 319) Inventory costing method by which the last costs into inventory are the first costs out to cost of goods sold. This method leaves the oldest costs—those of beginning inventory and the earliest purchases of the period—in ending inventory.

lower-of-cost-or-market (LCM) rule (p. 324) Requires that an asset be reported in the financial statements at whichever

is lower—its historical cost or its market value (current replacement cost for inventory).

periodic inventory system (p. 314) An inventory system in which the business does not keep a continuous record of the inventory on hand. Instead, at the end of the period, the business makes a physical count of the inventory on hand and applies the appropriate unit costs to determine the cost of the ending inventory.

perpetual inventory system (p. 314) An inventory system in which the business keeps a continuous record for each inventory item to show the inventory on hand at all times.

purchase allowance (p. 315) A decrease in the cost of purchases because the seller has granted the buyer a subtraction (an allowance) from the amount owed.

purchase discount (p. 316) A decrease in the cost of purchases earned by making an early payment to the vendor.

purchase return (p. 315) A decrease in the cost of purchases because the buyer returned the goods to the seller.

specific-unit-cost method (p. 317) Inventory cost method based on the specific cost of particular units of inventory.

weighted-average method (p. 318) Another name for the *average-cost method*.

 # Assess Your Progress

Some of the following exercises and problems are available as Excel questions in MyAccountingLab.

Ethics Check

EC6-1 Identify ethical principle violated

For each of the situations listed, identify which of three principles (integrity, objectivity, and independence, or due care) from the AICPA Code of Professional Conduct that is violated. Assume all persons listed in the situations are members of the AICPA. (Note: Refer to the AICPA Code of Professional Conduct contained on pages 29–30 in Chapter 1 for descriptions of the principles.)

a. Mariah's company is switching to FIFO, after using the LIFO method for several years. Mariah does not remember how to apply the FIFO method, but is too busy to review the technique. She figures the auditors will catch anything she does wrong.

b. Xun is the chief accountant for a furniture manufacturer. Two years ago, Xun changed the company's inventory method to FIFO. This year, Xun is changing back to LIFO. The motivation for the changes is solely to manipulate net income.

c. Eboni is an auditor at a public accounting firm. She is auditing one of her firm's largest clients. Her aunt is the CEO of this client. Eboni does not mention the relationship to her manager.

d. A fire at Sean's company has destroyed most of the accounting records and a significant amount of inventory. He finds some partial records to be able to reconstruct most of the financial records using the gross profit method. He has the opportunity to substitute a higher number for the quantity on hand so that insurance will pay the company more than the actual loss. He knows that the quantity on hand was much lower than he reports on the insurance claim form, but rationalizes that his company has paid insurance premiums for many years.

Short Exercises

S6-1. (*Learning Objective 1: Show how to account for inventory transactions*) Cozelle, Inc., purchased inventory costing $125,000 and sold 80% of the goods for $200,000. All purchases and sales were on account. Cozelle later collected 25% of the accounts receivable. Assume that sales returns are nonexistent.

1. Journalize these transactions for Cozelle, which uses the perpetual inventory system.
2. For these transactions, show what Cozelle will report for inventory, revenues, and expenses on its financial statements at the end of the month. Report gross profit on the appropriate statement.

LO 1

S6-2. (*Learning Objective 1: Show how to account for inventory transactions*) Rootstown Company sold 10,000 jars of its organic honey in the most current year for $8 per jar. The company had paid $3.50 per jar of honey. (Assume that sales returns are nonexistent.) Calculate the following:

1. Sales revenue
2. Cost of goods sold
3. Gross margin

LO 1

S6-3. (*Learning Objective 1: Show how to account for inventory transactions*) Trinkets Unlimited made total purchases of $250,000 in the most current year. It paid freight in of $3,000 on its purchases. Freight out (the cost to deliver the merchandise to its customers) totaled $7,000. Of the total purchases, Trinkets Unlimited returned $22,000 of the merchandise. Trinkets Unlimited took advantage of $2,000 of purchase discounts offered by its vendors. What was Trinkets Unlimited's cost of inventory?

LO 1

S6-4. (*Learning Objective 2: Apply the average, FIFO, and LIFO methods*) McDonough Copy Center sells laser printers and supplies. Assume McDonough Copy Center started the year with 100 containers of ink (average cost of $8.00 each, FIFO cost of $8.60 each, LIFO cost of $7.90 each). During the year, McDonough Copy Center purchased 600 containers of ink at $9.90 and sold 570 units for $20.00 each. McDonough Copy Center paid operating expenses throughout the year, a total of $5,500. Ignore income taxes for this exercise.

Prepare McDonough Copy Center's income statement for the current year ended December 31 under the average, FIFO, and LIFO inventory costing methods. Include a complete statement heading.

LO 2

S6-5. (*Learning Objective 2: Compare income tax effects of the inventory costing methods*) This exercise should be used in conjunction with S6-4. McDonough Copy Center is a corporation subject to a 30% income tax. Compute McDonough Copy Center's income tax expense under the average, FIFO, and LIFO inventory costing methods. Which method would you select to (a) maximize income before tax and (b) minimize income tax expense?

LO 2

S6-6. (*Learning Objective 2: Compare income and income tax effects of LIFO*) Marley Corporation uses the LIFO method to account for inventory. Marley is having an unusually good year, with net income well above expectations. The company's inventory costs are rising rapidly. What can Marley do immediately before the end of the year to decrease net income? Explain how this action decreases reported income, and tell why Marley might want to decrease its net income.

LO 2

Short Exercises S6-7 through S6-9 use the following data of Cowell Corporation:

	A	B	C	D
		Quantity	Unit Cost	Total
1				
2	Beginning inventory	100	$ 5.00	$ 500
3	Purchases	150	$ 8.00	$ 1,200
4	Goods available for sale	250		
5	Ending inventory	90		
6	Cost of goods sold	160		
7				

LO 2 **S6-7.** (*Learning Objective 2: Apply the average-cost method*) Using the average-cost method, calculate the cost of ending inventory and cost of goods sold for Cowell Corporation.

LO 2 **S6-8.** (*Learning Objective 2: Apply the FIFO method*) Using the FIFO method, calculate the cost of ending inventory and cost of goods sold for Cowell Corporation.

LO 2 **S6-9.** (*Learning Objective 2: Apply the LIFO method*) Using the LIFO method, calculate the cost of ending inventory and cost of goods sold for Cowell Corporation.

LO 2 **S6-10.** (*Learning Objective 2: Compare income, tax, and other effects of the inventory methods*) This exercise tests your understanding of the four inventory methods. List the name of the inventory method that best fits the description. Assume that the cost of inventory is rising.
1. _____ Results in an old measure of the cost of ending inventory
2. _____ Provides a middle-ground measure of ending inventory and cost of goods sold
3. _____ Enables a company to keep reported income from dropping lower by liquidating older layers of inventory
4. _____ Writes inventory down when current replacement cost drops below historical cost
5. _____ Matches the most current cost of goods sold against sales revenue
6. _____ Maximizes reported income
7. _____ Used to account for automobiles, jewelry, and art objects
8. _____ Results in a cost of ending inventory that is close to the current cost of replacing the inventory
9. _____ Generally associated with saving income taxes
10. _____ Enables a company to buy high-cost inventory at year-end and thereby decrease reported income and income tax

LO 3 **S6-11.** (*Learning Objective 3: Apply the lower-of-cost-or-market rule to inventory*) It is December 31, the end of the year, and the controller of Saxton Corporation is applying the lower-of-cost-or-market (LCM) rule to inventories. Before any year-end adjustments, Saxton reports the following data:

Cost of goods sold..	$445,000
Historical cost of ending inventory, as determined by a physical count...............	58,000

Saxton determines that the current replacement cost of ending inventory is $45,000. Show what Saxton should report for ending inventory and for cost of goods sold. Identify the financial statement where each item appears.

LO 4 **S6-12.** (*Learning Objective 4: Compute ratio data to evaluate operations*) Spritzer Company made sales of $24,000 million during 2016. Cost of goods sold for the year totaled $11,040 million. At the end of 2015, Spritzer's inventory stood at $1,000 million, and Spritzer ended 2016 with inventory of $1,400 million. Compute Spritzer's gross profit percentage and rate of inventory turnover for 2016.

S6-13. *(Learning Objective 5: Estimate ending inventory by the gross profit method)* Metro Technology began the year with inventory of $299,000 and purchased $1,820,000 of goods during the year. Sales for the year are $3,887,500, and Metro Technology's gross profit percentage is 60% of sales. Compute Metro Technology's estimated cost of ending inventory by using the gross profit method.

LO 5

S6-14. *(Learning Objective 5: Evaluate management decisions)* Determine whether each of the following actions in buying, selling, and accounting for inventories is ethical or unethical. Give your reason for each answer.

LO 5

1. In applying the lower-of-cost-or-market rule to inventories, Blue Mountain Coffee Company recorded an excessively low value for its ending inventory (below both cost and market). This action allowed the company to pay less income tax for the year.
2. Rosalind Sales, Inc., delayed the purchase of inventory until after December 31, 2016, to keep 2016's cost of goods sold from growing too large. The delay in purchasing inventory helped net income of 2016 to reach the level of profit demanded by the company's investors.
3. Carlson Pharmaceuticals purchased a large amount of inventory shortly before year-end to increase the LIFO cost of goods sold and decrease reported income for the year.
4. Glacier Corporation deliberately overstated purchases to produce a high figure for cost of goods sold (low amount of net income). The real reason was to decrease the company's income tax payments to the government.
5. Farley Sales Company deliberately overstated ending inventory in order to report higher profits (net income).

S6-15. *(Learning Objective 6: Analyze the effect of an inventory error on two years)* Richardson Supply's $3.9 million cost of inventory at the end of last year was understated by $1.2 million.

LO 6

1. Was last year's reported gross profit of $2.9 million overstated, understated, or correct? What was the correct amount of gross profit last year?
2. Is this year's gross profit of $3.6 million overstated, understated, or correct? What is the correct amount of gross profit for the current year?
3. Was last year's reported cost of goods sold of $5.4 million overstated, understated, or correct? What was the correct amount of cost of goods sold last year?
4. Is this year's cost of goods sold of $5.7 million overstated, understated, or correct? What is the correct amount of cost of goods sold for this year?

S6-16. *(Learning Objective 6: Analyze the effect of an inventory error on multiple years)* Here is the original schedule of cost of goods sold for Truman Company for the years of 2014 through 2017:

LO 6

A1					
	A	**B**	**C**	**D**	**E**
1		**2017**	**2016**	**2015**	**2014**
2	Beginning inventory	$ 350	$ 500	$ 600	$ 400
3	+ Purchases	1,250	1,450	1,100	1,000
4	= Cost of goods available	$ 1,600	$ 1,950	$ 1,700	$ 1,400
5	− Ending inventory	450	350	500	600
6	= Cost of goods sold	$ 1,150	$ 1,600	$ 1,200	$ 800
7					

During the preparation of its 2017 financial statements, Truman Company discovered that its 2015 ending inventory was understated by $200. Make the correction to the 2015 ending inventory and all other numbers in the schedule of cost of goods sold for any years affected.

1. What is the corrected cost of goods sold for 2015?
2. Did the understatement of ending inventory in 2015 cause the 2015 cost of goods sold to be *overstated* or *understated*?
3. What is the corrected cost of goods sold for 2016?

4. Did the understatement of ending inventory in 2015 cause the 2016 cost of goods sold to be *overstated* or *understated*?

5. Were any other years impacted by the 2015 $200 understatement of ending inventory? Why or why not?

Exercises MyAccountingLab

Group A

LO 1 2

E6-17A. *(Learning Objectives 1, 2: Show how to account for inventory transactions; apply the FIFO cost method)* Accounting records for Ontario Corporation yield the following data for the year ended June 30, 2016 (assume sales returns are non-existent):

Inventory, June 30, 2015...	$ 8,000
Purchases of inventory (on account)..	66,000
Sales of inventory—81% on account; 19% for cash (cost $52,000).........	99,000
Inventory at FIFO, June 30, 2016	22,000

Requirements

1. Journalize Ontario's inventory transactions for the year under the perpetual system.
2. Report ending inventory, sales, cost of goods sold, and gross profit on the appropriate financial statement.

LO 1 2

E6-18A. *(Learning Objectives 1, 2: Show how to account for inventory transactions; apply the FIFO cost method)* Cranwell Company's inventory records for a particular development program show the following at May 31:

May 1	Beginning inventory	6 units @ $150	=	$ 900
15	Purchase.................................	4 units @ 151	=	$ 604
26	Purchase.................................	14 units @ 160	=	$2,240

At May 31, 10 of these units are on hand. Journalize the following for Cranwell Company under the perpetual system:

1. Total May purchases in one summary entry. All purchases were on credit.
2. Total May sales and cost of goods sold in two summary entries. The selling price was $550 per unit, and all sales were on credit. Assume that Cranwell uses the FIFO inventory method.
3. Under FIFO, how much gross profit would Cranwell earn on these transactions? What is the FIFO cost of Cranwell Company's ending inventory?

LO 2

E6-19A. *(Learning Objective 2: Compare ending inventory and cost of goods sold by four methods)* Use the data for Cranwell Company in E6-18A to answer the following.

Requirements

1. Compute cost of goods sold and ending inventory, using each of the following methods:
   a. Specific unit cost, with five $150 units and five $160 units still on hand at the end
   b. Average cost
   c. FIFO
   d. LIFO
2. Which method produces the highest cost of goods sold? Which method produces the lowest cost of goods sold? What causes the difference in cost of goods sold?

E6-20A. *(Learning Objective 2: Compare the tax advantage of LIFO over FIFO)* Use the data for Cranwell Company in E6-18A to illustrate Cranwell's income tax advantage from using LIFO over FIFO. Sales revenue is $7,700, operating expenses are $1,400, and the income tax rate is 25%. How much in taxes would Cranwell Company save by using the LIFO method versus FIFO?

`LO 2`

E6-21A. *(Learning Objective 2: Apply the average, FIFO, and LIFO methods)* Spicer Company's inventory records for the most recent year contain the following data:

`LO 2`

	A	B	C
		Quantity	Unit Cost
1			
2	Beginning inventory	5,000	$ 10.00
3	Purchases during year	15,000	$ 12.00
4			

Spicer Company sold a total of 19,100 units during the year.

Requirements

1. Using the average-cost method, compute the cost of goods sold and ending inventory for the year.
2. Using the FIFO method, compute the cost of goods sold and ending inventory for the year.
3. Using the LIFO method, compute the cost of goods sold and ending inventory for the year.

E6-22A. *(Learning Objective 2: Compare ending inventory and cost of goods sold—FIFO vs. LIFO)* MusicPlace specializes in sound equipment. Because each inventory item is expensive, MusicPlace uses a perpetual inventory system. Company records indicate the following data for a line of speakers:

`LO 2`

Date		Item	Quantity	Unit Cost	Sale Price
Jun	1	Balance..................	15	$42	
	2	Purchase...............	7	73	
	7	Sale	6		$118
	13	Sale	4		111

Requirements

1. Determine the amounts that MusicPlace should report for cost of goods sold and ending inventory two ways:
   a. FIFO
   b. LIFO
2. MusicPlace uses the FIFO method. Prepare MusicPlace's income statement for the month ended June 30, 2016, reporting gross profit. Operating expenses totaled $280, and the income tax rate was 40%.

E6-23A. *(Learning Objective 2: Compare gross profit—FIFO vs. LIFO—falling prices)* Suppose a Costco store in Gainesville, Missouri, ended May 2016 with 1,000,000 units of merchandise that cost $8 each. Suppose the store then sold 100,000 units for $850,000 during June. Further, assume the store made two large purchases during June as follows:

`LO 2`

Jun	5	45,000 units @ $6.10	=	$274,500
	25	30,000 units @ $5.20	=	$156,000

Requirements

1. Calculate the store's gross profit under both FIFO and LIFO at June 30.
2. What caused the FIFO and LIFO gross profit figures to differ?

LO 3   **E6-24A.** *(Learning Objective 3: Apply the lower-of-cost-or-market rule to inventories)* Gordon Garden Supplies uses a perpetual inventory system. Gordon Garden Supplies has these account balances at January 31, 2016, prior to making the year-end adjustments:

Inventory	Cost of Goods Sold	Sales Revenue
Beg bal 11,500		
End bal 13,500	Bal 69,000	Bal 118,000

A year ago, the current replacement cost of ending inventory was $12,000, which exceeded the cost of $11,500. Gordon Garden Supplies has determined that the replacement cost of the January 31, 2016, ending inventory is $13,000.

Requirement

1. Prepare Gordon Garden Supplies' 2016 income statement through gross profit to show how the company would apply the lower-of-cost-or-market rule to its inventories.

LO 5   **E6-25A.** *(Learning Objective 5: Compute cost of goods sold and gross profit)* Supply the missing income statement amounts for each of the following companies:

Company	Net Sales	Beginning Inventory	Net Purchases	Ending Inventory	Cost of Goods Sold	Gross Profit
Arnold	$106,000	$19,000	$60,000	$17,000	(a)	(b)
Donahue	132,000	27,000	(c)	26,000	(d)	40,000
Allen	(e)	(f)	57,000	22,000	63,000	32,000
Nugent	86,000	8,000	32,000	(g)	35,000	(h)

Requirement

1. Prepare the income statement for Arnold Company for the year ended December 31, 2016. Use the cost-of-goods-sold model to compute cost of goods sold. Arnold's operating and other expenses for the year were $41,000. Ignore income tax.

Note: E6-26A builds on E6-25A with a profitability analysis of these companies.

LO 4   **E6-26A.** *(Learning Objective 4: Evaluate profitability and inventory turnover)* Refer to the data in E6-25A. Compute all ratio values to answer the following questions:
- Which company has the highest and which company has the lowest gross profit percentage?
- Which company has the highest and which has the lowest rate of inventory turnover?

Based on your figures, which company appears to be the most profitable?

LO 4   **E6-27A.** *(Learning Objective 4: Compute and evaluate gross profit percentage and inventory turnover)* Burner & Brett, a partnership, had the following inventory data:

	2015	2016
Ending inventory at:		
FIFO Cost...............	$24,920	$ 33,500
LIFO Cost...............	12,500	20,160
Cost of goods sold at:		
FIFO Cost...............		$ 87,630
LIFO Cost...............		97,980
Sales revenue...............		138,000

Burner & Brett need to know the company's gross profit percentage and rate of inventory turnover for 2016 under

1. FIFO.
2. LIFO.

Which method produces a higher gross profit percentage? Inventory turnover?

E6-28A. *(Learning Objective 5: Use the COGS model to make management decisions)* Toyland prepares budgets to help manage the company. Toyland is budgeting for the fiscal year ended January 31, 2016. During the preceding year ended January 31, 2015, sales totaled $9,600 million and cost of goods sold was $6,800 million. At January 31, 2015, inventory was $1,600 million. During the upcoming 2016 year, suppose Toyland expects cost of goods sold to increase by 14%. The company budgets next year's ending inventory at $1,900 million.

LO 5

Requirement

1. One of the most important decisions a manager makes is how much inventory to buy. How much inventory should Toyland purchase during the upcoming year to reach its budget?

E6-29A. *(Learning Objective 5: Use the COGS model to make management decisions)* Yoder Farm Supply, Inc., began January with inventory of $45,300. The business made net purchases of $37,200 and had net sales of $77,100 before a fire destroyed the company's inventory. For the past several years, Yoder Farm Supply's gross profit percentage has been 40%. Estimate the cost of the inventory destroyed by the fire. Identify another reason that owners and managers use the gross profit method to estimate inventory.

LO 5

E6-30A. *(Learning Objective 6: Analyze the effect of an inventory error)* By the Bay Marine Supply reported the following comparative income statements for the years ended November 30, 2016, and 2015:

LO 6

A1					
	A	**B**	**C**	**D**	**E**
1	**By the Bay Marine Supply** **Income Statements** **For the Years Ended November 30, 2016 and 2015**				
2			**2016**		**2015**
3	Sales revenue		$ 135,000		$ 122,000
4	Cost of goods sold:				
5	Beginning inventory	$ 14,500		$ 14,000	
6	Net purchases	76,000		75,000	
7	Cost of goods available	90,500		89,000	
8	Ending inventory	(19,000)		(14,500)	
9	Cost of goods sold		71,500		74,500
10	Gross profit		63,500		47,500
11	Operating expenses		30,000		23,000
12	Net income		$ 33,500		$ 24,500
13					

By the Bay's president and shareholders are thrilled by the company's boost in sales and net income during 2016. Then the accountants for the company discover that ending 2015 inventory was understated by $9,000. Prepare the corrected comparative income statements for the two-year period, complete with a heading for the statements. How well did By the Bay Marine Supply really perform in 2016 as compared with 2015?

Group B

LO **1** **2**

E6-31B. *(Learning Objectives 1, 2: Show how to account for inventory transactions; apply the FIFO cost method)* Accounting records for Dundas Corporation yield the following data for the year ended June 30, 2016:

Inventory, June 30, 2015...	$ 7,000
Purchases of inventory (on account)..	60,000
Sales of inventory—79% on account; 21% for cash (cost $40,000).........	90,000
Inventory at FIFO, June 30, 2016	27,000

Requirements

1. Journalize Dundas' inventory transactions for the year under the perpetual system.
2. Report ending inventory, sales, cost of goods sold, and gross profit on the appropriate financial statement.

LO **1** **2**

E6-32B. *(Learning Objectives 1, 2: Show how to account for inventory transactions; apply the FIFO cost method)* Arrow Corporation's inventory records for a particular development program show the following at March 31:

Mar	1	Beginning inventory	9 units @	$165	=	$1,485
	15	Purchase.................................	5 units @	166	=	830
	26	Purchase.................................	13 units @	175	=	2,275

At March 31, 11 of these units are on hand. Journalize the following for Arrow Corporation under the perpetual system:

1. Total March purchases in one summary entry. All purchases were on credit.
2. Total March sales and cost of goods sold in two summary entries. The selling price was $500 per unit, and all sales were on credit. Assume that Arrow uses the FIFO inventory method.
3. Under FIFO, how much gross profit would Arrow earn on these transactions? What is the FIFO cost of Arrow Corporation's ending inventory?

LO **2**

E6-33B. *(Learning Objective 2: Compare ending inventory and cost of goods sold by four methods)* Use the data for Arrow Corporation in E6-32B to answer the following.

Requirements

1. Compute cost of goods sold and ending inventory using each of the following methods:
   a. Specific unit cost, with seven $165 units and four $175 units still on hand at the end
   b. Average cost
   c. FIFO
   d. LIFO
2. Which method produces the highest cost of goods sold? Which method produces the lowest cost of goods sold? What causes the difference in cost of goods sold?

LO **2**

E6-34B. *(Learning Objective 2: Compare the tax advantage of LIFO over FIFO)* Use the data for Arrow Corporation in E6-32B to illustrate Arrow's income tax advantage from using LIFO over FIFO. Sales revenue is $8,000, operating expenses are $1,400, and the income tax rate is 30%. How much in taxes would Arrow Corporation save by using the LIFO method versus FIFO?

E6-35B. *(Learning Objective 2: Apply the average, FIFO, and LIFO methods)* Calder
Company's inventory records for the most recent year contain the following data:

A1 ↕			
	A	B	C
1		Quantity	Unit Cost
2	Beginning inventory	10,000	$ 12.00
3	Purchases during year	30,000	$ 15.00
4			

Calder Company sold a total of 38,000 units during the year.

Requirements

1. Using the average-cost method, compute the cost of goods sold and ending inventory for the year.
2. Using the FIFO method, compute the cost of goods sold and ending inventory for the year.
3. Using the LIFO method, compute the cost of goods sold and ending inventory for the year.

E6-36B. *(Learning Objective 2: Compare ending inventory and cost of goods sold—FIFO vs. LIFO)* MusicMagic.net specializes in sound equipment. Because each inventory item is expensive, MusicMagic uses a perpetual inventory system. Company records indicate the following data for a line of speakers:

Date	Item	Quantity	Unit Cost	Sale Price
Mar 1	Balance..................	11	$46	
2	Purchase................	7	68	
7	Sale	6		$91
13	Sale	4		91

Requirements

1. Determine the amounts that MusicMagic should report for cost of goods sold and ending inventory two ways:

   a. FIFO
   b. LIFO

2. MusicMagic uses the FIFO method. Prepare MusicMagic's income statement for the month ended March 31, 2016, reporting gross profit. Operating expenses totaled $330, and the income tax rate was 35%.

E6-37B. *(Learning Objective 2: Compare gross profit—FIFO vs. LIFO—falling prices)* Suppose a Sam's Club store in Champaign, Illinois, ended January 2016 with 800,000 units of merchandise that cost $5.00 each. Suppose the store then sold 100,000 units for $510,000 during February. Further, assume the store made two large purchases during February as follows:

Feb 5	45,000 units @ $3.10	=	$139,500
28	40,000 units @ $2.20	=	$88,000

Requirements

1. Calculate the store's gross profit under FIFO and LIFO at February 29.
2. What caused the FIFO and LIFO gross profit figures to differ?

LO **3** **E6-38B.** *(Learning Objective 3: Apply the lower-of-cost-or-market rule to inventories)* Erie Garden Supplies uses a perpetual inventory system. Erie Garden Supplies has these account balances at August 31, 2016, prior to making the year-end adjustments:

Inventory	Cost of Goods Sold	Sales Revenue
Beg bal 12,500		
End bal 13,000	Bal 73,000	Bal 116,000

A year ago, the current replacement cost of ending inventory was $12,600, which exceeded the cost of $12,500. Erie Garden Supplies has determined that the replacement cost of the August 31, 2016, ending inventory is $11,500.

Requirement

1. Prepare Erie Garden Supplies' 2016 income statement through gross profit to show how the company would apply the lower-of-cost-or-market rule to its inventories.

LO **5** **E6-39B.** *(Learning Objective 5: Compute cost of goods sold and gross profit)* Supply the missing amounts for each of the following companies:

Company	Net Sales	Beginning Inventory	Net Purchases	Ending Inventory	Cost of Goods Sold	Gross Profit
Baker	$106,000	$22,000	$62,000	$20,000	(a)	(b)
Johnson	136,000	26,000	(c)	21,000	(d)	41,000
Ethan	(e)	(f)	57,000	25,000	64,000	27,000
Thomas	85,000	9,000	33,000	(g)	29,000	(h)

Requirement

1. Prepare the income statement for Baker Company for the year ended December 31, 2016. Use the cost-of-goods-sold model to compute cost of goods sold. Baker's operating and other expenses for the year were $40,000. Ignore income tax.

Note: E6-40B builds on E6-39B with a profitability analysis of these companies.

LO **4** **E6-40B.** *(Learning Objective 4: Evaluate profitability and inventory turnover)* Refer to the data in E6-39B. Compute all ratio values to answer the following questions:
- Which company has the highest and which company has the lowest gross profit percentage?
- Which company has the highest and which has the lowest rate of inventory turnover?

Based on your figures, which company appears to be the most profitable?

LO **4** **E6-41B.** *(Learning Objective 4: Compute and evaluate gross profit percentage and inventory turnover)* Thurston & Talty, a partnership, had the following inventory data:

	2015	2016
Ending inventory at:		
FIFO Cost	$23,700	$ 28,150
LIFO Cost	11,200	18,000
Cost of goods sold at:		
FIFO Cost		$ 82,960
LIFO Cost		99,280
Sales revenue		136,000

Thurston & Talty need to know the company's gross profit percentage and rate of inventory turnover for 2016 under

1. FIFO.
2. LIFO.

Which method produces a higher gross profit percentage? Inventory turnover?

E6-42B. *(Learning Objective 5: Use the COGS model to make management decisions)* FunToys prepares budgets to help manage the company. FunToys is budgeting for the fiscal year ended January 31, 2016. During the preceding year ended January 31, 2015, sales totaled $9,900 million and cost of goods sold was $6,900 million. At January 31, 2015, inventory was $1,800 million. During the upcoming 2016 year, suppose FunToys expects cost of goods sold to increase by 14%. The company budgets next year's ending inventory at $2,100 million.

 LO 5

Requirement

1. One of the most important decisions a manager makes is how much inventory to buy. How much inventory should FunToys purchase during the upcoming year to reach its budget?

E6-43B. *(Learning Objective 5: Use the COGS model to make management decisions)* Ontario Farm Products began March with inventory of $49,300. The business made net purchases of $61,000 and had net sales of $82,000 before a fire destroyed the company's inventory. For the past several years, Ontario's gross profit percentage has been 40%. Estimate the cost of the inventory destroyed by the fire. Identify another reason that owners and managers use the gross profit method to estimate inventory.

LO 5

E6-44B. *(Learning Objective 6: Analyze the effect of an inventory error)* Blue Sky Marine Supply reported the following comparative income statements for the years ended April 30, 2016, and 2015:

LO 6

	A	B	C	D	E
	Blue Sky Marine Supply				
	Income Statements				
1	**For the Years Ended April 30, 2016 and 2015**				
2			**2016**		**2015**
3	Sales revenue		$ 144,000		$ 115,000
4	Cost of goods sold:				
5	Beginning inventory	$ 16,000		$ 9,000	
6	Net purchases	77,000		73,000	
7	Cost of goods available	93,000		82,000	
8	Ending inventory	(16,000)		(16,000)	
9	Cost of goods sold		77,000		66,000
10	Gross profit		67,000		49,000
11	Operating expenses		25,000		22,000
12	Net income		$ 42,000		$ 27,000
13					

Blue Sky's president and shareholders are thrilled by the company's boost in sales and net income during 2016. Then the accountants for the company discover that ending 2015 inventory was understated by $9,500. Prepare the corrected comparative income statements for the two-year period, complete with a heading for the statements. How well did Blue Sky really perform in 2016 as compared with 2015?

Quiz

Test your understanding of accounting for inventory by answering the following questions. Select the best choice from among the possible answers given.

Q6-45. Riverview Software began January with $3,700 of merchandise inventory. During January, Riverview made the following entries for its inventory transactions:

	A	B	C	D
		A1 ⬍		
1		Inventory	6,600	
2		Accounts Payable		6,600
3				
4		Accounts Receivable	7,300	
5		Sales Revenue		7,300
6				
7		Cost of Goods Sold	5,200	
8		Inventory		5,200
9				

How much was Riverview's inventory at the end of January?
a. $5,100
b. $ − 0 −
c. $6,600
d. $10,300

Q6-46. What was Riverview's gross profit for January?
a. $ − 0 −
b. $5,200
c. $7,300
d. $2,100

Q6-47. When does the cost of inventory become an expense?
a. When inventory is delivered to a customer
b. When inventory is purchased from the supplier
c. When payment is made to the supplier
d. When cash is collected from the customer

The next two questions use the following facts. Leading Edge Frame Shop wants to know the effect of different inventory costing methods on its financial statements. Inventory and purchases data for June are:

			Units	Unit Cost	Total Cost
Jun 1		Beginning inventory	2,400	$18.00	$43,200
4		Purchase	1,500	$18.30	27,450
9		Sale	(1,800)		

Q6-48. If Leading Edge Frame Shop uses the FIFO method, the *cost of the ending inventory* will be
a. $32,400.   c. $32,700.
b. $27,450.   d. $38,250.

Q6-49. If Leading Edge Frame Shop uses the LIFO method, *cost of goods sold* will be
a. $27,450.   c. $32,700.
b. $32,850.   d. $32,400.

Q6-50. In a period of rising prices,
a. cost of goods sold under LIFO will be less than under FIFO.
b. LIFO inventory will be greater than FIFO inventory.
c. gross profit under FIFO will be higher than under LIFO.
d. net income under LIFO will be higher than under FIFO.

Q6-51. The income statement for Good Heart Foods shows gross profit of $149,000, operating expenses of $124,000, and cost of goods sold of $218,000. What is the amount of net sales revenue?
a. $342,000
b. $491,000
c. $367,000
d. $273,000

Q6-52. The word *market* as used in "the lower of cost or market" generally means
a. liquidation price.
b. original cost.
c. retail market price.
d. current replacement cost.

Q6-53. The sum of ending inventory and cost of goods sold is
a. gross profit.
b. cost of goods available (or cost of goods available for sale).
c. net purchases.
d. beginning inventory.

Q6-54. The following data come from the inventory records of Dapper Company:

Net sales revenue	$624,000
Beginning inventory	64,000
Ending inventory	43,000
Net purchases	400,000

Based on these facts, the gross profit for Dapper Company is
a. $224,000.
b. $193,000.
c. $150,000.
d. $203,000.

Q6-55. Patterson Company ended the month of March with inventory of $20,000. Patterson expects to end April with inventory of $13,000 after selling goods with a cost of $93,000. How much inventory must Patterson purchase during April in order to accomplish these results?
a. $106,000
b. $126,000
c. $100,000
d. $86,000

Q6-56. Two financial ratios that clearly distinguish a discount chain such as Walmart from a high-end retailer such as Gucci are the gross profit percentage and the rate of inventory turnover. Which set of relationships is most likely for Gucci?

	Gross profit percentage	Inventory turnover
a.	High	High
b.	Low	Low
c.	Low	High
d.	High	Low

Q6-57. Sales are $500,000 and cost of goods sold is $320,000. Beginning and ending inventories are $28,000 and $38,000, respectively. How many times did the company turn its inventory over during this period?
a. 9.7 times
b. 6.4 times
c. 15.2 times
d. 5.5 times

Q6-58. Trudell, Inc., reported the following data:

Freight in......................	$ 26,000	Dividends..................	$ 4,000
Purchases	207,000	Purchase returns........	6,300
Beginning inventory	52,000	Sales revenue.............	446,000
Purchase discounts	4,300	Ending inventory.......	47,000

Trudell's gross profit percentage is
    a. 51.0.
    b. 48.0.
                                 c. 49.0.
                                 d. 55.7.

Q6-59. Crystal Aquarium Supplies had the following beginning inventory, net purchases, net sales, and gross profit percentage for the first quarter of 2016:

Beginning inventory, $57,000	Net purchases, $72,000
Net sales revenue, $92,000	Gross profit rate, 20%

By the gross profit method, the ending inventory should be
    a. $110,600.
    b. $55,400.
                                 c. $129,000.
                                 d. $73,600.

Q6-60. An error understated Bowerston Corporation's December 31, 2016, ending inventory by $54,000. What effect will this error have on total assets and net income for 2016?

Assets	**Net income**
a. No effect	Overstate
b. No effect	No effect
c. Understate	Understate
d. Understate	No effect

Q6-61. An error understated Grand Company's December 31, 2016, ending inventory by $27,000. What effect will this error have on net income for 2017?
    a. Understate
    b. No effect
    c. Overstate

Problems MyAccountingLab

Group A

P6-62A. *(Learning Objectives 1, 2: Show how to account for inventory in a perpetual system using the average-costing method)* Big Box purchases inventory in crates of merchandise; each crate of inventory is a unit. The fiscal year of Big Box ends each January 31. Assume you are dealing with a single Big Box store in Rosedale, Minnesota. The Rosedale store began the year with an inventory of 23,000 units that cost a total of $1,219,000. During the year, the store purchased merchandise on account as follows:

Jul (30,000 units at $58)..	$1,740,000
Nov (50,000 units at $62)......................................	3,100,000
Dec (60,000 units at $68).......................................	4,080,000
Total purchases..	$8,920,000

Cash payments on account totaled $8,592,000. During fiscal year 2016, the store sold 151,000 units of merchandise for $15,477,500, of which $5,300,000 was for cash and the balance was on account. Big Box uses the average-cost method for inventories. Operating expenses for the year were $2,500,000. Big Box paid 70% in cash and accrued the rest as accrued liabilities. The store accrued income tax at the rate of 30%.

Requirements

1. Make summary journal entries to record the store's transactions for the year ended January 31, 2016. Big Box uses a perpetual inventory system. Round average cost per unit to two decimal places and round all other amounts to the nearest dollar.
2. Prepare a T-account to show the activity in the Inventory account.
3. Prepare the store's income statement for the year ended January 31, 2016. Show totals for gross profit, income before tax, and net income.

P6-63A. *(Learning Objective 2: Apply various inventory costing methods)* Assume a Watercrest Sports outlet store began October 2016 with 47 pairs of running shoes that cost the store $38 each. The sale price of these shoes was $67. During October, the store completed these inventory transactions:

		Units	Unit Cost	Unit Sale Price
Oct 2	Sale	19	$38	$67
9	Purchase......	83	40	
13	Sale	28	38	67
18	Sale	10	40	68
22	Sale	34	40	68
29	Purchase......	24	42	

Requirements

1. The preceding data are taken from the store's perpetual inventory records. Which cost method does the store use? Explain how you arrived at your answer.
2. Determine the store's cost of goods sold for October. Also compute gross profit for October.
3. What is the cost of the store's October 31 inventory of running shoes?

P6-64A. *(Learning Objective 2: Compare inventory by three methods)* Armed Forces Surplus began March 2016 with 80 tents that cost $15 each. During the month, Armed Forces Surplus made the following purchases at cost:

March 6	100 tents @ $20 = $2,000
18	120 tents @ $25 = 3,000
26	50 tents @ $30 = 1,500

Armed Forces Surplus sold 296 tents, and at March 31, the ending inventory consists of 54 tents. The sale price of each tent was $45.

Requirements

1. Determine the cost of goods sold and ending inventory amounts for March under the average cost, FIFO cost, and LIFO cost. Round average cost per unit to two decimal places, and round all other amounts to the nearest dollar.
2. Explain why cost of goods sold is highest under LIFO. Be specific.
3. Prepare the Armed Forces Surplus income statement for March. Report gross profit. Operating expenses totaled $5,000. Armed Forces Surplus uses average costing for inventory. The income tax rate is 35%.

LO 2

P6-65A. *(Learning Objective 2: Compare various inventory costing methods)* The records of Aldrin Aviation include the following accounts for inventory of aviation parts at July 31 of the current year:

Inventory			
Aug 1	Balance	700 units @ $6.00	$ 4,200
Nov 5	Purchase	400 units @ $7.00	2,800
Jan 24	Purchase	8,400 units @ $7.50	63,000
Apr 8	Purchase	500 units @ $8.00	4,000

Sales Revenue		
Jul 31	9,050 units	$133,035

Requirements

1. Prepare a partial income statement through gross profit under the average, FIFO, and LIFO methods. Round average cost per unit to two decimal places and all other amounts to the nearest dollar.
2. Which inventory method would you use to minimize income tax? Explain why this method causes income tax to be the lowest.

LO 3

P6-66A. *(Learning Objective 3: Explain GAAP and apply the lower-of-cost-or-market rule to inventories)* Dixson Trade Mart has recently had lackluster sales. The rate of inventory turnover has dropped, and the merchandise is gathering dust. At the same time, competition has forced Dixson's suppliers to lower the prices that Dixson will pay when it replaces its inventory. It is now December 31, 2016, and the current replacement cost of Dixson's ending inventory is $90,000 below what Dixson actually paid for the goods, which was $260,000. Before any adjustments at the end of the period, the Cost of Goods Sold account has a balance of $770,000.

   a. What accounting action should Dixson take in this situation?
   b. Give any journal entry required.
   c. At what amount should Dixson report Inventory on the balance sheet?
   d. At what amount should the company report Cost of Goods Sold on the income statement?
   e. Discuss the accounting principle or concept that is most relevant to this situation.

LO 4

P6-67A. *(Learning Objective 4: Compute and evaluate gross margin and inventory turnover)* Pastry People, Inc., and Captain Coffee Corporation are both specialty food chains. The two companies reported these figures, in millions:

	A	B	C
	A1		
1	**Pastry People, Inc.** **Income Statements (Adapted)** **Years Ended December 31**		
2	**(Amounts in millions)**	**2016**	**2015**
3	Revenues:		
4	Net sales	$ 600	$ 704
5			
6	Costs and Expenses:		
7	Cost of goods sold	540	590
8	Selling, general, and administrative expenses	62	51
9			

A1		
	A	**B**	**C**

	A	B	C
1	**Pastry People, Inc.** **Balance Sheets (Adapted)** **December 31**		
2	**(Amounts in millions)**	**2016**	**2015**
3	**Assets**		
4	Current assets:		
5	Cash and cash equivalents	$ 12	$ 23
6	Receivables	22	32
7	Inventories	15	25
8			

A1		
	A	**B**	**C**

	A	B	C
1	**Captain Coffee Corporation** **Income Statements (Adapted)** **Years Ended December 31**		
2	**(Amounts in millions)**	**2016**	**2015**
3	Net sales	$ 7,000	$ 6,360
4	Cost of goods sold	3,500	2,600
5	Selling, general, and administrative expenses	2,925	2,390
6			

A1		
	A	**B**	**C**

	A	B	C
1	**Captain Coffee Corporation** **Balance Sheets (Adapted)** **December 31**		
2	**(Amounts in millions)**	**2016**	**2015**
3	**Assets**		
4	Current assets:		
5	Cash and temporary investments	$ 316	$ 176
6	Receivables, net	220	188
7	Inventories	700	550
8			

Requirements

1. Compute the gross profit percentage and the rate of inventory turnover for Pastry People and Captain Coffee for 2016.
2. Based on these statistics, which company looks more profitable? Why? What other expense category should we consider in evaluating these two companies?

LO 4 5 **P6-68A.** *(Learning Objectives 4, 5: Compute gross profit; use the COGS model to make management decisions, and estimate inventory by the gross profit method)* Assume Watertown Company, a camera store, lost some inventory in a fire on March 15. To file an insurance claim, Watertown Company must estimate its March 15 inventory by the gross profit method. Assume that for the past two years Watertown Company's gross profit has averaged 39% of net sales. Suppose that Watertown Company's inventory records reveal the following data:

Inventory, March 1	$ 57,400
Transactions March 1–15:	
Purchases	490,300
Purchase discounts	11,000
Purchase returns.......................	70,800
Sales..	647,000

Requirements

1. Estimate the cost of the lost inventory using the gross profit method.
2. Prepare the income statement for March 1 to March 15 for this product through gross profit. Show the detailed computations of cost of goods sold in a separate schedule.

LO 5 **P6-69A.** *(Learning Objective 5: Use the COGS model to make management decisions, and estimate amount of inventory to purchase)* Gary's Convenience Stores' income statement for the year ended December 31, 2015, and its balance sheet as of December 31, 2015, reported the following:

	A	B
1	**Gary's Convenience Stores** **Income Statement** **Year Ended December 31, 2015**	
2	Sales	$ 961,000
3	Cost of sales	724,000
4	Gross profit	237,000
5	Operating expenses	106,000
6	Net income	$ 131,000
7		

	A	B	C	D
1	**Gary's Convenience Stores** **Balance Sheet** **December 31, 2015**			
2	**Assets**		**Liabilities and Capital**	
3	Cash	$ 43,000	Accounts payable	$ 32,000
4	Inventories	64,000	Note payable	191,000
5	Land and		Total liabilities	223,000
6	buildings, net	269,000	Owner, capital	153,000
7			Total liabilities	
8	Total assets	$ 376,000	and capital	$ 376,000
9				

The business is organized as a proprietorship, so it pays no corporate income tax. The owner is budgeting for 2016 and expects sales and cost of goods sold to increase by 10%. To meet customer demand, ending inventory will need to be $82,000 at December 31, 2016. The owner hopes to earn a net income of $158,000 next year.

Requirements

1. One of the most important decisions a manager makes is the amount of inventory to purchase. Show how to determine the amount of inventory to purchase in 2016.
2. Prepare the store's budgeted income statement for 2016 to reach the target net income of $158,000. To reach this goal, operating expenses must decrease by $3,300.

P6-70A. *(Learning Objective 6: Analyze the effects of inventory errors)* The accounting records of Brilliant Home Store show these data (in millions). The shareholders are very happy with Brilliant's steady increase in net income.

LO 6

	2016	2015	2014
Net sales revenue...........................	$42	$39	$36
Cost of goods sold:			
Beginning inventory	$ 10	$ 9	$ 8
Net purchases	30	28	26
Cost of goods available..............	40	37	34
Less ending inventory................	(11)	(10)	(9)
Cost of goods sold	29	27	25
Gross profit.....................................	13	12	11
Operating expenses	6	6	6
Net income.....................................	$ 7	$ 6	$ 5

Auditors discovered that the ending inventory for 2014 was understated by $4 million and that the ending inventory for 2015 was understated by $5 million. The ending inventory at December 31, 2016, was correct.

Requirements

1. Show corrected income statements for each of the three years.
2. How much did these assumed corrections add to or take away from Brilliant's total net income over the three-year period? How did the corrections affect the trend of net income?
3. Will Brilliant's shareholders still be happy with the company's trend of net income? Give the reason for your answer.

Group B

P6-71B. *(Learning Objectives 1, 2: Show how to account for inventory in a perpetual system using the average-costing method)* Super Value purchases inventory in crates of merchandise; each crate of inventory is a unit. The fiscal year of Super Value ends each January 31. Assume you are dealing with a single Super Value store in Madison, Wisconsin. The Madison store began the year with an inventory of 14,000 units that cost a total of $742,000. During the year, the store purchased merchandise on account as follows:

LO 1 2

July (31,000 units at $55)	$1,705,000
November (51,000 units at $59)..........................	3,009,000
December (61,000 units at $65)...........................	3,965,000
Total purchases..	$8,679,000

Cash payments on account totaled $8,351,000. During fiscal year 2016, the store sold 149,000 units of merchandise for $15,272,500, of which $5,200,000 was for cash and the balance was on account. Super Value uses the average-cost method for inventories. Operating expenses for the year were $3,250,000. Super Value paid 70% in cash and accrued the rest as accrued liabilities. The store accrued income tax at the rate of 35%.

Requirements

1. Make summary journal entries to record the store's transactions for the year ended June 30, 2016. Super Value uses a perpetual inventory system. Round average cost per unit to two decimal places and round all other amounts to the nearest dollar.
2. Prepare a T-account to show the activity in the Inventory account.
3. Prepare the store's income statement for the year ended January 31, 2016. Show totals for gross profit, income before tax, and net income.

LO 2 **P6-72B.** *(Learning Objective 2: Apply various inventory costing methods)* Assume a Cross Country Sports outlet store began March 2016 with 49 pairs of running shoes that cost the store $35 each. The sale price of these shoes was $70. During March, the store completed these inventory transactions:

			Units	Unit Cost	Unit Sale Price
Mar	2	Sale	17	$35	$70
	9	Purchase......	83	37	
	13	Sale	32	35	70
	18	Sale	12	37	71
	22	Sale	34	37	71
	29	Purchase......	18	39	

Requirements

1. The preceding data are taken from the store's perpetual inventory records. Which cost method does the store use? Explain how you arrived at your answer.
2. Determine the store's cost of goods sold for March. Also compute gross profit for March.
3. What is the cost of the store's March 31 inventory of running shoes?

LO 2 **P6-73B.** *(Learning Objective 2: Compare inventory by three methods)* Military Surplus began May 2016 with 80 stoves that cost $20 each. During the month, Military Surplus made the following purchases at cost:

May 6	100 stoves @ $25 = $2,500
18	120 stoves @ $30 = 3,600
26	50 stoves @ $35 = 1,750

Military Surplus sold 286 stoves, and at May 31, the ending inventory consists of 64 stoves. The sale price of each stove was $45.

Requirements

1. Determine the cost of goods sold and ending inventory amounts for May under the average cost, FIFO cost, and LIFO cost. Round the average cost per unit to two decimal places, and round all other amounts to the nearest dollar.
2. Explain why cost of goods sold is highest under LIFO. Be specific.
3. Prepare Military Surplus's income statement for May. Report gross profit. Operating expenses totaled $3,500. Military Surplus uses average costing for inventory. The income tax rate is 30%.

LO 2 **P6-74B.** *(Learning Objective 2: Compare various inventory costing methods)* The records of Buzz Aviation include the following accounts for inventory of aviation parts at July 31 of the current year:

Inventory				
Aug 1	Balance	600 units @ $5.50	$ 3,300	
Nov 5	Purchase	500 units @ $7.20	3,600	
Jan 24	Purchase 7,000 units @ $7.50	52,500	
Apr 8	Purchase	900 units @ $8.00	7,200	

Sales Revenue			
	Jul 31	8,090 units	$114,878

Requirements

1. Prepare a partial income statement through gross profit under the average, FIFO, and LIFO methods. Round average cost per unit to two decimal places and all other amounts to the nearest whole dollar.
2. Which inventory method would you use to minimize income tax? Explain why this method causes income tax to be the lowest.

P6-75B. *(Learning Objective 3: Explain GAAP and apply the lower-of-cost-or-market rule to inventories)* Mahtomedi Trade Mart has recently had lackluster sales. The rate of inventory turnover has dropped, and the merchandise is gathering dust. At the same time, competition has forced Mahtomedi's suppliers to lower the prices that Mahtomedi will pay when it replaces its inventory. It is now December 31, 2016, and the current replacement cost of Mahtomedi's ending inventory is $75,000 below what Mahtomedi actually paid for the goods, which was $270,000. Before any adjustments at the end of the period, the Cost of Goods Sold account has a balance of $820,000.

LO **3**

    a. What accounting action should Mahtomedi take in this situation?
    b. Give any journal entry required.
    c. At what amount should Mahtomedi report Inventory on the balance sheet?
    d. At what amount should the company report Cost of Goods Sold on the income statement?
    e. Discuss the accounting principle or concept that is most relevant to this situation.

P6-76B. *(Learning Objective 4: Compute and evaluate gross margin and inventory turnover)* Frosted Donut, Inc., and Coffee Bean Corporation are both specialty food chains. The two companies reported these figures, in millions:

LO **4**

A1 ⬍		
A	**B**	**C**
Frosted Donut, Inc. **Income Statements (Adapted)** **Years Ended December 31**		
2 (Amounts in millions)	**2016**	**2015**
3 Revenues:		
4 Net sales	$ 700	$ 708
5		
6 Costs and Expenses:		
7 Cost of goods sold	560	594
8 Selling, general, and administrative expenses	64	55
9		

A1 ⬍		
A	**B**	**C**
Frosted Donut, Inc. **Balance Sheets (Adapted)** **December 31**		
2 (Amounts in millions)	**2016**	**2015**
3 **Assets**		
4 Current assets:		
5 Cash and temporary investments	$ 19	$ 28
6 Receivables	20	36
7 Inventories	30	70
8		

	A	B	C
1	**Coffee Bean Corporation** **Income Statements (Adapted)** **Years Ended December 31**		
2	**(Amounts in millions)**	**2016**	**2015**
3	Net sales	$ 6,000	$ 6,370
4	Cost of goods sold	2,700	2,601
5	Selling, general, and administrative expenses	2,925	2,363
6			

	A	B	C
1	**Coffee Bean Corporation** **Balance Sheets (Adapted)** **December 31**		
2	**(Amounts in millions)**	**2016**	**2015**
3	**Assets**		
4	Current assets:		
5	Cash and temporary investments	$ 313	$ 172
6	Receivables, net	225	191
7	Inventories	650	550
8			

Requirements

1. Compute the gross profit percentage and the rate of inventory turnover for Frosted Donut and Coffee Bean for 2016.
2. Based on these statistics, which company looks more profitable? Why? What other expense category should we consider in evaluating these two companies?

LO 4 5   **P6-77B.** *(Learning Objectives 4, 5: Compute gross profit; use the COGS model to make management decisions, and estimate inventory by the gross profit method)* Assume Thompson Company, a camera store, lost some inventory in a fire on July 15. To file an insurance claim, Thompson Company must estimate its July 15 inventory by the gross profit method. Assume that for the past two years, Thompson Company's gross profit has averaged 44% of net sales. Suppose that Thompson Company's inventory records reveal the following data:

Inventory, July 1	$ 57,600
Transactions July 1–15:	
Purchases	490,600
Purchase discounts	14,000
Purchase returns.......................	70,300
Sales..	648,000

Requirements

1. Estimate the cost of the lost inventory using the gross profit method.
2. Prepare the income statement for July 1 through July 15 for this product through gross profit. Show the detailed computation of cost of goods sold in a separate schedule.

LO 5   **P6-78B.** *(Learning Objective 5: Use the COGS model to make management decisions, and estimate amount of inventory to purchase)* Maroney's Convenience Stores' income statement for the year ended December 31, 2015, and its balance sheet as of December 31, 2015, reported the following:

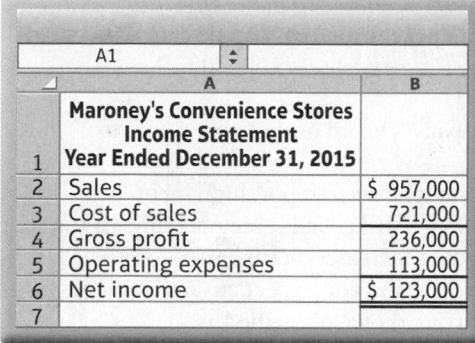

	A	B
1	**Maroney's Convenience Stores Income Statement Year Ended December 31, 2015**	
2	Sales	$ 957,000
3	Cost of sales	721,000
4	Gross profit	236,000
5	Operating expenses	113,000
6	Net income	$ 123,000
7		

	A	B	C	D
1	**Maroney's Convenience Stores Balance Sheet December 31, 2015**			
2	**Assets**		**Liabilities and Capital**	
3	Cash	$ 42,000	Accounts payable	$ 34,000
4	Inventories	66,000	Note payable	190,000
5	Land and		Total liabilities	224,000
6	buildings, net	268,000	Owner, capital	152,000
7			Total liabilities	
8	Total assets	$ 376,000	and capital	$ 376,000
9				

The business is organized as a proprietorship, so it pays no corporate income tax. The owner is budgeting for 2016 and expects sales and cost of goods sold to increase by 5%. To meet customer demand, ending inventory will need to be $77,000 at December 31, 2016. The owner hopes to earn a net income of $154,000 next year.

Requirements

1. One of the most important decisions a manager makes is the amount of inventory to purchase. Show how to determine the amount of inventory to purchase in 2016.
2. Prepare the store's budgeted income statement for 2016 to reach the target net income of $154,000. To reach this goal, operating expenses must decrease by $19,200.

P6-79B. (*Learning Objective 6: Analyze the effects of inventory errors*) The accounting records of Columbia Home Store show these data (in millions). The shareholders are very happy with Columbia's steady increase in net income.

	2016	2015	2014
Net sales revenue............................	$39	$36	$33
Cost of goods sold:			
Beginning inventory	$ 9	$ 8	$ 7
Net purchases	26	24	22
Cost of goods available	35	32	29
Less ending inventory................	(10)	(9)	(8)
Cost of goods sold	25	23	21
Gross profit....................................	14	13	12
Operating expenses	9	9	9
Net income....................................	$ 5	$ 4	$ 3

Auditors discovered that the ending inventory for 2014 was understated by $6 million and that the ending inventory for 2015 was understated by $4 million. The ending inventory at December 31, 2016, was correct.

Requirements

1. Show corrected income statements for each of the three years.
2. How much did these assumed corrections add to or take away from Columbia's total net income over the three-year period? How did the corrections affect the trend of net income?
3. Will Columbia's shareholders still be happy with the company's trend of net income? Give the reason for your answer.

Challenge Exercises and Problem

LO 2

E6-80. *(Learning Objective 2: Apply various inventory methods to make inventory policy decisions)* For each of the following situations, identify the inventory method that you would use; or, given the use of a particular method, state the strategy that you would follow to accomplish your goal.

a. Inventory costs are *decreasing*, and your company's board of directors wants to minimize income taxes.

b. Inventory costs are *increasing*, and the company prefers to report high income.

c. Suppliers of your inventory are threatening a labor strike, and it may be difficult for your company to obtain inventory. This situation could increase your income taxes.

d. Inventory costs have been stable for several years, and you expect costs to remain stable for the indefinite future. (Give the reason for your choice of method.)

e. Inventory costs are increasing. Your company uses LIFO and is having an unexpectedly good year. It is near year-end, and you need to keep net income from increasing too much in order to save on income tax.

f. Company management, like that of Apple and Pottery Barn, prefers a middle-of-the-road inventory policy that avoids extremes.

LO 2

E6-81. *(Learning Objective 2: Measure the effect of a LIFO liquidation)* Suppose Uptown Fashions, a specialty retailer, had these records for evening gowns during 2016:

Beginning inventory (36 @ $1,050)....................	$ 37,800
Purchase in February (24 @ $1,200)	28,800
Purchase in June (46 @ $1,250)	57,500
Purchase in December (35 @ $1,400)................	49,000
Cost of goods available for sale.........................	$173,100

Assume that Uptown sold 131 gowns during 2016 and uses the LIFO method to account for inventory. The income tax rate is 35%.

Requirements

1. Compute Uptown's cost of goods sold for evening gowns in 2016.

2. Compute what cost of goods sold would have been if Uptown had purchased enough inventory in December—at $1,400 per evening gown—to keep year-end inventory at the same level it was at the beginning of the year.

LO 4

E6-82. *(Learning Objective 4: Evaluate profitability)* A Mart, Inc., declared bankruptcy. Let's see why. A Mart reported these figures:

A	B	C	D	E
A Mart, Inc. **Statements of Income** **Years Ended December 31**				
Millions	**2016**	**2015**	**2014**	**2013**
Sales	$ 37.9	$ 36.8	$ 34.5	
Cost of sales	30.7	29.2	27.2	
Selling expenses	7.5	6.3	6.2	
Other expenses	0.1	0.9	0.7	
Net income (net loss)	$ (0.4)	$ 0.4	$ 0.4	
Additional data:				
Ending inventory	$ 8.4	$ 7.2	$ 7.0	$ 6.0

Requirement

1. Evaluate the trend of A Mart's results of operations during 2014 through 2016. Consider the trends of sales, gross profit, and net income. Track the gross profit percentage and the rate of inventory turnover in each year. Also discuss the role that selling expenses must have played in A Mart's difficulties.

P6-83. *(Learning Objectives 1, 2, 4: Account for inventory; analyze two companies that use different inventory methods)* Rollyson Financial Management believes that the biotechnology industry is a good investment and is considering investing in one of two companies. However, one company, FutureNow, Inc., uses the FIFO method of inventory, and another company, LifeTech, Inc., uses LIFO. The following information about the two companies is available from their annual reports:

FutureNow, Inc.	2015	2014
Inventory..	$ 90,000	$ 80,000
Cost of goods sold..	1,020,000	852,000
Sales..	1,500,000	1,420,000
Net income..	194,000	187,000

LifeTech, Inc.	2015	2014
Inventory (See Note)	$ 348,000	$ 309,000
Cost of goods sold..	3,921,000	3,982,500
Sales..	7,000,000	6,750,000
Net income..	900,000	780,000

Notes to the Financial Statement. If LifeTech had used the FIFO method, inventory would have been $21,000 higher at the end of 2014 and $22,000 higher at the end of 2015.

The income of the two companies is difficult to compare because LifeTech is a much larger company and uses a different inventory method. To better compare the two companies, Rollyson wants you to prepare the following analysis.

Requirements

1. Show the computation of LifeTech's cost of goods sold in 2015 using the LIFO method. Refer to Appendix 6B for an illustration.
2. Prepare summary journal entries for 2015 for LifeTech's purchases of inventory (assume all purchases are on account), sales (assume all are on account), and cost of goods sold. Prepare a T-account for inventory and post these transactions into the T-account. The company uses the perpetual inventory method.
3. Show the computation of LifeTech's cost of goods sold for 2015 using the FIFO method.
4. Compute the gross profit percentage for 2015 for both FutureNow and LifeTech using FIFO figures for both.
5. Compute the inventory turnover for 2015 for both FutureNow and LifeTech using FIFO figures for both.
6. Which company appears stronger? Support your answer.

APPLY YOUR KNOWLEDGE

Decision Cases

LO 2

Case 1. *(Learning Objective 2: Apply and compare various inventory methods, and assess the impact of a year-end purchase of inventory)* Jubilee Corporation is nearing the end of its first year of operations. Jubilee made inventory purchases of $745,000 during the year, as follows:

January	1,000 units @	$100.00	=	$100,000
July	4,000	121.25		485,000
November	1,000	160.00		160,000
Totals	6,000			$745,000

Sales for the year are 5,000 units for $1,200,000 of revenue. Expenses other than cost of goods sold and income taxes total $200,000. The president of the company is undecided about whether to adopt the FIFO method or the LIFO method for inventories. The income tax rate is 40%.

Requirements

1. To aid company decision making, prepare income statements under FIFO and under LIFO.
2. Compare the net income under FIFO with net income under LIFO. Which method produces the higher net income? What causes this difference? Be specific.

LO 2 3

Case 2. *(Learning Objectives 2, 3: Apply and compare various inventory cost methods; apply underlying GAAP for inventory)* The inventory costing method a company chooses can affect the financial statements and thus the decisions of the people who use those statements.

Requirements

1. Company A uses the LIFO inventory method and discloses its use of the LIFO method in notes to the financial statements. Company B uses the FIFO method to account for its inventory. Company B does *not* disclose which inventory method it uses. Company B reports a higher net income than Company A. In which company would you prefer to invest? Give your reason.
2. Representational faithfulness is an accepted accounting concept. Would you want management to be faithful in representing its accounting for inventory if you were a shareholder or a creditor of a company? Give your reason.

Ethical Issue

During 2016, Vanguard, Inc., changed to the LIFO method of accounting for inventory. Suppose that during 2015, Vanguard changes back to the FIFO method and the following year Vanguard switches back to LIFO again.

Requirements

1. What would you think of a company's ethics if it changed accounting methods every year?
2. What accounting principle would changing methods every year violate?
3. Who can be harmed when a company changes its accounting methods too often? How?

Focus on Financials | Apple Inc.

(Learning Objectives 1, 4: Show how to account for inventories; compute and evaluate gross profit and inventory turnover) The notes are part of the financial statements. They give details that would clutter the statements. This case will help you learn to use a company's inventory notes. Refer to **Apple Inc.**'s consolidated financial statements and related notes in Appendix A and online in the filings section of **http://www.sec.gov**. and answer the following questions:

LO **1 4**

Requirements

1. How much was Apple Inc.'s merchandise inventory at September 27, 2014? At September 28, 2013? Does Apple Inc. include all inventory that it handles in the inventory account on its balance sheet?
2. Refer to Note 1, Summary of Significant Accounting Policies, Inventories section. How does Apple Inc. *value* its inventories? Which *cost* method does the company use?
3. Using the cost-of-goods-sold model, compute Apple Inc.'s purchases of inventory during the year ended September 27, 2014.
4. Did Apple Inc.'s gross profit percentage on company sales improve or deteriorate in the year ended September 27, 2014, compared to the previous year?
5. For this part, assume that beginning inventory on September 30, 2012, was $791 million. Compute inventory turnover for 2014 and 2013. Would you rate Apple Inc.'s rate of inventory turnover for the years ended September 27, 2014, and September 28, 2013, as fast or slow in comparison to most other companies in its industry? Explain your answer.
6. Go to the SEC's website (**http://www.sec.gov**). Find Apple Inc.'s consolidated balance sheet and consolidated statement of operations for the fiscal year ended September 26, 2015. What has happened to the company's inventory turnover and gross profit percentages since September 27, 2014? Can you explain the reasons? Where would you find the company's explanations for these changes? (Challenge)

Focus on Analysis | Under Armour, Inc.

(Learning Objectives 1, 2, 4: Show how to account for inventory; explain GAAP for inventory; compute and evaluate gross profit and inventory turnover) Refer to **Under Armour, Inc.'s,** consolidated financial statements in Appendix B and online in the filings section of **http://www.sec.gov**. Show amounts in millions and round to the nearest $1 million.

LO **1 2 4**

Requirements

1. Three important pieces of inventory information are (a) the cost of inventory on hand, (b) the cost of goods sold, and (c) the cost of inventory purchases. Identify or compute each of these items for Under Armour, Inc., at December 31, 2014.
2. Which item in requirement 1 is most directly related to cash flow? Why? (Challenge)
3. Assume that all inventory purchases were made on account and that only inventory purchases increased Accounts Payable. Compute Under Armour, Inc.'s, cash payments for inventory during 2014.
4. See Note 2 Summary of Significant Accounting Policies, Inventories section. How does Under Armour, Inc., *value* its inventories? Which *costing* method does Under Armour, Inc., use?
5. Did Under Armour, Inc.'s gross profit percentage and rate of inventory turnover improve or deteriorate in 2014 (versus 2013)? Consider the overall effect of these two ratios. Did Under Armour, Inc., improve during 2014? How did these factors affect the net income for 2014? (Note: Under Armour, Inc.'s inventories totaled $319 million at the end of fiscal 2012.) Round answers to three decimal places.

Group Projects

(Learning Objective 4: Evaluate inventory turnover ratios) Obtain the annual reports of 10 companies, 2 from each of five different industries. Most companies' financial statements can be downloaded from their websites.

LO **4**

Requirements

1. Compute each company's gross profit percentage and rate of inventory turnover for the most recent two years. If annual reports are unavailable or do not provide enough data for multiple-year computations, you can gather financial statement data from *Moody's Industrial Manual.*

2. For the industries of the companies you are analyzing, obtain the industry averages for gross profit percentage and inventory turnover from Robert Morris Associates, *Annual Statement Studies;* Dun and Bradstreet, *Industry Norms and Key Business Ratios;* or Leo Troy, *Almanac of Business and Industrial Financial Ratios.*

3. How well does each of your companies compare to the other company in its industry? How well do your companies compare to the average for their industry? What insight about your companies can you glean from these ratios?

4. Write a memo to summarize your findings, stating whether your group would invest in each of the companies it has analyzed.

Quick Check Answers

1. *a*	7. *c*	13. *a*($160,000 − $72,000)/$160,000
2. *d*	8. *d*	
3. *e*	9. *a*	14. *c* [$72,000 ÷ ([$26,000 + $29,000]/2)]
4. *b*[(25 × $6) + (35 × $8)]	10. *c*($117,000 − $46,000)	
5. *c*[(25 + 39 + 12 − 60) × $6]	11. *b*($150,000 + $28,000 − $13,000)	15. *c*[$110,000 + $220,000 − [$500,000 × (1 − 0.35)]]
6. *c*[16 × ($150 + $312 + $108) ÷ 76]	12. *c*($26,000 + $80,000 + $3,000 − $8,000 − $29,000)	16. *d*

APPENDIX 6A

ACCOUNTING FOR INVENTORY IN THE PERIODIC SYSTEM

In the periodic inventory system, the business keeps no running record of the merchandise. Instead, at the end of the period, the business counts inventory on hand and applies the unit costs to determine the cost of ending inventory. This inventory figure appears on the balance sheet and is used to compute cost of goods sold.

Recording Transactions in the Periodic System

In the periodic system, the Inventory account carries the beginning balance left over from the preceding period throughout the current period. The business records purchases of inventory in the Purchases account (an expense). Then, at the end of the period, the Inventory account must be updated for the financial statements. A journal entry removes the beginning balance by crediting Inventory and debiting Cost of Goods Sold. A second journal entry sets up (debits) the ending inventory balance, based on the physical count, and credits Cost of Goods Sold. The final entry in this sequence transfers the amount of Purchases to Cost of Goods Sold, crediting Purchases and debiting Cost of Goods Sold. These end-of-period entries can be made during the closing process.

Exhibit 6A-1 illustrates the accounting in the periodic system. After the process is complete, Inventory has its correct ending balance of $120,000, and Cost of Goods Sold shows $540,000.

Exhibit 6A-1 | Recording and Reporting Inventories—Periodic System (All amounts assumed)

PANEL A—Recording Transactions and the T-accounts (All amounts are assumed)

	A	B	C	D
	A1			
1	1.	Purchases	560,000	
2		Accounts Payable		560,000
3		Purchased inventory on account.		
4				
5	2.	Accounts Receivable	900,000	
6		Sales Revenue		900,000
7		Sold inventory on account.		
8				
9	3.	End-of-period entries to update Inventory and record Cost of Goods Sold:		
10	a.	Cost of Goods Sold	100,000	
11		Inventory (beginning balance)		100,000
12		Transferred beginning inventory to COGS.		
13				
14	b.	Inventory (ending balance)	120,000	
15		Cost of Goods Sold		120,000
16		Set up ending inventory based on physical count.		
17				
18	c.	Cost of Goods Sold	560,000	
19		Purchases		560,000
20		Transferred purchases to COGS.		
21				

The T-accounts show the following:

Inventory		Cost of Goods Sold	
100,000*	100,000	100,000	120,000
120,000		560,000	
		540,000	

*Beginning inventory was $100,000

PANEL B—Reporting in the Financial Statements

Income Statement (Partial)			Ending Balance Sheet (Partial)	
Sales revenue		$900,000	Current assets:	
Cost of goods sold:			Cash	$ XXX
Beginning inventory	$ 100,000		Short-term investments	XXX
Purchases	560,000		Accounts receivable	XXX
Cost of goods available	660,000		Inventory	120,000
Ending inventory	(120,000)		Prepaid expenses	XXX
Cost of goods sold		540,000		
Gross profit		$360,000		

APPENDIX ASSIGNMENTS

Short Exercises

S6A-1. *(Record inventory transactions in the periodic system)* Wexton Technologies began the year with inventory of $560. During the year, Wexton purchased inventory costing $1,160 and sold goods for $2,600, with all transactions on account. Wexton ended the year with inventory of $640. Journalize all the necessary transactions under the periodic inventory system.

S6A-2. *(Compute cost of goods sold and prepare the income statement—periodic system)*
Use the data in S6A-1 to do the following for Wexton Technologies.

➤ **Requirements**

1. Post to the Inventory and Cost of Goods Sold accounts.
2. Compute cost of goods sold by the cost-of-goods-sold model.
3. Prepare the income statement of Wexton Technologies through gross profit.

Exercises

E6A-3. *(Compute amounts for the GAAP inventory methods—periodic system)* Suppose
Synthetix Corporation's inventory records for a particular computer chip indicate the following
at October 31:

Oct 1	Beginning inventory	4 units @ $60 =	$240
8	Purchase................................	3 units @ $60 =	180
15	Purchase................................	12 units @ $70 =	840
26	Purchase................................	1 units @ $80 =	80

The physical count of inventory at October 31 indicates that five units of inventory are on hand.

➤ **Requirements**

Compute ending inventory and cost of goods sold, using each of the following methods:
1. Specific unit cost, assuming three $60 units and two $70 units are on hand
2. Average cost (round average unit cost to the nearest cent)
3. First-in, first-out
4. Last-in, first-out

E6A-4. *(Journal inventory transactions in the periodic system; Compute cost of goods sold)* Use the data in E6A-3.

➤ **Requirements**

Journalize the following for the periodic system:
1. Total October purchases in one summary entry. All purchases were on credit.
2. Total October sales in a summary entry. Assume that the selling price was $275 per unit and that all sales were on credit.
3. October 31 entries for inventory. Synthetix uses LIFO. Post to the Cost of Goods Sold T-account to show how this amount is determined. Label each item in the account.
4. Show the computation of cost of goods sold by the cost-of-goods-sold model.

Problems

P6A-5. *(Compute cost of goods sold and gross profit on sales—periodic system)* Assume a
Championship outlet store began July 2016 with 52 units of inventory that cost $18 each. The
sale price of these units was $75. During July, the store completed these inventory transactions:

		Units	Unit Cost	Unit Sale Price
July 3	Sale	18	$18	$75
8	Purchase......	86	19	77
11	Sale	34	18	75
19	Sale	2	19	77
24	Sale	33	19	77
30	Purchase......	22	20	78
31	Sale	3	19	77

➤ **Requirements**

1. Determine the store's cost of goods sold for July under the periodic inventory system. Assume the FIFO method.
2. Compute gross profit for July.

P6A-6. *(Record transactions in the periodic system; report inventory items in the financial statements)* Accounting records for Just Desserts, Inc., yield the following data for the year ended December 31, 2016 (amounts in thousands):

Inventory, Dec 31, 2015...	$ 510
Purchases of inventory (on account)..	1,180
Sales of inventory—80% on account, 20% for cash.......................................	3,400
Inventory at the lower of FIFO cost or market, Dec 31, 2016	690

➤ **Requirements**

1. Journalize Just Desserts's inventory transactions for the year under the periodic system. Show all amounts in thousands.
2. Report ending inventory, sales, cost of goods sold, and gross profit on the appropriate financial statement (amounts in thousands). Show the computation of cost of goods sold.

APPENDIX 6B

THE LIFO RESERVE—CONVERTING A LIFO COMPANY'S NET INCOME TO THE FIFO BASIS

Suppose you are a financial analyst and it is your job to recommend stocks for your clients to purchase as investments. You have narrowed your choice to **Mega-Mart Stores, Inc. (a hypothetical company)** and **Kohl's Corporation.** Assume that Mega-Mart uses the LIFO method for inventories, and Kohl's uses FIFO. The two companies' net incomes are not comparable because they use different inventory methods. To compare the two companies, you need to place them on the same footing.

The Internal Revenue Service allows companies to use LIFO for income tax purposes only if they use LIFO for financial reporting. Companies that use LIFO inventories also report supplemental FIFO inventory information in the footnotes to the financial statements, allowing the investor to convert a company's net income from the LIFO basis to what the income would have been if the business had used FIFO. Companies that use LIFO usually report the FIFO cost, as well as a LIFO Reserve, in the footnotes of their financial statements. The LIFO Reserve[4] is the difference between the LIFO cost of an inventory and what the cost of that inventory would be under FIFO. In our example, assume that that our hypothetical Mega-Mart reports the following amounts:

Mega-Mart Stores, Inc. Uses LIFO		
	(In millions)	
	2015	**2014**
From the Mega-Mart balance sheet:		
Inventories (approximate FIFO cost)...............	$ 25,056	$22,749
Less LIFO reserve...	(165)	(135)
LIFO cost...	24,891	22,614
From the Mega-Mart income statement:		
Cost of goods sold...	$191,838	
Net income...	8,039	
Income tax rate	35%	

---

[4]The LIFO Reserve account is widely used in practice even though the word reserve is poor terminology.

Converting Mega-Mart's 2015 net income to the FIFO basis focuses on the LIFO Reserve because the reserve captures the difference between Mega-Mart's ending inventory costed at LIFO and at FIFO. Observe that during each year, the FIFO cost of ending inventory exceeded the LIFO cost. During 2015, the LIFO Reserve increased by $30 million ($165 million − $135 million). *The LIFO Reserve can increase only when inventory costs are rising.* Recall that during a period of rising costs, LIFO produces the highest cost of goods sold and the lowest net income. Therefore, for 2015, Mega-Mart's cost of goods sold would have been lower if the company had used the FIFO method for inventories. Mega-Mart's net income would have been higher, as the following computations show:

If Mega-Mart Had Used FIFO in 2015	
	(In millions)
Cost of goods sold, as reported under LIFO	$191,838
− Increase in LIFO Reserve ($165 − $135)	(30)
= Cost of goods sold, if Mega-Mart had used FIFO	$191,808
Lower cost of goods sold → Higher pretax income by	$ 30
Minus income taxes (35%)	11
Higher net income under FIFO	19
Net income as reported under LIFO	8,039
Net income Mega-Mart would have reported for 2015 if using FIFO	$ 8,058

Now you can compare Mega-Mart's net income with that of Kohl's Corporation. All the ratios used for the analysis—current ratio, inventory turnover, and so on—can be compared between the two companies as long as we use the FIFO figures for Cost of Goods Sold and Inventories for Mega-Mart.

The LIFO Reserve provides another opportunity for managers and investors to answer a key question about a company.

How much income tax has the company saved over its lifetime by using the LIFO method to account for inventory?

Using Mega-Mart as an example, the computation at the end of 2015 is as follows (amounts in millions):

Income tax saved by using LIFO = LIFO Reserve × Income tax rate
$$\$58 \quad = \quad \$165 \quad \times \quad .35$$

With these price changes, by the end of 2015, Mega-Mart has saved a total of $58 million by using the LIFO method to account for its merchandise inventory. Had Mega-Mart used the FIFO method, Mega-Mart would have almost $58 million less cash to invest in the opening of new stores.

In recent years, some companies have experienced declines in the carrying value of their inventories, either due to decreasing physical quantities or decreasing unit prices. When this happens, LIFO reserves can decline or even reverse. This ultimately makes gross profit and net income less under FIFO than LIFO. The details of this topic are reserved for more advanced accounting classes.

7 Plant Assets, Natural Resources, & Intangibles

Lee Snider/Alamy

SPOTLIGHT | FedEx Corporation

If you need a document or package delivered across the country overnight or any of a number of other business services, FedEx can handle it. **FedEx Corporation** sets a high standard for quick delivery, as well as other transportation, e-commerce, and business services. For this reason, FedEx has, for the last decade, consistently made the list as one of the "World's Most Admired Companies" by *Fortune* magazine. As you can see from the company's Consolidated Balance Sheets on the following page, FedEx moves packages using property and equipment, such as aircraft, package-handling equipment, computers, and vehicles. These are FedEx's most important resources (lines 11–15). The company owns over $40 billion of property and equipment as of May 31, 2014 (line 16), which is actually a little over $7.6 billion more than total assets (line 23)! How can this be? Notice that over the estimated useful lives of these assets, the company has built up accumulated depreciation of about $21.1 billion (line 17), indicating that the assets are more than half used up as of that date ($21,141/$40,691 = 52%). The net book value of FedEx's property and equipment is about $19.6 billion (line 18). The company also owns about $3.8 billion in goodwill and other tangible and intangible long-term assets (line 22). When you complete this chapter, you will understand better what these terms and concepts mean. ●

A1		

	A	B	C
1	**FedEx Corporation** **Consolidated Balance Sheets (Partial, Adapted)**		
2	**(In millions of $)**	**May 31, 2014**	**May 31, 2013**
3	**CURRENT ASSETS**		
4	Cash and cash equivalents	$ 2,908	$ 4,917
5	Receivables, less allowances of $164 and $176	5,460	5,044
6	Spare parts, supplies and fuel, less allowances	463	457
7	Deferred income taxes	522	533
8	Prepaid expenses and other	330	323
9	Total current assets	9,683	11,274
10	**PROPERTY AND EQUIPMENT, AT COST**		
11	Aircraft and related equipment	15,632	14,716
12	Package handling and ground support equipment	7,196	6,452
13	Computer and electronic equipment	5,169	4,958
14	Vehicles	4,400	4,080
15	Facilities and other	8,294	7,903
16	Gross property and equipment	40,691	38,109
17	Less accumulated depreciation and amortization	(21,141)	(19,625)
18	Net property and equipment	19,550	18,484
19	**OTHER LONG-TERM ASSETS**		
20	Goodwill	2,790	2,755
21	Other assets	1,047	1,054
22	Total other long-term assets	3,837	3,809
23	TOTAL ASSETS	$ 33,070	$ 33,567
24			

This chapter covers the measurement and reporting principles for long-term tangible fixed assets (also known as *plant assets* or *property and equipment*), **as well as intangible assets.** Unlike inventories that are typically bought, manufactured, and sold, fixed tangible and intangible assets are used in the business to earn a profit. This chapter also briefly covers measurement and reporting principles for natural resources, which begin as long-term assets. Then, as they are extracted or depleted, their cost is transferred to the income statement as an expense. The latter part of the chapter covers the rate of return on total assets, an important ratio that measures how profitably a company employs its assets.

LEARNING OBJECTIVES

1 **Measure and account for** the cost of plant assets

2 **Distinguish** a capital expenditure from an immediate expense

3 **Measure and record** depreciation on plant assets

4 **Analyze** the effect of a plant asset disposal

5 **Apply** GAAP for natural resources and intangible assets

6 **Explain** the effect of an asset impairment on the financial statements

7 **Analyze** rate of return on assets

8 **Analyze** the cash flow impact of long-lived asset transactions

You can access the most current annual report of FedEx Corporation in Excel format at **http://www.sec.gov**. Using the "FILINGS" link on the toolbar at the top of the home page, select "Company Filings Search." This will take you to the "EDGAR Company Filings" page. Type "FedEx" in the company name box, and select "Search." This will produce the "EDGAR Search Results" page showing the company name. Click on the "CIK" link beside the company name. This will pull up a list of the reports the company has filed with the SEC. Under the "Filing Type" box, type "10-K" and click the search box. Form 10-K is the SEC form for the company's annual report. Find the year that you wish to view. Click on the "Interactive Data" box, which takes you to the "View Filing Data" page. Find and click on the "View Excel Document" link at the top of this page. You may choose to either open or download the Excel files containing the company's most recent financial statements.

Businesses use several types of long-lived assets. We show these assets in Exhibit 7-1, along with the expense account that is typically associated with each one. For example, buildings, airplanes, and equipment depreciate. Natural resources deplete (often through cost of goods sold), and intangible assets are amortized.

Exhibit 7-1 | Long-Lived Assets and Related Expense Accounts

Asset Account (Balance Sheet)	Related Expense Account (Income Statement)
Plant Assets	
Land	None
Buildings, Machinery, and Equipment	Depreciation Expense
Furniture and Fixtures	Depreciation Expense
Land Improvements	Depreciation Expense
Natural Resources	Depletion Expense (through cost of goods sold)
Intangible Assets	Amortization Expense

■ *Plant assets* (also known as *property, plant, and equipment* or *fixed assets*) are long-lived assets that are tangible—for instance, land, buildings, and equipment. The expense associated with plant assets is called *depreciation expense*. Of the plant assets, land is unique. Land is not expensed over time because its usefulness does not decrease. Most companies report plant assets as property, plant, and equipment on the balance sheet. **FedEx** uses the heading Property and Equipment in its balance sheet shown on page 372 (lines 10–18).

■ *Natural resources* such as oil and gas reserves, coal mines, or stands of timber, are accounted for as long-term assets when they are purchased or developed. As the natural resource is extracted, its cost is transferred to inventory. Later, as the inventory is sold, its cost is transferred to cost of goods sold in a manner similar to that described in Chapter 6.

■ *Intangible assets* are useful because of the special rights they carry. They have no physical form. Patents, copyrights, and trademarks are intangible assets, as is goodwill. Accounting for intangibles is similar to accounting for plant assets. FedEx reports Goodwill and Other Assets on its balance sheet (lines 20 and 21).

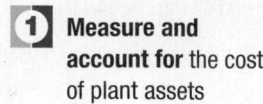

Measure and account for the cost of plant assets

MEASURE AND ACCOUNT FOR THE COST OF PLANT ASSETS

Here is the basic working rule for measuring the cost of an asset:

The cost of any asset is the sum of all the costs incurred to bring the asset to its intended use.

The cost of a plant asset includes purchase price, plus any taxes, commissions, and other amounts paid to make the asset ready for use. Because the specific costs differ for the various types of plant assets, we discuss the major groups individually.

Land

The cost of land includes its purchase price (cash plus any note payable given); brokerage commission, survey fees, legal fees; and any back property taxes that the purchaser pays. Land cost also includes expenditures for grading and clearing the land and for removing unwanted buildings.

The cost of land does *not* include the cost of fencing, paving, security systems, and lighting. These are separate plant assets—called *land improvements*—and they are subject to depreciation.

Suppose FedEx signs a $300,000 note payable to purchase 20 acres of land for a new shipping site. FedEx also pays $10,000 for real estate commission, $8,000 of back property tax, $5,000 for removal of an old building, a $1,000 survey fee, and $260,000 to pave the parking lot—all in cash. What is FedEx's cost of this land?

Purchase price of land		$300,000
Add related costs:		
Real estate commission	$10,000	
Back property tax........................	8,000	
Removal of building....................	5,000	
Survey fee....................................	1,000	
Total related costs......................		24,000
Total cost of land..........................		$324,000

Note that the cost to pave the parking lot, $260,000, is *not* included in the land's cost, because the pavement is a land improvement. FedEx would record the purchase of this land as follows:

	A	B	C	D
1		Land	324,000	
2		Note Payable		300,000
3		Cash		24,000
4				

Assets	=	Liabilities	+	Stockholders' Equity
+ 324,000 − 24,000	=	+ 300,000	+	0

This purchase of land increases both assets and liabilities. There is no effect on equity.

Buildings, Machinery, and Equipment

The cost of constructing a building includes architectural fees, building permits, contractors' charges, and payments for material, labor, and overhead. If the company constructs its own building, the cost will also include the cost of interest on money borrowed to finance the construction.

When an existing building (new or old) is purchased, its cost includes the purchase price, brokerage commission, sales and other taxes paid, and all expenditures to repair and renovate the building for its intended purpose.

The cost of FedEx's package-handling equipment includes its purchase price (less any discounts), plus transportation from the seller to FedEx, insurance while in transit, sales and other taxes, purchase commission, installation costs, and any expenditures to test the asset before it's placed in service. The equipment cost will also include the cost of any special platforms. Then, after the asset is up and running, insurance, taxes, and maintenance costs are recorded as expenses, not as part of the asset's cost.

Land Improvements and Leasehold Improvements

For a FedEx shipping terminal, the cost to pave a parking lot ($260,000) would be recorded in a separate account entitled Land Improvements. This account includes costs for such other items as driveways, signs, fences, and sprinkler systems. Although these assets are located on the land, they are subject to decay, and their cost should therefore be depreciated.

FedEx may lease some of its airplanes and other assets. The company customizes these assets for its special needs. For example, FedEx paints its logo on delivery trucks. These improvements are assets of FedEx even though the company may not own the truck. The cost of leasehold improvements should be depreciated over the shorter of the useful life of the improvement or the term of the lease. Most companies call the depreciation on leasehold improvements *amortization*, which is a similar concept to *depreciation*.

Lump-Sum (or Basket) Purchases of Assets

Businesses often purchase several assets as a group, or a "basket," for a single lump-sum amount. For example, FedEx may pay one price for land and a building. The company must identify the cost of each asset. The total cost is divided among the assets according to their relative sales (or market) values. This technique is called the *relative-sales-value method*.

Suppose FedEx purchases land and a building in Denver. The building sits on two acres of land, and the combined purchase price of land and building is $2,800,000. An appraisal indicates that the land's market value is $300,000 and that the building's market value is $2,700,000.

FedEx first figures the ratio of each asset's market value to the total market value. Total appraised value is $2,700,000 + $300,000 = $3,000,000. Thus, the land, valued at $300,000, is 10% of the total market value. The building's appraised value is 90% of the total. These percentages are then used to determine the cost of each asset:

Asset	Market (Sales) Value		Total Market Value		Percentage of Total Market Value		Total Cost	Cost of Each Asset
Land	$ 300,000	÷	$3,000,000	=	10%	× $2,800,000		$ 280,000
Building	2,700,000	÷	3,000,000	=	90%	× $2,800,000		2,520,000
Total	$3,000,000				100%			$2,800,000

If FedEx pays cash, the entry to record the purchase of the land and building is

	A1	◆				
	A		B		C	D
1		Land			280,000	
2		Building			2,520,000	
3		Cash				2,800,000
4						

Assets	=	Liabilities	+	Stockholders' Equity
+ 280,000	=			
+ 2,520,000	=	0	+	0
− 2,800,000	=			

Total assets don't change—it is merely the makeup of FedEx's assets that changes.

Try It

How would FedEx divide a $120,000 lump-sum purchase price for land, building, and equipment with estimated market values of $40,000, $95,000, and $15,000, respectively?

Answer:

	Estimated Market Value	Percentage of Total Market Value	×	Total Cost	=	Cost of Each Asset
Land..................	$ 40,000	26.7%*	×	$120,000	=	$ 32,040
Building.............	95,000	63.3%	×	$120,000	=	75,960
Equipment.........	15,000	10.0%	×	$120,000	=	12,000
Total	$150,000	100.0%				$120,000

*$40,000/$150,000 = 0.267, and so on

DISTINGUISH A CAPITAL EXPENDITURE FROM AN IMMEDIATE EXPENSE

2 **Distinguish** a capital expenditure from an immediate expense

When a company spends money on a plant asset, it must decide whether to record an asset or an expense. Examples of these expenditures range from FedEx's purchase of an airplane to replacing the tires on a FedEx truck.

Expenditures that increase the asset's capacity or extend its useful life are called **capital expenditures**. For example, the cost of a major overhaul that extends the useful life of a FedEx truck is a capital expenditure. Capital expenditures are said to be *capitalized, which means the cost is added to an asset account* and not expensed immediately. A major decision in accounting for plant assets is whether to capitalize or to expense a certain cost.

Costs that do not extend the asset's capacity or its useful life, but merely maintain the asset or restore it to working order, are recorded as expenses. For example, Repair Expense is reported on the income statement and matched against revenue. The costs of repainting a FedEx delivery truck, repairing a dented fender, and replacing tires are also expensed immediately. Exhibit 7-2 shows the distinction between capital expenditures and immediate expenses for ordinary repairs.

Exhibit 7-2 | Capital Expenditures vs. Immediate Expenses

Record an Asset for Capital Expenditures	Record Repair and Maintenance Expense (Not an Asset) for an Expense
Extraordinary repairs:	Ordinary repairs:
Major engine overhaul	Repair of transmission or other mechanism
Modification of body for new use of truck	Oil change, lubrication, and so on
Addition to storage capacity of truck	Replacement of tires and windshield, or a paint job

The distinction between a capital expenditure (a long-term asset) and an immediate expense requires judgment: Does the cost extend the asset's usefulness or its useful life? If so, record an asset. If the cost merely maintains the asset in its present condition or returns it to its prior condition, then record an expense.

Most companies expense all small (immaterial) costs (say, below $1,000) regardless of whether the costs are capital in nature. For larger (material) costs, they follow the capitalization rule stated in the previous paragraph. A conservative policy is one that avoids overstating assets and profits. A company that overstates its assets may eventually have to defend itself in court if investors or creditors lose money because of the company's improper accounting practices.

Accounting errors sometimes occur for plant asset costs. For example, a company may

- expense a cost that should have been capitalized. This error overstates expenses and understates net income in the year of the error.

- capitalize a cost that should have been expensed. This error understates expenses and overstates net income in the year of the error.

COOKING THE BOOKS
by Improper Capitalization

WorldCom

It is one thing to accidentally capitalize a plant asset instead of expensing it, but quite another to do it intentionally, thus deliberately overstating assets, understating expenses, and overstating net income. One well-known company committed one of the biggest financial statement frauds in U.S. history in this way.

In 2002, WorldCom, Inc., was one of the largest telecommunications service providers in the world. The company had grown rapidly from a small, regional telephone company in 1983 to a giant corporation in 2002 by acquiring an ever-increasing number of other such companies. But 2002 was a bad year for WorldCom, as well as for many others in the telecom industry. The United States was reeling from the effects of a deep economic recession spawned by the "bursting dot-com bubble" in 2000 and intensified by the terrorist attacks on U.S. soil in 2001. Wall Street was looking high and low for positive signs, pressuring public companies to keep profits trending upward in order to support share prices, without much success, at least for the honest companies.

Bernard J. ("Bernie") Ebbers, WorldCom's chief executive officer, was worried. He began to press his chief financial officer, Scott Sullivan, to find a way to make the company's income statement look healthier. After all legitimate attempts to improve earnings failed, Sullivan concocted a scheme to cook the books.

Like all telecommunications companies, WorldCom had signed contracts with other telephone companies, paying them fees so that WorldCom customers could use their lines for telephone calls and Internet activity. Generally accepted accounting principles (GAAP) require such fees to be expensed as incurred, rather than capitalized. Overestimating the growth of its business, WorldCom had incurred billions of dollars in such costs, about 15% more than its customers would ever use.

In direct violation of GAAP, Sullivan rationalized that the excessive amounts WorldCom had spent on line costs would eventually lead to the company's recognizing revenue in future years (thus extending their usefulness and justifying, in his mind, their classification as assets). Sullivan directed the accountants working under him to reclassify line costs as property, plant, and equipment assets, rather than as expenses, and to amortize (spread) the costs over several years rather than to expense them in the periods in which they were incurred. Over several quarters, Mr. Sullivan and his assistants transferred a total of $3.1 billion in such charges from operating expense accounts to property, plant, and equipment, resulting in the transformation of what would have been a net loss for all of 2001 and the first quarter of 2002 into a sizeable profit. It was the largest single fraud in U.S. history to that point.

Sullivan's fraudulent scheme was discovered by the company's internal audit staff during a routine spot-check of the company's records for capital expenditures. The staff members reported Sullivan's (and his staff's) fraudulent activities to the head of the company's audit committee and its external auditor, setting in motion a chain of events that resulted in Ebbers' and Sullivan's firings and the company's eventual bankruptcy. Ebbers, Sullivan, and several of their assistants went to prison for their participation in this fraudulent scheme.

Shareholders of WorldCom lost billions of dollars in share value when the company went down, and more than 500,000 people lost their jobs.

The WorldCom scandal rocked the financial world, causing global stock markets to plummet from lack of confidence. This prompted action on the part of the U.S. Congress and President George W. Bush that eventually led to the passage of the Sarbanes-Oxley Act of 2002, the most significant piece of shareholder protection legislation since the Great Depression in the 1930s.

MEASURE AND RECORD DEPRECIATION ON PLANT ASSETS

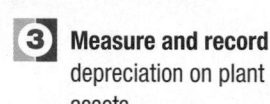
3 **Measure and record** depreciation on plant assets

As we've seen in previous chapters, plant assets are reported on the balance sheet at book value, which is calculated as follows:

$$\text{Book Value of a Plant Asset} = \text{Cost} - \text{Accumulated Depreciation}$$

Plant assets wear out, grow obsolete, and lose value over time. To account for this process, we allocate a plant asset's cost to expense over its life—a process called *depreciation*. The depreciation process follows the expense recognition principle discussed in Chapter 3. Depreciation apportions the cost of using a fixed asset over time by allocating a portion of that cost against the revenue the asset helps earn each period. Exhibit 7-3 illustrates the accounting for a Boeing 737 jet by FedEx.

Exhibit 7-3 | Depreciation: Allocating Costs to Periods in Which Revenues Are Generated

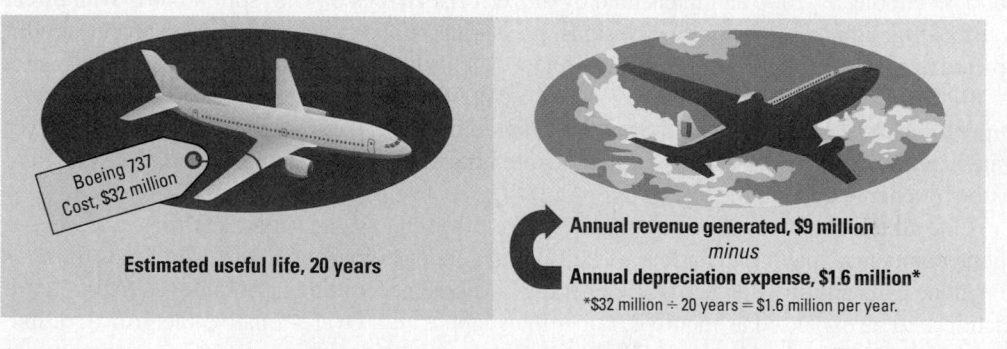

Recall that depreciation expense (not accumulated depreciation) is reported on the income statement.

Only land has an unlimited life and is not depreciated for accounting purposes. For most plant assets, depreciation is caused by one of the following:

- *Physical wear and tear.* For example, physical deterioration takes its toll on the usefulness of FedEx airplanes, equipment, delivery trucks, and buildings.

- *Obsolescence.* Computers and other electronic equipment may become *obsolete* before they deteriorate. An asset is obsolete when another asset can do the job more efficiently. An asset's useful life may be shorter than its physical life. FedEx and other companies depreciate their computers over a short period of time—perhaps four years—even though the computers will remain in working condition much longer.

Suppose FedEx buys a computer for use in tracking packages. FedEx believes it will get four years of service from the computer, which will then be worthless. Under straight-line depreciation, FedEx expenses one-quarter of the asset's cost in each of its four years of use.

You've just seen what depreciation is. Let's see what depreciation is *not*.

1. *Depreciation is not a process of valuation.* Businesses do *not* record depreciation based on changes in the market value of their plant assets. Instead, businesses allocate the asset's *cost* to the periods of its useful life.

2. *Depreciation does not mean setting aside cash to replace assets as they wear out.* Any cash fund is entirely separate from depreciation.

How to Measure Depreciation

To measure depreciation for a plant asset, we must know three things about it:

1. Cost
2. Estimated useful life
3. Estimated residual value

We have discussed cost, which is a known amount. The other two factors must be estimated.

Estimated useful life is the length of service expected from using the asset. Useful life may be expressed in years, units of output, miles, or some other measure. For example, the useful life of a building is stated in years. The useful life of a FedEx airplane or delivery truck may be expressed as the number of miles the vehicle is expected to travel. Companies base these estimates on their experience and on trade publications.

Estimated residual value—also called *scrap value* or *salvage value*—is the expected cash value of an asset at the end of its useful life. For example, FedEx may believe that a package-handling machine will be useful for seven years. After that time, FedEx may expect to sell the machine as scrap metal. The amount FedEx believes it can get for the machine at disposal is the estimated residual value. In computing depreciation, the estimated residual value is *not* depreciated because FedEx expects to receive this amount from selling the asset. If there's no expected residual value, the full cost of the asset is depreciated. A plant asset's **depreciable cost** is measured as follows:

$$\text{Depreciable Cost} = \text{Asset's cost} - \text{Estimated residual value}$$

Depreciation Methods

There are three main depreciation methods:

- Straight line
- Units of production
- Double-declining balance—an accelerated depreciation method

These methods allocate different amounts of depreciation to each period. However, they all result in the same total amount of depreciation, which is the asset's depreciable cost. Exhibit 7-4 presents the data we use to illustrate depreciation computations for a FedEx truck.

Exhibit 7-4 | Depreciation Computation Data

Data Item	Amount
Cost of truck..	$41,000
Less: Estimated residual value...............	(1,000)
Depreciable cost....................................	$40,000
Estimated useful life:	
Years..	5 years
Units of production	100,000 units [miles]

Straight-Line Method. In the **straight-line method**, an equal amount of depreciation is assigned to each year (or period) of asset use. Depreciable cost is divided by useful life in years to determine the annual depreciation expense. Applied to the FedEx truck data from Exhibit 7-4, straight-line depreciation is

$$\text{Straight-line depreciation per year} = \frac{\text{Cost} - \text{Residual value}}{\text{Useful life, in years}}$$

$$= \frac{\$41,000 - \$1,000}{5}$$

$$= \$8,000$$

The entry to record depreciation is

	A	B	C	D
1		Depreciation Expense—Truck	8,000	
2		Accumulated Depreciation—Truck		8,000
3				

Assets	=	Liabilities	+	Stockholders' Equity	−	Expenses
− 8,000	=	0				− 8,000

Observe that depreciation decreases the asset (through Accumulated Depreciation) and also decreases equity (through Depreciation Expense). Let's assume that FedEx purchased this truck on January 1, 2013. Assume that FedEx's accounting year ends on December 31. Exhibit 7-5 gives a *straight-line depreciation schedule* for the truck. The final column of the exhibit shows the *asset's book value*, which is cost less accumulated depreciation.

Exhibit 7-5 | Straight-Line Depreciation Schedule for Truck

	A	B	C	D	E	F	G
1	Date	Cost	Rate*	Depreciable Cost	Yearly Expense	Accum. Deprec.	Book Value
2	1/1/2013	41,000		40,000			41,000
3	12/31/2013		0.2	40,000	8,000	8,000	33,000
4	12/31/2014		0.2	40,000	8,000	16,000	25,000
5	12/31/2015		0.2	40,000	8,000	24,000	17,000
6	12/31/2016		0.2	40,000	8,000	32,000	9,000
7	12/31/2017		0.2	40,000	8,000	40,000	1,000
8							

*1/years of useful life = 1/5 = 0.2

As an asset is used in operations,

- accumulated depreciation increases.
- the book value of the asset decreases.

You can estimate the age (or the "used up" amount) of a plant asset by calculating the ratio between accumulated depreciation on a straight-line basis and cost. For example, if accumulated depreciation is $500,000 and cost is $1,000,000, the plant asset is approximately half used up. An asset's final book value is its *residual value* ($1,000 in Exhibit 7-5). At the end of its useful life, the asset is said to be *fully depreciated*.

Building depreciation schedules such as the one in Exhibit 7-5 is easy with Excel. Use the information in Exhibit 7-4 and the formula on page 380 to help you program the cells. To construct Exhibit 7-5 in Excel:

1. Open a new workbook. In cells A1 through G1, insert column headings to correspond to those of Exhibit 7-5. You will have to adjust the column width of your spreadsheet to accommodate the headings.

2. In cells B2 and G2 (asset cost and book value), type in the original gross cost (41,000). The remainder of the cells in column B should be blank.

3. In cell A2, type in the original purchase date (1/1/2013). In cells A3 through A7, type in the year-end dates of 12/31/2013 through 12/31/2017, respectively. Change the formatting of these cells to "date."

4. In cells C3 through C7, enter the depreciation rate for each year, which is the reciprocal of the asset's useful life (1/5, or 20%). Enter .2 in cell C3 and copy this value down through cell C7.

5. In cell D2, calculate the depreciable cost of $40,000. Enter =B2−1000. Copy this value down through cell D7.

6. In cell E3, enter the formula =C3*D3. The value $8,000 should appear. Copy this formula to cells E4 through E7.

7. Column F keeps a running sum of accumulated depreciation. Start with cell F3. Enter the formula =F2+E3. $8,000 (accumulated depreciation at the end of year 1) should appear. Copy cell F3 down to cells F4 through F7. You should get the same values as you see in Exhibit 7-5.

8. Column G keeps a running calculation of the declining net book value of the asset. Start with cell G3. Freeze the value of the original cost of the asset ($41,000) in cell G2 by entering "$" before both the column and row. Then subtract the value of accumulated depreciation (cell F3). The formula in cell G3 becomes =$G$2−F3. The result should be $33,000 ($41,000 − $8,000). Copy cell G3 down through cell G7.

A FedEx sorting machine that cost $10,000 with a useful life of five years and a residual value of $2,000 was purchased on January 1. What is straight-line depreciation for each year?

Answer:

$$\$1,600 = (\$10,000 - \$2,000)/5$$

Units-of-Production Method. In the **units-of-production (UOP) method**, a fixed amount of depreciation is assigned to each *unit of output*, or service, produced by the asset. Depreciable cost is divided by useful life—in units of production—to determine this amount. This per unit depreciation expense is then multiplied by the number of units produced each period to compute depreciation. The UOP depreciation per unit of output (mile) for the FedEx truck data in Exhibit 7-4 (p. 379) is

$$\text{Units-of-production depreciation per unit of output} = \frac{\text{Cost} - \text{Residual value}}{\text{Useful life, in units of production}}$$

$$= \frac{\$41,000 - \$1,000}{100,000 \text{ miles}} = \$0.40 \text{ per mile}$$

Assume that FedEx expects to drive the truck 20,000 miles during the first year, 30,000 during the second, 25,000 during the third, 15,000 during the fourth, and 10,000 during the fifth. Exhibit 7-6 shows the UOP depreciation schedule.

Exhibit 7-6 | Units-of-Production (UOP) Depreciation Schedule for Truck

	A	B	C	D	E	F	G
1	Date	Cost	Rate per unit	Number Units	Yearly Expense	Accum. Deprec.	Book Value
2	1/1/2013	41,000					41,000
3	12/31/2013		0.4	20,000	8,000	8,000	33,000
4	12/31/2014		0.4	30,000	12,000	20,000	21,000
5	12/31/2015		0.4	25,000	10,000	30,000	11,000
6	12/31/2016		0.4	15,000	6,000	36,000	5,000
7	12/31/2017		0.4	10,000	4,000	40,000	1,000
8							

The amount of UOP depreciation varies with the number of units the asset produces. In our example, the total number of units (miles) produced is 100,000. UOP depreciation does not depend directly on time, as with the other methods.

Try It in Excel®

If you built the straight-line depreciation schedule in Exhibit 7-5 with Excel, changing the spreadsheet for units-of-production depreciation is a snap. Steps 1–3 and 6–8 are identical. Only steps 4 and 5, dealing with columns C and D, change. You might want to start by opening the straight-line schedule you prepared and saving it under another name: "units-of-production depreciation." Next, change the column headings for column C and column D. Column C should be labeled "Rate per unit." Column D should be labeled "Number Units." Assuming you do this, here are the modified steps 4 and 5 of the process we used before:

4. In column C, calculate a per unit (rather than per year as we did with straight-line) depreciation rate by dividing the depreciable cost ($41,000 − $1,000 in Exhibit 7-4) by the number of units (100,000 miles) to get a fixed depreciation rate per mile ($0.40). Enter .4 in cell C3 and copy down through cell C7.
5. In cells D3 through D7, respectively, enter the number of miles driven in years one through five of the asset's useful life. These are 20,000, 30,000, 25,000, 15,000, and 10,000, respectively.

All of the other amounts in the table will automatically recalculate to reflect units-of-production depreciation, exactly as shown in Exhibit 7-6.

Double-Declining-Balance Method. An **accelerated depreciation method** writes off a larger amount of the asset's cost near the start of its useful life than the straight-line method does. The **double-declining-balance (DDB) method** is the most frequently used accelerated depreciation method. It computes annual depreciation by multiplying the asset's declining book value at the beginning of the year by a constant percentage, which is two times the straight-line depreciation rate. DDB rates are computed as follows:

$$\text{DDB depreciation rate per year} = \frac{1}{\text{Useful life, in years}} \times 2$$

$$= \frac{1}{5 \text{ years}} \times 2$$

$$= 20\% \times 2 = 40\%$$

- *First*, compute the straight-line depreciation rate per year. A truck with a 5-year useful life has a straight-line depreciation rate of 1/5, or 20%, each year. An asset with a 10-year useful life has a straight-line depreciation rate of 1/10, or 10%, and so on.

- *Second*, multiply the straight-line rate by 2 to compute the DDB rate. For a 5-year asset, the DDB rate is 40% (20% × 2). A 10-year asset has a DDB rate of 20% (10% × 2). The DDB rate for the FedEx truck in our example (p. 379) is 40%.

- *Third*, multiply the DDB rate by the period's *beginning* asset book value (cost less accumulated depreciation). Under the DDB method, ignore the residual value of the asset in computing depreciation, except during the last year.

- *Fourth*, determine the final year's depreciation amount, that is, the amount needed to reduce the asset's book value to its residual value. In Exhibit 7-7, the fifth and final year's DDB depreciation is $4,314—book value, end of year (2016) of $5,314 less the $1,000 residual value. *The residual value should not be depreciated* but should remain on the books until the asset is disposed of.

Exhibit 7-7 | Double-Declining-Balance (DDB) Depreciation Schedule for Truck

	A	B	C	D	E	F
	Date	**Cost**	**DDB Rate**	**Yearly Expense**	**Accum. Deprec.**	**Book Value**
1						
2	1/1/2013	41,000				41,000
3	12/31/2013		0.4	16,400	16,400	24,600
4	12/31/2014		0.4	9,840	26,240	14,760
5	12/31/2015		0.4	5,904	32,144	8,856
6	12/31/2016		0.4	3,542	35,686	5,314
7	12/31/2017		0.4	4,314	40,000	1,000*
8						

* Final-year depreciation is a plug amount needed to reduce asset book value to estimated salvage value

Try it in Excel®

If you built the straight-line and UOP depreciation schedules in Exhibits 7-5 and 7-6 with Excel, changing the spreadsheet for double-declining-balance (DDB) depreciation is easy. Steps 1–3 and 7–8 are identical. The other steps differ only slightly. You might want to start by opening the straight-line schedule you prepared and saving it under another name: "DDB depreciation." Next, change the column heading for column C to "DDB Rate." Right-click on column D (labeled "depreciable cost" in Exhibit 7-5) and delete the entire column. This moves the "yearly expense" over to column D. Here are modified steps 4 and 5 of the process we used for the straight-line rate, which replace steps 4–6 for the straight-line method:

4. In column C, calculate a new depreciation rate, which is double the straight-line rate. In our example, the straight-line rate is 20% per year. The DDB rate is 40% (2 × 20%). Enter .4 in cell C3 and copy down through cell C7.

5. Column D now contains a calculated amount for yearly depreciation expense. The yearly depreciation expense is the product of the previous book value of the asset (in column F) times the DDB rate (in column C). For 2013, depreciation expense is $16,400, which is calculated in Excel as =F2*C3. Enter this formula in cell D3. Your result should be $16,400. Copy this formula down through cell D6 (*not* cell D7, for reasons explained on the next page).

All of the other amounts in the table through line 6 will automatically recalculate to reflect DDB depreciation, exactly as shown in Exhibit 7-7.

The DDB method differs from the other methods in two ways:

1. Residual value is ignored initially; first-year depreciation is computed on the asset's full cost.

2. Depreciation expense in the final year is the "plug" amount needed to reduce the asset's book value to the residual amount. For this reason, depreciation expense in cell D7 of your Excel table should be 4,314, which is the amount needed to reduce the final book value to the residual amount of $1,000.

»» Try It

What is the DDB depreciation each year for the asset in the Try It on page 381?

Answers:

Yr. 1: $4,000 ($10,000 × 40%)
Yr. 2: $2,400 ($6,000 × 40%)
Yr. 3: $1,440 ($3,600 × 40%)
Yr. 4: $160 ($10,000 − $4,000 − $2,400 − $1,440 − $2,000 = $160)*
Yr. 5: $0

*The asset is not depreciated below residual value of $2,000.

Comparing Depreciation Methods

Let's compare the three methods in terms of the yearly amount of depreciation. The yearly amount varies by method, but the total $40,000 depreciable cost is the same under all methods.

	Amount of Depreciation per Year		
Year	Straight-Line	Units-of-Production	Accelerated Method Double-Declining Balance
1	$ 8,000	$ 8,000	$16,400
2	8,000	12,000	9,840
3	8,000	10,000	5,904
4	8,000	6,000	3,542
5	8,000	4,000	4,314
Total	$40,000	$40,000	$40,000

GAAP requires expense recognition in such a way as to match an asset's depreciation against the revenue the asset produces. For a plant asset that generates revenue evenly over time, the straight-line method best meets the expense recognition principle. The units-of-production method best meets the principle for those assets that wear out because of physical use rather than obsolescence. The accelerated method (DDB) best meets the principle for those assets that generate more revenue earlier in their useful lives and less in later years.

Exhibit 7-8 graphs annual depreciation amounts for the straight-line, units-of-production, and accelerated depreciation (DDB) methods. The graph of straight-line depreciation is flat through time because annual depreciation is the same in all periods. Units-of-production depreciation follows no particular pattern because annual depreciation depends on the use of the asset. Accelerated depreciation is greatest in the first year and less in the later years.

Exhibit 7-8 | Depreciation Patterns Through Time

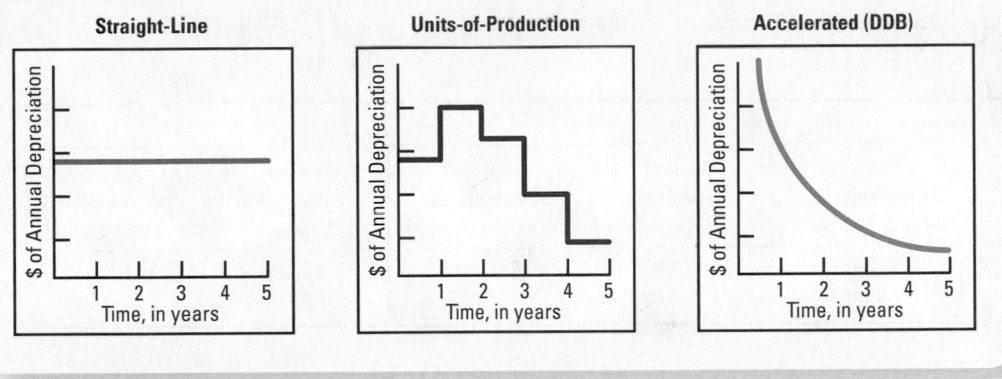

Exhibit 7-9 shows the percentage of companies that use each depreciation method from a recent survey of 600 companies conducted by the American Institute of Certified Public Accountants (AICPA).

Exhibit 7-9 | Depreciation Methods Used by 600 Companies

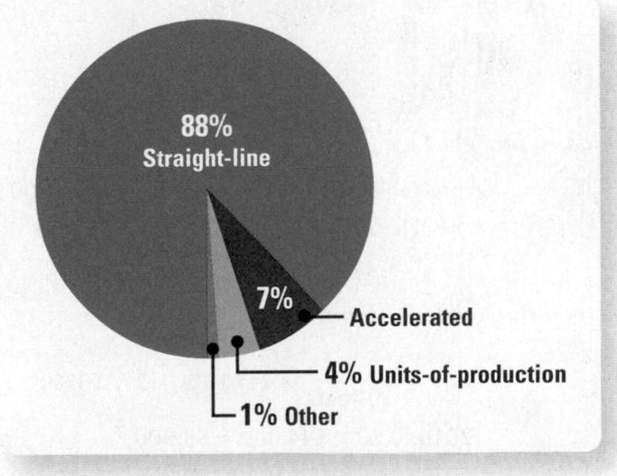

For reporting in the financial statements, straight-line depreciation is the most popular method. As we shall see, however, accelerated depreciation is most popular for income tax purposes.

Suppose FedEx purchased equipment on January 1, 2016, for $44,000. The expected useful life of the equipment is 10 years or 100,000 units of production, and its residual value is $4,000. Under three depreciation methods, the annual depreciation expense and the balance of accumulated depreciation at the end of 2016 and 2017 are

	Method A		Method B		Method C	
Year	Annual Depreciation Expense	Accumulated Depreciation	Annual Depreciation Expense	Accumulated Depreciation	Annual Depreciation Expense	Accumulated Depreciation
2016	$4,000	$4,000	$8,800	$ 8,800	$1,200	$1,200
2017	4,000	8,000	7,040	15,840	5,600	6,800

Requirements

1. Identify the depreciation method used in each instance, and show the equation and computation for each; round to the nearest dollar.

2. Assume continued use of the same method through year 2018. Determine the annual depreciation expense, accumulated depreciation, and book value of the equipment for 2016 through 2018 under each method, assuming 12,000 units of production in 2018.

Answers
Requirement 1

Method A: Straight-Line

Depreciable cost = $40,000($44,000 − $4,000)

Each year: $40,000/10 years = $4,000

Method B: Double-Declining-Balance

$$\text{Rate} = \frac{1}{10 \text{ years}} \times 2 = 10\% \times 2 = 20\%$$

2016: 0.20 × $44,000 = $8,800

2017: 0.20 × ($44,000 − $8,800) = $7,040

Method C: Units-of-Production

$$\text{Depreciation per unit} = \frac{\$44,000 - \$4,000}{100,000 \text{ units}} = \$0.40$$

2016: $0.40 × 3,000 units = $1,200

2017: $0.40 × 14,000 units = $5,600

Requirement 2

	Method A: Straight-Line		
Year	Annual Depreciation Expense	Accumulated Depreciation	Book Value
Start			$44,000
2016	$4,000	$ 4,000	40,000
2017	4,000	8,000	36,000
2018	4,000	12,000	32,000

	Method B: Double-Declining-Balance		
Year	Annual Depreciation Expense	Accumulated Depreciation	Book Value
Start			$44,000
2016	$8,800	$ 8,800	35,200
2017	7,040	15,840	28,160
2018	5,632	21,472	22,528

	Method C: Units-of-Production		
Year	Annual Depreciation Expense	Accumulated Depreciation	Book Value
Start			$44,000
2016	$1,200	$ 1,200	42,800
2017	5,600	6,800	37,200
2018	4,800	11,600	32,400

Computations for 2018	
Straight-line	$40,000/10 years = $4,000
Double-declining-balance	$28,160 × 0.20 = $5,632
Units-of-production	12,000 units × $0.40 = $4,800

Other Issues in Accounting for Plant Assets

Plant assets are complex because

- they have long lives.
- depreciation affects income taxes.
- companies may have gains or losses when they sell plant assets.
- international accounting changes in the future may affect the recognition as well as the carrying values of assets.

Depreciation for Tax Purposes

FedEx and most other companies use straight-line depreciation for reporting to stockholders and creditors on their financial statements. However, for income tax purposes they also keep a separate set of depreciation records, based on accelerated depreciation methods in the Internal Revenue Code (IRC) developed by the Internal Revenue Service (IRS). This is legal, ethical, and honest; U.S. tax law not only permits it, but expects it. The reason that different methods are typically used for financial statement and income tax purposes is that the objectives of GAAP are different from the tax-reporting objectives of the IRC. The objective of GAAP is to provide useful information for making economic decisions. The objective of the IRC is to raise sufficient revenue to pay for federal government expenditures.

CASH FLOW

Suppose you are a business manager and the IRS allows an accelerated depreciation method. Why do FedEx managers prefer accelerated over straight-line depreciation for income tax purposes? Accelerated depreciation provides the fastest tax deductions, thus decreasing immediate tax payments. FedEx can reinvest the tax savings back into the business. FedEx has a choice—pay taxes or buy equipment. This choice is easy.

To understand the relationships between cash flow, depreciation, and income tax, recall our depreciation example of a FedEx truck:

■ First-year depreciation is $8,000 under straight-line and $16,400 under double-declining-balance (DDB) method.

■ DDB is permitted for income tax purposes.

Assume that this FedEx office has $400,000 in revenue and $300,000 in cash operating expenses during the truck's first year and an income tax rate of 30%. The cash flow analysis appears in Exhibit 7-10.

Exhibit 7-10 | The Cash Flow Advantage of Accelerated Depreciation for Tax Purposes

		SL	Accelerated
1	Cash revenue	$400,000	$400,000
2	Cash operating expenses	300,000	300,000
3	Net cash provided by operations before income tax	100,000	100,000
4	Depreciation expense (a noncash expense)	8,000	16,400
5	Income before income tax	$ 92,000	$ 83,600
6	Income tax expense (30%)	$ 27,600	$ 25,080
	Cash-flow analysis:		
7	Net cash provided by operations before tax	$100,000	$100,000
8	Income tax expense	27,600	25,080
9	Net cash provided by operations	$ 72,400	$ 74,920
10	Extra cash available for investment if DDB is used ($74,920 − $72,400)		$ 2,520

You can see that, for income tax purposes, accelerated depreciation helps conserve cash for the business. That's why virtually all companies use accelerated depreciation to compute their income taxes.

There is a special depreciation method—used only for income tax purposes—called the **Modified Accelerated Cost Recovery System (MACRS)**. Under MACRS, each fixed asset is classified into one of eight classes identified by asset life (Exhibit 7-11 on the following page). Depreciation for the first four classes is computed by the double-declining-balance method. Depreciation for 15-year assets and 20-year assets is computed by the 150% declining-balance method. Under 150% DB, annual depreciation is computed by multiplying the straight-line rate by 1.50 (instead of 2.00, as for DDB). For a 20-year asset, the straight-line rate is 0.05 per year (1/20 = 0.05), so the annual MACRS depreciation rate is 0.075 (0.05 × 1.50). The taxpayer computes annual depreciation by multiplying asset book value at the beginning of the year by 0.075 in a manner similar to the way that DDB works.

The IRC permits several other rapid depreciation methods that, in some cases, permit companies to take additional "bonus depreciation" on "tangible personal property" (fixed assets that are not real estate) for tax purposes in the year of initial purchase. In other cases, a certain amount of investment in these types of fixed assets may be deducted entirely from taxable income rather than capitalized and depreciated. All of these methods are intended to provide incentives for businesses to continually reinvest in new plant and equipment, saving them cash in tax outlays and providing stimulus for the U.S. economy.

Exhibit 7-11 | Modified Accelerated Cost Recovery System (MACRS)

Class Identified by Asset Life (years)	Representative Assets	Depreciation Method
3	Race horses	DDB
5	Automobiles, light trucks, computers	DDB
7	Office furniture, fixtures	DDB
10	Other equipment	DDB
15	Sewage-treatment plants	150% DB
20	Certain real estate	150% DB
27½	Residential rental property	SL
39	Nonresidential rental property	SL

Most real estate is depreciated by the straight-line method (see the last two categories in Exhibit 7-11).

Depreciation for Partial Years

Companies purchase plant assets whenever they need them, not just at the beginning of the year. Therefore, companies must compute *depreciation for partial years*. Suppose FedEx purchases a warehouse building on September 1 for $500,000. The building's estimated life is 20 years, and its estimated residual value is $80,000. FedEx's accounting year ends on May 31. Let's consider how FedEx computes depreciation for September through May.

- First, compute depreciation for a full year (unless you are using the units-of-production method, which automatically adjusts for partial periods by merely accounting for the number of units produced in the period).

- Second, multiply full-year depreciation by the fraction of the year that you held the asset—in this case, 9/12. Assuming the straight-line method, the partial year's depreciation for this FedEx building is $15,750, calculated as follows:

$$\text{Full-year depreciation} \qquad \frac{\$500,000 - \$80,000}{20} = \$21,000$$

$$\text{Partial year depreciation} \qquad \$21,000 \times 9/12 = \$15,750$$

What if FedEx bought the asset on September 18? Many businesses record no monthly depreciation on assets purchased after the 15th of the month, and they record a full month's depreciation on an asset bought on or before the 15th.

Most companies use computerized systems to account for fixed assets. Each asset has a unique identification number, and the system will automatically calculate the asset's depreciation expense. Accumulated Depreciation is automatically updated.

Changing the Useful Life of a Depreciable Asset

After an asset is in use, managers may change its useful life on the basis of experience and new information. **The Walt Disney Company** made such a change, called a *change in accounting estimate*, several years ago. The company recalculated depreciation on the basis of revised useful lives of several of its theme park assets. The following note in the company's financial statements that year reported this change in accounting estimate:

Note 5
. . . [T]he Company extended the estimated useful lives of certain theme park ride and attraction assets based upon historical data and engineering studies. The effect of this change was to decrease depreciation by approximately $8 million (an increase in net income of approximately $4.2 million. . .).

Source: From Disney Enterprises, Inc.'s Financial Statements, 2014.

Assume that a Disney hot dog stand cost $50,000 and that the company originally believed the asset had a 10-year useful life with no residual value. Using the straight-line method, the company would record $5,000 depreciation each year ($50,000/10 years = $5,000). Suppose Disney used the asset for four years. Accumulated depreciation reached $20,000, leaving a remaining depreciable book value (cost less accumulated depreciation less residual value) of $30,000 ($50,000 − $20,000). From its experience, management believes the asset will remain useful for an *additional* 10 years. The company would spread the remaining depreciable book value over the asset's remaining life as follows:

Asset's remaining depreciable book value	÷	(New) Estimated useful life remaining	=	(New) Annual depreciation
$30,000	÷	10 years	=	$3,000

The yearly depreciation entry based on the new estimated useful life is as follows:

	A		C	D	G
1			Depreciation Expense—Hot Dog Stand	3,000	
2			Accumulated Depreciation—Hot Dog Stand		3,000
3					

Cell reference: A1

Depreciation decreases both assets and equity.

Assets	=	Liabilities	+	Stockholders' Equity	−	Expenses
− 3,000	=	0				− 3,000

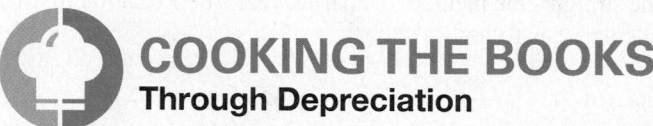

COOKING THE BOOKS
Through Depreciation

Waste Management

Since plant assets usually involve relatively large amounts and relatively large numbers of assets, sometimes a seemingly subtle change in the way they are accounted for can have a tremendous impact on the financial statements. When these changes are made in order to cook the books, the results can be devastating.

Waste Management, Inc., is North America's largest integrated waste service company, providing collection, transfer, recycling, disposal, and waste-to-energy services for commercial, industrial, municipal, and residential customers from coast to coast.

Starting in 1992, six top executives of the company, including its founder and chairman of the board, its chief financial officer, its corporate controller, its top lawyer, and its vice president of finance, decided that the company's profits were not growing fast enough to meet "earnings targets," which were tied to their executive bonuses. Among several fraudulent financial tactics these top executives employed to cook the books were (1) assigning unsupported and inflated salvage values to garbage trucks, (2) unjustifiably extending the estimated useful lives of their garbage trucks, and (3) assigning arbitrary salvage values to other fixed assets that previously had no salvage values. All of these tactics had the effect of decreasing the amount of depreciation expense in the income statements and increasing net income by a corresponding amount. While practices like this might seem relatively subtle and even insignificant when performed on an individual asset, remember that there were thousands of trash trucks and dumpsters involved, so the dollar amount grew huge in a short time. In addition, the company continued these practices for five years, overstating earnings by $1.7 billion.

The Waste Management fraud was the largest of its kind in history until the WorldCom scandal, discussed earlier in this chapter. In 1997, the company fired the officers involved and hired a new CEO who ordered a review of these practices, which uncovered the fraud. In the meantime, these dishonest executives had profited handsomely, receiving performance-based bonuses based on the company's inflated earnings, retaining their high-paying jobs, and receiving enhanced retirement benefits. One of the executives took the fraud to another level. Just 10 days before the fraud was disclosed, he enriched himself with a tax benefit by donating inflated company stock to his alma mater to fund a building in his name! Although the men involved were sued for monetary damages, none of them ever went to jail.

When the fraud was disclosed, Waste Management shareholders lost over $6 billion in the market value of their investments as the stock price plummeted by more than 33%. The company and these officers eventually settled civil lawsuits for approximately $700 million because of the fraud.

You might ask, "Where were the auditors while this was occurring?" The company's auditor was Arthur Andersen, LLP, whose partners involved on the audit engagement were eventually found to be complicit in the scheme. In fact, a few of the Waste Management officers who perpetrated the scheme had been ex-partners of the audit firm. As it turns out, the auditors actually identified many of the improper accounting practices of Waste Management. However, rather than insisting that the company fix the errors, or risk exposure, they merely "persuaded" management to agree not to repeat these practices in the future and entered into an agreement with them to write off the accumulated balance sheet overstatement over a period of 10 years. In June 2001, the SEC fined Arthur Andersen $7 million for "knowingly and recklessly issuing false and misleading audit reports" for Waste Management from 1993 through 1996.

In October 2001, immediately on the heels of these disclosures, the notorious Enron scandal broke. Enron, as well as WorldCom, were Arthur Andersen clients at the time. The Enron scandal finally put the firm out of business. Many people feel that, had it not been for Andersen's involvement in the Waste Management affair, the SEC might have been more lenient toward the company in the Enron scandal.

The Enron scandal is discussed in Chapter 10.

Fully Depreciated Assets

A *fully depreciated asset* is one that has reached the end of its estimated useful life. Suppose FedEx has fully depreciated equipment with zero residual value (cost was $60,000). FedEx accounts will appear as follows:

Equipment			Accumulated Depreciation			
60,000		−		60,000	=	Book value $0

The equipment's book value is zero, but that doesn't mean the equipment is worthless. FedEx may use the equipment for a few more years, but FedEx will not record any more depreciation on a fully depreciated asset.

When FedEx disposes of the equipment, FedEx will remove both the asset's cost ($60,000) and its accumulated depreciation ($60,000) from the books. The next section shows how to account for plant asset disposals.

ANALYZE THE EFFECT OF A PLANT ASSET DISPOSAL

Eventually, a plant asset ceases to serve a company's needs. The asset may wear out or become obsolete. Before accounting for the disposal of the asset, the business should bring depreciation up to date to

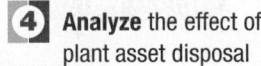 **4** **Analyze** the effect of a plant asset disposal

- measure the asset's final book value, and
- record the expense up to the date of disposal.

Disposing of a Fully Depreciated Asset for No Proceeds

To account for disposal, remove the asset and its related accumulated depreciation from the books. Suppose the final year's depreciation expense has just been recorded for a machine that cost $60,000 and is estimated to have zero residual value. The machine's accumulated depreciation thus totals $60,000. Assuming that this asset is junked, the entry to record its disposal is as follows:

	A	C	D	G
1		Accumulated Depreciation—Machinery	60,000	
2		Machinery		60,000
3		To dispose of a fully depreciated machine.		
4				

Assets	=	Liabilities	+	Stockholders' Equity
+ 60,000	=	0	+	0
− 60,000				

There is no gain or loss on this disposal, and there's no effect on total assets, liabilities, or equity.

If assets are disposed of for no proceeds before being fully depreciated, the company incurs a loss on the disposal in the amount of the asset's net book value. Suppose FedEx disposes of equipment that cost $60,000. This asset's accumulated depreciation is $50,000, and book value is, therefore, $10,000. Junking this equipment results in a loss equal to the book value of the asset:

	A	C	D	G
1		Accumulated Depreciation—Equipment	50,000	
2		Loss on Disposal of Equipment	10,000	
3		Equipment		60,000
4		To dispose of equipment.		
5				

Assets	=	Liabilities	+	Stockholders' Equity	−	Losses
+ 50,000	=	0				− 10,000
− 60,000						

FedEx disposed of an asset with $10,000 book value and received nothing. The result is a $10,000 loss, which decreases both total assets and equity.

The Loss on Disposal of Equipment is reported as Other income (expense) on the income statement. Losses decrease net income exactly as expenses do. Gains increase net income the same as revenues.

Selling a Plant Asset

Suppose FedEx sells equipment on September 30, 2016, for $7,300 cash. The equipment cost $10,000 when purchased on January 1, 2013, and has been depreciated straight-line. FedEx estimated a 10-year useful life and no residual value. Prior to recording the sale, FedEx accountants must update the asset's depreciation. Assume that FedEx uses the calendar year as its accounting period. Partial-year depreciation must be recorded for the asset's depreciation from January 1, 2016, to the sale date. The straight-line depreciation entry at September 30, 2016, is

	A1		
	A	C	D	G
1	Sep 30	Depreciation Expense ($10,000/10 years × 9/12)	750	
2		Accumulated Depreciation—Equipment		750
3		*To update depreciation.*		
4				

The Equipment account and the Accumulated Depreciation—Equipment account appear as follows. Observe that the equipment's book value is $6,250 ($10,000 − $3,750).

Equipment		Accumulated Depreciation—Equipment	
Jan 1, 2013 10,000	−	Dec 31, 2013 1,000	
		Dec 31, 2014 1,000	= Book value
		Dec 31, 2015 1,000	$6,250
		Sep 30, 2016 750	
		Balance 3,750	

The gain on the sale of the equipment for $7,300 is $1,050, computed as

Cash received from sale of the asset		$7,300
Book value of asset sold:		
Cost	$10,000	
Less: Accumulated depreciation	(3,750)	6,250
Gain on sale of the asset................................		$1,050

The entry to record sale of the equipment is

	A1		
	A	C	D	G
1	Sep 30	Cash	7,300	
2		Accumulated Depreciation—Equipment	3,750	
3		Equipment		10,000
4		Gain on Sale of Equipment		1,050
5		*To sell equipment.*		
6				

Total assets increase, and so does equity—by the amount of the gain.

Assets	=	Liabilities	−	Stockholders' Equity	+	Gains
+ 7,300						
+ 3,750	=	0			+	1,050
−10,000						

Gains and losses on asset disposals appear as Other income (expense), or Other gains (losses), on the income statement.

Exchanging a Plant Asset

Managers often trade in old assets for new ones. This is called a *nonmonetary exchange*. The accounting for nonmonetary exchanges is based on the *fair values of the assets involved*. Thus, the cost of an asset like plant and equipment received in a nonmonetary exchange is equal to the fair values of the assets given up (including the old asset and any cash paid). Any difference between the fair value of the old asset from its book value is recognized as gain (fair value of old asset exceeds book value) or loss (book value of old asset exceeds fair value) on the exchange. For example, assume Papa John's Pizza's

- old delivery car cost $9,000 and has accumulated depreciation of $8,000. Thus, the old car's book value is $1,000.

Assume Papa John's trades in the old automobile for a new one with a fair market value of $15,000 and pays cash of $10,000. Thus, the implied fair value of the old car is $5,000 ($15,000 − $10,000). This amount is treated as cash received by the business for the old vehicle.

- The cost of the new delivery car is $15,000 (fair value of the old asset, $5,000, plus cash paid, $10,000).

The pizzeria records the exchange transaction:

	A1				
	A	C		D	G
1		Delivery Auto (new)		15,000	
2		Accumulated Depreciation—Delivery Auto (old)		8,000	
3		Delivery Auto (old)			9,000
4		Cash			10,000
5		Gain on Exchange of Delivery Auto			4,000
6		*Traded in old delivery car for new auto.*			
7					

Assets	=	Liabilities	+	Stockholders' Equity	+	Gains
+15,000						
+ 8,000	=	0			+	4,000
− 9,000						
−10,000						

There was a net increase in total assets of $4,000 and a corresponding increase in stockholders' equity to reflect the gain on the exchange. Notice that this amount represents the excess of the fair value of the old asset ($5,000) over its book value ($1,000). Some special rules may apply here, but they are reserved for more advanced courses.

T-Accounts for Analyzing Plant Asset Transactions

You can perform quite a bit of analysis if you know how transactions affect the plant asset accounts. Here are the accounts with descriptions of the activity in each account.

Building (or Equipment)	
Beg bal	
Cost of assets purchased	Cost of assets disposed of
End bal	

Accumulated Depreciation	
Accumulated depreciation of assets disposed of	Beg bal
	Depreciation expense for the current period
	End bal

Cash	
Cash proceeds for assets disposed of	Cash paid for assets purchased

Long-Term Debt	
	New Debt incurred for assets purchased

Depreciation Expense	
Depreciation expense for the current period	

Gain on Sale of Building (or Equipment)	
	Gain on sale

Loss on Sale of Building (or Equipment)	
Loss on sale	

You can analyze transactions as they flow through these accounts to answer very useful questions such as the amount of cash paid to purchase new plant assets, the amount of cash proceeds from disposal of plant assets, the cost of assets purchased, and the gross cost as well as net book value of assets disposed of.

Example: Suppose you started the year with buildings that cost $100,000. During the year, you bought another building for $150,000 and ended the year with buildings that cost $180,000. What was the cost of the building you sold?

Building			
Beg bal	100,000		
Cost of assets purchased	150,000	Cost of assets sold	X = 70,000*
End bal	180,000		

*X = 100,000 + 150,000 − 180,000

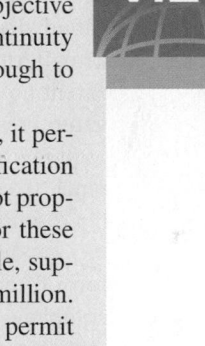

GLOBAL VIEW

One of the most significant differences between U.S. GAAP and International Financial Reporting Standards (IFRS) is the permitted reported carrying values of property, plant, and equipment. Recall from Chapter 1 that U.S. GAAP has long advocated the historical cost principle as most appropriate for plant assets because it results in a more objective (nonbiased) and therefore more reliable (auditable) figure. It also supports the continuity assumption, which states that we expect the entity to remain in business long enough to recover the cost of its plant assets through depreciation.

In contrast, while historical cost is the primary basis of accounting under IFRS, it permits the periodic revaluation of plant assets to fair market value. The primary justification for this position is that the historical cost of plant assets purchased years ago does not properly reflect their current values. Thus, the amounts shown on the balance sheet for these assets do not reflect a relevant measure of what these assets are worth. For example, suppose a business bought a building in downtown Orlando, Florida, in 1960 for $1 million. Assume that this year the building has been appraised for $20 million. IFRS would permit the company periodically to revalue the building on its balance sheet. In this case, the building account would be debited for $19 million, and an offsetting credit would be made to "revaluation surplus" which is a separate account in stockholders' equity. Depreciation from this point forward would be based on the revalued amount in the asset account. In the future, if the fair value of the building goes down, the building account could be credited, and revaluation surplus reduced by an offsetting amount.

The primary objection to the use of fair values on the balance sheet for plant assets is that these values are subjective and subject to change, sometimes quite rapidly. Consider, for example, residential and commercial real estate in California during the credit crisis of 2008 and 2009. The fair market values of these assets dropped by double-digit percentages in a period of less than one year. If these assets had been valued at fair market values on the books of the companies that held them, assets would have to have been adjusted accordingly, causing the balance sheet amounts to fluctuate wildly. Furthermore, if the assets had been depreciated, it is likely that both the depreciation expense and accumulated depreciation would also have had to be adjusted more frequently.

IFRS also differs substantially from U.S. GAAP with respect to accounting for depreciation. Whereas U.S. GAAP depreciates each asset as a composite whole (a building, manufactured equipment, an aircraft, etc.), IFRS uses a "components" approach. For example, suppose a company builds and owns a building that it is using for its operations. The total cost of the building, including all components (air-conditioning systems, roofing, duct work, plumbing, lighting systems, etc.) is $15 million. U.S. GAAP usually treats the building as a single composite asset within the class of buildings, with an estimated useful life of about 40 years that it depreciates using straight-line depreciation (about $375,000 per year). In contrast, IFRS does not view the building as a single composite asset, but recognizes the separate components of it—each with a different useful life and potentially accounted for with a different depreciation method. Thus, the frame of the building, the roof, air-conditioning systems, duct work, plumbing, light fixtures, and all other major components of the building each might have a different useful life (most being far less than 40 years) and be depreciated using a different method over shorter periods of time. Each has to be set up on the books as a separate plant asset with separate amounts of depreciation expense and accumulated depreciation. Converting a large enterprise's accounting system to a component approach for depreciation requires a massive one-time expenditure in information technology, as well as more extensive ongoing record-keeping requirements.

APPLY GAAP FOR NATURAL RESOURCES AND INTANGIBLE ASSETS

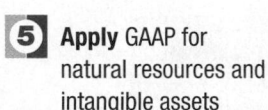

5 Apply GAAP for natural resources and intangible assets

Accounting for Natural Resources

Natural resources are long-term assets of a special type, such as iron ore, petroleum (oil), and timber. These resources are often called *wasting assets* because, in contrast to property and equipment, they are actually physically used up over time. The process by which this occurs is called **depletion**. Depletion is distinctively different from depreciation because it involves actually tracking the flow of a natural resource from its raw state, through inventory (to the extent not sold), to cost of goods sold or some other expense on the income statement. When a natural resource is acquired or developed, the entity follows the cost principle, similarly to that used in accounting for a plant asset. When the asset is extracted, the entity follows an approach much like the units-of-production depreciation method to account for the production. If all of the resource extracted is regarded as sold (as in the case of a drilling and exploration company), the amount depleted is transferred directly from long-term assets to the income statement in the form of an expense (such as depletion expense). However, as in the case of an integrated oil company (one with both production and refining operations), if a portion of the extracted resource is not immediately sold, it becomes saleable inventory (a current asset). Then, as the inventory is sold, its cost is transferred to an expense such as cost of goods sold, as discussed in Chapter 6.

For example, an oil reserve may cost **ExxonMobil** $100,000,000 and contain an estimated 10,000,000 barrels of oil. ExxonMobil is an integrated oil company, meaning it both drills for oil and refines it, so the company retains some inventory rather than selling all it produces. Upon purchase or development of the oil reserve (assuming the company paid cash), ExxonMobil makes the following entry:

	A	C	D	G
A1				
1		Oil Reserve	100,000,000	
2		Cash		100,000,000
3				

The depletion rate is $10 per barrel ($100,000,000/10,000,000 barrels). If 3,000,000 barrels are extracted and 1,000,000 barrels are sold, the company's different divisions might make the following entries. First, the oil reserve (long-term asset) is depleted by $30,000,000 (3,000,000 barrels × $10 per barrel) and $30,000,000 is transferred to inventory. The depletion entry is:

	A	C	D	G
1		Oil Inventory (3,000,000 barrels × $10)	30,000,000	
2		Oil Reserve		30,000,000
3				

The following week, as the oil is sold, ExxonMobil makes the following entry:

	A	C	D	G
1		Cost of Oil Sold (1,000,000 barrels × $10)	10,000,000	
2		Oil Inventory		10,000,000
3				

This would assign $10 million to Cost of Oil Sold (an expense) and leave $20 million in Oil Inventory (a current asset). The net book value of the oil reserve (the long-term asset) after these entries is $70 million ($100 million − $30 million).

Accounting for Intangible Assets

As we've seen, **intangible assets** are long-lived assets with no physical form. Intangibles are valuable because they carry special rights, and include patents, copyrights, trademarks, franchises, leaseholds, and goodwill. Like buildings and equipment, an intangible asset is recorded at its acquisition cost. Intangibles are the most valuable assets of high-tech companies and those that depend on research and development. The residual value of most intangibles is zero.

Intangible assets fall into two categories:

- Intangibles with *finite lives* that can be measured. We record amortization for these intangibles annually. **Amortization** expense is the title of the expense associated with intangibles. Amortization works like depreciation and is usually computed on a straight-line basis. Amortization can be credited directly to the asset account. Intangible assets with finite lives are amortized over the shorter of legal or useful life.

- Intangibles with *indefinite lives*. Record no amortization for these intangibles. Instead, check them annually for any loss in value (impairment), and record a loss when it occurs. Goodwill is the most prominent example of an intangible asset with an indefinite life.

In the following discussions, we illustrate the accounting for both categories of intangibles.

Accounting for Specific Intangibles

Each type of intangible asset is unique, and the accounting can vary from one asset to another.

Patents. **Patents** are federal government grants that give the holder the exclusive right for 20 years to produce and sell an invention. The invention may be a product or a process—for example, the Sony Blu-Ray disc players and the Dolby Laboratories surround-sound process. Like any other asset, a patent may be purchased. Suppose **Sony** pays $170,000 to acquire a patent on January 1, and the business believes the expected useful life of the patent is 5 years—not the entire 20-year period. Amortization expense is $34,000 per year ($170,000/5 years). Sony records the acquisition and amortization for this patent:

	A	C	D	G
1	Jan 1	Patents	170,000	
2		Cash		170,000
3		*To acquire a patent.*		
4				

	A	C	D	G
1	Dec 31	Amortization Expense—Patents ($170,000/5)	34,000	
2		Patents		34,000
3		*To amortize the cost of a patent.*		
4				

Assets	=	Liabilities	+	Stockholders' Equity	−	Expenses
− 34,000	=	0				− 34,000

You can see that we credited the Patents account directly (no Accumulated Amortization account). Amortization for an intangible decreases both assets and equity exactly as depreciation does for equipment or a building.

Copyrights. **Copyrights** are exclusive rights to reproduce and sell a book, musical composition, film, or other work of art. Copyrights also protect computer software programs, such as **Microsoft**'s Windows and Excel. Issued by the federal government, copyrights extend 70 years beyond the author's (composer's, artist's, or programmer's) life. The cost of obtaining a copyright from the government is low, but a company may pay a large sum to purchase an existing copyright from the owner. For example, a publisher may pay the author of a popular novel $1 million or more for the book copyright. Because the useful life of a copyright is usually no longer than two or three years, each period's amortization amount is a high proportion of the copyright cost.

Trademarks and Trade Names. **Trademarks** and **trade names** (or *brand names*) are distinctive identifications of products or services. The "eye" symbol that flashes across our television screens is the trademark that identifies the **CBS** television network. You are probably also familiar with **NBC**'s peacock. Advertising slogans that are legally protected include **American Airlines**' "AAdvantage" program and **Coca Cola Co.**'s "Make It Happy" slogan. These are distinctive identifications of products or services, marked with the symbol ™ or ®.

Some trademarks may have a definite useful life set by contract. We should amortize the cost of this type of trademark over its useful life. But a trademark or a trade name may have an indefinite life and not be amortized.

Franchises and Licenses. **Franchises** and **licenses** are privileges granted by a private business or a government to sell a product or service in accordance with specified conditions. The Chicago Cubs baseball organization is a franchise granted to its owner by the National League. **McDonald's** restaurants and **Holiday Inns** are popular franchises. The useful lives of many franchises and licenses are indefinite and, therefore, not amortized.

Goodwill. In accounting, **goodwill** has a very specific meaning:

> Goodwill is defined as the excess of the cost of purchasing another company over the sum of the market values of the acquired company's net assets (assets minus liabilities).

A purchaser is willing to pay for goodwill when the purchaser buys another company that has abnormal earning power.

FedEx operates in several foreign countries. Suppose FedEx acquires Europa Company at a cost of $10 million. Europa's assets have a market value of $9 million, and the market value of its liabilities total $2 million, so Europa's net assets total $7 million at current market value. In this case, FedEx paid $3 million for goodwill:

Purchase price paid for Europa Company		$10 million
Sum of the market values of Europa Company's assets	$9 million	
Less: Market values of Europa Company's liabilities...........	(2 million)	
Market value of Europa Company's net assets....................		7 million
Excess is called *goodwill*		$ 3 million

FedEx's entry to record the acquisition of Europa Company, including its goodwill, would be

	A	C	D	G
		A1		
1		Assets (Cash, Receivables, Inventories, Plant Assets,		
2		all at market value)	9,000,000	
3		Goodwill	3,000,000	
4		Liabilities		2,000,000
5		Cash		10,000,000
6				

Goodwill in accounting has special features:

1. Goodwill is recorded *only* when it is purchased in the acquisition of another company. A purchase transaction provides objective evidence of the value of goodwill. Companies never record goodwill that they create for their own business.

2. According to GAAP, goodwill is not amortized because the goodwill of many entities increases in value. Rather, each year, companies with goodwill on their financial statements are required to perform a special impairment test for goodwill, similar (but not identical) to the impairment test for other long-term assets described in the next section. If the test shows that goodwill is impaired, it must be written down to the impaired value. The details of this impairment test are beyond the scope of this text and are reserved for later courses.

Accounting for Research and Development Costs

Accounting for research and development (R&D) costs is one of the most difficult issues in accounting. R&D is the lifeblood of companies such as **Procter & Gamble, General Electric, Intel,** and **Boeing.** R&D is one of these companies' most valuable intangible assets. However, in general, U.S. companies do not report R&D assets on their balance sheets. Rather, they expense R&D costs as they are incurred.

EXPLAIN THE EFFECT OF AN ASSET IMPAIRMENT ON THE FINANCIAL STATEMENTS

Generally accepted accounting principles require that management of companies test both tangible and intangible long-term assets for impairment yearly. **Impairment** occurs when the expected future cash flows (which approximate the expected future benefits) from a long-term asset fall below the asset's net book (carrying) value (cost minus accumulated depreciation or amortization). If an asset is impaired, the company is required to adjust the carrying value downward from its

 Explain the effect of an asset impairment on the financial statements

book value to its **fair value**. In this case, fair value is based not on the expected future cash flows, but on the asset's estimated market value at the date of the impairment test. Exhibit 7-12 displays both the normal relationship and an impaired relationship between net book value, future cash flows, and fair value.

Exhibit 7-12 | Normal Relationship and Impaired Relationship Among Values of an Asset

	Normal		Impaired
Largest:	Future cash flows	Largest:	Net book value
Middle:	Fair value	Middle:	Future cash flows
Smallest:	Net book value	Smallest:	Fair value

In a normal relationship, estimated future cash flows represent the largest of the three amounts, followed by fair value, and then net book value. An impaired relationship exists if net book value exceeds estimated future cash flows. The process of accounting for asset impairment requires two steps:

Step 1 Test the asset for impairment.
  ▪ **If net book value > Estimated future cash flows, then the asset is impaired.**

Step 2 If the asset is impaired under step 1, compute the impairment loss.
  ▪ **Impairment loss = Net book value − Fair value**

To illustrate, let's assume that FedEx has a long-term asset with the following information as of May 31, 2014:

- **Net book value** $100 million
- **Estimated future cash flows**   80 million
- **Fair (market) value**   70 million

The two-stage impairment process is

Step 1 Impairment test: Is net book value > estimated future cash flows? (Answer: Yes, so the asset is impaired.)

Step 2 Impairment loss = Net book value ($100) − Fair value ($70) = $30

FedEx will make the following entry (in millions):

	A		C	D	G
1	2014				
2	May 31		Impairment Loss on Long-term Asset ($100 − $70)	30	
3			Long-term Asset		30
4					

			Stockholders'		
Assets	=	Liabilities	+	Equity	− Losses
− 30	=	0			− 30

Both long-term assets and equity decrease (through the Loss account). Under U.S. GAAP, once a long-term asset has been written down because of impairment, it may never again be written back up, should it increase in value.

GLOBAL VIEW

Unlike U.S. GAAP, IFRS records impairments for long-lived assets based on a one-step impairment process. The details of this process are covered in more advanced accounting courses. Also unlike U.S. GAAP, asset impairments under IFRS may be reversed in future periods for some types of long-term assets, in the event that the market price recovers. Thus, under IFRS, a company can record an impairment loss on certain long-term assets in one period and then write the asset back up with a corresponding gain in a later period.

Accounting for research and development costs represents another prominent difference between U.S. GAAP and IFRS. Whereas under U.S. GAAP, in general, both research and development costs are expensed as incurred, under IFRS, costs associated with the creation of intangible assets are classified into research-phase costs and development-phase costs. Costs in the research phase are always expensed. However, costs in the development phase are capitalized if the company can demonstrate meeting the following six criteria:

- The technical feasibility of completing the intangible asset
- The intention to complete the intangible asset
- The ability to use or sell the intangible asset
- The future economic benefits (e.g., the existence of a market or, if for internal use, the usefulness of the intangible asset)
- The availability of adequate resources to complete development of the asset
- The ability to reliably measure the expenditure attributable to the intangible asset during its development

Thus, IFRS are generally more permissive than U.S. GAAP toward capitalization of research and development costs. Adoption of IFRS should result in generally higher reported incomes for companies that incur research and development costs in periods in which these costs are incurred.

The Financial Accounting Standards Board (FASB) is currently working on a new accounting standard aimed at eliminating the differences between U.S. GAAP and IFRS in the area of research and development costs.

Still another difference between IFRS and U.S. GAAP lies in the capitalization of internally generated intangible assets such as brand names and patents. U.S. GAAP only permits capitalization of these when they are purchased from a source outside the company. The cost of internally generated brand names and patents must be expensed on the income statement. In contrast, IFRS allows the capitalization of internally generated intangible assets like these as long as it is probable (i.e., more likely than not) that the company will receive future benefits from them. Adoption of IFRS by U.S. companies is therefore expected to result in the recognition of more intangible assets on their balance sheets than presently exist. These assets may be either amortized over the assets' estimated useful lives or tested for impairment as they are held, depending on the asset.

ANALYZE RATE OF RETURN ON ASSETS

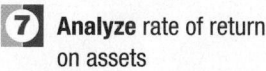

7 Analyze rate of return on assets

Evaluating company performance is a key goal of financial statement analysis. Shareholders entrust managers with the responsibility of developing a business strategy that utilizes company assets in a manner that both effectively and efficiently generates a profit. In this chapter, we begin to develop a framework by which company performance can be evaluated. The most basic framework for this purpose is **return on assets (ROA)**.

ROA, also known as *rate* of return on assets, measures how profitably management has used the assets that stockholders and creditors have provided the company. The basic formula for the ROA ratio is

$$ROA = \frac{\text{Net income}^1}{\text{Average total assets}}$$

where Average total assets = (Beginning total assets + Ending total assets)/2

ROA measures how much the entity earned for each dollar of assets invested by both stockholders and creditors. Companies with high ROA have both selected assets and managed them more successfully than companies with low ROA. ROA is often computed on a divisional or product-line basis to help identify less profitable segments and improve their performance.

DuPont Analysis: A More Detailed View of ROA

To better understand why ROA increased or decreased over time, companies often perform a **DuPont Analysis**,[2] which breaks ROA down into two component ratios that drive it:

$$\text{Net profit margin ratio} = \frac{\text{Net income}}{\text{Net sales}}$$

$$\text{Total asset turnover} = \frac{\text{Net sales}}{\text{Average total assets}}$$

Net profit margin ratio measures how much every sales dollar generates in profit. Net profit margin ratio can be increased in one of three ways: (1) increasing sales volume, or the amount of goods sold or services performed; (2) increasing sales prices; or (3) decreasing cost of goods sold and operating expenses.

Total asset turnover measures how many sales dollars are generated for each dollar of assets invested. This is a measure of how efficiently the company manages its assets. Asset turnover can be increased by (1) increasing sales in the ways just described; (2) keeping less inventory on hand; or (3) closing unproductive or low-performing facilities, selling idle assets, and consolidating operations to fewer places to reduce the amount of plant assets needed and focus efforts on the more profitable areas of the business.

ROA is the product of net profit margin ratio and total asset turnover:

$$ROA = \text{Net profit margin ratio} \times \text{Total asset turnover}$$

$$ROA = \frac{\text{Net income}}{\text{Net sales}} \times \frac{\text{Net sales}}{\text{Average total assets}} = \frac{\text{Net income}}{\text{Average total assets}}$$

By influencing the drivers of net profit margin ratio and total asset turnover, management devises strategies to improve each one, thus increasing ROA. Successful companies often choose between a mixture of two different strategies: *product differentiation* or *low cost*. A company that follows a high product differentiation strategy usually spends a great deal on research and development and advertising to convince customers that the company's products (usually higher priced) are worth the investment. **Apple Inc.,** our spotlight company in Appendix A as well as Chapters 5 and 13, follows a product differentiation strategy, introducing innovative and

---

[1]For companies with significant debt, some analysts may add interest expense to net income. While it is theoretically correct to do so, in order to illustrate DuPont analysis, we do not. Adding back interest makes a material difference to ROA only when interest expense is relatively high compared to net income.

[2]The full DuPont Analysis model actually illustrates a way to compute Return on Common Stockholders' Equity (ROE), which is the product of three component ratios: net profit margin ratio, total asset turnover, and leverage. In this chapter, we discuss a partial version of the full DuPont model, ROA, which is the product of the first two component ratios. In Chapter 9 we introduce the third component ratio (leverage) and in Chapter 10 we illustrate how the leverage ratio is used to convert ROA to ROE.

attractive technology in the marketplace before any other competitor and always at a higher price. Alternatively, a low-cost strategy usually relies on efficient management of inventory and productive assets to produce a high asset turnover. **Dell, Inc.**, a competitor of Apple's, follows a low-cost strategy. Of course, all companies would like to have the best of both worlds by maximizing both net profit margin ratio and asset turnover, but some companies have to settle for one or the other.

To illustrate, let's consider **FedEx Corporation's** ROA, using DuPont analysis.

FedEx Corporation Selected (Adapted) Financial Data		
	(Amounts in millions)	
	2013	2014
Net sales.....................................	$44,287	$45,567
Net income.................................	1,561	2,097
Average total assets....................	31,735	33,319

FedEx Corporation DuPont Analysis				
	Net profit margin ratio × (Net income/Net sales) ×		Total asset turnover (Net sales/Average total assets) =	=	ROA (Net income/Average total assets)
2013	$\dfrac{\$1,561}{\$44,287}$	×	$\dfrac{\$44,287}{\$31,735}$	=	4.9%
2014	$\dfrac{\$2,097}{\$45,567}$	×	$\dfrac{\$45,567}{\$33,319}$	=	6.3%

In 2013, the company's net profit margin ratio was 3.5% ($1,561 million/$44,287 million), which means that for each dollar of net sales, the company earned 3.5 cents in net profit (income). Its asset turnover was 1.396 ($44,287 million/$31,735 million), meaning that it earned $1.396 of sales revenue for every $1 of assets invested. In 2014, the company significantly improved its net profit margin ratio to 4.6% ($2,097 million/$45,567 million) by increasing sales while holding operating and other expenses down. At the same time, FedEx's asset turnover slowed to 1.368 times ($45,567 million/$33,319 million). FedEx purchased proportionately more property and equipment during that year than the increase it experienced in net sales. Thus, the company was more effective (profitable) in 2014 than 2013, but its efficiency declined slightly during the same period. Fortunately, the increase in profits outweighed the decrease in efficiency, so ROA increased from 4.9% to 6.3%.

Return on assets is the first of several ratios we will introduce over the next few chapters to show how analysts dissect financial statements to get behind the numbers, discover management's strategies, and evaluate their performance. In Chapters 9 and 10 we will add the component of financial leverage to the DuPont Analysis model and explain how it is combined with ROA to calculate return on common stockholders' equity (ROE).

ANALYZE THE CASH FLOW IMPACT OF LONG-LIVED ASSET TRANSACTIONS

Three main types of long-lived asset transactions appear on the statement of cash flows:

 Analyze the cash flow impact of long-lived asset transactions

- acquisitions,
- sales, and
- depreciation (as well as amortization).

Acquisitions and sales of long-term assets are *investing* activities. Capital expenditures are examples of investing activities (outflows) that appear on the statement of cash flows. The disposition of plant and other long-term assets results in a cash inflow in the investing activities section. Sometimes cash outflows and inflows from various investing activities are netted, as illustrated in Exhibit 7-13, which excerpts data from the cash flow statement of FedEx Corporation. Depreciation, acquisitions, capital expenditures, and sales (dispositions) of long-term capital assets are denoted in color (lines 7, 11, and 12).

Exhibit 7-13 | Reporting Investing Activities on FedEx Corporation's Statement of Cash Flows

	A	B
	A1 ◆	
1	**FedEx Corporation** **Statement of Cash Flows (Partial, Adapted)** **Year Ended May 31, 2014**	
2		**(In millions)**
3	**Cash Flows from Operating Activities:**	
4	Net income	$ 2,097
5	Adjustments to reconcile net income	
6	to net cash provided by operating activities:	
7	Depreciation and amortization	2,587
8	Other items (summarized)	(420)
9	Net cash provided by operating activities	4,264
10	**Cash Flows from Investing Activities:**	
11	Capital expenditures, net	(3,533)
12	Other asset acquisitions and dispositions, net	(18)
13	Net cash (used in) investing activities	(3,551)
14	**Cash Flows from Financing Activities:**	
15	Net cash (used in) financing activities	(2,719)
16	Effect of exchange rate changes on cash	(3)
17	**Net (decrease) in cash and cash equivalents**	(2,009)
18	**Cash and cash equivalents, beginning of period**	4,917
19	**Cash and cash equivalents, end of period**	$ 2,908
20		

Let's examine FedEx's investing activities first. During 2014, FedEx invested $3,533 million in capital expenditures (line 11). FedEx also engaged in net acquisition and disposition of other long-term assets, spending another $18 million (line 12). FedEx's statement of cash flows reports Depreciation and amortization (line 7) of $2,587 million. Observe that Depreciation and amortization is listed as a positive item under Adjustments to reconcile net income to net cash provided by operating activities. Since depreciation and amortization do not affect cash, you may be wondering why these amounts appear on the statement of cash flows. In this format, the operating activities section of the statement of cash flows starts with net income (line 4) and reconciles to net cash provided by operating activities (line 9). Depreciation and amortization decrease net income but do not affect cash. Depreciation and amortization are therefore added back to net income to measure cash flow from operations. The add-back of depreciation and amortization to net income offsets the earlier subtraction of these expenses. The sum of net income plus depreciation and amortization, therefore, helps to reconcile net income (on the accrual basis) to net cash flow from operations (a cash-basis amount). We revisit this topic in the full context of the statement of cash flows in Chapter 12.

FedEx's cash flows for fiscal 2014 were strong. Net cash provided by operating activities exceeded net income by $2.167 billion ($4.264 billion − $2.097 billion). With this excess, the company made sizeable capital expenditures, signaling that it invested in new plant and equipment and other long-term assets needed to expand and run its business. In addition, as reflected in the financing activities section, the company paid down long-term debt as well as made payments to shareholders in the amount of $2.719 billion. Although cash and cash equivalents decreased by a little over $2 billion from 2013, the company's cash and cash equivalents position at the end of fiscal 2014, in the amount of $2.908 billion, was still very strong.

 # DECISION GUIDELINES

PLANT ASSETS AND RELATED EXPENSES

FedEx Corporation, like all other companies, must make some decisions about how to account for its plant assets and intangibles. Let's review some of these decisions.

Decision	Guidelines
Capitalize or expense a cost?	General rule: Capitalize all costs that provide *future benefit for the business such as a new package-handling system. Expense all costs that provide no future benefit, such as a repair to an airplane.*
Capitalize or expense:	
• Cost associated with a new asset?	Capitalize all costs that bring the asset to its intended use, including asset purchase price, transportation charges, and taxes paid to acquire the asset.
• Cost associated with an existing asset?	Capitalize only those costs that add to the asset's capacity or to its useful life. Expense all other costs as maintenance or repairs.
Which depreciation method to use:	
• For financial reporting?	Use the method that best allocates the cost of an asset through depreciation expense against the revenues produced by the asset. Most companies use the straight-line method.
• For income tax?	Use the method that produces the fastest tax deductions (MACRS). A company can use different depreciation methods for financial reporting and for income tax purposes. In the United States, this practice is both legal and ethical.
How to account for natural resources?	Capitalize the asset's acquisition cost and all later costs that add to the natural resource's future benefit. Record depletion by the units-of-production method by transferring the amount extracted to inventory and eventually to cost of goods sold.
How to account for intangibles?	Capitalize acquisition cost and all later costs that add to the asset's future benefit. For intangibles with finite lives, record amortization expense. For intangibles with indefinite lives, measure impairment in value and record a loss for that amount.
How to record impairments in long-term assets?	Every year, conduct a two-step impairment process for long-term assets:
	STEP 1: Compare net book value with expected cash flows from the asset. If net book value > expected cash flows, the asset is impaired. Otherwise, the asset is not impaired.
	STEP 2: For all impaired assets under step 1, reduce the carrying value of the asset from net book value to fair value. Record a loss for the difference.
How profitable is the company?	Return on assets (ROA) = Net profit margin ratio × Total asset turnover = (Net income/Net sales) × (Net sales/Average total assets)

The figures that follow appear in the Answers to the Mid-Chapter Summary Problem, Requirement 2, on page 387.

	Method A: Straight-Line			Method B: Double-Declining-Balance		
Year	Annual Depreciation Expense	Accumulated Depreciation	Book Value	Annual Depreciation Expense	Accumulated Depreciation	Book Value
Start			$44,000			$44,000
2016	$4,000	$ 4,000	40,000	$8,800	$ 8,800	35,200
2017	4,000	8,000	36,000	7,040	15,840	28,160
2018	4,000	12,000	32,000	5,632	21,472	22,528

Requirements

1. Suppose the income tax authorities permitted a choice between these two depreciation methods. Which method would FedEx select for income tax purposes? Why?

2. Suppose FedEx purchased the equipment described in the table on January 1, 2016. Management has depreciated the equipment by using the double-declining-balance method. On July 1, 2018, FedEx sold the equipment for $27,000 cash.

Record depreciation for 2018 and the sale of the equipment on July 1, 2018.

Answers

Requirement 1

For tax purposes, most companies select the accelerated method because it results in the most depreciation in the earliest years of the asset's life. Accelerated depreciation minimizes income tax payments in the early years of the asset's life. That maximizes the business's cash at the earliest possible time.

Requirement 2

Entries to record depreciation to date of sale, and then the sale of the equipment, follow:

	A	B	C	D
1	2018			
2	Jul 1	Depreciation Expense—Equipment ($5,632 X 1/2 year)	2,816	
3		Accumulated Depreciation—Equipment		2,816
4		*To update depreciation.*		
5				
6	Jul 1	Cash	27,000	
7		Accumulated Depreciation—Equipment		
8		($15,840 + $2,816)	18,656	
9		Equipment		44,000
10		Gain on Sale of Equipment		1,656
11		*To record sale of equipment.*		
12				

REVIEW | Plant Assets & Intangibles

Quick Check (Answers are given on page 437.)

1. Baker, Inc., purchased a tract of land, a small office building, and some equipment for $1,700,000. The appraised value of the land was $1,100,000, the building $660,000, and the equipment $440,000. What is the cost of the land?
   - **a.** $850,000
   - **b.** $1,100,000
   - **c.** $566,667
   - **d.** None of the above

2. Which statement is false?
   - **a.** Depreciation creates a fund to replace the asset at the end of its useful life.
   - **b.** The cost of a plant asset minus accumulated depreciation equals the asset's book value.
   - **c.** Depreciation is based on the expense recognition principle because it apportions the cost of the asset against the revenue generated over the asset's useful life.
   - **d.** Depreciation is a process of allocating the cost of a plant asset over its useful life.

   Use the following data for questions 3–6.

   On July 1, 2016, Roam Communications purchased a new piece of equipment that cost $45,000. The estimated useful life is 10 years and estimated residual value is $7,500.

3. What is the depreciation expense for 2016 if Roam uses the straight-line method?
   - **a.** $2,250
   - **b.** $4,500
   - **c.** $1,875
   - **d.** $3,750

4. Assume Roam Communications purchased the equipment on January 1, 2016. If Roam uses the straight-line method for depreciation, what is the asset's book value at the end of 2017?
   - **a.** $37,500
   - **b.** $36,000
   - **c.** $45,000
   - **d.** $30,000

5. Assume Roam Communications purchased the equipment on January 1, 2016. If Roam uses the double-declining-balance method, what is depreciation for 2017?
   - **a.** $9,000
   - **b.** $6,000
   - **c.** $7,200
   - **d.** $16,200

6. Return to Roam's original purchase date of July 1, 2016. Assume that Roam uses the straight-line method of depreciation and sells the equipment for $32,000 on July 1, 2020. The result of the sale of the equipment is a gain (loss) of
   - **a.** ($11,000).
   - **b.** $2,000.
   - **c.** $5,000
   - **d.** $0.

7. A company bought a new machine for $26,000 on January 1. The machine is expected to last four years and to have a residual value of $3,000. If the company uses the double-declining-balance method, accumulated depreciation at the end of year two will be
   - **a.** $17,250.
   - **b.** $26,000.
   - **c.** $19,500.
   - **d.** $23,000.

8. Which of the following is *not* a capital expenditure?
   - **a.** A complete overhaul of an air-conditioning system
   - **b.** The addition of a building wing
   - **c.** Replacement of an old motor with a new one in a piece of equipment
   - **d.** A tune-up of a company vehicle
   - **e.** The cost of installing a piece of equipment

9. Which of the following assets is *not* subject to a decreasing book value through depreciation, depletion, or amortization?

   a. Land improvements   c. Natural resources

   b. Goodwill   d. Intangibles

10. Why would a business select an accelerated method of depreciation for tax purposes?

    a. MACRS depreciation follows a specific pattern of depreciation.

    b. Accelerated depreciation generates a greater amount of depreciation over the life of the asset than does straight-line depreciation.

    c. Accelerated depreciation is easier to calculate because salvage value is ignored.

    d. Accelerated depreciation generates higher depreciation expense immediately and therefore lowers tax payments in the early years of the asset's life.

11. A company purchased an oil well for $270,000. It estimates that the well contains 90,000 barrels, has an eight-year life, and no salvage value. If the company extracts and sells 7,000 barrels of oil in the first year, how much in cost of sales should be recorded?

    a. $27,000   c. $33,750

    b. $135,000   d. $21,000

12. Which item among the following is *not* an intangible asset?

    a. A patent   d. A copyright

    b. Goodwill   e. All of the listed choices are intangible assets.

    c. A trademark

13. An important measure of profitability is

    a. return on assets (ROA).   c. net sales.

    b. quick (acid test) ratio.   d. inventory turnover.

14. In 2016, total asset turnover for Jabber Company has increased. This means that the

    a. company has become more effective.

    b. company has neither become more effective nor more efficient.

    c. company has become more efficient.

    d. company has become more effective and more efficient.

Accounting Vocabulary

accelerated depreciation methods (p. 382) A depreciation method that writes off a relatively larger amount of the asset's cost nearer the start of its useful life than the straight-line method does.

amortization (p. 397) The systematic reduction of a lump-sum amount. Expense that applies to intangible assets in the same way depreciation applies to plant assets and depletion applies to natural resources.

capital expenditure (p. 376) Expenditure that increases an asset's capacity or extends its useful life. Capital expenditures are debited to an asset account.

copyright (p. 398) Exclusive right to reproduce and sell a book, musical composition, film, other work of art, or computer program. Issued by the federal government, copyrights extend 70 years beyond the author's life.

depletion (p. 396) That portion of a natural resource's cost that is used up in a particular period. Depletion expense is computed in the same way as units-of-production

depreciation. A depleted asset usually flows into inventory and eventually to cost of goods sold as the resource is sold.

depreciable cost (p. 379) The cost of a plant asset minus its estimated residual value.

double-declining-balance (DDB) method (p. 382) An accelerated depreciation method that computes annual depreciation by multiplying the asset's decreasing book value at the beginning of the year by a constant percentage, which is two times the straight-line rate.

DuPont Analysis (p. 402) A detailed approach to measuring rate of return on equity (see Chapter 10). In this chapter, we confine our discussion to return on assets, comprising the first two components of return on equity, calculated as follows: Net profit margin ratio (Net income/Net sales) × Total asset turnover (Net sales/Average total assets).

estimated residual value (p. 379) Expected cash value of an asset at the end of its useful life. Also called *residual value, scrap value*, or *salvage value*.

estimated useful life (p. 379) Length of service that a business expects to get from an asset. May be expressed in years, units of output, miles, or other measures.

fair value (p. 400) The asset's estimated market value at a particular date.

franchises and licenses (p. 398) Privileges granted by a private business or a government to sell a product or service in accordance with specified conditions.

goodwill (p. 398) Excess of the cost of an acquired company over the sum of the market values of its net assets (assets minus liabilities).

impairment (p. 399) The condition that exists when the carrying amount of a long-lived asset exceeds the amount of the future cash flows from the asset. Whenever long-term assets have been impaired, they have to be written down to fair values using a two-step process. Under U.S. GAAP, once impaired, the carrying value of a long-lived asset may never again be increased. Under IFRS, if the fair value of impaired assets recovers in the future, the values may be increased.

intangible asset (p. 397) An asset with no physical form—a special right to current and expected future benefits.

Modified Accelerated Cost Recovery System (MACRS) (p. 388) A special depreciation method used only for income tax purposes. Assets are grouped into classes, and for a given class, depreciation is computed by the double-declining-balance method, the 150% declining-balance method, or, for most real estate, the straight-line method.

natural resources (p. 396) Assets such as oil and gas reserves, coal mines, or stands of timber, accounted for as long-term assets when purchased or developed; their cost is transferred to expense through a process called depletion.

net profit margin ratio (p. 402) Computed by the formula Net income/Net sales. This ratio measures the portion of each net sales dollar generated in net profit.

patent (p. 397) A federal government grant giving the holder the exclusive right for 20 years to produce and sell an invention.

plant assets (p. 373) Long-lived assets, such as land, buildings, and equipment, used in the operation of the business. Also called *fixed assets* or *property and equipment*.

return on assets (ROA) (p. 401) Also known as *rate of return on assets*. Measures how profitably management has used the assets that stockholders and creditors have provided the company.

straight-line (SL) method (p. 380) Depreciation method in which an equal amount of depreciation expense is assigned to each year of asset use.

total asset turnover (p. 402) A measure of efficiency in usage of total assets. The ratio calculates how many times per year average total assets are covered by net sales. Formula: Net sales/Average total assets. Also known as *asset turnover*.

trademark, trade name (p. 398) A distinctive identification of a product or service. Also called a *brand name*.

units-of-production (UOP) method (p. 381) Depreciation method by which a fixed amount of depreciation is assigned to each unit of output produced by the plant asset.

ASSESS YOUR PROGRESS

Some of the following exercises and problems are available as Excel questions in MyAccountingLab.

Ethics Check

EC7-1. Identify ethical principle violated

For each of the situations listed, identify which of three principles (integrity, objectivity and independence, or due care) from the AICPA Code of Professional Conduct that is violated. Assume all persons listed in the situations are members of the AICPA. (Note: Refer to the AICPA Code of Professional Conduct contained on pages 29–30 in Chapter 1 for descriptions of the principles.)

    a. Oliver is aware that his company will receive tax benefits for recording depreciation expense. He depreciates a new asset using the double-declining-balance method in the first year. In the second year, he switches to the units-of-production method, but does not account for the depreciation he already expensed last year. This action on Oliver's part means that the company will recognize a higher amount of depreciation expense on its tax return in the second year than if he would have done the depreciation calculation correctly.

b. Currently, AirTravel Airlines uses the straight-line method of depreciation to depreciate its airplanes. Jamie's boss would like to see if switching to the units-of-production method would be a tax savings strategy for the company. Jamie does not remember how to calculate depreciation using the units-of-production method, so she makes up numbers to show her boss based on what she thinks might be right.

c. Frank is an audit manager at a local auditing firm. The firm is looking to outsource its payroll function. Frank strongly urges his firm to select the Speedy Payroll Company, but does not disclose that his son is a co-owner of the company.

d. In order to increase the tax benefits to her company, Tara categorizes the survey fees and grading and clearing expenditures associated with getting a plot of land ready for building as land improvements instead of including those expenditures in the cost of the land.

Short Exercises

LO 1

S7-1. *(Learning Objective 1: Measure the cost and book value of a company's plant assets)*
Examine the excerpt of a footnote from Red Rock's September 30, 2016, annual report to follow.

A1				
	A		B	C
1	Balances of Major Classes of Property and Equipment Are as Follows (in thousands)			
2			Sep. 30, 2016	Sep. 30, 2015
3	Land		$ 76,597	$ 48,922
4	Buildings and leasehold improvements		2,219,767	1,958,617
5	Capitalized real estate leases		24,869	24,264
6	Fixtures and equipment		1,674,089	1,387,110
7	Construction in progress and equipment not yet in service		53,328	118,933
8			4,048,650	3,537,846
9	Less accumulated depreciation and amortization		(1,853,963)	(1,644,414)
10			$ 2,194,687	$ 1,893,432
11				

1. What are Red Rock's largest two categories of property and equipment as of September 30, 2016? Describe in general terms the types of expenditures included in these categories.
2. What was Red Rock's gross cost of property and equipment at September 30, 2016? What was the book value of property and equipment on this date? Why is book value less than cost?

LO 1

S7-2. *(Learning Objective 1: Measure and record the cost of individual assets in a lump-sum purchase of assets)* Pittsfield Sound Center pays $330,000 for a group purchase of land, building, and equipment. At the time of acquisition, the land has a current market value of $54,000, the building's current market value is $90,000, and the equipment's current market value is $216,000. Journalize the lump-sum purchase of the three assets for the total cost of $330,000. The business signs a note payable for this amount.

S7-3. (*Learning Objective 2: Distinguish a capital expenditure from an immediate expense*)
Identify each of the following items as either a capital expenditure (C), expense on the income
statement (E), or neither (N):

LO 2

Type of Expenditure (C, E, or N)	Transaction
	1. Paid property taxes of $75,000 for the first year the new building is occupied.
	2. Paid interest on construction note for new plant building, $550,000.
	3. Repaired plumbing in main plant, paying $270,000 cash.
	4. Purchased equipment for new manufacturing plant, $6,000,000; financed with long-term note.
	5. Paid dividends of $40,000.
	6. Purchased a computer and peripheral equipment for $29,000 cash.
	7. Paved a parking lot on leased property for $300,000.
	8. Paid $90,000 in cash for installation of equipment in (4).
	9. Paid $148,000 to tear down old building on new plant site.
	10. Paid $31,000 maintenance on equipment in (4) during its first year of use.

S7-4. (*Learning Objective 3: Compute depreciation and book value by three methods—
first year only*) Assume that at the beginning of 2015 QuickAir purchased a used Jumbo 747
aircraft at a cost of $56,700,000. QuickAir expects the plane to remain useful for five years
(5,000,000 miles) and to have a residual value of $4,700,000. QuickAir expects to fly the plane
775,000 miles the first year, 1,200,000 miles each year during the second, third, and fourth
years, and 625,000 miles the last year.

LO 3

1. Compute QuickAir's depreciation for the first two years on the plane using the following
   methods:
   a. Straight-line method
   b. Units-of-production method (round depreciation per mile to the closest cent)
   c. Double-declining-balance method
2. Show the airplane's book value at the end of the first year under each depreciation method.

S7-5. (*Learning Objective 3: Select the best depreciation method for income tax purposes*)
This exercise uses the QuickAir data from S7-4. Assume QuickAir is trying to decide which
depreciation method to use for income tax purposes. The company can choose from among the
following methods: (a) straight-line, (b) units-of-production, or (c) double-declining-balance
methods.

LO 3

1. Which depreciation method offers the tax advantage for the first year? Describe the nature
   of the tax advantage.
2. How much income tax will QuickAir save for the first year of the airplane's use under the
   method you just selected as compared with using the straight-line depreciation method?
   The income tax rate is 35%. Ignore any earnings from investing the extra cash.

The following data should be used for S7-6 through S7-8.
Dazzle, Inc., purchased a new car for use in its business on January 1, 2015. It paid $25,000 for
the car. Dazzle expects the car to have a useful life of four years with an estimated residual value
of zero at the end of the four years. Dazzle expects to drive the car 60,000 miles during 2015,
65,000 miles during 2016, 40,000 miles in 2017, and 35,000 miles in 2018, for total expected
miles of 200,000.

LO 3

S7-6. (*Learning Objective 3: Compute depreciation using straight-line method with zero residual value*) Using the straight-line method of depreciation, calculate the following amounts for the car for each of the four years of its expected life:
  a. Depreciation expense
  b. Accumulated depreciation balance
  c. Book value

LO 3

S7-7. (*Learning Objective 3: Compute depreciation using units-of-production method with zero residual value*) Using the units-of-production method of depreciation (with miles as the production unit), calculate the following amounts for the car for each of the four years of its expected life (do not round here; use three decimal places for the depreciation cost per mile)
  a. Depreciation expense
  b. Accumulated depreciation balance
  c. Book value

LO 3

S7-8. (*Learning Objective 3: Compute depreciation using double-declining-balance method with zero residual value*) Using the double-declining-balance method of depreciation, calculate the following amounts for the car for each of the four years of its expected life:
  a. Depreciation expense
  b. Accumulated depreciation balance
  c. Book value

The following data should be used for S7-9 through S7-11.
Lovell, Inc., purchased a used van for use in its business on January 1, 2015. It paid $13,000 for the van. Lovell expects the van to have a useful life of four years, with an estimated residual value of $1,000 at the end of the four years. Lovell expects to drive the van 35,000 miles during 2015, 40,000 miles during 2016, 25,000 miles in 2017, and 20,000 miles in 2018, for total expected miles of 120,000.

LO 3

S7-9. (*Learning Objective 3: Compute depreciation using straight-line method with residual value*) Using the straight-line method of depreciation, calculate the following amounts for the van for each of the four years of its expected life:
  a. Depreciation expense
  b. Accumulated depreciation balance
  c. Book value

LO 3

S7-10. (*Learning Objective 3: Compute depreciation using units-of-production method with residual value*) Using the units-of-production method of depreciation (with miles as the production unit), calculate the following amounts for the van for each of the four years of its expected life:
  a. Depreciation expense
  b. Accumulated depreciation balance
  c. Book value

LO 3

S7-11. (*Learning Objective 3: Compute depreciation using double-declining-balance method with residual value*) Using the double-declining-balance method of depreciation, calculate the following amounts for the van for each of the four years of its expected life:
  a. Depreciation expense
  b. Accumulated depreciation balance
  c. Book value

LO 3

S7-12. (*Learning Objective 3: Compute partial year depreciation, and select the best depreciation method*) Assume that on September 30, 2015, LuxAir, an international airline based in Germany, purchased a Jumbo aircraft at a cost of €42,500,000 (€ is the symbol for the euro). LuxAir expects the plane to remain useful for five years (5,000,000 miles) and to have a residual value of €5,200,000. LuxAir will fly the plane 350,000 miles during the remainder of 2015. Compute LuxAir's depreciation on the plane for the year ended December 31, 2015, using the following methods:

    a. Straight-line

    b. Units-of-production

    c. Double-declining-balance

Which method would produce the highest net income for 2015? Which method produces the lowest net income?

S7-13. *(Learning Objective 3: Compute and record depreciation after a change in useful life of the asset)* Happy Times Amusement Park paid $180,000 for a concession stand. Happy Times started out depreciating the building using the straight-line method over ten years with zero residual value. After using the concession stand for three years, Happy Times determines that the building will remain useful for only two more years. Record Happy Times' depreciation on the concession stand for year four by the straight-line method.

LO **3**

S7-14. *(Learning Objectives 3, 4: Compute depreciation; record a gain or loss on disposal)* On January 1, 2015, Global Manufacturing purchased a machine for $920,000 that it expected to have a useful life of five years. The company estimated that the residual value of the machine was $70,000. Global Manufacturing used the machine for two years and sold it on January 1, 2017, for $250,000. As of December 31, 2016, the accumulated depreciation on the machine was $340,000.

LO **3 4**

    1. Calculate the gain or loss on the sale of the machinery.

    2. Record the sale of the machine on January 1, 2017.

S7-15. *(Learning Objective 5: Account for the depletion of a company's natural resources)* BB Petroleum, a giant oil company, holds reserves of oil and gas assets. At the end of 2016, assume the cost of BB Petroleum's oil reserves totaled $208 billion, representing 16 billion barrels of oil in the ground.

LO **5**

    1. Which depreciation method is similar to the depletion method that BB Petroleum and other oil companies use to compute their annual depletion expense for the oil removed from the ground?

    2. Suppose the company removed 1,000 million barrels of oil during 2017. Record this event. Show amounts in billions.

    3. Assume that, of the amount removed in (2), the company sold 900 million barrels. Make the cost of sales entry.

S7-16. *(Learning Objective 5: Measure and record goodwill)* Crunchies, Inc., dominates the snack-food industry with its Salty Chip brand. Assume that Crunchies, Inc., purchased Healthy Snacks, Inc., for $5.8 million cash. The market value of Healthy Snacks' assets is $7 million, and Healthy Snacks has liabilities with a market value of $6.0 million.

LO **5**

Requirements

    1. Compute the cost of the goodwill purchased by Crunchies.

    2. Explain how Crunchies will account for goodwill in future years.

S7-17. *(Learning Objective 6: Explain the effect of asset impairment on financial statements)* For each of the following scenarios, indicate whether a long-term asset has been impaired (Y for yes and N for no) and, if so, the amount of the loss that should be recorded.

LO **6**

Asset	Book Value	Estimated Future Cash Flows	Fair Value	Impaired? (Y or N)	Amount of Loss
a. Equipment	$180,000	$140,000	$100,000		
b. Trademark	$320,000	$460,000	$375,000		
c. Land	$52,000	$24,000	$21,000		
d. Factory building	$9 million	$9 million	$7 million		

LO 7 **S7-18.** *(Learning Objective 7: Calculate return on assets)* In 2016, Amici, Inc., reported $800 million in sales, $33 million in net income, and average total assets of $300 million. What is Amici's return on assets in 2016?

LO 7 **S7-19.** *(Learning Objective 7: Calculate return on assets)* Oswald Optical, Inc., provides a full line of designer eyewear to optical dispensaries. Oswald reported the following information for 2016 and 2015:

	2016	2015
Sales revenue.................................	$560,000	$430,000
Net income....................................	$ 46,800	$ 33,000
Average total assets.....................	$260,000	$220,000

Compute return on assets (ROA) for 2016 and 2015. Using the DuPont model, identify the components and state whether each improved or worsened from 2015 to 2016.

LO 8 **S7-20.** *(Learning Objective 8: Analyze the cash flow impact of investing activities on the statement of cash flows)* During 2016, Northwest Satellite Systems, Inc., purchased two other companies for $13 million in cash. Also during 2016, Northwest made capital expenditures of $11.3 million in cash to expand its market share. During the year, Northwest sold its North American operations, receiving cash of $11.4 million. Overall, Northwest reported a net income of $2.6 million during 2016.

Show what Northwest would report for cash flows from investing activities on its statement of cash flows for 2016. Report a total amount for net cash provided by (used in) investing activities.

Exercises MyAccountingLab

Group A

LO 1 **E7-21A.** *(Learning Objective 1: Measure the cost of plant assets)* Pawtucket Self Storage purchased land, paying $150,000 cash as a down payment and signing a $170,000 note payable for the balance. Pawtucket also had to pay delinquent property tax of $3,000, title insurance costing $4,500, and $7,000 to level the land and remove an unwanted building. The company paid $54,000 to add soil for the foundation and then constructed an office building at a cost of $800,000. It also paid $48,000 for a fence around the property, $19,000 for the company sign near the property entrance, and $10,000 for lighting of the grounds. What is the capitalized cost of each of Pawtucket's land, land improvements, and building?

LO 1 4 **E7-22A.** *(Learning Objectives 1, 4: Allocate costs to assets acquired in a lump-sum purchase; dispose of a plant asset)* Eastwood Manufacturing bought three used machines in a $209,000 lump-sum purchase. An independent appraiser valued the machines as shown:

Machine No.	Appraised Value
1	$ 73,100
2	120,400
3	21,500

What is each machine's individual cost? Immediately after making this purchase, Eastwood sold machine 3 for its appraised value. What is the result of the sale? (Round decimals to three places when calculating proportions, and use your computed percentages throughout.)

E7-23A. *(Learning Objective 2: Distinguish capital expenditures from expenses)* Assume Akro Products, Inc., purchased conveyor-belt machinery. Classify each of the following expenditures as a capital expenditure or an immediate expense related to machinery:

LO 2

    a. Major overhaul to extend the machinery's useful life by five years
    b. Periodic lubrication after the machinery is placed in service
    c. Purchase price
    d. Training of personnel for initial operation of the machinery
    e. Special reinforcement to the machinery platform
    f. Transportation and insurance while machinery is in transit from seller to buyer
    g. Ordinary repairs to keep the machinery in good working order
    h. Lubrication of the machinery before it is placed in service
    i. Sales tax paid on the purchase price
    j. Installation of the conveyor-belt machinery
    k. Income tax paid on income earned from the sale of products manufactured by the machinery

E7-24A. *(Learning Objectives 1, 3: Measure, depreciate, and report plant assets)* During 2016, Chun's Book Store paid $485,000 for land and built a store in Cleveland. Prior to construction, the city of Cleveland charged Chun's $1,400 for a building permit, which Chun's paid. Chun's also paid $15,320 for architect's fees. The construction cost of $690,000 was financed by a long-term note payable, with interest cost of $28,300 paid at completion of the project. The building was completed June 30, 2016. Chun's depreciates the building by the straight-line method over 35 years, with estimated residual value of $337,000.

LO 1 3

    1. Journalize transactions for the following:
        a. Purchase of the land
        b. All the costs chargeable to the building in a single entry
        c. Depreciation on the building for 2016

Explanations are not required.

    2. Report Chun's Book Store's plant assets on the company's balance sheet at December 31, 2016.
    3. What will Chun's income statement for the year ended December 31, 2016, report for these facts?

E7-25A. *(Learning Objective 3: Determine depreciation amounts by three methods)* Piccadilly Pizza bought a used Toyota delivery van on January 2, 2016, for $19,200. The van was expected to remain in service for four years (71,200 miles). At the end of its useful life, Piccadilly officials estimated that the van's residual value would be $1,400. The van traveled 28,000 miles the first year, 20,500 miles the second year, 18,500 miles the third year, and 4,200 miles in the fourth year.

LO 3

Requirements

    1. Prepare a schedule of depreciation expense per year for the van under the three depreciation methods discussed in this chapter. (For units-of-production and double-declining-balance methods, round to the nearest two decimal places after each step of the calculation.)
    2. Which method best tracks the wear and tear on the van?
    3. Which method would Piccadilly prefer to use for income tax purposes? Explain in detail why Piccadilly would prefer this method.

E7-26A. *(Learning Objectives 1, 3, 8: Report plant assets, depreciation, and investing cash flows)* Assume that on January 1, 2016, Merriman Steakhouse restaurant purchased a building, paying $55,000 cash and signing a $108,000 note payable. The restaurant paid another $66,000 to remodel the building. Furniture and fixtures cost $58,000, and dishes and supplies— a current asset—were obtained for $9,000. All expenditures were for cash. Assume that all of these expenditures occurred on January 1, 2016.

LO 1 3 8

    Merriman Steakhouse is depreciating the building over 25 years by the straight-line method, with estimated residual value of $59,000. The furniture and fixtures will be replaced at the end of five years and are being depreciated by the double-declining-balance method, with zero residual value. At the end of the first year, the restaurant still has dishes and supplies worth $1,500.

Show what the restaurant will report for supplies, plant assets, and cash flows at the end of the first year on its

- income statement,
- balance sheet, and
- statement of cash flows (investing only).

Note: The purchase of dishes and supplies is an operating cash flow because supplies are a current asset.

LO 3

E7-27A. *(Learning Objective 3: Change a plant asset's useful life)* Assume McGregor Consultants purchased a building for $445,000 and depreciated it on a straight-line basis over 40 years. The estimated residual value was $90,000. After using the building for 20 years, McGregor realized that the building will remain useful only 14 more years. Starting with the 21st year, McGregor began depreciating the building over a revised total life of 34 years and decreased the residual value to $15,500. Record depreciation expense on the building for years 20 and 21.

LO 3 4

E7-28A. *(Learning Objectives 3, 4: Compute depreciation; record a gain or loss on disposal)* On January 1, 2015, Alpha Manufacturing purchased a machine for $920,000. The company expects the machine to remain useful for eight years and to have a residual value of $70,000. Alpha Manufacturing uses the straight-line method to depreciate its machinery. Alpha Manufacturing used the machine for four years and sold it on January 1, 2019, for $400,000.

1. Compute accumulated depreciation on the machine at January 1, 2019 (same as December 31, 2018).
2. Record the sale of the machine on January 1, 2019.

LO 3 4

E7-29A. *(Learning Objectives 3, 4: Measure DDB depreciation; analyze the effect of a sale of a plant asset)* Assume that on January 2, 2016, Sonoma-Maine Furniture purchased fixtures for $8,200 cash, expecting the fixtures to remain in service for five years. Sonoma-Maine has depreciated the fixtures on a double-declining-balance basis, with $1,200 estimated residual value. On August 31, 2017, Sonoma-Maine sold the fixtures for $2,200 cash. Record both the depreciation expense on the fixtures for 2017 and the sale of the fixtures. Apart from your journal entry, also show how to compute the gain or loss on Sonoma-Maine's disposal of these fixtures.

LO 1 3 4

E7-30A. *(Learning Objectives 1, 3, 4: Measure a plant asset's cost; calculate UOP depreciation; analyze the effect of a used asset trade-in)* Covenant Truck Company is a large trucking company that operates throughout the United States. Covenant Truck Company uses the units-of-production (UOP) method to depreciate its trucks. The company trades in trucks often to keep driver morale high and to maximize fuel economy. Consider these facts about one Mack truck in the company's fleet: When acquired in 2016, the tractor-trailer rig cost $400,000 and was expected to remain in service for 10 years or 1,000,000 miles. Estimated residual value was $90,000. During 2016, the truck was driven 85,000 miles; during 2017, 165,000 miles; and during 2018, 175,000 miles. After 41,000 miles in 2019, the company traded in the Mack truck for a less-expensive Freightliner with a sticker price (fair market value) of $230,000. Covenant Truck Company paid cash of $29,000. Determine Covenant's gain or loss on the transaction. Prepare the journal entry to record the trade-in of the old truck on the new one.

LO 5

E7-31A. *(Learning Objective 5: Record natural resource assets and depletion)* Goldstein Mines paid $424,000 for the right to extract ore from a 200,000-ton mineral deposit. In addition to the purchase price, Goldstein Mines also paid a $100 filing fee, a $1,900 license fee to the state of Colorado, and $50,000 for a geologic survey of the property. Because the company purchased the rights to the minerals only, it expects the asset to have zero residual value when fully depleted. During the first year of production, Goldstein Mines removed 30,000 tons of ore, of which it sold 25,000 tons. Make journal entries to record (a) purchase of the mineral rights, (b) payment of fees and other costs, (c) depletion for first-year production, and (d) sales of ore. Round depletion per unit to the closest cent.

E7-32A. *(Learning Objectives 5, 6: Record intangibles, amortization, and impairment)*   LO **5** **6**

1. Maynard Printers incurred external costs of $800,000 for a patent for a new laser printer. Although the patent gives legal protection for 20 years, it is expected to provide Maynard Printers with a competitive advantage for only eight years. Assuming the straight-line method of amortization, make journal entries to record (a) the purchase of the patent and (b) amortization for year 1.

2. After using the patent for four years, Maynard Printers learns at an industry trade show that Sonic Printers is designing a more efficient printer. On the basis of this new information, Maynard Printers determines that the expected future cash flows from the patent are only $310,000. Its fair value on the open market is zero. Is this asset impaired? If so, make the impairment adjusting entry.

E7-33A. *(Learning Objectives 5, 6: Compute and account for goodwill and impairment)*   LO **5** **6**
Assume Caltron Co. paid $19 million to purchase Burton Industries. Assume further that Burton Industries had the following summarized data at the time of the Caltron Co. acquisition (amounts in millions):

Burton Industries			
Assets		**Liabilities and Equity**	
Current assets	$15	Total liabilities	$29
Long-term assets	21	Stockholders' equity	7
	$36		$36

Burton Industries' current assets had a current market value of $15 million, long-term assets had a current market value of only $17 million, and liabilities had a market value of $29 million.

Requirements

1. Compute the cost of goodwill purchased by Caltron Co.
2. Journalize Caltron Co.'s purchase of Burton Industries.
3. Explain how Caltron Co. will account for goodwill.

E7-34A. *(Learning Objective 7: Calculate return on assets)* Gunny Stores, Inc., one of the   LO **7**
nation's largest grocery retailers, reported the following information (adapted) in its comparative financial statements for the fiscal year ended January 31, 2015:

	January 31, 2015	January 31, 2014
Net sales.....................................	$75,000	$73,600
Net earnings.............................	$ 3,600	$ 3,300
Average total assets..................	$60,000	$59,400

Requirements

1. Compute net profit margin ratio for the years ended January 31, 2015, and 2014. Did it improve or worsen in 2015?
2. Compute asset turnover for the years ended January 31, 2015, and 2014. Did it improve or worsen in 2015?
3. Compute return on assets for the years ended January 31, 2015, and 2014. Did it improve or worsen in 2015? Which component (net profit margin ratio or asset turnover) was mostly responsible?

LO 8 **E7-35A.** *(Learning Objective 8: Report cash flows for plant assets)* Assume Abbey Corporation completed the following transactions:

    a. Sold a store building for $650,000. The building had cost Abbey $1,400,000, and at the time of the sale, its accumulated depreciation totaled $750,000.

    b. Lost a store building in a fire. The building cost $370,000 and had accumulated depreciation of $200,000. The insurance proceeds received by Abbey totaled $180,000.

    c. Renovated a store at a cost of $190,000 (cash).

    d. Purchased store fixtures for $50,000 (cash). The fixtures are expected to remain in service for ten years and then be sold for $50,000. Abbey uses the straight-line depreciation method.

For each transaction, show what Abbey would report for investing activities on its statement of cash flows. Show negative amounts in parentheses.

Group B

LO 1 **E7-36B.** *(Learning Objective 1: Measure the cost of plant assets)* Pierce Self Storage purchased land, paying $145,000 cash as a down payment and signing a $175,000 note payable for the balance. Pierce also had to pay delinquent property tax of $1,000, title insurance costing $2,500, and $4,000 to level the land and remove an unwanted building. The company paid $55,000 to add soil for the foundation and then constructed an office building at a cost of $800,000. It also paid $53,000 for a fence around the property, $19,000 for the company sign near the property entrance, and $11,000 for lighting of the grounds. What is the capitalized cost of each of Pierce's land, land improvements, and building?

LO 1 4 **E7-37B.** *(Learning Objectives 1, 4: Allocate costs to assets acquired in a lump-sum purchase; dispose of a plant asset)* Boltwood Manufacturing bought three used machines in a $148,000 lump-sum purchase. An independent appraiser valued the machines as shown:

Machine No.	Appraised Value
1	$30,000
2	$75,000
3	$45,000

What is each machine's individual cost? Immediately after making this purchase, Boltwood sold machine 3 for its appraised value. What is the result of the sale? (Round decimals to three places when calculating proportions, and use your computed percentages throughout.)

LO 2 **E7-38B.** *(Learning Objective 2: Distinguish capital expenditures from expenses)* Assume Blynn Athletic Products, Inc., purchased conveyor-belt machinery. Classify each of the following expenditures as a capital expenditure or an immediate expense related to machinery:

    a. Major overhaul to extend the machinery's useful life by four years

    b. Periodic lubrication after the machinery is placed in service

    c. Purchase price

    d. Installation of conveyor-belt machinery

    e. Lubrication of the machinery before it is placed in service

    f. Training of personnel for initial operation of the machinery

    g. Special reinforcement to the machinery platform

    h. Ordinary repairs to keep the machinery in good working order

    i. Transportation and insurance while machinery is in transit from seller to buyer

    j. Sales tax paid on the purchase price

    k. Income tax paid on income earned from the sale of products manufactured by the machinery

LO 1 3 **E7-39B.** *(Learning Objectives 1, 3: Measure, depreciate, and report plant assets)* During 2016, Liang's Book Store paid $484,000 for land and built a store in Georgetown. Prior to construction, the city of Georgetown charged Liang's $1,300 for a building permit, which

Liang's paid. Liang's also paid $15,300 for architect's fees. The construction cost of $685,000 was financed by a long-term note payable, with interest cost of $28,220 paid at completion of the project. The building was completed June 30, 2016. Liang's depreciates the building by the straight-line method over 35 years, with estimated residual value of $336,000.

1. Journalize transactions for the following:
   a. Purchase of the land
   b. All the costs chargeable to the building in a single entry
   c. Depreciation on the building for 2016

Explanations are not required.

2. Report Liang's Book Store's plant assets on the company's balance sheet at December 31, 2016.
3. What will Liang's income statement for the year ended December 31, 2016, report for this situation?

E7-40B. *(Learning Objective 3: Determine depreciation amounts by three methods)* Langley Pizza bought a used Chevrolet delivery van on January 2, 2016, for $18,600. The van was expected to remain in service for four years (57,000 miles). At the end of its useful life, Langley officials estimated that the van's residual value would be $1,500. The van traveled 20,500 miles the first year, 16,000 miles the second year, 15,400 miles the third year, and 5,100 miles in the fourth year.

Requirements

1. Prepare a schedule of depreciation expense per year for the van under the three depreciation methods discussed in this chapter. (For units-of-production and double-declining-balance methods, round to the nearest two decimal places after each step of the calculation.)
2. Which method best tracks the wear and tear on the van?
3. Which method would Langley prefer to use for income tax purposes? Explain in detail why Langley would prefer this method.

E7-41B. *(Learning Objectives 1, 3, 8: Report plant assets, depreciation, and investing cash flows)* Assume that on January 1, 2016, Shipley Sushi purchased a building, paying $56,000 cash and signing a $101,000 note payable. The restaurant paid another $63,000 to remodel the building. Furniture and fixtures cost $58,000, and dishes and supplies—a current asset—were obtained for $9,800. All expenditures were for cash. Assume that all of these expenditures occurred on January 1, 2016.

Shipley Sushi is depreciating the building over 25 years by the straight-line method, with estimated residual value of $50,000. The furniture and fixtures will be replaced at the end of five years and are being depreciated by the double-declining-balance method, with zero residual value. At the end of the first year, the restaurant still has dishes and supplies worth $1,800.

Show what the restaurant will report for supplies, plant assets, and cash flows at the end of the first year on its
- income statement,
- balance sheet, and
- statement of cash flows (investing only).

Note: The purchase of dishes and supplies is an operating cash flow because supplies are a current asset.

E7-42B. *(Learning Objective 3: Change a plant asset's useful life)* Assume Franklin Security Consultants purchased a building for $430,000 and depreciated it on a straight-line basis over 40 years. The estimated residual value was $70,000. After using the building for 20 years, Franklin realized that the building will remain useful only 14 more years. Starting with the 21st year, Franklin began depreciating the building over the newly revised total life of 34 years and decreased the estimated residual value to $12,980. Record depreciation expense on the building for years 20 and 21.

LO **3** **4**

E7-43B. *(Learning Objectives 3, 4: Compute depreciation; record a gain or loss on disposal)* On January 1, 2013, Regal Manufacturing purchased a machine for $850,000. Regal Manufacturing expects the machine to remain useful for eight years and to have a residual value of $40,000. Regal Manufacturing uses the straight-line method to depreciate its machinery. Regal Manufacturing used the machine for five years and sold it on January 1, 2018, for $325,000.

1. Compute accumulated depreciation on the machine at January 1, 2018 (same as December 31, 2017).
2. Record the sale of the machine on January 1, 2018.

LO **3** **4**

E7-44B. *(Learning Objectives 3, 4: Measure DDB depreciation; analyze the effect of a sale of a plant asset)* Assume that on January 2, 2016, Drake-Neiman purchased fixtures for $8,000 cash, expecting the fixtures to remain in service for five years. Drake-Neiman has depreciated the fixtures on a double-declining-balance basis, with $1,500 estimated residual value. On September 30, 2017, Drake-Neiman sold the fixtures for $2,200 cash. Record both the depreciation expense on the fixtures for 2017 and the sale of the fixtures. Apart from your journal entry, also show how to compute the gain or loss on Drake-Neiman's disposal of these fixtures.

LO **1** **3** **4**

E7-45B. *(Learning Objectives 1, 3, 4: Measure a plant asset's cost; calculate UOP depreciation; analyze the effect of a used asset trade-in)* Carson Truck Company is a large trucking company that operates throughout the United States. Carson Truck Company uses the units-of-production method to depreciate its trucks.

Carson Truck Company trades in trucks often to keep driver morale high and to maximize fuel economy. Consider these facts about one Mack truck in the company's fleet: When acquired in 2016, the tractor-trailer cost $390,000 and was expected to remain in service for 10 years or 1,000,000 miles. Estimated residual value was $70,000. During 2016, the truck was driven 79,000 miles; during 2017, 159,000 miles; and during 2018, 189,000 miles. After 36,000 miles in 2019, the company traded in the Mack truck for a less-expensive Freightliner with a sticker price (fair market value) of $240,000. Carson Truck Company paid cash of $24,000. Determine Carson Trucks' gain or loss on the transaction. Prepare the journal entry to record the trade-in of the old truck on the new one.

LO **5**

E7-46B. *(Learning Objective 5: Record natural resource assets and depletion)* Nero Mines paid $432,000 for the right to extract ore from a 425,000-ton mineral deposit. In addition to the purchase price, Nero Mines also paid a $150 filing fee, a $2,700 license fee to the state of Utah, and $92,150 for a geologic survey of the property. Because the company purchased the rights to the minerals only, it expected the asset to have zero residual value when fully depleted. During the first year of production, Nero Mines removed 70,000 tons of ore, of which it sold 64,000 tons. Make journal entries to record (a) purchase of the mineral rights, (b) payment of fees and other costs, (c) depletion for first-year production, and (d) sales of ore. Round depletion per unit to the closest cent.

LO **5** **6**

E7-47B. *(Learning Objectives 5, 6: Record intangibles, amortization, and impairment)*

1. Midway Printers incurred external costs of $600,000 for a patent for a new laser printer. Although the patent gives legal protection for 20 years, it is expected to provide Midway Printers with a competitive advantage for only ten years. Assuming the straight-line method of amortization, make journal entries to record (a) the purchase of the patent and (b) amortization for year 1.
2. After using the patent for five years, Midway Printers learns at an industry trade show that Superb Printers is designing a more efficient printer. On the basis of this new information, Midway Printers determines that the expected future cash flows from the patent are only $230,000 and that the patent is worthless on the open market. Is this asset impaired? If so, record the impairment adjusting entry.

E7-48B. *(Learning Objectives 5, 6: Compute and account for goodwill and impairment)*
Assume Doltron Co. paid $18 million to purchase Bailey Industries. Assume further that
Bailey Industries had the following summarized data at the time of the Doltron Co. acquisition
(amounts in millions):

Bailey Industries			
Assets		**Liabilities and Equity**	
Current assets	$17	Total liabilities	$24
Long-term assets	26	Stockholders' equity	19
	$43		$43

Bailey Industries' current assets had a current market value of $17 million, long-term assets had
a current market value of only $21 million, and liabilities had a market value of $24 million.

Requirements

1. Compute the cost of goodwill purchased by Doltron Co.
2. Journalize Doltron Co.'s purchase of Bailey Industries.
3. Explain how Doltron Co. will account for goodwill.

E7-49B. *(Learning Objective 7: Calculate return on assets)* Kirby, Inc., one of the largest
home improvement retailers, reported the following information (adapted) in its comparative
financial statements for the fiscal year ended January 31, 2015:

	January 31, 2015	January 31, 2014
Net sales....................................	$75,000	$73,600
Net earnings..............................	$ 3,600	$ 3,450
Average total assets..................	$60,000	$59,300

Requirements

1. Compute net profit margin ratio for the years ended January 31, 2015 and 2014. Did it
   improve or worsen in 2015?
2. Compute asset turnover for the years ended January 31, 2015 and 2014. Did it improve or
   worsen in 2015?
3. Compute return on assets for the years ended January 31, 2015 and 2014. Did it improve or
   worsen in 2015? Which component (net profit margin ratio or asset turnover) was mostly
   responsible?

E7-50B. *(Learning Objective 8: Report cash flows for plant assets)* Assume Thomas
Manufacturing Corporation completed the following transactions:
  a. Sold a store building for $600,000. The building had cost Thomas Manufacturing
     $1,300,000, and at the time of the sale, its accumulated depreciation totaled
     $700,000.
  b. Lost a store building in a fire. The building cost $340,000 and had accumulated
     depreciation of $160,000. The insurance proceeds received by Thomas Manufacturing
     totaled $130,000.
  c. Renovated a store at a cost of $140,000 (cash).
  d. Purchased store fixtures for $130,000 (cash). The fixtures are expected to remain in
     service for ten years and then be sold for $30,000. Thomas Manufacturing uses the
     straight-line depreciation method.

For each transaction, show what Thomas Manufacturing would report for investing activities on
its statement of cash flows. Show negative amounts in parentheses.

Quiz

Test your understanding of accounting for plant assets, natural resources, and intangibles by answering the following questions. Select the best choice from among the possible answers given.

Q7-51. A capital expenditure
  a. is expensed immediately.
  b. is a credit like capital (owners' equity).
  c. adds to an asset.
  d. records additional capital.

Q7-52. Which of the following items should be accounted for as a capital expenditure?
  a. Costs incurred to repair leaks in the building roof
  b. Maintenance fees paid with funds provided by the company's capital
  c. Taxes paid in conjunction with the purchase of office equipment
  d. The monthly rental cost of an office building

Q7-53. Suppose you buy land for $3,000,000 and spend $1,500,000 to develop the property. You then divide the land into lots as follows:

Category	Sale Price per Lot
15 Hilltop lots................	$575,000
15 Valley lots	$143,750

How much did each Hilltop lot cost you?
  a. $60,000
  b. $50,000
  c. $575,000
  d. $240,000

Q7-54. Which statement about depreciation is false?
  a. Depreciation is a process of allocating the cost of an asset to expense over its useful life.
  b. A major objective of depreciation accounting is to allocate the cost of using an asset against the revenues it helps to generate.
  c. Depreciation should not be recorded in years in which the market value of the asset has increased.
  d. Obsolescence as well as physical wear and tear should be considered when determining the period over which an asset should be depreciated.

Q7-55. At the beginning of last year, Brentwood Corporation purchased a piece of heavy equipment for $88,000. The equipment has a life of five years or 100,000 hours. The estimated residual value is $8,000. Brentwood used the equipment for 19,000 hours last year and 22,000 hours this year. Depreciation expense for year two using double-declining-balance (DDB) and units-of-production methods would be as follows:

	DDB	**UOP**
a.	$19,200	$19,360
b.	$19,200	$17,600
c.	$21,120	$19,360
d.	$21,120	$17,600

Q7-56. Tulsa Corporation acquired a machine for $27,000 and has recorded depreciation for two years using the straight-line method over a five-year life and $9,000 residual value. At the start of the third year of use, Tulsa revised the estimated useful life to a total of 10 years. Estimated residual value declined to $0.

How much depreciation should Tulsa record in each of the asset's last eight years (that is, year 3 through year 10), following the revision?
  a. $2,475
  b. $10,800
  c. $2,700
  d. Some other amount

Q7-57. Kline Company failed to record depreciation of equipment. How does this omission affect Kline's financial statements?
  a. Net income is understated and assets are overstated.
  b. Net income is overstated and assets are understated.
  c. Net income is understated and assets are understated.
  d. Net income is overstated and assets are overstated.

Q7-58. Acton, Inc., uses the double-declining-balance method for depreciation on its computers. Which item is *not* needed to compute depreciation for the first year?
  a. Estimated residual value   **c.** Original cost
  b. Expected useful life in years   **d.** All the items listed are needed.

Q7-59. Which of the following costs are reported on a company's income statement and balance sheet?

Income statement	Balance sheet
a. Cost of goods sold	Accumulated depreciation
b. Accumulated deprecation	Land
c. Goodwill	Accounts payable
d. Gain on sale of land	Cost of goods sold

Use the following information to answer questions 7-60 through 7-61.
Hamilton Company purchased a machine for $11,800 on January 1, 2016. The machine has been depreciated using the straight-line method over a four-year life with a $1,600 residual value. Hamilton sold the machine on January 1, 2018, for $8,000.

Q7-60. What is straight-line depreciation for the year ended December 31, 2016, and what is the book value on December 31, 2017?

Q7-61. What gain or loss should Hamilton record on the sale?
  a. Gain, $1,300   **c.** Loss, $1,300
  b. Loss, $1,250   **d.** Gain, $2,200

Q7-62. A company purchased mineral assets costing $889,000 with estimated residual value of $70,000 and holding approximately 260,000 tons of ore. During the first year, 53,000 tons are extracted and sold. What is the amount of depletion for the first year?
  a. $166,950   **d.** Cannot be determined from the data
  b. $181,219   given
  c. $151,850

Q7-63. Suppose AmerEx pays $72 million to buy Lone Star Overnight. The fair value of Lone Star's assets is $86 million, and the fair value of its liabilities is $21 million. How much goodwill did AmerEx purchase in its acquisition of Lone Star Overnight?
  a. $7 million   **c.** $51 million
  b. $21 million   **d.** $35 million

Q7-64. Harper, Inc., was reviewing its assets for impairment at the end of the current year. Information about one of its assets is as follows:

Net book value........................	$ 900,000
Estimated future cash flows......	$ 670,000
Fair (market) value..................	$ 645,000

Harper should report an impairment loss for the current year of
  a. $0.   **c.** $25,000.
  b. $230,000.   **d.** $255,000.

Q7-65. Data World, Inc., reported sales revenue of $480,000, net income of $36,000, and average total assets of $300,000. Data World's return on assets is
  a. 7.5%.   **c.** 62.5%.
  b. 1.6%.   **d.** 12.0%.

Problems MyAccountingLab

Group A

 **P7-66A.** *(Learning Objectives 1, 2, 3: Measure and account for plant assets; distinguish a capital expenditure from an expense; measure and record depreciation)* Assume Bowler Supply, Inc., opened an office in Dublin, Ohio. Bowler Supply incurred the following costs in acquiring land, making land improvements, and constructing and furnishing the new sales building:

a. Purchase price of land, including an old building that will be used for a garage (land market value is $315,000; building market value is $85,000)..	$360,000
b. Grading (leveling) land...	8,800
c. Fence around the land..	31,100
d. Attorney fee for title search on the land	600
e. Delinquent real estate taxes on the land to be paid by Bowler Supply	5,500
f. Company signs at entrance to the property	1,000
g. Building permit for the sales building..	300
h. Architect fee for the design of the sales building....................................	45,220
i. Masonry, carpentry, and roofing of the sales building.............................	510,000
j. Renovation of the garage building..	32,980
k. Interest cost on construction loan for sales building...............................	9,200
l. Landscaping (trees and shrubs)	6,700
m. Parking lot and concrete walks on the property	52,100
n. Lights for the parking lot and walkways..	7,300
o. Salary of construction supervisor (84% to sales building; 10% to land improvements; and 6% to garage building renovations)..............	42,000
p. Office furniture for the sales building..	79,600
q. Transportation and installation of furniture...	800

Assume Bowler Supply depreciates buildings over 30 years, land improvements over 15 years, and furniture over 12 years, all on a straight-line basis with zero residual value.

Requirements

1. Show how to account for each of Bowler Supply's costs by listing the cost under the correct account. Determine the total cost of each asset.
2. All construction was complete and the assets were placed in service on April 2. Record depreciation for the year ended December 31. Round to the nearest dollar.
3. How will what you learned in this problem help you manage a business?

 **P7-67A.** *(Learning Objectives 1, 3: Measure and account for the cost of plant assets; measure and record depreciation under DDB)* Romano Lake Resort reported the following on its balance sheet at December 31, 2016:

Property, plant, and equipment, at cost:	
Land...	$ 141,000
Buildings	702,000
Less: Accumulated depreciation	(340,000)
Equipment..	407,000
Less: Accumulated depreciation	(264,000)

In early July 2017, the resort expanded operations and purchased additional equipment for cash at a cost of $105,000. The company depreciates buildings by the straight-line method over 20 years with residual value of $87,000. Due to obsolescence, the equipment has a useful life of only 10 years and is being depreciated by the double-declining-balance method with zero residual value.

Requirements

1. Journalize Romano Lake Resort's plant asset purchase and depreciation transactions for 2017.
2. Report plant assets on the December 31, 2017, balance sheet.

P7-68A. *(Learning Objectives 1, 3, 4: Measure and account for the cost of plant assets and depreciation; analyze and record a plant asset disposal)* Carr, Inc., has the following plant asset accounts: Land, Buildings, and Equipment, with a separate accumulated depreciation account for each of these except Land. Carr completed the following transactions:

Jan 3	Traded in equipment with accumulated depreciation of $61,000 (cost of $136,000) for similar new equipment with a cash cost of $183,000. Received a trade-in allowance of $76,000 on the old equipment and paid $107,000 in cash.
Jun 30	Sold a building that had a cost of $655,000 and had accumulated depreciation of $160,000 through December 31 of the preceding year. Depreciation is computed on a straight-line basis. The building has a 40-year useful life and a residual value of $275,000. Carr received $140,000 cash and a $350,250 note receivable.
Oct 31	Purchased land and a building for a single price of $310,000 cash. An independent appraisal valued the land at $50,250 and the building at $284,750.
Dec 31	Recorded depreciation as follows: Equipment has an expected useful life of five years and an estimated residual value of 11% of cost. Depreciation is computed on the double-declining-balance method. Depreciation on buildings is computed by the straight-line method. The new building carries a 40-year useful life and a residual value equal to 20% of its cost.

Requirement

1. Record the transactions in Carr, Inc.'s, journal.

P7-69A. *(Learning Objectives 1, 3, 8: Measure and account for the cost of a plant asset; measure depreciation by three methods; identify the cash flow advantage of accelerated depreciation for tax purposes)* On January 3, 2016, Wayne Co. paid $280,000 for a computer system. In addition to the basic purchase price, the company paid a setup fee of $1,900, sales tax of $7,000, and $28,600 for a special platform on which to place the computer. Wayne's management estimates that the computer will remain in service for five years and have a residual value of $35,500. The computer will process 25,000 documents the first year, with annual processing decreasing by 2,500 documents during each of the next four years (that is, 22,500 documents in 2017; 20,000 documents in 2018; and so on). In trying to decide which depreciation method to use, the company president has requested a depreciation schedule for each of the three depreciation methods (straight-line, units-of-production, and double-declining-balance methods).

Requirements

1. For each of the generally accepted depreciation methods, prepare a depreciation schedule showing asset cost, depreciation expense, accumulated depreciation, and asset book value.
2. Wayne reports to stockholders and creditors in the financial statements using the depreciation method that maximizes reported income in the early years of asset use. For income tax purposes, the company uses the depreciation method that minimizes income tax payments in those early years. Consider the first year Wayne Co. uses the computer. Identify the depreciation methods that meet Wayne's objectives, assuming the income tax authorities permit the use of any of the methods.
3. Net cash provided by operations before income tax is $155,000 for the computer's first year. The income tax rate is 40%. For the two depreciation methods identified in requirement 2, compare the net income and net cash provided by operations (cash flow). Show which method gives the net income advantage and which method gives the cash flow advantage.

P7-70A. *(Learning Objectives 1, 3, 4, 6, 8: Analyze plant asset transactions from a company's financial statements)* Sweet Stores, Inc., sells electronics and appliances. The excerpts that follow are adapted from Sweet Stores' financial statements for 2016 and 2015.

	March 31,	
Balance Sheet (dollars in millions)	2016	2015
Assets		
Total current assets	$7,980	$6,907
Property, plant, and equipment................	4,836	4,194
Less: Accumulated depreciation	2,121	1,726
Goodwill..	553	515

	Year Ended March 31,	
Statement of Cash Flows (dollars in millions)	2016	2015
Operating activities:		
Net income	$1,142	$988
Noncash items affecting net income:		
Depreciation	459	459
Gain on sale of property, plant and equipment..........	(131)	0
Investing activities:		
Additions to property, plant, and equipment	(720)	(615)
Sale of property, plant and equipment........................	145	0

Requirements

1. How much was Sweet Stores' cost of plant assets at March 31, 2016? How much was the book value of plant assets? Show computations.
2. The financial statements give three evidences that Sweet Stores purchased plant assets and goodwill during fiscal year 2016. What are they?
3. Prepare T-accounts for Property, Plant, and Equipment; Accumulated Depreciation; and Goodwill. Then fill in the T-accounts with information from the comparative balance sheets and cash flow statements. Label each increase or decrease and give its dollar amount.
4. Prepare the journal entry for the sale of property, plant, and equipment in 2016.

P7-71A. *(Learning Objective 5: Account for natural resources)* Southwestern Energy Company's balance sheet includes the asset Iron Ore Rights. Southwestern Energy paid $2.2 million cash for the right to work a mine that contained an estimated 190,000 tons of ore. The company paid $61,000 to remove unwanted buildings from the land and $71,000 to prepare the surface for mining. Southwestern Energy also signed a $24,000 note payable to a landscaping company to return the land surface to its original condition after the rights to work the mine end. During the first year, Southwestern Energy removed 31,500 tons of ore, of which it sold 24,400 tons on account for $31 per ton. Operating expenses for the first year totaled $242,000, all paid in cash. In addition, the company accrued income tax at the tax rate of 25%.

Requirements

1. Record all of Southwestern Energy's transactions for the year. Round depletion per unit to the closest cent.

2. Prepare the company's single-step income statement for its iron ore operations for the first year. Evaluate the profitability of the company's operations.
3. What balances should appear from these transactions on Southwestern Energy's balance sheet at the end of its first year of operations?

P7-72A. *(Learning Objectives 1, 4, 8: Analyze the effect of a plant asset addition and disposal; Report plant asset transactions on the financial statements)* At the end of 2015, Chesapeake Energy had total assets of $17.2 billion and total liabilities of $9.8 billion. Included among the assets were property, plant, and equipment with a cost of $4.7 billion and accumulated depreciation of $2.8 billion. Chesapeake Energy completed the following selected transactions during 2016: The company earned total revenues of $26.9 billion and incurred total expenses of $21.5 billion, which included depreciation of $1.3 billion. During the year, Chesapeake Energy paid $1.8 billion for new property, plant, and equipment and sold old plant assets for $0.3 billion. The cost of the assets sold was $1.0 billion, and their accumulated depreciation was $0.4 billion.

LO 1 4 8

Requirements

1. Explain how to determine whether Chesapeake Energy had a gain or loss on the sale of old plant assets during the year. What was the amount of the gain or loss, if any?
2. Show how Chesapeake Energy would report property, plant, and equipment on the balance sheet at December 31, 2016, after all the year's activity. What was the book value of property, plant, and equipment?
3. Show how Chesapeake Energy would report its operating activities and investing activities on its statement of cash flows for 2016. Ignore gains and losses.

P7-73A. *(Learning Objective 7: Calculate return on assets)* Shopper's World operates general merchandise and food discount stores in the United States. The company reported the following information for the three years ending December 31, 2015:

LO 7

A1				
	A	**B**	**C**	**D**
1	**Shopper's World** **Consolidated Statements of Operations (Adapted)**			
2		For the year ended December 31		
3	**In millions of USD**	**2015**	**2014**	**2013**
4	Total net revenue	$ 75,000	$ 62,000	$ 61,000
5	Cost of sales	27,000	21,700	21,350
6	Selling, general and administrative expenses	43,950	35,020	36,120
7	Net income from operations	4,050	5,280	3,530
8	Other revenue (expense)	(770)	(800)	(840)
9	Net income before income taxes	3,280	4,480	2,690
10	Income tax expense	(850)	(2,230)	(570)
11	Net income	$ 2,430	$ 2,250	$ 2,120
12				

A1				
	A	**B**	**C**	**D**
1	**Shopper's World** **Partial Balance Sheets (Condensed)**			
2	**In millions of USD**	**Dec. 31, 2015**	**Dec. 31, 2014**	**Dec. 31, 2013**
3	Total current assets	$ 29,530	$ 28,590	$ 4,570
4	Property, plant and equipment, net	30,000	25,800	25,100
5	Other assets	970	810	830
6	Total assets	$ 60,500	$ 55,200	$ 30,500
7				

Requirements

1. Compute net profit margin ratio for Shopper's World for the years ended December 31, 2015, and December 31, 2014.
2. Compute asset turnover for Shopper's World for the years ended December 31, 2015, and December 31, 2014.
3. Compute return on assets for Shopper's World for the years ended December 31, 2015, and December 31, 2014.
4. What factors contributed to the change in return on assets during the year?

 **P7-74A.** *(Learning Objectives 4, 8: Analyze the effect of a plant asset disposal and the cash flow impact of long-lived asset transactions)* Cook Corporation reported the following related to property and equipment (all in millions):

From the balance sheets:

	12/31/16	12/31/15
Property and equipment	$26,430	$24,220
Accumulated depreciation	(16,045)	(15,210)

From the investing activities section of the 2016 cash flow statement:

Cash used to purchase property and equipment	($2,820)
Proceeds from sale of property and equipment	43

From the 2016 income statement:

Depreciation expense	$1,145
Gain or loss on the sale of equipment	??

Requirements

1. Draw T-accounts for Property and Equipment and Accumulated Depreciation. Enter information as presented and solve for the unknown in each account. (*Hint*: Recall the types of transactions that make each of the two accounts increase and decrease. You are solving for the cost of Property and Equipment sold and the Accumulated Depreciation on those assets.)
2. Based on your calculations in requirement 1, calculate the book value of assets sold during 2016. What is the difference between the sales price and the book value?
3. Prepare the journal entry for the sale of property and equipment during 2016. Describe the effect of this transaction on the financial statements. Compare the sales price and the book value in the journal entry, and compare this to the difference you calculated in requirement 2. Describe briefly.
4. Prepare a T-account for Property and Equipment, Net. Repeat requirement 1.

Group B

P7-75B. *(Learning Objectives 1, 2, 3: Measure and account for plant assets; distinguish a capital expenditure from an expense; measure and record depreciation)* Assume Royale House, Inc., opened an office in Urbana, Illinois. Royale House incurred the following costs in acquiring land, making land improvements, and constructing and furnishing the new sales building:

a. Purchase price of land, including an old building that will be used for a garage (land market value is $315,000; building market value is $85,000)...	$360,000
b. Grading (leveling) land...	8,100
c. Fence around the land...	31,900
d. Attorney fee for title search on the land	700
e. Delinquent real estate taxes on the land to be paid by Royale House............	5,100
f. Company signs at entrance to the property	1,100
g. Building permit for the sales building.......................................	500
h. Architect fee for the design of the sales building......................	26,050
i. Masonry, carpentry, and roofing of the sales building...............	513,000
j. Renovation of the garage building...	31,650
k. Interest cost on construction loan for sales building................	9,000
l. Landscaping (trees and shrubs)	6,600
m. Parking lot and concrete walks on the property	52,300
n. Lights for the parking lot and walkways...................................	7,000
o. Salary of construction supervisor (85% to sales building; 10% to land improvements; and 5% to garage building renovations)...............	37,000
p. Office furniture for the sales building......................................	79,800
q. Transportation and installation of furniture.............................	2,600

Assume Royale House depreciates buildings over 50 years, land improvements over 25 years, and furniture over 12 years, all on a straight-line basis with zero residual value.

Requirements

1. Show how to account for each of Royale House's costs by listing the cost under the correct account. Determine the total cost of each asset.
2. All construction was complete and the assets were placed in service on April 2. Record depreciation for the year ended December 31. Round to the nearest dollar.
3. How will what you learned in this problem help you manage a business?

P7-76B. (Learning Objectives 1, 3: Measure and account for the cost of plant assets; measure and record depreciation under DDB) Donatello Lake Resort reported the following on its balance sheet at December 31, 2016:

LO 1 3

Property, plant, and equipment, at cost:	
Land..	$ 145,000
Buildings	700,000
Less: Accumulated depreciation	(348,000)
Equipment...	401,000
Less: Accumulated depreciation	(261,000)

In early July 2017, the resort expanded operations and purchased additional equipment for cash at a cost of $109,000. The company depreciates buildings by the straight-line method over 20 years with residual value of $84,000. Due to obsolescence, the equipment has a useful life of only 10 years and is being depreciated by the double-declining-balance method with zero residual value.

Requirements

1. Journalize Donatello Lake Resort's plant asset purchase and depreciation transactions for 2017.
2. Report plant assets on the December 31, 2017, balance sheet.

 **P7-77B.** *(Learning Objectives 1, 3, 4: Measure and account for the cost of plant assets and depreciation; analyze and record a plant asset disposal)* Tucker, Inc., has the following plant asset accounts: Land, Buildings, and Equipment, with a separate accumulated depreciation account for each of these except Land. Tucker completed the following transactions:

Jan 3	Traded in equipment with accumulated depreciation of $61,000 (cost of $131,000) for similar new equipment with a cash cost of $177,000. Received a trade-in allowance of $76,000 on the old equipment and paid $101,000 in cash.
Jun 30	Sold a building that had a cost of $640,000 and had accumulated depreciation of $150,000 through December 31 of the preceding year. Depreciation is computed on a straight-line basis. The building has a 40-year useful life and a residual value of $240,000. Tucker received $125,000 cash and a $360,000 note receivable.
Oct 31	Purchased land and a building for a single price of $350,000 cash. An independent appraisal valued the land at $127,400 and the building at $236,600.
Dec 31	Recorded depreciation as follows:
	Equipment has an expected useful life of eight years and an estimated residual value of 12% of cost. Depreciation is computed on the double-declining-balance method.
	Depreciation on buildings is computed by the straight-line method. The new building carries a 40-year useful life and a residual value equal to 20% of its cost.

Requirement

1. Record the transactions in Tucker, Inc.'s, journal.

 **P7-78B.** *(Learning Objectives 1, 3, 8: Measure and account for the cost of a plant asset; measure depreciation by three methods; identify the cash flow advantage of accelerated depreciation for tax purposes)* On January 2, 2016, Smythe Co. paid $255,000 for a computer system. In addition to the basic purchase price, the company paid a setup fee of $1,500, sales tax of $6,600, and $31,900 for a special platform on which to place the computer. Smythe's management estimates that the computer will remain in service for five years and have a residual value of $30,000. The computer will process 55,000 documents the first year, with annual processing decreasing by 2,500 documents during each of the next four years (that is, 52,500 documents in year 2017, 50,000 documents in year 2018, and so on). In trying to decide which depreciation method to use, the company president has requested a depreciation schedule for each of the three depreciation methods (straight-line, units-of-production, and double-declining-balance methods).

Requirements

1. For each of the generally accepted depreciation methods, prepare a depreciation schedule showing asset cost, depreciation expense, accumulated depreciation, and asset book value.
2. Smythe reports to stockholders and creditors in the financial statements using the depreciation method that maximizes reported income in the early years of asset use. For income tax purposes, the company uses the depreciation method that minimizes income tax payments in those early years. Consider the first year Smythe Co. uses the computer. Identify the depreciation methods that meet Smythe's objectives, assuming the income tax authorities permit the use of any of the methods.
3. Net cash provided by operations before income tax is $157,000 for the computer's first year. The income tax rate is 40%. For the two depreciation methods identified in requirement 2, compare the net income and net cash provided by operations (cash flow). Show which method gives the net income advantage and which method gives the cash flow advantage.

 **P7-79B.** *(Learning Objectives 1, 3, 4, 6, 8: Analyze plant asset transactions from a company's financial statements)* Hometown Sales, Inc., sells electronics and appliances. The excerpts that follow are adapted from Hometown Sales' financial statements for 2016 and 2015:

Balance Sheet (dollars in millions)	April 30,	
	2016	2015
Assets		
Total current assets	$7,987	$6,906
Property, plant, and equipment...............	4,833	4,198
Less: Accumulated depreciation	2,121	1,725
Goodwill...	559	510

Statement of Cash Flows (dollars in millions)	Year Ended April 30,	
	2016	2015
Operating activities:		
Net income	$1,140	$983
Noncash items affecting net income:		
Depreciation	462	457
Gain on sale of property, plant and equipment	(124)	0
Investing activities:		
Additions to property, plant, and equipment	(712)	(615)
Sale of property, plant and equipment	135	0

Requirements

1. How much was Hometown Sales's cost of plant assets at April 30, 2016? How much was the book value of plant assets? Show computations.
2. The financial statements give three pieces of evidence that Hometown Sales purchased plant assets and goodwill during fiscal year 2016. What are they?
3. Prepare T-accounts for Property, Plant, and Equipment; Accumulated Depreciation; and Goodwill. Then fill in the T-accounts with information from the comparative balance sheets and cash flow statements. Label each increase or decrease and give its dollar amount.
4. Prepare the journal entry for the sale of property, plant, and equipment in 2016.

P7-80B. *(Learning Objective 5: Account for natural resources)* Northeastern Energy Company's balance sheet includes the asset Iron Ore Rights. Northeastern Energy paid $2.9 million cash for the right to work a mine that contained an estimated 225,000 tons of ore. The company paid $68,000 to remove unwanted buildings from the land and $78,000 to prepare the surface for mining. Northeastern Energy also signed a $38,750 note payable to a landscaping company to return the land surface to its original condition after the rights to work the mine end. During the first year, Northeastern Energy removed 35,000 tons of ore, of which it sold 27,500 tons on account for $38 per ton. Operating expenses for the first year totaled $256,000, all paid in cash. In addition, the company accrued income tax at the tax rate of 40%.

LO 5

Requirements

1. Record all of Northeastern Energy's transactions for the year. Round depletion per unit to the closest cent.
2. Prepare the company's single-step income statement for its iron ore operations for the first year. Evaluate the profitability of the company's operations.
3. What balances should appear from these transactions on Northeastern Energy's balance sheet at the end of its first year of operations?

P7-81B. (*Learning Objectives 1, 4, 8: Analyze the effect of a plant asset addition and disposal; report plant asset transactions on the financial statements*) At the end of 2015, Standard Power had total assets of $17.5 billion and total liabilities of $9.6 billion. Included among the assets were property, plant, and equipment with a cost of $4.7 billion and accumulated depreciation of $2.9 billion.

Standard Power completed the following selected transactions during 2016: The company earned total revenues of $26.8 billion and incurred total expenses of $22.0 billion, which included depreciation of $1.0 billion. During the year, Standard Power paid $2.1 billion for new property, plant, and equipment and sold old plant assets for $0.9 billion. The cost of the assets sold was $1.5 billion, and their accumulated depreciation was $1.0 billion.

Requirements

1. Explain how to determine whether Standard Power had a gain or loss on the sale of old plant assets during the year. What was the amount of the gain or loss, if any?
2. Show how Standard Power would report property, plant, and equipment on the balance sheet at December 31, 2016, after all the year's activity. What was the book value of property, plant, and equipment?
3. Show how Standard Power would report its operating activities and investing activities on its statement of cash flows for 2016. Ignore gains and losses.

P7-82B. (*Learning Objective 7: Calculate return on assets*) Bargain Hut Corporation operates general merchandise and food discount stores in the United States. The company reported the following information for the three years ending February 28, 2015:

A1		

	A	B	C	D
1	**Bargain Hut Corporation** **Consolidated Statements of Operations (Adapted)**			
2	In millions of USD	For the year ended February 28,		
3		2015	2014	2013
4	Total net revenue	$ 75,000	$ 62,000	$ 60,000
5	Cost of sales	27,000	21,700	21,000
6	Selling, general and administrative expenses	43,950	36,392	34,440
7	Net income from operations	4,050	3,908	4,560
8	Other revenue (expense)	(770)	(870)	(860)
9	Net income before income taxes	3,280	3,038	3,700
10	Income tax expense	(850)	(788)	(600)
11	Net income	$ 2,430	$ 2,250	$ 3,100
12				

A1		

	A	B	C	D
1	**Bargain Hut Corporation** **Partial Balance Sheets (Condensed)**			
2	In millions of USD	Feb. 28, 2015	Feb. 28, 2014	Feb. 28, 2013
3	Total current assets	$ 32,690	$ 28,820	$ 1,340
4	Property, plant and equipment, net	26,900	25,500	25,800
5	Other assets	910	880	860
6	Total assets	$ 60,500	$ 55,200	$ 28,000
7				

Requirements

1. Compute net profit margin ratio for Bargain Hut Corporation for the years ended February 28, 2015, and February 28, 2014.
2. Compute asset turnover for Bargain Hut Corporation for the years ended February 28, 2015, and February 28, 2014.

3. Compute return on assets for Bargain Hut Corporation for the years ended February 28, 2015, and February 28, 2014.
4. What factors contributed to the change in return on assets during the year?

P7-83B. *(Learning Objectives 4, 8: Analyze the effect of a plant asset disposal and the cash flow impact of long-lived asset transactions)* Morgan Corporation reported the following related to property and equipment (all in millions):

LO 4 8

From the balance sheets:

	12/31/16	**12/31/15**
Property and equipment	$23,530	$21,350
Accumulated depreciation	(18,395)	(17,530)

From the investing activities section of the 2016 cash flow statement:

Cash used to purchase property and equipment	($2,820)
Proceeds from sale of property and equipment	56

From the 2016 income statement:

Depreciation expense	$1,145
Gain or loss on the sale of equipment	??

Requirements

1. Draw T-accounts for Property and Equipment and Accumulated Depreciation. Enter information as presented and solve for the unknown in each account. (*Hint*: Recall the types of transactions that make each of the two accounts increase and decrease. You are solving for the cost of Property and Equipment sold and the Accumulated Depreciation on those assets.)
2. Based on your calculations in requirement 1, calculate the book value of assets sold during 2016. What is the difference between the sales price and the book value?
3. Prepare the journal entry for the sale of property and equipment during 2016. Describe the effect of this transaction on the financial statements. Compare the sales price and the book value in the journal entry, and compare this to the difference you calculated in requirement 2. Describe briefly.
4. Prepare a T-account for Property and Equipment, Net. Repeat requirement 1.

Challenge Exercises and Problem

E7-84. *(Learning Objective 3: Determine the effect on net income of a change in the depreciation method)* Yentun, Inc., has a popular line of boogie boards. Yentun reported net income of $62 million for 2016. Depreciation expense for the year totaled $28 million. Yentun, Inc., depreciates plant assets over eight years using the straight-line method and no residual value.

LO 3

Yentun, Inc., paid $224 million for plant assets at the beginning of 2016. At the start of 2017, Yentun changed its method of accounting for depreciation to the double-declining-balance method. The year 2017 is expected to be the same as 2016, except for the change in depreciation method. If Yentun had been using double-declining-balance method of depreciation all along, how much net income can Yentun, Inc., expect to earn during 2017? Ignore income tax.

E7-85. *(Learning Objective 2: Distinguish a capital expenditure from an expense, and measure the financial statement effects of an expensing error)* Acorn-France is a major telecommunication conglomerate. Assume that early in year one, Acorn-France purchased equipment at a cost of 5 million euros (€5 million). Management expects the equipment to remain in service for four years and the estimated residual value to be negligible. Acorn-France uses the straight-line depreciation method. *Through an accounting error, Acorn-France expensed the entire cost of the equipment at the time of purchase.* Because Acorn-France is operated as a partnership, it pays no income tax.

LO 2

Requirements

Prepare a schedule to show the overstatement or understatement in the following items at the end of each year over the four-year life of the equipment:

1. Total current assets
2. Equipment, net
3. Net income

LO 4

P7-86. *(Learning Objective 4: Determine plant and equipment transactions for an actual company)* FedEx Corporation provides a broad portfolio of transportation, e-commerce, and business services. FedEx reported the following information in its 2015 annual report:

A1		
	A	B	C
1	FedEx Corporation Partial Consolidated Balance Sheets		
2		May 31	
3	(in millions)	2015	2014
4	**PROPERTY AND EQUIPMENT, AT COST**		
5	Aircraft and related equipment	$ 16,186	$ 15,632
6	Package handling and ground support equipment	6,725	7,196
7	Computer and electronic equipment	5,208	5,169
8	Vehicles	5,816	4,400
9	Facilities and other	8,929	8,294
10	Gross property and equipment	42,864	40,691
11	Less accumulated depreciation and amortization	(21,989)	(21,141)
12	Net property and equipment	$ 20,875	$ 19,550
13			

A1		
	A	B	C
1	FedEx Corporation Partial Statements of Cash Flows		
2	(In millions)	May 31	
3		2015	2014
4	**Investing Activities**		
5	Capital expenditures	$ (4,347)	$ (3,533)
6	Business acquisitions	(1,429)	(36)
7	Proceeds from asset dispositions and other	24	18
8	Cash used in investing activities	$ (5,752)	$ (3,551)
9			

NOTE 1: DESCRIPTION OF BUSINESS AND SUMMARY OF SIGNIFICANT ACCOUNTING POLICIES

Property and equipment (excerpted):

For financial reporting purposes, we record depreciation and amortization of property and equipment on a straight-line basis over the asset's service life or related lease term, if shorter. For income tax purposes, depreciation is computed using accelerated methods when applicable... Depreciation expense, excluding gains and losses on sales of property and equipment used in operations, was $2.6 billion in 2015 and 2014, and $2.3 billion in 2013.

In May 2015, we retired from service seven Boeing MD11 aircraft and 12 related engines, four Airbus A310-300 aircraft and three related engines, three Airbus A300-600 aircraft and three related engines and one Boeing MD10-10 aircraft and three related engines, and related parts. As a consequence of this decision, impairment and related charges of $276 million ... were recorded in the fourth quarter.

Requirements

1. Using the information provided from the balance sheet and statement of cash flows for FedEx, reconstruct the Property and Equipment and Accumulated Depreciation accounts. You will not have to account for individual asset categories, but only for the gross cost of property and equipment and accumulated depreciation. You will have to solve for the original gross cost and accumulated depreciation of the plant and equipment sold. Ignore business acquisitions for purposes of this part.
2. Prepare the journal entries to record total capital expenditures, total depreciation expense, and total sales of property, plant, and equipment. You will have to compute an implied gain or loss on equipment sold based on the information given.

APPLY YOUR KNOWLEDGE

Decision Cases

Case 1. *(Learning Objective 3: Measure profitability based on different inventory and depreciation methods)* Suppose you are considering investing in two businesses, La Petite France Bakery and Burgers Ahoy. The two companies are virtually identical, and both began operations at the beginning of the current year. During the year, each company purchased inventory:

Jan	4	10,000 units at $4 =	40,000
Apr	6	5,000 units at 5 =	25,000
Aug	9	7,000 units at 6 =	42,000
Nov	27	10,000 units at 7 =	70,000
	Totals	32,000	$177,000

During the first year, both companies sold 25,000 units of inventory.

In early January, both companies purchased equipment costing $150,000 that had a 10-year estimated useful life and a $20,000 residual value. La Petite France uses the inventory and depreciation methods that maximize reported income. By contrast, Burgers Ahoy uses the inventory and depreciation methods that minimize income tax payments. Assume that both companies' trial balances at December 31 included the following:

Sales revenue	$350,000
Operating expenses*	50,000

*Does not include depreciation expense

The income tax rate is 40%.

Requirements

1. Prepare both companies' multiple-step income statements.
2. Write an investment newsletter to address the following questions: Which company appears to be more profitable? Which company has more cash to invest in promising projects? If prices continue rising over the long term, which company would you prefer to invest in? Why? (Challenge)

Case 2. *(Learning Objectives 2, 5: Distinguish between capital expenditures and expense; account for plant assets and intangible assets)* The following questions are unrelated except that they all apply to plant assets and intangible assets:

1. The manager of Wired Connections Inc. regularly buys plant assets and debits the cost to Repairs and Maintenance Expense. Why would he do that, since he knows this action violates GAAP?
2. The manager of Alpine Homes debits the cost of repairs and maintenance of plant assets to Plant and Equipment. Why would she do that, since she knows she is violating GAAP?
3. It has been suggested that because many intangible assets have no value except to the company that owns them, they should be valued at $1.00 or zero on the balance sheet. Many accountants disagree with this view. Which view do you support? Why?

 ## Ethical Issue

Dellroy National Bank purchased land and a building for the lump sum of $6 million. To get the maximum tax deduction, the bank's managers allocated 80% of the purchase price to the building and only 20% to the land. A more realistic allocation would have been 60% to the building and 40% to the land.

Requirements

1. What is the ethical issue in this situation?
2. Who are the stakeholders? What are the possible consequences to each?
3. Analyze the alternatives from the following standpoints: (a) economic, (b) legal, and (c) ethical.
4. What would you do? How would you justify your decision?

Focus on Financials | Apple Inc.

 (*Learning Objectives 2, 3, 6: Analyze activity in plant assets*) Refer to **Apple Inc.'s** Consolidated Financial Statements in Appendix A and online in the filings section of **http://www.sec.gov.**, and answer the following questions:

Requirements

1. Refer to Note 1 and Note 3 of the Notes to Consolidated Financial Statements. What kinds of assets are included in the Property, Plant and Equipment of Apple Inc.?
2. Refer to Note 1, Property, Plant and Equipment section. Which depreciation method does Apple Inc., use for reporting to stockholders and creditors in the financial statements? What type of depreciation method does the company probably use for income tax purposes? Why is this method preferable for tax purposes?
3. Depreciation expense is embedded in operating expense accounts listed on the income statement, so you can't break out the actual figure for depreciation in that way. Refer to the section on Property, Plant and Equipment in Note 1. How much was Apple Inc.'s depreciation and amortization expense on plant assets during 2014? What did this figure include? Now refer to Note 3—Consolidated Financial Statement Details. How much was Apple Inc.'s accumulated depreciation on fixed assets at the end of 2014? Explain why accumulated depreciation exceeds depreciation expense for the current year.
4. Refer to Notes 1 and 4 of the Notes to Consolidated Financial Statements. What are Apple Inc.'s intangible assets? How does the company account for each of these intangibles over its lifetime?

Focus on Analysis | Under Armour, Inc.

 (*Learning Objectives 1, 5, 6, 7, 8: Measure the cost of plant assets; explain plant asset activity; apply GAAP for intangible assets, explain an asset impairment, analyze rate of return on assets; analyze the cash flow impact of long-lived asset transactions*) Refer to the **Under Armour, Inc.,** Consolidated Financial Statements in Appendix B and online in the filings section of **http://www.sec.gov**. This case leads you through an analysis of the activity for some of Under Armour, Inc.'s, long-term assets, as well as the calculation of its rate of return on total assets.

Requirements

1. On the statement of cash flows, how much did Under Armour, Inc., pay for property and equipment during 2014? In what section of the cash flows statement do you find this amount?
2. Which depreciation method does Under Armour, Inc., use? Over what range of useful lives does Under Armour, Inc., depreciate various types of fixed assets? You can find discussions of this in Note 2 (Summary of Significant Accounting Policies).

3. Review the information in Note 4 (Property and Equipment, Net). List the categories of Under Armour, Inc.'s, property and equipment as of December 31, 2014, and December 31, 2013. How much depreciation expense is included in the calculation of net income for these two fiscal years? Does it appear that Under Armour, Inc.'s, property and equipment was proportionately newer or older at the end of 2014 (vs. 2013)? Explain your answer. (Challenge)

4. Examine Note 5 (Goodwill and Intangible Assets, Net) and Note 2. Briefly describe Under Armour, Inc.'s, accounting for goodwill and other intangible assets. What other types of intangible assets did Under Armour, Inc., own as of December 31, 2014?

5. Using DuPont Analysis, calculate Under Armour, Inc.'s, rate of return on total assets for fiscal 2014 and fiscal 2013. Total assets at December 31, 2012 (the end of its 2012 fiscal year), were $1,157 million. Did the company perform better or worse in 2014 than in 2013?

Group Project

Visit a local business and do the following.

Requirements

1. List all its plant assets.
2. If possible, interview the manager. Gain as much information as you can about the business's plant assets. For example, try to determine the assets' costs, the depreciation method the company is using, and the estimated useful life of each asset category. If an interview is impossible, then develop your own estimates of the assets' costs, useful lives, and book values, assuming an appropriate depreciation method.
3. Determine whether the business has any intangible assets. If so, list them and gain as much information as possible about their nature, cost, and estimated useful lives.
4. Write a detailed report of your findings and be prepared to present your results to the class.

Quick Check Answers

1. a {[$1,100/($1,100 + $660 + $440)] × $1,700 = $850}

2. a

3. c ($45,000 − $7,500)/10 × 6/12 = $1,875

4. a [($45,000 − $7,500)/10 × 2 = $7,500; $45,000 − $7,500 = $37,500]

5. c [$45,000 × 0.2 = $9,000; ($45,000 − $9,000) × 0.2 = $7,200]

6. b [($45,000 − $7,500)/10 × 4 = $15,000; $45,000 − $15,000 = $30,000; $32,000 − $30,000 = gain of $2,000]

7. c [$26,000 × 2/4 = $13,000; ($26,000 − $13,000) × 2/4 = $6,500; $13,000 + $6,500 = $19,500]

8. d

9. b

10. d

11. d [$270,000 × (7,000/90,000) = $21,000]

12. e

13. a

14. c

8 Long-Term Investments & the Time Value of Money

SPOTLIGHT | Intel Holds Several Different Types of Investments

Is it too early for you to start thinking about retirement? If you're smart, you'll start saving for retirement with your very first job out of college. You may use mutual funds, a savings plan at work, or make some investments on your own. The reasons people purchase long-term investments (stocks, bonds, and real estate, for example) are for current income (interest and dividends) and appreciation of the investment's value. Some very wealthy individuals invest in a wide variety of traditional and nontraditional investments in order to obtain significant influence over, or even to control, corporate entities and to maximize their wealth.

Businesses such as **Intel, Apple, General Electric**, and **Coca-Cola** invest for the same reasons. In this chapter you'll learn how to account for long-term investments of several types. We use Intel Corporation as our example company because Intel has so many interesting investments. You'll also learn about the time value of money, which is an essential factor in valuing some types of long-term investments as well as long-term liabilities (covered in Chapter 9).

What comes to mind when you think of Intel? Computer processors and microchips? Yes, but interestingly, 22.4% [($2,430 million + $9,063 million + $7,097 million + $2,023 million)/$91,956 million] of Intel's assets are tied up in investments in other companies. The assets section of Intel's 2014 balance sheet reports these investments on lines 5, 6, 12, and 13. ●

	A	B	C
	A1		
1	**Intel Corporation** **Consolidated Partial Balance Sheet (Partial, Adapted)**		
2	**In Millions**	**Dec. 27, 2014**	**Dec. 28, 2013**
3	**Current assets:**		
4	Cash and cash equivalents	$ 2,561	$ 5,674
5	Short-term investments	2,430	5,972
6	Trading assets	9,063	8,441
7	Accounts receivable, net	4,427	3,582
8	Inventories	4,273	4,172
9	Other current assets	4,976	4,243
10	Total current assets	27,730	32,084
11	Property, plant, and equipment, net	33,238	31,428
12	Marketable equity securities	7,097	6,221
13	Other long-term investments	2,023	1,473
14	Goodwill	10,861	10,513
15	Identified intangible assets, net	4,446	5,150
16	Other long-term assets	6,561	5,489
17	Total assets	$ 91,956	$ 92,358
18			

Throughout this course, you've become increasingly familiar with the financial statements of companies such as **The Walt Disney Company, Apple Inc., Under Armour, Inc.,** and **FedEx**. You've seen most of the items that appear in a set of financial statements. One of your learning goals should be to develop the ability to analyze whatever you encounter in real-company statements. This chapter will help you advance toward that goal.

The first half of this chapter shows how to account for long-term investments, including a brief overview of consolidated financial statements and the translation of financial statements of U.S.-owned foreign companies into U.S. dollars. The second half of the chapter covers the impact of the time value of money on the valuation of investments.

LEARNING OBJECTIVES

1 **Analyze and report** investments in held-to-maturity debt securities

2 **Analyze and report** investments in available-for-sale securities

3 **Analyze and report** investments in affiliated companies using the equity method

4 **Analyze and report** controlling interests in other corporations using consolidated financial statements

5 **Report** investing activities on the statement of cash flows

6 **Explain** the impact of the time value of money on certain types of investments

You can access the most current annual report of Intel Corporation in Excel format at **http://www.sec.gov**. Using the "FILINGS" link on the toolbar at the top of the home page, select "Company Filings Search." This will take you to the "Edgar Company Filings" page. Type "Intel" in the company name box, and select "Search." This will produce the "EDGAR Search Results" page showing the company name. Click on the "CIK" link beside the company name. This will pull up a list of the reports the company has filed with the SEC. Under the "Filing Type" box, type "10-K" and click the search box. Form 10-K is the SEC form for the company's annual report. Find the year that you wish to view. Click on the "Interactive Data" box, which takes you to the "View Filing Data" page. Find and click on the "View Excel Document" link at the top of this page. You may choose to either open or download the Excel files containing the company's most recent financial statements.

Investments come in all sizes and shapes—ranging from a few shares of stock to a controlling interest in multiple corporations, or interests in other types of investments such as corporate or municipal bonds or real estate. In later chapters, we will discuss stocks and bonds from the perspective of the company that issues the securities. In this chapter, we examine *long-term investments* from the perspective of the purchaser, or investor.

To consider investments, we need to define two key terms. The entity that owns stock or bonds of a corporation or other entity is the *investor*. The corporation or other entity that issues the stock or bond is the *investee*. A corporation or other entity, such as a municipality, that issues bonds is a *debtor*. If you own some shares of Intel common stock, you are an investor and Intel is the investee. If you own Intel bonds, you are an investor/creditor and Intel is the investee/debtor.

Stock and Bond Prices

You can log on to the Internet to learn Intel's current stock price or the current trading value of its publicly held debt. Exhibit 8-1 presents recent information from a popular financial website about Intel's stock on a particular day. During the previous 52 weeks, Intel common stock had a high price of $37.90 per share and a low of $24.92 per share. The annual cash dividend for the most recent full year was $0.90 per share. During the previous day, 64.78 million shares of Intel common stock were traded. At day's end, the price of the stock closed at $31.31, up $0.57 from the closing price of the preceding day.

Exhibit 8-1 | Intel Corporation Common Stock Information

52-Week						
Hi	Lo	Stock (sym)	Div	Avg. Volume	Close	Net Change
$37.90	$24.92	INTC	$0.90	64,780,000	$31.31	+0.57

Reporting Investments on the Balance Sheet

An investment is an asset to the investor. The investment may be short-term or long-term. **Short-term investments** in marketable equity or debt securities are current assets. They can be classified as *trading*, *held-to-maturity*, or *available-for-sale*, depending on management's intent and ability to hold rather than liquidate (sell) them. To be listed as short-term on the balance sheet,

- the investment must be *liquid* (readily convertible to cash), and
- the investor must intend either to convert the investment to cash within one year or operating cycle, whichever is longer, or to use it to pay a current liability.

We saw how to account for short-term investments in Chapter 5.

Investments that aren't short-term are listed as **long-term investments**, a category of non-current assets. Long-term investments include stocks and bonds that the investor expects to hold for longer than one year or operating cycle, whichever is longer. Exhibit 8-2 shows where short-term and long-term investments appear on the balance sheet.

Exhibit 8-2 | Reporting Investments on the Balance Sheet

	A1			A	B	C
1	**Current Assets:**					
2		Cash			$ X	
3		Short-term investments			X	
4		Accounts receivable			X	
5		Inventories			X	
6		Prepaid expenses			X	
7			Total current assets			X
8	Property, plant, and equipment					X
9	Long-term investments [or simply Investments]					X
10	Intangible assets					X
11	Other assets					X
12						

Assets are generally listed on the balance sheet in the order of liquidity. Long-term investments are less liquid than short-term investments because the company neither intends nor has the ability to liquidate them within the current year or operating cycle. Intel reports short-term investments as current assets, immediately after cash and cash equivalents (p. 439, lines 5 and 6). The company reports long-term investments in both debt securities (bonds) and equity securities (stock) in the non-current asset section of the balance sheet (p. 439, lines 12 and 13). We now discuss the financial reporting for each of these types of long-term investments.

ANALYZE AND REPORT INVESTMENTS IN HELD-TO-MATURITY DEBT SECURITIES

The major investors in debt securities such as bonds are financial institutions—pension funds, mutual funds, and insurance companies such as Intel Capital. The relationship between the issuing corporation and the investor (bondholder) may be diagrammed as follows:

1 **Analyze and report** investments in held-to-maturity debt securities

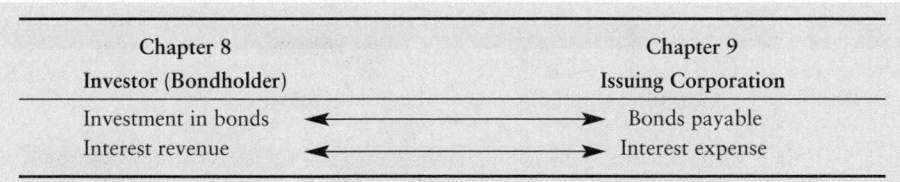

Chapter 8	Chapter 9
Investor (Bondholder)	**Issuing Corporation**
Investment in bonds ⟷	Bonds payable
Interest revenue ⟷	Interest expense

If the investor company intends to hold debt securities longer than a year, but not until maturity, they are categorized as available-for-sale securities and accounted for under the fair value method, described in the next section. If the investing company intends to hold a debt security until maturity, it accounts for the security at amortized cost, as a **held-to-maturity investment**, as described in this section.

Bonds of publicly traded companies are traded on the open market, just as stocks are. Like other forms of debt, bonds pay investors interest, usually semiannually (twice a year). The (face) interest rate of a particular bond is quoted on the face of the instrument and determines the cash amount of semiannual interest the debtor company pays. Bonds are usually issued in $1,000 face (par) denominations, but they typically do not sell at par value. The price of a bond at a particular time is quoted as a percentage of its par value. Market prices of bonds fluctuate inversely with market interest rates. If market rates on competing instruments are higher than the face rate of interest on a particular bond, the bond sells at a discount (below 100% of par, or face value). For example, a quoted bond price of 96.5 means that the $1,000 bond is selling for 96.5% of par, or $965 (discounted from par value). If market rates are lower than the face rate of interest on the bond being considered, the bond sells at a premium (above 100% of par). For example, a quoted bond price of 102.5 means that the bond is selling for 102.5% of par, or $1,025 (a premium over par value).

Held-to-maturity investments are reported by the *amortized cost method*, which determines the carrying amount. Bond investments are initially recorded at cost (market price as a percentage × par value of bonds issued). At each semiannual interest payment date, the investor records interest revenue (one-half the annual face interest rate × the face amount of the bond). In addition, whenever there is an issue premium or discount, it is amortized by adjusting the carrying amount of the bond upward or downward toward its par or face value, with an offsetting entry being made to interest revenue. Years later, at maturity, the carrying amount will have been adjusted from the original issue amount to its par or face value, and the investor will receive the face amount upon redemption of the bond.

As an example, assume that Intel Capital purchases $10,000 of 6% CBS bonds at a price of 95.2 on April 1, 2016. Intel Capital intends to hold the bonds until their maturity date, April 1, 2020. Interest dates are semiannual, on April 1 and October 1. Because these bonds mature on April 1, 2020, they will be outstanding for four years (48 months). In this case, Intel Capital pays a discount price for the bonds (95.2% of face value), because the market rates of interest for other similar instruments are higher than 6%.[1] The initial purchase price and carrying value of the investment is $9,520 (95.2% × $10,000). Intel Capital must amortize the discount of $480 and thus adjust the bonds' carrying amount from cost of $9,520 up to $10,000 over their 48-month term to maturity. Assume Intel Capital amortizes discount on the bonds by the straight-line method. Following are the entries for this bond investment on April 1 and October 1, 2016, the issue date and the first interest payment date:

	A	B	C	D
1	2016			
2	Apr 1	Held-to-Maturity Investment in Bonds ($10,000 × 0.952)	9,520	
3		Cash		9,520
4		*To purchase bond investment.*		
5				
6	Oct 1	Cash ($10,000 × 0.06 × 6/12)	300	
7		Interest Revenue		300
8		*To receive semiannual interest.*		
9				
10	Oct 1	Held-to-Maturity Investment in Bonds [($10,000 − $9,520)/48] × 6	60	
11		Interest Revenue		60
12		*To amortize discount on bond investment.*		
13				

At December 31, 2016, Intel Capital's year-end adjustments are

	A	B	C	D
1	2016			
2	Dec 31	Interest Receivable ($10,000 × 0.06 × 3/12)	150	
3		Interest Revenue		150
4		*To accrue interest revenue.*		
5				
6	Dec 31	Held-to-Maturity Investment in Bonds [($10,000 − $9,520)/48] × 3	30	
7		Interest Revenue		30
8		*To amortize discount on bond investment.*		
9				

---

[1]We will discuss how the time value of money impacts the price of an investment in the second half of this chapter.

This amortization entry has two effects:

- It increases the Held-to-Maturity Investment in Bonds account on its march toward maturity value, which will be $10,000 on April 1, 2020.
- It records the interest revenue earned from the increase in the carrying amount of the investment.

The financial statements of Intel Capital at December 31, 2016, would report the following for this investment in bonds:

Balance sheet at December 31, 2016:
Current assets:
Interest receivable... $ 150
Long-term assets:
Property, plant, and equipment .... X,XXX
Held-to-maturity investment in bonds ($9,520 + $60 + $30) 9,610
Income statement for the year ended December 31, 2016:
Other revenues:
Interest revenue ($300 + $60 + $150 + $30) .... $ 540

By April 1, 2020, the maturity date of the bonds, the carrying value will have been adjusted to equal the face value of $10,000, and Intel Capital will redeem the bonds for this amount.

If market interest rates are below the face rate on these bonds on the date of purchase, they will sell at a premium, with an initial carrying value of something above $10,000. On each interest payment date, as interest revenue is recorded, the premium on the bonds will be amortized as well, reducing the amount of interest revenue and gradually reducing the carrying value of the bonds over the period of the investment to its maturity value of $10,000.

ANALYZE AND REPORT INVESTMENTS IN AVAILABLE-FOR-SALE SECURITIES

Long-term **available-for-sale securities** may be debt securities not held to maturity or equity (stock) securities other than trading securities. *Cost* is used only as the initial amount for recording the purchase of these investments. At the end of each reporting period, these securities are adjusted to their current **fair values** because the company expects to sell the investments at these values at some point in the future, although not within the next year.

2 **Analyze and report** investments in available-for-sale securities

Accounting Methods for Long-Term Stock Investments

The accounting rules for long-term investments in equity securities (stock) depend on the percentage of ownership by the investor, as shown in Exhibit 8-3:

Exhibit 8-3 | Accounting Methods for Long-Term Stock Investments by Percentage of Ownership

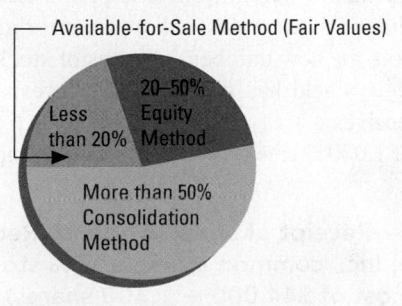

An investment less than 20% is considered available-for-sale because the investor usually has little or no influence on the investee, in which case the strategy would be to hold the investment, making it available for sale in periods beyond the end of the fiscal year. Ownership of 20% to 50% provides the investor with the opportunity to significantly influence the investee's operating decisions and policies over the long run. An investment above 50% allows the investor a great deal of long-term influence—perhaps control—over the investee company. The methods of accounting for 20% or more equity interests are discussed in the two sections that follow. In this section, we discuss securities accounted for as available-for-sale investments. Let's begin with an example.

Suppose Intel purchases 1,000 shares of **Advent Software, Inc.,** common stock at the market price of $44 per share. Intel intends to hold this investment for longer than a year, and therefore treats it as a long-term available-for-sale security (AFSS). Intel's entry to record the investment is

A1			
	A	B	C	D
1	2016			
2	Oct 23	Investment in AFSS (1,000 × $44)	44,000	
3		Cash		44,000
4		*Purchased investment.*		
5				

Assets	=	Liabilities	+	Stockholders' Equity
+ 44,000	=	0	+	0
− 44,000				

Assume that Intel receives a $0.20 cash dividend per share on the Advent Software stock. Intel's entry to record receipt of the dividend is

A1			
	A	B	C	D
1	2016			
2	Nov 14	Cash (1,000 × $0.20)	200	
3		Dividend Revenue		200
4		*Received cash dividend.*		
5				

Assets	=	Liabilities	+	Stockholders' Equity	+	Revenues
+200	=	0	+			+200

Receipt of a *stock* dividend is different from receipt of a cash dividend. For a stock dividend, the investor records no dividend revenue. Instead, the investor makes a memorandum entry in the accounting records to denote the new number of shares of stock held as an investment. Because the number of shares of stock held has increased, the investor's cost per share decreases. To illustrate, suppose Intel receives a 10% stock dividend from Advent Software, Inc. Intel would receive 100 shares (10% of 1,000 shares previously held) and make this memorandum entry in its accounting records:

MEMORANDUM—Receipt of stock dividend: Received 100 shares of Advent Software, Inc., common stock in 10% stock dividend. New cost per share is $40.00 (cost of $44,000 ÷ 1,100 shares).

In all future transactions affecting this investment, Intel's cost per share is now $40.

The Fair Value Adjustment

Generally accepted accounting principles (GAAP) require that companies adjust their portfolios of available-for-sale securities to *fair value* as of the balance sheet date. Fair value of an asset is the amount that would be received for the securities in an "orderly sale." GAAP recognizes three different approaches:

- Level 1: Quoted prices in active markets for identical assets
- Level 2: Estimates based on other observable inputs (e.g., prices for similar assets)
- Level 3: Estimates based on unobservable estimates (the company's own estimates based on certain assumptions)

Fair value should be determined using the most reliable method available. Level 1 is preferable because it is considered easiest to verify. If no quoted prices in active markets are available, the investor moves to levels 2 and 3, in that order, to make the fair value adjustment. Companies must disclose the aggregate amounts of fair value for both trading and available-for-sale investments determined under each of these three levels in the financial statement footnotes. In our example of the investment in Advent Software, Inc., stock, a level 1 fair value is available, because the stock has a quoted market price as of the end of the year. Returning to our original example before the stock dividend, assume that the quoted market price of the stock is $46.50, making fair value of the 1,000 shares of Advent Software, Inc., common stock $46,500 on December 31, 2016. In this case, Intel makes the following entry to adjust the investment to fair value:

	A	B	C	D
1	2016			
2	Dec 31	Allowance to Adjust Investment in AFSS to Market*		
3		($46,500 – $44,000)	2,500	
4		Unrealized Gain on Investment in AFSS		2,500
5		*Adjusted investment to fair value.*		
6				

*Alternatively, the entry may be made directly to the Investment in AFSS account.

The increase in the investment's fair value creates additional equity for the investor.

Assets	=	Liabilities	+	Stockholders' Equity
+ 2,500	=	0		+ 2,500

The Allowance to Adjust Investment in AFSS to Market is an optional companion account to the Investment in AFSS. Rather than use the allowance account, the company may make periodic adjustments directly to the Investment in AFSS account, as shown in Exhibit 5-2. In either case, the investment's cost ($44,000) plus the market adjustment ($2,500) equals the investment fair value carrying amount ($46,500), as follows:

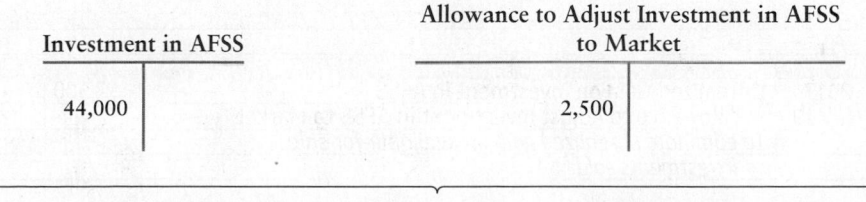

Investment carrying amount = Fair value of $46,500

Here the allowance has a debit balance because the fair value of the investment increased. If the investment's fair value declines, the allowance is credited. In that case, the carrying amount is its cost minus the allowance.

The other side of this adjustment entry is a credit to Unrealized Gain on Investment in AFSS. If the fair value of the investment declines, the company debits Unrealized Loss on Investment in AFSS. *Unrealized* gains and losses result from changes in fair value, not from sales of investments. For available-for-sale investments, the Unrealized Gain on Investment in AFSS account or the Unrealized Loss on Investment in AFSS account is reported as an element of *other comprehensive income*, which is a change in owners' equity that bypasses net income. The unrealized gain or loss is reported in a separate statement of comprehensive income or in a separate section of the income statement below net income in a combined statement of income and comprehensive income.

The statement of comprehensive income is covered more thoroughly in Chapter 11. The following display shows one of the ways that Intel could report its regular net income plus other comprehensive income from the unrealized gain in its combined Statement of Income and Other Comprehensive Income at the end of 2016 (all other figures are assumed for this illustration):

	A	B	C
1	**Intel Corporation** **Consolidated Statement of Comprehensive Income** **For Year Ended December 29, 2016**		
2	**(figures assumed, not actual)**		
3	Revenues		$ 50,000
4	Expenses, including income tax		36,000
5	Net income		$ 14,000
6	Other comprehensive income:		
7	Unrealized gain on investment in AFSS	$ 2,500	
8	Less Income tax 40%	(1,000)	1,500
9	Comprehensive income		$ 15,500
10			

The preceding example assumes that the investor holds an investment in only one equity security: stock of another company. Usually, companies invest in a portfolio of securities (both equity and debt securities of more than one company). In this case, the periodic adjustment to fair value must be made for the portfolio as a whole. See the "Try It" exercise at the end of this section (p. 447) for an example.

Selling an Available-for-Sale Investment

The sale of an available-for-sale investment usually results in a *realized* gain or loss. When an available-for-sale asset that has been revalued is subsequently sold, the amount of unrealized gain or loss existing on the asset at the date of sale is reversed, effectively returning the carrying value of the portion of the asset sold to its original cost. Realized gains and losses on the investment are then measured as the difference between the amount received from the sale and the cost of the investment.

Suppose Intel sells its entire investment in Advent Software, Inc., stock for $43,000 during 2017. Intel would record the sale as follows:

	A	B	C	D
1	2017	Unrealized Gain on Investment in AFSS	2,500	
2	May 19	Allowance to Adjust Investment in AFSS to Market		2,500
3		*To eliminate unrealized gain on available-for-sale*		
4		*investments sold.*		
5				
6	May 19	Cash	43,000	
7		Loss on Sale of Investment in AFSS	1,000	
8		Investment in AFSS (cost)		44,000
9		*Sold investment.*		
10				

Assets	=	Liabilities	+	Stockholders' Equity	−	Losses
− 2,500				− 2,500		
+ 43,000	=			0	−	1,000
− 44,000						

Intel would report Loss on Sale of Investment in AFSS as a realized loss in "Other income or loss" on the income statement.

Suppose Intel Corporation holds the following available-for-sale securities as long-term investments at December 31, 2017:

Stock	Cost	Level 1 Fair Value
The Coca-Cola Company.........	$ 85,000	$71,000
General Electric Company........	16,000	12,000
	$101,000	$83,000

Show how Intel will report long-term investments on its December 31, 2017, balance sheet.

Answer:

Assets	
Investments in AFSS...	$83,000

ANALYZE AND REPORT INVESTMENTS IN AFFILIATED COMPANIES USING THE EQUITY METHOD

Buying a Large Stake in Another Company

An investor owning between 20% and 50% of the investee's voting stock or other ownership interests may significantly influence the business activities of the investee. Such an investor can probably affect dividend policies, product lines, and other important matters. The investor company will more than likely hold one or more seats on the board of directors of the investee company. As shown in Exhibit 8-3, we use the **equity method** to account for these types of investments.

Intel holds equity-method investments in IM Flash Technologies, LLC, and Intel-GE Care Innovations, LLC. These investee companies are referred to as *affiliates* because the investor has a sufficient ownership percentage in them to significantly influence their operations. Because Intel has a voice in shaping the policy and operations of IM Flash Technologies, LLC, some measure of its profits and losses should be included in Intel's income.

 Analyze and report investments in affiliated companies using the equity method

Accounting for Equity-Method Investments

Investments accounted for by the equity method are recorded initially at cost. Suppose that, on January 1, 2016, Intel pays $490 million for 49% of the ownership of IM Flash Technologies, LLC. Intel's entry to record the purchase of this investment follows (in millions):

	A	B	C	D
1	2016			
2	Jan 1	Equity-method Investment	490	
3		Cash		490
4		*To purchase equity–method investment.*		
5				

Assets = Liabilities + Stockholders' Equity

+ 490 = 0 + 0

− 490

The Investor's Percentage of Investee Income. Under the equity method, Intel, as the investor, applies its percentage of ownership—49% in our example—in recording its share of the investee's net income and dividends. If IM Flash Technologies reports net income of $300 million for 2016, Intel records 49% of this amount as follows (in millions):

	A	B	C	D
1	2016			
2	Dec 31	Equity-method Investment (300×0.49)	147	
3		Equity-method Investment Revenue		147
4		*To record investment revenue.*		
5				

		Stockholders' Equity
Assets =	Liabilities +	(Revenue)

+ 147 = 0 + 147

Because of the close relationship between Intel and IM Flash Technologies, Intel, the investor, increases the Equity-method Investment account and records Equity-method Investment Revenue when IM Flash Technologies, the investee, reports income. As IM Flash's stockholders' equity increases, so does the Equity-method Investment account on Intel's books.

Receiving Dividends Under the Equity Method. Intel records its proportionate part of cash dividends received from IM Flash. When IM Flash declares and pays a cash dividend of $200 million, Intel receives 49% of this dividend and records this entry (in millions):

	A	B	C	D
1	2016			
2	Dec 31	Cash $(\$200 \times 0.49)$	98	
3		Equity-method Investment		98
4		*To receive cash dividend on equity-method investment.*		
5				

Assets = Liabilities + Stockholders' Equity

+ 98 = 0 + 0

− 98

The Equity-method Investment account is *decreased* for the receipt of a dividend on an equity-method investment. Why? Because the dividend decreases the investee's owners' equity and thus the investor's investment.

After the preceding entries are posted, Intel's Equity-method Investment account at December 31, 2016, shows Intel's equity in the net assets of IM Flash Technologies (in millions):

Equity-method Investment

Jan 1	Purchase	490	Dec 31	Dividends	98
Dec 31	Net income	147			
Dec 31	Balance	539			

On December 31, 2016, Intel would report the Equity-method investment on the balance sheet and the Equity-method investment revenue on the income statement as follows:

	Millions
Balance sheet (partial):	
Assets	
Total current assets...	$XXX
Property, plant, and equipment, net...................	XXX
Equity-method investment.................................	539
Income statement (partial):	
Income from operations.....................................	$XXX
Other revenue:	
Equity-method investment revenue................	147
Net income...	$XXX

Gain or loss on the sale of an equity-method investment is measured as the difference between the sale proceeds and the carrying amount of the investment. For example, Intel's sale of 20% of the IM Flash Technologies common stock for $100 million on January 1, 2017 would be recorded as follows (in millions):

	A	B	C	D
	A1			
1	2017			
2	Jan 1	Cash	100.0	
3		Loss on Sale of Equity-method Investment	7.8	
4		Equity-method Investment ($539 × 0.20)		107.8
5		*Sold 20% of investment.*		
6				

Assets	=	Liabilities	+	Stockholders' Equity	−	Losses
+ 100	=	0			−	7.8
− 107.8						

Summary of the Equity Method. The following T-account illustrates the accounting for equity-method investments:

Equity-method Investment

Original cost	Share of losses
Share of income	Share of dividends
Balance	

ANALYZE AND REPORT CONTROLLING INTERESTS IN OTHER CORPORATIONS USING CONSOLIDATED FINANCIAL STATEMENTS

4 **Analyze and report** controlling interests in other corporations using consolidated financial statements

In this section, we cover the situation in which an investing corporation buys more than 50% of the voting stock of another company, permitting the investor to actually *control* the investee. Intel's ownership of Intel Capital is an example.

Why Buy Controlling Interest in Another Company?

Most large corporations own controlling interests in other companies. A **controlling (or majority) interest** is the ownership of more than 50% of the investee's voting stock. Such an investment enables the investor to elect a majority of the members of the investee's board of directors and thus control the investee's policies, such as its production, distribution (supply chain), financing, and investing decisions. The investor is called the **parent company**, and the investee company is called the **subsidiary**. For example, **McAfee, Inc.**, a computer data security company, is a subsidiary of Intel Corporation, the parent. Therefore, the stockholders of Intel control McAfee, Inc., as diagrammed in Exhibit 8-4.

Exhibit 8-4 | Ownership Structure of Intel Corporation and McAfee, Inc.

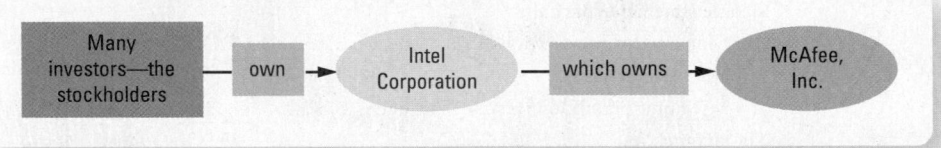

Intel Corporation owned controlling interests in 29 other subsidiary corporations as of the end of fiscal 2014. Exhibit 8-5 shows some of these other subsidiaries.

Exhibit 8-5 | Selected Subsidiaries of Intel Corporation

Intel Capital	Intel Americas, Inc.
Componentes Intel de Costa Rica, S.A.	Intel Europe, Inc.
Intel Asia Holding Limited	Wind River Systems, Inc.

Consolidation Accounting

Consolidation accounting is a method of combining the financial statements of all the companies controlled by the same stockholders. This method reports a single set of financial statements for the consolidated entity, which carries the name of the parent company.

Consolidated financial statements combine the balance sheets, income statements, statements of stockholders' equity, and cash flow statements of the parent company with those of its subsidiaries. The result is a single set of statements as if the parent and its subsidiaries were one company. Investors can gain a better perspective on total operations than they could by examining the reports of the parent and each individual subsidiary.

In consolidated financial statements, the assets, liabilities, revenues, and expenses of each subsidiary are added to the parent's accounts. For example, the balance in Intel Capital's Cash account is added to the balance in the Intel Corporation's Cash account and to the cash of all other subsidiaries. The sum of all of the cash amounts is presented as a single amount in the Intel consolidated balance sheet. Each account balance of a subsidiary, such as Intel Capital or Intel Europe, Inc., loses its identity in the consolidated statements, which bear the name of the parent, Intel Corporation. After a subsidiary's financial statements become consolidated into the parent company's statements, the subsidiary's statements are no longer available to the public.

Exhibit 8-6 diagrams a corporate structure for a parent corporation that owns controlling interests in five subsidiaries and an equity-method investment in another investee company.

Exhibit 8-6 | Parent Company with Consolidated Subsidiaries and an Equity-Method Investment

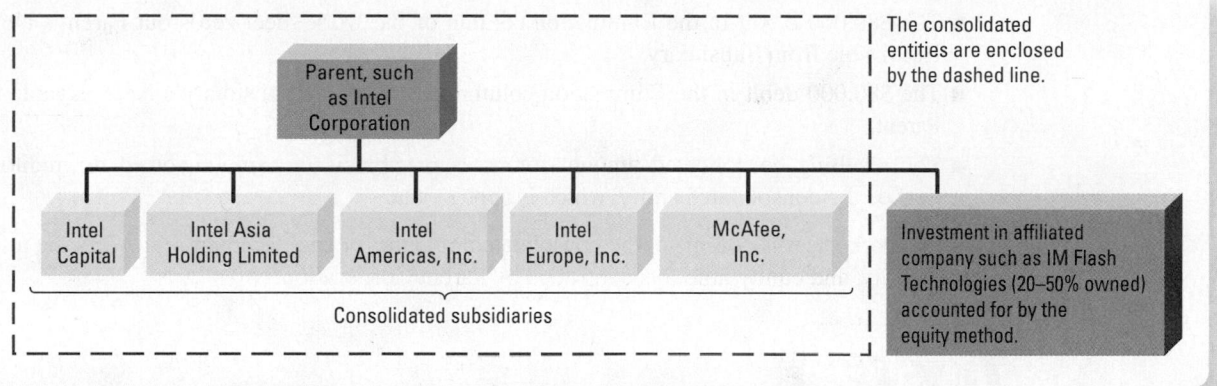

The Consolidated Balance Sheet and the Related Work Sheet

Intel Corporation owns all (100%) of the outstanding voting common stock of McAfee, Inc. Both Intel and McAfee, Inc., keep separate sets of books. Intel, the parent company, uses a work sheet to prepare the consolidated statements of Intel and its consolidated subsidiaries. Then Intel's consolidated balance sheet shows the combined assets and liabilities of Intel and all its subsidiaries.

Exhibit 8-7 shows the work sheet for consolidating the balance sheets of Parent Corporation and Subsidiary Corporation. We use these hypothetical entities to illustrate the consolidation process. Consider elimination entry (a) for the parent-subsidiary ownership accounts. Entry (a) credits the parent's Investment account to eliminate its debit balance. Entry (a) also eliminates the subsidiary's stockholders' equity accounts by debiting the subsidiary's Common Stock and Retained Earnings for their full balances. Without this elimination, the consolidated financial statements would include both the parent company's investment in the subsidiary and the subsidiary company's equity. But these accounts represent the same thing—Subsidiary's equity—and so they must be eliminated from the consolidated totals. If they weren't, the same resources would be counted twice.

Exhibit 8-7 | Work Sheet for a Consolidated Balance Sheet

A1					
A	**B**	**C**	**D**	**E**	**F**
1	Parent Corporation	Subsidiary Corporation	Eliminations Debit	Eliminations Credit	Parent and Subsidiary Consolidated Amounts
2					
3 **Assets**					
4 Cash	12,000	18,000			30,000
5 Note receivable from Subsidiary	80,000	—		(b) 80,000	—
6 Inventory	104,000	91,000			195,000
7 Investment in Subsidiary	150,000	—		(a) 150,000	—
8 Other assets	218,000	138,000			356,000
9 Total	564,000	247,000			581,000
10 **Liabilities and Stockholders' Equity**					
11 Accounts payable	43,000	17,000			60,000
12 Notes payable	190,000	80,000	(b) 80,000		190,000
13 Common stock	176,000	100,000	(a) 100,000		176,000
14 Retained earnings	155,000	50,000	(a) 50,000		155,000
15 Total	564,000	247,000	230,000	230,000	581,000
16					

The resulting Parent and Subsidiary consolidated balance sheet (far-right column) reports no Investment in Subsidiary account. Moreover, the consolidated totals for Common Stock and Retained Earnings are those of Parent Corporation only. Study the final column of the consolidation work sheet.

In this example, Parent Corporation has an $80,000 note receivable from Subsidiary, and Subsidiary has a note payable to Parent. The parent's receivable and the subsidiary's payable represent the same resources—all entirely within the consolidated entity. Both, therefore, must be eliminated, and entry (b) accomplishes this.

- The $80,000 credit in the Elimination column of the work sheet zeros out Parent's Note Receivable from Subsidiary.
- The $80,000 debit in the Elimination column zeros out the Subsidiary's Note Payable to Parent.
- The resulting consolidated amount for notes payable is the amount owed to creditors outside the consolidated entity, which is appropriate.

After the work sheet is complete, the consolidated amount for each account represents the total asset, liability, and equity amounts controlled by Parent Corporation.

>>

Examine Exhibit 8-7. Why does the consolidated stockholders' equity ($176,000 + $155,000) *exclude* the equity of Subsidiary Corporation?

Answer:

The stockholders' equity of the consolidated entity is that of the parent only. To include the stockholders' equity of the subsidiary as well as the investment in the subsidiary on the parent's books would be double counting.

Goodwill and Noncontrolling Interest

Goodwill and Noncontrolling (minority) Interest are two accounts that only a consolidated entity can have. As we saw in Chapter 7, goodwill is the intangible asset of the parent company that represents the parent company's excess payment over and above the fair market value of net assets of the acquired subsidiary.

Noncontrolling (minority) interest arises when a parent company owns less than 100% of the stock of a subsidiary. For example, General Electric (GE) owns less than 100% of some of the companies it controls. The remainder of the subsidiaries' stock is noncontrolling (minority) interest to GE. Noncontrolling Interest is reported as a separate account in the stockholders' equity section of the consolidated balance sheet of the parent company. The amount of noncontrolling interest in subsidiaries' stock must be clearly identified and labeled as such. GE reports noncontrolling interest in the stockholders' equity section on its balance sheet. By contrast, Intel reports no noncontrolling interest, which suggests that Intel owns 100% of all its subsidiaries.

Income of a Consolidated Entity

The income of a consolidated entity is the net income of the parent plus the parent's proportion of the subsidiaries' net income. Suppose Parent Company owns all the stock of Subsidiary S-1 and 60% of the stock of Subsidiary S-2. During the year just ended, Parent earned net income of $330,000, S-1 earned $150,000, and S-2 had a net loss of $100,000. Parent Company would report net income of $420,000, computed as

	Net Income (Net Loss) of Each Company		Parent's Ownership of Each Company		Parent's Consolidated Net Income (Net Loss)
Parent Company	$330,000	×	100%	=	$330,000
Subsidiary S-1	150,000	×	100%	=	150,000
Subsidiary S-2	(100,000)	×	60%	=	(60,000)
Consolidated net income					$420,000

COOKING THE BOOKS
with Investments and Debt

Enron Corporation

In 2000, Enron Corporation in Houston, Texas, employed approximately 22,000 people and was one of the world's leading electricity, natural gas, pulp and paper, and communications companies, with reported revenues of nearly $101 billion. *Fortune* had named Enron "America's Most Innovative Company" for six consecutive years. To many outside observers, Enron was the model corporation.

Enron's financial statements showed that the company was making a lot of money, but in reality, most of its profits were merely on paper. Rather than from operations, the great majority of the cash Enron needed to operate on a day-to-day basis came from bank loans. It was very important, therefore, that Enron keep its debt ratio (discussed in Chapter 3), as well as its return on assets (ROA, discussed in Chapter 7), at acceptable levels so the banks would continue to view the company as creditworthy. Enron's balance sheets contained large misstatements in the liabilities and stockholders' equity sections over a period of years. Many of the offsetting misstatements were in long-term assets. Specifically, Enron owned numerous long-term investments, including power plants; water rights; broadband cable; and sophisticated, complex, and somewhat dubious derivative financial instruments in such unusual things as the weather! Many of these investments actually had questionable value, but Enron had abused fair market value accounting to estimate them at grossly inflated values.

To create paper profits, Andrew Fastow, Enron's chief financial officer, created a veritable maze of "special purpose entities" (SPEs), financed with bank debt. He valued the investments mentioned above using "mark-to-market" (fair value accounting), using unrealistic assumptions that created inflated asset values on the financial statements. He then "sold" the dubious investments to the SPEs to get them off Enron's books. Enron recorded millions of dollars in "profits" from these transactions. Fastow then used Enron stock to collateralize the bank debt of the SPEs, making the transactions entirely circular. Unknown to Enron's board of directors, Fastow or members of his own family owned most of these entities, making them related parties to Enron. Enron was, in fact, the owner of the assets of the SPEs, and was, in fact, obligated for the debts of the SPEs since those debts were collateralized with Enron stock.

When Enron's fraud was discovered in late 2001, the company was forced to consolidate the assets of the SPEs, as well as all of their bank debt, into its own financial statements. The inflated assets had to be written down to impaired market values. The end result of the restatement impacted Enron's debt ratio and ROA so much that the banks refused to loan the company any more money to operate. Enron's energy trading business virtually dried up overnight, and it was bankrupt within 60 days. An estimated $60 billion in shareholder value, and 22,000 jobs, were lost. Enron's CEO, Jeffrey Skilling; its CFO, Andrew Fastow; and board chairman, Kenneth Lay, were all convicted of fraud. Skilling and Fastow both went to prison. Lay died suddenly of a heart attack before being sentenced.

Enron's audit firm, Arthur Andersen, was accused of trying to cover up its knowledge of Enron's practices by shredding documents. The firm was indicted by the U.S. Justice Department in March 2002. Because of the indictment, Andersen lost all of its public clients and was forced out of business. As a result, over 58,000 persons lost their jobs worldwide. A U.S. Supreme Court decision in 2005 eventually led to the withdrawal of the indictment, but it came much too late for the once "gold-plated" CPA firm. Allegations about the lack of quality of its work on Enron, as well as other well-publicized cases such as Waste Management (p. 390–391) and WorldCom (p. 377–378), who were also clients, doomed Arthur Andersen.

 **DECISION GUIDELINES**

ACCOUNTING METHODS FOR LONG-TERM INVESTMENTS

These guidelines show which accounting method to use for each type of long-term investment.

Intel has all types of investments—stocks, bonds, 25% interests, and controlling interests. How should Intel account for its various investments?

Type of Long-Term Investment	Accounting Method
Intel owns bonds that it intends to hold to maturity.	Amortized cost
Intel owns a portfolio of bond and other debt securities as well as equity securities in companies (less than 20%) that it intends to hold long-term.	Available-for-sale; fair value
Intel owns between 20% and 50% of investee/affiliate stock.	Equity
Intel owns more than 50% of investee stock.	Consolidation

Mid-Chapter | Summary Problem

1. Identify the appropriate accounting method for each of the following situations:
   a. Investment in 25% of investee's stock
   b. Investment in 10% of available-for-sale stock
   c. Investment in more than 50% of investee's stock

2. At what amount should the following long-term available-for-sale investment portfolio be reported on the December 31 balance sheet? All the investments are less than 5% of the investee's stock. Journalize any adjusting entry required by these data.

Stock	Investment Cost	Current Market Value
DuPont	$ 5,000	$ 5,500
ExxonMobil	61,200	53,000
Procter & Gamble	3,680	6,230

3. Investor paid $67,900 to acquire a 40% equity-method investment in the common stock of Investee. At the end of the first year, Investee's net income was $80,000, and Investee declared and paid cash dividends of $55,000. What is Investor's ending balance in its Equity-Method Investment account? Use a T-account to answer.

4. Parent company paid $85,000 for all the common stock of Subsidiary Company, and Parent owes Subsidiary $20,000 on a note payable. Complete the following consolidation work sheet:

	A1					
	A	B	C	D	E	F
1		Parent Company	Subsidiary Company	Eliminations Debit	Credit	Consolidated Amounts
2	**Assets**					
3	Cash	7,000	4,000			
4	Note receivable from Parent	—	20,000			
5	Investment in Subsidiary	85,000	—			
6	Other assets	108,000	99,000			
7	Total	200,000	123,000			
8	**Liabilities and Stockholders' Equity**					
9	Accounts payable	15,000	8,000			
10	Notes payable	20,000	30,000			
11	Common stock	120,000	60,000			
12	Retained earnings	45,000	25,000			
13	Total	200,000	123,000			
14						

Answers

1. a. Equity method

   b. Available-for-sale, adjusted to fair value at end of each reporting period

   c. Consolidation

2. Report the investments in available-for-sale securities (AFSS) at fair value, $64,730, as follows:

Stock	Investment Cost	Current Market Value
DuPont	$ 5,000	$ 5,500
ExxonMobil	61,200	53,000
Procter & Gamble	3,680	6,230
Totals	$69,880	$64,730

Adjusting entry:

	A1			
	A	B	C	D
1		Unrealized Loss on Investment in AFSS ($69,880 − $64,730)	5,150	
2		Allowance to Adjust Investment in AFSS to Market		5,150
3		*To adjust investments to fair value.*		
4				

3.

Equity-method Investment

Cost	67,900	Dividends	22,000**
Income	32,000*		
Balance	77,900		

* $80,000 × .40 = $32,000
** $55,000 × .40 = $22,000

4. Consolidation work sheet:

A1						
	A	B	C	D	E	F
		Parent Company	Subsidiary Company	Eliminations Debit	Credit	Consolidated Amounts
1						
2	**Assets**					
3	Cash	7,000	4,000			11,000
4	Note receivable from Parent	—	20,000		(a) 20,000	—
5	Investment in Subsidiary	85,000	—		(b) 85,000	—
6	Other assets	108,000	99,000			207,000
7	Total	200,000	123,000			218,000
8	**Liabilities and Stockholders' Equity**					
9	Accounts payable	15,000	8,000			23,000
10	Notes payable	20,000	30,000	(a) 20,000		30,000
11	Common stock	120,000	60,000	(b) 60,000		120,000
12	Retained earnings	45,000	25,000	(b) 25,000		45,000
13	Total	200,000	123,000	105,000	105,000	218,000
14						

Consolidation of Foreign Subsidiaries

GLOBAL VIEW

Many U.S. companies conduct a large part of their business abroad. Intel, General Electric, and PepsiCo, among others, are more active in other countries than they are in the United States. In fact, Intel earns 84% of its revenue outside the United States. Exhibit 8-8 shows the approximate percentages of international revenues for these companies.

Exhibit 8-8 | Extent of International Business

Company	Percentage of International Revenues
Intel...	84%
General Electric........................	54%
PepsiCo	40%

Foreign Currencies and Exchange Rates

Most countries use their own national currency. An exception is the European Union nations: France, Germany, Italy, Belgium, and others, use a common currency, the *euro*, whose symbol is €. If Intel, a U.S. company, sells computer processors to software developers in France, will Intel receive U.S. dollars or euros? If the transaction is in dollars, the company in France must buy dollars to pay Intel in U.S. currency. If the transaction is in euros, then Intel will collect euros and must sell euros for dollars.

The price of one nation's currency can be stated in terms of another country's monetary unit. This measure of one currency against another is called the **foreign-currency exchange rate**. In Exhibit 8-9, the dollar value of a euro is $1.06 as of April 15, 2015. This means that one euro can be bought for $1.06. Other currencies are also listed in Exhibit 8-9. These exchange rates vary daily.

Exhibit 8-9 | Foreign-Currency Exchange Rates as of April 15, 2015

Country	Monetary Unit	U.S. Dollar Value	Country	Monetary Unit	U.S. Dollar Value
Brazil............	Real (R)........................	$0.33	United Kingdom.......	Pound (£).........	$1.48
Canada.........	Canadian Dollar (C$)...	1.24	China	Yuan (元).........	0.16
France..........	Euro (€)........................	1.06	Japan........................	Yen (¥).............	0.010
Germany......	Euro (€)........................	1.06	Mexico....................	Peso (P)............	0.06

Source: *From The Treasury Reporting Rates of Exchange from https://www.fiscal.treasury.gov/fsreports/rpt/treasRptRateExch/current Rates.htm.*

We can convert the cost of an item stated in one currency to its cost in a second currency on a given date. We call this conversion a *translation*. Suppose an item purchased on April 15, 2015, costs 200 euros. To compute its cost in dollars, we multiply the euro amount by the conversion rate: 200 euros × $1.06 = $212.

Two main factors affect the price (the exchange rate) of a particular currency:

1. The ratio of a country's imports to its exports
2. The rate of return available in the country's capital markets

The Import/Export Ratio. Japanese exports often exceed Japan's imports. Customers of Japanese companies must buy yen (the Japanese unit of currency) to pay for their purchases denominated in yen. This strong demand for yen drives up the price of the yen. In contrast, the United States imports more goods than it exports. Americans must sell dollars to buy the foreign currencies needed to pay for the foreign goods. As the supply of dollars increases, the price of the dollar falls relative to other currencies.

The Rate of Return. The rate of return available in a country's capital markets affects the amount of investment funds flowing into the country. When rates of return are high in a politically stable country such as the United States, international investors buy stocks, bonds, and real estate in that country. This activity increases the demand for the nation's currency and drives up its exchange rate.

Currencies are often described as "strong" or "weak." The exchange rate of a **strong currency** is rising relative to other nations' currencies. The exchange rate of a **weak currency** is falling relative to other currencies.

The exchange rate for the British pound was $1.48 on April 15, 2015. On October 17, that rate may rise to $1.62. We would say that the dollar has weakened against the pound. The pound has thus become more expensive, making travel and conducting business in England more expensive for Americans.

The Foreign-Currency Translation Adjustment

The process of translating a foreign subsidiary's financial statements into dollars usually creates a **foreign-currency translation adjustment**. This item appears in the consolidated financial statements of most multinational companies and is reported as part of other comprehensive income. The statement of comprehensive income will be discussed in Chapter 11.

A translation adjustment arises due to changes in the foreign exchange rate over time. In general,

- *assets* and *liabilities* are translated into dollars at the current exchange rate on the date of the statements.
- *stockholders' equity* is translated into dollars at older, historical exchange rates. Paid-in capital accounts are translated at the historical exchange rate when the subsidiary was acquired. Retained earnings are translated at the average exchange rates applicable over the period in which interest in the subsidiary has been held.

This difference in exchange rates creates an out-of-balance condition on the balance sheet. The translation adjustment brings the balance sheet back into balance. Let's see how the translation adjustment works.

Suppose Intel has an Italian subsidiary whose financial statements are expressed in euros (the European currency). Intel must consolidate the Italian subsidiary's financials into its own statements. When Intel acquired the Italian company in 2009, a euro was worth $1.35 (assumed). When the Italian firm earned its retained income during 2009–2014, the average exchange rate was $1.30 (assumed). On the balance sheet date in 2014, a euro is worth only $1.20 (assumed). Exhibit 8-10 shows how to translate the Italian company's balance sheet into dollars.

Exhibit 8-10 | Translation of a Foreign-Currency Balance Sheet into Dollars

	A	B	C	D
			A1	
	Italian Imports, Inc., Accounts	**Euros**	**Exchange Rate**	**Dollars**
1				
2				
3	Assets	€ 800,000	$ 1.20	$ 960,000
4				
5	Liabilities	€ 500,000	1.20	$ 600,000
6	Stockholders' equity			
7	Common stock	100,000	1.35	135,000
8	Retained earnings	200,000	1.30	260,000
9	Accumulated other comprehensive income:			
10	Foreign-currency translation adjustment			(35,000)
11		€ 800,000		$ 960,000
12				

The *foreign-currency translation adjustment* is the balancing amount that brings the dollar amount of total liabilities and equity of a foreign subsidiary into agreement with the dollar amount of total assets (in Exhibit 8-10, total assets equal $960,000). Only after the translation adjustment of $35,000 do total liabilities and equity equal total assets stated in dollars.

What caused the negative translation adjustment? The euro weakened after the acquisition of the Italian company.

- When Intel acquired the foreign subsidiary in 2009, a euro was worth $1.35.

- When the Italian company earned its income during 2009 through 2014, the average exchange rate was $1.30.

- On the balance sheet date in 2014, a euro is worth only $1.20.

- Thus, the Italian company's equity (assets minus liabilities) is translated into only $360,000 ($960,000 − $600,000).

- To bring stockholders' equity to $360,000 requires a $35,000 negative adjustment.

A negative translation adjustment is like a loss, reported as a negative item in the statement of comprehensive income. Losses and gains from translation adjustments eventually are transferred to accumulated other comprehensive income in the stockholders' equity section of the balance sheet, as shown in Exhibit 8-10. The Italian firm's dollar figures in Exhibit 8-10 reflect what Intel would include in its consolidated balance sheet. The consolidation procedures would follow those illustrated in Exhibit 8-7.

REPORT INVESTING ACTIVITIES ON THE STATEMENT OF CASH FLOWS

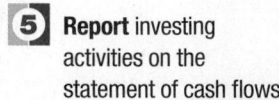

5 **Report** investing activities on the statement of cash flows

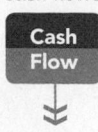

Cash Flow

Investing activities include many types of transactions. In Chapter 7, we covered the purchase and sale of long-term assets such as plant and equipment. In this chapter, we examine investments in stocks and bonds.

Exhibit 8-11 provides excerpts from Intel's 2014 consolidated statement of cash flows. During 2014, Intel sold available-for-sale investments for $1.2 billion. They purchased available-for-sale investments for $7 billion. Other available-for-sale investments matured and brought in additional cash of $8.9 billion. They purchased trading assets for $14.4 billion and sold other trading assets for $13.2 billion. They purchased nonmarketable equity investments for $1.4 billion, spent $10.1 billion for property, plant, and equipment, and spent another 0.3 billion in other investing activities. Overall, investing activities consumed $9.9 billion of Intel Corporation's cash in 2014.

Exhibit 8-11 | Intel Corporation's Investing Activities on the Statement of Cash Flows

	A	B
	Intel Corporation	
1	**Consolidated Statement of Cash Flows (Partial, Adapted)**	
2	**(In billions)**	**2014**
3	**Cash flows provided by (used for) investing activities:**	
4	Sales of available-for-sale investments	$ 1.2
5	Purchases of available-for-sale investments	(7.0)
6	Maturity of available-for-sale investments	8.9
7	Purchase of trading assets	(14.4)
8	Sale of trading assets	13.2
9	Purchase of non-marketable equity investments	(1.4)
10	Additions to property, plant, and equipment	(10.1)
11	Other investing activities	(0.3)
12	**Net cash (used for) investing activities**	$ (9.9)
13		

EXPLAIN THE IMPACT OF THE TIME VALUE OF MONEY ON CERTAIN TYPES OF INVESTMENTS

Which would you rather have: $1,000 received today, or $1,000 received a year from now? A logical person would answer: "I'd rather have the cash now, because if I get it now, I can invest it at some interest rate so that a year in the future I'll have more." The term **future value** means the sum of money that a given current investment will be "worth" at a specified time in the future, assuming a certain interest rate. The term *time value of money* refers to the fact that money earns interest over time. *Interest* is the cost of using money. To borrowers, interest is the fee paid to the lender for the period of the loan. To lenders, interest is the revenue earned from allowing someone else to use their money for a period of time.

> **6** **Explain** the impact of the time value of money on certain types of investments

Whether making investments or borrowing money long-term, we must always recognize the interest we receive or pay. Otherwise, we overlook an important part of the transaction. Suppose you invest $4,545 in corporate bonds that pay 10% interest (based on the original amount invested) each year. After one year, the value of your investment has grown to $5,000, as shown in Exhibit 8-12:

Exhibit 8-12 | Future Value of an Investment

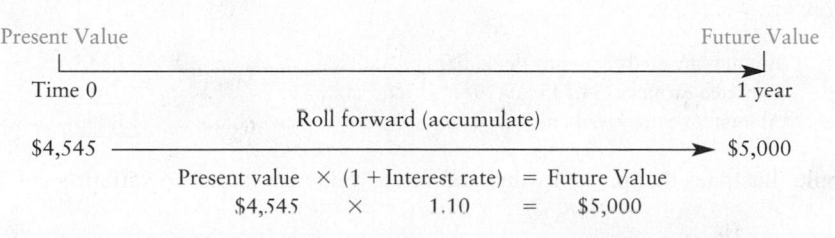

Present Value   Future Value

Time 0   1 year

Roll forward (accumulate)

$4,545 ──────────────────► $5,000

Present value × (1 + Interest rate) = Future Value
$4,545   ×   1.10   = $5,000

The difference between your original (present) investment ($4,545) and the future value of the investment ($5,000) is the amount of interest revenue you will earn during the year ($455).

Interest becomes more important as the time period lengthens because the amount of interest depends on the span of time the money is invested. The time value of money plays a key role in measuring the value of certain long-term investments as well as long-term debt.

If the money were invested for five years, you would have to perform five calculations like the one described above. You would also have to consider the compound interest that your investment is earning. *Compound interest* is not only the interest you earn on your principal amount but also the interest you receive on the interest you have already earned. Most business applications include compound interest.

To calculate the future value of an investment, we need three inputs: (1) the *amount of initial payment* (or *receipt*), (2) the length of *time* between investment and future receipt (or *payment*), and (3) the *interest rate*. The following table shows the interest revenue earned on the original $4,545 investment each year for five years at 10%:

End of Year	Interest	Future Value
0	—	$4,545
1	$4,545 × 0.10 = $455	5,000
2	5,000 × 0.10 = 500	5,500
3	5,500 × 0.10 = 550	6,050
4	6,050 × 0.10 = 605	6,655
5	6,655 × 0.10 = 666	7,321

As shown in the table, earning 10% compounded annually, a $4,545 investment grows to $5,000 at the end of one year, to $5,500 at the end of two years, and to $7,321 at the end of five years.

Present Value

Often a person knows or is able to estimate a future amount and needs to determine the related present value (PV). The term **present value** means the value on a given date of a future payment or series of future payments, discounted to reflect the time value of money. In Exhibit 8-12, present value and future value are on opposite ends of the same timeline. Suppose an investment promises to pay you $5,000 at the *end* of one year. How much would you pay *now* to acquire this investment? You would be willing to pay the present value of the $5,000 future amount, which, at 10% interest, is $4,545.

Like future value, present value depends on three factors: (1) the *amount of payment* (or *receipt*), (2) the length of *time* between investment and future receipt (or *payment*), and (3) the *interest rate*. The process of computing a present value is called *discounting* because the present value is *less* than the future value.

In our investment example, the future receipt is $5,000. The investment period is one year. Assume that you demand an annual interest rate of 10% on your investment. With all three factors specified, you can compute the present value of $5,000 at 10% for one year:

$$\text{Present value} = \frac{\text{Future value}}{1 + \text{Interest rate}} = \frac{\$5,000}{1.10} = \$4,545$$

By turning the data around into a future-value problem, we can verify the present-value computation:

Amount invested (present value)	$4,545
Expected earnings ($4,545 × 0.10)	455
Amount to be received one year from now (future value)..............	$5,000

This example illustrates that present value and future value are based on variations of the same equation:

$$\text{Future value} = \text{Present value} \times (1 + \text{Interest rate})^n$$

$$\text{Present value} = \frac{\text{Future value}}{(1 + \text{Interest rate})^n}$$

Where n = number of periods

If the $5,000 is to be received two years from now, you will pay only $4,132 for the investment, as shown in Exhibit 8-13. By turning the data around, we verify that $4,132 accumulates to $5,000 at 10% for two years:

Amount invested (present value)	$4,132
Expected earnings for first year ($4,132 × 0.10)..........................	413
Value of investment after one year	4,545
Expected earnings for second year ($4,545 × 0.10)	455
Amount to be received two years from now (future value)	$5,000

$$\text{Formula: Present value} = \frac{\text{Future value}}{(1 + \text{Interest rate})^n}$$

$$4,132 = \frac{5,000}{(1 + 0.10)^2}$$

$$\text{Future value} = \text{Present value} \times (1 + \text{Interest rate})^n$$

$$5,000 = \$4,132 \times (1 + 0.10)^2$$

Exhibit 8-13 | Present Value: An Example

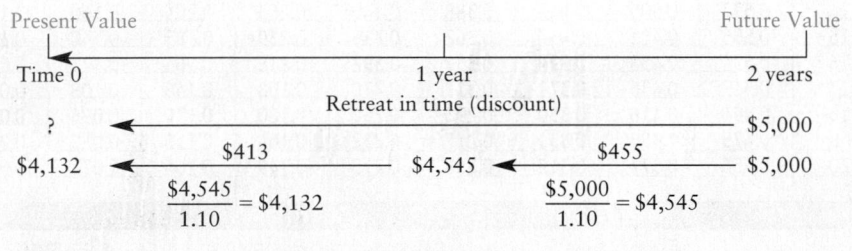

You would pay $4,132—the present value of $5,000—to receive the $5,000 future amount at the end of two years at 10% per year. The $868 difference between the amount invested ($4,132) and the amount to be received ($5,000) is the return on the investment, the sum of the two interest receipts: $413 + $455 = $868.

Present-Value Tables

We have shown the simple formula for computing present value. However, figuring present value "by hand" for investments spanning many years is time-consuming and presents too many opportunities for arithmetic errors. Present-value tables simplify our work. Let's review our examples of present value by using Exhibit 8-14, Present Value of $1.

Exhibit 8-14 | Present Value of $1

	A	B	C	D	E	F	G	H	I	J
1					Present Value of $1					
2	Periods	4%	5%	6%	7%	8%	10%	12%	14%	16%
3										
4	1	0.962	0.952	0.943	0.935	0.926	0.909	0.893	0.877	0.862
5	2	0.925	0.907	0.890	0.873	0.857	0.826	0.797	0.769	0.743
6	3	0.889	0.864	0.840	0.816	0.794	0.751	0.712	0.675	0.641
7	4	0.855	0.823	0.792	0.763	0.735	0.683	0.636	0.592	0.552
8	5	0.822	0.784	0.747	0.713	0.681	0.621	0.567	0.519	0.476
9	6	0.790	0.746	0.705	0.666	0.630	0.564	0.507	0.456	0.410
10	7	0.760	0.711	0.665	0.623	0.583	0.513	0.452	0.400	0.354
11	8	0.731	0.677	0.627	0.582	0.540	0.467	0.404	0.351	0.305
12	9	0.703	0.645	0.592	0.544	0.500	0.424	0.361	0.308	0.263
13	10	0.676	0.614	0.558	0.508	0.463	0.386	0.322	0.270	0.227
14	11	0.650	0.585	0.527	0.475	0.429	0.350	0.287	0.237	0.195
15	12	0.625	0.557	0.497	0.444	0.397	0.319	0.257	0.208	0.168
16	13	0.601	0.530	0.469	0.415	0.368	0.290	0.229	0.182	0.145
17	14	0.577	0.505	0.442	0.388	0.340	0.263	0.205	0.160	0.125
18	15	0.555	0.481	0.417	0.362	0.315	0.239	0.183	0.140	0.108
19	16	0.534	0.458	0.394	0.339	0.292	0.218	0.163	0.123	0.093
20	17	0.513	0.436	0.371	0.317	0.270	0.198	0.146	0.108	0.080
21	18	0.494	0.416	0.350	0.296	0.250	0.180	0.130	0.095	0.069
22	19	0.475	0.396	0.331	0.277	0.232	0.164	0.116	0.083	0.060
23	20	0.456	0.377	0.312	0.258	0.215	0.149	0.104	0.073	0.051
24										

For the 10% investment for one year, we find the junction of the 10% column and row 4 (corresponding to period 1) in Exhibit 8-14. The figure 0.909 is computed as follows: 1/1.10 = 0.909. This work has been done for us, and only the present value factors are given in the table. To figure the present value for $5,000, we multiply 0.909 by $5,000. The result is $4,545, which matches the result we obtained by hand.

For the two-year investment, we read down the 10% column and across row 5 (corresponding to period 2). We multiply 0.826 (computed as 0.909/1.10 = 0.826) by $5,000 and get $4,130, which confirms our earlier computation of $4,132 (the difference is due to rounding in the present-value table). Using the table, we can compute the present value of any single future amount.

Present Value of an Ordinary Annuity

Return to the investment example at the top of page 461. That investment provided the investor with only a single future receipt ($5,000 at the end of two years). *Ordinary annuity investments* provide multiple receipts of an equal amount at fixed year-end intervals over the investment's duration.

Consider an investment that promises *annual* cash receipts of $10,000 to be received at the end of each year for three years. Assume that you demand a 12% return on your investment. What is the investment's present value? That is, what would you pay today to acquire the investment? The investment spans three periods, and you would pay the sum of three present values. The computation follows:

Year	Annual Cash Receipt	Present Value of $1 at 12% (Exhibit 8-14)	Present Value of Annual Cash Receipt
1	$10,000	0.893	$ 8,930
2	10,000	0.797	7,970
3	10,000	0.712	7,120
Total present value of investment...............			$24,020

The present value of this annuity is $24,020. By paying this amount today, you will receive $10,000 at the end of each of the three years while earning 12% on your investment.

This example illustrates repetitive computations of the three future amounts, a time-consuming process. One way to ease the computational burden is to add the three successive present value factors (0.893 + 0.797 + 0.712) and multiply their sum (2.402) by the annual cash receipt ($10,000) to obtain the present value of the annuity ($10,000 × 2.402 = $24,020).

An easier approach is to use a present value of an ordinary annuity table. Exhibit 8-15 shows the present value of $1 to be received periodically for a given number of periods, at the end of each period. The present value of a three-period annuity at 12% is 2.402 (the junction of row 6 [corresponding to period 3] and the 12% column). Thus, $10,000 received annually at the end of each of three years, discounted at 12%, is $24,020 ($10,000 × 2.402), which is the present value.

Exhibit 8-15 | Present Value of Ordinary Annuity of $1

	A	B	C	D	E	F	G	H	I	J
1				**Present Value of Ordinary Annuity of $1**						
2	**Periods**	**4%**	**5%**	**6%**	**7%**	**8%**	**10%**	**12%**	**14%**	**16%**
3										
4	1	0.962	0.952	0.943	0.935	0.926	0.909	0.893	0.877	0.862
5	2	1.886	1.859	1.833	1.808	1.783	1.736	1.690	1.647	1.605
6	3	2.775	2.723	2.673	2.624	2.577	2.487	2.402	2.322	2.246
7	4	3.630	3.546	3.465	3.387	3.312	3.170	3.037	2.914	2.798
8	5	4.452	4.329	4.212	4.100	3.993	3.791	3.605	3.433	3.274
9	6	5.242	5.076	4.917	4.767	4.623	4.355	4.111	3.889	3.685
10	7	6.002	5.786	5.582	5.389	5.206	4.868	4.564	4.288	4.039
11	8	6.733	6.463	6.210	5.971	5.747	5.335	4.968	4.639	4.344
12	9	7.435	7.108	6.802	6.515	6.247	5.759	5.328	4.946	4.608
13	10	8.111	7.722	7.360	7.024	6.710	6.145	5.650	5.216	4.833
14	11	8.760	8.306	7.887	7.499	7.139	6.495	5.938	5.453	5.029
15	12	9.385	8.863	8.384	7.943	7.536	6.814	6.194	5.660	5.197
16	13	9.986	9.394	8.853	8.358	7.904	7.103	6.424	5.842	5.342
17	14	10.563	9.899	9.295	8.745	8.244	7.367	6.628	6.002	5.468
18	15	11.118	10.380	9.712	9.108	8.559	7.606	6.811	6.142	5.575
19	16	11.652	10.838	10.106	9.447	8.851	7.824	6.974	6.265	5.668
20	17	12.166	11.274	10.477	9.763	9.122	8.022	7.120	6.373	5.749
21	18	12.659	11.690	10.828	10.059	9.372	8.201	7.250	6.467	5.818
22	19	13.134	12.085	11.158	10.336	9.604	8.365	7.366	6.550	5.877
23	20	13.590	12.462	11.470	10.594	9.818	8.514	7.469	6.623	5.929
24										

Using Microsoft Excel to Calculate Present Value

While tables such as Exhibits 8-14 and 8-15 are helpful, they are limited to the interest rates in the columns or the periods of time in the rows. Using a computer program like Microsoft Excel provides an infinite range of interest rates and periods. For that reason, most businesspeople solve present-value problems quickly and easily using Excel rather than tables.

■ *To compute the present value of a single payment*, the following formula applies:

$$= \text{Payment}/(1 + i)^n$$

where i = interest rate
n = number of periods

■ In Excel, we use the ^ symbol to indicate the exponent. To illustrate, suppose you are expecting to receive a $500,000 payment four years from now, and suppose that market interest rates are 8%. You would enter the following formula in Excel:

$$= 500000/(1.08)\text{^}4$$

You should calculate a present value of $367,514.93 (rounded to $367,515).

■ *To compute the present value of an annuity (stream of payments)*, open an Excel spreadsheet to a blank cell. Click the insert function button (f_x). Then select the "Financial" category from the drop-down box. The following box will appear:

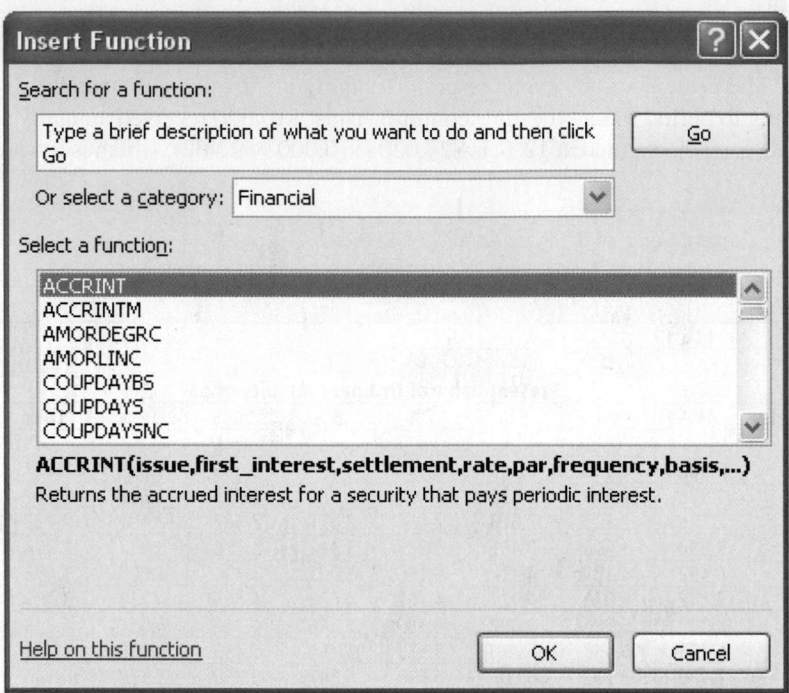

Scroll down the function list and select "PV." A description of the PV function will display beneath the function list, along with the following line: **PV (rate, nper, pmt, fv, type)**. Double-click PV, and the following box will appear:

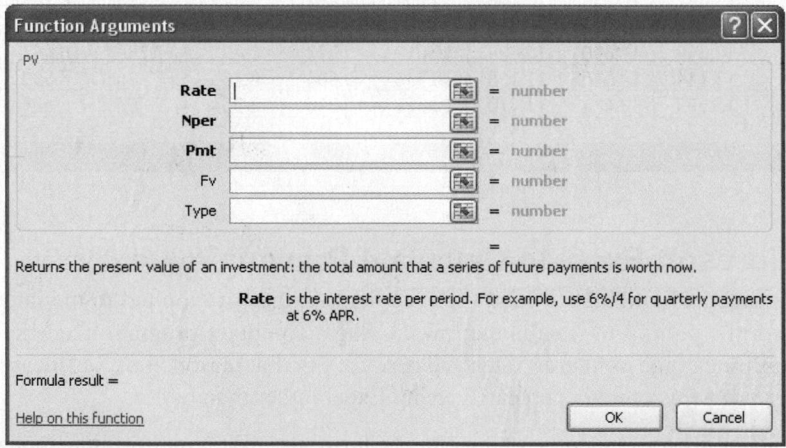

Enter the interest rate, the number of periods, and the payment (as a negative number). The present value of the annuity will appear at the bottom of the box after the "=" sign.

To illustrate, notice that we have assumed an investment that is expected to return $20,000 per year for 20 years and a market interest rate of 8%. The net present value of this annuity (rounded to the nearest cent) is $196,362.95, computed with Excel as follows:

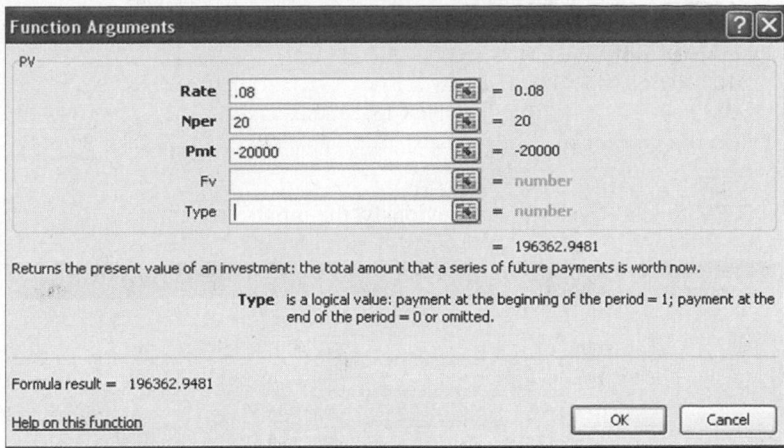

Using the PV Model to Compute Fair Value of Available-for-Sale Investments

Earlier in the chapter, we discussed GAAP for available-for-sale investments. Recall that, at the end of each year, investors are required to adjust the portfolio of these types of investments to fair values, using one of three different approaches (in this order of preference):

- Level 1: Quoted prices in active markets for identical assets
- Level 2: Estimates based on other observable inputs (e.g., prices for similar assets)
- Level 3: Estimates based on unobservable estimates (the company's own estimates based on certain assumptions)

Some types of investments (publicly traded stocks and bonds) have quoted prices in active markets. Determining fair value for these investments is easy: Merely obtain the quoted price from the financial media (usually the Internet or *Wall Street Journal* on the year-end). Other types of nontraditional investments (e.g., notes, bonds or stocks, contracts, annuities) may not have daily quoted market prices in active markets. Therefore, the company may use financial models that predict expected cash flows from these investments over a period of time and discount those cash flows back to the balance-sheet date. These are called level 2 or level 3 approaches to asset valuation. Use of these models may require a great deal of sophisticated judgment about the amount and timing of cash flows and sometimes a number of subjective estimates such as interest rates. Models such as these are quite sensitive to changes in these judgments and estimates. Let's illustrate with a simple example.

Present Value of an Investment in Bonds

The present value of a bond—its market price—is the present value of the future principal amount at maturity plus the present value of the future stated interest payments. The principal is a *single amount* to be received by the investor and paid by the debtor at maturity. The interest is an *annuity* because it occurs periodically.

Let's compute the present value of 9% five-year bonds of **Southwest Airlines** from the standpoint of an investor. The face value of the bonds is $100,000, and the face interest rate is 9% annually. Since bonds typically pay interest twice per year, these bonds pay 4.5% interest semiannually. At issuance, the market interest rate is assumed to be 10% annually, but it is computed at 5% semiannually (again, because the bonds pay interest twice a year). Therefore, the effective (market) interest rate for each of the 10 semiannual periods is 5%. We thus use 5% in computing the present value of the sum of the principal and of the stream of interest payments. The market price of these bonds is $96,149 as calculated on the next page:

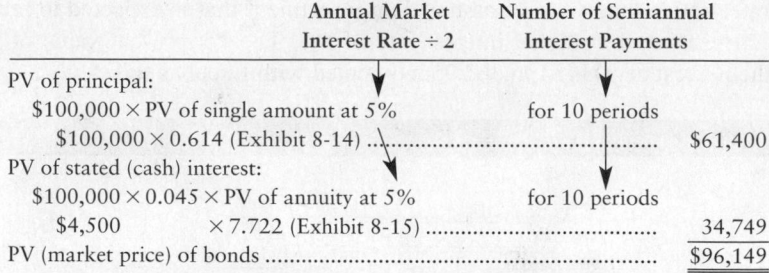

	Annual Market Interest Rate ÷ 2	Number of Semiannual Interest Payments	
PV of principal:			
$100,000 × PV of single amount at 5%		for 10 periods	
$100,000 × 0.614 (Exhibit 8-14)			$61,400
PV of stated (cash) interest:			
$100,000 × 0.045 × PV of annuity at 5%		for 10 periods	
$4,500 × 7.722 (Exhibit 8-15)			34,749
PV (market price) of bonds			$96,149

Using the Excel PV function as outlined previously, the inputs are[2]

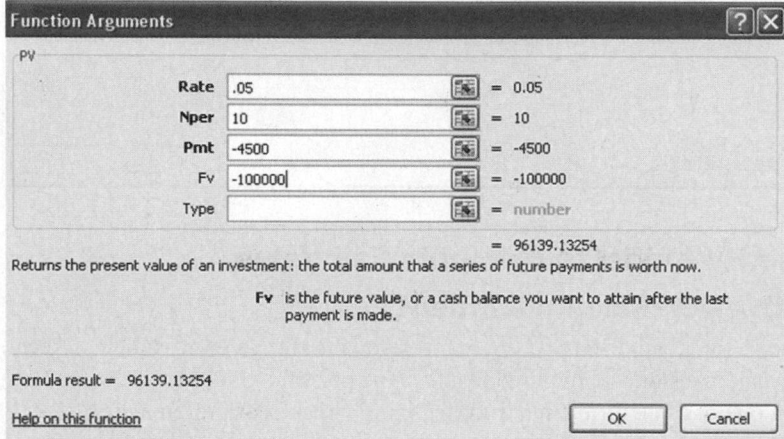

The fair value of the Southwest bonds on the investor's balance sheet would be $96,139 using Excel.[3] Amounts calculated from the PV tables ($96,149) and Excel ($96,139) differ merely by rounding. We discuss accounting for these bonds from the debtor's point of view in Chapter 9 on pages 512–515. It may be helpful for you to reread this section before you study those pages.

Intel reports the fair value of its long-term investments and other assets in a (partial) footnote to its 2014 financial statements as follows (in millions):

	Level 1	Level 2	Level 3
Marketable equity securities	$7,097	$ 0	$ 0
Other long-term assets	717	1,540	39

Some of the level 2 and level 3 fair value estimates use discounted cash flow projections such as the ones we have described in this section.

---

[2] Assume that all payments of interest and principal occur at the end of the period, rather than the beginning. Therefore, it is appropriate to leave the Excel table field labeled "Type" blank.

[3] In the real world, bond investments in public companies are typically classified as level 1 investments because they are usually traded in active markets with quoted prices. We use an investment in bonds here to illustrate the valuation computation for level 3 investments because bonds are easier to understand than the more complex types of level 3 investments. The process of estimating fair value using discounted cash flow models is similar for all types of investments.

1. Translate the balance sheet of the Brazilian subsidiary of **Wrangler Corporation**, a U.S. company, into dollars. When Wrangler acquired this subsidiary, the exchange rate of the Brazilian currency, the real, was $0.40. The average exchange rate applicable to retained earnings is $0.41. The real's current exchange rate is $0.43.

   Before performing the translation, predict whether the translation adjustment will be positive or negative. Does this situation generate a foreign-currency translation gain or loss? Give your reasons.

	Reals
Assets..	900,000
Liabilities	600,000
Stockholders' equity:	
Common stock...	30,000
Retained earnings......................................	270,000
	900,000

Answers

Translation of foreign-currency balance sheet: This situation will generate a *positive* translation adjustment, which is like a gain. The gain occurs because the real's current exchange rate, which is used to translate net assets (assets minus liabilities), exceeds the historical exchange rates used for stockholders' equity.

   The calculation follows:

	Reals	Exchange Rate	Dollars
Assets..	900,000	0.43	$387,000
Liabilities	600,000	0.43	$258,000
Stockholders' equity:			
Common stock.....................	30,000	0.40	12,000
Retained earnings.................	270,000	0.41	110,700
Accumulated other comprehensive income:			
Foreign-currency translation adjustment	—		6,300
	900,000		$387,000

2. You have invested in a commercial building that you are leasing to a national retail chain. The tenant has signed a 10-year lease agreement that cannot be canceled. You expect to collect $8,000 per month for the full term of the lease. What is the present value of this investment if prevailing interest rates are 12%, compounded monthly?

Answers

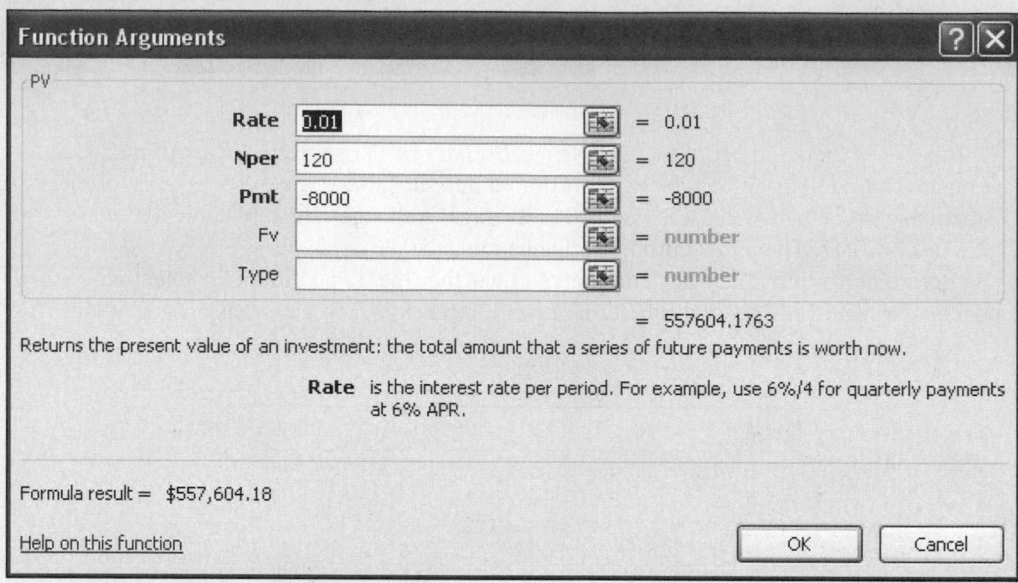

The interest compounds monthly, so it is appropriate to use 120 periods, the number of months in the lease, rather than 10 years. In addition, the yearly interest rate must be adjusted to a monthly rate of 1% (12% ÷ 12). The net present value of this lease is $557,604. Note that you cannot use Exhibit 8-15 since it does not include 1% and does not have 120 periods. The Excel PV function easily gives the result.

Review | Long-Term Investments & the Time Value of Money

Quick Check (Answers are given on page 491.)

1. Crandall's investment in less than 2% of Mobil's stock, which Crandall expects to hold for three years and then sell, is what type of investment?

    a. Trading
    b. Equity

    c. Available-for-sale
    d. Consolidation

2. Jacques Corporation purchased an available-for-sale investment in 2,000 shares of North Supplies stock for $20 per share. On the next balance-sheet date, North Supplies stock is quoted at $21 per share. Jacques' *balance sheet* should report

    a. investments of $42,000.
    b. investments of $40,000.

    c. unrealized gain of $40,000.
    d. unrealized loss of $2,000.

3. Use the Jacques Corporation data in question 2. Jacques' *income statement* should report

    a. investments of $40,000.
    b. unrealized gain of $2,000.
    c. unrealized loss of $2,000.
    d. nothing, because Jacques hasn't sold the investment.

4. Use the Jacques Corporation data in question 2. Jacques sold the North Supplies stock for $50,000 two months later. Jacques's *income statement* for the period of the sale should report a(n)

   a. investments of $50,000.

   b. gain on sale of $10,000.

   c. loss on sale of $10,000.

   d. unrealized gain of $2,000.

5. William Moving & Storage Co. paid $150,000 for 20% of the common stock of Welton Co. at the beginning of the year. During the year, Welton earned net income of $40,000 and paid dividends of $25,000. The carrying value of William's investment in Welton at the end of the year is

   a. $153,000

   b. $150,000

   c. $165,000

   d. $190,000

6. Tarrant, Inc., owns 80% of Boulder Corporation, and Boulder owns 80% of Corby Company. During 2016, these companies' net incomes are as follows before any consolidations:

   - Tarrant, $180,000
   - Boulder, $66,000
   - Corby, $45,000

   How much net income should Tarrant report for 2016?

   a. $291,000

   b. $180,000

   c. $268,800

   d. $261,600

7. Majestic, Inc., holds an investment in Cromwell bonds that pays interest each October 31. Majestic's *balance sheet* at December 31 should report

   a. interest expense.

   b. interest revenue.

   c. interest payable.

   d. interest receivable.

8. You are taking a vacation to Germany and you buy euros for $1.65. On your return, you cash in your unused euros for $1.40. During your vacation,

   a. the euro rose against the dollar.

   b. the dollar rose against the euro.

   c. the dollar lost value.

   d. the euro gained value.

9. Raymond Financing leases airplanes to airline companies. Raymond has just signed a 20-year lease agreement that requires annual year-end lease payments of $900,000. What is the present value of the lease using a 10% interest rate?

   a. $134,100

   b. $1,341,000

   c. $7,662,600

   d. $76,626,000

10. Sunnyside owns numerous foreign subsidiary companies. When Sunnyside consolidates its Swiss subsidiary, Sunnyside should translate the subsidiary's assets into dollars at the

    a. average exchange rate during the period Sunnyside owned the Swiss subsidiary.

    b. current exchange rate.

    c. historical exchange rate when Sunnyside purchased the Swiss company.

    d. none of the above; there's no need to translate the subsidiary's assets into dollars.

Accounting Vocabulary

available-for-sale securities (p. 443) All investments not classified as held-to-maturity or trading securities.

consolidated financial statements (p. 450) Financial statements of the parent company plus those of more than 50%-owned subsidiaries as if the combination were a single legal entity.

controlling (majority) interest (p. 450) Ownership of more than 50% of an investee company's voting stock.

equity method (p. 447) The method used to account for investments in which the investor has 20% to 50% of the investee's voting stock and can significantly influence the decisions of the investee.

fair value (p. 443) The amount that a seller would receive on the sale of an investment to a willing purchaser on a given date. Available-for-sale securities and trading securities are valued at fair market values on the balance-sheet date.

foreign-currency exchange rate (p. 456) The measure of one country's currency against another country's currency.

foreign-currency translation adjustment (p. 457) The balancing figure that brings the dollar amount of the total liabilities and stockholders' equity of the foreign subsidiary into agreement with the dollar amount of its total assets.

future value (p. 459) Measures the future sum of money that a given current investment is "worth" at a specified time in the future assuming a certain interest rate.

held-to-maturity investments (p. 441) Bonds and notes that an investor intends to hold until maturity.

long-term investments (p. 441) Any investment that does not meet the criteria of a short-term investment; any investment that the investor expects to hold longer than a year or that is not readily marketable.

noncontrolling (minority) interest (p. 452) A subsidiary company's equity that is held by stockholders other than the parent company (i.e., less than 50%).

parent company (p. 450) An investor company that owns more than 50% of the voting stock of a subsidiary company.

present value (p. 460) The value on a given date of a future payment or series of future payments, discounted to reflect the time value of money.

short-term investments (p. 440) Investment that a company plans to hold for one year or less and the investment is liquid (readily convertible to cash). Also called *marketable securities*.

strong currency (p. 457) A currency whose exchange rate is rising relative to other nations' currencies.

subsidiary (p. 450) An investee company in which a parent company owns more than 50% of the voting stock.

weak currency (p. 457) A currency whose exchange rate is falling relative to that of other nations' currencies.

Assess Your Progress

Some of the following exercises and problems are available as Excel questions in MyAccountingLab.

Ethics Check

EC8-1. Identify ethical principle violated

For each of the situations listed, identify which of three principles (integrity, objectivity and independence, or due care) from the AICPA Code of Professional Conduct that is violated. Assume all persons listed in the situations are members of the AICPA. (Note: Refer to the AICPA Code of Professional Conduct contained on pages 29–30, Chapter 1 for descriptions of the principles.)

    a. Nature Creations, Inc., recently purchased 100% of the outstanding voting stock of TimberCare, Inc. Both Nature Creations and TimberCare will continue to keep their own separate set of books. Nature Creations has an accounts receivable due from TimberCare, while TimberCare carries a liability due to Nature Creations on its books. Kerrie, the staff accountant for Nature Creations, does not know how to create elimination entries for the two companies since this is Nature Creations' first acquisition. Kerrie decides to add the balances of each balance sheet and income statement together, hoping that the elimination entries would not be material.

    b. Justin is a new partner in the firm of Pagano & Vitetta. He uses his influence to have the firm change its investment accounts to the Vito Brokerage House. Justin does not disclose that his mother is a senior investment advisor at Vito.

    c. Due to a downturn in the local economy, Jubilee Attractions, an amusement park, is experiencing lower ticket sales revenue than it had budgeted. To keep its investors happy, the controller, Maria, booked an unrealized gain on investments as a realized gain, therefore increasing net income. Maria rationalizes that the investment will eventually be sold at a gain so it is acceptable to book the gain as realized now.

    d. Corrigan Company purchases $200,000 of bonds that have a maturity date of May 1, 2026. Although Corrigan Company management intends to hold these bonds until the maturity date, Albert, the controller, classifies this bond investment as a trading security because Corrigan Company's ratios will appear stronger with the bond investment classified as a trading security.

Short Exercises

S8-1. *(Learning Objective 1: Record a held-to-maturity bond investment and interest when issued at par)* On January 1, 2016, Midtown Industries purchased $10,000 of 5% BRS bonds at a price of 100 (par.) Midtown intends to hold the bonds until their maturity date of January 1, 2021. The bonds pay interest semiannually on each January 1 and July 1. Record the initial purchase of the bonds on January 1, 2016, and the receipt of the interest on the first interest payment date of July 1, 2016.

LO 1

S8-2. *(Learning Objective 1: Record a held-to-maturity bond investment and interest when issued at a discount)* Broadbent Insurance purchased $100,000 of 5.5% DGM bonds on January 1, 2016, at a price of 90 when the market rate of interest was 8%. Broadbent intends to hold the bonds until their maturity date of January 1, 2021. The bonds pay interest semiannually on each January 1 and July 1. Record the initial purchase of the bonds by Broadbent on January 1, 2016, and the receipt of the interest on the first interest payment date of July 1, 2016.

LO 1

S8-3. *(Learning Objective 1: Calculate and record interest on a bond investment issued at a discount)* Using the data from S8-2, calculate the amount of discount amortization (using the straight-linc amortization method) on July 1, 2016, and record the related journal entry. What is the total interest revenue for the first six months of 2016? (Hint: include both the interest received in S8-2 and the discount amortization from this exercise.)

LO 1

S8-4. *(Learning Objective 1: Report a bond investment issued at a discount)* Using the data from S8-2, make the adjusting entry that Broadbent Insurance would need to make on December 31, 2016, related to the investment in DGM bonds. How would the bonds be reported on Broadbent Insurance's balance sheet as of December 31, 2016? What amount of interest revenue would be reported on Broadbent Insurance's income statement for the year ended December 31, 2016, related to the DGM bonds?

LO 1

S8-5. *(Learning Objective 1: Calculate and record interest on a bond investment issued at a premium)* Sunshine Pools purchased $100,000 of 12% BHT bonds on January 1, 2016, at a price of 107.5 when the market rate of interest was 10%. Sunshine intends to hold the bonds until their maturity date of January 1, 2021. The bonds pay interest semiannually on each January 1 and July 1. Calculate the amount of premium amortization (using the straight-line amortization method) on July 1, 2016, and record the related journal entry. What is the total interest revenue for the first six months of 2016?

LO 1

S8-6. *(Learning Objective 1: Report a bond investment issued at a premium)* Using the data from S8-5, make the adjusting entries that Sunshine Pools would need to make on December 31, 2016, related to the investment in BHT bonds. How would the bonds be reported on Sunshine Pools' balance sheet as of December 31, 2016? What amount of interest revenue would be reported on Sunshine Pools' income statement for the year ended December 31, 2016, related to the BHT bonds?

LO 1

S8-7. *(Learning Objective 1: Analyze and report investments in held-to-maturity securities)* Helio Ward (HW) owns vast amounts of corporate bonds. Suppose that on June 30, 2016, HW buys $1,300,000 of Amexon bonds at a price of 103. The Amexon bonds pay cash interest semiannually on June 30 and December 31 at the annual rate of 5% and mature at the end of five years.
  1. How much did HW pay to purchase the bond investment? How much will HW collect when the bond investment matures?
  2. How much cash interest will HW receive each year from Amexon?
  3. Will HW's annual interest revenue on the bond investment be more or less than the amount of cash interest received each year? Give your reason.
  4. Compute HW's annual interest revenue on this bond investment. Use the straight-line method to amortize the premium on the investment.

LO 1

LO **1** **S8-8.** (*Learning Objective 1: Record held-to-maturity investment transactions*) Return to S8-7, the Helio Ward (HW) investment in Amexon bonds. Journalize the following on HW's books:

    a. Purchase of the bond investment on June 30, 2016. HW expects to hold the investment to maturity.

    b. Receipt of semiannual cash interest on December 31, 2016.

    c. Amortization of the premium on the bonds on December 31, 2016. Use the straight-line method.

    d. Collection of the investment's face value at the maturity date on June 30, 2021. (Assume the receipt of 2021 interest and the amortization of bonds for 2021 have already been recorded, so ignore these entries.)

LO **2** **S8-9.** (*Learning Objective 2: Record an available-for-sale investment and related dividend revenue*) Williams Company purchases 1,000 shares of American Express common stock at the market price of $81.34 on March 23, 2016. (The equity method does not apply in this situation.) Williams intends to hold this investment for more than one year. On June 22, 2016, Williams receives a cash dividend of $0.29 per share of the American Express stock. Write the entries to (1) record the initial investment; and (2) record the receipt of the cash dividend.

LO **2** **S8-10.** (*Learning Objective 2: Adjust an available-for-sale investment to fair value*) Use the data from S8-9 for this exercise. At year-end on December 31, 2016, the American Express common stock that Williams Company holds has a quoted market price of $84.16 per share. Assuming that Williams Company has no other investments, record the entry to adjust the American Express common stock to fair value.

LO **2** **S8-11.** (*Learning Objective 2: Record the sale of an available-for-sale investment*) Use the data from S8-9 and S8-10 for this exercise. Williams Company sells its entire investment in American Express common stock on November 22, 2017, for a total of $74,500. Record the entries for the sale.

LO **2** **S8-12.** (*Learning Objective 2: Analyze and report an available-for-sale investment*) Hilton Company completed these long-term available-for-sale investment transactions during 2016:

2016	
Apr 10	Purchased 300 shares of Microscape stock, paying $20 per share. Hilton Company intends to hold the investment for the indefinite future.
Jul 22	Received a cash dividend of $1.29 per share on the Microscape stock.
Dec 31	Adjusted the Microscape investment to its current market value of $5,800.

1. Journalize Hilton Company's investment transactions. Explanations are not required.
2. Assume the Microscape Co. stock is Hilton Company's only investment. Explain how these transactions will be reflected on Hilton Company's income statement and its statement of comprehensive income.
3. Show how to report the investment and any unrealized gain or loss on Hilton Company's balance sheet at December 31, 2016. Ignore income tax.

LO **2** **S8-13.** (*Learning Objective 2: Account for the sale of an available-for-sale investment*) Use the data given in S8-12. On May 21, 2017, Hilton Company sold its investment in Microscape Co. stock for $30 per share.

1. Journalize the sale. No explanation is required.
2. How does the gain or loss that you recorded here differ from the gain or loss that was recorded at December 31, 2016?

S8-14. *(Learning Objective 3: Analyze and report an investment in an affiliate)* Suppose on January 1, 2016, Eastern Motors paid $430 million for a 30% investment in Tripp Motors. Assume Tripp earned net income of $80 million and declared and paid cash dividends of $40 million during 2016. **LO 3**

1. What method should Eastern Motors use to account for the investment in Tripp? Give your reason.
2. Journalize these three transactions on the books of Eastern Motors. Show all amounts in millions of dollars (rounded to the closest million), and include an explanation for each entry.
3. Post to the Equity-Method Investment T-account. What is its balance after all the transactions are posted?

S8-15. *(Learning Objective 3: Account for the sale of an equity-method investment)* Use the data given in S8-14. Assume that on January 1, 2017, Eastern Motors sold half its investment in Tripp Motors. The sale price was $125 million. Compute Eastern Motors' gain or loss on the sale. **LO 3**

S8-16. *(Learning Objective 4: Define and explain controlling interests and consolidated financial statements)* Answer these questions about consolidation accounting: **LO 4**

1. Define "parent company." Define "subsidiary company."
2. How do consolidated financial statements differ from the financial statements of a single company?
3. Which company's name appears on the consolidated financial statements? How much of the subsidiary's shares must the parent own before reporting consolidated statements?

S8-17. *(Learning Objective 4: Explain goodwill and noncontrolling interests)* Two accounts that arise from consolidation accounting are goodwill and noncontrolling interest. **LO 4**

1. What is goodwill, and how does it arise? Which company reports goodwill, the parent or the subsidiary? Where is goodwill reported?
2. What is noncontrolling interest, and which company reports it, the parent or the subsidiary? Where is noncontrolling interest reported?

S8-18. *(Learning Objective 5: Report investing transactions on the statement of cash flows)* Companies divide their cash flows into three categories for reporting on the cash flow statement. **LO 5**

1. List the three categories of cash flows in the order they appear on the cash flow statement. Which category of cash flows is most closely related to this chapter?
2. Identify two types of transactions that companies report as cash flows from investing activities.

LO 5   **S8-19.** *(Learning Objective 5: Using a statement of cash flows)* Excerpts from The Ink Spot Company statement of cash flows, as adapted, appear as follows:

	A	B	C
1	**The Ink Spot Company and Subsidiaries** **Consolidated Statement of Cash Flows** **(Adapted)**		
2	**(In millions)**	**Years Ended December 31,** **2016**	**2015**
3	**Operating Activities**		
4	Net cash provided by operating activities	$ 5,404	$ 1,498
5	**Investing Activities**		
6	Purchases of property, plant, and equipment	(1,001)	(951)
7	Acquisitions and investments, principally		
8	trademarks and bottling companies	(851)	(521)
9	Purchases of investments	(590)	(668)
10	Proceeds from disposals of investments	608	384
11	Proceeds from disposals of property, plant,		
12	and equipment	128	72
13	Other investing activities	183	178
14	Net cash used in investing activities	(1,523)	(1,506)
15	**Financing Activities**		
16	Issuances of debt (borrowing)	3,867	4,704
17	Payments of debt	(5,142)	(5,477)
18	Issuances of stock	220	438
19	Purchases of stock for treasury	(358)	(186)
20	Dividends	(2,298)	(2,172)
21	Net cash used in financing activities	(3,711)	(2,693)
22			

As the chief executive officer of The Ink Spot Company, your duty is to write the management letter to your stockholders explaining Ink Spot's major investing activities during 2016. Compare the company's level of investment with previous years, and indicate how the company financed its investments during 2016. Net income for 2016 was $4,123 million.

LO 6   **S8-20.** *(Learning Objective 6: Calculate present value)* Calculate the present value of the following amounts:
1. $12,000 at the end of five years at 10%
2. $12,000 a year at the end of the next five years at 10%

LO 6   **S8-21.** *(Learning Objective 6: Calculate the present value of an investment)* Chaplin Leasing leased a car to a customer. Chaplin will receive $150 a month for 60 months.
1. What is the present value of the lease if the annual interest rate in the lease is 12%? Use the PV function in Excel to compute the present value.
2. What is the present value of the lease if the car can likely be sold for $7,500 at the end of five years?

Exercises MyAccountingLab

Group A

LO 1   **E8-22A.** *(Learning Objective 1: Analyze and report held-to-maturity security transactions)* Assume that on September 30, 2016, Rentex, Inc., purchased 6% bonds of Morin Corporation at 97 as a long-term, held-to-maturity investment. The maturity value of the bonds will be $30,000 on September 30, 2021. The bonds pay interest on March 31 and September 30.

Requirements

1. What method should Rentex use to account for its investment in the Morin Corp. bonds?
2. Using the straight-line method of amortizing the discount on bonds, journalize all of Rentex's transactions on the bonds for 2016.
3. Show how Rentex would report everything related to the bond investment on its balance sheet at its year-end, December 31, 2016.

E8-23A. *(Learning Objective 2: Record transactions for available-for-sale securities)*
Journalize the following long-term, available-for-sale security transactions of Isley Department Stores:

    a. Purchased 400 shares of Howell Fine Foods common stock at $35 per share, with the intent of holding the stock for the indefinite future.
    b. Received a cash dividend of $1.60 per share on the Howell Fine Foods investment.
    c. At year-end, adjusted the investment account to fair value of $42 per share.
    d. Sold the Howell Fine Foods stock for the price of $25 per share.

E8-24A. *(Learning Objective 2: Analyze and report investments in available-for-sale securities)* During the most recent year, Michael Co. bought 3,800 shares of Canada common stock at $38, 640 shares of Brazil stock at $47.25, and 1,500 shares of Russian stock at $77—all as available-for-sale investments. At December 31, Hoover's Online reports Canada stock at $29.125, Brazil at $49.25, and Russian at $69.50.

Requirements

1. Determine the cost and the fair value of the long-term investment portfolio at December 31.
2. Record Michael's adjusting entry at December 31.
3. What would Michael Co. report on its statement of comprehensive income and balance sheet at year-end for the information given? Make the necessary disclosures. Ignore income tax.

E8-25A. *(Learning Objective 3: Account for transactions using the equity method)* Nelson
Corporation owns equity-method investments in several companies. Suppose Nelson paid $1,500,000 to acquire a 40% investment in Simpson Software Company. Simpson Software reported net income of $670,000 for the first year and declared and paid cash dividends of $440,000.

Requirements

1. Record the following in Nelson's journal: (a) purchase of the investment, (b) Nelson's proportion of Simpson Software's net income, and (c) receipt of the cash dividends.
2. What is the ending balance in Nelson's investment account?

E8-26A. *(Learning Objective 3: Analyze gains or losses on equity-method investments)* Without making journal entries, record the transactions of E8-25A directly in the Nelson T-account, Equity-method Investment. Assume that after all the noted transactions took place, Nelson sold its entire investment in Simpson Software for cash of $1,500,000. How much is Nelson's gain or loss on the sale of the investment?

E8-27A. *(Learning Objective 3: Apply the appropriate accounting method for a 30% investment)* Ashcroft Financial paid $500,000 for a 30% investment in the common stock of Magic, Inc. For the first year, Magic reported net income of $220,000 and at year-end declared and paid cash dividends of $140,000. On the balance-sheet date, the fair value of Ashcroft's investment in Magic stock was $430,000.

Requirements

1. Which method is appropriate for Ashcroft Financial to use in accounting for its investment in Magic, Inc.? Why?
2. Show everything that Ashcroft would report for the investment and any investment revenue in its year-end financial statements.

LO 4 **E8-28A.** *(Learning Objective 4: Prepare a consolidated balance sheet)* Nutone, Inc., owns Othello Corp. The two companies' individual balance sheets follow:

	A	B	C	D	E	F
	A1					
1	**Nutone, Inc.** **Consolidation Work Sheet**					
2		**Nutone, Inc.**	**Othello Corp.**	**Elimination** **Debit**	**Credit**	**Consolidated amounts**
3	Cash	$ 46,000	$ 20,000			
4	Accounts receivable, net	81,000	53,000			
5	Note receivable from Nutone	—	42,000			
6	Inventory	59,000	84,000			
7	Plant assets, net	289,000	91,000			
8	Investment in Othello	107,000	—			
9	Other assets	29,000	10,000			
10	Total	$ 611,000	$ 300,000			
11						
12						
13	Accounts payable	$ 48,000	$ 20,000			
14	Notes payable	145,000	39,000			
15	Other liabilities	77,000	134,000			
16	Common stock	105,000	85,000			
17	Retained earnings	236,000	22,000			
18	Total	$ 611,000	$ 300,000			
19						

Requirements

1. Prepare a consolidated balance sheet of Nutone, Inc. It is sufficient to complete the consolidation work sheet. Use Exhibit 8-7 as a model.
2. What is the amount of stockholders' equity for the consolidated entity?

LO 4 **E8-29A.** *(Learning Objective 4: Translate a foreign-currency balance sheet into dollars)* Translate into dollars the balance sheet of North Carolina Leather Goods' German subsidiary. When North Carolina Leather Goods acquired the foreign subsidiary, a euro was worth $1.06. The current exchange rate is $1.326. During the period when retained earnings were earned, the average exchange rate was $1.19 per euro.

	Euros
Assets......................................	650,000
Liabilities	300,000
Stockholders' equity:	
Common stock....................	55,000
Retained earnings...............	295,000
	650,000

During the period covered by this scenario, which currency was stronger, the dollar or the euro?

LO 5 **E8-30A.** *(Learning Objective 5: Prepare and use the statement of cash flows)* During fiscal year 2016, Honey Bakery reported a net income of $132.4 million. Honey Bakery received $1.4 million from the sale of other businesses. Honey Bakery made capital expenditures of $10.0 million and sold property, plant, and equipment for $7.3 million. The company purchased long-term investments at a cost of $11.5 million and sold other long-term investments for $2.5 million.

Requirement

1. Prepare the investing activities section of Honey Bakery's statement of cash flows. Based solely on Honey Bakery's investing activities, does it appear that the company is growing or shrinking? How can you tell?

E8-31A. *(Learning Objective 5: Use the statement of cash flows)* At the end of the year, Cityside Properties' statement of cash flows reported the following for investment activities:

A	B
A1	
Cityside Properties Consolidated Statement of Cash Flows (Partial)	
2 Cash flows from Investing Activities:	
3 Notes receivable collected	$ 3,116,000
4 Purchases of short-term investments	(3,465,000)
5 Proceeds from sales of equipment	1,409,000*
6 Proceeds from sales of investments (cost of $500,000)	515,000
7 Expenditures for property and equipment	(1,770,000)
8 Net cash used by investing activities	$ (195,000)
9	

*Cost $5,100,000; Accumulated depreciation, $3,691,000.

Requirement

1. For each item listed, make the journal entry that placed the item on Cityside Properties' statement of cash flows.

E8-32A. *(Learning Objective 6: Calculate the present value of a bond investment)* Stockman Corp. purchased ten $1,000 6% bonds of Voltgo Corporation when the market rate of interest was 7%. Interest is paid semiannually, and the bonds, and the bonds will mature in eight years. Using the PV function in Excel, compute the price Stockman paid (the present value) for the bond investment.

Group B

E8-33B. *(Learning Objective 1: Analyze and report held-to-maturity security transactions)* Assume that on September 30, 2016, Baytex, Inc., purchased 5% bonds of Hartley Corporation at 97 as a long-term, held-to-maturity investment. The maturity value of the bonds will be $46,000 on September 30, 2021. The bonds pay interest on March 31 and September 30.

Requirements

1. What method should Baytex use to account for its investment in the Hartley Corp. bonds?
2. Using the straight-line method of amortizing the discount on bonds, journalize all of Baytex's transactions on the bonds for 2016.
3. Show how Baytex would report everything related to the bond investment on its balance sheet at its year-end, December 31, 2016.

E8-34B. *(Learning Objective 2: Record transactions for available-for-sale securities)* Journalize the following long-term, available-for-sale investment transactions of Hammond Department Stores:

a. Purchased 410 shares of Potter Fine Foods common stock at $31 per share, with the intent of holding the stock for the indefinite future.
b. Received a cash dividend of $1.10 per share on the Potter Fine Foods investment.
c. At year-end, adjusted the investment account to fair value of $36 per share.
d. Sold the Potter Fine Foods stock for the price of $27 per share.

LO 2 **E8-35B.** *(Learning Objective 2: Analyze and report investments in available-for-sale securities)* During the most recent year, Ogden Co. bought 2,800 shares of Dublin common stock at $35, 590 shares of Chile stock at $45.50, and 1,000 shares of Russian stock at $70—all as available-for-sale investments. At December 31, Hoover's Online reports Dublin stock at $28.125, Chile at $48.00, and Russian at $63.25.

Requirements

1. Determine the cost and the fair value of the long-term investment portfolio at December 31.
2. Record Ogden Co.'s adjusting entry at December 31.
3. What would Ogden Co. report on its statement of comprehensive income and balance sheet at year-end for the information given? Make the necessary disclosures. Ignore income tax.

LO 3 **E8-36B.** *(Learning Objective 3: Account for transactions using the equity method)* Watson Corporation owns equity-method investments in several companies. Suppose Watson paid $1,300,000 to acquire a 30% investment in Smith Software Company. Smith Software reported net income of $680,000 for the first year and declared and paid cash dividends of $450,000.

Requirements

1. Record the following in Watson's journal: (a) purchase of the investment, (b) Watson's proportion of Smith Software's net income, and (c) receipt of the cash dividends.
2. What is the ending balance in Watson's investment account?

LO 3 **E8-37B.** *(Learning Objective 3: Analyze gains or losses on equity-method investments)* Without making journal entries, record the transactions of E8-36B directly in the Watson T-account, Equity-method Investment. Assume that after all the noted transactions took place, Watson sold its entire investment in Smith Software for cash of $1,000,000. How much is Watson's gain or loss on the sale of the investment?

LO 3 **E8-38B.** *(Learning Objective 3: Apply the appropriate accounting method for a 45% investment)* Agani Financial paid $570,000 for a 45% investment in the common stock of Sonic, Inc. For the first year, Sonic reported net income of $260,000 and at year-end declared and paid cash dividends of $135,000. On the balance-sheet date, the fair value of Agani's investment in Sonic stock was $430,000.

Requirements

1. Which method is appropriate for Agani Financial to use in its accounting for its investment in Sonic, Inc.? Why?
2. Show everything that Agani would report for the investment and any investment revenue in its year-end financial statements.

E8-39B. *(Learning Objective 4: Prepare a consolidated balance sheet)* Gamma, Inc., owns Cressida Corp. These two companies' individual balance sheets follow:

	A1	▲▼				
	A	**B**	**C**	**D**	**E**	**F**
1	**Gamma, Inc. Consolidation Work Sheet**					
2		**Gamma, Inc.**	**Cressida Corp.**	**Elimination** Debit	Credit	**Consolidated amounts**
3	Cash	$ 54,000	$ 14,000			
4	Accounts receivable, net	80,000	55,000			
5	Note receivable from Gamma	—	40,000			
6	Inventory	53,000	84,000			
7	Plant assets, net	290,000	99,000			
8	Investment in Cressida	98,000	—			
9	Other assets	24,000	8,000			
10	Total	$ 599,000	$ 300,000			
11						
12						
13	Accounts payable	$ 46,000	$ 28,000			
14	Notes payable	154,000	36,000			
15	Other liabilities	78,000	138,000			
16	Common stock	113,000	85,000			
17	Retained earnings	208,000	13,000			
18	Total	$ 599,000	$ 300,000			
19						

Requirements

1. Prepare a consolidated balance sheet of Gamma, Inc. It is sufficient to complete the consolidation work sheet. Use Exhibit 8-7 as a model.
2. What is the amount of stockholders' equity for the consolidated entity?

E8-40B. *(Learning Objective 4: Translate a foreign-currency balance sheet into dollars)* Translate into dollars the balance sheet of Ohio Leather Goods' Greek subsidiary. When Ohio Leather Goods acquired the foreign subsidiary, a euro was worth $1.06. The current exchange rate is $1.36. During the period when retained earnings were earned, the average exchange rate was $1.17 per euro.

	Euros
Assets	600,000
Liabilities	200,000
Stockholders' equity:	
Common stock	45,000
Retained earnings	355,000
	600,000

During the period covered by this situation, which currency was stronger, the dollar or the euro?

E8-41B. *(Learning Objective 5: Prepare and use the statement of cash flows)* During fiscal year 2016, Ellis Bakery reported a net income of $130.7 million. Ellis Bakery received $1.4 million from the sale of other businesses. Ellis Bakery made capital expenditures of $10.6 million and sold property, plant, and equipment for $7.5 million. The company purchased long-term investments at a cost of $12.1 million and sold other long-term investments for $3.1 million.

Requirement

1. Prepare the investing activities section of Ellis Bakery's statement of cash flows. Based solely on Ellis Bakery's investing activities, does it appear that the company is growing or shrinking? How can you tell?

LO 5 **E8-42B.** *(Learning Objective 5: Use the statement of cash flows)* At the end of the year, Blue Moon Properties' statement of cash flows reported the following for investing activities:

A1		
	A	B
1	**Blue Moon Properties** **Consolidated Statement of Cash Flows (Partial)**	
2	Cash flows from Investing Activities:	
3	Notes receivable collected	$ 3,117,000
4	Purchases of short-term investments	(3,460,000)
5	Proceeds from sales of equipment	1,399,000*
6	Proceeds from sales of investments (cost of $460,000)	468,000
7	Expenditures for property and equipment	(1,731,000)
8	Net cash used by investing activities	$ (207,000)
9		

*Cost $5,100,000; Accumulated depreciation, $3,701,000.

Requirement

1. For each item listed, make the journal entry that placed the item on Blue Moon's statement of cash flows.

LO 6 **E8-43B.** *(Learning Objective 6: Calculate the present value of a bond investment)* Shriver Corp. purchased five $1,000 7% bonds of Geotherm Corporation when the market rate of interest was 8%. Interest is paid semiannually, and the bonds will mature in five years. Using the PV function in Excel, compute the price Shriver paid (the present value) for the bond investment.

Quiz

Test your understanding of long-term investments and international operations by answering the following questions. Select the best choice from among the possible answers given.

Questions 44–46 use the following data:

Assume that Clear Networks owns the following long-term available-for-sale investments:

Company	Number of Shares	Cost per Share	Year-end Fair Value per Share	Dividend per Share
Harper Corp.	800	$58	$74	$2.10
Weston, Inc.	250	9	13	1.30
Rainglow Ltd.	400	24	26	0.90

Q8-44. Clear's balance sheet at year-end should report
a. investments of $58,250.
b. dividend revenue of $2,365.
c. investments of $72,850.
d. unrealized loss of $11,600.

Q8-45. Clear's income statement for the year should report
a. gain on sale of investment of $14,600.
b. investments of $72,850.
c. dividend revenue of $2,365.
d. unrealized loss of $14,600.

Q8-46. Suppose that, before year-end, Clear sells the Harper stock for $74 per share. Journalize the sale.

Q8-47. Dividends received on an equity-method investment
a. increase dividend revenue.
b. increase the investment account.
c. decrease the investment account.
d. increase owners' equity.

Q8-48. The starting point in accounting for all investments is
a. market value on the balance-sheet date.
b. cost minus dividends.
c. equity value.
d. cost.

Q8-49. Consolidation accounting
a. combines the accounts of the parent company and those of the subsidiary companies.
b. reports the receivables and payables of the parent company only.
c. eliminates all liabilities.
d. all of the above.

Q8-50. On January 1, 2016, Macrostore, Inc., purchased $100,000 face value of the 5% bonds of Service Express, Inc., at 110. The bonds mature on January 1, 2021. For the year ended December 31, 2019, Macrostore received cash interest of
a. $5,500.   c. $3,000.
b. $7,000.   d. $5,000.

Q8-51. Return to Macrostore, Inc.'s bond investment in the preceding question. For the year ended December 31, 2017, Macrostore received cash interest of $5,000. What was the interest revenue that Macrostore earned in this year?
a. $2,000   c. $7,000
b. $5,000   d. $3,000

Q8-52. The present value of $2,000 at the end of four years at 8% interest is
a. $6,624   c. $1,470.
b. $1,228.   d. $2,000.

Q8-53. Which of the following is not needed to compute the present value of an investment?
a. The length of time between the investment and future receipt
b. The rate of inflation
c. The interest rate
d. The amount of the receipt

Q8-54. What is the present value of bonds with a face value of $2,000, a stated interest rate of 6%, a market rate of 9%, and a maturity date six years in the future? Interest is paid semiannually. Use Excel.
a. $1,010   c. $2,456
b. $1,726   d. $2,000

Q8-55. Consolidation of a foreign subsidiary usually results in a
a. gain or loss on consolidation.
b. foreign-currency translation adjustment.
c. foreign-currency transaction gain or loss.
d. LIFO/FIFO difference.

Problems MyAccountingLab

Group A

LO **1**

P8-56A. (*Learning Objective 1: Analyze and report held-to-maturity investments purchased at a premium*) Insurance companies and pension plans hold large quantities of bond investments. Bolton Insurance Corp. purchased $2,800,000 of 9% bonds of Souza, Inc., for 112 on January 1, 2016. These bonds pay interest on January 1 and July 1 each year. They mature on January 1, 2020. At October 31, 2016, the end of the company's fiscal year, the market price of the bonds is 105.

Requirements

1. Journalize Bolton's purchase of the bonds as a long-term investment on January 1, 2016 (to be held to maturity), receipt of cash interest, and amortization of the bond premium at July 1, 2016. The straight-line method is appropriate for amortizing the bond investment.
2. Journalize the accrual of interest receivable and amortization of premium on October 31, 2016 (round the answer to the nearest whole number).
3. Show all financial statement effects of this long-term bond investment on Bolton Insurance Corp.'s balance sheet at October 31, 2016, and income statement for the year ending October 31, 2016.

LO **2 3**

P8-57A. (*Learning Objectives 2, 3: Analyze and report various long-term investment transactions on the balance sheet and income statement*) Delaware Exchange Company completed the following long-term investment transactions during 2016:

2016	
May 12	Purchased 18,200 shares, which make up 25% of the common stock of Nashua Corporation at total cost of $340,000.
Jul 9	Received annual cash dividend of $1.23 per share on the Nashua investment.
Sep 16	Purchased 1,000 shares of Columbus, Inc., common stock as an available-for-sale investment, paying $41.50 per share.
Oct 30	Received cash dividend of $0.33 per share on the Columbus investment.
Dec 31	Received annual report from Nashua Corporation. Net income for the year was $540,000.

At year-end, the fair value of the Columbus stock is $30,100. The fair value of the Nashua stock is $658,000.

Requirements

1. For which investment is fair value used in the accounting? Why is fair value used for one investment and not the other?
2. Show what Delaware Exchange would report on its year-end balance sheet, income statement, and statement of comprehensive income for these investment transactions. It is helpful to use a T-account for the Equity-method Investment account. Ignore income tax.

LO **2 3**

P8-58A. (*Learning Objectives 2, 3: Analyze and report available-for-sale and equity-method investments*) The beginning balance sheet of Robideau Corporation included the following:

Equity-method Investment in FUN Software.. $610,000

Robideau Corporation completed the following investment transactions during the year:

Mar 16	Purchased 1,400 shares of Orange, Inc., common stock as a long-term available-for-sale investment, paying $12.75 per share.
May 21	Received cash dividend of $2.25 per share on the Orange investment.
Aug 17	Received cash dividend of $90,000 from FUN Software.
Dec 31	Received annual reports from FUN Software; net income for the year was $530,000. Of this amount, Robideau's portion is 20%.

At year-end, the fair values of Robideau Corporation's investments are as follows: Orange, $26,200; FUN, $746,000.

Requirements

1. Record the transactions in the journal of Robideau Corporation.
2. Post entries to the T-account for Equity-method Investment in FUN Software, and determine its balance at December 31.
3. Show how to report the Investment in Available-for-Sale Securities and the Equity-method Investment in FUN Software accounts on Robideau Corporation's balance sheet at December 31.

P8-59A. *(Learning Objective 4: Analyze consolidated financial statements)* This problem demonstrates the dramatic effect that consolidation accounting can have on a company's ratios. Spindler Motor Company (Spindler) owns 100% of Spindler Motor Credit Corporation (SMCC), its financing subsidiary. Spindler's main operations consist of manufacturing automotive products. SMCC mainly helps people finance the purchase of automobiles from Spindler and its dealers. The two companies' individual balance sheets are adapted and summarized as follows (amounts in billions):

LO 4

	Spindler (Parent)	SMCC (Subsidiary)
Total assets	$85.1	$169.2
Total liabilities	$65.3	$155.9
Total stockholders' equity	19.8	13.3
Total liabilities and equity	$85.1	$169.2

Assume that SMCC's liabilities include $1.3 billion owed to Spindler, the parent company.

Requirements

1. Compute the debt ratio of Spindler Motor Company considered alone.
2. Determine the consolidated total assets, total liabilities, and stockholders' equity of Spindler Motor Company after consolidating the financial statements of SMCC into the totals of Spindler, the parent company.
3. Recompute the debt ratio of the consolidated entity. Why do companies prefer not to consolidate their financing subsidiaries into their own financial statements?

LO 4 **P8-60A.** *(Learning Objective 4: Consolidate a wholly owned subsidiary)* Assume Ronny, Inc., paid $362,000 to acquire all the common stock of Bircher Corporation and Bircher owes Ronny $194,000 on a note payable. Immediately after the purchase on September 30, 2016, the two companies' balance sheets appear as follows:

	Ronny	Bircher
Assets		
Cash	$ 54,000	$ 20,000
Accounts receivable, net	196,000	88,000
Note receivable from Bircher	194,000	—
Inventory	346,000	469,000
Plant assets, net	381,000	484,000
Investment in Bircher	362,000	—
Total	$1,533,000	$1,061,000
Liabilities and Stockholders' Equity		
Accounts payable	$ 126,000	$ 75,000
Notes payable	400,000	330,000
Other liabilities	231,000	294,000
Common stock	588,000	254,000
Retained earnings	188,000	108,000
Total	$1,533,000	$1,061,000

Requirement

1. Prepare the work sheet for the consolidated balance sheet of Ronny, Inc. Use Exhibit 8-7 as a model.

LO 6 **P8-61A.** *(Learning Objective 6: Explain the impact of the time value of money on valuation of investments)* Annual cash inflows from two competing investment opportunities are given. Each investment opportunity will require the same initial investment.

	Investment	
Year	A	B
1	$ 7,000	$10,000
2	9,000	10,000
3	14,000	10,000
	$30,000	$30,000

Requirement

1. Assuming a 14% interest rate, which investment opportunity would you choose?

LO 4 **P8-62A.** *(Learning Objective 4: Consolidate a foreign subsidiary)* Assume that Mason Corporation has a subsidiary company based in Japan.

	Yen
Assets	¥410,000,000
Liabilities	¥145,000,000
Stockholders' equity:	
Common stock	25,000,000
Retained earnings	240,000,000
	¥410,000,000

Requirements

1. Translate into dollars the foreign-currency balance sheet of the Japanese subsidiary of Mason. When Mason acquired this subsidiary, the Japanese yen was worth $0.0075. The current exchange rate is $0.0090. During the period when the subsidiary earned its income, the average exchange rate was $0.0088 per yen. Before you perform the foreign-currency translation calculations, indicate whether Mason has experienced a positive or a negative translation adjustment. State whether the adjustment is a gain or a loss, and show where it is reported in the financial statements.
2. To which company does the foreign-currency translation adjustment "belong"? In which company's financial statements will the translation adjustment be reported?

Group B

P8-63B. (*Learning Objective 1: Analyze and report held-to-maturity investments purchased at a premium*) Insurance companies and pension plans hold large quantities of bond investments. Variety Insurance Corp. purchased $3,900,000 of 4% bonds of Sherman, Inc., for 114 on January 1, 2016. These bonds pay interest on January 1 and July 1 each year. They mature on January 1, 2020. At October 31, 2016, the end of the company's fiscal year, the market price of the bonds is 101.

Requirements

1. Journalize Variety's purchase of the bonds as a long-term investment on January 1, 2016 (to be held to maturity), receipt of cash interest, and amortization of the bond premium at July 1, 2016. The straight-line method is appropriate for amortizing the bond investment.
2. Journalize the accrual of interest receivable and amortization of premium on October 31, 2016 (round answer to the nearest whole number).
3. Show all financial statement effects of this long-term bond investment on Variety Insurance Corp.'s balance sheet at October 31, 2016, and income statement for the year ending October 31, 2016.

P8-64B. (*Learning Objectives 2, 3: Analyze and report various long-term investment transactions on the balance sheet and income statement*) Utah Exchange Company completed the following long-term investment transactions during 2016:

2016	
May 12	Purchased 21,000 shares, which make up 45% of the common stock of Exeter Corporation at total cost of $340,000.
Jul 9	Received annual cash dividend of $1.21 per share on Exeter investment.
Sep 16	Purchased 1,100 shares of Amsterdam, Inc., common stock as an available-for-sale investment, paying $42.25 per share.
Oct 30	Received cash dividend of $0.34 per share on the Amsterdam investment.
Dec 31	Received annual report from Exeter Corporation. Net income for the year was $580,000.

At year-end, the fair value of the Amsterdam stock is $30,900. The fair value of the Exeter stock is $652,000.

Requirements

1. For which investment is fair value used in the accounting? Why is fair value used for one investment and not the other?
2. Show what Utah Exchange would report on its year-end balance sheet, income statement, and statement of comprehensive income for these investment transactions. It is helpful to use a T-account for the Equity-method Investment account. Ignore income tax.

LO **2** **3**   **P8-65B.** *(Learning Objectives 2, 3: Analyze and report available-for-sale and equity-method investments)* The beginning balance sheet of Landeau Corporation included the following:

Equity-method Investment in NEW Software..	$614,000

Landeau Corporation completed the following investment transactions during the year:

Mar 16	Purchased 2,200 shares of Hubbardston, Inc., common stock as a long-term available-for-sale investment, paying $12.00 per share.
May 21	Received cash dividend of $2.50 per share on the Hubbardston investment.
Aug 17	Received cash dividend of $85,000 from NEW Software.
Dec 31	Received annual reports from NEW Software; net income for the year was $550,000. Of this amount, Landeau's proportion is 26%.

At year-end, the fair values of Landeau Corporation's investments are as follows: Hubbardston, $26,600; NEW, $745,000.

Requirements

1. Record the transactions in the journal of Landeau Corporation.
2. Post entries to the T-account for Equity-method Investment in NEW Software, and determine its balance at December 31.
3. Show how to report the Investment in Available-for-Sale Securities and the Equity-method Investment in NEW Software accounts on Landeau Corporation's balance sheet at December 31.

LO **4**   **P8-66B.** *(Learning Objective 4: Analyze consolidated financial statements)* This problem demonstrates the dramatic effect that consolidation accounting can have on a company's ratios. Randall Motor Company (Randall) owns 100% of Randall Motor Credit Corporation (RMCC), its financing subsidiary. Randall's main operations consist of manufacturing automotive products. RMCC mainly helps people finance the purchase of automobiles from Randall and its dealers. The two companies' individual balance sheets are adapted and summarized as follows (amounts in billions):

	Randall (Parent)	RMCC (Subsidiary)
Total assets	$80.6	$164.8
Total liabilities	$63.9	$155.4
Total stockholders' equity	16.7	9.4
Total liabilities and equity................	$80.6	$164.8

Assume that RMCC's liabilities include $1.6 billion owed to Randall, the parent company.

Requirements

1. Compute the debt ratio of Randall Motor Company considered alone.
2. Determine the consolidated total assets, total liabilities, and stockholders' equity of Randall Motor Company after consolidating the financial statements of RMCC into the totals of Randall, the parent company.
3. Recompute the debt ratio of the consolidated entity. Why do companies prefer not to consolidate their financing subsidiaries into their own financial statements?

P8-67B. *(Learning Objective 4: Consolidate a wholly owned subsidiary)* Assume Robertson, Inc., paid $289,000 to acquire all the common stock of Dinette Corporation and Dinette owes Robertson $197,000 on a note payable. Immediately after the purchase on September 30, 2016, the two companies' balance sheets are as follows:

	Robertson	Dinette
Assets		
Cash..	$ 59,000	$ 57,000
Accounts receivable, net.........................	199,000	87,000
Note receivable from Dinette	197,000	—
Inventory...	294,000	412,000
Plant assets, net.....................................	388,000	441,000
Investment in Dinette	289,000	—
Total	$1,426,000	$ 997,000
Liabilities and Stockholders' Equity		
Accounts payable	$ 121,000	$ 77,000
Notes payable	405,000	335,000
Other liabilities	212,000	296,000
Common stock......................................	550,000	272,000
Retained earnings.................................	138,000	17,000
Total	$1,426,000	$ 997,000

Requirement

1. Prepare the work sheet for the consolidated balance sheet of Robertson, Inc. Use Exhibit 8-7 as a model.

P8-68B. *(Learning Objective 6: Explain the impact of the time value of money on the valuation of investments)* Annual cash inflows from two competing investment opportunities are given. Each investment opportunity will require the same initial investment.

	Investment	
Year	X	Y
1	$ 8,000	$10,000
2	5,000	10,000
3	17,000	10,000
	$30,000	$30,000

Requirement

1. Assuming an 8% interest rate, which investment opportunity would you choose?

P8-69B. *(Learning Objective 4: Consolidate a foreign subsidiary)* Assume that Lundgren Corporation has a subsidiary company based in Japan.

	Yen
Assets......................................	¥410,000,000
Liabilities	¥115,000,000
Stockholders' equity:	
Common stock....................	35,000,000
Retained earnings...............	260,000,000
	¥410,000,000

Requirements

1. Translate into dollars the foreign-currency balance sheet of the Japanese subsidiary of Lundgren. When Lundgren acquired this subsidiary, the Japanese yen was worth $0.0095. The current exchange rate is $0.0110. During the period when the subsidiary earned its income, the average exchange rate was $0.0100 per yen. Before you perform the foreign-currency translation calculations, indicate whether Lundgren has experienced a positive or a negative translation adjustment. State whether the adjustment is a gain or a loss, and show where it is reported in the financial statements.

2. To which company does the foreign-currency translation adjustment "belong"? In which company's financial statements will the translation adjustment be reported?

Challenge Exercises and Problem

E8-70. *(Learning Objectives 1, 2, 3, 5: Accounting for various types of investments)* Suppose PlaySpace owns the following investments at December 31, 2016:

    a. 100% of the common stock of PlaySpace United Kingdom, which holds assets of £700,000 and owes a total of £400,000. At December 31, 2016, the current exchange rate of the pound (£) is £1 = $1.99. The translation rate of the pound applicable to stockholders' equity is £1 = $1.61. During 2016, PlaySpace United Kingdom earned net income of £110,000, and the average exchange rate for the year was £1 = $1.90. PlaySpace United Kingdom declared and paid cash dividends of £60,000 during 2016.

    b. Investments that PlaySpace is holding to sell beyond the current period. These investments compose less than 20% of the voting stock in the investee. They cost $750,000 and declined in value by $300,000 during 2016, but they paid cash dividends of $18,000 to PlaySpace. One year ago, at December 31, 2015, the fair value of these investments was $1,000,000.

    c. 45% of the common stock of PlaySpace Financing Associates. During 2016, PlaySpace Financing earned net income of $1,000,000 and declared and paid cash dividends of $50,000. The carrying amount of this investment was $700,000 at December 31, 2015.

Requirements

1. Which method is used to account for each investment?
2. By how much did each of these investments increase or decrease PlaySpace's net income during 2016?
3. For investments b and c, show how PlaySpace would report these investments on its balance sheet at December 31, 2016.

E8-71. *(Learning Objectives 2, 4: Explain and analyze accumulated other comprehensive income)* Big-Box Retail Corporation reported stockholders' equity on its balance sheet at December 31:

	A	B
	Big-Box Retail Corporation	
	Balance Sheet (Partial)	
1	**December 31, 2017**	
2	Stockholders' equity: (in millions)	
3	Common stock, $0.20 par value—	
4	1,200 million shares authorized	
5	600 million shares issued	$ 120
6	Additional paid-in capital	1,100
7	Retained earnings	6,200
8	Accumulated other comprehensive (loss)	(?)
9	Less: Treasury stock, at cost	(100)
10		

Requirements

1. Identify the two components that typically make up accumulated other comprehensive income.
2. For each component of accumulated other comprehensive income, describe the event that can cause a *positive* balance. Also describe the events that can cause a *negative* balance for each component.
3. At December 31, 2016, Big-Box Retail's accumulated other comprehensive loss was $58 million. Then during 2017, Big-Box Retail had a positive foreign-currency translation adjustment of $22 million and an unrealized loss of $15 million on available-for-sale investments. What was Big-Box Retail's balance of accumulated other comprehensive income (loss) at December 31, 2017?

E8-72. *(Learning Objective 6: Calculate present values of competing investments)* Which option is better: receive $120,000 now or $25,000, $45,000, $35,000, $15,000, and $50,000, respectively, over the next five years?

Requirements

1. Assuming an 8% interest rate, which investment opportunity would you choose?
2. If you could earn 10%, would your choice change?
3. Assuming a 10% interest rate, what would the cash flow in year 5 have to be in order for you to be indifferent to the two plans?

APPLY YOUR KNOWLEDGE

Decision Cases

Case 1. *(Learning Objectives 2, 4: Make an investment decision)* Infografix Corporation's consolidated sales for 2016 were $26.6 billion, and expenses totaled $24.8 billion. Infografix operates worldwide and conducts 37% of its business outside the United States. During 2016, Infografix reported the following items in its financial statements (amounts in billions):

Foreign-currency translation adjustments...	$(202)
Unrealized holding _____ on available-for-sale investments.............	(328)

As you consider an investment in Infografix stock, some concerns arise. Answer each of the following questions:

1. What do the parentheses around the two dollar amounts signify?
2. Are these items reported as assets, liabilities, stockholders' equity, revenues, or expenses? Are they normal-balance accounts, or are they contra accounts?
3. Did Infografix include these items in net income? In retained earnings? In the final analysis, how much net income did Infografix report for 2016?
4. Should these items scare you away from investing in Infografix stock? Why or why not? (Challenge)

Case 2. *(Learning Objectives 1, 2, 5: Make an investment sale decision)* Cathy Talbert is the general manager of Barham Company, which provides data-management services for physicians in the Columbus, Ohio, area. Barham Company is having a rough year. Net income trails projections for the year by almost $75,000. This shortfall is especially important. Barham plans to issue stock early next year and needs to show investors that the company can meet its earnings targets.

Barham holds several investments purchased a few years ago. Even though investing in stocks is outside Barham's core business of data-management services, Talbert thinks these investments may hold the key to helping the company meet its net income goal for the year. She is considering what to do with the following investments:

1. Barham owns 50% of the common stock of Ohio Office Systems, which provides the business forms that Barham uses. Ohio Office Systems has lost money for the past two years but still has a retained earnings balance of $550,000. Talbert thinks she can get Ohio's treasurer to declare a $160,000 cash dividend, half of which would go to Barham.

2. Barham owns a bond investment purchased eight years ago for $250,000. The purchase price represents a discount from the bonds' maturity value of $400,000. These bonds mature two years from now, and Barham purchased them as a long-term investment intending to hold them until they matured. Their current market value is $380,000. Ms. Talbert has checked with a **Charles Schwab** investment representative, and she is considering selling the bonds. Schwab would charge a 1% commission on the sale transaction.

3. Barham owns 5,000 shares of **Microsoft** stock valued at $53 per share as a long-term investment. One year ago, Microsoft stock was worth only $28 per share. Barham purchased the Microsoft stock for $37 per share. Talbert wonders whether Barham should sell the Microsoft stock.

Requirement

1. Evaluate all three actions as a way for Barham Company to generate the needed amount of income. Recommend the best way for Barham to achieve its net income goal.

Ethical Issue

Media One owns 18% of the voting stock of Web Talk, Inc. The remainder of the Web Talk stock is held by numerous investors with small holdings. Austin Cohen, president of Media One and a member of Web Talk's board of directors, heavily influences Web Talk's policies.

Under the fair value method of accounting for investments, Media One's net income increases as it receives dividend revenue from Web Talk. Media One pays President Cohen a bonus computed as a percentage of Media One's net income. Therefore, Cohen can control his personal bonus to a certain extent by influencing Web Talk's dividends.

A recession occurs in 2016, and Media One's income is low. Cohen uses his power to have Web Talk pay a large cash dividend. The action requires Web Talk to borrow in order to pay the dividend.

Requirements

1. What are the ethical issues in the Media One case?
2. Who are the stakeholders? What are the possible consequences to each?
3. What are the alternatives for Austin Cohen to consider? Analyze each alternative from the following standpoints: (a) economic, (b) legal, (c) ethical.
4. If you were Cohen, what would you do?
5. Discuss how using the equity method of accounting for the investment would decrease Cohen's potential for manipulating his bonus.

Focus on Financials | Apple Inc.

(*Learning Objectives 2, 3, 4: Analyze investments, consolidated subsidiaries, and international operations*) The consolidated financial statements of **Apple Inc.** are given in Appendix A and online in the filings section of **http://www.sec.gov**.

Requirements

1. Refer to Note 1—Summary of Significant Accounting Policies, under *Cash Equivalents and Marketable Securities*. How does the company classify its investments?
2. Refer to Note 1 under Cash Equivalents and Marketable Securities. Does Apple Inc. adjust for periodic changes in fair value of these investments? If so, where do these adjustments appear?

3. Refer to Note 2—Financial Instruments, under *Cash, Cash Equivalents and Marketable Securities*. What does Apple Inc.'s investment policy require of its investments? What is the reasoning for this?

Focus on Analysis | Under Armour, Inc.

(Learning Objectives 2, 3, 4: Analyze and report available-for-sale investments; analyze consolidated statements and international operations) This case is based on the consolidated financial statements of **Under Armour, Inc.**, given in Appendix B and online in the filings section of **http://www.sec.gov**.

LO **2** **3** **4**

Requirements

1. Read Note 16—Segment Data and Related Information. What are Under Armour, Inc.'s three main product categories? Which of these product categories brought in the most revenue in 2014?
2. Read Note 16—Segment Data and Related Information. The company lists six geographic operating regions worldwide. List these regions. Which region brings in the most revenue?
3. Read Note 2—Summary of Significant Accounting Policies—Basis of Presentation. Which entities does Under Armour, Inc., consolidate? How does it treat intercompany balances and transactions?

Group Project

Pick a stock from *The Wall Street Journal* or another database or publication. Assume that your group purchases 1,000 shares of the stock as a long-term investment and that your 1,000 shares are less than 20% of the company's outstanding stock. Research the stock in *Value Line, Moody's Investor Record*, or another source to determine whether the company pays cash dividends and, if so, how much and at what intervals.

Requirements

1. Track the stock for a period assigned by your professor. Over the specified period, keep a daily record of the price of the stock to see how well your investment has performed. Each day, search the Corporate Dividend News in *The Wall Street Journal* to keep a record of any dividends you've received. End the period of your analysis at a month-end, such as September 30 or December 31.
2. Journalize all transactions that you have experienced, including the stock purchase, dividends received (both cash dividends and stock dividends), and any year-end adjustment required by the accounting method that is appropriate for your situation. Assume you will prepare financial statements on the ending date of your study.
3. Show what you will report on your company's balance sheet, income statement, and statement of cash flows as a result of your investment transactions.

Quick Check Answers

1. *c*

2. *a* (2,000 shares × $21 = $42,000)

3. *d*

4. *b* ($50,000 − $40,000 original cost) = $10,000

5. *a* [$150,000 + 0.20($40,000 − $25,000) − $153,000]

6. *d* [$180,000 + 0.80($66,000) + 0.64($45,000) = $261,600]

7. *d*

8. *b*

9. *c* [8.514 × $900,000]

10. *b*

9 | Liabilities

✓ SPOTLIGHT | Southwest Airlines: Flying High!

Southwest Airlines has been charting its own course in the airline industry for 45 years. The company began operating as a short-haul, no-frills carrier in 1971, with only three Boeing 737 aircraft serving Dallas, Houston, and San Antonio, Texas, business commuters with peanuts and drinks rather than lunch or dinner between stops. The company has gained a reputation through the years of providing reliable, low-cost travel from close-in, smaller airports that are convenient for many business commuters or vacationers. Through the years, Southwest's business strategy has been to keep operating costs lower than other carriers, passing the savings on to customers in the form of low fares. As of December 31, 2012, Southwest was the largest domestic air carrier in the United States. It served 93 destinations in 41 states, the District of Columbia, Puerto Rico, and six "near-international countries," including Mexico, Jamaica, the Bahamas, Aruba, the Dominican Republic, and Bermuda, with a fleet of 687 aircraft. Despite turbulence in a very volatile industry, Southwest has managed to remain consistently profitable while other airlines have struggled. In 2014, the company earned $1.136 billion on operating revenue of $18.6 billion. The company has also retained more liquidity (cash) than other airlines. In 2011, Southwest purchased AirTran Airways, a competitor, largely with cash and stock.

So why focus on its liabilities? Like other airlines, Southwest has reported some interesting liabilities on the face of its balance sheet, as seen on the next page. For example, Southwest's Rapid Rewards program awards points for paid miles flown that can be redeemed by customers for free flights in the future. Southwest accrues a frequent-flier liability for this program and reports "Accrued liabilities" on the company's consolidated balance sheets. Southwest also collects cash in advance for tickets sold that will be used at a later time. This creates unearned revenue that Southwest reports as "Air traffic liability," to be transferred to Passenger revenue later as customers redeem their tickets. Both of these types of liabilities are shown in the current liability

E.J. Baumeister Jr/Alamy

section of the balance sheets. Southwest also reports "Long-term debt," which consists of notes and bonds payable. The company has incurred these liabilities to finance purchases of its largest class of assets, which is the fleet of purchased aircraft.

One of the most interesting things about Southwest's obligations is not so much those that are reported as current or long-term liabilities on the face of the balance sheet, but those items that are not. The footnotes to the financial statements disclose that the company leases its terminal operations space, as well as some of its aircraft, for which it has future obligations to make lease payments. Most of these obligations are not recorded as liabilities, because the terms of the lease contracts are written in such a way that the company does not have ownership in the assets after the lease obligations are satisfied. In addition, the company has signed agreements with **Boeing Corporation** that obligate it to purchase a certain number of new aircraft per year for a number of years into the future. Although these obligations have not yet occurred, the company is required to disclose them in the footnotes. ●

	A1 ⬍		
	A	**B**	**C**
1	**Southwest Airlines Company** **Consolidated Balance Sheets (Adapted)**		
2		**Dec. 31, 2014**	**Dec. 31, 2013**
3	**(In Millions of $)**		
4	**Current assets**		
5	Cash and cash equivalents	$ 1,282	$ 1,355
6	Short-term investments	1,706	1,797
7	Accounts and other receivables	365	419
8	Inventories of parts and supplies	342	467
9	Deferred income taxes	477	168
10	Prepaid expenses and other	232	250
11	Total current assets	4,404	4,456
12	Property and equipment, at cost		
13	Flight equipment	18,473	16,937
14	Ground property and equipment	2,853	2,666
15	Other property and equipment	1,187	1,217
16	Property and equipment, at cost	22,513	20,820
17	Less allowance for depreciation and amortization	(8,221)	(7,431)
18	Property and equipment, net	14,292	13,389
19	Goodwill	970	970
20	Other assets	534	530
21	**Total assets**	$ 20,200	$ 19,345
22	**Current liabilities**		
23	Accounts payable	$ 1,203	$ 1,247
24	Accrued liabilities	1,565	1,229
25	Air traffic liability	2,897	2,571
26	Current maturities of long-term debt	258	629
27	Total current liabilities	5,923	5,676
28	Long-term debt less current maturities	2,434	2,191
29	Deferred income taxes	3,259	2,934
30	Other noncurrent liabilities	1,809	1,208
31	**Total liabilities**	13,425	12,009
32	**Stockholders' equity**		
33	Common stock	808	808
34	Capital in excess of par value	1,315	1,231
35	Retained earnings	7,416	6,431
36	Accumulated other comprehensive (loss)	(738)	(3)
37	Treasury stock, at cost	(2,026)	(1,131)
38	**Total stockholders' equity**	6,775	7,336
39	**Total liabilities and stockholders' equity**	$ 20,200	$ 19,345
40			

This chapter shows how to account for liabilities—both current and long-term—and those obligations that are merely footnote disclosures. We begin with current liabilities.

LEARNING OBJECTIVES

1 **Account for** current and contingent liabilities

2 **Account for** bonds payable and interest expense with straight-line amortization

3 **Account for** bonds payable and interest expense with effective interest amortization

4 **Analyze and differentiate** financing with debt vs. equity

5 **Understand** other long-term liabilities

6 **Report** liabilities on the financial statements

›› Try It in Excel®

You can access the most current annual report of Southwest Airlines Company in Excel format at **http://www.sec.gov**. Using the "FILINGS" link on the toolbar at the top of the home page, select "Company Filings Search." This will take you to the "Edgar Company Filings" page. Type "Southwest Airlines" in the company name box, and select "Search." This will produce the "EDGAR Search Results" page showing the company name. Click on the "CIK" link beside the company name. This will pull up a list of the reports the company has filed with the SEC. Under the "Filing Type" box, type "10-K" and click the search box. Form 10-K is the SEC form for the company's annual report. Find the year that you wish to view. Click on the "Interactive Data" box, which takes you to the "View Filing Data" page. Find and click on the "View Excel Document" link at the top of this page. You may choose to either open or download the Excel files containing the company's most recent financial statements.

ACCOUNT FOR CURRENT AND CONTINGENT LIABILITIES

1 **Account for** current and contingent liabilities

Current liabilities are obligations due within one year or within the company's normal operating cycle if longer than a year. Obligations due beyond that period of time are classified as *long-term liabilities*.

Current liabilities are of two kinds:

- Known amounts
- Estimated amounts

We look first at current liabilities of a known amount.

Current Liabilities of Known Amount

Current liabilities of known amount include accounts payable, short-term notes payable, sales tax payable, accrued liabilities, payroll liabilities, unearned revenues, and the current portion of long-term debt.

Accounts Payable. Amounts owed for products or services purchased on account are *accounts payable*. Southwest Airlines Co. reported Accounts Payable of $1,203 million at December 31, 2014 (line 23 on page 493). For example, Southwest Airlines purchases soft drinks and napkins as well as spare parts for aircraft maintenance on accounts payable. We have seen many other accounts payable examples in preceding chapters. One of a merchandiser's most common transactions is the credit purchase of inventory. Walmart Stores, Inc., and Target Corp. buy their inventory on account.

Accounts Payable Turnover. An important measure of liquidity for a retail business is **accounts payable turnover**, which measures the number of times a year a company is able to pay its accounts payable. The ratio is computed as follows:

$$\text{Accounts payable turnover (T/O)} = \text{Purchases from suppliers (assumed all on credit)}$$
$$\div \text{Average accounts payable}$$
$$\text{Turnover expressed in days} = 365 \div \text{T/O (computed above)}$$

The difficulty of computing this ratio is that "purchases from suppliers" is not normally reflected in any number on the financial statements. Therefore, it must be computed. In a merchandising company, inventory purchases can be computed by analyzing the activity in the inventory account and solving for merchandise purchases, as follows:

Inventory	
Beginning balance (from balance sheet)	Cost of goods sold (from income statement)
Purchases from suppliers*	
Ending balance (from balance sheet)	

*Purchases from suppliers (assumed all on credit) = Cost of goods sold (from income statement) + Ending inventory (from comparative balance sheet) – Beginning inventory (from comparative balance sheet)

Once the turnover is computed, it is usually expressed in number of days, or **days' payable outstanding (DPO)**, by dividing the turnover into 365. Here are comparative ratios for accounts payable turnover for Walmart Stores, Inc., and Target Corp. from their 2014 financial statements:

	Walmart Stores, Inc.	Target Corp.
Cost of goods sold	$ 358,069	$ 51,278
+ Ending inventory	+ 44,858	+ 8,790
− Beginning inventory	− 43,803	− 8,278
= Purchases	= 359,124	= 51,790
÷ Average accounts payable	÷ 37,748	÷ 7,547
= Accounts payable turnover	= 9.51	= 6.86
Days' payable outstanding (365/turnover)	38 days	53 days

If there is not a material difference between beginning and ending inventories (i.e., if they haven't increased or decreased very much during the year), it is not necessary to adjust for inventory amounts, as the difference has zero effect on the turnover ratio. This makes the computation easier; simply divide cost of goods sold by average accounts payable to compute accounts payable turnover, then divide the turnover ratio into 365 for DPO.

Walmart pays its accounts payable in about 38 days, whereas Target takes 53 days to pay its accounts payable. If you were a supplier of these two giant companies, which would you rather do business with, on the basis of this ratio? If cash collections are important to you in order to pay your own bills, the obvious answer is Walmart, based strictly on this ratio.

What makes an accounts payable turnover ratio strong or weak in the eyes of creditors and investors? Generally, a high turnover ratio (short period in days) is better than a low turnover ratio. Companies with shorter payment periods are generally better credit risks than those with longer payment periods. However, some companies with strong credit ratings strategically follow shrewd cash management policies, withholding payments to suppliers as long as possible, while speeding up collections, in order to conserve cash. For example, Walmart's accounts payable turnover of about 38 days and Target's 53 days are longer than a typical 30-day credit period. These huge companies strategically stretch payment periods in order to maximize returns on excess cash, which is tough on suppliers. However, because of their size, market share, and buying power, few suppliers can afford not to do business with Walmart and Target.

To be sure, credit and sales decisions are based on far more information than accounts payable turnover, so it's wise not to oversimplify. However, combined with inventory turnover (discussed in Chapter 6) and accounts receivable turnover (discussed in Chapter 5), all expressed in days, accounts payable turnover is an important ingredient in computing the *cash conversion cycle*, which is an overall measure of liquidity. Combined with the current ratio (discussed in Chapter 3) and the quick ratio (discussed in Chapter 5), studying the cash conversion cycle helps users of financial statements determine the overall liquidity of a company. We will discuss the cash conversion cycle in more depth in Chapter 13.

It is not possible to compute turnover ratios for inventory or accounts payable for a service business, because service businesses have neither cost of goods sold nor inventory. For example, Southwest Airlines, being a service company, has no cost of goods sold account on its financial statements. Although the company reports a small inventory of parts and supplies on its balance sheet, these are not comparable to inventories in a retail business. Therefore, neither inventory turnover nor accounts payable turnover for Southwest Airlines would be meaningful.

Short-Term Notes Payable. Short-term notes payable, a common form of financing, are notes payable due within one year. **Starbucks** lists its short-term notes payable as *short-term borrowings*. Starbucks may issue short-term notes payable to borrow cash or to purchase assets. On its notes payable, Starbucks must accrue interest expense and interest payable at the end of the period. The following sequence of entries covers the purchase of inventory, accrual of interest expense, and payment of a 10% short-term note payable that's due in one year:

	A	B	C	D
1	2016			
2	Jan 1	Inventory	8,000	
3		Note Payable, Short-Term		8,000
4		*Purchase of inventory by issuing a note payable.*		
5				

This transaction increases both an asset and a liability.

Assets	=	Liabilities	+	Stockholders' Equity
+ 8,000	=	+ 8,000	+	0

The Starbucks fiscal year ends each September 30. At year-end, Starbucks must accrue interest expense at 10% for January through September:

	A	B	C	D
1	Sep 30	Interest Expense ($8,000 × 0.10 × 9/12)	600	
2		Interest Payable		600
3		*Accrual of interest expense at year-end.*		
4				

Liabilities increase and equity decreases because of the expense.

Assets	=	Liabilities	+	Stockholders' Equity	−	Expenses
0	=	+ 600				− 600

The balance sheet at year-end will report the Note Payable of $8,000 and the related Interest Payable of $600 as current liabilities. The income statement will report interest expense of $600.

The following entry records the note's payment at maturity on January 1, 2017:

	A	B	C	D
1	2017			
2	Jan 1	Note Payable, Short-Term	8,000	
3		Interest Payable	600	
4		Interest Expense ($8,000 × 0.10 × 3/12)	200	
5		Cash [$8,000 + ($8,000 × 0.10)]		8,800
6		*Payment of a note payable and interest at maturity.*		
7				
8				

The debits zero out the payables and also record Starbucks' interest expense for October, November, and December.

Sales Tax Payable. Most states levy a sales tax on retail sales. Retailers collect the tax from customers and thus owe the state for the sales tax collected. Suppose one Saturday's sales at a Home Depot store totaled $200,000 (assume this is all in cash). Home Depot collected an additional 5% ($10,000) of sales tax. The store would record that day's sales as follows:

	A	B	C
1	Cash ($200,000 × 1.05)	210,000	
2	Sales Revenue		200,000
3	Sales Tax Payable ($200,000 × 0.05)		10,000
4	*To record cash sales and the related sales tax.*		
5			

Assets, liabilities, and equity all increase—equity because of the revenues.

Assets	=	Liabilities	+	Stockholders' Equity	+	Revenues
+ 210,000	=	+ 10,000				+ 200,000

Accrued Liabilities (Accrued Expenses). An **accrued liability** usually results from an expense that the business has incurred but not yet paid. Therefore, an accrued expense creates a liability, which explains why it is also called an **accrued expense**. Southwest Airlines Co. reported Accrued liabilities of $1,565 million at December 31, 2014 (line 24 on page 493).

For example, Southwest Airlines' salary expense and salary payable occur as employees work for the company. Interest expense accrues with the passage of time. There are several categories of accrued expenses:

- Salaries and Wages Payable
- Interest Payable
- Payroll Taxes Payable

Salaries and Wages Payable is the liability for salaries and wages expenses not yet paid at the end of the period. *Interest Payable* is the company's interest payable on notes payable. *Payroll Taxes Payable* include payroll taxes withheld from employee paychecks and the employer's share of employee taxes.

Payroll Liabilities. **Payroll**, also called *employee compensation*, is a major expense. For service organizations—such as law firms, real estate companies, and airlines—compensation is *the* major expense, just as cost of goods sold is the largest expense for a merchandising company.

Employee compensation takes many different forms. A *salary* is employee pay stated at a monthly or yearly rate. A *wage* is employee pay stated at an hourly rate. Sales employees earn a *commission*, which is a percentage of the sales the employee has made. A *bonus* is an amount over and above regular compensation. Accounting for all forms of compensation follows the pattern illustrated in Exhibit 9-1 (using assumed figures):

Exhibit 9-1 | Accounting for Payroll Expenses and Liabilities

	A	B	C
	A1 ⬍		
1	Salary Expense	10,000	
2	Employee Income Tax Payable		1,200
3	FICA Tax Payable		800
4	Salary Payable [take-home pay]		8,000
5	*To record salary expense.*		
6			

Every expense accrual has the same effect: Liabilities increase and equity decreases because of the expense. The accounting equation shows these effects.

$$
\begin{array}{ccccccc}
\textbf{Assets} & = & \textbf{Liabilities} & + & \textbf{Stockholders' Equity} & - & \textbf{Expenses} \\
 & & +\,1{,}200 & & & & -\,10{,}000 \\
0 & = & +\,800 & & & & \\
 & & +\,8{,}000 & & & &
\end{array}
$$

Salary expense represents *gross pay* (that is, employee pay before subtractions for taxes and other deductions). Salary expense creates several payroll liabilities:

- *Employee Income Tax Payable* is the employees' income tax that has been withheld from paychecks.

- *FICA Tax Payable* includes the employees' Social Security tax and Medicare tax, which also are withheld from paychecks. (FICA stands for the Federal Insurance Contributions Act, which created the Social Security tax.)

- *Salary Payable* is employees' net (take-home) pay.

Companies must also pay some *employer* payroll taxes and expenses for employee benefits. Accounting for these expenses is similar to the illustration in Exhibit 9-1.

Unearned Revenues. *Unearned revenues* are also called *deferred revenues* and *revenues collected in advance*. For all unearned revenue, the business has received cash from customers before earning the revenue. The company has a liability—an obligation to provide goods or services to the customer. Let's consider an example.

Southwest Airlines sells tickets and collects cash in advance. Southwest therefore reports unearned ticket revenue (which it calls Air traffic liability) for airline tickets sold in advance. At December 31, 2014, Southwest owed customers $2,897 million of air travel (see line 25 on page 493). Let's see how Southwest accounts for its Air traffic liability.

To illustrate with a transaction during 2016, assume that, on December 15, Southwest collects $300 for a round-trip ticket from Dallas to Los Angeles. Southwest records the cash collection and related liability as follows:

	A	B	C	D
	A1 ⬍			
1	2016			
2	Dec 15	Cash	300	
3		Air traffic liability		300
4		*Received cash in advance for ticket sale.*		
5				

```
              Air traffic liability
                              |
                              |   300
```

Suppose the customer flies to Los Angeles late in December. Southwest records the revenue earned as follows:

	A	B	C	D
1	2016			
2	Dec 28	Air traffic liability	150	
3		Ticket Revenue ($300 × 1/2)		150
4		*Earned revenue that was collected in advance.*		
5				

```
        Air traffic liability              Ticket Revenue
    150  |        300                          |    150
         |   Bal  150
```

The liability decreases and the revenue increases.

At year-end, Southwest reports

- $150 of Air traffic liability on the balance sheet, and
- $150 of ticket revenue on the income statement.

The customer returns to Dallas in January 2017, and Southwest records the revenue earned with this journal entry:

	A	B	C	D
1	2017			
2	Jan 4	Air traffic liability	150	
3		Ticket Revenue ($300 × 1/2)		150
4		*Earned revenue that was collected in advance.*		
5				

Now the liability balance is zero because Southwest has earned all the revenue it collected in advance.

```
              Air traffic liability
          150  |        300
          150  |
               |   Bal     0
```

Current Portion of Long-Term Debt. Some long-term debt must be paid in installments. The **current portion of long-term debt** (also called *current maturity* or *current installment*) is the amount of the principal that is payable within one year. At the end of each year, a company reclassifies (from long-term debt to a current liability) the amount of its long-term debt that must be paid next year.

Southwest Airlines reports Current maturities of long-term debt in the amount of $258 million as of December 31, 2014 (line 26 on page 493). Southwest also reports a long-term liability (line 28) in the amount of $2,434 million for Long-term debt, which excludes the current maturities. *Long-term debt* refers to long-term notes payable and bonds payable, which we cover in the second half of this chapter.

Current Liabilities That Must Be Estimated

A business may know that a liability exists but not know its exact amount. The business must report the liability on the balance sheet. Estimated liabilities vary among companies. Let's look first at Estimated Warranty Payable, a liability account that most merchandisers have.

Estimated Warranty Payable. Many companies guarantee their products under *warranty agreements*. The warranty period may extend for 90 days to a year for consumer products. Automobile companies—like **General Motors, BMW**, and **Toyota**—accrue liabilities for vehicle warranties.

Whatever the warranty's life, the expense recognition (matching) principle demands that the company record the *warranty expense* in the same period that the business records sales revenue. After all, the warranty motivates customers to buy products, so the company must record warranty expense in the period of sale. At the time of the sale, however, the company doesn't know which products are defective. The exact amount of warranty expense cannot be known with certainty, so the business must estimate warranty expense and the related liability.

Assume that **Black & Decker**, which manufactures power tools, made sales of $100,000 subject to product warranties. Assume that in past years between 2% and 4% of products proved defective. Black & Decker could estimate that 3% of sales will require repair or replacement. In this case, Black & Decker would estimate warranty expense of $3,000 ($100,000 × 0.03) for the year and make the following entry:

	A1 ⬍			
	A	**B**	**C**	**D**
1		Warranty Expense	3,000	
2		Estimated Warranty Payable		3,000
3		*To accrue warranty expense.*		
4				

Estimated Warranty Payable

	3,000

Assume that defects add up to $2,800, and Black & Decker will replace the defective products. Black & Decker then records the following:

	A1 ⬍			
	A	**B**	**C**	**D**
1		Estimated Warranty Payable	2,800	
2		Inventory		2,800
3		*To replace defective products sold under warranty.*		
4				

Estimated Warranty Payable

2,800	3,000
	Bal 200

At the end of the year, Black & Decker will report Estimated Warranty Payable of $200 as a current liability. The income statement reports Warranty Expense of $3,000 for the year. Then, next year Black & Decker will repeat this process. The Estimated Warranty Payable account probably won't ever zero out. If Black & Decker paid cash to satisfy the warranty, then the credit would be to Cash rather than to Inventory.

Vacation pay is another expense that must be estimated. And income taxes must be estimated because the final amount isn't determined until early the next year.

Contingent Liabilities

A *contingent liability* is not an actual liability. Instead, it's a potential liability that depends on the future outcome of past events. Examples of contingent liabilities are future obligations that may arise because of lawsuits, tax disputes, or alleged violations of environmental protection laws. The principle of representational faithfulness, discussed in Chapter 1, requires that companies disclose the substance of their financial positions and results of operations in a way that is as transparent and complete as possible. With liabilities, that principle implies: "When in doubt, disclose. When necessary, accrue." The Financial Accounting Standards Board (FASB) provides these guidelines to account for contingent liabilities:

1. *Accrue* (i.e., make an adjusting journal entry for) a contingent liability if, in management's opinion, it's *probable* that the loss (or expense) will occur *and* the *amount can be reasonably estimated*. Warranty expense, illustrated previously, is an example. Another example is a lawsuit that Southwest Airlines will probably lose at an estimated settlement amount of $1 million.

2. *Disclose* a contingency in a financial statement note if it's *reasonably possible* (less than probable but more than remote) that a loss (or expense) will occur. Lawsuits in progress are a prime example. Southwest Airlines includes a note in its 2014 financial statements to report contingent liabilities from examinations of its past income tax returns by the IRS.

> **Note 17, Contingencies**
>
> The Company is subject to various legal proceedings [...] including [...] examinations by the Internal Revenue Service (IRS). The IRS regularly examines the Company's federal income tax returns and, in the course thereof, proposes adjustments to the Company's federal income tax liability reported on such returns. The Company's management does not expect that [...] any of its currently ongoing legal proceedings or [...] any proposed adjustments [...] by the IRS [...] will have a material adverse effect on the Company's financial condition, results of operations, or cash flow.

Source: From Southwest Airlines, 2014 Financial Statements, http://www.sec.gov/Archives/edgar/data/92380/000009238003000025/q3_200310q.htm.

3. There is no need to report a contingent loss that is unlikely to occur. Instead, wait until an actual transaction clears up the situation. For example, suppose **Del Monte Foods** grows vegetables in Nicaragua, and the Nicaraguan government threatens to confiscate the assets of all foreign companies. Del Monte will report nothing about the contingency if the probability of a loss is considered remote.

A contingent liability may arise from lawsuits that claim wrongdoing by the company. The plaintiff may seek damages through the courts. If the court rules in favor of Southwest, there is no liability. But if the ruling favors the plaintiff, then Southwest will have an actual liability. It would be unethical to omit these disclosures from the financial statements because investors need this information to properly evaluate a company.

Commitments. Disclosure of contractual commitments often fall in the same category as contingencies, although they are slightly different. Commitments represent contractual promises a company has made to enter into transactions in the future and thus obligate the company to commit resources toward a certain purpose. Note 4 of Southwest Airlines Company's financial statements (the same note that describes contingencies) also includes a chart that describes the company's contractual purchase commitments to take delivery of 521 new Boeing 737 aircraft during years 2016 through 2027. It would not be proper to accrue commitments because the transactions have not yet occurred as of the balance-sheet date. However, because of the substantial amount of money required to fulfill these commitments (one plane costs $50–$70 million), Southwest is obligated to disclose them to shareholders and creditors, because they will have a substantial impact on the company's financial statements in future years.

The international accounting standard for loss contingencies contains different language and different requirements for accrual than the U.S. standard. Specifically, the term *contingency* is defined as a possible obligation that arises from a past event and whose existence will be confirmed only by the occurrence or nonoccurrence of one or more future events that are beyond the control of the entity. Contingencies are not considered "probable" to occur in the future. Therefore, contingencies can, by definition, only be disclosed in the financial statement footnotes. However, if it is "more likely than not" (i.e., greater than a 50% probability) that an obligation is going to arise, and if an estimate can be made of the amount, IFRS requires that a "provision" be recorded by making an accrual journal entry. Therefore, the circumstances for accrual of possible obligations are slightly different under IFRS than under U.S. generally accepted accounting principles (GAAP). Further details on this concept are covered in more advanced accounting texts.

Appendix E summarizes differences between U.S. GAAP and international financial reporting standards (IFRS), cross-referenced by chapter.

Are All Liabilities Reported on the Balance Sheet?

The big danger with liabilities is that you may fail to report a large debt on your balance sheet. What is the consequence of missing a large liability? You will definitely understate your liabilities and your debt ratio. By failing to accrue interest on the liability, you'll probably overstate your net income as well. In short, your financial statements will make you look better off than you really are. Any such error, if significant, hurts a company's credibility.

Contingent liabilities are very easy to overlook because they aren't actual debts at the present time. How would you feel if you owned stock in a company that failed to report a contingency that put the company out of business? If you had known of the contingency, you could have sold the stock and avoided the loss. In this case, you would hire a lawyer to file suit against the company for negligent financial reporting.

COOKING THE BOOKS
with Liabilities

Crazy Eddie, Inc.

Accidentally understating liabilities is one thing, but doing it intentionally is quite another. When unethical management decides to cook the books in the area of liabilities, its strategy is to *deliberately understate recorded liabilities*. This can be done by intentionally underrecording the amount of existing liabilities or by omitting certain liabilities altogether.

Crazy Eddie, Inc., first discussed in Chapter 6, used *multiple tactics* to overstate its financial position over a period of four consecutive years. In addition to overstating inventory (thus understating cost of goods sold and overstating income), the management of the company deliberately *understated accounts payable* by issuing fictitious (false) debit memoranda for suppliers (vendors). A debit memo is issued for goods returned to a vendor, such as Sony. When a debit memorandum is issued, accounts payable are debited (reduced), thus reducing current liabilities and increasing the current ratio. Eventually, expenses are also decreased, and profits are correspondingly increased through reduction of expenses. Crazy Eddie, Inc., issued $3 million of fictitious debit memoranda in one year, making the company's current ratio and debt ratio look better than they actually were, as well as overstating profits.

Summary of Current Liabilities

Let's summarize what we've covered thus far. A company can report its current liabilities on the balance sheet as follows:

	A	B	C	D
	A1 ⬍			
1	**Accounting, Inc.** **Balance Sheet** **December 31, 2016**			
2	**Assets**		**Liabilities**	
3	Current Assets:		Current liabilities:	
4	Cash		Accounts payable	
5	Short-term investments		Salary payable*	
6	Etc.		Interest payable*	
7			Payroll taxes payable*	
8	Property, plant, and equipment:		Unearned revenue	
9	Land		Estimated warranty payable*	
10	Etc.		Notes payable, short-term	
11			Current portion of long-term debt	
12	Other assets		**Total current liabilities**	
13			Long-term liabilities	
14				
15			**Stockholders' Equity**	
16			Common stock	
17			Retained earnings	
18			Total stockholders' equity	
19			Total liabilities and	
20	Total assets	$XXX	stockholders' equity	$XXX
21				

*These amounts are often combined and reported in a single total as "Accrued liabilities."

On its income statement this company would report the following:

- *Expenses* related to some of the current liabilities. Examples include Salary Expense, Interest Expense, Income Tax Expense, and Warranty Expense.
- *Revenue* related to the unearned revenue. Examples include Service Revenue and Sales Revenue that were collected in advance, but subsequently earned.

Mid-Chapter | Summary Problem

Assume that the **Estée Lauder Companies, Inc.**, faced the following liability situations at June 30, 2016, the end of the company's fiscal year. Show how Estée Lauder would report these liabilities on its balance sheet at June 30, 2016.

a. Salary expense for the last payroll period of the year was $900,000. Of this amount, employees' withheld income tax totaled $88,000 and FICA taxes were $61,000. These payroll amounts will be paid in early July.

b. On fiscal-year 2016 sales of $400 million, management estimates warranty expense of 2%. One year ago, at June 30, 2015, Estimated Warranty Payable stood at $3 million. Warranty payments were $9 million during the year ended June 30, 2016.

c. The company pays royalties on its purchased trademarks. Royalties for the trademarks are equal to a percentage of Estée Lauder's sales. Assume that sales in fiscal year 2016 were $400 million and were subject to a royalty rate of 3%. At June 30, 2016, Estée Lauder owes two-thirds of the year's royalty, to be paid in July.

d. Long-term debt, outstanding since 2014, totals $100 million and is payable in annual installments of $10 million each. The interest rate on the debt is 7%, and the interest is paid each December 31.

Answer

Liabilities at June 30, 2016:	
a. Current liabilities:	
Salary payable ($900,000 − $88,000 − $61,000).	$ 751,000
Employee income tax payable	88,000
FICA tax payable	61,000
b. Current liabilities:	
Estimated warranty payable	2,000,000
[$3,000,000 + ($400,000,000 × 0.02) − $9,000,000]	
c. Current liabilities:	
Royalties payable ($400,000,000 × 0.03 × 2/3)	8,000,000
d. Current liabilities:	
Current installment of long-term debt	10,000,000
Interest payable ($100,000,000 × 0.07 × 6/12)	3,500,000
Long-term debt ($100,000,000 − $10,000,000)	90,000,000

ACCOUNT FOR BONDS PAYABLE AND INTEREST EXPENSE WITH STRAIGHT-LINE AMORTIZATION

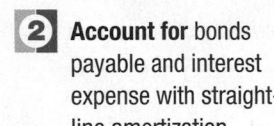

Account for bonds payable and interest expense with straight-line amortization

In Chapter 8 , we discussed bonds and notes from the standpoint of the investor, as held-to-maturity or available-for-sale investments (long-term assets). In this chapter, we examine bonds and notes from the flip-side, or the standpoint of the borrower, on whose balance sheets the bonds and notes will appear as long-term liabilities. We treat bonds payable and notes payable together because the accounting for each is virtually identical.

Large companies such as Southwest Airlines, Apple Inc., and **Toyota** cannot borrow billions from a single lender. So how do corporations borrow huge amounts? They issue (sell) bonds to the public. **Bonds payable** are groups of debt securities issued to multiple lenders, called *bondholders*. Southwest Airlines needs airplanes and can borrow large amounts by issuing bonds to thousands of individual and institutional investors, who each lend Southwest a smaller amount. Southwest receives the cash it needs, and each investor limits investment risk by diversifying—not putting all the "eggs in one basket."

Bonds: An Introduction

Bonds payable are debts of the issuing company. Purchasers of bonds receive a bond certificate, which carries the issuing company's name. The certificate also states the *principal*, which is typically stated in units of $1,000; principal is also called the bond's *face value*, *maturity value*, or *par value*. The bond obligates the issuing company to pay the debt at a specific future time called the *maturity date*.

Interest is the fee paid by a borrower for the use of someone else's money. The bond certificate states the interest rate that the issuer will pay the holder and the dates that the interest payments are due (generally, twice a year). Exhibit 9-2 shows an actual bond certificate.

Exhibit 9-2 | Bond Certificate (Adapted)

Issuing corporation

Annual Interest rate

Semiannual interest payments on January 1 and July 1 of each year

Maturity date July 1, 2017

Principal amount

Source: From Nuclear Project No.1 Revenue Bond, Series 1976B, Washington Public Power Supply System.

Issuing bonds usually requires the services of a securities firm, such as J.P. Morgan Chase or Merrill Lynch (a unit of Bank of America), to act as the underwriter of the bond issue. The **underwriter** purchases the bonds from the issuing company and resells them to its clients, or it may sell the bonds to its clients and earn a commission on the sale.

Types of Bonds. All the bonds in a particular issue may mature at the same time (**term bonds**) or in installments over a period of time (**serial bonds**). Serial bonds are like installment notes payable. Some of Southwest Airlines' long-term debts are serial in nature because they are payable in installments.

Secured, or *mortgage*, *bonds* give the bondholder the right to assume ownership of specified assets of the issuer if the company *defaults*—that is, fails to pay interest or principal. *Unsecured bonds*, called **debentures**, are backed only by the good faith of the borrower. Debentures carry a higher rate of interest than secured bonds because debentures are riskier investments.

Bond Prices. Investors may buy and sell bonds through bond markets. Bond prices are quoted at a percentage of their maturity (also called face or par) value. For example,

■ a $1,000 bond quoted at 100 is bought or sold for $1,000, which is 100% of its face value.

■ The same bond quoted at 101.5 has a market price of $1,015 (101.5% of face value = $1,000 × 1.015).

■ A $1,000 bond quoted at 88.375 is priced at $883.75 ($1,000 × 0.88375).

Bond Premium and Bond Discount. A bond issued at a price above its face (par) value is said to be issued at a **premium**, and a bond issued at a price below face (par) value has a **discount**. Premium on Bonds Payable has a *credit* balance and Discount on Bonds Payable carries a *debit* balance. Discount on Bonds Payable is therefore a contra liability account.

As a bond nears maturity, its market price moves toward face (par) value. Therefore, the price of a bond issued at a

■ premium decreases toward face or maturity value.

■ discount increases toward face or maturity value.

On the maturity date, a bond's market value exactly equals its face value because the company that issued the bond pays that amount to retire the bond.

The Time Value of Money. We discussed the time value of money in Chapter 8. You should refresh your understanding of that material at this point because we will use it extensively in accounting for bonds payable and related interest expense. Let's examine how the *time value of money* affects the pricing of bonds, using the same example provided in Chapter 8—except this time, from the issuer (or debtor's) point of view.

Bond Interest Rates Determine Bond Prices. Bonds are always sold at their *market price*, which is the amount investors will pay for the bond. *Market price is the bond's present value*, which equals the present value of the principal payment of the bond at the end of its term plus the present value of the stream of cash interest payments from date of issuance until the maturity date. Interest is usually paid semiannually (twice a year). Some companies pay interest annually or quarterly.

As discussed in Chapter 8, two interest rates work to set the price of a bond:

■ The **stated interest rate**, also called the coupon rate, is the interest rate printed on the bond certificate. The stated interest rate determines the amount of cash interest the borrower pays—and the investor receives—each year. As shown in the example in Chapter 8, suppose Southwest Airlines bonds have a stated interest rate of 9%. Southwest would pay $9,000 of interest annually on $100,000 of bonds. Each semiannual payment would be $4,500 ($100,000 × 0.09 × 6/12).

■ The **market interest rate**, or *effective interest rate*, is the rate that investors demand for loaning their money. The market interest rate varies by the minute.

A company may issue bonds with a stated interest rate that differs from the prevailing market interest rate. In fact, because market rates of interest can fluctuate daily, the two interest rates usually differ.

Exhibit 9-3 shows how the stated interest rate and the market interest rate interact to determine the issue price of a bond payable for three separate cases.

Southwest Airlines may issue 9% bonds when the market rate has risen to 10%. Will the Southwest 9% bonds attract investors in this market? No, because investors can earn 10% on other bonds of similar risk. Therefore, investors will purchase Southwest bonds only at a price less than their face value. The difference between the lower price and face value is a *discount* (Case B in Exhibit 9-3). Conversely, if the market interest rate is 8%, Southwest's 9% bonds will be so attractive that investors will pay more than face value to purchase them. The difference between the higher price and face value is a *premium* (Case C in Exhibit 9-3).

Exhibit 9-3 | How Stated Interest Rates and Market Interest Rates Interact to Determine the Price of a Bond

Issue Price of Bonds Payable

Case A:

Stated interest rate on a bond payable	equals	Market interest rate	Therefore,	Price of face (par, or maturity) value
Example: 9%	=	9%	→	*Par: $1,000 bond issued for $1,000*

Case B:

Stated interest rate on a bond payable	less than	Market interest rate	Therefore,	Discount price (price below face value)
Example: 9%		10%	→	*Discount: $1,000 bond issued for a price below $1,000*

Case C:

Stated interest rate on a bond payable	greater than	Market interest rate	Therefore,	Premium price (price above face value)
Example: 9%		8%	→	*Premium: $1,000 bond issued for a price above $1,000*

Issuing Bonds Payable at Par (Face Value)

We start with the most straightforward situation—issuing bonds at their par value (Case A in Exhibit 9-3). There is no premium or discount on these bonds payable.

Suppose Southwest Airlines issues $100,000 of 9% bonds payable that mature in five years. Assume that Southwest issues these bonds at par on January 1, 2016. This means that the stated rate of interest on the bonds exactly equals the market rate on January 1, 2016. The issuance entry is as follows:

	A	B	C	D
1	2016			
2	Jan 1	Cash	100,000	
3		Bonds Payable		100,000
4		To issue bonds at par.		
5				

Bonds Payable
| 100,000

Assets and liabilities increase when a company issues bonds payable.

Assets	=	Liabilities	+	Stockholders' Equity
+ 100,000	=	+ 100,000	+	0

Southwest, the borrower, makes a one-time entry to record the receipt of cash and the issuance of bonds. Afterward, investors buy and sell the bonds through the bond markets. These later buy-and-sell transactions between outside investors do *not* involve Southwest at all.

Interest payments occur each January 1 and July 1. Southwest's entry to record the first semi-annual interest payment is as follows:

	A	B	C	D
1	2016			
2	Jul 1	Interest Expense ($100,000 × 0.09 × 6/12)	4,500	
3		Cash		4,500
4		*To pay semiannual interest.*		
5				

The payment of interest expense decreases assets and equity. Bonds Payable is not affected.

Assets	=	Liabilities	+	Stockholders' Equity	−	Expenses
− 4,500	=	0	+			− 4,500

At year-end, Southwest accrues interest expense and interest payable for six months (July through December), as follows:

	A	B	C	D
1	2016			
2	Dec 31	Interest Expense ($100,000 × 0.09 × 6/12)	4,500	
3		Interest Payable		4,500
4		*To accrue interest.*		
5				

Liabilities increase, and equity decreases.

Assets	=	Liabilities	+	Stockholders' Equity	−	Expenses
0	=	+ 4,500	+			− 4,500

On January 1, Southwest will pay the interest, debiting Interest Payable and crediting Cash. This process continues throughout the five-year term of the bonds. Then, on the maturity date (January 1, 2021), Southwest pays off the bonds and makes the following entry:

	A	B	C	D
1	2021			
2	Jan 1	Bonds Payable	100,000	
3		Cash		100,000
4		*To pay bonds payable at maturity.*		
5				

Bonds Payable

100,000	100,000
	Bal 0

Assets	=	Liabilities	+	Stockholders' Equity
− 100,000	=	− 100,000		

Issuing Bonds Payable at a Discount

Market conditions may force a company to issue bonds at a discount. Suppose Southwest Airlines issues $100,000 of 9%, five-year bonds when the market interest rate is 10%. Interest payments occur semiannually, each January 1 and July 1. The market price of the bonds drops from 100 to 96.15 (96.15% of par), and Southwest receives $96,150[1] at issuance ($100,000 × 0.9615). The transaction is recorded as follows:

	A	B	C	D
		A1		
1	2016			
2	Jan 1	Cash	96,150	
3		Discount on Bonds Payable	3,850	
4		Bonds Payable		100,000
5		*To issue bonds at a discount.*		
6				

The accounting equation shows:

Assets	=	Liabilities	+	Stockholders' Equity
+ 96,150	=	− 3,850	+	0
		+ 100,000		

The Bonds Payable accounts have an initial carrying value of $96,150 as follows:

Bonds Payable		Discount on Bonds Payable		Net carrying value
	100,000	−	3,850	= of bonds payable $96,150

Southwest's balance sheet immediately after issuance of the bonds would report the following:

Total current liabilities		$ XXX
Long-term liabilities:		
Bonds payable, 9%, due 2021	$100,000	
Less: Discount on bonds payable...............	(3,850)	96,150

Discount on Bonds Payable is a contra account to Bonds Payable, a decrease in the company's liabilities. Subtracting the discount from Bonds Payable yields the *carrying amount* of the bonds.

Each semiannual *cash interest payment* is set by the bond contract and therefore remains constant over the life of the bonds:

$$\text{Semiannual interest payment} = \$100,000 \times 0.09 \times 6/12$$
$$= \$4,500$$

But Southwest's *interest expense* must be increased each period in order to account for the fact that the bonds were issued at a *discount*, which represents an additional cost of borrowing. This discount must be *amortized*, over the term of the bonds, assigning a portion to each interest period as additional interest expense.

The *straight-line amortization method* divides a bond discount into equal amounts over the bond's term. The amount of interest expense is therefore the same for each interest period.

---

[1]The example in Chapter 8 on page 466 shows how to determine the price of this bond as follows: (1) the present value of $100,000 paid 10 periods in the future, discounted at the market rate of 5% (0.10 annual rate ÷ 2), plus (2) the present value of an annuity, ten interest payments of $4,500 each (100,000 × face rate of 0.045 each period) discounted at 5%. The price is $96,149. To simplify computations in this example, we round up to $96,150.

Let's apply the straight-line amortization method to the Southwest Airlines bonds issued at a price of 96.150:

Semiannual cash interest payment ($100,000 × 0.09 × 6/12)		$4,500
+ Semiannual amortization of discount ($3,850 ÷ 10)...........................		385
= Estimated semiannual interest expense		$4,885

(Remember that the "10" in the calculation is the number of periods that interest will be paid for these bonds. The Southwest Airlines bonds are five-year bonds that pay interest semiannually, or twice per year. Therefore, the number of periods is 5 years × 2, or 10.) The straight-line amortization method uses these same amounts every period over the term of the bonds. Southwest's entry to record interest expense on July 1, 2016 (the first interest payment period) using the straight-line amortization method is as follows:

	A1				
	A	B		C	D
1	2016				
2	Jul 1	Interest Expense		4,885	
3		Discount on Bonds Payable			385
4		Cash			4,500
5		*To pay semiannual interest and amortize bond discount.*			
6					

After this entry is posted, the bonds would have a carrying value of $96,535, calculated as follows:

Bonds Payable		–	Discount on Bonds Payable				=	Carrying value
	01/01/16 100,000		01/01/16 3,850	07/01/16 385				96,535
			Bal. 3,465					

Each interest period, the discount on bonds payable is decreased by $385, and the carrying value of the bonds correspondingly increases by $385 until the carrying value of the bond reaches $100,000 face value at maturity, and the bonds are paid off with cash.

Issuing Bonds Payable at a Premium

Suppose the $100,000 face amount of Southwest Airlines bonds in the last example is issued at a price of 103.85. In this case, the stated rate of interest of the bonds is greater than the market rate, producing a bond premium. Each bond sells for 103.85% of par, or $1,038.50. The initial carrying value of the bonds is $103,850, comprised of $100,000 in face value of Bonds Payable plus $3,850 in Premium on Bonds Payable.

Bonds Payable		+	Premium on Bonds Payable		=	Carrying value
	01/01/16 $100,000			01/01/16 $3,850		$103,850

Using the straight line method, amortization of the premium over the term of the bonds is computed exactly the same way as discount amortization. However, as the premium is amortized, it reduces the amount of interest expense recognized each period because the issuing price was greater than the face value of the bonds. Bond premium is reduced, as is the carrying value of the bonds, until it reaches the face amount at maturity. Each semiannual interest payment remains at $4,500 as computed before. However, one-tenth of the bond premium ($385) must be amortized each interest payment date, resulting in interest expense of $4,115 ($4,500 − $385). Again, 10 periods are used in the calculation because the bonds are five year bonds paying interest twice per year, or 5 × 2 = 10. The entry to record the first interest payment on July 1, 2016, is:

	A1	⇕			
	A	**B**		**C**	**D**
1	2016				
2	Jul 1	Interest Expense		4,115	
3		Premium on Bonds Payable		385	
4		Cash			4,500
5		*To pay semi-annual interest and amortize bond premium*			
6					

After the first interest payment is posted to the accounts, premium on bonds payable is reduced to $3,465, and the bond carrying value is reduced to $103,465.

Bonds Payable		+	**Premium on Bonds Payable**		=	Carrying value
01/01/16	100,000		07/01/16 385	01/01/16 3,850		103,465
				Bal. 3,465		

Premium on bonds payable is decreased by $385 each interest payment date, and the carrying value of the bonds is correspondingly reduced by $385 for 10 periods until finally the carrying value of the bonds reaches $100,000 face amount at maturity, and the bonds are paid off with cash.

Generally accepted accounting principles (GAAP) permit the straight-line amortization method only when its amounts do not differ significantly from the amounts determined by the more precise and theoretically correct effective-interest method, discussed next.

The following graph shows the carrying value of bonds originally issued at (a) a discount price of 96.15, shown by the red line, and (b) a premium price of 103.85, shown by the blue line, and how the carrying value eventually amortizes on a straight line basis over five years, or 10 semiannual interest periods, to par or face value at maturity (the green line). The carrying value of bonds issued at par or face value, of course, remains constant over the term of the bonds.

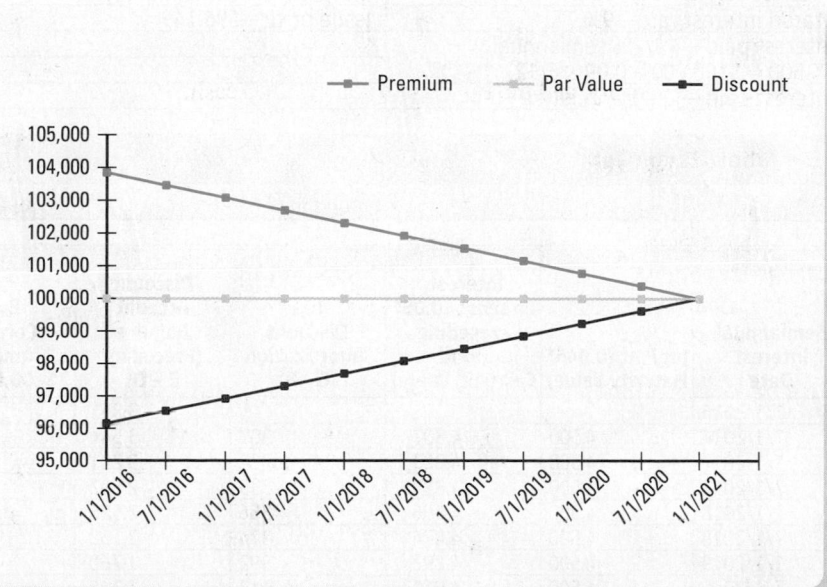

ACCOUNT FOR BONDS PAYABLE AND INTEREST EXPENSE WITH EFFECTIVE INTEREST AMORTIZATION

3 Account for bonds payable and interest expense with effective interest amortization

The *effective-interest method* is the most theoretically correct method of amortizing bond discount or premium because it recognizes the impact of the time value of money on interest expense recognized each interest payment period. Unlike the straight-line method, interest expense under the effective-interest method is different each interest payment period. The steps in the method are:

1. Determine the exact price of the bonds at issuance, taking into account the market rate of interest, the periodic interest payments based on the face amount multiplied by the face interest rate, and the maturity value of the bonds. This step can be performed most efficiently by using the present value (PV) function of Excel, as explained in Chapter 8.

2. Build an amortization table showing interest payments, interest expense, discount or premium amortization, discount or premium balance, and carrying value of the bonds. Again, Excel is the recommended tool to create an amortization table.

Issuing Bonds Payable at a Discount

Panel A of Exhibit 9-4 repeats the Southwest Airlines bond data we've been using when the bonds are issued at a discount. Panel B provides an amortization table that does two things:

- It determines the periodic interest expense (column C).
- It shows the bond carrying amount (column F).

Study the exhibit carefully because the amounts we'll be using come directly from the amortization table. We will discuss the meaning of the information in each column as we discuss the construction of the table on the next page.

Exhibit 9-4 | Amortization of Bond Discount

Panel A—Bond Data

	A	B
	A1	
	A	B
1	Issue date—January 1, 2016	Maturity date—January 1, 2021
2	Face (par or *maturity*) value—$100,000	Market interest rate at time of issue—10% annually, 5% semiannually
3	Stated interest rate—9%	Issue price—$96,149
4	Interest paid—4 1/2% semiannually, $4,500 = $100,000 × 0.09 × 6/12	
5	Interest paid—Jan. 1 and July 1	
6		

Panel B—Amortization Table

	A1					
	A	B	C	D	E	F
1	Semiannual Interest Date	Int Pmt (0.045* Maturity Value)	Interest Expense (0.05* Preceding Bond Carrying Value)	Discount Amortization (C – B)	Discount Account Balance (Preceding E – D)	Bond Carrying Amount ($100,000 – E)
2	1/1/2016				3,851	96,149
3	7/1/2016	4,500	4,807	307	3,544	96,456
4	1/1/2017	4,500	4,823	323	3,221	96,779
5	7/1/2017	4,500	4,839	339	2,882	97,118
6	1/1/2018	4,500	4,856	356	2,526	97,474
7	7/1/2018	4,500	4,874	374	2,152	97,848
8	1/1/2019	4,500	4,892	392	1,760	98,240
9	7/1/2019	4,500	4,912	412	1,348	98,652
10	1/1/2020	4,500	4,933	433	915	99,085
11	7/1/2020	4,500	4,954	454	461	99,539
12	1/1/2021	4,500	4,961**	461	0	100,000
13						

*Indicates multiplication in Excel.
**Adjusted for the effects of rounding.

Bond amortization tables are a snap when you prepare them in Excel. Open a blank Excel spreadsheet.

- In line 1, label the columns as shown in Panel B of Exhibit 9-4.

- Column A. Starting in line 2, enter the issue date (1/1/2016) followed by each of the semiannual interest payment dates. This will continue through line 12 with the last interest payment on January 1, 2021. Highlight all cell values in rows 2 through 12 of column A, and click on the drop down box in the "number" field on the ruler at the top of the spreadsheet. Choose the "date" category and click OK to change all cell values in Column A to the date format.

- Line 2, column E (bond discount). Enter 3851 in cell E2. Enter the formula $=100000-E2$ in cell F2. The calculated value of 96149 should appear in cell F2, representing the initial carrying value of the bond.

- Line 3, column B (semiannual cash interest payments, fixed by contract). Enter formula $=.045*100000$ in cell B3. A calculated value of 4500 should appear, representing the amount of the first cash interest payment.

- Line 3, column C (interest expense, calculated as the market rate of 5% x previous period's carrying amount of the bond). In cell C3, enter formula $=.05*F2$. A calculated value of 4807 should appear, representing the calculated amount of interest expense. If the cell shows a decimal fraction, use the "decrease decimal" command in the "number" field of the toolbar to reduce the decimals to none. This will round the value to the nearest dollar.

- Line 3, column D (discount amortization, which is the excess of interest expense in column C over the interest payment in column B). In cell D3, enter formula $=C3-B3$. A value of 307 should appear, representing the amount of discount amortization included in interest expense on the first interest payment date.

- Line 3, column E (unamortized discount account balance, which decreases as it is amortized). In cell E3, enter formula $=E2-D3$. A value of 3544 should appear, representing the unamortized discount remaining after the first interest payment.

- Line 3, column F (bond carrying amount). In cell F3, enter formula $=100000-E3$. A value of 96456 should appear, representing the adjusted carrying value of the bond after the first interest payment.

- For columns B through F, copy line 3 down through line 12. All of the numbers in the table should fill in. Line 12 will have to be adjusted for rounding by taking the remaining unamortized discount from cell E11 (461) and substituting that value in cell D12 (discount amortization). Also, substitute 4961 for interest expense in cell C12. This will adjust the final bond carrying amount to the maturity value of $100,000 and the unamortized discount to 0.

- Highlight cells B2 through F12, and insert commas to make the table easier to read. When you insert the commas, Excel automatically inserts two decimals and zeros, so use the "decrease decimal" key to format the table to whole dollars.

Interest Expense on Bonds Issued at a Discount

In Exhibit 9-4, Southwest Airlines borrowed $96,149 cash but must pay $100,000 when the bonds mature. What happens to the $3,851 balance of the discount account over the life of the bond issue?

The $3,851 is additional interest expense to Southwest over and above the stated interest that Southwest pays each six months. Exhibit 9-5 graphs the interest expense (column C in Exhibit 9-4) and the interest payment (column B in Exhibit 9-4) on the Southwest bonds over their lifetime. Observe that the semiannual interest payment is fixed—by contract—at $4,500. But the amount of interest expense increases as the discount bond marches upward toward maturity.

Exhibit 9-5 | Interest Expense on Bonds Payable Issued at a Discount

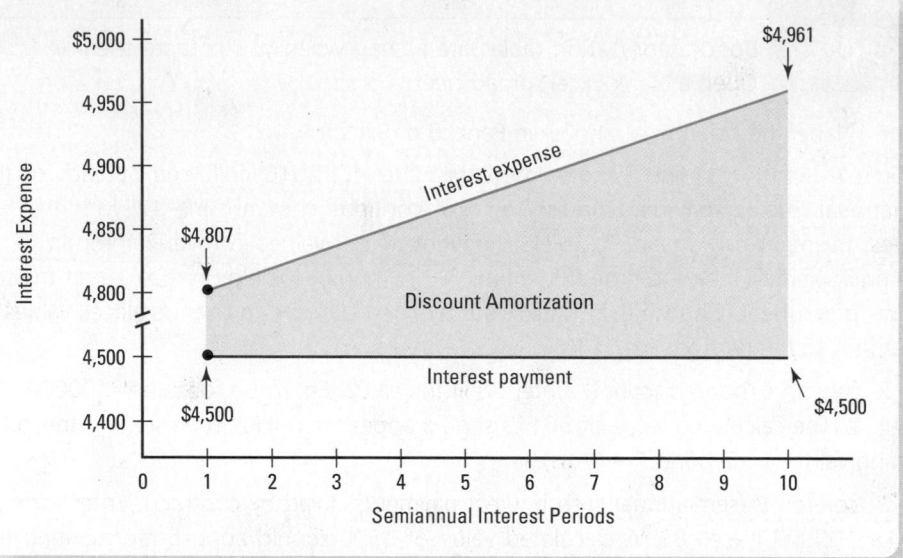

The discount is allocated to interest expense through amortization over the term of the bonds. Exhibit 9-6 illustrates the amortization of the bond discount, so the carrying value of the bonds increases from $96,149 at the start to $100,000 at maturity. These amounts come from Exhibit 9-4, column F (p. 512).

Exhibit 9-6 | Amortizing Discount on Bonds Payable

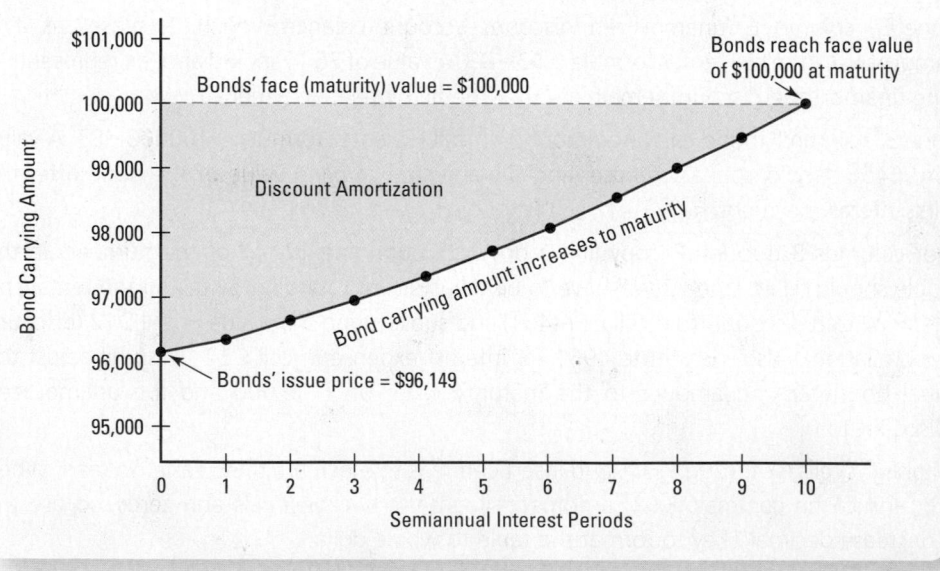

Now let's see how Southwest would account for these bonds each interest payment period. In our example, Southwest issued its bonds on January 1, 2016. On July 1, Southwest makes the first semiannual interest payment. But Southwest's interest expense is greater than its payment of $4,500. Southwest's journal entry to record interest expense and the interest payment for the first six months is seen on the following page (with all amounts taken from Exhibit 9-4):

	A	B	C	D
1	2016			
2	Jul 1	Interest Expense	4,807	
3		Discount on Bonds Payable		307
4		Cash		4,500
5		*To pay semiannual interest and amortize bond discount.*		
6				

The credit to Discount on Bonds Payable accomplishes two purposes:

- It adjusts the carrying value of the bonds as they march upward toward maturity value.
- It amortizes the discount to interest expense.

At December 31, 2016, Southwest accrues interest and amortizes the bond discount for July through December with this entry (amounts from Exhibit 9-4, page 512):

	A	B	C	D
1	2016			
2	Dec 31	Interest Expense	4,823	
3		Discount on Bonds Payable		323
4		Interest Payable		4,500
5		*To accrue semiannual interest and amortize bond discount.*		
6				

At December 31, 2016, Southwest's bond accounts appear as follows:

Bonds Payable		Discount on Bonds Payable		
	100,000	3,851	307	
			323	
		Bal 3,221		

Bond carrying amount, $96,779 = $100,000 − $3,221 from Exhibit 9-4, page 512.

≫ *Try It*

What would Southwest Airlines' 2016 income statement and year-end balance sheet report for these bonds?

Answer:

Income Statement for 2016

Interest expense ($4,807 + $4,823)	$ 9,630

Balance Sheet at December 31, 2016

Current liabilities:
Interest payable		$ 4,500

Long-term liabilities:
| Bonds payable .... | $100,000 | |
| Less: Discount on bonds payable............... | (3,221) | 96,779 |

At maturity on January 1, 2021, the discount will have been amortized to zero, and the bonds' carrying amount will be face value of $100,000. Southwest will retire the bonds by paying $100,000 to the bondholders.

Partial-Period Interest Amounts

Companies don't always issue bonds at the beginning or the end of their accounting year. They issue bonds when market conditions are most favorable, and that may be on May 16, August 1, or any other date. To illustrate partial-period interest, assume **Google, Inc.**, issues $100,000 of 8% bonds payable at 96 on August 31, 2016. The market rate of interest was 9%, and these bonds pay semiannual interest on February 28 and August 31 each year. The first few lines of Google's amortization table are as follows:

Semiannual Interest Date	4% Interest Payment	4 ½% Interest Expense	Discount Amortization	Discount Account Balance	Bond Carrying Amount
Aug 31, 2016				$4,000	$96,000
Feb 28, 2017	$4,000	$4,320	$320	3,680	96,320
Aug 31, 2017	4,000	4,334	334	3,346	96,654

Google's accounting year ends on December 31, so at year-end Google must accrue interest and amortize bond discount for four months (September through December). At December 31, 2016, Google will make this entry:

	A	B	C	D
1	2016			
2	Dec 31	Interest Expense ($4,320 × 4/6)	2,880	
3		Discount on Bonds Payable ($320 × 4/6)		213
4		Interest Payable ($4,000 × 4/6)		2,667
5		*To accrue interest and amortize discount at year-end.*		
6				

The year-end entry at December 31, 2016, uses 4/6 of the upcoming semiannual amounts at February 28, 2017. This example clearly illustrates the benefit of an amortization schedule.

Issuing Bonds Payable at a Premium

Let's modify the Southwest Airlines bond example to illustrate issuance of the bonds at a premium. Assume that, on January 1, 2016, Southwest issues $100,000 of five-year, 9% bonds that pay interest semiannually. If the 9% bonds are issued when the market interest rate is 8%, their issue price is $104,100.[2] The premium on these bonds is $4,100, and Exhibit 9-7 shows how to amortize the bonds by the effective-interest method. In practice, bond premiums are rare because few companies issue their bonds to pay cash interest above the market interest rate. We cover bond premiums for completeness.

Southwest's entry to record the issuance of the bonds on January 1, 2016, is as follows:

	A	B	C	D
1	2016			
2	Jan 1	Cash	104,100	
3		Bonds Payable		100,000
4		Premium on Bonds Payable		4,100
5		*To issue bonds at a premium.*		
6				

---

[2] You can use the same concepts in the example in Chapter 8 to determine the price of this bond.

At the beginning, Southwest's liability is $104,100—not $100,000. The accounting equation makes this clear.

Assets	=	Liabilities	+	Stockholders' Equity
+ 104,100	=	+ 100,000	+	0
		+ 4,100		

Exhibit 9-7 | Amortization of Bond Premium

Panel A—Bond Data

A1

	A	B
1	Issue date—January 1, 2016	Maturity date—January 1, 2021
2	Face (par or *maturity*) value—$100,000	Market interest rate at time of issue—8% annually, 4% semiannually
3	Stated interest rate—9%	Issue price—$104,100
4	Interest paid—4 1/2% semiannually, $4,500 = $100,000 × 0.09 × 6/12	
5	Interest paid—Jan. 1 and July 1	
6		

Panel B—Amortization Table

A1

	A Semiannual Interest Date	B Int Pmt (0.045* Maturity Value)	C Interest Expense (0.04* Preceding Bond Carrying Value)	D Premium Amortization (B − C)	E Premium Account Balance (Preceding E − D)	F Bond Carrying Amount ($100,000 + E)
2	1/1/2016				4,100	104,100
3	7/1/2016	4,500	4,164	336	3,764	103,764
4	1/1/2017	4,500	4,151	349	3,415	103,415
5	7/1/2017	4,500	4,137	363	3,052	103,052
6	1/1/2018	4,500	4,122	378	2,674	102,674
7	7/1/2018	4,500	4,107	393	2,281	102,281
8	1/1/2019	4,500	4,091	409	1,872	101,872
9	7/1/2019	4,500	4,075	425	1,447	101,447
10	1/1/2020	4,500	4,058	442	1,005	101,005
11	7/1/2020	4,500	4,040	460	545	100,545
12	1/1/2021	4,500	3,955**	545	0	100,000
13						

*Indicates multiplication in Excel.
**Adjusted for the effects of rounding.

If you prepared a debt amortization table for bond discount with Excel (Exhibit 9-4), it's easy to prepare an amortization table for bond premium. Open a blank Excel spreadsheet.

- In line 1, label the columns as shown in Panel B of Exhibit 9-7.

- Column A. Starting in line 2, enter the issue date (1/1/2016) followed by each of the semiannual interest payment dates. This will continue through line 12 with the last interest payment on January 1, 2021. Highlight all cell values in rows 2 through 12 of column A, and click on the drop-down box in the "number" field on the ruler at the top of the spreadsheet. Choose the "date" category and click OK to change all cell values in Column A to the date format.

- Line 2, column E (bond premium). Enter 4100 in cell E2. Enter the formula =100000+E2 in cell F2. The calculated value of 104100 should appear in cell F2, representing the initial carrying value of the bond.

■ Line 3, column B (semiannual interest payments, fixed by contract). In cell B3, enter formula =.045*100000. A calculated value of 4500 should appear, representing the first cash interest payment.

■ Line 3, column C (interest expense, calculated as the market rate of 4% x previous period's carrying amount of the bond). In cell C3, enter formula =.04*F2. A calculated value of 4164 should appear, representing interest expense recognized on the first interest payment date. If the cell shows a decimal fraction, use the "decrease decimal" command in the "number" field of the toolbar to reduce the decimals to none. This will round the value to the nearest dollar.

■ Line 3, column D (premium amortization, which is the excess of interest payment in column B over the interest expense in column C). In cell D3, enter formula =B3−C3. A value of 336 should appear, representing the amount of premium amortization deducted from interest expense on the first interest payment date.

■ Line 3, column E (unamortized premium account balance, which decreases as it is amortized). In cell E3, enter formula =E2−D3. A value of 3764 should appear, representing the remaining unamortized premium after the first interest payment.

■ Line 3, column F (bond carrying amount). In cell F3, enter formula =100000+E3. A value of 103764 should appear, representing the adjusted carrying value of the bond after the first interest payment.

■ For columns B to F, copy line 3 down through line 12. All of the numbers in the table should fill in. Line 12 will have to be adjusted for rounding by taking the remaining unamortized premium from cell E11 (544) and substituting that value in cell D12 (premium amortization). Also, substitute 3955 for interest expense in cell C12. This will adjust the final bond carrying amount to the maturity value of $100,000 and the unamortized premium to 0. Your Excel table may be $1 off in some places because of rounding.

■ Highlight cells B2 through F12 and format them for commas but no decimals, as you did for Exhibit 9-4.

Immediately after issuing the bonds at a premium on January 1, 2016, Southwest would report the bonds payable on the balance sheet as follows:

Total current liabilities.................................		$	XXX
Long-term liabilities:			
Bonds payable...	$100,000		
Premium on bonds payable.....................	4,100	104,100	

A premium is *added* to the balance of bonds payable to determine the carrying amount.

In Exhibit 9-7, Southwest borrowed $104,100 cash but must pay back only $100,000 at maturity. Amortization of the $4,100 premium will result in a reduction in Southwest's interest expense over the term of the bonds. The first interest payment on July 1, 2016, follows:

	A	B	C	D
	A1			
1	2016			
2	Jul 1	Interest Expense (from Exhibit 9-7)	4,164	
3		Premium on Bonds Payable	336	
4		Cash		4,500
5		*To pay semiannual interest and amortize bond premium.*		
6				

This entry shows that amortization of the premium over the first six months results in reducing interest expense to $4,164 ($4,500 − $336) while the cash interest paid remains at $4,500. Exhibit 9-8 graphs Southwest's interest payments (column B from Exhibit 9-7) and interest expense (column C).

Exhibit 9-8 | Interest Expense on Bonds Payable Issued at a Premium

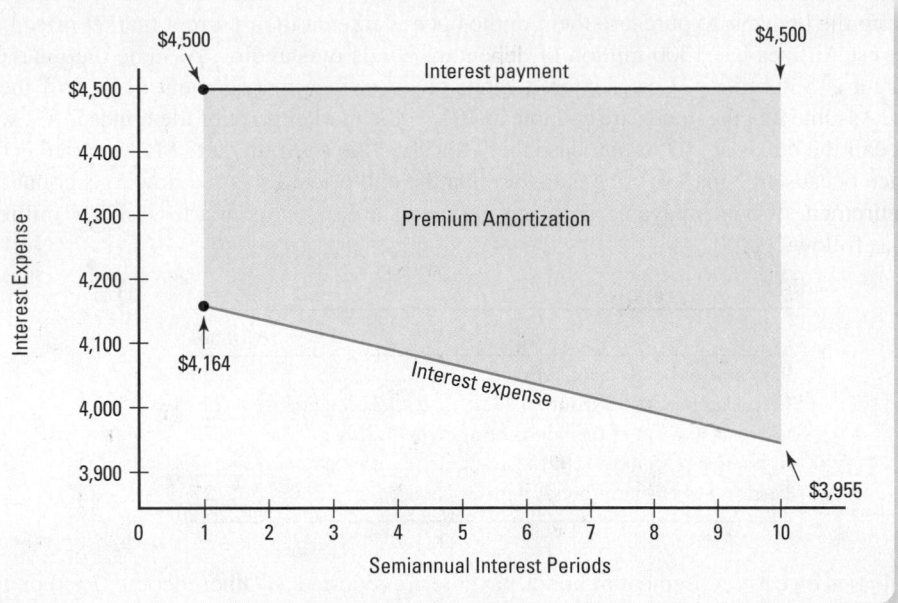

Through amortization, the premium decreases interest expense each period over the term of the bonds. Exhibit 9-9 diagrams the amortization of the bond premium so the carrying value of the bonds decreases from the issue price of $104,100 to maturity value of $100,000. All amounts are taken from Exhibit 9-7.

Exhibit 9-9 | Amortizing Premium on Bonds Payable

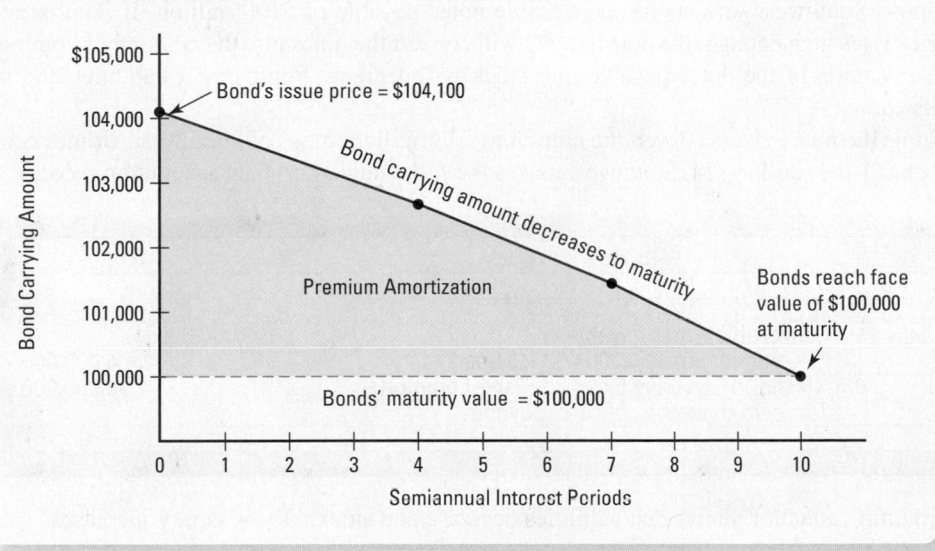

Should We Retire Bonds Payable Before Their Maturity?

Normally, companies wait until maturity to pay off, or *retire*, their bonds payable. But companies sometimes retire bonds early. The main reason for retiring bonds early is to relieve the pressure of making high interest payments. Also, the company may be able to borrow at a lower interest rate.

Some bonds are **callable**, which means that the issuer may *call*, or pay off, those bonds at a prearranged price (this is the *call price*) whenever the issuer chooses. The call price is often a percentage point or two above the par value, perhaps 101 or 102. Callable bonds give the issuer the benefit of being able to pay off the bonds whenever it is most favorable to do so. The alternative to calling the bonds is to purchase them in the open market at their current market price.

Southwest Airlines has $300 million of debenture bonds outstanding. Assume the unamortized discount is $30 million. Lower interest rates may convince management to pay off these bonds now. Assume that the bonds are callable at 101. If the market price of the bonds is 99, will Southwest call the bonds at 101 or purchase them for 99 in the open market? Market price is the better choice because the market price is lower than the call price. Let's see how to account for an early retirement of bonds payable. Retiring the bonds at 99 results in a loss of $27 million, computed as follows:

	Millions
Par value of bonds being retired	$300
Less: Unamortized discount	(30)
Carrying amount of the bonds being retired	270
Market price ($300 × 0.99)	297
Loss on retirement of bonds payable	$ 27

Gains and losses on early retirement of bonds payable are reported as Other income (loss) on the income statement.

Convertible Bonds and Notes

Some corporate bonds may be converted into the issuing company's common stock. These bonds are called **convertible bonds** (or **convertible notes**). For investors, these bonds combine the safety of (a) assured receipt of interest and principal on the bonds with (b) the opportunity for gains on the stock. The conversion feature is so attractive that investors usually accept a lower interest rate than they would on nonconvertible bonds. The lower cash interest payments benefit the issuer. If the market price of the issuing company's stock gets high enough, the bondholders will convert the bonds into stock.

Suppose Southwest Airlines has convertible notes payable of $100 million. If Southwest's stock price rises high enough, the note holders will convert the notes into the company's common stock. Conversion of the notes payable into stock will decrease Southwest's liabilities and increase its equity.

Assume the note holders convert the notes into four million shares of Southwest Airlines common stock ($1 par) on May 14. Southwest makes the following entry in its accounting records:

	A	B	C	D
	A1			
1	May 14	Convertible Notes Payable	100,000,000	
2		Common Stock (4,000,000 × $1 par)		4,000,000
3		Paid-in Capital in Excess of Par—Common		96,000,000
4		*To record conversion of notes payable.*		
5				

The accounting equation shows that liabilities decrease and stockholders' equity increases.

Assets	=	Liabilities	+	Stockholders' Equity
0	=	(100,000,000)		+ 4,000,000 + 96,000,000

The carrying amount of the notes ($100 million) ceases to be debt and becomes stockholders' equity. Common Stock is recorded at its *par value*, which is a dollar amount assigned to each share of stock. In this case, the credit to Common Stock is $4,000,000 (4,000,000 shares × $1 par value per share). The extra carrying amount of the notes payable ($96,000,000) is credited to another stockholders' equity account, Paid-in Capital in Excess of Par—Common. We'll be using this account in various ways in the next chapter.

ANALYZE AND DIFFERENTIATE FINANCING WITH DEBT VERSUS EQUITY

Managers must decide how to get the money they need to pay for assets. There are three main ways to finance operations:

- by retained earnings
- by issuing equity (stock)
- by issuing bonds (or notes) payable

Each strategy has its advantages and disadvantages.

> **4** **Analyze and differentiate** financing with debt vs. equity

1. *Financed by retained earnings* means that the company has enough cash from profitable operations to purchase the needed assets. There's no need to issue more stock or to borrow money. This strategy is low risk to the company.

2. *Issuing equity (stock)* creates no liabilities or interest expense and is less risky to the issuing corporation. But issuing stock is more costly, as we shall see.

3. *Issuing bonds or notes payable* does not dilute control of the corporation. It often results in higher earnings per share because the earnings on borrowed money usually exceed interest expense. But creating more debt increases the risk of the company.

Earnings per share (EPS) is the amount of a company's net income for each share of its common stock. EPS is the single most important statistic for evaluating companies because EPS is a standard measure of operating performance that applies to companies of different sizes and from different industries.

Suppose Southwest Airlines needs $500,000 for expansion. Assume Southwest has net income of $300,000 and 100,000 shares of common stock outstanding. Management is considering two financing plans. Plan 1 is to issue $500,000 of 6% bonds payable, and plan 2 is to issue 50,000 shares of common stock for $500,000. Management believes the new cash can be invested in operations to earn income of $200,000 before interest and taxes.

Exhibit 9-10 shows the relative earnings-per-share advantage of borrowing. As you can see, Southwest's EPS amount is higher if the company borrows by issuing bonds (compare lines 12 and 13). Southwest earns more on the investment ($102,000) than the interest it pays on the bonds ($30,000). This is called **trading on the equity**, or using **leverage**. It is widely used to increase earnings per share of common stock.

Exhibit 9-10 | Relative Advantage of Borrowing

	A	B	C	D	E
	A1				
1		Plan 1		Plan 2	
2		Borrow $500,000 at 6%		Issue 50,000 Shares of Common Stock for $500,000	
3	Net income before expansion		$ 300,000		$ 300,000
4	Expected project income before interest and				
5	income tax	$ 200,000		$ 200,000	
6	Less interest expense ($500,000 × 0.06)	(30,000)		0	
7	Expected project income before income tax	170,000		200,000	
8	Less income tax expense (40%)	(68,000)		(80,000)	
9	Expected project net income		102,000		120,000
10	Total company net income		$ 402,000		$ 420,000
11	Earnings per share after expansion:				
12	Plan 1 Borrow ($402,000/100,000 shares)		$ 4.02		
13	Plan 2 Issue Stock ($420,000/150,000 shares)				$ 2.80
14					

In this case, borrowing results in higher earnings per share than issuing stock. Borrowing has its disadvantages, however. Interest expense may be high enough to eliminate net income and lead to losses. Also, borrowing creates liabilities that must be paid during bad years as well as good years. In contrast, a company that issues stock can omit its dividends during a bad year. The Decision Guidelines provide some help in deciding how to finance operations.

 # DECISION GUIDELINES

FINANCING WITH DEBT OR WITH STOCK

El Chico is one of the oldest chains of Tex-Mex restaurants in the United States, begun by the Cuellar family in the Dallas area in 1940. Suppose El Chico is expanding into neighboring states. Take the role of Miguel Cuellar and assume you must make some key decisions about how to finance the expansion.

Decision	Guidelines
How will you finance El Chico's expansion?	Your financing plan depends on El Chico's ability to generate cash flow, your willingness to give up some control of the business, the amount of financing risk you are willing to take, and El Chico's credit rating.
Do El Chico's operations generate enough cash to meet all its financing needs?	If yes, the business needs little outside financing. There is no need to borrow. If no, the business will need to issue additional stock or borrow the money.
Are you willing to give up some of your control of the business?	If yes, then issue stock to other stockholders, who can vote their shares to elect the company's directors. If no, then borrow from bondholders, who have no vote in the management of the company.
How much leverage (financing risk) are you willing or able to take?	If much, then borrow as much as you can, and you may increase El Chico's earnings per share. But this will increase the business's debt ratio and the risk of being unable to pay its debts. If little, then borrow sparingly. This will hold the debt ratio down and reduce the risk of default on borrowing agreements. But El Chico's earnings per share may be lower than if you were to borrow.
How good is the business's credit rating?	The better the credit rating, the easier it is to borrow on favorable terms. A good credit rating also makes it easier to issue stock. Neither stockholders nor creditors will entrust their money to a company with a bad credit rating.

The Leverage Ratio

As discussed and illustrated in the previous section, financing with debt can be advantageous, but management of a company must be careful not to incur too much debt. Chapter 3 discussed the debt ratio, which measures the proportion of total liabilities to total assets:

$$\text{Debt ratio} = \frac{\text{Total debt (liabilities)}}{\text{Total assets}}$$

We can rearrange this relationship between total assets, total liabilities, and stockholders' equity in a different manner to illustrate the impact that leverage can have on profitability. The **leverage ratio** is calculated as follows:

$$\text{Leverage ratio} = \frac{\text{Average total assets}}{\text{Average common stockholders' equity}}$$

Also known as the **equity multiplier**, this ratio shows a company's average total assets per dollar of average common stockholder equity. A leverage ratio of exactly 1.0 would mean a company has no debt, because total assets would exactly equal total stockholders' equity. This condition is almost nonexistent, because virtually all companies have liabilities and, therefore, have leverage ratios in excess of 1.0. The more debt a company accumulates, the less the relative amount of total assets that are financed with stockholders' equity; thus, the denominator of the fraction decreases, increasing the leverage ratio. As we have shown previously, having a healthy amount of debt can actually enhance a company's profitability, in terms of the shareholders' investment. The leverage ratio is the third element of the *DuPont Analysis* model, introduced in the discussion of return on assets in Chapter 7.[3] The higher the leverage ratio, the more it magnifies return on stockholders' equity (Net income/Average stockholders' equity, or ROE). If net income is positive, return on assets (ROA) is positive. The leverage ratio magnifies this positive return to make return on equity (ROE) even more positive. This is because the company is using borrowed money to earn a profit (a concept known as *trading on the equity*).

However, if earnings are negative (losses), ROA is negative, and the leverage ratio makes ROE even more negative. We will discuss DuPont Analysis and ROE in more detail as we discuss stockholders' equity in Chapter 10. For now, let's focus on understanding the meaning of the leverage ratio by looking at Southwest Airlines in comparison with one of its competitors, United Continental Holdings (parent company of United Airlines and Continental Airlines). Here are the leverage ratios and debt ratios for the two companies at the end of 2014:

(In millions) for 2014	Southwest	United Continental
1. Average total assets	$19,773	$37,083
2. Average common stockholders' equity	$ 7,056	$ 2,690
3. Leverage ratio (1 ÷ 2)	2.80	13.79
4. Total liabilities (debt)	$13,425	$34,386
5. Total assets	$20,200	$37,353
6. Debt ratio (4 ÷ 5)	66.5%	92.1%

These figures show that Southwest has $2.80 of average total assets for each dollar of average stockholders' equity. Southwest's debt ratio is 66.5%, which we learned in Chapter 3 is about normal for many companies, and relatively low for the airline industry. In comparison, United Continental has a leverage ratio of 13.79 and a debt ratio of 92.1%, which are quite high. A quick search of the SEC website for the balance sheets of American Airlines Group, Inc. (the holding company of American Airlines) and Delta Airlines, Inc., showed that both these companies were in similar straits. Southwest truly does stand alone in comparison with other major airlines from a leverage standpoint!

The Times-Interest-Earned Ratio

Analysts use a second ratio—the **times-interest-earned ratio**—to relate income to interest expense. To compute this ratio, we divide *income from operations* (also called *operating income*) by interest expense. This ratio measures the number of times that operating income can *cover* interest

---

[3]The DuPont analysis model provides a detailed analysis of return on equity (ROE). It is the product of three elements: (Net income/Net sales) × (Net sales/Average total assets) × (Average total assets/Average common stockholders' equity). Notice that elements cross-cancel so that the model reduces to Net income/Average common stockholders' equity. See Chapter 10 for a more complete discussion of ROE. A modified version of the model considers only the first two elements to calculate return on assets (ROA), as discussed in Chapter 7.

expense. The times-interest-earned ratio is also called the **interest-coverage ratio**. A high times-interest-earned ratio indicates ease in paying interest expense; a low value suggests difficulty. Let's see how our competing airlines, Southwest and United Continental, compare on the times-interest-earned ratio (dollar amounts in millions taken from the companies' 2014 financial statements):

$$\text{Times-interest-earned ratio} = \frac{\text{Operating income}}{\text{Interest expense}}$$

$$\text{Southwest} \qquad \frac{\$2,225}{\$130} = 17.1 \text{ times}$$

$$\text{United Continental} \qquad \frac{\$2,373}{\$735} = 3.23 \text{ times}$$

Southwest's income from operations covers its interest expense 17.1 times, which is quite comfortable, especially for an airline company. In contrast, United Continental's operating earnings cover its interest expense 3.23 times. This is much improved over past years, but is still not nearly as strong as Southwest.

UNDERSTAND OTHER LONG-TERM LIABILITIES

Leases

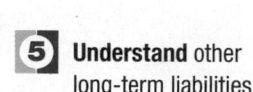
Understand other long-term liabilities

A **lease** is a rental agreement in which the tenant (**lessee**) agrees to make rent payments to the property owner (**lessor**) in exchange for the use of the asset. Leasing allows the lessee to acquire the use of a needed asset without having to make the large up-front payment that purchase agreements require. Accountants distinguish between two types of leases: operating leases and capital leases.

Types of Leases

Operating leases are sometimes short-term or cancelable. However, often operating lease agreements are noncancelable and require the lessee to commit funds to pay the lessor for the use of property for years. They give the lessee the right to use the asset but provide no continuing rights to the asset. Instead, the lessor retains the usual risks and rewards of owning the leased asset. To account for an operating lease, the lessee debits Rent Expense (or Lease Expense) and credits Cash for the amount of the lease payment. Operating leases require the lessee to make rent payments, so an operating lease creates a liability even though that liability does not appear on the lessee's balance sheet. In recent years, Southwest Airlines has begun to lease most of its facilities (hangars, buildings, and equipment, including airplanes) under operating lease agreements. Following is an excerpt from Note 8 of Southwest's 2014 financial statements:

Note 8 Leases (partial)
Total rental expense for operating leases, both aircraft and other, charged to operations in 2014, 2013, and 2012 was $931 million, $997 million, and $943 million, respectively. The majority of the Company's terminal operations space, as well as 174 aircraft, were under operating leases at December 31, 2014. Future minimum lease payments under noncancelable operating leases with initial or remaining terms in excess of one year at December 31, 2014, were (in millions) as follows:

2015	$ 684
2016	636
2017	592
2018	496
2019	430
Thereafter	2,317
Total	$5,155

Source: From Southwest's 2014 Financial Statements, http://www.sec.gov/Archives/edgar/data/92380/000009238015000027/R16.htm.

This essentially means that, although the company has merely signed rental agreements for these assets, it has an obligation over several years for over $5.1 billion to the companies from which it is leasing these assets. Neither the obligation nor the associated assets are included in Southwest's balance sheet. This is an example of what is called "off-balance-sheet financing."

Capital leases are often used to finance the acquisition of long-term assets. A **capital lease** is a long-term, noncancelable debt. How do we distinguish a capital lease from an operating lease? The FASB provides the U.S. GAAP guidelines. To be classified as a capital lease, the lease must meet any *one* of the following criteria:

1. The lease transfers title of the leased asset to the lessee at the end of the lease term. Thus, the lessee becomes the legal owner of the leased asset.

2. The lease contains a *bargain purchase option*. The lessee can be expected to purchase the leased asset and become its legal owner.

3. The lease term is 75% or more of the estimated useful life of the leased asset. The lessee uses up most of the leased asset's service potential.

4. The present value of the lease payments is 90% or more of the market value of the leased asset. In effect, the lease payments are the same as installment payments for the leased asset.

If the lease does not meet one of these exact criteria, it is classified as an operating lease by default.

Accounting for a capital lease is much like accounting for the purchase of an asset. The lessee enters the asset into the lessee's long-term asset accounts at the present value of the future cash outflows from the lease contact and records a long-term lease liability at the beginning of the lease term. Thus, the lessee capitalizes the asset even though the lessee may never take legal title to it, because the lease agreement, in substance, makes the lessee assume the risks and rewards of ownership of the assets and the associated obligations. In lieu of rent expense, the lessee of the capital asset records depreciation expense on the asset (as required of an owner) and interest expense on the lease obligation each period. Both of these expenses are recorded over the term of the lease obligation.

At December 31, 2014, Southwest Airlines reported its capital leases in Note 8 of its financial statements, excerpted as follows:

The Company had 16 aircraft classified as capital leases at December 31, 2014, compared with four aircraft classified as capital leases at December 31, 2013. Amounts applicable to these aircraft that are included in property and equipment were:

(in millions)	2014	2013
Flight equipment	$ 214	$69
Less: accumulated amortization	22	12
	$ 192	$ 57

The note shows that as of December 31, 2014, Southwest had 16 aircraft classified as capital leased assets. This number was up from four aircraft as of December 31, 2013, but down from many more than that in previous years. In contrast, Southwest leases 174 aircraft on an operating lease basis as of December 31, 2014.

Do Lessees Prefer Operating Leases or Capital Leases?

Suppose you were the chief financial officer (CFO) of Southwest Airlines. Southwest leases 174 of its 665 aircraft under operating leases. Suppose the leases can be structured either as operating leases or as capital leases. Which type of lease would you prefer for Southwest? Why? Consider what would happen to Southwest's debt ratio if its operating leases in Note 8 were capitalized and the related liabilities recognized. Computing Southwest's debt ratio two ways (*operating* leases versus reclassifying them as *capital* leases) will make your decision clear (using Southwest's actual figures in millions):

			Operating Leases as Stated	Operating Leases Reclassified as Capital Leases		
Debt ratio	=	$\dfrac{\text{Total liabilities}}{\text{Total assets}}$	= $\dfrac{\$13,425}{\$20,200}$	$\dfrac{\$13,425 + \$5,155}{\$20,200 + \$5,155}$	=	$\dfrac{\$18,580}{\$25,355}$
			= 0.665		=	0.733

You can see that capital leases increase the debt ratio—by almost seven percentage points for Southwest. By contrast, notice that operating leases don't affect the debt ratio that's currently calculated from the balance sheet. For this reason, companies prefer operating leases. It is easy to see why Southwest's long-term commitment for operating leases, as disclosed in Note 8, far outweighs that of its capital lease agreements.

Ethical Challenge. Because of the relatively mechanical nature of the accounting criteria for capitalization of leases, it is possible under existing U.S. GAAP to purposely structure a company's lease agreements so that they barely miss meeting the third criterion (75% test) or the fourth criterion (90% test) for capitalization. Many U.S. companies have taken advantage of these mechanical rules, quite legally, to their economic advantage, thus obtaining almost all the same economic benefits associated with ownership of long-term assets, but avoiding the detrimental impact that recording those assets and obligations can have on their debt ratios.

GLOBAL VIEW

In contrast to U.S. GAAP, with its mechanical, or "bright line," tests for capitalization of leases, IFRS adopts a much broader approach. Rather than rules, IFRS employs "guidance" that focuses on the overall substance of the transaction, rather than on the mechanical form, and that leaves more to the judgment of the preparer of the financial statement. If, in the judgment of the company's accountants, the lease transfers "substantially all of the risks and rewards of ownership to the lessee," IFRS says the lease should be capitalized. Otherwise, the lease should be expensed as an operating lease.

As of the date of this text, the FASB and IASB have issued a final exposure draft for a new standard on long-term leases that will, for the great majority of such agreements, require capital lease treatment. This will essentially end the practice of operating leases and off-balance-sheet financing for leased property. The new standard is expected to take effect sometime after 2016. When that happens, Southwest Airlines and many other companies with long-term operating leases for fixed assets could be forced to add billions of dollars to their long-term assets, as well as their long-term liabilities, with results as we just showed on their debt and other ratios.

Pensions and Postretirement Liabilities

Most companies have retirement plans for their employees. A **pension** is employee compensation that will be received during retirement. Companies also provide postretirement benefits, such as medical insurance for retired former employees. Because employees earn these benefits by their service, the company records pension and retirement-benefit expense while employees work for the company.

Pensions are one of the most complex areas of accounting. As employees earn their pensions and the company pays into the pension plan, the plan's assets grow. The obligation for future pension payments to employees also accumulates. At the end of each period, the company compares

- the fair market value of the assets in the retirement plans—cash and investments—with

- the plans' *projected benefit obligation*, which is the present value of promised future payments to retirees.

If the plan assets exceed the projected benefit obligation, the plan is said to be *overfunded*. In this case, the company must report the excess asset on its balance sheet. However, if the projected benefit obligation (the liability) exceeds plan assets, the plan is *underfunded*, and the company must report the excess liability on its balance sheet.

Southwest Airlines' retirement plans don't create large liabilities for Southwest. To illustrate pension liabilities, let's see the pension plan of American Airlines Group, Inc., the parent company of American Airlines. At December 31, 2014, the retirement plans of American Airlines were underfunded. They had

- assets with a fair market value of $10,986 million.

- projected benefit obligations totaling $17,594 million.

American Airline Group, Inc.'s, balance sheet, therefore, included a Pension and Post-Retirement Liability of $6,608 million ($17,594 million − $10,986 million). This liability was split between current and long-term liabilities, in accordance with the due dates for the obligations.

REPORT LIABILITIES ON THE FINANCIAL STATEMENTS

Reporting on the Balance Sheet This chapter began with the liabilities reported on the consolidated balance sheets of Southwest Airlines. Exhibit 9-11 shows a standard way for Southwest to report its current liabilities and long-term debt.

Exhibit 9-11 includes Note 6 from Southwest's consolidated financial statements. The note gives additional details about the company's liabilities. Note 6 shows the interest rates and the maturity dates of Southwest's long-term debt. Investors need these data to evaluate the company. The note also reports

 6 **Report** liabilities on the financial statements

- current maturities of long-term debt ($258 million) as a current liability.

- long-term debt (less current maturities) of $2,434 million.

Trace these amounts from the note to the balance sheet. Working back and forth between the financial statements and the related notes is an important part of financial analysis. You now have the tools to understand the liabilities reported on an actual balance sheet.

Exhibit 9-11 | Reporting the Liabilities of Southwest Airlines Co.

	A	B	C	D	E
	Southwest Airlines Co. Consolidated Balance Sheet (Partial, Adapted)	Dec. 31, 2014		Note 6 Long-term debt (In millions) (Adapted)	Dec. 31, 2014
1					
2	Liabilities (in millions)				
3	Current Liabilities:			Term loans due 2019–20	$ 923
4	Accounts payable	$ 1,203		Pass-through certificates due 2022	355
5	Accrued liabilities	1,565		Floating rate aircraft notes	300
6	Air traffic liability	2,897		7 3/8% debentures due 2027	134
7	Current maturities of			Convertible senior notes due 2016	113
8	long-term debt	258 ◄		5 3/4% notes due 2016	313
9	Total current liabilities	5,923		5 1/8% notes due 2017	316
10	Long-term debt, less current			Capital leases	199
11	maturities	2,434 ◄		Other long-term debt	60
12	Other long-term liabilities	5,068		Total long-term debt	2,713
13				Less current maturities	(258)
14	Total liabilities	$ 13,425		Less debt discounted and	
15				issuance costs	(21)
16				Long-term debt	$ 2,434
17					

Disclosing the Fair Value of Long-Term Debt

Generally accepted accounting principles require companies to report the fair value of their long-term debt. At December 31, 2014, Southwest Airlines' Note 11 included this excerpt (adapted, details omitted):

> The estimated fair value of the Company's long-term debt, including current maturities, was $2,843 million.

Overall, the fair value of Southwest's long-term debt, including current maturities, is about $151 million more than its carrying amount on the books ($2,692 million). Fair values of publicly traded debt are based on quoted market prices (level 1 measures, as discussed in Chapter 8), which fluctuate with interest rates and overall market conditions. Therefore, at any one time, fair values for various obligations can either exceed or be less than their carrying amounts.

Reporting Financing Activities on the Statement of Cash Flows

CASH FLOW

Let's examine Southwest's financing activities as reported on its statement of cash flows. Exhibit 9-12 is an excerpt from Southwest's consolidated statement of cash flows.

Exhibit 9-12 | Consolidated Statement of Cash Flows (Partial, Adapted) for Southwest Airlines Co.

	A	B
1	**Southwest Airlines Co.** **Consolidated Statement of Cash Flows (Adapted)**	
2	**(In millions)**	**Year Ended December 31, 2014**
3	Cash Flow from Operating Activities:	
4	Net cash provided by operating activities	$ 2,902
5	Cash Flow from Investing Activities:	
6	Net cash used for investing activities	(1,727)
7	Cash Flow from Financing Activities:	
8	Payments of long-term debt and capital lease obligations	(561)
9	Repurchase of common stock	(955)
10	Proceeds from issuance of long-term debt	300
11	Payments of cash dividends	(139)
12	Other financing sources (net)	107
13	Net cash used for financing activities	(1,248)
14	Net change in cash and cash equivalents	$ (73)
15		

Southwest has provided $2.9 billion more cash from operations than it used in 2014. The company has a long history of good financial management, and it is the most liquid and profitable airline company in the industry. With the excess cash generated from operations, Southwest has net investing activities of about $1.73 billion in property and equipment and investments of various types. In contrast, the company borrowed $300 million in long-term debt and spent $561 million in payments on long-term debt and capital lease obligations. It spent $955 million repurchasing common stock and paid $139 million in dividends, topics we will cover in Chapter 10. Southwest has borrowed rather heavily in order to finance its growth and refurbish its fleet of aircraft. This is evident in the long-term debt footnote in Exhibit 9-11. Much of that debt has not yet come due as of the end of 2014. About $2.7 billion of the debt still remains, with current maturities of about $258 million and the remainder extending to 2027. Over the next several years, the company will have to pay the debt off as it comes due, in installments, with cash provided by operations.

The Cessna Aircraft Company has outstanding an issue of 4% convertible bonds that mature October 1, 2024. Suppose the bonds are dated October 1, 2016, and pay interest each April 1 and October 1.

Bond Data

Maturity (face) value—$100,000

Stated interest rate—4%

Interest paid—2% semiannually, $2,000 ($100,000 × 0.04 × 6/12)

Market interest rate at the time of issue—5% annually, $2\frac{1}{2}$% semiannually

Requirements

1. Assume the bonds are issued at a price of 93.5. Using the straight-line method of amortization for bond discount:

   a. Calculate interest expense on bonds payable for each semiannual interest payment period.

   b. Calculate the amount of accrued interest payable on the December 31, 2016, financial statements.

   c. Prepare the journal entry required as of December 31, 2016, to accrue interest on the bonds payable.

2. Use Excel to build an amortization table through October 1, 2018. Use Excel to obtain the issue price. Use the effective interest method of amortization.

3. Using the amortization table, record the following transactions:

   a. Issuance of the bonds on October 1, 2016.

   b. Accrual of interest and amortization of the bond discount on December 31, 2016.

   c. Payment of interest and amortization of the bond discount on April 1, 2017.

   d. Conversion of one-third of the bonds payable into no-par stock on October 2, 2018. For no-par stock, transfer the bond carrying amount into the Common Stock account. There is no Additional Paid-in Capital account.

   e. Retirement of two-thirds of the bonds payable on October 2, 2018. Purchase price of the bonds is based on their call price of 102.

Answers
Requirement 1

	A	B	C	D	E
	A1				
1	1 (a):				
2	(a) Face amount of bonds			$ 100,000	
3	× Issue price			× .935	
4	(b) Proceeds			$ 93,500	
5	(c) Discount ((a) − (b))			$ 6,500	
6	Number of semiannual interest payment periods (8 × 2)			16	
7	Straight-line amortization per interest period ($6,500/16)			$ 406.25	
8	Interest paid each interest period (.02 × $100,000)			$2,000.00	
9	Total interest expense each interest period			$2,406.25	
10	1 (b):				
11	Accrued interest payable as of 12/31/2016:				
12	Interest paid each interest period (.02 × $100,000)			$2,000.00	
13	× portion of period between 10/1/2016 and 12/31/2016			× 3/6	
14	Accrued interest payable as of 12/31/2016			$1,000.00	
15	1(c):				
16	Interest Expense ($2,406.25 × .5)			1,203.13	
17	Discount on Bonds Payable ($406.25 × .5)				203.13
18	Interest Payable ($2,000 × .5)				1,000.00
19					

Requirement 2

	A	B	C	D	E	F
1	Amortization Table Cessna Aircraft Company					
2	Semiannual Interest Payment Date	Interest Payment (2% of Maturity Amount)	Interest Expense (2.5% of Preceding Bond Carrying Amount)*	Discount Amortization (C − B)*	Discount Account Balance (Preceding E − D)*	Bond Carrying Amount ($100,000 − E)*
3	10/1/2016				$ 6,528	$ 93,472
4	4/1/2017	$ 2,000	$ 2,337	$ 337	$ 6,191	$ 93,809
5	10/1/2017	$ 2,000	$ 2,345	$ 345	$ 5,846	$ 94,154
6	4/1/2018	$ 2,000	$ 2,354	$ 354	$ 5,492	$ 94,508
7	10/1/2018	$ 2,000	$ 2,363	$ 363	$ 5,129	$ 94,871
8						
9	Issue price	$ 93,472				
10						

*amounts may vary by $1 because of rounding

Requirement 3

	A	B	C	D	E
1		2016		**Debit**	**Credit**
2	a.	1-Oct	Cash	93,472	
3			Discount on Bonds Payable	6,528	
4			Bonds Payable		100,000
5			*To issue bonds at a discount.*		
6					
7	b.	31-Dec	Interest expense (2,337 × 3/6)	1,169	
8			Discount on Bonds Payable (337 × 3/6)		169
9			Interest Payable (2,000 × 3/6)		1,000
10			*To accrue interest and amortize bond discount.*		
11		2017			
12	c.	1-Apr	Interest expense (2,337 × 3/6)	1,168	
13			Interest payable	1,000	
14			Discount on Bonds Payable (337 × 3/6)		168
15			Cash		2,000
16			*To pay semiannual interest, part of which*		
17			*was accrued, and amortize bond discount.*		
18					
19	d.	2018			
20		2-Oct	Bonds Payable (100,000 × 1/3)	33,333	
21			Discount on Bonds Payable (5,129 × 1/3)		1,710
22			Common Stock (94,871 × 1/3)		31,623
23			*To convert one-third of bonds to common stock.*		
24					
25	e.	2-Oct	Bonds Payable (100,000 × 2/3)	66,667	
26			Loss on Retirement of Bonds	4,752	
27			Discount on Bonds Payable (5,129 × 2/3)		3,419
28			Cash (100,000 × 2/3 × 1.02)		68,000
29			*To retire bonds payable before maturity at 102.*		
30					

REVIEW | Liabilities

Quick Check (Answers are given on page 563.)

1. Which of the following is *not* an estimated liability?

   a. Vacation pay

   b. Allowance for bad debts

   c. Income taxes

   d. Product warranties

2. The current pay period ends on Friday, January 2, yet the company's fiscal year-end is on Wednesday, December 31. If the company does not make the proper adjusting entry to accrue payroll expenses at year-end, what would be the impact?

   a. Understate assets

   b. Overstate operating income

   c. Understate stockholders' equity

   d. Overstate liabilities

3. Accounts payable turnover for Big Blue, Inc., increased from 10 to 12 during 2016. Which of the following statements best describes what this means?

   a. The company paid its accounts payable more quickly in 2016, signaling a stronger liquidity position.

   b. The company paid its accounts payable more slowly in 2016, signaling a weaker liquidity position.

   c. Inventory turned over faster in 2016, meaning sales increased.

   d. Not enough information is provided to form a conclusion.

4. Outback Co. was organized to sell a single product that carries a 45-day warranty against defects. Engineering estimates indicate that 3% of the units sold will prove defective and require an average repair cost of $45 per unit. During Outback's first month of operations, total sales were 1,100 units; by the end of the month, seven defective units had been repaired. The liability for product warranties at month-end should be

   a. $315.

   b. $1,800.

   c. $1,170.

   d. $1,485.

   e. none of these.

5. A contingent liability should be recorded in the accounts

   a. if the amount can be reasonably estimated.

   b. if the amount is due in cash within one year.

   c. if the related future event will probably occur.

   d. both b and c.

   e. both a and c.

6. An unsecured bond is a

   a. term bond.

   b. mortgage bond.

   c. registered bond.

   d. serial bond.

   e. debenture bond.

7. The Discount on Bonds Payable account

   a. is expensed at the bond's maturity.

   b. is a miscellaneous revenue account.

   c. is an expense account.

   d. is a contra account to Bonds Payable.

   e. has a normal credit balance.

8. The discount on a bond payable becomes

   a. a reduction in interest expense the year the bonds mature.

   b. a reduction in interest expense over the life of the bonds.

   c. additional interest expense over the life of the bonds.

   d. additional interest expense the year the bonds are sold.

   e. a liability in the year the bonds are sold.

9. A bond that matures in installments is called a

   a. term bond.

   b. zero coupon.

   c. callable bond.

   d. secured bond.

   e. serial bond.

10. The carrying value of Bonds Payable equals

    a. Bonds Payable − Premium on Bonds Payable.

    b. Bonds Payable plus Accrued Interest.

    c. Bonds Payable plus Discount on Bonds Payable.

    d. Bonds Payable minus Discount on Bonds Payable.

11. Dart Corporation's leverage ratio increased from 2.5 in 2015 to 3.0 in 2016. Without looking at the financial statements, which statement best describes what may have occurred?

    a. The company incurred new debt financing in 2016, but it may or may not have been more profitable.

    b. The company incurred new debt financing in 2016, making it more profitable.

    c. The company incurred new equity financing in 2016, making it less profitable.

    d. The company incurred new equity financing in 2016, but it may or may not have been more profitable.

Use this information to answer questions 12–17.

McLennan Corporation issued $250,000 of 6.5%, 10-year bonds. The bonds are dated and sold on January 1, 2016. Interest payment dates are January 1 and July 1. The bonds are issued to yield the market interest rate of 7%. Use the effective-interest method for questions 12-16.

12. Using the PV function in Excel, the price of the bonds (amount raised from issuance) is
    a. $239,717.
    b. $250,000.
    c. $250,717.
    d. $241,117.

13. What is the amount of interest expense that McLennan Corporation will record on July 1, 2016, the first semiannual interest payment date? (All amounts rounded to the nearest dollar.)
    a. $10,525
    b. $314
    c. $8,125
    d. $8,439

14. What is the amount of discount amortization that McLennan Corporation will record on July 1, 2016, the first semiannual interest payment date?
    a. $314
    b. $8,125
    c. $0
    d. $8,439

15. What is the total cash payment for interest for each 12-month period? (All amounts are rounded to the nearest dollar.)
    a. $17,500
    b. $15,673
    c. $16,250
    d. $16,878

16. What is the carrying amount of the bonds on the January 1, 2017, balance sheet?
    a. $241,756
    b. $250,000
    c. $241,117
    d. $241,431

17. Assuming that the bonds were issued at the price calculated in question 12, if straight-line amortization were used instead of the effective interest method, the carrying amount of McLennan Corporation's bonds at December 31, 2016 (its fiscal year-end), is
    a. $240,673.
    b. $240,229.
    c. $241,561.
    d. $242,005.

Accounting Vocabulary

accounts payable turnover (p. 495) The number of times per year a company pays off its accounts payable.

accrued expense (p. 497) An expense incurred but not yet paid in cash. Also called *accrued liability*.

accrued liability (p. 497) A liability for an expense that has not yet been paid. Also called *accrued expense*.

bonds payable (p. 504) Groups of debt securities issued to multiple lenders called *bondholders*.

callable bond (p. 519) Bonds that are paid off early at a specified price at the option of the issuer.

capital lease (p. 525) Lease agreement in which the lessee assumes, in substance, the risks and rewards of asset ownership. In the United States, a lease is assumed to be a capital lease if it meets any one of four criteria: (1) The lease transfers title of the leased asset to the lessee. (2) The lease contains a bargain purchase option. (3) The lease term is 75% or more of the estimated useful life of the leased asset. (4) The

present value of the lease payments is 90% or more of the market value of the leased asset.

convertible bonds (or notes) (p. 520) Bonds or notes that may be converted into the issuing company's common stock at the investor's option.

current portion of long-term debt (p. 499) The amount of the principal that is payable within one year.

days' payable outstanding (DPO) (p. 495) Accounts payable turnover expressed in days (365/turnover).

debentures (p. 505) Unsecured bonds—bonds backed only by the good faith of the borrower.

discount (on a bond) (p. 506) Excess of a bond's face (par) value over its issue price.

earnings per share (EPS) (p. 521) Amount of a company's net income per share of its outstanding common stock.

equity multiplier (p. 523) Another name for *leverage ratio*.

interest-coverage ratio (p. 524) Another name for the *times-interest-earned ratio*.

lease (p. 524) Rental agreement in which the tenant (lessee) agrees to make rent payments to the property owner (lessor) in exchange for the use of the asset.

lessee (p. 524) Tenant in a lease agreement.

lessor (p. 524) Property owner in a lease agreement.

leverage (p. 521) Using borrowed funds to increase the return on equity. Successful use of leverage means earning more income on borrowed money than the related interest expense, thereby increasing the earnings for the owners of the business. Also called *trading on the equity*.

leverage ratio (p. 523) The ratio of average total assets ÷ average total common stockholders' equity, showing the proportion of average total assets to average total common stockholders' equity. This ratio, like the debt ratio introduced in Chapter 3, tells the mixture of a company's debt and equity financing and is useful in calculating rate of return on stockholders' equity (ROE) through the DuPont Model.

market interest rate (p. 506) Interest rate that investors demand for loaning their money. Also called *effective interest rate*.

operating lease (p. 524) A lease in which the lessee does not assume the risks or rewards of asset ownership.

payroll (p. 497) Employee compensation, a major expense of many businesses.

pension (p. 526) Employee compensation that will be received during retirement.

premium (on a bond) (p. 506) Excess of a bond's issue price over its face (par) value.

serial bonds (p. 505) Bonds that mature in installments over a period of time.

short-term notes payable (p. 496) Notes payable that are due within one year.

stated interest rate (p. 506) Interest rate that determines the amount of cash interest the borrower pays and the investor receives each year.

term bonds (p. 505) Bonds that all mature at the same time for a particular issue.

times-interest-earned ratio (p. 523) Ratio of income from operations to interest expense. Measures the number of times that operating income can cover interest expense. Also called the *interest-coverage ratio*.

trading on the equity (p. 521) Earning more income on borrowed money than the related interest expense, thereby increasing the earnings for the owners of the business. Also called *leverage*, the power of which is illustrated through the *leverage ratio*.

underwriter (p. 505) Organization that purchases the bonds from an issuing company and resells them to its clients or sells the bonds for a commission, agreeing to buy all unsold bonds.

ASSESS YOUR PROGRESS

Some of the following exercises and problems are available as Excel questions in MyAccountingLab.

Ethics Check

EC9-1 Identify ethical principle violated

For each of the situations listed, identify which of three principles (integrity, objectivity and independence, or due care) from the AICPA Code of Professional Conduct that is violated. Assume all persons listed in the situations are members of the AICPA. (Note: Refer to the AICPA Code of Professional Conduct contained on pages 29–30, Chapter 1 for descriptions of the principles)

    a. Nicole works in the payables department of Blue Steel, Inc. She noticed that her company's current ratio is a little lower than the industry average. In an attempt to improve the current ratio, she decides not to accrue wages payable for this month.

    b. Francis Candle Co. is a small, family-owned company that only employs one accountant, Jean. Since Jean is in charge of all areas of accounting and knows she will not get caught, she decides to create fictitious accounts payable entries at Francis Candle Co. for the company she owns, Candle Supply Inc.

    c. Louie recently graduated with an accounting degree and found a job in the payables department of Smith Sneaker Company. Louie is in charge of adjusting entries for accrued liabilities that have been paid, but he does not remember how to treat these entries because he has not seen them since one of his courses from his junior year in college. Louie assumes the accrued liabilities for this month are the same amounts as last month so he does not enter in the new accrual entries for this month and does not reverse last month's entries.

d. Jill is a newly-hired auditor for Jamestown & Blice, a CPA firm. Her father owns J&J Veterinary Supply. Jill is excited to be assigned to work on the account of J&J since she understands the business well from working part-time during summers there when she was growing up. Jill does not disclose that her father owns J&J because she knows she will not have any bias.

Short Exercises

S9-1. *(Learning Objective 1: Account for a short-term note payable)* Drexel Sports Authority purchased inventory costing $23,000 by signing a 10%, six-month, short-term note payable. The purchase occurred on January 1, 2016. Drexel will pay the entire note (principal and interest) on the note's maturity date of July 1, 2016. Journalize the company's (a) purchase of inventory; and (b) payment of the note plus interest on July 1, 2016.

LO 1

S9-2. *(Learning Objective 1: Analyze accounts payable turnover)* Wango Sales, Inc.'s, comparative income statements and balance sheets show the following selected information for 2015 and 2016:

LO 1

	2016	2015
Cost of goods sold	$2,850,000	$2,700,000
Ending inventory	$ 800,000	$ 600,000
Beginning inventory	$ 600,000	$ 400,000
Average accounts payable	$ 305,000	$ 255,000

Requirements

1. Calculate the company's accounts payable turnover and days' payable outstanding (DPO) for 2015 and 2016.
2. On the basis of this computation alone, has the company's liquidity position improved or deteriorated during 2016?

S9-3. *(Learning Objective 1: Account for warranty expense and estimated warranty payable)* Barnstormers USA guarantees tires against defects for five years or 60,000 miles, whichever comes first. Suppose Barnstormers USA can expect warranty costs during the five-year period to add up to 7% of sales. Assume that a Barnstormers USA dealer in St. Paul, Minnesota, made sales of $460,000 during 2016. Barnstormers USA received cash for 15% of the sales and took notes receivable for the remainder. Payments to satisfy customer warranty claims totaled $19,700 during 2016.

LO 1

1. Record the sales, warranty expense, and warranty payments for Barnstormers USA.
2. Post to the Estimated Warranty Payable T-account. The beginning balance was $16,000. At the end of 2016, how much in estimated warranty payable does Barnstormers USA owe to its customers?

S9-4. *(Learning Objective 1: Report warranties in the financial statements)* Refer to the data given in S9-3. What amount of warranty expense will Barnstormers USA report during 2016? Which accounting principle addresses this situation? Does the warranty expense for the year equal the year's cash payments for warranties? Explain the relevant accounting principle as it applies to measuring warranty expense.

LO 1

LO 1

S9-5. *(Learning Objective 1: Interpret a company's contingent liabilities)* Hamm Cycles, Inc., the motorcycle manufacturer, included the following note in its annual report:

NOTES TO CONSOLIDATED FINANCIAL STATEMENTS
7 (In Part): Commitments and Contingencies
  The Company self-insures its product liability losses in the United States up to $3.8 million (catastrophic coverage is maintained for individual claims in excess of $3.8 million up to $26.3 million). Outside the United States, the Company is insured for product liability up to $26.3 million per individual claim and in the aggregate.

---

1. Why are these *contingent* (versus *real*) liabilities?
2. In the United States, how can the contingent liability become a real liability for Hamm Cycles, Inc.? What are the limits to the company's product liabilities in the United States?
3. How can a contingency outside the United States become a real liability for the company? How does Hamm Cycles, Inc.'s potential liability differ for claims outside the United States?

LO 2

S9-6. *(Learning Objective 2: Review of bonds issued at a discount)* Read each statement below, indicate if it is true or false, and give a brief explanation of your answer.
1. When a bond is sold at a discount, the cash received is less than the present value of the future cash flows from the bond, based on the market rate of interest on the date of issue.
2. When a bond is issued at a discount, the semiannual cash interest payments are calculated using the market rate on the date of issue.
3. When a bond is issued at a discount, the semiannual amount of interest expense will be greater than the cash payment for interest.
4. When a bond is sold at a discount, the maturity value is less than the present value of the principal and interest payments, based on the market rate of interest on the date of issue.
5. The amortization of the discount on a bond payable results in additional interest expense recorded over the life of the bond.
6. When the year-end accrual of interest and amortization of discount is recorded, the carrying value of Bonds Payable on the balance sheet will increase.

LO 2

S9-7. *(Learning Objective 2: Determine bond prices at par, discount, or premium)* Determine whether the following bonds payable will be issued at par value, at a premium, or at a discount:
  a. Typecast Corporation issued 5% bonds when the market interest rate was 5%.
  b. Eugene Company issued bonds payable that pay stated interest of $6\frac{1}{4}\%$. At issuance, the market interest rate was $6\frac{3}{4}\%$.
  c. The market interest rate is 4%. Raintree Corp. issues bonds payable with a stated rate of $5\frac{1}{2}\%$.
  d. DoubleTyme, Inc., issued 3% bonds payable when the market rate was $3\frac{3}{4}\%$.

LO 2

S9-8. *(Learning Objective 2: Journalize basic bond payable transactions and bonds issued at par)* McQueen Corp. issued 7.5% seven-year bonds payable with a face amount of $90,000 when the market interest rate was 7.5%. Assume that the accounting year of McQueen ends on December 31 and that bonds pay interest on January 1 and July 1. Journalize the following transactions for McQueen. Include an explanation for each entry.
  a. Issuance of the bonds payable at par on July 1, 2016
  b. Accrual of interest expense on December 31, 2016 (rounded to the nearest dollar)
  c. Payment of cash interest on January 1, 2017
  d. Payment of the bonds payable at maturity (give the date)

LO 2

S9-9. *(Learning Objective 2: Determine bonds payable amounts with a discount; amortize bonds by the straight-line method)* Superior Drive-Ins Ltd. borrowed money by issuing $1,000,000 of 7% bonds payable at 96.5 on July 1, 2016. The bonds are 10-year bonds and pay interest each January 1 and July 1.
  1. How much cash did Superior receive when it issued the bonds payable? Journalize this transaction.

2. How much must Superior pay back at maturity? When is the maturity date?

3. How much cash interest will Superior pay each six months?

4. How much interest expense will Superior report each six months? Assume the straight-line amortization method. Journalize the entries for accrual of interest and amortization of discount on December 31, 2016, and payment of interest on January 1, 2017.

S9-10. *(Learning Objective 2: Determine bonds payable amounts with a premium; amortize bonds by the straight-line method)* Charley Company borrowed money by issuing $2,000,000 of 6% bonds payable at 101.5 on July 1, 2016. The bonds are five-year bonds and pay interest each January 1 and July 1. **LO 2**

1. How much cash did Charley receive when it issued the bonds payable? Journalize this transaction.

2. How much must Charley pay back at maturity? When is the maturity date?

3. How much cash interest will Charley pay each six months?

4. How much interest expense will Charley report each six months? Assume the straight-line amortization method. Journalize the entries for accrual of interest and amortization of premium on December 31, 2016, and payment of interest on January 1, 2017.

S9-11. *(Learning Objective 3: Issue bonds payable at a discount and amortize bonds using the effective-interest method)* Hartley Corporation issued $520,000 of 5%, 12-year bonds payable on March 31, 2016. The market interest rate at the date of issuance was 8%, and the Hartley Corporation bonds pay interest semiannually. Hartley Corporation's year-end is March 31. **LO 3**

1. Using the PV function in Excel, calculate the issue price of the bonds.

2. Prepare an effective-interest amortization table for the bonds through the first three interest payments. Round amounts to the nearest dollar.

3. Record Hartley Corporation's issuance of the bonds on March 31, 2016, and payment of the first semiannual interest amount and amortization of the bond discount on September 30, 2016. Explanations are not required.

S9-12. *(Learning Objective 3: Account for bonds payable issued at a discount using effective-interest method)* Use the amortization table that you prepared for Hartley Corporation's bonds in S9-11 to answer the following questions: **LO 3**

1. How much cash did Hartley Corporation borrow on March 31, 2016? How much cash will Hartley Corporation pay back at maturity on March 31, 2028?

2. How much cash interest will Hartley Corporation pay each six months?

3. How much interest expense will Hartley Corporation report on September 30, 2016, and on March 31, 2017? Why does the amount of interest expense increase each period?

S9-13. *(Learning Objective 3: Issue bonds payable at a premium and amortize bonds using the effective-interest method)* Jackson Corporation issued $600,000 of 6%, 10-year bonds payable on January 1, 2016. The market interest rate at the date of issuance was 4%, and the Jackson Corporation bonds pay interest semiannually. Jackson Corporation's year-end is June 30. **LO 3**

1. Using the PV function in Excel, calculate the issue price of the bonds.

2. Prepare an effective-interest amortization table for the bonds through the first three interest payments. Round amounts to the nearest dollar.

3. Record Jackson Corporation's issuance of the bonds on January 1, 2016, and payment of the first semiannual interest amount and amortization of the bond premium on June 30, 2016. (The bonds pay interest each June 30 and December 31.) Explanations are not required.

S9-14. *(Learning Objective 3: Account for bonds payable issued at a premium using effective interest method)* Use the amortization table that you prepared for Jackson Corporation's bonds in S9-13 to answer the following questions: **LO 3**

1. How much cash did Jackson Corporation borrow on January 1, 2016? How much cash will Jackson Corporation pay back at maturity?

2. How much cash interest will Jackson Corporation pay each six months?

3. How much interest expense will Jackson Corporation report on June 30, 2016, and on December 31, 2016? Does the amount of interest expense increase or decrease each period? Why?

LO 4 **S9-15.** *(Learning Objective 4: Calculate the leverage ratio, debt ratio, and times-interest-earned ratio, and evaluate debt-paying ability)* Examine the following selected financial information for Best Buy Co., Inc., and Walmart Stores, Inc., as of the end of their fiscal years ending in 2015:

(In millions)	Best Buy Co., Inc.	Walmart Stores, Inc.
1. Total assets	$15,256	$203,706
2. Total Stockholders' equity....................................	$ 4,995	$ 81,394
3. Operating income...	$ 1,450	$ 27,147
4. Interest expense...	$ 90	$ 2,348
5. Leverage ratio		
6. Total debt		
7. Debt ratio..		
8. Times interest earned		

1. Complete the table, calculating all the requested information for the two companies. Use year-end figures in place of averages where needed for the purpose of calculating ratios in this exercise.
2. Evaluate each company's long-term debt-paying ability (strong, medium, weak).

LO 4 **S9-16.** *(Learning Objective 4: Compute earnings-per-share effects of financing with bonds versus stock)* Nautical Marina needs to raise $1.0 million to expand the company. Nautical Marina is considering the issuance of either

- $1,000,000 of 8% bonds payable to borrow the money, or
- 100,000 shares of common stock at $10 per share.

Before any new financing, Nautical Marina expects to earn net income of $400,000, and the company already has 100,000 shares of common stock outstanding. Nautical Marina believes the expansion will increase income before interest and income tax by $100,000. The income tax rate is 40%.

Prepare an analysis to determine which plan is likely to result in the higher earnings per share. Based solely on the earnings-per-share comparison, which financing plan would you recommend for Nautical Marina?

LO 4 **S9-17.** *(Learning Objective 4: Compute and evaluate three ratios)* Jalbert Plumbing Products Ltd. reported the following data in 2016 (in millions):

	2016
Net operating revenues................	$ 31.8
Operating expenses	26.7
Operating income........................	5.1
Nonoperating items:	
Interest expense.......................	(0.6)
Other	(0.6)
Net income.................................	$ 3.9
Total assets	$200.0
Total stockholders' equity	74.0

Compute Jalbert's leverage ratio, debt ratio, and times-interest-earned ratio, and write a sentence to explain what those ratio values mean. Use year-end figures in place of averages where needed for the purpose of calculating ratios in this exercise. Would you be willing to lend Jalbert $1 million? State your reason.

S9-18. *(Learning Objective 5: Lease and pension vocabulary terms)* Complete the following statements with one of the terms listed here.

LO 5

Capital lease	Overfunded
Underfunded	Lessee
Pension	Operating lease
Lessor	Liability

1. A(n) _____ is an agreement that does not transfer the risks or rewards of asset ownership to the lessee.
2. An agreement in which the lessee assumes, essentially, the risks and rewards of asset ownership is a(n) _____.
3. A(n) _____ is compensation that an employee earns that will be received during the employee's retirement.
4. If the fair market value of the retirement plan assets is greater than the retirement plan's projected benefit obligation, the retirement plan is said to be _____.
5. The tenant in a lease arrangement is also known as the _____.
6. A(n) _____ retirement plan results when the fair market value of the plan assets are less than the plan's projected benefit obligation.
7. The _____ is the property owner who receives rent payments in exchange for use of the property.

S9-19. *(Learning Objective 6: Report liabilities)* LuxAll, Inc., includes the following selected accounts in its general ledger at December 31, 2016:

LO 6

Bonds payable (excluding current portion)	$450,000
Equipment	115,000
Current portion of bonds payable	50,000
Notes payable, long-term	300,000
Interest payable (due March 1, 2017)	1,200
Accounts payable	41,000
Discount on bonds payable (all long-term)	13,500
Accounts receivable	31,000

Prepare the liabilities section of LuxAll, Inc.'s, balance sheet at December 31, 2016, to show how the company would report these items. Report total current liabilities and total liabilities.

Exercises

Group A

E9-20A. *(Learning Objective 1: Account for a short-term note payable)* Ivanhoe Sports Authority purchased inventory costing $28,000 by signing a 7% short-term, one-year note payable. The purchase occurred on July 31, 2016. Ivanhoe pays annual interest each year on July 31. Journalize the company's (a) purchase of inventory; (b) accrual of interest expense on April 30, 2017, which is the year-end; and (c) payment of the note plus interest on July 31, 2017. (Round your answers to the nearest whole number.) (d) Show what the company would report for liabilities on its balance sheet at April 30, 2017, and on its income statement for the year ended on that date.

LO 1

E9-21A. *(Learning Objective 1: Account for warranty expense and the related liability)* The accounting records of Jim's Appliances included the following balances at the end of the period:

LO 1

Estimated Warranty Payable	Sales Revenue	Warranty Expense
Beg bal 5,000	106,000	

In the past, Jim's warranty expense has been 9% of sales. During the current period, the business paid $9,000 to satisfy the warranty claims.

Requirements

1. Journalize Jim's warranty expense for the period and the company's cash payments to satisfy warranty claims. Explanations are not required.
2. Show what Jim's will report on its income statement and balance sheet for this situation at the end of the period.
3. Which data item from requirement 2 will affect the current ratio? Will Jim's current ratio increase or decrease as a result of this item?

LO 1

E9-22A. (*Learning Objective 1: Record and report current liabilities*) TransWorld Publishing completed the following transactions for one subscriber during 2016:

Oct 1	Sold a one-year subscription, collecting cash of $2,000, plus sales tax of 8%.
Nov 15	Remitted (paid) the sales tax to the state of Ohio.
Dec 31	Made the necessary adjustment at year-end.

Requirement

1. Journalize these transactions (explanations not required). Then report any liability on the company's balance sheet at December 31, 2016.

LO 1

E9-23A. (*Learning Objective 1: Account for payroll expense and liabilities*) Perrault has an annual payroll of $190,000. In addition, the company incurs payroll tax expense of 8%. At December 31, Perrault owes salaries of $8,200 and FICA and other payroll tax of $700. The company will pay these amounts early next year. Show what Perrault will report for the foregoing on its income statement for the year and on its year-end balance sheet.

LO 1

E9-24A. (*Learning Objective 1: Record note payable transactions*) Assume that Cart Sales Company completed the following note payable transactions:

2016		
Jul 1	Purchased delivery truck costing $57,000 by issuing a one-year, 6% note payable.	
Dec 31	Accrued interest on the note payable.	
2017		
Jul 1	Paid the note payable at maturity.	

Requirements

1. How much interest expense must be accrued at December 31, 2016? (Round your answer to the nearest whole dollar.)
2. Determine the amount of Cart Sales' final payment on July 1, 2017.
3. How much interest expense will Cart Sales report for 2016 and for 2017?

LO 1

E9-25A. (*Learning Objective 1: Account for income tax*) At December 31, 2016, Hawley Real Estate reported a current liability for income tax payable of $78,000. During 2017, Hawley earned income of $650,000 before income tax. The company's income tax rate during 2017 was 35%. Also during 2017, Hawley paid income taxes of $172,000.

How much income tax payable did Hawley Real Estate report on its balance sheet at December 31, 2017? How much income tax expense did Hawley report on its 2017 income statement?

LO 1 4

E9-26A. (*Learning Objectives 1, 4: Analyze current and long-term liabilities; evaluate debt-paying ability*) Earth Friendly Structures, Inc., builds environmentally sensitive structures. The company's 2016 revenues totaled $2,760 million. At December 31, 2016, and 2015, the company had, respectively, $658 million and $603 million in current assets. The December 31, 2016, and 2015, balance sheets and income statements reported the following amounts:

	A	B	C
		2016	2015
1	**At year-end (In millions)**	**2016**	**2015**
2	Liabilities and stockholders' equity		
3	Current liabilities		
4	Accounts payable	$ 144	$ 172
5	Accrued expenses	112	180
6	Employee compensation and benefits	45	32
7	Current portion of long-term debt	4	6
8	Total current liabilities	305	390
9	Long-term debt	1,842	1,321
10	Post-retirement benefits payable	77	116
11	Other liabilities	29	22
12	Stockholders' equity	2,418	1,785
13	Total liabilities and stockholders' equity	$ 4,671	$ 3,634
14	Year-end (in millions)		
15	Cost of goods sold	$ 1,580	$ 1,218
16			

Requirements

1. Describe each of Earth Friendly Structures, Inc.'s, liabilities and state how the liability arose.
2. What were the company's total assets at December 31, 2016? Evaluate the company's leverage and debt ratios at the end of 2015 and 2016. Use year-end figures in place of averages where needed for the purpose of calculating ratios in this exercise. Did the company improve, deteriorate, or remain about the same over the year?
3. Assume that beginning and ending inventories for both periods did not differ by a material amount. Accounts payable at the end of 2014 was $176 million. Calculate accounts payable turnover as a ratio and days' payable outstanding (DPO) for 2015 and 2016. Calculate current ratios for 2015 and 2016 as well. Evaluate whether the company improved or deteriorated from the standpoint of ability to cover accounts payable and current liabilities over the year.

E9-27A. *(Learning Objectives 1, 6: Report a contingent liability)* Barclay Systems' revenues for 2016 totaled $26.2 million. As with most companies, Barclay is a defendant in lawsuits related to its products. Note 14 of the Barclay annual report for 2016 reported the following:

> **14. Contingencies**
> The company is involved in various legal proceedings.... It is the Company's policy to accrue for amounts related to these legal matters if it is probable that a liability has been incurred and an amount is reasonably estimable.

LO **1** **6**

Requirements

1. Suppose Barclay's lawyers believe that a significant legal judgment against the company is reasonably possible. How should Barclay report this situation in its financial statements?
2. Suppose Barclay's lawyers believe it is probable that a $2.0 million judgment will be rendered against the company. Report this situation in Barclay's financial statements. Journalize any entry requirements by GAAP. Explanations are not required.

E9-28A. *(Learning Objectives 1, 6: Report current and long-term liabilities)* Assume that Banff Electronics completed these selected transactions during March 2016:

LO **1** **6**

    a. Sales of $2,100,000 are subject to estimated warranty cost of 2%. The estimated warranty payable at the beginning of the year was $35,000, and warranty payments for the year totaled $58,000.

b. On March 1, Banff Electronics signed a $45,000 note payable that requires annual payments of $9,000 plus 5% interest on the unpaid balance each March 2.

c. BuyMore, Inc., a chain of discount stores, ordered $105,000 worth of wireless speakers and related products. With its order, BuyMore, Inc., sent a check for $105,000 in advance, and Banff shipped $60,000 of the goods. Banff will ship the remainder of the goods on April 3, 2016.

d. The March payroll of $220,000 is subject to employee withheld income tax of $30,700 and FICA tax of 7.65%. On March 31, Banff pays employees their take-home pay and accrues all tax amounts.

Requirement

1. Report these items on Banff Electronics' balance sheet at March 31, 2016.

LO 2
E9-29A. *(Learning Objective 2: Issue bonds payable (discount), pay and accrue interest, and amortize bond discount by the straight-line method)* On January 31, 2016, Danvers Logistics, Inc., issued five-year, 7% bonds payable with a face value of $10,000,000. The bonds were issued at 96 and pay interest on January 31 and July 31. Danvers Logistics, Inc., amortizes bond discount by the straight-line method. Record (a) issuance of the bonds on January 31, 2016, (b) the semiannual interest payment and amortization of bond discount on July 31, 2016, and (c) the interest accrual and discount amortization on December 31, 2016.

LO 2
E9-30A. *(Learning Objective 2: Measure cash amounts for a bond payable (premium); amortize bond premium by the straight-line method)* County Bank has $300,000 of 7% debenture bonds outstanding. The bonds were issued at 103 in 2016 and mature in 2036. The bonds have annual interest payments.

Requirements

1. How much cash did County Bank receive when it issued these bonds?
2. How much cash in *total* will County Bank pay the bondholders through the maturity date of the bonds?
3. Calculate the difference between your answers to requirements 1 and 2. This difference represents County Bank's total interest expense over the life of the bonds.
4. Compute County Bank's annual interest expense by the straight-line amortization method. Multiply this amount by 20. Your 20-year total should be the same as your answer to requirement 3.

LO 3
E9-31A. *(Learning Objective 3: Issue bonds payable (discount); record interest payments and the related bond amortization using the effective-interest method)* Score Ltd. is authorized to issue $2,000,000 of 3%, 10-year bonds payable. On December 31, 2016, when the market interest rate is 7%, the company issues $1,600,000 of the bonds. Score Ltd. amortizes bond discount by the effective-interest method. The semiannual interest dates are June 30 and December 31.

Requirements

1. Use the PV function in Excel to calculate the issue price of the bonds.
2. Using Exhibit 9-4 as a model, prepare a bond amortization table for the term of the bonds.
3. Record issuance of the bonds payable on December 31, 2016; the first semiannual interest payment on June 30, 2017; and the second payment on December 31, 2017.

LO 3
E9-32A. *(Learning Objective 3: Issue bonds payable (premium); record interest payment and the related bond amortization using the effective-interest method)* On June 30, 2016, the market interest rate is 8%. Team Sports Ltd. issues $800,000 of 10%, 10-year bonds payable. The bonds pay interest on June 30 and December 31. Team Sports Ltd. amortizes bond premium by the effective-interest method.

Requirements

1. Use the PV function in Excel to calculate the issue price of the bonds.
2. Using Exhibit 9-7 as a model, prepare a bond amortization table for the term of the bonds.
3. Record the issuance of bonds payable on June 30, 2016; the payment of interest on December 31, 2016; and the payment of interest on June 30, 2017.

E9-33A. *(Learning Objectives 4, 5: Interpret an operating lease footnote)* Footnote 2 of Abercrombie and Fitch Co.'s financial statements for fiscal year 2014 (January 31, 2015) contains the following information:

> At January 31, 2015, the Company was committed to noncancelable leases with remaining terms of 1 to 16 years. A summary of operating lease commitments under noncancelable leases follows (thousands):
>
> | | |
> |---|---:|
> | Fiscal 2015 | $ 409,046 |
> | Fiscal 2016 | $ 366,909 |
> | Fiscal 2017 | $ 279,960 |
> | Fiscal 2018 | $ 210,674 |
> | Fiscal 2019 | $ 165,307 |
> | Thereafter | $ 525,286 |
> | Total | $1,957,182 |

Source: From Abercrombie and Fitch Co., Notes To Consolidated Financial Statements, http://www.sec.gov/Archives/edgar/data/1018840/000101884015000020/a201410-k.htm.

Requirements

1. Interpret the information in the footnote. Assume that the leases relate to the stores operated by the company. What rights does the company have? What obligations?
2. Are the rights and obligations discussed in requirement 1 reported in the liability section of the balance sheet? Why or why not? How does this impact the company's debt and leverage ratios?
3. How is this type of reporting likely to change in the future?

E9-34A. *(Learning Objective 4: Evaluate debt-paying ability)* Companies that operate in different industries may have very different financial ratio values. These differences may grow even wider when we compare companies located in different countries.

Compare three leading companies (Company F, Company K, and Company R) by calculating the following ratios: current ratio, debt ratio, leverage ratio, and times-interest-earned ratio. Use year-end figures in place of averages where needed for the purpose of calculating ratios in this exercise.

	A	C	D	E
	A1			
1	(Amounts in millions or billions)	Company F	Company K	Company R
2	Income data			
3	Total revenues	$ 9,724	¥ 7,907	€ 136,492
4	Operating income	239	224	5,692
5	Interest expense	46	33	736
6	Net income	23	15	448
7	**Assets and liability data**			
8	(Amounts in millions or billions)			
9	Total current assets	434	5,383	148,526
10	Long-term assets	114	405	49,525
11	Total current liabilities	207	2,197	72,600
12	Long-term liabilities	116	2,318	110,107
13	Stockholders' equity	225	1,273	15,344
14				

Based on your computed ratio values, which company looks the least risky?

E9-35A. *(Learning Objective 4, 6: Analyze alternative plans for raising money)* Green Nation Financial Services is considering two plans for raising $600,000 to expand operations. Plan A is to borrow at 5%, and plan B is to issue 100,000 shares of common stock at $6.00 per share. Before any new financing, Green Nation Financial Services has net income of $400,000 and 100,000 shares of common stock outstanding. Assume you own most of Green Nation Financial Services' existing stock. Management believes the company can use the new funds to earn additional income of $550,000 before interest and taxes. Green Nation Financial Services' income tax rate is 40%.

Requirements

1. Analyze Green Nation Financial Services' situation to determine which plan will result in higher earnings per share.
2. Which plan allows you to retain control of the company? Which plan creates more financial risk for the company? Which plan do you prefer? Why? Present your conclusion in a memo to Green Nation Financial Services' board of directors.

Group B

LO 1

E9-36B. (*Learning Objective 1: Account for a short-term note payable*) Kimball Sports Authority purchased inventory costing $22,500 by signing a 6% short-term, one-year note payable. The purchase occurred on July 31, 2016. Kimball pays annual interest each year on July 31. Journalize the company's (a) purchase of inventory; (b) accrual of interest expense on April 30, 2017, which is the year-end; and (c) payment of the note plus interest on July 31, 2017. (Round your answers to the nearest whole number.) (d) Show what the company would report for liabilities on its balance sheet at April 30, 2017, and on its income statement for the year ended on that date.

LO 1

E9-37B. (*Learning Objective 1: Account for warranty expense and the related liability*) The accounting records of Carmine Appliances included the following balances at the end of the period:

Estimated Warranty Payable		Sales Revenue		Warranty Expense	
	Beg bal 4,000		120,000		

In the past, Carmine's warranty expense has been 8% of sales. During the current period, the business paid $7,000 to satisfy the warranty claims.

Requirements

1. Journalize Carmine's warranty expense for the period and the company's cash payments to satisfy warranty claims. Explanations are not required.
2. Show what Carmine will report on its income statement and balance sheet for this situation at the end of the period.
3. Which data item from requirement 2 will affect the current ratio? Will Carmine's current ratio increase or decrease as a result of this item?

LO 1

E9-38B. (*Learning Objective 1: Record and report current liabilities*) Great White Publishing completed the following transactions for one subscriber during 2016:

Oct 1	Sold a one-year subscription, collecting cash of $1,400, plus sales tax of 8%.
Nov 15	Remitted (paid) the sales tax to the state of Minnesota.
Dec 31	Made the necessary adjustment at year-end.

Requirement

1. Journalize these transactions (explanations not required). Then report any liability on the company's balance sheet at December 31, 2016.

LO 1

E9-39B. (*Learning Objective 1: Account for payroll expense and liabilities*) Penske has an annual payroll of $215,000. In addition, the company incurs payroll tax expense of 12%. At December 31, Penske owes salaries of $7,800 and FICA and other payroll tax of $550. The company will pay these amounts early next year.

Show what Penske will report for the foregoing on its income statement for the year and on its year-end balance sheet.

E9-40B. *(Learning Objective 1: Record note payable transactions)* Assume that Boston Sales Company completed the following note payable transactions:

LO **1**

2016	
Apr 1	Purchased delivery truck costing $64,000 by issuing a one-year, 5% note payable.
Dec 31	Accrued interest on the note payable.
2017	
Apr 1	Paid the note payable at maturity.

Requirements

1. How much interest expense must be accrued at December 31, 2016? (Round your answer to the nearest whole dollar.)
2. Determine the amount of Boston Sales' final payment on April 1, 2017.
3. How much interest expense will Boston Sales report for 2016 and for 2017? (If needed, round your answer to the nearest whole dollar.)

E9-41B. *(Learning Objective 1: Account for income tax)* At December 31, 2016, Saglio Real Estate reported a current liability for income tax payable of $73,000. During 2017, Saglio earned income of $650,000 before income tax. The company's income tax rate during 2017 was 33%. Also during 2017, Saglio paid income taxes of $173,000.

LO **1**

How much income tax payable did Saglio Real Estate report on its balance sheet at December 31, 2017? How much income tax expense did Saglio report on its 2017 income statement?

E9-42B. *(Learning Objectives 1, 4: Analyze current and long-term liabilities; evaluate debt-paying ability)* Great Earth Homes, Inc., builds environmentally sensitive structures. The company's 2016 revenues totaled $2,770 million. At December 31, 2016 and 2015, the company had, respectively, $653 million and $583 million in current assets. The December 31, 2016, and 2015, balance sheets and income statements reported the following amounts:

LO **1** **4**

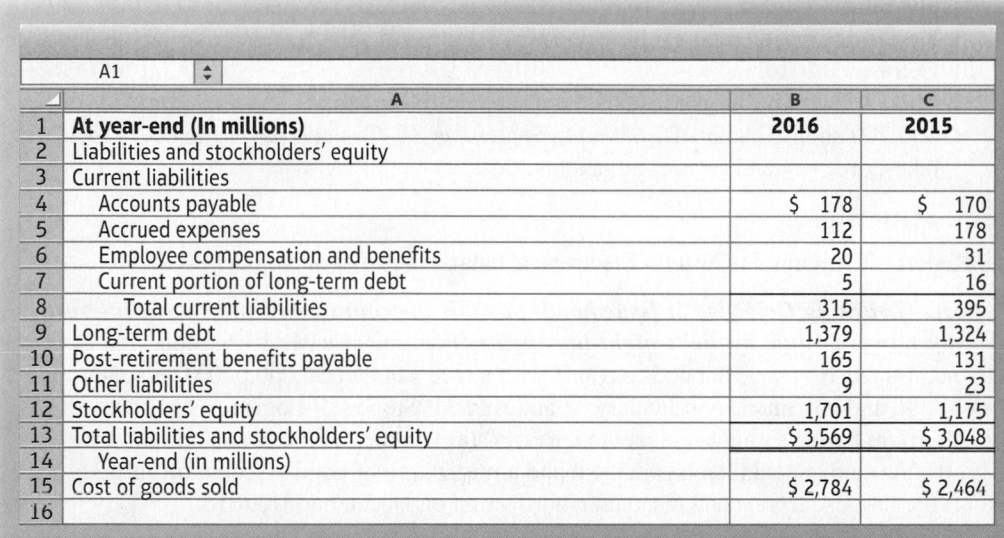

	A	B	C
		2016	**2015**
1	**At year-end (In millions)**		
2	Liabilities and stockholders' equity		
3	Current liabilities		
4	Accounts payable	$ 178	$ 170
5	Accrued expenses	112	178
6	Employee compensation and benefits	20	31
7	Current portion of long-term debt	5	16
8	Total current liabilities	315	395
9	Long-term debt	1,379	1,324
10	Post-retirement benefits payable	165	131
11	Other liabilities	9	23
12	Stockholders' equity	1,701	1,175
13	Total liabilities and stockholders' equity	$ 3,569	$ 3,048
14	Year-end (in millions)		
15	Cost of goods sold	$ 2,784	$ 2,464
16			

Requirements

1. Describe each of Great Earth Homes, Inc.'s, liabilities and state how the liability arose.
2. What were the company's total assets at December 31, 2016? Evaluate the company's leverage and debt ratios at the end of 2015 and 2016. Use year-end figures in place of averages where needed for the purpose of calculating ratios in this exercise. Did the company improve, deteriorate, or remain about the same over the year?

3. Assume that beginning and ending inventories for both periods did not differ by a material amount. Accounts payable at the end of 2014 was $182 million. Calculate accounts payable turnover as a ratio and days' payable outstanding (DPO) for 2015 and 2016. Calculate current ratios for 2015 and 2016 as well. Evaluate whether the company improved or deteriorated from the standpoint of ability to cover accounts payable and current liabilities over the year.

LO 1 6 **E9-43B.** *(Learning Objectives 1, 6: Report a contingent liability)* Crockett Security Systems' revenues for 2016 totaled $21.9 million. As with most companies, Crockett is a defendant in lawsuits related to its products. Note 14 of the Crockett annual report for 2016 reported the following:

> **14. Contingencies**
> The company is involved in various legal proceedings.... It is the Company's policy to accrue for amounts related to these legal matters if it is probable that a liability has been incurred and an amount is reasonably estimable.

Requirements

1. Suppose Crockett's lawyers believe that a significant legal judgment against the company is reasonably possible. How should Crockett report this situation in its financial statements?
2. Suppose Crockett's lawyers believe it is probable that a $1.7 million judgment will be rendered against the company. Report this situation in Crockett's financial statements. Journalize any entry required by GAAP. Explanations are not required.

LO 1 6 **E9-44B.** *(Learning Objectives 1, 6: Report current and long-term liabilities)* Assume Costello Electronics completed these selected transactions during September 2016:
   a. Sales of $2,500,000 are subject to estimated warranty cost of 3%. The estimated warranty payable at the beginning of the year was $36,000, and warranty payments for the year totaled $52,000.
   b. On September 1, Costello signed a $65,000 note payable that requires annual payments of $13,000 plus 5% interest on the unpaid balance each September 2.
   c. SaveMore, Inc., a chain of discount stores, ordered $110,000 worth of wireless speakers and related products. With its order, SaveMore, Inc., sent a check for $110,000, and Costello shipped $60,000 of the goods. Costello will ship the remainder of the goods on October 3, 2016.
   d. The September payroll of $200,000 is subject to employee withheld income tax of $30,700 and FICA tax of 7.65%. On September 30, Costello pays employees their take-home pay and accrues all tax amounts.

Requirement

1. Report these items on Costello Electronics' balance sheet at September 30, 2016.

LO 2 **E9-45B.** *(Learning Objective 2: Issue bonds payable (discount); pay and accrue interest; amortize bond discount by the straight-line method)* On January 31, 2016, Stonewall Logistics, Inc., issued 10-year, 5% bonds payable with a face value of $6,000,000. The bonds were issued at 96 and pay interest on January 31 and July 31. Stonewall Logistics, Inc., amortizes bond discount by the straight-line method. Record (a) issuance of the bonds on January 31, 2016, (b) the semiannual interest payment and amortization of bond discount on July 31, 2016, and (c) the interest accrual and discount amortization on December 31, 2016.

LO 2 **E9-46B.** *(Learning Objective 2: Measure cash amounts for a bond payable (premium); amortize bond premium by the straight-line method)* City Bank has $100,000 of 7% debenture bonds outstanding. The bonds were issued at 103 in 2016 and mature in 2036. The bonds have annual interest payments.

Requirements

1. How much cash did City Bank receive when it issued these bonds?
2. How much cash in *total* will City Bank pay the bondholders through the maturity date of the bonds?

3. Calculate the difference between your answers to requirements 1 and 2. This difference represents City Bank's total interest expense over the life of the bonds.

4. Compute City Bank's annual interest expense by the straight-line amortization method. Multiply this amount by 20. Your 20-year total should be the same as your answer to requirement 3.

E9-47B. *(Learning Objective 3: Issue bonds payable (discount); record interest payments and the related bond amortization using the effective-interest method)* ActiveGo Sports Ltd. is authorized to issue $5,000,000 of 4%, 10-year bonds payable. On December 31, 2016, when the market interest rate is 4.5%, the company issues $4,000,000 of the bonds. ActiveGo Sports amortizes bond discount by the effective-interest method. The semiannual interest dates are June 30 and December 31.

Requirements

1. Use the PV function in Excel to calculate the issue price of the bonds.
2. Using Exhibit 9-4 as a model, prepare a bond amortization table for the term of the bonds.
3. Record issuance of the bonds payable on December 31, 2016; the first semiannual interest payment on June 30, 2017; and the second payment on December 31, 2017.

E9-48B. *(Learning Objective 3: Issue bonds payable (premium); record interest payment and the related bond amortization using the effective-interest method)* On June 30, 2016, the market interest rate is 6%. Grommet Candies Ltd. issues $2,000,000 of 8%, 10-year bonds payable. The bonds pay interest on June 30 and December 31. Grommet Candies Ltd. amortizes bond premium by the effective-interest method.

Requirements

1. Use the PV function in Excel to calculate the issue price of the bonds.
2. Using Exhibit 9-7 as a model, prepare a bond amortization table for the term of the bonds.
3. Record the issuance of bonds payable on June 30, 2016; the payment of interest on December 31, 2016; and the payment of interest on June 30, 2017.

E9-49B. *(Learning Objectives 4, 5: Interpret an operating lease footnote)* Footnote 7 of Ann Taylor Stores Corp.'s financial statements for fiscal year 2014 contains the following information:

7. Commitments and Contingencies
Operating Leases

The Company occupies its retail stores and administrative facilities under operating leases, most of which are noncancelable. Some of the store leases grant the Company the right to extend the term for one or two additional five-year periods under substantially the same terms and conditions as the original leases. Some store leases also contain early termination options, which can be exercised by the Company under specific conditions. Most of the store leases require payment of a specified minimum rent, plus contingent rent based on a percentage of the store's net sales in excess of a specified threshold. The Company also leases certain office equipment for its corporate offices and store locations under noncancelable operating leases which generally have three-year terms.

Future minimum lease payments under noncancelable operating leases as of January 31, 2015, are as follows:

Fiscal Year	(in thousands)
2015	$ 211,182
2016	186,276
2017	171,203
2018	150,959
2019	132,921
Thereafter	363,047
Total	1,215,588
Sublease rentals	(7,688)
Net rentals	$1,207,900

Source: From Footnote 7 of Ann Taylor Stores Corp.'s Financial Statements, 2014.

Requirements

1. Interpret the information in the footnote. What rights does the company have? What obligations?
2. Are the rights and obligations discussed in requirement 1 reported in the liability section of the balance sheet? Why or why not? How does this impact the company's debt and leverage ratios?
3. How is this type of reporting likely to change in the future?

 E9-50B. *(Learning Objective 4: Evaluate debt-paying ability)* Companies that operate in different industries may have very different financial ratio values. These differences may grow even wider when we compare companies located in different countries.

Compare three leading companies (Company E, Company L, and Company R) by calculating the following ratios: current ratio, debt ratio, leverage ratio, and times-interest-earned ratio. Use year-end figures in place of averages where needed for the purpose of calculating ratios in this exercise.

	A1				
	A		B	C	D
1	(Amounts in millions or billions)		Company E	Company L	Company R
2	Income data				
3	Total revenues		$ 9,733	¥ 7,312	€ 136,390
4	Operating income		294	229	5,639
5	Interest expense		45	30	720
6	Net income		24	17	441
7	**Assets and liability data**				
8	(Amounts in millions or billions)				
9	Total current assets		434	5,383	155,364
10	Long-term assets		126	349	39,558
11	Total current liabilities		207	2,197	72,600
12	Long-term liabilities		127	2,331	110,627
13	Stockholders' equity		226	1,204	11,695
14					

Based on your computed ratio values, which company looks the least risky?

 **E9-51B.** *(Learning Objective 4, 6: Analyze alternative plans for raising money)* Stockwell Financial Services is considering two plans for raising $600,000 to expand operations. Plan A is to borrow at 6%, and plan B is to issue 125,000 shares of common stock at $4.80 per share. Before any new financing, Stockwell Financial Services has net income of $300,000 and 100,000 shares of common stock outstanding. Assume you own most of Stockwell Financial Services' existing stock. Management believes the company can use the new funds to earn additional income of $500,000 before interest and taxes. Stockwell Financial Services' income tax rate is 25%.

Requirements

1. Analyze Stockwell Financial Services' situation to determine which plan will result in the higher earnings per share.
2. Which plan allows you to retain control of the company? Which plan creates more financial risk for the company? Which plan do you prefer? Why? Present your conclusion in a memo to Stockwell Financial Services' board of directors.

Quiz

Test your understanding of accounting for liabilities by answering the following questions. Select the best choice from among the possible answers given.

Q9-52. For the purpose of classifying liabilities as current or noncurrent, the term *operating cycle* refers to

    a. the time period between purchase of merchandise and the conversion of this merchandise back to cash.

    b. a period of one year.

    c. the average time period between business recessions.

    d. the time period between date of sale and the date the related revenue is collected.

Q9-53. Failure to accrue interest expense results in

    a. an overstatement of net income and an understatement of liabilities.

    b. an overstatement of net income and an overstatement of liabilities.

    c. an understatement of net income and an overstatement of liabilities.

    d. an understatement of net income and an understatement of liabilities.

Q9-54. Tennis Shoe Warehouse operates in a state with a 6.5% sales tax. For convenience, Tennis Shoe Warehouse credits Sales Revenue for the total amount (selling price plus sales tax) collected from each customer. If Tennis Shoe Warehouse fails to make an adjustment for sales taxes,

    a. net income will be understated and liabilities will be understated.

    b. net income will be overstated and liabilities will be overstated.

    c. net income will be overstated and liabilities will be understated.

    d. net income will be understated and liabilities will be overstated.

Q9-55. What kind of account is Unearned Revenue?

    a. Asset account

    b. Revenue account

    c. Expense account

    d. Liability account

Q9-56. An end-of-period adjusting entry that debits Unearned Revenue most likely will credit

    a. an asset.

    b. a liability.

    c. a revenue.

    d. an expense.

Q9-57. Myron, Inc., manufactures and sells computer monitors with a three-year warranty. Warranty costs are expected to average 7% of sales during the warranty period. The following table shows the sales and actual warranty payments during the first two years of operations:

Year	Sales	Warranty Payments
2016	$500,000	$ 4,500
2017	800,000	40,000

Based on these facts, what amount of warranty liability should Myron, Inc., report on its balance sheet at December 31, 2017?

    a. $46,500

    b. $91,000

    c. $40,000

    d. $44,500

Q9-58. Maridell's Fashions has a debt that has been properly reported as a long-term liability up to the present year (2016). Some of this debt comes due in 2016. If Maridell's Fashions continues to report the current position as a long-term liability, the effect will be to

    a. understate the debt ratio.

    b. understate total liabilities.

    c. overstate the current ratio.

    d. overstate net income.

Q9-59. A bond with a face amount of $17,000 has a current price quote of 103.85. What is the bond's price?

a. $17,103.85

b. $176,545

c. $1,765.45

d. $17,654.50

Q9-60. Bond carrying value equals Bonds Payable

a. minus Premium on Bonds Payable.

b. plus Discount on Bonds Payable.

c. minus Discount on Bonds Payable.

d. plus Premium on Bonds Payable.

e. both a and b.

f. both c and d.

Q9-61. What type of account is Discount on Bonds Payable, and what is its normal balance?

a. Contra liability; Credit

b. Adjusting account; Credit

c. Contra liability; Debit

d. Reversing account; Debit

Questions 62–65 use the following data:

Sweetwater Company sells $300,000 of 13%, 15-year bonds for 96.8507 on April 1, 2016. The market rate of interest on that day is 13.5%. Interest is paid each year on April 1.

Q9-62. The entry to record the sale of the bonds on April 1 would be as follows:

	A	B	C	D
	A1			
1	a.	Cash	290,552	
2		Discount on Bonds Payable	9,448	
3		Bonds Payable		300,000
4				
5	b.	Cash	300,000	
6		Discount on Bonds Payable		9,448
7		Bonds Payable		290,552
8				
9	c.	Cash	300,000	
10		Bonds Payable		300,000
11				
12	d.	Cash	290,552	
13		Bonds Payable		290,552
14				

Q9-63. Sweetwater Company uses the straight-line amortization method. The amount of interest expense for each year will be

a. $39,000.

b. $41,130.

c. $19,815.

d. $39,630.

e. none of these.

Q9-64. Using straight-line amortization, write the adjusting entry required at December 31, 2016.

Q9-65. Using straight-line amortization, write the journal entry required at April 1, 2017.

Q9-66. McIntosh Corporation issued $100,000 of 12%, 20-year bonds payable on January 1, 2016. The market interest rate when the bonds were issued was 13%. Interest is paid semiannually on January 1 and July 1. The first interest payment is July 1, 2016. Using the effective-interest amortization method, how much interest expense will McIntosh record on July 1, 2016? Use Exhibit 9-4 as an example. Use Excel to calculate the issue price.

a. $6,040

b. $5,576

c. $6,500

d. $6,000

e. $40

Q9-67. Using the facts in the preceding question, McIntosh's entry to record the interest expense on July 1, 2016, will include a

    a. credit to Interest Expense.

    b. debit to Bonds Payable.

    c. credit to Discount on Bonds Payable.

    d. debit to Premium on Bonds Payable.

Q9-68. Amortizing the discount on bonds payable

    a. reduces the semiannual cash payment for interest.

    b. is necessary only if the bonds were issued at more than face value.

    c. increases the recorded amount of interest expense.

    d. reduces the carrying value of the bond liability.

Q9-69. The journal entry on the maturity date to record the payment of $2,500,000 of bonds payable that were issued at a $90,000 discount includes

    a. a debit to Discount on Bonds Payable for $90,000.

    b. a debit to Bonds Payable for $2,500,000.

    c. a credit to Cash for $2,590,000.

    d. all of the above.

Q9-70. Is the payment of the face amount of a bond on its maturity date regarded as an operating activity, an investing activity, or a financing activity?

    a. Operating activity

    b. Investing activity

    c. Financing activity

Problems MyAccountingLab

Group A

P9-71A. *(Learning Objective 1: Measure and report current liabilities)* Salt Air Marine experienced these events during the current year.

    a. December revenue totaled $110,000; and, in addition, Salt Air collected sales tax of 5%. The tax amount will be sent to the state of North Carolina early in January.

    b. On August 31, Salt Air signed a six-month, 9% note payable to purchase a boat costing $88,000. The note requires payment of principal and interest at maturity.

    c. On August 31, Salt Air received cash of $3,000 in advance for service revenue. This revenue will be earned evenly over six months.

    d. Revenues of $775,000 were covered by Salt Air's service warranty. At January 1, estimated warranty payable was $11,300. During the year, Salt Air recorded warranty expense of $31,000 and paid warranty claims of $34,300.

    e. Salt Air owes $75,000 on a long-term note payable. At December 31, 10% interest for the year plus $40,000 of this principal are payable within one year.

LO 1

Requirement

    1. For each item, indicate the account and the related amount to be reported as a current liability on the Salt Air Marine balance sheet at December 31.

LO **1** **P9-72A.** *(Learning Objective 1: Record liability-related transactions)* The following transactions of Smooth Notes Music Company occurred during 2016 and 2017:

2016	
Mar 3	Purchased a piano (inventory) for $50,000, signing a six-month, 4% note payable.
May 31	Borrowed $90,000 on an 8% note payable that calls for annual installment payments of $15,000 principal plus interest. Record the short-term note payable in a separate account from the long-term note payable.
Sep 3	Paid the six-month, 4% note at maturity.
Dec 31	Accrued warranty expense, which is estimated at 2.5% of sales of $196,000.
31	Accrued interest on the outstanding note payable.
2017	
May 31	Paid the first installment and interest for one year on the outstanding note payable.

Requirement

1. Record the transactions in Smooth Notes' journal. Explanations are not required.

LO **1** **2** **P9-73A.** *(Learning Objectives 1, 2: Record bond transactions [at par]; report bonds payable on the balance sheet)* The board of directors of Circuits Plus authorizes the issue of $9,000,000 of 8%, 25-year bonds payable. The semiannual interest dates are May 31 and November 30. The bonds are issued on May 31, 2016, at par.

Requirements

1. Journalize the following transactions:
   a. Issuance of half of the bonds on May 31, 2016
   b. Payment of interest on November 30, 2016
   c. Accrual of interest on December 31, 2016
   d. Payment of interest on May 31, 2017
2. Report interest payable and bonds payable as they would appear on the Circuits Plus balance sheet at December 31, 2016.

LO **1** **2** **6** **P9-74A.** *(Learning Objectives 1, 2, 6: Issue bonds at a discount; amortize by the straight-line method; report bonds payable and accrued interest payable on the balance sheet)* On February 28, 2016, Mackerel Corp. issues 6%, 20-year bonds payable with a face value of $1,800,000. The bonds pay interest on February 28 and August 31. Mackerel Corp. amortizes bond discount by the straight-line method.

Requirements

1. If the market interest rate is 5% when Mackerel Corp. issues its bonds, will the bonds be priced at par, at a premium, or at a discount? Explain.
2. If the market interest rate is 7% when Mackerel Corp. issues its bonds, will the bonds be priced at par, at a premium, or at a discount? Explain.
3. Assume that the issue price of the bonds is 96. Journalize the following bonds payable transactions.
   a. Issuance of the bonds on February 28, 2016
   b. Payment of interest and amortization of the bond discount on August 31, 2016
   c. Accrual of interest and amortization of the bond discount on December 31, 2016, the year-end
   d. Payment of interest and amortization of the bond discount on February 28, 2017
4. Report interest payable and bonds payable as they would appear on the Mackerel Corp. balance sheet at December 31, 2016.

P9-75A. *(Learning Objective 2: Account for bonds payable at a discount; amortize by the straight-line method)*

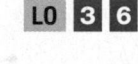

Requirements

1. Journalize the following transactions of Lamore Communications, Inc.:

2016		
Jan 1	Issued $3,000,000 of 6%, 10-year bonds payable at 94. Interest payment dates are July 1 and January 1.	
Jul 1	Paid semiannual interest and amortized bond discount by the straight-line method on the 6% bonds payable.	
Dec 31	Accrued semiannual interest expense and amortized the bond discount by the straight-line method on the 6% bonds payable.	
2017		
Jan 1	Paid semiannual interest.	
2026		
Jan 1	Paid the 6% bonds at maturity.	

2. At December 31, 2016, after all year-end adjustments, determine the carrying amount of Lamore Communications bonds payable, net.
3. For the six months ended July 1, 2016, determine the following for Lamore Communications, Inc.:
   a. Interest expense
   b. Cash interest paid
   What causes interest expense on the bonds to exceed cash interest paid?

P9-76A. *(Learning Objectives 3, 6: Analyze a company's long-term debt; report long-term debt on the balance sheet [effective-interest method])* The notes to the Mann Ltd. financial statements reported the following data on December 31, Year 1 (end of the fiscal year):

Note 6. Indebtedness

Bonds payable, 2% due on December 31, Year 8...	$4,000,000	
Less: Discount..	?	?
Notes payable, 6%, payable in $55,000 annual installments starting in Year 5...............................		330,000

Mann Ltd. amortizes bond discount by the effective-interest method and pays all interest amounts at December 31.

Requirements

1. Assume the market interest rate on January 1 of year 1, the date of issuance of the bonds, is 6%. Answer the following questions about Mann Ltd.'s long-term liabilities:
   a. Using the PV function in Excel, what is the issue price of the bonds?
   b. What is the maturity value of the 2% bonds?
   c. What is Mann Ltd.'s annual cash interest payment on the 2% bonds?
   d. What is the carrying amount of the 2% bonds at December 31, year 1?
2. Using Exhibit 9-4 as a model, prepare an amortization table through the maturity date for the 2% bonds. (Round all amounts to the nearest dollar.) How much is Mann Ltd.'s interest expense on the 2% bonds for the year ended December 31, Year 4?
3. Show how Mann Ltd. would report the 2% bonds payable and the 6% notes payable at December 31, Year 4.

LO **3** **6** **P9-77A.** *(Learning Objectives 3, 6: Issue convertible bonds at a discount, amortize by the effective-interest method, and convert bonds; report bonds payable on the balance sheet)* On December 31, 2016, Rugaboo Corp. issues 6%, 10-year convertible bonds payable with a maturity value of $4,000,000. The semiannual interest dates are June 30 and December 31. The market interest rate is 8%. Rugaboo Corp. amortizes bond discount by the effective-interest method.

Requirements

1. Use the PV function in Excel to calculate the issue price of the bonds.
2. Using Exhibit 9-4 as a model, prepare an effective-interest method amortization table for the term of the bonds.
3. Journalize the following transactions:
   a. Issuance of the bonds on December 31, 2016. Credit Convertible Bonds Payable.
   b. Payment of interest and amortization of the bond discount on June 30, 2017.
   c. Payment of interest and amortization of the bond discount on December 31, 2017.
   d. Conversion by the bondholders on July 1, 2018, of bonds with face value of $1,600,000 into 50,000 shares of Rugaboo Corp.'s $1-par common stock.
4. Show how Rugaboo Corp. would report the remaining bonds payable on its balance sheet at December 31, 2018.

LO **4** **P9-78A.** *(Learning Objective 4: Differentiate financing with debt vs. equity)* Mountainside Medical Goods is embarking on a massive expansion. Assume plans call for opening 20 new stores during the next two years. Each store is scheduled to be 30% larger than the company's existing locations, offering more items of inventory and with more elaborate displays. Management estimates that company operations will provide $1 million of the cash needed for expansion. Mountainside Medical must raise the remaining $4.5 million from outsiders.

The board of directors is considering obtaining the $4.5 million either through borrowing at 9% or by issuing an additional 500,000 shares of common stock. This year the company has earned $2.5 million before interest and taxes and has 500,000 shares of $1-par common stock outstanding. The market price of the company's stock is $9.00 per share. Assume that income before interest and taxes is expected to grow by 30% each year for the next two years. The company's marginal income tax rate is 20%.

Requirements

1. Use Excel to evaluate the effect of the above projected alternatives on net income and earnings per share two years from now.
2. Write a memo to Mountainside's management discussing the advantages and disadvantages of borrowing and of issuing common stock to raise the needed cash. Which method of raising the funds would you recommend?

LO **5** **6** **P9-79A.** *(Learning Objectives 5, 6: Report liabilities on the balance sheet; calculate the leverage ratio, debt ratio, and times-interest-earned ratio)* The accounting records of Brownfield Foods, Inc., include the following items at December 31, 2016:

Mortgage note payable,			Total assets	$4,600,000
current portion........................	$ 95,000		Accumulated depreciation,	
Projected pension			equipment	166,000
benefit obligation	455,000		Discount on bonds payable	
Bonds payable, long-term............	300,000		(all long-term)	23,000
Mortgage note payable,			Operating income...............	340,000
long-term	316,000		Equipment..........................	745,000
Bonds payable, current portion ...	200,000		Pension plan assets	
Interest expense..........................	226,000		(market value)................	405,000
			Interest payable..................	74,000

Requirements

1. Show how each relevant item would be reported on the Brownfield Foods, Inc., classified balance sheet, including headings and totals for current liabilities and long-term liabilities.
2. Answer the following questions about Brownfield Food's financial position at December 31, 2016:
   a. What is the carrying amount of the bonds payable (combine the current and long-term amounts)?
   b. Why is the interest-payable amount so much less than the amount of interest expense?
3. How many times did Brownfield Foods cover its interest expense during 2016?
4. Assume that all of the existing liabilities are included in the information provided. Calculate the leverage ratio and debt ratio of the company. Use year-end figures in place of averages where needed for the purpose of calculating ratios in this problem. Evaluate the health of the company from a leverage point of view. What other information would be helpful in making your evaluation?
5. Independent of your answer to (4), assume that Footnote 8 of the financial statements includes commitments for long-term operating leases over the next 15 years in the amount of $3,900,000. If the company had to capitalize these leases in 2016, how would it change the leverage ratio and the debt ratio? How would this impact your assessment of the company's health from a leverage point of view?

Group B

P9-80B. (*Learning Objective 1: Measure and report current liabilities*) Sea Spray Marine experienced these events during the current year.

  LO **1**

 a. December revenue totaled $130,000; and, in addition, Sea Spray collected sales tax of 5%. The tax amount will be sent to the state of Rhode Island early in January.
 b. On August 31, Sea Spray signed a six-month, 8% note payable to purchase a boat costing $80,000. The note requires payment of principal and interest at maturity.
 c. On August 31, Sea Spray received cash of $1,800 in advance for service revenue. This revenue will be earned evenly over six months.
 d. Revenues of $825,000 were covered by Sea Spray's service warranty. At January 1, estimated warranty payable was $11,400. During the year, Sea Spray recorded warranty expense of $33,000 and paid warranty claims of $34,500.
 e. Sea Spray owes $70,000 on a long-term note payable. At December 31, 6% interest for the year plus $25,000 of this principal are payable within one year.

Requirement

1. For each item, indicate the account and the related amount to be reported as a current liability on the Sea Spray Marine balance sheet at December 31.

P9-81B. (*Learning Objective 1: Record liability-related transactions*) The following transactions of Signature Music Company occurred during 2016 and 2017:

  LO **1**

2016	
Mar 3	Purchased a piano (inventory) for $70,000, signing a six-month, 10% note payable.
May 31	Borrowed $85,000 on a 5% note payable that calls for annual installment payments of $14,167 principal plus interest. Record the short-term note payable in a separate account from the long-term note payable.
Sep 3	Paid the six-month, 10% note at maturity.
Dec 31	Accrued warranty expense, which is estimated at 3% of sales of $193,000.
31	Accrued interest on the outstanding note payable.
2017	
May 31	Paid the first installment and interest for one year on the outstanding note payable.

Requirement

1. Record the transactions in Signature Music Company's journal. Explanations are not required.

LO 1 2

P9-82B. *(Learning Objectives 1, 2: Record bond transactions [at par]; report bonds payable on the balance sheet)* The board of directors of Laptops Plus authorizes the issue of $9,000,000 of 7%, 15-year bonds payable. The semiannual interest dates are May 31 and November 30. The bonds are issued on May 31, 2016, at par.

Requirements

1. Journalize the following transactions:
    a. Issuance of half of the bonds on May 31, 2016
    b. Payment of interest on November 30, 2016
    c. Accrual of interest on December 31, 2016
    d. Payment of interest on May 31, 2017
2. Report interest payable and bonds payable as they would appear on the Laptops Plus balance sheet at December 31, 2016.

LO 1 2 6

P9-83B. *(Learning Objectives 1, 2, 6: Issue bonds at a discount; amortize by the straight-line method; report bonds payable and accrued interest payable on the balance sheet)* On February 28, 2016, Marlin Corp. issues 8%, 10-year bonds payable with a face value of $900,000. The bonds pay interest on February 28 and August 31. Marlin Corp. amortizes bond discount by the straight-line method.

Requirements

1. If the market interest rate is 7% when Marlin Corp. issues its bonds, will the bonds be priced at par, at a premium, or at a discount? Explain.
2. If the market interest rate is 9% when Marlin Corp. issues its bonds, will the bonds be priced at par, at a premium, or at a discount? Explain.
3. Assume that the issue price of the bonds is 99. Journalize the following bond transactions.
    a. Issuance of the bonds on February 28, 2016
    b. Payment of interest and amortization of the bond discount on August 31, 2016
    c. Accrual of interest and amortization of the bond discount on December 31, 2016, the year-end
    d. Payment of interest and amortization of the bond discount on February 28, 2017
4. Report interest payable and bonds payable as they would appear on the Marlin Corp. balance sheet at December 31, 2016.

LO 2

P9-84B. *(Learning Objective 2: Account for bonds payable at a discount; amortize by the straight-line method)*

Requirements

1. Journalize the following transactions of Lamothe Communications, Inc.:

2016		
Jan	1	Issued $6,000,000 of 9%, 10-year bonds payable at 96. Interest payment dates are July 1 and January 1.
Jul	1	Paid semiannual interest and amortized the bond discount by the straight-line method on the 9% bonds payable.
Dec	31	Accrued semiannual interest expense and amortized the bond discount by the straight-line method on the 9% bonds payable.
2017		
Jan	1	Paid semiannual interest.
2026		
Jan	1	Paid the 9% bonds at maturity.

2. At December 31, 2016, after all year-end adjustments, determine the carrying amount of Lamothe Communications bonds payable, net.

3. For the six months ended July 1, 2016, determine the following for Lamothe Communications, Inc.:

    a. Interest expense

    b. Cash interest paid. What causes interest expense on the bonds to exceed cash interest paid?

P9-85B. *(Learning Objectives 3, 6: Analyze a company's long-term debt; report long-term debt on the balance sheet [effective-interest method])* The notes to the Friendship Ltd. financial statements reported the following data on December 31, Year 1 (end of the fiscal year):

```
Note 6. Indebtedness
    Bonds payable, 3% due December 31, Year 8 ........   $3,000,000
    Less: Discount .....................................        ?            ?
    Notes payable, 7%, payable in $50,000
        annual installments starting in Year 5 ..............          300,000
```

Friendship Ltd. amortizes bond discount by the effective-interest method and pays all interest amounts at December 31.

Requirements

1. Assume the market interest rate on January 1 of year 1, the date of issuance of the bonds, is 6%. Answer the following questions about Friendship Ltd.'s long-term liabilities:

    a. Using the PV function in Excel, what is the issue price of the bonds?

    b. What is the maturity value of the 3% bonds?

    c. What is Friendship Ltd.'s annual cash interest payment on the 3% bonds?

    d. What is the carrying amount of the 3% bonds at December 31, Year 1?

2. Using Exhibit 9-4 as a model, prepare an amortization table through the maturity date for the 3% bonds. (Round all amounts to the nearest dollar.) How much is Friendship Ltd.'s interest expense on the 3% bonds for the year ended December 31, Year 4?

3. Show how Friendship Ltd. would report the 3% bonds and the 7% notes payable at December 31, Year 4.

P9-86B. *(Learning Objectives 3, 6: Issue convertible bonds at a discount; amortize by the effective interest method; convert bonds; report bonds payable on the balance sheet)* On December 31, 2016, Zenith Corp. issues 7%, 10-year convertible bonds payable with a maturity value of $2,000,000. The semiannual interest dates are June 30 and December 31. The market interest rate is 9%. Zenith Corp. amortizes bond discount by the effective-interest method.

Requirements

1. Use the PV function in Excel to calculate the issue price of the bonds.

2. Using Exhibit 9-4 as a model, prepare an effective-interest method amortization table for the term of the bonds.

3. Journalize the following transactions:

    a. Issuance of the bonds on December 31, 2016. Credit Convertible Bonds Payable.

    b. Payment of interest and amortization of the bond discount on June 30, 2017.

    c. Payment of interest and amortization of the bond discount on December 31, 2017.

    d. Conversion by the bondholders on July 1, 2018, of bonds with face value of $800,000 into 70,000 shares of Zenith Corp. $1-par common stock.

4. Show how Zenith Corp. would report the remaining bonds payable on its balance sheet at December 31, 2018.

P9-87B. *(Learning Objective 4: Differentiate financing with debt vs. equity)* Summit Medical Goods is embarking on a massive expansion. Assume the plans call for opening 20 new stores during the next two years. Each store is scheduled to be 30% larger than the company's existing locations, offering more items of inventory and with more elaborate displays. Management estimates that company operations will provide $1.0 million of the cash needed for expansion. Summit Medical must raise the remaining $4.75 million from outsiders.

The board of directors is considering obtaining the $4.75 million either through borrowing at 3% or by issuing an additional 100,000 shares of common stock. This year the company has earned $1.5 million before interest and taxes and has 100,000 shares of $1-par common stock outstanding. The market price of the company's stock is $47.50 per share. Assume that income before interest and taxes is expected to grow by 10% each year for the next two years. The company's marginal income tax rate is 20%.

Requirements

1. Use Excel to evaluate the effect of the above projected alternatives on net income and earnings per share two years from now.
2. Write a memo to Summit's management discussing the advantages and disadvantages of borrowing and of issuing common stock to raise the needed cash. Which method of raising the funds would you recommend?

 **P9-88B.** *(Learning Objectives 5, 6: Report liabilities on the balance sheet; calculate the leverage ratio, debt ratio, and times-interest-earned ratio)* The accounting records of Brillhart Foods, Inc., include the following items at December 31, 2016:

Mortgage note payable,			Total assets	$4,600,000
current portion........................	$	98,000	Accumulated depreciation,	
Projected pension			equipment	168,000
benefit obligation		470,000	Discount on bonds payable	
Bonds payable, long-term............		300,000	(all long-term)	21,000
Mortgage note payable,			Operating income...............	390,000
long-term		312,000	Equipment..........................	745,000
Bonds payable, current portion ...		200,000	Pension plan assets	
Interest expense...........................		223,000	(market value).................	420,000
			Interest payable	75,000

Requirements

1. Show how each relevant item would be reported on the Brillhart Foods, Inc., classified balance sheet, including headings and totals for current liabilities and long-term liabilities.
2. Answer the following questions about Brillhart Food's financial position at December 31, 2016:
   a. What is the carrying amount of the bonds payable (combine the current and long-term amounts)?
   b. Why is the interest-payable amount so much less than the amount of interest expense?
3. How many times did Brillhart Foods cover its interest expense during 2016?
4. Assume that all of the existing liabilities are included in the information provided. Calculate the leverage ratio and debt ratio of the company. Use year-end figures in place of averages where needed for the purpose of calculating ratios in this problem. Evaluate the health of the company from a leverage point of view. What other information would be helpful in making your evaluation?
5. Independent of your answer to (4), assume that Footnote 8 of the financial statements includes commitments for long-term operating leases over the next 15 years in the amount of $3,800,000. If the company had to capitalize these leases in 2016, how would it change the leverage ratio and the debt ratio? How would this impact your assessment of the company's health from a leverage point of view?

Challenge Exercise and Problem

E9-89. *(Learning Objectives 1, 4, 6: Report current and long-term liabilities; evaluate leverage)* The top management of Parker Marketing Services examines the following company accounting records at August 29, immediately before the end of the year, August 31:

Total current assets.....................	$ 324,900
Noncurrent assets........................	1,074,000
	$1,398,900
Total current liabilities................	$ 173,700
Noncurrent liabilities	245,500
Stockholders' equity....................	979,700
	$1,398,900

1. Suppose Parker's management wants to achieve a current ratio of 2.8. How much in current liabilities should Parker pay off within the next two days in order to achieve its goal?
2. Calculate Parker's leverage ratio and debt ratio. Use year-end figures in place of averages where needed for the purpose of calculating ratios in this exercise. Evaluate the company's debt position. Is it low, high, or about average? What other information might help you to make a decision?

P9-90. *(Learning Objective 4: Understand how structuring debt transactions can affect a company)* The Organic Soda Company reported the following comparative information at December 31, 2016, and December 31, 2015 (amounts in millions and adapted):

	2016	2015
Current assets..	$20,900	$16,700
Total assets	72,800	46,500
Current liabilities	18,300	12,900
Total stockholders' equity	30,500	26,100
Net sales...	35,700	30,400
Net income..	11,312	6,510

Requirements

1. Calculate the following ratios for 2016 and 2015:
   a. Current ratio
   b. Debt ratio
2. During 2016, The Organic Soda Company issued $1,840 million of long-term debt that was used to retire short-term debt. What would the current ratio and debt ratio have been if this transaction had not been made?
3. The Organic Soda Company reports that its lease payments under operating leases will total $940 million in the future and $250 million will occur in the next year (2017). What would the current ratio and debt ratio have been in 2016 if these leases had been capitalized?

APPLY YOUR KNOWLEDGE

Decision Cases

Case 1. *(Learning Objective 4: Explore an actual bankruptcy; calculate leverage ratio, ROA, debt ratio, and times-interest-earned ratio)* In 2002, **Enron Corporation** filed for Chapter 11 bankruptcy protection, shocking the business community: How could a company this large and this successful go bankrupt? This case explores the causes and the effects of Enron's bankruptcy.

At December 31, 2000, and for the four years ended on that date, Enron reported the following (amounts in millions):

Balance Sheet (summarized)				
Total assets			$65,503	
Total liabilities			54,033	
Total stockholders' equity			11,470	

Income Statements (excerpts)				
	2000	1999	1998	1997
Net income	$ 979*	$893	$703	$105
Revenues	100,789			

*Operating income = $1,953
Interest expense = $838

Unknown to investors and lenders, Enron also controlled hundreds of partnerships that owed vast amounts of money. These special-purpose entities (SPEs) did not appear on the Enron financial statements. Assume that the SPEs' assets totaled $7,000 million and their liabilities stood at $6,900 million; assume a 10% interest rate on these liabilities.

During the four-year period up to December 31, 2000, Enron's stock price shot up from $17.50 to $90.56. Enron used its escalating stock price to finance the purchase of the SPEs by guaranteeing lenders that Enron would give them Enron stock if the SPEs could not pay their loans.

In 2001, the SEC launched an investigation into Enron's accounting practices. It was alleged that Enron should have been including the SPEs in its financial statements all along. Enron then restated net income for years up to 2000, wiping out nearly $600 million of total net income (and total assets) for this four-year period. Assume that $300 million of this loss applied to 2000. Enron's stock price tumbled, and the guarantees to the SPEs' lenders added millions to Enron's liabilities (assume the full amount of the SPEs' debt). To make matters worse, the assets of the SPEs lost much of their value; assume that their market value is only $500 million.

Requirements

1. Compute the debt ratio that Enron reported at the end of 2000. By using the DuPont Model, which we discussed in Chapter 7 (page 402), compute Enron's return on total assets (ROA) for 2000. For this purpose, use only total assets at the end of 2000, rather than the average of 1999 and 2000.
2. Compute Enron's leverage ratio for 2000. Use total assets and total stockholders' equity at the end of 2000. Now compute Enron's return on equity (ROE) by multiplying the ROA computed in Part 1 by the leverage ratio. Can you see anything unusual in these ratios that might have caused you to question them? Why or why not?
3. Add the asset and liability information about the SPEs to the reported amounts provided in the table. Recompute all ratios after including the SPEs in Enron's financial statements. Also compute Enron's times-interest-earned ratio both ways for 2000. Assume that the changes to Enron's financial position occurred during 2000.
4. Why does it appear that Enron failed to include the SPEs in its financial statements? How do you view Enron after including the SPEs in the company's financial statements? (Challenge)

LO 4 **Case 2.** *(Learning Objective 4: Analyze alternative ways of raising $5 million)* Business is going well for **Park 'N Fly**, the company that operates remote parking lots near major airports. The board of directors of this family-owned company believes that Park 'N Fly could earn an additional $1.5 million income before interest and taxes by expanding into new markets. However, the $5 million that the business needs for growth cannot be raised within the family. The directors, who strongly wish to retain family control of the company, must consider issuing securities to outsiders. The directors are considering three financing plans.

Plan A is to borrow at 6%. Plan B is to issue 100,000 shares of common stock. Plan C is to issue 100,000 shares of nonvoting, $3.75 preferred stock ($3.75 is the annual dividend paid on each share of preferred stock).[5] Park 'N Fly presently has net income of $3.5 million and 1 million shares of common stock outstanding. The company's income tax rate is 35%.

Requirements

1. Prepare an analysis to determine which plan will result in the highest earnings per share of common stock.
2. Recommend a plan to the board of directors. Give your reasons.

Ethical Issues

Issue 1. Microsoft Corporation is the defendant in numerous lawsuits claiming unfair trade practices. Microsoft has strong incentives not to disclose these contingent liabilities. However, GAAP requires that companies report their contingent liabilities.

Requirements

1. Why would a company prefer not to disclose its contingent liabilities?
2. Identify the parties involved in the decision and the potential consequences to each.
3. Analyze the issue of whether to report contingent liabilities from lawsuits from the following standpoints:
   a. Economic
   b. Legal
   c. Ethical
4. What impact will future changes in accounting standards, both at the U.S. level and the international level, likely have on the issue of disclosure of loss contingencies?

Issue 2. When is a lease a capital idea? Laurie Gocker, Inc., entered into a lease arrangement with Nathan Morgan Leasing Corporation for an industrial machine. Morgan's primary business is leasing. The cash purchase price of the machine is $1,000,000. Its economic life is six years.

Gocker's balance sheet reflects total assets of $10 million and total liabilities of $7.5 million. Among the liabilities is a $2.5 million long-term note outstanding at Last National Bank. The note carries a restrictive covenant that requires the company's debt ratio to be no higher than 75%. The company's revenues have been falling of late and the shareholders are concerned about profitability.

Gocker and Morgan are engaging in negotiations for terms of the lease. Some other relevant facts are as follows:

1. Morgan wants to take possession of the machine at the end of the initial lease term.
2. The term may run from four to five years, at Gocker's discretion.
3. Morgan estimates the machine will have no residual value, and Gocker will not purchase it at the end of the lease term.
4. The present value of minimum lease payments on the machine is $890,000.

Requirements

1. What is (are) the ethical issue(s) in this case?
2. Who are the stakeholders? Analyze the consequences for each stakeholder from the following standpoints: (a) economic, (b) legal, and (c) ethical.
3. How should Gocker structure the lease agreement?
4. As of the date of this text, the FASB and IASB have issued a joint exposure draft of a new standard on long-term leases that will require companies to capitalize most leases like this one. How will the analysis of this case change when this standard is issued?

---

[5]For a discussion of preferred stock, see Chapter 10.

Focus on Financials | Apple Inc.

(Learning Objectives 1, 2, 3, 4, 5, 6: Analyze current and long-term liabilities; evaluate debt-paying ability)

Refer to **Apple Inc.**'s consolidated financial statements in Appendix A and online in the filings section of **http://www.sec.gov**.

Requirements

1. Did accounts payable for Apple Inc., increase or decrease in 2014? Calculate accounts payable turnover for 2014. How many days does it take Apple Inc. to pay an average account payable? Comment on the length of the period in days.
2. Examine Note 5—Income Taxes—in the Notes to Consolidated Financial Statements. Income tax provision is another title for income tax expense. What was Apple Inc.'s income tax provision in 2014? Is the income tax provision likely to be equal to the amount Apple Inc. paid for its taxes in 2014? Why or why not? What was the company's effective tax rate in 2014?
3. Examine Note 6—Debt. Did Apple Inc., borrow more or pay off more long-term debt during 2014? How can you tell? What was the company's effective interest rate on its long-term debt? Why do you think this rate was so low? (Challenge)
4. Examine Note 10—Commitments and Contingencies—in the Notes to Consolidated Financial Statements. Describe some of Apple Inc.'s commitments and contingent liabilities as of September 27, 2014. Are any of these amounts included in the numbers in the balance sheet line items?
5. How would you rate Apple Inc.'s overall debt position—risky, safe, or average? Compute three ratios at September 27, 2014, and September 28, 2013, that help answer this question.

Focus on Analysis | Under Armour, Inc.

(Learning Objectives 1, 2, 3, 4, 5, 6: Analyze current liabilities and long-term debt) Refer to **Under Armour, Inc.'s,** consolidated financial statements in Appendix B and online in the filings section of **http://www.sec.gov**. These financial statements report a number of liabilities.

Requirements

1. The current liability section of Under Armour, Inc.'s, Consolidated Balance Sheet as of December 31, 2014, lists five different liabilities. List them and give a brief description of each.
2. Under Armour, Inc.'s current liability, revolving credit facility, was reduced to zero as of December 31, 2014. Refer to Note 6—Credit Facility and Long Term Debt. Describe what revolving credit facility means and why it was reduced to zero in 2014.
3. For 2014, calculate accounts payable turnover, both as a ratio and in number of days. Describe what this ratio means. Also compute the following other ratios for 2014 (if you have already computed them as part of your work in previous chapters, refer to them): (1) current ratio, (2) quick ratio, (3) days' sales to collection for accounts receivable, and (4) inventory turnover (express in days by dividing 365 by the turnover). How do you think you would combine the information in these ratios to assess Under Armour, Inc.'s, current debt-paying ability? (Challenge)
4. Refer to Note 6—Credit Facility and Long Term Debt, under *Other Long Term Debt*. What is Under Armour's weighted average interest rate on outstanding borrowings for 2014? How much in long-term debt obligations does Under Armour currently owe for 2015?
5. Refer to the note entitled "Commitments and Contingencies." Describe the contents of this footnote. Are any of these items included in the liabilities recorded in either the current or long-term section of the balance sheet? Why or why not?
6. Refer to Note 7—Commitments and Contingencies, under *Obligations Under Operating Leases*. Describe the company's commitments under operating lease arrangements. Calculate the impact on Under Armour, Inc.'s, ROA and debt ratios if the company's operating lease commitments as of the end of 2014 were capitalized.

7. For 2014, compute the company's debt ratio, leverage ratio, and times-interest-earned ratio. Would you evaluate Under Armour, Inc., as risky, safe, or average in terms of these ratios?

8. Access Under Armour, Inc.'s, most recent financial statements from http://www.sec.gov. Use the same method as described in the chapter opening for Southwest Airlines. What has happened to Under Armour, Inc.'s, debt position since the end of 2014? (Challenge)

Group Projects

Project 1. Consider three different businesses:
1. A bank
2. A magazine publisher
3. A department store

For each business, list all of its liabilities—both current and long-term. Then compare the three lists to identify the liabilities that the three businesses have in common. Also identify the liabilities that are unique to each type of business.

Project 2. Alcenon Corporation leases the majority of the assets that it uses in operations. Alcenon prefers operating leases (versus capital leases) in order to keep the lease liability off its balance sheet and maintain a low debt ratio.

Alcenon is negotiating a 10-year lease on an asset with an expected useful life of 15 years. The lease requires Alcenon to make 10 annual lease payments of $20,000 each, with the first payment due at the beginning of the lease term. The leased asset has a market value of $135,180. The lease agreement specifies no transfer of title to the lessee and includes no bargain purchase option.

Write a report for Alcenon's management to explain what conditions must be present for Alcenon to be able to account for this lease as an operating lease.

Quick Check Answers

1. *b*	5. *e*	12. *d*
2. *b*	6. *e*	13. *d*
3. *a*	7. *d*	14. *a*
4. *c* [1,100 × 0.03 × $45 = warranty expense of $1,485; repaired $45 × 7 = $315; year-end liability = $1,170 ($1,485 − $315)]	8. *c*	15. *c*
	9. *e*	16. *a*
	10. *d*	17. *d* [$241,117 + ($8,883/10)]
	11. *a*	

Amortization schedule for Quick Check Questions 12–17

A	B	C	D	E	F
	Int Pmt (0.0325 × Maturity Value)	Interest Expense (0.035 × Preceding Bond Carrying Value)	Discount Amortization (C − B)	Discount Account Balance (Preceding E − D)	Bond Carrying Amount ($250,000 − E)
1/1/2016				8,883	241,117
7/1/2016	8,125	8,439	314	8,569	241,431
1/1/2017	8,125	8,450	325	8,244	241,756
7/1/2017	8,125	8,461	336	7,908	242,092

10 Stockholders' Equity

Ian Dagnall/Alamy

SPOTLIGHT | The Home Depot: Building Toward Success

Founded in 1978, The Home Depot, Inc., is the world's largest home improvement specialty retailer. The Home Depot has more than 2,200 retail stores in the United States, its territories, Canada, and Mexico. The Home Depot's common stock is traded on the New York Stock Exchange (NYSE) under the stock symbol HD. The company is included in the Dow Jones Industrial Average and Standard & Poor's 500 Index.

During its 2014 fiscal year, The Home Depot reported 1.441 billion customer transactions that produced net sales of $83.2 billion, up 5.5% from fiscal year 2013; comparable store sales increased 5.3%. Virtually all of these sales were for cash. The average ticket price per customer in fiscal 2014 was $57.87, up 2% from 2013. This healthy increase in sales occurred in spite of a widely publicized security breach in the company's payment data system, causing them to incur millions of dollars in expenses to investigate and fix the problem. Basic Earnings per share on its common stock increased 25.4% to $4.74 per share. The company benefited from a continued strong recovery in the U.S. housing market in 2014.

Based on these strong earnings and cash flows, The Home Depot was able to increase its quarterly dividend at the end of 2014 to $0.59 per share, the fourth increase in as many years and the 116th consecutive quarter that the company has paid dividends. The company has a targeted dividend payout ratio (dividends ÷ earnings) of 50%. In 2014 this ratio was 50.8%. From February 2002 until February 2015, the company has returned more than $53.1 billion in cash to shareholders through repurchases of its stock. The company has a goal to maintain a high return on stockholders' equity (ROE), which reached 24.9%

for the year ended February 1, 2015. Below, you'll find the company's Consolidated Balance Sheets as of February 1, 2015 and February 2, 2014. ●

	A	B	C
	A1 ⬍		
1	**The Home Depot, Inc.** **Consolidated Balance Sheets (Adapted)**		
2	(In Millions, unless otherwise specified)	**Feb. 1, 2015**	**Feb. 2, 2014**
3	Total Current Assets	$ 15,302	$ 15,279
4	Property and Equipment, at cost	38,513	39,064
5	Less Accumulated Depreciation and Amortization	(15,793)	(15,716)
6	Net Property and Equipment	22,720	23,348
7	Goodwill	1,353	1,289
8	Other Assets	571	602
9	Total Assets	$ 39,946	$ 40,518
10	Total Current Liabilities	$ 11,269	$ 10,749
11	Long-Term Debt, excluding current installments	16,869	14,691
12	Other Long-Term Liabilities	1,844	2,042
13	Deferred Income Taxes	642	514
14	Total Liabilities	30,624	27,996
15	**STOCKHOLDERS' EQUITY**		
16	Common Stock, par value $0.05; authorized: 10 billion shares;		
17	issued: 1.768 billion shares at February 1, 2015 and 1.761		
18	billion shares at February 2, 2014; outstanding: 1.307		
19	billion shares at February 1, 2015 and 1.380 billion shares		
20	at February 2, 2014	88	88
21	Paid-In Capital	8,885	8,402
22	Retained Earnings	26,995	23,180
23	Accumulated Other Comprehensive Income (loss)	(452)	46
24	Treasury Stock, at cost, 461 million shares at February 1, 2015		
25	and 381 million shares at February 2, 2014	(26,194)	(19,194)
26	**Total Stockholders' Equity**	9,322	12,522
27	Total Liabilities and Stockholders' Equity	$ 39,946	$ 40,518
28			
29			

In this chapter, we focus on stockholders' equity. We'll show you how to account for the issuance of corporate capital stock to investors. We'll also cover the other elements of stockholders' equity—Additional Paid-in Capital, Retained Earnings, and Treasury Stock, plus dividends and stock splits. We'll conclude the chapter with a discussion of the Statement of Stockholders' Equity, in which we analyze the changes in all of the accounts in the stockholders' equity section of the balance sheet. By the time you finish this chapter, you may be ready to stop by a Home Depot store to get help in building something for yourself. Or you may find that you want to buy some stock in The Home Depot or one of its competitors.

In this chapter, we discuss some of the decisions a company faces when

▶ issuing stock,
▶ buying back its stock, and
▶ paying dividends.

In addition, we discuss the factors that influence the evaluation of profitability in relation to stockholders' investment.

Let's begin with the organization of a corporation.

LEARNING | OBJECTIVES

1 **Explain** the features of a corporation

2 **Account** for the issuance of stock

3 **Show** how treasury stock affects a company

4 **Account** for retained earnings, dividends, and splits

5 **Use** stock values in decision making

6 **Report** stockholders' equity transactions in the financial statements

》 *Try It* in *Excel*®

You can access the most current annual report of The Home Depot, Inc., in Excel format at **http://www.sec.gov**. Using the "FILINGS" link on the toolbar at the top of the home page, select "Company Filings Search." This will take you to the "Edgar Company Filings" page. Type "Home Depot" in the company name box, and select "Search." This will produce the "EDGAR Search Results" page showing the company name. Click on the "CIK" link beside the company name. This will pull up a list of the reports the company has filed with the SEC. Under the "Filing Type" box, type "10-K" and click the search box. Form 10-K is the SEC form for the company's annual report. Find the year that you wish to view. Click on the "Interactive Data" box, which takes you to the "View Filing Data" page. Find and click on the "View Excel Document" link at the top of this page. You may choose to either open or download the Excel files containing the company's most recent financial statements.

EXPLAIN THE FEATURES OF A CORPORATION

1 **Explain** the features of a corporation

Anyone starting a business must decide how to organize the company. Corporations differ from proprietorships and partnerships in several ways.

Separate Legal Entity. A corporation is a business entity formed under state law. It is a distinct entity—an artificial person that exists apart from its owners, the **stockholders**, or **shareholders**. The corporation has many of the rights that a person has. For example, a corporation may buy, own, and sell property. Assets and liabilities in the business belong to the corporation and not to its owners. The corporation may enter into contracts, sue, and be sued.

Nearly all large companies, such as The Home Depot, **Toyota**, and **Walmart**, are corporations. Their full names may include *Corporation* or *Incorporated* (abbreviated *Corp.* and *Inc.*) to indicate that they are corporations—like Intel Corporation and The Home Depot, Inc., for example. Corporations can also use the word *Company*, such as Southwest Airlines Company.

Continuous Life and Transferability of Ownership. Corporations have *continuous lives* regardless of changes in their ownership. The stockholders of a corporation may buy more of the stock, sell the stock to another person, give it away, or bequeath it in a will. The transfer of the stock from one person to another does not affect the continuity of the corporation. In contrast, proprietorships and partnerships terminate when their ownership changes.

Limited Liability. Stockholders have **limited liability** for the corporation's debts. They have no personal obligation for corporate liabilities. The most that a stockholder can lose on an investment in a corporation's stock is the cost of the investment. Limited liability is one of the most attractive features of the corporate form of organization. It enables corporations to raise more capital from a wider group of investors than proprietorships and partnerships can. By contrast, proprietors and partners are personally liable for all the debts of their businesses.[1]

Separation of Ownership and Management. Stockholders own the corporation, but the *board of directors*—elected by the stockholders—appoints officers to manage the business. Thus, stockholders may invest $1,000 or $1 million in the corporation without having to manage it.

Management's goal is to maximize the firm's value for the stockholders. But the separation between owners and managers may create problems. Without safeguards, corporate officers may try to run the business for their own benefit and not for the stockholders. They may engage in fraudulent financial reporting or misappropriate assets. Proper corporate governance practices, which include monitoring by internal and external auditors, as well as independent boards, can help prevent this type of activity.

Corporate Taxation. Corporations are separate taxable entities. They pay several taxes not borne by proprietorships or partnerships, including an annual franchise tax levied by the state. The franchise tax keeps the corporate charter in force. Corporations also pay federal and state income taxes.

Corporate earnings are subject to **double taxation** on their income to the extent they are distributed to shareholders in the form of dividends.

- First, corporations pay income taxes on their corporate income.
- Then stockholders pay income tax on the cash dividends received from corporations. Proprietorships and partnerships pay no business income tax. Instead, the business tax falls solely on the owners.

Government Regulation. Because stockholders have only limited liability for corporation debts, outsiders doing business with the corporation can look no further than the corporation if it fails to pay. To protect a corporation's creditors and stockholders, both federal and state governments monitor corporations. The regulations mainly ensure that corporations disclose the information that investors and creditors need to make informed decisions. Accounting provides much of this information.

Exhibit 10-1 summarizes the advantages and disadvantages of the corporate form of business organization.

Exhibit 10-1 | Advantages and Disadvantages of a Corporation

Advantages	Disadvantages
1. Can raise more capital than a proprietorship or partnership can	1. Separation of ownership and management
2. Continuous life	2. Double taxation of distributed profits
3. Ease of transferring ownership	3. Government regulation
4. Limited liability of stockholders	

Organizing a Corporation

The creation of a corporation begins when its organizers, called the *incorporators*, obtain a charter from the state. The charter includes the authorization for the corporation to issue a certain number of shares of stock. A share of stock is the basic unit of ownership for a corporation. The incorporators

- pay fees,
- sign the charter,
- file documents with the state, and
- agree to a set of **bylaws**, which act as the constitution for governing the company.

---

[1]Unless the business is organized as a limited-liability company (LLC) or a limited-liability partnership (LLP).

The corporation then comes into existence.

Ultimate control of the corporation rests with the stockholders, who elect a **board of directors** that sets company policy and appoints officers. The board elects a **chairperson**, who usually is the most powerful person in the organization. The chairperson of the board of directors often has the title chief executive officer (CEO). The board also designates the **president**, who is the chief operating officer (COO) in charge of day-to-day operations. Most corporations also have vice presidents in charge of sales, manufacturing, accounting and finance (the chief financial officer, or CFO), and other key areas. Exhibit 10-2 shows the authority structure in a corporation.

Exhibit 10-2 | Authority Structure of a Corporation

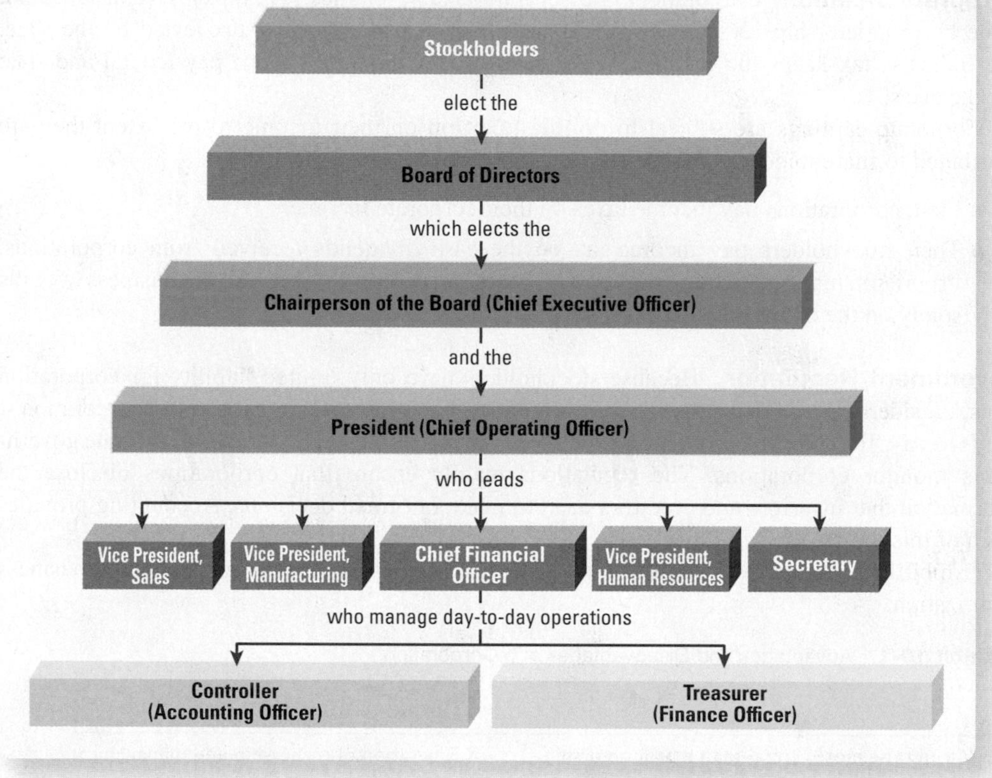

Stockholders' Rights

Ownership of stock entitles stockholders to four basic rights, as follows, unless a specific right is withheld by agreement with the stockholders:

1. *Vote.* The right to participate in management by voting on matters that come before the stockholders. This is the stockholder's sole voice in the management of the corporation. A stockholder gets one vote for each share of stock owned.

2. *Dividends.* The right to receive a proportionate part of any dividend. Each share of stock in a particular class receives an equal dividend.

3. *Liquidation.* The right to receive a proportionate share of any assets remaining after the corporation pays its liabilities in liquidation. Liquidation means to go out of business, sell the assets, pay all liabilities, and distribute any remaining cash to the owners.

4. *Preemption.* The right to maintain one's proportionate ownership in the corporation. Suppose you own 5% of a corporation's stock. If the corporation issues 100,000 new shares, it must offer you the opportunity to buy 5% (5,000) of the new shares. This right, called the *preemptive right*, is usually withheld from the stockholders.

Stockholders' Equity

As we saw in Chapter 1, **stockholders' equity** represents the stockholders' ownership interest in the assets of a corporation. Stockholders' equity is divided into two main parts:

1. **Paid-in capital**, also called **contributed capital**. This is the amount of stockholders' equity the stockholders have contributed to the corporation. Paid-in capital includes the stock accounts and any additional paid-in capital.

2. **Retained earnings**. This is the amount of stockholders' equity the corporation has earned through profitable operations and has not used for dividends.

Corporations report stockholders' equity by source. They report paid-in capital separately from retained earnings because most states prohibit the declaration of cash dividends from paid-in capital. Thus, cash dividends are declared from retained earnings.

The owners' equity of a corporation is divided into shares of **stock**. A corporation issues *stock certificates* to its owners when the company receives their investment in the business—usually cash. Because stock represents the corporation's capital, it is often called *capital stock*. The basic unit of capital stock is a *share*. A corporation may issue a stock certificate for any number of shares—1, 100, or any other number—but the total number of *authorized* shares is limited by charter. Exhibit 10-3 shows a stock certificate for a hypothetical corporation's common stock.

Exhibit 10-3 | Hypothetical Corporate Stock Certificate

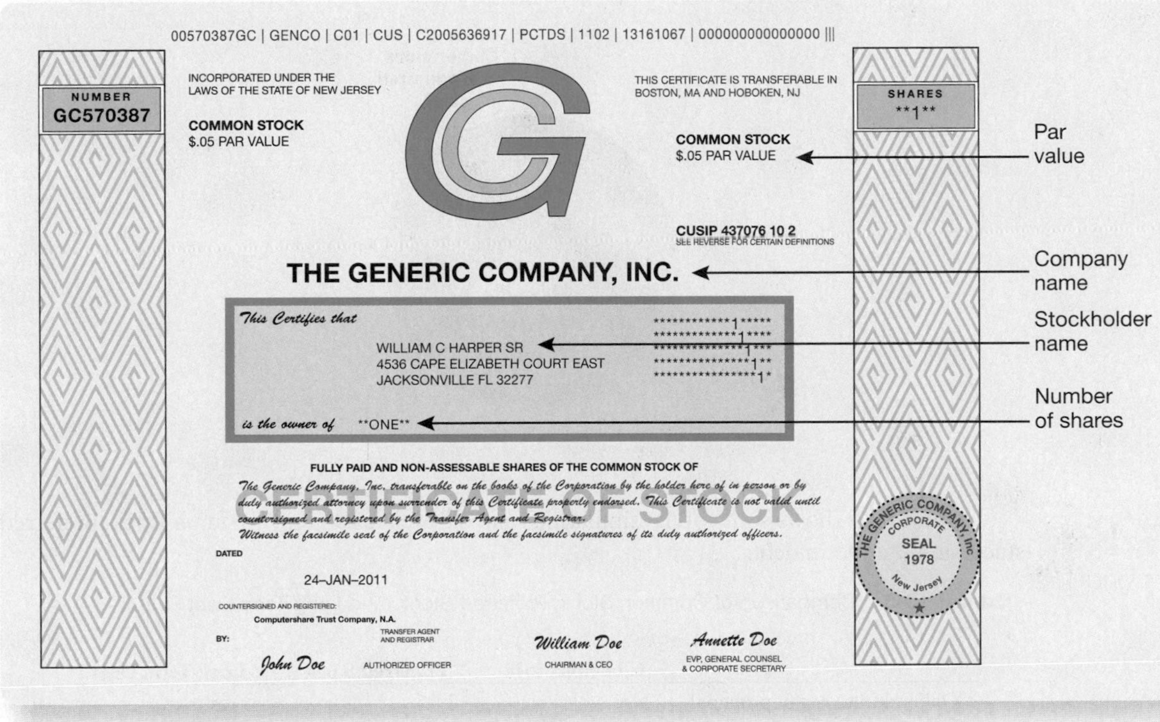

Stock in the hands of a stockholder is said to be *outstanding*. The total number of shares of stock outstanding at any time represents 100% ownership of the corporation.

Classes of Stock

Corporations issue different types of stock to appeal to a variety of investors. The stock of a corporation may be either

- common or preferred, and
- par or no-par.

Common and Preferred. Every corporation issues **common stock**, the basic form of capital stock. Unless designated otherwise, the word *stock* is understood to mean "common stock." Common stockholders have the four basic rights of stock ownership, unless a right is specifically withheld. The common stockholders are the owners of the corporation. They stand to benefit the most if the corporation succeeds because they take the most risk by investing in common stock.

Preferred stock gives its owners certain advantages over common stockholders. Preferred stockholders receive dividends before the common stockholders and they also receive assets before the common stockholders if the corporation liquidates. Owners of preferred stock also have the four basic stockholder rights, unless a right is specifically denied. Companies may issue different classes of preferred stock (Class A and Class B or Series A and Series B, for example). Each class of stock is recorded in a separate account. In most cases, the most preferred stockholders can expect to earn on their investments is a fixed dividend.

Preferred stock is a hybrid between common stock and long-term debt. Like interest on debt, preferred stock pays a fixed dividend. But, unlike interest on debt, the dividend is not required to be paid unless the board of directors declares the dividend. Also, companies have no obligation to pay back true preferred stock. Preferred stock that must be redeemed (paid back) by the corporation is a liability masquerading as a stock.

Preferred stock is rare. A recent survey of 600 corporations reveals that only 9% of them have issued preferred stock (Exhibit 10-4). In contrast, all corporations issue common stock. The balance sheet of The Home Depot (p. 565) does not reflect any preferred stock issued.

Exhibit 10-4 | Percentage of Corporations Issuing Preferred Stock

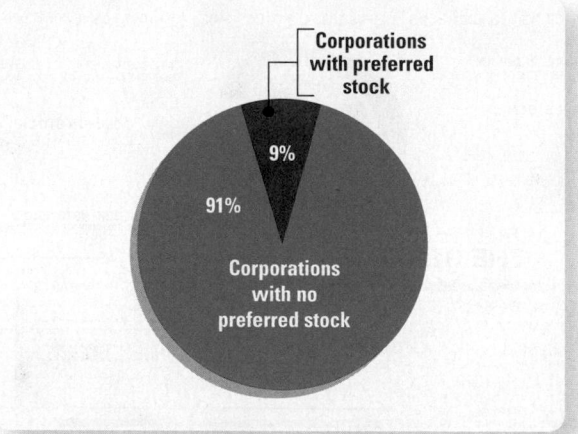

Exhibit 10-5 shows some of the similarities and differences among common stock, preferred stock, and long-term debt.

Exhibit 10-5 | Comparison of Common Stock, Preferred Stock, and Long-Term Debt

	Common Stock	Preferred Stock	Long-Term Debt
1. Obligation to repay principal	No	No	Yes
2. Dividends/interest	Dividends are not tax-deductible	Dividends are not tax-deductible	Interest expense is tax-deductible
3. Obligation to pay dividends/interest	Only after declaration	Only after declaration	At fixed rates and dates

Par Value and No-Par. Stock may be par-value stock or no-par stock. **Par value** is an arbitrary amount assigned by a company to a share of its stock upon original issuance. Most companies set the par value of their common stock low to avoid legal difficulties from issuing their stock below par. Most states require companies to maintain a minimum amount of stockholders' equity for the protection of creditors, and this minimum is often called the corporation's *legal capital*. For corporations with par-value stock, **legal capital** is the par value of the shares issued.

The par value of **PepsiCo** common stock is $0.0166 (1⅔ cents) per share. **Best Buy**'s and **Southwest Airlines Company**'s common stock all carry a par value of $1 per share. The Home Depot's common stock carries a par value of $0.05 per share.

No-par stock does not have a par value per share. Some no-par stock has a **stated value**, which makes it similar to par-value stock. The stated value is an arbitrary amount similar to par value. In a recent survey, only 9% of the companies had no-par stock outstanding. Krispy Kreme Doughnuts, Inc. and Sony Corporation have no-par stock.

ACCOUNT FOR THE ISSUANCE OF STOCK

Large corporations such as **The Home Depot, Inc., Google, Inc.,** and **Microsoft** sometimes need to raise huge amounts of money for specific purposes, such as operations or paying off long-term debt. The first time a private company issues stock to the public, it makes an **initial public offering (IPO)**. Corporations may sell stock directly to the stockholders or use the service of an *underwriter*, such as the investment banking firms **JP Morgan Chase & Co.** and **Goldman Sachs**. To attract investors, companies often advertise the issuance of their stock in the *Wall Street Journal* or the *Financial Times*. Let's see how a stock issuance works.

2 **Account** for the issuance of stock

Common Stock

Common Stock at Par. Assume that The Home Depot needs to raise $100 million through issuance of stock. Suppose The Home Depot's common stock had carried a par value equal to its issuance price of $10 per share. The entry for issuance of 10 million shares of stock at par would be

	A	B	C	D
	A1			
1	Jan 8	Cash (10,000,000 × $10)	100,000,000	
2		Common Stock		100,000,000
3		To issue common stock.		
4				

The Home Depot's assets and stockholders' equity increase by the same amount.

Assets	=	Liabilities	+	Stockholders' Equity
+ 100,000,000	=	0		+ 100,000,000

Common Stock Above Par. Most corporations set par value low and issue common stock for a price above par. Rather than $10 as in the assumed example above, The Home Depot's common stock has a par value of $0.05 per share. The $9.95 difference between issue price ($10) and par value ($0.05) is Paid-in Capital. Other names for this account are Additional Paid-in Capital or Paid-in Capital in Excess of Par. Both the par value of the stock and the additional amount are part of paid-in capital.

Because the entity is dealing with its own stockholders, a sale of stock does not result in gain, income, or profit to the corporation. This situation illustrates one of the fundamentals of accounting:

> **A company neither earns a profit nor incurs a loss when it sells its stock to, or buys its stock from, its own stockholders.**

With par value of $0.05 per share, The Home Depot's actual entry to record the issuance of common stock looked something like this:

	A	B	C	D
	A1			
1	Jul 23	Cash (10,000,000 × $10)	100,000,000	
2		Common Stock (10,000,000 × $0.05)		500,000
3		Paid-in Capital		
4		(10,000,000 × $9.95)		99,500,000
5		To issue common stock.		
6				

Both assets and stockholders' equity increase by the same amount.

Assets	=	Liabilities	+	Stockholders' Equity
+ 100,000,000 =		0		+ 500,000
				+ 99,500,000

The Paid-in Capital account is listed in the stockholders' equity section of the balance sheet immediately after the type of stock to which it relates (in the case of The Home Depot, common stock). Hypothetically, then, after the last entry on page 571, the Stockholders' Equity section of The Home Depot, Inc.'s, Balance Sheet might appear as follows (figures assumed):

	A1	⬍		
	A			**B**
1	**Stockholders' Equity**			
2	Common stock, $.05 par, 10 billion shares			
3	authorized, 10 million shares issued and outstanding			$ 500,000
4	Paid-in Capital			99,500,000
5	Total paid-in capital			100,000,000
6	Retained earnings			500,000,000
7	Total stockholders' equity			$ 600,000,000
8				

All the transactions in this section include a receipt of cash by the corporation as it issues *new* stock. The transactions we illustrate are different from those reported in the daily news. In those transactions, one stockholder sold stock to another investor. The corporation doesn't record those transactions because they were between two outside parties.

⟩⟩ *Try it*

Examine The Home Depot's consolidated balance sheet at February 1, 2015 (p. 565). Answer these questions about its actual stock transactions:

1. What was The Home Depot's total paid-in capital at February 1, 2015?

2. How many shares of common stock had The Home Depot issued through February 1, 2015?

3. What was the average issue price of The Home Depot's common stock that had been issued through February 1, 2015?

Answers:

		February 1, 2015
(1) Total paid-in capital (in millions)		$88 + $8,885 = $8,973
(2) Number of shares of common stock issued (in millions)		1,768

(3)

$$\frac{\text{Average issue price}}{\text{of common stock}} = \frac{\text{Total received from issuance of common stock (in millions)}}{\text{Common shares issued (in millions)}} = \frac{\$88 + \$8,885 = \$8,973}{1,768}$$

$$= \$5.08 \text{ per share}$$

The Home Depot has issued its common stock at an average price of $5.08 per share.

No-Par Common Stock. To record the issuance of no-par stock, the company debits the asset received and credits the Common Stock account for the cash or fair market value of the asset received. Suppose that, on April 1, 2015, Krispy Kreme Doughnuts, Inc., issues 64.926 million shares of no-par common stock for $310,768,000. Krispy Kreme's stock issuance entry is:

	A	B	C	D
	A1			
1	Apr. 1	Cash	310,768,000	
2		Common Stock		310,768,000
3		To issue no-par common stock.		
4				

Assets	=	Liabilities	+	Stockholders' Equity
+ 310,768,000 =		0		+ 310,768,000

Krispy Kreme's charter authorizes the company to issue 300 million shares of no-par stock, and the company has an accumulated deficit of $42.982 million in retained earnings and no accumulated other comprehensive income or treasury stock. Krispy Kreme Doughnuts, Inc., reports stockholders' equity on its balance sheet as follows (in millions):

	A	B
	A1	
1	**Stockholders' Equity**	
2	**(in millions)**	
3	Common stock, no par, 300,000,000 shares	
4	authorized, 64,926,000 shares issued and outstanding	$ 310,768,000
5	Accumulated deficit	(42,982,000)
6	Total stockholders' equity	$ 267,786,000
7		

You can see that a company with true no-par stock has no Additional Paid-in Capital account.

No-Par Common Stock with a Stated Value. Accounting for no-par stock with a stated value is identical to accounting for par-value stock. The excess over stated value is credited to Additional Paid-in Capital, or Paid-in Capital in Excess of Stated Value—Common.

Common Stock Issued for Assets Other Than Cash. When a corporation issues stock and receives assets other than cash, the company records the assets received at their current market value and credits the Common Stock and additional paid-in capital accounts accordingly. The assets' prior book values aren't relevant because the stockholder will demand stock equal to the market value of the asset given. On November 12, Kahn Corporation issued 15,000 shares of its $1 par common stock for equipment with a market value of $4,000 and a building with a market value of $120,000. Kahn's entry is

	A	B	C	D
	A1			
1	Nov 12	Equipment	4,000	
2		Building	120,000	
3		Common Stock (15,000 × $1)		15,000
4		Paid-in Capital in Excess of Par—Common		
5		($124,000 − $15,000)		109,000
6		To issue $1-par common stock in exchange for		
7		equipment and a building.		
8				

Assets and equity both increase by $124,000.

Assets	=	Liabilities	+	Stockholders' Equity
+ 4,000				+ 15,000
+ 120,000	=	0		+ 109,000

Common Stock Issued for Services. Sometimes a corporation will issue shares of common stock in exchange for services rendered, either by employees or outsiders. In this case, no cash is exchanged. However, the transaction is recognized at fair market value. The corporation usually recognizes an expense for the fair market value of the services rendered. Common stock is increased for its par value (if any), and additional paid-in capital is increased for any difference. For example, assume that Kahn Corporation engages an attorney to represent the company on a legal matter. The attorney bills the corporation $25,000 for services and agrees to accept 2,500 shares of $1 par common stock, rather than cash, in settlement of the fee. The fair market value of the stock is $10 per share. The journal entry to record the transaction is

	A	B	C	D
1		Legal Expense	25,000	
2		Common Stock (2,500 × $1 par)		2,500
3		Paid-in Capital in Excess of Par—Common		
4		($25,000 − $2,500)		22,500
5				

In this case, retained earnings (stockholders' equity) is eventually decreased (through legal expense) by $25,000, and paid-in capital (stockholders' equity) is increased for the same amount.

A Stock Issuance for Other Than Cash
Can Create an Ethical Challenge

Generally accepted accounting principles require a company to record the issuance of its stock at the fair market value of whatever the corporation receives in exchange for the stock. When the corporation receives cash, there is clear evidence of the value of the stock because cash is worth its face amount. But when the corporation receives an asset other than cash, the value of the asset can create an ethical challenge.

A computer whiz may start a new company by investing in computer software. The software may be market-tested or it may be new. The software may be worth millions, or it may be worthless. The corporation must record the asset received and the stock issued with a journal entry such as the following (assuming no-par stock is issued):

	A	B	C	D
1		Software	500,000	
2		Common Stock		500,000
3		Issued stock in exchange for software.		
4				

If the software is really worth $500,000, the accounting records are accurate. However, if the software is new and untested, both assets and stockholders' equity may be overstated.

Suppose your computer-whiz friend invites you to invest in the new business and shows you this balance sheet:

	A	B	C	D
1	**Gee-Whiz Computer Solutions, Inc.** **Balance Sheet** **December 31, 2016**			
2	**Assets**		**Liabilities and Stockholders' Equity**	
3	Computer software	$ 500,000	Total liabilities	$ -0-
4			**Stockholders' Equity**	
5			Common stock	500,000
6	Total assets	$ 500,000	Total liabilities and stockholders' equity	$ 500,000
7				

Companies like to report large asset and equity amounts on their balance sheets. That makes them look prosperous and creditworthy. Gee-Whiz looks debt free and appears to have a valuable asset. Will you invest in this new business? Here are two takeaway lessons:

- Some accounting values are more solid than others.
- Not all financial statements mean exactly what they say—unless they are audited by independent CPAs.

Preferred Stock

Accounting for preferred stock follows the same pattern we illustrated for common stock. When a company issues preferred stock, it credits Preferred Stock at its par value, with any excess credited to Paid-in Capital in Excess of Par—Preferred.

There may be separate accounts for paid-in capital in excess of par for preferred and common stock, but not necessarily. Some companies combine paid-in capital in excess of par from both preferred and common stock transactions into one account. Accounting for no-par preferred follows the pattern for no-par common stock. When reporting stockholders' equity on the balance sheet, a corporation lists its accounts in this order:

- Preferred stock
- Common stock
- Additional paid-in capital
- Retained earnings

In Chapter 9, we saw how to account for convertible bonds or notes payable (pp. 520–521). Companies also issue convertible preferred stock. The preferred stock is usually convertible into the company's common stock at the discretion of the preferred stockholders, as the price of the common stock, as well as its dividend, rises to an attractive level in the future. Here are some representative journal entries for convertible preferred stock, using assumed amounts:

- Convertible preferred stock $1 par, 50,000 shares issued at par value

	A	B	C	D
1	2016	Cash	50,000	
2		Convertible Preferred Stock		50,000
3		*Issued convertible preferred stock.*		
4				

- Converted preferred stock to common stock at the rate of 6.25 to 1 (8,000 shares of $1 par-value common stock issued in exchange for 50,000 shares of preferred stock)

	A	B	C	D
1	2016	Convertible Preferred Stock	50,000	
2		Common Stock		8,000
3		Paid-in Capital in Excess of Par—Common		42,000
4		*Investors converted preferred into common.*		
5				

As you can see, we simply remove Convertible Preferred Stock from the books and assign the new Common Stock the prior book value of the preferred.

Mid-Chapter Summary Problem

1. Test your understanding of the first half of this chapter by deciding whether each of the following statements is true or false.

   a. The policy-making body in a corporation is called the board of directors.

   b. The owner of 100 shares of preferred stock has greater voting rights than the owner of 100 shares of common stock.

   c. Par-value stock is worth more than no-par stock.

   d. Issuance of 1,000 shares of $5 par-value stock at $12 increases contributed capital by $12,000.

   e. The issuance of no-par stock with a stated value is fundamentally different from issuing par-value stock.

   f. A corporation issues its preferred stock in exchange for land and a building with a combined market value of $200,000. This transaction increases the corporation's owners' equity by $200,000 regardless of the assets' prior book values.

   g. Preferred stock is a riskier investment than common stock.

2. Adolfo Company has two classes of common stock. Only the Class A common stockholders are entitled to vote. The company's balance sheet included the following presentation:

	A	B
1	**Stockholders' Equity**	
2	Capital stock:	
3	Class A common stock, voting, $1 par value,	
4	authorized, issued and outstanding 1,260,000 shares	$ 1,260,000
5	Class B common stock, nonvoting, no par value,	
6	authorized, issued, and outstanding 46,200,000 shares	11,000,000
7		12,260,000
8	Additional paid-in capital	2,011,000
9	Retained earnings	872,403,000
10	Total stockholders' equity	$ 886,674,000
11		

Requirements

a. Record the issuance of the Class A common stock for cash. Use the Adolfo account titles.

b. Record the issuance of the Class B common stock for cash. Use the Adolfo account titles.

c. How much of Adolfo's stockholders' equity was contributed by the stockholders? How much was provided by profitable operations? Does this division of equity suggest that the company has been successful? Why or why not?

d. Write a sentence to describe what Adolfo's stockholders' equity means.

Answers

1. a. True;   b. False;   c. False;   d. True;   e. False;   f. True;   g. False

2. a.

A1				
	A	B	C	D
1		Cash	3,271,000	
2		Class A Common Stock		1,260,000
3		Additional Paid-in Capital		2,011,000
4		*To record issuance of Class A common stock.*		
5				

b.

A1				
	A	B	C	D
1		Cash	11,000,000	
2		Class B Common Stock		11,000,000
3		*To record issuance of Class B common stock.*		
4				

c. Contributed by the stockholders: $14,271,000 ($12,260,000 + $2,011,000). Provided by profitable operations: $872,403,000. This division suggests that the company has been successful because most of its stockholders' equity has come from profitable operations.

d. Adolfo's stockholders' equity of $886,674,000 means that the company's stockholders own $886,674,000 of the business's assets.

Authorized, Issued, and Outstanding Stock

It is important to distinguish among three distinctly different numbers of a company's stock. The following examples use The Home Depot's actual data from page 565.

- **Authorized stock** is the maximum number of shares the company can issue under its charter. As of February 1, 2015, The Home Depot was authorized to issue 10 billion shares of common stock.

- **Issued stock** is the number of shares the company has issued to its stockholders. This is a cumulative total from the company's beginning up through the current date, less any shares permanently retired. As of February 1, 2015, The Home Depot had issued 1.768 billion common shares.

- **Outstanding stock** is the number of shares that the stockholders own (that is, the number of shares outstanding in the hands of the stockholders). Outstanding stock is issued stock minus treasury stock. At February 1, 2015, The Home Depot had 1.307 billion shares of common stock outstanding, computed as

Issued shares (line 17, in billions)..................... 1.768
Less: Treasury shares (line 24, in billions) .... (0.461)
Outstanding shares (in billions) .... <u>1.307</u>

Now let's learn about treasury stock.

SHOW HOW TREASURY STOCK AFFECTS A COMPANY

3 **Show** how treasury stock affects a company

A company's own stock that it has issued and later reacquired is called **treasury stock**.[2] In effect, the corporation holds this stock in its treasury. Many public companies spend millions or even billions of dollars each year to buy back their own stock. Corporations purchase their own stock for several reasons:

1. The company has issued all its authorized stock and needs some stock for distributions to employees under stock purchase plans or compensation plans.

2. The business wants to increase net assets by buying its stock low and hoping to resell it for a higher price.

3. Management wants to avoid a takeover by an outside party.

4. Management wants to increase its reported earnings per share (EPS) of common stock (net income/number of common shares outstanding). Purchasing shares removes them from outstanding shares, thus decreasing the denominator of this fraction and increasing EPS. We cover the computation of EPS in more depth in Chapter 11.

5. Management uses a share repurchase program as a way to return excess cash to shareholders, in a manner similar to a dividend.

How Is Treasury Stock Recorded?

Treasury stock is recorded at cost (the market value of the stock on the date of the purchase) without regard to the stock's par value. Treasury stock is a *contra stockholders' equity* account; therefore, the treasury-stock account carries a debit balance, the opposite of the other equity accounts. It is reported beneath the Retained Earnings account on the balance sheet as a negative amount.

To understand the way treasury-stock transactions work, it is helpful to analyze the changes that occur in the treasury-stock account during the year. Let's start with The Home Depot's stockholders' equity at the end of the previous year, February 2, 2014 (we use rounded amounts in millions, except for shares):

	A	B
	A1	
1	**The Home Depot, Inc.** **Stockholders' Equity** **February 2, 2014**	
2	**(in millions)**	
3	Common stock	88
4	Paid-in capital	8,402
5	Retained earnings	23,180
6	Accumulated other comprehensive income	46
7	Treasury stock (381,000,000 shares)	(19,194)
8	Total stockholders' equity	$ 12,522
9		

[2]In this text, we illustrate the *cost* method of accounting for treasury stock because it is used most widely. Other methods are presented in intermediate accounting courses.

Notice that as of February 2, 2014, The Home Depot had spent $19,194 million to repurchase 381 million shares of its own stock. The average price it had paid for its shares through that date was about $50.38 per share ($19,194 million ÷ 381 million).

Repurchasing treasury stock provides a way for public companies to return cash to shareholders other than through dividends. The disadvantage to the shareholder of a share repurchase plan is that in order to receive cash, the shareholder has to surrender (dilute) his or her ownership in the company.

Note 6 of The Home Depot's financial statements gives more information about the company's accelerated share repurchase (ASR) program:

> In fiscal 2014, the Company entered into Accelerated Share Repurchase ("ASR") agreements with third-party financial institutions to repurchase $2.7 billion of the Company's common stock. Under the agreements, the Company paid $2.7 billion to the financial institutions and received a total of 34 million shares in fiscal 2014. The final number of shares delivered upon settlement of each agreement was determined with reference to the average price of the Company's common stock over the term of the applicable ASR agreement. The $2.7 billion of shares repurchased are included in Treasury Stock in the accompanying Consolidated Balance Sheets.

The footnote reflects that, under its ASR program, the company paid $2.7 billion to purchase 34 million shares from institutional investors and included those shares in treasury stock. The Consolidated Statement of Stockholders' Equity (Exhibit 10-9) reflects that a total of 80 million shares were purchased for $7 billion, so an additional 46 million shares must have been purchased on the open market. The average purchase price was $87.50 per share ($7 billion ÷ 80 million). The entry to record the aggregate of these purchases is

	A1	⬍			
	A	B		C	D
1	2014	Treasury Stock		7,000,000,000	
2	Various	Cash			7,000,000,000
3		Purchased treasury stock.			
4					

Assets	=	Liabilities	+	Stockholders' Equity
− 7,000,000,000	=	0		− 7,000,000,000

Notice that treasury stock is recorded at cost, which is the market price of the stock on the various days that The Home Depot purchased it. The financial statement impact of these transactions is decreased cash as well as stockholders' equity.

Retirement of Treasury Stock

A corporation may purchase its own stock and *retire* it by canceling the stock certificates. Retired stock cannot be reissued. Once the shares are repurchased, neither total assets nor total liabilities are affected, and a memorandum entry is made decreasing the number of shares issued in stockholders' equity.

Resale of Treasury Stock

Reselling treasury stock for cash grows assets and equity exactly as issuing new stock does. The sale increases assets and equity by the full amount of cash received. A company *never records gains or losses on transactions involving its own treasury stock.* Rather, amounts received in excess of amounts originally paid for treasury stock are recorded as Paid-in Capital from Treasury Stock Transactions, thus bypassing the income statement. If amounts received from resale of treasury stock were less than amounts originally paid, the difference would be debited to Paid-in Capital from Treasury Stock Transactions to the extent of that balance, and after that, to Retained Earnings. The Home Depot did not resell any of its treasury stock in fiscal 2014, but suppose that on July 22, 2014, it had resold a million shares of treasury stock for $90 per share. Assuming that the average cost of treasury shares is $87.50 (calculated on p. 579), the journal entry to record the resale of treasury shares would have been

	A	B	C	D
	A1			
1	2014			
2	Jul 22	Cash	90,000,000	
3		Treasury Stock		87,500,000
4		Paid-in Capital from Treasury Stock Transactions		2,500,000
5		*Sold treasury stock.*		
6				

Assets	=	Liabilities	+	Stockholders' Equity
+ 90,000,000	=	0		+ 87,500,000
				+ 2,500,000

Issuing Stock for Employee Compensation

Sometimes companies supplement employee salaries by granting shares of stock rather than cash. Sometimes they use treasury shares for this purpose and sometimes they grant newly issued shares for various reasons. The Consolidated Statement of Stockholders Equity (Exhibit 10-9 on page 592) shows that during the year ended February 1, 2015, The Home Depot issued 7 million new (not treasury) shares in conjunction with an employee stock compensation plan. Because the par value of the shares is only $0.05, the common stock account was impacted by only $350,000 (7,000,000 shares × 0.05 par value per share). Paid-in capital was credited for the remainder. The entry the company made was

	A	B	C	D
	A1			
1			**Debit**	**Credit**
2		Compensation Expense	122,000,000	
3		Common Stock (7,000,000 × .05)		350,000
4		Paid-in Capital		121,650,000
5		*To record stock-based compensation plan.*		
6				

Since items on the Statement of Stockholders' Equity are rounded to the nearest million, the impact on the common stock account is reflected as zero, and the entire credit ($122 million, rounded to the nearest million) is shown in paid-in capital.

Now let's take a look at The Home Depot's stockholders' equity as of February 1, 2015. For now, focus only on the treasury-stock account:

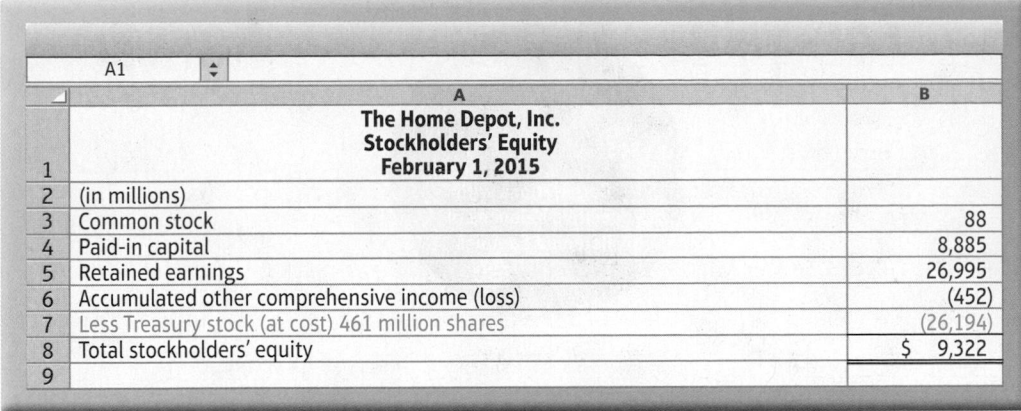

	A	B
1	**The Home Depot, Inc.** **Stockholders' Equity** **February 1, 2015**	
2	(in millions)	
3	Common stock	88
4	Paid-in capital	8,885
5	Retained earnings	26,995
6	Accumulated other comprehensive income (loss)	(452)
7	Less Treasury stock (at cost) 461 million shares	(26,194)
8	Total stockholders' equity	$ 9,322
9		

After treasury-stock transactions for the year ended February 1, 2015, have been recorded, the new number of treasury shares is 461 million. The balance in the treasury-stock account is $26,194 million. The new average purchase price of treasury shares is about $56.82 ($26,194 million ÷ 461 million).

Summary of Treasury-Stock Transactions

The types of treasury-stock transactions we have reviewed are as follows:

- Buying treasury stock. Assets and equity *decrease* by an amount equal to the cost of treasury stock purchased.

- Reselling treasury stock. Assets and equity *increase* by an amount equal to the sale price of the treasury stock sold.

- Retiring treasury stock, thus removing it from both common stock and from the treasury.

- Issuing stock for employee compensation. Expenses are increased, capital stock is increased for the par value of the shares, and additional paid-in capital is increased for the difference.

ACCOUNT FOR RETAINED EARNINGS, DIVIDENDS, AND SPLITS

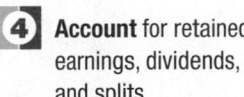

Account for retained earnings, dividends, and splits

The Retained Earnings account carries the balance of the business's net income, less its net losses, and less any declared dividends that have been accumulated over the corporation's lifetime. *Retained* means "held onto." Successful companies grow by reinvesting in the business the assets they generate through profitable operations. The Home Depot is an excellent example. Take another look at its stockholders' equity as of February 1, 2015, as seen at the top of this page. Notice that the Retained Earnings account ($26,995 million) is the largest account balance in stockholders' equity as of that date. In fact, because historically the company has spent so much money repurchasing treasury stock, retained earnings actually *exceeds* total stockholders' equity ($9,322 million).

The Retained Earnings account is not a reservoir of cash for paying dividends to the stockholders. In fact, the corporation may have a large balance in Retained Earnings but not have enough cash to pay a dividend. Cash and Retained Earnings are two entirely separate accounts with no particular relationship. Retained Earnings says nothing about the company's cash balance.

A *credit* balance in Retained Earnings is normal, indicating that the corporation's lifetime earnings exceed lifetime losses and dividends. A *debit* balance in Retained Earnings arises when a corporation's lifetime losses and dividends exceed lifetime earnings. Called a **deficit**, this amount is subtracted to determine total stockholders' equity. In a recent survey, 15.5% of companies had a retained earnings deficit (Exhibit 10-6).

Exhibit 10-6 | Percentage of Companies with Positive Retained Earnings, Deficits

Should the Company Declare and Pay Cash Dividends?

A **dividend** is a distribution by a corporation to its stockholders, usually based on earnings. Dividends usually take one of three forms:

- Cash
- Stock
- Noncash assets

In this section we focus on cash dividends and stock dividends because noncash dividends are rare. For a noncash asset dividend, debit Retained Earnings and credit the asset (for example, Investment in Available-for-Sale Securities) for the current market value of the asset given.

Cash Dividends

Most dividends are cash dividends. Finance courses discuss how a company decides on its dividend policy. Accounting tells a company if it can pay a dividend. To do so, a company must have both

- enough retained earnings to *declare* the dividend, and
- enough cash to *pay* the dividend.

A corporation declares a dividend before paying it. Only the board of directors has the authority to declare a dividend. The corporation has no obligation to pay a dividend until the board declares one, but once declared, the dividend becomes a legal liability of the corporation. There are three relevant dates for dividends (using assumed dates and amounts):

1. *Declaration date, June 19.* On the declaration date, the board of directors announces the dividend. Declaration of the dividend creates a liability for the corporation. Declaration is recorded by debiting Retained Earnings and crediting Dividends Payable. Assume a $50,000 dividend is declared.

	A	B	C	D
	A1			
1	Jun 19	Retained Earnings[3]	50,000	
2		Dividends Payable		50,000
3		*Declared a cash dividend.*		
4				

---

[3]In the early part of this book, we debited a Dividends account to clearly identify the purpose of the payment. From here on, we follow the more common practice of debiting the Retained Earnings account for dividend declarations.

Liabilities increase and stockholders' equity decreases.

Assets	=	Liabilities	+	Stockholders' Equity
0	=	+ 50,000		− 50,000

2. *Date of record, July 1.* As part of the declaration, the corporation announces the record date, which follows the declaration date by a few weeks. The stockholders on the record date will receive the dividend. There is no journal entry for the date of record.

3. *Payment date, July 10.* Payment of the dividend usually follows the record date by a week or two. Payment is recorded by debiting Dividends Payable and crediting Cash.

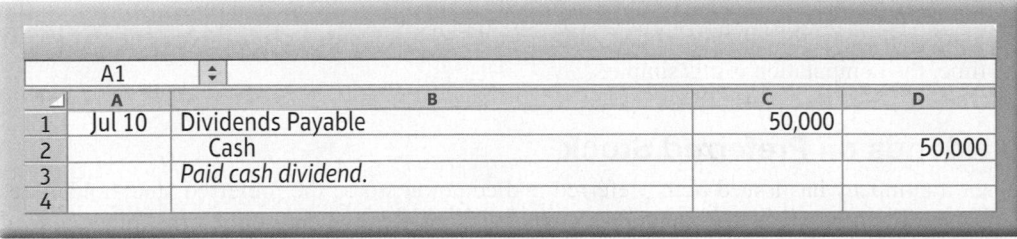

	A	B	C	D
		A1 ⬦		
1	Jul 10	Dividends Payable	50,000	
2		Cash		50,000
3		*Paid cash dividend.*		
4				

Both assets and liabilities decrease.

Assets	=	Liabilities	+	Stockholders' Equity
− 50,000	=	− 50,000		

The net effect of a dividend declaration and its payment, as shown in steps 1, 2, and 3, is a decrease in assets and a corresponding decrease in stockholders' equity.

Analyzing the Stockholders' Equity Accounts

By knowing accounting, you can look at a company's comparative year-to-year financial statements and tell a lot about what the company did during the current year. For example, The Home Depot reported the following for Retained Earnings (in millions):

	Feb. 1, 2015	Feb. 2, 2014
Retained Earnings	$26,995	$23,180

What do these figures tell you about The Home Depot's results of operations during the year ended February 1, 2015—did it earn net income or a net loss? How can you tell? Remember that

- net income is the only item that increases retained earnings;
- net losses decrease retained earnings;
- dividends declared decrease retained earnings; and
- other adjustments to retained earnings are usually relatively minor and relatively rare.

In most cases, if you know the amount of either net income or dividends, but not both, and if you know both beginning and ending balances of retained earnings, you can figure out the amount you don't know by analyzing the Retained Earnings account.

Let's analyze The Home Depot's Retained Earnings account for the year ended February 1, 2015. As shown previously, the balance of Retained Earnings was $23,180 million on February 2, 2014. Net income for the year ended February 1, 2015, according to the company's consolidated statement of income, was $6,345 million. If there were no other changes in Retained Earnings besides dividends, how much in dividends did the company declare?

If you know to use accounting, you can compute The Home Depot's dividend declarations during the year ended February 1, 2015, by analyzing the changes in the Retained Earnings account as follows (in millions):

		Retained earnings	
		Beg bal	23,180
Dividends	X	Net income	6,345
		End bal	26,995

Dividends (X) are \$2,530 million (\$23,180 million + \$6,345 million − X = \$26,995 million); X = \$2,530 million. It really helps to be able to use accounting in this way!

Sometimes it doesn't work out this simply. From time to time, some corporations might record prior-period adjustments or other nonrecurring items to retained earnings. However, the two major elements that affect retained earnings are net income (loss) and dividends, so most of the time, the computation is this simple.

Dividends on Preferred Stock

When a company has issued both preferred and common stock, the preferred stockholders receive their dividends first. The common stockholders receive dividends only if the total dividend is large enough to pay the preferred stockholders first.

Avant Garde, Inc., has 100,000 shares of \$1.50 preferred stock outstanding in addition to its common stock. The \$1.50 designation means that the preferred stockholders receive an annual cash dividend of \$1.50 per share. In 2016, Avant Garde declares an annual dividend of \$500,000. The allocation to preferred and common stockholders is:

Preferred dividend (100,000 shares × \$1.50 per share).............	\$150,000
Common dividend (remainder: \$500,000 − \$150,000)............	350,000
Total dividend..	\$500,000

If Avant Garde declares only a \$200,000 dividend, preferred stockholders receive \$150,000, and the common stockholders get the remainder, \$50,000 (\$200,000 − \$150,000).

Two Ways to Express the Dividend Rate on Preferred Stock. Dividends on preferred stock are stated either as a

- percent of par value, or
- dollar amount per share.

For example, preferred stock may be "6% preferred," which means that owners of the preferred stock receive an annual dividend equal to 6% of the stock's par value. If par value is \$100 per share, preferred stockholders receive an annual cash dividend of \$6 per share (6% of \$100). Alternatively, the preferred stock may be "\$3 preferred," which means that the preferred stockholders receive an annual dividend of \$3 per share regardless of the stock's par value. The dividend rate on no-par preferred stock is stated in a dollar amount per share.

Dividends on Cumulative and Noncumulative Preferred Stock. The balance-sheet classification of preferred stock, as well as the allocation of dividends, may be complex if the preferred stock is *cumulative*. Why? Corporations sometimes fail to pay a dividend to cumulative preferred stockholders. This is called *passing the dividend*, and the passed dividends are said to be *in arrears*. The owners of **cumulative preferred stock** must receive all dividends in arrears plus the current year's dividend before any dividends go to the common stockholders. In this sense, cumulative dividends almost take on the flavor of accrued interest on long-term debt, but not quite. Although cumulative dividends must be paid before other dividends, they must still be declared by the company's board of directors. *In most states, preferred stock is cumulative unless it is specifically labeled as noncumulative.*

Here's an example of how cumulative dividends work. Let's assume that the preferred stock of Avant Garde, Inc., is cumulative. Suppose Avant Garde passed the preferred dividend of \$150,000 in 2015. Before paying dividends to common in 2016, Avant Garde must first pay preferred dividends of $150,000 for both 2015 and 2016—a total of $300,000. On September 6, 2016, Avant Garde declares a $500,000 dividend. The entry to record the declaration is as follows:

	A1	⇕			
	A	B		C	D
1	Sep 6	Retained Earnings		500,000	
2		Dividends Payable, Preferred ($150,000 × 2)			300,000
3		Dividends Payable, Common ($500,000 − $300,000)			200,000
4		*To declare a cash dividend.*			
5					

If the preferred stock is *noncumulative*, the corporation is not obligated to pay passed dividends.

Stock Dividends

A **stock dividend** is a proportional distribution by a corporation of its own stock to its stockholders. Stock dividends increase the Common Stock account, the Paid-in Capital in Excess of Par—Common and decrease Retained Earnings. Total equity is unchanged, and no asset or liability is affected.

The corporation distributes stock dividends to stockholders in proportion to the number of shares they already own. If you own 300 shares of The Home Depot common stock and the corporation distributes a 10% common stock dividend, you get 30 (300 × 0.10) additional shares. You would then own 330 shares of the common stock. All other The Home Depot stockholders would also receive 10% more shares, leaving all common stockholders' proportionate ownership unchanged.

In distributing a stock dividend, the corporation gives up no assets. Why, then, do companies issue stock dividends? A corporation may choose to distribute stock dividends for these reasons:

1. *To continue dividends but conserve cash.* A company may need to conserve cash and yet wish to continue dividends in some form. So the corporation may distribute a stock dividend. Stockholders pay no income tax on stock dividends.

2. *To reduce the per-share market price of its stock.* Distribution of a stock dividend usually causes the stock's market price to fall because of the increased number of outstanding shares that result from it. The objective is to make the stock less expensive and therefore attractive to more investors.

Generally accepted accounting principles (GAAP) label a stock dividend of 25% or less of outstanding common shares as *small* and require that the dividend be recorded at the market value of the shares distributed. Suppose The Home Depot declared and distributed a 10% common stock dividend on February 3, 2015. At the time, The Home Depot had approximately 1,307 million shares of common stock outstanding, and the corporation's stock was trading for $106 per share. The Home Depot would have recorded this stock dividend as follows:

	A1	⇕			
	A	B		C	D
1	2015	Retained Earnings[4] (1,307,000,000 shares of			
2	Feb. 3	common outstanding × 0.10 stock dividend × $106			
3		market value per share of common)		13,854,200,000	
4		Common Stock (1,307,000,000 × 0.10 × $0.05			
5		par value per share)			6,535,000
6		Paid-in Capital			13,847,665,000
7		*Declared and distributed a 10% stock dividend.*			
8					

---

[4]Many companies debit Additional Paid-in Capital for their stock dividends.

The accounting equation clearly shows that a stock dividend has no effect on total assets, liabilities, or equity. The increases in equity offset the decreases, and the net effect is zero.

Assets	=	Liabilities	+	Stockholders' Equity
0	=	0		− 13,854,200,000
				+ 6,535,000
				+ 13,847,665,000

GAAP identifies stock dividends above 25% of outstanding common shares as *large* and permits large stock dividends to be recorded at par value. For a large stock dividend, therefore, The Home Depot, Inc., would debit Retained Earnings and credit Common Stock for the par value of the shares distributed in the dividend.

Stock Splits

A **stock split** is an increase in the number of shares of stock issued and outstanding, coupled with a proportionate reduction in the stock's par value. For example, if the company splits its stock 2 for 1, the number of outstanding shares is doubled and each share's par value is halved. A stock split, like a large stock dividend, decreases the market price of the stock—with the intention of making the stock more attractive in the market. Most leading companies in the United States—including **International Business Machines Corp.**, **PepsiCo, Inc.**, Apple, Inc., and The Home Depot, Inc.—have split their stock. The Home Depot, Inc.'s, stock price has split 13 times since the company's initial IPO in 1978.

Assume the market price of a share of The Home Depot, Inc.'s, common stock is approximately $100 per share. Assume that The Home Depot wishes to decrease the market price to approximately $50 per share. The Home Depot can split its common stock 2 for 1, and the stock price will fall to around $50. A 2-for-1 stock split means that

- the company will have twice as many shares of stock issued and outstanding after the split as it had before, and
- each share's par value will be cut in half.

Assume that, before the split, The Home Depot, Inc., had approximately 500 million shares of $0.10 (10 cents) par common stock issued and outstanding. Compare The Home Depot, Inc.'s, stockholders' equity before and after a 2-for-1 stock split (assumed, not actual numbers):

A1				
	A	**B**	**C**	**D**
1	**The Home Depot, Inc., Stockholders' Equity (Adapted, Assumed Numbers)**			
2	**Before 2-for-1 Stock Split**	**(In millions)**	**After 2-for-1 Stock Split**	**(In millions)**
3	Common stock, $0.10 par, 1,000		Common stock, $0.05 par, 1,000	
4	shares authorized, 500 shares		shares authorized, 1,000 shares	
5	issued and outstanding	$ 50	issued and outstanding	$ 50
6	Additional paid-in capital	643	Additional paid-in capital	643
7	Retained earnings	4,304	Retained earnings	4,304
8	Other equity	260	Other equity	260
9	Total stockholders' equity	$ 5,257	Total stockholders' equity	$ 5,257
10				

All account balances are the same after the stock split as before. Only three items are affected:

- Par value per share drops from $0.10 to $0.05.
- Shares *issued* double from 500 to 1,000 (both in millions).
- Shares *outstanding* double from 500 to 1,000 (both in millions).

Total equity doesn't change, nor do any assets or liabilities.

Summary of the Effects on Assets, Liabilities, and Stockholders' Equity

We've seen how to account for the basic stockholders' equity transactions:

- Issuance of stock—common and preferred (pp. 571–576)
- Purchase and sale of treasury stock (pp. 578–581)
- Cash dividends (pp. 582–585)
- Stock dividends and stock splits (pp. 585–586)

How do these transactions affect assets, liabilities, and equity? Exhibit 10-7 provides a helpful summary.

Exhibit 10-7 | Effects of Stock Transactions

	Effect on Total		
Transaction	Assets =	Liabilities +	Stockholders' Equity
Issuance of stock—common and preferred	Increase	No effect	Increase
Purchase of treasury stock	Decrease	No effect	Decrease
Sale of treasury stock	Increase	No effect	Increase
Declaration of cash dividend	No effect	Increase	Decrease
Payment of cash dividend	Decrease	Decrease	No effect
Stock dividend—large and small	No effect	No effect	No effect*
Stock split	No effect	No effect	No effect

*The stock accounts increase and retained earnings decrease by offsetting amounts that net to zero.

USE STOCK VALUES IN DECISION MAKING

The business community measures *stock values* in various ways, depending on the purpose of the measurement. These values include market value, redemption value, liquidation value, and book value.

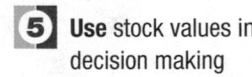

5 **Use** stock values in decision making

Market, Redemption, Liquidation, and Book Value

A stock's **market value**, or **market capitalization** *(market cap)*, is the market price of one share of the common stock at a given date, multiplied by the number of shares of common stock outstanding. Market price varies with the corporation's net income, financial position, and future prospects, and with general economic conditions. *In almost all cases, stockholders are more concerned about the market value of a stock than any other value.* The overall market assessment of the worth of a share of common stock is reflected in the **price-earnings ratio**, expressed as

$$\text{Price-earnings ratio} = \frac{\text{Market price of one share of common stock}}{\text{Earnings per share of common stock}}$$

For example, on February 1, 2015, the market price of one share of The Home Depot, Inc.'s, common stock was $104.42. The latest reported earnings per common share (basic) on its consolidated statement of earnings for the year ended February 1, 2015 was $4.74. Therefore, its price-earnings ratio on February 1, 2015 was 22.03 ($104.42 ÷ $4.74). The company reported 1,307 million shares of common stock outstanding (1,768 million shares issued − 461 million shares in treasury). Therefore, the market value (market capitalization) of The Home Depot, Inc., as of February 1, 2015, was approximately $136,477 million (1,307 million shares × $104.42). We will discuss the concept of market capitalization further, in relation to investment decisions, in Chapter 11.

Preferred stock that requires the company to redeem the stock at a set price is called **redeemable preferred stock**. The company is *obligated* to redeem (pay to retire) the preferred stock. Therefore, redeemable preferred stock is really not stockholders' equity. Instead, it's a liability. The price the corporation agrees to pay for the stock, set when the stock is issued, is called the **redemption value**. **Liquidation value** is the amount that a company must pay a preferred stockholder in the event the company liquidates (sells out) and goes out of business.

The **book value per share** of common stock is the amount of common stockholders' equity on the company's books for each share of its stock. If the company has only common stock outstanding, its book value is computed by dividing total shareholders' equity by the number of shares of common stock *outstanding*. Recall that *outstanding* stock is *issued* stock minus *treasury* stock. For example, a company with only common stockholders' equity of $150,000 and 5,000 shares of common stock outstanding has a book value of $30 per share ($150,000 ÷ 5,000 shares).

If the company has both preferred and common outstanding, the preferred stockholders have the first claim to owners' equity, and thus preferred equity should be deducted from the numerator of the book value per share. Preferred stock often has a specified redemption value. In the book-value-per-share ratio, the preferred equity is its redemption value plus any cumulative preferred dividends in arrears plus the current year dividend. Book value per share of common stock is then computed as follows:

$$\frac{\text{Book value per}}{\text{share of common stock}} = \frac{\text{Total stockholders' equity} - \text{Preferred equity}}{\text{Number of shares of common stock outstanding}}$$

Consider a hypothetical example. Crusader Corporation's balance sheet reports the following amounts:

	A	B
	Stockholders' Equity	
1		
2	Preferred stock, 5% cumulative, $100 par, 400 shares issued, and outstanding,	
3	redemption value $130 per share	$ 40,000
4	Common stock, $10 par, 5,500 shares issued, 5,000 shares outstanding	55,000
5	Additional paid-in capital—common	72,000
6	Retained earnings	88,000
7	Treasury stock—common, 500 shares at cost	(15,000)
8	Total stockholders' equity	$ 240,000
9		

Cumulative preferred dividends are in arrears for four years (including the current year). Crusader's preferred stock has a redemption value of $130 per share. The book-value-per-share computations for Crusader Corporation are

Preferred Equity

Redemption value (400 shares × $130)	$52,000
Cumulative dividends ($40,000 × 0.05 × 4 years)	8,000
Preferred equity...	$60,000*

Common Equity

Total stockholders' equity..	$240,000
Less preferred equity	(60,000)
Common equity	$180,000
Book value per share [$180,000 ÷ 5,000 shares outstanding (5,500 shares issued minus 500 treasury shares)]	$ 36.00

*If the preferred stock had no redemption value, then preferred equity would be $40,000 + preferred dividends in arrears.

Some investors search for stocks whose market price is below book value. They believe this indicates a good buy. Financial analysts often shy away from companies with a stock price at or below book value. To these analysts such a company is in trouble. As you can see, not all investors and analysts agree on a stock's value. In fact, wise investors base their decisions on more than a single ratio. In Chapter 13 you'll see the full range of financial ratios, plus more analytical techniques.

ROE: Relating Profitability to Stockholder Investment

Investors search for companies whose stocks are likely to increase in value. They're constantly comparing companies. But a comparison of The Home Depot, Inc., with a start-up company is not meaningful. The Home Depot's profits run into the millions, far exceeding a new company's net income. In addition, management of the company has spent years investing in assets and managing both borrowed resources and stockholders' invested capital. Does this automatically make The Home Depot, Inc., a better investment? Not necessarily. To compare the profitability of companies of different sizes, investors use some standard profitability measures, including

- return on assets and
- return on equity.

DuPont Analysis, discussed earlier in Chapter 7 and 9, provides a convenient and meaningful way to analyze the various elements of profitability, as shown in the following diagram:

ROA				Leverage Ratio	=	ROE
Net Profit Margin Ratio	×	Asset Turnover Ratio	×	Leverage Ratio	=	Return on Equity
$\dfrac{\text{Net income*}}{\text{Net sales}}$	×	$\dfrac{\text{Net sales}}{\text{Average total assets}}$	×	$\dfrac{\text{Average total assets}}{\text{Average common stockholders' equity}}$	=	$\dfrac{\text{Net income*}}{\text{Average common stockholders' equity}}$

* minus preferred dividends

The left-hand side of the diagram shows that **rate of return on total assets** or **return on assets (ROA)** is the product of two drivers: *net profit margin ratio* and *asset turnover*. Net profit margin ratio measures how effectively the company has earned revenue while controlling costs. Asset turnover measures how efficiently the company has managed its assets. We discussed these ratios as well as strategies that management uses to improve them in Chapter 7 (pp. 401–403). In Chapter 9 (p. 523), we introduced the *leverage ratio*, or *equity multiplier*, which shows the impact of the use of debt, or leverage, to magnify ROA. Together, the three ratios combine to measure **rate of return on common stockholders' equity**, or **return on equity (ROE)**, in the last column on the right-hand side of the diagram.

ROE shows the relationship between net income and common stockholders' equity. Return on equity is computed only on common stock because the return to preferred stockholders is usually limited to a specified dividend (for example, 5%). The numerator of ROE is net income minus preferred dividends, if any. The denominator is *average common stockholders' equity*—the average of total stockholders' equity minus preferred equity, if any. Since most companies do not have preferred stock, adjustments for preferred dividends and preferred equity are usually not necessary.

Let's use the DuPont Analysis model to analyze The Home Depot, Inc.'s, ROE as of February 1, 2015. All balance sheet computations in this paragraph are based on figures taken from the company's comparative Consolidated Balance Sheets on page 565. You should recompute the ratios and confirm the computations as you read. From its consolidated statements of earnings (**http://www.sec.gov**) (not reproduced in this chapter) we find that the company earned $6,345 million net income on $83,176 million in net sales for the year ended February 1, 2015, for a net profit margin ratio of 7.628%. This ratio is then combined with the balance-sheet information (in millions) to compute ROA and ROE as follows:

	ROA		$\times$	**Leverage Ratio**	=	ROE
Net Profit Margin Ratio	$\times$	Asset Turnover Ratio	$\times$	Leverage Ratio	=	Return on Equity
$\dfrac{\text{Net income*}}{\text{Net sales}}$	$\times$	$\dfrac{\text{Net sales}}{\text{Average total assets}}$	$\times$	$\dfrac{\text{Average total assets}}{\text{Average common stockholders' equity}}$	=	$\dfrac{\text{Net income*}}{\text{Average common stockholders' equity}}$
$\dfrac{\$6{,}345}{\$83{,}176}$	$\times$	$\dfrac{\$83{,}176}{\$40{,}232}$	$\times$	$\dfrac{\$40{,}232}{\$10{,}922}$	=	$\dfrac{\$6{,}345}{\$10{,}922}$
$\{7.628\%\}$	$\times$	$\{2.067\}$	$\times$	$\{3.6836\}$	=	$\{58.1\%\}$
	$\{$ROA $= 15.77\%\}$					

* minus preferred dividends

Each dollar of sales has resulted in about 7.628 cents of net profit. The company's asset turnover was 2.067, meaning that it earned $2.067 in sales for each average dollar invested in total assets. A leverage ratio of 3.6836 to 1 means that the company owns about $3.68 of assets for each dollar of stockholders' equity invested. Average total liabilities are $29,310 million, so the debt ratio for the company (based on average total liabilities to average total assets) is about 73% ($29,310/$40,232). The leverage ratio of 3.6836, multiplied by ROA of 15.77%, magnifies profitability on shareholder investment to 58.1%.

Are these returns strong, weak, or somewhere in between? To answer that question, it is necessary to have other information, such as

- comparative returns for The Home Depot, Inc., for prior years and
- comparative returns for other companies in the same industry.

For example, the following diagram compares The Home Depot, Inc.'s, fiscal 2014 and 2013 ROE. It also compares The Home Depot, Inc.'s, ROE for the year ended February 1, 2015, with that of a competitor, **Lowes Companies, Inc.**

	Net Profit Margin Ratio	$\times$	Asset Turnover Ratio	$\times$	Leverage Ratio	=	Return on Equity
The Home Depot, Inc. 2015	7.628%	$\times$	2.067	$\times$	3.6836	=	58.1%
The Home Depot, Inc. 2014	6.83%	$\times$	1.93	$\times$	2.69	=	35.5%
The Home Depot, Inc. 2013	6.07%	$\times$	1.83	$\times$	2.29	=	25.4%
Lowes Companies, Inc. 2015	4.80%	$\times$	1.74	$\times$	2.96	=	24.7%

In comparison with the year ended February 2, 2014, The Home Depot, Inc.'s, ROE for the year ended February 1, 2015, is substantially higher. Its net profit margin ratio in fiscal 2015 rose to 7.628% from 6.83% in fiscal 2014, meaning the company was more profitable on each dollar of sales. Eight-tenths of one percent improvement may not seem like much at first, but when multiplied by over $83 billion in sales, it calculates to an extra $664 million in net profit! In addition, asset turnover increased from 1.93 to 2.067, which means the company earned more in sales per dollar invested and so was more efficient in fiscal 2015 than in fiscal 2014. The leverage ratio increased to 3.68 during fiscal 2015 from 2.69 during fiscal 2014, indicating the company was using more debt financing in fiscal 2015 than in the previous year. With interest rates at all-time lows, the period from 2013 through 2015 was a good period to incur debt, as long as it could be repaid in a timely manner and as long as the company was earning more on the borrowed funds than those funds cost in terms of interest. In summary, the company has been more effective (profitable), more efficient (smaller relative investment in assets), and more highly leveraged (debt) in the past three years. All of this activity combined amounted to a boost in ROE to 58.1% in the year ended February 1, 2015—good news for investors, and good news for the company's share price, which increased from $67.30 at January 31, 2013 to $104.43 at February 1, 2015.

In comparison with ROE data for Lowes Companies, Inc., The Home Depot, Inc.'s, results in fiscal 2015 were higher in every dimension. Its net profit margin ratio (7.628%) bested Lowes by 2.8%, meaning The Home Depot stores were significantly more profitable per dollar of sales. The likely explanation for this is that The Home Depot's costs per dollar of sales were lower. The Home Depot, Inc., turned assets over more efficiently than Lowes in fiscal 2015 (2.067 vs. 1.74). Finally, The Home Depot, Inc., has significantly more leverage in its capital structure (3.6836 vs. 2.96), thus magnifying its ROA from 15.77% to an ROE of 58.1%, compared to an ROE of only 24.7% for Lowes Companies, Inc.

What is a good rate of return on total assets? Ten percent is considered a strong benchmark in most industries. However, rates of return on assets vary by industry because the components of ROA are different across industries. Some high-technology companies earn much higher returns than do utility companies, grocery stores, and manufacturers of consumer goods such as toothpaste and paper towels. Companies that are efficient, generating a large amount of sales per dollar of assets invested, or companies that can differentiate their products and earn higher gross profit margins on them, have higher ROA than companies that do not have these attributes.

You can see by studying the DuPont model that whenever ROA is positive, ROE is always higher than ROA because of the leverage ratio (or equity multiplier). This also makes sense from an economic standpoint. Stockholders take a lot more investment risk than creditors, so the stockholders demand that ROE exceed ROA. They expect the return on their investment to exceed the cost of borrowed funds. Investors and creditors compare companies' ROE in much the same way they compare ROA. The higher the rate of return, the more successful the company. In many industries, 15% is considered a good ROE. The Home Depot, Inc.'s, ROE of 58.1% for the year ended February 1, 2015 is exceptionally high.

The Decision Guidelines at the end of the chapter (p. 594) offer suggestions for what to consider when investing in stock. You will also use all of these ratios more in Chapter 13.

REPORT STOCKHOLDERS' EQUITY TRANSACTIONS IN THE FINANCIAL STATEMENTS

The details of transactions impacting the various accounts in stockholders' equity are reported on the statement of cash flows as well as on the statement of stockholders' equity.

 Report stockholders' equity transactions in the financial statements

Statement of Cash Flows

Many of the transactions we've covered are reported on the statement of cash flows. Equity transactions are *financing activities* because the company is dealing with its owners. Financing transactions that affect both cash and equity fall into three main categories:

- Issuance of stock
- Treasury stock
- Dividends

Financing activities from the Consolidated Statement of Cash Flows for The Home Depot, Inc., for the year ended February 1, 2015, are reported in Exhibit 10-8.

Issuances of Stock. The Home Depot, Inc., received cash of $252 million in conjunction with the issuance of new common stock during the year ended February 1, 2015.

Treasury Stock. During the year ended February 1, 2015, The Home Depot, Inc., spent $7 billion in cash to repurchase shares of treasury stock and reported the payment as a financing activity.

Dividends. Most mature companies, including The Home Depot, Inc., pay cash dividends to their stockholders. Dividend payments are a type of financing transaction because the company is paying its stockholders for the use of their money. During the year ended February 1, 2015, The Home Depot paid $2,530 million in cash dividends. Stock dividends are not reported on the statement of cash flows because the company pays no cash for them.

In Exhibit 10-8, cash payments for the purchase of treasury stock and dividends appear as negative amounts, denoted by parentheses. Issuance of stock appears as a positive amount.

Exhibit 10-8 | The Home Depot, Inc.'s, Financing Activities Related to Stockholders' Equity

	A	B
	A1	
	A	**B**
1	**Cash Flows from Financing Activities**	**(In millions)**
2	Repurchases of common stock	(7,000)
3	Proceeds from sale of common stock	252
4	Cash Dividends Paid to Stockholders	(2,530)
5		

Statement of Stockholders' Equity

Businesses may report stockholders' equity in a way that differs from our examples. We use a detailed format in this book to help you learn all the components of stockholders' equity. Exhibit 10-9 contains the Consolidated Statements of Stockholders' Equity for The Home Depot, Inc., for the two fiscal years ended February 1, 2015.

Exhibit 10-9 | The Home Depot, Inc.'s, Consolidated Statements of Stockholders' Equity

	A	B	C	D	E	F	G	H	I
1	**The Home Depot, Inc. Consolidated Statements of Stockholders' Equity (Adapted)**								
2	**In Millions**	**Total**	**Common Stock**	**Shares**	**Paid-in Capital**	**Retained Earnings**	**Accumulated Other Comprehensive Income (Loss)**	**Treasury Stock**	**Shares**
3	BALANCE at Feb. 03, 2013	$ 17,777	$ 88	1,754	$ 7,948	$ 20,038	$ 397	$ (10,694)	270
4	Net Earnings	5,385				5,385			
5	Shares Issued Under Employee Stock Plans, shares	103		7	103				
6	Tax Effect of Stock-Based Compensation	123			123				
7	Foreign-Currency Translation Adjustments	(329)					(329)		
8	Cash Flow Hedges, net of tax	(12)					(12)		
9	Stock Options, Awards and Amortization of Restricted Stock	228			228				
10	Repurchases of Common Stock	(8,500)						(8,500)	111
11	Cash Dividends	(2,243)				(2,243)			
12	Other	(10)					(10)		
13	BALANCE at Feb. 02, 2014	$ 12,522	$ 88	1,761	$ 8,402	$ 23,180	$ 46	$ (19,194)	381
14	Net Earnings	6,345				6,345			
15	Shares Issued Under Employee Stock Plans, shares	122		7	122				
16	Tax Effect of Stock-Based Compensation	136			136				
17	Foreign-Currency Translation Adjustments	(510)					(510)		
18	Cash Flow Hedges, net of tax	11					11		
19	Stock Options, Awards and Amortization of Restricted Stock	225			225				
20	Repurchases of Common Stock	(7,000)						(7,000)	80
21	Cash Dividends	(2,530)				(2,530)			
22	Other	1					1		
23	BALANCE at Feb. 01, 2015	$ 9,322	$ 88	1,768	$ 8,885	$ 26,995	$ (452)	$ (26,194)	461
24									

Notice that, in contrast to the balance-sheet presentation (shown on p. 565), the Statement of Stockholders' Equity presents a detailed vertical analysis of the activity in each separate account in the Stockholders' Equity section over multiple years (usually three years, although, for space purposes, our illustration covers only two). There are separate columns for each account in stockholders' equity: Common Stock (both dollar amounts and number of shares); Paid-in Capital; Retained Earnings; and Treasury Stock (both dollar amounts and number of shares). The statement also contains another column entitled Accumulated Other Comprehensive Income (Loss), which summarizes changes in the few elements of income that are permitted to bypass the income statement. These include foreign-currency translation adjustments resulting from consolidation of foreign subsidiaries and unrealized gains or losses on available-for-sale securities. Both of these were discussed in Chapter 8. Other comprehensive income will be covered again in Chapter 11.

A Detailed Stockholders' Equity Section of the Balance Sheet

One of the most important skills you will take from this course is the ability to understand the financial statements of real companies. Exhibit 10-10 presents a side-by-side comparison of the stockholders' equity section of the balance sheet using our general teaching format and the format you are likely to encounter in real-world balance sheets, such as that of The Home Depot, Inc. All amounts are assumed for this illustration.

Exhibit 10-10 | Formats for Reporting Stockholders' Equity

	A	B	C	D
1	**General Teaching Format**		**Real-World Format**	
2	**Stockholders' Equity**		**Stockholders' Equity**	
3				
4	Paid-in capital:		Preferred stock, 8%, $10 par, 30,000	
5	Preferred stock, 8%, $10 par, 30,000		shares authorized, issued, and outstanding	$ 330,000
6	shares authorized, issued, and outstanding	$ 300,000	Common stock, $1 par, 100,000 shares	
7	Paid-in capital in excess of		authorized, 60,000 shares issued,	60,000
8	par—preferred	30,000	58,600 shares outstanding	
9	Common stock, $1 par, 100,000 shares		Additional paid-in capital	2,150,000
10	authorized, 60,000 shares issued,	60,000	Retained earnings	1,500,000
11	58,600 shares outstanding		Less treasury stock, common	
12	Paid-in capital in excess of		(1,400 shares at cost)	(40,000)
13	par—common	2,100,000	Accumulated other comprehensive income	200,000
14	Paid-in capital from treasury stock		Total stockholders' equity	$ 4,200,000
15	transactions, common	20,000		
17	Paid-in capital from retirement of			
18	preferred stock	30,000		
19	Total paid-in capital	2,540,000		
20	Retained earnings	1,500,000		
21	Subtotal	4,040,000		
22	Less treasury stock, common			
23	(1,400 shares at cost)	(40,000)		
24	Accumulated other comprehensive income	200,000		
25	Total stockholders' equity	$ 4,200,000		
26				

In general,

- Preferred stock (whenever it exists) comes first and is usually reported as a single amount.

- Common stock lists par value per share, the number of shares authorized, the number of shares issued, and the number of shares outstanding. The balance of the Common Stock account is determined as

Common stock = Number of shares *issued* × Par value per share

- Additional paid-in capital combines Paid-in capital in excess of par plus Paid-in capital from other sources. Additional paid-in capital belongs to the common stockholders.

- Outstanding stock equals issued stock minus treasury stock.
- Retained earnings comes after the paid-in capital accounts.
- Treasury stock is reported, usually at cost, as a deduction.
- Accumulated other comprehensive income is added (or accumulated other comprehensive loss is deducted). This account may be listed either before or after Treasury Stock.

 # DECISION GUIDELINES

INVESTING IN STOCK

Suppose you've saved $5,000 to invest. You visit a nearby **Edward Jones** office, where the broker probes for your risk tolerance. Are you investing mainly for dividends or for growth in the stock price? You must make some key decisions.

Investor Decision	Guidelines
Which category of stock to buy for:	
• A safe investment?	Preferred stock is safer than common, but for even more safety, invest in high-grade corporate bonds or government securities.
• Steady dividends?	Cumulative preferred stock. However, the company is not obligated to declare preferred dividends, and the dividends are unlikely to increase.
• Increasing dividends?	Common stock, as long as the company's net income is increasing and the company has adequate cash flow to pay a dividend after meeting all obligations and other cash demands.
• Increasing stock price?	Common stock, but again only if the company's net income and cash flow are increasing.
How to identify a good stock to buy?	There are many ways to pick stock investments. One strategy that works reasonably well is to invest in companies that consistently earn higher rates of return on assets and on equity than competing firms in the same industry. Also, select industries that are expected to grow.

1. The balance sheet of Newline Corp. reported the following at December 31, 2016. The company has no transactions that produce other comprehensive income or loss.

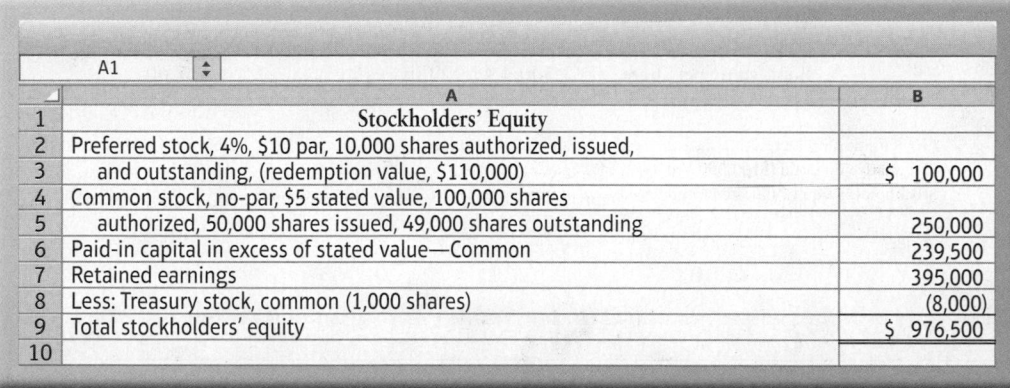

	A	B
1	Stockholders' Equity	
2	Preferred stock, 4%, $10 par, 10,000 shares authorized, issued,	
3	and outstanding, (redemption value, $110,000)	$ 100,000
4	Common stock, no-par, $5 stated value, 100,000 shares	
5	authorized, 50,000 shares issued, 49,000 shares outstanding	250,000
6	Paid-in capital in excess of stated value—Common	239,500
7	Retained earnings	395,000
8	Less: Treasury stock, common (1,000 shares)	(8,000)
9	Total stockholders' equity	$ 976,500
10		

Requirements

a. Is the preferred stock cumulative or noncumulative? How can you tell?
b. What is the total amount of the annual preferred dividend?
c. How many shares of common stock are outstanding?
d. Compute the book value per share of the common stock. No preferred dividends are in arrears, and Newline has not yet declared the 2016 dividend.

2. Use the following accounts and related balances to prepare the classified balance sheet of Whitewing, Inc., at September 30, 2016. Use the account format of the balance sheet.

Common stock, $1 par,		Long-term note payable	$ 80,000
50,000 shares authorized,		Inventory	85,000
20,000 shares issued	$ 20,000	Property, plant, and	
Dividends payable	4,000	equipment, net	226,000
Cash	9,000	Accounts receivable, net	23,000
Accounts payable	28,000	Preferred stock, $3.75, no-par,	
Paid-in capital in excess		10,000 shares authorized,	
of par—common	115,000	2,000 shares issued	24,000
Treasury stock, common,		Accrued liabilities	3,000
1,000 shares at cost	6,000	Retained earnings	75,000

Answers

1. a. The preferred stock is cumulative because it is not specifically labeled otherwise.
   b. Total annual preferred dividend: $4,000 ($100,000 × 0.04).
   c. Common shares outstanding: 49,000 (50,000 issued − 1,000 treasury).
   d. Book value per share of common stock:

Common:	
Total stockholders' equity	$976,500
Less stockholders' equity allocated to preferred	(114,000)*
Stockholders' equity allocated to common	$862,500
Book value per share ($862,500 ÷ 49,000 shares)	$17.60

*Redemption value	$110,000
Cumulative dividend ($100,000 × 0.04)	4,000
Stockholders' equity allocated to preferred	$114,000

2.

	A	B	C	D	E
1	**Whitewing, Inc.** **Balance Sheet** **September 30, 2016**				
2	**Assets**		**Liabilities**		
3	Current Assets		Current Liabilities		
4	Cash	$ 9,000	Account payable		$ 28,000
5	Accounts receivable, net	23,000	Dividends payable		4,000
6	Inventory	85,000	Accrued liabilities		3,000
7	Total current assets	117,000	Total current liabilities		35,000
8	Property, plant, and		Long-term note payable		80,000
9	equipment, net	226,000	Total liabilities		115,000
10					
11			**Stockholders' Equity**		
12			Preferred stock, $3.75, no par,		
13			10,000 shares authorized,		
14			2,000 shares issued and		
15			outstanding	$ 24,000	
16			Common stock, $1 par,		
17			50,000 shares authorized,		
18			20,000 shares issued,		
19			19,000 shares outstanding	20,000	
20			Paid-in capital in excess of		
21			par—common	115,000	
22			Retained earnings	75,000	
23			Treasury stock, common,		
24			1,000 shares at cost	(6,000)	
25			Total stockholders' equity		228,000
26			Total liabilities and		
27	Total assets	$ 343,000	stockholders' equity		$ 343,000
28					

Review | Stockholders' Equity

Quick Check (Answers are given on page 630.)

1. Cooper Company is authorized to issue 60,000 shares of $1 par common stock. On March 30, 2016, Cooper issued 30,000 shares at $11 per share. Cooper's journal entry to record these facts should include a

   a. debit to Common Stock for $330,000.
   b. credit to Paid-in Capital in Excess of Par for $330,000.
   c. credit to Common Stock for $30,000.
   d. Both a and c.

Questions 2–5 use the following account balances of Machado Co. at August 31, 2016:

Dividends Payable.........................	$ 10,000	Cash..	$136,000
Preferred Stock, $50 par...............	25,000	Common Stock, $10 par...............	1,800,000
Paid-in Capital in Excess of Par—		Retained Earnings........................	225,000
Common.................................	180,000		

2. How many shares of common stock has Machado issued?

   a. 136,000   c. 1,980,000
   b. 180,000   d. Some other amount

3. Machado's total paid-in capital at August 31, 2016, is

   a. $2,005,000   c. $180,000
   b. $1,995,000   d. $2,220,000

4. Machado's total stockholders' equity as of August 31, 2016, is

   a. $2,230,000   c. $2,356,000
   b. $2,005,000   d. $850,000

5. What would Machado's total stockholders' equity be if Machado had $20,000 of treasury stock?

   a. $2,356,000   c. $2,210,000
   b. $2,005,000   d. $2,220,000

6. BOGO Corporation purchased treasury stock in 2016 at a price of $22 per share and resold the treasury stock in 2017 at a price of $42 per share. What amount should BOGO report on its income statement for 2017?

   a. $20 gain per share   c. $42 gain per share
   b. $22 gain per share   d. $0

7. The stockholders' equity section of a corporation's balance sheet reports

	Discount on Bonds Payable	*Treasury Stock*
a.	No	Yes
b.	Yes	Yes
c.	Yes	No
d.	No	No

8. The purchase of treasury stock

   a. increases one asset and decreases another asset.
   b. decreases total assets and increases total stockholders' equity.
   c. has no effect on total assets, total liabilities, or total stockholders' equity.
   d. decreases total assets and decreases total stockholders' equity.

9. When does a cash dividend become a legal liability?
   - **a.** On date of payment
   - **b.** On date of record
   - **c.** On date of declaration
   - **d.** Never, because it is paid

10. When do dividends increase stockholders' equity?
    - **a.** On date of payment
    - **b.** On date of record
    - **c.** On date of declaration
    - **d.** Never

11. Forest Run Mall, Inc., has 3,000 shares of 10%, $30 par cumulative preferred stock and 180,000 shares of $5 par common stock outstanding. At the beginning of the current year, preferred dividends were four years in arrears. Forest Run's board of directors wants to pay a $5.25 cash dividend on each share of outstanding common stock in the current year. To accomplish this, what total amount of dividends must Forest Run declare?
    - **a.** $981,000
    - **b.** $990,000
    - **c.** $945,000
    - **d.** Some other amount

12. Stock dividends
    - **a.** increase the corporation's total liabilities.
    - **b.** reduce the total assets of the company.
    - **c.** have no effect on total stockholders' equity.
    - **d.** are distributions of cash to stockholders.

13. What is the effect of a stock dividend and a stock split on total assets?

	Stock Dividend	Stock Split
a.	No effect	No effect
b.	Decrease	Decrease
c.	No effect	Decrease
d.	Decrease	No effect

14. A 2-for-1 stock split has the same effect on the number of shares being issued as a
    - **a.** 200% stock dividend.
    - **b.** 100% stock dividend.
    - **c.** 20% stock dividend.
    - **d.** 50% stock dividend.

15. The numerator for computing the rate of return on total assets is
    - **a.** net income plus depreciation expense.
    - **b.** net income minus preferred dividends.
    - **c.** gross margin.
    - **d.** net income.

16. The denominator for computing the rate of return on equity is
    - **a.** average common stockholders' equity.
    - **b.** net sales.
    - **c.** average total assets.
    - **d.** net income.

Accounting Vocabulary

authorized stock (p. 577) Maximum number of shares a corporation can issue under its charter.

board of directors (p. 568) Group elected by the stockholders to set policy for a corporation and to appoint its officers.

book value per share (p. 588) Amount of common stockholders' equity on the company's books for each share of its stock.

bylaws (p. 567) Constitution for governing a corporation.

chairperson (p. 568) Elected by a corporation's board of directors, usually the most powerful person in the corporation.

common stock (p. 570) The most basic form of capital stock. The common stockholders own a corporation.

contributed capital (p. 569) The amount of stockholders' equity that stockholders have contributed to the corporation. Also called *paid-in capital*.

cumulative preferred stock (p. 584) Preferred stock whose owners must receive all dividends in arrears plus current year dividends before the corporation can pay dividends to the common stockholders.

deficit (p. 581) Debit balance in the Retained Earnings account.

dividend (p. 582) Distribution (usually cash) by a corporation to its stockholders.

double taxation (p. 567) Corporations pay income taxes on corporate income, then the stockholders pay personal income tax on the cash dividends that they receive from corporations.

DuPont Analysis (p. 589) A detailed approach to measuring rate of return on equity (ROE), calculated as follows: Net profit margin ratio (net income minus preferred dividends/net sales) × Total asset turnover (net sales/average total assets) × Leverage ratio (average total assets/average common stockholders' equity). The first two components of the model comprise return on assets (ROA).

initial public offering (IPO) (p. 571) The first time a corporation issues stock to the public, which causes the number of issued and outstanding shares of stock to increase.

issued stock (p. 577) Number of shares a corporation has issued to its stockholders.

legal capital (p. 570) Minimum amount of stockholders' equity that a corporation must maintain for the protection of creditors. For corporations with par-value stock, legal capital is the par value of the stock issued.

limited liability (p. 566) No personal obligation of a stockholder for corporation debts. A stockholder can lose no more on an investment in a corporation's stock than the cost of the investment.

liquidation value (p. 588) The amount a corporation must pay a preferred stockholder in the event the company liquidates and goes out of business.

market capitalization (p. 587) The market price of one share of common stock × the total number of common shares outstanding at a particular date.

market value (of a stock) (p. 587) Price for which a person could buy or sell a share of stock.

outstanding stock (p. 577) Stock in the hands of stockholders.

paid-in capital (p. 569) The amount of stockholders' equity that stockholders have contributed to the corporation. Also called *contributed capital*.

par value (p. 570) Arbitrary amount assigned by a company to a share of its stock.

preferred stock (p. 570) Stock that gives its owners certain advantages, such as the priority to receive dividends before the common stockholders and the priority to receive assets before the common stockholders if the corporation liquidates.

president (p. 568) Chief operating officer in charge of managing the day-to-day operations of a corporation.

price-earnings (P/E) ratio (p. 587) The ratio of the market price of a share of common stock to its earnings per share.

rate of return on common stockholders' equity (p. 589) Net income minus preferred dividends, divided by average common stockholders' equity. A measure of profitability. Also called *return on equity*.

rate of return on total assets (p. 589) Net income minus preferred dividends divided by average total assets. This ratio measures a company's success in using its assets to earn income for the persons who finance the business. Also called *return on assets*.

redeemable preferred stock (p. 588) A corporation reserves the right to buy an issue of stock back from its shareholders, with the intent to retire the stock.

redemption value (p. 588) The price a corporation agrees to eventually pay for its redeemable preferred stock, set when the stock is issued.

retained earnings (p. 569) The amount of stockholders' equity that the corporation has earned through profitable operation of the business and has not given back to stockholders.

return on assets (ROA) (p. 589) Another name for *rate of return on total assets*.

return on equity (ROE) (p. 589) Another name for *rate of return on common stockholders' equity*.

shareholders (p. 566) Persons or other entities that own stock in a corporation. Also called *stockholders*.

stated value (p. 571) An arbitrary amount assigned to no-par stock; similar to par value.

stock (p. 569) Shares into which the owners' equity of a corporation is divided.

stock dividend (p. 585) A proportional distribution by a corporation of its own stock to its stockholders.

stock split (p. 586) An increase in the number of issued and outstanding shares of stock coupled with a proportionate reduction in the stock's par value.

stockholder (p. 566) A person who owns stock in a corporation. Also called a *shareholder*.

stockholders' equity (p. 569) The stockholders' ownership interest in the assets of a corporation.

treasury stock (p. 578) A corporation's own stock that it has issued and later reacquired.

Assess Your Progress

Some of the following exercises and problems are available as Excel questions in MyAccountingLab.

Ethics Check

EC10-1. Identify ethical principle violated
For each of the situations listed, identify which of three principles (integrity, objectivity and independence, or due care) from the AICPA Code of Professional Conduct that is violated. Assume all persons listed in the situations are members of the AICPA. (Note: Refer to the AICPA Code of Professional Conduct contained on pages 29–30, Chapter 1 for descriptions of the principles.)

    a. Henry is the CFO for Front Street Coffee Corporation and is going to take the company public within the next six months. In an effort to make the stock look more appealing and therefore sell at a higher price, Henry overrides the system controls and records fictitious sales entries.

    b. Heather is a senior auditor for Lenardi & Calwell and has worked on its client, New Iron, Inc., for the past few years. A few months ago, New Iron, Inc., offered Heather a position in its internal audit department. Heather accepted the position and works very closely with the external auditors. In fact, she often prepares the work papers for the external auditor since she knows the systems better than the new auditors.

    c. Lauren's company, Tombolo Technologies, recently decided to repurchase stock from its shareholders. Lauren is in charge of booking the entries for this new treasury stock. However, she does not know how to record treasury stock transactions, so she just deducts the amount repurchased from Common Stock.

    d. Evan is a senior manager at Firth & Wells, a regional public accounting firm. Firth & Wells recently obtained a new client, Gatmut, Inc. Evan's sister is the CEO of Gamut, a fact that he did not disclose to the board.

Short Exercises

LO 1
S10-1. *(Learning Objective 1: Explain advantages and disadvantages of a corporation)*
What are two main advantages that a corporation has over a proprietorship and a partnership? What are two main disadvantages of a corporation? Describe the authority structure of a corporation. Who holds ultimate power?

LO 1
S10-2. *(Learning Objective 1: Describe characteristics of preferred and common stock)*
Answer the following questions about the characteristics of a corporation's stock:
1. Who are the real owners of a corporation?
2. What privileges do preferred stockholders have over common stockholders?
3. Which class of stockholders reaps greater benefits from a highly profitable corporation? Explain your answer.

LO 2
S10-3. *(Learning Objective 2: Describe the effect of a stock issuance on paid-in capital)*
Mitchell Corporation received $11,500,000 for the issuance of its stock on May 14. The par value of the Mitchell Corporation stock was only $11,500. Was the excess amount of $11,488,500 a profit to Mitchell Corporation? If not, what was it?

Suppose the par value of the Mitchell Corporation stock had been $2 per share, $4 per share, or $7 per share. Would a change in the par value of the company's stock affect Mitchell Corporation's total paid-in capital? Give the reason for your answer.

LO 2
S10-4. *(Learning Objective 2: Issue stock—par-value stock and no-par stock)* At fiscal year-end 2016, Martin Legal Services and Kramer Doughnuts reported these adapted amounts on their balance sheets (all amounts in millions except for par value per share):

	A	B	C
	A1		
1		Martin Legal Services:	
2		Common stock, $0.01 par value, 2,100 shares issued	$ 21
3		Additional paid-in capital	17,700
4			

	A	B	C
	A1		
1		Kramer Doughnuts:	
2		Common stock, no par value, 67 shares issued	$ 294
3			

Assume each company issued its stock in a single transaction. Journalize each company's issuance of its stock, using its actual account titles. Explanations are not required.

S10-5. *(Learning Objective 2: Record issuance of stock for cash and for services)* On January 14, Roland Corporation issued 100,000 shares of its $0.01 par-value common stock for the market price of $13.50 per share. Attorney Christie Mann invoiced Roland Corporation for $28,000 and has agreed to accept 2,000 shares of its $0.01 par-value common stock in full payment for this invoice. Roland Corporation issues the common stock to Attorney Mann on January 29 when the market price of the common stock was $13.70. Record the stock-issuance transactions for Roland Corporation.

LO 2

S10-6. *(Learning Objective 2: Issue stock to finance the purchase of assets)* This short exercise demonstrates the similarity and the difference between two ways to acquire plant assets.

LO 2

Case A—Issue stock and buy the assets in separate transactions:

Livingston, Inc., issued 11,000 shares of its $15 par common stock for cash of $750,000. In a separate transaction, Livingston used the cash to purchase a building for $525,000 and equipment for $225,000. Journalize the two transactions.

Case B—Issue stock to acquire the assets in a single transaction:

Livingston, Inc., issued 11,000 shares of its $15 par common stock to acquire a building with a market value of $525,000 and equipment with a market value of $225,000. Journalize this transaction.

Compare the balances in all the accounts after making both sets of entries. Are the account balances similar or different?

S10-7. *(Learning Objective 2: Prepare the stockholders' equity section of a balance sheet)* The financial statements of Hillcrest Employment Services, Inc., reported the following accounts (adapted, with dollar amounts in thousands except for par value):

LO 2

Paid-in capital in excess of par	$166	Total revenues	$1,370
Notes payable (short-term)	110	Accounts payable	510
Common stock, $0.01 par,		Retained earnings	646
900,000 shares issued	9	Other current liabilities	2,452
Long-term debt	22	Total expenses	959

Prepare the stockholders' equity section of Hillcrest's balance sheet. Net income has already been closed to Retained Earnings.

LO 5 **S10-8.** *(Learning Objective 5: Use stockholders' equity data)* Refer to the data in S10-7. Using only year-end figures rather than averages, compute the following for Hillcrest Employment Services:
   a. Net income
   b. Total liabilities
   c. Total assets (use the accounting equation)
   d. Net profit margin ratio
   e. Asset turnover
   f. Leverage ratio
   g. Return on equity

What additional information do you need before you can use this data to make decisions?

LO 3 **S10-9.** *(Learning Objective 3: Account for the purchase and sale of treasury stock)* On January 10, 2016, Jenson Corporation purchased treasury stock at a cost of $21 million. On July 3, 2016, Jenson Corporation resold some of the treasury stock for $12 million; this resold treasury stock had cost Jenson Corporation $4 million. Record the purchase and resale of Jenson Corporation's treasury stock. Overall, how much did stockholders' equity increase or decrease as a result of the two treasury-stock transactions?

LO 3 **S10-10.** *(Learning Objective 3: Explain purchase of treasury stock to fight off a takeover of the corporation)* Lucinda Lowery Exports, Inc., is located in Clancy, New Mexico. Lowery is the only company with reliable sources for its imported gifts. The company does a brisk business with specialty stores such as Neiman Marcus. Lowery's recent success has made the company a prime target for a takeover. An investment group named Alberton is attempting to buy 52% of Lowery's outstanding stock against the wishes of Lowery's board of directors. Board members are convinced that the Alberton investors would sell the most desirable pieces of the business and leave little of value.

At the most recent board meeting, several suggestions were advanced to fight off the hostile takeover bid. The suggestion with the most promise is to purchase a huge quantity of treasury stock. Lowery has the cash to carry out this plan.

Requirements

1. Suppose you are a significant stockholder of Lucinda Lowery Exports, Inc. Write a memorandum to explain to the board how the purchase of treasury stock would make it difficult for the Alberton group to take over Lowery. Include in your memo a discussion of the effect that purchasing treasury stock would have on stock outstanding and on the size of the corporation.
2. Suppose Lowery management is successful in fighting off the takeover bid and later sells the treasury stock at prices greater than the purchase price. Explain what effect these sales will have on assets, stockholders' equity, and net income.

LO 4 **S10-11.** *(Learning Objective 4: Account for cash dividends)* On February 5, 2016, Jubilee Rental Corporation's board of directors declared a dividend of $0.24, to be paid on March 18, 2016, to the shareholders of record as of the close of business on March 9, 2016. Jubilee has 2,000,000 shares of $0.01 par-value common stock authorized with 1,200,000 shares issued and outstanding. Jubilee has no preferred stock. Record the declaration of the dividend and the payment of the dividend. Include the proper dates with each journal entry.

LO 4 **S10-12.** *(Learning Objective 4: Account for cash dividends)* Greenwood Corporation earned net income of $90,000 during the year ended December 31, 2016. On December 15, Greenwood declared the annual cash dividend on its 2% preferred stock (15,000 shares with total par value of $150,000) and a $0.45 per share cash dividend on its common stock (50,000 shares with total par value of $500,000). Greenwood then paid the dividends on January 4, 2017.

Journalize the following for Greenwood Corporation:
  a. Declaring the cash dividends on December 15, 2016
  b. Paying the cash dividends on January 4, 2017

Did Retained Earnings increase or decrease during 2016? By how much?

S10-13. *(Learning Objective 4: Divide cash dividends between preferred and common stock)* LO 4
Baxter, Inc., has 25,000 shares of $1.35 preferred stock outstanding in addition to its common
stock. The $1.35 designation means that the preferred stockholders receive an annual cash
dividend of $1.35 per share. In 2016, Baxter declares an annual dividend of $500,000. The
allocation to preferred and common stockholders is

Preferred dividend (25,000 shares × $1.35 per share)................	$ 33,750
Common dividend (remainder: $500,000 − $33,750)	466,250
Total dividend..	$500,000

Answer these questions about Baxter's cash dividends.
  1. How much in dividends must Baxter declare each year before the common stockholders
     receive any cash dividends for the year?
  2. Suppose Baxter, Inc., declares cash dividends of $400,000 for 2016. How much of the
     dividends goes to preferred? How much goes to common?
  3. Is Baxter's preferred stock cumulative or noncumulative? How can you tell?
  4. Baxter, Inc., passed the preferred dividend in 2015 and 2016. Then in 2017, Baxter
     declares cash dividends of $1,300,000. How much of the dividends goes to preferred? How
     much goes to common?

S10-14. *(Learning Objective 4: Record a small stock dividend)* Downtown Bancshares has LO 4
40,000 shares of $8 par common stock outstanding. Suppose Downtown declares and distrib-
utes a 16% stock dividend when the market value of its stock is $20 per share.
  1. Journalize Downtown's declaration and distribution of the stock dividend on May 11. An
     explanation is not required.
  2. What was the overall effect of the stock dividend on Downtown's total assets? On total
     liabilities? On total stockholders' equity?

S10-15. *(Learning Objective 5: Compute book value per share)* Fresco Ambulatory, Inc., has LO 5
the following stockholders' equity:

Preferred stock, 1%, $4 par,	
34,000 shares authorized and issued.....................................	$ 136,000
Common stock, $4 par, 100,000 shares authorized,	
65,000 shares issued	260,000
Additional paid-in capital—Common	2,190,000
Retained earnings...	1,700,000
Less treasury stock, common (1,200 shares at cost)	(46,000)
Total stockholders' equity...	$4,240,000

The company has passed its preferred dividends for three years, including the current year.
Compute the book value per share of the company's common stock.

LO 5

S10-16. (*Learning Objective 5: Compute and explain return on assets and return on equity*) Give the DuPont model formula for computing (a) rate of return on total assets (ROA) and (b) rate of return on common stockholders' equity (ROE). Then answer these questions about the rate-of-return computations.

1. Explain the meaning of the component driver ratios in the computation of ROA.
2. What impact does the leverage ratio have on ROA?
3. Under what circumstances will ROE be higher than ROA? Under what circumstances would ROE be lower than ROA?

LO 5

S10-17. (*Learning Objective 5: Compute return on assets and return on equity for a leading company*) Nestor Corporation's 2016 financial statements reported the following items, with 2015 figures given for comparison (adapted, and in millions):

A	B	C	D
		2016	**2015**
	Balance Sheet		
	Total assets	¥ 10,616	¥ 9,507
	Total liabilities	¥ 7,406	¥ 6,631
	Total stockholders' equity (all common)	3,210	2,876
	Total liabilities and stockholders' equity	¥ 10,616	¥ 9,507
	Income Statement		
	Net sales revenue	¥ 7,629	
	Operating expense	7,292	
	Interest expense	31	
	Other expense	196	
	Net income	¥ 110	

Use the DuPont model to compute Nestor's return on assets and return on common equity for 2016. Evaluate the rates of return as strong or weak. What additional information would be helpful in making this decision? (¥ is the symbol for the Japanese yen.)

LO 5

S10-18. (*Learning Objective 5: Define and use various stock values*) Wallace Corporation is conducting a special meeting of its board of directors to address some concerns raised by the stockholders. Stockholders have submitted the following questions. Answer each question.

1. What is the difference between the redemption value and the liquidation value of preferred stock?
2. Suzanne Gibson, a Wallace shareholder, proposes to transfer some land she owns to the company in exchange for shares of the company stock. What value should Wallace Corporation use to determine the number of shares of our stock to issue for the land?
3. Preferred shares generally are preferred with respect to dividends and in the event of our liquidation. Why would investors buy our common stock when preferred stock is available?
4. What does the redemption value of our preferred stock require us to do?
5. One of our stockholders owns 200 shares of Wallace stock and someone has offered to buy his shares for the company's book value. Our stockholder asks us the formula for computing the book value of his stock.

LO 6

S10-19. (*Learning Objective 6: Measure cash flows from financing activities*) During 2016, Advantage Corporation earned net income of $5.8 billion and paid off $2.7 billion of long-term notes payable. Advantage raised $1.4 billion by issuing common stock, paid $3.0 billion to purchase treasury stock, and paid cash dividends of $1.7 billion. Report Advantage's *cash flows from financing* activities on the statement of cash flows for 2016.

S10-20. *(Learning Objective 6: Analyze a basic statement of stockholders' equity)* Use the following statement of stockholders' equity to answer the following questions about Beckett Corporation:

LO 6

	A	B	C	D	E	F
1	**Beckett Corporation** **Statement of Stockholders' Equity** **For the Year Ended December 31, 2016**					
2		**Common Stock $4 Par**	**Additional Paid-in Capital**	**Retained Earnings**	**Treasury Stock**	**Total Stockholders' Equity**
3	Balance, December 31, 2015	$ 40,000	$ 11,000	$ 140,000	$ (25,000)	$ 166,000
4	Issuance of stock	128,000	580,000			708,000
5	Net income			120,000		120,000
6	Cash dividends			(25,000)		(25,000)
7	Purchase of treasury stock				(15,000)	(15,000)
8	Sale of treasury stock		7,000		6,000	13,000
9	Balance, December 31, 2016	$ 168,000	$ 598,000	$ 235,000	$ (34,000)	$ 967,000
10						

1. How much cash did the issuance of common stock bring in during 2016?
2. How much in dividends did Beckett declare during 2016?
3. What was the effect of the dividends on Beckett's retained earnings? On total paid-in capital? On total stockholders' equity? On total assets?
4. What was the cost of the treasury stock that Beckett purchased during 2016?
5. What was the cost of the treasury stock that Beckett sold during the year? For how much did Beckett sell the treasury stock during 2016?
6. How much was Beckett's net income?
7. What is Beckett's total stockholders' equity as of December 31, 2016?

S10-21. *(Learning Objective 6: Analyze a statement of stockholders' equity including stock dividends and other comprehensive income)* The statement of stockholders' equity for Hammer Corporation follows.

LO 6

	A	B	C	D	E	F	G
1	**Hammer Corporation** **Statement of Stockholders' Equity** **For the Year Ended December 31, 2016**						
2		**Common Stock $4 Par**	**Additional Paid-in Capital**	**Retained Earnings**	**Treasury Stock**	**Accumulated Other Comprehensive Income**	**Total Stockholders' Equity**
3	Balance, December 31, 2015	$ 40,000	$ 12,000	$ 140,000	$ (23,000)	$ 10,000	$ 179,000
4	Issuance of stock	128,000	530,000				658,000
5	Net income			84,500			84,500
6	Cash dividends			(21,000)			(21,000)
7	Stock dividends—10%	16,800	29,200	(46,000)			0
8	Purchase of treasury stock				(7,000)		(7,000)
9	Sale of treasury stock		8,000		3,000		11,000
10	Other comprehensive income					12,000	12,000
11	Balance, December 31, 2016	$ 184,800	$ 579,200	$ 157,500	$ (27,000)	$ 22,000	$ 916,500
12							

Use Hammer Corporation's statement to answer the questions:

1. How much cash did the issuance of common stock bring in during 2016?
2. What was the effect of the stock dividends on Hammer's retained earnings? On total paid-in capital? On total stockholders' equity? On total assets?
3. What was the cost of the treasury stock that Hammer purchased during 2016? What was the cost of the treasury stock that Hammer sold during the year? For how much did Hammer sell the treasury stock during 2016?
4. Hammer revalued available-for-sale investments during the year, resulting in an unrealized gain of $9,000. It also consolidated a foreign subsidiary, resulting in a foreign currency translation gain of $3,000. How much was comprehensive income? How much should be added to Hammer's Accumulated Other Comprehensive Income? Is Accumulated Other Comprehensive Income included in Hammer's net income?

Exercises MyAccountingLab

Group A

LO 2 6

E10-22A. *(Learning Objectives 2, 6: Account for issuance of stock; prepare the stockholders' equity section of a balance sheet)* Pinkerton Stores is authorized to issue 13,000 shares of common stock. During a two-month period, Pinkerton completed these stock-issuance transactions:

Mar 23	Issued 3,000 shares of $6.00 par common stock for cash of $15.50 per share.
Apr 12	Received inventory with a market value of $20,000 and equipment with market value of $39,000 for 3,100 shares of the $6.00 par common stock.

Requirements

1. Journalize the transactions.
2. Prepare the stockholders' equity section of Pinkerton Stores' balance sheet for the transactions given in this exercise. Retained Earnings has a balance of $46,000.

LO 2

E10-23A. *(Learning Objective 2: Measure paid-in capital of a corporation)* Journey Publishing was recently organized. The company issued common stock to an attorney who provided legal services worth $15,000 to help organize the corporation. Journey Publishing also issued common stock to an inventor in exchange for her patent with a market value of $78,000. In addition, Journey received cash both for the issuance of 9,000 shares of its preferred stock at $110 per share and for the issuance of 18,000 of its common shares at $2 per share. During the first year of operations, Journey Publishing earned net income of $94,000 and declared a cash dividend of $25,000. Without making journal entries, determine the total paid-in capital created by these transactions.

LO 2

E10-24A. *(Learning Objective 2: Prepare the stockholders' equity section of a balance sheet)* The financial statements of Wellman Employment Services, Inc., reported the following accounts (adapted, with dollar amounts in thousands except for par value):

Paid-in capital in excess of par	$192	Total revenues	$1,390
Other stockholders' equity (negative)	(22)	Accounts payable	470
Common stock, $0.01 par,		Retained earnings	648
300,000 shares issued	3	Other current liabilities	2,568
Long-term debt	24	Total expenses	556

Prepare the stockholders' equity section of Wellman's balance sheet. Net income has already been closed to Retained Earnings.

E10-25A. (*Learning Objectives 3, 6: Show how treasury stock affects a company; prepare the stockholders' equity section of a balance sheet*) Alistair Software had the following selected account balances at December 31, 2016 (all numbers and amounts are in thousands, except par value per share):

LO 3 6

Inventory	$ 654	Common stock, $2.50 par	
Property, plant, and		per share, 800 shares	
equipment, net	950	authorized, 250 shares	
Paid-in capital in excess of par	900	issued	$ 625
Treasury stock,		Retained earnings	2,222
140 shares at cost	1,890	Accounts receivable, net	600
Accumulated other		Notes payable	1,166
comprehensive income (loss)	(730)*		

*Debit balance

Requirements

1. Prepare the stockholders' equity section of Alistair's balance sheet (in thousands).
2. How can Alistair have a larger balance of treasury stock than the sum of Common Stock and Paid-in Capital in Excess of Par?

E10-26A. (*Learning Objective 3: Account for the purchase and sale of treasury stock*) Cinders Marketing Corporation reported the following stockholders' equity at December 31 (adapted and in millions):

LO 3

Common stock	$ 281
Additional paid-in capital	275
Retained earnings	2,129
Treasury stock	(611)
Total stockholders' equity	$2,074

During the next year, Cinders Marketing purchased treasury stock at a cost of $28 million and resold treasury stock for $9 million (this treasury stock had cost Cinders Marketing $3 million). Record the purchase and resale of Cinders Marketing's treasury stock. Overall, how much did stockholders' equity increase or decrease as a result of the two treasury-stock transactions?

E10-27A. (*Learning Objectives 2, 3, 4: Account for issuance of stock; show how treasury stock affects a company; account for dividends*) At December 31, 2016, Sidestep Corporation reported the stockholders' equity accounts shown here (with dollar amounts in millions, except per-share amounts).

LO 2 3 4

Common stock $1.00 par value per share,	
26 million shares issued	$ 26
Paid-in capital in excess of par value	91
Retained earnings	270
Treasury stock, at cost	(40)
Total stockholders' equity	$347

Sidestep's 2017 transactions included
- **a.** Net income, $446 million
- **b.** Issuance of 6 million shares of common stock for $12.50 per share
- **c.** Purchase of 11 million shares of treasury stock for $121 million
- **d.** Sold 5 million of the treasury shares purchased in part c for $60 million
- **e.** Declaration and payment of cash dividends of $36 million

Requirements

1. Journalize Sidestep's transactions in parts b, c, d, and e. Explanations are not required.
2. What was the overall effect of these transactions (parts a–e) on Sidestep's stockholders' equity?

LO 6

E10-28A. *(Learning Objective 6: Report stockholders' equity after a sequence of transactions)* Use the Sidestep Corporation data in E10-27A to prepare the stockholders' equity section of the company's balance sheet at December 31, 2017.

LO 2 3 4 6

E10-29A. *(Learning Objectives 2, 3, 4, 6: Infer transactions from a company's comparative stockholders' equity)* Quanto Products Company reported the following stockholders' equity on its balance sheet:

	A	B	C
		December 31,	
1	**Stockholders' Equity** **(Dollars and shares in millions except for par value)**	**2017**	**2016**
2	Convertible preferred stock—$1.00 par value; authorized 65 shares;		
3	issued and outstanding:		
4	2017 and 2016—4 and 8 shares, respectively	$ 4	$ 8
5	Common stock—$1.00 per share par value; authorized		
6	1,500 shares; issued: 2017 and 2016—200		
7	and 100 shares, respectively	200	100
8	Additional paid-in capital	700	278
9	Retained earnings	6,300	5,025
10	Treasury stock, common—at cost		
11	2017—38 shares; 2016—8 shares	(874)	(152)
12	Total stockholders' equity	6,330	5,259
13	Total liabilities and stockholders' equity	$ 46,955	$ 44,009
14			

Requirements

1. What caused Quanto's preferred stock to decrease during 2017? Cite all possible causes.
2. What caused Quanto's common stock to increase during 2017? Identify all possible causes.
3. How many shares of Quanto's common stock were outstanding at December 31, 2017?
4. Quanto's net income during 2017 was $1,380 million. How much were Quanto's dividends during the year?
5. During 2017, Quanto sold no treasury stock. What average price per share did Quanto pay for the treasury stock that the company purchased during the year?

LO 4

E10-30A. *(Learning Objective 4: Compute dividends on preferred and common stock)* Supreme Manufacturing, Inc., reported the following at December 31, 2016, and December 31, 2017:

	A	B
1	**Stockholders' Equity**	
2	Preferred stock, cumulative, $4.00 par, 7%, 65,000 shares issued	$ 260,000
3	Common stock, $0.35 par, 9,090,000 shares issued	3,181,500
4		

Supreme Manufacturing has paid all preferred dividends through 2013.

Requirement

1. Compute the total amounts of dividends to both preferred and common for 2016 and 2017 if total dividends are $120,000 in 2016 and $204,000 in 2017.

E10-31A. *(Learning Objectives 4, 6: Record a stock dividend and report stockholders' equity)* The stockholders' equity for Rightwell Corporation on June 16, 2017, follows:

	A	B
1	**Stockholders' Equity**	
2	Common stock, $0.40 par, 2,300,000 shares	
3	authorized, 400,000 shares issued	$ 160,000
4	Paid-in capital in excess of par—common	861,013
5	Retained earnings	7,133,000
6	Accumulated other comprehensive income (loss)	(190,000)
7	Total stockholders' equity	$ 7,964,013
8		

On June 16, 2017, the market price of Rightwell common stock was $18 per share. Assume Rightwell declared and distributed a 12% stock dividend on this date.

Requirements

1. Journalize the declaration and distribution of the stock dividend.
2. Prepare the stockholders' equity section of the balance sheet after the stock dividend.
3. Why is total stockholders' equity unchanged by the stock dividend?
4. Suppose Rightwell had a cash balance of $550,000 on June 17, 2017. What is the maximum amount of cash dividends Rightwell can declare?

E10-32A. *(Learning Objectives 2, 3, 4: Measure the effects of stock issuance, dividends, splits, and treasury-stock transactions)* Identify the effects—both the direction and the dollar amount—of these assumed transactions on the total stockholders' equity of Ashby Corporation. Each transaction is independent.

    a. Declaration of cash dividends of $78 million.
    b. Payment of the cash dividend in (a).
    c. A 20% stock dividend. Before the dividend, 68 million shares of $4.00 par common stock were outstanding; the market value was $16.47 at the time of the dividend.
    d. A 30% stock dividend. Before the dividend, 68 million shares of $4.00 par common stock were outstanding; the market value was $20.25 at the time of the dividend.
    e. Purchase of 2,300 shares of treasury stock (par value $4.00) at $15.25 per share.
    f. Sale of 400 shares of the treasury stock for $18.00 per share. Cost of the treasury stock was $15.25 per share.
    g. A 3-for-1 stock split. Prior to the split, 68 million shares of $4.00 par common stock were outstanding.

E10-33A. *(Learning Objective 5: Measure book value per share of common stock)* The balance sheet of Eclectic Rug Company reported the following:

Redeemable preferred stock, 8%, $100 par value,
    redemption value $25,000; outstanding 200 shares................ $20,000
Common stockholders' equity:
    4,000 shares issued and outstanding 70,000
Total stockholders' equity... $90,000

Requirements

1. Compute the book value per share for the common stock, assuming all preferred dividends are fully paid up including the current year (none in arrears).
2. Compute the book value per share of the common stock, assuming that three years' cumulative preferred dividends, including the current year, are in arrears.
3. Eclectic Rug's common stock recently traded at a market price of $14.75 per share. Does this mean that Eclectic Rug's stock is a good buy at that price?

LO 5

E10-34A. *(Learning Objective 5: Evaluate profitability)* York Company included the following items in its financial statements for 2016, the current year (amounts in millions):

Payment of long-term debt..........	$17,075	Dividends paid......................	$ 205
Proceeds from issuance		Net sales:	
of common stock....................	8,415	Current year.....................	80,000
Total liabilities:		Preceding year.................	67,000
Current year-end....................	32,311	Net income:	
Preceding year-end.................	38,029	Current year.....................	2,379
Total stockholders' equity:		Preceding year.................	2,007
Current year-end....................	23,475	Operating income:	
Preceding year-end.................	14,045	Current year.....................	4,878
Borrowings...............................	6,590	Preceding year.................	3,998

Requirements

1. Use DuPont Analysis to compute York's return on assets and return on common equity during 2016 (the current year). York has no preferred stock outstanding.
2. Do the company's rates of return look strong or weak? Give your reason.
3. What additional information do you need to make the decision in requirement 2?

LO 6

E10-35A. *(Learning Objective 6: Report cash flows from financing activities)* Use the York Company data in E10-34A to show how the company reported cash flows from financing activities during 2016 (the current year).

LO 6

E10-36A. *(Learning Objective 6: Use a company's statement of stockholders' equity)* Seaside Water Company reported the following items on its statement of shareholders' equity for the year ended December 31, 2016 (amounts in thousands of dollars):

	$1.00 Par Common Stock	Additional Paid-in Capital	Retained Earnings	Accumulated Other Comprehensive Income	Total Shareholders' Equity
Balance, December 31, 2015.............	$395	$1,630	$4,500	$7	$6,532
Net earnings.......................................			1,110		
Other comprehensive income............				1	
Issuance of stock..............................	100	290			
Cash dividends...................................			(75)		
Balance, December 31, 2016.............					

Requirements

1. Determine the December 31, 2016, balances in Seaside Water's shareholders' equity accounts and total shareholders' equity on this date.
2. Seaside Water's total liabilities on December 31, 2016, are $7,800. What is Seaside Water's debt ratio on this date?
3. Was there a profit or a loss for the year ended December 31, 2016? How can you tell?
4. At what price per share did Seaside Water issue common stock during 2016?

Group B

LO 2 6

E10-37B. *(Learning Objectives 2, 6: Account for issuance of stock; prepare the stockholders' equity section of a balance sheet)* Tropical Goods is authorized to issue 10,000 shares of common stock. During a two-month period, Tropical completed these stock-issuance transactions:

Feb 23	Issued 1,700 shares of $2.00 par common stock for cash of $15.00 per share.
Mar 12	Received inventory with a market value of $19,000 and equipment with market value of $46,000 for 3,200 shares of the $2.00 par common stock.

Requirements

1. Journalize the transactions.
2. Prepare the stockholders' equity section of Tropical Sporting Goods' balance sheet for the transactions given in this exercise. Retained Earnings has a balance of $45,000.

E10-38B. *(Learning Objective 2: Measure paid-in capital of a corporation)* Nationwide Publishing was recently organized. The company issued common stock to an attorney who provided legal services worth $27,000 to help organize the corporation. Nationwide Publishing also issued common stock to an inventor in exchange for her patent with a market value of $83,000. In addition, Nationwide received cash both for the issuance of 10,000 shares of its preferred stock at $70 per share and for the issuance of 17,000 shares of its common shares at $8 per share. During the first year of operations, Nationwide Publishing earned net income of $72,000 and declared a cash dividend of $28,000. Without making journal entries, determine the total paid-in capital created by these transactions.

LO 2

E10-39B. *(Learning Objective 2: Prepare the stockholders' equity section of a balance sheet)* The financial statements of Royal Employment Services, Inc., reported the following accounts (adapted, with dollar amounts in thousands except for par value):

LO 2

Paid-in capital in excess of par	$207	Total revenues	$1,450
Other stockholders' equity (negative)	(27)	Accounts payable	460
Common stock, $0.01 par,		Retained earnings	643
900,000 shares issued	9	Other current liabilities	2,562
Long-term debt	23	Total expenses	836

Prepare the stockholders' equity section of Royal's balance sheet. Net income has already been closed to Retained Earnings.

S10-40B. *(Learning Objectives 3, 6: Show how treasury stock affects a company; prepare the stockholders' equity section of a balance sheet)* Patterson Software had the following selected account balances at December 31, 2016 (all numbers and amounts are in thousands, except par value per share):

LO 3 6

Inventory	$ 653	Common stock, $2.00 par	
Property, plant, and		per share, 800 shares	
equipment, net	903	authorized, 400 shares	
Paid-in capital in excess of par	899	issued	$ 800
Treasury stock,		Retained earnings	2,240
160 shares at cost	1,840	Accounts receivable, net	1,100
Accumulated other		Notes payable	1,254
comprehensive income (loss)	(730)*		

*Debit balance

Requirements

1. Prepare the stockholders' equity section of Patterson Software's balance sheet (in thousands).
2. How can Patterson have a larger balance of treasury stock than the sum of Common Stock and Paid-in Capital in Excess of Par?

E10-41B. *(Learning Objective 3: Account for the purchase and sale of treasury stock)* Raintree Marketing Corporation reported the following stockholders' equity at December 31 (adapted and in millions):

LO 3

Common stock	$ 365
Additional paid-in capital	286
Retained earnings	3,190
Treasury stock	(690)
Total stockholders' equity	$3,151

During the next year, Raintree Marketing purchased treasury stock at a cost of $34 million and resold treasury stock for $15 million (this treasury stock had cost Raintree Marketing $6 million). Record the purchase and resale of Raintree Marketing's treasury stock. Overall, how much did stockholders' equity increase or decrease as a result of the two treasury-stock transactions?

LO 2 3 4

S10-42B. *(Learning Objectives 2, 3, 4: Account for issuance of stock; show how treasury stock affects a company; account for dividends)* At December 31, 2016, Pioneer Corporation reported the stockholders' equity accounts shown here (with dollar amounts in millions, except per-share amounts).

Common stock $3.00 par value per share, 22 million shares issued....................	$ 66
Paid-in capital in excess of par value.....	33
Retained earnings.................................	250
Treasury stock, at cost	(100)
Total stockholders' equity................	$249

Pioneer's 2017 transactions included
  a. Net income, $447 million
  b. Issuance of 10 million shares of common stock for $14 per share
  c. Purchase of 5 million shares of treasury stock for $65 million
  d. Sold 4 million of the treasury shares purchased in part c for $56 million
  e. Declaration and payment of cash dividends of $33 million

Requirements

1. Journalize Pioneer's transactions in parts b, c, d, and e. Explanations are not required.
2. What was the overall effect of these transactions (parts a through e) on Pioneer Corporation's stockholders' equity?

LO 6

E10-43B. *(Learning Objective 6: Report stockholders' equity after a sequence of transactions)* Use the Pioneer Corporation data in E10-42B to prepare the stockholders' equity section of the company's balance sheet at December 31, 2017.

LO 2 3 4 6

E10-44B. *(Learning Objectives 2, 3, 4, 6: Infer transactions from a company's comparative stockholders' equity)* Crogan Products Company reported the following stockholders' equity on its balance sheet:

	A	B	C
		December 31,	
1	**Stockholders' Equity** (Dollars and shares in millions except for par value)	**2017**	**2016**
2	Convertible preferred stock—$2.50 par value; authorized 70 shares;		
3	issued and outstanding:		
4	2017 and 2016—6 and 12 shares, respectively	$ 15	$ 30
5	Common stock—$3.00 per share par value; authorized		
6	1,300 shares; issued: 2017 and 2016—300		
7	and 200 shares, respectively	900	600
8	Additional paid-in capital	1,200	655
9	Retained earnings	6,300	5,075
10	Treasury stock, common—at cost		
11	2017—57 shares; 2016—12 shares	(1,254)	(228)
12	Total stockholders' equity	7,161	6,132
13	Total liabilities and stockholders' equity	$ 47,686	$ 44,932
14			

Requirements

1. What caused Crogan's preferred stock to decrease during 2017? Cite all possible causes.
2. What caused Crogan's common stock to increase during 2017? Identify all possible causes.

3. How many shares of Crogan's common stock were outstanding at December 31, 2017?
4. Crogan's net income during 2017 was $1,430 million. How much were Crogan's dividends during the year?
5. During 2017, Crogan sold no treasury stock. What average price per share did Crogan pay for the treasury stock that the company purchased during the year?

E10-45B. *(Learning Objective 4: Compute dividends on preferred and common stock)* **LO 4**
Ontario Manufacturing, Inc., reported the following at December 31, 2016, and December 31, 2017:

	A	B
1	**Stockholders' Equity**	
2	Preferred stock, cumulative, $2.50 par, 4%, 55,000 shares issued	$ 137,500
3	Common stock, $0.15 par, 9,070,000 shares issued	1,360,500
4		

Ontario Manufacturing has paid all preferred dividends through 2013.

Requirement

1. Compute the total amounts of dividends to both preferred and common for 2016 and 2017 if total dividends are $90,000 in 2016 and $225,000 in 2017.

E10-46B. *(Learning Objectives 4, 6: Record a stock dividend and report stockholders' equity)* The stockholders' equity for Little Wonders Company on August 13, 2017, follows: **LO 4 6**

	A	B
1	**Stockholders' Equity**	
2	Common stock, $0.60 par, 2,100,000 shares	
3	authorized, 700,000 shares issued	$ 420,000
4	Paid-in capital in excess of par—common	1,506,773
5	Retained earnings	7,111,000
6	Accumulated comprehensive income (loss)	(185,000)
7	Total stockholders' equity	$ 8,852,773
8		

On August 13, 2017, the market price of Little Wonders common stock was $20 per share. Assume Little Wonders declared and distributed a 25% stock dividend on this date. (Treat the stock dividend as a small stock dividend.)

Requirements

1. Journalize the declaration and distribution of the stock dividend.
2. Prepare the stockholders' equity section of the balance sheet after the stock dividend.
3. Why is total stockholders' equity unchanged by the stock dividend?
4. Suppose Little Wonders had a cash balance of $530,000 on August 14, 2017. What is the maximum amount of cash dividends Little Wonders can declare?

E10-47B. *(Learning Objectives 2, 3, 4: Measure the effects of stock issuance, dividends, splits, and treasury-stock transactions)* Identify the effects—both the direction and the dollar amount—of these assumed transactions on the total stockholders' equity of Newberry Corporation. Each transaction is independent.  **LO 2 3 4**

    a. Declaration of cash dividends of $82 million.
    b. Payment of the cash dividend in (a).
    c. A 25% stock dividend. Before the dividend, 73 million shares of $1.00 par common stock were outstanding; the market value was $19.88 at the time of the dividend.

d. A 30% stock dividend. Before the dividend, 73 million shares of $1.00 par common stock were outstanding; the market value was $18.50 at the time of the dividend.

e. Purchase of 1,700 shares of treasury stock (par value $1.00) at $17.25 per share.

f. Sale of 600 shares of the treasury stock for $19.00 per share. Cost of the treasury stock was $17.25 per share.

g. A 2-for-1 stock split. Prior to the split, 73 million shares of $1.00 par common stock were outstanding.

LO 5 **E10-48B.** *(Learning Objective 5: Measure book value per share of common stock)* The balance sheet of Walton Wallcoverings Company reported the following:

Redeemable preferred stock, 6%, $90 par value, redemption value $25,000; outstanding 200 shares................	$18,000
Common stockholders' equity:	
4,000 shares issued and outstanding	60,000
Total stockholders' equity..	$78,000

Requirements

1. Compute the book value per share for the common stock, assuming all preferred dividends are fully paid up including the current year (none in arrears.)
2. Compute the book value per share of the common stock, assuming that three years' cumulative preferred dividends, including the current year, are in arrears.
3. Walton Wallcoverings' common stock recently traded at a market price of $10.75 per share. Does this mean that Walton Wallcoverings' stock is a good buy at that price?

LO 5 **E10-49B.** *(Learning Objective 5: Evaluate profitability)* Easton Company included the following items in its financial statements for 2016, the current year (amounts in millions):

Payment of long-term debt..........	$ 17,055	Dividends paid	$	195
Proceeds from issuance		Net sales:		
of common stock.....................	8,425	Current year.....................		60,000
Total liabilities:		Preceding year.................		67,000
Current year-end....................	32,311	Net income:		
Preceding year-end	38,025	Current year.....................		6,488
Total stockholders' equity:		Preceding year.................		2,003
Current year-end.....................	23,483	Operating income:		
Preceding year-end	14,039	Current year.....................		10,054
Borrowings................................	6,500	Preceding year.................		4,012

Requirements

1. Use DuPont Analysis to compute Easton's return on assets and return on common equity during 2016 (the current year). Easton has no preferred stock outstanding.
2. Do the company's rates of return look strong or weak? Give your reason.
3. What additional information do you need to make the decision in requirement 2?

LO 6 **E10-50B.** *(Learning Objective 6: Report cash flows from financing activities)* Use the Easton data in E10-49B to show how the company reported cash flows from financing activities during 2016 (the current year).

LO 6 **E10-51B.** *(Learning Objective 6: Use a company's statement of stockholders' equity)* Rickett Water Company reported the following items on its statement of shareholders' equity for the year ended December 31, 2016 (amounts in thousands of dollars):

	$2 Par Common Stock	Additional Paid-in Capital	Retained Earnings	Accumulated Other Comprehensive Income	Total Shareholders' Equity
Balance, December 31, 2015.............	$370	$1,730	$4,500	$9	$6,609
Net earnings.....................................			1,310		
Other comprehensive income				1	
Issuance of stock	160	230			
Cash dividends..................................			(85)		
Balance, December 31, 2016.............					

Requirements

1. Determine the December 31, 2016, balances in Rickett Water's shareholders' equity accounts and total shareholders' equity on this date.
2. Rickett Water's total liabilities on December 31, 2016, are $7,000. What is Rickett Water's debt ratio on this date?
3. Was there a profit or a loss for the year ended December 31, 2016? How can you tell?
4. At what price per share did Rickett Water issue common stock during 2016?

Quiz

Test your understanding of stockholders' equity by answering the following questions. Select the best choice from among the possible answers given.

Q10-52. Which of the following is a characteristic of a corporation?
  a. Limited liability of stockholders   **c.** Mutual agency
  b. No income tax   **d.** Both b and c

Q10-53. Fair Play, Inc., issues 250,000 shares of no-par common stock for $5 per share. The journal entry is which of the following?

	A	B	C	D
1	a.	Cash	1,250,000	
2		Common Stock		250,000
3		Gain on the Sale of Stock		1,000,000
4				
5	b.	Cash	250,000	
6		Common Stock		250,000
7				
8	c.	Cash	1,250,000	
9		Common Stock		1,250,000
10				
11	d.	Cash	1,250,000	
12		Common Stock		500,000
13		Paid-in Capital in Excess of Par		750,000
14				

Q10-54. Par value
  a. may exist for common stock but not for preferred stock.
  b. is an arbitrary amount that establishes the legal capital for each share.
  c. represents the original selling price for a share of stock.
  d. is established for a share of stock after it is issued.
  e. represents what a share of stock is worth.

Q10-55. The paid-in capital portion of stockholders' equity does not include
  a. Paid-in Capital in Excess of Par Value.   **d.** Preferred Stock.
  b. Common Stock.   **e.** both c and d.
  c. Retained Earnings.

Q10-56. Preferred stock is least likely to have which of the following characteristics?

    a. The right of the holder to convert to common stock

    b. Preference as to dividends

    c. Preference as to voting

    d. Preference as to assets on liquidation of the corporation

Q10-57. Which of the following classifications represents the most shares of common stock?

    a. Issued shares   **d.** Unissued shares

    b. Outstanding shares   **e.** Authorized shares

    c. Treasury shares

Use the following information for questions Q10-58 to Q10-60:

These account balances at December 31 relate to Sportstuff, Inc.:

Accounts Payable	$ 51,600	Paid-in Capital in Excess	
Accounts Receivable	81,450	of Par—Common	$270,000
Common Stock	318,000	Preferred Stock, 10%, $100 Par	89,000
Treasury Stock	5,900	Retained Earnings	71,200
Bonds Payable	3,800	Notes Receivable	12,600

Q10-58. What is total paid-in capital for Sportstuff, Inc.? (Assume that treasury stock does not reduce total paid-in capital.)

    a. $682,900   **d.** $677,000

    b. $671,100   **e.** None of the above

    c. $748,200

Q10-59. What is total stockholders' equity for Sportstuff, Inc.?

    a. $742,300   **d.** $754,100

    b. $677,000   **e.** None of the above

    c. $748,200

Q10-60. Sportstuff's net income for the period is $119,200 and beginning common stockholders' equity is $681,700. Sportstuff's return on common stockholders' equity is closest to:

    a. 18.6%   **c.** 17.9%

    b. 16.7%   **d.** 16.5%

Q10-61. A company paid $28 per share to purchase 900 shares of its common stock as treasury stock. The stock was originally issued at $12 per share. Which of the following is the journal entry to record the purchase of the treasury stock?

	A	B	C	D
	A1			
1	a.	Treasury Stock	25,200	
2		Cash		25,200
3				
4	b.	Treasury Stock	10,800	
5		Retained Earnings	14,400	
6		Cash		25,200
7				
8	c.	Common Stock	25,200	
9		Cash		25,200
10				
11	d.	Treasury Stock	10,800	
12		Paid-in Capital in Excess of Par	14,400	
13		Cash		25,200
14				

Q10-62. When treasury stock is sold for less than its cost, the entry should include a debit to

    a. Gain on Sale of Treasury Stock.   **c.** Retained Earnings.

    b. Loss on Sale of Treasury Stock.   **d.** Paid-in Capital in Excess of Par.

Q10-63. A company purchased 100 shares of its common stock at $46 per share. It then sells 45 of the treasury shares at $76 per share. The entry to sell the treasury stock includes a
 a. credit to Retained Earnings for $3,000.
 b. debit to Retained Earnings for $1,350.
 c. credit to Cash for $3,420.
 d. credit to Paid-in Capital from Treasury Stock Transactions for $1,350.
 e. credit to Treasury Stock for $3,420.

Q10-64. Stockholders are eligible for a dividend if they own the stock on the date of
 a. issuance.   **c.** record.
 b. payment.   **d.** declaration.

Q10-65. Paul's Foods has outstanding 500 shares of 9% preferred stock, $100 par value; and 1,700 shares of common stock, $20 par value. Paul's declares dividends of $20,500. Which of the following is the correct entry?

	A	B	C	D
	A1			
1	a.	Dividends Payable, Preferred	4,500	
2		Dividends Payable, Common	16,000	
3		Cash		20,500
4				
5	b.	Retained Earnings	20,500	
6		Dividends Payable, Preferred		4,500
7		Dividends Payable, Common		16,000
8				
9	c.	Retained Earnings	20,500	
10		Dividends Payable, Preferred		10,250
11		Dividends Payable, Common		10,250
12				
13	d.	Dividends Expense	20,500	
14		Cash		20,500
15				

Q10-66. A corporation has 50,000 shares of 12% preferred stock outstanding. Also, there are 50,000 shares of common stock outstanding. Par value for each is $100. If a $900,000 dividend is paid, how much goes to the preferred stockholders?
 a. None   **d.** $108,000
 b. $600,000   **e.** $900,000
 c. $580,000

Q10-67. Assume the same facts as in Q10-66. What is the amount of dividends per share on common stock?
 a. $12.00   **d.** $18.00
 b. $6.00   **e.** None of these
 c. $3.00

Q10-68. Which of the following is *not* true about a 10% stock dividend?
 a. Retained Earnings decreases.
 b. The market value of the stock is needed to record the stock dividend.
 c. Total stockholders' equity remains the same.
 d. Par value decreases.
 e. Paid-in Capital increases.

Q10-69. A company declares a 5% stock dividend. The debit to Retained Earnings is an amount equal to
 a. the market value of the shares to be issued.
 b. the excess of the market price over the original issue price of the shares to be issued.
 c. the par value of the shares to be issued.
 d. the book value of the shares to be issued.

Q10-70. Which of the following statements is *not* true about a 3-for-1 stock split?
 a. Par value is reduced to one-third of what it was before the split.
 b. Retained Earnings remains the same.
 c. Total stockholders' equity increases.
 d. The market price of each share of stock will decrease.
 e. A stockholder with 10 shares before the split owns 30 shares after the split.

Q10-71. Dellanova Company's net income and net sales are $25,000 and $1,150,000, respectively, and average total assets are $120,000. What is Dellanova's return on assets?
 a. 20.8%   c. 9.8%
 b. 2.8%   d. 22.8%

Problems MyAccountingLab

Group A

LO 2 6

P10-72A. *(Learning Objectives 2, 6: Account for stock issuance; report stockholders' equity)* The partners who own Lane Rafts wished to avoid the unlimited personal liability of the partnership form of business, so they incorporated as Lane Rafts, Inc. The charter from the state of California authorizes the corporation to issue 160,000 shares of $6 par common stock. In its first month, Lane Rafts completed the following transactions:

Mar 6	Issued 1,000 shares of common stock to the promoter for assistance with issuance of the common stock. The promotional fee was $27,000. Debit Organization Expense.
9	Issued 10,000 shares of common stock to Jenny Collins and 20,000 shares to Pam Lane in return for cash equal to the stock's market value of $10 per share. The two women were partners in Lane Rafts Co.
26	Issued 1,500 shares of common stock for $22 cash per share.

Requirements

1. Record the transactions in the journal.
2. Prepare the stockholders' equity section of the Lane Rafts, Inc., balance sheet at March 31, 2017. The ending balance of Retained Earnings is $90,000.

LO 6

P10-73A. *(Learning Objective 6: Report stockholders' equity)* Rollo Corp. has the following stockholders' equity information:

Rollo's charter authorizes the company to issue 5,000 shares of 7% preferred stock with par value of $110 and 650,000 shares of no-par common stock. The company issued 2,500 shares of the preferred stock at $110 per share. It issued 65,000 shares of the common stock for a total of $511,000. The company's retained earnings balance at the beginning of 2016 was $79,000, and net income for the year was $95,000. During 2016, Rollo declared the specified dividend on preferred and a $0.60 per-share dividend on common. Preferred dividends for 2015 were in arrears.

Requirement

1. Prepare the stockholders' equity section of Rollo Corp.'s balance sheet at December 31, 2016. Show the computation of all amounts. Journal entries are not required.

P10-74A. *(Learning Objectives 2, 4: Analyze stockholders' equity and dividends of a corporation)* Yoder Outdoor Furniture Company included the following stockholders' equity on its year-end balance sheet at February 28, 2017:

Stockholders' Equity	
Preferred stock, 6% cumulative—par value $35 per share; authorized 120,000 shares in each class	
Class A—issued 72,000 shares	$ 2,520,000
Class B—issued 89,000 shares...............................	3,115,000
Common stock—$6 par value: authorized 1,500,000 shares,	
issued 310,000 shares...	1,860,000
Additional paid-in capital—common	5,570,000
Retained earnings...	8,370,000
	$21,435,000

Requirements

1. Identify the different issues of stock that Yoder Outdoor Furniture Company has outstanding.
2. Give the summary entries to record issuance of all the Yoder stock. Assume that all the stock was issued for cash. Explanations are not required.
3. Suppose Yoder passed its preferred dividends for three years. Would the company have to pay those dividends in arrears before paying dividends to the common stockholders? Give your reason.
4. What amount of preferred dividends must Yoder declare and pay each year to avoid having preferred dividends in arrears?
5. Assume that preferred dividends are in arrears for 2016. Journalize the declaration of an $820,000 dividend on February 28, 2017. An explanation is not required.

P10-75A. *(Learning Objectives 2, 3, 4: Account for stock issuance, dividends, and treasury stock)* Walker Jewelry Company reported the following summarized balance sheet at December 31, 2016:

Assets	
Current assets..	$ 34,500
Property and equipment, net	93,200
Total assets...	$127,700
Liabilities and Equity	
Liabilities	$ 38,000
Stockholders' equity:	
$0.40 cumulative preferred stock, $15 par, 200 shares issued ...	3,000
Common stock, $7 par, 6,300 shares issued.........................	44,100
Paid-in capital in excess of par—common	17,600
Retained earnings...	25,000
Total liabilities and equity..	$127,700

During 2017, Walker Jewelry completed these transactions that affected stockholders' equity:

Feb	13	Issued 5,700 shares of common stock for $10 per share.
Jun	7	Declared the regular cash dividend on the preferred stock.
	24	Paid the cash dividend.
Aug	9	Declared and distributed a 10% stock dividend on the common stock. Market price of the common stock was $14 per share.
Oct	26	Reacquired 900 shares of common stock as treasury stock, paying $16 per share.
Nov	20	Sold 300 shares of the treasury stock for $21 per share.
Dec	31	Declared a cash dividend of $0.25 per share on the outstanding common stock; dividends will be paid in January, 2018.

Requirements

1. Journalize Walker Jewelry's transactions. Explanations are not required.
2. Report Walker Jewelry's stockholders' equity at December 31, 2017. Net income for 2017 was $27,000.

 **P10-76A.** *(Learning Objectives 3, 4, 6: Measure the effects of stock-related transactions on a company)* Assume Dairy Freeze, Inc., completed the following transactions during 2016, the company's 10th year of operations:

Feb	3	Issued 17,000 shares of common stock ($2.00 par) for cash of $510,000.
Mar	19	Purchased 2,800 shares of the company's own common stock at $21 per share.
Apr	24	Sold 1,900 shares of treasury common stock for $29 per share.
Aug	15	Declared a cash dividend on the 13,000 shares of $0.70 no-par preferred stock.
Sep	1	Paid the cash dividends.
Nov	22	Declared and distributed a 15% stock dividend on the 92,000 shares of $2.00 par common stock outstanding. The market value of the common stock was $27 per share.

Requirements

1. Analyze each transaction in terms of its effect on the accounting equation of Dairy Freeze, Inc.
2. What impact did each transaction have on cash flows?

P10-77A. *(Learning Objectives 4, 5: Prepare a corporation's balance sheet; measure profitability)* The following accounts and related balances of Seagull Designers, Inc., as of December 31, 2016, are arranged in no particular order:

Cash	$ 42,000	Interest expense	$ 16,300
Accounts receivable, net	20,000	Property, plant, and	
Paid-in capital in excess		equipment, net	354,000
of par—common	22,000	Common stock, $1 par,	
Accrued liabilities	25,000	1,250,000 shares authorized,	
Long-term note payable	98,000	118,000 shares issued	118,000
Inventory	89,000	Prepaid expenses	22,000
Dividends payable	11,000	Common stockholders'	
Retained earnings	?	equity, December 31, 2015	226,000
Accounts payable	145,000	Net income	90,000
Trademarks, net	11,000	Total assets,	
Goodwill	16,000	December 31, 2015	494,000
		Treasury stock,	
		23,000 shares at cost	32,000
		Net sales	950,000

Requirements

1. Prepare Seagull's classified balance sheet in the account format at December 31, 2016.
2. Use DuPont Analysis to compute rate of return on total assets and rate of return on common stockholders' equity for the year ended December 31, 2016.
3. Do these rates of return suggest strength or weakness? Give your reason. What additional information might help you make your decision?

P10-78A. *(Learning Objective 6: Analyze a statement of stockholders' equity)* Paulus Specialties, Inc., reported the following statement of stockholders' equity for the year ended October 31, 2016:

A1						
	A	**B**	**C**	**D**	**E**	**F**
1	Paulus Specialties, Inc. Statement of Stockholders' Equity For the Year Ended October 31, 2016					
2	(In millions)	Common Stock	Additional Paid-in Capital	Retained Earnings	Treasury Stock	Total
3	Balance, October 31, 2015	$ 460	$ 1,600	$ 909	$ (116)	$ 2,853
4	Net income			350		350
5	Cash dividends			(192)		(192)
6	Issuance of stock (100 shares)	100	300			400
7	Stock dividend	112	210	(322)		—
8	Sale of treasury stock		17		5	22
9	Balance, October 31, 2016	$ 672	$ 2,127	$ 745	$ (111)	$ 3,433
10						

Requirements

Answer these questions about Paulus Specialties' stockholders' equity transactions.

1. What is the par value of the company's common stock?
2. At what price per share did Paulus Specialties issue its common stock during the year?
3. What was the cost of treasury stock sold during the year? What was the selling price of the treasury stock sold? What was the increase in total stockholders' equity?
4. Paulus Specialties' statement of stockholders' equity lists the stock transactions in the order in which they occurred. What was the percentage of the stock dividend? Round to the nearest percentage. (Ignore treasury stock in answering this question.)

Group B

P10-79B. *(Learning Objectives 2, 6: Account for stock issuance; report stockholders' equity)* The partners who own Canal Kayaks wished to avoid the unlimited personal liability of the partnership form of business, so they incorporated as Canal Kayaks, Inc. The charter from the state of Nevada authorizes the corporation to issue 125,000 shares of $15 par common stock. In its first month, Canal Kayaks completed the following transactions:

Jan	6	Issued 100 shares of common stock to the promoter for assistance with issuance of common stock. The promotional fee was $1,800. Debit Organization Expense.
	9	Issued 11,000 shares of common stock to Debby Evrard and 15,000 shares to Kathy Priesto in return for cash equal to the stock's market value of $22 per share. The two women were partners in Canal Kayaks.
	26	Issued 1,400 shares of common stock for $22 cash per share.

Requirements

1. Record the transactions in the journal.
2. Prepare the stockholders' equity section of Canal Kayaks, Inc., balance sheet at January 31, 2017. The ending balance of Retained Earnings is $65,000.

LO **6**

P10-80B. *(Learning Objective 6: Report stockholders' equity)* Jackson Corp. has the following stockholders' equity information:

Jackson's charter authorizes the company to issue 9,000 shares of 6% preferred stock with par value of $110 and 450,000 shares of no-par common stock. The company issued 2,250 shares of the preferred stock at $110 per share. It issued 112,500 shares of the common stock for a total of $515,000. The company's retained earnings balance at the beginning of 2016 was $73,000, and net income for the year was $96,000. During 2016, Jackson declared the specified dividend on preferred and a $0.40 per-share dividend on common. Preferred dividends for 2015 were in arrears.

Requirement

1. Prepare the stockholders' equity section of Jackson Corp.'s balance sheet at December 31, 2016. Show the computation of all amounts. Journal entries are not required.

LO **2** **4**

P10-81B. *(Learning Objectives 2, 4: Analyze stockholders' equity and dividends of a corporation)* Classic Outdoor Furniture Company included the following stockholders' equity on its year-end balance sheet at February 28, 2017:

Stockholders' Equity	
Preferred stock, 6.0% cumulative—par value $35 per share; authorized 130,000 shares in each class	
Class A—issued 79,000 shares	$ 2,765,000
Class B—issued 89,000 shares	3,115,000
Common stock—$5 par value: authorized 1,750,000 shares,	
issued 240,000 shares	1,200,000
Additional paid-in capital—common	5,540,000
Retained earnings	8,350,000
	$20,970,000

Requirements

1. Identify the different issues of stock that Classic Outdoor Furniture Company has outstanding.
2. Give the summary entries to record issuance of all the Classic stock. Assume that all the stock was issued for cash. Explanations are not required.
3. Suppose Classic passed its preferred dividends for three years. Would the company have to pay those dividends in arrears before paying dividends to the common stockholders? Give your reasons.
4. What amount of preferred dividends must Classic declare and pay each year to avoid having preferred dividends in arrears?
5. Assume that preferred dividends are in arrears for 2016. Journalize the declaration of an $870,000 dividend on February 28, 2017. An explanation is not required.

LO **2** **3** **4**

P10-82B. *(Learning Objectives 2, 3, 4: Account for stock issuance, dividends, and treasury stock)* Dublin Jewelry Company reported the following summarized balance sheet at December 31, 2016:

Assets	
Current assets	$ 33,700
Property and equipment, net	84,700
Total assets	$118,400
Liabilities and Equity	
Liabilities	$ 37,600
Stockholders' equity:	
$0.90 cumulative preferred stock, $20 par, 200 shares issued	4,000
Common stock, $5 par, 6,100 shares issued	30,500
Paid-in capital in excess of par—common	17,300
Retained earnings	29,000
Total liabilities and equity	$118,400

During 2017, Dublin Jewelry completed these transactions that affected stockholders' equity:

Feb	13	Issued 4,900 shares of common stock for $8 per share.
Jun	7	Declared the regular cash dividend on the preferred stock.
	24	Paid the cash dividend.
Aug	9	Declared and distributed a 15% stock dividend on the common stock. Market price of the common stock was $9 per share.
Oct	26	Reacquired 1,000 shares of common stock as treasury stock, paying $14 per share.
Nov	20	Sold 800 shares of the treasury stock for $19 per share.
Dec	31	Declared a cash dividend of $0.25 per share on the outstanding common stock; dividends will be paid in January, 2018.

Requirements

1. Journalize Dublin Jewelry's transactions. Explanations are not required.
2. Report Dublin Jewelry's stockholders' equity at December 31, 2017. Net income for 2017 was $23,000.

P10-83B. *(Learning Objectives 3, 4, 6: Measure the effects of stock-related transactions on a company)* Assume Sweet Treats, Inc., completed the following transactions during 2016, the company's 10th year of operations:

Feb	3	Issued 13,000 shares of common stock ($2.00 par) for cash of $416,000.
Mar	19	Purchased 2,200 shares of the company's own common stock at $27 per share.
Apr	24	Sold 1,300 shares of treasury stock for $30 per share.
Aug	15	Declared a cash dividend on the 16,000 shares of $0.60 no-par preferred stock.
Sep	1	Paid the cash dividends.
Nov	22	Declared and distributed a 15% stock dividend on the 98,000 shares of $2.00 par common stock outstanding. The market value of the common stock was $29 per share.

Requirements

1. Analyze each transaction in terms of its effect on the accounting equation of Sweet Treats, Inc.
2. What impact did each transaction have on cash flows?

LO 4 5   **P10-84B.** *(Learning Objectives 4, 5: Prepare a corporation's balance sheet; measure profitability)* The following accounts and related balances of Ginger Designers, Inc., as of December 31, 2016, are arranged in no particular order:

Cash..	$50,000	Interest expense...........................	$ 16,200
Accounts receivable, net...............	23,000	Property, plant, and	
Paid-in capital in excess		equipment, net	363,000
of par—common.......................	16,000	Common stock, $2 par,	
Accrued liabilities..........................	26,000	1,500,000 shares authorized,	
Long-term note payable	95,000	112,000 shares issued.............	224,000
Inventory.......................................	89,000	Prepaid expenses	16,000
Dividends payable.........................	5,000	Common stockholders'	
Retained earnings.........................	?	equity, December 31, 2015	247,000
Accounts payable	130,000	Net income.................................	32,000
Trademarks, net............................	6,000	Total assets,	
Goodwill.......................................	16,000	December 31, 2015................	492,000
		Treasury stock,	
		9,000 shares at cost................	25,000
		Net sales....................................	650,000

Requirements

1. Prepare Ginger's classified balance sheet in the account format at December 31, 2016.
2. Use DuPont Analysis to compute rate of return on total assets and rate of return on common stockholders' equity for the year ended December 31, 2016.
3. Do these rates of return suggest strength or weakness? Give your reason. What additional information might help you make your decision?

LO 6   **P10-85B.** *(Learning Objective 6: Analyze a statement of stockholders' equity)* Fall River Specialties, Inc., reported the following statement of stockholders' equity for the year ended October 31, 2016:

	A	B	C	D	E	F
1	**Fall River Specialties, Inc.** **Statement of Stockholders' Equity** **For the Year Ended October 31, 2016**					
2	(In millions)	**Common Stock**	**Additional Paid-in Capital**	**Retained Earnings**	**Treasury Stock**	**Total**
3						
4	**Balance, October 31, 2015**	$ 430	$ 1,640	$ 904	$ (115)	$ 2,859
5	Net income			480		480
6	Cash dividends			(190)		(190)
7	Issuance of stock (200 shares)	100	120			220
8	Stock dividend	106	127	(233)		—
9	Sale of treasury stock		11		7	18
10	**Balance, October 31, 2016**	$ 636	$ 1,898	$ 961	$ (108)	$ 3,387
11						

Requirements

Answer these questions about Fall River Specialties' stockholders' equity transactions.
1. What is the par value of the company's common stock?
2. At what price per share did Fall River Specialties issue its common stock during the year?
3. What was the cost of treasury stock sold during the year? What was the selling price of the treasury stock sold? What was the increase in total stockholders' equity?

4. Fall River Specialties' statement of stockholders' equity lists the stock transactions in the order in which they occurred. What was the percentage of the stock dividend? Round to the nearest percentage. (Ignore treasury stock in answering this question.)

Challenge Exercises and Problem

E10-86. (*Learning Objectives 2, 3, 4: Reconstruct transactions from the financial statements*) Dolson Networking Solutions began operations on January 1, 2016, and immediately issued its stock, receiving cash. Dolson's balance sheet at December 31, 2016, reported the following stockholders' equity:

Common stock, $1 par......................	$ 52,000
Additional paid-in capital..................	260,300
Retained earnings.............................	27,000
Treasury stock, 1,200 shares.............	(13,200)
Total stockholders' equity............	$326,100

During 2016, Dolson
    a. issued stock for $6 per share.
    b. purchased 1,300 shares of treasury stock, paying $11 per share.
    c. resold some of the treasury stock.
    d. declared and paid cash dividends.

Requirement

1. Journalize all of Dolson's stockholders' equity transactions during the year. Dolson's entry to close net income to Retained Earnings was

	A	B	C	D
		A1		
	A	**B**	**C**	**D**
1		Revenues	171,000	
2		Expenses		119,000
3		Retained Earnings		52,000
4				

E10-87. (*Learning Objective 6: Report financing activities on the statement of cash flows*) **LO 6**
Use the Dolson Networking Solutions data in E10-86 to show how the company reported cash flows from financing activities during 2016.

E10-88. (*Learning Objectives 2, 3, 4: Account for issuance of stock and treasury stock; explain the changes in stockholders' equity*) Atlantic Corporation reported the following **LO 2 3 4**
stockholders' equity data (all dollars in millions except par value per share):

	A	B	C
	A1		
		December 31,	
1		**2016**	**2015**
2	Preferred stock	$ 606	$ 730
3	Common stock, $1 par value	906	884
4	Additional paid-in capital—common	1,512	1,468
5	Retained earnings	20,650	19,108
6	Treasury stock, common	(2,800)	(2,605)
7			

Atlantic earned net income of $2,940 during 2016. For each account except Retained Earnings, one transaction explains the change from the December 31, 2015, balance to the December 31, 2016, balance. Two transactions affected Retained Earnings. Give a full explanation, including the dollar amount, for the change in each account.

LO 2 3 4

E10-89. *(Learning Objectives 2, 3, 4: Account for issuance of stock, treasury stock, and other changes in stockholders' equity)* Fandom, Inc., ended 2016 with 9 million shares of $1 par common stock issued and outstanding. Beginning additional paid-in capital was $9 million, and retained earnings totaled $36 million.

- In April 2017, Fandom issued 4 million shares of common stock at a price of $2 per share.
- In June, the company declared and distributed a 10% stock dividend at a time when Fandom's common stock had a market value of $10 per share.
- Then in September, Fandom's stock price dropped to $1 per share and the company purchased 4 million shares of treasury stock.
- For the year, Fandom earned net income of $29 million and declared cash dividends of $13 million.

Requirement

1. Complete the following tabulation to show what Fandom, Inc., should report for stockholders' equity at December 31, 2017. Journal entries are not required.

(Amounts in millions)	Common Stock	+	Additional Paid-In Capital	+	Retained Earnings	−	Treasury Stock	=	Total Equity
Balance, Dec 31, 2016.............	$9		$9		$36		0		$54
Issuance of stock									
Stock dividend............................									
Purchase of treasury stock............									
Net income.................................									
Cash dividends									
Balance, Dec 31, 2017................									

LO 5

E10-90. *(Learning Objective 5: Analyze information from stockholders' equity)* The stockholders' equity of Akron Uniforms as of December 31, 2016 and 2015, follows:

	2016	2015
Common stock, 2,000,000 shares authorized, 1,000,000 and 900,000 shares issued, respectively	$ 350,000	$ 315,000
Paid-in capital in excess of par	34,850,000	30,115,000
Paid-in capital-treasury stock transactions	53,000	50,000
Retained earnings	64,500,000	55,000,000
Treasury stock, at cost, 40,000 and 45,000 shares, respectively	(1,528,000)	(1,719,000)
Total stockholders' equity	$98,225,000	$83,761,000

Requirements

1. What is the par value of the common stock?
2. How many shares of common stock were outstanding at the end of 2016?
3. As of December 31, 2016, what was the average price that stockholders paid for all common stock when issued?
4. Prepare a summary journal entry to record the change in common stock during the year.
5. What was the average price that stockholders paid for the common stock issued in 2016?
6. What was the average price paid by Akron Uniforms for the treasury stock at December 31, 2016?
7. Prepare a summary journal entry to record the change in treasury stock during the year.
8. Assuming net income for 2016 was $11,000,000, prepare a summary journal entry to record the dividends declared during 2016.

APPLY YOUR KNOWLEDGE

Decision Cases

Case 1. *(Learning Objectives 2, 6: Evaluate alternative ways of raising capital)* Nate Smith and Darla Jones have written a computer program for a virtual reality video game system; it is expected to be more popular than any other gaming system on the market currently. They need additional capital to market the product, and they plan to incorporate their business. Smith and Jones are considering alternative capital structures for the corporation. Their primary goal is to raise as much capital as possible without giving up control of the business. Smith and Jones plan to receive 50,000 shares of the corporation's common stock in return for the net assets of their old business. After the old company's books are closed and the assets are adjusted to current market value, Smith's and Jones's capital balances will each be $25,000.

The corporation's plans for a charter include an authorization to issue 10,000 shares of preferred stock and 500,000 shares of $1 par common stock. Smith and Jones are uncertain about the most desirable features for the preferred stock. Prior to incorporating, Smith and Jones are discussing their plans with two investment groups. The corporation can obtain capital from outside investors under either of the following plans:

- *Plan 1.* Group 1 will invest $80,000 to acquire 800 shares of 6%, $100 par, nonvoting, preferred stock.
- *Plan 2.* Group 2 will invest $55,000 to acquire 500 shares of $5, no-par preferred stock and $35,000 to acquire 35,000 shares of common stock. Each preferred share receives 50 votes on matters that come before the stockholders.

Requirements

Assume that the corporation is chartered.
1. Journalize the issuance of common stock to Smith and Jones. Debit each person's capital account for its balance.
2. Journalize the issuance of stock to the outsiders under both plans.
3. Assume that net income for the first year is $120,000 and total dividends are $30,000. Prepare the stockholders' equity section of the corporation's balance sheet under both plans.
4. Recommend one of the plans to Smith and Jones. Give your reasons. (Challenge)

Case 2. *(Learning Objective 4: Analyze cash dividends and stock dividends)* **United Parcel Service (UPS), Inc.**, had the following stockholders' equity amounts on December 31, 2016 (adapted, in millions):

Common stock and additional paid-in capital; 1,135 shares issued..............	$ 278
Retained earnings...	9,457
Total stockholders' equity	$9,735

During 2016, UPS paid a cash dividend of $0.715 per share. Assume that, after paying the cash dividends, UPS distributed a 10% stock dividend. Assume also that during the following year, UPS declared and paid a cash dividend of $0.65 per share.

Suppose you own 10,000 shares of UPS common stock, acquired three years ago, prior to the 10% stock dividend. The market price of UPS stock was $61.02 per share before the stock dividend.

Requirements

1. How does the stock dividend affect your proportionate ownership in UPS? Explain.
2. What amount of cash dividends did you receive last year? What amount of cash dividends will you receive after the above dividend action?
3. Assume that immediately after the stock dividend was distributed, the market value of UPS's stock decreased from $61.02 per share to $55.473 per share. Does this decrease represent a loss to you? Explain.

4. Suppose UPS announces at the time of the stock dividend that the company will continue to pay the annual $0.715 *cash* dividend per share, even after distributing the *stock* dividend. Would you expect the market price of the stock to decrease to $55.473 per share as in requirement 3? Explain.

Ethical Issues

Ethical Issue 1. (*Note:* This case is based on a real situation.) George Campbell paid $50,000 for a franchise that entitled him to market Success Associates software programs in the countries of the European Union. Campbell intended to sell individual franchises for the major language groups of western Europe—German, French, English, Spanish, and Italian. Naturally, investors considering buying a franchise from Campbell asked to see the financial statements of his business.

Believing the value of the franchise to be greater than $50,000, Campbell sought to capitalize his own franchise at $500,000. The law firm of McDonald & LaDue helped Campbell form a corporation chartered to issue 500,000 shares of common stock with par value of $1 per share. Attorneys suggested the following chain of transactions:

   a. A third party borrows $500,000 and purchases the franchise from Campbell.
   b. Campbell pays the corporation $500,000 to acquire all its stock.
   c. The corporation buys the franchise from the third party, who repays the loan.

In the final analysis, the third party is debt-free and out of the picture. Campbell owns all of the corporation's stock, and the corporation owns the franchise. The corporation balance sheet lists a franchise acquired at a cost of $500,000. This balance sheet is Campbell's most valuable marketing tool.

Requirements

1. What is the ethical issue in this situation?
2. Who are the stakeholders in the suggested transaction?
3. Analyze this case from the following standpoints: (a) economic, (b) legal, and (c) ethical. What are the consequences to each stakeholder?
4. How should the transaction be reported?

Ethical Issue 2. St. Genevieve Petroleum Company is an independent oil producer in Baton Parish, Louisiana. In February, company geologists discovered a pool of oil that tripled the company's proven reserves. Prior to disclosing the new oil to the public, St. Genevieve quietly bought most of its stock as treasury stock. After the discovery was announced, the company's stock price increased from $6 to $27.

Requirements

1. What is the ethical issue in this situation? What accounting principle is involved?
2. Who are the stakeholders?
3. Analyze the facts from the following standpoints: (a) economic, (b) legal, and (c) ethical. What is the impact on each stakeholder?
4. What decision would you have made?

Focus on Financials | Apple Inc.

(*Learning Objectives 2, 3, 5: Analyze common stock, retained earnings, return on equity, and return on assets*) **Apple Inc.'s** consolidated financial statements appear in Appendix A and online in the filings section of **http://www.sec.gov**.

Requirements

1. Refer to Apple's Consolidated Balance Sheets and Note 7 (Shareholders' Equity). Describe the class of stock that Apple Inc. has authorized. How many shares of that stock have been issued as of September 27, 2014? How many are outstanding as of September 27, 2014?

2. Refer to the Consolidated Balance Sheets and the Consolidated Statements of Stockholders' Equity. How many shares of treasury stock did the company purchase during the year ended September 27, 2014? What was the cost of the treasury stock? How much per share?

3. Examine Apple Inc.'s Consolidated Statement of Stockholders' Equity. Analyze the change that occurred in the company's Retained Earnings account during the year ended September 27, 2014. Can you trace the change to any of its other financial statements? Is this a good thing or a bad thing?

4. Use DuPont Analysis to compute Apple Inc.'s return on equity and return on assets for 2014. Pick a company that is a competitor of Apple Inc. and compute these ratios for the competitor. Which ratios are similar? Which are different? Which company do you think is more profitable? Explain.

Focus on Analysis | Under Armour, Inc.

(Learning Objectives 2, 3, 4: Analyze treasury stock and retained earnings) This case is based on the consolidated financial statements of **Under Armour, Inc.**, given in Appendix B and online in the filings section of **http://www.sec.gov**. In particular, this case uses Under Armour, Inc.'s, Consolidated Balance Sheets and Consolidated Statements of Stockholders' Equity for the year 2014.

Requirements

1. As of the end of December 31, 2014, how many shares of common stock does Under Armour, Inc., have authorized? Issued? Outstanding?

2. Refer to Note 8—Stockholders' Equity and the Consolidated Statement of Stockholders' Equity for the year 2014. What is the difference between Under Armour's Class A Common Stock and Class B Convertible Common Stock? Are there any restrictions on who can own Class B stock?

3. Did Under Armour, Inc., issue any new shares of Class A Common Stock during 2014? How can you tell? (Challenge)

4. Prepare a T-account to show the beginning and ending balances plus all the activity in Retained Earnings for 2014.

Group Project in Ethics

The global economic recession that started in 2007, and that persists in certain sectors, has impacted every business, but it was especially hard on banks, automobile manufacturing, and retail companies. Banks were largely responsible for the recession. Some of the biggest banks made excessively risky investments collateralized by real estate mortgages, and many of these investments soured when the real estate markets collapsed. When banks had to write these investments down to market values, the regulatory authorities notified them that they had inadequate capital ratios on their balance sheets to operate. Banks stopped lending money. Because stock prices were depressed, companies could not raise capital by selling stock. With both debt and stock financing frozen, many businesses had to close their doors.

Fearing collapse of the whole economy, the central governments of the United States and several European nations loaned money to banks to prop up their capital ratios and keep them open. The government also loaned massive amounts to the largest insurance company in the United States (AIG) as well as to General Motors and Chrysler to help them stay in business. When asked why, many in government replied "these businesses were too important to fail." In several cases, the U.S. government has taken an "equity stake" in some banks and businesses by taking preferred stock in exchange for the cash infusion.

Because of the recession, corporate downsizing has occurred on a massive scale throughout the world. Although companies in the retail sector provide more jobs than the banking and automobile industry combined, the government has not chosen to "bail out" any retail businesses. Each company or industry mentioned in this book has pared down plant and equipment, laid off employees, or restructured operations. Some companies have been forced out of business altogether.

Requirements

1. Identify all the stakeholders of a corporation. A *stakeholder* is a person or a group who has an interest (that is, a stake) in the success of the organization.
2. Do you believe that some entities are "too important to fail"? Should the federal government help certain businesses to stay afloat during economic recessions and allow others to fail?
3. Identify several measures by which a company may be considered deficient and in need of downsizing. How can downsizing help to solve this problem?
4. Debate the bailout issue. One group of students takes the perspective of the company and its stockholders, and another group of students takes the perspective of the other stakeholders of the company (the community in which the company operates and society at large).
5. What is the problem with the government taking an equity position such as preferred stock in a private enterprise?

Quick Check Answers

1. *c* (30,000 shares × $1 = $30,000)

2. *b* ($1,800,000/$10 par = 180,000 shares)

3. *a* ($180,000 + $25,000 + $1,800,000)

4. *a* ($180,000 + $25,000 + $1,800,000 + $225,000)

5. *c* ($2,230,000−$20,000)

6. *d* (No gain or loss [for the income statement] on treasury-stock transactions)

7. *a*

8. *d*

9. *c*

10. *d*

11. *b* [First, annual preferred dividend = $9,000 (3,000 × $30 × 0.10)]. Five years of preferred dividends must be paid (four in arrears plus the current year). [($9,000 × 5) + (180,000 × $5.25 per share common dividend) = $990,000]

12. *c*

13. *a*

14. *b*

15. *b*

16. *a*

Evaluating Performance: Earnings Quality, the Income Statement, & the Statement of Comprehensive Income

11

The Gap, Inc., is truly a case study in how a company has to adapt to changing market conditions in order to prosper in a highly competitive global retail economy. Many factors influence a company's performance, some of which (such as product development, purchasing, and marketing) stem from management's strategic choices, and some others, such as global marketing trends and the relative value of the U.S. dollar in global markets, are beyond the company's control. The Gap, Inc., operates in a highly competitive global "fashion forward" market. Management must make fast decisions regarding the type of merchandise to purchase based on fashion trends in the highly volatile market for teen and young adult clothing and accessories. The Gap, Inc., operates company-owned stores in the United States as well as nine foreign countries. In addition, the company has franchise agreements with other unaffiliated companies to operate Gap, Banana Republic, and Old Navy stores in many other countries around the world. The company's products are also available to online customers worldwide through company-owned websites. Many of the company's sales and purchases often have to be made in the currencies of foreign countries. Settling transactions in currencies other than the U.S. dollar can have a significant impact on reported profits.

Joe Raedle/Getty Images

In his letter to shareholders in the company's 2014 annual report, Art Peck, the company's new chairman and CEO, stated that the company's focus for 2015 and beyond is on four priorities: global growth, product, experience, and talent.[1] Exhibit 11-1 on the next page presents the company's consolidated statements of earnings for the fiscal year 2014 (endcd January 31, 2015) in comparison with two previous fiscal years. During fiscal 2014, the company reported net sales that were 1.8% ahead of fiscal 2013, while cost of goods sold and occupancy

[1] The Gap, Inc., 2014 Annual Report, Shareholder's letter.

expenses increased by 3%. As a result, gross margin slipped by almost 1 percentage point, from 39% of net sales to about 38%. Operating expenses were up 1.5% in fiscal 2014 over fiscal 2013, causing operating income to fall by 3.1%. Because operating results from The Gap, Inc., have followed a see-saw pattern, rather than a steady, even climb for several years, the market may not view The Gap, Inc., as favorably as some other companies as an investment.

Exhibit 11-1 | The Gap, Inc., Consolidated Statements of Income

	A	B	C	D
	A1			
	The Gap, Inc.			
1	**Consolidated Statements of Income (Adapted)**	**Fiscal 2014**	**Fiscal 2013**	**Fiscal 2012**
2		**12 Months Ended**		
3	**($ and shares in millions, except per share amounts)**	**Jan. 31, 2015**	**Feb. 01, 2014**	**Feb. 02, 2013**
4	Net sales	$ 16,435	$ 16,148	$ 15,651
5	Cost of goods sold and occupancy expenses	10,146	9,855	9,480
6	Gross profit	6,289	6,293	6,171
7	Operating expenses	4,206	4,144	4,229
8	Operating income	2,083	2,149	1,942
9	Interest (expense)	(75)	(61)	(87)
10	Interest income	5	5	6
11	Income before income taxes	2,013	2,093	1,861
12	Income taxes	751	813	726
13	Net income	$ 1,262	$ 1,280	$ 1,135
14				
15	Weighted-average number of shares—basic	435	461	482
16	Weighted-average number of shares—diluted	440	467	488
17				
18	Earnings per share—basic (in dollars per share)	$ 2.90	$ 2.78	$ 2.35
19	Earnings per share—diluted (in dollars per share)	$ 2.87	$ 2.74	$ 2.33
20				
21	Cash dividends declared and paid per share	$ 0.91	$ 0.61	$ 0.50
22				

An interesting fact you may not know about The Gap, Inc., is the significant work the company is doing in the area of corporate social responsibility (CSR), a nonfinancial measure of performance that is becoming more important as a perceived measure of success. The company has set goals in four key areas to measure and improve its performance in being a good corporate citizen: the environment, its employees, human rights, and community investment. Each year, The Gap, Inc., along with many other companies such as **The Home Depot, Inc**. (the focus company in Chapter 10), issues a separate report on CSR. ●

When you finish this chapter, you will have a better understanding of earnings quality and how you can use a company's income statement (including footnotes) to estimate it. In addition, you'll learn about some other emerging ways to measure a company's performance that are not directly related to a company's earnings.

This chapter builds on your understanding of the corporate income statement. After studying this chapter, you will have seen all the types of items that typically appear on an income statement. You'll study the components of *income from continuing operations*, which is the basis for many analysts' predictions about companies' future operations, as well as their current values. You'll learn to use information in the current financial statements, as well as the footnotes, to help decide whether to invest in a particular stock. You'll learn about how and why companies typically report income from discontinued operations separately from income from continuing operations. You'll also learn how conducting international business transactions in foreign currencies impacts net income. The chapter provides information about earnings per share, the most often-mentioned statistic in business, and about how to construct the statement of comprehensive income, which includes certain gains and losses that are allowed to bypass the income statement and eventually be reported as a separate element of stockholders' equity. Finally, you'll have a chance to see some reports issued by management and the company's auditors regarding both financial and nonfinancial measures of performance. The knowledge you get from this chapter will help you analyze financial statements and use the information in decision making.

We begin with a basic question: How do we evaluate the quality of a company's earnings? The term *quality of earnings* refers to the characteristics of an earnings number that make it most useful for decision making.

LEARNING OBJECTIVES

① **Evaluate** quality of earnings

② **Account** for foreign-currency gains and losses

③ **Account** for other items on the income statement

④ **Compute** earnings per share

⑤ **Analyze** the statement of comprehensive income, footnotes, and supplemental disclosures

⑥ **Differentiate** management's and auditors' reporting responsibilities

EVALUATE QUALITY OF EARNINGS

A corporation's net income, or net earnings (including earnings per share), receives more attention than any other single item in the financial statements. To stockholders, the larger the net income, the greater the likelihood of dividends. In addition, a steady and upward trend in *persistent* earnings generally translates sooner or later to a higher stock price.

Suppose you are considering investing in either the stock of **The Gap, Inc.**, or another major retailer. How do you make the decision? A knowledgeable investor will want to assess each company's **earnings quality**. The higher the quality of earnings in the current period as compared to its recent past, the more likely it is that the company is executing a successful business strategy to generate healthy earnings in the future, which is a key component in its stock price.

There are many components of earnings quality. Among the most prominent are (1) proper revenue and expense recognition, (2) high and persistently improving gross margin/sales ratio, (3) declining or stable operating expenses compared to sales, and (4) high and persistently improving operating earnings/sales ratio. To explore the makeup and the quality of earnings, let's examine its various sources. Exhibit 11-1 shows the Consolidated Statements of Income of The Gap, Inc., for fiscal years 2014, 2013, and 2012. We'll use these statements as a basis for our discussion of earnings quality.

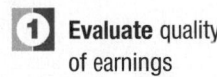

① **Evaluate** quality of earnings

You can access the most current annual report of The Gap, Inc., in Excel format at **http://www.sec.gov**. Using the "FILINGS" link on the toolbar at the top of the home page, select "Company Filings Search." This will take you to the "Edgar Company Filings" page. Type "Gap" in the company name box, and select "Search." This will produce the "EDGAR Search Results" page showing the company name. Click on the "CIK" link beside the company name. This will pull up a list of the reports the company has filed with the Securities and Exchange Commission (SEC). Under the "Filing Type" box, type "10-K" and click the search box. Form 10-K is the SEC form for the company's annual report. Find the year that you wish to view. Click on the "Interactive Data" box, which takes you to the "View Filing Data" page. Find and click on the "View Excel Document" link at the top of this page. You may choose to either open or download the Excel files containing the company's most recent financial statements.

Revenue Recognition

The first component of earnings quality is proper recognition of net revenue, or *net sales*. You learned about revenue in Chapters 3 through 5. The *revenue principle*, discussed in Chapter 3 (pp. 124–125), states that, under accrual accounting, revenue should be recognized when it is *earned*. For a retail business, revenue is generally considered earned when the selling business has fulfilled its obligation to either deliver the product or the service to the customer. In recognizing revenue, several important events usually have to occur: (1) The seller delivers the product or service to the customer; (2) the customer takes ownership of the product or service; and (3) the seller either collects cash or is reasonably assured of collecting the cash in the near future. In Chapter 4 (pp. 221–222), you learned about the importance of internal controls over the processes by which revenue is recognized and by which cash collections are entered into the accounting system. In Chapter 5 (pp. 261–263), you learned that net sales is the difference between gross sales and reductions made by sales returns and sales discounts. You also learned that credit sales, or sales on account, have to go through the process of collection, that some will ultimately not be collectible, and that a company must make an allowance for doubtful accounts. You studied the concept of *free on board* (FOB) terms, which governs the issue of who owns the goods during the shipment process, and therefore the timing of revenue. You must understand all of these concepts in order to grasp the meaning of proper revenue recognition.

Proper revenue recognition in a retail business like The Gap, Inc., is relatively straightforward. As explained in its Notes to Consolidated Financial Statements, The Gap, Inc., recognizes revenue as well as related cost of goods sold at the time customers receive the products. In the stores, revenue is recognized at the registers when the customers receive and pay for merchandise. For online sales (which in fiscal 2014 comprise about $2.5 billion, or 15% of total net sales), the company has to estimate how long it takes the merchandise to reach customers by mail or courier. For both over-the-counter and online sales, the company estimates an allowance for returns and deducts it from gross sales to report *net sales*.

Let's examine Exhibit 11-1 and analyze the trend in The Gap's Net sales (in millions, line 4). Notice that, over the past three years, Net sales for the company as a whole have trended slightly upward. From fiscal year 2012 to 2013, Net sales increased from $15,651 million to $16,148 million (about 3.2%). In fiscal 2014, net sales increased to $16,435 million (1.8% over 2013 and 5% over 2012). The smaller percentage increase in 2014 was significantly impacted by the fact that the increasing strength in the U.S. dollar relative to currencies of other countries during the year made Gap brand merchandise more expensive, thus reducing demand for its products overseas. If that fact were ignored, net sales would have increased 3% in fiscal 2014. Comparable store sales for the flagship Gap stores division, a key factor in growth for retail stores, were down 5% in 2014 compared with fiscal 2013. However, this was offset by a 5% increase in comparable store sales for Old Navy, the division that sells lower-cost merchandise. This made overall comparable store sales flat in fiscal 2014 compared with fiscal 2013. Therefore, the 1.8% increase in sales came from opening new stores rather than increasing sales from existing stores. The company opened 30 Althea stores, 37 Gap and outlet stores in Asia, and 17 Old Navy stores in Asia. All of these changes were obtained from reading the footnotes to the financial statements.

The real key to The Gap, Inc.'s future as an investment is whether it can continue growing the top line (net sales) in its Consolidated Statement of Net Income. Intense competition from other specialty retailers, as well as the frenetic pace of specialty fashion retailing, present challenges to revenue growth. The Gap, Inc.'s, stock price, like that of other specialty retailers, has been no exception, fluctuating from a low of about $15.60 per share to a high of more than $46 per share over the three-year period.

The Financial Accounting Standards Board (FASB) and International Accounting Standards Board (IASB) have reached agreement on a new standard, to be implemented in 2017, that will bring the revenue recognition standards of the two bodies into much closer harmony and consistency than existed under previous standards. This newly adopted standard, discussed in depth in Chapters 3 and 5, has very little impact on the material covered in this course since the standards for revenue recognition in the retail industry were already closely aligned globally. You may cover the new standard in more detail in later accounting courses.

COOKING THE BOOKS
with Revenue

Research has shown that roughly one-half of all financial statement fraud over the past two decades has involved improper revenue recognition.[2] Several of the more significant revenue recognition issues involving fraud, from the SEC's files follow:

- *Recognizing revenue prematurely (before it is earned).* One of the common fraud techniques is **channel stuffing**, in which a company may ship inventory to regular customers in excess of amounts ordered. **Bristol-Myers Squibb**, a global pharmaceuticals company, was sued by the SEC in 2004 for channel stuffing during 2000 and 2001. The company allegedly stuffed its distribution channels with excess inventory near the end of every quarter in amounts sufficient to meet company sales targets (tied to executive bonuses), overstating revenue by about $1.5 billion. The company paid a civil fine of $100 million and established a $50 million fund to compensate shareholders for their losses.[3]

- *Providing incentives for customers to purchase more inventory than is needed.* Incentives are given in exchange for future discounts and other benefits.

- *Reporting revenue when significant services are still to be performed or goods are still to be delivered.*

- *Reporting sales to fictitious or nonexistent customers.* This may include falsified shipping and inventory records.

Cost of Goods Sold and Gross Profit (Gross Margin)

After revenue, the next two important components in earnings quality are cost of goods sold and the resulting gross profit. Before we get to these components, however, it is important to emphasize that, just as avoiding premature or improper revenue recognition is important, it is equally important to make sure that *all expenses are accurately, completely, and transparently included*

---

[2]*CPA Letter* (February 2003). American Institute of Certified Public Accountants. See www.aicpa.org/pubs/cpaltr/feb2003/financial.htm.

[3]Accounting and Auditing Enforcement Release No. 2075, August 4, 2004. *Securities and Exchange Commission v. Bristol-Myers Squibb Company*, 04-3680 DNJ (2004). See www.sec.gov/news/press/2004-105.htm.

in the computation of net income. We saw with the example of the WorldCom fraud in Chapter 7 what can happen when a company manipulates reported earnings by deliberately understating expenses. Without the integrity that comes through full and complete disclosures of all existing expenses, and without recognizing those expenses in the proper periods, trends in earnings are at best meaningless and, at worst, downright misleading.

Cost of Goods Sold. As we learned in Chapter 6, cost of goods sold represents the direct cost of the goods sold to customers. In the case of The Gap, Inc., Cost of goods sold also includes the cost of occupying the space used to sell the product, or store rent. As shown on line 5 of Exhibit 11-1, Cost of goods sold and occupancy expenses represents the largest single operating expense for The Gap, Inc. Cost of goods sold and occupancy expenses as a percentage of net sales remained flat at about 61% in fiscal 2012 and 2013 and rose slightly to about 62% in fiscal 2014. In general, assuming cost of goods sold is accurately measured each period, maintaining stability of cost of goods sold as a percentage of net sales revenue is generally regarded as a sign of high earnings quality. Maintaining control of costs is usually accomplished through development of effective marketing strategies, establishment of a consistent supply chain for inventory purchases, and promoting long-term relationships with reliable vendors. Like other major retailers, The Gap, Inc.'s, Cost of goods sold includes store occupancy expenses (rent). Controlling occupancy expense is usually a matter of effectively negotiating leases for new and established stores.

Gross Profit (Gross Margin). Gross profit (Gross margin) represents the difference between Net sales and Cost of goods sold. Therefore, all other things equal, an increase in cost of goods sold from one period to the next signals a decline in gross profit over that same period. For The Gap, Inc., Gross profit decreased from 39% ($6,293/$16,148) in fiscal 2013 to 38% ($6,289/$16,435) in fiscal 2014 (line 6 of Exhibit 11-1, all dollar amounts in millions). Gross profit percentages for The Gap, Inc., have remained fairly constant, fluctuating between 36% and 40% of net sales, for the last decade.

Operating and Other Expenses

As implied in the title, operating expenses are the ongoing expenses incurred by the entity other than direct expenses for merchandise and other costs directly related to sales. The largest operating expenses generally include salaries, wages, utilities, and supplies. Again, given that the entity takes care to accurately measure operating expenses, the lower these costs are relative to sales, we can assume management is operating the business more efficiently and, therefore, more profitably. As shown in line 7 of Exhibit 11-1, operating expenses of The Gap, Inc., have followed a rather stable pattern in relation to sales over the three-year period. From fiscal 2012 through fiscal 2014, operating expenses (in millions) were $4,229; $4,144; and $4,206, respectively. As a percentage of net sales, however, operating expenses have declined over the three-year period from 27% to 25.6%, which is a positive trend. When companies experience revenue challenges, it is wise to try to trim fat from operations by cutting back on costs. The trick is knowing when and how much to cut, because indiscriminate cost cutting can erode perceived quality of the company's product or service, further damaging the bottom line. The Gap, Inc., apparently figured this out years ago, because its operating expenses as a percentage of net sales have consistently ranged from 25% to 28% for several years.

Operating Income (Earnings)

Given the integrity that comes with accuracy and transparency of reported revenues and expenses, a trend of high and persistently improving operating earnings in relation to net sales reflects increasing earnings quality. Operating income is a function of all of its individual elements: sales revenue, cost of goods sold, gross margin (gross profit), and operating expenses. For The Gap, Inc., because the relationship between Net sales and Cost of goods sold and occupancy expenses have fluctuated, Operating income has also fluctuated. In fiscal 2012, it was $1,942 million (12.4% of net sales); in fiscal 2013, it rose to $2,149 million (13.3% of net sales); in fiscal 2014, it fell back to $2,083 million (12.7% of net sales). However, for reasons we have discussed throughout this section, some of which are due to management decisions and some of which are beyond management's control, there are doubts as to whether the company can continue to improve its operating earnings over the long term. As a matter of fact, if you analyzed the trend for the five years preceding fiscal 2014, you would see that the trend in the company's operating earnings has been rather erratic.

ACCOUNT FOR FOREIGN-CURRENCY GAINS AND LOSSES

International transactions are common in many businesses and can significantly influence reported earnings. Manufacturing of all kinds of products has migrated to places such as China, India, Mexico, Central America, and Southeast Asia, where labor and materials are less costly. Transportation and communications systems, as well as manufacturing processes, have improved to the point at which it has become convenient and cost-effective for retailers to purchase virtually all items for resale from companies in these developing countries. According to The Gap, Inc.'s, annual report, the company purchases nearly all of its inventories from sources outside the United States. Sometimes those purchases are made in currencies other than U.S. dollars, such as the Chinese yuan. The Gap, Inc., owns and operates stores in Canada, the United Kingdom, France, Ireland, Japan, China, and Italy. In addition, it has franchise agreements with unaffiliated companies to operate Gap and Banana Republic stores in many other countries around the world.

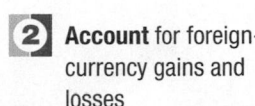 **Account** for foreign-currency gains and losses

Dollars Versus Foreign Currency

Assume The Gap, Inc., ships clothing and accessories to Republica, an unaffiliated franchise operation with stores in Mexico City, Monterrey, Guadalajara, and Cancun, Mexico. The sale can be made in dollars or in pesos. If Republica agrees to pay in dollars, The Gap, Inc., avoids the complication of dealing in a foreign currency, and the transaction is the same as selling to a Banana Republic store in San Francisco. But suppose Republica orders 1 million pesos (approximately $65,000) worth of inventory from The Gap, Inc., requests to pay in pesos, and The Gap, Inc., agrees to receive pesos in payment of its receivable instead of dollars.

The Gap, Inc., will need to convert the pesos to dollars; so the transaction poses a challenge. What if the peso weakens before The Gap, Inc., collects from the Mexican chain? In that case, The Gap, Inc., will not collect as many dollars as expected. The following example shows how to account for **foreign-currency exchange rate** gains and losses.

The Gap, Inc., sells goods to Republica on account for a price of 1 million pesos on July 28. On that date, a peso is worth $0.065. One month later, on August 28, the peso has weakened against the dollar so that a peso is worth only $0.062. The Gap, Inc., receives 1 million pesos from Republica on August 28, but the dollar value of The Gap, Inc.'s, cash receipt is $3,000 less than expected. The Gap, Inc., ends up earning less than hoped for on the transaction. The following journal entries show how The Gap, Inc., would account for these transactions (ignore cost of goods sold):

	A1			
	A	B	C	D
1	Jul 28	Accounts Receivable—Republica (1,000,000 pesos × $0.065)	65,000	
2		Sales Revenue		65,000
3		*Sale on account.*		
4				

	A1			
	A	B	C	D
1	Aug 28	Cash (1,000,000 pesos × $0.062)	62,000	
2		Foreign-Currency Transaction Loss	3,000	
3		Accounts Receivable—Republica		65,000
4		*Collection on account.*		
5				

If The Gap, Inc., had required Republica to pay at the time of the sale, it would have received pesos worth $65,000. But by selling on account, The Gap, Inc., exposed itself to foreign-currency exchange risk. It therefore had a $3,000 *foreign-currency transaction loss* when it received $3,000 less cash than expected. If the peso had increased in value relative to the dollar, The Gap, Inc., would have had a *foreign-currency transaction gain.*

When a company holds a receivable denominated in a foreign currency, it wants the foreign currency to strengthen so that it can be converted into more dollars. Unfortunately, that did not occur for The Gap, Inc., on the sale in this example.

Purchasing in a foreign currency also exposes a company to foreign-currency exchange risk. To illustrate, assume The Gap, Inc., buys a shipment of watches on account from Excel, Ltd., a Swiss company. The price is 20,000 Swiss francs. On September 15, The Gap, Inc., receives the goods and the Swiss franc is quoted at $1.10. When The Gap, Inc., pays two weeks later, the Swiss franc has weakened against the dollar—to $1.05. The Gap, Inc., would record the purchase and payment as follows:

	A1		B	C	D
	A		B	C	D
1	Sep 15	Inventory (20,000 Swiss francs × $1.10)		22,000	
2		Accounts Payable—Excel, Ltd.			22,000
3		*Purchase on account.*			
4					

	A1		B	C	D
	A		B	C	D
1	Sep 29	Accounts Payable—Excel, Ltd.		22,000	
2		Cash (20,000 Swiss francs × $1.05)			21,000
3		Foreign-Currency Transaction Gain			1,000
4		*Payment on account.*			
5					

The Swiss franc could have strengthened against the dollar, and The Gap, Inc., would have had a foreign-currency transaction loss. A company with a payable denominated in a foreign currency wants the dollar to get stronger: The payment then costs fewer dollars when the transaction is settled.

Reporting Foreign-Currency Gains and Losses on the Income Statement

The foreign-currency transaction gain account holds gains on transactions settled in a foreign currency. Likewise, the foreign-currency transaction loss account holds losses on transactions conducted in foreign currencies. Companies report the *net amount* of these two accounts on the income statement as Other Revenues and Gains, or Other Expenses and Losses, as the case may be. For example, assuming the two transactions we just described were the only two during the year, The Gap, Inc., would combine its $3,000 foreign-currency loss and the $1,000 gain and report the net loss of $2,000 on the income statement as

Other Expenses and Losses:
Foreign-currency transaction loss, net .... $(2,000)

These gains and losses fall into the "Other" category because they arise from buying and selling foreign currencies, not from the company's main business. The Gap, Inc.'s, foreign-currency losses amounted to $34 million in fiscal 2014, according to financial statement footnotes.

Reporting Foreign-Currency Exchange Gains and Losses on Cash and Cash Equivalents in the Statement of Cash Flows

Companies like The Gap, Inc., that maintain cash and cash equivalent balances denominated in foreign currencies are required to report the impact of foreign-currency exchange gains and losses on those balances as a separate line item on the statement of cash flows, directly after net cash provided by financing activities. We will cover this topic further in Chapter 12.

Should We Hedge Our Foreign-Currency Transaction Risk?

One way for U.S. companies to avoid foreign-currency transaction losses is to insist that international transactions be settled in dollars. This requirement puts the burden of foreign-currency gains and losses on the foreign party. But this approach may alienate customers and decrease sales. Another way for a company to protect itself is by hedging. **Hedging** enables the entity to protect itself from losing money in one transaction by engaging in a counterbalancing transaction.

A U.S. company selling goods to be collected in Mexican pesos expects to receive a fixed number of pesos. If the peso is losing value, the U.S. company would expect the pesos to be worth fewer dollars than the amount of the receivable—an expected-loss situation, as we saw for The Gap, Inc.

The U.S. company may have accumulated payables in a foreign currency, such as The Gap, Inc.'s, payable to the Swiss company. Losses on pesos may be offset by gains on Swiss francs. Most companies do not have equal amounts of receivables and payables in foreign currencies. To obtain a more precise hedge, companies can buy *futures contracts*. These are contracts for foreign currencies to be received in the future. Futures contracts can create a payable to exactly offset a receivable, and vice versa. Many companies that do business internationally use hedging techniques. The Gap, Inc., made gains on hedging in the amount of $28 million and used them to offset its foreign currency transaction losses of $34 million, for a net loss of only $6 million in fiscal 2014, according to the financial statement footnote 1.

ACCOUNT FOR OTHER ITEMS ON THE INCOME STATEMENT

Interest Expense and Interest Income

Covered in Chapters 5, 8, and 9, interest income represents the amount earned on invested money, and interest expense represents the cost of borrowed money. These items are not related to the company's operating activities, but to financing activities. Thus, they are segregated and reported in a separate section of the income statement. Note 5 to The Gap, Inc.'s, consolidated financial statements indicates that the company owes approximately $1.35 billion in long-term debt outstanding as of January 31, 2015. Line 9 of the company's Consolidated Statements of Income reports $75 million, $61 million, and $87 million in interest expense for fiscal 2014, 2013, and 2012, respectively. Line 10 reports a very minor amount of interest income.

 Account for other items on the income statement

Corporate Income Taxes

The next important ingredient of reported earnings on the statement of income is corporate income tax expense, which must be subtracted to arrive at net income. The current maximum federal income tax rate for corporations is 35%. In addition, state income taxes run about 5% in many states. The Gap, Inc.'s, fiscal 2014 income tax provision (expense) of $751 million amounts to about 37.3% of earnings before income taxes. Thus, we use a rate of 40% to approximate income taxes in the illustrations that follow.

To account for income tax, the corporation measures

- *income tax expense*, an expense on the income statement. Income tax expense helps measure net income.
- *income tax payable*, a current liability on the balance sheet. Income tax payable is the amount of tax to be paid to the government based on the company's income tax return.

Accounting for income tax follows the principles of accrual accounting. Suppose, at the end of fiscal 2016, The Gap, Inc., reports income before tax (also called **pre-tax accounting income**) of $2 billion. As we saw previously, The Gap, Inc.'s combined income tax rate is close to 40%. To start this discussion, assume income tax expense and income tax payable are the same. Then on January 28, 2017 (the end of its 2016 fiscal year) The Gap, Inc., would record income tax for the year as follows (amounts in millions):

	A	B	C	D
	A1			
1	2017	(In millions)		
2	Jan 28	Income Tax Expense ($2,000 × 0.40)	800	
3		Income Tax Payable		800
4		*Recorded income tax for the year.*		
5				

The Gap, Inc.'s, financial statements for fiscal 2016 would report these figures (partial, in millions):

Income statement (in millions)		Balance sheet (in millions)	
Income before income tax	$2,000	Current liabilities:	
Income tax expense	(800)	Income tax payable	$800
Net income................................	$1,200		

In general, income tax expense and income tax payable can be computed as

$$\begin{matrix} \text{Income} \\ \text{tax} \\ \textit{expense} \end{matrix} = \begin{matrix} \text{Income before} \\ \text{income tax} \\ \text{(from the} \\ \textit{income} \\ \textit{statement}) \end{matrix} \times \begin{matrix} \text{Income} \\ \text{tax} \\ \text{rate} \end{matrix} \qquad \begin{matrix} \text{Income} \\ \text{tax} \\ \textit{payable} \end{matrix} = \begin{matrix} \text{Taxable} \\ \text{income (from} \\ \text{the } \textit{income tax} \\ \textit{return} \text{ filed with} \\ \text{the IRS)} \end{matrix} \times \begin{matrix} \text{Income} \\ \text{tax} \\ \text{rate} \end{matrix}$$

The income statement and the income tax return are entirely separate documents:

- The *income statement* reports the results of operations.
- The *income tax return* is filed with the Internal Revenue Service (IRS) to measure how much tax to pay the government.

For most companies, income tax expense and income tax payable differ. Some revenues and expenses affect income differently for accounting and for tax purposes. The most common difference between accounting income and **taxable income** occurs when a corporation uses straight-line depreciation in its financial statements and accelerated depreciation for the tax return.

Continuing with the The Gap, Inc., illustration, suppose for fiscal 2016 that it had

- pre-tax accounting income of $2 billion on its income statement, and
- taxable income of $1,600 million on its income tax return.

Taxable income is less than accounting income because The Gap, Inc., uses

- straight-line depreciation for accounting purposes (say, $200 million), and
- accelerated depreciation for tax purposes (say, $600 million).

The Gap, Inc., would record income tax for fiscal 2016 as follows (dollar amounts in millions and an income tax rate of 40%):

	A	B	C	D
	A1			
1	2017	(In millions)		
2	Jan 28	Income Tax Expense ($2,000 × 0.40)	800	
3		Income Tax Payable ($1,600 × 0.40)		640
4		Deferred Tax Liability		160
5		*Recorded income tax for the year.*		
6				

Deferred Tax Liability is usually long-term.

The Gap, Inc.'s financial statements for fiscal 2016 will report

Income statement (in millions)		Balance sheet (in millions)	
Income before income tax	$2,000	Current liabilities:	
Income tax expense	(800)	Income tax payable	$640
Net income.................................	$1,200	Long-term liabilities:	
		Deferred tax liability	160*

*Assuming the beginning balance of Deferred tax liability was zero.

In March 2017, The Gap, Inc., would pay income tax payable of $640 million because this is a current liability. The deferred tax liability can be paid later.

For a given year, Income Tax Payable can exceed Income Tax Expense. This occurs when, because of differences in revenue and expenses for book and tax purposes, taxable income exceeds book income. When that occurs, the company debits a Deferred Tax Asset. The remainder of this topic is reserved for a more advanced course.

Effective tax planning, both by in-house tax staff and externally through the counsel of the company's independent outside accountants and attorneys, can help lower the company's tax burden and can contribute substantially to improved operating profits.

Which Income Number Predicts Future Profits?

How is income from continuing operations used in investment analysis? Suppose Kimberly Kuhl, an analyst with **Morgan Stanley**, is estimating the value of The Gap, Inc.'s, common stock. Kuhl believes that The Gap, Inc., can earn annual income each year equal to its income from ongoing (continuing) operations after tax—$1,262 million for fiscal 2014 for The Gap, Inc.

To estimate the value of The Gap, Inc.'s, common stock, financial analysts use a method similar to that described in Chapter 8 to determine the present value of The Gap, Inc.'s, stream of future income. Ms. Kuhl must use some interest rate to compute the present value. Assume that an appropriate interest rate (i) for the valuation of The Gap, Inc., is 10%. This rate is often based on the company's **weighted-average cost of capital** (WACC), which is a measure of the average returns that creditors and investors demand from the company. WACC is a major focus in corporate finance courses, so we do not discuss how it is computed in detail. However, you should know that WACC is influenced by the risk that a company might not be able to sustain a certain rate of return into the indefinite future. The higher the risk associated with an investment, the higher the rate of return demanded by investors and creditors, and vice versa. This rate is also called an **investment capitalization rate** because it is used to estimate the value of an investment. Assuming the capitalization rate is reasonable, and that the company can continue to earn this amount of income for an infinite period into the future, a simple way to estimate the value of the stock of The Gap, Inc., is

$$\text{Estimated value of The Gap, Inc., common stock} = \frac{\text{Estimated annual income in the future}}{\text{Investment capitalization rate}} = \frac{\$1{,}262 \text{ million}}{0.10} = \$12.62 \text{ billion}$$

Kuhl thus estimates that The Gap, Inc., as a company is worth $12.62 billion. She then computes the company's market capitalization based on its stock price at fiscal year end. The Gap, Inc.'s balance sheet at January 31, 2015, reports that the company has 421 million shares of common stock outstanding. The market price of The Gap, Inc., common stock on February 2, 2015 is $41.18 per share. (The market price on January 31, 2015 is not available because it is not a trading day, so we use the next trading day which is February 2, 2015.) The market value of The Gap, Inc., as a company (market capitalization) as of that date is

$$\begin{array}{ccc}
\text{Market} & & \text{Number of shares} & \text{Market price} \\
\text{value of the} & = & \text{of common stock} \times & \text{per share} \\
\text{company} & & \text{outstanding} & \\
\end{array}$$

$$\text{\$17.34 billion} = \quad 421 \text{ million} \quad \times \quad \text{\$41.18}$$

The investment decision rule is

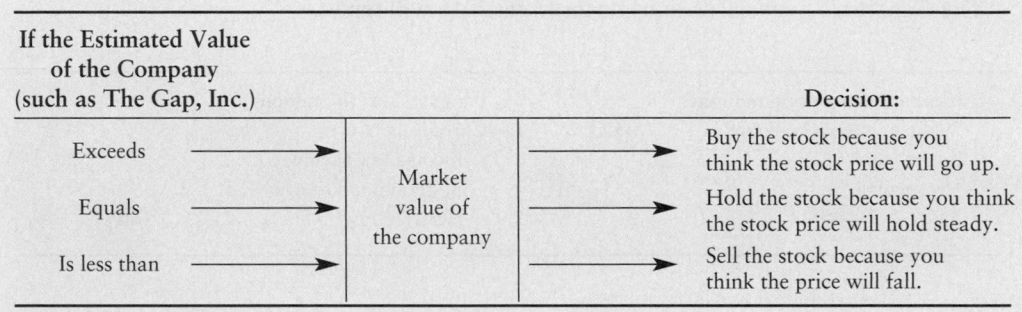

If the Estimated Value of the Company (such as The Gap, Inc.)		Decision:
Exceeds	Market value of the company	Buy the stock because you think the stock price will go up.
Equals		Hold the stock because you think the stock price will hold steady.
Is less than		Sell the stock because you think the price will fall.

In this case,

				Decision:
Estimated Value of The Gap, Inc. $12.62 billion	Is less than	Market value of The Gap, Inc. $17.34 billion		Sell the stock
$29.98 per share*	Is less than	$41.18 per share		Sell the stock

*$12.62 billion/421 million shares

The February price of the stock ($41.18 per share) exceeds its estimated value ($29.98 per share) so Kuhl believes The Gap, Inc.'s, stock price may drop from its February market value of $41.18 to somewhere in a range near $30 per share. Based on this analysis, Morgan Stanley would issue a "sell" decision on The Gap, Inc., common stock in February. Tracking the stock over time reveals whether Morgan Stanley's investment recommendation was correct. On November 3, 2015, shares of The Gap, Inc. closed at a price of $28.27 per share. Therefore, Kuhl's decision in February to sell the stock at a price of $41.18 appears to have been a wise one. You should use caution in making these types of estimates because they do not include information about the company that might emerge at a later time or other market uncertainties. In reality, such estimates are only educated guesses. It is very difficult to predict stock price trends. Although some experts have better track records than others, even the experts can't predict stock prices perfectly!

Discontinued Operations

Most large companies engage in several lines of business. For example, The Gap, Inc., owns Gap stores, its mid-line store, as well as **Old Navy** (its less-expensive lines), **Banana Republic** (its upscale lines) and **Piperlime**, a specialty line of women's shoes and handbags. **General Electric** makes household appliances and jet engines and owns **NBC**, the media network. We call each identifiable part of a company a *segment* of the business.

A company may sell or discontinue segments of its business from time to time. This did not happen to The Gap, Inc., during the fiscal years covered in Exhibit 11-1. However, in January

2015, the company announced the decision to discontinue its smallest brand, Piperlime, including its online platform and its single store in New York, by the end of the first quarter of fiscal 2015. Piperlime's results of operations will be disclosed as discontinued operations in 2015. As another prominent example, during the second quarter of 2012, another well-known international company, **Nike, Inc.**, announced the sale of two of its major brands, Umbro and Cole Haan. Nike completed the sale of the assets of Umbro to Iconix Brand group for $225 million. The company reported a loss from discontinued operations of $107 million (net of the tax benefit it received from deducting the loss on its tax return) in the income statement of the second quarter of 2012. Also during the quarter, Nike reached an agreement to sell Cole Haan to Apax Partners for $570 million. The actual sale did not occur until 2013, but because it had agreed to sell this brand in 2012, Nike was entitled to report its loss from discontinued operations (net of tax benefit) in Loss from Discontinued Operations in 2012. Note that the caption "Discontinued Operations" includes *both* operating income or loss of the segment during the divestiture period *and* gains or losses on the transaction at the point of sale of the segment.

All gains and losses from discontinued operations are shown "net of tax"—that is, the income tax expense (or savings) from the gain (or loss) is subtracted from the item before reporting it in the income statement. *Financial analysts typically do not include discontinued operations in predictions of future corporate income because the discontinued segments will not continue to generate income for the company.* The end-of-chapter summary problem (pp. 651–652) contains an example and illustration of reporting for discontinued operations. The details of this topic are covered in more advanced accounting classes.

Accounting Changes

Companies sometimes voluntarily change from one accounting method to another, such as from double-declining-balance (DDB) to straight-line depreciation, or from first-in, first-out (FIFO) to average cost for inventory. From time to time, companies might also be required to make accounting changes whenever the FASB issues new accounting pronouncements. An accounting change makes it difficult to compare one period with preceding periods. Without detailed information, investors can be misled into thinking that the current year is better or worse than the preceding year, when in fact the only difference is a change in the accounting method.

Two types of accounting changes are most relevant to introductory accounting:

1. *Changes in accounting estimates* include changing the estimated life of a building or equipment and the estimated percent of uncollectible receivables. For these changes, companies report amounts for the *current and future* periods on the new basis. There is no looking back to the past. A change in depreciation method is treated as a change in estimate.

2. *Changes in accounting principles* include most changes in accounting methods, such as from FIFO to average cost for inventory and from one method to another for a revenue or an expense. For these changes, the company reports figures for all periods presented in the income statement—*past as well as current*—on the new basis. The company *retrospectively restates* (looks back and restates) all prior-period amounts that are presented for comparative purposes with the current year, as though the new accounting method had been in effect all along. This lets investors compare all periods that are presented on the same accounting basis. Other times, companies might discover errors they have made in applying accounting principles that must be corrected, requiring a change from the erroneous principle to one that is generally accepted.

   If an accounting change impacts periods prior to the earliest one presented in the current income statement, an adjustment, called a **prior-period adjustment**, must be made to the beginning balance of retained earnings in the current period's statement of stockholders' equity. The summary problem at the end of this chapter (pp. 651–652) contains an example of how this is done.

A detailed discussion of accounting changes is reserved for future accounting courses.

COMPUTE EARNINGS PER SHARE

4 Compute earnings per share

The final segment of the income statement reports **earnings per share** (**EPS**), which is the amount of a company's net income per share of its *outstanding common stock*. EPS is a key measure of a business's success because it shows how much income the company earned for each share of stock. Stock prices are quoted at an amount per share, and investors buy a certain number of shares. EPS is used to help determine the value of a share of stock. EPS is computed as

$$\text{Earnings per share} = \frac{\text{Net income} - \text{Preferred dividends}}{\text{Weighted-average number of shares of common stock outstanding}}$$

The corporation lists its various sources of income separately: continuing operations, discontinued operations, and net income. It also lists the EPS figure for each of these elements of net income. Consider the EPS of The Gap, Inc., The final section of Exhibit 11-1 (lines 18 through 19) shows how companies report EPS. Notice that two EPS computations are made: one for "basic" (the currently outstanding shares) and one for "diluted" (which takes into account potential increases in outstanding shares). Companies must first compute a weighted-average number of shares outstanding. This computation, which is beyond the scope of this textbook, takes into account the changes that might occur in the number of shares outstanding during the year from such things as treasury-stock purchases or reissuances. According to Exhibit 11-1, The Gap, Inc., has a "basic" weighted average of 435 million shares of common stock outstanding as of the end of fiscal 2014 (line 15) and "basic" EPS of $2.90 (line 18).

15	Weighted-average number of shares—basic....................................	435 million
18	Earnings per share—basic ($1,262 million/435 million).................	$2.90

Effect of Preferred Dividends on Earnings per Share. Recall that EPS is earnings per share of *common* stock. But the holders of preferred stock have first claim on dividends. Therefore, preferred dividends must be subtracted from net income and income from continuing operations to compute EPS. Preferred dividends are not subtracted from discontinued operations.

Like the vast majority of corporations, The Gap, Inc., has only one type of stock, which is common stock. However, for illustrative purposes only, suppose that The Gap, Inc., had 5,000,000 shares of preferred stock outstanding, each with a $1.00 dividend. The Gap, Inc.'s, annual preferred dividends would be $5,000,000 (5,000,000 × $1.00). The $5,000,000 is subtracted from net income, resulting in the following EPS amount (recall that The Gap, Inc., has a weighted average of 435 million shares of common stock outstanding):

Basic earnings per share of common stock (435 weighted-average shares outstanding) (in millions): ($1,262 − $5)/435..	$2.89

Earnings per Share Dilution. Some corporations have contingent plans that might eventually call for issuance of additional common shares. For example, a corporation might have convertible preferred stock, which may be exchanged for common stock. When preferred is converted to common, the EPS is *diluted*—reduced—because more common shares are divided into net income. Other potential transactions might also dilute EPS. For example, according to the financial statement footnotes, The Gap, Inc. could potentially issue an additional 5 million common shares as part of a stock-based compensation plan for employees. Corporations with complex capital structures like this present two sets of EPS figures:

- EPS based on actual outstanding common shares (*basic* EPS)
- EPS based on outstanding common shares plus the additional shares that can arise from conversion of the preferred stock into common stock or other dilutive securities (*diluted* EPS)

The Gap, Inc.'s, weighted-average diluted number of shares for the year ended January 31, 2015, is 440 million (435 million + 5 million shares in the stock option plan). Therefore, the EPS on a diluted basis is reduced by about $0.03 per share to account for the additional shares outstanding on a diluted basis (line 19 of Exhibit 11-1).

ANALYZE THE STATEMENT OF COMPREHENSIVE INCOME, FOOTNOTES, AND SUPPLEMENTAL DISCLOSURES

Reporting Comprehensive Income

All companies report net income or net loss on their income statements. As we saw in Chapter 8, companies with unrealized gains and losses on certain investments and foreign-currency translation adjustments also report another income figure. **Comprehensive income** is the company's change in total stockholders' equity from all sources other than from the owners of the business. Comprehensive income includes net income plus

- unrealized gains (losses) on available-for-sale investments, and
- foreign-currency translation gains/losses.

These types of other comprehensive income were discussed in Chapter 8. There are others, but discussion of them is reserved for later courses.

> *Items of comprehensive income, other than net income, do not enter into the determination of earnings per share.*

Generally accepted accounting principles require that comprehensive income for a company be presented either alone in a separate **statement of comprehensive income** or combined with the "regular" income statement into a unified statement of comprehensive income. Exhibit 11-2 presents The Gap, Inc.'s separate Consolidated Statements of Comprehensive Income for the three fiscal years ended January 31, 2015. Notice that it starts on line 4 with net income of $1,262 million, $1,280 million, and $1,135 million for the three fiscal years from line 13 of the Consolidated Statements of Earnings in Exhibit 11-1. Lines 6 and 7 add foreign-currency translation gains (losses) (net of tax) for the three fiscal years. Lines 8 through 10 include adjustments for unrealized changes in fair value of derivative financial instruments (a type of available-for-sale investment) for the three fiscal years. Lines 11 through 13 make reclassifications from other comprehensive income to net income for realized gains and losses on derivative financial instruments sold during the three fiscal years.

From this point, net income and other comprehensive income (lines 4 and 14, respectively) follow separate paths to the Stockholders' Equity section of the balance sheet. Net income from line 4 is added to Retained Earnings in the company's Consolidated Statements of Stockholders' Equity. Other Comprehensive Income (Loss) (net of tax) from line 14 is added to (subtracted from) Accumulated Other Comprehensive Income (Loss) in the company's Consolidated Statements of Stockholders' Equity.

5 **Analyze** the statement of comprehensive income, footnotes, and supplemental disclosures

Exhibit 11-2 | The Gap, Inc., Consolidated Statements of Comprehensive Income

	A	B	C	D
	A1			
1	**The Gap, Inc.** **Consolidated Statements of Comprehensive Income**			
2			**12 Months Ended**	
3	**(in millions of USD)**	**Jan. 31, 2015**	**Feb. 1, 2014**	**Feb. 2, 2013**
4	Net income	$ 1,262	$ 1,280	$ 1,135
5	Other comprehensive income (loss), net of tax:			
6	Foreign-currency translation, net of tax (tax benefit)			
7	of $(2), $5, and $-	(47)	(51)	(71)
8	Change in fair value of derivative			
9	financial instruments, net of tax (tax benefit)			
10	of $48, $30, and $18	118	48	28
11	Reclassification adjustment for realized (gains) losses			
12	on derivative financial instruments, net of tax			
13	of $(20), $(27), and $(4)	(41)	(43)	(5)
14	Other comprehensive income (loss), net of tax	30	(46)	(48)
15	Comprehensive income	$ 1,292	$ 1,234	$ 1,087
16				

For Additional Details, Don't Forget the Footnotes

To fully understand the impact of information in the financial statements, and to form a more accurate opinion about the quality of a company's earnings, you need to become familiar with additional details found in the financial statement footnotes.

Footnote 1 of every public company's financial statements contains a summary of significant accounting policies used to prepare them. For example, in Note 1 of The Gap, Inc.'s, consolidated financial statements, you can find the following information in narrative format that you may need to fully understand how The Gap, Inc., computes net income:

- Its organization
- Its principles of consolidation
- How it determines its fiscal year reporting period
- Its revenue recognition policy
- The types of costs it includes in cost of goods sold and operating expenses
- How it calculates rent, advertising, share-based compensation of employees, gift card revenue, earnings per share, foreign-currency gains and losses, comprehensive income, and income taxes
- The impact of recently issued accounting principles that might impact comparability of reported income and that might have required accounting changes

Other footnotes contain additional detail supporting reported information for balance sheet and income statement information. Here are some examples from The Gap, Inc.'s, financial statement footnotes that impact the computation of net income and other comprehensive income:

- Note 2: Additional financial statement information, including details about property and equipment (including depreciation), accumulated other comprehensive income, and sales returns and allowances
- Note 3: Details of an acquisition the company made during fiscal 2014
- Note 4: Goodwill and intangible assets, including amortization expense
- Note 5: Long-term debt, including interest expense
- Note 10: Accumulated Other Comprehensive Income
- Note 11: Share-based compensation
- Note 12: Leases
- Note 13: Income taxes
- Note 14: Employee benefit plans
- Note 15: Earnings per share
- Note 16: Commitments and contingencies
- Note 17: Segment information

The last item in the list deserves special attention. Whenever it is relevant, companies have to break down key information (such as sales, operating income, and assets) by **segment**. For this purpose, a segment is defined as a division or subset of a business's operations. To be considered a segment, the division or operating unit must directly earn revenue for the company. Segments may be created by product line, type of business, geographic areas, or other logical divisions. Internally, each segment's revenues and expenses are accounted for separately.

The objective of requiring disclosures about operating information by segments is to provide the user with more detailed information about the different types of business activities in which a company engages and the different economic environments in which it operates. Seeing this detailed information helps users of financial statements to (a) better understand the company's performance, (b) better assess the company's prospects for future net cash flows, and (c) make more informed judgments about the company as a whole. For purposes of reporting segment information, companies are allowed to tailor the information toward their particular "management approach"; that is, they may define segments in the same way they manage and evaluate their business activities (i.e., by geographic region, brand, type of revenue, etc.).

Exhibit 11-3 shows an excerpt from Note 17 of The Gap, Inc.'s, consolidated financial statements showing the breakdown of net sales by its four management-defined segments.

After reading this footnote, you should be much more informed of the geographic regions of the world where The Gap, Inc., earns its revenue, the brands (Gap, Old Navy, Banana Republic, and Other) that produce its revenue, and the amount of sales growth from each of its brands over its fiscal 2014 year. Totals of this detailed information tie back to total consolidated net sales reported in Exhibit 11-1 (p. 632). For example, you can readily see that 77% of total consolidated Net sales is earned in the United States and 23% is earned from stores in other countries. The segment with the highest reported sales growth over the latest fiscal year (8%) is the "other" category, which includes Piperlime, Althea and Intermix. The major segment with the highest sales growth (6%) was Old Navy Global. However, the flagship stores (Gap Global) experienced a 3% decline in sales. This footnote contains many more details than we can discuss here, including comparative information from prior years, enabling the analyst to compute trends over time. This detailed information should allow a more accurate prediction of the direction the company may be headed in the future, as well as its prospects for growth and added share value.

Exhibit 11-3 | Excerpt of Note 17: Segment Information for Sales

We identify our operating segments according to how our business activities are managed and evaluated. As of January 31, 2015, we had four operating segments: Gap Global, Old Navy Global, Banana Republic Global, and Growth, Innovation, and Digital ("GID"). Each brand's specialty, outlet, online, and franchise operations were managed by global brand presidents and Piperlime, Athleta, and Intermix were managed by the president of the GID division. Each of our brands serves customers through its store and online channels, allowing us to execute on our omni-channel strategy where customers can shop seamlessly in retail stores and online through desktop or mobile devices. We have determined that each of our operating segments share similar economic and other qualitative characteristics, and therefore the results of our operating segments are aggregated into one reportable segment as of January 31, 2015.

Net sales by brand and region are as follows:

A1						
	A	**B**	**C**	**D**	**E**	**F**	**G**
1	**($ in millions)**						
2	**Fiscal 2014**	**GAP Global**	**Old Navy Global**	**Banana Republic Global**	**Other (2)**	**Total**	**Percentage of Net Sales**
3	U.S. (1)	$ 3,575	$ 5,967	$ 2,405	$ 725	$ 12,672	77%
4	Canada	384	500	249	4	1,137	7
5	Europe	824	—	93	—	917	6
6	Asia	1,208	149	145	—	1,502	9
7	Other regions	174	3	30	—	207	1
8	Total Sales	$ 6,165	$ 6,619	$ 2,922	$ 729	16,435	100%
9							
10	Sales growth (decline)	(3)%	6%	2%	8%	2%	
11							

(1) U.S. includes the United States, Puerto Rico, and Guam.

(2) Includes Piperlime, Althea, and Intermix

Total online sales were $2.5 billion, $2.3 billion, and $1.9 billion in fiscal 2014, 2013, and 2012, respectively.

Nonfinancial Reports

A growing number of companies now issue annual reports covering their performance in such nonfinancial areas as **corporate social responsibility** (CSR). For example, many of the focus companies in this textbook, such as **The Gap, Inc.**, **The Walt Disney Company**, **Apple Inc.**, and **The Home Depot, Inc.**, issue annual **CSR reports**. These reports contain voluntary disclosures on how companies are conducting and governing their businesses in ways that benefit not only their shareholders but also the environment, their employees, and society as a whole. The Global Reporting Initiative (GRI) is an independent institution formed in 1997 to develop a common framework for sustainability reporting. Many of the world's largest businesses now issue CSR reports under GRI's strict guidelines. While reporting under this framework is voluntary rather than mandatory in the United States, the SEC has endorsed these types of reports. Other countries, such as France, South Africa, and The Netherlands, now mandate some form of CSR reporting in order to be listed on their stock exchanges.

You can find The Gap, Inc.'s, CSR report at the following web address: **http://www.letsdomore .com/**. Check it out! Reading this report may make you feel better about doing business at The Gap, Inc., or investing in its stock.

DIFFERENTIATE MANAGEMENT'S AND AUDITORS' RESPONSIBILITIES IN FINANCIAL REPORTING

Management's Responsibility

Differentiate management's and auditors' reporting responsibilities

Management issues a report on internal control over financial reporting along with the company's financial statements. Exhibit 11-4 is an excerpt from the report of management for The Gap, Inc.

Management declares its responsibility for the internal controls over financial reporting in accordance with the Sarbanes-Oxley Act of 2002. Management also states that it has conducted an assessment of internal controls over financial reporting based on the framework established by the Committee of Sponsoring Organizations (COSO) of the Treadway Commission and has concluded that, as of January 31, 2015, internal controls over financial reporting are effective. In addition, management states that the internal controls of the company have been audited by the company's outside auditors and refers to their report, which can be found in the company's annual report on the website of the U.S. Securities and Exchange Commission (**http://www.sec.gov**). See Try It in Excel on page 634 for explicit instructions on how to access The Gap, Inc.'s, most recent annual report. Exhibit 11-5 contains excerpts of the independent auditors' combined report on the financial statements as well as the internal controls of a hypothetical public company.

Exhibit 11-4 | Statement of Management's Responsibility

> Our management is responsible for establishing and maintaining an adequate system of internal control over financial reporting, as defined in Exchange Act Rule 13a-15(f). Management conducted an assessment of our internal control over financial reporting based on the framework established by the Committee of Sponsoring Organizations of the Treadway Commission in Internal Control—Integrated Framework (released in 2013). Based on the assessment, management concluded that as of January 31, 2015, our internal control over financial reporting is effective. The Company's internal control over financial reporting as of January 31, 2015 has been audited by (....) an independent registered public accounting firm, as stated in their report which is included herein.

Auditor Report

The Securities Exchange Act of 1934 requires companies that issue their stock publicly to file audited financial statements with the SEC. Companies engage outside auditors who are certified public accountants to examine their financial statements as well as their internal controls over

Exhibit 11-5 | Excerpts of Independent Auditors' Report for Hypothetical Public Company

To the Board of Directors and Stockholders of Superior Clothing, Inc.

We have audited the accompanying consolidated balance sheets of Superior Clothing, Inc., and subsidiaries (the "Company") as of January 31, 2015, and February 1,2014, and the related consolidated statements of earnings, comprehensive income, stockholders' equity, and cash flows for each of the three fiscal years in the period ended January 31, 2015. We also have audited the Company's internal control over financial reporting as of January 31, 2015, based on criteria established by *Internal Control—Integrated Framework* issued by the Committee of Sponsoring Organizations of the Treadway Commission. The Company's management is responsible for these financial statements, for maintaining effective internal control over financial reporting, and for its assessment of the effectiveness of internal control over financial reporting, included in the accompanying Management's Report on Internal Control over Financial Reporting. Our responsibility is to express an opinion on these financial statements and opinion on the Company's internal control over financial reporting based on our audits.

We conducted our audits in accordance with the standards of the Public Company Accounting Oversight Board (United States). Those standards require that we plan and perform the audit to obtain reasonable assurance about whether the financial statements are free from material misstatements and whether effective internal control over financial reporting was maintained in all material respects...We believe that our audits provide a reasonable basis for our opinions.

A company's internal control over financial reporting is a process designed by, or under the supervision of, the company's...financial officers...and effected by the Company's board of directors...to provide reasonable assurance regarding the reliability of financial reporting and the preparation of financial statements...in accordance with generally accepted accounting principles.

Because of the inherent limitations of internal control over financial reporting, including the possibility of collusion or improper management override of controls, material misstatements due to error or fraud may not be prevented or detected on a timely basis. Also, projections of any evaluation of the effectiveness of internal control over financial reporting to future periods are subject to the risk that the controls may become inadequate because of changes in conditions, or that the degree of compliance with the policies or procedures may deteriorate.

In our opinion, the consolidated financial statement referred to above present fairly, in all material respects, the financial position of Superior Clothing, Inc., and subsidiaries as of January 31, 2015, and February 1, 2014, and the results of their operations and their cash flows for each of the three years in the period ended January 31, 2015, in conformity with accounting principles generally accepted in the United States of America. Also, in our opinion, the Company maintained, in all material respects, effective internal control over financial reporting as of January 31, 2015, based on the criteria established in *Internal Control—Integrated Framework* issued by the Committee of Sponsoring Organizations of the Treadway Commission.

/s/ Independent Auditing Firm

Anytown, U.S.A.

March 15, 2015

Source: Based on Kimberly-Clark Corporation Report of Independent Registered Public Accounting Firm, http://www.sec.gov/Archives/edgar/data/55/85/000119312506252528/ dex995.htm.

financial reporting. The independent auditors decide whether the company's financial statements comply with GAAP. They must also decide whether the internal controls of the company meet certain standards. The firm then issues a combined audit report on both the financial statements and the company's system of internal controls over financial reporting.

The audit report is addressed to the board of directors and stockholders of the company. A partner of the auditing firm signs the firm's name to the report.

The combined audit report on financial statements and internal control over financial reporting typically contains five paragraphs:

- The first paragraph identifies the audited financial statements as well as the company being audited. It also states the responsibility of the company's management as well as the auditor's responsibilities.

- The second paragraph describes how the audit was performed in accordance with generally accepted auditing standards of the Public Company Accounting Oversight Board (an independent regulatory body with SEC oversight). These are the standards used by auditors as the benchmark for evaluating audit quality.

- The third paragraph describes in detail what a system of internal controls is, noting that it should be designed to provide reasonable assurance that transactions are recorded to permit preparation of financial statements that are fairly presented in conformity with GAAP.

- The fourth paragraph describes inherent limitations in the system of internal controls and notes that, at best, the system of internal controls can only provide reasonable assurance that financial statements are fairly presented.

- The fifth paragraph expresses the auditor's combined opinion on both the fairness of financial statements, in all material respects, in conformity with GAAP and the effectiveness of the company's internal controls over financial reporting. The auditing firm is expressing an **unqualified (clean) opinion** on both the fairness of the financial statements and the effectiveness of the company's internal controls. The unqualified opinion is the highest statement of assurance that an independent certified public accountant can express.

The independent audit adds credibility to the financial statements of a company as well as to its system of internal controls. It is no accident that financial reporting and auditing are more advanced in the United States than anywhere else in the world and that U.S. capital markets are the envy of the world.

 # DECISION GUIDELINES

USING THE INCOME STATEMENT AND RELATED NOTES IN INVESTMENT ANALYSIS

Suppose you've completed your studies, taken a job, and have been fortunate to save $10,000. Now you are ready to start investing. These guidelines provide a framework for using accounting information for investment analysis.

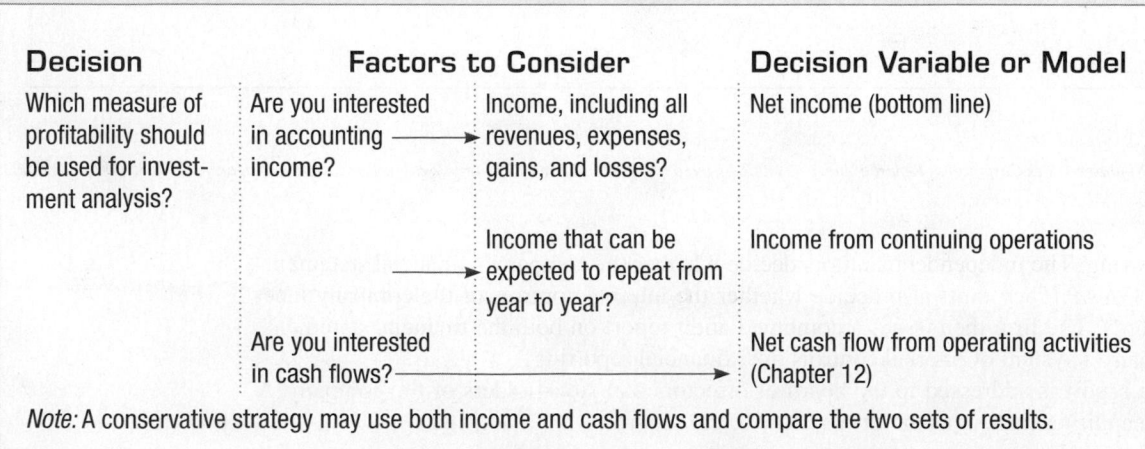

Decision	Factors to Consider		Decision Variable or Model
Which measure of profitability should be used for investment analysis?	Are you interested in accounting income? →	Income, including all revenues, expenses, gains, and losses?	Net income (bottom line)
	→	Income that can be expected to repeat from year to year?	Income from continuing operations
	Are you interested in cash flows? →		Net cash flow from operating activities (Chapter 12)

Note: A conservative strategy may use both income and cash flows and compare the two sets of results.

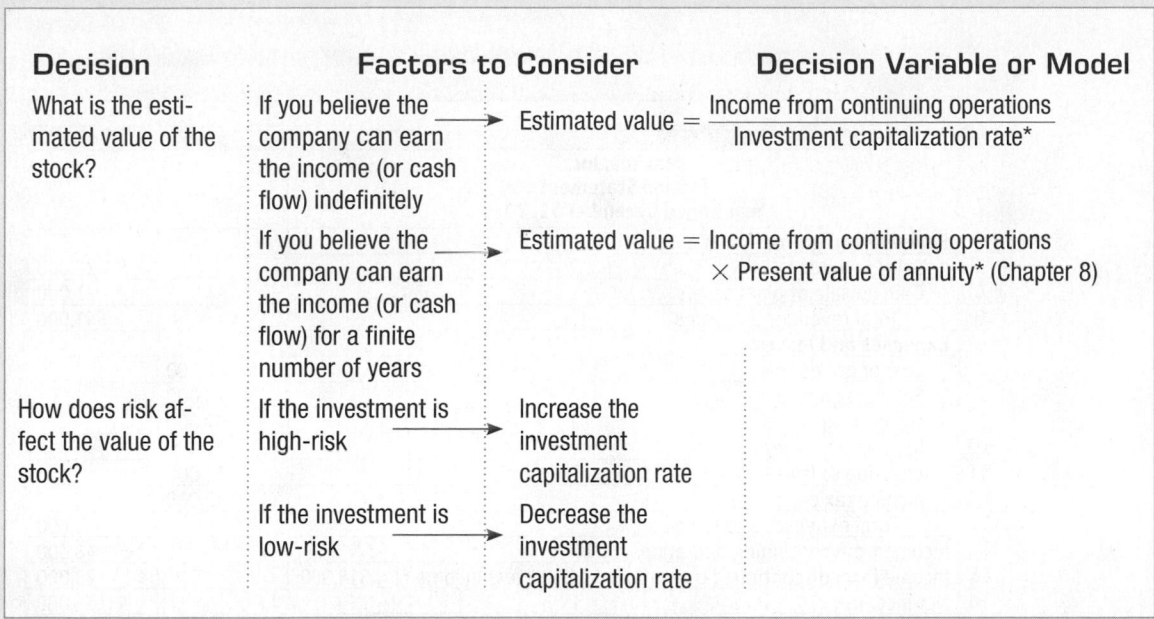

Decision	Factors to Consider	Decision Variable or Model
What is the estimated value of the stock?	If you believe the company can earn the income (or cash flow) indefinitely →	Estimated value = $\dfrac{\text{Income from continuing operations}}{\text{Investment capitalization rate*}}$
	If you believe the company can earn the income (or cash flow) for a finite number of years →	Estimated value = Income from continuing operations × Present value of annuity* (Chapter 8)
How does risk affect the value of the stock?	If the investment is high-risk →	Increase the investment capitalization rate
	If the investment is low-risk →	Decrease the investment capitalization rate

*Use rate approximates the company's weighted-average cost of capital.

End-of-Chapter Summary Problems

The following information was taken from the ledger of Maxima, Inc.:

Prior-period adjustment—net of tax:			Treasury stock, common	
credit to Retained Earnings	$ 5,000		(5,000 shares at cost)	$ 25,000
Gain on sale of plant assets	21,000		Selling expenses	78,000
Cost of goods sold	380,000		Common stock, no par,	
Income tax expense:			45,000 shares issued	180,000
Continuing operations	32,000		Sales revenue	620,000
Discontinued operations	18,000		Interest expense	30,000
Preferred stock, 8%, $100 par,			Income from discontinued	
500 shares issued	50,000		operations	46,000
Dividends declared	16,000		Loss due to lawsuit	11,000
Retained earnings, beginning,			General expenses	62,000
as originally reported	103,000			

Requirement

1. Prepare a single-step income statement (with all revenues and gains grouped together) and a statement of retained earnings for Maxima, Inc., for the current year ended December 31, 2016. Include the earnings-per-share presentation and show computations. Assume no changes in the stock accounts during the year.

Answers

	A	B	C
1	**Maxima, Inc.** **Income Statement** **Year Ended December 31, 2016**		
2	**Revenue and gains:**		
3	Sales revenue		$ 620,000
4	Gain on sale of plant assets		21,000
5	Total revenues and gains		641,000
6	**Expenses and losses:**		
7	Cost of goods sold	$ 380,000	
8	Selling expenses	78,000	
9	General expenses	62,000	
10	Interest expense	30,000	
11	Loss due to lawsuit	11,000	
12	Income tax expense	32,000	
13	Total expenses and losses		593,000
14	Income from continuing operations		48,000
15	Income from discontinued operations, $46,000, less income tax, $18,000		28,000
16	Net income		$ 76,000
17	**Earnings per share:***		
18	Income from continuing operations		
19	[($48,000 − $4,000)/40,000 shares]		$ 1.10
20	Income from discontinued operations		
21	($28,000/40,000 shares)		0.70
22	Net income [($76,000 − $4,000)/40,000 shares]		$ 1.80
23			

*Computations:

$$EPS = \frac{\text{Income} - \text{Preferred dividends}}{\text{Common shares outstanding}}$$

Preferred dividends: $50,000 × 0.08 = $4,000
Common shares outstanding:
  45,000 shares issued − 5,000 treasury shares = 40,000 shares outstanding

	A	B
1	**Maxima, Inc.** **Statement of Retained Earnings** **Year Ended December 31, 2016**	
2	Retained earnings balance, beginning, as originally reported	$ 103,000
3	Prior-period adjustment—credit	5,000
4	Retained earnings balance, beginning, as adjusted	108,000
5	Net income for current year	76,000
6		184,000
7	Dividends for current year	(16,000)
8	Retained earnings balance, ending	$ 168,000
9		

Note: The Statement of Retained Earnings is usually incorporated into the Statement of Stockholders' Equity. See Chapter 10 for a more complete discussion.

Review | The Income Statement

Quick Check (Answers are given on page 677.)

1. The quality of earnings suggests that

   a. stockholders want the corporation to earn enough income to be able to pay its debts.

   b. net income is the best measure of the results of operations.

   c. continuing operations and one-time transactions are of equal importance.

   d. income from continuing operations is a more relevant predictor of future performance than income from one-time transactions.

2. Which statement is true?

   a. All prior-period adjustments are combined with continuing operations on the income statement.

   b. Discontinued operations are a separate category on the income statement.

   c. Prior-period adjustments are part of discontinued operations.

   d. All of the above are true.

3. Neylon Corporation earned $5.94 per share on its common stock. Suppose you capitalize Neylon's income at 6%. How much are you willing to pay for a share of Neylon stock?

   a. $5.94

   b. $35.64

   c. $99.00

   d. $50.00

4. The following is a selected portion of Trendy Trinkets' income statement:

| | Year Ended | | |
	2017	2016	2015
Income (loss) from continuing operations	$(20,000)	$62,000	$120,000
Income (loss) from discontinued operations	(8,000)	(4,500)	2,500
Net income (loss)	$(28,000)	$57,500	$122,500
Earnings (loss) per share from continuing operations:			
Basic...	$ (0.20)	$ 0.60	$ 1.12
Earnings (loss) per share from discontinued operations:			
Basic...	$ (0.08)	$ (0.04)	$ 0.02
Earnings (loss) per share:			
Basic...	$ (0.28)	$ 0.56	$ 1.14

Trendy Trinkets has no preferred stock outstanding. How many shares of common stock did Trendy Trinkets have outstanding during fiscal year 2017?

   a. 100,000 shares

   b. 71,429 shares

   c. 140,000 shares

   d. 102,500 shares

5. You are taking a vacation to Italy, and you buy euros for $1.20. On your return, you cash in your unused euros for $1.00. During your vacation,

   a. the dollar lost value.

   b. the euro gained value.

   c. the dollar rose against the euro.

   d. the euro rose against the dollar.

6. Allen County, Indiana, purchased earth-moving equipment from a Canadian company. The cost was $1,600,000 Canadian, and the Canadian dollar was quoted at $0.97. A month later, Allen County paid its debt, and the Canadian dollar was quoted at $0.96. What was Allen County's cost of the equipment?

   a. $1,616,000   **c.** $16,000

   b. $1,552,000   **d.** $1,536,000

7. Why is it important for companies to report their accounting changes to the public?

   a. Accounting changes affect dividends, and investors want dividends.

   b. Some accounting changes are more extraordinary than others.

   c. It is important for the results of operations to be compared between periods.

   d. Most accounting changes increase net income, and investors need to know why the increase in net income occurred.

8. Other comprehensive income

   a. includes unrealized gains and losses on available-for-sale investments.

   b. affects earnings per share.

   c. includes gains and losses on sale of equipment.

   d. has no effect on income tax.

9. Mattison Corporation earned income before tax of $180,000. Taxable income was $150,000, and the income tax rate was 32%. The journal entry to record Mattison's income tax expense and income tax liability was:

	A	B	C	D
	A1			
1	a.	Income Tax Payable	57,600	
2		Income Tax Expense		48,000
3		Deferred Tax Liability		9,600
4	b.	Income Tax Expense	48,000	
5		Income Tax Payable		48,000
6	c.	Income Tax Expense	57,600	
7		Income Tax Payable		57,600
8	d.	Income Tax Expense	57,600	
9		Income Tax Payable		48,000
10		Deferred Tax Liability		9,600
11				

10. Deferred Tax Liability is usually

	Type of Account	*Reported on the Statement*
a.	Short-term	Income statement
b.	Long-term	Balance sheet
c.	Long-term	Income statement
d.	Short-term	Statement of stockholders' equity

11. The main purpose of the statement of stockholders' equity is to report

   a. comprehensive income.

   b. financial position.

   c. reasons for changes in the equity accounts.

   d. results of operations.

12. An auditors' report by independent accountants

   a. gives investors assurance that the company's financial statements conform to GAAP.

   b. is ultimately the responsibility of the management of the client company.

   c. ensures that the financial statements are error-free.

   d. gives investors assurance that the company's stock is a safe investment.

Accounting Vocabulary

channel stuffing (p. 635) A type of financial statement fraud that is accomplished by shipping more to customers (usually around the end of the year) than they ordered, with the expectation that they may return some or all of it. The objective is to record more revenue than the company has actually earned with legitimate sales and shipments.

clean opinion (p. 650) An *unqualified opinion.*

comprehensive income (p. 645) A company's change in total stockholders' equity from all sources other than from the owners of the business (including distributions to owners).

corporate social responsibility (CSR) (p. 648) A nonfinancial measure of a company's performance, including its investment in corporate governance, environmental conservation, and other socially responsible programs that benefit society as a whole.

earnings per share (EPS) (p. 644) Amount of a company's net income per share of its outstanding common stock.

earnings quality (p. 633) The characteristics of an earnings number that make it most useful for decision making; the degree to which earnings are an accurate reflection of underlying economic events for both revenues and expenses, and the extent to which earnings from a company's core operations are improving over time. Assuming that revenues and expenses are measured accurately, high-quality earnings are reflected in steadily improving sales and steadily declining costs over time, so that income from continuing operations follows a high and improving pattern over time.

foreign-currency exchange rate (p. 637) The measure of one country's currency against another country's currency.

hedging (p. 639) To protect oneself from losing money in one transaction by engaging in a counterbalancing transaction.

investment capitalization rate (p. 641) An assumed rate of return used to estimate the value of an investment in stock. This rate should approximate the weighted-average cost of capital (see below).

pre-tax accounting income (p. 640) Income before tax on the income statement.

prior-period adjustment (p. 643) A correction to the beginning balance of retained earnings for an error of an earlier period.

segment (p. 646) A division or subset of a business's operations, especially in large corporations. For a division to be considered a segment, it must directly earn revenue for the company. Segments may be created by product line, by type of business, by geographic areas, or other logical divisions for the corporation. Internally, each segment's revenues and expenses are accounted for separately.

statement of comprehensive income (p. 645) A statement showing all of the changes in stockholders' equity during a period other than transactions with owners. The statement of comprehensive income includes net income as well as other comprehensive income, such as unrealized gains/losses on available-for-sale securities and foreign-currency translation gains/losses.

taxable income (p. 640) The basis for computing the amount of tax to pay the government.

unqualified (clean) opinion (p. 650) An audit opinion stating that the financial statements are presented fairly, in all material respects, in accordance with generally accepted accounting principles.

weighted-average cost of capital (p. 641) The combined rate of return expected for a company by its creditors and investors. In general, the higher the risk associated with the company, the greater the expected returns by creditors and investors.

ASSESS YOUR PROGRESS

Some of the following exercises and problems are available as Excel questions in MyAccountingLab

Ethics Check

EC11-1 Identify the ethical principle violated

For each of the situations listed, identify which of three principles (integrity, objectivity and independence, or due care) from the AICPA Code of Professional Conduct that is violated. Assume all persons listed in the situations are members of the AICPA. (Note: Refer to the AICPA Code of Professional Conduct contained on pages 29–30, Chapter 1 for descriptions of the principles.)

    a. Brianna is the CEO of Scuba Systems and is preparing for the independent public accounting firm that is performing the year-end audit of Scuba Systems. Brianna has been swamped with work and forgot to conduct an assessment of internal controls. To save time, she quickly writes the report, using last year's report on internal control over financial reporting as a guide. She changes some words to update the report but does not do any assessment of the internal control system.

b. Matthew is a first-year auditor for a large accounting firm. He is assigned to test cash for the firm's largest client, Transport Global. Matthew is not sure what type of testing he should perform so he just copies the work papers from last year and changes the date.

c. Ashley is a new audit manager at Smith & Associates. She owns stock in Overpass Systems, a client of Smith & Associates. She does not disclose her stock ownership to Smith & Associates because she knows she would not be influenced by her stock ownership while performing her audit work at Overpass Systems.

d. Jared is in charge of preparing the Notes to Financial Statements for Gearbox, Inc. Jared knows that Gearbox is currently facing a reasonably possible loss of over $100 million due to a lawsuit, but does not want the company's share price to drop because he owns stock options. Instead of disclosing the lawsuit in the notes as required, Jared decides to exclude it.

Short Exercises

LO 1

S11-1. (*Learning Objective 1: Evaluate quality of earnings*) Research has shown that over 50% of financial statement frauds are committed by companies that recognize revenue improperly. What does this mean? Describe the most common ways companies improperly recognize revenue.

LO 1 3

S11-2. (*Learning Objective 1, 3: Evaluate quality of earnings*) Study the 2016 income statement of Kurzic Imports, Inc., and answer these questions about the company:

	A1			

	A	B	C
1	**Kurzic Imports, Inc.** **Consolidated Statement of Operations (Adapted)**		
2			**Year Ended**
3	**(In thousands except per share amounts)**	**2016**	**2015**
4			
5	Net sales	$ 1,806,092	$ 1,825,975
6	Operating costs and expenses:		
7	Cost of sales (including buying and store occupancy costs)	1,045,880	1,121,690
8	Selling, general, and administrative expenses	526,060	549,850
9	Depreciation and amortization	48,750	55,675
10	Total operating costs and expenses	1,620,690	1,727,215
11	Operating income (loss)	185,402	98,760
12	Nonoperating (income) and expenses:		
13	Interest and investment income	(2,740)	(2,675)
14	Interest expense	1,640	1,725
15	Interest income, net	(1,100)	(950)
16	Income (loss) from continuing operations before income taxes	186,502	99,710
17	Provision (benefit) for income taxes	69,315	34,700
18	Income (loss) from continuing operations	$ 117,187	$ 65,010
19	Discontinued operations:		
20	Income (loss) from discontinued operations	210	(2,300)
21	Net income (loss)	$ 117,397	$ 62,710
22			
23	Earnings (loss) per share from continuing operations: Basic	$ 1.52	$ 0.85
24			
25	Earnings (loss) per share from discontinued operations: Basic	$ 0.00	$ (0.03)
26			
27	Earnings (loss) per share: Basic	$ 1.52	$ 0.83
28			

1. How much gross profit did Kurzic Imports earn on the sale of its products in 2016? How much was income from continuing operations? Net income?
2. At the end of 2016, what dollar amount of net income would most sophisticated investors use to predict Kurzic Imports' net income for 2017 and beyond? Name this item, give its amount, and state your reason.

S11-3. *(Learning Objective 1: Prepare a complex income statement)* Musicality, Inc., reported the following items, listed in no particular order, at December 31, 2016 (in thousands):

LO 1

Other gains (losses)	$(23,000)	Cost of goods sold	74,000
Net sales revenue	195,000	Operating expenses	66,000
Loss on discontinued		Accounts receivable	22,000
operations	10,000		

Income tax of 40% applies to all items.

Prepare Musicality's multistep income statement for the year ended December 31, 2016. Omit earnings per share.

S11-4. *(Learning Objective 1: Value a company's stock)* For fiscal year 2016, Orange Computer, Inc., reported net sales of $19,320 million, net income of $1,991 million, and no significant discontinued operations or accounting changes. Earnings per share was $2.10. At a capitalization rate of 10%, how much should one share of Orange stock be worth? Compare your estimated stock price with the market price of $71.04 as quoted in the newspaper. Based on your estimated market value, should you buy, hold, or sell Orange stock?

LO 1

S11-5. *(Learning Objective 2: Account for foreign-currency gains and losses)* Suppose Natural Soda Corp. sells soft-drink syrup on account to a Russian company on September 12. Natural Soda Corp. agrees to accept 200,000 Russian rubles. On the date of sale, the ruble is quoted at $0.36. Natural Soda Corp. collects half the receivable on October 18 when the ruble is worth $0.31. Then on November 15, when the foreign-exchange rate of the ruble is $0.39, Natural Soda Corp. collects the final amount.

Journalize these three transactions for Natural Soda Corp. Ignore cost of goods sold.

LO 2

S11-6. *(Learning Objective 2: Account for foreign-currency gains and losses)* Industrial Belting sells goods on account for 700,000 Mexican pesos. The foreign-exchange rate for a peso is $0.092 on the date of sale. Industrial Belting then collects cash on April 24 when the exchange rate for a peso is $0.096. Record Industrial Belting's cash collection. Ignore cost of goods sold.

Industrial Belting buys inventory on account for 29,000 Swiss francs. A Swiss franc costs $0.78 on the purchase date. Record Industrial Belting's payment of cash on October 25, when the exchange rate for a Swiss franc is $0.83.

In these two scenarios, which currencies strengthened? Which currencies weakened?

LO 2

S11-7. *(Learning Objective 3: Use other information on an income statement)* Juneau Cruise Lines, Inc., reported the following income statement for the year ended December 31, 2016:

LO 3

	Millions
Operating revenues	$95,500
Operating expenses	84,100
Operating income	$11,400
Other revenue (expense), net	1,000
Income from continuing operations	$12,400
Discontinued operations, net of tax	1,100
Net income	$13,500

Requirements

1. Were Juneau Cruise Line's discontinued operations more like an expense or revenue? How can you tell?
2. Should the discontinued operations of Juneau Cruise Lines be included in or excluded from net income? State your reason.
3. Suppose you are working as a financial analyst and your job is to predict Juneau Cruise Line's net income for 2017 and beyond. Which item from the income statement will you use for your prediction? Identify its amount. Why will you use this item?

LO 3   **S11-8.** *(Learning Objective 3: Account for a corporation's income tax)* Colossal Marine, Inc., had income before income tax of $171,000 and taxable income of $148,000 for 2016, the company's first year of operations. The income tax rate is 40%.

1. Make the entry to record Colossal Marine's income taxes for 2016.
2. Show what Colossal Marine will report on its 2016 income statement, starting with income before income tax. Also show what Colossal Marine will report for current and long-term liabilities on its December 31, 2016, balance sheet.

LO 4   **S11-9.** *(Learning Objective 4: Interpret earnings-per-share data)* Weather Seal Windows Company has preferred stock outstanding and issued additional common stock during the year.

1. Give the basic equation to compute earnings per share of common stock for net income.
2. List the income items for which Weather Seal Windows must report earnings-per-share data.
3. What makes earnings per share useful as a business statistic?

LO 4   **S11-10.** *(Learning Objective 4: Compute earnings per share)* Return to the Musicality data in S11-3. Musicality had 10,000 shares of common stock outstanding during 2016. Musicality declared and paid preferred dividends of $1,000 during 2016. Report Musicality's earnings per share on the income statement. (Round all calculations to two decimal places.)

LO 5   **S11-11.** *(Learning Objective 5: Report comprehensive income)* Use the Musicality data in S11-3. In addition, Musicality had unrealized gains of $2,100 on available-for-sale investments and a $3,200 foreign-currency translation adjustment (a gain) during 2016. Both amounts are net of tax and in thousands. Start with Musicality's net income from S11-3 and show how the company could report other comprehensive income on its 2016 financial statements.

Should Musicality report earnings per share for other comprehensive income? State why or why not.

LO 5   **S11-12.** *(Learning Objective 5: Report a prior-period adjustment)* iWorld, Inc., was set to report the following statement of retained earnings for the year ended December 31, 2016:

	A	B
	A1	
1	**iWorld, Inc.** **Statement of Retained Earnings** **Year Ended December 31, 2016**	
2	Retained earnings, December 31, 2015	$ 55,000
3	Net income for 2016	67,000
4	Dividends declared for 2016	(26,000)
5	Retained earnings, December 31, 2016	$ 96,000
6		

Before issuing its 2016 financial statements, iWorld learned that net income of 2015 was overstated by $10,000. Prepare iWorld's 2016 statement of retained earnings to show the correction of the error—that is, the prior-period adjustment. (*Hint*: Use the end-of-chapter summary problem as an example.)

S11-13. *(Learning Objective 5: Analyze segment information)* Worldwide Electronics Corporation, based in New Jersey, sells electronics equipment through 150 retail and 25 outlet stores across the United States and in 18 different foreign countries. In addition, the company has a well-designed website through which it markets its products. The company manages and evaluates the retail, outlet, and Internet businesses through three separate divisions, each with its own management.

1. Define a "segment" of a business. What would be a logical way for Worldwide Electronics Corporation to segment its business for financial reporting purposes?
2. What is the purpose of segment reporting? In what ways might segment reporting benefit prospective investors in Worldwide Electronics?

S11-14. *(Learning Objective 6: Differentiate responsibility for financial statements)* The annual report of Meinike Computer, Inc., included the following:

> *Management's Annual Report on Internal Control over Financial Reporting*
>
> The Company's management is responsible for establishing and maintaining adequate control over financial reporting [....] Management conducted an evaluation of the effectiveness of the Company's internal control over financial reporting [....] Based on this evaluation, management has concluded that the Company's internal control over financial reporting was effective as of September 30, 2016....

> Report of Independent Registered Public Accounting Firm
> The Board of Directors and Shareholders
> Meinike Computer, Inc.:
>
> We have audited the accompanying consolidated balance sheets of Meinike Computer, Inc., and subsidiaries (the Company) as of September 30, 2016, and September 30, 2015, and the related consolidated statements of operations, comprehensive income, shareholders' equity, and cash flows for each of the years in the three-year period ended September 30, 2016. We have also audited the company's internal control over financial reporting. These consolidated financial statements are the responsibility of the Company's management. Our responsibility is to express an opinion on these consolidated financial statements based on our audits and an opinion on the company's internal control over financial reporting based on our audits.
>
> We conducted our audits in accordance with the standards of the Public Company Accounting Oversight Board (United States)....
>
> In our opinion, the consolidated financial statements referred to above present fairly, in all material respects, the financial position of the Company as of September 30, 2016, and September 30, 2015, and the results of its operations and its cash flows for each of the years in the three-year period ended September 30, 2016, in conformity with accounting principles generally accepted in the United States of America. Also, in our opinion the company maintained effective internal control over financial reporting.
>
> SLMA LLP
>
> Aurora, Colorado
> December 28, 2016

1. Who is responsible for Meinike's financial statements?
2. By what accounting standards are the financial statements prepared?
3. Identify one concrete action that Meinike management takes to fulfill its responsibility for the reliability of the company's financial information.
4. Which entity gave an outside, independent opinion on the Meinike financial statements? Where was this entity located, and when did it release its opinion to the public?
5. Exactly what did the audit cover? Give names and dates.
6. By what standards did the auditor conduct the audit?
7. What was the auditor's opinion of Meinike's financial statements?

Exercises MyAccountingLab

Group A

LO 1

E11-15A. *(Learning Objective 1: Prepare and use a complex income statement; prepare a statement of comprehensive income)* Suppose Searstown Cycles, Inc., reported a number of special items on its income statement. The following data, listed in no particular order, came from Searstown's financial statements (amounts in thousands):

Income tax expense (savings):		Net sales..................................	$13,500
Continuing operations..................	$305	Foreign-currency translation	
Discontinued operations..............	58	gain, net of taxes..............................	350
Unrealized gain on		Income from discontinued operations	290
available-for-sale investments,		Dividends declared and paid	650
net of taxes..................................	36	Total operating expenses........................	12,200
Short-term investments....................	20		

Requirements

1. Show how the Searstown Cycles, Inc., multistep income statement for the year ended September 30, 2016, should appear. Omit earnings per share. Use the end-of-chapter summary problem as an example.
2. Prepare the Statement of Comprehensive Income for Searstown Cycles, Inc., for the year ended September 30, 2016. Use Exhibit 11-2 as an example.

LO 1 4

E11-16A. *(Learning Objectives 1, 4: Prepare an income statement; compute earnings per share; evaluate quality of earnings; evaluate a company as an investment)* The Hooper Book Company accounting records include the following for 2016 (in thousands):

Other revenues...	$ 1,600
Income tax expense	5,640
Sales revenue...	122,000
Total operating expenses...	104,800

Requirements

1. Prepare Hooper Book Company's single-step income statement for the year ended December 31, 2016, including EPS. Hooper had 1,000,000 shares of common stock and no preferred stock outstanding during the year.
2. Assume Hooper Book Company's income from operations reflects that its core business has been steadily increasing by about 10% per year over the past three years and that none of its operations have been discontinued. What does this say about the quality of its earnings?
3. Assume investors capitalize Hooper Book Company's earnings from continuing operations at 7%. Estimate the price of one share of the company's stock.

LO 1

E11-17A. *(Learning Objective 1: Use income data for investment analysis)* During 2016, Flash Bytes, Inc., had sales of $7.66 billion, operating profit of $2.10 billion, and net income of $3.00 billion. EPS was $4.70. On January 2, 2017, one share of Flash Bytes common stock was priced at $54.00 on the New York Stock Exchange.

What investment capitalization rate did investors appear to be using to determine the value of one share of Flash Bytes stock? The formula for the value of one share of stock uses EPS in the calculation.

E11-18A. (*Learning Objective 2: Account for foreign-currency gains and losses*) Assume that Holloway Stores completed the following foreign-currency transactions:

May 9	Purchased various inventory items on account from Toyita, a Japanese company. The price was 700,000 yen, and the exchange rate of the yen was $0.0092.
Jun 18	Paid Toyita when the exchange rate was $0.0085.
22	Sold merchandise on account to Magnificente, a French company, at a price of 40,000 euros. The exchange rate was $1.22. Ignore cost of goods sold.
28	Collected from Magnificente when the exchange rate was $1.18.

Requirements

1. Journalize these transactions for Holloway. Focus on the gains and losses caused by changes in foreign-currency rates. Round your answers to the nearest whole dollar.
2. On May 10, immediately after the purchase, and on June 23, immediately after the sale, which currencies did Holloway want to strengthen? Which currencies did in fact strengthen? Explain your reasoning.

E11-19A. (*Learning Objective 3: Account for income tax by a corporation*) During 2016, the Martell Heights Corp. income statement reported income of $320,000 before tax. The company's income tax return filed with the IRS showed taxable income of $280,000. During 2016, Martell Heights was subject to an income tax rate of 25%.

Requirements

1. Journalize Martell Heights' income taxes for 2016.
2. How much income tax did Martell Heights have to pay for the year 2016?
3. At the beginning of 2016, Martell Heights' balance of Deferred Tax Liability was $31,000. How much Deferred Tax Liability did Martell Heights report on its balance sheet at December 31, 2016?

E11-20A. (*Learning Objective 4: Compute earnings per share*) Altar Loan Company's balance sheet at December 31, 2016, reports the following:

Preferred stock, $100 par value, 6%, 9,000 shares issued	$ 900,000
Common stock, $0.75 par, 900,000 shares issued	675,000
Treasury stock, common, 70,000 shares at cost	630,000

During 2016, Altar Loan earned net income of $6,200,000. Compute Altar Loan's earnings per common share (EPS) for 2016; round EPS to two decimal places. Assume the number of shares issued and outstanding did not change during the year.

E11-21A. (*Learning Objective 4: Compute and use earnings per share*) Athens Holding Company operates numerous businesses, including motel, auto rental, and real estate companies. The year 2016 was interesting for Athens, which reported the following on its income statement (in millions):

Net revenues	$3,931
Total expenses and other	3,355
Income from continuing operations	$ 576
Loss from discontinued operations, net of tax	(85)
Net income	$ 491

During 2016, Athens had the following (in millions, except for par value per share):

Common stock, $0.05 par value, 600 shares issued	$	30
Treasury stock, 200 shares at cost..		(3,700)

Requirement

1. Using the end-of-chapter summary problem as an example, show how Athens should report earnings per share for 2016; round EPS to the nearest cent.

LO 5 **E11-22A.** *(Learning Objective 5: Report a prior-period adjustment on the statement of retained earnings)* EcoClean, Inc., a household products chain, reported a prior-period adjustment in 2016. An accounting error caused net income of 2015 to be understated by $13 million. Retained earnings at December 31, 2015, as previously reported, was $344 million. Net income for 2016 was $97 million, and 2016 dividends declared were $68 million.

Requirement

1. Using the end-of-chapter summary problem as an example, prepare the company's statement of retained earnings for the year ended December 31, 2016. How does the prior-period adjustment affect EcoClean's net income for 2016?

LO 5 **E11-23A.** *(Learning Objective 5: Prepare a statement of comprehensive income)* During the year ended December 31, 2016, Bacarella International Corporation earned $3,600,000 in net income after taxes. The company reported $120,000 of net unrealized gains on available-for-sale securities, net of taxes, and $160,000 in foreign-currency translation gains from consolidation of its Mexican subsidiary company, net of taxes.

Requirements

1. Prepare the Statement of Comprehensive Income for Bacarella International Corporation for the year ended December 31, 2016. Use Exhibit 11-2 as an example.
2. Explain where the following items will appear in Bacarella International Corporation's Statement of Stockholder's Equity for the year ended December 31, 2016:
   a. Net income
   b. Net unrealized gains from available-for-sale securities, net of taxes
   c. Foreign-currency translation gains from consolidation of Mexican subsidiary, net of taxes

LO 5 **E11-24A.** *(Learning Objective 5: Analyze segment information)* The following information appears in a footnote to the 2014 financial statements of The Procter & Gamble Company (the information has been adapted for this exercise):

SUMMARY OF SEGMENT DATA

.....Our five reportable segments are comprised of:

- Beauty: Beauty Care (Antiperspirant and Deodorant, Cosmetics, Personal Cleansing, Skin Care); Hair Care and Color; Prestige (SKII, Fragrances); Salon Professional;

- Grooming: Shave Care (Blades and Razors, Pre- and Post-Shave Products); Appliances;

- Health Care: Personal Health Care (Gastrointestinal, Rapid Diagnostics, Respiratory, Other Personal Health Care, Vitamins/Minerals/Supplements); Oral Care (Toothbrush, Toothpaste, Other Oral Care);

- Fabric Care and Home Care: Fabric Care (Laundry Additives, Fabric Enhancers, Laundry Detergents); Home Care (Air Care, Dish Care, Surface Care); Personal Power (Batteries); Professional;

- Baby, Feminine and Family Care: Baby Care (Baby Wipes, Diapers and Pants); Feminine Care (Feminine Care, Incontinence); Family Care (Paper Towels, Tissues, Toilet Paper).

	A	B	C	D	E
A1					
1	**Global Segment Results** *(In millions)*		**Net Sales**	**Earnings/(Loss) from Continuing Operations Before Income Taxes**	**Net Earnings/(Loss) from Continuing Operations**
2	BEAUTY	**2014**	$ **19,507**	$ **3,530**	$ **2,739**
3		2013	19,956	3,215	2,474
4		2012	20,318	3,196	2,390
5					
6	GROOMING	**2014**	**8,009**	**2,589**	**1,954**
7		2013	8,038	2,458	1,837
8		2012	8,339	2,395	1,807
9					
10	HEALTH CARE	**2014**	**7,798**	**1,597**	**1,083**
11		2013	7,684	1,582	1,093
12		2012	7,235	1,520	1,022
13					
14	FABRIC CARE AND HOME CARE	**2014**	**26,060**	**4,678**	**3,039**
15		2013	25,862	4,757	3,089
16		2012	25,580	4,485	2,816
17					
18	BABY, FEMININE, AND FAMILY CARE	**2014**	**20,950**	**4,310**	**2,940**
19		2013	20,479	4,507	3,047
20		2012	19,714	4,271	2,927
21					
22	TOTAL COMPANY*	**2014**	**83,062**	**14,885**	**11,707**
23		2013	82,581	14,692	11,301
24		2012	82,006	12,528	9,150
25					

*The segments shown here do not sum to Total Company figures because Total Company includes depreciation and amortization, and financial results from discontinued/sold segments.

Requirements

1. What are The Procter & Gamble Company's segments as of the end of its 2014 fiscal year?
2. Which segments appear to be performing better in 2014 than they did in 2013?
3. Which segments were the most profitable in 2014? Least profitable? Evaluate the overall profitability of The Procter & Gamble Company as of the close of 2014.
4. What can you learn from analyzing this segment information that helps make you a more prospective investor in The Procter & Gamble Company?

Group B

E11-25B. *(Learning Objective 1: Prepare and use a complex income statement; prepare a statement of comprehensive income)* Suppose Victor Cycles, Inc., reported a number of special items on its income statement. The following data, listed in no particular order, came from Victor's financial statements (amounts in thousands):

LO **1**

Income tax expense (savings):		Net sales..	$13,300
Continuing operations.................	$295	Foreign-currency translation	
Discontinued operations..............	56	gain, net of taxes................................	300
Unrealized gain on		Income from discontinued operations	280
available-for-sale investments,		Dividends declared and paid..................	620
net of taxes....................................	35	Total operating expenses........................	12,200
Short-term investments....................	20		

Requirements

1. Show how the Victor Cycles, Inc., multistep income statement for the year ended September 30, 2016, should appear. Omit earnings per share. Use the end-of-chapter summary problem as an example.
2. Prepare the Statement of Comprehensive Income for Victor Cycles, Inc., for the year ended September 30, 2016. Use Exhibit 11-2 as an example.

LO 1 4

E11-26B. *(Learning Objectives 1, 4: Prepare an income statement; compute earnings per share; evaluate quality of earnings; evaluate a company as an investment)* The Calloway Book Company's accounting records include the following for 2016 (in thousands):

Other revenues...	$ 2,300
Income tax expense..	7,950
Sales revenue...	129,000
Total operating expenses...	104,800

Requirements

1. Prepare Calloway Book's single-step income statement for the year ended December 31, 2016, including EPS. Calloway Book had 1,000,000 shares of common stock and no preferred stock outstanding during the year.
2. Assume Calloway Book Company's income from operations reflects that its core business been steadily increasing by about 10% per year over the past three years and that none of its operations have been discontinued. What does this say about the quality of its earnings?
3. Assume investors capitalize Calloway Book earnings from continuing operations at 8%. Estimate the price of one share of the company's stock.

LO 1

E11-27B. *(Learning Objective 1: Use income data for investment analysis)* During 2016, Rondell, Inc., had sales of $6.96 billion, operating profit of $2.0 billion, and net income of $3.0 billion. EPS was $4.30. On January 3, 2017, one share of Rondell common stock was priced at $54.10 on the New York Stock Exchange.

What investment capitalization rate did investors appear to be using to determine the value of one share of Rondell stock? The formula for the value of one share of stock uses EPS in the calculation.

LO 2

E11-28B. *(Learning Objective 2: Account for foreign-currency gains and losses)* Assume that Newman Stores completed the following foreign-currency transactions:

May 9	Purchased various inventory items on account from Harajuku, a Japanese company. The price was 800,000 yen, and the exchange rate of the yen was $0.0088.
Jun 18	Paid Harajuku when the exchange rate was $0.0081.
22	Sold merchandise on account to Le Fleur, a French company, at a price of 50,000 euros. The exchange rate was $1.21. Ignore cost of goods sold.
28	Collected from Le Fleur when the exchange rate was $1.13.

Requirements

1. Journalize these transactions for Newman. Focus on the gains and losses caused by changes in foreign-currency rates; round your answers to the nearest whole dollar.
2. On May 10, immediately after the purchase, and on June 23, immediately after the sale, which currencies did Newman want to strengthen? Which currencies did in fact strengthen? Explain your reasoning.

E11-29B. *(Learning Objective 3: Account for income tax by a corporation)* During 2016, Botto Heights Corp.'s income statement reported income of $420,000 before tax. The company's income tax return filed with the IRS showed taxable income of $390,000. During 2016, Botto Heights was subject to an income tax rate of 40%.

Requirements

1. Journalize Botto Heights' income taxes for 2016.
2. How much income tax did Botto Heights have to pay for the year 2016?
3. At the beginning of 2016, Botto Heights' balance of Deferred Tax Liability was $37,000. How much Deferred Tax Liability did Botto Heights report on its balance sheet at December 31, 2016?

E11-30B. *(Learning Objective 4: Compute earnings per share)* Prestige Loan Company's balance sheet at December 31, 2016, reports the following:

Preferred stock, $50 par value, 10%, 10,000 shares issued	$ 500,000
Common stock, $0.75 par, 1,000,000 shares issued.....................	750,000
Treasury stock, common, 80,000 shares at cost	720,000

During 2016, Prestige Loan earned net income of $6,300,000. Compute Prestige Loan's earnings per common share (EPS) for 2016. (Round EPS to two decimal places.) Assume the number of shares issued and outstanding did not change during the year.

E11-31B. *(Learning Objective 4: Compute and use earnings per share)* Crocker Holding Company operates numerous businesses, including motel, auto rental, and real estate companies. The year 2016 was interesting for Crocker, which reported the following on its income statement (in millions):

Net revenues	$3,936
Total expenses and other...	3,360
Income from continuing operations...............................	$ 576
Income from discontinued operations,	
net of tax..	84
Net income..	$ 660

During 2016, Crocker had the following (in millions, except for par value per share):

Common stock, $0.15 par value, 1,300 shares issued	$ 195
Treasury stock, 500 shares at cost...	(3,649)

Requirement

1. Using the end-of-chapter summary problem as an example, show how Crocker should report earnings per share for 2016; round EPS to the nearest cent.

E11-32B. *(Learning Objective 5: Report a prior-period adjustment on the statement of retained earnings)* EverClean, Inc., a household products chain, reported a prior-period adjustment in 2016. An accounting error caused net income of 2015 to be overstated by $12 million. Retained earnings at December 31, 2015, as previously reported, was $345 million. Net income for 2016 was $99 million, and 2016 dividends declared were $65 million.

Requirement

1. Using the end-of-chapter summary problem as an example, prepare the company's statement of retained earnings for the year ended December 31, 2016. How does the prior-period adjustment affect EverClean's net income for 2016?

LO 5

E11-33B. *(Learning Objective 5: Prepare a statement of comprehensive income)* During the year ended December 31, 2016, Martinson International Corporation earned $4,200,000 in net income after taxes. The company reported $180,000 of net unrealized losses on available-for-sale securities, net of taxes, and $180,000 in foreign-currency translation losses from consolidation of its Brazilian subsidiary company, net of taxes.

Requirements

1. Prepare the Statement of Comprehensive Income for Martinson International Corporation for the year ended December 31, 2016. Use Exhibit 11-2 as an example.
2. Explain where the following items will appear in Martinson International Corporation's Statement of Stockholder's Equity for the year ended December 31, 2016:
   a. Net income
   b. Net unrealized losses from available-for-sale securities, net of taxes
   c. Foreign-currency translation losses from consolidation of Brazilian subsidiary, net of taxes

LO 5

E11-34B. *(Learning Objective 5: Analyze segment information)* The following information appears in a footnote to the 2014 financial statements of Nike, Inc.:

	A1				
	A		**B**	**C**	**D**
1				Year Ended May 31,	
2	(In millions)		2014	2013	2012
3	**REVENUE**				
4	North America		$ 12,299	$ 11,158	$ 9,538
5	Western Europe		4,979	4,193	4,212
6	Central & Eastern Europe		1,387	1,229	1,146
7	Greater China		2,602	2,478	2,561
8	Japan		771	876	920
9	Emerging Markets		3,949	3,832	3,523
10	Global Brand Divisions		125	115	111
11	Total NIKE Brand		26,112	23,881	22,011
12	Converse		1,684	1,449	1,324
13	Corporate		3	(17)	(4)
14	**TOTAL NIKE CONSOLIDATED REVENUES**		**$ 27,799**	**$ 25,313**	**$ 23,331**
15	**EARNINGS BEFORE INTEREST AND TAXES**				
16	North America		$ 3,075	$ 2,641	$ 2,092
17	Western Europe		855	643	599
18	Central & Eastern Europe		279	234	209
19	Greater China		816	813	913
20	Japan		131	139	135
21	Emerging Markets		955	988	826
22	Global Brand Divisions		(2,021)	(1,746)	(1,479)
23	Total NIKE Brand		4,090	3,712	3,295
24	Converse		496	425	394
25	Corporate		(1,009)	(884)	(674)
26	Total NIKE Consolidated Earnings Before Interest and Taxes		$ 3,577	$ 3,253	$ 3,015
27					

Requirements

1. Based on this information, what do you think are Nike, Inc.'s, reportable segments as of the end of its 2014 fiscal year?
2. Which segments appear to be growing fastest in 2014? Slowest?
3. Which segments were the most profitable in 2014? Least profitable? Evaluate the overall profitability of Nike, Inc., as of the close of 2014.
4. What can you learn from analyzing this segment information that helps make you a more prospective investor in Nike, Inc.?

Quiz

Test your understanding of the corporate income statement and the statement of stockholders' equity by answering the following questions. Select the best choice from among the possible answers given.

Q11-35. What is the most relevant net income figure on a corporate multistep income statement for predicting future profits and for use in investment valuation?

    a. Prior-period adjustments

    b. Gain on sale of plant assets

    c. Income from continuing operations

    d. Income from discontinued operations

Q11-36. Marva's Lotion Company reports several earnings numbers on its current-year income statement (parentheses indicate a loss):

Gross profit	$140,000	Income from continuing operations	$ 38,000
Net income	40,000	Discontinued operations	(12,000)
Income before income tax	76,000		

How much net income would most investment analysts predict for Marva's to earn next year?

    a. $38,000   **c.** $76,000

    b. $40,000   **d.** $26,000

Q11-37. Return to the preceding question. Suppose you are evaluating Marva's Lotion Company stock as an investment. You require a 10% rate of return on investments, so you capitalize Marva's earnings at 10%. How much are you willing to pay for all of Marva's stock?

    a. $400,000   **c.** $1,400,000

    b. $760,000   **d.** $380,000

Q11-38. Providence Systems purchased inventory on account from Megaplex. The price was ¥150,000, and a yen was quoted at $0.0088. Providence paid the debt in yen a month later when the price of a yen was $0.0093. Providence

    a. debited Inventory for $1,320.

    b. recorded a foreign-currency transaction gain of $75.

    c. debited Inventory for $1,395.

    d. None of the above.

Q11-39. One way to hedge a foreign-currency transaction loss is to

    a. pay debts as late as possible.

    b. pay in the foreign currency.

    c. offset foreign-currency inventory and plant assets.

    d. collect in your own currency.

Q11-40. Foreign-currency transaction gains and losses are reported on the

    a. income statement.   **c.** statement of cash flows.

    b. balance sheet.   **d.** consolidation work sheet.

Q11-41. Earnings per share is *not* reported for

    a. income from discontinued operations.   **c.** income from continuing operations.

    b. comprehensive income.

Q11-42. Copyking Corporation has income before income tax of $200,000 and taxable income of $120,000. The income tax rate is 25%. Copyking's income statement will report net income of

    a. $30,000.   **c.** $120,000.

    b. $50,000.   **d.** $150,000.

Q11-43. Copyking Corporation in the preceding question must immediately pay income tax of
  a. $120,000.
  b. $50,000.
  c. $90,000.
  d. $30,000.

Q11-44. Use the Copyking Corporation data in Q11-42 and Q11-43. At the end of its first year of operations, Copyking's deferred tax liability is
  a. $20,000.
  b. $30,000.
  c. $50,000.
  d. $120,000.

Q11-45. Which of the following items is most closely related to prior-period adjustments?
  a. Preferred stock dividends
  b. Retained earnings
  c. Treasury stock
  d. Earnings per share

Q11-46. Segment information is reported in a company's
  a. income statement.
  b. financial statement footnotes.
  c. balance sheet.
  d. statement of stockholders' equity.

Q11-47. Which statement is true?
  a. Management audits the financial statements.
  b. Auditors of public companies audit financial statements as well as internal controls.
  c. GAAP requires companies to issue reports on corporate social responsibility (CSR).
  d. Independent auditors prepare the financial statements.

Problems MyAccountingLab

Group A

 **P11-48A.** *(Learning Objectives 1, 3, 4: Prepare a complex income statement, including earnings per share; evaluate quality of earnings)* The following information was taken from the records of Daughtry Cosmetics, Inc., at December 31, 2016:

Prior-period adjustment—net of taxes		Interest expense	$ 21,000
debit to Retained Earnings	$ 5,000	Gain on lawsuit settlement	6,000
Income tax expense (savings):		Dividend revenue	12,000
Continuing operations	27,600	Treasury stock, common	
Income from discontinued		(1,000 shares at cost)	16,000
operations	4,800	General expenses	70,900
Loss on sale of plant assets	10,000	Sales revenue	536,000
Income from discontinued		Retained earnings, beginning,	
operations	12,000	as originally reported	196,000
Preferred stock, 6%, $25 par,		Selling expenses	81,000
1,000 shares issued	25,000	Common stock, no par,	
Cost of goods sold	302,000	21,000 shares authorized	
Dividends declared on common stock	28,000	and issued	350,000

Requirements

1. Using the End-of-Chapter Summary Problem as an example, prepare Daughtry Cosmetics' single-step income statement, which lists all revenues together and all expenses together, for the fiscal year ended December 31, 2016. Include earnings-per-share data. For purposes of earnings per share, assume dividends have been declared on preferred stock as of December 31.
2. Evaluate income for the year ended December 31, 2016. Daughtry's top managers hoped to earn income from continuing operations equal to 7% of sales.

P11-49A. *(Learning Objective 5: Preparing a statement of retained earnings)* Use the data in P11-48A to prepare the Daughtry Cosmetics statement of retained earnings for the year ended December 31, 2016. Use the Statement of Retained Earnings in the End-of-Chapter Summary Problem as a model.

LO 5

P11-50A. *(Learning Objective 1: Use income data to make an investment decision)* Daughtry Cosmetics in P11-48A holds significant promise for carving a niche in its industry. A group of Irish investors is considering purchasing the company's outstanding common stock. Daughtry's stock is currently selling for $24 per share.

LO 1

A *BetterLife Magazine* story predicted the company's income is bound to grow. It appears that Daughtry can earn at least its current level of income for the indefinite future. Based on this information, the investors think that an appropriate investment capitalization rate for estimating the value of Daughtry's common stock is 10%. How much will this belief lead the investors to offer for Daughtry Cosmetics? Will Daughtry's existing stockholders be likely to accept this offer? Explain your answers.

P11-51A. *(Learning Objective 2: Account for foreign-currency gains or losses)* Suppose Lyndell Corporation completed the following international transactions:

LO 2

May	1	Sold inventory on account to Polito, an Italian automaker, for €80,000. The exchange rate of the euro was $1.34, and Polito demands to pay in euros. Ignore cost of goods sold.
	10	Purchased supplies on account from a Canadian company at a price of Canadian $59,000. The exchange rate of the Canadian dollar was $0.77, and the payment will be in Canadian dollars.
	17	Sold inventory on account to an English firm for 138,000 British pounds. Payment will be in pounds, and the exchange rate of the pound was $1.93. Ignore cost of goods sold.
	22	Collected from Polito. The exchange rate is €1 = $1.37.
Jun	18	Paid the Canadian company. The exchange rate of the Canadian dollar is $0.76.
	24	Collected from the English firm. The exchange rate of the British pound was $1.90.

Requirements

1. Record these transactions in Lyndell's journal and show how to report the foreign-currency transaction gain or loss on the income statement.
2. How will what you learned in this problem help you structure international transactions?

P11-52A. *(Learning Objectives 1, 3, 4: Evaluate quality of earnings; compute earnings per share; estimate the price of a stock)* Better Ventures, Ltd. (BVL), specializes in taking under-performing companies to a higher level of performance. BVL's capital structure at December 31, 2015, included 12,000 shares of $2.20 preferred stock and 130,000 shares of common stock. During 2016, BVL issued common stock and ended the year with 140,000 shares of common stock outstanding. Average common shares outstanding during 2016 were 134,000. Income from continuing operations during 2016 was $225,000. The company discontinued a segment of the business at a loss of $66,000. All amounts are after income tax. Assume the number of preferred shares outstanding did not change in 2016.

LO 1 3 4

Requirements

1. Compute BVL's earnings per share. Start with income from continuing operations.
2. Analysts believe BVL can earn its current level of income for the indefinite future. Estimate the market price of a share of BVL common stock at investment capitalization rates of 8%, 10%, and 12%. Which estimate presumes an investment in BVL is the most risky? How can you tell?

P11-53A. *(Learning Objectives 3, 4, 5: Prepare an income statement; compute earnings per share; prepare a statement of comprehensive income)* Megan Hodge, accountant for Natural Foods, Inc., was injured in a skiing accident. While she was recuperating, another, inexperienced employee prepared the following income statement for the fiscal year ended June 30, 2016:

	A	B	C
	A1 ⬍		
1	**Natural Foods, Inc.** **Income Statement** **June 30, 2016**		
2	**Revenue and gains:**		
3	Sales		$ 870,000
4	Paid-in capital in excess of par—common		14,000
5	Total revenues and gains		884,000
6	**Expenses and losses:**		
7	Cost of goods sold	$ 385,000	
8	Selling expenses	104,000	
9	General expenses	96,000	
10	Unrealized loss on available-for-sale investments	10,000	
11	Dividends paid	12,000	
12	Income tax expense	85,500	
13	Total expenses and losses		692,500
14	Income from operations		$ 191,500
15	**Other gains and losses:**		
16	Loss on discontinued operations		(25,000)
17	Net income		$ 166,500
18	Earnings per share		$ 11.10
19			

The individual *amounts* listed on the income statement are correct. However, some *accounts* are reported incorrectly, and some accounts do not belong on the income statement at all. The income tax rate of 30% has not been applied to Discontinued Operations. Natural Foods issued 15,000 shares of common stock back in 2004 and held 5,000 shares as treasury stock all during the fiscal year 2016.

Requirements

1. Using the End-of-Chapter Summary Problem as an example, prepare a corrected income statement for Natural Foods, Inc., for the fiscal year ended June 30, 2016. Use the single-step format, which lists all revenues together and all expenses together. Also prepare the earnings-per-share section of the statement.

2. Using Exhibit 11-2 as an example, prepare a Statement of Comprehensive Income for Natural Foods, Inc., for the fiscal year ended June 30, 2016. Start with net income, as computed in Requirement 1.

P11-54A. *(Learning Objective 3: Account for a corporation's income tax)* The accounting (not the income tax) records of Elemental Publications, Inc., provide the income statement for the year ended December 31, 2016.

	2016
Total revenue	$910,000
Expenses:	
Cost of goods sold...............................	$480,000
Operating expenses	200,000
Total expenses before tax....................	$680,000
Pretax accounting income	$230,000

Taxable income for 2016 includes these modifications from pre-tax accounting income:
  a. Additional taxable income of $13,000 earned in 2017 but taxed in 2016

b. Additional depreciation expense of $33,000 for Modified Accelerated Cost Recovery System (MACRS) tax depreciation in 2016

The income tax rate is 32%.

Requirements

1. Compute Elemental's taxable income for 2016.
2. Journalize the corporation's income taxes for 2016.
3. Prepare the corporation's single-step income statement for 2016.

Group B

P11-55B. (*Learning Objectives 1, 4: Prepare a complex income statement, including earnings per share; evaluate quality of earnings*) The following information was taken from the records of Clark Cosmetics, Inc., at December 31, 2016:

Prior-period adjustment—net of taxes		Interest expense	$ 24,000
debit to Retained Earnings	$ 8,000	Gain on lawsuit settlement	8,000
Income tax expense (savings):		Dividend revenue	14,000
Continuing operations	26,440	Treasury stock, common	
Income from discontinued		(1,000 shares at cost)	17,000
operations	6,320	General expenses	72,900
Loss on sale of plant assets	12,000	Sales revenue	542,000
Income from discontinued		Retained earnings, beginning,	
operations	16,000	as originally reported	198,000
Preferred stock, 10%, $10 par,		Selling expenses	83,000
4,000 shares issued	40,000	Common stock, no par,	
Cost of goods sold	306,000	23,000 shares authorized	
Dividends declared on common stock	27,000	and issued	370,000

Requirements

1. Using the End-of-Chapter Summary Problem as an example, prepare Clark Cosmetics' single-step income statement, which lists all revenues together and all expenses together, for the fiscal year ended December 31, 2016. Include earnings-per-share data. For purposes of earnings per share, assume dividends have been declared on preferred stock as of December 31.
2. Evaluate income for the year ended December 31, 2016. Clark's top managers hoped to earn income from continuing operations equal to 6% of sales.

P11-56B. (*Learning Objective 5: Prepare a statement of retained earnings*) Use the data in P11-55B to prepare the Clark Cosmetics statement of retained earnings for the year ended December 31, 2016. Use the Statement of Retained Earnings in the End-of-Chapter Summary Problem as a model.

P11-57B. (*Learning Objective 1: Use income data to make an investment decision*) Clark Cosmetics in Problem P11-55B holds significant promise for carving a niche in its industry. A group of Irish investors is considering purchasing the company's outstanding common stock. Clark's stock is currently selling for $21 per share.

A *Better Life Magazine* story predicted the company's income is bound to grow. It appears that Clark can earn at least its current level of income for the indefinite future. Based on this information, the investors think that an appropriate investment capitalization rate for estimating the value of Clark's common stock is 10%. How much will this belief lead the investors to offer for Clark Cosmetics? Will Clark's existing stockholders be likely to accept this offer? Explain your answers.

LO **2** **P11-58B.** *(Learning Objective 2: Account for foreign-currency gains or losses)* Suppose Taupe Corporation completed the following international transactions:

May	1	Sold inventory on account to Aromando, an Italian automaker, for €100,000. The exchange rate of the euro was $1.37, and Aromando demands to pay in euros. Ignore cost of goods sold.
	10	Purchased supplies on account from a Canadian company at a price of Canadian $53,000. The exchange rate of the Canadian dollar was $0.73, and the payment will be in Canadian dollars.
	17	Sold inventory on account to an English firm for 132,000 British pounds. Payment will be in pounds, and the exchange rate of the pound was $1.95. Ignore cost of goods sold.
	22	Collected from Aromando. The exchange rate is €1 = $1.40.
Jun	18	Paid the Canadian company. The exchange rate of the Canadian dollar is $0.72.
	24	Collected from the English firm. The exchange rate of the British pound was $1.92.

Requirements

1. Record these transactions in Taupe's journal and show how to report the foreign-currency transaction gain or loss on the income statement.
2. How will what you learned in this problem help you structure international transactions?

LO **1** **3** **4** **P11-59B.** *(Learning Objectives 1, 3, 4: Evaluate quality of earnings; compute earnings per share; estimate the price of a stock)* Turnover Specialists, Ltd. (TSL), specializes in taking underperforming companies to a higher level of performance. TSL's capital structure at December 31, 2015, included 11,000 shares of $2.30 preferred stock and 125,000 shares of common stock. During 2016, TSL issued common stock and ended the year with 135,000 shares of common stock outstanding. Average common shares outstanding during 2016 were 131,000. Income from continuing operations during 2016 was $220,000. The company discontinued a segment of the business at a gain of $67,000. All amounts are after income tax. Assume the number of preferred shares outstanding did not change in 2016.

Requirements

1. Compute TSL's earnings per share. Start with income from continuing operations.
2. Analysts believe TSL can earn its current level of income for the indefinite future. Estimate the market price of a share of TSL common stock at investment capitalization rates of 6%, 8%, and 10%. Which estimate presumes an investment in TSL is the most risky? How can you tell?

LO **3** **4** **5** **P11-60B.** *(Learning Objectives 3, 4, 5: Prepare an income statement; compute earnings per share; prepare a statement of comprehensive income)* Sophie Miller, accountant for Northern Foods, Inc., was injured in a snowboarding accident. While she was recuperating, another, inexperienced employee prepared the following income statement for the fiscal year ended June 30, 2016:

	A	B	C
1	**Northern Foods, Inc.** **Income Statement** **June 30, 2016**		
2	**Revenue and gains:**		
3	Sales		$ 864,000
4	Paid-in capital in excess of par—common		12,000
5	Total revenues and gains		876,000
6	**Expenses and losses:**		
7	Cost of goods sold	$ 387,000	
8	Selling expenses	104,000	
9	General expenses	99,000	
10	Unrealized loss on available-for-sale investments	13,000	
11	Dividends paid	15,000	
12	Income tax expense	109,600	
13	Total expenses and losses		727,600
14	Income from operations		$ 148,400
15	**Other gains and losses:**		
16	Income from discontinued operations		27,000
17	Net income		$ 175,400
18	Earnings per share		$ 11.69
19			

The individual *amounts* listed on the income statement are correct. However, some *accounts* are reported incorrectly, and some accounts do not belong on the income statement at all. The income tax rate of 40% has not been applied to Discontinued Operations. Northern Foods issued 15,000 shares of common stock back in 2004 and held 5,000 shares as treasury stock all during the fiscal year 2016.

Requirements

1. Using the End-of-Chapter Summary Problem as an example, prepare a corrected income statement for Northern Foods, Inc., for the fiscal year ended June 30, 2016. Use the single-step format, which lists all revenues together and all expenses together. Also prepare the earnings-per-share section of the statement.
2. Using Exhibit 11-2 as an example, prepare a Statement of Comprehensive Income for Northern Foods, Inc., for the fiscal year ended June 30, 2016. Start with net income, as computed in Requirement 1.

P11-61B. *(Learning Objective 3: Account for a corporation's income tax)* The accounting (not the income tax) records of Consolidated Publications, Inc., provide the income statement for the year ended December 31, 2016.

LO 3

	2016
Total revenue	$900,000
Expenses:	
Cost of goods sold..............................	$480,000
Operating expenses	220,000
Total expenses before tax....................	700,000
Pretax accounting income	$200,000

Taxable income for 2016 includes these modifications from pre-tax accounting income:
a. Additional taxable income of $17,000 earned in 2017 but taxed in 2016
b. Additional depreciation expense of $33,000 for Modified Accelerated Cost Recovery System (MACRS) tax depreciation in 2016

The income tax rate is 30%.

Requirements

1. Compute Consolidated's taxable income for 2016.
2. Journalize the corporation's income taxes for 2016.
3. Prepare the corporation's single-step income statement for 2016.

Challenge Problem

P11-62. *(Learning Objectives 1, 2, 4, 5: Analyze how various transactions affect the income statement and EPS)* Windy City Fashions, Inc., operates as a retailer of casual apparel. A recent, condensed income statement for Windy City Fashions follows:

	A	B	C
	A1		
1	**Income Statement** **For the Year Ended January 31, 2015**		
2	Sales revenue		$ 2,255,000
3	Operating expenses:		
4	Cost of goods sold	$ 1,100,000	
5	Selling and administrative expenses	500,000	1,600,000
6	Operating income		655,000
7	Other revenue (expenses)		25,000
8	Income before tax		680,000
9	Income tax expense (25% tax rate)		170,000
10	Net income		$ 510,000
11	Earnings per share (30,000 shares)		$ 17.00
12			

Requirements

1. Assume that the following transactions were inadvertently omitted at the end of the year. Using the categories in the table, indicate the effect of each of the transactions on each category; use + for increase, − for decrease, and NE for no effect. Provide dollar amounts for each column except Earnings per Share.

Transaction	Operating Income	Income Before Tax	Net Income	Earnings per Share
Unadjusted balances	655,000	680,000	510,000	
a.				
b.				
c.				
d.				
e.				
f.				
g.				
h.				
i.				
Totals				

a. Purchased inventory on account from a German company. The price was 140,000 euros. The exchange rate of the euro was $1.20.

b. Sold inventory on account, $100,000 (cost of inventory, $30,000).

c. Corrected a $60,000 overstatement of depreciation expense from a previous year.

d. Paid the German company for the inventory purchased when the exchange rate was $1.46.

e. Distributed 2,100 shares in a 7% stock dividend. The market value of the stock was $45.

f. Recorded additional administrative expense, $3,000.

    g. Recorded interest earned, $15,000.

    h. Declared dividends on preferred stock, $60,000.

    i. Issued additional 2,100 shares of common stock, $98,700.

2. Determine the amount of Operating Income, Income Before Tax, Net Income, and Earnings Per Share after recording these transactions. Assume transactions (e) and (i) occurred on January 1.

APPLY YOUR KNOWLEDGE

Decision Cases

Case 1. *(Learning Objective 1: Evaluate quality of earnings)* Prudhoe Bay Oil Co. is having its initial public offering (IPO) of company stock. To create public interest in its stock, Prudhoe Bay's chief financial officer has blitzed the media with press releases. One in particular caught your eye. On November 19, Prudhoe Bay announced unaudited earnings per share (EPS) of $1.19—up 89% from last year's EPS of $0.63. An 89% increase in EPS is outstanding!

    Before deciding to buy Prudhoe Bay stock, you investigated further and found that the company omitted several items from the determination of unaudited EPS:

- Unrealized loss on available-for-sale investments, $0.06 per share
- Gain on sale of building, $0.05 per share
- Prior-period adjustment, increase in retained earnings, $1.10 per share
- Restructuring expenses, $0.29 per share
- Loss on settlement of lawsuit begun five years ago, $0.12 per share
- Lost income due to employee labor strike, $0.24 per share
- Income from discontinued operations, $0.09 per share

Wondering how to treat these "special items," you called your stockbroker at **Merrill Lynch**. She thinks that these items are nonrecurring and outside Prudhoe Bay's core operations. Furthermore, she suggests that you ignore the items and consider Prudhoe Bay's earnings of $1.19 per share to be a good estimate of long-term profitability.

Requirement

1. What EPS number will you use to predict Prudhoe Bay's future profits? Show your work, and explain your reasoning for each item.

Case 2. *(Learning Objective 1: Evaluate quality of earnings)* Mike Magid Toyota is an automobile dealership. Magid's annual report includes Note 1—Summary of Significant Accounting Policies as follows:

> **Income Recognition**
>
> **Sales are recognized when cash payment is received or, in the case of credit sales, which represent the majority of . . . sales, when a down payment is received and the customer enters into an installment sales contract. These installment sales contracts . . . are normally collectible over 36 to 60 months . . .**
>
> **Revenue from auto insurance policies sold to customers are recognized as income over the life of the contracts.**

> *Source: From Clayton Homes, INC.Annual Report, http://www.sec.gov/Archives/edgar/containers/fix014/ 719547/0000950144-96-006864.txt.*

Bay Area Nissan, a competitor of Mike Magid Toyota, includes the following note in its Summary of Significant Accounting Policies:

> **Accounting Policies for Revenues**
>
> **Sales are recognized when cash payment is received or, in the case of credit sales, which represent the majority of . . . sales, when the customer enters into an installment sales contract. Customer down payments are rare. Most of these installment sales contracts are**

normally collectible over 36 to 60 months. . . Revenue from auto insurance policies sold to customers are recognized when the customer signs an insurance contract. Expenses are recognized over the life of the insurance contracts.

Source: From Clayton Homes, INC.Annual Report, http://www.sec.gov/Archives/edgar/containers/fix014/719547/ 0000950144-96-006864.txt.

Requirement

Suppose you have decided to invest in an auto dealership, and you've narrowed your choices to Magid and Bay Area. Which company's earnings are of higher quality? Why? Will their accounting policies affect your investment decision? If so, how? Mention specific accounts in the financial statements that will differ between the two companies. (Challenge)

Ethical Issue

Ethical Issue. The income statement of Royal Bank of Singapore reported the following results of operations:

Income before income taxes	$187,046
Income tax expense	72,947
Income from continuing operations	114,099
Income from discontinued operations, net of income tax	419,557
Net earnings	$533,656

Suppose Royal Bank's management, in violation of International Financial Reporting Standards (IFRS), had reported the company's results of operations in this manner:

Earnings before income taxes	$706,603
Income tax expense	172,947
Net earnings	$533,656

Requirements

1. Identify the ethical issue in this situation.
2. Who are the stakeholders?
3. Evaluate the issue from the standpoint of (a) economic, (b) legal or regulatory, and (c) ethical dimensions. What are the possible effects on all stakeholders you identified?
4. Put yourself in the position of the controller of the bank. Your boss, the CEO, tries to pressure you to make the disclosure that violates IFRS. What would you do? What are the potential consequences?

Focus on Financials | Apple Inc.

 (Learning Objective 1: Evaluate quality of earnings; evaluate an investment) Refer to the **Apple Inc.,** consolidated financial statements in Appendix A and online in the filings section of **http://www.sec.gov**.

Requirements

1. Apple Inc.'s consolidated statements of operations do not mention income from continuing operations. Why not? Focus your attention on the company's Consolidated Statements of Operations for the three years ended September 27, 2014, as well as the footnotes to financial statements and other materials. What clues do you find that help you evaluate the quality of Apple Inc.'s earnings?
2. Assume the role of an investor. Suppose you are determining the price to pay for a share of Apple Inc. stock. Assume you are considering three investment capitalization rates that depend on the risk of an investment in Apple Inc.: 5%, 6%, and 7%. Compute your estimated value of a share of Apple Inc., stock, using each of the three capitalization rates. For the sake of simplicity for this activity, use net income for the fiscal year ending September 27, 2014 as the estimated annual income in the future. Which estimated value would you base your investment strategy on if you rate Apple Inc. risky? If you consider Apple Inc. a safe investment?
3. Go to Apple Inc.'s website and compare your computed estimates to its actual stock price. Which of your prices is most realistic? (Challenge)

Focus on Analysis | Under Armour, Inc.

(Learning Objectives 1, 5: Evaluate quality of earnings; evaluate an investment; analyze **LO 1 5**
supplemental disclosures) This case is based on the **Under Armour, Inc.**, consolidated
financial statements in Appendix B and online in the filings section of **http://www.sec.gov**.

Requirements

1. Focus on the company's Consolidated Statements of Income for the three years ended
   December 31, 2014, as well as Note 2 summarizing the company's significant accounting
   policies. What is your evaluation of the quality of Under Armour, Inc.'s, earnings? Explain
   how you formed your opinion.
2. Refer to Note 16 to the Consolidated Financial Statements. How does Under Armour,
   Inc.'s, management define its operating regions? Which financial statement information
   does the company report by operating region? Which region appears to be the largest?
   What does this tell you about the international nature of Under Armour, Inc.'s, business?
3. At the end of 2014, how much would you have been willing to pay for one share of Under
   Armour, Inc.'s, stock if you had rated the investment as high risk? As low risk? Use even-
   numbered investment capitalization rates in the range of 4%–10% for your analysis, and
   use basic earnings per share for continuing operations.
4. Go to Under Armour, Inc.'s, website and get the current price of a share of its common
   stock. Which value that you estimated in requirement 3 is closest to the company's actual
   stock price? (Challenge)

Group Project

Select a company and research its business. Search the Internet for articles about this company.
Obtain its latest available annual report from the company's website or from **http://www.sec.gov**.
Click "Filings." Then, use the link entitled "Company Filings Search."

Requirements

1. Based on your group's analysis, come to class prepared to instruct the class on six interesting facts about the company that can be found in its financial statements and the related
   notes. Your group can mention only the obvious, such as net sales or total revenue, net income, total assets, total liabilities, total stockholders' equity, and dividends, in conjunction
   with other terms. Once you use an obvious item, you may not use that item again.
2. The group should write a paper discussing the facts that it has uncovered. Limit the paper
   to two double-spaced typed pages.

Quick Check Answers

1. *d*	5. *c*	9. *d*
2. *b*	6. *b* ($1,600,000 × $0.97)	10. *b*
3. *c* ($5.94/0.06)	7. *c*	11. *c*
4. *a* ([$28,000]/[0.28])	8. *a*	12. *a*

12

The Statement of Cash Flows

⬤ SPOTLIGHT | Google: The Ultimate Answer (and Cash) Machine

What Internet search engine do you use? When you're looking for an answer to a question, like most people, you may "just Google it." Google is the world's most popular search engine. Created by Larry Page and Sergey Brin when they were students at Stanford University, Google has grown from small beginnings to become a global technology leader that has helped transform the way people obtain all sorts of information. The company generates revenue primarily by delivering cost-effective online advertising. Google maintains an index of billions of web pages, which it makes freely available via its search engine to anyone with an Internet connection. Google stock has been a "hit" on Wall Street since its initial public offering (IPO). Recently, a share of Google, Inc., traded at over $500 per share!

The beauty of Google is that it's so easy to use. Access the Internet at **http://www.google.com**, and you can simply enter what you want to find in the search box; you get a list of helpful websites. The world is literally at your fingertips. Google may be the ultimate answer machine and, in recent years, it has become a cash machine as well! In 2014, its Net cash provided by operating activities exceeded its Net income by almost $8 billion, and the company finished the year with about $18.3 billion in Cash and cash equivalents on the books! ⬤

Stillfx/Fotolia

678

	A1		A	B	C
1			**Google, Inc.** **Consolidated Statements of Cash Flows (Adapted)**		
2				**12 Months Ended**	
3			**(In millions of $)**	**Dec. 31, 2014**	**Dec. 31, 2013**
4			**Operating activities**		
5			Net income	$ 14,444	$ 12,920
6			Adjustments:		
7			Depreciation expense and loss on disposal of property and equipment	3,523	2,781
8			Amortization and impairment of intangible and other assets	1,456	1,158
9			Stock-based compensation, net of taxes	3,631	2,862
10			Deferred income taxes	(938)	(437)
11			Other gains and losses	(104)	(594)
12			Changes in current assets and liabilities		
13			Accounts receivable	(1,641)	(1,307)
14			Income taxes, net	283	401
15			Prepaid revenue, expenses and other assets	459	(930)
16			Accounts payable	436	605
17			Accrued expenses and other liabilities	757	713
18			Accrued revenue share	245	254
19			Deferred revenue	(175)	233
20			Net cash provided by operating activities	22,376	18,659
21			**Investing activities**		
22			Purchases of property and equipment	(10,959)	(7,358)
23			Purchases of marketable securities	(56,310)	(45,444)
24			Maturities and sales of marketable securities	51,315	38,314
25			Other investments, net	(213)	2,257
26			Acquisitions of other companies	(4,888)	(1,448)
27			Net cash used in investing activities	(21,055)	(13,679)
28			**Financing activities**		
29			Net payments related to stock-based compensation, net of taxes	(1,421)	(300)
30			Proceeds from issuance of debt, net of costs	11,625	10,768
31			Repayment of debt	(11,643)	(11,325)
32			Net cash (used in) financing activities	(1,439)	(857)
33			Effect of exchange rate changes on cash and cash equivalents	(433)	(3)
34			Net increase (decrease) in cash and cash equivalents	(551)	4,120
35			Cash and cash equivalents at beginning of year	18,898	14,778
36			Cash and cash equivalents at end of year	$ 18,347	$ 18,898
37			Supplemental disclosures of cash flow information		
38			Cash paid for interest	$ 86	$ 72
39			Cash paid for taxes	2,819	1,932
40			Noncash financing activities	2,314	433
41					

In preceding chapters, we covered cash flows as they related to various topics: receivables, plant assets, and so on. **In this chapter, we show you how to prepare and use the statement of cash flows**. We begin with the statement format used by the vast majority of companies, the *indirect method*. We end with the alternate format of the statement of cash flows, the *direct method*, which is used by a minority of companies but is considered by many to be more informative. After working through this chapter, you will be able to analyze the cash flows of actual companies using both approaches.

This chapter has three sections:

▶ Introduction, consisting of Learning Objectives 1 and 2, beginning on the next page.

▶ Preparing the Statement of Cash Flows: Indirect Method (Learning Objective 3), pages 683–693.

▶ Preparing the Statement of Cash Flows: Direct Method (Learning Objective 4), pages 697–705.

The introduction applies to all the cash flow topics. Professors who wish to cover only the indirect method can assign Learning Objectives 1, 2, and 3 of the chapter. Those interested only in the direct method can proceed from the introduction, which ends on page 683, to the direct method (Learning Objective 4), on page 697.

LEARNING OBJECTIVES

1 **Identify** the purposes of the statement of cash flows

2 **Distinguish** among operating, investing, and financing activities

3 **Prepare** a statement of cash flows by the indirect method

4 **Prepare** a statement of cash flows by the direct method

» Try It in Excel®

You can access the most current annual report of Google, Inc. in Excel format at **http://www.sec.gov**. Using the "FILINGS" link on the toolbar at the top of the home page, select "Company Filings Search." This will take you to the "Edgar Company Filings" page. Type "Google" in the company name box, and select "Search." This will produce the "EDGAR Search Results" page showing the company name. Click on the "CIK" link beside the company name. This will pull up a list of the reports the company has filed with the SEC. Under the "Filing Type" box, type "10-K" and click the search box. Form 10-K is the SEC form for the company's annual report. Find the year that you wish to view. Click on the "Interactive Data" box, which takes you to the "View Filing Data" page. Find and click on the "View Excel Document" link at the top of this page. You may choose to either open or download the Excel files containing the company's most recent financial statements.

IDENTIFY THE PURPOSES OF THE STATEMENT OF CASH FLOWS

1 **Identify** the purposes of the statement of cash flows

The balance sheet reports a company's financial position, and balance sheets from two periods show whether cash increased or decreased. But that doesn't explain *why* the cash balance changed. The income statement reports net income and offers clues about cash, but the income statement doesn't tell *why* cash increased or decreased. We need a third financial statement.

The **statement of cash flows** reports **cash flows**—cash receipts and cash payments—in other words, where cash came from (receipts) and how it was spent (payments). The statement covers a span of time and therefore is dated "Year Ended December 31, 2016" or "Month Ended June 30, 2016." Exhibit 12-1 illustrates the relative timing of the four basic statements.

The statement of cash flows serves these purposes:

1. *Predicts future cash flows.* Past cash receipts and payments are reasonably good predictors of future cash flows.

2. *Evaluates management decisions.* Businesses that make wise decisions prosper, and those that make unwise decisions suffer losses. The statement of cash flows reports how managers got cash and how they used cash to run the business.

Exhibit 12-1 | Timing of the Financial Statements

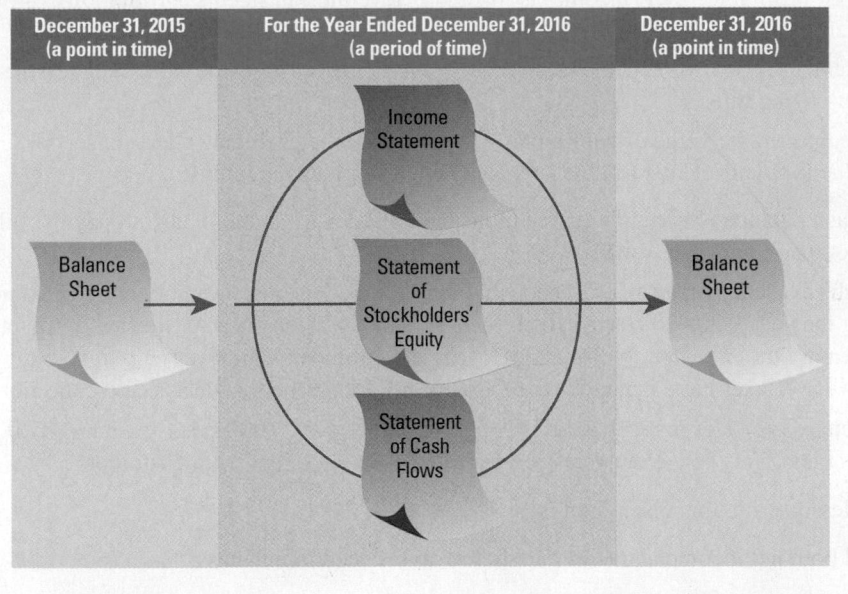

3. *Determines ability to pay dividends and interest.* Stockholders want dividends on their investments. Creditors demand interest and principal on their loans. The statement of cash flows reports on the ability to make these payments.

4. *Shows the relationship of net income to cash flows.* Usually, high net income eventually leads to an increase in cash, and vice versa. But cash flow can suffer even when net income is high.

On a statement of cash flows, *cash* means more than just cash in the bank. It includes **cash equivalents**, which are highly liquid short-term investments that can be converted into cash immediately. Examples include money-market accounts and investments in U.S. government securities. Throughout this chapter, the term *cash* refers to cash and cash equivalents.

How's Your Cash Flow? Telltale Signs of Financial Difficulty

Companies want to earn net income because profit measures success. Without net income, a business sinks. There will be no dividends, and the stock price suffers. High net income attracts investors, but you can't pay bills with net income. That requires cash.

A company needs both net income and strong cash flow. Income and cash flow usually move together because net income eventually generates cash. Sometimes, however, net income and cash flow take different paths. To illustrate, consider Fastech Company:

	A	B
1	**Fastech Company** **Income Statement** **Year Ended December 31, 2016**	
2	Sales revenue	$ 100,000
3	Cost of goods sold	30,000
4	Operating expenses	10,000
5	Net income	$ 60,000
6		

	A	B	C	D
1	**Fastech Company** **Balance Sheet** **December 31, 2016**			
2	Cash	$ 3,000	Total current liabilities	$ 50,000
3	Receivables	37,000	Long-term liabilities	20,000
4	Inventory	40,000		
5	Plant assets, net	60,000	Stockholders' equity	70,000
6	Total assets	$ 140,000	Total liabilities and equity	$ 140,000
7				

What can we glean from Fastech's income statement and balance sheet?

- Fastech is profitable. Net income is 60% of revenue. Fastech's profitability looks outstanding.
- The current ratio is 1.6, and the debt ratio is only 50%. These measures suggest little trouble in paying bills.
- But Fastech is on the verge of bankruptcy. Can you spot the problem? Can you see what is causing the problem? Three trouble spots leap out to a financial analyst.

1. The cash balance is very low. Three thousand dollars isn't enough cash to pay the bills of a company with sales of $100,000.
2. Fastech isn't selling inventory fast enough. Fastech turned over its inventory only 0.75 times during the year ($30,000 cost of goods sold ÷ $40,000 inventory). As we saw in Chapter 6, inventory turnover rates of 3–8 times a year are common. A turnover ratio of 0.75 times means that it takes Fastech far too long to sell its inventory, and that delays cash collections.
3. Fastech's days' sales in receivables is 135 days (365 ÷ ($100,000 sales revenue /$37,000 receivables). Very few companies can wait that long to collect from customers.

The takeaway lesson from this discussion is

- you need both net income and strong cash flow to succeed in business.

Let's turn now to the different categories of cash flows.

DISTINGUISH AMONG OPERATING, INVESTING, AND FINANCING ACTIVITIES

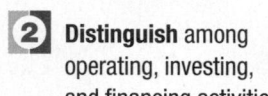

A business engages in three types of business activities:

- Operating activities
- Investing activities
- Financing activities

Google's statement of cash flows reports cash flows under these three headings, as shown on page 679.

Operating activities create revenues, expenses, gains, and losses—*net income*, which is a product of accrual basis accounting. The statement of cash flows reports on operating activities. Operating activities are the most important of the three categories because they reflect the core of the organization. *A successful business must generate most of its cash from operating activities.*

Investing activities increase and decrease *long-term assets*, such as computers, land, buildings, equipment, and investments in other companies. Purchases and sales of these assets are investing activities. Investing activities are important, but they are less critical than operating activities.

Financing activities obtain cash from investors and creditors. Issuing stock, borrowing money, buying and selling treasury stock, and paying cash dividends are financing activities. Paying off a loan is another example. Financing cash flows relate to *long-term liabilities and stockholders' equity*. They are the least important of the three categories of cash flows, and that's why they come last. Exhibit 12-2 shows how operating, investing, and financing activities relate to the various parts of the balance sheet.

Exhibit 12-2 | How Operating, Investing, and Financing Activities Affect the Balance Sheet

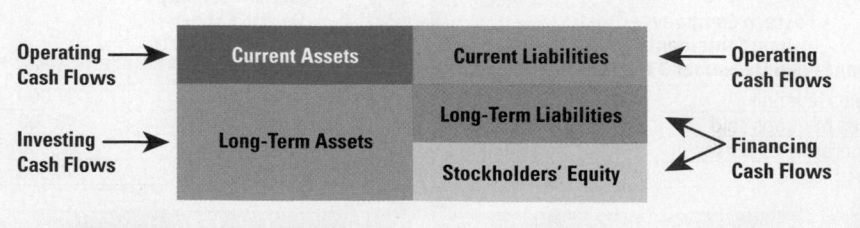

Examine Google's statement of cash flows on page 679. Focus on the final line of each section: Operating, Investing, and Financing. Google has very strong cash flows. During 2014, Google's operating activities provided about $22.4 billion of cash (line 20). Of that cash, $14.4 billion came from net income (line 5). We will explain the other adjustments later. Then, Google invested in the following: about $11 billion in property and equipment (line 22); about $56 billion in marketable securities (line 23); and about $5 billion in other companies (line 26). The company sold another $51 billion in marketable securities or received maturity values (line 24). Finally, it used about $1.4 billion in net financing (it paid out cash related to stock-based compensation in the amount of about $1.4 billion, borrowed $11.6 billion, and repaid $11.6 billion of debt [lines 29, 30, and 31, respectively]). These figures show that

- *operations* are Google's largest source of cash.
- the company is *investing* in the future.
- other companies, banks, and individuals are willing to *finance* Google by lending money to the company.

Two Formats for Operating Activities

There are two ways to format operating activities on the statement of cash flows:

- **Indirect method**—reconciles from net income to net cash provided by operating activities (pp. 683–693)
- **Direct method**—reports all cash receipts and cash payments from operating activities (pp. 697–705)

The two methods use different computations, but they produce the same figure for Net cash provided by *operating activities*. The two methods do not affect *investing* or *financing activities*. The following table summarizes the differences between the indirect and direct methods:

Indirect Method		Direct Method	
Net income.....................................	$600	Collections from customers..........	$2,000
Adjustments:		*Deductions:*	
Depreciation, etc.	300	Payments to suppliers, etc.	(1,100)
Net cash provided by		Net cash provided by	
operating activities	$900	operating activities	$ 900

———— same ————

We begin with the indirect method because the vast majority of companies use it.

PREPARE A STATEMENT OF CASH FLOWS BY THE INDIRECT METHOD

To illustrate the statement of cash flows, we use **The Roadster Factory, Inc. (TRF)**, a dealer in auto parts for sports cars. Proceed as follows to prepare the statement of cash flows by using the indirect method:

Step 1 Lay out the template as shown in Part 1 of Exhibit 12-3 (p. 684). The exhibit is comprehensive. The diagram in Part 2 (p. 685) gives a visual picture of the statement.

Step 2 Use the balance sheet to determine the increase or decrease in cash during the period. The change in cash is the "check figure" for the statement of cash flows. Exhibit 12-4 (p. 686) shows The Roadster Factory's (TRF's) comparative balance sheets, with Cash highlighted. TRF's cash decreased by $8,000 during 2016. *Why* did Cash decrease? The statement of cash flows will provide the answer.

3 **Prepare** a statement of cash flows by the indirect method

Step 3 From the income statement, take Net income; Depreciation, depletion, and amortization expense; and any Gains or Losses on the sale of long-term assets. Insert these items on the statement of cash flows. Exhibit 12-5 (p. 686) gives TRF's income statement, with relevant items highlighted.

Step 4 Use the income statement and balance-sheet data to prepare the statement of cash flows. The statement of cash flows is complete only after you have explained the year-to-year changes in all the balance-sheet accounts.

Exhibit 12-3 | Part 1: Template of the Statement of Cash Flows: Indirect Method

	A1	

	A
1	**The Roadster Factory, Inc. (TRF)** **Statement of Cash Flows** **Year Ended December 31, 2016**
2	**Cash flows from operating activities:**
3	Net income
4	Adjustments to reconcile net income to net cash provided by operating activities:
5	+ Depreciation/depletion/amortization expense
6	+ Loss on sale of long-term assets
7	– Gain on sale of long-term assets
8	– Increases in current assets other than cash
9	+ Decreases in current assets other than cash
10	+ Increases in current liabilities
11	– Decreases in current liabilities
12	Net cash provided by (used for) operating activities
13	**Cash flows from investing activities:**
14	+ Sales of long-term assets (investments, land, building, equipment, and so on)
15	– Purchases of long-term assets
16	+ Collections of notes receivable
17	– Loans to others
18	Net cash provided by (used for) investing activities
19	**Cash flows from financing activities:**
20	+ Issuance of stock
21	+ Sale of treasury stock
22	– Purchase of treasury stock
23	+ Borrowing (issuance of notes or bonds payable)
24	– Payment of notes or bonds payable
25	– Payment of dividends
26	Net cash provided by (used for) financing activities
27	**Net increase (decrease) in cash during the year**
28	+ Cash at December 31, 2015
29	= Cash at December 31, 2016
30	

Exhibit 12-3 | Part 2: Positive and Negative Items on the Statement of Cash Flows: Indirect Method

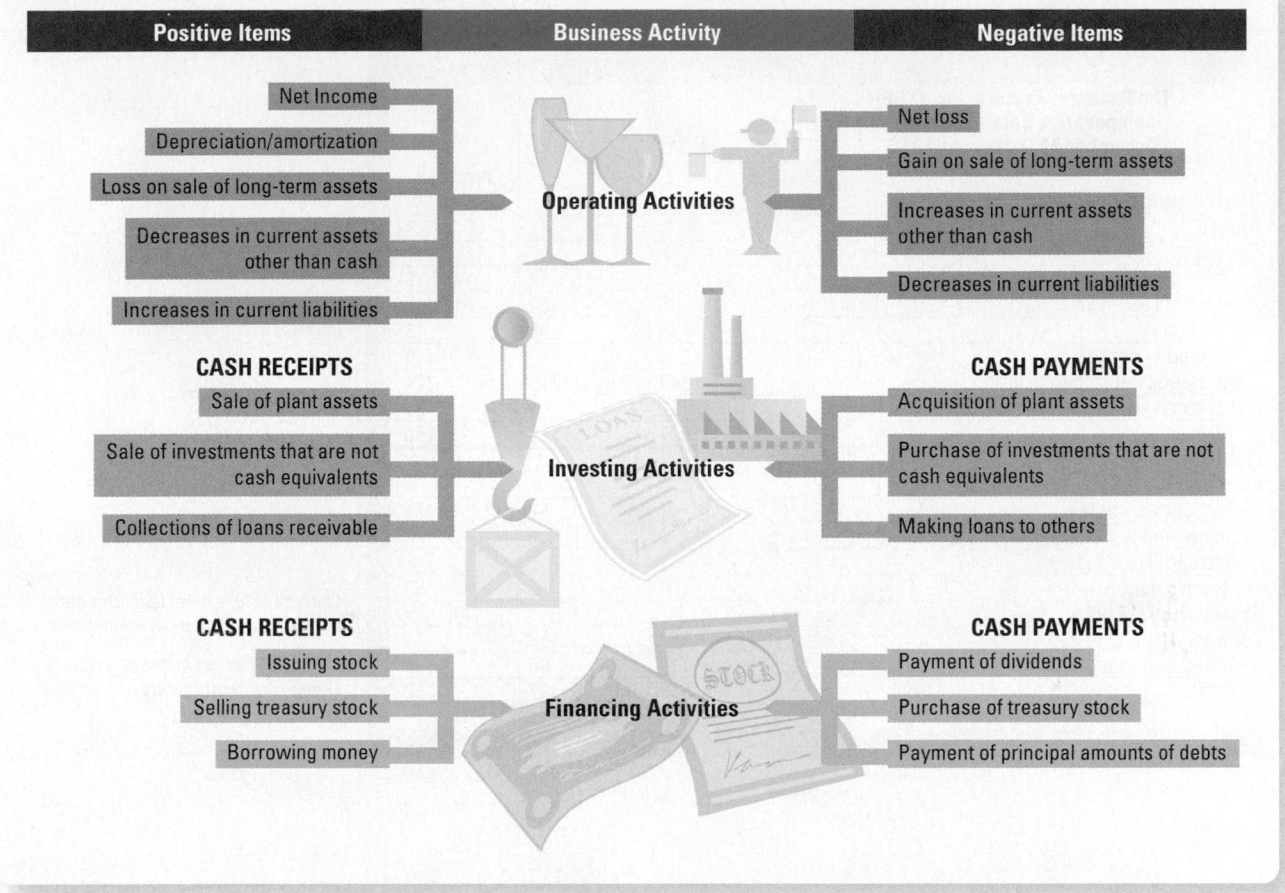

Cash Flows from Operating Activities

Operating activities are related to the transactions that make up net income.

Go to "Cash Flows from Operating Activities" in Exhibit 12-6 on page 687.

The operating section of the Statement of Cash Flows (Exhibit 12-6) begins with Net income, taken from the Income Statement (Exhibit 12-5) and is followed by "Adjustments to reconcile net income to net cash provided by operating activities." Let's discuss these adjustments.

(A) **Depreciation, Depletion, and Amortization Expenses.** These expenses are added back to net income to convert net income to cash flow. Let's see why. Depreciation is recorded as Depreciation Expense and has no effect on cash. But depreciation, like all other expenses, decreases net income. Therefore, to convert net income to cash flows, we add depreciation back to net income. The add-back cancels the earlier deduction.

	A	B	C
1	Depreciation Expense	18,000	
2	Accumulated Depreciation		18,000
3			

Exhibit 12-4 | Comparative Balance Sheets

	A	B	C	D	
	A1				
1	**The Roadster Factory, Inc. (TRF)** **Comparative Balance Sheets** **December 31, 2016 and 2015**				
2	**(In thousands)**	**2016**	**2015**	**Increase (Decrease)**	
3	**Assets**				
4	Current:				
5	Cash	$ 34	$ 42	$ (8)	
6	Accounts receivable	96	81	15	
7	Inventory	35	38	(3)	— Changes in current assets—*Operating*
8	Prepaid expenses	8	7	1	
9	Plant assets, net of depreciation	343	219	124	
10	Notes receivable	21	—	21	— Changes in noncurrent assets—*Investing*
11	Total	$ 537	$ 387	$ 150	
12	**Liabilities**				
13	Current:				
14	Accounts payable	$ 91	$ 57	$ 34	
15	Salary and wage payable	4	6	(2)	— Changes in current liabilities—*Operating*
16	Accrued liabilities	1	3	(2)	
17	Long-term debt	160	77	83	Changes in long-term liabilities and
18	**Stockholders' Equity**				paid-in capital accounts—*Financing*
19	Common stock	162	158	4	
20	Retained earnings	119	86	33	— Change due to net income—*Operating*
21	Total	$ 537	$ 387	$ 150	Change due to dividends—*Financing*
22					

Exhibit 12-5 | Income Statement

	A	B	C
	A1		
1	**The Roadster Factory, Inc. (TRF)** **Income Statement** **Year Ended December 31, 2016**		
2		**(In thousands)**	
3			
4	Revenues and gains:		
5	Sales revenue	$ 303	
6	Interest revenue	2	
7	Gain on sale of plant assets	8	
8	Total revenues and gains		$ 313
9	Expenses:		
10	Cost of goods sold	$ 150	
11	Salary and wage expense	56	
12	Depreciation expense	18	
13	Other operating expense	17	
14	Income tax expense	15	
15	Interest expense	7	
16	Total expenses		263
17	Net income		$ 50
18			

Exhibit 12-6 | Statement of Cash Flows—Operating Activities—Indirect Method

	A	B	C
	The Roadster Factory, Inc. (TRF)		
	Partial Statement of Cash Flows (Indirect Method)		
1	**For the Year Ended December 31, 2016**		
2		**(In thousands)**	
3	**Cash flows from operating activities:**		
4	Net income		$ 50
5	Adjustments to reconcile net income to net cash		
6	provided by operating activities:		
7	Ⓐ Depreciation	$ 18	
8	Ⓑ Gain on sale of plant assets	(8)	
9	Increase in accounts receivable	(15)	
10	Decrease in inventory	3	
11	Ⓒ Increase in prepaid expenses	(1)	
12	Increase in accounts payable	34	
13	Decrease in salary and wage payable	(2)	
14	Decrease in accrued liabilities	(2)	27
15	Net cash provided by operating activities		$ 77
16			

Example: Suppose you had only two transactions, a $1,000 cash sale and depreciation expense of $300. Net cash flow from operations is $1,000, and Net income is $700 ($1,000 − $300). To go from net income ($700) to cash flow ($1,000), we add back the depreciation ($300). Depletion and amortization are treated like depreciation.

Ⓑ **Gains and Losses on the Sale of Long-Term Assets.** Sales of long-term assets are *investing* activities, and there's often a gain or loss on the sale. On the statement of cash flows, the gain or loss is an adjustment to net income. Exhibit 12-6 includes an adjustment for a gain. During 2016, The Roadster Factory sold equipment for $62,000. The book value was $54,000, so there was a gain of $8,000.

The $62,000 cash received from the sale is an investing activity (Exhibit 12-7, page 688), and the $62,000 includes the $8,000 gain. Net income also includes the gain, so we must subtract the gain from net cash provided by operations so that it may be added to the net book value of equipment sold in the investing section ($54,000 + $8,000 = $62,000). We explain investing activities in the next section.

A loss on the sale of plant assets also creates an adjustment in the operating section. Since the cash received from the sale of a long-term asset at a loss is less than the asset's book value, the amount of cash received reflects the loss. Losses are deducted from net income. Therefore, in order to show the amount of cash received from the sale of the asset in the investing section, losses are *added back* to net income in the operating section to compute Net cash flow from operations.

Ⓒ **Changes in the Current Asset and Current Liability Accounts, Excluding Cash.** Most current assets and current liabilities result from operating activities. For example, accounts receivable result from sales, inventory relates to cost of goods sold, and so on. Except for Cash, changes in the current accounts are adjustments to net income on the cash flow statement. The reasoning is as follows:

1. *An increase in a noncash current asset decreases cash.* It takes cash to acquire assets. Suppose you make a sale on account. Accounts receivable are increased, but cash isn't affected yet. Exhibit 12-4 (p. 686) reports that during 2016, The Roadster Factory's Accounts Receivable increased by $15,000. To compute cash flow from operations, we must subtract the $15,000 increase in Accounts Receivable, as shown in Exhibit 12-6. The reason is this: We have *not* collected this $15,000 in cash. Similar logic applies to all the other current assets. If they increase, cash decreases.

2. *A decrease in a noncash current asset increases cash.* Suppose TRF's Accounts Receivable balance decreased by $4,000. Cash receipts caused Accounts Receivable to decrease, so we add decreases in Accounts Receivable and the other current assets to net income.

3. *A decrease in a current liability decreases cash.* Payment of a current liability decreases both cash and the liability, so we subtract decreases in current liabilities from net income. In Exhibit 12-6, the $2,000 decrease in Accrued Liabilities is *subtracted* to compute Net cash provided by operations.

4. *An increase in a current liability increases cash.* The Roadster Factory's Accounts Payable increased. That can occur only if cash was not spent to pay this debt. Cash payments are therefore less than expenses, and TRF has more cash on hand. Thus, increases in current liabilities increase cash.

Evaluating Cash Flows from Operating Activities. Let's step back and evaluate The Roadster Factory's operating cash flows during 2016. TRF's operations provided net cash flow of $77,000. This amount exceeds net income, which is one sign of a healthy company. Now let's examine TRF's investing and financing activities, as reported in Exhibit 12-7.

Exhibit 12-7 | Statement of Cash Flows—Indirect Method

	A	B	C
	A1		
1	The Roadster Factory, Inc. (TRF) Statement of Cash Flows (Indirect Method) For the Year Ended December 31, 2016		
2		(In thousands)	
3	**Cash flows from operating activities:**		
4	Net income		$ 50
5	Adjustments to reconcile net income to net cash		
6	provided by operating activities:		
7	Ⓐ Depreciation	$ 18	
8	Ⓑ Gain on sale of plant assets	(8)	
9	Increase in accounts receivable	(15)	
10	Decrease in inventory	3	
11	Ⓒ Increase in prepaid expenses	(1)	
12	Increase in accounts payable	34	
13	Decrease in salary and wage payable	(2)	
14	Decrease in accrued liabilities	(2)	27
15	Net cash provided by operating activities		77
16	**Cash flows from investing activities:**		
17	Acquisition of plant assets	$ (196)	
18	Loan to another company	(21)	
19	Proceeds from sale of plant assets	62	
20	Net cash used for investing activities		(155)
21	**Cash flows from financing activities:**		
22	Proceeds from issuance of long-term debt	$ 94	
23	Proceeds from issuance of common stock	4	
24	Payment of long-term debt	(11)	
25	Payment of dividends	(17)	
26	Net cash provided by financing activities		70
27	**Net (decrease) in cash**		$ (8)
28	Cash balance, December 31, 2015		42
29	Cash balance, December 31, 2016		$ 34
30			

Cash Flows from Investing Activities

Investing activities affect long-term assets, such as Plant Assets and long-term Investments such as debt and equity securities of other companies. Increases in these accounts represent purchases of these assets and are offset by decreases to cash. Decreases to these accounts represent sales of these assets and are offset by increases to cash.

Most of the data come from the balance sheet.

Computing Purchases and Sales of Plant Assets. Companies keep a separate account for each plant asset. But for computing cash flows, it is helpful to combine all the plant assets into a single summary account. Also, we subtract accumulated depreciation and use the net figure. It's easier to work with a single plant asset account.

To illustrate, observe that The Roadster Factory's

- balance sheet reports beginning plant assets, net of accumulated depreciation, of $219,000. The ending balance is $343,000 (Exhibit 12-4).
- income statement shows depreciation expense of $18,000 and an $8,000 gain on sale of plant assets (Exhibit 12-5).

TRF's purchases of plant assets total $196,000 (take this amount as given; see Exhibit 12-7). How much, then, are the proceeds from the sale of plant assets? First, we must determine the book value of the plant assets sold:

Plant Assets, Net

Beginning balance	+	Acquisitions	−	Depreciation expense	−	Book value of assets sold	=	Ending balance
$219,000	+	$196,000	−	$18,000		−X	=	$343,000
						−X	=	$343,000 − $219,000 − $196,000 + $18,000
						X	=	$54,000

The sale proceeds are $62,000, determined as follows:

Sale proceeds	=	Book value of assets sold	+	Gain	−	Loss
X	=	$54,000	+	$8,000	−	$0
X	=	$62,000				

Trace the sale proceeds of $62,000 to the statement of cash flows in Exhibit 12-7. The Plant Assets T-account provides another look at the computation of the book value of the assets sold.

Plant Assets, Net

Beginning balance	219,000	Depreciation expense	18,000
Acquisitions	196,000	Book value of assets sold	54,000
Ending balance	343,000		

If the sale resulted in a loss of $3,000, the sale proceeds would be $51,000 ($54,000 − $3,000), and the statement of cash flows would report $51,000 as a cash receipt from this investing activity.

Computing Purchases and Sales of Investments, and Loans and Collections. The cash amounts of investment transactions can be computed in the manner illustrated for plant assets. TRF does not have investments but we assume they do in this illustration. Investments are easier because there is no depreciation, as shown in the following equation:

Investments (amounts assumed for illustration only)

Beginning balance	+	Purchases	−	Book value of investments sold	=	Ending balance
$100,000	+	$50,000		−X	=	$140,000
				−X	=	$140,000 − $100,000 − $50,000
				X	=	$10,000

The Investments T-account provides another look (amounts assumed).

Investments

Beginning balance	100,000		
Purchases	50,000	Book value of investments sold	10,000
Ending balance	140,000		

The Roadster Factory has a long-term receivable, and the cash flows from loan transactions on notes receivable can be determined as follows (data from Exhibit 12-4):

Notes Receivable

Beginning balance	+	New loans made	−	Collections	=	Ending balance
$0	+	X		−0	=	$21,000
		X			=	$21,000

Notes Receivable

Beginning balance	0		
New loans made	21,000	Collections	0
Ending balance	21,000		

Please refer to the investing section of the Statement of Cash Flows (Exhibit 12-7) to see all the investing activities listed together for TRF. Exhibit 12-8 summarizes the cash flows from investing activities, highlighted in color.

Cash Flows from Financing Activities

Financing activities affect liabilities and stockholders' equity, such as Notes Payable, Bonds Payable, Long-Term Debt, Common Stock, Paid-in Capital in Excess of Par, and Retained Earnings. Most of the data come from the balance sheet. Increases in these accounts, excluding Retained Earnings, are offset by increases in cash. Decreases in these accounts are offset by decreases in cash.

Computing Issuances and Payments of Long-Term Debt. The beginning and ending balances of Long-Term Debt, Notes Payable, or Bonds Payable come from the balance sheet. If either new issuances or payments are known, the other amount can be computed. Assume that proceeds from The Roadster Factory's new long-term debt issuances (represented as an increase

Exhibit 12-8 | Computing Cash Flows from Investing Activities

Receipts

From sale of plant assets	Beginning plant assets, net	+	Acquisition cost	−	Depreciation expense	−	Book value of assets sold	=	Ending plant assets, net
	Cash received	=	Book value of assets sold	+ or −	Gain on sale Loss on sale				
From sale of investments	Beginning investments	+	Purchase cost of investments	−	Book value of investments sold	=	Ending investments		
	Cash received	=	Book value of investments sold	+ or −	Gain on sale Loss on sale				
From collection of notes receivable	Beginning notes receivable	+	New loans made	−	Collections	=	Ending notes receivable		

Payments

For acquisition of plant assets	Beginning plant assets, net	+	Acquisition cost	−	Depreciation expense	−	Book value of assets sold	=	Ending plant assets, net
For purchase of investments	Beginning investments	+	Purchase cost of investments	−	Book value of investments sold	=	Ending investments		
For new loans made	Beginning notes receivable	+	New loans made	−	Collections	−	Ending notes receivable		

in cash) total $94,000 (take this amount as given in Exhibit 12-7). Debt payments (represented by a decrease in cash) are computed by performing an analysis of the Long-Term Debt account (see Exhibit 12-4).

Long-Term Debt (Notes Payable, Bonds Payable)

Beginning balance	+	Issuance of new debt	−	Payments of debt	=	Ending balance
$77,000	+	$94,000		−X	=	$160,000
				−X	=	$160,000 − $77,000 − $94,000
				X	=	$11,000

Long-Term Debt

		Beginning balance	77,000
Payments	11,000	Issuance of new debt	94,000
		Ending balance	160,000

Computing Issuances of Stock and Purchases of Treasury Stock. These cash flows can be determined from the stock accounts. For example, cash received from issuing common stock is computed from Common Stock and Paid-in Capital in Excess of Par. We use a single summary Common Stock account as we do for plant assets. The Roadster Factory data are

Common Stock

Beginning balance	+	Issuance of new stock	=	Ending balance
$158,000	+	$4,000	=	$162,000

Common Stock

Beginning balance	158,000
Issuance of new stock	4,000
Ending balance	162,000

Increases in common stock and related additional paid-in capital are represented by offsetting increases in Cash.

The Roadster Factory has no treasury stock, but cash flows from purchasing treasury stock can be computed as follows (using assumed amounts):

Treasury Stock (amounts assumed for illustration only)

Beginning balance	+	Purchase of treasury stock	=	Ending balance
$16,000	+	$3,000	=	$19,000

Treasury Stock

Beginning balance	16,000
Purchase of treasury stock	3,000
Ending balance	19,000

Increases (purchases) of treasury stock are represented by offsetting decreases in cash. If treasury stock is reissued for cash, the decrease in treasury stock is offset by an increase in cash.

Computing Dividend Declarations and Payments. If dividend declarations and payments are not given elsewhere, they can be computed. For The Roadster Factory, this computation is as follows:

Retained Earnings

Beginning balance	+	Net income	−	Dividend declarations and payments	=	Ending balance
$86,000	+	$50,000		−X	=	$119,000
				−X	=	$119,000 − $86,000 − $50,000
				X	=	$17,000

The T-account also shows the dividend computation. Dividends paid, represented by decreases in retained earnings, are offset by decreases in cash.

Retained Earnings

Dividend declarations and payments	17,000	Beginning balance	86,000
		Net income	50,000
		Ending balance	119,000

Please refer to the financing section of the Statement of Cash Flows (Exhibit 12-7) to see all the financing activities listed together for TRF.

Exhibit 12-9 summarizes the cash flows from financing activities, highlighted in color.

Exhibit 12-9 | Computing Cash Flows from Financing Activities

Receipts

From borrowing—issuance of long-term debt (notes payable)	Beginning long-term debt (notes payable)	+	Cash received from issuance of long-term debt	− Payment of debt =	Ending long-term debt (notes payable)
From issuance of stock	Beginning stock	+	Cash received from issuance of new stock	=	Ending stock

Payments

Of long-term debt	Beginning long-term debt (notes payable)	+	Cash received from issuance of long-term debt	− Payment of debt =	Ending long-term debt (notes payable)
To purchase treasury stock	Beginning treasury stock + Purchase cost of treasury stock = Ending treasury stock				
Of dividends	Beginning retained earnings + Net income − Dividend declarations and payments = Ending retained earnings				

Classify each of the following as an operating activity, an investing activity, or a financing activity as reported on the statement of cash flows prepared by the *indirect* method.

a. Issuance of stock

b. Borrowing long-term

c. Sales revenue

d. Payment of dividends

e. Purchase of land with cash

f. Purchase of treasury stock

g. Paying bonds payable

h. Interest expense

i. Sale of equipment

j. Cost of goods sold

k. Purchase of another company with cash

l. Making a loan

Answers:

a. Financing

b. Financing

c. Operating (included in net income)

d. Financing

e. Investing

f. Financing

g. Financing

h. Operating (included in net income)

i. Investing

j. Operating (included in net income)

k. Investing

l. Investing

Noncash Investing and Financing Activities

Companies make investments that do not require cash. They also obtain financing other than cash. Our examples have included none of these transactions. Now suppose The Roadster Factory issued common stock valued at $300,000 to acquire a warehouse. TRF would journalize this transaction as

	A1 $\updownarrow$		
	A	**B**	**C**
1	Warehouse Building	300,000	
2	Common Stock		300,000
3			

This transaction would not be reported as a cash payment because TRF paid no cash. But the investment in the warehouse and the issuance of stock are important. These noncash investing and financing activities should be reported in a separate schedule under the statement of cash flows. Exhibit 12-10 illustrates noncash investing and financing activities (all amounts are assumed).

Exhibit 12-10 | Noncash Investing and Financing Activities

	A1 $\updownarrow$	
	A	**B**
1		**Thousands**
2		
3	**Noncash investing and financing activities:**	
4	Acquisition of building by issuing common stock	$ 300
5	Acquisition of land by issuing note payable	70
6	Payment of long-term debt by issuing common stock	100
7	Total noncash investing and financing activities	$ 470
8		

Now let's apply what you've learned about the statement of cash flows prepared by the indirect method.

Lucas Corporation reported the following income statement and comparative balance sheets, along with transaction data for 2016:

	A	B	C
1	**Lucas Corporation** **Income Statement** **Year Ended December 31, 2016**		
2	Sales revenue		$ 662,000
3	Cost of goods sold		560,000
4	Gross profit		102,000
5	Operating expenses		
6	Salary expenses	$ 46,000	
7	Depreciation expense—equipment	7,000	
8	Amortization expense—patent	3,000	
9	Rent expense	2,000	
10	Total operating expenses		58,000
11	Income from operations		44,000
12	Other items:		
13	Loss on sale of equipment		(2,000)
14	Income before income tax		42,000
15	Income tax expense		16,000
16	Net income		$ 26,000
17			

	A	B	C	D	E	F
1	**Lucas Corporation** **Comparative Balance Sheets** **December 31, 2016 and 2015**					
2	**Assets**	**2016**	**2015**	**Liabilities**	**2016**	**2015**
3	Current:			Current:		
4	Cash and cash equivalents	$ 19,000	$ 3,000	Accounts payable	$ 35,000	$ 26,000
5	Accounts receivable	22,000	23,000	Accrued liabilities	7,000	9,000
6	Inventories	34,000	31,000	Income tax payable	10,000	10,000
7	Prepaid expenses	1,000	3,000	Total current liabilities	52,000	45,000
8	Total current assets	76,000	60,000	Long-term note payable	44,000	—
9	Equipment, net	67,000	52,000	Bonds payable	40,000	53,000
10	Long-term investments	18,000	10,000	**Stockholders' Equity**		
11	Patent, net	44,000	10,000	Common stock	52,000	20,000
12				Retained earnings	27,000	19,000
13				Less: Treasury stock	(10,000)	(5,000)
14	Total assets	$ 205,000	$ 132,000	Total liabilities and Stockholders' equity	$ 205,000	$ 132,000
15						

Transaction Data for 2016:

Purchase of equipment with cash	$ 98,000	Issuance of long-term note payable	
Payment of cash dividends	18,000	to purchase patent	$ 37,000
Issuance of common stock to		Issuance of long-term note payable to	
retire bonds payable	13,000	borrow cash	7,000
Purchase of long-term investment		Issuance of common stock for cash	19,000
with cash	8,000	Proceeds from sale of equipment	
Purchase of treasury stock	5,000	(book value, $76,000)	74,000

Requirement

1. Prepare Lucas Corporation's statement of cash flows (indirect method) for the year ended December 31, 2016. Follow the four steps outlined below. For Step 4, prepare a T-account to show the transaction activity in each long-term balance-sheet account. For each plant asset, use a single account, net of accumulated depreciation (for example: Equipment, Net).

   Step 1 Lay out the template of the statement of cash flows.

   Step 2 From the comparative balance sheets, determine the increase in cash and cash equivalents during the year, $16,000.

   Step 3 From the income statement, take net income, depreciation, amortization, and the loss on sale of equipment to the statement of cash flows.

   Step 4 Complete the statement of cash flows. Account for the year-to-year change in each balance-sheet account.

Answer:

A1

	A	B	C
1	**Lucas Corporation** **Statement of Cash Flows** **Year Ended December 31, 2016**		
2	**Cash flows from operating activities:**		
3	Net income		$ 26,000
4	Adjustments to reconcile net income to		
5	net cash provided by operating activities:		
6	Depreciation	$ 7,000	
7	Amortization	3,000	
8	Loss on sale of equipment	2,000	
9	Decrease in accounts receivable	1,000	
10	Increase in inventories	(3,000)	
11	Decrease in prepaid expenses	2,000	
12	Increase in accounts payable	9,000	
13	Decrease in accrued liabilities	(2,000)	19,000
14	Net cash provided by operating activities		45,000
15	**Cash flows from investing activities:**		
16	Purchase of equipment	$ (98,000)	
17	Sale of equipment	74,000	
18	Purchase of long-term investment	(8,000)	
19	Net cash used for investing activities		(32,000)
20	**Cash flows from financing activities:**		
21	Issuance of common stock	$ 19,000	
22	Payment of cash dividends	(18,000)	
23	Issuance of long-term note payable	7,000	
24	Purchase of treasury stock	(5,000)	
25	Net cash provided by financing activities		3,000
26	**Net increase in cash and cash equivalents**		**16,000**
27	Cash and cash equivalents balance, December 31, 2015		3,000
28	Cash and cash equivalents balance, December 31, 2016		$ 19,000
29	**Noncash investing and financing activities:**		
30	Issuance of long-term note payable to purchase patent		$ 37,000
31	Issuance of common stock to retire bonds payable		13,000
32	Total noncash investing and financing activities		$ 50,000
33			

Equipment, Net

Bal	52,000		
	98,000	76,000	
		7,000	
Bal	67,000		

Long-Term Investments

Bal	10,000		
	8,000		
Bal	18,000		

Patent, Net

Bal	10,000		
	37,000	3,000	
Bal	44,000		

Long-Term Note Payable

		Bal	0
			37,000
			7,000
		Bal	44,000

Bonds Payable

		Bal	53,000
	13,000		
		Bal	40,000

Common Stock

		Bal	20,000
			13,000
			19,000
		Bal	52,000

Retained Earnings

		Bal	19,000
	18,000		26,000
		Bal	27,000

Treasury Stock

Bal	5,000		
	5,000		
Bal	10,000		

PREPARE A STATEMENT OF CASH FLOWS
BY THE DIRECT METHOD

The Financial Accounting Standards Board (FASB) and the International Accounting Standards Board (IASB) prefer the direct method of reporting operating cash flows because it provides clearer information about the sources and uses of cash. However, only a very small percentage of companies use this method because it requires more computations than the indirect method. Investing and financing cash flows are unaffected by the method used.

4 **Prepare** a statement of cash flows by the direct method

To illustrate the statement of cash flows, we use The Roadster Factory, Inc. (TRF), a dealer in auto parts for sports cars. To prepare the statement of cash flows by the direct method, proceed as follows:

Step 1 Lay out the template of the statement of cash flows by the direct method, as shown in Part 1 of Exhibit 12-11. Part 2 (p. 698) gives a visual presentation of the statement.

Step 2 Use the balance sheet to determine the increase or decrease in cash during the period. The change in cash is the "check figure" for the statement of cash flows. The Roadster Factory's comparative balance sheets show that cash decreased by $8,000 during 2016 (Exhibit 12-4, p. 686). *Why* did cash decrease during 2016? The statement of cash flows explains.

Exhibit 12-11 | Part 1: Template of the Statement of Cash Flows—Direct Method

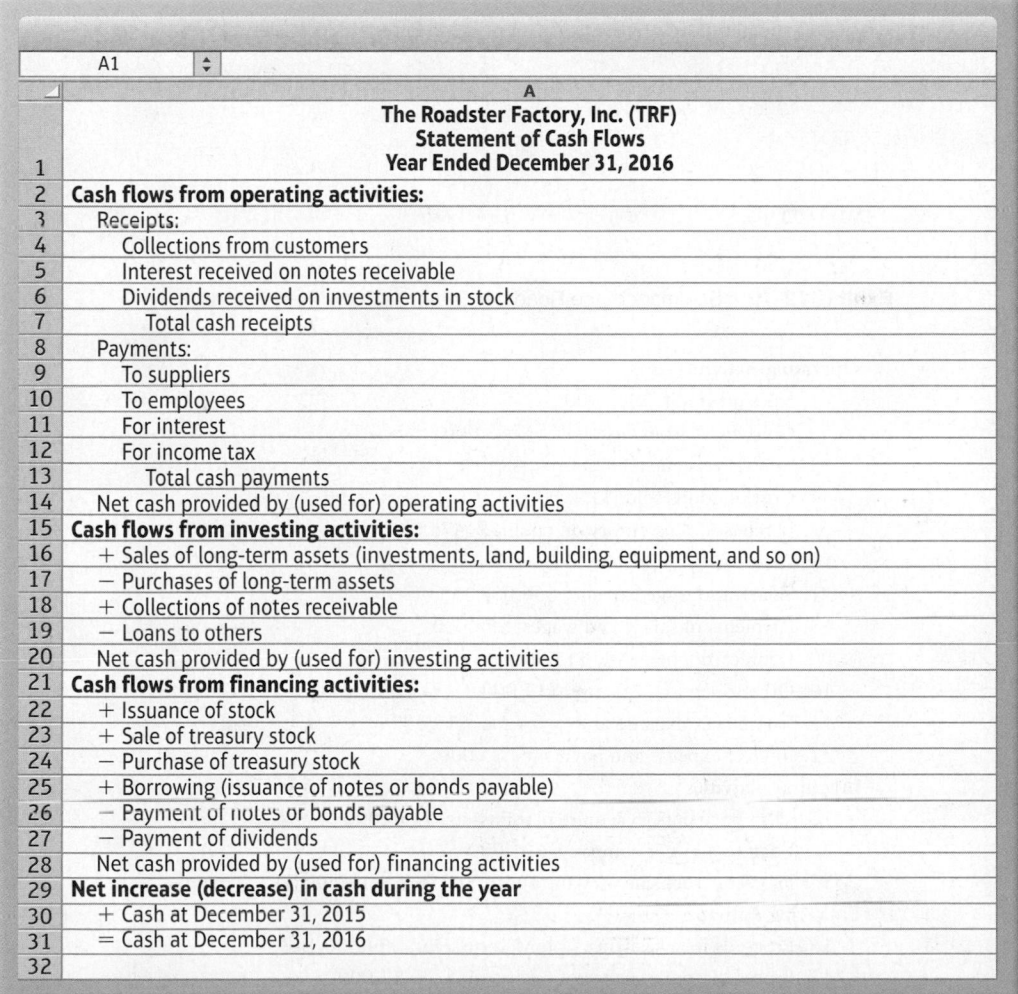

	A
	The Roadster Factory, Inc. (TRF)
	Statement of Cash Flows
1	Year Ended December 31, 2016
2	**Cash flows from operating activities:**
3	Receipts:
4	Collections from customers
5	Interest received on notes receivable
6	Dividends received on investments in stock
7	Total cash receipts
8	Payments:
9	To suppliers
10	To employees
11	For interest
12	For income tax
13	Total cash payments
14	Net cash provided by (used for) operating activities
15	**Cash flows from investing activities:**
16	+ Sales of long-term assets (investments, land, building, equipment, and so on)
17	− Purchases of long-term assets
18	+ Collections of notes receivable
19	− Loans to others
20	Net cash provided by (used for) investing activities
21	**Cash flows from financing activities:**
22	+ Issuance of stock
23	+ Sale of treasury stock
24	− Purchase of treasury stock
25	+ Borrowing (issuance of notes or bonds payable)
26	− Payment of notes or bonds payable
27	− Payment of dividends
28	Net cash provided by (used for) financing activities
29	**Net increase (decrease) in cash during the year**
30	+ Cash at December 31, 2015
31	= Cash at December 31, 2016
32	

Exhibit 12-11 | Part 2: Cash Receipts and Cash Payments on the Statement of Cash Flows—Direct Method

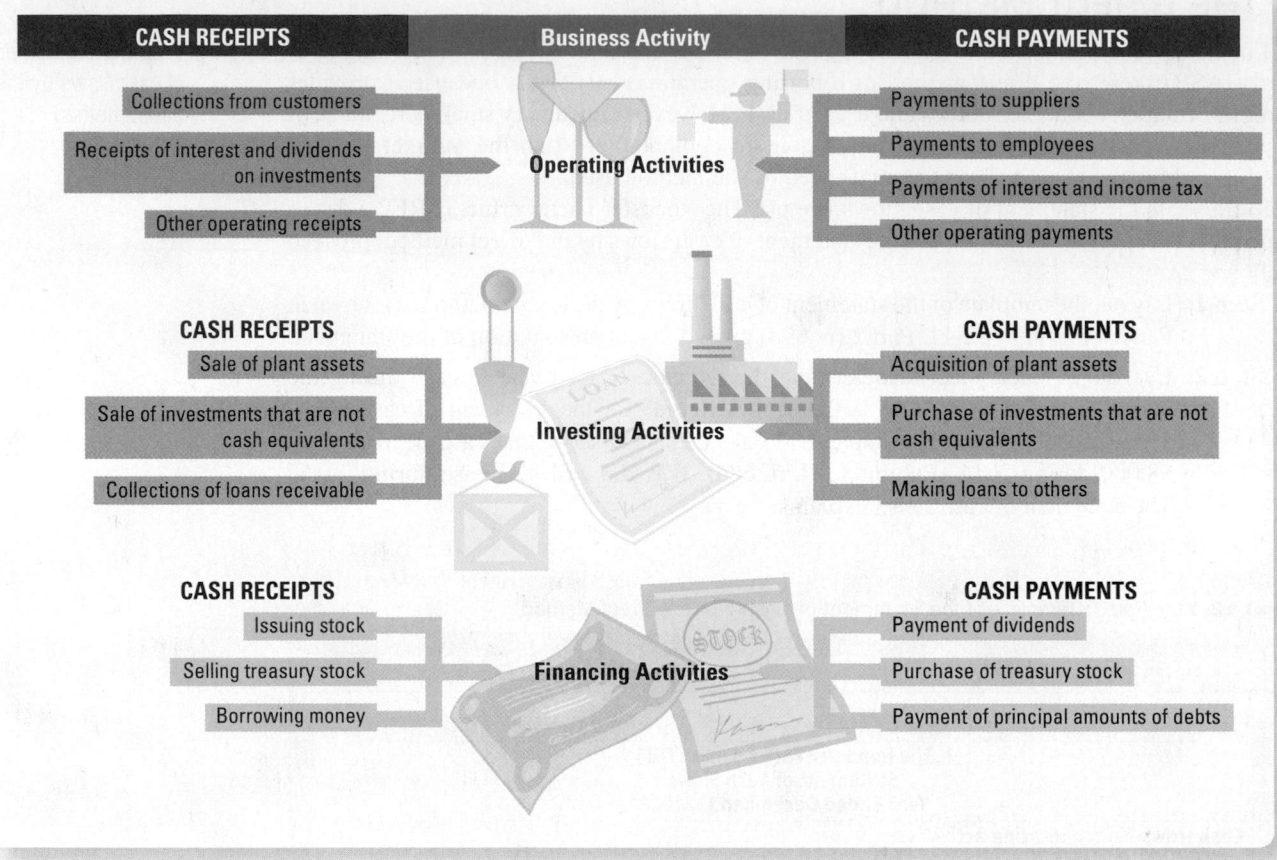

Exhibit 12-12 | Summary of the Roadster Factory's 2016 Transactions

Operating Activities

1. Sales on credit, $303,000
*2. Collections from customers, $288,000
*3. Interest revenue and receipts, $2,000
4. Cost of goods sold, $150,000
5. Purchases of inventory on credit, $147,000
*6. Payments to suppliers, $133,000
7. Salary and wage expense, $56,000
*8. Payments of salary and wages, $58,000
9. Depreciation expense, $18,000
10. Other operating expense, $17,000
*11. Income tax expense and payments, $15,000
*12. Interest expense and payments, $7,000

Investing Activities

*13. Cash payments to acquire plant assets, $196,000
*14. Loan to another company, $21,000
*15. Proceeds from sale of plant assets, $62,000, including $8,000 gain

Financing Activities

*16. Proceeds from issuance of long-term debt, $94,000
*17. Proceeds from issuance of common stock, $4,000
*18. Payment of long-term debt, $11,000
*19. Declaration and payment of cash dividends, $17,000

*Indicates a cash flow to be reported on the statement of cash flows.
Note: Income statement data are taken from Exhibit 12-16, page 702.

Step 3 Use the available data to prepare the statement of cash flows. The Roadster Factory's transaction data appear in Exhibit 12-12 on page 698. These transactions affected both the income statement (Exhibit 12-5, p. 686) and the statement of cash flows. Some transactions in Exhibit 12-12 affect one statement and some affect the other. For example, sales (item 1) are reported on the income statement. Cash collections (item 2) go on the statement of cash flows. Other transactions, such as interest expense and payments (item 12), affect both statements. *The statement of cash flows reports only those transactions with cash effects* (those with an asterisk in Exhibit 12-12). Exhibit 12-13 (on this page below) gives The Roadster Factory's statement of cash flows for 2016.

Cash Flows from Operating Activities

Operating cash flows are listed first because they are the most important. Exhibit 12-13 shows that The Roadster Factory is sound; operating activities were the largest source of cash.

Cash Collections from Customers. Both cash sales and collections of accounts receivable are reported on the statement of cash flows as "Collections from customers ... $288,000" in Exhibit 12-13.

Cash Receipts of Interest and Dividends. The income statement reports interest revenue and dividend revenue. Only the cash receipts of interest and dividends appear on the statement of cash flows—$2,000 of interest received in Exhibit 12-13. The Roadster Factory, Inc., received no revenue from dividends in 2016.

Payments to Suppliers. Payments to suppliers include all expenditures for inventory and operating expenses except employee pay, interest, and income taxes. *Suppliers* are those entities that provide inventory and essential services. For example, a clothing store's suppliers may include

Exhibit 12-13 | Statement of Cash Flows—Direct Method

	A	B	C
1	**The Roadster Factory, Inc. (TRF)** **Statement of Cash Flows (Direct Method)** **For Year Ended December 31, 2016**		
2		**(In thousands)**	
3	**Cash flows from operating activities:**		
4	Receipts:		
5	Collections from customers	$ 288	
6	Interest received	2	
7	Total cash receipts		$ 290
8	Payments:		
9	To suppliers	$ (133)	
10	To employees	(58)	
11	For income tax	(15)	
12	For interest	(7)	
13	Total cash payments		(213)
14	Net cash provided by operating activities		77
15	**Cash flows from investing activities:**		
16	Acquisition of plant assets	$ (196)	
17	Loan to another company	(21)	
18	Proceeds from sale of plant assets	62	
19	Net cash used for investing activities		(155)
20	**Cash flows from financing activities:**		
21	Proceeds from issuance of long-term debt	$ 94	
22	Proceeds from issuance of common stock	4	
23	Payment of long-term debt	(11)	
24	Payment of dividends	(17)	
25	Net cash provided by financing activities		70
26	**Net (decrease) in cash**		(8)
27	Cash balance, December 31, 2015		42
28	Cash balance, December 31, 2016		$ 34
29			

Tommy Hilfiger, Adidas, and **Ralph Lauren**. Other suppliers provide advertising, utilities, and office supplies. Exhibit 12-13 shows that The Roadster Factory paid suppliers $133,000.

Payments to Employees. This category includes salaries, wages, and other forms of employee pay. Accrued amounts are excluded because they have not yet been paid. The statement of cash flows reports only the cash payments of $58,000.

Payments for Interest Expense and Income Tax Expense. Interest and income tax payments are reported separately. The Roadster Factory paid cash for all its interest and income taxes. Therefore, the same amount goes on the income statement and the statement of cash flows. These payments are operating cash flows because the interest and income tax are expenses.

Depreciation, Depletion, and Amortization Expense

These expenses are *not* listed on the direct-method statement of cash flows because they do not affect cash.

Cash Flows from Investing Activities

Investing is critical because a company's investments affect the future. Large purchases of plant assets signal expansion. Meager investing activity means the business is not growing.

Purchasing Plant Assets and Investments and Making Loans to Other Companies. These cash payments acquire long-term assets. The Roadster Factory's first investing activity in Exhibit 12-13 is the purchase of plant assets ($196,000). TRF also made a $21,000 loan and thus got a note receivable.

Proceeds from Selling Plant Assets and Investments and from Collecting Notes Receivable. These cash receipts are also investing activities. The sale of the plant assets needs explanation. The Roadster Factory received $62,000 cash from the sale of plant assets, and there was an $8,000 gain on this transaction. What is the appropriate amount to show on the cash flow statement? It is $62,000, the cash received from the sale, not the $8,000 gain.

Investors are often critical of a company that sells large amounts of its plant assets. That may signal an emergency. For example, problems in the airline industry have caused some companies to sell airplanes to generate cash.

Cash Flows from Financing Activities

Cash flows from financing activities include the following:

Proceeds from Issuance of Stock and Debt (Notes and Bonds Payable). Issuing stock and borrowing money are two ways to finance a company. In Exhibit 12-13, The Roadster Factory received $4,000 when it issued common stock. TRF also received $94,000 cash when it issued long-term debt (such as a note payable) to borrow money.

Payment of Debt and Purchasing the Company's Own Stock. Paying debt (notes payable) is the opposite of borrowing. TRF reports long-term debt payments of $11,000. The purchase of treasury stock is another example of a use of cash.

Payment of Cash Dividends. Paying cash dividends is a financing activity, as shown by The Roadster Factory's $17,000 payment in Exhibit 12-13. A *stock* dividend has no effect on Cash and is *not* reported on the cash flow statement.

Noncash Investing and Financing Activities

Companies make investments that do not require cash. They also obtain financing other than cash. Our examples thus far have included none of these transactions. Now suppose that The

Roadster Factory issued common stock valued at $300,000 to acquire a warehouse. TRF would journalize this transaction as

A1				
	A	B	C
1	Warehouse Building	300,000	
2	Common Stock		300,000
3			

This transaction would not be reported as a cash payment because TRF paid no cash. But the investment in the warehouse and the issuance of stock are important. These noncash investing and financing activities can be reported in a separate schedule under the statement of cash flows. Exhibit 12-14 illustrates noncash investing and financing activities (all amounts are assumed).

Exhibit 12-14 | Noncash Investing and Financing Activities

A1		
	A	B
1		**Thousands**
2		
3	**Noncash investing and financing activities:**	
4	Acquisition of building by issuing common stock	$ 300
5	Acquisition of land by issuing note payable	70
6	Payment of long-term debt by issuing common stock	100
7	Total noncash investing and financing activities	$ 470
8		

Try It

Using the direct method, classify each of the following as an operating activity, an investing activity, or a financing activity. Also identify those items that are not reported on the statement of cash flows prepared by the *direct* method.

a. Net income
b. Payment of dividends
c. Borrowing long-term
d. Payment of cash to suppliers
e. Making a loan
f. Sale of treasury stock
g. Depreciation expense
h. Purchase of equipment with cash

i. Issuance of stock
j. Purchase of another company with cash
k. Payment of a long-term note payable
l. Payment of income taxes
m. Collections from customers
n. Accrual of interest revenue
o. Expiration of prepaid expense
p. Receipt of cash dividends

Answers:

a. Not reported
b. Financing
c. Financing
d. Operating
e. Investing
f. Financing
g. Not reported
h. Investing

i. Financing
j. Investing
k. Financing
l. Operating
m. Operating
n. Not reported
o. Not reported
p. Operating

Now let's see how to compute the operating cash flows by the direct method.

Computing Operating Cash Flows by the Direct Method

To compute operating cash flows by the direct method, we use the income statement and the *changes* in the balance-sheet accounts. Exhibit 12-15 diagrams the process. Exhibit 12-16 is The Roadster Factory's income statement, and Exhibit 12-17 shows the comparative balance sheets.

Exhibit 12-15 | Direct Method of Computing Cash Flows from Operating Activities

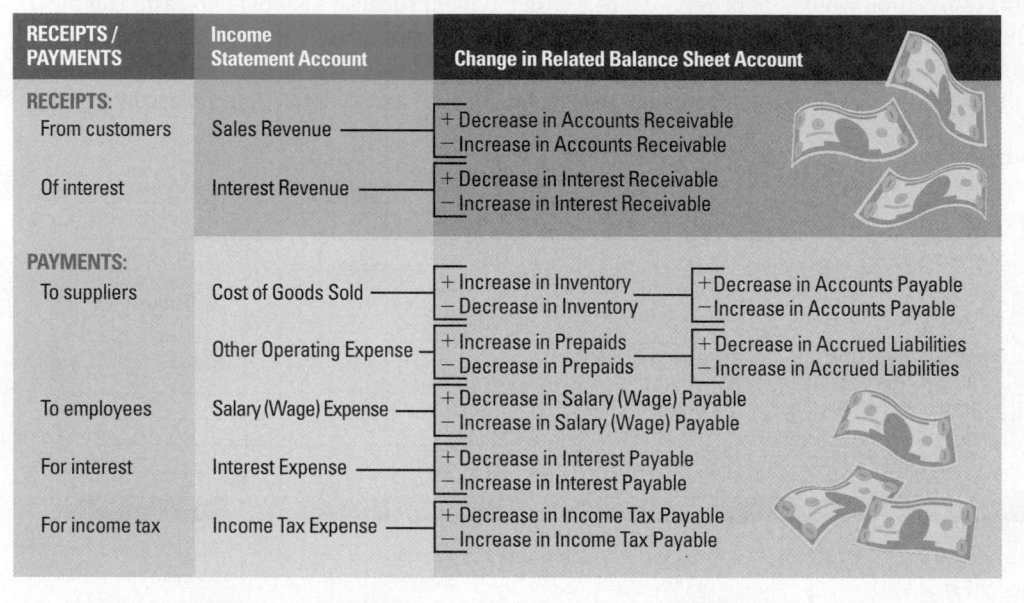

Exhibit 12-16 | Income Statement

	A	B	C
	A1		
1	**The Roadster Factory, Inc. (TRF)** **Income Statement** **Year Ended December 31, 2016**		
2		**(In thousands)**	
3	Revenues and gains:		
4	Sales revenue	$ 303	
5	Interest revenue	2	
6	Gain on sale of plant assets	8	
7	Total revenues and gains		$ 313
8	Expenses:		
9	Cost of goods sold	$ 150	
10	Salary and wage expense	56	
11	Depreciation expense	18	
12	Other operating expense	17	
13	Income tax expense	15	
14	Interest expense	7	
15	Total expenses		263
16	Net income		$ 50
17			

Exhibit 12-17 | Comparative Balance Sheets

	A	B	C	D	
				Increase	
	The Roadster Factory, Inc. (TRF) **Comparative Balance Sheets** **December 31, 2016 and 2015**				
1					
2	(In thousands)	**2016**	**2015**	(Decrease)	
3	**Assets**				
4	Current:				
5	Cash	$ 34	$ 42	$ (8)	
6	Accounts receivable	96	81	15	— Changes in noncash current assets—*Operating*
7	Inventory	35	38	(3)	
8	Prepaid expenses	8	7	1	
9	Plant assets, net of depreciation	343	219	124	— Changes in noncurrent assets—*Investing*
10	Notes receivable	21	—	21	
11	Total	$ 537	$ 387	$ 150	
12	**Liabilities**				
13	Current:				
14	Accounts payable	$ 91	$ 57	$ 34	
15	Salary and wage payable	4	6	(2)	— Changes in current liabilities—*Operating*
16	Accrued liabilities	1	3	(2)	
17	Long-term debt	160	77	83	
18	**Stockholders' Equity**				*Changes in long-term liabilities and*
19	Common stock	162	158	4	*paid-in capital accounts—Financing*
20	Retained earnings	119	86	33	*Change due to net income—Operating*
21	Total	$ 537	$ 387	$ 150	*Change due to dividends—Financing*
22					

Computing Cash Collections from Customers. Collections start with sales revenue (an accrual basis amount). The Roadster Factory's income statement (Exhibit 12-16) reports sales of $303,000. Accounts receivable increased from $81,000 at the beginning of the year to $96,000 at year-end, a $15,000 increase (Exhibit 12-17). Based on those amounts, Cash Collections equal $288,000, as follows. We must solve for cash collections (X):

Accounts Receivable

Beginning balance	+	Sales	−	Collections	=	Ending balance
$81,000	+	$303,000		−X	=	$96,000
				−X	=	$96,000 − $81,000 − $303,000
				X	=	$288,000

The T-account for Accounts Receivable provides another view of the same computation.

Accounts Receivable

Beginning balance	81,000		
Sales	303,000	Collections	288,000
Ending balance	96,000		

Accounts Receivable increased, so collections must be less than sales.

All collections of receivables are computed this way. Let's turn now to cash receipts of interest revenue. In our example, The Roadster Factory earned interest revenue and collected cash of $2,000. The amounts of interest revenue and cash receipts of interest often differ, and Exhibit 12-15 shows how to make this computation.

Computing Payments to Suppliers. This computation includes two parts:

■ Payments for inventory

■ Payments for operating expenses (other than salaries and wages)

Payments for inventory are computed by converting cost of goods sold to the cash basis. We use Cost of Goods Sold, Inventory, and Accounts Payable. First, we must solve for purchases. All the amounts come from Exhibits 12-16 and 12-17.

Cost of Goods Sold

Beginning inventory	+	Purchases	−	Ending inventory	=	Cost of goods sold
$38,000	+	X	−	$35,000	=	$150,000
		X			=	$150,000 − $38,000 + $35,000
		X			=	$147,000

Now we can compute cash payments for inventory (Y), as follows:

Accounts Payable

Beginning balance	+	Purchases	−	Payments for inventory	=	Ending balance
$57,000	+	$147,000	−Y		=	$91,000
			−Y		=	$91,000 − $57,000 − $147,000
			Y		=	$113,000

The T-accounts show where the data come from. Start with Cost of Goods Sold.

Cost of Goods Sold				Accounts Payable		
Beg inventory	38,000	End inventory	35,000	Payments for inventory	113,000	Beg bal 57,000
Purchases	147,000					Purchases 147,000
Cost of goods sold	150,000					End bal 91,000

Accounts Payable increased, so payments for inventory are less than purchases.

Computing Payments for Other Operating Expenses. Payments for operating expenses other than salaries and wages are computed from three accounts: Prepaid Expenses, Accrued Liabilities, and Other Operating Expenses. All The Roadster Factory data come from Exhibits 12-16 and 12-17.

Prepaid Expenses

Beginning balance	+	Payments	−	Expiration of prepaid expense (assumed)	=	Ending balance
$7,000	+	X	−	$7,000	=	$8,000
		X			=	$8,000 − $7,000 + $7,000
		X			=	$8,000

Accrued Liabilities

Beginning balance	+	Accrual of expense at year-end (assumed)	−	Payments	=	Ending balance
$3,000	+	$1,000	−X		=	$1,000
			−X		=	$1,000 − $3,000 − $1,000
			X		=	$3,000

Other Operating Expenses

Accrual of expense at year-end	+	Expiration of prepaid expense	+	Payments	=	Ending balance
$1,000	+	$7,000	+	X	=	$17,000
				X	=	$17,000 − $1,000 − $7,000
				X	=	$9,000
		Total payments for other operating expenses			=	$8,000 + $3,000 + $9,000
					=	$20,000

The T-accounts give another picture of the same data.

Prepaid Expenses				
Beg bal	7,000	Expiration of		
Payments	8,000	prepaid		
		expense	7,000	
End bal	8,000			

Accrued Liabilities			
		Beg bal	3,000
Payment	3,000	Accrual of	
		expense at	
		year-end	1,000
		End bal	1,000

Other Operating Expenses		
Accrual of	1,000	
expense at		
year-end		
Expiration of		
prepaid		
expense	7,000	
Payments	9,000	
End bal	17,000	

Total payments for other operating expenses = $20,000 ($8,000 + $3,000 + $9,000)

Now we can compute Payments to Suppliers:

Payments to suppliers	=	Payments for inventory	+	Payments for other operating expenses
$133,000	=	$113,000	+	$20,000

Computing Payments to Employees. It is convenient to combine all payments to employees into one account, Salary and Wage Expense. We then adjust the expense for the change in Salary and Wage Payable, as shown here:

Salary and Wage Payable

Beginning balance	+	Salary and wage expense	−	Payments	=	Ending balance
$6,000	+	$56,000	−	−X	=	$4,000
				−X	=	$4,000 − $6,000 − $56,000
				X	=	$58,000

Salary and Wage Payable

Payments to employees	58,000	Beginning balance	6,000
		Salary and wage expense	56,000
		Ending balance	4,000

Computing Payments of Interest and Income Taxes. The Roadster Factory's expense and payment amounts are the same for interest and income tax, so no analysis is required. If the expense and the payment differ, the payment can be computed as shown in Exhibit 12-15.

Computing Investing and Financing Cash Flows

Investing and financing activities are explained on pages 689–692. These computations are the same for both the direct and the indirect methods.

Fidelity Company reported the following for 2016 and 2015 (in millions):

At December 31,	2016	2015
Receivables, net..........................	$3,500	$3,900
Inventory....................................	5,200	5,000
Accounts payable	900	1,200
Income taxes payable	600	700

Year Ended December 31,	2016
Revenues......................................	$23,000
Cost of goods sold........................	14,100
Income tax expense......................	900

Based on these figures, how much cash did
• Fidelity collect from customers during 2016?
• Fidelity pay for inventory during 2016?
• Fidelity pay for income taxes during 2016?

Answers:

		Beginning receivables	+	Revenues	−	Collections	=	Ending receivables
Collections from customers	= $23,400:	$3,900	+	$23,000	−	$23,400	=	$3,500

		Cost of goods sold	+	Increase in inventory	+	Decrease in accounts payable	=	Payments
Payments for inventory	= $14,600:	$14,100	+	($5,200 − $5,000)	+	($1,200 − $900)	=	$14,600

		Beginning income taxes payable	+	Income tax expense	−	Payment	=	Ending income taxes payable
Payment of income taxes	= $1,000:	$700	+	$900	−	$1,000	=	$600

Measuring Cash Adequacy: Free Cash Flow

Throughout this chapter, we have focused on cash flows from operating, investing, and financing activities. Some investors want to know how much cash a company can "free up" for new opportunities. **Free cash flow** is the amount of cash available from operations after paying for planned investments in plant assets. Free cash flow can be computed as follows:

$$\text{Free cash flow} = \frac{\text{Net cash provided}}{\text{by operating activities}} - \frac{\text{Cash payments earmarked for}}{\text{investments in plant assets}}$$

PepsiCo, Inc., uses free cash flow to manage its operations. Suppose PepsiCo expects net cash inflow of $2.3 billion from operations. Assume PepsiCo plans to spend $1.9 billion to modernize its bottling plants. In this case, PepsiCo's free cash flow would be $0.4 billion ($2.3 billion − $1.9 billion). If a good investment opportunity comes along, PepsiCo should have $0.4 billion to invest in the other company. **Shell Oil Company** also uses free cash flow analysis. A large amount of free cash flow is preferable because it means that a lot of cash is available for new investments. The Decision Guidelines that follow show some ways to use cash flow and income data for investment and credit analysis.

 # DECISION GUIDELINES

INVESTORS' AND CREDITORS' USE OF CASH FLOW AND RELATED INFORMATION

Jan Childres is a private investor. Through years of experience, she has devised some guidelines for evaluating both stock investments and bond investments. Childres uses a combination of accrual accounting data and cash flow information. Here are her decision guidelines for both investors and creditors.

➤ INVESTORS

Questions	Factors to Consider	Financial Statement Predictor/ Decision Model*
1. How much in dividends can I expect to receive from an investment in stock?	Expected future net income	Income from continuing operations**
	Expected future cash balance	Net cash flows from (in order) • operating activities • investing activities • financing activities
	Future dividend policy	Current and past dividend policy
2. Is the stock price likely to increase or decrease?	Expected future net income	Income from continuing operations**
	Expected future cash flows from operating activities	Income from continuing operations** Net cash flow from operating activities
3. What is the future stock price likely to be?	Expected future income from	
	• continuing operations, and	$$\text{Expected future price of a share of stock} = \frac{\text{Income from continuing operations per share**}}{\text{Investment capitalization rate**}}$$
	• cash flow from operating activities	$$\text{Expected future price of a share of stock} = \frac{\text{Net cash flow from operations per share}}{\text{Investment capitalization rate**}}$$

➤ CREDITORS

Question	Factors to Consider	Financial Statement Predictor
Can the company pay the interest and principal at the maturity of a loan?	Expected future net cash flow from operating activities	Income from continuing operations** Net cash flow from operating activities

---

*There are many other factors to consider in making these decisions. These are some of the more common.

**See Chapter 11.

Adeva Health Foods, Inc., reported the following comparative balance sheets for 2016 and 2015 and the income statement for 2016:

A1		
A	**B**	**C**
Adeva Health Foods, Inc. **Comparative Balance Sheets** **December 31, 2016 and 2015**		
	2016	**2015**
Cash	$ 19,000	$ 3,000
Accounts receivable	22,000	23,000
Inventories	34,000	31,000
Prepaid expenses	1,000	3,000
Equipment, net	90,000	79,000
Intangible assets	9,000	9,000
	$ 175,000	$ 148,000
Accounts payable	$ 14,000	$ 9,000
Accrued liabilities	16,000	19,000
Income tax payable	14,000	12,000
Notes payable	45,000	50,000
Common stock	31,000	20,000
Retained earnings	64,000	40,000
Treasury stock	(9,000)	(2,000)
	$ 175,000	$ 148,000

A1	
A	**B**
Adeva Health Foods, Inc. **Income Statement** **Year Ended December 31, 2016**	
Sales revenue	$ 190,000
Gain on sale of equipment	6,000
Total revenue and gains	196,000
Cost of goods sold	85,000
Depreciation expense	19,000
Other operating expenses	36,000
Total expenses	140,000
Income before income tax	56,000
Income tax expense	18,000
Net income	$ 38,000

Assume that **Berkshire Hathaway** is considering buying Adeva. Berkshire Hathaway requests the following cash flow data for 2016. There were no noncash investing and financing activities.

a. Collections from customers.

b. Cash payments for inventory.

c. Cash payments for other operating expenses.

d. Cash payment for income tax.

e. Cash received from the sale of equipment. Adeva paid $40,000 for new equipment during the year.

f. Issuance of common stock.

g. Issuance of notes payable. Adeva paid off $20,000 during the year.

h. Cash dividends. There were no stock dividends.

Provide the requested data. Show your work.

Answers

a. Analyze Accounts Receivable: Let X = Collections from customers:

Beginning Accounts Receivable	+	Sales	–	Collections	=	Ending Accounts Receivable
$23,000	+	$190,000	–	X	=	$22,000
				X	=	$191,000

b. Analyze Inventory and Accounts Payable: Let X = Purchases, and let Y = Payments for inventory:

Beginning Inventory	+	Purchases	–	Cost of Goods Sold	=	Ending Inventory
$31,000	+	X	–	$85,000	=	$34,000
		X			=	$88,000

Beginning Accounts Payable	+	Purchases	–	Payments	=	Ending Accounts Payable
$9,000	+	$88,000	–	Y	=	$14,000
				Y	=	$83,000

c. Start with Other Operating Expenses, and adjust for the changes in Prepaid Expenses and Accrued Liabilities:

Other Operating Expenses	– Decrease in Prepaid Expenses	+ Decrease in Accrued Liabilities	=	Payments for Other Operating Expenses
$36,000	– $2,000	+ $3,000	=	$37,000

d. Analyze Income Tax Payable: Let X = Payment of income tax:

Beginning Income Tax Payable	+	Income Tax Expense	–	Payments	=	Ending Income Tax Payable
$12,000	+	$18,000	–	X	=	$14,000
				X	=	$16,000

e. Analyze Equipment, Net: Let X = Book value of equipment sold. Then combine with the gain or loss to compute cash received from the sale:

Beginning Equipment, net	+	Acquisitions	−	Depreciation Expense	−	Book Value Sold	=	Ending Equipment, net
$79,000	+	$40,000	−	$19,000	−	X	=	$90,000
						X	=	$10,000

Cash Received from Sale	=	Book Value Sold	+	Gain on Sale
$16,000	=	$10,000	+	$6,000

f. Analyze Common Stock: Let X = Issuance:

Beginning Common Stock	+	Issuance	=	Ending Common Stock
$20,000	+	X	=	$31,000
		X	=	$11,000

g. Analyze Notes Payable: Let X = Issuance:

Beginning Notes Payable	+	Issuance	−	Payment	=	Ending Notes Payable
$50,000	+	X	−	$20,000	=	$45,000
		X			=	$15,000

h. Analyze Retained Earnings: Let X = Dividends:

Beginning Retained Earnings	+	Net Income	−	Dividends	=	Ending Retained Earnings
$40,000	+	$38,000	−	X	=	$64,000
				X	=	$14,000

Review | Statement of Cash Flows

Quick Check (Answers are given on page 749.)

1. All except which of the following activities are reported on the statement of cash flows?
   a. Marketing activities
   b. Financing activities
   c. Investing activities
   d. Operating activities

2. On the statement of cash flows, activities that create long-term liabilities are usually
   a. financing activities.
   b. operating activities.
   c. investing activities.
   d. noncash investing and financing activities.

3. On the statement of cash flows, activities affecting long-term assets are
   a. operating activities.
   b. marketing activities.
   c. investing activities.
   d. financing activities.

4. In 2016, Merrill Corporation borrowed $90,000, paid dividends of $34,000, issued 14,000 shares of stock for $35 per share, purchased land for $20,000, and received dividends of $7,000. Net income was $90,000, and depreciation for the year totaled $12,000. Accounts receivable increased by $9,000. How much should be reported as net cash provided by operating activities by the indirect method?
   a. $102,000
   b. $635,000
   c. $75,000
   d. $93,000

5. On the statement of cash flows, activities that obtain the cash needed to launch and sustain a company are

   a. investing activities.
   b. income activities.

   c. marketing activities.
   d. financing activities.

6. On the statement of cash flows, the exchange of stock for land would be reported as which of the following?

   a. Investing activities
   b. Exchanges are not reported on the statement of cash flows
   c. Noncash investing and financing activities
   d. Financing activities

Use the following Sutherland Corporation information for questions 7–10.

Net income..	$70,000	Increase in accounts payable	$ 12,000
Depreciation expense	13,000	Acquisition of equipment	
Payment of dividends	5,000	with cash............................	23,000
Increase in accounts receivable	2,000	Sale of treasury stock	4,000
Collection of long-term notes receivable..........	7,000	Payment of long-term debt.........	8,000
Loss on sale of land..	9,000	Proceeds from sale of land..........	39,000
		Decrease in inventories...............	1,000

7. Under the indirect method, net cash provided by operating activities would be

   a. $105,000.
   b. $117,000.

   c. $103,000.
   d. $119,000.

8. Net cash provided by (used for) investing activities would be

   a. $119,000.
   b. $23,000.

   c. $105,000.
   d. $(117,000).

9. Net cash provided by (used for) financing activities would be

   a. $5,000.
   b. $(1,000).

   c. $(9,000).
   d. $119,000.

10. The net book value of land sold must have been

   a. $30,000.
   b. $39,000.
   c. $48,000.
   d. Cannot be determined from the data given.

11. Stoddard's Ice Cream began the year with $40,000 in accounts receivable and ended the year with $30,000 in accounts receivable. If credit sales for the year were $625,000, the cash collected from customers during the year amounted to

   a. $665,000.
   b. $615,000.

   c. $635,000.
   d. $655,000.

12. Merrimack Farms, Ltd., made sales of $760,000 and had cost of goods sold of $380,000. Inventory decreased by $15,000, and accounts payable decreased by $10,000. Operating expenses were $150,000. How much was Merrimack Farms' net income for the year?

   a. $230,000
   b. $215,000

   c. $380,000
   d. $220,000

13. Use the Merrimack Farms data from question 12. Accounts payable relates solely to the purchase of inventory. How much cash did Merrimack Farms pay for inventory during the year?

   a. $380,000
   b. $390,000

   c. $215,000
   d. $375,000

Accounting Vocabulary

cash equivalents (p. 681) Highly liquid short-term investments that can be converted into cash immediately.

cash flows (p. 680) Cash receipts and cash payments (disbursements).

direct method (p. 683) Format of the operating activities section of the statement of cash flows; lists the major categories of operating cash receipts (collections from customers and receipts of interest and dividends) and cash disbursements (payments to suppliers and employees, and for interest and income taxes).

financing activities (p. 682) Activities that obtain from investors and creditors the cash needed to launch and sustain the business; a section of the statement of cash flows.

free cash flow (p. 706) The amount of cash available from operations after paying for planned investments in plant assets.

indirect method (p. 683) Format of the operating activities section of the statement of cash flows; starts with net income and reconciles to net cash flow from operating activities.

investing activities (p. 682) Activities that increase or decrease the long-term assets available to the business; a section of the statement of cash flows.

operating activities (p. 682) Activities that create revenues, expenses, gains and losses; a section of the statement of cash flows. Operating activities affect the income statement.

statement of cash flows (p. 680) Reports cash receipts and cash payments classified according to the entity's major activities: operating, investing, and financing.

ASSESS YOUR PROGRESS

Some of the following exercises and problems are available as Excel questions in MyAccountingLab.

Ethics Check

EC12-1 Identify ethical principle violated

For each of the situations listed, identify which of three principles (integrity, objectivity and independence, or due care) from the AICPA Code of Professional Conduct is violated. Assume all persons listed in the situations are members of the AICPA. (Note: Refer to the AICPA Code of Professional Conduct contained on pages 29–30, Chapter 1 for descriptions of the principles.)

   a. Sandy is a newly hired accountant at Driver Systems. Her responsibilities include preparing all of the company's financial statements including its statement of cash flows. Driver Systems uses the direct method to prepare its statement of cash flows. Sandy has not prepared a statement of cash flows in many years and cannot remember how to prepare it using the direct method. Sandy prepares the statement of cash flows using the indirect method and hopes that no one will notice.

   b. Richard is an accountant who is close to retirement at Canvas Industries. Since he does not have much time left with the company, he has been a little careless with the preparation of the company's statement of cash flows. The ending cash balance does not match the cash balance on the balance sheet, but Richard forces it to balance with a plug figure.

   c. Erin is the accounting manager of Velo, Inc., and has approved the acquisition of expensive, new equipment without approval from her boss. She knows her boss will find out when her boss looks at the financial statements so Erin asks one of the staff accountants to hide the cash flow in another category where it will not be noticed.

   d. Julie has been the CFO of Sola Technologies for 15 years, and has never uncovered any material mistakes or fraud on its financial statements. Julie is sure this year that nothing has changed, so she signs off on the financial statements without reviewing them first because she has more urgent matters demanding her attention.

Short Exercises

S12-1. *(Learning Objective 1: Explain the purposes of the statement of cash flows)* State how the statement of cash flows helps investors and creditors perform each of the following functions:

a. Predict future cash flows

b. Evaluate management decisions

LO 1

S12-2. *(Learning Objective 1: Explain the purposes of the statement of cash flows)* Sowell Enterprises, Inc., has experienced an unbroken string of nine years of growth in net income. Nevertheless, the company is facing bankruptcy. Creditors are calling all of Sowell's loans for immediate payment, and the cash is simply not available. It is clear that the company's top managers overemphasized profits and gave too little attention to cash flows.

Write a brief memo, in your own words, to explain to the managers of Sowell Enterprises, Inc., the purposes of the statement of cash flows.

LO 1

S12-3. *(Learning Objective 2: Evaluate operating cash flows—indirect method)* Examine the statement of cash flows of Chadwell Company.

LO 2

	A	B	C
	A1		
1	**Chadwell Company** **Consolidated Statement of Cash Flows (Adapted, In Millions)** **Year Ended December 31, 2016**		
2	**Cash flows from operating activities:**		
3	Net income	$ 875	
4	Adjustment to reconcile net income to net cash		
5	used in operating activities:		
6	Depreciation and amortization	222	
7	Change in assets and liabilities, net of acquired businesses:		
8	Increase in Accounts receivable	(470)	
9	Increase in Other current assets	(160)	
10	Decrease in Accounts payable	(167)	
11	Decrease in Accrued expenses and other liabilities	(238)	
12	Increase in Unearned revenue	25	
13	Decrease in Income taxes payable	(266)	
14	Increase in Other, net	26	
15	Net cash used in operating activities		$ (153)
16	**Cash flows from investing activities:**		
17	Purchase of property and equipment	$ (1,593)	
18	Purchase of investments	(21,282)	
19	Sale of investments	19,286	
20	Acquisitions of other companies	(363)	
21	Net cash used in investing activities		$ (3,952)
22	**Cash flows from financing activities:**		
23	Proceeds from the issuance of common stock, net	$ 835	
24	Other financing activities, net	378	
25	Net cash provided by financing activities		$ 1,213
26	Impact of foreign currency translation		18
27	Net increase (decrease) in cash and cash equivalents		$ (2,874)
28	Cash and cash equivalents at beginning of year		4,155
29	Cash and cash equivalents at end of year		$ 1,281
30			

Suppose Chadwell's operating activities *provided*, rather than *used*, cash. Identify three things under the indirect method that could cause operating cash flows to be positive.

LO 2 **S12-4.** *(Learning Objective 2: Use cash flow data to evaluate performance)* The CEO and CFO from Jolson Hotels, Inc., are reviewing company performance for 2016. The income statement reports a 20% increase in net income over 2015. However, most of the increase resulted from a gain on insurance proceeds from fire damage to a building. The balance sheet shows a large increase in receivables. The cash flows statement, in summarized form, reports the following:

Net cash used for operating activities......................	$(63,500)
Net cash provided by investing activities................	42,000
Net cash provided by financing activities	29,100
Increase in cash during 2016.................................	$ 7,600

Write a memo giving Jolson Hotels' top executives your assessment of 2016 operations and your outlook for the future. Focus on the information content of the cash flows data.

LO 3 **S12-5.** *(Learning Objective 3: Report cash flows from operating activities—indirect method)* Smythe Transportation began 2016 with accounts receivable, inventory, and prepaid expenses totaling $60,000. At the end of the year, Smythe had a total of $62,000 for these current assets. At the beginning of 2016, Smythe owed current liabilities of $35,000, and at year-end current liabilities totaled $31,000.

Net income for the year was $21,000. Included in net income were a $3,000 gain on the sale of land and depreciation expense of $5,000.

Show how Smythe should report cash flows from operating activities for 2016. Smythe uses the *indirect* method.

LO 2 **S12-6.** *(Learning Objective 2: Distinguish among operating, financing, and investing activities—indirect method)* Peabody Cruiselines is preparing its statement of cash flows (*indirect* method) for the year ended March 31, 2016. Consider the following items in preparing the company's statement of cash flows. Identify each item as an operating activity—addition to net income (O+) or subtraction from net income (O−), an investing activity (I), a financing activity (F), or an activity that is not used to prepare the cash flows statement by the indirect method (N). Place the appropriate symbol in the blank space.

☐	**a.** Increase in accounts payable
☐	**b.** Decrease in accounts receivable
☐	**c.** Gain on sale of building
☐	**d.** Loss on sale of land
☐	**e.** Depreciation expense
☐	**f.** Increase in inventory
☐	**g.** Issuance of common stock
☐	**h.** Decrease in accrued liabilities
☐	**i.** Net income
☐	**j.** Decrease in prepaid expense
☐	**k.** Collection of cash from customers
☐	**l.** Purchase of equipment with cash
☐	**m.** Retained earnings
☐	**n.** Payment of dividends

S12-7. (*Learning Objective 3: Prepare operating cash flows—indirect method*) Williams Corporation accountants have assembled the following data for the year ended June 30, 2016:

LO 3

Net income.................................	$?	Cost of goods sold....................	$116,000
Payment of dividends...............	6,100	Other operating expenses.........	34,000
Proceeds from the issuance		Purchase of equipment	
of common stock	18,000	with cash.........................	42,000
Sales revenue............................	225,000	Increase in current liabilities.....	10,000
Increase in current assets		Payment of note payable	30,000
other than cash	29,000	Proceeds from sale of land........	27,000
Purchase of treasury stock........	7,000	Depreciation expense	5,000

Prepare the *operating activities section* of Williams' statement of cash flows for the year ended June 30, 2016. Williams Corporation uses the *indirect* method for operating cash flows.

S12-8. (*Learning Objective 3: Prepare a statement of cash flows—indirect method*) Use the data in SE12-7 to prepare Williams Corporation's statement of cash flows for the year ended June 30, 2016. Williams uses the *indirect* method for operating activities.

LO 3

S12-9. (*Learning Objective 3: Compute investing cash flows*) Pratt Computer Sales, Inc., reported the following financial statements for 2016:

LO 3

	A	B
	A1	
1	**Pratt Computer Sales, Inc.** **Income Statement** **Year Ended December 31, 2016**	
2	**(In thousands)**	
3	Service revenue	$ 770
4	Cost of goods sold	310
5	Salary expense	50
6	Depreciation expense	40
7	Other expenses	140
8	Total expenses	540
9	Net income	$ 230
10		

	A	B	C	D	E	F
	A1					
1	**Pratt Computer Sales, Inc.** **Comparative Balance Sheets** **December 31, 2016 and 2015**					
2	**(In thousands)**					
3	**Assets**	**2016**	**2015**	**Liabilities**	**2016**	**2015**
4	Current:			Current:		
5	Cash	$ 20	$ 17	Accounts payable	$ 53	$ 42
6	Accounts receivable	56	45	Salary payable	30	26
7	Inventory	71	87	Accrued liabilities	12	15
8	Prepaid expenses	6	5	Long-term note payable	64	53
9	Plant assets, net	226	180			
10	Long-term investments	52	71	**Stockholders' Equity**		
11				Common stock	41	30
12				Retained earnings	231	239
13	Total	$ 431	$ 405	Total	$ 431	$ 405
14						

Compute the following investing cash flows; enter all amounts in thousands.
- **a.** Acquisitions of plant assets (all were for cash). Pratt Computer Sales sold no plant assets.
- **b.** Proceeds from the sale of investments. Pratt Computer Sales purchased no investments.

LO 3 **S12-10.** *(Learning Objective 3: Compute financing cash flows)* Use the Pratt Computer Sales data in SE12-9 to compute the following; enter all amounts in thousands.
- **a.** New borrowing or payment of long-term notes payable. Pratt Computer Sales had only one long-term note payable transaction during the year.
- **b.** Issuance of common stock or retirement of common stock. Pratt Computer Sales had only one common stock transaction during the year.
- **c.** Payment of cash dividends (same as dividends declared).

LO 4 **S12-11.** *(Learning Objective 4: Compute operating cash flows—direct method)* Use the Pratt Computer Sales data in SE12-9 to compute the following; enter all amounts in thousands.
- **a.** Collections from customers
- **b.** Payments for inventory

LO 4 **S12-12.** *(Learning Objective 4: Compute operating cash flows—direct method)* Use the Pratt Computer Sales data in SE12-9 to compute the following; enter all amounts in thousands.
- **a.** Payments to employees
- **b.** Payments of other expenses

LO 4 **S12-13.** *(Learning Objective 4: Prepare a statement of cash flows—direct method)* Laughlin Horse Farms, Inc., began 2016 with cash of $190,000. During the year, Laughlin earned service revenue of $591,000 and collected $570,000 from customers. Expenses for the year totaled $425,000, with $410,000 paid in cash to suppliers and employees. Laughlin also paid $137,000 to purchase equipment and a cash dividend of $45,000 to stockholders. During 2016, Laughlin borrowed $24,000 by issuing a note payable. Prepare the company's statement of cash flows for the year ending December 31, 2016. Format operating activities by the *direct* method.

LO 4 **S12-14.** *(Learning Objective 4: Computing operating cash flows—direct method)* Mulberry Golf Club, Inc., has assembled the following data for the year ended September 30, 2016:

Cost of goods sold............................	$107,000	Payment of dividends.........................	$ 7,500
Payments to suppliers.......................	111,000	Proceeds from issuance	
Purchase of equipment with cash	43,000	of common stock	17,000
Payments to employees....................	74,000	Sales revenue.....................................	217,000
Payment of note payable	23,000	Collections from customers...............	202,000
Proceeds from sale of land...............	62,000	Payment of income tax......................	15,000
Depreciation expense	5,000	Purchase of treasury stock.................	5,500

Prepare the *operating activities* section of Mulberry Golf Club, Inc.'s, statement of cash flows for the year ended September 30, 2016. Mulberry Golf Club uses the *direct* method for operating cash flows.

LO 4 **S12-15.** *(Learning Objective 4: Preparing a statement of cash flows—direct method)* Use the data in SE12-14 to prepare Mulberry Golf Club, Inc.'s, statement of cash flows for the year ended September 30, 2016. The company uses the *direct* method for operating cash flows.

Exercises MyAccountingLab

Group A

LO 2 3 **E12-16A.** *(Learning Objectives 2, 3: Distinguish among operating, investing, and financing activities for the statement of cash flows—indirect method)* Bloomfield Investments specializes in low-risk government bonds. Identify each of Bloomfield's transactions as operating (O), investing (I), financing (F), noncash investing and financing (NIF), or a transaction that is not reported on the statement of cash flows (N). Indicate whether each item increases (+) or decreases (−) cash. The *indirect* method is used for operating activities.

☐	a. Payment of long-term debt
☐	b. Increase in salary payable
☐	c. Cash sale of land
☐	d. Sale of long-term investment
☐	e. Acquisition of building by cash payment
☐	f. Net income
☐	g. Issuance of common stock for cash
☐	h. Payment of cash dividend
☐	i. Acquisition of equipment by issuance of note payable
☐	j. Purchase of long-term investment with cash
☐	k. Issuance of long-term note payable to borrow cash
☐	l. Increase in prepaid expenses
☐	m. Decrease in accrued liabilities
☐	n. Loss of sale of equipment
☐	o. Decrease in accounts receivable
☐	p. Depreciation of equipment
☐	q. Increase in accounts payable
☐	r. Amortization of intangible assets
☐	s. Purchase of treasury stock

E12-17A. *(Learning Objectives 2, 3: Distinguish among operating, investing, and financing activities for the statement of cash flows—indirect method)* A company uses the indirect method to prepare the statement of cash flows. Indicate whether each of the following transactions affects an operating activity, an investing activity, a financing activity, or a noncash investing and financing activity:

LO 2 3

	A	B	C	D	E	F	G	H
		A1						
1	a.	Equipment	28,000		h.	Dividends Payable	25,000	
2		Cash		28,000		Cash		25,000
3	b.	Bonds Payable	70,000		i.	Treasury Stock	12,000	
4		Cash		70,000		Cash		12,000
5	c.	Cash	110,000		j.	Land	123,000	
6		Common Stock		17,000		Cash		123,000
7		Paid-in Capital in Excess of Par		93,000	k.	Cash	74,000	
8	d.	Depreciation Expense	16,000			Accounts Receivable	13,000	
9		Accumulated Depreciation		16,000		Service Revenue		87,000
10	e.	Loss on Disposal of Equipment	2,000		l.	Salary Expense	36,000	
11		Equipment, Net		2,000		Cash		36,000
12	f.	Building	235,000		m.	Furniture and Fixtures	36,000	
13		Note Payable, Long-Term		235,000		Cash		36,000
14	g.	Cash	10,000					
15		Long-Term Investment		10,000					
16								

E12-18A. *(Learning Objective 3: Compute cash flows from operating activities—indirect method)* The accounting records of Midwest Distributors, Inc., reveal the following:

LO 3

Net income...	$ 40,000	Depreciation expense	$ 17,000
Collection of dividend revenue	7,700	Decrease in current liabilities..........	23,000
Payment of interest............................	15,000	Decrease in current assets	
Sales revenue......................................	180,000	other than cash	28,000
Loss on sale of land............................	27,000	Payment of dividends	7,600
Acquisition of land with cash............	44,000	Payment of income tax...................	12,000

Requirement

1. Prepare the cash flows from operating activities by section of the statement of cash flows using the *indirect* method. Use the format of the operating activities section of Exhibit 12-6. Also evaluate the operating cash flow of Midwest Distributors. Give the reason for your evaluation.

LO 3

E12-19A. *(Learning Objective 3: Compute cash flows from operating activities—indirect method)* The accounting records of the Wisconsin Trading Post Company include these accounts:

Cash				Accounts Receivable				Inventory		
Jul 1	80,000			Jul 1	8,000			Jul 1	6,000	
Receipts	468,000	Payments	450,000	Credit sales	522,000	Collections	418,000	Purchases	433,000	Cost of Sales 333,000
Jul 31	98,000			Jul 31	112,000			Jul 31	106,000	

Equipment			Accumulated Deprec.—Equipment				Accounts Payable		
Jul 1	186,000				Jul 1	45,000		Jul 1	11,000
Acquisition	8,000				Depreciation	2,000	Payments 330,000	Purchases	433,000
Jul 31	194,000				Jul 31	47,000		Jul 31	114,000

Accrued Liabilities			Retained Earnings			
		Jul 1	14,000	Quarterly	Jul 1	64,000
Payments 33,000		Accruals	29,000	Dividend 16,000	Net Income 10,000	
		Jul 31	10,000		Jul 31	58,000

Requirement

1. Prepare the company's net cash provided by (used for) operating activities section of the statement of cash flows for the month of July. Use the *indirect* method. Do you see any potential problems in the company's cash flows from operations? How can you tell?

LO 3

E12-20A. *(Learning Objective 3: Prepare the statement of cash flows—indirect method)* The income statement and additional data of Nyman Travel Products, Inc., follow:

	A	B	C
	A1		
	Nyman Travel Products, Inc.		
	Income Statement		
1	**Year Ended December 31, 2016**		
2	Revenues:		
3	Service revenue	$ 234,000	
4	Dividend revenue	8,300	$ 242,300
5	Expenses:		
6	Cost of goods sold	103,000	
7	Salary expense	62,000	
8	Depreciation expense	33,000	
9	Advertising expense	4,300	
10	Interest expense	2,100	
11	Income tax expense	8,000	212,400
12	Net income		$ 29,900
13			

Additional data:

   a. Acquisition of plant assets was $134,000. Of this amount, $90,000 was paid in cash and $44,000 by signing a note payable.

   b. Proceeds from sale of land totaled $34,000.

   c. Proceeds from issuance of common stock totaled $60,000.

   d. Payment of long-term note payable was $14,000.

   e. Payment of dividends was $12,000.

   f. From the balance sheets:

A1				
	A		B	C
1			December 31,	
2			2016	2015
3	**Current assets:**			
4	Cash		$ 165,000	$ 68,000
5	Accounts receivable		42,000	56,000
6	Inventory		48,000	61,000
7	Prepaid expenses		9,600	8,700
8				
9	**Current liabilities:**			
10	Accounts payable		$ 38,000	$ 25,000
11	Accrued liabilities		99,000	82,000
12				

Requirements

   1. Prepare Nyman's statement of cash flows for the year ended December 31, 2016, using the *indirect* method.

   2. Evaluate Nyman's cash flows for the year. In your evaluation, mention all three categories of cash flows and give the reason for your evaluation.

E12-21A. *(Learning Objective 3: Evaluate a statement of cash flows—indirect method)*   **LO 3**
Consider three independent cases for the cash flows of Sharma Merchandising Corp. For each case, identify from the statement of cash flows how Sharma Merchandising Corp. generated the cash to acquire new plant assets. Rank the three cases from the most healthy financially to the least healthy.

A1				
	A	B	C	D
1		Case A	Case B	Case C
2	Cash flows from operating activities:			
3	Net income	$ 14,000	$ 14,000	$ 14,000
4	Depreciation and amortization	17,000	17,000	17,000
5	Increase in current assets	(3,000)	(1,000)	(7,000)
6	Decrease in current liabilities	(4,000)	(3,000)	(27,000)
7		24,000	27,000	(3,000)
8	Cash flows from investing activities:			
9	Acquisition of plant assets	(141,000)	(141,000)	(141,000)
10	Sales of plant assets	47,000	148,000	28,000
11		(94,000)	7,000	(113,000)
12	Cash flows from financing activities:			
13	Issuance of stock	104,000	26,000	149,000
14	Payment of debt	(45,000)	(38,000)	(28,000)
15		59,000	(12,000)	121,000
16	Net increase (decrease) in cash	$ (11,000)	$ 22,000	$ 5,000
17				

LO **3** **4**   **E12-22A.** *(Learning Objectives 3, 4: Compute investing and financing amounts for the statement of cash flows)* Compute the following items for the statement of cash flows:

    a. Beginning and ending Plant Assets, Net, are $120,000 and $115,000, respectively. Depreciation for the period was $13,000, and purchases of new plant assets were $15,000. Plant assets were sold at a $5,000 loss. What were the cash proceeds of the sale?

    b. Beginning and ending Retained Earnings are $44,000 and $69,000, respectively. Net income for the period was $59,000, and stock dividends were $6,000. How much were cash dividends?

LO **4**   **E12-23A.** *(Learning Objective 4: Compute cash flows from operating activities—direct method)* The accounting records of Pelham Pharmaceuticals, Inc., reveal the following:

Payment of salaries and wages	$36,000	Net income		$20,000
Depreciation expense	26,000	Payment of income tax		8,000
Decrease in current liabilities	11,000	Collection of dividend revenue		9,000
		Payment of interest		20,000
Decrease in current assets other than cash	21,000	Cash sales		45,000
		Gain on sale of land		6,000
Payment of dividends	7,000	Acquisition of land with cash		32,000
Collection of accounts receivable	90,000	Payment of accounts payable		54,000

Requirement

    1. Prepare cash flows from operating activities using the *direct* method. Also evaluate Pelham's operating cash flow. Give the reason for your evaluation.

LO **4**   **E12-24A.** *(Learning Objective 4: Identify items for the statement of cash flows—direct method)* Selected accounts of Downtown Galleries show the following:

Salary Payable

		Beginning bal	11,000
Payments	15,000	Salary expense	32,000
		Ending bal	28,000

Buildings

Beginning bal	75,000	Depreciation	17,000
Acquisitions with cash	116,000	Book value of building sold	88,000*
Ending bal	86,000		

*Sale price was $120,000.

Notes Payable

		Beginning bal	183,000
Payments	54,000	Issuance of note payable for cash	68,000
		Ending bal	197,000

Requirement

    1. For each account, identify the item or items that should appear on a statement of cash flows prepared by the *direct* method. State where to report the item.

E12-25A. *(Learning Objective 4: Prepare the statement of cash flows—direct method)* The income statement and additional data of Value World, Inc., follow:

	A	B	C
	Value World, Inc.		
	Income Statement		
1	**Year Ended June 30, 2016**		
2	**Revenues:**		
3	Sales revenue	$ 275,000	
4	Dividend revenue	8,500	$ 283,500
5	**Expenses:**		
6	Cost of goods sold	110,000	
7	Salary expense	60,000	
8	Depreciation expense	22,000	
9	Advertising expense	13,000	
10	Interest expense	2,200	
11	Income tax expense	8,000	215,200
12	Net income		$ 68,300
13			

Additional data:

    a. Collections from customers are $12,000 less than sales.

    b. Payments to suppliers are $2,300 less than the sum of cost of goods sold plus advertising expense.

    c. Payments to employees are $1,500 more than salary expense.

    d. Dividend revenue, interest expense, and income tax expense equal their cash amounts.

    e. Acquisition of plant assets is $210,000. Of this amount, $110,000 is paid in cash and $100,000 by signing a long-term note payable.

    f. Proceeds from sale of land total $29,000.

    g. Proceeds from issuance of common stock total $31,000.

    h. Payment of a long-term note payable is $17,000.

    i. Payment of dividends is $12,500.

    j. Cash balance, June 30, 2015, was $25,000.

Requirements

    1. Prepare Value World, Inc.'s, statement of cash flows and accompanying schedule of non-cash investing and financing activities. Report operating activities by the *direct* method.

    2. Evaluate Value World's cash flows for the year. In your evaluation, mention all three categories of cash flows and give the reason for your evaluation.

E12-26A. *(Learning Objective 4: Compute amounts for the statement of cash flows—direct method)* Compute the following items for the statement of cash flows:

    a. Beginning and ending Accounts Receivable are $47,000 and $53,000, respectively. Credit sales for the period total $141,000. How much are cash collections from customers?

    b. Cost of Goods Sold is $76,000. Beginning Inventory balance is $39,000, and Ending Inventory balance is $35,000. Beginning and ending Accounts Payable are $29,000 and $32,000, respectively. How much are cash payments for inventory?

Group B

E12-27B. *(Learning Objectives 2, 3: Distinguish among operating, investing, and financing activities for the statement of cash flows—indirect method)* McDowell Investments specializes in low-risk government bonds. Identify each of McDowell's transactions as operating (O), investing (I), financing (F), noncash investing and financing (NIF), or a transaction that is not reported on the statement of cash flows (N). Indicate whether each item increases (+) or decreases (−) cash. The *indirect* method is used for operating activities.

	a. Increase in salary payable
	b. Depreciation of equipment
	c. Sale of long-term investment
	d. Issuance of common stock for cash
	e. Decrease in accrued liabilities
	f. Amortization of intangible assets
	g. Acquisition of building by cash payment
	h. Payment of long-term debt
	i. Issuance of long-term note payable to borrow cash
	j. Purchase of treasury stock
	k. Net income
	l. Loss on sale of equipment
	m. Decrease in accounts receivable
	n. Acquisition of equipment by issuance of note payable
	o. Increase in accounts payable
	p. Payment of cash dividend
	q. Purchase of long-term investment with cash
	r. Cash sale of land
	s. Increase in prepaid expenses

LO 2 3

E12-28B. *(Learning Objectives 2, 3: Distinguish among operating, investing, and financing activities for the statement of cash flows—indirect method)* A company uses the indirect method to prepare the statement of cash flows. Indicate whether each of the following transactions affects an operating activity, an investing activity, a financing activity, or a noncash investing and financing activity.

A1

	A	B	C	D	E	F	G	H
1	a.	Cash	61,000		h.	Equipment	11,000	
2		Common Stock		10,000		Cash		11,000
3		Paid-in Capital in Excess of Par		51,000	i.	Furniture and Fixtures	18,000	
4	b.	Dividends Payable	13,000			Cash		18,000
5		Cash		13,000	j.	Cash	52,000	
6	c.	Cash	7,000			Accounts Receivable	11,000	
7		Long-Term Investment		7,000		Service Revenue		63,000
8	d.	Building	105,000		k.	Salary Expense	14,000	
9		Note Payable—Long-Term		105,000		Cash		14,000
10	e.	Treasury Stock	12,000		l.	Loss on Disposal of Equipment	1,000	
11		Cash		12,000		Equipment, Net		1,000
12	f.	Depreciation Expense	5,000		m.	Bonds Payable	35,000	
13		Accumulated Depreciation		5,000		Cash		35,000
14	g.	Land	15,000					
15		Cash		15,000					
16								

LO 3

E12-29B. *(Learning Objective 3: Compute cash flows from operating activities—indirect method)* The accounting records of Central Distributors, Inc., reveal the following:

Net income..	$ 13,000	Depreciation expense	$ 9,000
Collection of dividend revenue..........	7,200	Increase in current liabilities...........	22,000
Payment of interest............................	12,000	Increase in current assets	
Sales revenue	208,000	other than cash	26,000
Loss on sale of land...........................	20,000	Payment of dividends	7,300
Acquisition of land with cash............	42,000	Payment of income tax....................	5,000

Requirement

1. Prepare the cash flows from operating activities section of the statement of cash flows using the *indirect* method. Use the format of the operating activities section of Exhibit 12-6. Also evaluate the operating cash flow of Central Distributors. Give the reason for your evaluation.

E12-30B. (*Learning Objective 3: Compute cash flows from operating activities—indirect*
method) The accounting records of The Dakota Trading Post Company include these accounts:

Cash			Accounts Receivable			Inventory		
Oct 1	90,000		Oct 1	1,000		Oct 1	3,000	
Receipts	460,000	Payments 445,000	Credit sales 540,000		Collections 440,000	Purchases	438,000	Cost of Sales 336,000
Oct 31	105,000		Oct 31	101,000		Oct 31	105,000	

Equipment			Accumulated Deprec.—Equipment			Accounts Payable		
Oct 1	182,000			Oct 1	57,000		Oct 1	13,000
Acquisition 3,000				Depreciation 1,000	Payments 332,000		Purchases	438,000
Oct 31	185,000			Oct 31	58,000		Oct 31	119,000

Accrued Liabilities			Retained Earnings		
		Oct 1	19,000	Quarterly	Oct 1	64,000
Payments 30,000	Accruals	27,000	Dividend	17,000	Net Income 35,000
	Oct 31	16,000		Oct 31	82,000

Requirement

1. Prepare the company's net cash provided by (used for) operating activities section of the statement of cash flows for the month of October. Use the *indirect* method. Do you see any potential problems in the company's cash flows from operations? How can you tell?

E12-31B. (*Learning Objective 3: Prepare the statement of cash flows—indirect method*)
The income statement and additional data of Norman Travel Products, Inc., follow:

	A	B	C
	Norman Travel Products, Inc.		
	Income Statement		
1	**Year Ended December 31, 2016**		
2	Revenues:		
3	Service revenue	$ 234,000	
4	Dividend revenue	8,100	$ 242,100
5	Expenses:		
6	Cost of goods sold	94,000	
7	Salary expense	62,000	
8	Depreciation expense	26,000	
9	Advertising expense	4,300	
10	Interest expense	1,900	
11	Income tax expense	7,000	195,200
12	Net income		$ 46,900
13			

Additional data:

  a. Acquisition of plant assets was $150,000. Of this amount, $99,000 was paid in cash and $51,000 by signing a note payable.

  b. Proceeds from sale of land totaled $25,000.

  c. Proceeds from issuance of common stock totaled $47,000.

  d. Payment of a long-term note payable was $17,000.

e. Payment of dividends was $12,000.

f. From the balance sheets:

	December 31, 2016	December 31, 2015
Current assets:		
Cash	$ 90,000	$ 83,800
Accounts receivable	38,000	55,000
Inventory	104,000	91,000
Prepaid expenses	9,000	8,300
Current liabilities:		
Accounts payable	$ 34,000	$ 23,000
Accrued liabilities	18,000	43,000

Requirements

1. Prepare Norman's statement of cash flows for the year ended December 31, 2016, using the *indirect* method.
2. Evaluate Norman's cash flows for the year. In your evaluation, mention all three categories of cash flows and give the reason for your evaluation.

LO 3

E12-32B. *(Learning Objective 3: Evaluate a statement of cash flows—indirect method)* Consider three independent cases for the cash flows of Loader Company. For each case, identify from the statement of cash flows how Loader Company generated the cash to acquire new plant assets. Rank the three cases from the most healthy financially to the least healthy.

	Case A	Case B	Case C
Cash flows from operating activities:			
Net income	$ 25,000	$ 25,000	$ 25,000
Depreciation and amortization	11,000	11,000	11,000
Increase in current assets	(2,000)	(14,000)	(27,000)
Decrease in current liabilities	(5,000)	(1,000)	(12,000)
	29,000	21,000	(3,000)
Cash flows from investing activities:			
Acquisition of plant assets	(102,000)	(102,000)	(102,000)
Sales of plant assets	46,000	111,000	11,000
	(56,000)	9,000	(91,000)
Cash flows from financing activities:			
Issuance of stock	76,000	18,000	119,000
Payment of debt	(47,000)	(28,000)	(27,000)
	29,000	(10,000)	92,000
Net increase (decrease) in cash	$ 2,000	$ 20,000	$ (2,000)

LO 3 4

E12-33B. *(Learning Objectives 3, 4: Compute investing and financing amounts for the statement of cash flows)* Compute the following items for the statement of cash flows:

a. Beginning and ending Plant Assets, Net, are $120,000 and $112,000, respectively. Depreciation for the period was $16,000, and purchases of new plant assets were $26,000. Plant assets were sold at an $8,000 loss. What were the cash proceeds of the sale?

b. Beginning and ending Retained Earnings are $48,000 and $73,000, respectively. Net income for the period was $61,000, and stock dividends were $6,000. How much were cash dividends?

E12-34B. *(Learning Objective 4: Compute cash flows from operating activities—direct method)* The accounting records of Stanley Pharmaceuticals, Inc., reveal the following:

Payment of salaries		Net income..................................	$60,000
and wages........................	$ 38,000	Payment of income tax..............	24,000
Depreciation expense	26,000	Collection of dividend	
Increase in current		revenue	8,000
liabilities..........................	5,000	Payment of interest.....................	18,000
Increase in current assets		Cash sales....................................	34,000
other than cash	15,000	Loss on sale of land	6,000
Payment of dividends	4,000	Acquisition of land with cash.....	33,000
Collection of accounts		Payment of accounts	
receivable........................	125,000	payable	53,000

Requirement

1. Prepare cash flows from operating activities using the *direct* method. Also evaluate Stanley's operating cash flow. Give the reason for your evaluation.

E12-35B. *(Learning Objective 4: Identify items for the statement of cash flows—direct method)* Selected accounts of Rosemont Golf Company show the following:

Salary Payable

		Beginning bal	8,000
Payments	23,000	Salary expense	21,000
		Ending bal	6,000

Buildings

Beginning bal	60,000	Depreciation	15,000
Acquisitions with cash	90,000	Book value of building sold	89,000*
Ending bal	46,000		

*Sale price was $112,000.

Notes Payable

		Beginning bal	176,000
Payments	50,000	Issuance of note payable for cash	56,000
		Ending bal	182,000

Requirement

1. For each account, identify the item or items that should appear on a statement of cash flows prepared by the *direct* method. State where to report the item.

LO 4   E12-36B. (*Learning Objective 4: Prepare the statement of cash flows—direct method*) The income statement and additional data of One Stop, Inc., follow:

A1			
	A	**B**	**C**
1	**One Stop, Inc.** **Income Statement** **Year Ended June 30, 2016**		
2	**Revenues:**		
3	Sales revenue	$ 265,000	
4	Dividend revenue	11,000	$ 276,000
5	**Expenses:**		
6	Cost of goods sold	109,000	
7	Salary expense	52,000	
8	Depreciation expense	32,000	
9	Advertising expense	7,000	
10	Interest expense	2,500	
11	Income tax expense	11,500	214,000
12	Net income		$ 62,000
13			

Additional data:

a. Collections from customers are $15,000 more than sales.
b. Payments to suppliers are $2,300 more than the sum of cost of goods sold plus advertising expense.
c. Payments to employees are $2,300 less than salary expense.
d. Dividend revenue, interest expense, and income tax expense equal their cash amounts.
e. Acquisition of plant assets is $161,000. Of this amount, $133,000 is paid in cash and $28,000 by signing a long-term note payable.
f. Proceeds from sale of land total $25,000.
g. Proceeds from issuance of common stock total $93,000.
h. Payment of a long-term note payable is $29,000.
i. Payment of dividends is $10,000.
j. Cash balance, June 30, 2015, was $42,000.

Requirements

1. Prepare One Stop, Inc.'s, statement of cash flows and accompanying schedule of noncash investing and financing activities. Report operating activities by the *direct* method.
2. Evaluate One Stop's cash flows for the year. In your evaluation, mention all three categories of cash flows and give the reason for your evaluation.

LO 4   E12-37B. (*Learning Objective 4: Compute amounts for the statement of cash flows—direct method*) Compute the following items for the statement of cash flows:

a. Beginning and ending Accounts Receivable are $42,000 and $35,000, respectively. Credit sales for the period total $139,000. How much are cash collections from customers?
b. Cost of Goods Sold is $67,000. Beginning Inventory was $56,000, and Ending Inventory balance is $59,000. Beginning and ending Accounts Payable are $24,000 and $26,000, respectively. How much are cash payments for inventory?

Quiz

Test your understanding of the statement of cash flows by answering the following questions. Select the best choice from among the possible answers given.

Q12-38. Paying off bonds payable is reported on the statement of cash flows under
  a. investing activities.
  b. noncash investing and financing activities.
  c. financing activities.
  d. operating activities.

Q12-39. The sale of inventory for cash is reported on the statement of cash flows under
  a. noncash investing and financing activities.
  b. operating activities.
  c. investing activities.
  d. financing activities.

Q12-40. Selling equipment for cash is reported on the statement of cash flows under
  a. operating activities.
  b. noncash investing and financing activities.
  c. investing activities.
  d. financing activities.

Q12-41. Which of the following terms appears on a statement of cash flows—indirect method?
  a. Depreciation expense   **c.** Cash receipt of interest revenue
  b. Collections from customers   **d.** Payments to suppliers

Q12-42. On an indirect method statement of cash flows, an increase in a prepaid insurance would be
  a. added to increases in current assets.   **c.** deducted from net income.
  b. added to net income.   **d.** included in payments to suppliers.

Q12-43. On an indirect method statement of cash flows, an increase in accounts payable would be
  a. reported in the financing activities section.
  b. added to net income in the operating activities section.
  c. deducted from net income in the operating activities section.
  d. reported in the investing activities section.

Q12-44. On an indirect method statement of cash flows, a gain on the sale of plant assets would be
  a. reported in the investing activities section.
  b. deducted from net income in the operating activities section.
  c. ignored, since the gain did not generate any cash.
  d. added to net income in the operating activities section.

Q12-45. A company uses the direct method to prepare the statement of cash flows. Select an activity for each of the following transactions:
  1. Receiving cash dividends is a/an _____ activity.
  2. Paying cash dividends is a/an _____ activity.

Q12-46. Innovations Camera Co. sold equipment with a cost of $18,000 and accumulated depreciation of $6,000 for an amount that resulted in a gain of $4,000. What amount should Innovations report on the statement of cash flows as "proceeds from sale of plant assets"?
  a. $14,000   **c.** $15,000
  b. $16,000   **d.** Some other amount

Questions 47–57 use the following data. Sheehan Corporation formats operating cash flows by the *indirect* method in questions 47–55. Sheehan uses the direct method in questions 56–57.

	A	B	C
	A1 ⬍		
1	**Sheehan's Income Statement for 2016**		
2	Sales revenue	$ 175,000	
3	Gain on sale of equipment	6,000*	$ 181,000
4	Cost of goods sold	108,000	
5	Depreciation	6,500	
6	Other operating expenses	26,000	140,500
7	Net income		$ 40,500
8			

*The book value of equipment sold during 2016 was $20,000.

	A	B	C	D	E	F
	A1 ⬍					
1	**Sheehan's Comparative Balance Sheets December 31, 2016 and 2015**					
2		**2016**	**2015**		**2016**	**2015**
3	Cash	$ 5,500	$ 1,500	Accounts payable	$ 4,000	$ 5,000
4	Accounts receivable	7,000	18,000	Accrued liabilities	8,000	3,000
5	Inventory	12,000	11,000	Common stock	24,000	12,000
6	Plant and equipment, net	91,000	67,000	Retained earnings	79,500	77,500
7		$ 115,500	$ 97,500		$ 115,500	$ 97,500
8						

Q12-47. How many items enter the computation of Sheehan's net cash provided by operating activities?

    a. 2   **c.** 5

    b. 7   **d.** 3

Q12-48. How do Sheehan's accrued liabilities affect the company's statement of cash flows for 2016?

    a. Increase in cash used by financing activities

    b. They don't because the accrued liabilities are not yet paid

    c. Increase in cash used by investing activities

    d. Increase in cash provided by operating activities

Q12-49. How do accounts receivable affect Sheehan's cash flows from operating activities for 2016?

    a. Increase in cash provided by operating activities

    b. Decrease in cash provided by operating activities

    c. They don't because accounts receivable result from investing activities

    d. Decrease in cash used by investing activities

Q12-50. Sheehan's net cash provided by operating activities during 2016 was

    a. $55,000.   **c.** $61,000.

    b. $58,000.   **d.** $52,000.

Q12-51. How many items enter the computation of Sheehan's net cash flow from investing activities for 2016?

    a. 5   **c.** 7

    b. 3   **d.** 2

Q12-52. The book value of equipment sold during 2016 was $20,000. Sheehan's net cash flow from investing activities for 2016 was

    a. net cash used of $52,000.

    b. net cash used of $58,000.

    c. net cash used of $24,500.

    d. net cash used of $61,000.

Q12-53. How many items enter the computation of Sheehan's net cash flow from financing activities for 2016?

    a. 2

    b. 7

    c. 3

    d. 5

Q12-54. Sheehan's largest financing cash flow for 2016 resulted from (assume no stock dividends were distributed)

    a. issuance of common stock.

    b. payment of dividends.

    c. purchase of equipment.

    d. sale of equipment.

Q12-55. Sheehan's net cash flow from financing activities for 2016 was (assume no stock dividends were distributed)

    a. net cash used of $37,500.

    b. net cash used of $26,500.

    c. net cash provided of $12,000.

    d. net cash used of $56,000.

Q12-56. Assume Sheehan uses the direct method to prepare the statement of cash flows. Credit sales totaled $850,000, accounts receivable increased by $60,000, and accounts payable decreased by $20,000. How much cash did the company collect from customers?

    a. $850,000

    b. $910,000

    c. $790,000

    d. $810,000

Q12-57. Assume Sheehan uses the direct method to prepare the statement of cash flows. Income tax payable was $4,000 at the end of the year and $3,000 at the beginning. Income tax expense for the year totaled $59,700. What amount of cash did the company pay for income tax during the year?

    a. $58,700

    b. $62,700

    c. $60,700

    d. $59,700

Problems MyAccountingLab

Group A

P12-58A. (*Learning Objectives 2, 3: Prepare an income statement, balance sheet, and statement of cash flows—indirect method*) Klaben Motors, Inc., was formed on January 1, 2016. The following transactions occurred during 2016:

    On January 1, 2016, Klaben issued its common stock for $510,000. Early in January, Klaben made the following cash payments:

    a. $220,000 for equipment

    b. $243,000 for inventory (nine cars at $27,000 each)

    c. $25,000 for 2016 rent on a store building

    In February, Klaben purchased three cars for inventory on account. Cost of this inventory was $117,000 ($39,000 each). Before year-end, Klaben paid $70,200 of this debt. The company uses the first-in, first-out (FIFO) method to account for inventory.

    During 2016, Klaben sold 11 autos for a total of $649,000. Before year-end, it had collected 80% of this amount.

    The business employs two people. The combined annual payroll is $151,000, of which Klaben owes $1,000 at year-end. At the end of the year, Klaben paid income tax of $22,000.

    Late in 2016, Klaben declared and paid cash dividends of $11,000.

    For equipment, Klaben uses the straight-line depreciation method, over five years, with zero residual value.

LO **2** **3**

Requirements

1. Prepare Klaben Motors, Inc.'s, income statement for the year ended December 31, 2016. Use the single-step format, with all revenues listed together and all expenses together.
2. Prepare Klaben's balance sheet at December 31, 2016.
3. Prepare Klaben's statement of cash flows for the year ended December 31, 2016. Format cash flows from operating activities by using the *indirect* method.

LO 2 4   **P12-59A.** *(Learning Objectives 2, 4: Prepare an income statement, balance sheet, and statement of cash flows—direct method)* Use the Klaben Motors, Inc., data from P12-58A.

Requirements

1. Prepare Klaben's income statement for the year ended December 31, 2016. Use the single-step format, with all revenues listed together and all expenses together.
2. Prepare Klaben's balance sheet at December 31, 2016.
3. Prepare Klaben's statement of cash flows for the year ended December 31, 2016. Format cash flows from operating activities by using the *direct* method.

LO 2 3   **P12-60A.** *(Learning Objectives 2, 3: Prepare the statement of cash flows—indirect method)* Carlson Software Corp. has assembled the following data for the years ending December 31, 2016 and 2015.

A1	⬍		
	A	B	C
1		December 31,	
2		2016	2015
3	**Current Accounts:**		
4	Current assets:		
5	Cash and cash equivalents	$ 105,800	$ 20,000
6	Accounts receivable	18,000	64,100
7	Inventories	8,600	86,000
8	Prepaid expenses	2,900	1,600
9	Current liabilities:		
10	Accounts payable	$ 9,300	$ 55,400
11	Income tax payable	28,600	16,600
12	Accrued liabilities	15,000	27,400
13			

Transaction Data for 2016:

Acquisition of land by issuing long-term note payable	$202,000	Purchase of treasury stock	$14,100
		Loss on sale of equipment	32,000
Stock dividends	34,900	Payment of cash dividends	46,000
Collection of loan..................	12,400	Issuance of long-term note	
Depreciation expense	19,000	payable to borrow cash.....	52,200
Purchase of building		Net income.........................	58,000
with cash...........................	159,000	Issuance of common stock	
Retirement of bonds payable		for cash	83,100
by issuing common stock	80,000	Proceeds from sale of	
Purchase of long-term		equipment	12,300
investment with cash.........	45,300	Amortization expense..........	5,500

Requirement

1. Prepare Carlson Software Corp.'s statement of cash flows using the *indirect* method to report operating activities. Include an accompanying schedule of noncash investing and financing activities.

P12-61A. *(Learning Objectives 2, 3: Prepare the statement of cash flows—indirect method)* LO  2 3
The comparative balance sheets of Canton Movie Theater Company at June 30, 2016, and 2015, reported the following:

A	B	C
A1		
A	**B**	**C**
1		June 30,	
2		2016	2015
3	**Current assets:**		
4	Cash and cash equivalents	$ 45,400	$ 14,500
5	Accounts receivable	14,500	22,200
6	Inventories	63,800	61,200
7	Prepaid expenses	3,100	2,200
8	**Current liabilities:**		
9	Accounts payable	$ 57,300	$ 55,600
10	Accrued liabilities	32,700	46,700
11	Income tax payable	9,800	10,900
12			

Canton Movie Theater's transactions during the year ended June 30, 2016, included:

Acquisition of land		Proceeds from sale of long-	
by issuing note payable	$104,000	term investment	$15,500
Amortization expense............	5,000	Depreciation expense	15,200
Payment of cash dividend......	28,000	Cash purchase of building.....	44,000
Cash purchase of		Net income............................	54,000
equipment	34,600	Issuance of common	
Issuance of long-term note		stock for cash	10,000
payable to borrow cash.....	47,000	Stock dividend.......................	12,000

Requirements

1. Prepare Canton Movie Theater Company's statement of cash flows for the year ended June 30, 2016, using the *indirect* method to report cash flows from operating activities. Report noncash investing and financing activities in an accompanying schedule.
2. Evaluate Canton Movie Theater's cash flows for the year. Mention all three categories of cash flows, and give the reason for your evaluation.

LO **2** **3**

P12-62A. *(Learning Objectives 2, 3: Prepare the statement of cash flows—indirect method)* The 2016 and 2015 comparative balance sheets and 2016 income statement of King Supply Corp. follow:

	A	B	C	D
	A1			
1	**King Supply Corp.** **Comparative Balance Sheets**			
2		**December 31,**		**Increase**
3		**2016**	**2015**	**(Decrease)**
4	Current assets:			
5	Cash and cash equivalents	$ 17,300	$ 4,000	$ 13,300
6	Accounts receivable	56,000	55,000	1,000
7	Inventories	66,600	52,200	14,400
8	Prepaid expenses	1,800	3,900	(2,100)
9	Plant assets:			
10	Land	63,600	20,000	43,600
11	Equipment, net	53,100	49,900	3,200
12	Total assets	$ 258,400	$ 185,000	$ 73,400
13	Current liabilities:			
14	Accounts payable	$ 35,400	$ 26,900	$ 8,500
15	Salary payable	24,000	16,000	8,000
16	Other accrued liabilities	22,100	24,200	(2,100)
17	Long-term liabilities:			
18	Notes payable	49,000	25,000	24,000
19	Stockholders' equity:			
20	Common stock, no-par	88,100	65,900	22,200
21	Retained earnings	39,800	27,000	12,800
22	Total liabilities and stockholders' equity	$ 258,400	$ 185,000	$ 73,400
23				

	A	B	C
	A1		
1	**King Supply Corp.** **Income Statement** **Year Ended December 31, 2016**		
2	Revenues:		
3	Sales revenue		$ 442,000
4	Expenses:		
5	Cost of goods sold	$ 186,500	
6	Salary expense	76,000	
7	Depreciation expense	15,000	
8	Other operating expense	50,300	
9	Interest expense	24,200	
10	Income tax expense	29,000	
11	Total expenses		381,000
12	Net income		$ 61,000
13			

King Supply had no noncash investing and financing transactions during 2016. During the year, there were no sales of land or equipment, no payment of notes payable, no retirements of stock, and no treasury stock transactions.

Requirements

1. Prepare the 2016 statement of cash flows, formatting operating activities by using the *indirect* method.
2. How will what you learned in this problem help you evaluate an investment?

P12-63A. *(Learning Objectives 2, 4: Prepare the statement of cash flows—direct method)*
Use the King Supply Corp. data from P12-62A.

Requirements

1. Prepare the 2016 statement of cash flows by using the *direct* method.
2. How will what you learned in this problem help you evaluate an investment?

P12-64A. *(Learning Objectives 2, 4: Prepare the statement of cash flows—direct method)*
Crutchfield Furniture Gallery, Inc., provided the following data from the company's records for the year ended October 31, 2017:

  a. Credit sales, $584,200
  b. Loan to another company, $12,800
  c. Cash payments to purchase plant assets, $44,400
  d. Cost of goods sold, $403,000
  e. Proceeds from issuance of common stock, $7,000
  f. Payment of cash dividends, $48,700
  g. Collection of interest, $4,500
  h. Acquisition of equipment by issuing short-term note payable, $16,300
  i. Payments of salaries, $93,700
  j. Proceeds from sale of plant assets, $22,300, including $6,700 loss
  k. Collections on accounts receivable, $406,000
  l. Interest revenue, $3,000
  m. Cash receipt of dividend revenue, $4,700
  n. Payments to suppliers, $368,000
  o. Cash sales, $182,700
  p. Depreciation expense, $49,600
  q. Proceeds from issuance of note payable, $20,200
  r. Payments of long-term notes payable, $71,000
  s. Interest expense and payments, $13,400
  t. Salary expense, $91,900
  u. Loan collections, $11,200
  v. Proceeds from sale of investments, $9,500, including $3,100 gain
  w. Payment of short-term note payable by issuing long-term note payable, $41,000
  x. Amortization expenses, $4,800
  y. Income tax expense and payments, $38,300
  z. Cash balance: October 31, 2016, $40,200; October 31, 2017, $18,000

Requirements

1. Prepare Crutchfield Furniture Gallery, Inc.'s, statement of cash flows for the year ended October 31, 2017. Use the *direct* method for cash flows from operating activities. Include an accompanying schedule of noncash investing and financing activities.
2. Evaluate 2017 from a cash flows standpoint. Give your reasons.

 **P12-65A.** *(Learning Objectives 2, 3, 4: Prepare the statement of cash flows—direct and indirect methods)* To prepare the statement of cash flows, accountants for Percy Electric Company have summarized 2016 activity in two accounts:

Cash

Beginning bal	71,500	Payments on accounts payable	446,000
Sale of long-term investment	21,300	Payments of dividends	27,900
Collections from customers	661,500	Payments of salaries and wages	139,200
Issuance of common stock	47,600	Payments of interest	25,500
Receipts of dividends	16,900	Purchase of equipment	31,700
		Payments of other operating expenses	34,100
		Payment of long-term note payable	41,100
		Purchase of treasury stock	25,700
		Payment of income tax	19,100
Ending Bal	28,500		

Common Stock

Beginning bal	84,100
Issuance for cash	47,600
Issuance to acquire land	80,300
Issuance to retire note payable	20,000
Ending bal	232,000

Percy Electric's 2016 income statement and balance sheet data follow:

	A	B	C
A1			
1	**Percy Electric Company** **Income Statement** **Year Ended December 31, 2016**		
2	Revenues:		
3	Sales revenue		$ 689,200
4	Dividend revenue		16,900
5	Total revenue		706,100
6	Expenses and losses:		
7	Cost of goods sold	$ 447,200	
8	Salary and wage expense	131,400	
9	Depreciation expense	19,900	
10	Other operating expense	49,400	
11	Interest expense	27,800	
12	Income tax expense	17,100	
13	Loss on sale of investments	1,100	
14	Total expenses and losses		693,900
15	Net income		$ 12,200
16			

A1 ‡	
A	**B**
Percy Electric Company **Selected Balance Sheet Data** **December 31, 2016**	
	Increase (Decrease)
3 Current assets:	
4 Cash and cash equivalents	$ (43,000)
5 Accounts receivable	27,700
6 Inventories	(9,000)
7 Prepaid expenses	(5,000)
8 Land	80,300
9 Equipment, net	11,800
10 Long-term investments	(22,400)
11 Current liabilities:	
12 Accounts payable	(7,800)
13 Interest payable	2,300
14 Salary payable	(7,800)
15 Other accrued liabilities	10,300
16 Income tax payable	(2,000)
17 Long-term note payable	(61,100)
18 Common stock	147,900
19 Retained earnings	(15,700)
20 Treasury stock	25,700
21	

Requirements

1. Prepare the statement of cash flows of Percy Electric Company for the year ended December 31, 2016, using the *direct* method to report operating activities. Also prepare the accompanying schedule of noncash investing and financing activities.
2. Use Percy Electric's 2016 income statement and information from its selected balance sheet data to prepare a supplementary schedule of cash flows from operating activities by using the *indirect* method.

P12-66A. *(Learning Objectives 2, 3, 4: Prepare the statement of cash flows—indirect and direct methods)* The comparative balance sheets of Donna Dunn Design Studio, Inc., at June 30, 2016, and 2015, and transaction data for fiscal 2016, are as follows:

	A1				
	A		**B**	**C**	**D**
1	**Donna Dunn Design Studio, Inc.** **Comparative Balance Sheets**				
2				June 30,	Increase
3				2016	2015	(Decrease)
4	Current assets:				
5	Cash		$ 28,400	$ 8,100	$ 20,300
6	Accounts receivable		48,600	22,100	26,500
7	Inventories		98,200	62,900	35,300
8	Prepaid expenses		1,300	2,600	(1,300)
9	Land		36,900	102,300	(65,400)
10	Equipment, net		74,400	73,500	900
11	Long-term investment		19,200	5,800	13,400
12			$ 307,000	$ 277,300	$ 29,700
13	Current liabilities:				
14	Notes payable, short-term		$ 13,100	$ 18,700	$ (5,600)
15	Accounts payable		29,500	40,500	(11,000)
16	Income tax payable		13,600	14,600	(1,000)
17	Accrued liabilities		18,200	9,600	8,600
18	Interest payable		3,600	2,800	800
19	Salary payable		4,700	4,400	300
20	Long-term note payable		47,300	94,400	(47,100)
21	Common stock		68,900	47,300	21,600
22	Retained earnings		108,100	45,000	63,100
23			$ 307,000	$ 277,300	$ 29,700
24					

Transaction data for the year ended June 30, 2016, follows:

    a. Net income, $70,600
    b. Depreciation expense on equipment, $13,500
    c. Purchased long-term investment with cash, $13,400
    d. Sold land for $58,200, including $7,200 loss
    e. Acquired equipment by issuing long-term note payable, $14,400
    f. Paid long-term note payable, $61,500
    g. Received cash for issuance of common stock, $16,000
    h. Paid cash dividends, $7,500
    i. Paid short-term note payable by issuing common stock, $5,600

Requirements

1. Prepare the statement of cash flows of Donna Dunn Design Studio, Inc., for the year ended June 30, 2016, using the *indirect* method to report operating activities. Also prepare the accompanying schedule of noncash investing and financing activities. All current accounts except Notes Payable, short-term, result from operating transactions.
2. Prepare a supplementary schedule showing cash flows from operations by the *direct* method. The accounting records provide the following: collections from customers, $239,000; interest received, $1,500; payments to suppliers, $146,900; payments to employees, $48,100; payments for income tax, $12,000; and payment of interest, $5,000.

Group B

P12-67B. *(Learning Objectives 2, 3: Prepare an income statement, balance sheet, and statement of cash flows—indirect method)* Pruitt Motors, Inc., was formed on January 1, 2016. The following transactions occurred during 2016:

LO 2 3

On January 1, 2016, Pruitt issued its common stock for $440,000. Early in January, Pruitt made the following cash payments:

a. $180,000 for equipment
b. $203,000 for inventory (seven cars at $29,000 each)
c. $17,000 for 2016 rent on a store building

In February, Pruitt purchased two cars for inventory on account. Cost of this inventory was $80,000 ($40,000 each). Before year-end, Pruitt paid $24,000 of this debt. The company uses the first-in, first-out (FIFO) method to account for inventory.

During 2016, Pruitt sold eight autos for a total of $488,000. Before year-end, it had collected 80% of this amount.

The business employs five people. The combined annual payroll is $125,000, of which Pruitt owes $3,000 at year-end. At the end of the year, Pruitt paid income tax of $12,600.

Late in 2016, Pruitt declared and paid cash dividends of $19,000.

For equipment, Pruitt uses the straight-line depreciation method, over five years, with zero residual value.

Requirements

1. Prepare Pruitt Motors, Inc.'s, income statement for the year ended December 31, 2016. Use the single-step format, with all revenues listed together and all expenses together.
2. Prepare Pruitt's balance sheet at December 31, 2016.
3. Prepare Pruitt's statement of cash flows for the year ended December 31, 2016. Format cash flows from operating activities by using the *indirect* method.

P12-68B. *(Learning Objectives 2, 4: Prepare an income statement, balance sheet, and statement of cash flows—direct method)* Use the Pruitt Motors, Inc., data from P12-67B.

LO 2 4

Requirements

1. Prepare Pruitt's income statement for the year ended December 31, 2016. Use the single-step format, with all revenues listed together and all expenses together.
2. Prepare Pruitt's balance sheet at December 31, 2016.
3. Prepare Pruitt's statement of cash flows for the year ended December 31, 2016. Format cash flows from operating activities by using the *direct* method.

P12-69B. *(Learning Objectives 2, 3: Prepare the statement of cash flows—indirect method)* Johnson Software Corp. has assembled the following data for the years ending December 31, 2016 and 2015:

LO 2 3

A1		
	A	B	C
1		December 31,	
2		2016	2015
3	**Current Accounts:**		
4	Current assets:		
5	Cash and cash equivalents	$ 67,000	$ 30,000
6	Accounts receivable	21,000	64,100
7	Inventories	8,800	81,000
8	Prepaid expenses	3,100	1,700
9	Current liabilities:		
10	Accounts payable	$ 9,100	$ 55,600
11	Income tax payable	18,700	16,600
12	Accrued liabilities	15,500	27,400
13			

Transaction Data for 2016:

Acquisition of land by issuing long-term note payable	$197,000	Purchase of treasury stock	$10,700
		Gain on sale of equipment.....	3,500
Stock dividends	40,100	Payment of cash dividends	18,100
Collection of loan..................	10,100	Issuance of long-term note	
Depreciation expense	21,000	payable to borrow cash.....	34,700
Purchase of building		Net income..........................	5,700
with cash...........................	109,000	Issuance of common stock	
Retirement of bonds payable		for cash	37,000
by issuing common stock	64,000	Proceeds from sale of	
Purchase of long-term		equipment	53,000
investment with cash.........	45,200	Amortization expense..........	4,400

Requirement

1. Prepare Johnson Software Corp.'s statement of cash flows using the *indirect* method to report operating activities. Include an accompanying schedule of noncash investing and financing activities.

 **P12-70B.** *(Learning Objectives 2, 3: Prepare the statement of cash flows—indirect method)* The comparative balance sheets of Barberton Movie Theater Company at September 30, 2016 and 2015, reported the following:

	A	B	C
	A1		
	A	September 30,	
1		2016	2015
2			
3	**Current assets:**		
4	Cash and cash equivalents	$ 33,800	$ 16,000
5	Accounts receivable	14,500	21,600
6	Inventories	63,900	60,400
7	Prepaid expenses	17,200	1,500
8	**Current liabilities:**		
9	Accounts payable	$ 58,000	$ 56,000
10	Accrued liabilities	47,200	37,200
11	Income tax payable	3,300	10,300
12			

Barberton's transactions during the year ended September 30, 2016, included the following:

Acquisition of land by issuing note payable	$109,000	Proceeds from sale of long-term investment	$ 16,300
Amortization expense............	6,000	Depreciation expense	15,700
Payment of cash dividend......	28,000	Cash purchase of building.....	44,000
Cash purchase of equipment	59,100	Net income..........................	58,000
Issuance of long-term note payable to borrow cash.....	45,000	Issuance of common stock for cash....................	15,000
		Stock dividend.......................	17,000

Requirements

1. Prepare Barberton Movie Theater Company's statement of cash flows for the year ended September 30, 2016, using the *indirect* method to report cash flows from operating activities. Report noncash investing and financing activities in an accompanying schedule.
2. Evaluate Barberton's cash flows for the year. Mention all three categories of cash flows, and give the reason for your evaluation.

P12-71B. *(Learning Objectives 2, 3: Prepare the statement of cash flows—indirect method)*  The 2016 and 2015 comparative balance sheets and 2016 income statement of Lombardi Supply Corp. follow:

A1				
	A	**B**	**C**	**D**
1	**Lombardi Supply Corp.** **Comparative Balance Sheets**			
2		**December 31,**		**Increase**
3		**2016**	**2015**	**(Decrease)**
4	Current assets:			
5	Cash and cash equivalents	$ 17,900	$ 14,000	$ 3,900
6	Accounts receivable	56,700	60,000	(3,300)
7	Inventories	37,700	52,200	(14,500)
8	Prepaid expenses	1,700	3,900	(2,200)
9	Plant assets:			
10	Land	69,100	22,100	47,000
11	Equipment, net	62,100	49,300	12,800
12	Total assets	$ 245,200	$ 201,500	$ 43,700
13	Current liabilities:			
14	Accounts payable	$ 35,500	$ 31,300	$ 4,200
15	Salary payable	30,000	21,100	8,900
16	Other accrued liabilities	22,800	24,100	(1,300)
17	Long-term liabilities:			
18	Notes payable	52,000	38,000	14,000
19	Stockholders' equity:			
20	Common stock, no-par	88,200	64,000	24,200
21	Retained earnings	16,700	23,000	(6,300)
22	Total liabilities and stockholders' equity	$ 245,200	$ 201,500	$ 43,700
23				

A1			
	A	**B**	**C**
1	**Lombardi Supply Corp.** **Income Statement** **Year Ended December 31, 2016**		
2	Revenues:		
3	Sales revenue		$ 438,000
4	Expenses:		
5	Cost of goods sold	$ 185,100	
6	Salary expense	76,900	
7	Depreciation expense	16,100	
8	Other operating expense	50,100	
9	Interest expense	24,600	
10	Income tax expense	29,300	
11	Total expenses		382,100
12	Net income		$ 55,900
13			

Lombardi Supply had no noncash investing and financing transactions during 2016. During the year, there were no sales of land or equipment, no payment of notes payable, no retirements of stock, and no treasury stock transactions.

Requirements

1. Prepare the 2016 statement of cash flows, formatting operating activities by using the *indirect* method.
2. How will what you learned in this problem help you evaluate an investment?

LO 2 4 **P12-72B.** *(Learning Objectives 2, 4: Prepare the statement of cash flows—direct method)*
Use the Lombardi Supply Corp. data from P12-71B.

Requirements

1. Prepare the 2016 statement of cash flows by using the *direct* method.
2. How will what you learned in this problem help you evaluate an investment?

LO 2 4 **P12-73B.** *(Learning Objectives 2, 4: Prepare the statement of cash flows—direct method)*
Driscoll Furniture Gallery, Inc., provided the following data from the company's records for the
year ended December 31, 2016:

   a. Credit sales, $600,000
   b. Loan to another company, $9,900
   c. Cash payments to purchase plant assets, $59,200
   d. Cost of goods sold, $282,900
   e. Proceeds from issuance of common stock, $20,000
   f. Payment of cash dividends, $48,600
   g. Collection of interest, $4,300
   h. Acquisition of equipment by issuing short-term note payable, $16,400
   i. Payments of salaries, $88,800
   j. Proceeds from sale of plant assets, $22,500, including $6,900 loss
   k. Collections on accounts receivable, $395,000
   l. Interest revenue, $3,700
   m. Cash receipt of dividend revenue, $8,900
   n. Payments to suppliers, $368,200
   o. Cash sales, $191,300
   p. Depreciation expense, $49,900
   q. Proceeds from issuance of note payable, $20,000
   r. Payments of long-term notes payable, $57,000
   s. Interest expense and payments, $13,800
   t. Salary expense, $86,800
   u. Loan collections, $8,500
   v. Proceeds from sale of investments, $11,200, including $3,700 gain
   w. Payment of short-term note payable by issuing long-term note payable, $59,000
   x. Amortization expenses, $1,400
   y. Income tax expense and payments, $38,000
   z. Cash balance: December 31, 2015, $19,100; December 31, 2016, $17,300

Requirements

1. Prepare Driscoll Furniture Gallery, Inc.'s, statement of cash flows for the year ended
   December 31, 2016. Use the *direct* method for cash flows from operating activities.
   Include an accompanying schedule of noncash investing and financing activities.
2. Evaluate 2016 from a cash flows standpoint. Give your reasons.

P12-74B. *(Learning Objectives 2, 3, 4: Prepare the statement of cash flows—direct and indirect methods)* To prepare the statement of cash flows, accountants for Franklin Electric Company have summarized 2016 activity in two accounts:

Cash

Beginning bal	9,100	Payments on accounts payable	387,000
Sale of long-term investment	21,000	Payments of dividends	27,800
Collections from customers	661,800	Payments of salaries and wages	132,800
Issuance of common stock	47,100	Payments of interest	26,800
Receipts of dividends	16,600	Purchase of equipment	31,600
		Payments of other operating expenses	34,300
		Payment of long-term note payable	41,700
		Purchase of treasury stock	19,000
		Payment of income tax	19,300
Ending Bal	35,300		

Common Stock

Beginning bal	54,000
Issuance for cash	47,100
Issuance to acquire land	51,000
Issuance to retire note payable	24,000
Ending bal	176,100

Franklin Electric's 2016 income statement and balance sheet data follow:

	A	B	C
	Franklin Electric Company		
	Income Statement		
1	**Year Ended December 31, 2016**		
2	Revenues:		
3	Sales revenue		$ 691,800
4	Dividend revenue		16,600
5	Total revenue		708,400
6	Expenses and losses:		
7	Cost of goods sold	$ 398,700	
8	Salary and wage expense	125,000	
9	Depreciation expense	41,700	
10	Other operating expense	23,800	
11	Interest expense	24,400	
12	Income tax expense	16,100	
13	Loss on sale of investments	1,400	
14	Total expenses and losses		631,100
15	Net income		$ 77,300
16			

	A	B
A1		
	Franklin Electric Company **Selected Balance Sheet Data** **December 31, 2016**	
1		
2		**Increase** **(Decrease)**
3	Current assets:	
4	Cash and cash equivalents	$ 26,200
5	Accounts receivable	30,000
6	Inventories	(12,900)
7	Prepaid expenses	(300)
8	Land	51,000
9	Equipment, net	(10,100)
10	Long-term investments	(22,400)
11	Current liabilities:	
12	Accounts payable	(1,200)
13	Interest payable	(2,400)
14	Salary payable	(7,800)
15	Other accrued liabilities	(10,800)
16	Income tax payable	(3,200)
17	Long-term note payable	(65,700)
18	Common stock	122,100
19	Retained earnings	49,500
20	Treasury stock	19,000
21		

Requirements

1. Prepare the statement of cash flows of Franklin Electric Company for the year ended December 31, 2016, using the *direct* method to report operating activities. Also prepare the accompanying schedule of noncash investing and financing activities.
2. Use Franklin Electric's 2016 income statement and information from its selected balance sheet data to prepare a supplementary schedule of cash flows from operating activities by using the *indirect* method.

P12-75B. *(Learning Objectives 2, 3, 4: Prepare the statement of cash flows—indirect and direct methods)* The comparative balance sheets of Sally Fagan Design Studio, Inc., at June 30, 2016, and 2015, and transaction data for fiscal 2016, are as follows:

A1 ◆			
	A	**B**	**C**	**D**
1	**Sally Fagan Design Studio, Inc.** **Comparative Balance Sheets**			
2		**June 30,**		**Increase**
3		**2016**	**2015**	**(Decrease)**
4	Current assets:			
5	Cash	$ 28,400	$ 10,800	$ 17,600
6	Accounts receivable	48,800	31,500	17,300
7	Inventories	68,500	62,900	5,600
8	Prepaid expenses	400	2,400	(2,000)
9	Land	43,100	89,900	(46,800)
10	Equipment, net	74,100	73,700	400
11	Long-term investment	19,200	4,600	14,600
12		$ 282,500	$ 275,800	$ 6,700
13	Current liabilities:			
14	Notes payable, short-term	$ 13,200	$ 20,200	$ (7,000)
15	Accounts payable	29,400	40,400	(11,000)
16	Income tax payable	13,800	14,700	(900)
17	Accrued liabilities	38,100	14,900	23,200
18	Interest payable	4,100	2,500	1,600
19	Salary payable	4,300	4,900	(600)
20	Long-term note payable	48,800	94,200	(45,400)
21	Common stock	65,100	51,200	13,900
22	Retained earnings	65,700	32,800	32,900
23		$ 282,500	$ 275,800	$ 6,700
24				

Transaction data for the year ended June 30, 2016, follows:
- **a.** Net income, $70,600
- **b.** Depreciation expense on equipment, $13,200
- **c.** Purchased long-term investment with cash, $14,600
- **d.** Sold land for $39,900, including $6,900 loss
- **e.** Acquired equipment by issuing long-term note payable, $13,600
- **f.** Paid long-term note payable, $59,000
- **g.** Received cash for issuance of common stock, $6,900
- **h.** Paid cash dividends, $37,700
- **i.** Paid short-term note payable by issuing common stock, $7,000

Requirements

1. Prepare the statement of cash flows of Sally Fagan Design Studio, Inc., for the year ended June 30, 2016, using the *indirect* method to report operating activities. Also prepare the accompanying schedule of noncash investing and financing activities. All current accounts except Notes Payable, short-term, result from operating transactions.
2. Prepare a supplementary schedule showing cash flows from operations by the *direct* method. The accounting records provide the following: collections from customers, $231,600; interest received, $1,200; payments to suppliers, $95,100; payments to employees, $39,100; payments for income tax, $12,100; and payment of interest, $4,400.

Challenge Exercises and Problem

LO 3 4

E12-76. *(Learning Objectives 3, 4: Compute cash flow amounts)* Top Notch, Inc., reported the following in its financial statements for the year ended May 31, 2016 (in thousands):

	A	B 2016	C 2015
1		**2016**	**2015**
2	Income Statement		
3	Net sales	$ 23,984	$ 21,115
4	Cost of sales	18,088	15,333
5	Depreciation	259	234
6	Other operating expenses	3,880	4,248
7	Income tax expense	536	485
8	Net income	$ 1,221	$ 815
9	Balance Sheet		
10	Cash and cash equivalents	$ 15	$ 14
11	Accounts receivable	597	609
12	Inventory	3,060	2,790
13	Property and equipment, net	4,345	3,425
14	Accounts payable	1,549	1,366
15	Accrued liabilities	942	639
16	Income tax payable	201	190
17	Long-term liabilities	476	463
18	Common stock	520	446
19	Retained earnings	4,329	3,734
20			

Requirement

1. Determine the following cash receipts and payments for Top Notch, Inc., during 2016 (enter all amounts in thousands):
   a. Collections from customers
   b. Payments for inventory
   c. Payments for other operating expenses
   d. Payment of income tax
   e. Proceeds from issuance of common stock
   f. Payment of cash dividends

LO 3

E12-77. *(Learning Objective 3: Use the balance sheet and the statement of cash flows together)* Crown Specialties reported the following at December 31, 2016 (in thousands):

	A	B 2016	C 2015
1		**2016**	**2015**
2	From the comparative balance sheet:		
3	Property and equipment, net	$ 11,000	$ 9,640
4	Long-term notes payable	4,100	3,010
5	From the statement of cash flows:		
6	Depreciation	$ 1,890	
7	Capital expenditures	(4,130)	
8	Proceeds from sale of property and equipment	800	
9	Proceeds from issuance of long-term note payable	1,175	
10	Payment of long-term note payable	(150)	
11	Issuance of common stock	386	
12			

Requirement

1. Determine the following items for Crown Specialties during 2016:
   a. Gain or loss on the sale of property and equipment
   b. Amount of long-term debt issued for something other than cash

P12-78. *(Learning Objectives 2, 3: Prepare a balance sheet from a statement of cash flows)*
The December 31, 2015, balance sheet and the 2016 statement of cash flows for Northtown, Inc., follow:

	A	B
1	**Northtown, Inc.** **Balance Sheet** **December 31, 2015**	
2	**Assets:**	
3	Cash	$ 14,000
4	Accounts receivable (net)	95,000
5	Inventory	60,500
6	Prepaid expenses	2,600
7	Land	99,800
8	Machinery and equipment (net)	73,600
9	Total assets	$ 345,500
10	**Liabilities:**	
11	Accounts payable	$ 40,300
12	Unearned revenue	9,000
13	Income taxes payable	6,000
14	Long-term debt	84,100
15	**Total liabilities**	139,400
16	**Stockholders' equity:**	
17	Common stock, no par	47,300
18	Retained earnings	158,800
19	Total stockholders' equity	206,100
20	Total liabilities and stockholders' equity	$ 345,500
21		

	A	B	C
	Northtown, Inc.		
	Statement of Cash Flows		
1	**Year Ended December 31, 2016**		
2	**Cash flows from operating activities:**		
3	Net income		$ 15,600
4	Adjustments to reconcile net income to net cash		
5	provided by operating activities:		
6	Depreciation	$ 13,600	
7	Loss on sale of equipment	8,000	
8	Gain on sale of land	(6,800)	
9	Change in assets and liabilities:		
10	Decrease in Accounts receivable	66,300	
11	Increase in Inventory	(17,900)	
12	Increase in Prepaid expenses	(1,300)	
13	Increase in Accounts payable	1,000	
14	Decrease in Taxes payable	(4,700)	
15	Increase in Unearned revenue	15,000	73,200
16	Net cash provided by operating activities		$ 88,800
17	**Cash flows from investing activities:**		
18	Purchase of equipment	(28,000)	
19	Sale of equipment	5,000	
20	Sale of land	69,700	
21	Net cash provided by investing activities		46,700
22	**Cash flows from financing activities:**		
23	Repayment of long-term debt	(15,000)	
24	Issuance of common stock	22,000	
25	Dividends paid (dividends declared, $9,000)	(3,000)	
26	Net cash provided by financing activities		4,000
27	Increase (decrease) in cash		139,500
28	Cash balance, December 31, 2015		14,000
29	Cash balance, December 31, 2016		$ 153,500
30			

Requirement

1. Prepare the December 31, 2016, balance sheet for Northtown, Inc.

APPLY YOUR KNOWLEDGE

Decision Cases

LO 3

Case 1. *(Learning Objective 3: Prepare and use the statement of cash flows to evaluate operations)* The 2016 income statement and the 2016 comparative balance sheet of T-Bar-M Camp, Inc., have just been distributed at a meeting of the camp's board of directors. The directors raise a fundamental question: Why is the cash balance so low? This question is especially troublesome since 2016 showed record profits. As the controller of the company, you must answer the question.

A1		
	A	**B**
1	**T–Bar–M Camp, Inc.** **Income Statement** **Year Ended December 31, 2016**	
2	**(In thousands)**	
3	Revenues:	
4	Sales revenue	$ 436
5	Expenses:	
6	Cost of goods sold	221
7	Salary expense	48
8	Depreciation expense	46
9	Interest expense	13
10	Amortization expense	11
11	Total expenses	339
12	Net income	$ 97
13		

A1			
	A	**B**	**C**
1	**T–Bar–M Camp, Inc.** **Comparative Balance Sheets** **December 31, 2016 and 2015**		
2	**(In thousands)**	**2016**	**2015**
3	**Assets:**		
4	Cash	$ 17	$ 63
5	Accounts receivable, net	72	61
6	Inventories	194	181
7	Property, plant, and equipment	369	259
8	Accumulated depreciation	(244)	(198)
9	Long-term investments	31	0
10	Patents	177	188
11	Totals	$ 616	$ 554
12	**Liabilities and owners' equity:**		
13	Accounts payable	$ 63	$ 56
14	Accrued liabilities	12	17
15	Notes payable, long-term	179	264
16	Common stock, no par	149	61
17	Retained earnings	213	156
18	Totals	$ 616	$ 554
19			

Requirements

1. Prepare a statement of cash flows for 2016 in the format that best shows the relationship between net income and operating cash flow. The company sold no plant assets or long-term investments and issued no notes payable during 2016. There were *no* noncash investing and financing transactions during the year. Show all amounts in thousands.

2. Answer the board members' question: Why is the cash balance so low? Point out the two largest cash payments during 2016. (Challenge)

3. Considering net income and the company's cash flows during 2016, was it a good year or a bad year? Give your reasons.

Case 2. (*Learning Objectives 1, 2: Use cash flow data to evaluate an investment*) Applied Technology, Inc., and Four-Star Catering are asking you to recommend their stock to your clients. Because Applied and Four-Star earn about the same net income and have similar financial positions, your decision depends on their statements of cash flows, summarized as follows:

	Applied		Four–Star	
Net cash provided by operating activities:......................		$ 30,000		$ 70,000
Cash provided by (used for) investing activities:				
Purchase of plant assets	$(20,000)		$(100,000)	
Sale of plant assets..	40,000	20,000	10,000	(90,000)
Cash provided by (used for) financing activities:				
Issuance of common stock		—		30,000
Paying off long-term debt		(40,000)		—
Net increase in cash..		$ 10,000		$10,000

Requirement

1. Based on their cash flows, which company looks better? Give your reasons. Challenge

Ethical Issues

Columbia Motors is having a bad year. Net income is only $37,000. Also, two important overseas customers are falling behind in their payments to Columbia, and Columbia's accounts receivable are ballooning. The company desperately needs a loan. The Columbia board of directors is considering ways to put the best face on the company's financial statements. Columbia's bank closely examines cash flow from operations. Darlene McCardell, Columbia's controller, suggests reclassifying as long-term the receivables from the slow-paying clients. She explains to the board that removing the $80,000 rise in accounts receivable from current assets will increase net cash provided by operations. This approach may help Columbia get the loan.

Requirements

1. Using only the amounts given, compute net cash provided by operations, both without and with the reclassification of the receivables. Which reporting makes Columbia look better?
2. Identify the ethical issue(s).
3. Who are the stakeholders?
4. Analyze the issue from the (a) economic, (b) legal, and (c) ethical standpoints. What is the potential impact on all stakeholders?
5. What should the board do?
6. Under what conditions would the reclassification of the receivables be considered ethical?

Focus on Financials | Apple Inc.

(*Learning Objectives 1, 2, 3, 4: Use the statement of cash flows*) Use **Apple Inc.'s** consolidated statement of cash flows along with the company's other consolidated financial statements, all in Appendix A and online in the filings section of **http://www.sec.gov**, to answer the following questions.

Requirements

1. By which method does Apple Inc. report cash flows from operating activities? How can you tell?
2. What type of activity (operating, financing, or investing) generated the most cash flows for Apple in 2014? Which activity type(s) used cash in 2014? Judging by the statement of cash flows only, is Apple a healthy company? Explain your answer.
3. Suppose Apple Inc., reported net cash flows from operating activities by using the direct method. Compute the following amounts for the year ended December 31, 2014 (ignore the statement of cash flows, and use only Apple Inc.'s income statement and balance sheet).
   a. Calculate collections from customers and others. Prepare a T-account for Gross Accounts Receivable. Prepare another T-account for Allowance for Doubtful Accounts. Calculate the beginning and ending gross amounts of Gross Accounts Receivable by adding the beginning and ending balances of Allowance for Doubtful Accounts ($99 million and $86 million, respectively) to the net accounts receivable at both the beginning and end of the year.

Assume that all sales are on account. Also assume that the company uses the percentage of net sales method for estimating doubtful accounts expense and that the company estimates this amount at 0.5%.

b. Calculate payments to suppliers. Apple Inc. calls its cost of goods sold "Cost of Sales." Assume all inventory is purchased on account and that all cash payments to suppliers are made from accounts payable.

c. Evaluate 2014 for Apple Inc. in terms of net income, total assets, stockholders' equity, cash flows from operating activities, and overall results. Be specific. (Challenge)

Focus on Analysis | Under Armour, Inc.

(Learning Objectives 1, 2, 3, 4: Analyze cash flows) Refer to the **Under Armour, Inc.'s**, consolidated financial statements in Appendix B and online in the filings section of **http://www .sec.gov**. Focus on the year ended December 31, 2014.

LO 1 2 3 4

Requirements

1. What is(are) Under Armour, Inc.'s, main source(s) of cash? Is this good news or bad news to its managers, stockholders, and creditors? What is Under Armour, Inc.'s, main use of cash? Is this good news or bad news? Discuss your reasoning.
2. Explain briefly the three most significant differences between net cash provided by operating activities and net income.
3. Did Under Armour, Inc., buy or sell more plant assets during 2014 than in the previous two years? How can you tell?
4. Identify the largest item in the financing activities section of the Consolidated Statement of Cash Flows. Explain the company's probable reasoning behind this activity.
5. Evaluate Under Armour, Inc.'s, overall performance for 2014 in terms of cash flows. Be as specific as you can. What other information would be helpful to you in making your evaluation?

Group Projects

Project 1. Each member of the group should obtain the annual report of a different company. Select companies in different industries. Evaluate each company's trend of cash flows for the most recent two years. In your evaluation of the companies' cash flows, you may use any other information that is publicly available—for example, the other financial statements (income statement, balance sheet, statement of stockholders' equity, and the related notes), and news stories from magazines and newspapers. Rank the companies' cash flows from best to worst, and write a two-page report on your findings.

Project 2. Select a company and obtain its annual report, including all the financial statements. Focus on the statement of cash flows and, in particular, the cash flows from operating activities. Specify whether the company uses the direct method or the indirect method to report operating cash flows. As necessary, use the other financial statements (income statement, balance sheet, and statement of stockholders' equity) and the notes to prepare the company's cash flows from operating activities by using the *other* method.

Quick Check Answers

1. *a*
2. *a*
3. *c*
4. *d* ($90,000 + $12,000 − $9,000)
5. *d*
6. *c*
7. *c* ($70,000 + $13,000 − $2,000 + $9,000 + $12,000 + $1,000)
8. *b* ($7,000 − $23,000 + $39,000)
9. *c* (− $8,000 + $4,000 − $5,000)
10. *c* ($39,000 + $9,000)
11. *c* ($40,000 + $625,000 − $30,000)
12. *a* ($760,000 − $380,000 − $150,000)
13. *d* ($380,000 − $15,000 + $10,000)

13 Financial Statement Analysis

SPOTLIGHT | Under Armour, Inc., is a "Red-Hot" Competitor!

Throughout this book we have shown how to account for the financial position, results of operations, and cash flows, of such well-known companies as **The Walt Disney Company**, **Apple Inc.**, **Under Armour, Inc.**, **FedEx Corporation**, **Intel Corporation**, **Southwest Airlines Company**, **The Gap, Inc.**, and **Google, Inc.** Only one aspect of the course remains: financial statement analysis. In the first half of this chapter, armed with information about the industry, the company, and its business strategy, we use horizontal, vertical, and cash flow analysis to help analyze the financial statements of Under Armour, Inc., our Appendix B focus company. Under Armour, Inc. was also featured in the discussion of inventories and cost of goods sold in Chapter 6. In the second half of the chapter, we illustrate the use of ratios in financial statement analysis of Apple Inc., our Appendix A focus company, also featured in the discussion of short-term investments and receivables in Chapter 5. When you finish this chapter, you should be able to understand the relationships among the data that reflect the financial position, results of operations, and cash flows of two of the world's most important companies. In addition, the skills you develop in this chapter are transferrable, allowing you to deeply understand and interpret the financial statements of any other company of your choosing. This is truly what makes accounting such a valuable business tool!

Under Armour, Inc., is a red-hot competitor that is clearly "playing to win" in the athletic apparel game. Share prices of Under Armour, Inc., rose in value by an incredible 70% during its fiscal year ended December 31, 2014. Over a longer time period, the company's stock price has performed at "Olympian" growth levels—850% over 5 years, and 1,400% in 10 years!

A big part of Under Armour, Inc.'s business strategy is innovation. Like so many other great companies, Under Armour, Inc., started with a simple idea: to make a superior T-shirt. Founder and CEO Kevin Plank, a former University of Maryland football player, founded Under Armour, Inc., from the basement of his mother's home in 1996. Plank's goal was developing an innovative new alternative to the traditional cotton T-shirt that provided compression and wicked perspiration off the skin rather than absorbed it. The result was a line of apparel engineered to keep athletes cool, dry, and light throughout the course of a game, practice, or workout. The technology behind Under Armour's diverse product assortment for men, women, and youth is complex, but the program for reaping the benefits is simple: Wear athletic gear that is suited to the seasons—hot, cold, and in-between.

Besides making its mark in the apparel industry, Under Armour is making big inroads into "connected fitness" with recent acquisitions of Endomonto, MyFitnessPal, and MapMyFitness. The company's Connected Fitness community now has over 130 million unique users across its combined electronic platforms, representing the largest digital health and fitness community in the world. Latest technological innovations include "wearable computing," integrating sensors into its products to measure speed, calories burned, heart rate, and other statistics to assist the athlete in evaluating his or her performance over time.

Just how well is all of this innovation working from a financial viewpoint? We can answer that question by financial statement analysis, beginning with Under Armour, Inc.'s, comparative Consolidated Statements of Operations for the years ended December 31, 2014, 2013, and 2012. In 2014, Under Armour generated net revenues of about $3 billion. Is that positive or negative news? To answer that question, we need not only to analyze the trend in net revenues, but also to compare it with the trends in key expenses over the three years. We also need to compare, or benchmark, Under Armour's results with those of its major competitor. ●

	A	B	C	D
	Under Armour, Inc.			
1	**Consolidated Statements of Income (Adapted)**	**12 Months Ended**		
2	In thousands of $	Dec. 31, 2014	Dec. 31, 2013	Dec. 31, 2012
3	Net revenues	$ 3,084,370	$ 2,332,051	$ 1,834,921
4	Cost of goods sold	1,572,164	1,195,381	955,624
5	Gross profit	1,512,206	1,136,670	879,297
6	Selling, general and administrative expenses	1,158,251	871,572	670,602
7	Income from operations	353,955	265,098	208,695
8	Interest expense, net	(5,335)	(2,933)	(5,183)
9	Other expense, net	(6,410)	(1,172)	(73)
10	Income before income taxes	342,210	260,993	203,439
11	Provision for income taxes	134,168	98,663	74,661
12	Net income	$ 208,042	$ 162,330	$ 128,778
13	Net income available per common share			
14	Basic (USD Per Share)	$ 0.98	$ 0.77	$ 0.62
15	Diluted (USD Per Share)	0.95	0.75	0.61
16	Weighted average common shares outstanding			
17	Basic (In Shares)	213,227	210,696	208,686
18	Diluted (In Shares)	219,380	215,958	212,760
19				

This chapter covers the basic tools of financial statement analysis. The first part of the chapter shows how to evaluate Under Armour, Inc., from year to year and how to compare it to other companies that are in the same lines of business. For this comparison, we use **Nike, Inc.**, which is generally regarded as the major competitor in the athletic apparel space. The second part of the chapter discusses the most widely used financial ratios for Apple Inc., which is our focus company in Appendix A. You have seen most of these ratios in earlier chapters. However, we have yet to use all of them in a comprehensive analysis of a company. By studying all these ratios together,

- you will learn the basic tools of financial statement analysis.
- you will enhance your business education.

Regardless of your chosen field—marketing, management, finance, entrepreneurship, or accounting—you will find these analytical tools useful as you move through your career.

LEARNING | OBJECTIVES

1 **Perform** horizontal analysis

2 **Perform** vertical analysis

3 **Prepare** common-size financial statements

4 **Analyze** the statement of cash flows

5 **Use** ratios to make business decisions

6 **Use** other measures to make investment decisions

» Try It in Excel®

You can access the most current annual report of **Under Armour**, Inc., in Excel format at **http://www.sec.gov**. Using the "FILINGS" link on the toolbar at the top of the home page, select "Company Filings Search." This will take you to the "Edgar Company Filings" page. Type "Under Armour" in the company name box, and select "Search." This will produce the "EDGAR Search Results" page showing the company name. Click on the "CIK" link beside the company name. This will pull up all of the reports the company has filed with the SEC. Under the "Filing Type" box, type "10-K" and click the search box. Form 10-K is the SEC form for the company's annual report. Find the year that you wish to view. Click on the "Interactive Data" box, which takes you to the "View Filing Data" page. Find and click on the "View Excel Document" link at the top of this page. You may choose to either open or download the Excel files containing the company's most recent financial statements.

It Starts with the Big Picture

It is impossible to evaluate a company effectively by examining only one year's numerical data. Financial analysis involves more than just doing the math. Thorough analysis of the financial position and results of operations of a company begins with understanding the business and industry of the company—the big picture. This usually entails quite a bit of reading and research, using all kinds of media—the business press, trade journals, and other publications. You can often gain free access to this information via popular finance websites that you can research on the Internet. There are also some excellent "for pay" websites (such as the Motley fool, **http://www .fool.com**, and Hoovers, Inc., **http://www.hoovers.com**,) through which industry and company analyses may be purchased. Learning about what's happening in the industry, markets, general economic conditions, trends in product development, and specific company strategies puts the numbers in context and helps you understand why they turned out as they did. After all, accounting data should paint a picture of the results of implementing a particular business strategy.

The athletic apparel industry is enjoying a period of booming expansion as the worldwide economy recovers from a severe economic recession. Consumers are feeling comfortable again, opening their pocketbooks to purchase sporty and fashionable activewear. Increasingly, robust consumer confidence has lifted sales for makers and marketers of athletic wear, as well as for the retailers that sell it. In 2014, activewear sales growth exceeded that of the apparel market as a whole. Athletic gear is both comfortable and stylish. Manufacturers are giving attention to making fabrics in new colors and styles, making it appealing to wear athletic gear on the street as well as the gym. Under Armour, Inc., is enjoying its share of this boom.

For example, net revenues for Under Armour, Inc., grew from about $1.8 billion during the year ended December 31, 2012, to about $3.1 billion during the year ended December 31, 2014. This represents a remarkable 68% growth over 36 months. Furthermore, the company's performance was quite strong across all of its divisions. Overall revenues grew at a rate of more than 20% year over year during the company's most recent 20 consecutive quarters. In addition, in the first quarter of fiscal 2015, revenue for Under Armour, Inc., (not shown) continued to skyrocket. Apparel sales grew 21% over the first quarter of fiscal 2014; footwear revenues increased 41%, and international revenues jumped 74%. The Consolidated Statements of Operations on page 751 reveal that the company's income from operations has also steadily increased from about $208.7 million for the year ended December 31, 2012, to about $354 million for the year ended December 31, 2014.

Every public company's annual report filed with the SEC begins with a description of the company's business. This section of the annual report provides vital information on the company's products, its marketing and promotion, sales and distribution strategies, product design and development, manufacturing and quality assurance, and inventory management. Item 1 (Business) describes how a company views its own operations and lends insight into why company management makes certain strategic decisions. Also, in the Management's Discussion and Analysis (MD&A) section of Under Armour, Inc.'s, annual report, you will find management's explanations for trends in sales and shipments, cost of sales and gross profit, selling, general and administrative expenses, and income taxes. The trend in every line item of the Consolidated Statements of Operations on page 751 is explained by management in MD&A.

Once we have an understanding of the big picture, we can start to dig deeper into the numbers, and they begin to make more sense. Public companies' financial statements are comparative, that is, they cover at least two periods. Under Armour, Inc.'s, Consolidated Statements of Operations on page 751 cover three fiscal years. In fact, most financial analysis covers trends in reported data over 3 to 10 years. Since one of the goals of financial analysis is to predict the future, it makes sense to start by mapping the trends of the past. This is particularly true of income statement data such as net revenues and the various expenses that make up reported net income.

The graphs in Exhibit 13-1 show Under Armour, Inc.'s, three-year trend of net revenues and income from operations. Reading from left to right, Under Armour's net revenues (panel A) as well as its income from operations (panel B) increased at a healthy pace from 2012 through 2014. This is generally a good sign, because steadily increasing revenues and operating income demonstrate quality of earnings and often point the way to expansion and growth in company value in future years. How can we predict Under Armour, Inc.'s net sales and income from operations for 2015 and beyond? As we have seen, financial statement analysis is more than just finding a trend line. It also involves knowing key facts about the company's past actions, as well as its future plans. Let's do some horizontal analysis and see if we can discover more about Under Armour, Inc.'s story as we go.

Exhibit 13-1 | Comparative Net Revenues and Income from Operations for Under Armour (2012–2014)

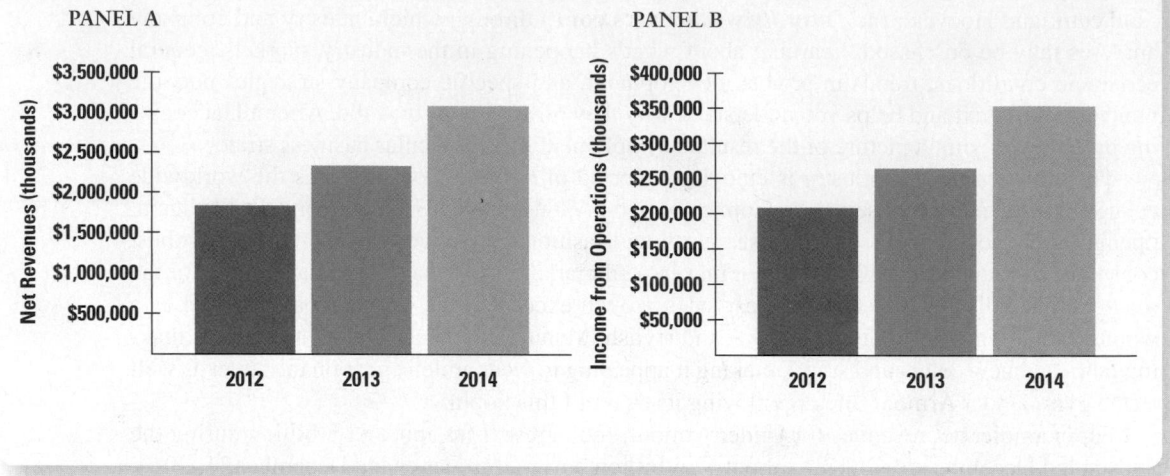

PERFORM HORIZONTAL ANALYSIS

① **Perform** horizontal analysis

Many decisions hinge on the trend of revenues, expenses, income from operations, and so on. Have revenues increased this year? By how much? Suppose net revenues have increased by $5 million this year. Is that a positive sign or not so positive? The response often is "compared to what?" The evaluation depends on net revenues last period and the period before that. For example, if the $5 million increase in net revenues this year represents a 20% increase from last year, and perhaps a 40% increase over a two-year period, this adds information that can improve the evaluation or decision.

The study of percentage changes from year to year is called **horizontal analysis**. Computing a percentage change takes two steps:

1. Compute the dollar amount of the change from one period (the base period) to the next.
2. Divide the dollar amount of change by the base-period amount.

Illustration: Under Armour, Inc.

Horizontal analysis is illustrated for Under Armour, Inc., as follows (using the 2013 to 2014 figures, dollars in thousands):

	2014	2013	Increase (Decrease)	
			Amount	Percentage
Net revenues	$3,084,370	$2,332,051	$752,319	32.3%

Under Armour's net revenues (in thousands) increased by 32.3% during 2014, computed as follows:

Step 1 Compute the dollar amount of change from 2013 to 2014:

2014		2013		Increase
$3,084,370	−	$2,332,051	=	$752,319

Step 2 Divide the dollar amount of change by the base-period amount. This computes the percentage change for the period:

$$\text{Percentage change} = \frac{\text{Dollar amount of change}}{\text{Base-year amount}}$$

$$= \frac{\$752,319}{\$2,332,051} = 32.3\%$$

Exhibit 13-2 presents a line-by-line detailed horizontal analysis of Under Armour, Inc.'s comparative Consolidated Statements of Operations over the two-year period from December 31, 2012, through December 31, 2014.

Exhibit 13-2 | Comparative Consolidated Statements of Operations—Horizontal Analysis

A1						
A	**B**	**C**	**D**	**E**	**F**	
Under Armour, Inc. **Comparative Horizontal Analysis of** **Consolidated Statements of Income**		**12 Months Ended**				
	Dec. 31, 2014	**% change** **2013–2014**	**Dec. 31, 2013**	**% change** **2012–2013**	**Dec. 31, 2012**	
3 (In thousands of $)						
4 Net revenues	$ 3,084,370	32.3%	$ 2,332,051	27.1%	$ 1,834,921	
5 Cost of goods sold	1,572,164	31.5%	1,195,381	25.1%	955,624	
6 Gross profit	1,512,206	33.0%	1,136,670	29.3%	879,297	
7 Selling, general and administrative expenses	1,158,251	32.9%	871,572	30.0%	670,602	
8 Income from operations	353,955	33.5%	265,098	27.0%	208,695	
9 Interest expense, net	(5,335)	81.9%	(2,933)	(43.4%)	(5,183)	
10 Other expense, net	(6,410)	446.9%	(1,172)	1,505.5%	(73)	
11 Income before income taxes	342,210	31.1%	260,993	28.3%	203,439	
12 Provision for income taxes	134,168	36.0%	98,663	32.1%	74,661	
13 Net income	$ 208,042	28.2%	$ 162,330	26.1%	$ 128,778	
14						

» Try It in Excel®

Formatting comparative financial statements for horizontal analysis when the financial statements are in Excel format is quite easy. Try reconstructing Exhibit 13-2 in Excel.

1. Start with the Consolidated Statements of Operations in the opening figure of the chapter.
2. Change the labels to correspond with Exhibit 13-2. Your spreadsheet might be slightly different from Exhibit 13-2, so the cells in which you start to enter formulas might have to be modified accordingly.
3. Insert one column between the 2014 and 2013 columns and another column between the 2013 and 2012 columns. Label these "% change."
4. Compute the percentage change as follows. We start in cell C4 (blank). Change the format of the data in the cell to % by clicking on the % box in the number field in the top toolbar. In cell C4, type the following: =(B4–D4)/D4. The result of 32.3% should appear in the cell. Copy this cell formula through line 13 of the sheet to perform this computation for all other income and expenses.
5. Repeat the process in (4) using blank cell E4 and using the formula: =(D4–F4)/F4. Copy this formula through line 13.
6. Pat yourself on the back. You've just performed horizontal analysis using Excel!

Now focus on the "% change" column from 2013 to 2014 in Exhibit 13-2. A chart from the MD&A section of the company's annual report includes a more detailed discussion of these changes by category. Let's analyze the change in net revenues by category first:

	A	B	C	D	E
	A1				
1		Year ended December 31			
2	(In thousands)	2014	2013	$ Change	% Change
3	Apparel	$2,291,520	$1,762,150	$529,370	30.0%
4					
5	Footwear	430,987	298,825	132,162	44.2%
6					
7	Accessories	275,425	216,098	59,327	27.5%
8					
9	Total product sales	2,997,932	2,277,073	720,859	31.7%
10					
11	License and other revenues	86,438	54,978	31,460	57.2%
12					
13	Total net revenues	$3,084,370	$2,332,051	$752,319	32.3%

The figure above shows that Under Armour, Inc.'s, net revenue consists of net sales of products (apparel, footwear, and accessories) as well as license and other revenues. Product sales are generated primarily from the wholesale of products to national, regional, independent, and specialty retailers, as well as direct sales through factory outlet stores. The overall 32.3% increase in net revenues by category was comprised of a 30% increase in apparel sales, a 44.2% increase in footwear, and a 27.5% increase in accessories. License and other revenues, although the smallest category of total net revenues, grew by the largest percentage (57.2%) during the year. License revenues come from agreements the company has made with third parties such as professional sports teams to market Under Armour branded apparel and accessories. The company also sold digital fitness platform licenses and subscriptions, along with digital advertising through MapMyFitness, Inc., which the company acquired in 2013.

Cost of goods sold (Exhibit 13-2, line 5) measures the direct cost of various products sold. Gross profit (line 6) measures the difference between net revenues and cost of goods sold. Exhibit 13-2 shows that cost of goods sold increased by 31.5% in 2014. This allowed gross profit to increase by 33% over 2013. In MD&A, management explains that this increase was caused largely by a decreased sales mix of "excess inventory" through the company's factory outlet stores. Excess inventory are products that typically move slower. The company has to cut the selling prices of these products in order to sell them, thus lowering gross profit. The company's inventory of such products was less in 2014 than 2013, enabling it to maintain higher sales prices and gross profits.

Selling, general, and administrative expenses in 2014 (Exhibit 13-2, line 7) increased by 32.9% over 2013. MD&A reveals that these expenses consist of marketing costs such as global sponsorship of professional teams and athletes; selling costs such as distribution, product innovation and supply chain costs; and the cost of corporate services such as personnel and other administrative costs. These costs rose over the year, but not at as high a rate as gross profit, enabling the company's income from operations (line 8) to grow by a still larger percentage (33.5%).

Interest expense for 2014 (Exhibit 13-2, line 9) grew by 81.9% over 2013, primarily due to new long-term debt the company incurred during the year, which we will see when we analyze the balance sheet later. Other expenses (line 10) consisted mostly of foreign currency exchange losses due to a relatively strong U.S. dollar. Line 12 contains the company's provision for income taxes. Under Armour, Inc's, income tax provision rose by 36% in 2014, which is roughly consistent with the increased profits the company has reported. You can read more about all of these expenses in Chapter 11.

Overall, Under Armour, Inc.'s, profits have continued to rise from 2012 through 2014, driven principally by increased net revenues fueled by increased demand for Under Armour's products. At the same time, the company has managed to maintain control over its costs of products as well as selling, general and administrative expenses, resulting in "bottom line" profits that have

Exhibit 13-3 | Horizontal Analysis: Consolidated Balance Sheets

	A	B	C	D	E
	A1				
1	**Under Armour,Inc.** **Consolidated Balance Sheets (in thousands of USD)**				
2				Increase (decrease)	
3	**Assets**	Dec. 31, 2014	Dec. 31, 2013	Amount	Percentage
4	Cash and cash equivalents	$ 593,175	$ 347,489	$ 245,686	70.7%
5	Accounts receivable, net	279,835	209,952	69,883	33.3%
6	Inventories	536,714	469,006	67,708	14.4%
7	Prepaid expenses and other current assets	87,177	63,987	23,190	36.2%
8	Deferred income taxes	52,498	38,377	14,121	36.8%
9	Total current assets	1,549,399	1,128,811	420,588	37.3%
10	Property and equipment, net	305,564	223,952	81,612	36.4%
11	Goodwill	123,256	122,244	1,012	0.8%
12	Intangible assets, net	26,230	24,097	2,133	8.9%
13	Deferred income taxes	33,570	31,094	2,476	8.0%
14	Other long-term assets	57,064	47,543	9,521	20.0%
15	Total assets	$ 2,095,083	$ 1,577,741	$ 517,342	32.8%
16	**Liabilities and Stockholders' Equity**				
17	Revolving credit facility	$ –	$ 100,000	$ (100,000)	(100.0)%
18	Accounts payable	210,432	165,456	44,976	27.2%
19	Accrued expenses	147,681	133,729	13,952	10.4%
20	Current maturities of long-term debt	28,951	4,972	23,979	482.3%
21	Other current liabilities	34,563	22,473	12,090	53.8%
22	Total current liabilities	421,627	426,630	(5,003)	(1.2)%
23	Long-term debt, net of current maturities	255,250	47,951	207,299	432.3%
24	Other long-term liabilities	67,906	49,806	18,100	36.3%
25	Total liabilities	744,783	524,387	220,396	42.0%
26	Commitments and contingencies (see Note 7)				
27	Stockholders' equity				
28	Class A Common Stock	59	57	2	3.5%
29	Class B Convertible Common Stock	12	13	(1)	(7.7)%
30	Additional paid-in capital	508,350	397,248	111,102	28.0%
31	Retained earnings	856,687	653,842	202,845	31.0%
32	Accumulated other comprehensive income (loss)	(14,808)	2,194	(17,002)	(774.9)%
33	Total stockholders' equity	1,350,300	1,053,354	296,946	28.2%
34	Total liabilities and stockholders' equity	$ 2,095,083	$ 1,577,741	$ 517,342	32.8%
35					

increased at almost the same rate as revenues. These facts help explain why the company's stock has been such a "hot commodity."

Studying year-to-year changes in balance-sheet accounts can enhance our total understanding of the current and long-term financial position of the entity. Let's look at a few balance-sheet changes in Exhibit 13-3.

First, cash and cash equivalents (line 4) increased by an impressive 70.7% in 2014. Accounts receivable, net increased by 33.3%, which roughly corresponds to the 32.3% increase in net revenues we saw in Exhibit 13-2. These changes indicate that the company's net revenues and accounts receivable grew during 2014, and that the company was collecting a significant amount of these revenues in cash. Inventories (line 6) increased by 14.4%, indicating that the company was building up inventories, anticipating increased sales in 2015. The company's revolving credit facility (line 17) was paid off completely during 2014, likely with the proceeds of new long-term debt (lines 20 and 23). Accounts payable (line 18) increased by 27.2%, not quite as much as cost of goods sold (31.5%, as shown in Exhibit 13-2, line 5). This indicates that the company's rate of payments to its creditors is improving. Overall, total current assets (line 9) increased at the rate of 37.3%, and total current liabilities (line 22) decreased by 1.2%. Net working capital (current assets − current liabilities) increased from $702.2 million in 2013 to $1.128 billion in 2014. The current ratio (current assets/current liabilities) was extremely strong in both years (2.65 in 2013, improving to 3.67 in 2014), indicating the company maintained a very strong ability to pay its short-term liabilities.

Property and equipment, net (line 10) increased by 36.4%, indicating that the company invested significant amounts in long-term assets such as warehouses and technology. Long-term debt (lines 20 and 23), which consists largely of amounts borrowed to finance these assets, as well as debt related to capital lease obligations, increased by $231 million (about $24 million in current liabilities and $207 million in long-term liabilities).

Reference to the Stockholders' Equity footnote as well as the Consolidated Statement of Stockholders' Equity indicates that the company has two classes of common stock (Class A and Class B): 400 million shares of Class A common stock and 36.6 million shares of Class B common stock are authorized. The Class B common stock is convertible to shares of Class A common stock. However, the par values of stock in each class are only $0.0003 1/3. As of December 31, 2014, 177.3 million shares of Class A stock with a par value of approximately $59,000 are outstanding. 36.6 million shares of Class B stock with a par value of approximately $12,000 are outstanding. The issue price of these shares has produced additional paid-in capital of $508,350,000 in 2014 (a 28% increase over 2013). This increase mainly occurred in connection with exercise of stock options by employees and others, as well as recognition of stock-based compensation expense. Finally, net income of $208 million, decreased by a reduction for shares withheld for stock-based compensation ($5.2 million) accounted for the net increase in retained earnings of $202.8 million.

Overall, it appears that as of December 31, 2014, Under Armour, Inc.'s, financial position is very healthy and growing, both from the current as well as the long-term standpoint. Management has invested significant resources in the growth of the company through the end of 2014. The company has also accumulated a substantial amount of cash and inventories and is ready to grow even more in 2015.

Trend Percentages

Trend percentages are a form of horizontal analysis. Trends indicate the direction a business is taking. How have revenues changed over a five-year period? What trend does net income show? These questions can be answered by trend percentages over a representative period, such as the most recent five years.

Trend percentages are computed by selecting a base year whose amounts are set equal to 100%. The amount for each following year is stated as a percentage of the base amount. To compute a trend percentage, divide an item for a later year by the base-year amount, and multiply by 100.

$$\text{Trend \%} = \frac{\text{Any year \$}}{\text{Base year \$}} \times 100$$

Recall that, in Chapter 11, we established that income from operations is often viewed as the primary measure of a company's earnings quality. This is because it represents a company's best predictor of the future net inflows from its core business units. Income from continuing operations is often used in estimating the current value of the business.

Under Armour, Inc., showed income from operations for 2012–2014 as follows:

(In millions)	2014	2013	2012 (Base)
Income from operations	$353,955	$265,098	$208,695

We want to calculate a trend for the period 2012 through 2014. The first year in the series (2012) is set as the base year. Trend percentages are computed by dividing each successive year's amount by the 2012 amount. The resulting trend percentages follow (2012 = 100%):

	2014	2013	2012 (Base)
Income from operations	170%	127%	100%

In 2013, Income from operations took a 27% jump, relative to the base year, and it took another 43% jump in 2014, to account for a total 70% increase relative to the base year. The cause for these results is largely attributable to the tremendous growth occurring in revenues over the two-year period. You can perform a trend analysis on any item you consider important. Trend analysis using income-statement data is widely used for predicting the future.

Horizontal analysis highlights changes over time in financial statement line items. However, no single technique gives a complete picture of a business.

PERFORM VERTICAL ANALYSIS

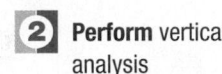 **Perform** vertical analysis

Vertical analysis shows the relationship of a financial statement item to its base, which is the 100% figure. All items on the particular financial statement are reported as a percentage of the base. For the income statement, net revenue (net sales) is usually the base. Suppose that investors have come to expect a company's net income to be greater than 8% of net sales revenue. A drop to 4% over a period of two years while general economic conditions are improving may cause investors to become disappointed in the performance of company management. Thus, they might sell the company's stock in favor of companies with more attractive earnings potential.

Illustration: Under Armour, Inc.

Exhibit 13-4 shows the vertical analysis of Under Armour, Inc.'s, Consolidated Statements of Operations. In this case,

$$\text{Vertical analysis } \% = \frac{\text{Each income statement item}}{\text{Net sales (revenue)}}$$

Exhibit 13-4 | Comparative Consolidated Statements of Operations—Vertical Analysis

A1							
	A	**B**	**C**	**D**	**E**	**F**	**G**
1	**Under Armour, Inc.** **Consolidated Statements of Income (Adapted)**	**Year ended**	**% of**	**Year ended**	**% of**	**Year ended**	**% of**
2	**($ in thousands)**	**Dec. 31, 2014**	**total**	**Dec. 31, 2013**	**total**	**Dec. 31, 2012**	**total**
3	Net revenues	$ 3,084,370	100.0%	$ 2,332,051	100.0%	$ 1,834,921	100.0%
4	Cost of goods sold	1,572,164	51.0%	1,195,381	51.3%	955,624	52.1%
5	Gross profit	1,512,206	49.0%	1,136,670	48.7%	879,297	47.9%
6	Selling, general and administrative expenses	1,158,251	37.6%	871,572	37.4%	670,602	36.5%
7	Income from operations	353,955	11.4%	265,098	11.4%	208,695	11.4%
8	Interest expense, net	(5,335)	(0.2)%	(2,933)	(0.1)%	(5,183)	(0.3)%
9	Other expense, net	(6,410)	(0.2)%	(1,172)	(0.1)%	(73)	0.0%
10	Income before income taxes	342,210	11.0%	260,993	11.2%	203,439	11.1%
11	Provision for income taxes	134,168	4.3%	98,663	4.2%	74,661	4.1%
12	Net income	$ 208,042	6.7%	$ 162,330	7.0%	$ 128,778	7.0%
13							

>> ***Try It** in **Excel**®*

Formatting comparative financial statements for vertical analysis when the financial statements are in Excel format is just as easy as it was for horizontal analysis. Try reconstructing Exhibit 13-4 in Excel.

1. Start with the Consolidated Statements of Operations in the opening figure of the chapter. You will be ahead of the game if you have already prepared this in Excel.
2. Change the labels to correspond with Exhibit 13-4. Your spreadsheet might be slightly different than Exhibit 13-4, so the cells in which you start to enter formulas might have to be modified accordingly.

3. We are preparing three years of comparative data, so insert columns after each of the 2014, 2013, and 2012 financial columns. In our example, these become columns C, E, and G with blank cells; label these "% of total."

4. Common-sized income statements set net revenues at 100% and express all other income and expenses as percentages of net revenues. To set net revenues at 100%, we start in cell C3 (blank). In the cell, type the following: =B3/$B$3. It is very important to insert the $ signs in the denominator both before and after the letter B. This "freezes" cell B3 to make it a constant denominator for the values in all other cells in the column. You may also use the F4 function key to freeze the cell value. The result of 100% should appear in the cell. To increase precision, use the "increase decimal" tab in the "number" field in the toolbar. We have adjusted to a precision of one decimal place. Copy this cell formula through line 12 of the sheet to perform this computation for all other income and expenses.

5. Repeat the process in (4) for the 2013 and 2012 figures columns by entering corresponding formulas in columns E and G. Copy these formulas through line 12. Use the "borders" tab (under "font" in the toolbar) to format the cells to extend the proper underscoring as shown in Exhibit 13-4.

6. Pat yourself on the back. You're learning to use Excel for the very valuable function of vertical analysis! Now let's dig into the numbers to interpret what they mean.

The vertical analysis format in Exhibit 13-4 permits us to study trends in key financial statistics such as gross profit, operating income, and net income over time. The absolute numbers are converted to percentages, permitting us to see fluctuations we might not see otherwise. Let's begin with gross profit and proceed through operating expenses.

Under Armour, Inc.'s, gross profit percentages over the three-year period have improved slightly (47.9% in 2012, 48.7% in 2013, and 49.0% in 2014). As we learned in Chapter 6, gross profit percentage measures the average percentage of profit generated per each dollar of sales. The company is improving in this area, meaning that it is controlling costs while slightly increasing its selling prices, perhaps to partially compensate for increased operating costs.

While gross profit improved, the company's operating expenses increased slightly from 36.5% of net revenues in 2012 to 37.6% of net revenues in 2014. This slightly negative trend had the impact of counteracting the slightly positive trend the company saw in gross profit. The result is remarkably consistent income from operations of 11.4% to 11.5% of net revenues. Notice that the overall picture of how the company is implementing its strategy over time is complementary to the picture we saw with horizontal analysis, except from a slightly different angle. Under Armour, Inc., appears to be a profitable and well-managed company from a financial standpoint as of the year ended December 31, 2014.

Exhibit 13-5 shows the vertical analysis of Under Armour, Inc.'s, Consolidated Balance Sheets. The base amount (100%) is total assets for each year. The vertical analysis of Under Armour, Inc.'s, balance sheet reveals several things about Under Armour's financial position at December 31, 2014, relative to December 31, 2013:

■ Cash and cash equivalents increased in 2014 by 70.7% from 2013 (Exhibit 13-3, p. 757), and it also increased as a percentage of total assets from 22.0% to 28.3% (line 4 in Exhibit 13-5).

■ Even though we saw from Exhibit 13-3, line 5, that accounts receivable, net increased by 33.3% from 2013 to 2014, line 5 of Exhibit 13-5 shows that it remained virtually constant as a percentage of total assets (13.4% in 2014 vs. 13.3% in 2013). As pointed out in the previous section, the percentage increase in accounts receivable year over year roughly matches the percentage increase in net sales from line 4 in Exhibit 13-2 (32.3%). This is a signal that the company's sales and receivables are following a consistent pattern of growth and that collections are holding steady.

Although inventories increased by 14.4% from 2013 to 2014 (Exhibit 13-3 line 6), they declined as a percentage of total assets, from 29.7% in 2013 to 25.6% in 2014 (Exhibit 13-5, line 6). Inventory turnover (cost of goods sold ÷ average inventory) increased slightly from about 3.03 times

Exhibit 13-5 | Comparative Consolidated Balance Sheets—Vertical Analysis

	A	B	C	D	E
1	**Under Armour, Inc.** **Consolidated Balance Sheets (in thousands of USD)**		**% of total**		**% of total**
2		**Dec. 31, 2014**		**Dec. 31, 2013**	
3	**Assets**				
4	Cash and cash equivalents	$ 593,175	28.3%	$ 347,489	22.0%
5	Accounts receivable, net	279,835	13.4%	209,952	13.3%
6	Inventories	536,714	25.6%	469,006	29.7%
7	Prepaid expenses and other current assets	87,177	4.2%	63,987	4.1%
8	Deferred income taxes	52,498	2.5%	38,377	2.4%
9	Total current assets	1,549,399	74.0%	1,128,811	71.5%
10	Property and equipment, net	305,564	14.6%	223,952	14.2%
11	Goodwill	123,256	5.9%	122,244	7.7%
12	Intangible assets, net	26,230	1.3%	24,097	1.5%
13	Deferred income taxes	33,570	1.6%	31,094	2.0%
14	Other long-term assets	57,064	2.7%	47,543	3.0%
15	Total assets	$ 2,095,083	100.0%	$ 1,577,741	100.0%
16	**Liabilities and Stockholders' Equity**				
17	Revolving credit facility	$ –		$ 100,000	6.3%
18	Accounts payable	210,432	10.0%	165,456	10.5%
19	Accrued expenses	147,681	7.0%	133,729	8.5%
20	Current maturities of long-term debt	28,951	1.4%	4,972	0.3%
21	Other current liabilities	34,563	1.6%	22,473	1.4%
22	Total current liabilities	421,627	20.1%	426,630	27.0%
23	Long-term debt, net of current maturities	255,250	12.2%	47,951	3.0%
24	Other long-term liabilities	67,906	3.2%	49,806	3.2%
25	Total liabilities	744,783	35.5%	524,387	33.2%
26	Commitments and contingencies (see Note 7)				
27	Stockholders' equity				
28	Class A Common Stock	59	0.0%	57	0.0%
29	Class B Convertible Common Stock	12	0.0%	13	0.0%
30	Additional paid-in capital	508,350	24.3%	397,248	25.2%
31	Retained earnings	856,687	40.9%	653,842	41.4%
32	Accumulated other comprehensive income (loss)	(14,808)	(0.7)%	2,194	0.1%
33	Total stockholders' equity	1,350,300	64.5%	1,053,354	66.8%
34	Total liabilities and stockholders' equity	$ 2,095,083	100.0%	$ 1,577,741	100.0%
35					

per year (once about every 120 days) in 2013 to about 3.126 times per year (once about every 117 days) in 2014.[2] Combining information from Exhibits 13-4 and 13-5, we see that gross profit improved slightly in 2014 (49% vs. 48.7%), and inventory turned over about 3 days faster in 2014 than 2013. This means that the company's products were both more profitable and sold faster in 2014 than 2013—a very good trend.

- Although Exhibit 13-3 line 10 shows that property, plant and equipment (net) increased by 36.4% in 2014 over 2013, it remained relatively consistent in terms of its proportion of total assets (14.6% vs. 14.2% in line 10 of Exhibit 13-5). Thus, the company's investment in property, plant and equipment grew proportionately with all other assets during 2014.

- The company's debt ratio (total liabilities ÷ total assets), reflected clearly in line 25, rose from 33.2% of total assets in 2013 to 35.5% of total assets in 2014. This increase was caused chiefly by an increase in long-term borrowing (line 23) in 2014 in order to finance expansion. As we discussed in Chapter 3, a debt ratio of 35.5% is considered quite low. This will allow the company to expand operations and service the debt as long as cash flow from operations remains healthy.

Overall, Under Armour, Inc.'s, financial position was very strong as of December 31, 2014. The company was highly liquid, well invested in inventory and fixed assets, and had a relatively low level of leverage (debt). It is no wonder that analysts have a high opinion of the future of this "red-hot" competitor in the athletic apparel industry!

---

[2]For computation of inventory turnover, see Chapter 6. Inventory as of December 31, 2012 was $319.3 million.

PREPARE COMMON-SIZE FINANCIAL STATEMENTS

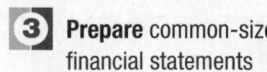

3 Prepare common-size
financial statements

Exhibits 13-4 and 13-5 can be modified to report only percentages (no dollar amounts). Such financial statements are called **common-size statements**. A common-size financial statement assists in the comparison of different companies because all amounts are stated in percentages, thus expressing the financial results of each comparative company in terms of a common denominator.

Calculate the common-size percentages for the following income statement:

Net sales..................................	$150,000
Cost of goods sold..................	60,000
Gross profit............................	90,000
Operating expense..................	40,000
Operating income..................	50,000
Income tax expense...............	15,000
Net income............................	$ 35,000

Answer:

Net sales..................................	100%	(= $150,000 ÷ $150,000)
Cost of goods sold..................	40	(= $ 60,000 ÷ $150,000)
Gross profit............................	60	(= $ 90,000 ÷ $150,000)
Operating expense..................	27	(= $ 40,000 ÷ $150,000)
Operating income..................	33	(= $ 50,000 ÷ $150,000)
Income tax expense...............	10	(= $ 15,000 ÷ $150,000)
Net income............................	23%	(= $ 35,000 ÷ $150,000)

Remember that you can use Excel, as pointed out earlier, to quickly and easily convert dollar-denominated data to percentages. You might want to practice doing this with the abbreviated data above to assure yourself that you have mastered it.

Benchmarking

Benchmarking compares a company to some standard set by others. The goal of benchmarking is improvement. Suppose you are a financial analyst for **Goldman Sachs**, a large investment bank. You are considering investing in one of two different retailers, say Under Armour, Inc., or Nike, Inc. A direct comparison of these companies' financial statements may not be meaningful, in part because Nike, Inc., is so much larger than Under Armour, Inc. However, you can convert both companies' income statements to common size and compare the percentages, making comparisons more meaningful.

Benchmarking Against a Key Competitor

Exhibit 13-6 presents the common-size income statement of Under Armour, Inc., benchmarked against the common-size income statement of Nike, Inc.

Exhibit 13-6 | Common-Size Income Statements Benchmarked Against Competitor

	A1			B	C
	Under Armour, Inc. Common-Size Income Statement for Comparison with Key Competitor (Adapted) Year Ended During 2014				
1					
2				Under Armour, Inc.	Nike, Inc.
3	Net sales			100.0%	100.0%
4	Cost of sales			51.0%	55.2%
5	Gross profit			49.0%	44.8%
6	Operating (selling, general and administrative) expenses			37.6%	35.1%
7	Operating income			11.4%	9.7%
8					

In this comparison, the results of operations of the two companies are strikingly similar. Because Nike, Inc., is so much larger than Under Armour, Inc., it sells to a wider range of customers, including big-box discount stores such as Wal-Mart and Target. It also sells a wider range of products than Under Armour. Therefore, Nike, Inc.'s, gross profit percentage (44.8%) is slightly below Under Armour, Inc.'s (49%). However, due to its size advantage, which produces economies of scale, Nike, Inc., has lower operating (selling, general, and administrative) expense percentages than Under Armour, Inc., partially compensating for its lower gross margin percentages. Operating incomes for the two companies (11.4% for Under Armour, Inc. vs. 9.7% for Nike, Inc.) are very comparable.

ANALYZE THE STATEMENT OF CASH FLOWS

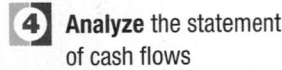

4 Analyze the statement of cash flows

This chapter has focused on the income statement and balance sheet. We may also perform horizontal analysis on the statement of cash flows. To continue our discussion of its role in decision making, let's use Exhibit 13-7, the comparative Consolidated Statements of Cash Flows of Under Armour, Inc. on page 764. We have modified the statements somewhat to illustrate selected horizontal percentage changes.

For 2014, net cash provided by operating activities was the major source of cash for the company ($219 million). Net cash provided by operations increased by 82.4% in 2014 over 2013. Also, for 2014, net cash provided by operating activities exceeded net income. The ability to generate most of its cash from operations is one sign of a healthy company.

Now focus on the investing section. Notice that the company has increased spending for property and equipment by 60% from 2013 to 2014. This is a signal that the company is plowing cash back into the business and that excess cash generated from operations is being invested in building future capacity. Finally, notice that the company is using long-term debt to finance the

Exhibit 13-7 | Under Armour, Inc., Comparative Consolidated Statements of Cash Flows

	A	B	C	D
		A1		
	Under Armour, Inc.	12 Months Ended		
1	Consolidated Statements of Cash Flows			
2	(in thousands of $)	Dec. 31, 2014	Dec. 31, 2013	% change
3	**Cash flows from operating activities**			
4	Net income	$ 208,042	$ 162,330	28.2%
5	Adjustments to reconcile net income to net cash provided by operating activities:			
6	Depreciation and amortization	72,093	50,549	
7	Unrealized foreign currency exchange rate losses (gains)	11,739	1,905	
8	Loss on disposal of property and equipment	261	332	
9	Stock-based compensation	50,812	43,184	
10	Deferred income taxes	(17,584)	(18,832)	
11	Changes in reserves and allowances	31,350	13,945	
12	Changes in operating assets and liabilities, net of effects of acquisitions:			
13	Accounts receivable	(101,057)	(35,960)	
14	Inventories	(84,658)	(156,900)	
15	Prepaid expenses and other assets	(33,345)	(19,049)	
16	Accounts payable	49,137	14,642	
17	Accrued expenses and other liabilities	28,856	56,481	
18	Income taxes payable and receivable	3,387	7,443	
19	Net cash provided by operating activities	219,033	120,070	82.4%
20	**Cash flows from investing activities**			
21	Purchases of property and equipment	(140,528)	(87,830)	60.0%
22	Purchase of business	(10,924)	(148,097)	
23	Purchases of other assets	(860)	(475)	
24	Change in loans receivable	–	(1,700)	
25	Net cash used in investing activities	(152,312)	(238,102)	
26	**Cash flows from financing activities**			
27	Proceeds from revolving credit facility	–	100,000	
28	Payments on revolving credit facility	(100,000)	–	
29	Proceeds from term loan	250,000	–	
30	Payments on term loan	(13,750)	–	
31	Payments on long-term debt	(4,972)	(5,471)	
32	Excess tax benefits from stock-based compensation arrangements	36,965	17,167	
33	Proceeds from exercise of stock options and other stock issuances	15,776	15,099	
34	Payments of debt-financing costs	(1,713)	–	
35	Net cash provided by financing activities	182,306	126,795	43.8%
36	Effect of exchange rate changes on cash and cash equivalents	(3,341)	(3,115)	
37	**Net increase in cash and cash equivalents**	$ 245,686	$5,648	
38	Cash and cash equivalents beginning of period	347,489	341,841	
39	Cash and cash equivalents end of period	$ 593,175	$ 347,489	
40				

portion of its growth that it cannot provide through operations. Interest rates were at historic lows during this time period, and the company had very low leverage, making borrowing an attractive means of financing for the future. Analysts may find the statement of cash flows as helpful for spotting weakness as for gauging success. Why? Because a *shortage* of cash can throw a company into bankruptcy, but lots of cash doesn't ensure success. Let's look at the cash flow statement of Unix Corporation. See if you can find signals of cash flow distress.

	A	B	C
	A1		
1	**Unix Corporation** **Statement of Cash Flows** **Year Ended June 30, 2016**		
2	**(In millions)**		
3	**Operating activities:**		
4	Net income		$ 35,000
5	Adjustments to reconcile net income to net cash provided by operating activities:		
6	Depreciation	$ 14,000	
7	Net increase in current assets other than cash	(24,000)	
8	Net increase in current liabilities	8,000	(2,000)
9	Net cash provided by operating activities		33,000
10	**Investing activities:**		
11	Sale of property, plant, and equipment	$ 91,000	
12	Net cash provided by investing activities		91,000
13	**Financing activities:**		
14	Borrowing	$ 22,000	
15	Payment of long-term debt	(90,000)	
16	Purchase of treasury stock	(9,000)	
17	Payment of dividends	(23,000)	
18	Net cash used for financing activities		(100,000)
19	Increase (decrease) in cash		$ 24,000
20			

Unix Corporation's statement of cash flows reveals the following:

■ Net cash provided by operating activities is less than net income. That's strange. Ordinarily, net cash provided by operating activities exceeds net income because of the add-back of depreciation and amortization. The increases in current assets and current liabilities should cancel out over time. For Unix Corporation, current assets increased far more than current liabilities during the year. This may be harmless. But it may signal difficulty in collecting receivables or selling inventory. Either event will cause trouble.

■ The sale of plant assets is Unix's major source of cash. This is okay if this is a one-time situation. Unix may be shifting from one line of business to another, and it may be selling off old assets. But if the sale of plant assets is the major source of cash for several periods, Unix will face a cash shortage. A company can't sell off its plant assets forever. Soon it will go out of business.

■ The only strength shown by the statement of cash flows is that Unix paid off more long-term debt than it borrowed. This will improve the debt ratio and Unix's credit standing.

In summary, here are some cash flow signs of a healthy company:

■ Net cash flow provided by operating activities exceeds net income.

■ Operations are the major *source* of cash (not a *use* of cash).

■ Investing activities include more purchases than sales of long-term assets.

■ Financing activities are not dominated by borrowing.

Perform a horizontal analysis and a vertical analysis of the comparative income statement of Hard Rock Products, Inc., which makes metal detectors. State whether 2016 was a good year or a bad year compared with 2015, and give your reasons. We encourage you to use Excel as a tool to perform your analysis.

A1

	A	B	C
1	**Hard Rock Products, Inc.** **Comparative Income Statements** **Years Ended December 31, 2016 and 2015**		
2		**2016**	**2015**
3	Total revenues	$ 275,000	$ 225,000
4	Expenses:		
5	Cost of goods sold	194,000	165,000
6	Engineering, selling, and administrative expenses	54,000	48,000
7	Interest expense	5,000	5,000
8	Income tax expense	9,000	3,000
9	Other expense (income)	1,000	(1,000)
10	Total expenses	263,000	220,000
11	Net income	$ 12,000	$ 5,000
12			

Answer

The horizontal analysis shows that total revenues increased 22.2%. This was greater than the 19.5% increase in total expenses, resulting in a 140% increase in net income.

A1

	A	B	C	D	E
1	**Hard Rock Products, Inc.** **Horizontal Analysis of Comparative Income Statements** **Years Ended December 31, 2016 and 2015**				
2		**2016**	**2015**	**Increase (Decrease)**	
				Amount	**Percent**
3	Total revenues	$ 275,000	$ 225,000	$ 50,000	22.2%
4	Expenses:				
5	Cost of goods sold	194,000	165,000	29,000	17.6
6	Engineering, selling, and				
7	administrative expenses	54,000	48,000	6,000	12.5
8	Interest expense	5,000	5,000	—	—
9	Income tax expense	9,000	3,000	6,000	200.0
10	Other expense (income)	1,000	(1,000)	2,000	—*
11	Total expenses	263,000	220,000	43,000	19.5
12	Net income	$ 12,000	$ 5,000	$ 7,000	140.0%
13					

*Percentage changes are typically not computed for shifts from a negative to a positive amount and vice versa.

The vertical analysis shows decreases in the percentages of net revenues consumed by the cost of goods sold (from 73.3% to 70.5%) and by the engineering, selling, and administrative expenses (from 21.3% to 19.6%). Because these two items are Hard Rock's largest dollar expenses, their percentage decreases are quite important. The relative reduction in expenses raised 2016 net income to 4.4% of revenues, compared with 2.2% the preceding year. The overall analysis indicates that 2016 was significantly better than 2015.

A1						
	A	**B**	**C**	**D**	**E**	
1	**Hard Rock Products, Inc.** **Vertical Analysis of Comparative Income Statements** **Years Ended December 31, 2016 and 2015**					
2		**2016**		**2015**		
		Amount	**Percent**	**Amount**	**Percent**	
3	Total revenues	$ 275,000	100.0 %	$ 225,000	100.0 %	
4	Expenses:					
5	Cost of goods sold	194,000	70.5	165,000	73.3	
6	Engineering, selling, and					
7	administrative expenses	54,000	19.6	48,000	21.3	
8	Interest expense	5,000	1.8	5,000	2.2	
9	Income tax expense	9,000	3.3	3,000	1.4 **	
10	Other expense (income)	1,000	0.4	(1,000)	(0.4)	
11	Total expenses	263,000	95.6	220,000	97.8	
12	Net income	$ 12,000	4.4 %	$ 5,000	2.2 %	
13						

**Number rounded up.

USE RATIOS TO MAKE BUSINESS DECISIONS

Ratios are a major tool of financial analysis. We have discussed the use of many ratios in financial analysis in various chapters throughout the book. A ratio expresses the relationship between various types of financial information. In this section, we review how ratios are computed and used to make business decisions, using Apple Inc., which was our spotlight company in Chapter 5, and which is also our focus company in Appendix A of the text.

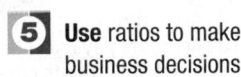 **Use** ratios to make business decisions

Many companies include ratios in a special section of their annual reports. Exhibit 13-8 shows a summary of selected data from previous Apple Inc., annual reports. Popular financial websites on the Internet report many of these ratios. Exhibit 13-8 has been prepared in Excel format, with formulas for most of the ratios we have studied in this text. This template can be used as a template for any company's financial statements, but has been tailor-made in this chapter for Apple Inc.

The ratios we discuss in this chapter are classified as follows:

1. Measuring ability to pay current liabilities

2. Measuring turnover and cash conversion cycle

3. Measuring leverage: overall ability to pay debts

4. Measuring profitability

5. Analyzing stock as an investment

You will find the skills you have acquired in earlier chapters in this book helpful when performing financial analysis using Microsoft Excel, as you work on the problems related to this section. Excel makes computation of financial ratios a breeze. However, interpretation of what the ratios mean and the use of the ratios to make decisions takes more time and effort! Now, let's analyze Apple Inc.

Exhibit 13-8 | Financial Summary: Apple Inc.

A1						
	A	**B**	**C**	**D**	**E**	**F**
1	**Apple Inc.** **Financial Summary and Key Ratios***					
2	In millions of $	**FY 2014**	**FY 2013**	**FY 2012**	**FY 2011**	**FY 2010**
3	**Results of operations**					
4	Net sales	$ 182,795	$ 170,910	$ 156,508	$ 108,249	$ 65,225
5	Cost of sales	112,258	106,606	87,846	64,431	39,541
6	Gross margin	70,537	64,304	68,662	43,818	25,684
7	Gross margin as percent of net sales	38.6%	37.6%	43.9%	40.5%	39.4%
8	Operating income	52,503	48,999	55,241	33,790	18,385
9	Operating income as percent of net sales	28.7%	28.7%	35.3%	31.2%	28.2%
10	Net income after taxes	39,510	37,037	41,733	25,922	14,013
11	Net income/sales (Return on Sales or ROS)	21.6%	21.7%	26.7%	23.9%	21.5%
12	ROA (line 11 x line 29)	18.0%	19.4%	28.6%	27.0%	22.9%
13	ROE (line 12 x line 40)	33.61%	30.73%	42.93%	41.58%	35.38%
14	Times interest earned	137	360	N/A	N/A	N/A
15	Common shares outstanding (000)	6,085,572	6,477,320	6,543,726	924,528	909,461
16	Earnings per common share, basic	$ 6.49	$ 5.72	$ 6.38	$ 28.05	$ 15.41
17	Price/earnings multiple	15.50	12.00	14.93	13.59	21.91
18	Cash dividends	11,126	10,564	2,523	–	–
19	Dividends per common share	1.82	1.64	2.65	–	–
20	**Financial position**					
21	Accounts receivable	17,460	13,102	10,930	5,369	5,510
22	Average accounts receivable	15,281	12,016	8,150	5,440	4,436
23	Inventories	2,111	1,764	791	776	1,051
24	Average inventories	1,937.5	1,277.5	783.5	913.5	753
25	Current assets	68,531	73,286	57,653	44,988	41,678
26	Quick assets	42,537	53,648	40,059	31,321	31,130
27	Total assets	231,839	207,000	176,064	116,371	75,183
28	Average total assets	219,420	191,532	146,218	95,777	61,342
29	Asset turnover (line 4/line 28)	0.833	0.892	1.070	1.130	1.063
30	Accounts payable	30,196	22,367	21,175	14,632	12,015
31	Average accounts payable	26,282	21,771	17,904	13,324	8,808
32	Current liabilities	63,448	43,658	38,542	27,970	20,722
33	Total liabilities	120,292	83,451	57,854	39,756	27,392
34	Working capital (line 25-line 32)	5,083	29,628	19,111	17,018	20,956
35	Current ratio (line 25/line 32)	1.08	1.68	1.50	1.61	2.01
36	Quick ratio (line 26/line 32)	0.67	1.23	1.04	1.12	1.50
37	Debt ratio (line 33/line 27)	0.52	0.40	0.33	0.34	0.36
38	Total stockholders' equity	111,547	123,549	118,210	76,615	47,791
39	Average stockholders' equity	117,548	120,880	97,413	62,203	39,716
40	Leverage ratio (line 28/line 39)	1.867	1.584	1.501	1.540	1.545
41	Inventory turnover (line 5/ line 24)	57.94	83.45	112.12	70.53	52.51
42	Days inventory outstanding (DIO)(365/line 41)	6.30	4.37	3.26	5.18	6.95
43	Accounts receivable turnover (line 4/line 22)	11.96	14.22	19.20	19.90	14.70
44	Days sales outstanding (DSO)(365/line 43)	30.52	25.67	19.01	18.34	24.83
45	Accounts payable turnover (line 5/line 31)	4.27	4.90	4.91	4.84	4.49
46	Days payable outstanding (DPO)(365/line 45)	85.48	74.49	74.34	75.41	81.29
47	Cash conversion cycle (line 42+line44-line 46)	(48.7)	(44.5)	(52.1)	(51.9)	(49.5)
48						

*There may be some slight variation in the calculations of ratios due to rounding.

Remember to Start at the Beginning: Company and Industry Information

As stated in the chapter opening, financial analysis is just massaging numbers unless we give the numbers a context. That comes from understanding the company and the industry and from knowing not only its history but where it appears to be headed in the future. Apple is known as perhaps the world's most innovative company. Founded as Apple Computer Company in Cupertino, California, in 1976 by two college dropouts, Steve Jobs and Michael Wozniak, the company first went public in 1977. For more than two decades, Apple was predominantly a manufacturer of personal computers. It faced intense competition from companies such as Dell, Inc., another upstart from Round Rock, Texas. Apple faced rocky sales and low market share during the 1990s. Jobs, who had been ousted from the company in 1985, returned to Apple in 1996 and shortly thereafter became the company's permanent CEO. Jobs subsequently instilled a new corporate philosophy of recognizable products and simple design, starting with the original iMac in 1998. Jobs died prematurely in 2011, but under an able team of senior management headed by CEO Tim Cook, the company continues to grow and prosper.

With the introduction of the successful iPod music player in 2001 and iTunes Music Store in 2003, Apple established itself as a leader in the consumer electronics and media sales industries, leading it to drop "Computer" from the company's name in 2007. The company is now also known for its iOS range of smart phone, media player, and tablet computer products that began with the iPhone, followed by the iPod Touch and then iPad. In 2015, the company launched both Apple TV and the Apple Watch. Apple TV is a device that directly links Internet programming to HDTVs, delivering streaming Internet-based content without the necessity of subscribing to cable. Apple TV is now the dominant player in the streaming video market. The Apple Watch is billed as Apple's most personal device yet. It is literally the world's first "wearable computer," incorporating all of Apple's unique technology and personal data tools into a device that travels with you wherever you go. The technological revolution continues to unfold, with some predicting that virtually every device that we use being connected to the Internet by 2020. Apple Inc., seems to be well positioned to prosper in this "brave new world" of technology because of its reputation as an innovator.

But how has all of this innovation impacted Apple Inc.'s shareholders? The discussion in the following paragraphs describes how the company's business strategy from 2012 through 2014 has impacted its numbers as seen in Exhibit 13-8. You can't fully understand the numbers without knowing the story.

As of the end of its September 29, 2012 fiscal year, Apple was the largest publicly traded corporation in the world by market capitalization, with an estimated value of $626 billion, larger than that of Google and Microsoft combined. As reflected in Exhibit 13-8, during the fiscal years 2010 through 2012, worldwide net sales revenues (line 4) for Apple Inc., grew by 2.4 times, from $65.2 billion to $156.5 billion. Net income after taxes (line 10) during this period almost tripled, growing from $14.0 billion to $41.7 billion. As of the end of its 2012 fiscal year, the company had generated an enormous stockpile of liquidity in cash and marketable securities, and had never paid a dollar of dividends to its shareholders or returned cash to them in any other form. Because it had so much cash, the company had no need to borrow money on a long-term basis. Consequently, its debt ratio was extremely low.

Shareholders of the company began to complain that, while the company was flush with profits and cash, the stockholders had not been allowed to participate adequately in the company's profitability through dividends or stock repurchases. Under pressure from the stockholders, the company's board of directors voted to pay Apple Inc.'s first dividend at the end of fiscal 2012, as well as to engage in an aggressive stock repurchase program over a period of several years, in order to allow shareholders to realize the pent-up appreciation in their shares' price, which was at that time in excess of $600 per share. However, there was a problem getting the cash out of the company to the shareholders. Most of the company's cash was sitting in banks of the company's profitable subsidiaries located in foreign countries that had much lower tax rates than the United States. In order to be distributed by Apple Inc. (the parent company), the cash and earnings would have to be "repatriated." That is, it would have to be distributed as dividends from the foreign subsidiaries and translated from foreign currencies to dollars. Repatriation of these earnings would have subjected them to U.S. corporate income taxes at rates exceeding 30%.

How could Apple make the required distributions and still avoid taxes? The company's finance team went to work and came up with an innovative solution: borrow the money to pay shareholder dividends and to repurchase their shares rather than transfer it from the foreign subsidiaries. Consequently, in spite of its tremendous stockpile of cash, Apple Inc. issued about $40 billion in long-term bonds during fiscal 2013 and 2014. The company combined the proceeds from the issuance of the bonds with those from the sale of some of the company's vast holdings in short-term available-for-sale marketable securities(refer to Chapter 5) in order to provide almost $90 billion in new cash to finance dividend payments and share repurchases over the 2013 and 2014 fiscal years. Because of the company's excellent credit rating, the bonds have been snapped up by institutional investors such as pension funds. The interest on the bonds (at historically low rates) is tax deductible (whereas dividend payments would not have been), and the company has avoided the heavy U.S. tax burden associated with repatriation of its earnings. In addition, the company declared a 7-for-1 stock split in 2014, distributing 7 shares for each share owned by its existing shareholders. This stock dividend increased the number of Apple's outstanding shares sevenfold, and reduced the market price of the stock from over $700 per share to less than $100 per share. The impact of these decisions on the company's liquidity and profitability ratios over the past two years has been significant, as you will see in the discussion that follows.

Now Let's Do the Numbers

Once you gain knowledge about a company and its industry, how do you determine whether the company's performance has been strong or weak, based on its current-period ratios? You can make that decision only if you have the following ratios to compare against the current period: (1) prior-year ratios, and (2) industry comparables, either in the form of an industry average or the ratios of a strong competitor. In the case of all the ratios in the following sections, we compare Apple's current year ratios with (1) its prior years' ratios (see Exhibit 13-8) and (2) ratios for the industry (if available), or ratios of one or more of Apple Inc.'s competitors.

Measuring Ability to Pay Current Liabilities

Working capital is defined as

$$\text{Working capital} = \text{Current assets} - \text{Current liabilities}$$

Working capital (also referred to as net working capital) measures the ability to pay current liabilities with current assets. In general, the larger the working capital, the better the ability to pay debts. Recall that capital is total assets minus total liabilities. Working capital is like a "current" version of total capital.

Consider two companies with equal working capital:

	Company	
	Jones	Smith
Current assets......................	$100,000	$200,000
Current liabilities	50,000	150,000
Working capital	$ 50,000	$ 50,000

Both companies have working capital of $50,000, but Jones's working capital is as large as its current liabilities. Smith's working capital is only one-third as large as current liabilities. Jones is in a better position because its working capital is a higher percentage of current liabilities.

As shown in Exhibit 13-8 (line 34), Apple Inc.'s working capital as of September 27, 2014 (the end of its 2014 fiscal year), was $5,083 million. This is down significantly from $29,628 million and $19,111 million at the end of its 2013 and 2012 fiscal years, respectively. As explained above, the company's reduction in working capital reflects its strategic decision to return cash to its shareholders starting in 2013. The company doubled its payments to shareholders in the form of stock repurchases from $22.9 billion in fiscal 2013 to $45 billion in fiscal 2014. The company also returned $11.1 billion more cash to shareholders in the form of cash dividends in 2014. This left Apple Inc.'s working capital substantially lower, but still not depleted to a critical level, because the company continues to generate billions of dollars in sales monthly, mostly for cash. Let's look at two key ratios now that help tell the rest of the story.

Current Ratio. The most common ratio evaluating current assets and current liabilities is the **current ratio**, which is current assets divided by current liabilities. As discussed in Chapter 3, the current ratio measures the ability to pay current liabilities with current assets. Exhibit 13-9 and Exhibit 13-10 show the Consolidated Statements of Operations and the Consolidated Balance Sheets of Apple Inc., respectively.

Exhibit 13-9 | Comparative Consolidated Statements of Operations—Apple Inc.

	A	B	C	D
		12 Months Ended		
1	**Apple Inc.** **Consolidated Statements of Operations**			
2	In millions, except share data	**Sep. 27, 2014**	**Sep. 28, 2013**	**Sep. 29, 2012**
3	Net sales	$ 182,795	$ 170,910	$ 156,508
4	Cost of sales	112,258	106,606	87,846
5	Gross margin	70,537	64,304	68,662
6	Operating expenses:			
7	Research and development	6,041	4,475	3,381
8	Selling, general and administrative	11,993	10,830	10,040
9	Total operating expenses	18,034	15,305	13,421
10	Operating income	52,503	48,999	55,241
11	Other income/(expense), net	980	1,156	522
12	Income before provision for income taxes	53,483	50,155	55,763
13	Provision for income taxes	13,973	13,118	14,030
14	Net income	$ 39,510	$ 37,037	$ 41,733
15	Earnings per share:			
16	Basic*	$ 6.49	$ 5.72	$ 6.38
17	Diluted*	$ 6.45	$ 5.68	$ 6.31
18	Shares used in computing earnings per share:			
19	Basic	6,085,572	6,477,320	6,543,726
20	Diluted	6,122,663	6,521,634	6,617,483
21	Cash dividends declared per common share	$ 1.82	$ 1.64	$ 0.38
22	*Restated in 2013 and 2012 to reflect 7:1 stock split in 2014			
23				

Using figures from Exhibit 13-10, the following are current ratios of Apple Inc., at September 27, 2014, and September 28, 2013:

	Apple Inc.'s Current Ratio	
Formula (figures in millions)	**2014**	**2013**
$\text{Current ratio} = \dfrac{\text{Current assets}}{\text{Current liabilities}}$	$\dfrac{\$68,531}{\$63,448} = 1.08$	$\dfrac{\$73,286}{\$43,658} = 1.68$

Apple Inc.'s current ratio decreased during 2014, from 1.68 to 1.08, for the same reason that its working capital decreased: use of excess cash to pay dividends and repurchase stock from shareholders. Line 35 of Exhibit 13-8 shows the current ratio declining significantly over the past five years from 2.01 in 2010 to 1.08 in 2014. Further examination of current assets and current liabilities in Exhibit 13-10 shows that current liabilities increased from $43,658 million to $63,448 million (about 45%) during 2014, while current assets declined from $73,286 million to $68,531 million (about 6.5%). Accounts payable increased from $22,367 million to $30,196 million (35.0%) in 2014 over 2013 and, according to Exhibit 13-8 (line 30), by 2.5 times in five years' time. This is a natural consequence of the growth the company has experienced. It is hardly a sign of trouble, especially since the current ratio is within the bounds of what is considered healthy from the standpoint of the ability to pay current liabilities. In general, a higher current ratio indicates a stronger financial position. Apple Inc., certainly has more than sufficient current assets to maintain its operations. Apple's current ratio of 1.08 is comparable to the current ratios of two competitors: IBM and Hewlett-Packard Company,

Company	Current Ratio
IBM..	1.25
Hewlett-Packard Company................	1.15

Exhibit 13-10 | Comparative Consolidated Balance Sheets—Apple Inc.

	A	B	C
	A1		
1	**Apple,Inc.** **Consolidated Balance Sheets**	**Sep. 27, 2014**	**Sep. 28, 2013**
2	In Millions of $, unless otherwise specified		
3	**Current assets:**		
4	Cash and cash equivalents	$ 13,844	$ 14,259
5	Short-term marketable securities	11,233	26,287
6	Accounts receivable, less allowances of $86 and $99, respectively	17,460	13,102
7	Inventories	2,111	1,764
8	Deferred tax assets	4,318	3,453
9	Vendor non-trade receivables	9,759	7,539
10	Other current assets	9,806	6,882
11	**Total current assets**	68,531	73,286
12	Long-term marketable securities	130,162	106,215
13	Property, plant and equipment, net	20,624	16,597
14	Goodwill	4,616	1,577
15	Acquired intangible assets, net	4,142	4,179
16	Other assets	3,764	5,146
17	**Total assets**	$ 231,839	$ 207,000
18	**Current liabilities:**		
19	Accounts payable	$ 30,196	$ 22,367
20	Accrued expenses	18,453	13,856
21	Deferred revenue	8,491	7,435
22	Commercial paper	6,308	–
23	**Total current liabilities**	63,448	43,658
24	Deferred revenue - non-current	3,031	2,625
25	Long-term debt	28,987	16,960
26	Other non-current liabilities	24,826	20,208
27	**Total liabilities**	120,292	83,451
28	Commitments and contingencies		
29	**Shareholders' equity:**		
30	Common stock and additional paid-in capital, $0.00001 par value;		
31	12,600,000 shares authorized; 5,866,161 and 6,294,494 shares		
32	issued and outstanding, respectively	23,313	19,764
33	Retained earnings	87,152	1,04,256
34	Accumulated other comprehensive income/(loss)	1,082	(471)
35	**Total shareholders' equity**	111,547	123,549
36	**Total liabilities and shareholders' equity**	$ 231,839	$ 207,000
37			

Quick (Acid-Test) Ratio. As discussed in Chapter 5, the **quick (acid-test) ratio** tells us whether the entity could pass the acid test of paying all its current liabilities if they came due immediately (quickly). The quick ratio uses a narrower base to measure liquidity than the current ratio does.

To compute the quick ratio, we add cash, short-term investments, and accounts receivable (net of allowances), and divide by current liabilities. Inventory and prepaid expenses are excluded because they are less liquid. A business may be unable to convert inventory to cash immediately.

Using the information in Exhibits 13-8 (line 36) and 13-10, Apple Inc.'s quick ratios for 2014 and 2013 are (in millions of $):

		Apple Inc.'s Quick Ratio	
	Formula	2014	2013
Quick ratio =	$\dfrac{\text{Cash and cash equivalents}+\text{Short-term investments}+\text{Net current receivables}}{\text{Current liabilities}}$	$\dfrac{\$13,844 + \$11,233 + \$17,460}{\$63,448} = 0.67$	$\dfrac{\$14,259 + \$26,287 + \$13,102}{\$43,658} = 1.23$

Like the current ratio, the company's quick ratio declined somewhat from 2010 through 2014 and was quite low at the end of 2014. However, because of Apple Inc.'s ability to generate cash quickly, a low quick ratio doesn't spell liquidity problems. In addition, Apple Inc. is still competitive with other major companies in its industry. Compare Apple Inc.'s quick ratio with the values of two leading competitors:

Company	Quick (Acid-Test) Ratio
IBM...	0.944
Hewlett-Packard Company................	0.73

A quick ratio of 0.90 to 1.00 is acceptable in most industries. How can many retail companies function with low quick ratios? Because their cash conversion cycles are so short. This points us to the next group of ratios, which measure turnover and the cash conversion cycle.

Measuring Turnover and the Cash Conversion Cycle

The ability to sell inventory and collect receivables, as well as effectively manage payments on accounts payable, is the lifeblood of any retail, wholesale, or manufacturing concern. In this section, we discuss three ratios that measure this ability—inventory turnover, accounts receivable turnover, and accounts payable turnover—as well as the relationship between them, called the *cash conversion cycle*.

Inventory Turnover. Companies generally strive to sell their inventory as quickly as possible. The faster inventory sells, the sooner cash comes in. **Inventory turnover**, discussed in Chapter 6, measures the number of times a company sells its average level of inventory during a year. A fast turnover indicates ease in selling inventory; a low turnover indicates difficulty. A value of 6 means that the company's average level of inventory has been sold six times during the year, and that's usually better than a turnover of three times. But too high a value can mean that the business is not keeping enough inventory on hand, which can lead to lost sales if the company can't fill orders. Therefore, a business strives for the most *profitable* rate of turnover, not necessarily the *highest* rate.

To compute inventory turnover, divide cost of goods sold by the average inventory for the period. We use the cost of goods sold—*not sales*—in the computation because both cost of goods sold and inventory are stated *at cost*. Apple Inc.'s inventory turnover for 2014 is

Formula	Apple Inc.'s Inventory Turnover	Competitor (Hewlett-Packard Co.)
Inventory turnover $= \dfrac{\text{Cost of goods sold}}{\text{Average inventory}}$	$\dfrac{\$112,258 \text{ million}}{\$1,937.5 \text{ million}} = 57.94$	9.06
Days' inventory outstanding (DIO) $= \dfrac{365}{\text{Turnover}}$	$\dfrac{365}{57.94} = 6.3 \text{ days}$	40.3 days

Cost of goods sold comes from the Consolidated Statements of Operations (Exhibit 13-9). Average inventory (from the balance sheets, Exhibit 13-10) is the average of beginning ($1,764 million) and ending inventory ($2,111 million). If inventory levels vary greatly from month to month, you may compute the monthly average by adding the 12 monthly balances and dividing the sum by 12.

Inventory turnover varies widely with the nature of the business. For example, Apple's inventory turned over 57.9 times in 2014. On a daily basis (days' inventory outstanding), that means once every 6.3 days (365/57.9)! In 2013, Apple Inc.'s inventory turned over 83.5 times. Line 41 in Exhibit 13-8 shows that inventory turnover more than doubled between 2010 and 2012 and has declined to about one-half of its 2012 rate as of the end of fiscal 2014. However, it is still quite high. In contrast, Hewlett-Packard Company's inventory turned over 9.06 times in 2014 (about once every 40.3 days). Computer and electronics manufacturers purposely keep very low inventory levels because of their ability to manufacture inventory quickly and because technology is subject to rapid obsolescence. Apple Inc., is exceptional, even by these standards.

To evaluate inventory turnover, compare the ratio over time as well as with industry averages or competitors. Steadily increasing inventory turnover is a positive sign, particularly if gross profits are also increasing. A sharp decline in inventory turnover suggests the need to take action to increase sales, usually by lowering prices. Unfortunately, this will reduce gross margins until excess inventory can be disposed of.

Accounts Receivable Turnover. **Accounts receivable turnover** measures the ability to collect cash from credit customers. In general, the higher this ratio, the better. However, a receivable turnover that is too high may indicate that credit is too tight, and that may cause a company to lose sales to good customers.

To compute accounts receivable turnover, divide net sales (assumed all on credit) by average net accounts receivable. The ratio tells how many times during the year average receivables were turned into cash. Apple Inc.'s accounts receivable turnover ratio for 2014 was

Formula		Apple Inc.'s Accounts Receivable Turnover	Competitor (Hewlett-Packard Co.)
Accounts receivable turnover	$= \dfrac{\text{Net credit sales}}{\text{Average net accounts receivable}}$	$\dfrac{\$182,795 \text{ million}}{\$15,281 \text{ million}} = 11.96$	7.50
Days' sales outstanding (DSO) (or days'-sales-in-receivables)	$= \dfrac{365}{\text{Turnover}}$	$\dfrac{365}{11.96} = 30.5 \text{ days}$	48.7 days

Net sales comes from Exhibit 13-9 and from line 4 of Exhibit 13-8. Average net accounts receivable (line 22 of Exhibit 13-8) is figured by adding beginning ($13,102 million) and ending receivables ($17,460 million) from Exhibit 13-10, then dividing by 2. If accounts receivable vary widely during the year, compute the average by using the 12 monthly balances. Apple Inc., collected its average accounts receivable 11.96 times during 2014. According to Exhibit 13-8 (line 43), accounts receivable turnover has been steadily decreasing, from 19.9 times in fiscal 2011 to 11.96 times in 2014. In comparison, Hewlett-Packard Company's accounts receivable turnover for 2014 was 7.5 times.

Apple Inc.'s accounts receivable turnover of 11.96 times per year is much faster than the industry average. Apple owns and operates a large number of retail stores, and much of its sales are for cash, which makes the receivables balance very low relative to the sales balance.

Days' Sales Outstanding. Businesses must convert accounts receivable to cash. All else being equal, the lower the receivable balance, the better the cash flow.

The *days' sales outstanding (DSO)*, or **days sales in receivables**, discussed in Chapter 5, shows how many days' sales remain in accounts receivable. Days' sales in receivables can be calculated two different ways, each of which produces the identical result. First, if you have already calculated receivables turnover (see the previous section), simply divide the turnover into 365. For Apple Inc., days' sales in receivables works out to about 30.5 days (365/11.96). Exhibit 13-8 (line 44) shows that DSO has increased by about 12 days since 2011, meaning the company collected cash on receivables 12 days slower in 2014 than it did in 2011. However, Apple's collection period on its receivables is still acceptable and approximately equals an average company's credit cycle of 30 days.

The second way to compute the ratio, described in Chapter 5, merely works from a different angle, by a two-step process:

1. Divide net sales by 365 days to figure average daily sales.

2. Divide average net receivables by average daily sales.

The data to compute this ratio for Apple Inc. are taken from the 2014 income statement (Exhibit 13-9) and balance sheet (Exhibit 13-10):

Formula	Apple Inc.'s Days' Sales in Accounts Receivable	Competitor (Hewlett-Packard Company)
Days' sales outstanding (DSO) or days' sales in receivables:		
1. Average daily sales $= \dfrac{\text{Net sales}}{365 \text{ days}}$	$\dfrac{\$182,795 \text{ million}}{365 \text{ days}} = \$500.8$ million	
2. Convert average daily sales to DSO $= \dfrac{\text{Average net accounts receivable}}{\text{Average daily sales}}$	$\dfrac{\$15,281 \text{ million}}{\$500.8 \text{ million}} = 30.5$ days	48.7 days

By comparison, Hewlett-Packard Company's, DSO in 2014 was 48.7 days (365/7.5 turnover). Hewlett-Packard sells fewer types of products than Apple and owns no retail outlets.

Accounts Payable Turnover. Discussed in Chapter 9, accounts payable turnover measures the number of times per year that the entity pays off its accounts payable. To compute accounts payable turnover, divide cost of goods sold by average accounts payable.[3] For Apple Inc., this ratio is

Formula	Apple Inc.'s Accounts Payable Turnover	Competitor (Hewlett-Packard Co.)
Accounts payable turnover $= \dfrac{\text{Cost of goods sold}}{\text{Average accounts payable}}$	$\dfrac{\$112,258 \text{ million}}{\$26,282 \text{ million}} = 4.27$	4.93
Days' payable outstanding (DPO) $= \dfrac{365}{\text{Turnover}}$	$\dfrac{365}{4.27} = 85.5$ days	74.0 days

Cost of goods sold comes from Exhibit 13-9 and line 5 of Exhibit 13-8, while average accounts payable comes from line 31 of Exhibit 13-8. On average, Apple Inc., pays off its accounts payable 4.27 times per year, which is about every 85.5 days. To convert accounts payable turnover to days' payable outstanding (DPO), divide the turnover into 365 (365 ÷ 4.27 = 85.5 days). In comparison, Hewlett-Packard Company's accounts payable turnover is 4.93 times per year, or about every 74 days. The financial summary (Exhibit 13-8, line 46) shows that DPO has increased by about 10 days during the past four years, indicating that in 2014 Apple Inc., is paying its suppliers about 10 days slower than it did in 2011.

Cash Conversion Cycle. By expressing the three turnover ratios in days, we can compute a company's **cash conversion cycle** as follows:

Formula	Apple Inc.'s Cash Conversion Cycle	Competitor (Hewlett-Packard Co.)
Cash conversion cycle $=$ DIO + DSO − DPO	$6.3 + 30.5 - 85.5 = -48.7$ days	15.0 days
where DIO $=$ Days' inventory outstanding		
DSO $=$ Days' sales outstanding		
DPO $=$ Days' payable outstanding		

At first glance, a negative amount for the cash conversion cycle looks odd. What does it mean? Apple Inc., is in the enviable position of being able to sell inventory and collect from its customers 48.7 days before it has to pay its suppliers who provided the parts and materials to produce

---

[3]For manufacturing or service-oriented companies, it is appropriate to use purchases rather than cost of goods sold as the numerator of the fraction. This requires adjusting cost of goods sold for the difference between beginning and ending inventories. See Chapter 9 for details. When inventories are small in relation to cost of goods sold, and/or when there is virtually no change between beginning and ending inventories (as is the case for Apple Inc.), this adjustment is insignificant. Therefore, to simplify, cost of goods sold may be used without adjustment.

those inventories. This means that Apple can stock less inventory and hold onto cash longer than other companies. It also helps explain why the company could afford to keep over $11 billion in short-term marketable securities (Exhibit 13-10) to "sop up" its excess cash, using it to make still more money while waiting to pay off suppliers. According to Exhibit 13-8, line 47, Apple's negative cash conversion cycle has decreased (become less favorable) by almost four days from 2011 through 2014. Apple's competitor, Hewlett-Packard Company, had a positive cash conversion cycle of 15.0 days in 2014.

Under Armour, Inc., featured earlier in this chapter, had a positive cash conversion cycle in 2014 of about 113 days, whereas Nike, Inc., a competitor of Under Armour's, has an 88.7 day cycle. These companies have a much slower inventory turnover ratio than Apple Inc. Retail companies that have a more "seasonal" inventory turnover (about four times per year, or about every 90 days) have cash conversion cycles in the range of 30 to 60 days, depending on how long it takes to collect from customers. The cash conversion cycle for service-oriented businesses consists only of (DSO – DPO) because service businesses typically do not carry inventory.

Measuring Leverage: Overall Ability to Pay Debts

The ratios discussed so far relate to current assets and current liabilities. They measure the ability to sell inventory, collect receivables, and pay current liabilities. Two indicators of the ability to pay total liabilities are the debt ratio and the times-interest-earned ratio.

Debt Ratio. Suppose you are a bank loan officer and you have received loan applications for $500,000 from two similar companies. The first company already owes $600,000, and the second owes only $250,000. Which company gets the loan? Company 2 may look like the stronger candidate, because it owes less.

This relationship between total liabilities and total assets is called the **debt ratio**. Discussed in Chapters 3 and 9, the debt ratio tells us the proportion of assets financed with debt. A debt ratio of 1 reveals that debt has financed all the assets. A debt ratio of 0.50 means that debt finances half the assets. The higher the debt ratio, the greater the pressure to pay interest and principal. The lower the debt ratio, the lower the company's credit risk.

The debt ratios for Apple Inc. in 2014 and 2013 follow ($ in millions):

		Apple Inc.'s Debt Ratio		Competitor
	Formula	2014	2013	(Hewlett-Packard Company)
Debt ratio $= \dfrac{\text{Total liabilities}}{\text{Total assets}}$		$\dfrac{\$120,292}{\$231,839} = 0.52$	$\dfrac{\$83,451}{\$207,000} = 0.40$	0.73

Although Apple Inc.'s debt ratio increased substantially during 2014, it is still low compared to its competitor and compared with many other public companies. The Risk Management Association reports that the average debt ratio for most companies ranges around 0.62, with relatively little variation from company to company. However, companies in certain industries such as airlines usually have higher debt ratios. The debt ratio is related to the leverage ratio discussed in the next section, which is used in DuPont Analysis to compute return on equity.

Times-Interest-Earned Ratio. Analysts use a second ratio—the **times-interest-earned ratio** (introduced in Chapter 9)—to relate operating income to interest expense. To compute the times-interest-earned ratio, divide income from operations (operating income) by interest expense. Interest expense is a component of other income (expense) and is disclosed separately in Note 3 of the financial statements. This ratio measures the number of times operating income can *cover* interest expense and is also called the *interest-coverage ratio*. A high ratio indicates ease in paying interest; a low value suggests difficulty.

		Apple Inc.'s Times-Interest-Earned Ratio		Competitor
	Formula	2014	2013	(Hewlett-Packard Company)
Times-interest-earned ratio $= \dfrac{\text{Income from operations}}{\text{Interest expense}}$		$\dfrac{\$52,503}{\$384} = 137$	$\dfrac{\$48,999}{\$136} = 360$	12

Apple Inc.'s interest expense for fiscal 2014 was $384 million, up from $136 million in 2013. Income from operations covered these amounts by 137 times and 360 times, respectively. The company's operating income is clearly sufficient to cover its interest charges. In comparison, Hewlett-Packard Company has a relatively high debt ratio (0.73), and its times-interest-earned ratio is quite a bit lower (12.). However, Hewlett-Packard Company is also quite capable of servicing its interest payments. In Chapter 9, we studied the financial statements of Southwest Airlines, with 17.1 times interest coverage, and United Continental with only 3.2 times interest coverage. In summary, the judgment about the adequacy of interest coverage, like so many other factors of financial statement analysis, is very much dependent on the industry, as well as the company being studied.

Measuring Profitability

The fundamental goal of business is to earn a profit, and so the ratios that measure profitability are reported widely.

Gross (Profit) Margin Percentage. In Chapter 6, we defined gross (profit) margin as net sales − cost of goods sold. That is, gross margin is the amount of profit that the entity makes from merely selling a product before other operating costs are subtracted. In Chapter 11, we emphasized that a persistently improving gross margin percentage is one important element of earnings quality. Let's look at Apple Inc.'s gross margin percentages (see Exhibits 13-8 [line 7] and 13-9 for details):

Formula	Apple Inc.'s Gross Margin % 2014	2013	Competitor (Hewlett-Packard Company)
Gross Margin % = $\frac{\text{Gross margin}}{\text{Net sales}}$	38.6%	37.6%	24.1%

Apple is known as *the* innovator in the technology field. The company is constantly inventing new technology that people literally stand in line to purchase! Do you remember the last time you visited an Apple store (perhaps when a new version of the iPhone was introduced)? How much were you willing to pay for your new iPhone, iPad, or iMac? Do you remember how crowded the store was? As we discussed in Chapter 7, because of the creative talents of their people, some companies have been able to adopt a "product differentiation" business strategy, which allows them to sell their products for more than their competitors. When everyone wants the product, they are usually willing to pay more for it. As shown in Exhibit 13-8, line 7, Apple's gross margin percentage of 38.6% in 2014 is 1% greater in 2014 than it was in 2013. However, notice that Apple Inc.'s gross margin percentage in 2014 is 5.3% less than it was in fiscal 2012. Although Apple Inc. is the recognized industry leader, it does not have a monopoly on smart computing devices. In recent years, competitive pressures from other smart phone and handheld-device companies like Samsung have forced Apple Inc. to lower prices, thus affecting its gross margins. However, in comparison, Hewlett-Packard Company has only a 24.1% gross margin percentage on its products.

Operating Income (Profit) Percentage. Operating income (profit) percentage is income from operations as a percentage of net sales. It is an important statistic because it measures the percentage of profit earned from each sales dollar in a company's core business operations. In Chapter 11, we pointed out that a persistently high operating income compared to net sales is an important determinant of earnings quality. The first component of high operating earnings is a high gross margin percentage. After that, maximizing operating income depends on keeping operating expenses as low as possible, given a specified level of desired product quality and customer service. Apple Inc.'s operating income percentages, compared with Hewlett-Packard Company, follow:

Formula	Apple Inc.'s Operating Income % 2014	2013	Competitor (Hewlett-Packard Company)
Operating Income % = $\frac{\text{Operating Income}}{\text{Net sales}}$	28.7%	28.7%	6.4%

Apple is far ahead of the competition on earnings from its core operations. However, according to Exhibit 13-8 (line 9), because of declines in gross margin percentage in recent years, the company's operating profit percentage has declined from its high of 35.3% in 2012 back to 2010 levels.

DuPont Analysis. In Chapters 7 (pp. 402–403) and 10 (pp. 589–591), we introduced the **DuPont Analysis**, which is a detailed computation of rate of return on total assets (ROA) and rate of return on common stockholders' equity (ROE). It might prove helpful to reread those pages before you proceed with the following material. In Exhibit 13-11, we review the basic driver ratios for DuPont Analysis to provide a template for the analysis by component.

Exhibit 13-11 | DuPont Analysis Model

		ROA		×	Leverage ratio (Equity multiplier)	=	ROE
Rate of return on sales (Net profit margin ratio)	×	Asset turnover ratio		×	Leverage ratio (Equity multiplier)	=	Return on equity (ROE)
$\dfrac{\text{Net income*}}{\text{Net sales}}$	×	$\dfrac{\text{Net sales}}{\text{Average total assets}}$		×	$\dfrac{\text{Average total assets}}{\text{Average common stockholders' equity}}$	=	$\dfrac{\text{Net income*}}{\text{Average common stockholders' equity}}$

*minus preferred dividends, if any

Notice that the ultimate goal of DuPont Analysis is to explain the rate of return on common stockholders' equity in a detailed fashion (far right-hand column) by breaking it down into its component elements: rate of return on sales, asset turnover, and leverage ratio. The first two components of the model combine to give rate of return on total assets (ROA). When the last component (leverage ratio) is incorporated into the model, it produces (by cross-cancellation) rate of return on common stockholders' equity (ROE). We now explain each component of the model, using figures for Apple Inc., to illustrate.

Rate of Return (Net Profit Margin) on Sales. In business, *return* refers to profitability. Consider the **rate of return on net sales**, or simply *return on sales* (ROS). (The word *net* is usually omitted for convenience.) In Chapter 7, we referred to this ratio as *net profit margin ratio*. The initial element of DuPont Analysis, this ratio shows the percentage of each sales dollar earned as net income. The return-on-sales ratios for Apple Inc. are as follows (using figures in millions from Exhibits 13-8 and 13-9):

			Apple Inc.'s Rate of Return on Sales		Competitor
	Formula		2014	2013	(Hewlett-Packard Company)
Rate of return on sales (Net profit margin ratio)	=	$\dfrac{\text{Net income} - \text{Preferred dividends}}{\text{Net sales}}$	$\dfrac{\$39,510}{\$182,795} = 21.6\%$	$\dfrac{\$37,037}{\$170,910} = 21.7\%$	4.5%

Companies strive for a high rate of return on sales. The higher the percentage, the more profit is being generated by sales dollars. According to Exhibit 13-8 (line 11), Apple Inc.'s return on sales was high in 2014 (21.6%), but again looking at the five-year trend, we see that it sank back to 2010 levels after reaching an all-time high in 2012 of 26.7%. This is principally because of the decline in gross margins in recent years, as discussed earlier. However, even considering recent declines, Apple Inc.'s return on sales is more than that of some other leading companies:

Company	Rate of Return on Sales
FedEx...	4.6%
PepsiCo..	9.8%
Intel..	20.9%
Hewlett-Packard Company......................	4.5%

Asset Turnover. As discussed in Chapter 7, **asset turnover** measures the amount of net sales generated for each dollar invested in assets. As such, it is a measure of how efficiently management is operating the company. Companies with high asset turnover tend to be more productive than companies with low asset turnover. Let's examine Apple Inc.'s asset turnover for 2014 compared with 2013 and then compare it to competitor Hewlett-Packard Company's asset turnover (see Exhibit 13-8, line 28, for average total assets).

	Formula	Apple Inc.'s Asset Turnover		Competitor
		2014	2013	(Hewlett Packard Company)
Asset turnover ratio =	$\dfrac{\text{Net sales}}{\text{Average total assets}}$	$\dfrac{\$182,795 \text{ million}}{219,420 \text{ million}} = 0.833$	$\dfrac{\$170,910 \text{ million}}{\$191,532 \text{ million}} = 0.892$	1.07

Compared to Hewlett-Packard, Apple has invested more in assets per dollar of sales. This is often the case with innovative companies, as opposed to companies that focus on low cost. To make major product innovations requires a significant investment in both tangible and intangible assets. So, while Apple Inc. is significantly more profitable than Hewlett-Packard Company, it is less efficiently managed, at least by this measure.

Rate of Return on Total Assets (ROA). Having computed the "driver ratios" (rate of return on net sales and asset turnover), we are now prepared to combine them into the first two elements of DuPont Analysis to compute **rate of return on assets** (ROA):[4]

Rate of return on assets (ROA)	Apple Inc.'s ROA		Competitor
	2014	2013	(Hewlett-Packard Company)
Rate of return on sales	21.6%	21.7%	4.5%
×	×	×	×
Asset turnover ratio	0.833	0.892	1.07
=	=	=	=
ROA	18.0%	19.4%	4.8%

Again, the raw figures for our computations are based on income and asset figures from Exhibits 13-8 (line 12), 13-9, and 13-10, but the component ratios are based on the previous two illustrations. We see from these computations that for Apple Inc., ROA is driven principally by its high profitability based on product differentiation, rather than efficiency. In contrast, Hewlett-Packard Company's ROA is based more on efficiency than profitability. Hewlett-Packard is a low-margin provider of basic computer technology, and as the low-cost provider, it is more efficient, generating more sales per dollar invested in total assets than Apple.

Leverage (Equity Multiplier) Ratio. The final element of DuPont Analysis is the **leverage ratio**, which measures the impact of debt financing on profitability. You learned in Chapters 9 and 10 that it can be advantageous to use borrowed capital to finance a business. Earlier, we expressed the debt ratio as the ratio of total liabilities to total assets. The leverage ratio, or equity multiplier, measures the number of dollars of assets provided by each dollar of invested capital in stockholders' equity. Since Total assets – Stockholders' equity = Total liabilities, the leverage ratio is a way of inversely expressing the debt ratio—it merely looks at financing from the other side of the fundamental accounting equation. Let's examine Apple Inc.'s leverage ratios for 2014 and 2013 compared with that of its competitor, Hewlett-Packard Company (see Exhibit 13-8, line 28, for average total assets and line 39 for average stockholders' equity).

	Formula	Apple Inc.'s Leverage Ratios		Competitor
		2014	2013	(Hewlett-Packard Company)
Leverage ratio =	$\dfrac{\text{Average total assets}}{\text{Average common stockholders' equity}}$	$\dfrac{\$219,420 \text{ million}}{\$117,548 \text{ million}} = 1.867$	$\dfrac{\$191,532 \text{ million}}{120,880 \text{ million}} = 1.584$	3.813

---

[4]Some analysts use net income before interest expense to compute ROA, since interest expense measures the return earned by creditors who provide the portion of total assets for which the company has used borrowed capital.

As we pointed out earlier, Apple Inc., has a comparatively low debt ratio (52% and 40% for 2014 and 2013, respectively). This translates to comparatively low leverage ratios for Apple Inc. (1.867 and 1.584 for 2014 and 2013, respectively). By comparison, Hewlett-Packard Company has a comparatively high debt ratio (73% for 2014). Therefore, Hewlett-Packard uses much more borrowed capital than equity capital to finance its operations, and its leverage ratio is much higher (3.813).

Rate of Return on Common Stockholders' Equity (ROE). A popular measure of profitability is **rate of return on common stockholders' equity**, often shortened to *return on equity* (ROE). Also discussed in Chapter 10, this ratio shows the relationship between net income and common stockholders' investment in the company—how much income is earned for every $1 invested by common stockholders.

To compute this ratio by itself, first subtract preferred dividends, if any, from net income to measure income available to the common stockholders. Then divide income available to common stockholders by average common equity during the year. Common equity is total equity minus preferred equity. The vast majority of companies have no preferred equity, so common equity makes up the total. The 2014 return on common stockholders' equity, computed the traditional way, for Apple Inc., is

Formula	Apple Inc.'s 2014 Rate of Return on Common Stockholders' Equity	Competitor (Hewlett-Packard Company)
$\dfrac{\text{Rate of return}}{\text{on common}} = \dfrac{\text{Net income} - \text{Preferred dividends}}{\text{Average common stockholders' equity}}$	$\dfrac{\$39{,}510 \text{ million} - \$0}{\$117{,}548 \text{ million}} = 33.6\%$	18.3%

DuPont Analysis ultimately reaches the same result (except for rounding error), but using it allows us to see much more information about the interaction between profitability (return on sales), asset utilization (turnover), and leverage:

Rate of Return on Stockholders' Equity (ROE)	Apple Inc.'s ROE 2014	2013	Competitor (Hewlett-Packard Company)
ROA	18.0	19.4%	4.8%
×	×	×	×
Leverage ratio	1.867	1.584	3.813
=	=	=	=
ROE	33.6%	30.7%	18.3%

Apple Inc., is by far a more profitable company than Hewlett-Packard Company. Hewlett-Packard is slightly more efficient in terms of asset turnover and more highly leveraged than Apple, having an asset turnover ratio of 1.07, a 73% debt ratio, and a leverage ratio of 3.81 ($3.81 of assets per dollar of stockholders' equity). To be sure, use of leverage is often a good thing, as long as it is kept within reasonable limits. The practice of using leverage is called **trading on the equity** because it acts as a compounding factor for ROA. Companies like Hewlett-Packard that finance operations with debt are said to *leverage* their positions. However, Apple's superior profitability makes ROA, and also ROE, much higher. As we pointed out in Chapter 10, leverage can hurt ROE as well as help. If profits and cash flows decline, debts still must be paid. Therefore, leverage is a double-edged sword. It increases profits during good times but also magnifies losses during bad times.

Following are some recent ROE figures for a few other well-known companies:

Company	Rate of Return on Common Equity
General Electric.................	11.7%
Google	15.1%
Starbucks	42.4%

Earnings per Share of Common Stock. As discussed in Chapters 9 and 11, *earnings per share of common stock*, or simply **earnings per share (EPS)**, is the amount of net income earned for each share of outstanding *common* stock. EPS is the most widely quoted of all financial statistics. It's the only ratio that appears on the income statement.

Earnings per share is computed by dividing net income available to common stockholders by the weighted-average number of common shares outstanding during the year. Preferred dividends are subtracted from net income because the preferred stockholders have a prior claim to their dividends. Like most other companies, Apple Inc., has no preferred stock and thus has no preferred dividends. The firm's EPS for 2014 and 2013 follow (based on Exhibits 13-8 (line 16) and 13-9):

		Apple Inc.'s Earnings per Share (Basic)	
	Formula	2014	2013 (restated for 7:1 stock split in 2014)
Earnings per share of common stock	$= \dfrac{\text{Net income} - \text{Preferred dividends (in thousands)}}{\text{Average number of shares of common stock outstanding (in thousands)}}$	$\dfrac{\$39,510,000 - \$0}{6,085,572} = \$6.49$	$\dfrac{\$37,037,000 - \$0}{6,477,320} = \$5.72$

We see that Apple Inc.'s EPS increased 13% ($6.49 vs. $5.72) during 2014. This exhibit restates EPS in 2013 to reflect a 7:1 stock split in 2014. Recall that Apple Inc. declared a 7:1 stock split in 2014, which increased the number of shares sevenfold, and decreased EPS proportionately. It also decreased the market value of the company's stock from over $634 per share to $93 per share. The stock split was a strategic move designed to increase the marketability of Apple Inc.'s shares, making them more affordable. Apple Inc.'s stockholders have been enjoying huge appreciation in their investment for many years. In mid-2015, Apple Inc.'s common shares sold for about $130 per share. That's almost 40% appreciation from the price of the stock immediately after the split. So with the stock fluctuating this wildly in price over a six-month period, would purchasing Apple Inc.'s shares at $130 per share be a wise business decision? Where is the stock headed in 2016 and beyond? That's the relevant question to which a prospective stockholder wants an answer. The next section gives you some information on how analysts make this decision.

Analyzing Stock as an Investment

Investors buy stock to earn a return on their investment. This return consists of two parts: (1) gains (or losses) from selling the stock and (2) dividends.

Price-Earnings Ratio (Multiple). The **price-earnings ratio (multiple)** is the ratio of common stock price per share to earnings per share. This ratio, abbreviated P/E, appears in the *Wall Street Journal* stock listings and online. It shows the market price of $1 of earnings. Exhibit 13-8 (line 17) shows historical P/E multiples of Apple Inc. stock at various times from 2010 through 2014.

Calculations for the P/E ratios of Apple Inc. follow. The market price of Apple's common stock was $100.75 at September 27, 2014 (the end of its 2014 fiscal year) and $482.75 at September 28, 2013 (the end of its 2013 fiscal year). Stock prices can be obtained from a company's website or various other financial websites.

		Apple Inc.'s Price/Earnings Ratio	
	Formula	2014	2013 (before restatement for 7:1 stock split in 2014)
P/E ratio $=$	$\dfrac{\text{Market price per share of common stock}}{\text{Earnings per share}}$	$\dfrac{\$100.75}{\$6.49} = 15.5$	$\dfrac{\$482.75}{\$40.03} = 12.1$

Given Apple Inc.'s 2014 P/E ratio of 15.5, we would say that the company's stock is selling at 15.5 times earnings. Each $1 of Apple's earnings is worth $15.50 to the stock market.

Stocks trade in ranges, and public companies report updated EPS quarterly. These earnings are annualized and projected for the upcoming year (quarterly earnings multiplied by 4). Since Apple's yearly earnings were reported in 2014, its stock has traded in the range of $100 to $131 per share. Things change fast in the technology industry. New competitors, like Samsung and Motorola (a subsidiary of Google, Inc.), are threatening Apple with smart devices that perform comparably for a lower price. Market prices of stocks are based on consensus estimations of what may happen in the future—health of the global economy, business cycles, competition, government policies (both here and abroad), new-product announcements, foreign trade deals, foreign currency fluctuations, and even the health of key company executives may significantly impact the estimates. Markets run on sentiment and are very difficult to predict. Some analysts study past trends in P/E multiples and try to estimate future trading ranges. If the P/E multiple of a particular stock drifts toward the low end of a range, and if its projected earnings are increasing, it means that the price of the stock is becoming more attractive, which is a signal to buy. As P/E multiples drift higher, given projected earnings, the stock becomes too expensive, and the analyst would recommend "hold" or "sell." Apple Inc.'s historical P/E multiple on May 29, 2015, was 16.2 (stock price was $131.08 per share). The projected (forward) P/E multiple for Apple Inc. from one popular website in September 2015 was 13.52. Projected earnings per share for fiscal 2015 from the same website, based on the estimates of many stock analysts, was about $9. Therefore, the projected price of Apple Inc.'s stock as of September 2015 would be $121.68 (13.52 × $9). That would make Apple Inc.'s shares appear overvalued at the price of $131.08 per share on May 29, 2015. Would you buy it, hold it, or sell it? A sell decision would have probably been best, because by October 17, 2015, Apple Inc. stock was trading for about $111 per share.

Dividend Yield. **Dividend yield** is the ratio of dividends per share of stock to the stock's market price per share. This ratio measures the percentage of a stock's market value returned annually to the stockholders as dividends. Although dividends are never guaranteed, some well-established companies have continued to pay dividends even through turbulent economic times. *Preferred* stockholders pay special attention to this ratio because they invest primarily to receive dividends. However, certain companies, such as General Electric, **Merck Pharmaceuticals**, IBM, or Apple, also pay attractive dividends on their common stock. In periods of low interest rates on certificates of deposit or money-market funds, dividend-paying stocks become more attractive alternatives for conservative investors.

Because of its legendary profitability and phenomenal cash flows, Apple Inc., paid the first quarterly dividend in its history ($2.65 per share) on August 16, 2012. Since that time, the company has paid regular dividends. For the year ended September 27, 2014, Apple Inc.'s stock paid $1.82 per share in dividends! Based on Apple Inc.'s stock price of $100.75 on September 27, 2014, the dividend yield for shareholders on Apple Inc.'s common stock on that date was

Formula	*Dividend Yield on Apple Inc. Common Stock* September 27, 2014
Dividend yield on common stock* $= \dfrac{\text{Dividend per share of common stock}}{\text{Market price per share of common stock}}$	$\dfrac{\$1.82}{\$100.75} = 0.018$

*Dividend yields may also be calculated for preferred stock in a similar manner.

The company's dividend yield at the end of its 2014 fiscal year was about 1.8%. If you think a dividend yield of 1.8% is low, you'd be correct, but compared to current yields on certificates of deposit or bonds, it's pretty attractive. Dividend yields vary widely. They are generally higher for older, established firms (such as **Procter & Gamble** and General Electric) and lower to nonexistent for young, growth-oriented companies. Investors in Apple Inc. have not historically purchased the stock for its dividend potential, but because the stock is known for its capital appreciation. However, Apple Inc.'s shareholders are now expecting both.

Book Value per Share of Common Stock. **Book value per share of common stock** is simply common stockholders' equity divided by the number of shares of common stock outstanding. Common equity equals total equity less preferred equity. Apple Inc. has no preferred stock outstanding. Calculations of its book value per share of common stock follow. Numbers are based on Exhibit 13-10 (line 35), and Exhibit 13-9 (line 19).

		Book Value per Share of Apple Inc. Common Stock	
Formula (figures in thousands)		2014	2013
Book value per share of common stock	$= \dfrac{\text{Total stockholders' equity} - \text{Preferred equity}}{\text{Number of shares of common stock outstanding (basic)}}$	$\dfrac{\$111{,}547{,}000 - \$0}{6{,}085{,}572} = \$18.33$	$\dfrac{\$123{,}549{,}000 - \$0}{6{,}477{,}320} = \$19.07$

Book value per share indicates the recorded accounting amount for each share of common stock outstanding. Many experts believe book value is not useful for investment analysis because it bears no relationship to market value and provides little information beyond what's reported on the balance sheet. But some investors base their investment decisions on book value. For example, some investors rank stocks by the ratio of market price per share to book value per share: the lower the ratio, the more attractive the stock. These investors are called "value" investors, as contrasted with "growth" investors, who focus more on trends in net income.

What is the outlook for Apple Inc.? Some have predicted that Apple has had its day and that the appeal of its stock may have peaked. But people have said that before about Apple, and they have been proven wrong because they failed to account for Apple's most valuable asset—its innovative and creative workforce. Apple's track record over the past decade is nothing short of astounding. Many people have made a lot of money from buying (and selling) its stock at the right time. Its earnings per share are solid, and its ROS, ROA, and ROE lead the industry. As of March 28, 2015 (the first two quarters of fiscal 2015), Apple had $132.6 billion in sales at a gross margin of 40.3%, and $33.5 billion in highly liquid assets on its books awaiting deployment in the creative process. From the standpoint of liquidity and leverage, the company is in great shape. It has a negative cash conversion cycle, meaning that it sells inventory and collects cash from customers weeks before accounts payable are due. As of the end of fiscal 2014, it has a low debt ratio and no problems servicing existing debt. The company's recent P/E ratio of about 13.5 is relatively low.

Beyond that, Apple Inc. is one of the largest, and perhaps the most innovative, companies in the world, continually producing new products that everyone wants. The future for the company in the "brave new world" of personal electronics depends on whether it can continue to provide the type of products that have so captured our fancy in the past. Stay tuned via your iPhone, iPad, or Apple Watch.

The Limitations of Ratio Analysis

Business decisions are made in a world of uncertainty. As useful as ratios are, they aren't a cure-all. Consider a physician's use of a thermometer. A reading of 102.0° Fahrenheit tells a doctor that something is wrong with the patient but doesn't indicate what the problem is or how to cure it.

In financial analysis, a sudden drop in the current ratio signals that *something* is wrong, but it doesn't identify the problem. A manager must analyze the figures to learn what caused the ratio to fall. A drop in current assets may mean a cash shortage or that sales are slow. The manager must evaluate all the ratios in the light of factors such as increased competition or a slowdown in the economy.

Legislation, international affairs, scandals, and other factors can turn profits into losses. To be useful, ratios should be analyzed over a period of years to consider all relevant factors. Any one year, or even any two years, may not represent the company's performance over the long term. The investment decision, whether in stocks, bonds, real estate, cash, or more exotic instruments, depends on one's tolerance for risk, and risk is the one factor that is always a certainty!

USE OTHER MEASURES TO MAKE INVESTMENT DECISIONS

Economic Value Added (EVA®)

6 Use other measures to make investment decisions

The top managers of **Coca-Cola**, **Quaker Oats**, and other leading companies use **economic value added (EVA®)** to evaluate operating performance. EVA® combines accounting and finance to measure whether operations have increased stockholders' wealth. EVA® can be computed as follows:

$$EVA® = \text{Net income before taxes} + \text{Interest expense} - \text{Capital charge}$$

$$\text{Capital charge} = \left(\underset{\text{payable}}{\text{Notes}} + \underset{\substack{\text{of long-} \\ \text{term debt}}}{\underset{\text{maturities}}{\text{Current}}} + \underset{\text{debt}}{\text{Long-term}} + \underset{\text{equity}}{\text{Stockholders'}} \right) \times \underset{\text{capital}}{\text{Cost of}}$$

(Beginning balances)

All amounts for the EVA® computation, except the cost of capital, come from the financial statements. The **weighted-average cost of capital**, discussed earlier in Chapter 11, is a weighted average of the returns demanded by the company's stockholders and lenders. Cost of capital varies with the company's level of risk. For example, stockholders would demand a higher return from a start-up company than from Under Armour, Inc., because the new company is untested and therefore riskier. Lenders would also charge the new company a higher interest rate because of its greater risk. Thus, the new company has a higher cost of capital than Under Armour, Inc.

The cost of capital is a major topic in finance classes. In the following discussions, we assume a value for the cost of capital (such as 10%, 12%, or 15%) to illustrate the computation of EVA®.

The idea behind EVA® is that the returns to the company's stockholders (net income) and to its creditors (interest expense) should exceed the company's capital charge. The **capital charge** is the amount that stockholders and lenders *charge* a company for the use of their money. A positive EVA® amount suggests an increase in stockholder wealth, and so the company's stock should remain attractive to investors. If EVA® is negative, stockholders will probably be unhappy with the company and sell its stock, resulting in a decrease in the stock's price. Different companies tailor the EVA® computation to meet their own needs.

Let's apply EVA® to Under Armour, Inc. The company's EVA® for 2014 (see Exhibit 13-2 and Exhibit 13-3 for inputs) can be computed as follows, using net income before taxes (NIBT) and assuming an 8% weighted-average cost of capital (dollars in millions):

$$
\begin{aligned}
\text{Under Armour, Inc.'s EVA®} &= \text{NIBT} + \underset{\text{expense}}{\text{Interest}} - \left(\underset{\text{borrowings}}{\text{Short-term}} + \underset{\text{debt}}{\text{Long-term}} + \underset{\text{equity}}{\text{Stockholders'}} \right) \times \underset{\text{capital}}{\text{Cost of}} \\
&\qquad\qquad\qquad\qquad\qquad\qquad (\text{Beginning balances}) \\
&= \$342 + \$5 - [(\$105 + \$48 + \$1{,}053) \times 0.08] \\
&= \$347 - \$1{,}206 \times 0.08 \\
&= \$347 - \$96 \\
&= 251
\end{aligned}
$$

By this measure, Under Armour, Inc.'s, operations added $251 million of value to its stockholders' wealth during 2014 after meeting the company's capital charge. This performance is considered strong, confirming our earlier conclusions about the performance of Under Armour, Inc., by more conventional methods.

Red Flags in Financial Statement Analysis

Recent accounting scandals have highlighted the importance of *red flags* in financial analysis. The following conditions may mean a company is very risky:

- *Earnings problems.* Have income from continuing operations and net income decreased for several years in a row? Has income turned into a loss? This may be okay for a company in a cyclical industry, such as an airline or a home builder, but a company such as Under Armour, Inc., may be unable to survive consecutive loss years.

- *Decreased cash flow.* Cash flow validates earnings. Is net cash provided by operations consistently lower than net income? Are the sales of plant assets a major source of cash? If so, the company may be facing a cash shortage.

- *Too much debt.* How does the company's debt ratio compare to that of major competitors and to the industry average? If the debt ratio is much higher than average, the company may be unable to pay debts during tough times. As we saw earlier, Apple Inc.'s debt ratio of 52% in 2014 was much lower than Hewlett-Packard Company's 73% debt ratio.

- *Inability to collect receivables.* Are days' sales in receivables growing faster than for other companies in the industry? A cash shortage may be looming. Apple Inc.'s cash collections from customers are very strong.

- *Buildup of inventories.* Is inventory turnover slowing down? If so, the company may be unable to move products, or it may be overstating inventory as reported on the balance sheet. Recall from the cost-of-goods-sold model that one of the easiest ways to overstate net income is to overstate ending inventory. Apple Inc. has no problem here.

- *Trends of sales, inventory, and receivables.* Sales, receivables, and inventory generally move together. Increased sales lead to higher receivables and require more inventory in order to meet demand. Strange movements among these items may spell trouble. Apple Inc.'s relationships look normal.

Efficient Markets

An **efficient capital market** is one in which market prices fully reflect all information available to the public. Because stock prices reflect all publicly accessible data, it can be argued that the stock market is efficient. Market efficiency has implications for management action and for investor decisions. It means that managers cannot fool the market with accounting gimmicks. If the information is available, the market as a whole can set a "fair" price for the company's stock.

Suppose you are the president of Vitacomp Corporation. Reported earnings per share are $2, and the stock price is $40—so the P/E ratio is 20. You believe Vitacomp's stock is underpriced. To correct this situation, you are considering changing your depreciation method from accelerated to straight-line. The accounting change will increase earnings per share to $3. Will the stock price then rise to $60? Probably not; the company's stock price will probably remain at $40 because the market can understand the accounting change. After all, the company merely changed its method of computing depreciation. There is no effect on Vitacomp's cash flows, and the company's economic position is unchanged. An efficient market interprets data in light of their true underlying meaning.

In an efficient market, the search for "underpriced" stock is fruitless unless the investor has relevant *private* information. But it is unlawful as well as unethical to invest on the basis of *inside* information. An appropriate strategy seeks to manage risk, diversify investments, and minimize transaction costs. Financial analysis helps mainly to identify the risks of various stocks and then to manage the risk.

The Decision Guidelines feature summarizes the most widely used ratios.

DECISION GUIDELINES

USING RATIOS IN FINANCIAL STATEMENT ANALYSIS

Bobby and Kaye Simpson operate a financial services firm. They manage other people's money and do most of their own financial statement analysis. How do they measure companies' ability to pay bills, sell inventory, collect receivables, and so on? They use the standard ratios we have covered throughout this book.

Ratio	Computation	Information Provided
Measuring ability to pay current liabilities:		
1. Current ratio	$$\frac{\text{Current assets}}{\text{Current liabilities}}$$	Measures ability to pay current liabilities with current assets
2. Quick (acid-test) ratio	$$\frac{\text{Cash and cash equivalents} + \text{Short-term investments} + \text{Net current receivables}}{\text{Current liabilities}}$$	Shows ability to pay all current liabilities if they come due immediately
Measuring turnover and cash conversion cycle:		
3. Inventory turnover and days' inventory outstanding (DIO)	$$\text{Inventory turnover} = \frac{\text{Cost of goods sold}}{\text{Average inventory}}$$ $$\text{Days' inventory outstanding (DIO)} = \frac{365}{\text{Inventory turnover}}$$	Indicates salability of inventory—the number of times a company sells its average level of inventory during a year. DIO converts inventory turnover to number of days it takes to sell average inventory.
4. Accounts receivable turnover	$$\frac{\text{Net credit sales}}{\text{Average net accounts receivable}}$$	Measures ability to collect cash from credit customers
5. Days' sales in receivables or days' sales outstanding (DSO)	$$\frac{\text{Average net accounts receivable}}{\text{Average daily sales}}$$ or $$\frac{365}{\text{Accounts receivable turnover}}$$	Shows how many days' sales remain in Accounts Receivable—how many days it takes to collect the average level of receivables
6. Accounts payable turnover and days' payable outstanding (DPO)	$$\text{Accounts payable turnover} = \frac{\text{Cost of goods sold}}{\text{Average accounts payable}}$$ Days' payable outstanding (DPO) = 365/Accounts payable turnover	Shows how many times a year accounts payable turn over and how many days it takes the company to pay off accounts payable
7. Cash conversion cycle	Cash conversion cycle = DIO + DSO − DPO where DIO = Days' inventory outstanding DSO = Days' sales outstanding DPO = Days' payable outstanding	Shows overall liquidity by computing the total days it takes to convert inventory to receivables and back to cash, less the days to pay off its suppliers
Measuring ability to pay long-term debt:		
8. Debt ratio	$$\frac{\text{Total liabilities}}{\text{Total assets}}$$	Indicates percentage of assets financed with debt
9. Times-interest-earned ratio	$$\frac{\text{Income from operations}}{\text{Interest expense}}$$	Measures the number of times operating income can cover interest expense

Ratio	Computation	Information Provided
Measuring profitability:		
10. Gross margin %	$\dfrac{\text{Gross margin}}{\text{Net sales}}$	Shows the percentage of profit that a company makes from merely selling the product, before any other operating costs are subtracted
11. Operating income %	$\dfrac{\text{Income from operations}}{\text{Net sales}}$	Shows the percentage of profit earned from each dollar of sales in the company's core business, after operating costs have been subtracted
12. DuPont model	Exhibit 13-11	A detailed analysis of return on assets (ROA) and return on common stockholders' equity (ROE)
13. Rate of return on net sales	$\dfrac{\text{Net income} - \text{Preferred dividends}}{\text{Net sales}}$	Shows the percentage of each sales dollar earned as net income
14. Asset turnover ratio	$\dfrac{\text{Net sales}}{\text{Average total assets}}$	Measures the amount of net sales generated for each dollar invested in assets
15. Rate of return on total assets	DuPont method: $\text{Rate of return on net sales} \times \text{Asset turnover}$ or $\dfrac{\text{Net income} - \text{Preferred dividends}}{\text{Average total assets}}$	Measures how profitably a company uses its assets
16. Leverage ratio	$\dfrac{\text{Average total assets}}{\text{Average common stockholders' equity}}$	Otherwise known as the *equity multiplier*, measures the ratio of average total assets to average common stockholders' equity
17. Rate of return on common stockholders' equity	DuPont method: $\text{ROA} \times \text{Leverage ratio}$ or $\dfrac{\text{Net income} - \text{Preferred dividends}}{\text{Average common stockholders' equity}}$	Measures how much income is earned for every dollar invested by the company's common shareholders
18. Earnings per share of common stock	$\dfrac{\text{Net income} - \text{Preferred dividends}}{\text{Average number of shares of common stock outstanding}}$	Measures the amount of net income earned for each share of the company's common stock outstanding
Analyzing stock as an investment:		
19. Price-earnings ratio	$\dfrac{\text{Market price per share of common stock}}{\text{Earnings per share}}$	Indicates the market price of $1 of earnings
20. Dividend yield	$\dfrac{\text{Dividend per share of common (or preferred) stock}}{\text{Market price per share of common (or preferred) stock}}$	Shows the percentage of a stock's market value returned as dividends to stockholders each period
21. Book value per share of common stock	$\dfrac{\text{Total stockholders' equity} - \text{Preferred equity}}{\text{Number of shares of common stock outstanding}}$	Indicates the recorded accounting amount for each share of common stock outstanding

The following financial data are adapted from the annual reports of Lear Corporation:

A1						
	A	B	C	D	E
1	**Lear Corporation** **Four-Year Selected Financial Data** **Years Ended January 31, 2016, 2015, 2014, and 2013**				
2	**Operating Results***	**2016**	**2015**	**2014**	**2013**
3	**Net Sales**	$ 13,848	$ 13,673	$ 11,635	$ 9,054
4	Cost of goods sold	8,715	8,599	6,775	5,318
5	Interest expense	109	75	45	46
6	Income from operations	1,675	1,445	1,817	1,333
7	Net earnings (net loss)	1,450	877	1,127	824
8	Cash dividends	76	75	76	77
9					
10	**Financial Position**				
11	Merchandise inventory	1,550	1,904	1,462	1,056
12	Total assets	7,591	7,012	5,189	3,963
13	Current ratio	1.48	0.95	1.25	1.20
14	Stockholders' equity	3,010	2,928	2,630	1,574
15	Average number of shares of				
16	common stock outstanding				
17	(in thousands)	850	879	895	576
18					

*Dollar amounts are in thousands.

Requirement

1. Compute the following ratios for 2014 through 2016, and evaluate Lear's operating results. Use the DuPont formula for ROA and ROE. Are operating results strong or weak? Did they improve or deteriorate during the three-year period?

   a. Inventory turnover

   b. Gross margin (profit) percentage

   c. Operating income (profit) percentage

   d. Rate of return on sales

   e. Asset turnover

   f. Rate of return on assets

   g. Leverage ratio

   h. Rate of return on stockholders' equity

   i. Times interest earned

   j. Earnings per share

Answer

	2016	2015	2014
a. Inventory turnover	$\dfrac{\$8,715}{(\$1,550 + \$1,904)/2} = 5.05$ times	$\dfrac{\$8,599}{(\$1,904 + \$1,462)/2} = 5.1$ times	$\dfrac{\$6,775}{(\$1,462 + \$1,056)/2} = 5.4$ times
b. Gross profit percentage	$\dfrac{\$13,848 - \$8,715}{\$13,848} = 37.1\%$	$\dfrac{\$13,673 - \$8,599}{\$13,673} = 37.1\%$	$\dfrac{\$11,635 - \$6,775}{\$11,635} = 41.8\%$
c. Operating income percentage	$\dfrac{\$1,675}{\$13,848} = 12.1\%$	$\dfrac{\$1,445}{\$13,673} = 10.6\%$	$\dfrac{\$1,817}{\$11,635} = 15.6\%$
d. Rate of return on sales	$\dfrac{\$1,450}{\$13,848} = 10.5\%$	$\dfrac{\$877}{\$13,673} = 6.4\%$	$\dfrac{\$1,127}{\$11,635} = 9.7\%$
e. Asset turnover	$\dfrac{\$13,848}{(\$7,591 + \$7,012)/2} = 1.897$	$\dfrac{\$13,673}{(\$7,012 + \$5,189)/2} = 2.241$	$\dfrac{\$11,635}{(\$5,189 + \$3,963)/2} = 2.543$
f. Rate of return on assets*	$10.5\% \times 1.897 = 19.9\%$	$6.4\% \times 2.241 = 14.3\%$	$9.7\% \times 2.543 = 24.7\%$
g. Leverage ratio	$\dfrac{\$7,301.50}{(\$3,010 + \$2,928)/2} = 2.459$	$\dfrac{\$6,100.50}{(\$2,928 + \$2,630)/2} = 2.195$	$\dfrac{\$4,576}{(\$2,630 + \$1,574)/2} = 2.177$
h. Rate of return on stockholders' equity*	$19.9\% \times 2.459 = 48.9\%$	$14.3\% \times 2.195 = 31.4\%$	$24.7\% \times 2.177 = 53.8\%$
i. Times-interest-earned ratio	$\dfrac{\$1,675}{\$109} = 15.4$ times	$\dfrac{\$1,445}{\$75} = 19.3$ times	$\dfrac{\$1,817}{\$45} = 40.4$ times
j. Earnings per share	$\dfrac{\$1,450}{850} = \$1.71$	$\dfrac{\$877}{879} = \$1.00$	$\dfrac{\$1,127}{895} = \$1.26$

* Used DuPont model in Exhibit 13-11.

Evaluation. After dipping a little in 2015, some of Lear's operating results started to recover in 2016. The gross profit percentage is consistent with 2015, and operating income percentage and all the return measures are improving in 2016. Asset turnover has fallen a little, but rate of return on assets is headed in the right direction because of the increases in profitability that the company has experienced in 2016. The final result in 2016 was a healthy net income and earnings per share for the year. This yielded a positive ROA and, because of leverage, an even more positive ROE.

Review | Financial Statement Analysis

Quick Check (Answers are given on page 828.)

Analyze Donovan Company's financial statements by answering the questions that follow. Donovan owns a chain of restaurants.

	A	B	C
A1 ⇕			
	Donovan Company **Consolidated Statements of Income (Adapted)** **Years Ended December 31, 2016 and 2015**	**2016**	**2015**
1			
2	(In millions, except per share data)	**2016**	**2015**
3	Revenues		
4	Sales by Company-operated restaurants	$ 12,900	$ 11,100
5	Revenues from franchised and affiliated restaurants	4,450	3,600
6	Total revenues	17,350	14,700
7	Food and paper (Cost of goods sold)	4,515	3,330
8	Payroll and employee benefits	3,800	3,500
9	Occupancy and other operating expenses	2,900	3,400
10	Franchised restaurants—occupancy expenses	946	840
11	Selling, general, and administrative expenses	1,840	1,740
12	Other operating expense, net	545	845
13	Total operating expenses	14,546	13,655
14	Operating income	2,804	1,045
15	Interest expense	360	385
16	Other nonoperating expense, net	97	58
17	Income before income taxes	2,347	602
18	Income tax expense	821	241
19	Net income	$ 1,526	$ 361
20	Per common share basic:		
21	Net income	$ 1.39	$ 0.38
22	Dividends per common share	$ 0.70	$ 0.50
23			

A1	◆		
	A	**B**	**C**
1	**Donovan Company** **Consolidated Balance Sheets** **December 31, 2016 and 2015**		
2	**(In millions, except per share data)**	**2016**	**2015**
3	**Assets**		
4	**Current assets:**		
5	Cash and equivalents	$ 590	$ 445
6	Accounts and notes receivable	760	826
7	Inventories, at cost, not in excess of market	140	126
8	Prepaid expense and other current assets	560	435
9	Total current assets	2,050	1,832
10	**Property and equipment:**		
11	Property and equipment, at cost	28,770	26,300
12	Accumulated depreciation and amortization	(8,870)	(7,300)
13	Net property and equipment	19,900	19,000
14	**Other assets:**		
15	Investments in affiliates	1,090	1,000
16	Goodwill, net	1,770	1,540
17	Miscellaneous	960	1,070
18	Total other assets	3,820	3,610
19	Total assets	$ 25,770	$ 24,442
20	**Liabilities and Stockholders' Equity**		
21	**Current liabilities:**		
22	Accounts payable	$ 560	$ 630
23	Income taxes	65	18
24	Other taxes	200	200
25	Accrued interest	183	194
26	Accrued restructuring and restaurant closing costs	115	325
27	Accrued payroll and other liabilities	910	735
28	Current maturities of long-term debt	380	275
29	Total current liabilities	2,413	2,377
30	Long-term debt	9,300	9,400
31	Other long-term liabilities and noncontrolling interests	710	540
32	Deferred income taxes	1,030	1,005
33	**Total liabilities**	$ 13,453	$ 13,322
34	**Stockholders' equity:**		
35	Preferred stock, no par value; authorized—140.0 million shares;		
36	issued—none	—	—
37	Common stock, $0.01 par value; authorized—2.0 billion shares;		
38	issued—1,400 million shares	14	14
39	Additional paid-in capital	2,531	2,432
40	Unearned ESOP compensation	(94)	(96)
41	Retained earnings	20,106	19,350
42	Accumulated other comprehensive income (loss)	(810)	(1,570)
43	Common stock in treasury, at cost; 300 and 450 million shares	(9,430)	(9,010)
44	Total stockholders' equity	12,317	11,120
45	Total liabilities and stockholders' equity	$ 25,770	$ 24,442
46			

1. Horizontal analysis of Donovan's income statement for 2016 would show which of the following for selling, general, and administrative expenses?

a. 0.11   **c.** 0.95

b. 5.75%   **d.** None of the above

2. Vertical analysis of Donovan's income statement for 2016 would show which of the following for selling, general, and administrative expenses (use total revenues as the base)?
   a. 10.61%   **c.** 12.60%
   b. 14.30%   **d.** None of the above

3. Which item on Donovan's income statement has the most favorable trend during 2015–2016?
   a. Net income   **c.** Food and paper costs
   b. Payroll and employee benefits   **d.** Total revenues

4. On Donovan's common-size balance sheet for 2016, Goodwill would appear as
   a. 10.20% of total revenues.   **c.** 6.9%.
   b. $1,770 million.   **d.** up by 14.9%.

5. A good benchmark for Donovan Company would be
   a. Microsoft.   **c.** Whataburger.
   b. Volvo.   **d.** all of the above.

6. Donovan's inventory turnover for 2016 was
   a. 34 times.   **c.** 84 times.
   b. 61 times.   **d.** 15 times.

7. Donovan's quick (acid-test) ratio at the end of 2016 was
   a. 0.85.   **c.** 0.56.
   b. 2.41.   **d.** 0.05.

8. In 2016, using total revenues, Donovan's average collection period for accounts and notes receivable is
   a. 32 days.   **c.** 1 day.
   b. 2 days.   **d.** 17 days.

9. The average debt ratio for most companies is around 0.62. In 2016, Donovan's total debt position looks
   a. middle-ground.   **c.** safe.
   b. risky.   **d.** Cannot tell from the financial statements

10. Donovan's return on total revenues for 2016 is
    a. 5.92%.   **c.** 8.8%.
    b. $2.18.   **d.** $1.39.

11. Donovan's return on stockholders' equity for 2016 is
    a. 5.92%.   **c.** 13.0%.
    b. $1,526 million.   **d.** 8.8%.

12. On December 31, 2016, Donovan's common stock sold for $34 per share. At that price, how much did investors say $1 of the company's net income was worth?
    a. $1.00   **c.** $34.00
    b. $24.46   **d.** $0.06

13. On December 31, 2016, Donovan's common stock sold for $34 per share, and dividends per share were $0.70. Compute Donovan's dividend yield during 2016.
    a. 7.0%   **c.** 2.1%
    b. 1.5%   **d.** 5.2%

14. How much EVA® did Donovan generate for investors during 2016? Assume the cost of capital was 6%.
    a. $1,459 million   **c.** $1,526 million
    b. $1,886 million   **d.** $566 million

Accounting Vocabulary

accounts payable turnover (p. 775) Measures the number of times per year a company pays off its accounts payable. Assuming all purchases are on credit, to compute accounts payable turnover, divide purchases (cost of goods sold + ending inventory − beginning inventory) by average accounts payable. When inventories are immaterial, or when there is very little difference between beginning and ending inventories, substitute cost of goods sold for purchases.

accounts receivable turnover (p. 774) Measures a company's ability to collect cash from credit customers. To compute accounts receivable turnover, divide net credit sales by average net accounts receivable.

acid-test ratio (p. 772) Ratio of the sum of cash plus short-term investments plus net current receivables to total current liabilities. Tells whether the entity can pay all its current liabilities if they come due immediately. Also called the *quick ratio*.

asset turnover (p. 779) The dollars of sales generated per dollar of assets invested. Formula is Net sales ÷ Average total assets.

benchmarking (p. 762) The comparison of a company to a standard set by other companies, with a view toward improvement.

book value per share of common stock (p. 782) Common stockholders' equity divided by the number of shares of common stock outstanding. The recorded amount for each share of common stock outstanding.

capital charge (p. 784) The amount that stockholders and lenders charge a company for the use of their money. Calculated as (Notes payable + Loans payable + Long-term debt + Stockholders' equity) × Cost of capital.

cash conversion cycle (p. 775) The number of days it takes to convert inventory to receivables, and receivables into cash, after paying off payables. The formula is Days' inventory outstanding + Days' sales outstanding − Days' payables outstanding.

common-size statement (p. 762) A financial statement that reports only percentages (no dollar amounts).

current ratio (p. 770) Current assets divided by current liabilities. Measures a company's ability to pay current liabilities with current assets.

days' sales in receivables (p. 774) Ratio of average net accounts receivable to one day's sales. Indicates how many days' sales remain in Accounts Receivable awaiting collection. Also called the *collection period* and *days' sales outstanding*.

debt ratio (p. 776) Ratio of total liabilities to total assets. States the proportion of a company's assets that is financed with debt.

dividend yield (p. 782) Ratio of dividends per share of stock to the stock's market price per share. Tells the percentage of a stock's market value that the company returns to stockholders as dividends.

DuPont Analysis (p. 778) Detailed method of analyzing rate of return on common stockholders' equity. Rate of return on sales × Asset turnover × Leverage = Return on average common stockholders' equity.

earnings per share (EPS) (p. 781) Amount of a company's net income earned for each share of its outstanding common stock.

economic value added (EVA®) (p. 784) Used to evaluate a company's operating performance. EVA® combines the concepts of accounting income and corporate finance to measure whether the company's operations have increased stockholders' wealth. EVA® = Net income before taxes + Interest expense − Capital charge.

efficient capital market (p. 785) A capital market in which market prices fully reflect all information available to the public.

horizontal analysis (p. 754) Study of percentage changes in line items on comparative financial statements.

inventory turnover (p. 773) Ratio of cost of goods sold to average inventory. Indicates how rapidly inventory is sold.

leverage ratio (p. 779) Ratio of average total assets to average common stockholders' equity. Measures the number of dollars of assets provided by each dollar of invested capital.

price-earnings ratio (p. 781) Ratio of the market price of a share of common stock to the company's earnings per share. Measures the value that the stock market places on $1 of a company's earnings.

quick (acid-test) ratio (p. 772) Another name for the *acid-test ratio*.

rate of return on assets (p. 779) Net income − preferred dividends ÷ average total assets. This ratio measures a company's success in using its assets to earn income for the persons who finance the business. Also called *return on total assets*. Can also be computed using the first two elements of DuPont Analysis (Rate of return on net sales × Asset turnover).

rate of return on common stockholders' equity (p. 780) Net income minus preferred dividends, divided by average common stockholders' equity. A measure of profitability. Also called *return on equity*. Also can be computed with DuPont Analysis.

rate of return on net sales (p. 778) Ratio of net income − preferred dividends to net sales. A measure of profitability. Also called *return on sales*.

times-interest-earned ratio (p. 776) Ratio of income from operations to interest expense. Measures the number of times that operating income can cover interest expense. Also called the *interest-coverage ratio*.

trading on the equity (p. 780) Another name for *leverage*.

trend percentages (p. 758) A form of horizontal analysis that indicates the direction a business is taking.

vertical analysis (p. 759) Analysis of a financial statement that reveals the relationship of each statement item to a specified base, which is the 100% figure.

weighted-average cost of capital (p. 784) A weighted average of the returns demanded by the company's stockholders and lenders. Often referred to as the *weighted-average cost of capital (WACC)*.

working capital (p. 770) Current assets minus current liabilities; measures a business's ability to meet its short-term obligations with its current assets. Also called *net working capital*.

ASSESS YOUR PROGRESS

Some of the following exercises and problems are available as Excel questions in MyAccountingLab.

Ethics Check

EC13-1. Identify ethical principle violated

For each of the situations listed, identify which of three principles (integrity, objectivity and independence, or due care) from the AICPA Code of Professional Conduct is violated. Assume all persons listed in the situations are members of the AICPA. (Note: Refer to the AICPA Code of Professional Conduct contained on pages 29–30. Chapter 1 for descriptions of the principles.)

    a. Tiffany is the senior accounting manager for Kiva Co. and is in charge of preparing quarterly reports for the CEO and CFO. These reports compare a variety of Kiva's financial ratios to industry averages. This quarter, Kiva has done poorly compared to its competitors, so some of its ratios were not favorable. Because of their legendary tempers, Tiffany does not want to upset the CEO and CFO. She decides to include only favorable ratios in her report.

    b. Jackie is an accountant for Widget, Inc., and is stressed by the amount of work her boss has been giving her. Yesterday, Jackie's boss asked that she perform a financial statement analysis on the company's previous five years of financial statements and write a report explaining any inconsistencies. Jackie is busy, so she quickly throws together the report, without double checking the data used and the related calculations.

    c. Amirali was recently hired as a senior audit manager at the firm of Moeini & Chaghervand, but did not disclose that his wife is the CFO for one of its clients.

    d. Miles is the accounting manager for Genesis Global and knows the company must maintain working capital in excess of $50,000 to stay in accordance with its debt covenants. This past year, Genesis's working capital fell below $50,000 for a short period of time. Miles created fictitious entries to hide the violation of its debt covenants.

Short Exercises

 S13-1. *(Learning Objective 1: Perform horizontal analysis of revenues and net income)*
Verifine Corporation reported the following amounts on its 2016 comparative income statements:

(In thousands)	2016	2015	2014
Revenues.........................	$20,289	$20,045	$18,449
Total expenses................	10,701	10,409	10,180

Perform a horizontal analysis of revenues and net income—both in dollar amounts and in percentages—for 2016 and 2015.

S13-2. *(Learning Objective 1: Perform trend analysis of sales and net income)* Breen, Inc., reported the following sales and net income amounts:

LO 1

(In thousands)	2016	2015	2014	2013
Sales............................	$10,962	$10,266	$9,570	$8,700
Net income.................	553	392	371	350

Show Breen's trend percentages for sales and net income. Use 2013 as the base year.

S13-3. *(Learning Objective 2: Perform vertical analysis to correct a cash shortage)* Crafton Software reported the following amounts on its balance sheets at December 31, 2016, 2015, and 2014:

LO 2

	2016	2015	2014
Cash.......................................	$ 14,750	$ 7,920	$ 7,245
Receivables, net....................	29,500	15,840	19,320
Inventory..............................	312,700	237,600	183,540
Prepaid expenses	35,400	42,240	33,810
Property, plant, and equipment, net	197,650	224,400	239,085
Total assets	$590,000	$528,000	$483,000

Sales and profits are high. Nevertheless, Crafton is experiencing a cash shortage. Perform a vertical analysis of Crafton Software's assets at the end of years 2016, 2015, and 2014. Use the analysis to explain the reason for the cash shortage.

S13-4. *(Learning Objective 3: Compare common-size income statements of two companies)* Carlton, Inc., and Lofton Corporation are competitors. Compare the two companies by converting their condensed income statements to common size.

LO 3

(In millions)	Carlton	Lofton
Net sales...	$16,000	$7,000
Cost of goods sold...	9,536	4,648
Selling and administrative expenses...............	4,448	1,414
Interest expense...	96	14
Other expenses...	32	42
Income tax expense..	672	154
Net income...	$ 1,216	$ 728

Which company earned more net income? Which company's net income was a higher percentage of its net sales? Explain your answer.

LO 5 **S13-5.** (*Learning Objective 5: Evaluate the trend in a company's current ratio*) Examine the financial data of Peterson Corporation.

Year Ended December 31	2016	2015	2014
Operating Results			
Net income..	$ 220	$ 310	$ 312
Earnings per common share	$1.23	$1.54	$1.85
Net income as a percent of sales..........................	19.6%	17.6%	19.6%
Return on average stockholders' equity................	21.0%	18.0%	19.0%
Financial Position			
Current assets..	$ 646	$ 596	$ 434
Current liabilities	$ 380	$ 400	$ 350
Working capital	$ 266	$ 196	$ 84
Current ratio..	1.70	1.49	1.24

Show how to compute Peterson's current ratio for each year 2014 through 2016. Is the company's ability to pay its current liabilities improving or deteriorating?

LO 5 **S13-6.** (*Learning Objective 5: Evaluate a company's quick [acid-test] ratio*) Use the Gagnon, Inc., balance-sheet data to answer the following questions.
1. Compute Gagnon, Inc.'s, quick (acid-test) ratio at December 31, 2016, and 2015.
2. Use the comparative information from the table given for Horner, Inc., Isaacson Company, and Jona Companies Limited. Is Gagnon, Inc.'s, quick (acid-test) ratio for 2016 and 2015 strong, average, or weak in comparison?

	A	B	C	D	E
	A1				
1	**Gagnon, Inc.** **Balance Sheets (Adapted)** **December 31, 2016 and 2015**				
2				Increase (Decrease)	
3	**(Dollar amounts in millions)**	**2016**	**2015**	**Amount**	**Percentage**
4	**Assets**				
5	Current assets:				
6	Cash and cash equivalents	$ 1,202	$ 902	$ 300	33.3%
7	Short-term investments	8	84	(76)	(90.5)
8	Receivables, net	246	256	(10)	(3.9)
9	Inventories	90	82	8	9.8
10	Prepaid expenses and other assets	242	344	(102)	(29.7)
11	Total current assets	1,788	1,668	120	7.2
12	Property, plant, and equipment, net	3,642	3,306	336	10.2
13	Intangible assets	1,010	858	152	17.7
14	Other assets	820	732	88	12.0
15	Total assets	$ 7,260	$ 6,564	$ 696	10.6%
16	**Liabilities and Stockholders' Equity**				
17	Current liabilities:				
18	Accounts payable	$ 978	$ 884	$ 94	10.6%
19	Income tax payable	40	70	(30)	(42.9)
20	Short-term debt	124	118	6	5.1
21	Other	70	72	(2)	(2.8)
22	Total current liabilities	1,212	1,144	68	5.9
23	Long-term debt	3,514	2,844	670	23.6
24	Other liabilities	1,168	1,076	92	8.6
25	Total liabilities	5,894	5,064	830	16.4
26	**Stockholders' equity:**				
27	Common stock	2	2	—	—
28	Retained earnings	1,532	1,670	(138)	(8.3)
29	Accumulated other comprehensive (loss)	(168)	(172)	4	(2.3)
30	Total stockholders' equity	1,366	1,500	(134)	(8.9)
31	Total liabilities and stockholders' equity	$ 7,260	$ 6,564	$ 696	10.6%
32					

Company	Quick (acid-test) Ratio
Horner, Inc. (Utility)	0.79
Isaacson Company (Department store)..................	0.68
Jona Companies Limited (Grocery store)	0.71

S13-7. *(Learning Objective 5: Compute and evaluate turnover and the cash conversion cycle)* Use the Gagnon 2016 income statement that follows and the balance sheet from S13-6 to compute the following:

LO 5

A1				
	A		**B**	**C**
1	**Gagnon, Inc.** **Statements of Income (Adapted)** **Year Ended December 31, 2016 and 2015**			
2	**(Dollar amounts in millions)**		**2016**	**2015**
3	Revenues		$ 9,505	$ 9,309
4	Expenses:			
5	Food and paper (Cost of goods sold)		2,519	2,634
6	Payroll and employee benefits		2,169	2,241
7	Occupancy and other operating expenses		2,443	2,745
8	General and administrative expenses		1,207	1,135
9	Interest expense		194	147
10	Other expense (income), net		21	(35)
11	Income before income taxes		952	442
12	Income tax expense		387	269
13	Net income		$ 565	$ 173
14				

a. Gagnon, Inc.'s, rate of inventory turnover and days' inventory outstanding for 2016.

b. Days' sales in average receivables (days' sales outstanding) during 2016 (round dollar amounts to one decimal place). Assume all sales are made on account.

c. Accounts payable turnover and days' payables outstanding for 2016. For this purpose, assume that the impact of inventories on cost of goods sold is immaterial, allowing you to use cost of goods sold rather than purchases in your computations.

d. Length of cash conversion cycle in days for 2016.

Do these measures look strong or weak? Give the reason for your answer.

S13-8. *(Learning Objective 5: Measure ability to pay long-term debt)* Use the financial statements of Gagnon, Inc., in S13-6 and S13-7.

LO 5

 1. Compute the company's debt ratio at December 31, 2016.

 2. Compute the company's times-interest-earned ratio for 2016. For operating income, use income before both interest expense and income taxes. You can simply add interest expense back to income before taxes.

 3. Is Gagnon's ability to pay liabilities and interest expense strong or weak? Comment on the value of each ratio computed for questions 1 and 2.

S13-9. *(Learning Objective 5: Measure profitability using DuPont Analysis)* Use the financial statements of Gagnon, Inc., in S13-6 and S13-7 to compute these profitability measures for 2016. Show each computation.

LO 5

  a. Rate of return on sales
  b. Asset turnover ratio
  c. Rate of return on total assets
  d. Leverage (equity multiplier) ratio
  e. Rate of return on common stockholders' equity
  f. Is Gagnon, Inc.'s, profitability strong, medium, or weak?

LO 5

S13-10. (*Learning Objective 5: Compute EPS and the price-earnings ratio*) The annual report of Ferguson Cars, Inc., for the year ended December 31, 2016, included the following items (in millions):

Preferred stock outstanding, 10%	$ 100
Net income	$1,200
Average number of shares of common stock outstanding	700

1. Compute earnings per share (EPS) and the price-earnings ratio for Ferguson Cars' stock. Round to the nearest cent. The price of a share of Ferguson Cars' stock is $19.98.
2. How much does the stock market say $1 of Ferguson Cars' net income is worth?

LO 5

S13-11. (*Learning Objective 5: Use ratio data to reconstruct an income statement*) A skeleton of Pine Florals' income statement appears as follows (amounts in thousands):

	A	B
1	**Income Statement**	
2	Net sales	$ 7,200
3	Cost of goods sold	(a)
4	Selling expenses	1,516
5	Administrative expenses	1,334
6	Interest expense	(b)
7	Other expenses	153
8	Income before taxes	1,045
9	Income tax expense	(c)
10	Net income	$ (d)
11		

Use the following ratio data to complete Pine Florals' income statement:
  a. Inventory turnover was 4 (beginning inventory was $780; ending inventory was $750).
  b. Rate of return on sales (after income taxes) is 0.10.

LO 5

S13-12. (*Learning Objective 5: Use ratio data to reconstruct a balance sheet*) A skeleton of Pine Florals' balance sheet appears as follows (amounts in thousands):

	A	B	C	D
1	**Balance Sheet**			
2	Cash	$ 260	Total current liabilities	$ 2,250
3	Receivables	(a)	Long-term debt	(e)
4	Inventories	750	Other long-term liabilities	980
5	Prepaid expenses	(b)		
6	Total current assets	(c)		
7	Plant assets, net	(d)	Common stock	160
8	Other assets	2,450	Retained earnings	2,570
9	Total assets	$ 6,500	Total liabilities and equity	$ (f)
10				

Use the following ratio data to complete Pine Florals' balance sheet:
  a. Debt ratio is 0.58.
  b. Current ratio is 1.10.
  c. Quick (acid-test) ratio is 0.200.

S13-13. *(Learning Objective 5: Analyze a company based on its ratios)* Take the role of an investment analyst at Cole Binder. It is your job to recommend investments for your client. The only information you have is the following ratio values for two companies in the graphics software industry:

Ratio	Tower.org	Graphics Imaging
Days' sales in receivables.............................	41	48
Inventory turnover......................................	7	11
Gross profit percentage	67%	58%
Net income as a percent of sales................	12%	13%
Times interest earned	19	13
Return on equity	35%	30%
Return on assets..	14%	19%

Write a report to the Cole Binder investment committee. Recommend one company's stock over the other. State the reasons for your recommendation.

S13-14. *(Learning Objective 6: Measure economic value added)* Compute economic value added (EVA®) for Beecher Software. The company's cost of capital is 12%. Net income before taxes was $730 thousand, interest expense $403 thousand, beginning long-term debt $750 thousand, and beginning stockholders' equity was $3,250 thousand. Round all amounts to the nearest thousand dollars. Should the company's stockholders be happy with the EVA®?

Exercises MyAccountingLab

Group A

E13-15A. *(Learning Objective 1: Compute year-to-year changes in working capital)* What were the dollar amounts of change and the percentage of each change in Majestic Mountain Lodge's net working capital during 2016 and 2015? Is this trend favorable or unfavorable?

	2016	2015	2014
Total current assets	$643,260	$299,000	$300,000
Total current liabilities	390,000	110,000	150,000

E13-16A. *(Learning Objective 1: Perform horizontal analysis of an income statement)* Prepare a horizontal analysis of the comparative income statements of Connor Music Co. Round percentage changes to the nearest one-tenth percent (three decimal places).

	A	B	C
A1			
1	**Connor Music Co.** **Comparative Income Statements** **Years Ended December 31, 2016 and 2015**		
2		**2016**	**2015**
3	Total revenue	$ 836,000	$ 938,000
4	Expenses:		
5	Cost of goods sold	$ 408,000	$ 409,350
6	Selling and general expenses	238,000	263,000
7	Interest expense	9,500	14,000
8	Income tax expense	79,000	85,750
9	Total expenses	734,500	772,100
10	Net income	$ 101,500	$ 165,900
11			

LO 1

E13-17A. *(Learning Objective 1: Compute trend percentages)* Compute trend percentages for Sagamore Valley Sales & Service's total revenue and net income for the following five-year period, using year 0 as the base year. Round to the nearest full percent.

(In thousands)	Year 4	Year 3	Year 2	Year 1	Year 0
Total revenue	$1,428	$1,242	$1,088	$1,021	$1,019
Net income	106	95	82	69	86

Which grew faster during the period, total revenue or net income?

LO 2

E13-18A. *(Learning Objective 2: Perform vertical analysis of a balance sheet)* Curtis Golf Company has requested that you perform a vertical analysis of its balance sheet to determine the component percentages of its assets, liabilities, and stockholders' equity.

	A	B
	Curtis Golf Company **Balance Sheet** **December 31, 2016**	
1		
2	**Assets**	
3	Total current assets	$ 41,440
4	Property, plant, and equipment, net	199,640
5	Other assets	38,920
6	Total assets	$ 280,000
7		
8	**Liabilities**	
9	Total current liabilities	$ 47,320
10	Long-term debt	106,120
11	Total liabilities	153,440
12		
13	**Stockholders' Equity**	
14	Total stockholders' equity	126,560
15	Total liabilities and stockholders' equity	$ 280,000
16		

LO 3

E13-19A. *(Learning Objective 3: Prepare a common-size income statement)* Prepare a comparative common-size income statement for Connor Music Co., using the 2016 and 2015 data of E13-16A and rounding to four decimal places.

E13-20A. *(Learning Objective 4: Analyze the statement of cash flows)* Identify any weaknesses revealed by the statement of cash flows of Beckwith Orchards, Inc.

	A	B	C
1	**Beckwith Orchards, Inc.** **Statement of Cash Flows** **For the Current Year**		
2	**Operating activities:**		
3	Net income		$ 72,100
4	Add (subtract) adjustments to reconcile net income to net cash provided by operating activities:		
5	Depreciation	$ 11,250	
6	Net increase in current assets other than cash	(53,500)	
7	Net decrease in current liabilities		
8	exclusive of short-term debt	(19,750)	(62,000)
9	Net cash provided by operating activities		10,100
10			
11	**Investing activities:**		
12	Sale of property, plant, and equipment		124,200
13	Net cash provided by investing activities		124,200
14			
15	**Financing activities:**		
16	Issuance of bonds payable	$ 117,050	
17	Payment of short-term debt	(180,525)	
18	Payment of long-term debt	(89,025)	
19	Payment of dividends	(39,500)	
20	Net cash used for financing activities		(192,000)
21	Increase (decrease) in cash		$ (57,700)
22			

E13-21A. *(Learning Objective 5: Compute ratios; evaluate turnover, liquidity, and current debt-paying ability)* The financial statements of Adventure News, Inc., include the following items:

	2016	2015	2014
Balance sheet:			
Cash	$ 24,000	$ 30,000	
Short-term investments	12,000	21,000	
Net receivables	58,000	71,000	40,000
Inventory	90,000	73,000	59,000
Prepaid expenses.........................	10,000	10,000	
Total current assets	194,000	205,000	
Accounts payable..........................	40,000	70,000	30,000
Total current liabilities.................	133,000	95,000	
Income statement:			
Net credit sales	$491,000	$506,000	
Cost of goods sold	277,000	288,000	

Requirements

1. Using Exhibit 13-8 as a model, compute the following ratios for 2016 and 2015:
   a. Current ratio
   b. Quick (acid-test) ratio
   c. Inventory turnover and days' inventory outstanding (DIO)
   d. Accounts receivable turnover
   e. Days' sales in average receivables or days' sales outstanding (DSO)
   f. Accounts payable turnover and days' payable outstanding (DPO). Use cost of goods sold in the formula for accounts payable turnover
   g. Cash conversion cycle (in days)
   When computing days, round your answer to the nearest whole number.

2. Evaluate the company's liquidity and current debt-paying ability for 2016. Has it improved or deteriorated from 2015?

3. As a manager of this company, what would you try to improve next year?

LO 6

E13-22A. *(Learning Objective 5: Analyze the ability to pay liabilities)* DuBois Furniture Company has requested that you determine whether the company's ability to pay its current liabilities and long-term debts improved or deteriorated during 2016. To answer this question, compute the following ratios for 2016 and 2015. Use Exhibit 13-8 as a model. Round your answers to two decimal places. Summarize the results of your analysis in a short paragraph.

    a. Net working capital
    b. Current ratio
    c. Quick (acid-test) ratio
    d. Debt ratio
    e. Times-interest-earned ratio

	2016	2015
Cash	$ 22,000	$ 51,000
Short-term investments	34,000	23,000
Net receivables	121,000	131,000
Inventory	238,000	273,000
Prepaid expenses	19,000	7,000
Total assets	570,000	490,000
Total current liabilities	227,000	272,000
Long-term debt	97,000	104,000
Income from operations	194,000	150,000
Interest expense	42,000	44,000

LO 5

E13-23A. *(Learning Objective 5: Analyze profitability)* For 2016 and 2015, compute return on sales (ROS), asset turnover (AT), return on assets (ROA), leverage (L), return on common stockholders' equity (ROE), gross profit percentage (GP), operating income percentage (OI), and earnings per share (EPS) to measure the ability to earn profits for Dominion Decor, Inc., whose comparative income statements follow. Use DuPont Analysis for ROA and ROE, and round each component ratio to three decimals; for other ratio computations, round to two decimals.

A1		
	A	**B**	**C**

	A	B	C
1	**Dominion Decor, Inc.** **Comparative Income Statements** **Years Ended December 31, 2016 and 2015**		
2		**2016**	**2015**
3	Net sales	$ 190,000	$ 240,000
4	Cost of goods sold	102,000	134,000
5	Gross profit	88,000	106,000
6	Selling and general expenses	44,000	49,000
7	Income from operations	44,000	57,000
8	Interest expense	9,000	7,000
9	Income before income tax	35,000	50,000
10	Income tax expense	12,000	16,000
11	Net income	$ 23,000	$ 34,000
12			

Additional data:

	2016	2015	2014
Total assets	$ 300,000	$ 270,000	$250,000
Common stockholders' equity	$ 104,000	$ 103,000	$102,000
Preferred dividends	$ 15,000	$ 14,000	$ 3,000
Average common shares outstanding during the year	24,000	23,000	22,000

Did the company's operating performance improve or deteriorate during 2016?

E13-24A. *(Learning Objectives 5, 6: Evaluate a stock as an investment)* Evaluate the common stock of Monroe Falls Distributing Company as an investment. Specifically, use the three common stock ratios to determine whether the common stock increased or decreased in attractiveness during the past year. (The number of common stock shares was the same in 2015 and 2016.) Round calculations and your final answer to three decimal places.

LO 5 6

	2016	2015
Net income	$ 114,000	$ 70,500
Dividends to common	11,000	18,000
Total stockholders' equity at year-end	300,000	510,000
(includes 43,500 shares of common stock)		
Preferred stock, 5%	105,000	105,000
Market price per share of common stock at year-end	$ 23.50	$ 17.25

E13-25A. *(Learning Objective 6: Use economic value added to measure corporate performance)* Two companies with different economic-value-added (EVA®) profiles are Emerson Company, Inc., and Farmers Bank Limited. Adapted versions of the two companies' financial statements are presented here (in millions):

LO 6

	Emerson Company, Inc.	Farmers Bank Limited
Balance sheet data (beginning of year):		
Total assets	$ 4,490	$13,590
Interest-bearing debt	$ 1,257	$ 3
All other liabilities	2,690	2,590
Stockholders' equity	543	10,997
Total liabilities and equity	$ 4,490	$13,590
Income statement data:		
Total revenue	$10,447	$ 3,819
Interest expense	79	5
Net income before taxes	$ 220	$ 1,121

Requirements

1. Before performing any calculations, which company do you think represents the better investment? Give your reason.
2. Compute the EVA® for each company, and then decide which company's stock you would rather hold as an investment. Assume that both companies' cost of capital is 9.5%.

Group B

LO 1

E13-26B. *(Learning Objective 1: Compute year-to-year changes in working capital)* What were the dollar amount of change and the percentage of each change in Blueberry Lane Lodge's net working capital during 2016 and 2015? Is this trend favorable or unfavorable?

	2016	2015	2014
Total current assets	$424,950	$259,800	$260,000
Total current liabilities	410,000	200,000	130,000

LO 1

E13-27B. *(Learning Objective 1: Perform horizontal analysis of an income statement)* Prepare a horizontal analysis of the comparative income statements of Mitchell Music Co. Round percentage changes to the nearest one-tenth percent (three decimal places).

	A	B	C
	A1		
1	**Mitchell Music Co.** **Comparative Income Statements** **Years Ended December 31, 2016 and 2015**		
2		**2016**	**2015**
3	Total revenue	$ 1,075,000	$ 915,000
4	Expenses:		
5	Cost of goods sold	$ 475,000	$ 406,250
6	Selling and general expenses	285,000	261,000
7	Interest expense	22,500	12,500
8	Income tax expense	104,500	82,150
9	Total expenses	887,000	761,900
10	Net income	$ 188,000	$ 153,100
11			

LO 1

E13-28B. *(Learning Objective 1: Compute trend percentages)* Compute trend percentages for Valley View Sales & Service's total revenue and net income for the following five-year period, using year 0 as the base year. Round to the nearest full percent.

(In thousands)	Year 4	Year 3	Year 2	Year 1	Year 0
Total revenue	$1,422	$1,263	$1,098	$1,020	$1,019
Net income	170	112	101	96	83

Which grew faster during the period, total revenue or net income?

E13-29B. *(Learning Objective 2: Perform vertical analysis of a balance sheet)* Fox Den Golf Company has requested that you perform a vertical analysis of its balance sheet to determine the component percentages of its assets, liabilities, and stockholders' equity.

 LO 2

A1		
	A	**B**
	Fox Den Golf Company	
	Balance Sheet	
1	**December 31, 2016**	
2	**Assets**	
3	Total current assets	$ 45,880
4	Property, plant, and equipment, net	222,580
5	Other assets	41,540
6	Total assets	$ 310,000
7		
8	**Liabilities**	
9	Total current liabilities	$ 50,530
10	Long-term debt	115,630
11	Total liabilities	166,160
12		
13	**Stockholders' Equity**	
14	Total stockholders' equity	143,840
15	Total liabilities and stockholders' equity	$ 310,000
16		

E13-30B. *(Learning Objective 3: Prepare a common-size income statement)* Prepare a comparative common-size income statement for Mitchell Music Co. using the 2016 and 2015 data of E13-27B and rounding to four decimal places.

LO 3

E13-31B. *(Learning Objective 4: Analyze the statement of cash flows)* Identify any weaknesses revealed by the statement of cash flows of Sunshine Fruit, Inc.

LO 4

A1			
	A	**B**	**C**
	Sunshine Fruit, Inc.		
	Statement of Cash Flows		
1	**For the Current Year**		
2	**Operating activities:**		
3	Net income		$ 104,000
4	Add (subtract) adjustments to reconcile net income to net cash provided by operating activities:		
5	Depreciation	$ 32,000	
6	Net increase in current assets other than cash	(65,000)	
7	Net decrease in current liabilities		
8	exclusive of short-term debt	(44,000)	(77,000)
9	Net cash provided by operating activities		27,000
10			
11	**Investing activities:**		
12	Sale of property, plant, and equipment		151,000
13	Net cash provided by investing activities		151,000
14			
15	**Financing activities:**		
16	Issuance of bonds payable	$ 110,000	
17	Payment of short-term debt	(186,000)	
18	Payment of long-term debt	(101,000)	
19	Payment of dividends	(56,000)	
20	Net cash used for financing activities		(233,000)
21	Increase (decrease) in cash		$ (55,000)
22			

LO **5**   **E13-32B.** *(Learning Objective 5: Compute ratios; evaluate turnover, liquidity, and current debt-paying ability)* The financial statements of Carver News, Inc., include the following items:

	2016	2015	2014
Balance sheet:			
Cash	$ 77,000	$ 103,000	
Short-term investments	13,000	27,000	
Net receivables	81,000	84,000	30,000
Inventory	88,000	75,000	60,000
Prepaid expenses...........................	12,000	6,000	
Total current assets	271,000	295,000	
Accounts payable...........................	85,000	70,000	50,000
Total current liabilities..................	138,000	96,000	
Income statement:			
Net credit sales	$491,000	$ 505,000	
Cost of goods sold	271,000	279,000	

Requirements

1. Using Exhibit 13-8 as a model, compute the following ratios for 2016 and 2015:
   a. Current ratio
   b. Quick (acid-test) ratio
   c. Inventory turnover and days' inventory outstanding (DIO)
   d. Accounts receivable turnover
   e. Days' sales in average receivables or days' sales outstanding (DSO)
   f. Accounts payable turnover and days' payable outstanding (DPO). Use cost of goods sold in the formula for accounts payable turnover
   g. Cash conversion cycle (in days)
   When computing days, round your answer to the nearest whole number.
2. Evaluate the company's liquidity and current debt-paying ability for 2016. Has it improved or deteriorated from 2015?
3. As a manager of this company, what would you try to improve next year?

LO **5**   **E13-33B.** *(Learning Objective 5: Analyze the ability to pay liabilities)* Irvin Furniture Company has requested that you determine whether the company's ability to pay its current liabilities and long-term debts improved or deteriorated during 2016. To answer this question, compute the following ratios for 2016 and 2015. Use Exhibit 13-8 as a model. Round your answers to two decimal places.

   a. Net working capital
   b. Current ratio
   c. Quick (acid-test) ratio

   d. Debt ratio
   e. Times-interest-earned ratio

Summarize the results of your analysis in a short paragraph.

	2016	2015
Cash..	$ 22,000	$ 48,000
Short-term investments.................	26,000	19,000
Net receivables	123,000	132,000
Inventory.......................................	235,000	269,000
Prepaid expenses	14,000	6,000
Total assets....................................	570,000	530,000
Total current liabilities	217,000	113,000
Long-term debt	77,000	303,000
Income from operations	250,000	130,000
Interest expense............................	38,000	46,000

E13-34B. *(Learning Objective 5: Analyze profitability)* For 2016 and 2015, compute return on sales (ROS), asset turnover (AT), return on assets (ROA), leverage (L), return on common stockholders' equity (ROE), gross profit percentage (GP), operating income percentage (OI), and earnings per share (EPS) to measure the ability to earn profits of Harmony Decor, Inc., whose comparative income statements follow. Use DuPont Analysis for ROA and ROE, and round each component ratio to three decimals; for other ratio computations, round to two decimals.

A1			
	A	B	C
1	**Harmony Decor, Inc.** **Comparative Income Statements** **Years Ended December 31, 2016 and 2015**		
2		**2016**	**2015**
3	Net sales	$ 250,000	$ 199,000
4	Cost of goods sold	123,000	102,000
5	Gross profit	127,000	97,000
6	Selling and general expenses	55,000	51,000
7	Income from operations	72,000	46,000
8	Interest expense	14,000	18,000
9	Income before income tax	58,000	28,000
10	Income tax expense	20,000	10,000
11	Net income	$ 38,000	$ 18,000
12			

Additional data:

	2016	2015	2014
Total assets..	$310,000	$305,000	$ 300,000
Common stockholders' equity.................	$196,000	$194,000	$ 192,000
Preferred dividends..................................	$ 2,000	$ 1,000	$ 0
Average common shares outstanding during the year	15,000	14,000	13,000

Did the company's operating performance improve or deteriorate during 2016?

LO 5 6 E13-35B. *(Learning Objectives 5, 6: Evaluate a stock as an investment)* Evaluate the common stock of Bastille Distributing Company as an investment. Specifically, use the three common stock ratios to determine whether the common stock increased or decreased in attractiveness during the past year. (The number of common stock shares was the same in 2015 and 2016.) Round calculations and your final answer to three decimal places.

	2016	2015
Net income...	$ 91,000	$ 98,700
Dividends to common	28,000	20,000
Total stockholders' equity at year-end................	575,000	495,000
(includes 96,250 shares of common stock)		
Preferred stock, 7%..	90,000	90,000
Market price per share of common		
stock at year-end	$ 22.00	$ 16.80

LO 6 E13-36B. *(Learning Objective 6: Use economic value added to measure corporate performance)* Two companies with different economic-value-added (EVA®) profiles are Daniels Company, Inc., and Granger Bank Limited. Adapted versions of the two companies' financial statements are presented here (in millions):

	Daniels Company, Inc.	Granger Bank Limited
Balance sheet data (beginning of year):		
Total assets	$ 4,430	$14,704
Interest-bearing debt	$ 1,244	$ 13
All other liabilities............................	2,550	2,600
Stockholders' equity	636	12,091
Total liabilities and equity................	$ 4,430	$14,704
Income statement data:		
Total revenue	$10,506	$ 3,800
Interest expense.................................	81	8
Net income before taxes....................	$ 195	$ 999

Requirements

1. Before performing any calculations, which company do you think represents the better investment? Give your reason.
2. Compute the EVA® for each company, and then decide which company's stock you would rather hold as an investment. Assume that both companies' cost of capital is 12.5%.

Quiz

Use the Miami Medical Corporation financial statements that follow to answer questions 13-37 through 13-48.

A1		

	A	B	C
1	**Miami Medical Corporation** **Consolidated Statements of Financial Position**		
2		**December 31,**	
3	**(In Millions)**	**2016**	**2015**
4	**Assets:**		
5	Current Assets		
6	Cash and cash equivalents	$ 4,369	$ 4,206
7	Short-term investments	850	523
8	Accounts and notes receivable	3,404	2,402
9	Inventories, at cost	433	404
10	Prepaid expense and other current assets	1,602	1,221
11	Total current assets	10,658	8,756
12	Property and equipment, net	1,545	938
13	Investments	6,681	5,328
14	Other non-current assets	302	122
15	Total assets	$ 19,186	$ 15,144
16	**Liabilities and stockholders' equity:**		
17	Current liabilities		
18	Accounts payable	$ 7,702	$ 6,000
19	Accrued and other liabilities	3,695	3,099
20	Total current liabilities	11,397	9,099
21	Long-term debt	306	307
22	Other non-current liabilities	1,701	1,175
23	Total liabilities	13,404	10,581
24	Stockholders' equity		
25	Preferred stock and capital in excess of $0.02 par value;		
26	shares issued and outstanding: none	—	—
27	Common stock and capital in excess of $0.05 par value;		
28	shares authorized: 6,000; shares issued: 1,402 and		
29	1,146, respectively	7,807	7,007
30	Treasury stock, at cost: 180 and 124 shares, respectively	(6,200)	(4,403)
31	Retained earnings	4,304	2,036
32	Other comprehensive loss	(91)	(29)
33	Other	(38)	(48)
34	Total stockholders' equity	5,782	4,563
35	Total liabilities and stockholders' equity	$ 19,186	$ 15,144
36			

	A	B	C	D
1	**Miami Medical Corporation** **Consolidated Statements of Income**			
2		**Year ended December 31,**		
3	**(In Millions, Except per Share Amounts)**	**2016**	**2015**	**2014**
4	Net Revenue	$ 42,041	$ 35,304	$ 31,191
5	Cost of goods sold	35,164	29,111	26,061
6	Gross profit	6,877	6,193	5,130
7	Operating expenses:			
8	Selling, general, and administrative	3,748	3,350	2,689
9	Research, development, and engineering	584	558	529
10	Special charges	—	—	500
11	Total operating expenses	4,332	3,908	3,718
12	Operating income	2,545	2,285	1,412
13	Investment and other income (loss), net	185	197	(78)
14	Income before income taxes	2,730	2,482	1,334
15	Income tax expense	1,137	950	473
16	Net income	$ 1,593	$ 1,532	$ 861
17	Earnings per common share:			
18	Basic	$ 1.42	$ 0.90	$ 0.37
19				

Q13-37. During 2016, Miami Medical's total assets

  a. increased by 26.7%.

  b. increased by $1,902 million.

  c. Both a and b

  d. increased by 21.1%.

Q13-38. Miami Medical's current ratio at year-end 2016 is closest to

  a. 1.2.

  b. 0.94.

  c. 0.739.

  d. 21.1

Q13-39. Miami Medical's quick (acid-test) ratio at year-end 2016 is closest to

  a. 0.46.

  b. $8,623 million.

  c. 0.76.

  d. 0.68.

Q13-40. What is the largest single item included in Miami Medical's debt ratio at December 31, 2016?

  a. Accounts payable

  b. Cash and cash equivalents

  c. Common stock

  d. Investments

Q13-41. Using the earliest year available as the base year, the trend percentage for Miami Medical's net revenue during 2016 was

  a. 135%.

  b. up by $10,850 million.

  c. 119%.

  d. up by 19.1%.

Q13-42. Miami Medical's common-size income statement for 2016 would report cost of goods sold as

  a. 134.9%.

  b. $35,164 million.

  c. 83.6%.

  d. up by 20.8%.

Q13-43. Assuming all sales were on account, Miami Medical's days' sales in receivables during 2016 was

  a. 134.9 days.

  b. 35 days.

  c. 20.8 days.

  d. 25 days.

Q13-44. Miami Medical's inventory turnover during fiscal year 2016 was

  a. 134.9 times.

  b. very slow.

  c. $835,164.

  d. 84 times.

Q13-45. Miami Medical's long-term debt bears interest at 11%. During the year ended December 31, 2016, Miami's times-interest-earned ratio was closest to:

  a. 20.8 times.

  b. 134.9 times.

  c. 75.6 times.

  d. 35,164.

Q13-46. Miami Medical's trend of return on sales is
    a. improving in 2016 as compared to 2014.
    b. declining.
    c. stuck at 21.1%.
    d. worrisome.

Q13-47. How many shares of common stock did Miami Medical have outstanding, on average, during 2016? (*Hint*: Compute earnings per share.)
    a. 35,164 million
    b. 1,122 million
    c. 20.8 million
    d. 134.9 million

Q13-48. Book value per share of Miami Medical's common stock outstanding at December 31, 2016, was
    a. 134.9.
    b. $4.73.
    c. 35,164.
    d. 20.8.

Problems MyAccountingLab

Group A

P13-49A. *(Learning Objectives 1, 5: Compute trend percentages, return on sales, asset turnover, and ROA and compare with industry)* Net sales, net income, and total assets for Abacus Shipping, Inc., for a five-year period follow:

LO **1** **5**

(In thousands)	2016	2015	2014	2013	2012
Net sales	$500	$418	$365	$309	$299
Net income	51	39	43	34	27
Total assets	298	262	249	223	201

Requirements

1. Compute trend percentages for each item for 2013 through 2016. Use 2012 as the base year and round to the nearest percent.
2. Compute the rate of return on net sales for 2014 through 2016, rounding to three decimal places. Explain what this means.
3. Compute asset turnover for 2014 through 2016. Explain what this means.
4. Use DuPont Analysis to compute rate of return on average total assets (ROA) for 2014 through 2016.
5. How does Abacus Shipping's return on net sales for 2016 compare with previous years? How does it compare with that of the industry? In the shipping industry, rates above 9% are considered good, and rates above 11% are outstanding.
6. Evaluate Abacus Shipping, Inc.'s, ROA for 2016, compared with previous years and against an 18% benchmark for the industry.

LO **3** **5**   **P13-50A.** *(Learning Objectives 3, 5: Prepare common-size statements; analyze profitability; make comparisons with the industry)* Top managers of Bryan Products, Inc., have asked for your help in comparing the company's profit performance and financial position with the average for the industry. The accountant has given you the company's income statement and balance sheet and also the following data for the industry:

A1				
	A		**B**	**C**
1	**Bryan Products, Inc.** **Income Statement Compared with Industry Average** **Year Ended December 31, 2016**			
2			**Bryan**	**Industry Average**
3	Net sales		$ 800,000	100.0%
4	Cost of goods sold		416,000	57.3
5	Gross profit		384,000	42.7
6	Operating expenses		176,000	29.4
7	Operating income		208,000	13.3
8	Other expenses		12,000	2.5
9	Net income		$ 196,000	10.8%
10				

A1				
	A		**B**	**C**
1	**Bryan Products, Inc.** **Balance Sheet Compared with Industry Average** **December 31, 2016**			
2			**Bryan**	**Industry Average**
3	Current assets		$ 531,300	72.1%
4	Fixed assets, net		127,650	19.0
5	Intangible assets, net		20,700	4.8
6	Other assets		10,350	4.1
7	Total		$ 690,000	100.0%
8				
9	Current liabilities		$ 317,400	47.2%
10	Long-term liabilities		144,900	21.0
11	Stockholders' equity		227,700	31.8
12	Total		$ 690,000	100.0%
13				

Requirements

1. Prepare a common-size income statement and balance sheet for Bryan Products. The first column of each statement should present Bryan Products' common-size statement, and the second column should show the industry averages.
2. For the profitability analysis, compare Bryan Products' (a) ratio of gross profit to net sales, (b) ratio of operating income to net sales, and (c) ratio of net income to net sales with the industry averages. Is Bryan Products' profit performance better or worse than the average for the industry?
3. For the analysis of financial position, compare Bryan Products' (a) ratios of current assets and current liabilities to total assets and (b) ratio of stockholders' equity to total assets. Compare these ratios with the industry averages. Is Bryan Products' financial position better or worse than the average for the industry?

P13-51A. *(Learning Objective 4: Use the statement of cash flows for decision making)* You are evaluating two companies as possible investments. The two companies, which are similar in size, are commuter airlines that fly passengers up and down the East Coast. All other available information has been analyzed, and your investment decision depends on the statements of cash flows.

LO 4

A	B	C	D	E
Chattanooga Flights, Inc. **Statements of Cash Flows** **Years Ended November 30, 2017 and 2016**				
		2017		**2016**
Operating activities:				
Net income (net loss)		$ (63,000)		$ 160,000
Adjustments to reconcile net income(loss) to net cash provided by operating activities:				
Total		79,000		(13,000)
Net cash provided by operating activities		16,000		147,000
Investing activities:				
Purchase of property, plant,				
and equipment	$ (67,000)		$ (140,000)	
Sale of long-term investments	58,000		9,000	
Net cash provided by (used for)				
investing activities		(9,000)		(131,000)
Financing activities:				
Issuance of short-term notes payable	$ 198,000		$ 218,000	
Payment of short-term notes payable	(246,000)		(183,000)	
Payment of cash dividends	(51,000)		(92,000)	
Net cash provided (used) by financing activities		(99,000)		(57,000)
Increase (decrease) in cash		$ (92,000)		$ (41,000)
Cash balance at beginning of year		106,000		147,000
Cash balance at end of year		$ 14,000		$ 106,000

A	B	C	D	E
Eastern Airlines **Statements of Cash Flows** **Years Ended September 30, 2017 and 2016**				
		2017		**2016**
Operating activities:				
Net income		$ 264,000		$ 193,000
Adjustments to reconcile net income to net cash provided by operating activities:				
Total		67,000		79,000
Net cash provided by operating activities		331,000		272,000
Investing activities:				
Purchase of property, plant,				
and equipment	$ (395,000)		$ (610,000)	
Sale of property, plant, and equipment	69,000		119,000	
Net cash used for investing activities		(326,000)		(491,000)
Financing activities:				
Issuance of long-term notes payable	$ 198,000		$ 131,000	
Payment of short-term notes payable	(95,000)		(26,000)	
Net cash provided by financing activities		103,000		105,000
Increase (decrease) in cash		$ 108,000		$ (114,000)
Cash balance at beginning of year		176,000		290,000
Cash balance at end of year		$ 284,000		$ 176,000

Requirement

1. Discuss the relative strengths and weaknesses of Chattanooga Flights, Inc., and Eastern Airlines. Conclude your discussion by recommending one of the companies' stocks as an investment.

LO 5

P13-52A. *(Learning Objective 5: Compute effects of business transactions on selected ratios)* Financial statement data of Morgan Engineering include the following items:

Cash	$ 30,000	Accounts payable	$107,000
Short-term investments..............	32,000	Accrued liabilities......................	31,000
Accounts receivable, net............	86,000	Long-term notes payable...........	163,000
Inventories	147,000	Other long-term liabilities.........	31,000
Prepaid expenses	5,000	Net income................................	91,000
Total assets	673,000	Number of common	
Short-term notes payable...........	48,000	shares outstanding...........	50,000

Requirements

1. Compute Morgan's current ratio, debt ratio, and earnings per share. Round all ratios to two decimal places.
2. Compute the three ratios after evaluating the effect of each transaction that follows. Consider each transaction *separately.*
   a. Borrowed $160,000 on a long-term note payable
   b. On January 1, issued 18,000 shares of common stock, receiving cash of $308,000
   c. Paid short-term notes payable, $30,000
   d. Purchased merchandise of $8,000 on account, debiting Inventory
   e. Received cash on account, $24,000

LO 5

P13-53A. *(Learning Objective 5: Use ratios to evaluate a stock investment)* Comparative financial statement data of Sanfield Optical Mart follow:

	A1	⬍		
	A		B	C
1	Sanfield Optical Mart Comparative Income Statements Years Ended December 31, 2016 and 2015			
2			2016	2015
3	Net sales		$ 986,000	$ 892,000
4	Cost of goods sold		680,000	581,000
5	Gross profit		306,000	311,000
6	Operating expenses		127,000	148,000
7	Income from operations		179,000	163,000
8	Interest expense		30,000	50,000
9	Income before income tax		149,000	113,000
10	Income tax expense		41,000	41,000
11	Net income		$ 108,000	$ 72,000
12				

A	B	C	D
Sanfield Optical Mart **Comparative Balance Sheets** **December 31, 2016 and 2015**			
	2016	**2015**	**2014***
Current assets:			
Cash	$ 32,000	$ 82,000	
Current receivables, net	227,000	157,000	$ 200,000
Inventories	297,000	294,000	258,000
Prepaid expenses	7,000	29,000	
Total current assets	563,000	562,000	
Property, plant, and equipment, net	273,000	261,000	
Total assets	$ 836,000	$ 823,000	701,000
Accounts payable	$ 150,000	$ 105,000	112,000
Other current liabilities	135,000	187,000	
Total current liabilities	285,000	292,000	
Long-term liabilities	240,000	233,000	
Total liabilities	525,000	525,000	
Common stockholders' equity, no par	311,000	298,000	199,000
Total liabilities and stockholders' equity	$ 836,000	$ 823,000	

A1

*Selected 2014 amounts.

Other information:

1. Market price of Sanfield common stock: $89.38 at December 31, 2016, and $85.67 at December 31, 2015
2. Common shares outstanding: 15,000 during 2016 and 10,000 during 2015
3. All sales on credit

Requirements

1. Compute the following ratios for 2016 and 2015:
   a. Current ratio
   b. Quick (acid-test) ratio
   c. Receivables turnover and days' sales outstanding (DSO) (round to the nearest whole day)
   d. Inventory turnover and days' inventory outstanding (DIO) (round to the nearest whole day)
   e. Accounts payable turnover and days' payable outstanding (DPO) (use cost of goods sold in the numerator of the turnover ratio and round DPO to the nearest whole day).
   f. Cash conversion cycle (in days)
   g. Times-interest-earned ratio
   h. Return on assets (use DuPont Analysis)
   i. Return on common stockholders' equity (use DuPont Analysis)
   j. Earnings per share of common stock
   k. Price-earnings ratio
2. Decide whether (a) Sanfield's financial position improved or deteriorated during 2016 and (b) whether the investment attractiveness of Sanfield's common stock appears to have increased or decreased.
3. How will what you learned in this problem help you evaluate an investment?

P13-54A. *(Learning Objectives 5, 6: Use ratios to decide between two stock investments; measure economic value added)* Assume that you are considering purchasing stock as an investment. You have narrowed the choice to Star.com and Westlake Shops and have assembled the following data.

LO 5 6

Selected income statement data for the current year:

	Star.com	Westlake Shops
Net sales (all on credit).................	$602,000	$523,000
Cost of goods sold.........................	460,000	386,000
Income from operations	90,000	69,000
Interest expense............................	—	11,000
Net income....................................	68,000	35,000

Selected balance-sheet and market price data at the *end* of current year:

	Star.com	Westlake Shops
Current assets:		
Cash	$ 22,000	$ 36,000
Short-term investments	5,000	15,000
Current receivables, net	183,000	165,000
Inventories..	218,000	184,000
Prepaid expenses..	21,000	11,000
Total current assets	449,000	411,000
Total assets...	982,000	935,000
Total current liabilities	371,000	335,000
Total liabilities	670,000	688,000
Preferred stock, 10%, $150 par...........................		30,000
Common stock, $1 par (100,000 shares)................	100,000	
$5 par (15,000 shares)...................		75,000
Total stockholders' equity	312,000	247,000
Market price per share of common stock	$ 7.48	$ 36.21

Selected balance-sheet data at the *beginning* of current year:

	Star.com	Westlake Shops
Balance sheet:		
Current receivables, net..	$144,000	$195,000
Inventories	208,000	196,000
Total assets...	851,000	908,000
Long-term debt	—	310,000
Preferred stock, 10%, $150 par		30,000
Common stock, $1 par (100,000 shares).................	100,000	
$5 par (15,000 shares).................		75,000
Total stockholders' equity	265,000	221,000

Your strategy is to invest in companies that have low price-earnings ratios but appear to be in good shape financially. Assume that you have analyzed all other factors and that your decision depends on the results of ratio analysis.

Requirements

1. Compute the following ratios for both companies for the current year, and decide which company's stock better fits your investment strategy.
   a. Quick (acid-test) ratio
   b. Inventory turnover
   c. Days' sales in average receivables
   d. Debt ratio
   e. Times-interest-earned ratio
   f. Return on common stockholders' equity
   g. Earnings per share of common stock
   h. Price-earnings ratio

2. Compute each company's economic-value-added (EVA®) measure and determine whether the companies' EVA®s confirm or alter your investment decision. Each company's cost of capital is 10%. (For this requirement, ignore income taxes (use net income) when computing EVA®.)

Group B

P13-55B. *(Learning Objectives 1, 5: Compute trend percentages, return on sales, asset turnover, and ROA, and compare with industry)* Net sales, net income, and total assets for Urbana Shipping, Inc., for a five-year period follow:

(In thousands)	2016	2015	2014	2013	2012
Net sales.....................	$510	$400	$362	$314	$296
Net income................	53	47	50	37	24
Total assets	297	269	246	231	209

Requirements

1. Compute trend percentages for each item for 2013 through 2016. Use 2012 as the base year and round to the nearest percent.
2. Compute the rate of return on net sales for 2014 through 2016, rounding to three decimal places. Explain what this means.
3. Compute asset turnover for 2014 through 2016. Explain what this means.
4. Use DuPont Analysis to compute rate of return on average total assets (ROA) for 2014 through 2016.
5. How does Urbana Shipping's return on net sales for 2016 compare with previous years? How does it compare with that of the industry? In the shipping industry, rates above 9% are considered good, and rates above 11% are outstanding.
6. Evaluate Urbana Shipping, Inc.'s, ROA for 2016, compared with previous years and against an 18% benchmark for the industry.

P13-56B. *(Learning Objectives 3, 5: Prepare common-size statements; analyze profitability; make comparisons with the industry)* Top managers of Gordon Products, Inc., have asked for your help in comparing the company's profit performance and financial position with the average for the industry. The accountant has given you the company's income statement and balance sheet and also the following data for the industry:

	A	B	C
A1			
	Gordon Products, Inc.		
	Income Statement Compared with Industry Average		
1	**Year Ended December 31, 2016**		
2		**Gordon**	**Industry Average**
3	Net sales	$ 955,000	100.0%
4	Cost of goods sold	649,400	57.3
5	Gross profit	305,600	42.7
6	Operating expenses	210,100	29.4
7	Operating income	95,500	13.3
8	Other expenses	4,775	2.5
9	Net income	$ 90,725	10.8%
10			

	A	B	C
1	**Gordon Products, Inc.** **Balance Sheet Compared with Industry Average** **December 31, 2016**		
2		**Gordon**	**Industry Average**
3	Current assets	$ 531,300	72.1%
4	Fixed assets, net	129,720	19.0
5	Intangible assets, net	27,600	4.8
6	Other assets	1,380	4.1
7	Total	$ 690,000	100.0%
8			
9	Current liabilities	$ 271,860	47.2%
10	Long-term liabilities	146,280	21.0
11	Stockholders' equity	271,860	31.8
12	Total	$ 690,000	100.0%
13			

Requirements

1. Prepare a common-size income statement and balance sheet for Gordon Products. The first column of each statement should present Gordon Products' common-size statement, and the second column should show the industry averages.
2. For the profitability analysis, compare Gordon Products' (a) ratio of gross profit to net sales, (b) ratio of operating income to net sales, and (c) ratio of net income to net sales with the industry averages. Is Gordon Products' profit performance better or worse than the average for the industry?
3. For the analysis of financial position, compute Gordon Products' (a) ratios of current assets and current liabilities to total assets and (b) ratio of stockholders' equity to total assets. Compare these ratios with the industry averages. Is Gordon Products' financial position better or worse than the average for the industry?

LO 4

P13-57B. *(Learning Objective 4: Use the statement of cash flows for decision making)* You are evaluating two companies as possible investments. The two companies, which are similar in size, are commuter airlines that fly passengers up and down the West Coast. All other available information has been analyzed, and your investment decision depends on the statements of cash flows.

A1				
A	**B**	**C**	**D**	**E**
Western Air **Statements of Cash Flows** **Years Ended May 31, 2017 and 2016**				
		2017		**2016**
Operating activities:				
Net income (net loss)		$ (105,000)		$ 214,000
Adjustments to reconcile net income(loss) to net cash provided by operating activities:				
Total		118,000		(44,000)
Net cash provided by operating activities		13,000		170,000
Investing activities:				
Purchase of property, plant, and				
equipment	$ (94,000)		$ (147,000)	
Sale of long-term investments	98,000		29,000	
Net cash provided by (used for)				
investing activities		4,000		(118,000)
Financing activities:				
Issuance of short-term notes payable	$ 149,000		$ 185,000	
Payment of short-term notes payable	(256,000)		(134,000)	
Payment of cash dividends	(67,000)		(106,000)	
Net cash used for financing activities		(174,000)		(55,000)
Increase (decrease) in cash		$ (157,000)		$ (3,000)
Cash balance at beginning of year		168,000		171,000
Cash balance at end of year		$ 11,000		$ 168,000

A1				
A	**B**	**C**	**D**	**E**
Tech Flights **Statements of Cash Flows** **Years Ended May 31, 2017 and 2016**				
		2017		**2016**
Operating activities:				
Net income		$ 201,000		$ 147,000
Adjustments to reconcile net income to net cash provided by operating activities				
Total		92,000		66,000
Net cash provided by operating activities		293,000		213,000
Investing activities:				
Purchase of property, plant, and equipment	$ (448,000)		$(630,000)	
Sales of property, plant, and equipment	87,000		113,000	
Net cash used for investing activities		(361,000)		(517,000)
Financing activities:				
Issuance of long-term notes payable	$ 244,000		$ 168,000	
Payment of short-term notes payable	(107,000)		(16,000)	
Net cash provided by financing activities		137,000		152,000
Increase (decrease) in cash		$ 69,000		$ (152,000)
Cash balance at beginning of year		135,000		287,000
Cash balance at end of year		$ 204,000		$ 135,000

Requirement

1. Discuss the relative strengths and weaknesses of Western Air and Tech Flights. Conclude your discussion by recommending one of the companies' stocks as an investment.

LO 5 **P13-58B.** *(Learning Objective 5: Compute effects of business transactions on selected ratios)* Financial statement data of Eastland Engineering include the following items:

Cash	$ 27,000	Accounts payable	$100,000
Short-term investments..............	32,000	Accrued liabilities......................	34,000
Accounts receivable, net............	83,000	Long-term notes payable	162,000
Inventories	147,000	Other long-term liabilities	31,000
Prepaid expenses	9,000	Net income.................................	94,000
Total assets	677,000	Number of common	
Short-term notes payable...........	44,000	shares outstanding	46,000

Requirements

1. Compute Eastland's current ratio, debt ratio, and earnings per share. Round all ratios to two decimal places.
2. Compute the three ratios after evaluating the effect of each transaction that follows. Consider each transaction *separately*.
   a. Borrowed $100,000 on a long-term note payable
   b. On January 1, issued 20,000 shares of common stock, receiving cash of $362,000
   c. Paid short-term notes payable, $25,000
   d. Purchased merchandise of $45,000 on account, debiting Inventory
   e. Received cash on account, $16,000

LO 5 **P13-59B.** *(Learning Objective 5: Use ratios to evaluate a stock investment)* Comparative financial statement data of Arch Optical Mart follow:

	A	B	C
	A1		
1	**Arch Optical Mart** **Comparative Income Statements** **Years Ended December 31, 2016 and 2015**		
2		**2016**	**2015**
3	Net sales	$ 957,000	$ 875,000
4	Cost of goods sold	675,000	576,000
5	Gross profit	282,000	299,000
6	Operating expenses	129,000	142,000
7	Income from operations	153,000	157,000
8	Interest expense	37,000	45,000
9	Income before income tax	116,000	112,000
10	Income tax expense	40,000	39,000
11	Net income	$ 76,000	$ 73,000
12			

A1				
	A	**B**	**C**	**D**
1	**Arch Optical Mart** **Comparative Balance Sheets** **December 31, 2016 and 2015**			
2		**2016**	**2015**	**2014***
3	Current assets:			
4	Cash	$ 45,000	$ 49,000	
5	Current receivables, net	217,000	158,000	$200,000
6	Inventories	302,000	286,000	181,000
7	Prepaid expenses	4,000	29,000	
8	Total current assets	568,000	522,000	
9	Property, plant, and equipment, net	285,000	277,000	
10	Total assets	$853,000	$799,000	700,000
11				
12	Accounts payable	$160,000	$110,000	112,000
13	Other current liabilities	135,000	188,000	
14	Total current liabilities	295,000	298,000	
15	Long-term liabilities	243,000	231,000	
16	Total liabilities	538,000	529,000	
17	Common stockholders' equity, no par	315,000	270,000	199,000
18	Total liabilities and stockholders' equity	$853,000	$799,000	
19				

*Selected 2014 amounts.

Other information:
1. Market price of Arch common stock: $88.17 at December 31, 2016, and $77.01 at December 31, 2015
2. Common shares outstanding: 18,000 during 2016 and 17,800 during 2015
3. All sales on credit

Requirements

1. Compute the following ratios for 2016 and 2015:
   a. Current ratio
   b. Quick (acid-test) ratio
   c. Receivables turnover and days' sales outstanding (DSO); round to nearest whole day
   d. Inventory turnover and days' inventory outstanding (DIO); round to nearest whole day
   e. Accounts payable turnover and days' payable outstanding (DPO); use cost of goods sold in the turnover ratio and round DPO to nearest whole day
   f. Cash conversion cycle (in days)
   g. Times-interest-earned ratio
   h. Return on assets; use DuPont Analysis
   i. Return on common stockholders' equity; use DuPont Analysis
   j. Earnings per share of common stock
   k. Price-earnings ratio
2. Decide whether (a) Arch's financial position improved or deteriorated during 2016 and (b) whether the investment attractiveness of Arch's common stock appears to have increased or decreased.
3. How will what you learned in this problem help you evaluate an investment?

P13-60B. *(Learning Objectives 5, 6: Use ratios to decide between two stock investments; measure economic value added)* Assume that you are considering purchasing stock as an investment. You have narrowed the choice to Disc.com and Holiday Shops and have assembled the following data.

LO 5 6

Selected income statement data for current year:

	Disc.com	Holiday Shops
Net sales (all on credit).................	$595,000	$514,000
Cost of goods sold........................	458,000	390,000
Income from operations	86,000	79,000
Interest expense............................	—	16,000
Net income	64,000	39,000

Selected balance-sheet and market price data at the *end* of the current year:

	Disc.com	Holiday Shops
Current assets:		
Cash	$ 26,000	$ 42,000
Short-term investments	7,000	12,000
Current receivables, net	184,000	162,000
Inventories...	217,000	187,000
Prepaid expenses......................................	20,000	13,000
Total current assets	454,000	416,000
Total assets	982,000	932,000
Total current liabilities	365,000	335,000
Total liabilities	670,000	713,000
Preferred stock: 10%, $100 par...........................		20,000
Common stock, $1 par (100,000 shares)..............	100,000	
$5 par (10,000 shares)................		50,000
Total stockholders' equity	312,000	219,000
Market price per share of common stock	$ 6.40	$ 66.60

Selected balance-sheet data at the *beginning* of the current year:

	Disc.com	Holiday Shops
Balance sheet:		
Current receivables, net...	$141,000	$190,000
Inventories	203,000	194,000
Total assets..	845,000	908,000
Long-term debt	—	309,000
Preferred stock, 10%, $100 par		20,000
Common stock, $1 par (100,000 shares)................	100,000	
$5 par (10,000 shares).................		50,000
Total stockholders' equity	260,000	219,000

Your strategy is to invest in companies that have low price-earnings ratios but appear to be in good shape financially. Assume that you have analyzed all other factors and that your decision depends on the results of ratio analysis.

Requirements

1. Compute the following ratios for both companies for the current year, and decide which company's stock better fits your investment strategy.
   a. Quick (acid-test) ratio
   b. Inventory turnover
   c. Days' sales in average receivables
   d. Debt ratio
   e. Times-interest-earned ratio
   f. Return on common stockholders' equity

   g. Earnings per share of common stock

   h. Price-earnings ratio

2. Compute each company's economic-value-added (EVA®) measure and determine whether the companies' EVA®s confirm or alter your investment decision. Each company's cost of capital is 10%. (For this requirement, ignore income taxes (use net income) when computing EVA®.)

Challenge Exercises and Problem

E13-61. *(Learning Objectives 2, 3, 5: Use ratio data to reconstruct a company's balance sheet)* The following data (dollar amounts in millions) are taken from the financial statements of Burbick Industries, Inc.:

`LO 2 3 5`

Total liabilities	$12,500
Total current assets	$16,150
Accumulated depreciation	$ 900
Debt ratio	50%
Current ratio	1.90

Requirement

1. Complete the following condensed balance sheet. Report amounts to the nearest million dollars.

	(In millions)
Current assets	☐
Property, plant, and equipment	☐
Less: Accumulated depreciation	☐ ☐
Total assets	☐
Current liabilities	☐
Long-term liabilities	☐
Stockholders' equity	☐
Total liabilities and stockholders' equity	☐

E13-62. *(Learning Objectives 2, 3, 5: Use ratio data to reconstruct a company's income statement)* The following data (dollar amounts in millions) are from the financial statements of Valley Corporation:

`LO 2 3 5`

Average stockholders' equity	$3,200
Interest expense	$ 500
Operating income as a percent of sales	35%
Rate of return on stockholders' equity	25%
Income tax rate	36%

Requirement

1. Complete the following condensed income statement. Report amounts to the nearest million dollars.

Sales..	
Operating expense..................	
Operating income...................	
Interest expense......................	
Pretax income	
Income tax expense...............	
Net income............................	

LO 1 2 3 4

P13-63. *(Learning Objectives 1, 2, 3, 4: Use trend percentages, common-size percentages, and ratios to reconstruct financial statements)* An incomplete comparative income statement and balance sheet for Emore Corporation follow:

	A	B	C
	A1		
	A	**B**	**C**
1	**Emore Corporation** **Comparative income Statements** **Years Ended December 31, 2016 and 2015**		
2		**2016**	**2015**
3	Sales revenue	$2,100,000	$2,000,000
4	Cost of goods sold	?	1,100,000
5	Gross profit	?	900,000
6	Operating expense	?	700,000
7	Operating income	?	200,000
8	Interest expense	20,000	20,000
9	Income before income tax	?	180,000
10	Income tax expense (30%)	?	54,000
11	Net income	?	$ 126,000
12			

	A	B	C
	A1		
	A	**B**	**C**
1	**Emore Corporation** **Balance Sheet** **December 31, 2016 and 2015**		
2		**2016**	**2015**
3	ASSETS		
4	Current:		
5	Cash	$?	$ 28,000
6	Accounts receivable, net	?	145,000
7	Inventory	?	180,000
8	Total current assets	?	353,000
9	Plant and equipment, net	?	447,000
10	Total assets	$?	$800,000
11	LIABILITIES		
12	Current liabilities	$160,000	$160,000
13	10% Bonds payable	?	240,000
14	Total liabilities	?	400,000
15	STOCKHOLDERS' EQUITY		
16	Common stock, $5 par	?	203,200
17	Retained earnings	?	196,800
18	Total stockholders' equity	?	400,000
19	Total liabilities and stockholders' equity	$?	$800,000
20			

Requirement

1. Using the ratios, common-size percentages, and trend percentages given, complete the income statement and balance sheet for Emore for 2016. Additional information:

	A	B	C
		2016	2015
1	**Additional information:**	**2016**	**2015**
2	Common size cost of goods sold %:	75%	55%
3	Common size common stock %:	27%	25.4%
4	Trend percentage, Operating income	130%	100%
5	Asset turnover	2	
6	Accounts receivable turnover	15	
7	Quick (acid-test) ratio	1.30	
8	Current ratio	2.25	
9	Return on equity (DuPont model)	35%	
10			

APPLY YOUR KNOWLEDGE

Decision Cases

Case 1. *(Learning Objectives 5, 6: Assess the effects of transactions on a company)* Suppose American Cable and Entertainment, Inc., is having a bad year in 2016, as the company has incurred a $4.9 billion net loss. The loss has pushed most of the return measures into the negative column, and the current ratio dropped below 1.0. The company's debt ratio is still only 0.27. Assume top management of American Cable and Entertainment is pondering ways to improve the company's ratios. In particular, management is considering the following transactions:

LO **5 6**

1. Selling off the cable television segment of the business for $30 million (receiving half in cash and half in the form of a long-term note receivable). Book value of the cable television business is $27 million.
2. Borrowing $100 million on long-term debt.
3. Purchasing treasury stock for $500 million cash.
4. Writing off one-fourth of goodwill carried on the books at $128 million.
5. Selling advertising at the normal gross profit of 60%. The advertisements run immediately.
6. Purchasing trademarks from **NBC**, paying $20 million cash and signing a one-year note payable for $80 million.

Requirements

1. Top management wants to know the effects of these transactions (increase, decrease, or no effect) on the following ratios of American Cable and Entertainment:
   a. Current ratio
   b. Debt ratio
   c. Times-interest-earned ratio (measured as [Net income + Interest expense]/Interest expense)
   d. Return on equity
   e. Book value per share of common stock
2. Some of these transactions have an immediately positive effect on the company's financial condition. Some are definitely negative. Others have an effect that cannot be judged as clearly positive or negative. Evaluate each transaction's effect as positive, negative, or unclear. (Challenge)

Case 2. *(Learning Objectives 5, 6: Analyze the effects of an accounting difference on the ratios)* Assume that you are a financial analyst. You are trying to compare the financial statements of **Caterpillar, Inc.,** with those of **CNH Global,** an international company that uses

LO **5 6**

international financial reporting standards (IFRS). Caterpillar, Inc., uses the last-in, first-out (LIFO) method to account for its inventories. IFRS does not permit CNH Global to use LIFO, so it uses FIFO. Analyze the effect of this difference in accounting method on the two companies' ratio values. For each ratio discussed in this chapter, indicate which company will have the higher (and the lower) ratio value. Also identify those ratios that are unaffected by the FIFO/LIFO difference. Ignore the effects of income taxes, and assume inventory costs are increasing. Then, based on your analysis of the ratios, summarize your conclusions as to which company looks better overall.

LO 2 5

Case 3. *(Learning Objectives 2, 5: Identify action to cut losses and establish profitability)* Suppose you manage Outward Bound, Inc., a Vermont sporting goods store that lost money during the past year. To turn the business around, you must analyze the company and industry data for the current year to learn what is wrong. The company's data follow:

	A	B	C
	Outward Bound, Inc. **Common-Size Balance Sheet Data**		
1			
2		**Outward Bound**	**Industry Average**
3	Cash and short-term investments	3.0%	6.8%
4	Trade receivables, net	15.2	11.0
5	Inventory	64.2	60.5
6	Prepaid expenses	1.0	0.0
7	Total current assets	83.4%	78.3%
8	Fixed assets, net	12.6	15.2
9	Other assets	4.0	6.5
10	Total assets	100.0%	100.0%
11			
12	Notes payable, short-term, 12%	17.1%	14.0%
13	Accounts payable	21.1	25.1
14	Accrued liabilities	7.8	7.9
15	Total current liabilities	46.0	47.0
16	Long-term debt, 11%	19.7	16.4
17	Total liabilities	65.7	63.4
18	Common stockholders' equity	34.3	36.6
19	Total liabilities and stockholders' equity	100.0%	100.0%
20			

	A	B	C
	Outward Bound, Inc. **Common-Size Income Statement Data**		
1			
2		**Outward Bound**	**Industry Average**
3	Net sales	100.0%	100.0%
4	Cost of sales	(68.2)	(64.8)
5	Gross profit	31.8	35.2
6	Operating expense	(37.1)	(32.3)
7	Operating income (loss)	(5.3)	2.9
8	Interest expense	(5.8)	(1.3)
9	Other revenue	1.1	0.3
10	Income (loss) before income tax	(10.0)	1.9
11	Income tax (expense) saving	4.4	(0.8)
12	Net income (loss)	(5.6)%	1.1%
13			

Requirement

1. On the basis of your analysis of these figures, suggest four courses of action Outward Bound might take to reduce its losses and establish profitable operations. Give your reason for each suggestion. (Challenge)

Ethical Issues

Turnberry Golf Corporation's long-term debt agreements make certain demands on the business. For example, Turnberry may not purchase treasury stock in excess of the balance of retained earnings. Also, long-term debt may not exceed stockholders' equity, and the current ratio may not fall below 1.50. If Turnberry fails to meet any of these requirements, the company's lenders have the authority to take over management of the company.

Changes in consumer demand have made it hard for Turnberry to attract customers. Current liabilities have mounted faster than current assets, causing the current ratio to fall to 1.47. Before releasing financial statements, Turnberry management is scrambling to improve the current ratio. The controller points out that the company owns an investment that is currently classified as long-term. The investment can be classified as either long-term or short-term, depending on management's intention. By deciding to convert an investment to cash within one year, Turnberry can classify the investment as short-term—a current asset. On the controller's recommendation, Turnberry's board of directors votes to reclassify long-term investments as short-term.

Requirements

1. What is the accounting issue in this case? What ethical decision needs to be made?
2. Who are the stakeholders?
3. Analyze the potential impact on the stakeholders from the following standpoints: (a) economic, (b) legal, and (c) ethical.
4. Shortly after the financial statements are released, sales improve; so, too, does the current ratio. As a result, Turnberry management decides not to sell the investments it had reclassified as short-term. Accordingly, the company reclassifies the investments as long-term. Has management acted unethically? Give the reasoning underlying your answer.

Focus on Financials | Apple Inc.

*(**Learning Objectives 4, 5, 6:** Compute standard financial ratios; use the statement of cash flows; measure liquidity and profitability; analyze stock as an investment)* Use the consolidated financial statements and the data in **Apple Inc.'s** annual report in Appendix A and online in the filings section of **http://www.sec.gov** to evaluate the company's comparative performance for 2014 versus 2013.

Requirements

1. Perform horizontal and vertical analysis of the following information on the company's comparative income statements for 2014 and 2013:
   a. Net sales
   b. Gross margin
   c. Operating income
   d. Net income
   Did the company appear to be performing better or worse on these dimensions in 2014, relative to 2013? Explain.
2. Perform horizontal and vertical analysis of the company's balance sheets for 2014 and 2013. In what areas did the company's balance sheet appear to be improving? Deteriorating? Explain.
3. Compute trends in the major elements of the company's cash flow statement (operations, investing, and financing) for 2014 relative to 2013. From where does the company generate most of its cash? What did the company spend most of its cash on?
4. As explained in the narrative of this chapter, using fiscal 2014 year-end data, we predicted a stock price for Apple Inc. of about $121 per share. Using an Internet site such as Google Finance or Yahoo! Finance, perform research on events that have happened since then. Have these events positively or negatively impacted the company's stock price? Which events were controllable by the company, and which were not? Using this data, update the analysis given in this chapter regarding the potential of the company's stock as a long-term investment. Would Apple Inc. stock have been a good buy at $121 per share if purchased at the end of its fiscal year 2014? Explain. (Challenge)

Focus on Analysis | Under Armour, Inc.

(Learning Objectives 1, 5: Analyze trend data; compute the standard financial ratios and use them to make decisions) Use the **Under Armour, Inc.**, consolidated financial statements in Appendix B and online in the filings section of **http://www.sec.gov** to address the following questions.

Requirements

1. Compute ratios for 2013 and 2014 to determine the following for Under Armour, Inc.:
   a. The company's ability to pay its current liabilities. Was 2014 stronger or weaker than 2013?
   b. The company's inventory turnover and days inventory outstanding (DIO); accounts receivable turnover and days sales outstanding (DSO), accounts payable turnover and days payable outstanding (DPO), and the number of days in its cash conversion cycle (CCC). 2012 figures for the company are as follows (in thousands): Accounts receivable (net) $175,524; Inventories $319,286; Accounts payable $143,689. Was 2014 stronger or weaker than 2013 based on these measures? (Assume all sales were on account.)
   c. The company's rates of return on sales (ROS), average total assets (ROA), and average stockholders' equity (ROE), using DuPont analysis. For computation of averages, use the following amounts for 2012: total assets = $1,157,083; total stockholders' equity = $816,922. Did these ratios get stronger or weaker in 2014 compared to 2013?
2. Find Under Armour, Inc.'s, annual report for 2015 at **http://www.sec.gov**. Also perform research using an Internet site such as MSN Money or Yahoo! Finance to update the information from question 1. (Challenge)
3. What in your opinion is the company's outlook for the future? Would you buy the company's stock as an investment? Why or why not? (Challenge)

Group Projects

Project 1. Select an industry in which you are interested, and use the leading company in that industry as the benchmark. Then select two other companies in the same industry. For each category of ratios in the Decision Guidelines feature on pages 786–787, compute at least two ratios for all three companies. Write a two-page report that compares the two companies with the benchmark company.

Project 2. Select a company and obtain its financial statements. Convert the income statement and the balance sheet to common size and compare the company you selected to the industry average. **Risk Management Association's** *Annual Statement Studies*, **Dun & Bradstreet's** *Industry Norms & Key Business Ratios*, and **Prentice Hall's** *Almanac of Business and Industrial Financial Ratios* by Leo Troy publish common-size statements for most industries. You will find these and other resources in your campus library and on the Internet.

Quick Check Answers

1. *b* ($1,840 − $1,740)/$1,740 = 5.75%

2. *a* ($1,840/$17,350) = 10.61%

3. *a*

4. *c* ($1,770/$25,770) = 6.9%

5. *c*

6. *a* $\left[\dfrac{\$4,515}{(\$140 + \$126)/2}\right] = 34$ times

7. *c* [($590 + $760)/$2,413 = 0.56]

8. *d* $\left[\dfrac{((\$760 + \$826)/2)}{(\$17,350/365)}\right] = 17$ days

9. *c*

10. *c* ($1,526/$17,350 = 8.8%)

11. *c* $\left[\dfrac{\$1,526}{((\$12,317 + \$11,120)/2)}\right] = 13.0\%$

12. *b* ($34/$1.39) = $24.46

13. *c* ($0.70/$34) = 2.1%

14. *a* [$2,347 + $360 − ($275 + $9,400 + $11,120) × 0.06] = $1,459

COMPREHENSIVE FINANCIAL STATEMENT ANALYSIS PROJECT

The objective of this exercise is to develop your ability to perform a comprehensive analysis on a set of financial statements. Obtain a copy of the 2014 annual report (10-K) of Kohl's Corporation (year ended January 31, 2015) from **http://www.sec.gov**. (Note: The proper term to use in the company search box is "Kohls").

Requirement 1

Basic information (provide sources):
   a. Using a site such as Yahoo! Finance or Hoover's Inc., research the discount variety store industry. List two competitors of Kohl's Corporation.
   b. Describe Kohl's business and risk factors.
   c. List three Kohl's brands.
   d. What is Kohl's largest asset? Largest liability?
   e. How many shares of common stock are authorized? Issued? Outstanding?
   f. Did Kohl's repurchase any shares of common stock during the year? If so, how many?
   g. When does Kohl's record revenue?
   h. What inventory method does Kohl's use?
   i. What was Kohl's bad debt expense for the year?
   j. Does Kohl's have any business interests in foreign countries? Explain your answer.

Requirement 2

Evaluate profitability. Using information you have learned in the text and elsewhere, evaluate Kohl's profitability for 2014 compared with 2013. (Remember that the 2014 year-end is January 31, 2015.) In your analysis, you should compute the following ratios and then comment on what those ratios indicate. NOTE: You will have to look up the 10-K for 2013 to obtain total assets and stockholders' equity for 2012. See **http://www.sec.gov**.
   a. Rate of return on sales
   b. Asset turnover
   c. Return on assets (DuPont model)
   d. Leverage ratio
   e. Return on equity (DuPont model)
   f. Gross margin percentage
   g. Earnings per share (show computation)
   h. Book value per share

Requirement 3

Evaluate the company's ability to sell inventory and pay debts during 2014 and 2013. You should note that the company does not hold traditional accounts receivable because it sells all of its receivables to Capital One, which is a credit card company. Therefore, it is impossible to compute accounts receivable turnover and days sales to collection. However, in your analysis, you should compute the following ratios and then comment on what those ratios indicate. Since the 2014 annual report includes only the balance sheets for 2014 and 2013, you will need to look up the 10-K for 2013 for information about 2012 inventory and accounts payable.
   a. Inventory turnover and days' inventory outstanding (DIO)
   b. Accounts payable turnover and days' payable outstanding (DPO)
   c. Cash conversion cycle (DIO-DPO)
   d. Current ratio
   e. Quick (acid-test) ratio
   f. Debt ratio
   g. Times interest earned

Requirement 4

Evaluate Kohl's cash flow.

  a. For 2014, what are Kohl's two main sources of cash?
  b. For 2014, is Kohl's net cash flow from operations greater than or less than net income? What is the primary cause of the difference?
  c. For 2014, what is the primary source of cash from investing activities? Is this the same as in 2013 and 2012? If not, state the primary source(s) of cash from investing activities in 2013 and 2012.
  d. For 2014, what is the primary source of cash from financing activities? Is this the same as in 2013 and 2012? If not, state the primary source(s) of cash from financing activities in 2013 and 2012.
  e. What trend(s) do you detect from this analysis?

Requirement 5

Other financial analysis.

  a. Compute common-size percentages for sales, gross profit, operating income, and net income for 2011–2014. Comment on your results.
  b. Find the selected financial data in the 10-K where Kohl's reports selected information since 2011. Compute trend percentages, using 2011 as the base year, for total revenues and net earnings. Comment on your results.

Requirement 6

Evaluate Kohl's Corporation stock as an investment.

  a. What was the closing market price of Kohl's Corporation stock on February 2, 2015, the next trading day after the balance-sheet date of January 31, 2015?
  b. Compute the price-earnings ratio using your EPS calculation and the market price you just determined.
  c. Assume that Kohl's Corporation's weighted-average cost of capital, and therefore, the relevant capitalization rate for projected earnings from operations, is 8%. Using the methods you learned in Chapter 11, calculate a projected value of Kohl's Corporation as of February 2, 2015. Compare that calculated value with the company's market capitalization (market cap) as of that date. Based on comparison of these two computations, would you evaluate the company's stock as a "buy," "hold," or "sell"? State your reasons. Now compare the price of the stock as of the date you are making this evaluation (it will be later than February 2, 2015) with the price as of February 2, 2015. In retrospect, would your decision using the data as of February 2, 2015 have been a wise one? State your reasons.

2 0 1 4

Apple Inc.

A N N U A L   R E P O R T

Author's Note: Information in the narrative component of these financial statements has been greatly abbreviated, though should be sufficient to complete the requirements of the Focus on Financials activities.

To view the report in its entirety, visit:
http://www.sec.gov/Archives/edgar/data/320193/000119312514383437/d783162d10k.htm

Source: From Apple Inc., Annual Report 2014

UNITED STATES
SECURITIES AND EXCHANGE COMMISSION
Washington, D.C. 20549

Form 10-K

[…]

☒   **ANNUAL REPORT PURSUANT TO SECTION 13 OR 15(d) OF THE SECURITIES EXCHANGE ACT OF 1934**

For the fiscal year ended September 27, 2014

[…]

Commission file number: 000-10030

[…]

APPLE INC.

(Exact name of registrant as specified in its charter)

California	**94-2404110**
(State or other jurisdiction of incorporation or organization)	(I.R.S. Employer Identification No.)
1 Infinite Loop **Cupertino, California**	**95014**
(Address of principal executive offices)	(Zip Code)

Registrant's telephone number, including area code: **(408) 996-1010**

Securities registered pursuant to Section 12(b) of the Act:

Common Stock, $0.00001 par value per share	**The NASDAQ Stock Market LLC**
(Title of class)	(Name of exchange on which registered)

Securities registered pursuant to Section 12(g) of the Act: None

---

[…]

5,864,840,000 shares of common stock were issued and outstanding as of October 10, 2014.

DOCUMENTS INCORPORATED BY REFERENCE

[…]

PART I

Item 1. Business

Company Background

The Company designs, manufactures, and markets mobile communication and media devices, personal computers, and portable digital music players, and sells a variety of related software, services, accessories, networking solutions, and third-party digital content and applications. The Company's products and services include iPhone®, iPad®, Mac®, iPod®, Apple TV®, a portfolio of consumer and professional software applications, the iOS and OS X® operating systems, iCloud® , and a variety of accessory, service and support offerings. In September 2014, the Company announced Apple Watch™, which is expected to be available in early calendar year 2015, and Apple Pay™, which became available in the U.S. in October 2014. The Company also sells and delivers digital content and applications through the iTunes Store®, App Store™, iBooks Store™ and Mac App Store. The Company sells its products worldwide through its retail stores, online stores and direct sales force, as well as through third-party cellular network carriers, wholesalers, retailers and value-added resellers. In addition, the Company sells a variety of third-party iPhone, iPad, Mac and iPod compatible products, including application software, and various accessories, through its online and retail stores. The Company sells to consumers, small and mid-sized businesses ("SMB") and education, enterprise and government customers. The Company's fiscal year is the 52 or 53-week period that ends on the last Saturday of September. The Company is a California corporation established in 1977.

Business Strategy

The Company is committed to bringing the best user experience to its customers through its innovative hardware, software and services. The Company's business strategy leverages its unique ability to design and develop its own operating systems, hardware, application software and services to provide its customers products and solutions with innovative design, superior ease-of-use and seamless integration. As part of its strategy, the Company continues to expand its platform for the discovery and delivery of third-party digital content and applications through the iTunes Store. As part of the iTunes Store, the Company's App Store and iBooks Store allow customers to discover and download applications and books through either a Mac or Windows-based computer or through iPhone, iPad and iPod touch® devices ("iOS devices"). The Company's Mac App Store allows customers to easily discover, download and install Mac applications. The Company also supports a community for the development of third-party software and hardware products and digital content that complement the Company's offerings. The Company believes a high-quality buying experience with knowledgeable salespersons who can convey the value of the Company's products and services greatly enhances its ability to attract and retain customers. Therefore, the Company's strategy also includes building and expanding its own retail and online stores and its third-party distribution network to effectively reach more customers and provide them with a high-quality sales and post-sales support experience. The Company believes continual investment in research and development ("R&D"), marketing and advertising is critical to the development and sale of innovative products and technologies.

Business Organization

The Company manages its business primarily on a geographic basis. Accordingly, the Company determined its reportable operating segments, which are generally based on the nature and location of its customers, to be the Americas, Europe, Greater China, Japan, Rest of Asia Pacific and Retail. The Americas segment includes both North and South America. The Europe segment includes European countries, as well as India, the Middle East and Africa. The Greater China segment includes China, Hong Kong and Taiwan. The Rest of Asia Pacific segment includes Australia and Asian countries, other than those countries included in the Company's other operating segments. The results of the Company's geographic segments do not include the results of the Retail segment. Each operating segment provides similar hardware and software products and similar services. Further information regarding the Company's operating segments may be found in Part II, Item 7 of this Form 10-K under the subheading "Segment Operating Performance," and in Part II, Item 8 of this Form 10-K in the Notes to Consolidated Financial Statements in Note 11, "Segment Information and Geographic Data."
[…]

No single customer accounted for more than 10% of net sales in 2014, 2013 or 2012.

Competition

The markets for the Company's products and services are highly competitive and the Company is confronted by aggressive competition in all areas of its business. These markets are characterized by frequent product introductions and rapid technological advances that have substantially increased the capabilities and use of mobile communication and media devices, personal computers and other digital electronic devices. The Company's competitors who sell mobile devices and personal computers based on other operating systems have aggressively cut prices and lowered their product margins to gain or maintain market share. The Company's financial condition and operating results can be adversely affected by these and other industry-wide downward pressures on gross margins. Principal competitive factors important to the Company include price, product features, relative price/performance, product quality and reliability, design innovation, a strong third-party software and accessories ecosystem, marketing and distribution capability, service and support and corporate reputation.

The Company is focused on expanding its market opportunities related to personal computers and mobile communication and media devices. These markets are highly competitive and include many large, well-funded and experienced participants. The Company expects competition in these markets to intensify significantly as competitors attempt to imitate some of the features of the Company's products and applications within their own products or, alternatively, collaborate with each other to offer solutions that are more competitive than those they currently offer. These markets are characterized by aggressive pricing practices, frequent product introductions, evolving design approaches and technologies, rapid adoption of technological and product advancements by competitors and price sensitivity on the part of consumers and businesses.

The Company's digital content services have faced significant competition from other companies promoting their own digital music and content products and services, including those offering free peer-to-peer music and video services.

The Company's future financial condition and operating results depend on the Company's ability to continue to develop and offer new innovative products and services in each of the markets in which it competes. The Company believes it offers superior innovation and integration of the entire solution including the hardware (iPhone, iPad, Mac and iPod), software (iOS, OS X and iTunes), online services and distribution of digital content and applications (iTunes Store, App Store, iBooks Store and Mac App Store). Some of the Company's current and potential competitors have substantial resources and may be able to provide such products and services at little or no profit or even at a loss to compete with the Company's offerings.

Supply of Components

Although most components essential to the Company's business are generally available from multiple sources, a number of components are currently obtained from single or limited sources. In addition, the Company competes for various components with other participants in the markets for mobile communication and media devices and personal computers. Therefore, many components used by the Company, including those that are available from multiple sources, are at times subject to industry-wide shortage and significant pricing fluctuations that could materially adversely affect the Company's financial condition and operating results.
[…]

Foreign and Domestic Operations and Geographic Data

During 2014, the Company's domestic and international net sales accounted for 38% and 62%, respectively, of total net sales. Information regarding financial data by geographic segment is set forth in Part II, Item 7 of this Form 10-K under the subheading "Segment Operating Performance," and in Part II, Item 8 of this Form 10-K in the Notes to Consolidated Financial Statements in Note 11, "Segment Information and Geographic Data."

While substantially all of the Company's hardware products are currently manufactured by outsourcing partners that are located primarily in Asia, the Company also performs final assembly of certain products at its manufacturing facility in Ireland. The supply and manufacture of a number of components is performed by sole-sourced outsourcing partners in the U.S., Asia and Europe. Margins on sales of the Company's products in foreign countries and on sales of products that include components obtained from foreign suppliers, can be adversely affected by foreign currency exchange rate fluctuations and by international trade regulations, including tariffs and antidumping penalties. Information regarding concentration in the available sources of supply of materials and products is set forth in Part II, Item 8 of this Form 10-K in the Notes to Consolidated Financial Statements in Note 10, "Commitments and Contingencies."

Business Seasonality and Product Introductions

The Company has historically experienced higher net sales in its first quarter compared to other quarters in its fiscal year due in part to seasonal holiday demand. Additionally, new product introductions can significantly impact net sales, product costs and operating expenses. Product introductions can also impact the Company's net sales to its indirect distribution channels as these channels are filled with new product inventory following a product introduction, and often, channel inventory of a particular product declines as the next related major product launch approaches. Net sales can also be affected when consumers and distributors anticipate a product introduction. However, neither historical seasonal patterns nor historical patterns of product introductions should be considered reliable indicators of the Company's future pattern of product introductions, future net sales or financial performance.
[...]

Employees

As of September 27, 2014, the Company had approximately 92,600 full-time equivalent employees and an additional 4,400 full-time equivalent temporary employees and contractors. Approximately 46,200 of the total full-time equivalent employees worked in the Company's Retail segment.
[...]

CONSOLIDATED STATEMENTS OF OPERATIONS
(In millions, except number of shares which are reflected in thousands and per share amounts)

	Years ended		
	September 27, 2014	September 28, 2013	September 29, 2012
Net sales	$ 182,795	$ 170,910	$ 156,508
Cost of sales	112,258	106,606	87,846
Gross margin	70,537	64,304	68,662
Operating expenses:			
Research and development	6,041	4,475	3,381
Selling, general and administrative	11,993	10,830	10,040
Total operating expenses	18,034	15,305	13,421
Operating income	52,503	48,999	55,241
Other income/(expense), net	980	1,156	522
Income before provision for income taxes	53,483	50,155	55,763
Provision for income taxes	13,973	13,118	14,030
Net income	$ 39,510	$ 37,037	$ 41,733
Earnings per share:			
Basic	$ 6.49	$ 5.72	$ 6.38
Diluted	$ 6.45	$ 5.68	$ 6.31
Shares used in computing earnings per share:			
Basic	6,085,572	6,477,320	6,543,726
Diluted	6,122,663	6,521,634	6,617,483
Cash dividends declared per common share	$ 1.82	$ 1.64	$ 0.38

See accompanying Notes to Consolidated Financial Statements.

CONSOLIDATED STATEMENTS OF COMPREHENSIVE INCOME
(In millions)

	Years ended		
	September 27, 2014	September 28, 2013	September 29, 2012
Net income	$ 39,510	$ 37,037	$ 41,733
Other comprehensive income/(loss):			
Change in foreign currency translation, net of tax effects of $50, $35 and $13, respectively	(137)	(112)	(15)
Change in unrecognized gains/losses on derivative instruments:			
Change in fair value of derivatives, net of tax benefit/(expense) of $(297), $(351) and $73, respectively	1,390	522	(131)
Adjustment for net losses/(gains) realized and included in net income, net of tax expense/(benefit) of $(36), $255 and $220, respectively	149	(458)	(399)
Total change in unrecognized gains/losses on derivative instruments, net of tax	1,539	64	(530)
Change in unrealized gains/losses on marketable securities:			
Change in fair value of marketable securities, net of tax benefit/ (expense) of $(153), $458 and $(421), respectively	285	(791)	715
Adjustment for net losses/(gains) realized and included in net income, net of tax expense/(benefit) of $71, $82 and $68, respectively	(134)	(131)	(114)
Total change in unrealized gains/losses on marketable securities, net of tax	151	(922)	601
Total other comprehensive income/(loss)	1,553	(970)	56
Total comprehensive income	$ 41,063	$ 36,067	$ 41,789

See accompanying Notes to Consolidated Financial Statements.

CONSOLIDATED BALANCE SHEETS

(In millions, except number of shares which are reflected in thousands and par value)

	September 27, 2014	September 28, 2013
ASSETS:		
Current assets:		
Cash and cash equivalents	$ 13,844	$ 14,259
Short-term marketable securities	11,233	26,287
Accounts receivable, less allowances of $86 and $99, respectively	17,460	13,102
Inventories	2,111	1,764
Deferred tax assets	4,318	3,453
Vendor non-trade receivables	9,759	7,539
Other current assets	9,806	6,882
Total current assets	68,531	73,286
Long-term marketable securities	130,162	106,215
Property, plant and equipment, net	20,624	16,597
Goodwill	4,616	1,577
Acquired intangible assets, net	4,142	4,179
Other assets	3,764	5,146
Total assets	$ 231,839	$ 207,000
LIABILITIES AND SHAREHOLDERS' EQUITY:		
Current liabilities:		
Accounts payable	$ 30,196	$ 22,367
Accrued expenses	18,453	13,856
Deferred revenue	8,491	7,435
Commercial paper	6,308	0
Total current liabilities	63,448	43,658
Deferred revenue – non-current	3,031	2,625
Long-term debt	28,987	16,960
Other non-current liabilities	24,826	20,208
Total liabilities	120,292	83,451
Commitments and contingencies		
Shareholders' equity:		
Common stock and additional paid-in capital, $0.00001 par value; 12,600,000 shares authorized; 5,866,161 and 6,294,494 shares issued and outstanding, respectively	23,313	19,764
Retained earnings	87,152	104,256
Accumulated other comprehensive income/(loss)	1,082	(471)
Total shareholders' equity	111,547	123,549
Total liabilities and shareholders' equity	$ 231,839	$ 207,000

See accompanying Notes to Consolidated Financial Statements.

CONSOLIDATED STATEMENTS OF SHAREHOLDERS' EQUITY
(In millions, except number of shares which are reflected in thousands)

	Common Stock and Additional Paid-In Capital		Retained Earnings	Accumulated Other Comprehensive Income/(Loss)	Total Shareholders' Equity
	Shares	**Amount**			
Balances as of September 24, 2011	6,504,937	$ 13,331	$ 62,841	$ 443	$ 76,615
Net income	0	0	41,733	0	41,733
Other comprehensive income/(loss)	0	0	0	56	56
Dividends and dividend equivalents declared	0	0	(2,523)	0	(2,523)
Share-based compensation	0	1,740	0	0	1,740
Common stock issued, net of shares withheld for employee taxes	69,521	200	(762)	0	(562)
Tax benefit from equity awards, including transfer pricing adjustments	0	1,151	0	0	1,151
Balances as of September 29, 2012	6,574,458	16,422	101,289	499	118,210
Net income	0	0	37,037	0	37,037
Other comprehensive income/(loss)	0	0	0	(970)	(970)
Dividends and dividend equivalents declared	0	0	(10,676)	0	(10,676)
Repurchase of common stock	(328,837)	0	(22,950)	0	(22,950)
Share-based compensation	0	2,253	0	0	2,253
Common stock issued, net of shares withheld for employee taxes	48,873	(143)	(444)	0	(587)
Tax benefit from equity awards, including transfer pricing adjustments	0	1,232	0	0	1,232
Balances as of September 28, 2013	6,294,494	19,764	104,256	(471)	123,549
Net income	0	0	39,510	0	39,510
Other comprehensive income/(loss)	0	0	0	1,553	1,553
Dividends and dividend equivalents declared	0	0	(11,215)	0	(11,215)
Repurchase of common stock	(488,677)	0	(45,000)	0	(45,000)
Share-based compensation	0	2,863	0	0	2,863
Common stock issued, net of shares withheld for employee taxes	60,344	(49)	(399)	0	(448)
Tax benefit from equity awards, including transfer pricing adjustments	0	735	0	0	735
Balances as of September 27, 2014	5,866,161	$ 23,313	$ 87,152	$ 1,082	$ 111,547

See accompanying Notes to Consolidated Financial Statements.

CONSOLIDATED STATEMENTS OF CASH FLOWS
(In millions)

	Years ended		
	September 27, 2014	September 28, 2013	September 29, 2012
Cash and cash equivalents, beginning of the year	$ 14,259	$ 10,746	$ 9,815
Operating activities:			
Net income	39,510	37,037	41,733
Adjustments to reconcile net income to cash generated by operating activities:			
Depreciation and amortization	7,946	6,757	3,277
Share-based compensation expense	2,863	2,253	1,740
Deferred income tax expense	2,347	1,141	4,405
Changes in operating assets and liabilities:			
Accounts receivable, net	(4,232)	(2,172)	(5,551)
Inventories	(76)	(973)	(15)
Vendor non-trade receivables	(2,220)	223	(1,414)
Other current and non-current assets	167	1,080	(3,162)
Accounts payable	5,938	2,340	4,467
Deferred revenue	1,460	1,459	2,824
Other current and non-current liabilities	6,010	4,521	2,552
Cash generated by operating activities	59,713	53,666	50,856
Investing activities:			
Purchases of marketable securities	(217,128)	(148,489)	(151,232)
Proceeds from maturities of marketable securities	18,810	20,317	13,035
Proceeds from sales of marketable securities	189,301	104,130	99,770
Payments made in connection with business acquisitions, net	(3,765)	(496)	(350)
Payments for acquisition of property, plant and equipment	(9,571)	(8,165)	(8,295)
Payments for acquisition of intangible assets	(242)	(911)	(1,107)
Other	16	(160)	(48)
Cash used in investing activities	(22,579)	(33,774)	(48,227)
Financing activities:			
Proceeds from issuance of common stock	730	530	665
Excess tax benefits from equity awards	739	701	1,351
Taxes paid related to net share settlement of equity awards	(1,158)	(1,082)	(1,226)
Dividends and dividend equivalents paid	(11,126)	(10,564)	(2,488)
Repurchase of common stock	(45,000)	(22,860)	0
Proceeds from issuance of long-term debt, net	11,960	16,896	0
Proceeds from issuance of commercial paper, net	6,306	0	0
Cash used in financing activities	(37,549)	(16,379)	(1,698)
Increase/(decrease) in cash and cash equivalents	(415)	3,513	931
Cash and cash equivalents, end of the year	$ 13,844	$ 14,259	$ 10,746
Supplemental cash flow disclosure:			
Cash paid for income taxes, net	$ 10,026	$ 9,128	$ 7,682
Cash paid for interest	$ 339	$ 0	$ 0

See accompanying Notes to Consolidated Financial Statements.

Notes to Consolidated Financial Statements

Note 1 – Summary of Significant Accounting Policies

Apple Inc. and its wholly-owned subsidiaries (collectively "Apple" or the "Company") designs, manufactures and markets mobile communication and media devices, personal computers and portable digital music players, and sells a variety of related software, services, accessories, networking solutions and third-party digital content and applications. The Company sells its products worldwide through its retail stores, online stores and direct sales force, as well as through third-party cellular network carriers, wholesalers, retailers and value-added resellers. In addition, the Company sells a variety of third-party iPhone, iPad, Mac and iPod compatible products, including application software, and various accessories through its online and retail stores. The Company sells to consumers, small and mid-sized businesses, and education, enterprise and government customers.

Basis of Presentation and Preparation

The accompanying consolidated financial statements include the accounts of the Company. Intercompany accounts and transactions have been eliminated. The preparation of these consolidated financial statements in conformity with U.S. generally accepted accounting principles ("GAAP") requires management to make estimates and assumptions that affect the amounts reported in these consolidated financial statements and accompanying notes. Actual results could differ materially from those estimates.

The Company's fiscal year is the 52 or 53-week period that ends on the last Saturday of September. The Company's fiscal years 2014, 2013 and 2012 ended on September 27, 2014, September 28, 2013 and September 29, 2012, respectively. An additional week is included in the first fiscal quarter approximately every six years to realign fiscal quarters with calendar quarters. Fiscal years 2014 and 2013 spanned 52 weeks each. Fiscal year 2012 spanned 53 weeks, with a 14th week included in the first quarter of 2012. Unless otherwise stated, references to particular years, quarters, months and periods refer to the Company's fiscal years ended in September and the associated quarters, months and periods of those fiscal years.

[...]

Common Stock Split

On June 6, 2014, the Company effected a seven-for-one stock split to shareholders of record as of June 2, 2014. All share and per share information has been retroactively adjusted to reflect the stock split.

Revenue Recognition

Net sales consist primarily of revenue from the sale of hardware, software, digital content and applications, accessories and service and support contracts. The Company recognizes revenue when persuasive evidence of an arrangement exists, delivery has occurred, the sales price is fixed or determinable and collection is probable. Product is considered delivered to the customer once it has been shipped and title, risk of loss and rewards of ownership have been transferred. For most of the Company's product sales, these criteria are met at the time the product is shipped. For online sales to individuals, for some sales to education customers in the U.S., and for certain other sales, the Company defers revenue until the customer receives the product because the Company retains a portion of the risk of loss on these sales during transit. The Company recognizes revenue from the sale of hardware products, software bundled with hardware that is essential to the functionality of the hardware, and third-party digital content sold on the iTunes Store in accordance with general revenue recognition accounting guidance. The Company recognizes revenue in accordance with industry specific software accounting guidance for the following types of sales transactions: (i) standalone sales of software products, (ii) sales of software upgrades and (iii) sales of software bundled with hardware not essential to the functionality of the hardware.

For the sale of most third-party products, the Company recognizes revenue based on the gross amount billed to customers because the Company establishes its own pricing for such products, retains related inventory risk for physical products, is the primary obligor to the customer and assumes the credit risk for amounts billed to its customers. For third-party applications sold through the App Store and Mac App Store and certain digital content sold through the iTunes Store, the Company does not determine the selling price of the products and is not the primary obligor to the customer. Therefore, the Company accounts for such sales on a net basis by recognizing in net sales only the commission it retains from each sale. The portion of the gross amount billed to customers that is remitted by the Company to third-party app developers and certain digital content owners is not reflected in the Company's Consolidated Statements of Operations.

The Company records deferred revenue when it receives payments in advance of the delivery of products or the performance of services. This includes amounts that have been deferred for unspecified and specified software upgrade rights and non-software services that are attached to hardware and software products. The Company sells gift cards redeemable at its retail and online stores, and also sells gift cards redeemable on the iTunes Store for the purchase of digital content and software. The Company records deferred revenue upon the sale of the card, which is relieved upon redemption of the card by the customer. Revenue from AppleCare service and support contracts is deferred and recognized over the service coverage periods. AppleCare service and support contracts typically include extended phone support, repair services, web-based support resources and diagnostic tools offered under the Company's standard limited warranty.

The Company records reductions to revenue for estimated commitments related to price protection and other customer incentive programs. For transactions involving price protection, the Company recognizes revenue net of the estimated amount to be refunded. For the Company's other customer incentive programs, the estimated cost of these programs is recognized at the later of the date at which the Company has sold the product or the date at which the program is offered. The Company also records reductions to revenue for expected future product returns based on the Company's historical experience. Revenue is recorded net of taxes collected from customers that are remitted to governmental authorities, with the collected taxes recorded as current liabilities until remitted to the relevant government authority.
[…]

Shipping Costs

For all periods presented, amounts billed to customers related to shipping and handling are classified as revenue, and the Company's shipping and handling costs are included in cost of sales.

Warranty Costs

The Company generally provides for the estimated cost of hardware and software warranties at the time the related revenue is recognized. The Company assesses the adequacy of its pre-existing warranty liabilities and adjusts the amounts as necessary based on actual experience and changes in future estimates.

Software Development Costs

Research and development ("R&D") costs are expensed as incurred. Development costs of computer software to be sold, leased, or otherwise marketed are subject to capitalization beginning when a product's technological feasibility has been established and ending when a product is available for general release to customers. In most instances, the Company's products are released soon after technological feasibility has been established. Costs incurred subsequent to achievement of technological feasibility were not significant, and software development costs were expensed as incurred during 2014, 2013 and 2012.

Advertising Costs

Advertising costs are expensed as incurred and included in selling, general and administrative expenses. Advertising expense was $1.2 billion, $1.1 billion and $1.0 billion for 2014, 2013 and 2012, respectively.
[…]

Earnings Per Share

Basic earnings per share is computed by dividing income available to common shareholders by the weighted-average number of shares of common stock outstanding during the period. Diluted earnings per share is computed by dividing income available to common shareholders by the weighted-average number of shares of common stock outstanding during the period increased to include the number of additional shares of common stock that would have been outstanding if the potentially dilutive securities had been issued. Potentially dilutive securities include outstanding stock options, shares to be purchased under the Company's employee stock purchase plan, unvested restricted stock and unvested RSUs. The dilutive effect of potentially dilutive securities is reflected in diluted earnings per share by application of the treasury stock method. Under the treasury stock method, an increase in the fair market value of the Company's common stock can result in a greater dilutive effect from potentially dilutive securities.

The following table shows the computation of basic and diluted earnings per share for 2014, 2013 and 2012 (net income in millions and shares in thousands):

	2014	2013	2012
Numerator:			
Net income	$ 39,510	$ 37,037	$ 41,733
Denominator:			
Weighted-average shares outstanding	6,085,572	6,477,320	6,543,726
Effect of dilutive securities	37,091	44,314	73,757
Weighted-average diluted shares	6,122,663	6,521,634	6,617,483
Basic earnings per share	$ 6.49	$ 5.72	$ 6.38
Diluted earnings per share	$ 6.45	$ 5.68	$ 6.31

[...]

Financial Instruments

Cash Equivalents and Marketable Securities

All highly liquid investments with maturities of three months or less at the date of purchase are classified as cash equivalents. The Company's marketable debt and equity securities have been classified and accounted for as available-for-sale. Management determines the appropriate classification of its investments at the time of purchase and reevaluates the designations at each balance sheet date. The Company classifies its marketable debt securities as either short-term or long-term based on each instrument's underlying contractual maturity date. Marketable debt securities with maturities of 12 months or less are classified as short-term and marketable debt securities with maturities greater than 12 months are classified as long-term. The Company classifies its marketable equity securities, including mutual funds, as either short-term or long-term based on the nature of each security and its availability for use in current operations. The Company's marketable debt and equity securities are carried at fair value, with the unrealized gains and losses, net of taxes, reported as a component of shareholders' equity. The cost of securities sold is based upon the specific identification method.
[...]

Allowance for Doubtful Accounts

The Company records its allowance for doubtful accounts based upon its assessment of various factors. The Company considers historical experience, the age of the accounts receivable balances, credit quality of the Company's customers, current economic conditions and other factors that may affect customers' ability to pay.

Inventories

Inventories are stated at the lower of cost, computed using the first-in, first-out method, or market. If the cost of the inventories exceeds their market value, provisions are made currently for the difference between the cost and the market value.

Property, Plant and Equipment

Property, plant and equipment are stated at cost. Depreciation is computed by use of the straight-line method over the estimated useful lives of the assets, which for buildings is the lesser of 30 years or the remaining life of the underlying building; between two to five years for machinery and equipment, including product tooling and manufacturing process equipment; and the shorter of lease terms or ten years for leasehold improvements. The Company capitalizes eligible costs to acquire or develop internal-use software that are incurred subsequent to the preliminary project stage. Capitalized costs related to internal-use software are amortized using the straight-line method over the estimated useful lives of the assets, which range from three to five years. Depreciation and amortization expense on property and equipment was $6.9 billion, $5.8 billion and $2.6 billion during 2014, 2013 and 2012, respectively.

Long-Lived Assets Including Goodwill and Other Acquired Intangible Assets

The Company reviews property, plant and equipment, inventory component prepayments and certain identifiable intangibles, excluding goodwill, for impairment. Long-lived assets are reviewed for impairment whenever events or changes in circumstances indicate the carrying amount of an asset may not be recoverable. Recoverability of these assets is measured by comparison of their carrying amounts to future undiscounted cash flows the assets are expected to generate. If property, plant and equipment, inventory component prepayments and certain identifiable intangibles are considered to be impaired, the impairment to be recognized equals the amount by which the carrying value of the assets exceeds its fair value. The Company did not record any significant impairments during 2014, 2013 and 2012.

[…]

The Company amortizes its intangible assets with definite useful lives over their estimated useful lives and reviews these assets for impairment. The Company typically amortizes its acquired intangible assets with definite useful lives over periods from three to seven years.

Fair Value Measurements

The Company applies fair value accounting for all financial assets and liabilities and non-financial assets and liabilities that are recognized or disclosed at fair value in the financial statements on a recurring basis. The Company defines fair value as the price that would be received from selling an asset or paid to transfer a liability in an orderly transaction between market participants at the measurement date. When determining the fair value measurements for assets and liabilities, which are required to be recorded at fair value, the Company considers the principal or most advantageous market in which the Company would transact and the market-based risk measurements or assumptions that market participants would use in pricing the asset or liability, such as risks inherent in valuation techniques, transfer restrictions and credit risk. Fair value is estimated by applying the following hierarchy, which prioritizes the inputs used to measure fair value into three levels and bases the categorization within the hierarchy upon the lowest level of input that is available and significant to the fair value measurement:

Level 1 – Quoted prices in active markets for identical assets or liabilities.

Level 2 – Observable inputs other than quoted prices in active markets for identical assets and liabilities, quoted prices for identical or similar assets or liabilities in inactive markets, or other inputs that are observable or can be corroborated by observable market data for substantially the full term of the assets or liabilities.

Level 3 – Inputs that are generally unobservable and typically reflect management's estimate of assumptions that market participants would use in pricing the asset or liability.

The Company's valuation techniques used to measure the fair value of money market funds and certain marketable equity securities were derived from quoted prices in active markets for identical assets or liabilities. The valuation techniques used to measure the fair value of the Company's debt instruments and all other financial instruments, all of which have counterparties with high credit ratings, were valued based on quoted market prices or model driven valuations using significant inputs derived from or corroborated by observable market data.

[…]

Note 2 – Financial Instruments

Cash, Cash Equivalents and Marketable Securities

The following tables show the Company's cash and available-for-sale securities' adjusted cost, gross unrealized gains, gross unrealized losses and fair value by significant investment category recorded as cash and cash equivalents or short- or long-term marketable securities as of September 27, 2014 and September 28, 2013 (in millions):

	Adjusted Cost	Unrealized Gains	Unrealized Losses	Fair Value	Cash and Cash Equivalents	Short-Term Marketable Securities	Long-Term Marketable Securities
	2014						
Cash	$ 10,232	$ 0	$ 0	$ 10,232	$ 10,232	$ 0	$ 0
Level 1:							
Money market funds	1,546	0	0	1,546	1,546	0	0
Mutual funds	2,531	1	(132)	2,400	0	2,400	0
Subtotal	4,077	1	(132)	3,946	1,546	2,400	0
Level 2:							
U.S. Treasury securities	23,140	15	(9)	23,146	12	607	22,527
U.S. agency securities	7,373	3	(11)	7,365	652	157	6,556
Non-U.S. government securities	6,925	69	(69)	6,925	0	204	6,721
Certificates of deposit and time deposits	3,832	0	0	3,832	1,230	1,233	1,369
Commercial paper	475	0	0	475	166	309	0
Corporate securities	85,431	296	(241)	85,486	6	6,298	79,182
Municipal securities	940	8	0	948	0	0	948
Mortgage- and asset-backed securities	12,907	26	(49)	12,884	0	25	12,859
Subtotal	141,023	417	(379)	141,061	2,066	8,833	130,162
Total	$ 155,332	$ 418	$ (511)	$ 155,239	$ 13,844	$ 11,233	$ 130,162

[...]

As of September 27, 2014, the Company considers the declines in market value of its marketable securities investment portfolio to be temporary in nature and does not consider any of its investments other-than-temporarily impaired. The Company typically invests in highly-rated securities, and its investment policy limits the amount of credit exposure to any one issuer. The policy generally requires investments to be investment grade, with the primary objective of minimizing the potential risk of principal loss. Fair values were determined for each individual security in the investment portfolio. When evaluating an investment for other-than-temporary impairment, the Company reviews factors such as the length of time and extent to which fair value has been below its cost basis, the financial condition of the issuer and any changes thereto, changes in market interest rates, and the Company's intent to sell, or whether it is more likely than not it will be required to sell, the investment before recovery of the investment's cost basis. During 2014, 2013 and 2012 the Company did not recognize any significant impairment charges.
[...]

Accounts Receivable

Trade Receivables

The Company has considerable trade receivables outstanding with its third-party cellular network carriers, wholesalers, retailers, value-added resellers, small and mid-sized businesses, and education, enterprise and government customers. The Company generally does not require collateral from its customers; however, the Company will require collateral in certain instances to limit credit risk. In addition, when possible, the Company attempts to limit credit risk on trade receivables with credit insurance for certain customers or by requiring third-party financing, loans or leases to support credit exposure. These credit-financing arrangements are directly between the third-party financing company and the end customer. As such, the Company generally does not assume any recourse or credit risk sharing related to any of these arrangements.

As of September 27, 2014, the Company had two customers that represented 10% or more of total trade receivables, one of which accounted for 16% and the other 13%. As of September 28, 2013, the Company had two customers that represented 10% or more of total trade receivables, one of which accounted for 13% and the other 10%. The Company's cellular network carriers accounted for 72% and 68% of trade receivables as of September 27, 2014 and September 28, 2013, respectively. The additions and write-offs to the Company's allowance for doubtful accounts during 2014, 2013 and 2012 were not significant.
[...]

Note 3 – Consolidated Financial Statement Details

The following tables show the Company's consolidated balance sheet details as of September 27, 2014 and September 28, 2013 (in millions):

Inventories

	2014	2013
Components	$ 471	$ 683
Finished goods	1,640	1,081
Total inventories	$ 2,111	$ 1,764

Property, Plant and Equipment

	2014	2013
Land and buildings	$ 4,863	$ 3,309
Machinery, equipment and internal-use software	29,639	21,242
Leasehold improvements	4,513	3,968
Gross property, plant and equipment	39,015	28,519
Accumulated depreciation and amortization	(18,391)	(11,922)
Net property, plant and equipment	$ 20,624	$ 16,597

Accrued Expenses

	2014	2013
Accrued warranty and related costs	$ 4,159	$ 2,967
Accrued marketing and selling expenses	2,321	1,291
Accrued taxes	1,209	1,200
Accrued compensation and employee benefits	1,209	959
Deferred margin on component sales	1,057	1,262
Other current liabilities	8,498	6,177
Total accrued expenses	$ 18,453	$ 13,856

Non-Current Liabilities

	2014	2013
Deferred tax liabilities	$ 20,259	$ 16,489
Other non-current liabilities	4,567	3,719
Total other non-current liabilities	$ 24,826	$ 20,208

Other Income and Expense

The following table shows the detail of other income and expense for 2014, 2013 and 2012 (in millions):

	2014	2013	2012
Interest and dividend income	$ 1,795	$ 1,616	$ 1,088
Interest expense	(384)	(136)	0
Other expense, net	(431)	(324)	(566)
Total other income/(expense), net	$ 980	$ 1,156	$ 522

Note 4 – Goodwill and Other Intangible Assets

On July 31, 2014, the Company completed the acquisitions of Beats Music, LLC, which offers a subscription streaming music service, and Beats Electronics, LLC, which makes Beats® headphones, speakers and audio software (collectively, "Beats"). The total purchase price consideration for these acquisitions was $2.6 billion, which consisted primarily of cash, of which $2.2 billion was allocated to goodwill, $636 million to acquired intangible assets and $258 million to net liabilities assumed. Concurrent with the close of the acquisition, the Company repaid $295 million of existing Beats outstanding debt to third-party creditors. In conjunction with the Beats acquisitions, the Company issued approximately 5.1 million shares of its common stock to certain former equity holders of Beats. The restricted stock was valued at approximately $485 million based on the Company's common stock on the acquisition date. The majority of these shares, valued at approximately $417 million, will vest over time based on continued employment with Apple.

The Company also completed various other business acquisitions during 2014 for an aggregate cash consideration, net of cash acquired, of $957 million, of which $828 million was allocated to goodwill, $257 million to acquired intangible assets and $128 million to net liabilities assumed.

The Company completed various business acquisitions during 2013 for an aggregate cash consideration, net of cash acquired, of $496 million, of which $419 million was allocated to goodwill, $179 million to acquired intangible assets and $102 million to net liabilities assumed.

The Company's gross carrying amount of goodwill was $4.6 billion and $1.6 billion as of September 27, 2014 and September 28, 2013, respectively. The Company did not have any goodwill impairments during 2014, 2013 or 2012.

The following table summarizes the components of gross and net intangible asset balances as of September 27, 2014 and September 28, 2013 (in millions):

	2014			2013		
	Gross Carrying Amount	Accumulated Amortization	Net Carrying Amount	Gross Carrying Amount	Accumulated Amortization	Net Carrying Amount
Definite-lived and amortizable acquired intangible assets	$ 7,127	$ (3,085)	$ 4,042	$ 6,081	$ (2,002)	$ 4,079
Indefinite-lived and non-amortizable acquired intangible assets	100	0	100	100	0	100
Total acquired intangible assets	$ 7,227	$ (3,085)	$ 4,142	$ 6,181	$ (2,002)	$ 4,179

Amortization expense related to acquired intangible assets was $1.1 billion, $960 million and $605 million in 2014, 2013 and 2012, respectively. As of September 27, 2014, the remaining weighted-average amortization period for acquired intangible assets is 3.8 years. [...]
[...]

Note 5 – Income Taxes

The provision for income taxes for 2014, 2013 and 2012, consisted of the following (in millions):

	2014	2013	2012
Federal:			
Current	$ 8,624	$ 9,334	$ 7,240
Deferred	3,183	1,878	5,018
	11,807	11,212	12,258
State:			
Current	855	1,084	1,182
Deferred	(178)	(311)	(123)
	677	773	1,059
Foreign:			
Current	2,147	1,559	1,203
Deferred	(658)	(426)	(490)
	1,489	1,133	713
Provision for income taxes	$ 13,973	$ 13,118	$ 14,030

The foreign provision for income taxes is based on foreign pre-tax earnings of $33.6 billion, $30.5 billion and $36.8 billion in 2014, 2013 and 2012, respectively. The Company's consolidated financial statements provide for any related tax liability on undistributed earnings that the Company does not intend to be indefinitely reinvested outside the U.S. Substantially all of the Company's undistributed international earnings intended to be indefinitely reinvested in operations outside the U.S. were generated by subsidiaries organized in Ireland, which has a statutory tax rate of 12.5%. As of September 27, 2014, U.S. income taxes have not been provided on a cumulative total of $69.7 billion of such earnings. The amount of unrecognized deferred tax liability related to these temporary differences is estimated to be approximately $23.3 billion.

As of September 27, 2014 and September 28, 2013, $137.1 billion and $111.3 billion, respectively, of the Company's cash, cash equivalents and marketable securities were held by foreign subsidiaries and are generally based in U.S. dollar-denominated holdings. Amounts held by foreign subsidiaries are generally subject to U.S. income taxation on repatriation to the U.S.

A reconciliation of the provision for income taxes, with the amount computed by applying the statutory federal income tax rate (35% in 2014, 2013 and 2012) to income before provision for income taxes for 2014, 2013 and 2012, is as follows (dollars in millions):

	2014	2013	2012
Computed expected tax	$ 18,719	$ 17,554	$ 19,517
State taxes, net of federal effect	469	508	677
Indefinitely invested earnings of foreign subsidiaries	(4,744)	(4,614)	(5,895)
Research and development credit, net	(88)	(287)	(103)
Domestic production activities deduction	(495)	(308)	(328)
Other	112	265	162
Provision for income taxes	$ 13,973	$ 13,118	$ 14,030
Effective tax rate	26.1%	26.2%	25.2%

[…]

Note 6 – Debt

[…]

Long-Term Debt

In the third quarter of 2014 and 2013, the Company issued $12.0 billion and $17.0 billion of long-term debt, respectively. The debt issuances included floating- and fixed-rate notes with varying maturities for an aggregate principal amount of $29.0 billion (collectively the "Notes"). The Notes are senior unsecured obligations, and interest is payable in arrears, quarterly for the floating-rate notes and semi-annually for the fixed-rate notes.

The following table provides a summary of the Company's long-term debt as of September 27, 2014 and September 28, 2013:

	2014		2013	
	Amount (in millions)	Effective Interest Rate	Amount (in millions)	Effective Interest Rate
Floating-rate notes due 2016	$ 1,000	0.51%	$ 1,000	0.51%
Floating-rate notes due 2017	1,000	0.31%	0	0
Floating-rate notes due 2018	2,000	1.10%	2,000	1.10%
Floating-rate notes due 2019	1,000	0.54%	0	0
Fixed-rate 0.45% notes due 2016	1,500	0.51%	1,500	0.51%
Fixed-rate 1.05% notes due 2017	1,500	0.30%	0	0
Fixed-rate 1.00% notes due 2018	4,000	1.08%	4,000	1.08%
Fixed-rate 2.10% notes due 2019	2,000	0.53%	0	0
Fixed-rate 2.85% notes due 2021	3,000	0.79%	0	0
Fixed-rate 2.40% notes due 2023	5,500	2.44%	5,500	2.44%
Fixed-rate 3.45% notes due 2024	2,500	0.90%	0	0
Fixed-rate 3.85% notes due 2043	3,000	3.91%	3,000	3.91%
Fixed-rate 4.45% notes due 2044	1,000	4.48%	0	0
Total borrowings	29,000		17,000	
Unamortized discount	(52)		(40)	
Hedge accounting fair value adjustments	39		0	
Total long-term debt	$ 28,987		$ 16,960	

[…]

The effective rates for the Notes include the interest on the Notes, amortization of the discount and, if applicable, adjustments related to hedging. The Company recognized $381 million and $136 million of interest expense on its long-term debt for the years ended September 27, 2014 and September 28, 2013, respectively. The Company did not have any long-term debt in 2012.

[…]

Note 7 – Shareholders' Equity

Preferred and Common Stock

During the second quarter of 2014, the Company's shareholders approved amendments (the "Amendments") to the Company's Restated Articles of Incorporation. The Amendments included the elimination of the Board of Directors' authority to issue preferred stock and established a par value for the Company's common stock of $0.00001 per share.

Dividends

The Company declared and paid cash dividends per common share during the periods presented as follows:

	Dividends Per Share		Amount (in millions)	
2014:				
Fourth quarter	$	0.47	$	2,807
Third quarter		0.47		2,830
Second quarter		0.44		2,655
First quarter		0.44		2,739
Total	$	1.82	$	11,031
2013:				
Fourth quarter	$	0.44	$	2,763
Third quarter		0.44		2,789
Second quarter		0.38		2,490
First quarter		0.38		2,486
Total	$	1.64	$	10,528

The Company paid cash dividends of $0.38 per share, totaling $2.5 billion, during the fourth quarter of 2012. Future dividends are subject to declaration by the Board of Directors.

[…]

Note 10 – Commitments and Contingencies

Accrued Warranty and Indemnification

The Company offers a basic limited parts and labor warranty on its hardware products. The basic warranty period for hardware products is typically one year from the date of purchase by the end-user. The Company also offers a 90-day basic warranty for its service parts used to repair the Company's hardware products. The Company provides currently for the estimated cost that may be incurred under its basic limited product warranties at the time related revenue is recognized. Factors considered in determining appropriate accruals for product warranty obligations include the size of the installed base of products subject to warranty protection, historical and projected warranty claim rates, historical and projected cost-per-claim and knowledge of specific product failures that are outside of the Company's typical experience. The Company assesses the adequacy of its pre-existing warranty liabilities and adjusts the amounts as necessary based on actual experience and changes in future estimates.

The following table shows changes in the Company's accrued warranties and related costs for 2014, 2013 and 2012 (in millions):

	2014	2013	2012
Beginning accrued warranty and related costs	$ 2,967	$ 1,638	$ 1,240
Cost of warranty claims	(3,760)	(3,703)	(1,786)
Accruals for product warranty	4,952	5,032	2,184
Ending accrued warranty and related costs	$ 4,159	$ 2,967	$ 1,638

[...]

The Company has entered into indemnification agreements with its directors and executive officers. Under these agreements, the Company has agreed to indemnify such individuals to the fullest extent permitted by law against liabilities that arise by reason of their status as directors or officers and to advance expenses incurred by such individuals in connection with related legal proceedings. [...]
[...]

Operating Leases

The Company leases various equipment and facilities, including retail space, under noncancelable operating lease arrangements. The Company does not currently utilize any other off-balance sheet financing arrangements. The major facility leases are typically for terms not exceeding 10 years and generally contain multi-year renewal options. Leases for retail space are for terms ranging from five to 20 years, the majority of which are for 10 years, and often contain multi-year renewal options. As of September 27, 2014, the Company's total future minimum lease payments under noncancelable operating leases were $5.0 billion, of which $3.6 billion related to leases for retail space.

Rent expense under all operating leases, including both cancelable and noncancelable leases, was $717 million, $645 million and $488 million in 2014, 2013 and 2012, respectively. Future minimum lease payments under noncancelable operating leases having remaining terms in excess of one year as of September 27, 2014, are as follows (in millions):

2015	$ 662
2016	676
2017	645
2018	593
2019	534
Thereafter	1,877
Total	$ 4,987

[...]

Contingencies

The Company is subject to various legal proceedings and claims that have arisen in the ordinary course of business and that have not been fully adjudicated. In the opinion of management, there was not at least a reasonable possibility the Company may have incurred a material loss, or a material loss in excess of a recorded accrual, with respect to loss contingencies. However, the outcome of litigation is inherently uncertain. Therefore, although management considers the likelihood of such an outcome to be remote, if one or more of these legal matters were resolved against the Company in a reporting period for amounts in excess of management's expectations, the Company's consolidated financial statements for that reporting period could be materially adversely affected.
[...]

2 0 1 4

Under Armour, Inc.

A N N U A L   R E P O R T

Author's Note: Information in the narrative component of these financial statements has been greatly abbreviated, though should be sufficient to complete the requirements of the Focus on Analysis activities.

To view the report in its entirety, visit:
http://www.sec.gov/Archives/edgar/data/1336917/000133691715000006/ua-20141231x10k.htm

Source: From Under Armour Inc., Annual Report 2014

UNITED STATES
SECURITIES AND EXCHANGE COMMISSION
Washington, D.C. 20549

Form 10-K

[...]

☑ **ANNUAL REPORT PURSUANT TO SECTION 13 OR 15(d) OF THE SECURITIES EXCHANGE ACT OF 1934**

For the fiscal year ended December 31, 2014

[...]

Commission File No. 001-33202

[...]

UNDER ARMOUR, INC.
(Exact name of registrant as specified in its charter)

Maryland	**52-1990078**
(State or other jurisdiction of incorporation or organization)	(I.R.S. Employer Identification No.)
1020 Hull Street	
Baltimore, Maryland 21230	**(410) 454-6428**
(Address of principal executive offices) (Zip Code)	(Registrant's Telephone Number, Including Area Code)

Securities registered pursuant to Section 12(b) of the Act:

Class A Common Stock	**New York Stock Exchange**
(Title of each class)	(Name of each exchange on which registered)

[...]

DOCUMENTS INCORPORATED BY REFERENCE

[...]

ITEM 1.   BUSINESS

General

Our principal business activities are the development, marketing and distribution of branded performance apparel, footwear and accessories for men, women and youth. The brand's moisture-wicking fabrications are engineered [...] for wear in nearly every climate to provide a performance alternative to traditional products. Our products are sold worldwide and are worn by athletes at all levels, from youth to professional, on playing fields around the globe, as well as by consumers with active lifestyles.

Our net revenues are generated primarily from the wholesale sales of our products to national, regional, independent and specialty retailers. We also generate net revenue from the sale of our products through our direct to consumer sales channel, which includes our brand and factory house stores and websites, and from product licensing. A large majority of our products are sold in North America; however we believe that our products appeal to athletes and consumers with active lifestyles around the globe. Internationally, our net revenues are generated from a mix of wholesale sales to retailers and distributors and sales through our direct to consumer sales channels, and license revenue from sales by our third party licensee. We plan to continue to grow our business over the long term through increased sales of our apparel, footwear and accessories, expansion of our wholesale distribution, growth in our direct to consumer sales channel and expansion in international markets. Virtually all of our products are manufactured by [...] unaffiliated [...] manufacturers operating in 13 countries outside of the United States.

In December 2013, we acquired MapMyFitness, Inc. ("MapMyFitness"), a digital connected fitness company with users primarily in the U.S., and in January 2015, we acquired Endomondo, ApS. ("Endomondo") a digital connected fitness company with over 20 million registered users primarily in Europe and other regions outside the U.S. In February 2015, we entered into an agreement to acquire MyFitnessPal, Inc. ("MyFitnessPal"), a digital nutrition and connected fitness company with over 80 million registered users. [...] The acquisition is expected to close in the first quarter of 2015, subject to regulatory approval. These businesses will form the core of our Connected Fitness business and strategy.

Our Connected Fitness strategy is focused on connecting with our consumers and increasing awareness and sales of our existing product offerings through our global wholesale and direct to consumer channels. We plan to engage and grow this community by developing innovative applications, services and other digital solutions to impact how athletes and fitness-minded individuals train, perform and live.

We were incorporated as a Maryland corporation in 1996. [...]

Products

Our product offerings consist of apparel, footwear and accessories for men, women and youth. We [...] provide consumers with products that we believe are a superior alternative to traditional athletic products. In 2014, sales of apparel, footwear and accessories represented 74%, 14% and 9% of net revenues, respectively. Licensing arrangements, primarily for the sale of our products, and other revenue represented the remaining 3% of net revenues. [...]

Apparel

Our apparel is offered in a variety of styles and fits intended to enhance comfort and mobility, regulate body temperature and improve performance regardless of weather conditions. [...] Our three gearlines are marketed to tell a very simple story about our highly technical products and extend across the sporting goods, outdoor and active lifestyle markets. [...] HEATGEAR® when it is hot, COLDGEAR® when it is cold and ALLSEASONGEAR® between the extremes. [...]
[...]

Footwear

Our footwear offerings include football, baseball, lacrosse, softball and soccer cleats, slides and performance training, running, basketball and outdoor footwear. Our footwear is light, breathable and built with performance attributes for athletes. Our footwear is designed with innovative technologies which provide stabilization, directional cushioning and moisture management engineered to maximize the athlete's comfort and control.

Accessories

Accessories primarily includes the sale of headwear, bags and gloves. Our accessories include HEATGEAR® and COLDGEAR® technologies and are designed with advanced fabrications to provide the same level of performance as our other products.

License and Other

We have agreements with our licensees to develop Under Armour apparel and accessories. [...] During 2014, our licensees offered socks, team uniforms, baby and kids' apparel, eyewear and inflatable footballs and basketballs that feature performance advantages and functionality similar to our other product offerings.

We also offer digital fitness platform licenses and subscriptions, along with digital advertising through our MapMyFitness business. License and other revenues generated from the sale of apparel and accessories and the use of our MapMyFitness platforms are included in our net revenues.

Marketing and Promotion

We currently focus on marketing and selling our products to consumers primarily for use in athletics, fitness, training and outdoor activities. [...]

Sports Marketing

Our marketing and promotion strategy begins with providing and selling our products to high-performing athletes and teams on the high school, collegiate and professional levels. We execute this strategy through outfitting agreements, professional and collegiate sponsorships, individual athlete agreements and by providing and selling our products directly to team equipment managers and to individual athletes. As a result, our products are seen on the field, giving them exposure to various consumer audiences through the internet, television, magazines and live at sporting events. This exposure [...] helps us establish on-field authenticity as consumers can see our products being worn by high-performing athletes.

We are the official outfitter of athletic teams in several high-profile collegiate conferences. We are an official supplier of footwear and gloves to the National Football League ("NFL") and we are the official combine scouting partner to the NFL with the right to sell combine training apparel. We are the Official Performance Footwear Supplier of Major League Baseball and a partner with the National Basketball Association ("NBA") which allows us to market our NBA athletes in game uniforms in connection with our basketball footwear.

Internationally, we sponsor and sell our products to European and Latin America soccer and rugby teams. [...] [...]

Media

We feature our products in a variety of national digital, broadcast, and print media outlets. We also utilize social and mobile media to engage consumers and promote conversation around our brand and our products.

Retail Presentation

The primary component of our retail marketing strategy is to increase and brand floor space dedicated to our products within our major retail accounts. The design and funding of Under Armour concept shops within our major retail accounts has been a key initiative for securing prime floor space, educating the consumer and creating an exciting environment for the consumer to experience our brand. Under Armour concept shops enhance our brand's presentation within our major retail accounts with a shop-in-shop approach, using dedicated floor space exclusively for our products, including flooring, lighting, walls, displays and images.

Sales and Distribution

The majority of our sales are generated through wholesale channels, which include national and regional sporting goods chains, independent and specialty retailers, department store chains, institutional athletic departments and leagues and teams. [...]

We also sell our products directly to consumers through our own network of brand and factory house stores in our North America, Latin America and Asia-Pacific operating segments, and through websites globally. [...] Through [...] stores, consumers experience our brand first-hand and have broader access to our performance products. In 2014, sales through our wholesale, direct to consumer and licensing channels represented 67%, 30% and 3% of net revenues, respectively.

[…]

Our primary business operates in four geographic segments: (1) North America, comprising the United States and Canada, (2) Europe, the Middle East and Africa ("EMEA"), (3) Asia-Pacific, and (4) Latin America. […] The following table presents net revenues by segment for each of the years ending December 31, 2014, 2013 and 2012:

	Year ended December 31,					
	2014		**2013**		**2012**	
		% of		**% of**		**% of**
(*In thousands*)	**Net Revenues**	**Net Revenues**	**Net Revenues**	**Net Revenues**	**Net Revenues**	**Net Revenues**
North America	$ 2,796,390	90.7%	$ 2,193,739	94.1%	$ 1,726,733	94.1%
Other foreign countries and businesses	287,980	9.3	138,312	5.9	108,188	5.9
Total net revenues	$ 3,084,370	100.0%	$ 2,332,051	100.0%	$ 1,834,921	100.0%

[…]

Competition

[…] Many of our competitors are large apparel and footwear companies with strong worldwide brand recognition and significantly greater resources than us, such as Nike and Adidas. We also compete with other manufacturers, including those specializing in outdoor apparel, and private label offerings of certain retailers, including some of our retail customers.

[…]

Under Armour, Inc. and Subsidiaries

Consolidated Balance Sheets
(In thousands, except share data)

	December 31, 2014	December 31, 2013
Assets		
Current assets		
Cash and cash equivalents	$ 593,175	$ 347,489
Accounts receivable, net	279,835	209,952
Inventories	536,714	469,006
Prepaid expenses and other current assets	87,177	63,987
Deferred income taxes	52,498	38,377
Total current assets	1,549,399	1,128,811
Property and equipment, net	305,564	223,952
Goodwill	123,256	122,244
Intangible assets, net	26,230	24,097
Deferred income taxes	33,570	31,094
Other long term assets	57,064	47,543
Total assets	$ 2,095,083	$ 1,577,741
Liabilities and Stockholders' Equity		
Current liabilities		
Revolving credit facility	$ —	$ 100,000
Accounts payable	210,432	165,456
Accrued expenses	147,681	133,729
Current maturities of long term debt	28,951	4,972
Other current liabilities	34,563	22,473
Total current liabilities	421,627	426,630
Long term debt, net of current maturities	255,250	47,951
Other long term liabilities	67,906	49,806
Total liabilities	744,783	524,387
Commitments and contingencies (see Note 7)		
Stockholders' equity		
Class A Common Stock, $0.0003 1/3 par value; 400,000,000 shares authorized as of December 31, 2014 and 2013; 177,295,988 shares issued and outstanding as of December 31, 2014 and 171,628,708 shares issued and outstanding as of December 31, 2013.	59	57
Class B Convertible Common Stock, $0.0003 1/3 par value; 36,600,000 shares authorized, issued and outstanding as of December 31, 2014 and 40,000,000 shares authorized, issued and outstanding as of December 31, 2013.	12	13
Additional paid-in capital	508,350	397,248
Retained earnings	856,687	653,842
Accumulated other comprehensive income (loss)	(14,808)	2,194
Total stockholders' equity	1,350,300	1,053,354
Total liabilities and stockholders' equity	$ 2,095,083	$ 1,577,741

See accompanying notes.

Under Armour, Inc. and Subsidiaries

Consolidated Statements of Income

(In thousands, except per share amounts)

	Year Ended December 31,		
	2014	**2013**	**2012**
Net revenues	$ 3,084,370	$ 2,332,051	$ 1,834,921
Cost of goods sold	1,572,164	1,195,381	955,624
Gross profit	1,512,206	1,136,670	879,297
Selling, general and administrative expenses	1,158,251	871,572	670,602
Income from operations	353,955	265,098	208,695
Interest expense, net	(5,335)	(2,933)	(5,183)
Other expense, net	(6,410)	(1,172)	(73)
Income before income taxes	342,210	260,993	203,439
Provision for income taxes	134,168	98,663	74,661
Net income	$ 208,042	$ 162,330	$ 128,778
Net income available per common share			
Basic	$ 0.98	$ 0.77	$ 0.62
Diluted	$ 0.95	$ 0.75	$ 0.61
Weighted average common shares outstanding			
Basic	213,227	210,696	208,686
Diluted	219,380	215,958	212,760

See accompanying notes.

Under Armour, Inc. and Subsidiaries

Consolidated Statements of Comprehensive Income

(In thousands)

	Year Ended December 31,		
	2014	**2013**	**2012**
Net income	$ 208,042	$ 162,330	$ 128,778
Other comprehensive income (loss):			
Foreign currency translation adjustment	(16,743)	(897)	423
Unrealized gain (loss) on cash flow hedge, net of tax of ($408), $505 and $58 for the years ended December 31, 2014, 2013 and 2012.	(259)	723	(83)
Total other comprehensive income (loss)	(17,002)	(174)	340
Comprehensive income	$ 191,040	$ 162,156	$ 129,118

See accompanying notes.

Under Armour, Inc. and Subsidiaries
Consolidated Statements of Stockholders' Equity
(In thousands)

	Class A Common Stock		Class B Convertible Common Stock		Additional Paid-In Capital	Retained Earnings	Accumulated Other Comprehensive Income (Loss)	Total Stockholders' Equity
	Shares	Amount	Shares	Amount				
				[...]				
Balance as of December 31, 2012	166,922	$ 56	42,600	$ 14	$321,303	$493,181	$ 2,368	$ 816,922
Exercise of stock options	1,822	—	—	—	12,159	—	—	12,159
Shares withheld in consideration of employee tax obligations relative to stock-based compensation arrangements	(47)	—	—	—	—	(1,669)	—	(1,669)
Issuance of Class A Common Stock, net of forfeitures	332	—	—	—	3,439	—	—	3,439
Class B Convertible Common Stock converted to Class A Common Stock	2,600	1	(2,600)	(1)	—	—	—	—
Stock-based compensation expense	—	—	—	—	43,184	—	—	43,184
Net excess tax benefits from stock-based compensation arrangements	—	—	—	—	17,163	—	—	17,163
Comprehensive income	—	—	—	—	—	162,330	(174)	162,156
Balance as of December 31, 2013	171,629	57	40,000	13	397,248	653,842	2,194	1,053,354
Exercise of stock options	1,454	1	—	—	11,258	—	—	11,259
Shares withheld in consideration of employee tax obligations relative to stock-based compensation arrangements	(95)	—	—	—	—	(5,197)	—	(5,197)
Issuance of Class A Common Stock, net of forfeitures	908	—	—	—	12,067	—	—	12,067
Class B Convertible Common Stock converted to Class A Common Stock	3,400	1	(3,400)	(1)	—	—	—	—
Stock-based compensation expense	—	—	—	—	50,812	—	—	50,812
Net excess tax benefits from stock-based compensation arrangements	—	—	—	—	36,965	—	—	36,965
Comprehensive income (loss)	—	—	—	—	—	208,042	(17,002)	191,040
Balance as of December 31, 2014	177,296	$ 59	36,600	$ 12	$508,350	$856,687	$(14,808)	$1,350,300

See accompanying notes.

Under Armour, Inc. and Subsidiaries

Consolidated Statements of Cash Flows

(In thousands)

	Year Ended December 31,		
	2014	**2013**	**2012**
Cash flows from operating activities			
Net income	$ 208,042	$ 162,330	$ 128,778
Adjustments to reconcile net income to net cash used in operating activities			
Depreciation and amortization	72,093	50,549	43,082
Unrealized foreign currency exchange rate losses (gains)	11,739	1,905	(2,464)
Loss on disposal of property and equipment	261	332	524
Stock-based compensation	50,812	43,184	19,845
Deferred income taxes	(17,584)	(18,832)	(12,973)
Changes in reserves and allowances	31,350	13,945	13,916
Changes in operating assets and liabilities, net of effects of acquisitions:			
Accounts receivable	(101,057)	(35,960)	(53,433)
Inventories	(84,658)	(156,900)	4,699
Prepaid expenses and other assets	(33,345)	(19,049)	(4,060)
Accounts payable	49,137	14,642	35,370
Accrued expenses and other liabilities	28,856	56,481	21,966
Income taxes payable and receivable	3,387	7,443	4,511
Net cash provided by operating activities	219,033	120,070	199,761
Cash flows from investing activities			
Purchases of property and equipment	(140,528)	(87,830)	(50,650)
Purchase of business	(10,924)	(148,097)	—
Purchases of other assets	(860)	(475)	(1,310)
Change in loans receivable	—	(1,700)	—
Change in restricted cash	—	—	5,029
Net cash used in investing activities	(152,312)	(238,102)	(46,931)
Cash flows from financing activities			
Proceeds from revolving credit facility	—	100,000	—
Payments on revolving credit facility	(100,000)	—	—
Proceeds from term loan	250,000	—	—
Payments on term loan	(13,750)	—	(25,000)
Proceeds from long term debt	—	—	50,000
Payments on long term debt	(4,972)	(5,471)	(44,330)
Excess tax benefits from stock-based compensation arrangements	36,965	17,167	17,868
Proceeds from exercise of stock options and other stock issuances	15,776	15,099	14,776
Payments of debt financing costs	(1,713)	—	(1,017)
Net cash provided by financing activities	182,306	126,795	12,297
Effect of exchange rate changes on cash and cash equivalents	(3,341)	(3,115)	1,330
Net increase in cash and cash equivalents	245,686	5,648	166,457
Cash and cash equivalents			
Beginning of period	347,489	341,841	175,384
End of period	$ 593,175	$ 347,489	$ 341,841
Non-cash investing and financing activities			
Increase in accrual for property and equipment	$ 4,922	$ 3,786	$ 12,137
Non-cash acquisition of business	11,233	—	—
Other supplemental information			
Cash paid for income taxes	103,284	85,570	57,739
Cash paid for interest, net of capitalized interest	4,146	1,505	3,306

See accompanying notes.

Under Armour, Inc. and Subsidiaries

Notes to the Audited Consolidated Financial Statements

1. Description of the Business

Under Armour, Inc. is a developer, marketer and distributor of branded performance apparel, footwear and accessories. These products are sold worldwide and worn by athletes at all levels, from youth to professional on playing fields around the globe, as well as by consumers with active lifestyles.

2. Summary of Significant Accounting Policies

Basis of Presentation

The accompanying consolidated financial statements include the accounts of Under Armour, Inc. and its wholly owned subsidiaries (the "Company"). All intercompany balances and transactions have been eliminated. The accompanying consolidated financial statements were prepared in accordance with accounting principles generally accepted in the United States of America.
[…]

Cash and Cash Equivalents

The Company considers all highly liquid investments with an original maturity of three months or less at date of inception to be cash and cash equivalents. Included in interest expense, net for the years ended December 31, 2014, 2013 and 2012 was interest income of $192.0 thousand, $23.7 thousand and $25.2 thousand, respectively, related to cash and cash equivalents.

Concentration of Credit Risk

[…] The majority of the Company's accounts receivable is due from large sporting goods retailers. Credit is extended based on an evaluation of the customer's financial condition and collateral is not required. The Company had two customers in North America that individually accounted for 23.4% and 11.1% of accounts receivable as of December 31, 2014. The Company's largest customer accounted for 14.4%, 16.6% and 16.6% of net revenues for the years ended December 31, 2014, 2013 and 2012, respectively.

Allowance for Doubtful Accounts

The Company makes ongoing estimates relating to the collectability of accounts receivable and maintains an allowance for estimated losses resulting from the inability of its customers to make required payments. In determining the amount of the reserve, the Company considers historical levels of credit losses and significant economic developments within the retail environment that could impact the ability of its customers to pay outstanding balances and makes judgments about the creditworthiness of significant customers based on ongoing credit evaluations. […] As of December 31, 2014 and 2013, the allowance for doubtful accounts was $3.7 million and $2.9 million, respectively.

Inventories

Inventories consist primarily of finished goods. Costs of finished goods inventories include all costs incurred to bring inventory to its current condition, including inbound freight, duties and other costs. The Company values its inventory at standard cost which approximates landed cost, using the first-in, first-out method of cost determination. Market value is estimated based upon assumptions made about future demand and retail market conditions. If the Company determines that the estimated market value of its inventory is less than the carrying value of such inventory, it records a charge to cost of goods sold to reflect the lower of cost or market. […]
[…]

Property and Equipment

Property and equipment are stated at cost, including the cost of internal labor for software customized for internal use, less accumulated depreciation and amortization. Property and equipment is depreciated using the straight-line method over the estimated useful lives of the assets: 3 to 10 years for furniture, office equipment, software and plant equipment and 10 to 35 years for site improvements, buildings and building equipment. Leasehold and tenant improvements are amortized over the shorter of the lease term or the estimated useful lives of the assets. The cost of in-store apparel and footwear fixtures and displays are capitalized, included in furniture, fixtures and displays, and depreciated over 3 years. The Company periodically reviews assets' estimated useful lives based upon actual experience and expected future utilization. A change in useful life is treated as a change in accounting estimate and is applied prospectively.

The Company capitalizes the cost of interest for long term property and equipment projects based on the Company's weighted average borrowing rates in place while the projects are in progress. Capitalized interest was $0.4 million and $0.4 million as of December 31, 2014 and 2013, respectively.

Upon retirement or disposition of property and equipment, the cost and accumulated depreciation are removed from the accounts and any resulting gain or loss is reflected in selling, general and administrative expenses for that period. Major additions and betterments are capitalized to the asset accounts while maintenance and repairs, which do not improve or extend the lives of assets, are expensed as incurred.

Goodwill, Intangible Assets and Long-Lived Assets

Goodwill and intangible assets are recorded at their estimated fair values at the date of acquisition and are allocated to the reporting units that are expected to receive the related benefits. Goodwill and indefinite lived intangible assets are not amortized and are required to be tested for impairment at least annually or sooner whenever events or changes in circumstances indicate that the assets may be impaired. [...] The Company performs its annual impairment tests in the fourth quarter of each fiscal year.

[...] When factors indicate that an asset should be evaluated for possible impairment, the Company reviews long-lived assets to assess recoverability from future operations using undiscounted cash flows. If future undiscounted cash flows are less than the carrying value, an impairment is recognized in earnings to the extent that the carrying value exceeds fair value.

Accrued Expenses

At December 31, 2014, accrued expenses primarily included $61.4 million and $14.0 million of accrued compensation and benefits and marketing expenses, respectively. At December 31, 2013, accrued expenses primarily included $56.7 million and $11.9 million of accrued compensation and benefits and marketing expenses, respectively.

Foreign Currency Translation and Transactions

The functional currency for each of the Company's wholly owned foreign subsidiaries is generally the applicable local currency. The translation of foreign currencies into U.S. dollars is performed for assets and liabilities using current foreign currency exchange rates in effect at the balance sheet date and for revenue and expense accounts using average foreign currency exchange rates during the period. Capital accounts are translated at historical foreign currency exchange rates. Translation gains and losses are included in stockholders' equity as a component of accumulated other comprehensive income. Adjustments that arise from foreign currency exchange rate changes on transactions, primarily driven by intercompany transactions, denominated in a currency other than the functional currency are included in other expense, net on the consolidated statements of income.
[...]

Revenue Recognition

The Company recognizes revenue pursuant to applicable accounting standards. Net revenues consist of both net sales and license and other revenues. Net sales are recognized upon transfer of ownership, including passage of title to the customer and transfer of risk of loss related to those goods. Transfer of title and risk of loss is based upon shipment under free on board shipping point for most goods or upon receipt by the customer depending on the country of the sale and the agreement with the customer. In some instances, transfer of title and risk of loss takes place at the point of sale, for example, at the Company's brand and factory house stores. The Company may also ship product directly from its supplier to the customer and recognize revenue when the product is delivered to and accepted by the customer. License and other revenues are primarily recognized based upon shipment of licensed products sold by the Company's licensees. Sales taxes imposed on the Company's revenues from product sales are presented on a net basis on the consolidated statements of income and therefore do not impact net revenues or costs of goods sold.

The Company records reductions to revenue for estimated customer returns, allowances, markdowns and discounts. The Company bases its estimates on historical rates of customer returns and allowances as well as the specific identification of outstanding returns, markdowns and allowances that have not yet been received by the Company. [...] As of December 31, 2014 and 2013, there were $68.9 million and $43.8 million, respectively, in reserves for customer returns, allowances, markdowns and discounts.
[...]

4. Property and Equipment, Net

Property and equipment consisted of the following:

(In thousands)	December 31, 2014	December 31, 2013
Leasehold and tenant improvements	$ 128,088	$ 97,776
Furniture, fixtures and displays	80,035	68,045
Buildings	46,419	45,903
Software	67,506	51,984
Office equipment	51,531	39,551
Plant equipment	70,317	45,509
Land	17,628	17,628
Construction in progress	57,677	28,471
Other	3,175	1,219
Subtotal property and equipment	522,376	396,086
Accumulated depreciation	(216,812)	(172,134)
Property and equipment, net	$ 305,564	$ 223,952

Construction in progress primarily includes costs incurred for software systems, leasehold improvements and in-store fixtures and displays not yet placed in use.

Depreciation expense related to property and equipment was $63.6 million, $48.3 million and $39.8 million for the years ended December 31, 2014, 2013 and 2012, respectively.

5. Goodwill and Intangible Assets, Net

The following table summarizes changes in the carrying amount of the Company's goodwill by reportable segment as of the periods indicated:

(In thousands)	North America	Other foreign countries and businesses	Total
Balance as of December 31, 2013	$ 119,799	$ 2,445	$ 122,244
Goodwill acquired	—	1,012	1,012
Balance as of December 31, 2014	$ 119,799	$ 3,457	$ 123,256

During 2014, the Company acquired $1.0 million of goodwill in connection with the acquisition of certain assets of its former distributor in Mexico, which was accounted for as a business combination.

The following table summarizes the Company's intangible assets as of the periods indicated:

(In thousands)	December 31, 2014 Gross Carrying Amount	December 31, 2014 Accumulated Amortization	December 31, 2014 Net Carrying Amount	December 31, 2013 Gross Carrying Amount	December 31, 2013 Accumulated Amortization	December 31, 2013 Net Carrying Amount
Intangible assets subject to amortization:						
Technology	$ 12,000	$ (1,907)	$ 10,093	$ 12,000	$ (126)	$ 11,874
Trade name	5,000	(1,353)	3,647	5,000	(53)	4,947
Customer relationships	11,927	(4,692)	7,235	3,600	(38)	3,562
Lease-related intangible assets	3,896	(2,762)	1,134	3,896	(2,605)	1,291
Other	2,196	(893)	1,303	1,266	(532)	734
Total	$ 35,019	$ (11,607)	$ 23,412	$ 25,762	$ (3,354)	$ 22,408
Indefinite-lived intangible assets			2,818			1,689
Intangible assets, net			$ 26,230			$ 24,097

Technology, trade-name and customer relationship intangible assets were acquired with the purchase of MapMyFitness and are amortized on a straight-line basis over 84 months, 48 months and 24 months, respectively. Customer relationship intangible assets were also acquired with the acquisition of certain assets of the Company's former distributor in Mexico and are amortized on a straight-line basis over 36 months. Lease-related intangible assets were acquired with the purchase of the Company's corporate headquarters and are amortized over the remaining third party lease terms, which ranged from 9 months to 15 years on the date of purchase. Other intangible assets are amortized using estimated useful lives of 55 months to 120 months with no residual value. Amortization expense, which is included in selling, general and administrative expenses, was $8.5 million, $1.6 million and $2.2 million for the years ended December 31, 2014, 2013 and 2012, respectively.

The following is the estimated amortization expense for the Company's intangible assets as of December 31, 2014:

(*In thousands*)	
2015	$ 7,862
2016	6,118
2017	3,236
2018	2,074
2019	1,966
2020 and thereafter	2,156
Amortization expense of intangible assets	$ 23,412

At December 31, 2014, 2013 and 2012, the Company determined that its goodwill and indefinite-lived intangible assets were not impaired.

6. Credit Facility and Long Term Debt

Credit Facility

In May 2014, the Company entered into a new unsecured $650.0 million credit facility and terminated its prior $325.0 million secured revolving credit facility. The credit agreement has a term of five years through May 2019, with permitted extensions under certain circumstances. The credit agreement provides for a committed revolving credit facility of $400.0 million, in addition to an aggregate term loan commitment of $250.0 million, consisting of a $150.0 million term loan, drawn at the closing of the credit agreement, and $100.0 million delayed draw term loan drawn in November 2014 for general corporate purposes. At the Company's request and the lenders' consent, the revolving credit facility or term loans may be increased by up to an additional $150.0 million. Borrowings under the revolving credit facility may be made in U.S. Dollars, Euros, Pounds Sterling, Japanese Yen and Canadian Dollars. Up to $50.0 million of the facility may be used for the issuance of letters of credit and up to $50.0 million of the facility may be used for the issuance of swingline loans. There were no significant letters of credit and no swingline loans outstanding as of December 31, 2014.
[…]

The Company used $100.0 million of the proceeds from the $150.0 million loan to repay the $100.0 million outstanding under the Company's prior revolving credit facility. The Company incurred and capitalized $1.7 million in deferred financing costs in connection with the credit facility.

Other Long Term Debt

The Company has long term debt agreements with various lenders to finance the acquisition or lease of qualifying capital investments. Loans under these agreements are collateralized by a first lien on the related assets acquired. At December 31, 2014, 2013 and 2012, the outstanding principal balance under these agreements was $2.0 million, $4.9 million and $11.9 million, respectively. Currently, advances under these agreements bear interest rates which are fixed at the time of each advance. The weighted average interest rates on outstanding borrowings were 3.1%, 3.3% and 3.7% for the years ended December 31, 2014, 2013 and 2012, respectively.
[…]

The following are the scheduled maturities of long term debt as of December 31, 2014:

(In thousands)	
2015	$ 28,951
2016	27,000
2017	27,000
2018	27,000
2019	138,250
2020 and thereafter	36,000
Total scheduled maturities of long term debt	284,201
Less current maturities of long term debt	(28,951)
Long term debt obligations	$ 255,250

Interest expense, net was $5.3 million, $2.9 million and $5.2 million for the years ended December 31, 2014, 2013 and 2012, respectively. Interest expense includes the amortization of deferred financing costs and interest expense under the credit and long term debt facilities.

The Company monitors the financial health and stability of its lenders under the credit and other long term debt facilities, however during any period of significant instability in the credit markets lenders could be negatively impacted in their ability to perform under these facilities.

7. Commitments and Contingencies

Obligations Under Operating Leases

The Company leases warehouse space, office facilities, space for its brand and factory house stores and certain equipment under non-cancelable operating leases. The leases expire at various dates through 2028, excluding extensions at the Company's option, and include provisions for rental adjustments. [...] The following is a schedule of future minimum lease payments for non-cancelable real property operating leases as of December 31, 2014 as well as significant operating lease agreements entered into during the period after December 31, 2014 through the date of this report:

(In thousands)	
2015	$ 56,452
2016	57,079
2017	52,172
2018	48,345
2019	44,313
2020 and thereafter	214,214
Total future minimum lease payments	$ 472,575

Included in selling, general and administrative expense was rent expense of $59.0 million, $41.8 million and $31.1 million for the years ended December 31, 2014, 2013 and 2012, respectively, under non-cancelable operating lease agreements. Included in these amounts was contingent rent expense of $11.0 million, $7.8 million and $6.2 million for the years ended December 31, 2014, 2013 and 2012, respectively.

Sponsorships and Other Marketing Commitments

Within the normal course of business, the Company enters into contractual commitments in order to promote the Company's brand and products. These commitments include sponsorship agreements with teams and athletes on the collegiate and professional levels, official supplier agreements, athletic event sponsorships and other marketing commitments. The following is a schedule of the Company's future minimum payments under its sponsorship and other marketing agreements as of December 31, 2014, as well as significant sponsorship and other marketing agreements entered into during the period after December 31, 2014 through the date of this report:

(*In thousands*)	
2015	$ 90,056
2016	71,654
2017	56,734
2018	44,982
2019	33,155
2020 and thereafter	96,345
Total future minimum sponsorship and other marketing payments	$ 392,926

The amounts listed above are the minimum obligations required to be paid under the Company's sponsorship and other marketing agreements. [...]

Other

From time to time, the Company is involved in litigation and other proceedings, including matters related to commercial and intellectual property disputes, as well as trade, regulatory and other claims related to its business. The Company believes that all current proceedings are routine in nature and incidental to the conduct of its business, and that the ultimate resolution of any such proceedings will not have a material adverse effect on its consolidated financial position, results of operations or cash flows.

In connection with various contracts and agreements, the Company has agreed to indemnify counterparties against certain third party claims relating to the infringement of intellectual property rights and other items. Generally, such indemnification obligations do not apply in situations in which the counterparties are grossly negligent, engage in willful misconduct, or act in bad faith. Based on the Company's historical experience and the estimated probability of future loss, the Company has determined that the fair value of such indemnifications is not material to its consolidated financial position or results of operations.

8. Stockholders' Equity

The Company's Class A Common Stock and Class B Convertible Common Stock have an authorized number of shares at December 31, 2014 of 400.0 million shares and 36.6 million shares, respectively, and each have a par value of $0.0003 1/3 per share. Holders of Class A Common Stock and Class B Convertible Common Stock have identical rights, including liquidation preferences, except that the holders of Class A Common Stock are entitled to one vote per share and holders of Class B Convertible Common Stock are entitled to 10 votes per share on all matters submitted to a stockholder vote. Class B Convertible Common Stock may only be held by Kevin Plank, the Company's founder and Chief Executive Officer, or a related party of Mr. Plank, as defined in the Company's charter. As a result, Mr. Plank has a majority voting control over the Company. Upon the transfer of shares of Class B Convertible Stock to a person other than Mr. Plank or a related party of Mr. Plank, the shares automatically convert into shares of Class A Common Stock on a one-for-one basis. In addition, all of the outstanding shares of Class B Convertible Common Stock will automatically convert into shares of Class A Common Stock on a one-for-one basis upon the death or disability of Mr. Plank or on the record date for any stockholders' meeting upon which the shares of Class A Common Stock and Class B Convertible Common Stock beneficially owned by Mr. Plank is less than 15% of the total shares of Class A Common Stock and Class B Convertible Common Stock outstanding. Holders of the Company's common stock are entitled to receive dividends when and if authorized and declared out of assets legally available for the payment of dividends.

During the year ended December 31, 2014, 3.4 million shares of Class B Convertible Common Stock were converted into shares of Class A Common Stock on a one-for-one basis in connection with stock sales.
[...]

16. Segment Data and Related Information

The Company's operating segments are based on how the Chief Operating Decision Maker ("CODM") makes decisions about allocating resources and assessing performance. As such, the CODM receives discrete financial information for the Company's principal business by geographic region based on the Company's strategy to become a global brand. These geographic regions include North America; Latin America; Europe, the Middle East and Africa ("EMEA"); and Asia-Pacific. Each geographic segment operates exclusively in one industry: the development, marketing and distribution of branded performance apparel, footwear and accessories. [...]

The net revenues and operating income (loss) associated with the Company's segments are summarized in the following tables. Net revenues represent sales to external customers for each segment. In addition to net revenues, operating income (loss) is a primary financial measure used by the Company to evaluate performance of each segment. Intercompany balances were eliminated for separate disclosure and the majority of corporate expenses within North America have not been allocated to other foreign countries and businesses.

	Year Ended December 31,		
(In thousands)	2014	2013	2012
Net revenues			
North America	$ 2,796,390	$ 2,193,739	$ 1,726,733
Other foreign countries and businesses	287,980	138,312	108,188
Total net revenues	$ 3,084,370	$ 2,332,051	$ 1,834,921

	Year Ended December 31,		
(In thousands)	2014	2013	2012
Operating income (loss)			
North America	$ 372,347	$ 271,338	$ 200,084
Other foreign countries and businesses	(18,392)	(6,240)	8,611
Total operating income	353,955	265,098	208,695
Interest expense, net	(5,335)	(2,933)	(5,183)
Other expense, net	(6,410)	(1,172)	(73)
Income before income taxes	$ 342,210	$ 260,993	$ 203,439

Net revenues by product category are as follows:

	Year Ended December 31,		
(In thousands)	2014	2013	2012
Apparel	$ 2,291,520	$ 1,762,150	$ 1,385,350
Footwear	430,987	298,825	238,955
Accessories	275,425	216,098	165,835
Total net sales	2,997,932	2,277,073	1,790,140
Licensing and other revenues	86,438	54,978	44,781
Total net revenues	$ 3,084,370	$ 2,332,051	$ 1,834,921

As of December 31, 2014 and 2013, the majority of the Company's long-lived assets were located in the United States. Net revenues in the United States were $2,670.4 million, $2,082.5 million and $1,650.4 million for the years ended December 31, 2014, 2013 and 2012, respectively.

[...]

TYPICAL CHARTS OF ACCOUNTS FOR DIFFERENT TYPES OF BUSINESSES

A Simple Service Corporation

Assets	Liabilities	Stockholders' Equity
Cash	Accounts Payable	Common Stock
Accounts Receivable	Notes Payable, Short-Term	Retained Earnings
Allowance for Uncollectible Accounts	Salary Payable	Dividends
Notes Receivable, Short-Term	Wages Payable	
Interest Receivable	Payroll Taxes Payable	**Revenues and Gains**
Supplies	Employee Benefits Payable	Service Revenue
Prepaid Rent	Interest Payable	Interest Revenue
Prepaid Insurance	Unearned Service Revenue	Gain on Sale of Land (Furniture, Equipment, or Building)
Notes Receivable, Long-Term	Notes Payable, Long-Term	
Land		**Expenses and Losses**
Building		Salary Expense
Accumulated Depreciation—Building		Payroll Tax Expense
Equipment		Employee Benefits Expense
Accumulated Depreciation—Equipment		Rent Expense
Furniture		Insurance Expense
Accumulated Depreciation—Furniture		Supplies Expense
		Uncollectible Accounts Expense
		Depreciation Expense—Furniture
		Depreciation Expense—Equipment
		Depreciation Expense—Building
		Income Tax Expense
		Interest Expense
		Miscellaneous Expense
		Loss on Sale (or Exchange) of Land (Furniture, Equipment, or Building)

A Service Partnership

Same as service corporation, except for owners' equity

Owners' Equity

Partner 1, Capital
Partner 2, Capital
.
.
.
Partner N, Capital

Partner 1, Drawing
Partner 2, Drawing
.
.
.
Partner N, Drawing

(continued)

TYPICAL CHARTS OF ACCOUNTS FOR DIFFERENT TYPES OF BUSINESSES (continued)

A Complex Merchandising Corporation

Assets	Liabilities	Stockholders' Equity

Assets	Liabilities	Stockholders' Equity	Expenses and Losses
Cash	Accounts Payable	Preferred Stock	
Investments in Trading Securities or Investments in Available-for-Sale Securities	Notes Payable, Short-Term	Paid-in Capital in Excess of Par—Preferred	Cost of Goods Sold
	Current Portion of Bonds Payable	Common Stock	Salary Expense
Accounts Receivable	Salary Payable	Paid-in Capital in Excess of Par—Common	Wage Expense
Allowance for Uncollectible Accounts	Wages Payable		Commission Expense
Notes Receivable, Short-Term	Payroll Taxes Payable	Paid-in Capital from Treasury Stock Transactions	Payroll Tax Expense
Interest Receivable	Employee Benefits Payable	Paid-in Capital from Retirement of Stock	Employee Benefits Expense
Inventory	Interest Payable		Rent Expense
Supplies	Income Tax Payable	Retained Earnings	Insurance Expense
Prepaid Rent	Unearned Sales Revenue	Accumulated Other Comprehensive Income (or Loss)	Supplies Expense
Prepaid Insurance	Notes Payable, Long-Term		Uncollectible Accounts Expense
Notes Receivable, Long-Term	Bonds Payable	Unrealized Gain (or Loss) on Investments in Available-for-Sale Securities	Depreciation Expense—Land Improvements
Equity-Method Investment	Lease Liability		Depreciation Expense—Furniture and Fixtures
Investments in Available-for-Sale Securities		Foreign Currency Translation Adjustment	Depreciation Expense—Equipment
Investment in Bonds Held-to-Maturity		Treasury Stock	Depreciation Expense—Buildings
Other Receivables, Long-Term		Noncontrolling Interest	Organization Expense
Land			Amortization Expense—Franchises
Land Improvements		**Revenues and Gains**	Amortization Expense—Leasehold Improvements
Buildings		Sales Revenue	Amortization Expense—Patent
Accumulated Depreciation—Buildings		Interest Revenue	Income Tax Expense
Equipment		Dividend Revenue	Unrealized Loss on Trading Securities
Accumulated Depreciation—Equipment		Equity-Method Investment Revenue	Loss on Sale of Investments
Furniture and Fixtures		Unrealized Gain on Trading Securities	Loss on Sale (or Exchange) of Land (Furniture and Fixtures, Equipment, or Buildings)
Accumulated Depreciation—Furniture and Fixtures		Gain on Sale of Investments	
Franchises		Gain on Sale of Land (Furniture and Fixtures, Equipment, or Buildings)	Discontinued Operations—Loss
Patents		Discontinued Operations—Gain	Extraordinary Losses
Leasehold Improvements		Extraordinary Gains	
Goodwill			

A Manufacturing Corporation

Same as merchandising corporation, except for assets

Assets

Inventories:
   Materials Inventories
   Work-in-Process Inventories
   Finished Goods Inventories
Factory Wages
Factory Overhead

APPENDIX D

SUMMARY OF GENERALLY ACCEPTED ACCOUNTING PRINCIPLES (GAAP)

Every technical area has professional associations and regulatory bodies that govern the practice of the profession. Accounting is no exception. In the United States, generally accepted accounting principles (GAAP) are written by the Financial Accounting Standards Board (FASB). The FASB has seven full-time members and a large staff. An independent organization with no government or professional affiliation, the FASB is subject to oversight by the Financial Accounting Foundation (FAF), which selects its members and funds its work. In order to ensure impartiality, FASB members are required to sever all ties to previous firms and institutions that they may have served prior to joining the FASB. Each member is appointed for a five-year term and is eligible for one additional five-year term.

FASB pronouncements are called *Statements of Financial Accounting Standards.* Once issued, these pronouncements are added to the *Accounting Standards Codification™,* which is the single source of authoritative nongovernmental U.S. GAAP. The codification organizes the many pronouncements that constitute U.S. GAAP—each of which specifies how to measure and report a particular type of business event or transaction—into a consistent, searchable format. GAAP is the "accounting law of the land." In the same way that our laws draw authority from their acceptance by the people, GAAP depends on general acceptance by the business community. Throughout this book, we refer to GAAP as the proper way to measure and report business activity.

In 2002, the FASB and the International Accounting Standards Board (IASB) announced a convergence project, whereby both bodies agreed to combine international financial reporting standards (IFRS) and U.S. GAAP into one set of global, compatible, high-quality standards. All new FASB and IASB standards written since that time have been written to measure and report various types of business activities in compatible (if not identical) ways. However, some differences between the two sets of standards still exist. Those differences are discussed in Appendix E.

The U.S. Congress has given the Securities and Exchange Commission (SEC), a government organization that regulates the trading of investments, ultimate responsibility for establishing accounting rules for companies that are owned by the general investing public. However, the SEC has delegated much of its rule-making power to the FASB. Exhibit D-1 outlines the flow of authority for developing GAAP.

Exhibit D-1 | Flow of Authority for Developing GAAP

| United States Congress | Securities and Exchange Commission | Financial Accounting Standards Board | Pronouncements that make up generally accepted accounting principles (GAAP) |

The Objective of Financial Reporting

The basic objective of financial reporting is to provide information that is useful in making investment and lending decisions. The FASB believes that accounting information can be useful in decision making only if it is *relevant* and if it *faithfully represents* economic reality.

Relevant information is useful in making predictions and for evaluating past performance—that is, the information has feedback value. For example, PepsiCo's disclosure of the profitability of each of its lines of business is relevant for investor evaluations of the company. To be relevant, information must be timely. To faithfully represent, the information must be complete, neutral (free from bias), and without material error (accurate). Accounting information must focus on the *economic substance* of a transaction, event, or circumstance, which may or may not always be the same as its legal form. Faithful representation makes the information *reliable* to users. Exhibit 1-3 on page 7 of Chapter 1 presents the objective of accounting, its fundamental and enhancing qualitative characteristics, and its constraint. These characteristics and constraint combine to shape the concepts and principles that make up GAAP. Exhibit D-2 summarizes the assumptions, concepts, and principles that accounting has developed to provide useful information for decision making.

Exhibit D-2 | Summary of Important Accounting Concepts, Principles, and Financial Statements

Assumptions, Concepts, Principles, and Financial Statements	Quick Summary	Text Reference
Assumptions and Concepts		
Entity assumption	Accounting draws a boundary around each organization to be accounted for.	Chapter 1, page 8
Continuity (going-concern) assumption	Accountants assume the business will continue operating for the foreseeable future.	Chapter 1, page 8
Stable-monetary-unit assumption	Accounting information is expressed primarily in monetary terms that ignore the effects of inflation.	Chapter 1, page 9
Time-period concept	Ensures that accounting information is reported at regular intervals.	Chapter 3, page 124
Principles		
Historical cost principle	Assets are recorded at their actual historical cost.	Chapter 1, page 9
Revenue principle	Tells accountants when to record revenue (only after it has been earned) and the amount of revenue to record (the cash value of what has been received).	Chapter 3, page 124; Chapter 5, page 258; and Chapter 11, page 634
Expense recognition (matching) principle	Directs accountants to (1) identify and measure all expenses incurred during the period and (2) match the expenses against the revenues earned during the period. The goal is to measure net income.	Chapter 3, page 125
Consistency principle	Businesses should use the same accounting methods from period to period.	Chapter 6, page 324
Disclosure principle	A company's financial statements should report enough information for outsiders to make informed decisions about the company.	Chapter 6, page 324
Financial Statements		
Balance sheet	Assets = Liabilities + Owners' Equity at a point in time.	Chapter 1
Income statement	Revenues and gains − Expenses and losses = Net income or net loss for the period	Chapters 1 and 11
Statement of cash flows	Cash receipts − Cash payments = Increase or decrease in cash during the period, grouped under operating, investing, and financing activities	Chapters 1 and 12
Statement of Comprehensive Income	Net income (from income statement) + Other comprehensive income − Other comprehensive loss = Comprehensive income	Chapter 11
Statement of retained earnings	Beginning retained earnings + Net income (or − Net loss) − Dividends Declared = Ending retained earnings	Chapters 1 and 10
Statement of stockholders' equity	Shows the reason for the change in each stockholders' equity account, including retained earnings.	Chapter 10, page 592
Financial statement notes	Provide information that cannot be reported conveniently on the face of the financial statements. The notes are an integral part of the statements.	Chapter 11, page 646

SUMMARY OF DIFFERENCES BETWEEN U.S. GAAP AND IFRS CROSS REFERENCED TO CHAPTER

The following table describes some of the current differences between U.S. generally accepted accounting principles (GAAP) and International Financial Reporting Standards (IFRS) that relate to topics (by chapter) covered in this textbook. Because of the globalization of business, there are theoretical advantages to adopting a single uniform set of global accounting standards. However, for practical reasons, achieving that goal has proven to be illusive. Nevertheless, some experts believe that the integration of GAAP and IFRS will eventually become a reality. The last column of the table explains what could happen if the U.S. GAAP of today were to switch to IFRS as they currently exist. This will help you assess the impact of these changes on U.S. financial statements.

Accounts	Topic	U.S. GAAP Position	IFRS Position	Implications of Switch to IFRS
Inventory and Cost of Goods Sold Chapter 6	Inventory costing	Companies can choose to use LIFO inventory costing, if desired. A large portion of U.S. companies currently use LIFO for its tax benefits.	LIFO is not allowed under any circumstances.	LIFO could be eliminated. Companies could still choose to use FIFO, average, or specific identification methods.
	Lower-of-cost-or market (LCM)	Market is usually determined to be replacement cost. LCM write-downs cannot be reversed.	Market is always net realizable value (fair market value). LCM write-downs can be reversed under certain conditions.	LCM write-downs may become less common, as selling prices are usually greater than replacement costs. Some write-downs might be reversed over time.
Property, Plant, and Equipment Chapter 7	Asset impairment and revaluation	If long-term assets are impaired, they are written down. Write-downs may not be reversed.	Long-term assets may be written up or down, based on fair market value (appraisals). Adjustments may be potentially reversed.	The cost principle might not apply to long-term assets as strongly. Assets could be evaluated by independent appraisers and adjusted either up or down.
	Depreciation	Assets are depreciated by classes (i.e., buildings, equipment, etc.).	Assets are depreciated by component (much more detailed than by classes).	Much more detailed records would have to be kept over depreciation.
Research and Development Chapter 7	Development costs	All research and development costs are expensed. Only exception is for computer software development costs, which can be capitalized and amortized over future sales revenues.	All research is expensed, but development costs are capitalized if six criteria are met, and amortized over future sales revenues.	Standards already developed by U.S. GAAP might be extended to apply to all development costs, not just computer software development.
Intangible Assets Chapter 7	Capitalization and recognition of intangible assets on balance sheet	Only recognized when purchased. Internally developed not recognized.	Recognized if future benefit is probable and reliably measurable (same criteria as recognition of contingencies). May be purchased or internally developed.	More intangible assets could be recognized on balance sheet. Adjusted for amortization or impairment over time.

(continued)

Accounts	Topic	U.S. GAAP Position	IFRS Position	Implications of Switch to IFRS
Contingent Liabilities Chapter 9	Recording of contingent liabilities	Accrued (recorded in journal entry) if probable and reliably measurable. Contingent liabilities that are reasonably possible are disclosed in notes to financial statements.	Both probable and possible contingent liabilities are recorded in journal entries. Contingencies are not considered "probable" to occur in the future. Therefore, they can, by definition, only be disclosed in the financial statement footnotes. However, if it is "more likely than not" (i.e., greater than a 50% probability) that an obligation is going to arise, and if an estimate can be made of the amount, IFRS requires that a "provision" be recorded by making an accrual journal entry.	More liabilities will likely be recorded, regardless of the outcome of proposals being studied by FASB and IASB.
Contingent Liabilities Chapter 9	Disclosure of contingencies	The FASB has proposed that the standard for disclosure of loss contingencies be increased to include all such matters that are expected to be resolved in the near term (i.e., within the next year) and that could have a severe impact (higher than material, disruptive to the business). In addition, the proposal requires a quantitative tabular reconciliation of accrued loss contingencies that includes increases or decreases in such amounts during the most recent year.	IASB is studying its present requirements with a view to increase required disclosures in the next few years.	More liabilities will likely be recorded, regardless of the outcome of proposals being studied by the FASB and IASB.
Lease Liabilities Chapter 9	Classification of leases	FASB and IASB are on the verge of issuing a new standard that will eliminate virtually all operating leases. The present value of all future payments on leased assets will be capitalized under the category of "right to use" assets. The related obligations will be reported as "future lease payment" long-term liabilities. The new standard is expected to be issued in 2016 to be effective for financial statements issued after December 15, 2018.	Same as U.S. GAAP Position.	More leases could be classified as capital leases, resulting in more frequent recognition of long-term assets as well as long-term liabilities.

Accounts	Topic	U.S. GAAP Position	IFRS Position	Implications of Switch to IFRS
Revenue Chapter 5 and 11	Revenue recognition	The FASB and IASB have have recently issued a new joint standard that recognizes revenue based on a 5-step model. Details of the model are covered in Chapter 5. The new standard, issued in 2015, will go into effect in 2018. For the retail industry (largely featured in this book), U.S. GAAP and IFRS for revenue recognition were already essentially identical.	The IASB's standard on revenue recognition is a joint standard with the FASB, so after the new standard is effective in 2018, the U.S. GAAP and IFRS positions on revenue recognition will be the same, thus eliminating this difference.	The new standard will standardize the way in which revenues are recognized globally.
Interest Revenue and Interest Expense Chapter 12	Indirect method cash flows statement presentation Direct method cash flows statement presentation	Interest revenue and interest expense are part of net income, and as such are included in operating activities (as part of net income) on an indirect method cash flows statement. Interest income is not reported under investing activities.	Interest revenue and interest expense are removed from net income (as an adjustment, similar to the adjustment for depreciation expense) in the operating activities section of the indirect method cash flows statement. Interest income is reported under investing activities, and interest expense is reported under financing activities for both direct and indirect methods.	Interest revenue and interest expense reclassified to different sections of the cash flows statement.

Company Index

Glindex A Combined Glossary and Subject Index

A

Above par common stock, 571–572

Accelerated depreciation. A depreciation method that writes off a relatively larger amount of the asset's cost nearer the start of its useful life than the straight-line method does, 382–384

Account. The record of the changes that have occurred in a particular asset, liability, or stockholders' equity during a period. The basic summary device of accounting, 62–64
  adjusting, 127–141. *See also* Adjustments to entries
  after posting to ledger, 84–85
  analyzing, 86–87
  asset accounts, 62
  chart of accounts, 87–88
  formats for, 88–89
  impact of transactions on, 75–78
  liability accounts, 63
  normal balance of, 88
  permanent, 148
  stockholders' equity accounts, 63–64
  temporary, 148
  types of, 62–64
  uncollectible, 266–273
  uncollectible, writing off, 270–271

Account format. A balance-sheet format that lists assets on the left and liabilities and stockholders' equity on the right, 151

Account numbers, list of, 87–88

Accounting. The information system that measures business activities, processes that information into reports and financial statements, and communicates the results to decision makers, 4. *See also* Accounting decisions; Accounting equation; Accounting information; Assumptions

Accounting cycle. The process by which financial statements are prepared, 4

Accounting decisions, 26–29

Accounting equation. The most basic tool of accounting: Assets = Liabilities + Owners' equity, 11–12
  account types and, 62–64
  impact of business transactions on, 64–72

Accounting errors, correcting, 87

Accounting estimates, changes in, 643

Accounting information
  accuracy of, 7
  comparability of, 8
  completeness of, 7
  conceptual foundations, 7
  disclosure of, 7
  economic substance, 7
  flow of, 4, 80–84
  free from bias, 7, 9
  global, 10–11
  and internal control, 207
  material, 7
  qualitative characteristics of, 7–8
  relevance, 7, 9
  reliability of, 7
  timeliness of, 8
  understandability of, 8
  users of, 4
  verifiability of, 8, 9

Accounting principles, 7
  vs. bookkeeping, 4
  changing methods of, 643

fair value, 9, 11
faithful representation, 7
financial, 5
generally accepted accounting principles (GAAP), 7–8, 10–11
historical cost principle, 9
management, 5
relevance, 7

Accounts payable, 12, 21, 63, 494

Accounts payable turnover. Measures the number of times per year a company pays off its accounts payable. Assuming all purchases are on credit, to compute accounts payable turnover, divide purchases (cost of goods sold + ending inventory – beginning inventory) by average accounts payable. When inventories are immaterial, or when there is very little difference between beginning and ending inventories, substitute cost of goods sold for purchases, 495–496, 775

Accounts receivable, 62

Accounts receivable turnover. Measures a company's ability to collect cash from credit customers. To compute accounts receivable turnover, divide net credit sales by average net accounts receivable, 278–279, 774

Accrual. An expense or a revenue that occurs before the business pays or receives cash. An accrual is the opposite of a deferral, 128

Accrual accounting. Accounting that records the impact of a business event as it occurs, regardless of whether the transaction affected cash and cash flows, 122
  cash-basis accounting vs., 122
  ethical issues in, 127

Accrued expense. An expense incurred but not yet paid in cash, 134–136, 497

Accrued liability. A liability for an expense that has not yet been paid by the company, 21, 63, 497

Accrued revenue. A revenue that has been earned but not yet received in cash, 135

Accumulated depreciation. The cumulative sum of all depreciation expense from the date of acquiring a plant asset, 21, 132

Accumulated depreciation account, 21, 132

Accumulated other comprehensive income. The cumulative amount of items reported as other comprehensive income; a separate category in the stockholders' equity section of the balance sheet, 256, 645

Acid-test ratio. Ratio of the sum of cash plus short-term investments plus net current receivables to total current liabilities. Tells whether the entity can pay all its current liabilities if they come due immediately. Also called the *quick ratio*, 278, 772–773

Adjusted trial balance. A list of all the ledger accounts with their adjusted balances, 140

Adjustments to entries
  accruals, 128
  accrued expenses, 134–136
  accrued revenues, 136
  deferrals, 128
  depreciation, 128
  prepaid expenses, 128–131
  summary of, 138–139
  trial balance, 140
  unearned revenue, 136–137

Aging-of-receivables. A way to estimate bad debts by analyzing individual accounts receivable according to the length of time they have been receivable from the customer, 269–270, 271

Allowance for Bad Debts, 267–271

Allowance for Doubtful Accounts. Another name for *Allowance for Uncollectible Accounts*, 267–271

Allowance for Uncollectible Accounts. The estimated amount of collection losses on accounts receivable. Another name for *Allowance for Doubtful Accounts*, 267–271

Allowance method. A method of recording collection losses based on estimates of how much money the business will not collect from its credit customers, 267–271

Amortization. The systematic reduction of a lump-sum amount. Expense that applies to intangible assets in the same way depreciation applies to plant assets and depletion applies to natural resources, 397
  for bond premium, 516–519
  depreciation on leasehold improvements, 375
  as expense item, 17
  intangible assets, 397
  revenue and, 20
  on statement of cash flows, 685, 687, 700
  straight-line method, 509–511

Amortized cost method, 442

Approvals, proper, for internal control, 209

Asset. An economic resource that is expected to be of benefit in the future, 11, 62. *See also* Intangible asset; Plant assets
  accounts receivable, 62
  asset accounts, 62
  asset transactions, 403–404
  assumptions about, 8–9
  basket purchases of, 375
  buildings, 62
  cash/cash equivalents, 20, 62
  classifying by liquidity, 150
  current, 20, 687–688
  current, liquidity of, 150
  depreciable, changing useful life of, 389–390
  equipment, furniture, fixtures, 62
  fixed, 12, 21
  fully depreciated, 391, 392
  impairment of, 399–401
  improper access to, 204
  intangible, 21
  inventory, 12, 20, 62
  investments, 21
  kinds of, 12
  land, 62
  long-term, 20–21
  long-term, liquidity of, 150
  prepaid expenses, 20, 21, 62
  property and equipment, 12, 21
  receivables, 20
  reporting, 150
  return on, 401–403
  safeguarding, 204
  sale of, 687
  wasting, 396

Asset turnover. The dollars of sales generated per dollar of assets invested. Formula is Net sales ÷ Average total assets, 402, 589, 779

Association for Certified Fraud Examiners (ACFE), 202

These items are reported either in a separate statement or in a combined statement of net income and comprehensive income. At the end of a period, items of comprehensive income for that period are reported as accumulated other comprehensive income, a separate category of stockholders' equity, 256, 446
Other receivables, 264
"Outsider claims," 11
Outstanding check. A check issued by the company and recorded on its books but not yet paid by its bank, 215
Outstanding stock. Stock in the hands of stockholders, 569, 577–578, 644
Overfunded benefit plan, 527
Owners' equity. The claim of the owners of a business to the assets of the business. Also called *capital*, *stockholders' equity* or *net assets*, 11, 22
  and financing activities, 682
  paid-in capital, 12–13, 22
  of proprietorships and partnerships, 14
  retained earnings, 12–13, 22
Ownership, transferability of, 566

P

Paid-in capital. The amount of stockholders' equity that stockholders have contributed to the corporation. Also called *contributed capital*, 12–13, 22, 569
Par value. Arbitrary amount assigned by a company to a share of its stock, 504, 570
  of common stock. *See under* Common stock
  issuing bonds at, 507–508
Parent company. An investor company that owns more than 50% of the voting stock of a subsidiary company, 450
Partial years, depreciation for, 389
Partial-period interest amounts, 516
Partnership. An association of two or more persons who co-own a business for profit, 6
  owners' equity in, 14
Password. A special set of characters that must be provided by the user of a computerized program or data files to prevent unauthorized access to those files, 209, 210
Patent. A federal government grant giving the holder the exclusive right for 20 years to produce and sell an invention, 397–398
Payments, to suppliers, 699, 704
Payroll. Employee compensation, a major expense of many businesses, 497–498
Payroll liabilities, 134–136, 497–498
Pension. Employee compensation that will be received during retirement, 526–527
Percent-of-sales method. Computes uncollectible-account expense as a percentage of net sales. Also called the *income-statement approach* because it focuses on the amount of expense to be reported on the income statement, 268–269, 271
Periodic inventory system. An inventory system in which the business does not keep a continuous record of the inventory on hand. Instead, at the end of the period, the business makes a physical count of the inventory on hand and applies the appropriate unit costs to determine the cost of the ending inventory, 314, 332, 366–367
Permanent accounts. Asset, liability, and stockholders' equity accounts that are not closed at the end of the period, 148

Perpetual inventory system. An inventory system in which the business keeps a continuous record for each inventory item to show the inventory on hand at all times, 314–316, 320–321, 332
Petty cash. Fund containing a small amount of cash that is used to pay minor amounts, 224
Phish. Creating bogus websites for the purpose of stealing unauthorized data, such as names, addresses, Social Security numbers, bank account, and credit card numbers, 210
Phishing expeditions, 210
Physical wear and tear, 378
Plant assets. Long-lived assets, such as land, buildings, and equipment, used in the operation of the business. Also called *fixed assets* or *property and equipment*, 131, 373
  accounting for, 387
  analyzing transactions, 394–395
  book value of, 133
  buildings, machinery, and equipment, 21, 62, 374–375
  cash flow impact, 403–404
  depreciable cost of, 379
  depreciation for tax purposes, 387–389
  depreciation of, 131–133, 378–385
  disposing of for no proceeds, 392
  effects of disposal of, 391–395
  exchanging, 393–394
  land, 62, 373, 374
  land improvements and leasehold improvements, 375
  lump-sum purchases of assets, 375
  purchases and sales of, 689, 700
  selling, 392–393
Posting. Copying amounts from the journal to the ledger, 79
Postretirement liabilities, 526–527
Preemption, 568
Preferred dividends, effect on earnings per share, 644, 782
Preferred stock. Stock that gives its owners certain advantages, such as the priority to receive dividends before the common stockholders and the priority to receive assets before the common stockholders if the corporation liquidates, 570, 575–576
  dividends on, 584–585, 644
  redeemable, 588
Premium (on a bond). Excess of bond's issue price over its face (par) value, 506
  issuing bonds payable at, 510–511, 516–519
Prepaid expense. A category of miscellaneous assets that typically expire or get used up in the near future. Examples include prepaid rent, prepaid insurance, and supplies, 128
  adjusting entries, 128–131
  on balance sheet, 19, 20
  prepaid rent, 129
  supplies, 130
Present value. The value on a given date of a future payment or series of future payments, discounted to reflect the time value of money, 460
  of an annuity, 462–463
  of available-for-sale investments, 465
  calculating with Microsoft Excel, 463–465
  of investments in bonds, 465–466
  of money, 460–461
Present-value tables, 461–462
President. Chief operating officer in charge of managing the day-to-day operations of a corporation, 568

Pre-tax accounting income. Income before tax on the income statement, 640
Price-earnings (P/E) ratio. Ratio of the market price of a share of common stock to the company's earnings per share. Measures the value that the stock market places on $1 of a company's earnings, 587, 781–782
Principal. The amount borrowed by a debtor and lent by a creditor, 273, 274, 504
Prior-period adjustment. A correction to the beginning balance of retained earnings for an error of an earlier period, 643
Production costs, 20
Profit margin. *See* Gross margin
Profitability, and stockholder investment, 589–591
Projected benefit obligation, 526
Promissory notes, 264, 274
Proper approvals, and internal control, 209
Property and equipment. *See* Plant assets
Proprietorship. A business with a single owner, 5
  owners' equity in, 14
Public Company Accounting Oversight Board, 205
Public interest principle, 29
Purchase allowance. A decrease in the cost of purchases because the seller has granted the buyer a subtraction (an allowance) from the amount owed, 315
Purchase discount. A decrease in the cost of purchases earned by making an early payment to the vendor, 316
Purchase return. A decrease in the cost of purchases because the buyer returned the goods to the seller, 315
Purchases, budgeted, 329
Purchasing department, 209

Q

Quality of earnings. *See* Earnings quality
Quick ratio. Another name for the *acid-test ratio*, 278, 772–773
Quitting concern, 8

R

Rate of return, foreign currencies and exchange rates, 457
Rate of return on assets (ROA). Net income – preferred dividends divided by average total assets. This ratio measures a company's success in using its assets to earn income for the persons who finance the business. Also called *return on total assets*. Can also be computed using the first two elements of DuPont Analysis (Rate of return on net sales × Asset turnover), 779
Rate of return on common stockholders' equity. Net income minus preferred dividends, divided by average common stockholders' equity. A measure of profitability. Also called *return on equity*, 589, 780
Rate of return on net sales. Ratio of net income – preferred dividends to net sales. A measure of profitability. Also called *return on sales*, 778
Rate of return on total assets. Net income minus preferred dividends divided by average total assets. This ratio measures a company's success in using its assets to earn income for the persons who finance the business. Also called *return on assets*, 401–403, 589, 779